RED COLLAR WHITE COLLAR CRIME

Corporate, Predatory & Violent Fraud Offenders

Frank S. Perri

About the Author

Frank S. Perri, JD, CPA, CFE, is an attorney with over 25 years of criminal law experience. The author travels throughout the country lecturing to businesses, universities, law enforcement, certified public accountants, certified fraud examiners, forensic accountants, and certified internal auditors. He publishes and lectures in the area of white-collar crime, organizational misconduct, offender profiling, corporate governance, red-collar crime, and forensic accounting in legal, behavioral, accounting, and criminological journals. Perri also coined the term red-collar crime.

The author received his law degree from the University of Illinois College of Law, his Master in Business Administration from Case Western Reserve University and his bachelor's degree in Economics from Union College located in Schenectady, New York. The author is a Certified Public Accountant, a Certified Fraud Examiner, and a member of the Association of Certified Fraud Examiners.

Summary of Contents

Table of Contents

6

Chapter 1

White Collar Crime

Despite the trillions of dollars lost to white-collar crime, comparatively the white-collar offender has escaped the type of in-depth scrutiny and academic analysis non-white-collar offenders are subjected to due to an implied credibility about their character they have received from academia, the criminal justice system, and society at large. Instead of digging deeper to understand and refine their criminal profile, we ended up relying on outdated and unfounded assumptions to construct opinions about their character traits that are more likely than not inaccurate. This insight actually exposes people and organizations to being victimized time and again because assumptions are not based on fact, but myth. Consider that just because these offenders aggress against others in a manner not reflective of traditional notions of criminality, or in ways that are easily recognizable by the general public, does not mean they are not capable of inflicting harm to others due to how they perceive exploitable opportunities. White-collar offenders are not a homogenous offender class in terms of the extent of their criminality, why they offend, the number of victims created, and the methods they go about to offend.

There appears to be an imbalance between how white-collar criminals are perceived as offenders and what they truly represent in terms of harboring a criminal mindset that is open to exploiting others and organizations. On the one hand they are considered offenders who would not have engaged in misconduct at their organization but for financial pressures such as trying to get through an economic downturn. However, on the other hand, research confirms that there are offenders who go out of their way to exploit an organization to satisfy their motives that is not dependent on any type of pressure except that they are criminal entrepreneurs no different than a street-level offender setting up a narcotics distribution apparatus. What is lacking in our understanding of white-collar offenders is that just as there is a continuum of criminality with non-white-collar offenders, the same holds true in white-collar offenses. In some cases non-white-collar offenders are deemed low-level offenders because they break the law on minor matters, but are not engaged in severe, harmful acts towards others. Yet in other cases some offenders target children to exploit or those who are serial burglars that go from one home to another thieving.

The same dynamic holds true for white-collar offenders—they too engage in different types of fraud schemes that may be more financially devastating than others together with targeting different victims to satisfy their motives. We may have an employee exploiting weak internal controls at work to embezzle low amounts of money that cannot be easily traced to his or her actions. Alternatively, corporate leaders encourage financial statement fraud in the billions of dollars by artificially inflating income to give the impression to outsiders that their business is more successful than it actually is. However they also personally profited at the expense of the organization, employees, and shareholders by selling their stock options at artificially inflated prices because of the false accounting information they provided to the securities market. Moreover, we observe predatory fraud offenders who specifically target individuals and infiltrate organizations, both for and not-for-profit, to financially exploit without remorse leaving victims penniless and organizations bankrupt. In addition, white-collar offenders are more than willing to resort to violence as a solution to a perceived problem, this subgroup of violent fraud offenders are referred to as red collar criminals in that they are motivated to resort to violence in order to prevent the detection and or disclosure of their fraud scheme. Red-collar offenders, with cold ease, kill family members, friends, co-workers and those who investigate their fraud schemes such as regulators.

Furthermore, people typically do not hesitate in unequivocally denouncing offenses that appear obvious, such as murder, terrorism, and sexual assault because they do not experience moral ambiguity about the unacceptability of these offenses accompanied by public condemnation. Yet moral ambiguity appears to have uniquely attached itself to white-collar offenders because how we intellectually understand them and how we feel about them may be at odds, which ultimately impacts our response to their misconduct. We may denounce their behavior, but at the same time refer to them as "good people who did a bad thing" or labeled "accidental offenders" because it was never their true desire to engage in fraud despite the financial and emotional damage caused. Would we attribute the character trait of goodness to a rapist or terrorist or label them as accidental offenders knowing the planning that went into their crimes? Yet, this moral ambiguity persistently cloaks the white-collar crime classification, ultimately influencing the perception that a different kind of offender exists. Moral ambiguity is preserved because there is a viewpoint that in some circumstances government tolerates corporate offenders by balancing the harm they cause against the perceived greater good they provide such as economic growth, employment opportunities, and the political stability maintained by not compromising the efficiency of the market place that provides tax revenue. If we hope to diminish the impact of moral ambiguity, the gap between what we want to believe about these offenders and what the evidence tells us about what they actually represent must be bridged.

In order to properly assess their risk to society, an updated offender profile based on a better understanding of their behavioral traits is needed. For decades, we generally relied upon sociological and criminological scholars to educate us on this crime classification and specifically on the issue of corporate misconduct, but without in-depth scholarship about the offenders themselves. Although their insights were invaluable in exposing corporate misconduct, in the past other disciplines such as the legal, accounting, and behavioral sciences were not actively involved in white-collar crime scholarship, but today they are because a multiple disciplinary approach to studying white-collar crime is needed. Greater collaboration among disciplines allows for improved offender profiling, and fraud prevention and detection amongst practitioners to reduce the risk inherent in this crime. A more in-depth analysis of white-collar offenders by offering a framework that brings different academic disciplines into the conversation is needed so that we can understand them in a more holistic manner, how their criminality facilitates corporate and predatory fraud and red collar offenses.

Often books on white-collar crime tend to be one dimensional, meaning they just examine criminological aspects of white-collar crime while others focus solely on the technical aspects of how fraud schemes are perpetrated. Without a multiple disciplinary approach, there are simply too many questions about white-collar crime, corporate and predatory fraud offenders for one discipline to answer in more complete terms. When we do not enlist the help of other disciplines to fill in the gaps to unanswered questions, we end up speculating about this offender's criminal and behavioral profile based on what we want to believe about them. Yet, by offering diverse disciplinary perspectives, one begins to appreciate the synergy created on how these different insights fit together to explain why white-collar crime, its offenders, and corporate fraud thrives, thus ultimately relying less and less on offender profile speculations. Practically, not applying a holistic approach to studying white-collar crime is where we have fallen short for decades explaining in part why people and organizations are repeatedly victimized.

As a result, there appears to be a perception, albeit erroneous, that white-collar offenders reflect a homogenous offender group in terms of the extent of their criminality while displaying a value system reflecting a virtuous lifestyle. We often believe that fraud offenders commit crimes outside their character, however their offenses are very much within their character especially since on balance their crimes are planned and can occur over a period of months and years. Moreover, it is assumed fraud offenders are characteristically and optically different because they are better educated, employed, and engage in civically-minded behaviors, thus they do not reflect the unstable, unemployed street-level offender many people equate with being criminally inclined. Unfortunately people are seduced by offender socioeconomic status distinctions and interpret such differences as representative of whether someone is at risk to break the law. Although distinctions between white-collar and non-white-collar offenders matters, what is more important are the similarities of how they manifest their criminal thinking to exploit vulnerable situations regardless of the crime they prefer to engage in. What is known about these offenders is that they manifest their aggression in a different form against others and organizations to satisfy their motive for financial gain, while relying on their own unique rationalizations to morally distance themselves from their misconduct, yet creating victims nonetheless no differently than non white collar offenders. Acknowledging the similarities of how fraud offenders think about exploitable opportunities is the first step in diluting the moral ambiguity surrounding their profile.

Understanding personality traits is important especially as it relates to those that occupy leadership positions because of the impact they have on leadership style, the tone they set for the organization influencing their culture, and how subordinates respond to incidences of misconduct. We learn how corrupt leadership displays certain reoccurring behavioral patterns that increase the risk they will find fraud an acceptable solution to problems such as how to maintain profitability. Furthermore, we find both intriguing and concerning the possibility that certain personality traits promote both occupational success in organizations and facilitate criminal tendencies at the same time. Of course, this does not mean that corporate leaders are by definition corrupt, but it does suggest that harboring antisocial attitudes does not disqualify one from entering the higher ranks of the corporate world—working class citizens may, and do, exhibit these traits. Moreover, understanding personality is important because of its impact on how offenders perceive risk-taking and whether certain types of personalities are more prone to rely on unethical and criminal behavior to satisfy their motives.

Similarly, although it is unfortunate that corporate misconduct occurs at all, there is a normalcy to its pervasiveness. While normalcy should not be interpreted to mean that its existence is condoned, there are risk factors that come together creating a strong negative synergy increasing the probability that organizational misconduct will occur, be tolerated, and even celebrated at times. The reality is the majority of people work in an organizational setting, thus it is useful to learn how organizations facilitate fraudulent behaviors from its leadership all the way to its subordinates. At the organizational level, we need to appreciate the influence of group dynamics that serves as a risk factor increasing the probability that people who might not have any motivation to engage in white-collar crime do engage in it once they are in a group setting. What is it about a group setting that makes people more susceptible to engage in misconduct? When we understand those individual and organizational risk factors coming together, we now have a framework to rely on to explain why misconduct is so foreseeable especially when we observe similar characteristics of how misconduct keeps reoccurring regardless of the industry.

Moreover, we examine why regulatory agencies might fail in detecting blatant fraud especially how Bernard Madoff manipulated the United States Securities and Exchange Commission for years even after the Commission was put on notice on numerous occasions by numerous experts about his crime occurring in plain sight coupled with Madoff's own suspicious behaviors that should have triggered a more surgical investigative response into his business affairs. In addition, we need to understand why the Bernard Madoffs of the world are skilled predatory offenders taking advantage of the investing public, especially those considered well-educated and traditionally not thought of as being at risk for exploitation. If these schemes repeat themselves so often, why are we still beguiled by these offenders only to become their victims? What predatory skill base and tactics do offenders rely on facilitating the ease in which victims happily give them money?

Lastly, people often work in toxic organizations lacking integrity, impacting not only the quality of one's work, but their mindset. This book assists us to better interpret our experiences when immersed in such environments where misconduct thrives. Now this multiple disciplinary framework facilitates the understanding of the people we are surrounded by, how they impact organizational culture, which ultimately impacts how we react to situations—for better or for worse. Moreover, the book can help protect one from going down the proverbial slippery slope of potentially engaging in fraud when we may not think we are engaging in it. People may believe that they engaged in unethical, but not criminal behavior, only to find themselves facing criminal charges because they did not understand the dynamics that lead to them engaging in more than just unethical behavior in the first place.

White Collar Crime Criminological Considerations

The sinful heart is ever the same, but sin changes in quality as society develops.

Edward Ross

Over the past several years, ongoing scandals at public corporations such as Enron, Wells Fargo, and WorldCom to name a few, and the Bernard Madoff Ponzi scheme, raised public awareness of the economic, societal, and personal harm that can result from fraud offenses (O'Donnell & Willing, 2003). White-collar crimes cause substantial social harm by undermining the economy, exacerbating the divide between poverty and wealth, eroding institutional trust, and depriving individuals of time and resources (Ford, 2007). The actions of a few corrupt public officials and business people can affect the livelihoods of thousands. A research study on fraudulent financial reporting, defined as the intentional misrepresentation of a corporation's financial statements or a lack of financial disclosure, found that between 1998 and 2007, 347 U.S. public corporations studied suffered a cumulative fraud-induced financial loss of $120 billion (COSO, 2010). Moreover the 2018 *Report to the Nations*, prepared by the Association of Certified Fraud Examiners (ACFE), conservatively estimates that fraud costs the global economy more than $3 trillion. Consider the 2015 scandal when car maker Volkswagen admitted that 11 million of its vehicles were equipped with software used to manipulate emissions test results.

The software sensed when the car was being tested and then activated equipment that reduced emissions. After testing, during regular driving, the software ignored increased emissions far above legal limits. This was done to save fuel and improve the car's acceleration. The purpose of limiting emissions was to reduce the risks of triggering emphysema, bronchitis and other respiratory diseases. In 2017, manufacturer Kobe Steel disclosed that for up to a decade employees falsified data when producing metal parts used in aircraft, automobiles, railway, and nuclear power plants potentially impacting the safety of the public (Fuse, 2017). Kobe corporate culture encouraged employees to ignore misconduct when falsification occurred. Also in 2017, it became well known that employees of one of the biggest U.S. banks, Wells Fargo, secretly issued credit cards without customer consent by forging customer signatures on paperwork and creating fake e-mail accounts to register customers for online banking services without their knowledge. Employees also falsified bank records, and funded sham accounts with their own money, or money from a customer's account without their knowledge, which served no customer financial need (Wells Fargo, 2017).

In many cases, customers only noticed when they received a letter in the mail congratulating them for opening a new account while accumulating fees. Yet white-collar crime is not limited to for-profit organizations; it occurs in government as well. Consider the case of comptroller and treasurer of Dixon, Illinois, Rita Crundwell, who worked in this capacity from 1983-2012 (Jenco, 2013). The Federal Bureau of Investigation (FBI) revealed that Crundwell embezzled an estimated $53 million over 22 years to support a lavish lifestyle including a horse-breeding business, luxury homes and vehicles. To justify payment of Dixon municipal funds to her secret bank account, Crundwell created almost 180 fake invoices over two decades to make it appear as though the State of Illinois was billing the city for work completed in Dixon. External finance auditors for Dixon failed to notice Crundwell's fake invoices nor did they follow the standard practice of verifying alleged projects by calling the state or visually inspecting the alleged projects. Even though white-collar crime is often devastating for individuals, for-profit, nonprofit, and government organizations, many consider it to be less serious than other types of crimes. Perhaps a partial explanation is that street-level offenses are perceived to more likely threaten our personal security and the safety of loved ones. Such emotional reactions typically are not associated with white-collar crime; we are more likely to be confused and angered than fearful of it. This perception of the lack of seriousness white-collar crime engenders is ironic given that the total financial cost of white-collar crime far exceeds that of street crime, including intangible costs, such as emotional devastation and stress-induced health problems (Friedrich, 2007).

Moreover, the likelihood of becoming a victim of white-collar crime is far greater than that of becoming a victim of a serious street-level crime and every bit as devastating to one's quality of life (Friedrichs, 2007).

Despite the relative magnitude of the cost of white-collar crime that dwarf the cost of non-white-collar crime, researchers have empirically demonstrated that the concept of white-collar crime has been underrepresented in criminological and criminal justice literature, and a sizeable scholarship imbalance still exists (McGurrin et al., 2013). In part, this is due to public perceptions and fear of street-level crimes that disproportionately fueled the attention of researchers towards violent crimes, while ignoring white-collar crimes and its offenders (Van Slyke et al., 2016). Consequently, the focus of academia and the criminal justice system has been on explaining, preventing, and responding to street-level offenses (Holtfreter et al., 2008). With minimal quality scholarship on white-collar crime and its offenders, for decades we have relied on creating in our minds, erroneously and to our detriment, a misperception of white-collar crime, including how we perceive offenders, their value system, their character, and why they exploit others and organizations for their benefit (Perri et al., 2014a). Bluntly put, scholarship on white-collar crime and its offenders has been neglected, which has created and perpetuated a distorted white-collar offender profile (Goldstraw, 2005). For purposes of this book, the concept of profiling generally refers to the analysis of a person's behavioral characteristics used to determine whether they are at risk to commit a crime.

As an example, noted crime scholar James Q. Wilson—famous for the phrase 'broken windows' suggesting that public order is fragile and if proverbially the first 'broken window' is not fixed soon more windows will be broken—wrote a *Wall Street Journal* article titled, "Hard Times, Fewer Crimes" (Wilson, 2011). In this paper, Wilson states that in the U.S. violent crimes reached a forty-year low together with property-related crimes in 2010, while also commenting on non-white-collar crime victimology. However, it is ironic that white-collar crime, which is exposed almost daily within this international paper, was never mentioned by Wilson, supporting the notion that white-collar crime, its offenders, and victims are understudied. Even in criminological textbooks and criminology doctoral programs, coverage of white-collar crime is underrepresented (McGurrin et al., 2013). Moreover, this lack of research revealing the truth about these offenders influenced the criminal justice system, including prosecutorial offices and the judiciary, which at times treats white-collar crimes as less serious because a victim may not be as obvious when contrasted to a victim of violence. There is a subtle implication that either no one feels the injury or that the injury is substantially more indirect, intangible, and spread out over a large number of people, as opposed to the individualized, direct injury experienced in a violent crime (Gustafson, 2007). Consequently, this inaccurate, minimized degree of perceived harm suffered by victims of white-collar crimes appears insignificant when compared to the harms suffered by victims of street crimes, the largely accepted conventional construction of crime in the public conscious (Croall, 2007a). The perceived faceless quality of this offense is perpetuated by the fact that victimology scholarship often did not include white-collar crime victims in their surveys.

The lack of rigorous criminological and behavioral scholarship on refining the white-collar offender profile enhanced the misperception that these offenders are somehow less criminally inclined to exploit others and organizations when compared to non-white-collar offenders who are more likely to be perceived as predators. Typically, white-collar offenders are perceived as engaging in fraud because they are responding to some kind of pressure such as too much debt or a need to help an organization get through a difficult financial period rather than engaging in this offense in a predatory, planned manner. People can relate to these pressures because they can plausibly see themselves committing fraud if they were in the offender's situation. Generally, law abiding citizens have a more difficult time relating to criminals who exploit the weak, or children as examples. Thus, even if the end result of their offense is financially devastating to a large number of people, the misconduct can be rationalized away, where there is never an acceptable, digestible reason to exploit children. Although limited there is quality scholarship on white-collar crime and its offenders, much of the scholarship is either inaccurate, incomplete, or non-existent which contributes to the perception that these offenders display something other than criminality even though the evidence suggests otherwise. White-collar offenders display criminal attributes that are no different than non-white-collar criminals. They simply manifest their aggression against others in a different form to satisfy their motives by relying on their own particular rationalizations while creating victims nonetheless.

Moreover, white-collar offenders may not display criminality in ways easily recognized by the general public, but this does not mean they do not harbor criminal thinking patterns that facilitate offender decision making. Just as criminal thinking patterns are applied to non-white-collar offenders, their application to white collar offenders explaining why they are at risk for offending is a logical extension, but one that has been woefully ignored to our detriment. Unfortunately, the diminished application of criminological insights to these offenders prolonged the myth that somehow these offenses are described as "out of character." Without an adequate framework to understand these offenders and the risk factors that facilitate white-collar offending, antifraud professionals, including the judicial system, erroneously ascribed inaccurate character traits to them. This factor can impact professional skepticism inherent in audits, how these offenders' impact organizations especially those in leadership positions, how they are punished, fraud investigation protocol, and academia's description of the white-collar offender profile.

In this chapter, common misperceptions of the white-collar offender profile are challenged by providing a framework of how they, in fact, think no differently than non-white-collar criminals who seek out exploitable opportunities. In addition, it is equally important to understand their antisocial interpersonal strategies, specifically how they interact with others to gain advantages over them. This is especially critical when exploring the interpersonal strategies used by corrupt corporate leadership. Furthermore, we examine the contributions and limitations of Edwin Sutherland's scholarship, how to think about white-collar crime as a criminological discipline, together with exploring the different rationalizations offenders use to morally distance themselves from their conduct. Also, we address the application of the psychological concept known as projection bias to advance a plausible partial explanation as to why white-collar criminals appear to represent a different type of offender in terms of the implied credibility they receive together with character attributes assigned to this offender group. For example, both academia and antifraud professionals project their values onto these offenders which facilitate the creation and perpetuation of the myth of what these offenders erroneously represent. Examining this question is pivotal to addressing why antifraud practitioners and scholars, at times, are unable to fully appreciate the character of those encountered on a daily basis given the billions of dollars lost to fraudulent behaviors as well as their violent impulses. For example, so often fraud offenders are deemed non-violent because the white-collar classification is described as non-violent, yet as we shall study in great depth, white-collar offenders are equally capable of resorting to violence as a solution to a perceived problem.

Lastly, we explore offender motives and their worldviews which influence their decision to engage in white-collar crime together with debunking the myth that this crime classification represents a homogenous offender group in terms of the extent of their deviancy. These offenders are not homogenous in their methods of offending, the extent of their exploitation, or the victims they prey upon just as non-white-collar offenders are not homogenous in terms of the above characteristics. White-collar offenders come in different flavors no differently than non-white-collar offenders. Some white-collar offenders are predatory in their exploitations of who they target no differently than sexual predators are in terms of who they target. Some street-level offenders specialize in narcotics distribution while some white-collar offenders specialize in securities fraud. Regardless of the crime classification, we observe similarities in how offenders think about exploitable opportunities.

Edwin Sutherland and White-collar Crime

It would be difficult to write about white-collar crime without bringing scholar Edwin Sutherland into the conversation because his seminal work on white-collar crime influenced criminological research in the twentieth century and beyond. By focusing on white-collar crime, Sutherland "altered the study of crime throughout the world in fundamental ways by focusing attention upon a form of lawbreaking that had previously been ignored by criminological scholars" (Lilly et al., 2011, p. 277). Recall, however, that prior to Sutherland, many other writers referred to predatory fraud offenders who take victims' money through stock-swindling and fraudulent brokerage practices as "white-collar bandits" (Van Slyke et al., 2016, p. 27). Although Sutherland was not the first to comment and publish on issues surrounding white-collar crime, he "was the one that put the concept front and center in the world of social science" through the media and professional attention he received (Schoepfer & Tibbetts, 2012, p. 68). As a pioneer in the field, Sutherland "wished to debunk the myth" and challenge biases that criminality was reserved for those from the lower rungs of society, maintaining that educated, socioeconomically well-off individuals also engaged in crime (Lilly et al., 2011, p. 274). It was Sutherland's view that white-collar offenders display motives and rationalizations to morally distant themselves from criminal acts that may be different from those offered by conventional street-level criminals.

As a result, professional, educated, and affluent people who commit serious crimes against society should not be immune from criminological study due to their more advantageous socioeconomic status or because bias blinds us from seeing them for who they are. Sutherland was able to debunk "misleading and incorrect" perceptions of white-collar offenders by discarding accepted notions of what these offenders represent in terms of harboring criminal mindsets (Soltes, 2016, p. 17). Sutherland was inspired, in part, to study educated, economically well-off people engaging in professional misconduct by reading Edward A. Ross's book *Sin and Society* (1907), where he came across the concept of the "criminaloid" which describes individuals from the upper-echelons of society who participates in illicit schemes causing harm to others (Soltes, 2016, p. 19). Ross was one of the first to voice his concern in a compelling manner warning that the United States was experiencing a lag in public reaction to threats posed by emerging industrial societies pertaining to white-collar offenses and laws needed to address such threats (Ross, 1907). Thus, many of the problems observable today such as corruption in business practices, deceptions in financial information, and distribution of products that are harmful to the public, to name a few, were also prevalent over a hundred years ago when Ross wrote about his observations. Consequently, the lag in time between recognizing the threat and doing something about it allowed offenders to escape accountability.

At the same time Ross observed that these offenders give the impression that they are respectable members of society, and avoided the label of criminal because they were not prosecuted as vigorously or punished in proportion to the harm caused (Soltes, 2016). These offenders may have been guilty in the eyes of the law, but since they are not as culpable in the eyes of the public, they were not considered capable of harboring a criminal nature like the stereotypical street-level offender. Ross further recognized that while the law may make their misdeeds crimes, as long as the public notion of morality does not condemn their behaviors as they would other types of criminal conduct, they escape both punishment and public disapproval. In essence, according to Ross, the real weakness was in the public's attitude toward these types of offenders that has yet to attach a harsh disapproval of their conduct (Ross, 1907). For example, there is generally a harsh societal disapproval of homicide or sexual assault believing it is morally wrong to engage in such behavior. Yet this type of definitive societal disapproval of white-collar crime as contrasted with these other crimes is not as solidified in the public's moral conscience. Moreover, Ross went on to observe that we are not always aware of white-collar victimization because such criminal acts are committed in secret, and cloaked in respectability by hiding behind a veneer of virtue even though the damage to society can be on a large scale (Ross, 1907).

In building on Ross's insights and considering the trillions of dollars lost to white-collar crime, Sutherland recognized early on that white-collar offenders, "are by far the most dangerous to society of any type of criminals from the point of view of effects on private property and social institutions" (Sutherland, 1934, p. 32). Consider the comments of a reviewer on Sutherland's ground-breaking 1949 book titled *White-collar Crime* supporting Sutherland's insight noting that, "institutional crimes can never have the emotional impact of personal crimes, though the former may be just as—or more—reprehensible and injurious to society" (Soltes, 2016, p. 24). Sutherland accurately observed that companies are effectively organized to engage in crime if they so choose to exploit opportunities for financial gain under the veil of corporate secrecy while employing their own particular rationalizations to justify their illegal behaviors (Sutherland, 1949). As a result of being able to operate in secrecy, the general public is not particularly sensitized to white-collar crime or its prevention further observing, "white-collar crimes continue because of this lack of organization on the part of the public" to act as a countermeasure to these offenders' agendas (Sutherland, 1983, p. 257).

Because the general public is not well-organized to challenge white-collar crime at the corporate level, it is not in a favorable position to counter management's illegal actions before they occur or the culture of crime they encourage both implicitly by organizational norms and explicitly through direct orders from corporate leadership. This is due to an imbalance of insider management information who know the risk factors triggering misconduct versus insignificant public knowledge of corrupt management actions until scandals erupt and actually harms the public forcing government to investigate the misconduct after the fact. Except for a few scholars such as Sutherland whose career spanned mostly from the 1920s through the 1940s, corporate misconduct was overlooked by criminologists and those in the legal profession as a topic worth studying. Because of the perception that corporate misconduct in general was not injurious to others, coupled with the fact that corporate misconduct was not regulated, this further perpetuated the belief that if there is no regulation to mitigate the harms of corporate deviance, then there is no harm (Soltes, 2016). Moreover, except for a few regulations prohibiting the sale of adulterated products and laws regulating competition and the sale of securities, the federal government left it up to the individual states to enact their own regulations to protect consumers and investors.

There appeared to be wide-spread acceptance of the view that the public is indifferent to or ambivalent about business crimes, in general, and thus lack sufficient moral outrage to organize and counter corporate misconduct (Cullen et al., 2008). Following the second world war of the 1940s and into the 1950s, the public was not as concerned with corporate deviance as they were following the stock market crash of 1929 and the economic depression that followed in the 1930s which impacted millions of lives (Soltes, 2016). In fact, surveys conducted during the 1950s reflect indifference to corporate deviance. For example, participants of a 1958 survey condemned a firm for not paying respectable wages more harshly than they did others who committed white-collar crime (Soltes, 2016). When summarizing the public's views on white-collar crime, an academician suggested survey respondents in 1958 were less concerned about the moral consequences of another's behavior, than "if what is offered can be sold at a profit, then it is legitimate" (Soltes, 2016, p. 25). Corporate practices deplorable to Sutherland were not necessarily deplorable to others; at times the public "even sympathizes with offenders when they have been caught" (Soltes, 2016, p. 30).

Corporate misconduct was simply tolerated and not a public priority coupled with the fact that white-collar crime lacked the sensational appeal that made front-page news. This was due to a lack of technical knowledge journalists needed to write about the complexities of white-collar litigation (Soltes, 2016). Writing about street-level offenses is simply easier since more can identify and empathize with victims quicker than they could understand the complexities of accounting fraud, for example, or its impact to society. In addition, from a law enforcement perspective, the general unwritten policy until a few decades ago was not to prosecute lawyers, accountants, and executives on the grounds that they are valuable members of society. To prosecute them was considered too harsh coupled with the fact that law enforcement and academia did not consider white-collar crimes, such as financial statement fraud, a crime in the same category of seriousness as non-white-collar crime. Although white-collar crime might be thought of as a legal category, for the most part it is neither a legal category nor a specific offense unless law makers explicitly outline what types of crimes are considered white-collar. There is no discrete group of offenses which can readily be identified as white-collar crime because it is more of a symbolic term used to differentiate crimes that are not of the traditional street-level variety.

Further there are socioeconomic disparities, and differences in how the crimes are committed (Freiberg, 2000). Yet, the fact that white-collar offenders may not share similar socioeconomic traits with street-level offenders is irrelevant; it is the thinking behind their conduct that determines the pervasiveness of their antisocial and criminal mindset they rely on to justify exploiting people, organizations, or both (Perri et al., 2014a). As it currently stands, at least within the academic community, there will be no agreement as to a precise definition of what white-collar crime means, but the term should be preserved in light of its powerful cultural impact (Green, 2007). Thus, those seeking a single, universal, and easily applied definition of white-collar crime will be disappointed. White-collar crime today can only be defined as a practical term, "a speculative formulation serving as a guide in the investigation…of a problem, or an 'umbrella' term, a broad term encompassing a wide range of different activities" (Rorie, 2020, p. 17). The "premise here is that at this late stage in the history of the term white-collar crime, it is thoroughly unrealistic and accordingly dysfunctional to imagine that one can insist on a sharply drawn and widely acceptable definition of such crime" (p. 17).

Conceptual ambiguity exists because white-collar crime is a loosely-defined term with many interpretations which makes it difficult to empirically measure. As stated by one scholar in a similar forum, "If we can't define it, we can't measure it; if we can't measure it, we can't explain it" (Schoepfer & Tibbetts, 2012, p. 80). The consequence of this inability to engage in empirical measurement due to definitional imprecision gives rise to legal ambiguity in that we are not sure what acts are in fact crimes versus acts that are simply deviant from a social science perspective (Payne, 2013). If the concept of white-collar crime is to maintain relevancy to legal and social science communities, then there must be a trade off from accepting definitional ambiguity of what the term white-collar crime actually means. Thus, there will be no particular viewpoint as to the "right" white-collar crime definition, only the definition that is right for the purpose intended by the person employing it (Green,

2007). It is, however, vital to understand what the term means to the person who is using it in order to understand what they are actually saying because the definition impacts what questions are asked, what kinds of answers are meaningful, and where researchers look for answers. The definition of white-collar crime is and will continue to be controversial due to disputes on whether the term ought to be defined on the basis of the nature of the offense itself or on the socioeconomic characteristics of the offender. That said, white-collar crime can be defined in many ways, and it is appropriate to do so (Croall, 2001).

As a result, there are advantages and disadvantages to using offender-based versus offense-based definitions. However, the fact that there are advantages and disadvantages to examining white-collar crime from different viewpoints should not be a reason to become bogged down in definitional sparring when we can contemporaneously consider both approaches without sacrificing much needed scholarship. Sutherland defined white-collar crime by invoking the social status of the offender as "a crime committed by a person of respectability and high socioeconomic status in the course of their occupation" (Sutherland, 1983, p. 7). The disadvantage with Sutherland's definition of white-collar crime is that invoking the socioeconomic status of the offender makes it difficult to apply. For example, who qualifies as being from the upper echelons of society? How much money does one need to earn to be considered eligible for white-collar classification? Inserting the condition that white-collar crimes must have been perpetrated by someone with high social status is too difficult a condition to meet. There would be no agreement as to what conditions should be required in order for someone to be labeled as having a high socioeconomic status. When Sutherland was asked to elaborate on the characteristics of white-collar offenders, he responded, "he was not sure" (Perri et al., 2014, p. 79).

For purposes of this book, the author does not adopt the narrower profile of white-collar offenders that Sutherland referred to decades ago because current criminological research does not support this sociological position when in fact offenders from different class stratifications, such as the middle class, engage in white-collar crime (Weisburd et al., 2001). However, this does not mean the socioeconomic aspects of an offender are not important because this book is about understanding the different types of white-collar offenders. In fact, Sutherland was correct in singling out the high socioeconomic status of some offenders worthy of studying given the enormous damage they are capable of exacting on organizations especially when they are in corporate leadership positions. In addition, by studying the offender, we tend to increase the likelihood for finding patterns of behavioral risk factors that increase the probability that an offender would engage in white-collar crime (Benson & Manchak, 2014). By understanding these risk factors, we can begin constructing a more precise white-collar offender profile(s) that may help organizations identify individuals by the behaviors they exhibit to determine if they are at risk for engaging in fraud and help law enforcement with the investigation of such offenders. Moreover, law enforcement communities, including prosecutorial offices, tend to refer to white-collar crimes as financial or economic crimes and do not define white-collar crime from the perspective of the socioeconomic status of the offender no more than they would define a homicide by that criteria. As a result, there is no advocacy for any particular interpretation of the term, thus the term white-collar crime is used in the widest possible sense so as not to exclude any of the various disciplines from the discussion.

That being said, legal circles generally view white-collar crime as illegal acts perpetrated by an individual, organization, or both which are characterized by deceit, concealment, or violation of trust for financial gain and which are not dependent upon the application or threat of physical force or violence (Van Slyke et al., 2016). Individuals and organizations commit these acts to obtain money, property, or services, to avoid the payment or loss of money or services, or to secure personal or business advantage (Edelhetz, 1970). White-collar crime is better thought of as having a family of characteristics or traits, rather than as a single definition with inflexible conditions (Green, 2007). The term white-collar crime should display an "umbrella-like" quality in that it can encompass different types of crimes and deviant acts that are not only criminal in nature but might have financial penalties attached to them—such as regulatory infractions—because they display a deceptive quality of trying to circumvent laws, rules, and regulations. There are some who believe the definition should take into account environmental harms, unsafe working conditions, and dangerous consumer products. For example, Sutherland not only considered crime as we know it, where there is punishment for breaking the law, he also looked at regulatory infractions, unfair labor practices, violations of patents, and misbranding of foods and drugs (Green, 2007). Let us explore another crime classification that has an umbrella-like quality even though it displays more definitional clarity.

Although making the analogy of white-collar crime to homicide is not perfect, it helps to illustrate the point being made. Homicide is generally defined as the unjustifiable killing of another person. While homicides come in many different forms, they all fall under the umbrella of the homicide concept. Thus there are homicides referred to as parricides, felony murder, second-degree murder, reckless homicide, and infanticide, to name a few. They are different because the factual characteristics of the murders are different. Some entail a child killing a parent which is a parricide or a parent killing a child which is infanticide. Felony murder is a murder committed during the commission of a felony, such as a bank robbery. In this case, while in the process of committing a felony, which is the robbery, for example, a teller is killed because he or she refused to give the robbers money when demanded. These murders are factually technically different, yet what they have in common is the fact that there is a dead body that would not have been dead but for the unjustifiable act of killing a person. Analogously, we should look for common traits that fit into a category labeled white-collar crime. The term white-collar crime should be understood to refer to a loosely-defined collection of criminal offenses, various forms of deviance, different kinds of offenders, and ethical and legal concepts that share a series of similarities and relationships (Green, 2007). What we mean by ethical and legal concepts is the blameworthiness of the act in terms of whether the criminal state of mind required to prosecute an offender includes evidence of 1) intent and knowledge of the act, 2) the degree of harmfulness of the act, 3) the risks inherent in the act, and 4) is there a sense that societal moral norms have been violated, such as trust, and legal requirements, such as fiduciary duties to the corporation and shareholders (Green, 2007).

By examining some of these conditions, we can determine whether certain acts should be included under the umbrella of white-collar crime and whether a particular offense resembles other offenses within a given category. For example, the exploitation of trust is seen as a distinctive feature of white-collar crime taking the form of 1) abuse of a professional position of authority, 2) by use of specialized knowledge obtained from employment to facilitate particular types of crime, and 3) defrauding the public or an employer (Freiberg, 2000). Generally, the exploitation of trust is not part of a street-level offense such as participating in a robbery of another person whom the offender does not typically even know. A legal approach offers some advantages because it provides a more precise standardized working definition encompassing a large array of frauds to obtain property and financial gain through deception and misrepresentation involving antitrust violations, securities fraud, occupational fraud, bribery, kickbacks, tax fraud, extortion, trade-secret thefts, and bank fraud (Brody & Kiehl, 2010). Legal definitions must be more precise because under most societal jurisdictions, a criminal code has to tell citizens what is and is not considered illegal so they can adjust behavior according to what is allowed under the law.

In addition, white-collar crime should include those illegal or unethical acts that violate fiduciary responsibility of public trust committed by an individual and/or organization, usually during the course of legitimate occupational activity for personal and/or organizational gain (Hasnas, 2005). Furthermore, white-collar crime is considered a broad category that includes high-level corporate misconduct, occupational fraud schemes by ordinary citizens as well as predatory, solo offenders who may or may not belong to an organization (Perri, 2011a). Some white-collar crimes are business crimes in that they are committed to further business interests, and financial scams such as Ponzi schemes perpetrated by predatory fraud offenders whose occupation it is to engage in white-collar crimes by exploiting others, especially their trust for financial gain (Simpson, 2013). Practically, because people have rather informal interpretations of the term, white-collar crime can refer to financial crimes, corporate malfeasance, crimes committed by organized crime that include money laundering and financial crimes committed by terrorist organizations funding their operations (Cliff & Desilets, 2014).

Also, the definition may include not only more traditional forms of white-collar crime that take place within an organization by those who may be perceived to be in a position of trust regardless of their employment title, but it also may include someone such as a high-level executive who has the power to commit fraud due to their position of authority (Shover & Hochstetler, 2006). Credit card, Internet, and telemarketing fraud are examples of white-collar crimes that might be committed by individuals other than corporate executives who may not have been the type of offender Sutherland profiled as his prototypical white-collar offender. Consider that some of these frauds do not necessarily take place within an organizational setting, and practically some of these frauds did not exist at the time Sutherland lectured on the white-collar crime concept. Thus, it is sufficient to say that white-collar criminals come from different socioeconomic strata, and their deceptions for financial gain are perpetrated in infinite fraud schemes that may or may not be perpetrated at the organizational level (Perri, 2011a). Moreover, the term "fraud" is used interchangeably with the term white-collar crime because when people think of the term fraud, they conceptualize it by some type of deception for monetary gain that is also reflective of the common use of the term white-collar crime.

Thus for flexibility, the term fraud and white-collar crime are used interchangeably, yet like the term white-collar crime, the use of the term fraud is both widespread and at times unclear (Green & Kugler, 2012). Fraud is a generic term embracing every conniving means by which human ingenuity can devise ways to take advantage of others by false representations including trickery, being cunning, and other unfair ways by which people can be cheated (Albrecht et al., 2012). At its core, fraud consists of the misappropriation of money or property by means of deceit, which involve violations of standards, rules and laws, while unethical behavior also includes violations of informal and implicit norms, such as the reciprocity of being trustworthy (Den Nieuwenboer & Kaptein 2008). Financial statement fraud, which is under the white-collar crime umbrella, is defined as a deliberate misrepresentation, misstatement or omission of financial statement data for the purpose of misleading the reader and creating a false impression of an organization's financial strength. Fraud is also often defined more broadly to include, 1) acts aimed at objects other than the misappropriation of property such as the deprivation of honest services, obstruction of government functions, and obtaining unjust advantage, and 2) acts committed by means other than deception such as breach of trust, conflicts of interest, and exploitation.

Projection Bias and the Distortion of the White-collar Criminal Profile

The great enemy of the truth is very often not the lie—deliberate, contrived and dishonest—but the myth, persistent, persuasive and unrealistic.

President John F. Kennedy

As a result of the many lost decades where we failed to refine the white-collar offender profile, antifraud professionals, including academicians, lack a more well-rounded framework to conceptualize criminal thought patterns and behavioral traits that facilitate offending. Consequently the void created due to a lack of a framework has been filled with erroneous, unsupported character and criminological assumptions, often shaped by personal biases about how this offender class is perceived (Perri et al., 2014a). Biases expose our preferences which can influence how we want to think about criminality, which further exacerbates our misunderstanding of criminality in general. This misunderstanding of fraud offenders further expose us and organizations to the risk of financial exploitations, and at times, violence. Bias about our perceptions concerning criminality and offenders persists because it feeds into and reinforces our belief system even if it is not fact-based. Bias invites misinterpretations about offender profiles that are not grounded in thoughtful analysis, but reflect what we wish these offenders represent or do not represent (Brody et al., 2012). We end up attaching character traits of goodness to an offender class that are based on speculation. Often academicians, and those in the criminal justice system, such as judges who sentence these offenders, refer to them as "good people who did a bad thing."

Consider that it is not uncommon for rapists, killers, drug dealers, and a variety of other offenders to proclaim their "goodness," because their actions were "out of character"—they were simply honest mistakes. Analogously, it would not be surprising if some who know terrorists proclaim their goodness because the terrorist loves their families despite the harm they cause with ease and without remorse. Would we characterize these people as "good people who did a bad thing"? If the answer is no, why do we have a need to extend this courtesy to fraud offenders who can inflict harm on others, albeit in a different form? The issue is not one of being overly critical of any particular offender, in this case fraud offenders, but questioning whether we create a distorted view of them by attributing qualities of goodness that is unwarranted. Often, we jump to conclusions about a person's underlying character and fail to sufficiently correct our beliefs by adjusting to the situation at hand, relying heavily instead on overly simplistic notions of "good" or "bad" character—both in our efforts to explain past and predict future behavior (Kim, 2005, p. 996). White-collar crime scholars struggle to understand why "good people do dirty work," or why what appear to be upstanding members of the business community resort to crime (Apel & Paternoster, 2009).

For example, in the Center for Audit Quality's paper titled *Deterring and Detecting Financial Reporting Fraud*, the authors' state that "even under extreme pressure, only a small percentage of senior management actually commits fraud…Why and how do good people start down the slippery slope to fraud" (CAQ, 2010, p. 5)? One report titled *Who Is the Typical Fraudster?* states, "the fraudster is deemed a very smart, hardworking, and honest employee" (KPMG, 2011a, p. 14). This statement is rather ironic in that if these employees were so honest, why are they committing fraud? One accounting academician who interviewed fraud offenders stated, "they are just ordinary people who made mistakes" (Goodman, 2010). This academician went on to assert "your idea of what you think a white-collar felon is, really isn't reality…most of the people I interview are really nice, everyday people. They could be anyone walking down the street" (Weigel, 2013).

Consider that narcotics dealers, arsonists, and rapists who have not been apprehended come across as charming, nice everyday people walking amongst us. Should our perception of what they actually represent be different because they come across as something other than a felon? We are reminded of the observations of a criminal psychologist with decades of experience in evaluating criminals who stated, "I've interviewed serial killers who, despite leaving dead bodies in their own view, say they are good people" (Samenow, 2009). Even forensic accounting and fraud examination textbooks perpetuate stereotypes which students internalize. This exacerbates the problem of not learning a more accurate profile of fraud offenders. Prolonged and entrenched misperceptions potentially impact how students think about and apply professional skepticism, especially in audits, and how they approach interviewing fraud suspects. For example, as the statement below referenced in a textbook illustrates, fraud offending is described, albeit erroneously, as reflecting an accidental quality:

> The common fraudster is depicted with the following characteristics: first time offender, middle-aged, male, well educated, married with children, trusted employee, in a position of responsibility, and possibly considered a "good citizen" through works in the community, or through a church organization. This individual is often described as having some non-shareable problems, typically financial in nature or that the problem can only be solved with money, which creates the perceived pressure. When aligned with opportunity and the ability to rationalize his other actions, the otherwise good citizen succumbs to pressure, develops one or more schemes, and misappropriates assets or commits an act involving some form of corruption. This person might be characterized as the "accidental fraudster". Notwithstanding the fraud act, the accidental fraudster is considered a good, law abiding person, who under normal circumstances would never consider theft, breaking important laws, or harming others. When discovered, family members, fellow employees, and other persons in the community are often surprised or even shocked by the alleged behavior of the perpetrator (Kranacher et al., 2011, p. 86).

The first error made in terming these offenders as "accidental" is that it contradicts the criminal liability these offenders face when breaking laws; "there is no such thing as accidental fraud or crime" (Albrecht et al., 2012, p. 307). One cannot be an accidental fraud offender and at the same time be criminally liable. An accident is when we do something in a negligent manner by not exercising the type of care that one would use in a given situation. For example, driving through a red light traffic signal because one did not pay attention to the signal and getting into a car crash is an accident. Would we describe a drug dealer selling narcotics to children as an "accidental drug dealer"? Is it not plausible that a drug dealer would know that it is easier to exploit the naiveté and weaknesses of a child's age to sell their product to get them addicted at an earlier age? Do not offenders deliberately look for weaknesses in an organization's internal controls to exploit for their financial gain?

Seeking out exploitable opportunities does not reflect an accidental quality. When we understand that part of the problem lies in studying fraud offenders in isolation from what criminality actually entails, it is not surprising that academia, the judicial system, and antifraud professionals advance, at times, an erroneous or incomplete description of these offenders. Those who are not exposed to real-life situations, such as interfacing with criminals on a daily basis, rely on their bias, most likely subconsciously, to build a homogenous image of what white-collar offender represent to them that does not reflect reality (Brody et al., 2012). They study fraud offenders from a distance which results in the creation of offender profiles that are sterile, abstract, inaccurate, and incomplete; they lack a sense of how fraud offenders actually operate. Consider the unsupported assumptions of an academician trying to explain that somehow there is an accidental, unintentional quality to the offender's fraudulent behaviors, "With few exceptions, no one leaves a leading business school or embarks on a new career with the aspiration of doing harm. And after becoming wealthy, most successful executives don't set out to engage in fraud" (Soltes, 2016, p. 9).

If the above statement above were true, why do so many wealthy executives go to prison for fraud when they had everything to lose by engaging in it? What are the few exceptions we are talking about? Why is it not possible that someone went to a leading business school with criminal inclinations already intact, but is simply waiting for an exploitable opportunity to present itself? In addition, why is there the assumption that executives became wealthy through legitimate means? Is it not possible that they started out acquiring wealth fraudulently and subsequently were caught? Alternatively, could they not have started out as a legitimate business, but engaged in financial statement fraud to enhance their wealth? Many drug dealers may start out poor, but end up with incredible wealth until their drug dealing scheme is detected, dismantled, and prosecuted. Fraud offenders appear to be granted an implied credibility as to how they are characterized because of the belief that it is not their natural, initial inclination to engage in crime because they do not resemble the street-level offenders most people equate with criminality. Perhaps a more accurate description than "accidental fraud offender" is the "unexpected fraud offender" label to describe those who present themselves in ways others would normally not equate with criminality due to an appearance of respectability (Perri, 2016, p. 64). Fortunately scholars, especially in the accounting field, are beginning to challenge vague, unsupported application of offender character traits perpetuated in academic and practitioner circles that advance offender profiles that are inaccurate, stating:

[T]here are those who may know offenders who have committed horrific homicides, sexual assaults, etc., and yet they indicate what a good person the offender is by pointing to admirable deeds they may have done. Would we attribute "good virtue" to an individual who preys on the weak such as children or the elderly in a violent manner? Why do we as a profession have a need to attribute good virtue to fraud offenders when whether they are good or not is irrelevant as to whether a crime was committed? Is it because we believe, albeit erroneously, that fraud offenders' may not have the typical negative behavioral, exploitative, disposition of conventional criminals that many cannot relate to? Or is it that fraud offenders have behavioral qualities, which we can relate to, that is admirable? Do we have a need to reduce our own anxiety made possible through projection bias, by diluting the negative behavioral traits about those that we are familiar with and similar to (Brody et al., 2012, p. 519)?

What is a plausible explanation for the disconnect between how we perceive these offenders and what they represent from a criminological perspective? A partial explanation is that professionals engage in the psychological concept of projection bias to fill the void that is created when a behavioral and criminological framework does not exist to understand this offender profile in a more holistic and accurate manner (Perri et al., 2014). Projection bias is a "psychological defense mechanism to reduce personal anxiety where an individual transfers their own attributes, thoughts, feelings, and emotions, usually to other people, given a set of circumstances" (Perri, 2016, p. 65). It is the tendency to assume that others share similar values, beliefs, or thoughts as your own when there may not be a competing framework to offer more accurate information to neutralize these erroneous assumptions about others. At times, people wrongly assume that others are incapable of antisocial behaviors because they themselves would not engage in some type of misconduct. This explains why we may be shocked when we learn that someone we know has committed a serious crime, be it white-collar or some other crime classification. What enhances the impact of relying on projection bias? Research suggests the more similar in various characteristics others are when compared to ourselves, the more we tend to believe that a person harbors a value system similar to our own (Burgoon et al., 2002).

For example, another person may be perceived as more trustworthy even though there is no evidence that similarity of characteristics, such as being educated, is a guarantee of parallel values (Burgoon et al., 2002). As a result, it may be surprising to learn that individuals who may look like us, have the same level of education, share the same sense of civic pride, attend the same religious gatherings, or that are considered trustworthy employees can behave dishonestly. Furthermore, academicians, criminal justice, and legal professionals, and at times the general public, engage in projection bias by thinking about how they would behave in a given situation and why they would not engage in white-collar crime as a solution to a problem but for some perceived pressure to do so. There is a bias that these offenders do not set out to commit fraud, but are somehow forced to in order to survive, thus they do not reflect what real criminality is about. Some scholars project their bias when they believe publicity about corporate criminal behavior serves as a deterrent to engage in fraud because, 1) executives do not want to embarrass themselves and their families, 2) they fear exposure and public shame, 3) they fear criminal and civil liability, and 4) they believe partaking in fraud will reduce the chances for legitimate advancement (Barnard, 1999). Consider this unsupported insight:

> For these individuals, in the rational weighing of the costs and benefits of crime, loss of respect weighs more heavily…than formal punishment. This is why shaming rituals, such as the corporate icon proceeding or the directors' woodshed proceeding, are likely to be effective. High status business leaders may be especially susceptible to shaming rituals. They are the people most likely to worry about public appearances, to be vulnerable to moralistic or judgmental social groups, to defer to authority and to be relatively conventional in attitudes toward law and order. They are people most likely to be concerned about maintaining the appearance of business competence and professional accomplishment. Consider, for example, a corporate executive who is deciding whether to bribe a public official or to dump toxic wastes. They might not care that much about what an auto mechanic in a remote part of town will think of them than if they're caught and word of their offense is broadcast to the community at large. But they probably care a lot about how their family, their colleagues, their firm's customers, their neighbors, and even the members of their health club feel about their actions (Barnard, 1999, p. 967).

There is an implied class bias in the above statement that these offenders have more to lose than an uneducated street-level offender, thus they are more inclined to be deterred from engaging in white-collar crime. If this insight were true, how is it possible that we experience financial losses in the billions of dollars that dwarf street-level losses if executives were so concerned about the public shame they would experience if they were caught? Where is the evidence that the risk of public exposure dampens executive motivations to engage in white-collar crime? Yet if this is the position we care to adopt, then it is reasonable to believe that misconduct should be low, but this is not the case as evidenced by the billions of dollars in fraud that occurs within organizations alone (Palmer, 2012). There exists a bias, whether conscious or not, that there is something inherently different about the white-collar offender profile prompting a different analysis than non-white-collar offenders instead of examining the similarities in their criminal attitudes (Brody et al., 2012). In some respects, part of the dynamic relies on debunking the perception that because white-collar offenders do not harbor the same optics of criminality associated with street-level criminals, then one does not adopt criminal attitudes as their own (Kanazawa, 2011). As Sutherland observed, the general public "does not think of the businessman as a criminal" because the person "does not fit the stereotype of the criminal" (Sutherland, 1983, p. 232).

Moreover, he warned of being seduced by offender appearances and attributing a value system to white-collar offenders based on some of the descriptions above such as being educated, appearing respectable, and generally being law abiding in other aspects of their life (Lilly et al., 2011). For some, the image white-collar offenders present relies on the optics of criminality as opposed to the personality of the offender, how they think

26

of exploitable opportunities, and what they actually ending up doing that is unethical and at worse criminal. Relying on the optics of criminality means people's perception of what is criminal is defined not necessarily only by a person's conduct, but also by their socioeconomic factors, such as educational level, physical appearances, employment status, social status, income level, citizenship, work histories, criminal histories, and charitable endeavors, to name a few. In essence, criminality is not just defined by the criminal act itself, but one has to display characteristics that are outside of the act itself to harbor an authentic criminal mindset. This insight parallels scholarship findings where white-collar and street-level offenders were "drawn from distinctly different sectors of the American population such as age, race, education levels, and gender" reinforcing stereotypes of what criminality should look like and not on the similarities of how they think of taking advantage of exploitable opportunities (Weisburd, 1991, p. 73).

Even white-collar offenders have bought into the myth that they are different because they do not resemble the typical street-level offender despite the fact that they caused serious harm to victims who have been deprived of their property. Consider one convicted white-collar offender's statement to a sentencing judge on how they perceive themselves to be different because of the optics attributed to criminality, "I have been sitting in jail now for two months and have experienced living in a cell with a poor ignorant illegal alien, a career criminal, a drug user and smuggler, and a killer…I can tell you without hesitation I am not at all similar. I don't look the same, talk the same, act the same, or feel the same" (Hare, 1999, p. 122). Another fraud offender, appealing to the optics of criminality to differentiate herself from other non-white-collar offenders stated, "I'm not tattooed and pierced" (Goodman, 2010). Securities fraud offender Justin Paperny considered himself different from other types of non-white collar offenders when he was in prison stating, "I felt different from most of the men around me. I could not relate to them. My background was too different. They had tattoos, meth teeth, and they could hardly string together two grammatically correct sentences. We think our education and background separates us from the other criminals around us" (Perri et al., 2014, p. 39).

Although those of the upper echelons of society and what is referred to as the "middle class" may not resemble the convicted criminals we are accustomed to equating with criminality because they are educated, their social class modifies the characteristics of the type of crime they engage. This is because white-collar crime compared to non-white-collar crime is less coarse, less dirty, and violent, but nonetheless more manipulative and indifferent to the impact they have on others especially since many offenders may not even believe they hurt anyone (Henderson, 1901, p. 250). Sutherland recognized the same flawed character assumptions the general public made about fraud offenders are reflected in the criminal justice system. Judges might "empathize with white-collar offenders at times" which explains why they are not punished in proportion to their misconduct and the resulting harm (Wang & Cheng, 2016, p. 545). For example, Sutherland illustrates this observation by citing comments made to convicted white-collar offenders by a sentencing judge who stated, "You are men of affairs, of experience, of refinement and culture, of excellent reputation and standing in the business and social world" (Sutherland, 1949, p. 8). Ostensibly, class bias is reflected in the above statement when commenting on the type of traits the defendants apparently possess implying they fail to fit the stereotypical image of a street-level criminal.

This class bias impacts what punishments are imposed which often results in making it difficult to sanction those who appear to share the same social class and assume to share the same values with those who enforce the law such as the judiciary (Rackmill, 1992). For example, one sentencing judge commenting on white-collar offenders questioned, "How is it possible that men who are basically moral and decent in their own families—perhaps even generous in civic and charitable contributions—are able to engage in corporate acts that have extraordinary inhumane consequences?" (Shover & Wright, 2001, p. 214). Another sentencing judge projected character traits to white-collar offenders suggesting basically they are "good people who have nevertheless done some bad things" (Haugh, 2014, p. 3145). Observe similar sentiments of a judge who sentenced CEO Michael Peppel in 2013 to seven days in jail for fraudulent financial statements, money laundering, and securities fraud which caused the business to collapse, and thirteen hundred employees to lose their jobs with investors who lost eighteen million dollars. Eventually the CEO went to prison for two years after the prosecution

27

appealed the judge's lenient sentence. However in the initial punishment of having to only serve seven days in jail, the sentencing judge justified the punishment by injecting her perception of the defendant by stating:

[t]he defendant was not just a man, but a remarkable good man (Gnau, 2013) noting that a lenient sentence was warranted because he was now "involved in a business venture that is apparently a growing success and provides a very much needed service to a large number of people...[is a] talented business man, entrepreneur...that it would be wasteful for the government to spend taxpayers' money to incarcerate someone that has the ability to create for his country and economy" (Moore et al., 2013, p. 16).

Offender Joe Collins engaged in fraud that destroyed a financial services company that incurred losses of $2.4 billion due to his misconduct. The sentencing judge believed that Collins' crimes did not truly reflect his character, and stated, "There's no doubt that, but for this matter, Mr. Collins is a certifiable saint" (Van Slyke et al., 2016, p. 662). Collins could have received a life-sentence, but instead the judge imposed a year and one day in prison. The judge sentenced CEO of General Reinsurance Corporation, Ronald Ferguson, to only two years stating, "We will never know why such a good man did such a bad thing" (Antilla, 2012). Consider the statement of fraud offender Rajat Gupta's sentencing judge where he stated, "This is a deepening mystery in my work...why do so many good people do bad things" (Soltes, 2016, p. 62). Of course the judge also referred to all the wonderful philanthropic efforts Rajat was involved in that would actually make these individuals the type that merit admiration from others despite their fraudulent behaviors.

Consequences of Projection Bias: Practical Insights

Understanding projection bias from a practical standpoint is crucial for those that are involved either directly or indirectly in fraud investigations, auditing, human resources, forensic accountants, academia, and law enforcement, to name a few. Because projection bias may distort our beliefs about a given situation, we need to ask ourselves how a distortion can impact one on a professional basis. Accountants, including auditors, are obligated to exercise due diligence which means they must approach their duties with a sense of seriousness and precision. Thus one of the requirements is to maintain a sense of professional skepticism when performing an audit, for example. If projection bias prevents an auditor from believing those whom they are auditing would not commit fraud, the commitment to due diligence is diluted and potentially compromised. In other words, engaging in projection bias unconsciously distorts our reality of who is and is not capable of engaging in fraud. Thus we might not ask pointed questions about the prevalence of fraud at an organization because of the belief that others who appear to share the same value system as ourselves would not engage in fraud. Moreover, questions evoking answers that might reveal an indicator of ongoing fraud are never asked even if our intuition may tell us that there are red-flags worthy of exploration. It is important to use one's creativity to think of areas where one's projection bias about a given topic might distort reality to their detriment. Some other areas that may be influenced by projection bias and that will be broached later on include, 1) the impact on audit risk assessments, 2) the risk of misinterpreting evidence, 3) the impact on planning an audit, 4) the risk of misinterpreting indicators to deception, 5) the impact of how crime scenes are interpreted, 6) the risk of being manipulated and, 7) the impact of how to conduct an interview and what interview strategies to employ.

Debunking the Myth of the Out of Character Offense

As a "group, white-collar offenders are not quite as upstanding and law-abiding as we had thought" (Benson & Simpson, 2009, p. 39). White collar criminals are adept at exploiting opportunities for organizational advancement as well as identifying relationships that could lead to power, success, wealth and admiration (Naso, 2012). Rarely satisfied by their achievements, they are excessively self-centered, narcissistic, willingly place their personal goals ahead of moral standards, seek power and success, and believe they are above the law as they commit crimes with impunity (Naso, 2012). It is not that white-collar offenders do not recognize ethical principles, yet they are not bound to them under certain conditions such as intense pressures to meet financial goals or in circumstances where detection is unlikely. Their value systems are situationally compromised, but not non-existent; they simply are willing to set aside their integrity when convenient to satisfy their motives. In essence, they are capable of recognizing what they are doing is wrong, but rationalize the permissibility of such an act because they are capable of displaying a value system that accommodates selective violations of moral standards. White-collar criminals, especially the predatory type, harbor a distorted attitude toward reality diminishing their obligation to others by taking refuge in their moral disengagement through rationalizations or simply being remorseless in their exploitation.

Individuals convicted of white-collar crimes might grudgingly acknowledge their antisocial behavior, but nonetheless deny criminal intent and the label of criminal. In short, unlike many street criminals, they resist ascribing a negative identity into their self-definition coupled with perceiving such a label as a personal insult. By denying the label of corrupt, such individuals avoid the adverse effects of an undesirable social identity. Yet ironically, a common perception is that white-collar crimes represent "out of character" offenses because offenders are generally educated, law abiding, employed, and exhibit ethical behavior in other facets of their lives; as a result they are perceived as being less apt to engage in crime (Brody et al., 2012). At times out of character is confused with doing something that is not within one's ordinary course of conduct. However, the fact that an offender chooses to engage in a crime that was not within their ordinary course of conduct or that the offender would have preferred an alternative path than having to resort to crime to satisfy a motive does not mean it was not within one's character (Perri et al., 2014a). Part of the difficulty in reconciling the perceptions of white-collar crime and the actual offender is that criminal thinking traits are not attributed to these offenders because their behaviors are viewed as resulting from temporary moral lapses. White-collar offenders are assumed to be one-shot offenders not likely to be processed in the criminal justice system on a repeat basis (Van Slyke et al., 2016).

Even though there has been a long tradition of scholarship dating back to Sutherland recognizing white-collar offenders as repeat offenders, the myth still exists that they are not likely to have much contact with the criminal justice system (Perri & Brody, 2013). Unlike street-level offenders who often are repeat offenders, many scholars assume that white-collar recidivism is the exception and not the norm (Shover & Wright, 2001). In addition, for laypersons not accustomed to criminality, in general, the term criminal does not simply refer to being involved in the criminal justice system, but rather evokes certain images of what criminality looks like and those who are more apt to perpetrate crime in order to preserve a certain identity of what they are not (Weisburd et al., 2001). The criminal label is intended to convey a great deal about who it is applied to together with summarizing a vast array of meaningful behaviors, lifestyles, and motives that communicate information to others. To put it bluntly, prototypical criminals are different, which is a comfortable moral position to adopt since it allows a separation of who we believe we are and are not even when committing crime, albeit fraud. Yet the error made when we adopt these positions is that it allows us to downplay our own misconduct because we can rely on a biased, predetermined image of what criminality looks like and not just the act that may rise to the level of criminality. Furthermore, by finding ways to distance ourselves from the criminal image, we are able to preserve an identity we have forged for ourselves which for many people—even those who break the law—is a portrait of an honest, law-abiding citizen.

We convince ourselves that by being a good citizen who works, pays taxes, belongs to a religious organization, and donates time and money to charities, our good qualities outweigh our bad qualities which further neutralizes the negative emotions associated with misconduct. In other words, the good we do far outweighs the bad we do, thus, on balance, we are not criminal; we do not display the criminal lifestyle to define who we are. Real criminals do not work or contribute to the good of their community; they take what they can by stealth or force. Also, they do not adhere to societal norms because if it did, they would not commit crime in the first place. The fact that one does not engage in crime on a day to day basis to support a certain lifestyle and does support societal norms does not mean that on balance one cannot engage in criminal activity. Furthermore, one's behavior of goodness does not neutralize one's antisocial behavior so that we can pretend it never happened. While some white-collar offenders may exhibit characteristics of conformity and stability that are not generally associated with criminality, there are many non-white-collar criminals who do not exhibit an overall criminal lifestyle either

29

(Shover & Wright, 2001). In essence, people get caught up in the label and image of what criminality looks like and not necessarily the underlying conduct that defines criminality and antisocial, unethical behaviors that may not technically be criminal, but can still hurt someone.

Consider that white-collar and non-white-collar criminals can have equally extensive criminal histories and exhibit the same tendency to exploit opportunities through criminal means (Shover & Wright, 2001).White-collar criminals can maintain positive attitudes towards social conformity and legality even when participating in misconduct, but believe they must do something they themselves define as wrong, as opposed to what the criminal justice system defines as wrong, in order to deal with some perceived crisis that threatens them, their families, or their companies (Shover & Wright, 2001). They acknowledge the importance of the law, but because of a perceived pressure or simply the desire to acquire more without any apparent pressure, they do not obey it. Yet "most, if not all, of us break laws, formal rules, and other social conventions at some point...most people will, under specific circumstances, allow themselves to violate norms that they accept as legitimate" (Shover & Wright, 2001, p. 148). Some scholars adopted this position as being one of situational morality or situational honesty stating:

> When faced with a moral conflict, people do not aspire to be saints but rather allow themselves a measure of deviation from what they consider proper behavior. Such deviation would not stem from a lack of knowledge or a distorted view of right behavior, nor would it stem from weakness of will or inability to resist temptation. The leeway a person gives themselves to deviate from the right course may be considered a decision guided by principal (Shover & Wright, 2001, p. 148).

From time to time, news accounts speak of regular, everyday people who unexpectedly commit hideous crimes that shock their communities including parents, spouses, relatives, friends, neighbors, work colleagues, and others who have close, even intimate relationships with people who are at a loss to understand what happened (Samenow, 2009). When they learn of the crime while watching the evening news or reading the newspaper, their first thought is that the person they know could not possibly be the perpetrator because it is totally out of character. When a particular crime is reported as being out of character, the reason given is because the perpetrator has no prior record, that they had an excellent employment history, or, perhaps, that they were a church or civic leader (Samenow, 2010). For example, in referencing the criminality of fraud offender Rajat Gupta, a colleague indicated that the crime is "wholly inconsistent with the character of the man I know", until an offender exploits a given situation, even though the offender rejects a criminal lifestyle as the norm (Rothfeld, 2012). One of Ponzi schemer Bernard Madoff's employees stated, "He appeared to believe in family, loyalty, and honesty…never in your wildest imagination would you think he was a fraudster" (Creswell & Thomas, 2009). Consider a colleague and a former Harvard Business School classmate of convicted Enron CEO Jeffrey Skilling, who stated, "the Jeffrey Skilling I knew…was a good man. He was smart, he worked hard, he loved his family…when his entire career unraveled with his conviction on multiple federal felony charges relating to Enron's financial collapse, it not only shocked me that he had gone wrong, but how spectacularly he had done so" (Soltes, 2016, p. 2).

What does the phrase "out of character" actually imply? According to criminal psychologist, Dr. Stanton Samenow, during multiple decades of research, evaluation, and treatment of humans, he has yet to find someone do something that is not within their character despite being surprised by what others do. Even if we are shocked by the seemingly off-balanced behavior of someone we know intimately, it does not mean that an offender's behavior is out of character (Perri et al., 2014a). Typically, "out of character" means that we lack information about the person; there are aspects of their behavior and thought processes that we lack knowledge of, thus there is more to the story than appears evident at the moment (Samenow, 2010). Samenow further adds, "there are thinking patterns that long have been present within the person predating the behavior at issue and these thinking patterns express themselves at a moment of opportunity…The crime is very much within the character of the perpetrator" (Perri et al., 2014a, p. 334). For example, in Samenow's book, *The Myth of the Out of Character Crime*, the author cites a case of a young man who committed a brutal rape of a high school girl (Samenow, 2010).

The perpetrator had no prior criminal record; he was known to the neighbors as the nice college kid who delivered vegetables from his family's garden in his wagon.

While his father asserted that what his son had done was completely out of character, he did not have complete information. The father was not aware that since his son was a young boy, he composed violent and pornographic stories; for years his mind had been laden with fantasies of violence and coerced sex. Nor did this parent know that his son followed young female work colleagues, parked outside their homes, and fantasized about assaulting them (Samenow, 2010). Only when the police came to the house with search warrants collecting evidence did they discover years of sexual fantasies that had incubated, chronicled in his stories, and hidden from view. Through the act of physical rape, his violent sexual fantasy rehearsals were finally converted to reality. While the above example may appear extreme, it is important to be aware and careful of what we think we may know about others, versus what they actually believe deep inside and what motivates them. Remember white-collar offenders, especially with their arsenal of rationalizations, downplay their behavior by trying to get others to believe they are just as susceptible to committing fraud.

Consider the statement of attorney Marc Dreier who engineered a Ponzi scheme in the hundreds of millions of dollars stating, "It is easy to say you would never cross the line, but the line is presented to very, very few people...How many could say for sure that they would never do what I did if they had the opportunity and thought they wouldn't get caught" (Soltes, 2016, p. 328)? What is Dreier's strategy in making this statement? Dreier's strategy is to get others to align with his plight and rationalization in that it is possible anyone could be in his position and commit crimes, so he is not considered to be as "bad" as he appears, even though he caused harm to others. The belief that somehow we are all co-equally programmed to engage in a crime of this magnitude is a falsehood. In fact we also see this position taken by academics in accounting where they claim that "we all have the propensity to commit a crime" (Carozza, 2018, p. 45). People exhibit different risk factors and confuse or do not understand the difference between possibility and probability. One could say that we are all capable of becoming serial killers and on its surface, such a statement may appear correct. Yet when we analyze such a statement, we reflect on the fact that there are risk factors that increase the probability that one will become a serial killer, but we are not all co-equally programmed or at risk of becoming one.

Let us consider another crime classification and ask Dreier's question applying a different crime classification and gauge your reaction. Assume that Dreier was a convicted arsonist. Would his opinion be acceptable to adopt as our own? That is, if we were in his position, would we also burn buildings down that might have people in them? Would we desire to be an arsonist if it were guaranteed that we would not be discovered and punished? What if Dreier sold narcotics to minors to get them addicted to support his lifestyle? Would we sell narcotics to children to support our lifestyle if we could be 100 percent certain that we would not be caught and punished? There are risk factors that may increase why one person is more likely to engage in crime than another. While many events in life are possible, it does not mean they are co-equally probable to occur. Situations require analysis of what might contribute and heighten the probability that an event will occur. What risk factors increase the probability that a person will engage in unethical or criminal conduct, in this case white-collar crime? We must be careful of fraud offenders such as Dreier because they are skilled at appearing to share similar character traits with non-offenders in order to appear as though they are no different than the average citizen who tries to do the right thing in life by following societal norms of acceptable behavior.

Moreover, do not be seduced by the type of crime that is being committed—whether street-level or white-collar—to assess whether the offense is out of character, or not. As previously stated, there seems to be an erroneous belief that people do not plan to commit fraud; there is an accidental quality where offenders do not premeditate their actions as reflected in the comments below made by professionals who advocate against fraudulent behaviors. One antifraud professional stated, "People don't wake up and say I think I'll become a criminal today...instead it's a slippery slope and we lose our footing one step at a time" (Rezaee & Riley, 2010, p. 89). Another individual who turned out to be an antifraud whistleblower stated, "No one decides to commit fraud one fine morning...These decisions are built on years of working to push the ethical envelop little by little each time" (Carozza, 2014, p. 36). This is not to state that there may not be those who take incremental steps toward fraud, but to proclaim that people are not capable of having the motivation to commit fraud from the beginning without first engaging in the proverbial slippery slope toward fraudulent behavior is not accurate. Consider the insight of this offender that stands in stark contrast to the belief that fraudsters are accidental offenders and who are opportunists willing to exploit weakness for financial gain:

> Some people will, by nature, take advantage of situations. I would say that I am always open to the chance of committing fraud. It's the way I am. I wasn't consumed by it, but I was just aware of little things. I notice little things. Someone's password...glitches in the system. It's just the way I am...And I fell into a group of others who were like me and were always on the lookout (Free & Murphy, 2015, p. 35).

The social backgrounds of convicted white-collar offenders are indeed different from the typical street offender sample with respect to race, age, education, employment history, age of onset of official criminality, career length, and frequency of offending (Weisburd et al., 2001). However in other important respects there is little to distinguish white-collar offenders, on average, from the prototypical street offender. Convicted fraud offenders, as a group, can be amoral and detached from normal relationships coupled with being "an unusually antisocial group in terms of lack of regard for others" (Blum, 1972, p. 50). Some of these fraud offenders reflect a pathological or predatory quality where they meticulously plan their financial exploitation no differently than a non-white-collar offender may plan the sexual assault of their preferred target (Dorminey et al., 2010). As Sutherland stated white-collar crime is "identical in its general characteristics with other crime rather than different from it" (Sutherland, 1941, p. 112). Individuals with a long-standing propensity for deviance and criminality are more likely to commit white-collar crime, regardless of an organization's ethical climate in which they work. For at least some white-collar offenders, the workplace is nothing more than an additional setting in which to unleash deviant impulses when the opportunity arises. The organization provides access to the situational requisites necessary to carry out specific white-collar offenses (Simpson & Weisburd, 2008). Sutherland warned that "many business and professional men engage in predatory activities that are no different than predators" who engage street-level crime (Sutherland, 1937, p. 207).

For example, predatory fraud offenders seek out individuals or organizations where they can quickly establish fraud schemes; they may be favorable to the concealment of fraud where weak internal controls can be exploited without detection (Dorminey et al., 2010). White-collar offenders may display a greater tendency toward irresponsibility and an inability to adhere to social norms of integrity and abide by rules set by organizations and the law (Van Slyke et al., 2016). They can exhibit risk-taking behaviors that are not intelligently thought through, poor work habits including a lack of conscientiousness and dependability coupled with having unstable or unclear work histories no differently than street-level offenders (Van Slyke et al., 2016). Adults convicted of white-collar crimes are often repeat offenders countering the erroneous belief held by scholars that white-collar offenders "do not have a commitment to crime as a way of life because the loss of social status, respectability, money, a job, and a comfortable home and family deters them from a criminal lifestyle unlike street-level offenders who have no concern about how criminality affects their future or status" (Shover & Wright, 2001, p. 369). They are not the proverbial "one-shot" offender not likely to be processed in the criminal justice system that many believe is representative of these offenders' criminal history profile (Van Slyke et al., 2016). Consequently, "white collar offenders do not form a homogenous group with respect to their pattern of offending, level of deviance, attitudes toward crime, or social identity" (Walters & Geyer, 2004, p. 280).

They display histories of violence, property offenses and substance abuse that are traditionally thought to be attributed mainly to uneducated, street-level offenders; their deviancy is indistinguishable from non-white-collar criminals, especially those that are chronic fraud offenders (Walters & Geyer, 2004). Studies have shown that even though first-time fraud offenders may exhibit less risk in being repeat offenders, those offenders with a criminal history display recidivism rates comparable to those robbery and firearm offenders (Weissmann & Block, 2007). Chronic white-collar offenders display a history of social instability that characterizes the backgrounds of street-level criminals, including unsteady employment, marital breakup, and substance abuse. Although they did

32

not fit traditional stereotypes of criminality, they are defined by a pattern of offending which suggests a willingness to seek out specific types of situational opportunities to exploit. Chronic offenders, especially those exploiting people's trust, 1) deceive, exploit, and manipulate others in order to achieve personal gain, 2) exhibit no genuine remorse for their actions, 3) blame their victims for being stupid or deserving of their fate, and 4) minimize the harmful consequences of their actions or they may simply display an arrogant indifference. Chronic fraud offenders represent an offending group referred to as opportunity seekers, seeking out opportunities to commit crime or, at times, create situations favorable to committing a specific type of offense (Weisburd et al., 2001).

Chronic offenders exhibit a strong commitment to breaking the law, but also display instability and low self-control in their lives (Weisburd et al., 2001). While they appear to lead conventional, normal lives, the chronic offending group's propensity to offend starts early in their lives not differing much from street offender backgrounds (Weisburd et al., 2001). Consider the history of one chronic fraud offender countering the belief that they are "one-shot" offenders, "He had been arrested ten times between 1966 and 1988. The arrests ranged from white-collar related crimes such as fraud, forgery, and theft of securities, to aggravated arson, a weapons offense, and, finally, distribution of cocaine" (Weisburd et al., 2001, p. 84). Moreover, first-time offender is often confused with offending only one time; a lack of a prior record is not synonymous with a lack of prior offending (Freiberg, 2000). Even though there are white-collar criminals with repeated arrests, many white-collar criminals do not have prior arrests; the absence of a record is seen as a distinctive difference between traditional criminals and white-collar criminals (Freiberg, 2000). Some frauds are a result of months of scheming and are not the result of one fraudulent act on one particular day, is characteristic of a street-level crime. For example, Bernard Madoff, the securities fraud offender was sentenced to prison for 150 years, can technically be classified as a first-time offender because this was his first arrest.

Yet Madoff's fraud extended over fifteen years and in fact the extensive and at times collusive, deliberately planned quality of the fraud is actually an aggravating factor (Freiberg, 2000). Consider the case of a fraud offender that went from one organization to another exploiting the organization's internal controls for financial gain. The accountant of a small business began embezzling money within a month from the start of her job (Sharma et al., 2009). Over a period of three and one-half years, she stole between $900,000 and $1.2 million. As the fraud was being perpetrated, the owner struggled, even considering bankruptcy while the accountant knew since she had access to the company's financial statements to manipulate. Because the accountant had so much independence over the financial records, she was able to conceal her fraud from the owner and the auditor who reviewed the company's financial statements. The accountant was eventually caught and prosecuted, but it was later revealed the fraud turned out to be at a minimum her fourth fraud scam. Fraud offenders are better educated and more sophisticated than most criminals engaging in misconduct with cold, careful calculation, thus they are rational offenders and most likely to weigh the risks of possible courses of action against the anticipated rewards of criminal behavior (Kim, 2005).

The rational choice argument of law-abiding behavior suggests people comply with the law because they decide, weighing the costs and benefits associated with possible alternative wrongful and rightful courses of action, to forego the criminal conduct. This calculation of risk includes the likelihood of being caught and the severity of punishment (Moorh, 2003). Many white-collar offenders "are highly skilled at cost-benefit analysis. They're highly intelligent. They've been to the best schools. They weigh the risk of being caught against the potential reward, and they decide it's worth the risk" (Van Slyke et al., 2016, p. 289). White-collar offenders do consider how they can advance their financial position at the expense of others without being caught. Even if such choices are based on imperfect information, they still make calculated decisions to obtain financial benefits through illegal means with minimal likelihood of being caught and punished (Tomlinson & Pozzuto, 2016). Thus, individuals choose to engage in white-collar crime when the perceived benefits of doing so appear to outweigh the perceived costs, relative to an alternative course of action. The perceived benefits might be higher revenues, higher stock values, or better bonuses.

Some research suggests that people, in general, are more apt to think of the upside to illegality being the perceived benefits versus the downside which is punishment if caught (Tomlinson & Pozzuto, 2016). Corporations, like individuals, may engage in a similar analysis where management, as a group, considers how they can get away with breaking laws and regulations that impact other people and organizations without getting caught (Van Slyke et al., 2016). To further expose the myth that they are somehow the 'kinder and gentler' offender, it is erroneously assumed that because white-collar crime is classified as a nonviolent offense, white-collar offenders are also non-violent by nature (Perri, 2011a). Law enforcement agencies, including the court system, have similar misperceptions that fraud offenders are non-violent and thus harmless (Brody & Kiehl, 2010). For example, one U.S. federal court judge stated, "White-collar criminals are not people who are threatening the lives of others. They are not violent people" (Wheeler et al., 1988, p. 63). According to one scholar, white-collar offenders are "neither violent [nor] antisocial" (Mauer, 1974, p. 152). Other academicians in their handbook stated, "There are some notable differences involved [with] white-collar criminals compared with...criminals on the lower rungs of the offense ladder. For one thing, white-collar criminals pose no physical danger...Violence is not their thing" (Hobbs & Wright, 2006, p. 79).

Again, we observe the bias from these authors that violence is the province of individuals from lower socioeconomic status relying on the optics of criminality to determine whether someone is at risk to engage in violence and not whether they harbor antisocial personality traits that may trigger violent responses depending on motives that need to be satisfied. Consider the conduct of former president of AFG Financial Group Alan Hand, who orchestrated a $100 million mortgage fraud scheme. Hand personally wanted to kill the witnesses that disclosed his fraud scheme to authorities, but could not because he was in jail (Perri, 2016). Hand attempted to hire a contract killer while in jail, but the person turned out to be an undercover law enforcement officer. Hand told the undercover officer, "I wish I was there to watch him suffer and kill the man's wife and children if they are home" (Perri, 2016, p. 64). Although committed by a subgroup of white-collar offenders, a tendency towards violence is not surprising considering many of them harbor deviant criminal personality traits no differently than non-white-collar offenders. White-collar criminals are capable of resorting to brutal violence which is the ultimate form of control over an individual(s) that interferes with their fraudulent goals (Perri, 2016). In circumstances where there is a threat of fraud detection, some white-collar criminals resort to violence in order to silence people who discovered or could detect their fraud, and to prevent such discovery from being disclosed to interested parties (Perri, 2016).

Consider the case of Wall Street securities fraud offender Ivan Boesky, who was involved in the Michael Milken of Drexel Burnham securities fraud scheme in the 1980s. Boesky's inside story deserves attention because it also illustrates the ease in which white-collar offenders can resort to violence under specific conditions. Boesky paid Wall Street investment banker Martin Siegel of Kidder, Peabody & Co. $800,000 for inside trading information plus a 5 percent kickback on profits Boesky would make from the use of the information for the benefit of his clients. Dennis Levine, managing director of Drexel Burnham, received a 5 percent kickback for inside information, but no cash. Moreover, Boesky would share the inside information he purchased with a close friend and Wall Street trader John Mulheren. Boesky eventually stopped making payments to Siegel when he learned that Levine was under investigation by the SEC and it was Levine who first implicated Boesky by cooperating with federal authorities.

In turn, Boesky cooperated with federal prosecutors by implicating Milken, Siegel, and Mulheren in a larger stock manipulation and inside trading scheme in order to receive a more lenient sentence. Siegel ended up serving only a few months in prison for inside trading and tax evasion for his cooperation implicating other well-known Wall Street investment banking operatives at Goldman Sachs & Co. Yet, Boesky feared for his physical safety when he implicated Milken and Mulheren. Boesky's fears were not unfounded when it was learned that Mulheren had a "mission: to kill the man behind his torment; someone he had once counted among his closest friends: Ivan Boesky" (Stewart, 1992, p. 422). Even though not directly referencing the concept of fraud detection homicide previously discussed, Gregory Stewart, author of the book *Den of Thieves*, supported the insight that violence as a solution to a problem permeates white-collar offender thinking when he stated: "Perhaps it would be inevitable, even within the confines of a white-collar scandal, that violence would erupt. The money and power at stake was immense; many have killed and been killed for far less. Siegel had feared Boesky would have him killed; Boesky feared Milken would have him killed; now Mulheren had actually set out to kill Boesky" (Stewart, 1992, p. 422).

Antisocial Personality Traits of White-collar Offenders

Joseph Wells, founder of the Association of Certified Fraud Examiners (ACFE), observed, "As a group…the majority of CPAs are still ignorant about fraud…for the last 80 years, untrained accounting graduates have been drafted to wage war against sophisticated liars and thieves…And as multi-billion dollar accounting failures have shown, it has not been much of a fight" (Ramamoorti, 2008, p. 522). What exactly is it that academic, non-academic professionals, and the general public may not understand about white-collar offenders that prompts such an observation by Wells? A partial answer is that white-collar offenders may not manifest their criminality in ways that are easily recognized by others, however this does not mean that they do not harbor criminal personality traits that facilitate criminal decision making. Sutherland was correct in that criminal personality reflects socioeconomic neutrality; offenders engage in different crimes to satisfy their motives despite differences in age, race, criminal histories, gender, educational level, and other socioeconomic traits. Both non-white-collar and white-collar offenders display consistent criminal thought patterns and attitudes about others and/or situations to exploit. Crime is not reserved for certain socioeconomic classes. Just because the secretive aspects of white-collar crime are less visible does not mean they do not display the same antisocial behavior as non-white-collar crimes. Moreover, fraud lacks the fear factor typically associated with street-level offenses; while it reflects a sterile, intangible, and emotionless quality, the lack of fear does not mean that it is harmless (Soltes, 2016). Furthermore, Wells correctly emphasized the necessity of understanding antisocial thinking stating, "while fraudsters may look like ordinary people, they're not…it is important to concentrate on how they think and their thought processes, especially high-level executives where there is a tendency to believe that elevated organizational rank equates to honesty" (Wells, 2012, p. 54). Plus, consider the insights of criminal psychologist Dr. Samenow supporting Wells' position on the importance of understanding criminal thought processes:

> Despite the difference in the manner in which they execute their crimes, the mentality of a person who robs a bank and a corporate executive who perpetrates fraud is the same; both pursue power and control at the expense of others. Both are able to shut off considerations of consequences and conscience long enough to do what they want. Neither has an operational concept of injury to others. Neither puts themselves in the place of others. The offense for which either offender is caught, more likely than not, represents just the tip of the iceberg of each offender's irresponsibility and illegal conduct. Both know right from wrong, but whatever they are doing at the time is "right" to their way of thinking. If apprehended…they will do their utmost to dispel responsibility by implicating or blaming others (Samenow, 2012a).

The problem, at least as it stands for many in the accounting profession, is that training does not incorporate instruction on understanding criminal mindsets even though they have significant responsibility for understanding fraud and the opportunity to interview those who could commit fraud. At the present time accountants are at a disadvantage when involved in antifraud measures given how little they understand of what constitutes criminality. As one fraud offender who was a certified public accountant stated, "the plain truth is that the accounting profession today, whether in the role of external auditor or individual auditor and accountant, does not have the sufficient education, training, skills, and experiences necessary to match wits with criminals" (Payne, 2016, p. 617). It is not surprising fraud is so rampant in society and undetected by institutions, both private and government, that are charged to protect society. Consider the insight of a convicted fraud offender referring to accountants, auditors and antifraud professionals explaining why they are at a disadvantage: "You are not getting courses in criminality or psychology. You are not getting courses in what motivates people like me to commit the crimes that I committed that are going to possibly destroy your careers. They are going to cause investors to lose hundreds of millions of dollars" (Ramamoorti, 2008, p. 522).

Accountants, auditors, and those in the fraud examination field are beginning to understand the value of receiving additional training as it pertains to the criminal personality. As one auditor stated advocating for educating auditors and those in the fraud investigation field, "If auditors end up getting trained in diverse fields such as behavioral finance and criminal profiling, it will only add to their arsenal…I am confident that it will increase the success rate of forensic auditors" in identifying fraudulent conduct (Simha & Satyanarayan, 2016, p. 38). Another forensic accountant stated, "training in criminal profiling and behavioral finance both help with fraud investigation teams…with specific investigations, where you need to go beyond the documents, the things you can't see with your eyes, you need to understand the person you are investigating, their psyche and personality" (Simha & Satyanarayan, 2016, p. 38). Furthermore, although laws are generally determined through society's moral consensus of what comprises unacceptable behavior, we do not simply consider violations of the law as the only basis on which to determine whether someone harbors antisocial traits. There are numerous ways to define antisocial conduct. At times, people believe that if conduct is not illegal then it is ethical and this position is far from the truth. Antisocial thinking traits are typically attached to criminal acts, but they also apply to acts that are not illegal, per se, but may be damaging to others including an organization because they are unethical in nature.

For example, antisocial behavior can reflect unethical behavior that violate traditional norms that are morally unacceptable to the larger community. Examples include cheating, lying, manipulations, and other forms of dishonesty, including behaviors such as bullying and its relation to facilitating fraudulent behaviors from subordinates. In and of itself, bullying may not be a criminal act, but it is considered an unethical and antisocial act as it transgresses norms of acceptable behavior when it comes to respecting personal boundaries. In addition, before exploring with specificity what is meant by antisocial/criminal thinking traits, let us first understand what is meant by prosocial behaviors so that a basis of comparison exists. Prosocial behavior means an individual exhibits traits of, 1) self-discipline, 2) a sense of humility and reliability, 3) being respectful toward others and earning the respect of others, 4) having a sense of personal responsibility and keeping one's word by fulfilling obligations because one is trustworthy, 5) not victimizing others for personal gain and respecting appropriate personal and proprietary boundaries. Other prosocial behaviors include helping others without expecting anything in return, sharing, volunteering, cooperating, and displaying concern for others. Generally speaking, and this is not to be interpreted in an absolute manner, people who have been raised in a prosocial environment of respecting the rule of law and social norms that respect appropriate boundaries are more likely to be deterred from engaging in criminal behavior.

This perspective stands in contrast to those individuals who have been socialized in an antisocial environment where they may have adopted attitudes that favor rule-breaking behaviors coupled with rejecting broader societal norms (Boduszek et al., 2012b). The reason that the phrase "generally speaking" is used is because many white-collar offenders come from environments where they are familiar with prosocial behaviors, but may in certain situations ignore them which explains why people Sutherland referred to who come from respectable backgrounds go to prison. Furthermore, it should not be assumed that individuals who appear to come from "respectable" families are not raised to think in antisocial and criminal ways. Many "respectable" families accumulated wealth through fraud schemes that eventually were exposed. The terms antisocial and criminal behaviors will be used interchangeably because they represent behaviors disapproved of by societal norms and laws that punish such behaviors.

Antisocial and Criminal Thinking Traits

Our thoughts become our words, our words become our actions our actions become our character and our character becomes our destiny.

Gandhi

Given the billions of dollars lost to white-collar crime, the display of criminal attitudes endorsing exploitation by these offenders should not be ignored. A body of research confirms "that individual norms,

36

attitudes, and values play an important role in offending decisions" (Simpson, 2013, p. 317). Scholars acknowledge white-collar offender attitudes are no longer anomalies to ignore given the destructive nature fraud plays within society (Ragatz & Fremouw, 2010). Moreover, criminal behavior cannot be understood without an understanding of the offender's thinking processes; today scholars have begun to apply criminal attitudes and thinking styles to white-collar offenders (Benson & Manchak, 2014). Yet, ironically, for decades scholars failed to apply criminal thinking traits to white-collar offenders because criminological scholarship focused on examining conventional, street-level offenses such as violent and property crimes (Lilly et al., 2011). Antisocial and criminal thinking has been conceptualized as distorted thinking patterns or thinking errors coupled with one's attitudes and values supported by rationalizations which justify law-breaking behavior; in other words beliefs supporting the position that it is alright to violate others and/or their property (Perri et al., 2014a). Criminal thinking posits that those who display antisocial behaviors engage in certain modes of thought that support their behavior ultimately leading to making bad life choices which further facilitates future criminal behavior. Moreover, criminal thinking distortions impact how we process information (Barbour, 2013). For example, criminal thinking would consider a trusting demeanor in others not as strength to admire, but as a weakness to take advantage of. Criminal thinking facilitates decisions that appear self-indulgent, rash, interpersonally invasive, and against social norms (Boduszek & Hyland, 2012a).

Harboring antisocial thoughts does not mean one will commit crime, but it is a risk factor that elevates the probability of engaging in antisocial behavior especially if crime is perceived as a solution to satisfy a motive. Some argue that we all exhibit antisocial traits at one point or another in our lives, but we should question how pervasive are they in our lives, how often do we display them, how comfortable do we feel engaging them to satisfy agendas, and do we rely on such traits to support a criminal lifestyle on an ongoing basis (Taxman et al., 2011)? Thus, a tolerant attitude towards violence is a factor identifying individuals at risk for resorting to violence. Also, intelligence does not determine whether someone harbors criminal attitudes. In fact, mental sharpness may determine how successful one is in engaging in criminal behaviors; one should not assume only low intelligent people engage in crime (Egan et al., 2000). Fraud offenders attending some of the best schools in the country can now be found in prison. Moreover, some of the largest criminal atrocities committed throughout history and crimes against humanity were perpetrated by highly intelligent, well-educated people who had no reservations in harming others on behalf of their leaders and for personal gain. Criminal thinking triggers the next phase which is acting on one's thoughts to satisfy personal needs and therefore it is correlated with criminal behavior. Also, criminal needs that require fulfillment lead one to, 1) manipulate and control others, 2) receive rewards through criminal conduct, 3) blame others for their own actions, 4) exercise impaired moral reasoning with a self-serving mindset, and 4) adopt antisocial moral codes which facilitate criminal behavior regardless of the crime classification.

White-collar offenders may not exhibit a perpetual criminal lifestyle typically associated with street-level criminals, but they do exhibit criminal thinking patterns (Ragatz et al., 2012). Edwin Sutherland was one of the first to ascribe criminal thinking to white-collar offenders within organizations (Bodeszek & Hyland, 2012a). Sutherland believed that criminal attitudes and thinking traits develop through associations with others who harbor such attitudes, whether white-collar crime or not. Those harboring antisocial thinking patterns are comfortable using deceit, manipulation, and violence to satisfy a motive together with an ownership attitude where people are things—objects to be possessed. White-collar offenders exploit weaknesses be it someone's trust and the internal controls of an organization while easily engaging in rationalizations to justify the harm they cause or readily deny the existence of victims, and punish those perceived as interfering with their fraud schemes (Perri et al., 2014a). Interestingly, many individuals engaged in white-collar crime tend not to abandon the values society encourages; they continue to value fairness, honesty, integrity, and so forth, even as they engage in misconduct. Criminal attitudes and thinking traits include, but are not limited to, weakness exploitations, a disregard for rules, norms, personal, and social boundaries, power orientation, sentimentality, and relying on rationalizations (Perri et al., 2014a).

Criminal thought processes may also include a sense of excitement and gratification from satisfying criminal motives and retribution toward those who interfere with offender goals also known as goal interference (Samenow, 1984). Furthermore, the trait of entitlement is a consistent risk factor; the attitude that a person has "a right to take whatever they want from whoever has what they desire" regardless of the imposition it may cause others (Bodeszek & Hyland, 2012a, p. 30). Other criminal traits include social identification with those who support their goals and emulate their conduct as a criminal role model. Consider the fact that when someone repeats antisocial and criminal acts, this should not be confused with someone displaying an uncontrollable impulsivity or urge that is outside of their ability to suppress when it actually reflects a habitual lifestyle of engaging in such acts (Samenow, 1984). These offenders are looking for opportunities to exploit. While they engaged in misconduct many times undetected does not mean they were impulsive. Impulsivity is an excuse used to remove accountability from the equation to hold someone responsible for their behavior by making statements such as they just "snapped" or they could not control themselves, thus they cannot be accountable for their behaviors. There is a calculation behind the act that may not be apparent, but the time and place to execute their acts is thought through even if their calculation was flawed. The fact that they may not be good at planning or risk assessment does not mean they are impulsive.

If offenders get caught, instead of reflecting on the wrong they committed, they return to the same criminal lifestyle because their antisocial attitudes are still justified and rationalized away (Boduszek & Hyland, 2012a). Fraud offenders, like any other type of offender, engage in a cost-benefit analysis or some type of risk assessment at the time and decide whether it is more advantageous to move forward with the crime than not to move forward (Shover & Wright, 2001). White-collar offenders are deliberate and calculating in their assessments of the cost and benefits of whether to commit a criminal act, often manipulating and taking advantage of weak regulatory environments and weak organizational internal controls (Simpson, 2013). Organizational crimes in particular require detailed planning that produce long-term benefits for individual offenders and their firms and some examples include accounting fraud, price fixing conspiracies, stock price manipulations, and mortgage frauds (Simpson, 2013). Many individuals learn to engage in crime through exposure to and adoption of attitudes favorable to breaking the law from other people within an organization that is open to committing fraud (Boduszek et al., 2012b). Moreover, a negative synergy is created increasing the probability of adopting a criminal lifestyle over time when we spend time with people who display aggressive, interpersonally hostile mannerisms, coupled with criminal attitudes, and a criminal history (Boduszek et al., 2011b).

A body of research suggests that individual norms, attitudes, and values play an important role in whether an individual engages in white-collar crime (Simpson, 2013). Moreover, criminal attitudes are not necessarily driven by a lack of empathy even though lacking empathy may facilitate criminal activity, but a lack of empathy is not a prerequisite to harboring criminal attitudes (Egan et al., 2000). Someone who is criminally minded may lack empathy when they commit the act, but may display empathy when interacting with their family. Individual differences do exist when it comes to understanding human forces that maintain motivations to disregard the rights and needs of others for one's own benefit. Criminals believe they are good and decent people, rejecting the thought that one is a criminal by performing sentimental acts toward others which enhance the criminal's view of oneself as good (Yochelson & Samenow, 1976). Moreover, there is a thoughtlessness to their behaviors, but the thoughtlessness should not be confused with a lack of risk assessment. Their thoughtlessness could be due to their unjustified optimism that they are so good at their criminal acts that they will not be caught. They may display super optimism believing their abilities set them above detection and being held accountable for their misconduct (Perri et al., 2014a).

They cut off facts that may interfere with their motivations in order to eliminate fear and doubt so that they maintain their belief that they are immune from apprehension. As a result, they approach criminal activity in a state of super confidence where there is not a doubt in their minds that the criminal act can be executed without detection. The antisocial and criminal thinking patterns outlined in Table 1 will receive further attention when applied to specific examples in future chapters. Yet for now, take the time to understand the concepts. Criminal thinking traits delineated below do not necessarily apply equally to all white-collar offenders in quantity or intensity at all times and more research is needed to refine their application. However, when we have a template to organize what constitutes criminal thinking, preferences, and attitudes, not only can we protect ourselves because we know how to better recognize individual antisocial behaviors, but when we are exposed to them, we also know how to better perform our duties be it as auditors or antifraud professionals.

Table 1	**Antisocial and Criminal Thinking Traits**
Weakness Exploitation	Taking advantage of others vulnerability and situations to satisfy a motive.
Goal Interference	Punishing and potentially harming those, in violent and non-violent ways, that get in the way of antisocial and criminal goals.
Social Identification	What group do we want to be identified with? Who do we look up to? Who do we want to emulate or be like?
Victim Mindset	View themselves as the victim. Blame others and/or circumstances.
Lack of Accountability	Not accepting responsibility for not fulfilling obligations or for disregarding rules, regulations, laws and social norms.
Excitement	Delight in duping others, enjoyment, gratification, pleasure, satisfaction when engaging in antisocial and criminal behaviors. Enjoyment may be derived from the harm inflicted on others be violent or non-violent.
Disregard of Rules	Disregarding of rules also entails disregarding laws, morals, norms and ethical standards. This trait reflects not respecting personal and proprietary boundaries reflecting a diminished sense of obligation to others.
Entitled Mindset	Belief one is entitled to what they desire regardless of the harm caused to others. Deserving special treatment or privileges justifiability of one's behavior.
Sentimentality	Sentimentality helps offenders give the impression to others that they are good people incapable of criminality or that their offenses were out of character.
Power Orientation	Views people as objects to control to satisfy their agenda. Controlling others and situations is more important than applying logic to thoughtfully engage in risk assessment. Manipulations and violence are tactics used to control.
Super Optimism	The belief that one cannot be held accountable because they are so good at exploiting opportunities without detection or punishment. The belief that they are immune from accountability for their behavior. They tend to reject or ignore facts that interfere with their view that their acts are not detectable. A sense of invulnerability inspite of risks and potential consequences.
Rationalizations	Used by white-collar and non-white-collar offenders, rationalizations are crime classification neutral. Rationalizations facilitate the offender's ability to morally distance themselves from their antisocial and criminal acts. Rationalizations neutralize accountability and reduce the guilt someone might experience. However criminals whether they are white or non-white-collar do not have to rely on rationalizations to commit crimes. Rationalizations can be used by those who commit unethical but not criminal acts.

Learning to recognize these thinking traits in others is not difficult. One method is to practice observing what people do and what they say. One can practice identifying these traits from people they personally interact with, but also when viewing, for example, television shows that have to do with criminality, films or what they read. Reflect on past interactions with people and ask yourself did they do or say something that appeared to be antisocial in nature, but that you did not have the vocabulary to describe what it was that you were personally experiencing or observing from a distance. Study the dialogue between people and see if you can identify which antisocial trait is on display. One can also practice when attempting to identify antisocial interpersonal strategies that are outlined below under the section on recognizing antisocial interpersonal strategies. For example, assume we observe someone bullying a subordinate at work, they are engaging in the antisocial trait of power orientation. Here the bully is trying to control someone by intimidating or threatening them in some manner making the subordinate feel very uncomfortable to the point they will comply with the bully's request. What if the bully demotes someone for not participating in a fraud scheme?

Then we observe the antisocial trait of goal interference in addition to power orientation. Here the person bullied decides not to participate in committing fraud ends up being unfairly punished by being demoted at work because they are viewed as interfering with the bully's agenda which is illegally obtaining money. Perhaps we overhear someone state they have not hurt anyone through their misconduct; we are observing the reliance on rationalizations to morally distance themselves from their misconduct. Understanding antisocial and criminal thinking traits is of immense importance especially when we exam interpersonal dynamics between senior management and subordinates within a corrupt corporate environment that participates in misconduct. Moreover, how are these thinking traits activated and enhanced by one's individual personality traits? Does one's personality traits facilitate the reliance on these criminal thinking traits to satisfy one's motive? The short answer is yes and we will be examining how personality traits can behave as a risk factor increasing the probability of relying on antisocial and criminal thinking that ultimately culminates into misconduct or a criminal act be it white-collar crime or non-white-collar crime.

Moreover, criminal thinking is likely to be activated when individuals associate with like-minded people who engage in crime. We observe this dynamic in organizations that engage in unethical and criminal behaviors on a large scale. Investigating the degree of identification with and approval of antisocial associates is a significant predictor of the influence that criminal associates have on a person which, in turn, contributes to repetitive criminal behavior. Individuals who spend time with others who harbor criminal attitudes are more apt to adopt those attitudes (Boduszek et al., 2011a; b). When combining criminal thinking traits outlined above, they become activated because the people they are associated with reinforce such attitudes with rationalizations that their behavior is justified (Boduszek et al., 2012b). For example, people who engage in narcotics trafficking may convince each other that they are simply earning a living. In addition, the more a person engages in criminal behavior and the more time spent in the criminal justice system, the more likely they will adopt and harbor criminal attitudes (Boduszek et al., 2011b). In essence a criminal lifestyle becomes normalized and actually doing the right thing by respecting the rule of law and respecting appropriate boundaries is rejected; doing the right thing may even be viewed as naïve and irresponsible.

In order to accelerate learning the different antisocial thinking traits available to build a template in understanding criminality, it is worth visualizing offenders as being on a continuum of deviancy as illustrated in Table 2. This continuum helps one conceptualize antisocial thinking traits; it is not meant to favor one trait over another. Also, the continuum is more of a visual aid to facilitate understanding of how one may be at greater risk to commit crime than another who harbors prosocial traits. Moreover, it is not necessary to harbor all the traits to display antisocial behaviors. For example, the continuum would assist in understanding those who are at risk for displaying deep-rooted antisocial traits versus those who do not reject criminal attitudes, but do not reflect a core antisocial personality approving of an overall criminal lifestyle (Perri, 2013b). What is difficult for many to accept is that there are individuals who naturally gravitate toward these traits and actually would rather rely on these traits to interact with others than display prosocial behaviors. Understanding that people may be represented on this continuum is important to know because it assists us in better assessing risk of being exploited, both financially and violently by people who harbor and rely on such traits to satisfy motives. The reality is these traits apply to white-collar offenders even though the thought that these offenders harbor such traits may be contrary to our intuition.

Table 2   Antisocial and Criminal Thinking Trait Continuum

COLUMN 1	COLUMN 2	COLUMN 3	COLUMN 4	COLUMN 5
Disregard Law	Disregard Law	Disregard Law	Disregard Law	Disregard Law
Rationalizations	Rationalizations	Rationalizations	Rationalizations	Rationalizations
	Immunity	Immunity	Immunity	Immunity
	Entitled	Entitled	Entitled	Entitled
		Excitement	Excitement	Excitement
		Victim Mindset	Victim Mindset	Victim Mindset
			Exploitative	Exploitative
			Sentimentality	Sentimentality
				Power Orientation
				Goal Interference
				Social Identification

Generally speaking, when moving from left to right, thus from column 1 moving along to column 4, the number of traits a person harbors increases the risk that they are more likely to engage in criminal and/or antisocial behaviors to satisfy a motive. However, this does not mean someone displaying traits in column four applies only to a street-level offender engaging in brutal acts of violence, although such offenders do exhibit these traits. A person harboring the traits in column four can be a predatory fraud offender especially given their remorseless and exploitative natures. Someone displaying traits from column one can move to the right and acquire other thinking traits especially if these risk factors are present: 1) they continue to engage in crime, 2) their personalities facilitate the emergence of these traits and, 3) one associates with others displaying these traits while endorsing and adopting their approach to committing antisocial acts.

Moreover, a person displaying column four traits may not have any criminal record, such as a high-level corporate executive who displays their aggression in a different form to satisfy their motive through fraud and unethical practices. They might engage in power orientation behaviors such as bullying subordinates to engage in fraud, display a victim mindset of blaming others for their misfortune when they get caught by law enforcement, believe that they are too smart to get caught committing fraud, and have an array of rationalizations available at their disposal to justify their actions. As we shall study in later chapters, consider the negative synergy produced elevating the risk of corporate misconduct when employees from the CEO to subordinates display these antisocial traits combined with individual personality traits such as psychopathy and narcissism that facilitate the natural acceptance and reliance on such traits.

In addition to these individual risk factors, consider how the risk of corporate misconduct is compounded by an organizational culture that actually rewards these antisocial behaviors because of the perceived financial benefit they bring to the organization (Perri, 2013b). When we examine column one, what kind of individual might these traits potentially apply to? Perhaps we visualize someone that engages in tax fraud when filing a tax return once a year. They rely on rationalizations to disregard the law and will not disclose information to prepare a tax return, but otherwise lead an overall law-abiding life. Another example might entail an owner not disclosing all revenue that was collected in cash because it is easier to not disclose because there is no documentation to reveal cash revenue was ever collected. They may disregard tax laws requiring disclosure, rely on rationalizations conveniently available to justify their tax fraud, and believe that they are relatively immune from detection. Although a person may not reflect a criminal lifestyle of engaging in criminal activity for all their needs, not displaying a criminal lifestyle in all aspects of one's life does not mean that they did not engage in an antisocial act. This is one of the major reasons why fraud offenders are capable of rationalizing away their behaviors so easily.

White-collar Criminal Success through Weakness Exploitation

Criminal thinking entails searching for vulnerable targets such as individuals and organizations as examples and to capitalize on exploitable opportunities (Samenow, 1984). Compared to non-white-collar offenders, white-collar criminals manifest their aggression differently toward others and organizations to satisfy a motive (Perri & Brody 2012). Weakness exploitation manifests itself in various forms such as a person who exhibits human virtues like honesty, giving others the benefit of the doubt, ethics and morals, or physical differences. It is necessary to spend some time explaining this concept of weakness exploitation because it is at the heart of understanding antisocial thinking as it relates to transgressing appropriate boundaries be it one's physicality, an organization's internal controls, or taking advantage of a person's trust. For example, a criminal who engages in violence may exploit a person who is weaker, younger, or frailer in comparison to themselves because they are easier to control. Children are frequent targets of sexual assault because not only are they easier to physically control, but also easier to emotionally manipulate. An individual motivated to rob someone is more apt to do so if the person is elderly because there is less resistance. The criminal in these cases understands that their targets or situations harbor weaknesses that are easier to exploit. Analogously, there are white-collar offenders who seek out organizations with weak internal controls because they can more easily exploit them to commit fraud and avoid detection than they could in organizations with more effective internal controls and stronger means of detection. We may also harbor weaknesses in our attitudes about how we perceive others as previously discussed under the projection bias topic.

Criminals take advantage of a person's goodwill that is rooted in projection bias where we give others an implied credibility simply because we believe they harbor values that we value. In other words, we give others credibility without having a basis to impute credibility. White-collar criminals rely on an implied credibility and the respect of other professionals which makes deception harder to detect (Gaetano, 2012). Thus are we able to, again, keep our projection bias in check? Consider the insights of Samuel (Sam) Antar who was part of a family conspiracy in that his entire family cheated the U.S. government and investors through its Crazy Eddies consumer electronics chain company (Wells, 2012). Sam, the cousin of Crazy Eddie founder Eddie Antar, joined the retail chain in the 1980s. As a CFO and certified public accountant, Sam participated in a multimillion-dollar fraud scheme which involved asset misappropriation and overstating income to inflate stock prices. The family fraud scheme unraveled because family members involved in a feud informed the Securities Exchange Commission (SEC) that the company overstated inventory by approximately $50 million. In return to receiving leniency in punishment, Sam provided key testimony on behalf of the prosecution against his cousin Eddie (Gaetano, 2012). What is interesting about Sam is that he started working for Crazy Eddies at age fourteen, and essentially trained from the beginning to be an effective fraud offender within this publicly traded company. He was encouraged to become an accountant with the anticipation that he would join the family business to eventually participate in financial statement fraud on behalf of Crazy Eddies (Antar, 2013).

As a result of his antisocial upbringing, Sam has an intuitive understanding of what the criminal mindset truly means and how it is displayed that other fraud offenders cannot articulate as well. When others engaged in fraud, it began well into their adulthood for reasons such as trying to save a business and personal financial problems, for example. Many did not engage in fraud, as Sam did, to run a criminogenic organization from the beginning by taking advantage of others for their own personal gain. Furthermore, Sam identifies two types of fraud offenders: the crossover and career fraud offenders. The crossover offender has lived a relatively normal life, but then falls to temptation and commits a crime when given an opportunity. The career criminal, like Sam himself, is not just tempted by opportunity, he or she does not see anything wrong with committing crime especially when they are skilled at it and victims are sufficiently vulnerable for exploitation. Consider Antar's insights as to the career criminal:

> When I was doing my crimes, I didn't think in terms of right or wrong. It was just my normal lifestyle...To the career criminal like me, there's no morality. There's nothing to understand. You have to take the morality out so you can understand the rationale of their actions. Take guys like Bernie Madoff...These are intelligent guys. Smart guys. Probably went to college. Took classes in ethics and

morality. Saw other criminals go to jail. Did it stop them? If Bernie Madoff went to jail for 150 years, would any other crimes in progress stop? Would career criminals stop? Find God and morality? Ain't gonna happen…So, most criminals don't get caught, and there could be dozens of Bernie Madoffs we just don't know about…When you go back to organized groups of criminals, you find they've been doing it for years (Gaetano, 2012).

Unlike other fraud offenders who rely on rationalizations to distance themselves away from their criminality, Antar makes no excuses for what his business was really about stating, "Crazy Eddie was built on deceit…We were nothing but cold-hearted and soulless criminals…We were two-bit thugs" (Knapp, 2009, p. 106). Sam further gives us insights on what they really thought of their behavior and it is obvious that they were basically criminal entrepreneurs believing that it was their job to make money illegally with no sense of guilt:

> Eddie Antar and I never had a single conversation about morality or right and wrong. We simply did not care about the victims of our crimes. Our conversations only focused on the successful execution of our cold-blooded schemes to defraud investors. At Crazy Eddie, we committed our crimes simply because we thought we could execute them successfully. We enjoyed being criminals and enjoyed the money. We had no empathy for the people we hurt. We didn't even need the money, just wanted more (Antar, 2013).

Generally, people are inclined to assume the best in others by giving them the benefit of the doubt and although that may be an admirable human quality, it is a poor defense against fraud offenders especially those that are predators (Gaetano, 2012). Many of the qualities that make people capable of being responsible actors in society are the same qualities that make people vulnerable to white-collar crime. Sam states that one's humanity may make them a better person, but it also makes it easier for criminals to commit their crimes because they have no constraints on their behavior and therefore do not feel obligated to reciprocate the victim's humanity. The offender interprets a victim's humanity not as a strength the way most people would, but as a weakness to exploit. In one study that examined the mindset of accountants who went to prison for defrauding their clients, which reflects this idea of exploiting the weakness of others, some of the accountants "claimed that if the victims were incapable of securing their assets, they deserved to have them stolen" (Dellaportas, 2013, p. 36). The question becomes what weakness are we actually referring to? The weakness in the eyes of the offender is the trust the victim has in the offender, but which is not reciprocated by the offender because they view this trust as an opportunity to exploit. Sam articulates the criminal thinking mindset of what exploiting human weakness means to satisfy their fraud scheme motives stating:

> White-collar criminals consider your humanity, ethics, and good intentions as weaknesses to be exploited in the execution of their crimes. We measure our effectiveness by the comfort level of our victims and we increase our victim's comfort level by building walls of false integrity around ourselves. We don't play fair. We have no respect for you. We have no respect for your laws. We don't have respect for your customs. In fact, your laws and customs make it easier for us to commit our crimes. It's a paradox. The more humane society is, the easier it is to commit the crimes. Humanity limits your behavior but it doesn't limit our behavior because we're immoral human beings. One's humanity might consist of one's morals, standards of conduct, good will, ethics, sense of fairness, giving one the benefit of the doubt, and belief in the rule of law. The things that make you a good person make me a more capable criminal (Antar, 2010; 2009).

Building Walls of False Integrity

As Sam indicated, fraud offenders build walls of false integrity to reduce the probability people will question their actions and to dilute suspicions that may exist about their behaviors to gain the trust of their victims (Antar, 2013). False integrity is created by participating and giving money to charities, receiving awards, exhibiting prosocial behaviors, displaying important professional titles such as being the CEO or CFO of a company, and belonging to civic and religious organizations. Participating in these prosocial activities allows the offender the opportunity to seduce others into believing and adopting a public image of the themselves as being a person of integrity and goodness that does not in reality exist—hence the name 'walls of false integrity' (Antar, 2010; 2009). The public image is used to deflect attention away from their true motives. As Sam further elaborated, "I walked old ladies across the street and gave huge sums of money to charity, while having no empathy whatsoever for the victims of my crimes" (Antar, 2010). As a result, stature, status, generosity, and good deeds gain the respect of their potential victims making it less likely victims will question their behavior. As Sam stated, "you never know who the real person is behind a criminal's carefully choreographed wall of false integrity" projecting an image contrary to who they are (Antar, 2013).

The Case of Fraud Offender Steven Hoffenberg

Once you start a Ponzi scheme you couldn't stop because you would wreck everything.

Steven Hoffenberg

In the 1980s, Steven Hoffenberg, CEO of Towers Financial Corporation, relied on a type of financing where Towers would purchase at a five percent discount from nursing homes, hospitals and other medical facilities, money that was owned to them by insurance companies (Soltes, 2016). This type of financing provides organizations the cash they immediately need by providing Towers with a method of making money by having the insurance pay the full amount owed to Towers. Thus if the insurance company owed a hospital $100, Towers paid the hospital $95 and he would get paid $100 from the insurance company. However, Towers had to come up with the money to pay the health care providers, thus he borrowed against the money the insurance companies were to pay in the future by issuing promissory notes. Thousands invested in buying Tower's promissory notes. The problem began when Towers bought the obligations owed to the hospitals, but they were of such poor quality that Towers was unable to collect on them from insurers (Soltes, 2016). Thus, Towers would pay the hospital the $95, but could not collect the $100, thus there was a loss of $95. This in turn caused Towers a problem because they could not pay off the investors that bought the promissory notes plus interest owed to them and as a result, the losses started to accumulate.

Towers knew that he had to keep borrowing money to pay off investors and the way to get others to keep buying Towers' promissory notes was by convincing investors that Towers was in fact making money giving the impression that Towers was not too risky a proposition. To give the appearance of profitability, Towers recognized revenue on money owed to them by insurance companies even though it was never collected or that it would never be collected plus recognized revenue on money owed even before the collection process began. When the money owed to Towers was past due its collection date, Towers would refresh the dates of the money due to it as being new and not past due. Consequently, Towers always looked like it was doing well because losses were never recorded. Eventually the firm collapsed in 1993 and Hoffenberg went to prison for twenty years owing investors over $470 million. Hoffenberg gave insights in running a deceptive enterprise as a pragmatic issue rather than a moral issue. Hoffenberg stated:

> Once you start a Ponzi scheme and go into the cash register, you can't get out. You eat up so much money going into the cash register that you need more and more money to feed it—so you're stuck. They were throwing money at me and the more business we did, the more losses we had…You couldn't stop because you would wreck everything. Morals go out the window when the pressure is on. When responsibility is there and you have to meet budgetary numbers, you can forget about morals. Circumstances over-rule morals (Soltes, 2016, p. 272).

In some respects the statement made by Hoffenberg, "circumstances over-rule morals", is reflective of the observation previously made where virtue is situational meaning that individual are willing to engage in a cost-benefit analysis that includes compromising their values if there is another interest that takes a priority over one's values (Heath, 2008). Consider Hoffenberg's opinion on whether he was remorseful for selling the promissory notes to investors to sustain the fraud that reflects this accepting a partial responsibility mindset stating, "I never sold securities. I'm a salesman and creator of innovative products. I'm on the road or on an airplane. I had nothing to do with selling the Ponzi and I didn't do the accounting. I'm culpable, but I'm not the one doing it" (Soltes, 2016, p. 273). What is interesting about Hoffenberg is that he perceives his actions in the abstract, not understanding the magnitude of his behavior on an emotional level. In part this has to do with how offenders engage in fraud at the organizational level generally entails recruiting others to help perpetrate the scheme—fraud schemes in large organizations typically require the assistance of multiple people. Thus in this case, Hoffenberg set the tone that allowed fraud to occur because he ordered it, but it was not that he was involved in the actual physical mechanics of the fraud by making adjustments to the financial statements to make them appear better than they were. It is as if he is a spectator of the fraud he ordered, but never getting his hands dirty in committing the fraud. The self-view that because one is not involved in the actual mechanics of perpetrating the fraud is a common view of upper level management that delegate the fraud to others to perpetrate. Hoffenberg was asked what he would change if he could do it all over again and he responded:

> Nothing…the model was perfect. It operated on eight cylinders and if not for the income-recognition wrong call [this is where he included revenue that was not earned as being earned on the financial statements], the company would have been a Fortune 1000 company. Keep in mind that Towers wasn't really a Ponzi. What the word Ponzi means is that you're taking new money to pay old money. That's not what Towers did. Towers invested this money and actually made a fortune on it, but we couldn't make the fortune quick enough and we turned left instead of right on offering documents (Soltes, 2016, p. 273).

Antisocial and Criminal Interpersonal Strategies of White-collar Criminals

Just as there are characteristics of how a prosocial person will interact with others, those that harbor an antisocial mindset also exhibit distinct interpersonal strategies. A prosocial interpersonal strategy would be answering a question honestly and directly. Another example would be to allow an individual to voice opinions without attacking them personally simply because they may not agree with a certain point of view. An antisocial interpersonal strategy is quite different and recognizable. The problem many people have when they experience someone's antisocial interpersonal mannerism is that they do not necessarily know how to react to the negative experience they have been subjected to because typically people experience on average more prosocial than antisocial interpersonal encounters. As a result, it is not uncommon to not know how to explain or react to the encounter because it tends to be experienced emotionally such as being angry, hurt, intimidated, threatened, and confused. Keep in mind these emotional reactions may be the exact end goal of the person relying on such interpersonal tactics.

Yet understanding these strategies is important to those that are antifraud professionals exposed to such strategies especially when studying how leadership uses antisocial interpersonal strategies to intimidate and bully subordinates into committing fraud. Moreover, these strategies do not necessarily have to be experienced in a negative manner because the motive with a positive interpersonal strategy is to make a person feel good about the relationship in order to reduce professional skepticism by an auditor as an example. For example, do we reduce our skepticism about whether to engage in a business dealing or whether an auditor is willing to overlook gathering evidence to support the client's representation because the interpersonal strategy used increased one's perceived trustworthiness even though due diligence requires one to maintain a skeptical mindset regardless whether the quality of relationship is good? Some of the more positively experienced antisocial interpersonal strategies include but are not limited to charm, altruism, false bonding, and agreeing with someone without meaning it. Furthermore, impression management is a goal directed interpersonal communication process in which people attempt to influence the perceptions of other people about a person, organization, or both as examples.

It is usually used synonymously with self-presentation in which a person tries to influence the perception of their image. The notion of impression management also refers to practices in professional communication and public relations, where the term is used to describe the process of formation of an organization's public image. There is nothing inherently wrong with impression management, however it can be used by criminals of all types for manipulative purposes. The impression can be for portraying a positive image by making others feel good about themselves, by generously dispensing compliments, or to instill fear in others through intimidation. Interpersonal strategies that will probably provoke a negative experience in another include but are not limited to resorting to engaging in personal attacks, putting others on the defensive, and accusing others of not understanding. Moreover, consider the negative antisocial interpersonal strategy relating to trying to understand the facts of a case as an example and one is instructed to interview such an individual perhaps during an audit or a fraud investigation.

What would these strategies look like? Some of them would be displays of, 1) vagueness and omitting facts, 2) pathological lying and manipulations, 3) a desire to minimize significant facts, 4) making a big deal over minor points, 5) appearing truthful by incorporating truthful statements with untruthful statement, 6) silence and stonewalling, and 7) distortions of the truth and selective attention. Let us examine how Sam Antar's interpersonal strategies interestingly dovetail those listed above in terms of how management reacts to earnings disappointments, criticism, skepticism and cynicism. Does management start by stating, "We take full responsibility and make no excuses, only to be followed by carefully worded innuendos, excuses and deflection…Do they question the integrity of those that ask questions" (Antar, 2007)? In addition, does management accentuate the positive then spin and deflect negative information by blaming others for the company's problems? Does management attempt to intimidate people who question areas they do not want probed with the goals of making people uncomfortable so they do not want to ask questions (Antar, 2007)? Some of Sam's own antisocial interpersonal strategies listed below with external parties such as auditors, fraud examiners, and law enforcement included:

- The kindness you show your adversaries will reduce their propensity to be skeptical of you.
- Make excuses as long as you can. Try to have your excuses based on at least one truthful fact even if the fact is unrelated to your actions and argument,
- Always say in words you take responsibility, but try to indirectly shift the blame on other people and factors. You need to portray yourself as a stand-up person,
- When you cannot defend your actions or arguments, attack the messenger to detract attention from your questionable actions,
- Always show your kindness by doing people favors. You will require the gratitude of such people to come to your aid and defend you,
- Build up your stature, integrity, and credibility by publicizing the good deeds you have done in areas unrelated to the subject of scrutiny,
- Build a strong base of support with those who will defend you. If you can, appear to take the high road and then have your surrogates do the dirty work for you,
- If you are under investigation, always say you will cooperate. However, use all means Necessary, legal or otherwise, to stifle the investigators,
- When facts cannot be disputed, accept them as true, but rationalize your actions. Making mistakes is acceptable as long as you have no wrongful intent,
- When called to testify, have selective memory about your actions. It is harder to be charged with perjury if you cannot remember what you have done rather than testify and lie about it.

The Case of Fraud Offender Marc Dreier

It is difficult to comprehend how someone can create losses in the millions and at times billions of dollars, yet when revealed, the magnitude of the deception is so overwhelming that accepting the fact that the fraud may have started out with the intention of being a legitimate business appears contradictory in nature

(Soltes, 2016). What starts as a small problem in a legitimate business remains unresolved becoming a bigger problem, but the person that is involved in Ponzi financing is beholden to the belief that with a little more time and changes in business conditions, the issues will resolve themselves and no one will get hurt. Far beyond the point where the fraud might be resolved through legitimate means, the offender cannot see exactly what has been created; in essence a monster that cannot be slain because it got too big to slay. After years of self-deception about what has been created, it is difficult to see the truth even when revealed by others because the fraud simply becomes so routinized that the normalcy of engaging in a scheme day in and day out is interpreted as legitimate and efficient. Consider the case of attorney Marc Dreier who, at least optically, created an innovative law firm of about 250 attorneys. However, to maintain such an enterprise, financial strain was expected and as the firm grew, the expenses began to outpace revenue.

Dreier borrowed heavily at high interest rates in order to meet expenses, but also to give outsiders the appearances that there were no financial problems at the firm which is what triggered the start of Ponzi financing. Dreier knew that he could not fund the firm by legitimate means alone so he began to sell debt to hedge funds under the false pretense that it was from a real estate firm known as Solow Reality. In the past, Dreier represented Sheldon Solow, owner of Solow Reality, thus given Solow's reputation, few hedge fund managers would question the credibility of Solow's debt notes. According to Dreier, "Solow was known as a very unorthodox, but successful real estate developer, which allowed me to convince investors that the notes were genuine" (Soltes, 2016, p. 263). Thus, Dreier produced false documents that appeared to be created by Solow Reality and presented them as authentic documents to hedge funds. Dreier first started with selling a fictitious $20 million note, then a $40 million note, then a $60 million note, and so on. However, the money was not just used to pay law firm expenses, but to support a lavish lifestyle in order to give the impression of being successful by entertaining on his yacht, at his glamorous apartments, at his beach house in the Hamptons, and even bought a restaurant in Los Angeles for the purpose of maintaining an image of success.

Dreier believed the firm would eventually earn enough money to pay off the fraudulent loans in a way that the firm could survive. Yet after awhile, it became more difficult to find hedge funds that would buy his debt and in order to attract buyers, he kept increasing the interest rate offered from eight percent to twelve percent. When the financial markets began to collapse in 2008, investors were demanding their money back, but it became impossible to pay off the investors because he could not find new investors that would be used to pay off old investors. Dreier was able to find an investor named Fortress Investment Group, because they had already bought about $100 million in fictitious Solow notes, to consider a $50 million note from the Ontario Teachers Pend Fund which is one of Dreier's clients. Fortress agreed to buy the note and Dreier fabricated the note as if it was from Ontario Teacher. The only issue was that Fortress wanted to have an in-person meeting with a representative from the Ontario Teachers Pension Fund. Dreier decided to impersonate an officer that was from Ontario Teachers. According to Dreier, he displayed the antisocial trait of super optimism and embellished abilities believing that he would not get caught stating:

> Because I had succeeded with some impersonations and brazen acts before, I entertained the possibility that I could somehow do it again, even though this particular impersonation was far riskier and even more ridiculous. As strange as it sounds, not getting caught just wasn't my main priority. My priority was still to find some way, even if it was far-fetched, to keep the debt current and keep the firm alive and keep my reputation. After I went through the impersonation in Toronto, I knew that the representative of the hedge fund at the signing had been suspicious. I left the airport where my chartered plane was waiting, but at the airport I received a call from the head of the fund telling me that they thought something was wrong. At that point I could have boarded the plane and fled. Instead I went back to the office of the Teachers Fund, thinking I could possibly talk my way out of it. It's a slippery slope once you surrender to ambition. I did not set out to steal hundreds of millions of dollars, but ended up doing so incrementally after crossing a line I could not retreat from…once I started, there seemed to be no way out other than to continue (p. 267).

After seven years and nearly $800 million in fabricated debt notes, he was arrested by the Canadian Police and sentenced to twenty years in a U.S. prison. It was easier to continue the scheme especially when he was respected by his employees and valued by his clients. For example, Dreier went on to state,

> For six-plus years I did manage to pay everyone everything that was owed to them, plus a very nice profit for them. I did this, of course, by victimizing new lenders who, inevitably, would suffer the loss, but I continued to believe that somehow I would turn the firm into such a money maker that I would be able to cover all the debt. I also believed, even if very irrationally, that I would not end up hurting people, because, in the end, everyone would be paid. I was keeping lots and lots of people employed at the firm and they were in a way unwittingly benefiting from my perpetuating the scheme, I tried to rationalize that the potential harm was offset by the current good and just hoped that it would somehow all work out (Soltes, 2016, p. 269).

The Fraud Triangle: Advantages and Limitations

From a criminology perspective white-collar crime like other crimes can best be explained by three factors: a supply of motivated offenders, the availability of suitable victims, and the absence of capable guardians—control systems or someone "to mind the store" (Ramamoorti, 2008). The fraud triangle is a framework designed to explain the reasoning behind a person's decision to commit white-collar crime especially in the workplace. The three prongs of the triangle can be summarized as pressure/incentives, opportunity, and rationalization. There have been attempts to improve on the fraud triangle by developing what is known as a fraud diamond that incorporates the elements of the fraud triangle, but also include the concept of offender capability (Dorminey et al., 2010). However, whether it is the fraud triangle or the fraud diamond, neither model addresses in enough detail criminological components of criminal thinking traits attributable to these offenders. As such generations of antifraud professionals, law enforcement, and those in academia, are not taught major elements of what constitutes the criminal personality illustrated by how they think about crime and individual behavioral traits facilitating negative outcomes.

The problem is that antifraud professionals get stuck believing the fraud triangle is all that is necessary to understand risk factors triggering offending. Although the fraud triangle is a respectable place to begin the analysis of how and why fraud actually occurs, the problem with the fraud triangle is that it fails to address the antisocial thinking process that led people down a corrupt path in the first place. Put differently, why would a person choose to resolve a problem criminally when legal options might be available? This is why a section on understanding antisocial and criminal thinking patterns was included in order to expand one's thinking on how to view offender's thought processes to supplement the fraud triangle. The fraud triangle in this respect is limited, however it is important to give the fraud triangle's uses the respect it deserves because it did start the process of understanding how to consider elements that trigger fraud offending. Let us explore the major points of the fraud triangle consisting of pressures, incentives, opportunities and rationalizations.

Incentives and Pressure that Encourage Fraud

Research suggests that many frauds are committed as a result of work-related financial pressures or some reflect a more personal, vice-related pressure such as an addiction or too much debt due to living beyond one's means (Albrecht et al., 2012). Other personal pressures unrelated to work include unpaid medical bills, addictions, family separations due to divorce, and a spouse losing their job. Work related pressures might include, 1) expectations from Wall Street who monitor publically traded corporations, 2) liquidity issues or commonly referred to as cash flow issues where a business may have difficulty paying bills because they do not have the cash to do so, 3) a declining industry where it is difficult to maintain sales levels, 4) managerial pressures that have nothing to do with the financial viability of an entity, but reflect unattainable growth targets, and 5) the inability to meet regulatory requirements that could force the organization to pay fines and potentially face criminal liability.

Seldom mentioned, but a very real pressure that deserves mentioning, is the belief that one has a duty of loyalty to commit fraud for the benefit of the organization and work colleagues. Under such circumstances, employees see themselves as forced into corruption due to loyalty issues and demands by superiors. Moreover, there are industry condition risk factors that may increase the probability of experiencing pressure and they include, 1) new accounting, statutory, or regulatory requirements that could impair the financial stability or profitability of the entity, 2) a high degree of competition or market saturation, accompanied by declining profit margins, 3) a declining industry with increasing business failures, and 4) rapid changes in the industry, such as significant declines in customer demand, high vulnerability to rapidly changing technology, or rapid product obsolescence. Consider the statement regarding pressure resulting in fraud at Heinz Corporation reflecting financial pressure:

> When we didn't meet our growth targets, the top brass really came down on us, recalls a former marketing official at the company's huge Heinz U.S.A. division. And everybody knew that if you missed the targets enough, you were out on your ear. In this environment, some harried managers apparently resorted to deceptive bookkeeping when they couldn't otherwise meet profit goals set by the company's top executives (Anand et al., 2004, p. 42).

Organizations need to carefully distinguish between expected high, but fair performance and those that demand excessive and ultimately unattainable levels of performance, however this principle is often ignored (Free et al., 2007). For example, Walmart's top management ordered its store managers to keep labor cost low by using the interpersonal strategy of threatening those who failed to comply with demotion and dismissal in order to establish Walmart as the industry's lowest price leader. This pressure caused managers to turn to illegal means by coercing employees to work off the clock to shave time off their payroll records. As one manager put it, "I screwed plenty of people in my career there. Honestly, you have to. It's either you do it, or there's the door. They told us in meetings, I can hire anyone off the street and pay them fifty thousand dollars to run the store" (Palmer, 2012, p. 186).

Opportunities to Engage in Fraud

A criminal opportunity arises whenever a motivated person or group of persons recognizes or perceives a suitable target is not adequately guarded; in essence there is a situation that is vulnerable and open to exploitation (Benson, 2015). Furthermore, these opportunities are presented by vulnerable environments and opportunistically interpretable scenarios that individuals and groups assess that offer the potential for reward with little risk of detection or punishment. In terms of white-collar crime opportunity, it is essentially a situation or combination of circumstances that create a pathway for fraud (Aguilera & Vadera, 2008). With regard to white-collar crime, the term 'suitable target' is conceived more broadly to include situations in which an individual or group of individuals can "pervert or distort legitimate economic business or professional activities so as to illegally benefit themselves" (Benson, 2015, p. 552). Some exploitable opportunities can be embedded in weak internal controls, a corporate culture that supports antisocial behaviors such as encouraging bribery to get business, and ineffective management. For the sake of white-collar crime, the style of opportunity highlighted can refer to situational factors of the industry itself, the corporate environment that workers are in, and the current financial health of the organization.

Trends show that firms in certain industries are correlated with being more likely to commit unethical practices and contain similar levels of criminal activity because of exploitable opportunities. Opportunity both facilitate and cause white-collar crime and in general criminal behavior is not as possible in the absence of criminal opportunities (Tomlinson & Pozzuto, 2016). Criminal motivation and skills do not provide access to opportunities, but they do prepare one to take advantage of opportunities should such prospects arise. With regard to white-collar crime, criminal opportunities arise or become available to potential offenders as a result of their holding certain occupational positions. The occupational position gives the offender legitimate access to some situation or opportunity in which the offender can advance their own interests at the expense of other individuals, organizations, or the market, in general (Benson & Simpson, 2009). For example, positions of trust that are acquired through employment may create opportunities to take advantage of. White-collar criminals stumble across opportunities in the course of their business dealings and through interactions with others; routine interactions between people and their environments create the necessary conditions for crime.

For example, by virtue of their positions in the health care system, physicians have access to various public and private health care insurance systems. Because of this legitimate access, physicians can submit fraudulent claims for payment for health care services never rendered. As another example, by virtue of their positions, the owners or highly placed executives in certain types of companies can conspire together to set prices in violation of antitrust laws. The degree to which occupations create or make available opportunities for white-collar crime depends on the laws, regulations, and rules governing occupations, industries, and types of economic activities. Offenders are attracted to exploitable opportunities that require little effort, offer low risks and high rewards coupled with rationalizations to explain away their behaviors. Employees gain this specialized knowledge by virtue of the fact that their position inside a business affords them legitimate access to sensitive parts of the business and this legitimacy is used by motivated employee thieves to complete, as well as to mask their criminal acts and at times to mask the acts of their co-conspirators (Benson & Simpson, 2009).

When in such positions, employees are in an optimal place to know where there are weaknesses within a business to exploit if they are engaging in fraud. In some occupations, it is expected that employees will take materials, information, and equipment home with them as needed to complete their jobs. In these situations trusted employees are guardians of the business's property and it is this trusted position that makes it easy for motivated employees to exploit their employer, customers, or both (Tomlinson & Pozzuto, 2016). For example, the buying and selling of securities is a legitimate economic activity that can be perverted when a corporate insider trades shares of their own company on the basis of nonpublic material information (Benson, 2015). Here, the activity of trading securities is the target. If that activity is not well regulated and supervised or guarded by government entities, then it becomes a suitable target by means of which a potential offender can take advantage of others information for personal financial gain. Yet another aspect of opportunity that facilitates white-collar crime is due to a lack of checks and balances and effective oversight (Antar, 2013).

Other opportunities represent themselves through, 1) inadequate internal controls to safeguard assets, 2) a disregard for regulations, 3) a poor tone at the top where leadership either ignores ethical and legal considerations or encourages their employees to engage in misconduct, 4) a high turnover rate where duties are not segregated, 5) a weak board of directorship that does not adequately assess the business risks management undertakes, 6) aggressive accounting used to engage in earnings management, 7) unusual and related party transactions that are not monitored, 8) significant accounting changes that do not offer a logical reason for the changes, and 9) being apathetic and ignorant about fraud opportunities. Rational choice theory asserts that those who commit crime first balance the potential risks and rewards. There are several factors that impact the rational choice theory including, 1) a person's opportunities to earn legitimate money, 2) how much of that legitimate money is available, 3) the amount of money they can gain from committing crime, 4) the likelihood of being caught, and 5) once caught, the probability of being punished. This theory, however, is just as individual as it is social, meaning factors in corporate culture can influence motivations to exploit opportunities for personal gain.

With rational choice in mind, most corporate crimes consist of an internal cost-benefit analysis that either persuades or dissuades people in moments of exploitable opportunities. Although people may engage in rational choice in a flawed manner where they may end up having their fraud scheme detected, this does not mean they do not engage in a risk assessment of the costs versus the benefits. The rational choice to exploit an opportunity does not always have to be primarily out of self-interest. Individuals maximize their own interests as they define their own interest and concepts such as "altruism, loyalty, vengefulness, and fairness are all motivations that can play a role in an individual's decisions under different circumstances" (Soltes, 2016, p. 94). Making trade-offs through cost-benefit analysis has long been regarded as a core competency in business. As a result, white-collar offenders engage in risk assessments after carefully calculating the benefits and costs (Soltes, 2016). Consider the perspectives of an accounting partner at KPMG who made a conscious decision not to register a tax shelter with the Internal Revenue Service (IRS) who went on to reassure his colleagues of the benefits of not registering and that they were simply following industry norms. The partner stated:

There are no tax products marketed to individuals by our competitors which are registered. First, the financial exposure to the Firm is minimal. Based upon on our analyses of the applicable penalty sections, we conclude that the penalties would be no greater than $14,000 per $100,000 in KPMG fees. Any financial exposure that may be applicable can be easily dealt with by setting up a reserve against fees collected. Given the relatively nominal amount of such potential penalties, the Firm's financial results should not be affected by this decision. The rewards of successful marketing of the tax structure product and the competitive disadvantage which may result from registration far exceed the financial exposure to penalties that may arise (p. 90).

Rationalizations Facilitating Fraudulent Behaviors

Fraud offenders, perhaps simplistically phrased, can be put into two categories: those who think they can get away with their crimes and those who believe they were committing an unethical, but not a criminal act. Yet both rely on rationalizations justifying their behaviors. An attribute of the criminal personality is the offender's tendency to make generous or self-serving use of rationalizations to distance themselves from their misconduct. For clarification purposes, there are differences in motivation and rationalization; usually motivation is what drives the act, the reasons behind the act, while rationalization nullifies or neutralizes the moral objection to the act (Goldstraw, 2005). The likelihood of offending is reduced if one perceives illegal acts as immoral, socially harmful, violates environmental protection norms, or one that carries negative social or reputational consequences for the person or the organization. However, the risk of offending increases if rationalizations surface dampening the perceived immorality of the offending. Rationalizations are also referred to as techniques of neutralization, which allow the offender to minimize the apparent conflict between their behavior and the prevailing societal norms of right and wrong.

Rationalizations are equally used by white-collar and non-white-collar offenders and are uniquely crafted to align with a particular crime. Historically, white-collar offender rationalizations were regarded by scholars as not being antisocial because they do not explicitly endorse lawbreaking. Rather due to extenuating circumstances, white-collar crime was perceived as permissible under certain conditions (Benson & Manchak, 2014). In addition, "moral ambiguity permeates the idea of white-collar crime, affecting both how we subjectively understand it and how we respond to it as a society" coupled with how we rationalize engaging in it (Simpson, 2013, p. 318). Rationalization is a common behavior among white-collar offenders because many offenders are raised to understand that theft is wrong, therefore rationalizations are needed to make sense of their actions (Wells, 2012). Rationalizations can be thought of as linguistic devices invoked by management and employees that blunt the moral force of the law and ethics which neutralize the guilt of participation to avoid damage to their self-image. For those who did not believe they were committing an unethical or criminal act, one of the traits criminals pick up through contact with other criminals are "definitions favorable to the violation of law"; in other words, ways of describing their actions that made them seem less wrong or to protect themselves from blame (Sutherland & Cressey, 1978, p. 81).

When asked to provide rationalizations for their actions, offenders "engage in narrative sense-making to align their actions with personal and cultural expectations of appropriate behavior…doing so allows them to manage the potential stigma that arises from violating norms" (Copes et al., 2013, p. 353). Almost without exception and regardless whether they come from the upper or middle reaches of the status hierarchy, convicted white-collar offenders deny having criminal intent (Benson & Manchak, 2014). Without criminal intent means that if it were not for certain circumstances which may have pressured them, they would not have engaged in fraud. Thus, if the business was not in financial trouble, they never would have resorted to fraud to help them through a difficult time. Offenders view themselves as generally moral, and they typically do not see themselves as being like real criminals, instead they tend to rationalize away their offenses as oversights, mistakes, or technical violations (Benson & Manchak, 2014). Of course not all white-collar offenders are oblivious to the illegality of their behavior. Some do recognize that certain actions violate the law and run counter to prevailing moral conventions, but convince themselves through rationalizations that the violations are acceptable, even necessary (Benson & Manchak, 2014).

The important characteristic about rationalizations is that they allow the offender to retain allegiance to the dominant system of societal norms and values which favors a virtuous character, while at the same time exempting their own actions from its obligations, thereby freeing them to pursue their self-interest in a relatively unconstrained fashion (Sykes & Matza, 1957). Moreover, simply because one is involved in a criminal subculture does not isolate them from the norms of behavior valued by larger society. Few offenders, whether white-collar or non-white-collar, live totally outside the demands for conformity by the dominant social order; even mafia bosses have family, have responsibilities, pay their bills, send their children to college, and often support their church and other social institutions (Cromwell & Bizer, 2012). The societal goals of being respected, appreciated, being valued as a human being, having self-worth, and admired permeates deviant culture too, although they may be distorted in practice. The use of rationalizations allow these individuals to justify their less commendable activities to the extent they appear socially acceptable, at least to themselves, and allows them to maintain a sense of social acceptance and self-esteem. Furthermore, by lessening any guilt from the commission of crimes and providing the individual with a positive self-image, the use of rationalizations facilitates further criminal acts. As one behavioral finance scholar stated:

> Nobody is ever a villain in their own narrative, so if someone takes actions that threaten to paint them as a bad person, they are more likely to change their opinion of what's right and wrong, rather than change their opinion of themselves. People can make poor decisions by getting gradually worse without realizing how far they've shifted (Soltes, 2016, p. 321).

Most persons, criminal or not, justify their behavior to themselves and others, thereby reducing or eliminating guilt, shame, and accountability for their actions through rationalizing. Rationalizations can serve a variety of purposes, not solely to allay one's conscience, but also to avoid or reduce moral or legal judgments from others. Individuals and groups are motivated to resolve the inherent ambiguity that often surrounds their behavior and outcomes in a manner that serves their self-interests and preserves one's social identity by reframing the meaning of their acts that are contrary to ethics and potentially the law. Rationalizations are common in everyday life; they are ritualized accounts that explain a variety of unethical acts and outcomes so as to reconcile them with societal norms. These factors suggest white-collar offenders do conform to normative roles and are self-interested in doing so because they have a greater stake in conformity than street-level offenders who may reject societal norms to a greater degree. Rationalizations are not always created spontaneously by individuals, but instead they are learned patterns of thought likely to be routinized within organizational cultures, subcultures, and groups, be it legitimate or illegitimate ones, and some are likely to be exclusive to the group in which they belong.

Rationalizations can be crime specific, thus arsonists and sexual predators will employ their own rationalizations in contrast to white-collar offenders. Organizational environments provide a source of learned and appropriate rationalizations, thus a major feature of the corporation, in general, is that the individual is isolated from the broader community. This may serve to insulate deviant ideas from critical scrutiny and harsher judgment. For rationalizations to be believable, they should be appropriate for the social position of the person asserting the rationalization which will likely vary based on the socioeconomic status of the offender and the type of offense. It is necessary for those who describe themselves as law-abiding and honorable citizens to justify their behaviors through rationalizations in order to mitigate the risk of losing face. Fraud offenders describe their crimes as part of a general display of irresponsibility for which they are not completely accountable which allows them to facilitate the avoidance of being labeled as adopting a criminal identity. Some white-collar offenders believe that it is beneath them to engage in street-level offenses like violence and property crimes to acquire people's money and it is street-level offenses they equate a criminal identity with even though they are depriving others of their money or property by using a different strategy. As one fraud offender stated:

You know, sometimes life's not easy. You just kind of have this pressure from everywhere. You know what I'm saying? Nobody ever really wants to commit crimes. Nobody likes to commit crime. I don't know if you understand that? Sometimes difficulties and circumstances make people do stuff. So yeah, I'm not the type, I mean, not a "crime person". It was just circumstances (Copes et al., 2013, p. 357).

Rationalizations allow individuals the ability to hold thoughts that are psychologically inconsistent with each other by seeking ways to reduce their inherent conflict by changing their beliefs about the rightness or wrongfulness of the behavior, or by acquiring new information or beliefs that will reduce such conflicts. As one psychologist observed, "We are creative narrators of stories that tend to allow us to do what we want and that justify what we have done...We believe our stories and thus believe that we are objective about ourselves" (Soltes, 2016, p. 258). Rationalizations can so ingrain themselves into one's self-image to the extent that one can lie to themselves and accept rationalizations as reality to prevent the conflict that stems from the incompatibility of what they do and who they think they are. Perhaps the best description of understanding rationalizations is not found in academic literature, but in George Orwell's novel, *1984* where he discusses the concept of doublethink. Orwell describes doublethink as:

The power of holding two contradictory beliefs in one's mind simultaneously, and accepting both of them....To tell deliberate lies while genuinely believing in them, to forget any fact that has become inconvenient, and then, when it becomes necessary again, to draw it back from oblivion for just so long as it is needed, to deny the existence of objective reality and all the while to take account of the reality which one denies (Orwell, 1949).

Doublethink is a mechanism through which the individual reduces uncomfortable mental conflicts when holding two contradictory beliefs simultaneously and accepting them both as morally viable (Palmer, 2012). The benefit of doublethink is that it allows two conflicting ideas to coexist, but still allows the offender to perceive themselves as a good person. Doublethink is also a self-protective mechanism resulting from extensive use of rationalizations that allows compartmentalizing and protecting one's identity of who they prefer to be given particular circumstances. Compartmentalization is a psychological defense strategy used to avoid the discomfort and anxiety caused by a person's values, emotions and beliefs that may be at conflict due to the inconsistency of the application of one's values to a given situation. However, we should not think that all fraud offenders need to rely on rationalizations and doublethinking to reduce anxieties associated with unethical and/or criminal behaviors. It is perhaps naïve to think that all people who commit offenses, heinous acts or fraud for that matter "feel bad" about their behaviors and require some form of rationalizations. Consider the insights of offender CFO Samuel Antar:

Most people think that we have to rationalize our crimes. Not true. We know what we're doing and simply do not care about our victims. I simply didn't. Rationalization is for sissy criminals. You have to take the moral compass out of the equation to really understand criminal behavior. Morality doesn't exist in the criminal world, except it helps us when the other person has morality (Antar, 2013).

Fraud offenders are more adept at sanitizing their actions than street-level offenders who are less educated and lack the communication and intellectual sophistication necessary to invent creative rationalization narratives. They create rationalizations acceptable to the audience they are trying to persuade by reflecting a value system more in line with middle class virtues and not those of conventional street-level offenders who may offer little in terms of parallel value systems. Thus, someone that asserts they engage in fraud to save the company from bankruptcy may be attractive to a business owner who has faced financial pressures before. However, it is equally important to give the impression that they do not support a criminal lifestyle as a way of making a living. Interestingly, street-level offenders might take responsibility for their acts more than white-collar offenders who deny they committed a crime altogether and in fact they tend to define their crimes in terms of a mistake or misunderstanding or as "illegal but not criminal" (Copes et al., 2013, p. 365). Securities fraud offender, Justin Paperny, reflects the above sentiments:

> White-collar offenders utter the same lines I once cried: I did not set out to do harm; my intentions were sound, however, the culture was corrupt; it was unethical, not illegal; any successful business person works out of gray areas; I knew it was wrong, yet the temptation to cheat was too great; everyone was doing it; and so on. I found solace in blaming the toxic culture that I claimed groomed me, or in blaming my senior partner (Perri et al., 2014a, p. 16).

In addition, one of the major differences between corporate crime and street crime is the frequency with which white-collar criminals simply deny the authority of the laws that they have broken. Often this is based on some variant of laissez-faire ideology which either contests the legitimacy, or denies the efficacy of any government interference in the market place (Clinard & Yeager, 1980). More sophisticated deniers appeal to the business judgment rule in order to condemn government interference in mere governance issues. The business judgment rule is derived from the doctrine in corporate law that courts defer to the business judgment of corporate executives to make decision they deem in the best interest of the organization they oversee as long as they carry out their duties with diligence and in good faith. Both arguments suggest government simply does not have the right to regulate certain forms of private transactions. As a result, individual business people need not appeal to any rationalizations in defense of their actions, they need only insist upon their rights. Recently investigators have begun to explore how white-collar neutralizations are structured by social class and gender as well as by the mechanics of offenses. Women are more likely to rationalize their crimes as the result of an unavoidable necessity to support family, whereas men are more likely to deny harm or to condemn their condemners (Benson & Manchak, 2014).

Comparing white-collar male professionals convicted of financial crimes with street-level offenders, both offender groups stressed the need to provide for others such as their families to justify their involvement in their offenses, but they displayed subtle differences. The socially privileged professionals presented a broader, more embellished view of their obligations, citing their responsibilities to employees and their creditors. Research identified a number of rationalizations employed by white-collar criminals and all of them provided a viewpoint on illegal behavior that enables white-collar offenders to violate the law without feeling or diminishing guilt or tarnishing their self-image as respectable people. According to one study that interviewed white-collar criminals in prison, they indicated they should not be in prison because they perceived their own behavior as non-criminal (Dhami, 2007). Typical responses as to how white-collar offenders neutralized their crimes included, "There's no victim in white-collar crime...white-collar crime isn't a danger to society...There was no visual damage, no physical damage, no none was hurt...It was mostly a financial matter" (Dhami, 2007, p. 70). They often blamed the victim in that they somehow deserved to have the fraud inflicted upon them especially if the victim was an organization.

In another study that specifically interviewed only accountants in prison for various frauds such as asset misappropriation, tax evasion, and taking money from client accounts, they provided rationalizations which included, 1) denying that they had the intent to commit fraud, 2) there was no injury because the insurance company covered any losses implying that the money really did not belong to anyone, 3) the money was there for the taking if a need should arise, 4) blaming the victim for their losses in that if victims could not protect their assets they deserved to have their money taken, 5) the money was going to be repaid, 6) the money was used to help others, and 7) no one was actually harmed from their fraud (Dellaportas, 2013). One accountant who took company assets believed that the employer deserved to have money embezzled from his company because of the unfair way he was treated. The offender will find self-deception facilitates regarding their own excuses as plausible if they are in a social environment in which such claims tend to be given credence, or where they are unlikely to encounter critical or dismissive voices.

Thus it is not uncommon to hear rationalizations such as everyone else is doing it, appealing to higher loyalties within an organization, and believing that one is entitled to engage in white-collar crime in order to offset a perceived injustice to them (Heath, 2008). Perhaps the offender acknowledges injury, but claims that the victim is unworthy of concern because, in some sense, they deserved it. For example, the crime is portrayed as retaliation for some offense committed by the victim or the organization. It is sometimes suggested that it is morally unacceptable for one individual to be punished for an offense, when others who have committed the same offense are not punished. Some offenders deny being motivated by self-interest, claiming that it was instead done out of obedience to some moral obligation. The fact of widespread misconduct by others may also be used to remove the moral stigma associated with an offense coupled with the goal of showing that the law is out of touch with social expectations, and therefore obedience to the law and its enforcement is outdated (Heath, 2008). The function of such environments is to create a social context in which certain types of excuses are given sympathetic understanding, or perhaps even encouraged. In this way, the offender finds it easier to live with the obvious contradiction between his own commitment to the moral standards of society and the criminality of his actions.

All of this creates an environment in which it is relatively easy for people to convince themselves that, rather than stealing, what they are really doing is taking what they are owed, or perhaps punishing their employer for treating employees poorly (Green, 1990). One survey found that "when employees felt exploited by the company…these workers were more involved in acts against the organization as a mechanism to correct perceptions of inequity or injustice" (Hollinger & Clark, 1983, p. 142). Also, if the corporation engaged in unethical or illegal practices, employees may regard their own theft as nothing but the seizure of resources owed to them anyways. Although rationalizations used by white-collar offenders are similar to those often studied among general offenders, they tend to center around the values, customs, and ideologies of the business world (Benson & Manchak, 2014). Furthermore, the use of rationalizations by white-collar offenders is known to be widespread, but it does not mean that offenders can pick and choose randomly among the rationalizations to interpret their own behavior. Offenders of all types offer a variety of rationalizations justifying their behaviors, but many do so in ways that reflect the expectations of the group. This explains why different rationalizations exist for different types of white-collar crimes (Copes et al., 2013). For example, antitrust offenses have a different history and are committed using different techniques than offenses such as financial statement fraud or income tax evasion (Benson & Manchak, 2014).

Moreover, collective rationalization highlights the ways in which organization members ignore identified or suspected deviance to insulate themselves or the organization from liability affecting organizational behavior by socializing individuals and organizations to actively avoid acknowledging information that confirms the existence of illegal activities (Rorie, 2020). The officers and directors of a firm have competing obligations both to root out illegal behavior and to ensure the firm achieves its goals despite internal or external challenges and obstacles. This can lead organization members to question the legitimacy of accusations made against other members. For example "leaders have diminished obligations to investigate charges against their own if the allegations come from outside sources with suspect motives" (Roric, 2020, p. 180). Competitive business environments triggers a natural suspicion about the motives of outsiders who raise questions about an organization's practices. Meeting this suspicion by willfully ignoring signs of deviance can send signals to other members of the organization that deviant behavior is at the very least ignored, if not outright accepted, so long as it benefits the firm.

Practicing collective rationalization, particularly when such practice becomes a part of normal organizational behavior, creates organizational norms supportive of silencing or hiding information that may harm the business. These practices may be viewed to be acceptable if blowing the whistle on internal deviance would substantially affect the achievement of organizational goals. Overarching goals of organizational performance can lead to organizational norms that support the suppression of negative information that may disrupt or inhibit goal attainment. It is also the case that organization members' uncertainty about the illegality of an organizational action or their inability to determine the best way to speak up about these issues inhibits whistleblowing and similar internal actions. However, whether they are formalized or simply a part of the informal structure of the organization, norms tolerant of concerted ignorance can become part of the culture or may help to define the climate of an organization when left unchecked. The organization's climate, and in turn employee behavior, is heavily affected by the types of behaviors and activities that are rewarded or sanctioned by the organization. Accordingly "managers develop interest in not enforcing their authority because deviance in their domains would reflect failure in their leadership" (Rorie, 2020, p. 181). This suggests that managers can create a climate conducive to the suppression of negative information and knowledge of deviant acts when admission of such behavior would not reflect well on the manager or the business. It is unclear whether this approach can be applied to issues of occupational offending that occur within the workplace, that may ultimately hurt the corporation, or organizational deviance that benefits the firm.

By exercising collective rationalization and ignoring deviant acts within the business, the company is allowed to profit from the deviant or criminal behavior without violating informal organizational norms. In these instances, overlooking or suppressing knowledge of deviant acts occurs not because managers or employees are actively ignoring illegal or unethical behavior, but rather because deviance has become part of the organization's normal behavior. Normalization of deviance highlights the ways in which certain acts can lose their deviant or criminal nature through their normal occurrence as part of otherwise legitimate organizational behavior. In essence, organization members do not see harmful acts as either deviant or criminal, nor do they see them as harmful to the organization. Rather, the normalization of deviance allows well intentioned people to engage in behaviors that in other circumstances would be recognized as deviant. Normalizing deviance within an organization allows members to create neutralizations or justifications for their behaviors that are accepted by other organization members.

At the same time, organization members who recognize patterns of deviance may be afraid to speak up because they are afraid of confronting co-workers about behaviors viewed within the group to be normal. This pattern of deviance normalization has its most impactful effects, internally and externally, when organization members normalize deviant behaviors that subvert processes designed to protect those who rely upon the organization for essential products or services. The external influence of normalized deviance can be substantial in other ways, as it can affect how an organization interacts with strategic partners during the course of business relationships. It has been argued that the normalization of deviance occurs because organizations are in search of new ways to achieve their goals of efficiency, increased productivity, and economic gain. In particular, it is an increased focus on achieving increases in these goals without a matching concern for the implementation of appropriate methods used to obtain the goal that leads to normalized deviance.

All that matters is the goal, and reward systems that emphasize goal attainment without a concomitant focus on emphasizing the proper ways to achieve that goal leave open opportunities for a normalization of deviant organizational activities. The normalization of deviance within organizations is not always a reflection of deviant intentions by organization members or attempts by the organization to find creative ways around regulations that may increase costs or seem onerous. Rather, deviance can become normalized over time as alternative processes or practices, which are ultimately deviant, replace accepted practices or processes that are either inefficient, ineffective, or flat out inhibit an organization's ability to achieve its goals. In other words deviance can rationalized as a form of efficiency—a way to get things done in a more efficient manner. Thus, the ends justify the means in that if deviance assisted in accomplishing organizational goals, then so be it. Deviance that becomes normalized can, therefore, simply be a result of misguided organizational adaptations to blocked goals or means of goal attainment. Let us examine some of the major rationalizations used by fraud offenders, both individually and collectively, in more detail.

Denial of Responsibility

Denial of responsibility refers to the individual who knows or suspects misconduct, but sees themselves as blameless even though they may have participated in the misconduct either directly by actually committing fraud or indirectly by putting subtle pressure on others to commit fraud. Generally, offenders deny responsibility by claiming their behavior is accidental because they have no choice but to engage in fraud due to circumstances beyond their control, such as management orders, peer pressure, dire financial straits, being deceived, that everyone else does it, and that they play a small part in the overall fraud scheme, and so on. For example, a manager who denies responsibility because they were taking orders might think, "What can I do? I just have to do what the boss says." This is an easily-adopted rationalization when experiencing intense pressure from management to meet revenue goals and more common when the crime is committed from within an organization by its employees (Benson & Manchak, 2014). Let us apply this rationalization in the context of a situation which occurred at B.F. Goodrich.

One of Goodrich's businesses entailed making wheels and brakes for aircraft, both civilian and military. Back in 1967 during the Vietnam War, Goodrich was contracted by the U.S. Air Force to make brakes for one of its fighter planes. A scandal ensued when a tight work schedule produced shortcuts in quality control and competition for the contract led to underestimation of the time required to complete it which, in turn, lead to pressure on supervisors to pass defective equipment as sound (Hoyk & Hersey, 2008). It turned out that the brake design was defective, but the manufacture of the brake went forward anyway because to start all over would be time consuming and costly. Conflict grew between those engineers who believed the brake defect should be disclosed instead of pretending the brake functioned correctly and those who did not believe they had any responsibility to disclose even though they were part of the team assigned to work on the brakes. When one of the engineering team members asked another team member if his conscience would bother him if during flight tests something should happen to the pilot like an injury or death due to defective brakes, the engineer answered back, "I learned a long time ago not to worry about things over which I have no control over. I have no control over this...Why should my conscience bother me?" (Vandivier, 2002, p. 157). Another example involves corporate officials marketing the dangerous intra-uterine contraceptive device (IUD) who stated the life-threatening infections were not caused by a design flaw, rather it was the result of improper use (Shover & Wright, 2001). Similarly, car makers blame road conditions and unsafe drivers for deaths and injuries rather than defective car design (Shover & Wright, 2001).

This rationalization facilitates the offender defining his conduct in a way that relieves him of responsibility, thereby mitigating both social disapproval, legal liability, and a personal sense of failure. The complexity of laws regulating many white-collar crimes and the hierarchical structure of companies offer offenders numerous ways to diffuse their responsibility because often participants collude for the fraud scheme to work. When using this rationale, individuals do not regard themselves as perpetrators of unethical acts, rather they view themselves as morally responsible individuals being forced into unethical acts. Consider the contradictory insights of Steven Garfinkel, CFO of medical equipment financing company DVI Inc., who believed fraudulent behavior exists when we actually engage in deception face to face but not when committed in a sterile manner such as filling out forms. On multiple occasions, Garfinkel would sign false collateral reports meaning he was stating that the company had more assets to use as collateral to borrow against than it actually did. This fraud sent Garfinkel to prison, yet in describing his behavior he stated: "I know this is going to sound bizarre, but when I was signing the documents, I didn't think of that as lying...There was a difference between filling out a form and flat out looking at someone in the eye and lying to them and saying no, there is nothing else you should know...I don't know why that seemed different, but it was" (Soltes, 2016, p. 125).

In an organizational context, this typically takes place by blaming the firm, superiors, or subordinates for our actions. This rationalization can also relate to blaming or assigning responsibility for unethical conduct on one's clients or customers. For example, consider the following interview conducted with former Swiss-based UBS banker Bradley Birkenfeld. The banker conveniently neglected to tell U.S. officials about his assistance in helping a U.S. client hide $200 million in revenues by introducing him to a consultant who specialized in creating shell companies that concealed the ownership of UBS accounts. Birkenfeld's response suggests that he was not responsible for any tax evasion: "I don't sign people's tax returns, so what they do with their taxes is not my business. I'm a banker...So you would steer them to somebody who would help them hide their money? You would recommend them to these service providers?' [the interviewer] asked. 'That's correct,' Birkenfeld said. 'You must have known deep down that it was illegal,' [the interviewer] remarked...'That's correct,' Birkenfeld said" (CBS, 2009).

Denial of Injury

Another technique for neutralizing the stigma of white-collar crime is the denial of injury or harm to anyone including organizations. In many white-collar crimes, such as insider trading or antitrust violations, there is no readily identifiable individual victim which makes it easy for offenders to downplay the seriousness of their crimes to the point of insignificance (Benson & Manchak, 2014). In one antitrust case, offenders simply refuse to believe price-fixing caused any harm as illustrated by an executive stating, "Illegal? Yes. But not criminal…I assumed that criminal action meant damaging someone, and we did not do that" (Geis, 1968). Often we will hear, "No one was really harmed…it could have been worse" (Anand et al., 2004, p. 41). The classic use of this technique is a fraud offender describing his actions as "borrowing" the money—by the offender's estimation, no one will be hurt because the money will be paid back at some point in the future. Consider this offender statement, "I figured that if you could use something and help yourself and replace it and not hurt anybody it was all right" (Shover & Wright, 2001, p. 343). Offenders also employ this rationalization when believing no one was really harmed because the organization is insured and can easily recover the costs, the actual damage is slight, and the organization does not appear to care are the harm is to the public or market as a whole.

A manager involved in a price fixing scandal illustrating this rationalization stated: "Since the spirit of such meetings only appeared to be correcting a horrible price level situation, that there was not an attempt to actually damage customers…there was no personal gain for me, the company did not seem actually to be defrauding…So I guess morally it did not seem quite so bad as might be inferred by the definition of the activity itself" (Geis, 1995, p. 156). It is easier to deny injury if the offended party does not react and organizations fail to punish employee fraud. These reactions implicitly reinforce the belief that fraud does not matter, thus no injury can be attached to their actions because injury is not visible as it would be with a street-level offense. For example, in a study of ongoing theft at an electronics factory, workers felt little guilt because no harm appeared to be done. As one worker put it, "It's a corporation…It's not like taking from one person…the people justify it that the corporation wouldn't be hurt by it…they just jack the price up and screw the customer. They're not losing anything. The Company told us that last year they lost $30,000…but that was for losses of all types. It gives them a nice big tax write-off. I'll bet you a goddamn day's pay that they jack that…write-off way up too (Anand et al., 2004, p. 42).

As previously indicated, rationalizations are not just applicable to white-collar offenders, they also apply to non-white-collar offenders. Consider the statement of one offender involved in theft by breaking into a large department store and cracking open the store's safe. Although the store belonged to a friend, the offender asserted no real damage was done stating, "He is completely covered by insurance. [The store owner] isn't going to lose a dime. One hour after they found the store was robbed, he had the insurance company's check for his loss—a lot more than what we got" (Cromwell & Birzer, 2012, p. 521). This offender was adept at arson by burning cars, houses, and businesses so that owners could collect insurance. In most of these cases, he reasoned he was simply engaging in a business transaction to assist those who needed cash. This offender further stated, "Arson is a victimless crime. Who gets hurt? Some fucking insurance company with a gazillion bucks. Little guy down here can't pay his mortgage or the payments on his car or whatever. A nickels worth of gas and a quart coke bottle and he's free and clear. I make a few dollars. No harm, no foul" (Cromwell & Birzer, 2012, p. 521). For example, identity theft offenders view this crime as not causing any harm and in fact their actions did not cause any real loss, financial or otherwise to individuals. Some identity theft offenders claim their crimes actually help the victims.

Consider the statement of one offender: "I convinced myself that I wasn't going to do anything bad to their credit or to them. It actually may have helped them. I would've gotten them a nice credit card with a high credit line and its going to help their credit and stuff like that and then I would close it" (Copes et al., 2013, p. 357). Here the rationalization assists the offender into believing that there cannot be any victim if in fact their behavior may have benefited them in some manner even though the victim never consented to such behavior. Others claimed they were just borrowing the money such as one offender stating she experienced no guilt because she needed the money as bad as the people she was scamming, plus she was going to pay the money back when her circumstances improved (Copes et al., 2013). Another identity theft offender stated: "With credit cards if you notify them that your credit card is missing then you are not liable. The same thing with forgeries and the bank. If you notify the bank, the consumer is not liable. The bank is going to be insured, so the bank is going to get their money back. The consumer is not gonna be hurt. Nobody really loses but the insurance companies. It's not taking from an individual per se, like burglary" (Copes et al., 2013, p. 357).

Denial of the Victim

One of the most identifiable features of white-collar crime is its often faceless quality to fraud perpetrators which facilitates permissive attitudes toward crime when the victim is unknown and will probably never meet or interact with those who are harmed by their actions (Landsheer et al., 1994). Denial of an identifiable victim usually takes two forms. One form is when the offender asserts that the victim's actions were inappropriate and therefore he, she or an organization deserved the harm thus there is no victim because they provoked the harm they experienced making them unworthy of concern (Heath, 2008). The offender might claim that the unethical activity can be characterized as a form of righteous justice or as a means to ensure the crimes or unethical activity of others be punished thus diminishing the existence of a victim. As a result, the offender claims rightful retaliation thus denying the victim's aggrieved status. For example, rather than referring to the act as stealing from the company, an employee takes property for personal use as a means to punish the employer for treating the employee or employees improperly or unfairly.

The other version of denying the victim is to depersonalize the victim into a faceless statistic facilitating the ability to psychologically distance themselves from their acts. Here the victim is absent, unknown, or abstract, which is often the case with property and economic crimes. At times this rationalization is also used by those that commit violent acts or atrocities where the victims in their view is simply a faceless statistic; unfortunate people who is simply in the wrong place at the wrong time. In this instance, the offender can minimize his internal culpability because there are no visible victims triggering the offender's moral conscience. This rationalization may be evident because often the harms of fraud are spread out over many people. For example, consider that most people carry automobile insurance. Part of the cost of insurance probably reflects the losses the insurance company incurred due to fraud that is passed down to the insurance customers where the loss is embedded in the cost of the insurance we pay. In the corporate world, antitrust actions or illegally copying software might take place since no one can identify the competitors or shareholders who would be affected. Executives of firms who attempt to evade taxes through various techniques can more easily justify the actions since it is difficult to identify the specific citizen harmed.

Condemnation of the Condemners

This rationalization involves an offender who legitimizes their behavior by pointing out the illegal or corrupt behavior of those in authority or in positions of respect in society the offender is taking advantage of. The condemnation of the condemners finds expression by denying the legitimacy of the law and government regulatory agencies that enforce in their mind unfair laws. Often organizational members insist that regulatory agencies not only invite cheating, but demand it (Shover & Wright, 2001). Legal sanctions may trigger anger and defiance especially if the legal and regulatory agencies are perceived to be unfair, biased, and stigmatizing (Simpson, 2013). For example, the business owner may argue that the tax code itself is unfair and unjust, hence it is not worthy of respect or obedience. Condemning condemners involves delegitimizing the legitimacy of those who claim certain behaviors as corrupt and those that are corrupt may characterize a disliked law as vague, complex, rarely enforced, punitive, or politically motivated such that enforcement is inconsistent or malicious. Offenders relying on this rationalization do not believe they have a moral obligation to obey the law by asserting its unfairness (Benson & Manchak, 2014). White-collar offenders shift attention away from their conduct on to the motives of other persons or groups, such as regulators, prosecutors, and government agencies as harboring a personal motive to single them out to make examples of them to enforce their regulations.

Telemarketing fraud offenders relying on this rationalization describe themselves as businesspersons and not offenders due to merely engaging in routine sales transactions asserting it is the victim's fault for being greedy or ignorant. Consider the insights of one thief who stole from his colleagues who he considered thieves or other professionals who he did favors for illustrating how he condemned those he took advantage of. When asked whether he felt remorseful about stealing from his associates, he replied, "No. Why should I? They were all a bunch of thieves too. Most of the money, they stole themselves…they had it coming. I hardly ever took something from an innocent person. They were thieves themselves, or degenerate gamblers, or crooked politicians" (Cromwell & Birzer, 2012, p. 521). The wrongfulness of an offender's own behavior is more easily diluted when he can point to the wrongfulness of another's misconduct. This neutralization technique takes many forms in white-collar cases: the offender calls his critics hypocrites, argues they are motivated by personal spite, and for political gain. The claim of selective enforcement or prosecution is particularly prominent in this neutralization. In addition, white-collar offenders may point to a biased regulatory system or an anti-capitalist government philosophy. Consider the application of this rationalization by this offender's viewpoint:

> The system is crooked and always has been. The little guy can't get a fair shake. Guy robs a convenience store of $20 gets 15, maybe 20 years [in prison]. The same judge that gives probation to somebody like that Milken guy who stole 3–4 billion and spent about 18 months in prison and kept a billion of what he stole…they act like they're the paragons of virtue (Cromwell & Birzer, 2012, p. 520).

Appeal to Higher Loyalties

Instead of denying responsibility or the existence of a victim, offenders sometimes appeal to a higher loyalty suggesting their conduct was not merely excusable, but actually the right thing to do under the circumstances. In other words, "the actors argue that their violation of norms is due to their attempt to realize a higher-order value" (Anand et al., 2004, p. 41). The most common higher purpose justifying white-collar crime appears to be group-based loyalty which involves framing one's actions so that they can be seen as serving a greater moral purpose other than themselves (Benson & Manchak, 2014). Rather than being based on pure self-interest, here the offender claims they were motivated by a higher moral obligation such as loyalty to others including family, managers, the firm, coworkers, customers, or society in general. For example, the owner of a small business may justify cheating on taxes by arguing that staying in business so as to protect the livelihood of his or her employees is more important than conforming to the tax code. The offender does not necessarily reject the norms he is violating, rather, he sees other priorities that are aligned with his group as more compelling. The offender asserts their violation of societal norms is due to their attempt to realize a higher purpose as illustrated by this offender statement, "We answered to a more important cause…I would not report it because of my loyalty to my boss" (Anand et al., 2004, p. 41).

Offenders rationalize their loyalty as necessity to protect a boss or employee, shore up a failing business, or maximize shareholder value are employing this neutralization technique. What is different in the business context, and what outsiders sometimes have difficulty comprehending, is the extent to which the corporation itself can serve as an object of higher loyalty. In and of itself loyalty is an important quality to display within an organization. Considerable effort on the part of management is aimed toward cultivation of these loyalties, from dramatic initiation rituals for new employees, on-site recreational and sports facilities, personal counseling services, to the widespread team building seminars and weekend retreats. However, an unintended consequence of the intense loyalties developed through such techniques is that employees believe they are excused from any accusation of criminality so long as their actions were undertaken for the sake of the firm rather than for reasons of self-interest. For example, one study of retired Fortune 500 Company managers showed widespread condemnation of whistleblowing on the grounds that it conflicted with the loyalty owed by employees to the firm. Many believed that, with certain exceptions such as safety violations, individuals who were unwilling to participate in illegal activities should simply quit their jobs or keep quiet, rather than "go to the government" (Clinard, 1983, p. 116).

It should be noted that managers will sometimes appeal to the fiduciary relationship that they hold toward shareholders or other stakeholders as an excuse for misconduct (Clinard & Yeager, 1980). The "we did it for the shareholders" excuse had a ring of plausibility to it, because agents are obliged to advance the interests of their principal as best as they can and this sometimes does require violations of conventional morality. Yet the loyalty argument is a false defense supporting crime as a solution because agency relationships cannot be used to justify illegal and unethical acts. For example, the actions of Chiquita Brand International executives demonstrated this rationalization when they were willing to pay millions to a terrorist organization in Colombia for the protection of employees who worked there, contrary to U.S. law (Cohen, 2007).

Metaphor of the Ledger

The metaphor of the ledger is differentiated from the appeal to higher loyalties rationalization in that the offender is not claiming his or her behavior is benefiting some greater good or some person or group to whom he owes greater loyalty. He or she admits the misconduct, but asserts that good deeds balance the misconduct—even tip the scales in his or her favor. As one scholar stated, "good in the credit column is balanced against evil in the debit column…acts of charity and benevolence offset entries of greed or selfishness" (Klockars, 1974, p. 152). By creating a behavioral balance sheet, the offender sees his current negative actions as heavily outweighed by a lifetime of good deeds, both personal and professional, minimizing moral guilt. For example, many white-collar criminal sentencings are preceded by a flood of letters to the court supportive of the defendant and attesting to his or her good deeds. Under the claim of entitlement, offenders rationalize their conduct on the grounds they deserve the fruits of their illegal behavior. The actors believe they are entitled to indulge in deviant behaviors because of the time and effort invested in their jobs such as believing, "We've earned the right…It's all right for me to use the internet for personal reasons at work. After all I do work overtime" (Anand et al., 2004, p. 41).

White-collar crime scholar Gilbert Geis, studying the antitrust case brought against heavy electrical equipment manufacturers in 1961, drew attention to the number of defendants who "took the line that their behavior, while technically criminal, had really served a worthwhile purpose by stabilizing prices" (Geis, 1968, p. 108). One offender, who spent a lifetime engaged in various non-white-collar crimes, rationalized that while he may have been involved in numerous criminal behaviors, he was also a good person stating, "I try to help somebody every day. There's not a day goes by…somebody comes to me and I help them" (Cromwell & Birzer, 2012, p. 519). This same offender related that he has always been a big tipper in bars and restaurants disclosing that a man came up to him and introduced himself as the son of a waitress in a restaurant that this offender regularly patronized. The man told the offender that it was his tips to his mother that allowed them to eat and keep a roof over their head. The offender stated, "I wish now that I had tipped her even better" (p. 519).

In another instance, he told of seeing a homeless family with two children standing on the street in the rain stating, "I picked them up…and took them to a motel and paid for a few days and bought them some food" (Cromwell & Birzer, 2012, p. 519). This offender also gave another example where a friend of his who owned a drug store experienced financial problems and asked for his help. The offender agreed to burn down his store so that the owner could collect the insurance, and a few months later the friend had a new store that was prospering. He received $20,000 from the insurance proceeds from the drugstore fire. The offender stated, "I dropped in to see my old pal at his new drugstore. It was doing a brisk business, and I noticed he had all of his old employees working there. They didn't know it but if not for me, they would all be in the unemployment line. I admired the results of my work. I had made a major contribution to the welfare of the community" (p. 520).

Normality and Social Comparison

Normality and social comparison entails an offender justifying their misconduct by comparing it to the misconduct of others. If "others are worse" or "everybody else is doing it," the offender, although acknowledging their misconduct, is able to minimize the attached moral stigma and view their behavior as aligned within a range of acceptable norms. Consider these statements reflecting social comparison between offenders, "You have no right to criticize us…Others are worse than we are" (Anand et al., 2004, p. 41). Some consider engaging in fraud and using this rationalization as legitimate business practice. As one consultant stated, "If you didn't do it, you weren't just stupid—you weren't behaving as a prudent businessman, which is the ground rule. You owed it to your partners, to your stockholders, to maximize profits. Everybody else was doing it" (Gobert & Punch, 2007, p. 105). Convicted CFO Whitacre of HealthSouth stated, "I didn't feel guilty about it then because I felt like the company was stealing so much money that mine was minuscule compared to what they were stealing…it really helped; it took some of the guilt away" (Wells, 2012, p. 55). Consider the statement of one fraud offender expressing the rationalization of social comparison: "I will never believe I have done anything criminally wrong. I did what is business. If I bent the rules, who doesn't? If you are going to punish me, sweep away the system. If I am guilty, there are many others who should be by my side in the dock" (Shover & Wright, 2001, p. 346).

Legality

Fraud offenders excuse corrupt practices on the grounds that they are not illegal, enthusiastically questioning their very applicability of the law when the law may be very applicable to their situation. This disconnect between behavior and rules provides latitude where some will conclude that whatever has not been labeled specifically illegal is acceptable. A prominent feature of corporate crime is the frequency business executives dispute the legitimacy of the law under which they are obligated to follow, or question the motives of the prosecutors who enforce them. Corporate criminals contest the very legitimacy of regulation by suggesting that the government, when it imposes constraints upon the marketplace, is beholden to special interests while the corporation represents the broader interests of the public. In essence, the corporation is a larger and more important constituency than the government, then it enjoys stronger democratic legitimacy than the government.

Necessity

"I did it for my family" remains one of the most popular excuses for occupational crime (Daly, 1989). Chronic fraud offender Barry Webne, a controller for a company stated, "I wanted to get my kids and my family everything they needed, material-wise, toys, stuffed animals, anything they wanted" (Wells, 2012, p. 55). Webne's fraud scheme was relatively simple; basically he set up a shell company at his place of work and directed payments to himself stealing an estimated $1.25 million. The direct payments to himself were classified on the company's financial statements as expenses, but in fact they were fictitious expenses. Webne stated his employer did not provide adequate oversight who further stated, "As long as the financial statements were turned in on time, nobody bothered us" (p. 55). White-collar scholar Gilbert Geis quotes one defendant in a heavy electrical antitrust case of 1961 excusing his actions in the following terms: "I thought that we were more or less working on a survival basis in order to try to make enough to keep our plant and our employees" (Geis, 1968, p. 108).

Here one can see the vocabulary of "survival" being used to blend the "necessity" defense into an appeal to higher loyalties and in this case, an altruistic concern for the plant's employees. The necessity rationalization is also intensified by the competitiveness of the marketplace and the workplace. This means that if one individual refuses to perform an illegal act, he may simply be replaced by someone else who will or if one firm refuses to pay a bribe, the business will simply go to some other firm that will. Consider a manager commenting on another manager engaged in financial statement fraud: "What he did was not unethical…he knew what he was doing. It's not that he did it out of ignorance of anything. What he did was he made the best of a situation without having to sacrifice the company's progress. If we couldn't have gotten the profits this way, I don't know how we would have gotten the money. We might have had to cut back on some things we didn't want to sacrifice, like our marketing budget, or on people. You know, I mean the alternatives to the decision were probably a lot uglier" (Yeager, 2007, p. 33).

Segregation of Duties

In some respect, the segregation of duties rationalization could be considered a form of denial of responsibility, however it appears to deserve its own category so that it would be more memorable for readers. Segregation of duties is the concept of requiring more than one person to complete a task. The concept is not practiced only in business, but also in government and the military as examples. In business the separation of duties is displayed by having more than one individual perform a task which is typically considered an internal control matter intended to prevent fraud and error. Segregation of duties is a basic building block of sustainable risk management and internal controls for an organization. The risk management goal of segregation of duties controls is to prevent unilateral actions from occurring in key processes where irreversible affects are beyond an organization's tolerance for error or fraud. With respect to a business, the separation of duties prohibits the assignment of responsibility to one person for asset acquisition, their custody, and the related record keeping.

Thus, for example, one person can place an order to buy an asset, but a different person must record the transaction in the accounting records. By separating duties, it is much more difficult to commit fraud, since at least two people must work together to do so, which makes fraud less likely than if one person is responsible for all aspects of an accounting transaction. Let us look at another example as it relates to cash. One person opens envelopes containing checks, and another person records the checks in the accounting system. Another example relates to inventory where one person orders goods from suppliers, and another person logs in the received goods in the accounting system. This keeps the purchasing person from diverting incoming goods for their own use. However, this internal control of duty segregation can be manipulated to be used as a rationalization to distance oneself from fraudulent behavior especially if there is collusion which neutralizes the benefits of having a segregation of duties system in place. We are apt to hear from offenders that because they are in control of a small aspect of the overall fraud scheme, they cannot be responsible especially if there was collusion. Typically a subordinate will state that they were taking orders from a superior to minimize their role.

Thus the segregation of duties concept is purposely distorted, acting as a buffer between the offender's actions and the consequences of engaging in fraud. What is not understood by fraud offenders is that legally, one does not have to commit the entire fraud act to be held accountable for the fraud in its entirety. That is why we see prosecutors charge individuals with conspiracy to commit fraud which neutralizes this rationalization. In conspiracies, especially when there is collusion between the parties, the act of one offender is adopted as an act of all the other offenders. Thus, in reference to fraud, if a senior executive colludes with a subordinate to commit financial statement fraud, even though the subordinate was the person that manipulated the internal controls to perpetrate the fraud, the subordinate's argument cannot be that they were just taking orders from there superior as a way to mitigate their role. Conversely, the executive cannot argue that they did not manipulate the internal controls, thus they did not participate in the fraud. The executive and the subordinate may have separate duties, however they cannot rely on the fact that they participated in only part of the fraud to claim innocence.

The Case of Fraud Offender Walter Pavlo

MCI was a telecommunications company that became the site and perpetrator of a number of financial statement frauds in the late 1990s and into the early 2000s. Problems surfaced at MCI because sales representatives signed up a large number of customers knowing they were not going to pay their bills, however by signing them up, the representatives earned more commissions regardless of whether the customer could pay or not. However, MCI did not want to write-off uncollectible account receivables because this would increase the probability that MCI would have to revise and reveal to the public how much money it really made which in turn meant its stock price would go down. MCI's finance unit, whose role it was to collect bad customer debts, complained to upper management about the sales practices, but management sided with the sales unit because they needed the sales team to generate large volumes of orders to maintain the appearance of growth. MCI's top management ordered the head of the firm's finance unit, Ralph McCumber, to delay writing off bad debt until the following fiscal year, however McCumber voiced strong objection to this request (Palmer, 2012).

McCumber eventually complied and relayed the order to collections manager and subordinate Walter Pavlo for implementation, who also objected. Moreover, MCI's top management established unrealistic targets for the amount of bad debt Pavlo's team had to collect each year and according to Pavlo and other co-conspirators who engaged in fraud, top management knew that the only way that they could meet such targets was through fraud. Most of Pavlo's collection efforts were fruitless and desperate to keep his job, he began to employ fraudulent accounting techniques to hide the unpaid debt that he could not collect. According to Pavlo, he did not begin his career at MCI with a plan to defraud the company stating, "If someone asked me on my first day at MCI, how I was going to steal U.S. $6 million…I would have said that I would never do such a thing and I wouldn't even know how to do it" (Jacka, 2004, p. 50). In addition, for Pavlo, no one thing led to the embezzlement of $6 million of MCI money, "it was a combination of the industry, the profit, the tone at the top, the friend, the external auditors, the internal auditors and many other small things" (Jacka, 2004, p. 52).

Moreover, Pavlo felt enormous pressure from within MCI and did not know how to meet MCI's debt collection mandates without cheating especially since his performance reviews were based entirely on how much of MCI's bad debt he collected eventually rationalizing that everyone else was committing fraud to make it, why should he not benefit (Bucy et al., 2008). Pavlo was taught how to hide the debts of some of MCI's worst performing customers so that his personal record would continue to look impressive. Pavlo thought his fraudulent accounting of bad debt and theft of MCI's money would never be discovered admitting that "I went through a stage of being afraid... then I became bitter about how life was going for me, so I was immune to how wrong it was to do what I was doing" (Bucy et al., 2008, p. 408). Pavlo eventually adopted an attitude of wanting what he thought was rightful revenge against MCI for what his job did to his life. Pavlo talked about how easy it was to cross the line and engage in misconduct stating, "I am a cautious person, but once someone opens the door, I will charge through it. I have been known to be pretty aggressive. I don't have a lot of fear in taking business risks, though I have more now. I see things pretty quickly, act quickly and don't think things all the way through" (Bucy et al., 2008, p. 408).

Pavlo would reclassify past due accounts by having customer's sign promissory notes where the customer would pay for this debt in the future even though such customers would never pay off their debts. In turn, MCI would reclassify the past-due accounts now classified as promissory notes as revenue even though it was not money that was ever going to be collected. Although renegotiating a past due bill is not unethical or fraudulent, if MCI had reason to believe that the bill would never be collected, then it was engaging in fraud because MCI is making a representation that it will be collected. In addition, Pavlo would accept a delinquent customer's stock as payment for outstanding bills. This was done without the approval of upper management who initially disapproved, but later went along with the scheme. Again, these schemes were not enough to make the uncollectible bills manageable, thus upper management ordered Pavlo to reclassify the past due bills into different time periods, namely into the future so that they were not in fact past due bills under this fraud scheme. Pavlo also engaged the accounts receivable department in a fraud practice known as lapping, which is posting payments received from one customer to another overdue account to make overdue accounts appear current in order to meet corporate's bad debt collection goals.

MCI's management encouraged and rewarded Pavlo for the scheme of lapping and many other inventive and illegal acts that helped MCI reach its projected financial numbers to increase the stock price. With the assistance of some fellow employees and a business associate named Harold Mann, who had been an MCI customer, they devised a plan in which Pavlo would threaten delinquent customer to either pay their account or have service immediately cut off. Mann, the co-conspirator, initiated the fraud by creating a dummy corporation named Orion. Then Mann, on behalf of Orion, offered to assume MCI customers' past due debt for an upfront fee and subsequent monthly payments. The customers were led to believe that Mann/Orion would negotiate with MCI to clear their debt by paying MCI in full or in part their debt. The customers expected that with their debt presumably cleared, they would be allowed to remain as MCI customers. In fact, the money paid to Orion was divided among the co-conspirators. Pavlo then would have to reconcile the MCI financial statements so that it would appear that past due bills were being paid down to keep them as customers. It is worthwhile to examine some of the rationalizations Pavlo used to make the concept tangible to the reader. What made the rationalizations seductive was that they appealed to Pavlo's emotions and intellect. For example, the rationalizations fed into Pavlo's emotional side in terms of how he felt he was being treated by MCI management who profited from his fraud. In addition, Mann knew how to use rationalizations to further feed into the seduction Pavlo experienced by enticing him to engage in the fraud scheme.

Consider that at one point in the fraud scheme, Pavlo was not making any additional money from the fraud he was perpetrating on behalf of management, thus why should he not also benefit. Some of the rationalizations Mann offered included the denial of injury. When Pavlo questioned whether MCI would be getting any of the money they collected, Mann stated, "if we don't pay MCI, it's not really anything. I mean you can't steal money MCI wasn't going to get anyway, right" (Palmer, 2012, p. 75)? Observe the denial of a victim rationalization offered by Mann to Pavlo where there is no victim or that the person or organization deserved to be defrauded. In this case Mann is addressing Pavlo's concerns about the wrongfulness of defrauding MCI and MCI customers who are late on paying their bills telling Pavlo, "Spare me the sermon...[they] are out-and-out deadbeats" (Palmer, 2012, p. 75). This rationalization reinforced Pavlo's negative opinion of MCI customers who used the services, but never had any intention of paying their bills. Mann also offered Pavlo the rationalization of social comparison where one's behavior is acceptable if there is the perception that another's behavior is even worse coupled with the metaphor of the ledger rationalization. As Mann went on to convince Pavlo about the righteousness of the fraud, Mann said to Pavlo, "Everybody cheats. That's the way the world works. Your problem, Wally, is that you haven't figured out how to make money at it." Pavlo went on to state,

> The scheme Mann was describing...was no worse than what MCI's customers were doing to MCI, or what MCI was doing to its shareholders...Mann's twisted logic made sense (*social comparison*). Money, tons of it, was being manipulated, lied about, misused, misplaced, stolen. By everybody...from the corporate chiefs above to the scumbag customers below (Pavlo, 2012, p. 77). If MCI had been paying him what he was worth, treated him fairly, he reasoned, he'd have less to complain about. But he was getting screwed, too (*metaphor of the ledger*). Sixty-three thousand dollars a year (his salary at the time) to play nanny to two billion! MCI had driven him away from his family and into the arms of cigarettes and booze. They were cooking the books and he was helping them do it, while enjoying none of the benefits (Palmer, 2012, p. 79).

Over a six month period, Pavlo and his colleague siphoned $6 million from poor-performing clients and hid the money in a Grand Cayman bank account. He began to live according to his new found wealth: an expensive new car, tailored suits, and vacations. Yet six months into the fraud, MCI's auditors noticed a strange series of transactions that involved Pavlo and an account in Grand Cayman. Pavlo resigned immediately, hoping that the company would write off the $6 million as bad debt and thereby avoid any adverse publicity that would inevitably follow an investigation, but MCI called the FBI and Pavlo eventually went to prison and since his release has expressed remorse for his behavior.

White-Collar Criminal Motives, Influences and Worldviews

Greed is an enduring attribute of the human experience because it serves, in part, to explain one's wants and needs that are reinforced and rewarded at all levels of society. However, greed becomes problematic for organizations and individuals when it motivates one to engage in unethical or criminal acts resulting in "the abuse of the public trust, fraud, theft and damages the well-being of others for personal gain" (Imoniana & Murcia, 2016, p. 148). Although greed is common explanation of why white-collar crime flourishes, it is also overly simplistic because many people are greedy, but law-abiding. If greed combined with opportunity really caused crime in any significant sense, then there would be a lot more crime, simply because greed is widespread as a human desire and the world is flooded with opportunity. Moreover, the mere presence of a financial incentive is not sufficient to explain criminal conduct since the vast majority of individuals confront such incentives on a regular basis and yet do not avail themselves of the opportunity to commit crimes. As a result, more well-rounded explanations are needed to understand motivational factors influencing offenders. We explore the theory of general strain as well as how a society's cultural expectations and an individual's worldviews might influence their decision to engage in fraud.

General Strain Theory and White-collar Crime

General strain theory is a partial explanation offering insights into criminal motivations in general and specifically white-collar crime. This theory asserts that society puts pressure on individuals to achieve socially acceptable goals though they lack the means to achieve them ultimately leading to strain which may trigger criminal behavior. Strain theory "proposes that societal norms affect individuals' aspirations for things like material goods and other indicators of success" (Zahra et al., 2005, p. 808). Strain theory was developed to explain what was thought to be the much higher rate of crime among lower socioeconomic class individuals who are encouraged to pursue the goal of upward mobility as contrasted to individuals from the upper echelons of society who appeared to exhibit less criminal behavior. Strain may be structural referring to the processes at the societal level which filter down and affect how the individual perceives their ability to achieve self-aspirations. For example, if particular social structures prevent individuals from upward mobility or there is inadequate regulation, this may facilitate the individual's perceptions of how crime can be a solution to a perceived pressure, stress, or obstacle.

Thus, it was believed lower socioeconomic class individuals frequently have more trouble achieving these goals through legitimate channels, experience strain or pressure, and "may seek to relieve this strain by using deviant means to achieve their desired ends" (Zahra et al., 2005, p. 813). Given these insights, it would appear that strain theory has little to contribute in offering reasons for white-collar crime since people typically who are in white-collar positions normally are not under financial pressures because they tend to earn higher incomes and benefit from other socioeconomic factors that give white-collar offenders an advantage such as access to better educational opportunities. However, what motivates people who are, generally speaking, considered to be educated, well-off, and middle class—many of whom are already quite wealthy—to risk everything just to gain, at times, a relatively marginal increase in income? Yet, "criminal activities are surprisingly common among elite groups that might be thought to have little to gain from such behavior" (Coleman, 1989, p. 243).

The existence of white-collar offending is sometimes taken as evidence against the application of strain theory to white-collar offenders, however it is actually quite relevant to the explanation of white-collar crime. Strain helps to explain why individual employees and corporations through management are more likely to turn to white-collar crime when they have trouble achieving their financial goals through legitimate channels. Some offenders state they were motivated by a desire for financial gain, although they more often state their offense was motivated by the socially acceptable desire to prevent financial loss to an organization and the hardship it might cause (Weisburd et al., 2001). For example, studies suggest that corporate crime is common in for-profit companies, companies experiencing the strain of relatively low profits, declining profits, companies in depressed industries, and companies suffering from other types of financial problems such as low sales and perceived threats from competitors (Albrecht et al., 2012). Let us explore different motivational strain characteristics attributable to individuals and organizations.

Individual Motivation and Strain Characteristics

An understanding of what motivates fraud offenders whether acting alone or in collusion with others, within or outside an organization, can go a long way in identifying risk factors that facilitate fraud offenses. An individual's motivation for fraud may have originated from not having needs met, greed, threat to continued goal attainment and so forth (Stotland, 1977). However, offenders may not always have one explicit motivation to engage in fraud. Indeed, one of the reasons we ascribe greed as an explanation for their behaviors is that we often find it difficult to explain their true motives because they are unknowable, thus we rely on greed as the catch-all motivation for their acts. Consider the statement of convicted fraud offender Mark Koenig from Enron trying to explain why he participated in fraud. During his trial, Koenig, former head of investor relations told jurors, "I wish I knew why I did it. I did it to keep my job, to keep the value that I had in the company, to keep working for the company. I didn't have a good reason" (Free et al., 2007). At times, white-collar crime "is an activity for its own sake, for its own pleasures and satisfaction" (Roberts, 2016).

66

Some fraud offenders, however, express a contemptuous delight in the fraud act itself rather than simply the outcome. As they found themselves successful at this crime, they begin to gain a secondary delight in the knowledge that they are fooling those they are taking advantage of in addition to displaying their perceived superiority to others. In addition, the gratification obtained from mastery of a situation may be particularly prevalent in more complex, long-term frauds where specialist skills are required which impacts one's perceived sense of power. The sensation of power over another individual(s) or organization represents a strong motivating force for some fraud offenders to the point that it becomes an end in itself. Research confirms the desire for control is positively and significantly related to intentions to engage in fraud (Piquero et al, 2005).

As such, corporate crime decision making is influenced by situational, individual, and personality characteristics of one's desire to control and manipulate events to successfully engage in fraud. Furthermore, there is no doubt that the vast majority of white-collar crime is motivated by what might broadly be referred to as financial incentives. Typically individuals who commit occupational crimes are seeking to enrich themselves personally, just as firms engaged in corporate crime aspire to improve their financial performance. It is crucial to know what it is that a fraud perpetrator desires, 1) money, bonuses, and stock-based compensation, 2) status, meaning to keep up with others' material gains, fame, or celebrity status, 3) perhaps revenge, a catch-me-if-you-can game, or parity with others, and 4) everybody else is doing it, why can't I? (Ramamoorti & Olsen, 2007, p. 54). When there is a widespread belief that "everyone is getting rich," many come to believe they are passing up opportunities for self-enrichment (Ramamoorti, 2008). A former city council person justifying corruption stated: "People…like me are expected to work full-time, without salaries, without staff, or even postage stamps. I for one couldn't afford such a situation. And that is where a businessman seeking special favors filled the gap…I came to the conclusion that I was missing out, that I could combine my real desire to give public service with what they call a piece of the action" (Shover & Wright, 2001, p. 346).

In addition, the motivation to fulfill self-interest through fraud is often ignored, but plays an important role in facilitating unethical behavior. Specifically, individuals who see gain in committing misconduct are more likely than others who may be deterred due to moral inhibitions or the fear of sanctions, to seize the opportunity and partake in misconduct (Shover & Wright, 2001). The benefits of engaging in misconduct include increased income, higher status within the organization, the thrill of engaging in misconduct, increasing market share, increased revenue, and reducing organizational expenses (Shover & Wright, 2001). One of the main reasons for not doing what we intend is because our self-interest dominates our actual behavior with a disregard for other ethical considerations due to compromising our sense of right and wrong in the process (Bazerman & Tenbrunsel, 2011). For example, when employees lie on their resume about their educational backgrounds, work experience, or both, it is clear that getting the job and serving their own self-interest outweighs ethical considerations of basic honesty.

Although short-sighted, and often self-sabotaging as evidenced by the number of fraud offenders who go to prison, the impact of self-interest causes people to sacrifice their moral compass and an organization's ethical standards, such as the company's code of ethics. In these situations, employees know what constitutes appropriate behavior, yet still fail to do so out of self-interest. Strain may embed itself at the individual level referring to the stresses experienced by an individual as they look for ways to satisfy their needs and, for some, fraud is perceived as a short-term solution to this problem. At the individual level, a range of work-related strains may contribute to white-collar crime, particularly crimes against the employee's company, such as embezzlement. This may be especially true if strains are viewed by employees as unfair thereby lowering inhibitions, creating a desire for revenge against the source of the strain, and reducing one's commitment to the company. Evidence suggests strain contributes to a range of negative outcomes, including job dissatisfaction, alcohol use, drug use, workplace aggression, and employee theft.

Reports among white-collar offenders studied suggests there are "occasional cases of revenge seekers who are unhappy with the way they have been treated by their companies and who justify stealing from them" (Wheeler, 1992, p. 118). Workers engaging in employee theft commonly justify their crime by claiming employers deserve what they have taken from them since they exploit workers. There are several types of stress factors influencing the motivation to engage in misconduct including but not limited to, 1) job role ambiguity such as unclear job expectations, 2) job role conflicts reflecting incompatible job demands and conflict between job and family demands, 3) job role overloads such as too much work, 4) lack of personnel or other resources to complete work, 5) high job demands in combination with low control of how to complete those demands, 6) insufficient rewards for one's efforts, 7) job insecurity and unpleasant working conditions, 8) low levels of skill utilization, and 9) interpersonal problems including discrimination, physical, sexual, and mental harassment.

a. Personal Strain

The most common workplace strains perceived to motivate unethical behavior include the pressure to meet, 1) unrealistic business objectives/deadlines, 2) the desire to further one's careers, 3) protect one's livelihoods, 4) meeting personal financial obligations, and 4) financial stability and success of one's company. Moreover, as an economy changes or a firm fails, people who have reached the heights of wealth, power, and success grab what they can get before their achievements are diluted. They perceive a financial problem can be resolved by temporarily relying on fraud and view themselves as making a minor decision that will maintain the status quo until there are improvements in economic circumstances. Entrepreneurs too may encounter adverse business conditions that place them in a position of financial vulnerability threatening the organization they have built for themselves in addition to the possibility of losing power, status, and pride (Duffield & Grabosky, 2001). Satisfying themselves or caring for their families was another motive for offending among a sample of convicted white-collar criminals for reasons including, 1) not meeting basic needs, such as the needs for food, shelter, and medical care, 2) making undesirable adjustments in response to financial problems, such as giving up medical insurance and taking second jobs, and 3) falling behind in paying bills (Weisburd et al., 2001).

Financial problems affect higher class individuals coupled with the emphasis on consumerism leading many middle and higher class individuals to spend beyond their means while accumulating unmanageable debt levels. Higher socioeconomic class individuals are not immune to financial crises brought on by such things as health problems, economic downturns, and unemployment. To illustrate, many upper middle-class male offenders rationalize their white-collar crimes stating economic recessions create serious financial problems for them and they wanted to protect their families, employees, and others from hardship (Willott et al., 2001). Individuals are motivated not only for financial success, but social status as well as attaining the respect and admiration of others. While many white-collar workers already reflect status in the eyes of the larger society, they may develop status goals beyond their reach. An inability to legitimately achieve one's desired monetary success is a specific type of strain, and "many middle and upper class people want more money than they can have and obtain through legitimate channels" (Agnew, 2001, p. 162). Financial strain is a subjective matter in that even those of above average wealth may feel economically deprived in comparison to what others possess.

Expectations we create for ourselves may trigger strain even when true financial deprivation may not exist. One area frequently neglected in the study of serious fraud is the importance of the relationship between managers and their employees where an employee perceives they are being treated unfairly by their employer which could motivate employees to commit fraud to balance out the perceived injustice. It can be due to circumstances including missing out on a promotion, inadequate compensation, perceived unfair treatment compared to coworkers, disciplinary action, or chronic resentment at a perceived lack of appreciation of talents and contributions. Under these conditions, disgruntlement may develop and vengeful employees could seek retribution for perceived slights and/or neglect through acts of white-collar crime through the deliberate misuse or misapplication of the organization's resources or assets (Holtfreter, 2005). In fact, interviewed convicted male fraud offenders stated that their primary motivation was dissatisfaction with an employer and underpayment for services (Goldstraw, 2005). For example, as one fraud offender stated, "I felt I deserved to get something additional for my work since I wasn't getting paid enough" (Shover & Wright, 2001, p. 346). Other sources of financial strain contributing to fraud as a solution to a problem may result from lifestyle choices frequently identified as a primary motivation for both genders (Sakurai & Smith, 2003).

In contemporary society, the cost and addictive properties of illicit and prescribed drugs may contribute to financial stress together with relationship breakdowns and expensive divorce settlements, custody or maintenance struggles and debt. In some cases, marital breakdown represents a sudden and dramatic decline in an individual's standard of living, along with feelings of powerlessness and resentment. One study examined the criminal attitudes of accountants who went to prison for various frauds including, tax fraud, asset misappropriation from organizations, and taking money from trust accounts (Dellaportas, 2013). Some of the explanations given were that it was the right decision to engage in fraud from a business perspective, but illegal to do so. The accountant's opportunity to engage in fraud resulted from exploiting weak internal controls, engaging in check fraud, and relationships with clients who put their trust in the accountant to oversee their finances were exploited. Motives for engaging in fraud ranged from, 1) gambling addictions, 2) financial pressure and family issues such as divorce, 3) investments were doing poorly due to market conditions, 4) hide business losses or business not performing well with potential bankruptcy on the horizon, 5) help a relative who is in financial distress, and 6) revenge toward employer for not being promoted.

b. Anticipated Strain

Strain may result not only from experienced stresses, but also from the anticipation that stress may be experienced in the future. Thus offenders try to preempt the stress and any anticipated losses that may occur from surfacing in the first place by engaging in fraud. Anticipated strain is relevant to white-collar crime because corporations and many white-collar workers devote much effort to the prediction and management of their future economic position, thus the fear of failing has been identified as a type of anticipated strain that may trigger misconduct. As a result, the motivation for their crime is not necessarily for more financial rewards, but rather the "fear of falling–of losing what they have worked so hard to gain such as their financial success and status" (Weisburd et al., 1991, p. 224). In addition, some offenders are motivated to make unethical decisions to preserve their professional reputation and institutional power (Duffield & Grabosky, 2001). Also, it has been said that high levels of environmental uncertainty, such as those associated with a complex or a rapidly changing business culture, enhances the perception that future profits are threatened, and could trigger the motivation to engage in white-collar crime. For example, some corporate officials engage in price fixing in order to reduce price uncertainty and fluctuations thereby protecting their future economic well-being.

c. Vicarious Strain

The concept of vicarious strain facilitates the understanding of what may trigger the motivation for white-collar crime where some offenders state their behavior was motivated not so much by their own personal strain or anticipation of strain, but by their desire to protect family, friends, employees, or organizations they work for from hardship. For example, an employee of a large bank embezzled over $35,000. When asked why she embezzled the money, she stated that her son was addicted to heroin at a cost of nearly $500 per day and because she could not stand to see him go through withdrawals—in essence she embezzled to support his habit (Albrecht et al., 2012). Moreover, given corporate crimes may have little to do with an individual employee's personal stresses, but a lot to do with organizational pressures, it is possible that some individuals closely identify with the corporation they work for where they vicariously experience the strains of the corporation itself. This does not mean that offenders do not benefit from such crimes such as advancing their position in the corporation, but it may not have been a primary motivation. As a result, an employee may engage in fraud on behalf of the organization to assist the organization to get through a difficult economic period.

Organizational Motivation and Strain Characteristics

Organizational pressures can facilitate the motive for corporate crime when legitimate means are insufficient to achieve corporate goals and these pressures are felt throughout the hierarchy of an organization. Corporate crime is common among companies with low, declining profits, companies in distressed industries, other types of financial problems unique to the organization, and the perceived threat of potential economic problems whether reasonable or not (Van Slyke et al., 2016). Regulations perceived as excessive or unreasonable may prompt corporate misconduct. Yet organizational crime may occur even when there are no financial stresses, but simply because of the inability to satisfy economic goals and the fear of losing the success already achieved. Anticipated strain also applies to organizations who foresee potential economic decline and attempt to preempt the impact on an organization of future losses. Furthermore, financial pressures may be self-inflicted because of poor decision making on the part of management. Corporations may have trouble achieving reasonable financial goals through legitimate channels due to competition from others, a lack of resources, and technological changes, thus experiencing their own version of strain.

Corporate managers experience pressure to achieve high profits for the company's shareholders and creditors, for stock market evaluations of the corporation's performance relative to their competitors, and because their own interests are linked with the company's success. Fluctuations in business cycles and unethical organizational cultures that conflict with accepted social, ethical, and legal norms of behavior correlate with increases in the rate of white-collar crime (Ramamoorti, 2008). An intense emphasis on monetary success leads to self-induced pressures that when coupled with a weak emphasis on rules or a philosophy that downplays the importance of laws and regulations plus an opportunity to commit fraud within an organization create a negative synergy increasing the risk of criminality. A corporate environment preoccupied with monetary success at any cost that implicitly or explicitly encourages corporate executives to exploit or disregard regulatory controls, also prompts the motivation to achieve success by any means. Reflecting the above sentiments, after noting the illegitimate earnings management misdeeds of organizations such as Enron, WorldCom and others: "Companies do not grow in a constant fashion with each quarter's results better than last. In the long run conforming to pressures to satisfy the market's desire for impossible predictability and unwise growth leads to the destruction of corporate value, shortened careers, humiliation, and damaged companies" (Chew & Gillan, 2009, p. 167).

Organizational and individual motivations can occur simultaneously. For example, otherwise honest executives resort to lying, cheating, and stealing in order to relieve the immense pressure to meet analyst expectations of unattainable performance, just to keep their jobs and thus, for self-preservation (Ramamoorti, 2008). For example, white-collar crime can often be attributed to managerial decisions that push employees to commit crimes out of fear and pressure placed on them to perform. Noted scholar Marshall Clinard concluded that "[u]ndue corporate pressures upon middle management may lead to their becoming engaged in illegal or unethical behavior" (Bucy et al., 2008, p. 412). Financial problems can motivate corporate actors if they are explicitly or implicitly threatened with job loss or limited advancement unless they engage in corporate crime. For example, an executive who took a strong stand against the manufacture of an unsafe car was told, "You're not a member of the team. Shut up or go looking for another job" (Coleman & Ramos, 1998, p. 18). While some corporate officials may be pressured into crime by their supervisors, others engage in crime out of a desire to prevent or reverse economic losses.

National Cultural Ethos: The American Dream

High-earning individuals possess abundant financial resources, but they also pursue financial goals and lifestyles beyond their reach. There are societal and cultural expectations that encourage wealth acquisition among the wealthy and poor alike. For example, the term "the American Dream" was introduced to the country's cultural ethos in 1931 by historian James Truslow Adams to describe a vision of a society open to individual achievement. The American dream is the belief that one can start from anywhere, become anything, and rise to heights no matter where or from what circumstances one began (Noonan, 2017). This cultural mindset distinguished America from old Europe where titles and inherited family wealth dictated social standing; if one was lucky enough to be born into the right family, they would always be on top, and if not, they would always be on the bottom. In essence, your position in life was predetermined regardless whether or not you had the ambition to better yourself.

The American dream was aspirational, a viewpoint that bred hope where with dedication and focus, one could move forward and hopefully for the better. However, the term became a slogan synonymous with achieving material success and individual opportunities for a middle class lifestyle such as attaining a home and a good retirement (Choo & Tan, 2007). Yet the American dream was not always about material gain even though material gain could be one of the interpretations of the philosophy. It was also about achieving a sense of flexibility within a society by bringing economic and social equality into the discussion. This cultural ethos as we know it tends to reflect more of a monetary complexion where within "the American dream, there is no final stopping point; the measure of 'monetary success' is conveniently indefinite and relative. At each income level…Americans want just about twenty-five percent more, but of course this 'just a bit more' continues to operate once it is obtained (Simpson & Weisburd, 2008, p. 41).

In some respect, the American dream is a mixed blessing providing rationalizations for the best and worst aspects of its society where "a cardinal American virtue, 'ambition', promotes a cardinal vice, 'deviant behavior'…The American Dream defining success is open ended in that the dream offers no final stopping point and it requires never ending achievement" (Choo & Tan, 2007, p. 210). Striving for monetary success dwarfs other worthy, legitimate goals; the desire to accumulate money is relentless, enticing corporate executives to pursue monetary goals by any means necessary while offering rationalizations for their success through corruption and fraud. Rationalizations facilitate encouraging and justifying a "bottom-line" or "all that matters are profits" mentality at the expense of disregarding rules and regulations, thus we should not be surprised that fraud occurs as often as it does and on such a colossal basis. To this day, the desire to accumulate endless wealth is alive and well with daily displays of commercials and media glorifying those that were able to acquire such wealth achieving the American Dream. Just as this cultural viewpoint can drive entrepreneurship, corporate expansion, social mobility, and technological innovation, it also contributes to triggering fraudulent and unethical behavior to achieve success "by any means necessary" (Choo & Tan, 2007, p. 209). Let us explore if a national cultural ethos encouraging wealth accumulation influenced these high-level fraud offenders who recall their childhood experience and the economic circumstance they encountered.

According to convicted fraud offender Barry Minkow and founder of ZZZZ Best Corporation, memories of his adolescence were dominated by feelings of "shame he felt at his family's sporadic poverty" (Palmer, 2012, p. 53). Consider that convicted CEOs Bernie Ebbers of WorldCom, CEO Dennis Kozlowski of Tyco and CEO Ken Lay of Enron came from modest backgrounds, yet displayed a ravenous desire to acquire wealth for wealth's sake and at any cost (Jennings, 2004). Convicted Tyco CEO Dennis Kozlowski stated that he hired people like himself who came from modest, poor backgrounds and wanted to be rich (Jennings 2004). Enron's CEO Kenneth Lay "grew up dirt poor…Acutely conscious of his family circumstances…The hardship honed Lay's ambition…cultivat[ing] a powerful sense of personal entitlement" (McLean & Elkind, 2003, p. 490). According to Lay, when people were unable to pay their mortgages and walked away from their homes, the bank looked to my father for repayment…My father was stuck with these vacant houses which he could not sell or rent out…I remember those years as a very difficult period" (Taubman, 2007, p. 3). It appeared that these experiences drove a desire to compensate for those difficult times when Lay told a friend, "I don't want to be rich, I want to be world-class rich" insisting that he eat his lunch on a silver plate (Cruver, 2002, p. 23).

Ideological Influences on Offender Motives

Ideology typically refers to a person's set of ideals that form the basis for their economic and political viewpoints. Ideological motivators allow the ends to justify the means where perpetrators commit fraud to satisfy some perceived legitimate motivation that is consistent with their viewpoints (Dorminey et al, 2010). There are lawyers, politicians, economists, journalists to name a few who are ideologically opposed to the regulation of business coupled with harboring a particular distaste for using criminal law to control business practices which they believe are better left to the free market (Gobert & Punch, 2007). There is also a category of business people who not only want minimal regulation with maximum freedom to do as they please, but who actively resent regulations and display contempt for regulators willing to break the law in an open manner. Consider the Van der Valks case in the Netherlands. The Van der Valks operated a successful, family run business in the hotel and restaurant sector where the family was well known for providing friendly services and quality products (Gobert &

Punch, 2007). However they failed to follow basic regulations and violated employment laws, hired illegal employees, and did not pay various taxes thus engaging in tax fraud.

They covered up their misconduct by maintaining poor or non-existent records and by the time their cases went to court, amounts reached around $100 million especially those involving tax fraud. The Van der Valks open deviance of the government was apparent and their defense was that the rules should not apply to successful entrepreneurs like themselves despite their years of rule-breaking. In their opinion, "regulators were pathetic bureaucrats who deserved to be treated with contempt" (Gobert & Punch, 2007, p. 103). Their attitude was that their family was powerful and that any locality would be pleased to have their business given the jobs they would create—law breaking simply became a profitable way of conducting their business. Underneath their misconduct was a genuine and deep contempt for rules and those that tried to enforce them. Among the many points the Van der Valks made, they argued that they already paid enough taxes, and that their helping young people from abroad earn a living, albeit illegal, was a form of social work.

Some of the public regarded them as heroes and not villains. One of the Van der Valks stated that "if running a business, managing to survive and working hard is criminal; then yes, we are criminals" (Gobert & Punch, 2007, p. 104). Occasionally, once identified, white-collar offenders seek out the media and give interviews believing their skills of persuasion are effective enough to convince the public that they have done nothing wrong and are being targeted unjustly by law enforcement (Babiak & O'Toole, 2012). They compared the tax authorities to the Nazi occupiers during the second world war branding them as "blackmailers and extortionists, who used arrest and interrogation methods associated with the Nazis in the war" (Gobert & Punch, 2007, p. 103). The implicit and not so subtle message of the Van der Valks was that, "real businessmen should be allowed to make money with as little hindrance from the state as possible: Do people want to destroy a healthy company? Crime in the Netherlands is rising at a disturbing pace. Isn't it better that they [the government] spend time on tackling that rather than people who with hard work have built up a healthy business (Gobert & Punch, 2007, p. 103)?

Moreover, white-collar criminals often appeal to societal ideologies of laissez faire capitalist philosophies claiming laws regulating economic activity are unjust where they pose more threat to the public good than the business practices they are trying to prevent. Ideological beliefs facilitate neutralizing a guilty mind further enforcing the belief that government regulations stifle the business person's right to make a profit regardless of how the profit is attained (Lilly et al., 2011). For example, when a group of business executives were asked how to reduce the level of corporate crime, the most common recommendation was for the government to "stop the drift to socialism and the restriction of freedom" to economic activity (Lane, 1953, p. 164). All of the other proposals made by these executives focused upon either increasing the quality or integrity of government, or else decriminalizing the relevant activities they were involved in. Not one made any suggestion that would have enhanced compliance with the existing body of law. Some assert capitalism promotes the belief in free enterprise that can be used against government regulations as illegitimate interference in their practices where regulations should be ignored. Yet the belief government has no role in regulating markets is a distorted interpretation about free market ideology (Duska et al., 2011).

If this were the case, then taking an extreme form of laissez faire ideology would mean that a person could sell what are now toxic drugs on the open market to anyone of any age without any government interference regardless of whom the drugs hurt. The original idea behind free markets focused on unleashing people's creativity to provide the public with goods and services the market demanded as long as the laws pertaining to such activity were followed. Even Adam Smith, the author of the book the *Wealth of Nations*, who is credited with the idea of pursing one's self-interest known as the invisible hand, did not advocate for ignoring laws in pursuit of one's self-interest. Smith stated, "Every man is left perfectly free to pursue his own interest, his own way, and to bring both his industry and capital into competition with those of any other man, or order of men, as long as he does not violate the laws of justice" (Duska et al., 2011, p. 172). Economics Noble Prize winner Milton Friedman, who was a fierce believer in the free markets paralleling Adam Smith stated, "The primary and only responsibility of business is to use its resources and engage in activities designed to increase its profits so long as it stays with the rules of the game, which is to say, engages in open and free competition without deception or fraud" (Duska et al., 2011, p. 170).

A common strategy of those advocating for less regulation is to pick out odd regulations, perhaps legitimately an ineffective regulation, and use it as grounds to denounce the need for regulation in general, or to question the competence of government in order to gain a political edge through lobbying efforts to lessen regulation (Clinard & Yeager, 1980). The other major strategy is to suggest that government is motivated by some type of anticapitalist ideology agenda especially when offenders are prosecuted for their crimes. Thus offender prosecution is seen as stemming not from considerations of justice but rather from some political ideology, something other than capitalism, that believes personal freedoms should be restricted. Ideology as a motivation is most often associated with frauds like tax evasion and more recently with terrorist financing which involves multiple fraud schemes to finance nefarious agendas (Perri, 2010b). For example, a tax evader may believe that government is not entitled to their money and a terrorist ideology legitimizes the commission of white-collar crime to finance their activities.

Consider the war against terrorism cannot be separated from the war against fraud; fraud analysis must be central to understanding terrorist behavioral patterns and that fraud analysis cannot be viewed as a side issue (Perri & Brody, 2011d). Although the perception may be that fraud is not linked to terrorism because white-collar crime issues are more the province of organized crime, the perception is misguided. Terrorists derive funding from a variety of criminal activities ranging in scale and sophistication from low-level crime, white-collar crime, narcotics smuggling, or from state sponsors of terrorism. Some fraud schemes include credit card fraud, bank fraud, mortgage fraud, charitable donation fraud, insurance fraud, identity theft, money laundering, immigration fraud, and tax evasion. Shell companies are used by terrorist groups to receive and distribute money; these companies provide a legitimate appearance and may engage in legitimate activities to establish a positive reputation in the business community.

A Culture of Competition Influencing Offender Motives

The perception of how one internalizes and what importance a person attaches to a culture of competition and their pursuit to surpass others in the accumulation of wealth and status enhances the motivation to engage in white-collar crime (Shover, 2007). The key motivators are the desire for wealth, success, and the fear of failure which grows stronger over time (Shover & Wright, 2001). Money is an objective, measureable, visible, tangible, standard of success which is also equated with acquisition of power to control others and situations. In capitalistic systems, competition is seen as building character; a powerful stimulus to individual achievement, and a test of personal self-worth. In "cultures of competition, individuals are driven to strive for success, whether it is fortune, fame, or respect, and they worry ceaselessly about conditions that might stand in their way" (Shover, 2007, p. 89). The widespread insecurity generated in competitive environments not only impacts interpersonal relationships and influences individual actions, but such environments trigger motivations to engage in misconduct; competition can become all-consuming. When one's importance within an organization is constantly compared with others, the drive to prevail can compromise personal values and other obligations. By elevating and rewarding success above other goals, competitive environments facilitate rationalizations and motives to be satisfied through misconduct.

However, even though offenders may find relief in winning a competition, the by-product of such intensity is the immergence of insecurity; there is always another battle to be waged the next day, so the competitive games continue as do the illegal means to win. White-collar offenders reveal that a culture of competition provided the impetus to push ethical boundaries and consequently criminal boundaries to engage in fraudulent acts. Consider the insights of one fraud offender who was impacted by this culture: "You could be selling a $10 thousand dollar, you could be selling a $49.95 ticket, and it's the same principle. It's the same rules, it's the same game. I like to win. I like to win in all games I play, you know. And the money is a reason to be there, and a reason I have that job. But winning is what I want to do. I want to beat everybody else in the office" (Shover, 2007, p. 89). Moreover, "in the financial arena, the name of the game is money—make it now, make it fast, make a lot. To some players in this financial game, the question of whether to play fairly or unfairly, legally

73

or illegally, is not debated. Their only issue of concern is how much, how fast, and what are the chances of being caught" (Bovi, 1994, p. 103).

The culture of competition is not only for capitalistic nations, but people may be more hypersensitized to its forces because it is encouraged and revered as a national philosophy within a capitalistic society where economic success supersedes the importance of loyalty to an ethical value system. Often those captive to the culture of competition rely on fraud to achieve success only in the end to sacrifice their futures and that of their families when they may be sent to prison for misconduct. How one interacts with a culture of competition in order to become successful is tied to how they view themselves and the identity they wish to cloak themselves with. Thus, becoming successful was more than simply one path a person could choose, "it was in a very real sense a badge of one's intrinsic worth" (Shover & Wright, 2001, p. 348). The competitive struggle is a battlefield where the most capable emerge victorious. Consider how a culture of competition influenced this individual:

> I sold to the first person I ever talked to on the phone. And it was just like that first shot of heroin. I'm not a heroin addict…I've only done heroin a couple of times before. But it was amazing…It was never about the money after that…Yeah, it was about the money initially, but when I realized that I could do this every day, it was no longer about the money. It was about the competition, you know. I wanted to be the best salesman, and I wanted to make the most money that day (Shover, 2007, p. 89).

Winners are admired for the ability and drive that made them successful. If one views themselves as participating in the competitive economic battlefield, how do they fight in such a battlefield? Do they see rules, law, regulations, and social norms regarding competition as obstacles to success? Is someone willing to engage in fraud to win in this competitive struggle at any price? There is a pervasive sense of insecurity; a powerful undercurrent is displayed in industrial capitalistic cultures where fear of failure permeates contemporary society from the upper to lower-echelons (Shover & Wright, 2001). White-collar workers may turn to crime when their status is threatened, especially when they are committed to a culture of competition that characterizes a capitalistic system. Individuals may prove themselves to be winners by using illegal means to advance their own position or use their position within a corporation to satisfy their motives. Consider that, "along with the desire for great wealth goes the desire to prove oneself by 'winning' the competitive struggles that play such a prominent role in our economic system. And this desire to be 'a winner' provides another powerful motivation for deviant behavior irrespective of any financial gain that may be involved" (Coleman & Ramos, 1998, p. 12). The culture of competition breeds a fear of failure mindset. This fear of failure is linked to the demand for success, and together they provide a powerful impetus that is central to directing economic behavior in favor of fulfilling ambitions, at times, through illegal means.

This same fear of failure in the competitive struggle for wealth and success is clearly reflected in the middle class world which relies on media. Through the media, we are constantly reminded to maintain a competitive drive and edge since there are others willing to engage in fraud in order to stay competitive. As these commentators observe, "the television's world is relentlessly upbeat, clean, and materialistic. With few exceptions, prime time programming features people who are preoccupied with personal ambition. If not utterly consumed by ambition and the fear of ending up as losers, these characters take both the ambition and the fear for granted" (Shover & Wright, 2001, p. 349). The motive to win is more important than how one wins. There is a need for personal affirmation displayed by some form of success obtained, perhaps, from committing fraud to distributing narcotics if necessary to acquire wealth. In essence, you are "somebody" when you can display wealth that proves to others that the dream has been fulfilled. Consider the insights of a street-level offender that would easily apply to achievement-oriented business executives reflecting the culture of competition:

> Full-time hustlers never relax…As is the case in any jungle, the hustler's every waking hour is lived with both the practical and subconscious knowledge that if he ever relaxes, if he ever slows down, the other hungry, restless foxes, ferrets, wolves, and vultures out there with him won't hesitate to make him their prey ((Shover & Wright, 2001, p. 349).

74

The Influence of One's Worldview on Offender Motives

A worldview is a mental framework in which individuals and groups define their perception of reality, the nature and purpose of life, and the laws that govern human relationships. Worldviews shape how we perceive, interpret, understand, and respond to the realities around us. They are shaped by life experiences, our upbringing, education, and religious exposure to name a few factors and they shape our approach to life, how we interact with others and how we approach problem solving. Worldviews become part of a person's identity of who they are, how they view themselves, how they view others, how they want others to view them, and what is important to them. We all harbor worldviews whether we are aware of it or not. Let us explore examples of what worldviews might entail. A conflict-oriented worldview considers conflict to be normal and acceptable. In this case, people believe in a win-lose relationship orientation instead of a win-win approach. This means some people believe that for someone to get ahead, someone else has to lose. For example, the son of a banker, age 16, illustrated this worldview stated, "business isn't just about beating the other guy, it's about fucking and destroying him if you can" (Naso, 2012, p. 252).

Another example would be that if I do not cheat someone out of their money, they will cheat me out of mine. Some might believe that one is either the victimizer or the victim in life, thus they must choose between the two. Generally speaking, western cultures tend to adopt a worldview that the path to a better life is through personal effort and initiative, but people from other countries may harbor worldviews that are in direct contrast to westerners where they are more likely to believe a better life is obtained through dishonesty and corruption (Rothstein & Uslaner, 2005). Let us revisit the statement of convicted Enron CEO Jeffrey Skilling who stated, "I've thought about this alot, and all that matters is money" (McLean & Elkind, 2003, p. 55). On its face, we could plausibly argue that there is nothing to analyze from such a statement because it is reflective of one person's opinion of how they view money. Yet, let us change the statement and ask whether we are as indifferent to the person's beliefs. "All that matters to me is to kill as many people who do not practice religion the way I do." "All that matters to me is that I assassinate this politician because they do not believe what I believe." How do we interpret this statement: "All that matters to me is the destruction of the United States." Our emotional reaction to the statements above is predictably not positive.

This may be an extreme example, but we have seen how people's beliefs in the terrorist world can be so engrained into their worldview that they are willing to engage in violence to satisfy their belief system. What is one willing to do to make their belief become a reality? If someone like Skilling makes this comment as CEO of Enron, is their belief so strong that they are willing to participate in some type of white-collar crime to satisfy their beliefs? Are we willing to give bribes, accept bribes, engage in financial statement fraud, securities fraud, or insider trading, participate in kickback schemes, as examples, to obtain money if money is all that is important? People's personal beliefs should not be ignored as simply personal opinions because they do influence how they perform their job duties, especially in leadership roles. Skilling's worldview that "all that matters is money" appears to be constant whether as a student at Harvard or as CEO, as was underscored by one of his teachers at the Harvard Business School. Professor John LeBoutillier, asked Skilling when he was a young man at Harvard "what he would do if his company were producing a product that might cause harm—or even death—to the customer that used it" (Hoyk & Hersey, 2011, p. 54). Skilling reportedly responded, although denied by him, "I'd keep making and selling the product. My job as a businessman is to be a profit center and to maximize return to the shareholders" (p. 54).

Personal beliefs matter because they reveal how people view others and situations to potentially exploit, especially if they naturally lack empathy. Moreover, belonging to an organization can increase the significance of culturally shared definitions, and influence an individual's worldview in ways that could change how they interpret situations, and either the likelihood of engaging in crime or the frequency of crime. Through interaction with other organizational members, employees are socialized into the culture where they learn motivations, rationalizations, and how to "filter deviant acts through a sanitizing, ideological prism, which gives them the appearance of not being criminal" (Shover & Wright, 2001, p. 214). If an individual harbors a worldview that does not reject corruption as a means to succeed, and the organizational culture rewards those who engage in it, in essence the organization facilitates the intensification and legitimization of one's worldview that corruption is an acceptable means of achieving goals. Some of the strongest evidence of the impact of organizational culture on influencing one's worldview comes from white-collar offenders themselves who have acknowledged, even though using rationalizations to neutralize the moral aspect of their actions, that their former worldview justified engaging in white-collar crime making it appear necessary, even heroic within an organization. In summary, worldviews can facilitate the emergence of motivations to engage in good or bad conduct.

Victimization and White-collar Crime

While "studies of victimization from white-collar crime have been largely absent from criminological discussions of policies supporting the victims of crime, a considerable amount of recent research indicates that many offenses have a severe and long lasting impact and that victims are much in need of support and are less different from victims of violence than often assumed" (Van Slyke et al., 2016, p. 66). What we do know is that white-collar crime has serious economic, physical, and emotional effects on individuals as well as enormous national economic and social costs that exceed those of conventional street-level crimes. Consider this fraud victim's experience after learning about the Ponzi scheme Bernard Madoff perpetrated: "I had felt very depressed for many, many months. It was hard to accept such losses. I felt that I had lost my identity, along with my self-respect…I felt crushed and anonymous, as if I had become transparent, and just didn't count anymore." His wife wrote to the court about her "fear and anxiety," "major depression" daily, and, elsewhere, about how she thought that suicide was the only answer to stopping the pain" (Lewis, 2011a, p. 170).

The impact of serious frauds, such as company bankruptcies and environmental disasters on communities, include loss of employment and revenue from commerce, and public health problems. Crimes characterized as victimless, such as tax evasion, drain resources from local and national governments and deprive citizens of tax revenue benefits. Some commentators have argued that white-collar crime's biggest cost is the flood of cynicism, distrust, and loss of confidence in major institutions that follows each incident. This has a profoundly negative impact on how people look at investing and buying from legitimate organizations. The observance of misconduct and corruption gives the impression that markets are unfair, erodes public trust, and places a drag on long-term economic development (Van Slyke et al., 2016). Victimization can vary from incidents that are annoying, but negligible, to those that are life-changing and, at times, life threatening. Fraud victims may experience actual or threatened loss of their home, an ability to plan for retirement, a need to work longer hours, or an inability to support their families. These situations often have a psychological impact, such as stress, anxiety, and depression, with actual and attempted suicides being reported. In cases where spouses are unaware of the loss of money due to fraud, family disintegration may follow, such as divorce. It is especially difficult for elderly victims who have less time to recoup losses—it destroys the security they saved for.

Victimization may also involve a sense of betrayal and embarrassment. Some victims may blame themselves giving credence to the Latin legal term *caveat emptor* (Van Slyke et al., 2016). Caveat emptor means that it is a buyer's responsibility to inspect the quality of an item before purchasing it. Thus some fraud victims blame themselves believing they did not exercise enough due diligence before partaking in a financial opportunity. They blame themselves for being careless and some outside observers blame the victim for being greedy—thus deserving to be taken advantage of. Other victims may experience a betrayal of trust when an employer is involved. Victim support groups generally do not deal with white-collar victims and as a result victims experience confusion on how to navigate the court system, prosecution offices, and regulatory bodies, such as the Securities and Exchange Commission (SEC), to obtain some kind of restitution and justice for their victimization (Van Slyke et al., 2016). Sadly, victims might experience more anger and dissatisfaction with the criminal justice system than the perpetrators due to frustration caused by navigating a bureaucratic maze.

Conclusion

Many years have been lost in not studying white-collar offenders as thoughtfully as we should have in order to construct a more realistic profile of their behaviors and risk factors that trigger the probability of engaging in fraud and at times violence. However, it is never too late to start given there are no indications that fraud will decline any time soon. The first step in understanding fraud offenders is to debunk longstanding myths and reject personal biases of how we perceive them. Moreover, the importance of understanding how criminals think about exploitable opportunities cannot be overstated. Criminals are opportunists who prey on weakness, whether it is non-white-collar or white-collar offenses they intend to commit. White-collar offenders aggress in a different form to satisfy their motives, but create victims nonetheless.

The fact that fraud offenders may not present themselves in a way that fits our perception of what a criminal should look like is where we get into trouble. Do not be seduced by outward appearances of normalcy—it is how the person thinks that matters. Listen to what people have to say about questionable scenarios that display an ethical and legal component. Do we hear people trying to rely on a rationalization to neutralize their behaviors? Learn to recognize antisocial traits and interpersonal strategies by listening to people in everyday life situations. This practice helps hone one's ability to recognize such traits and learn how people think. Moreover, people reveal opinions, worldviews, even inadvertently, about matters that reflect how they truly think about a situations and others. Personal opinions should not be systematically disregarded because they may reflect deeper motives and worldviews that facilitate their desire to exploit others and organizations.

Chapter 2

Red Collar Crime

Fredric Tokars displayed the appearance of success as a former Atlanta prosecutor and prominent criminal defense attorney who also participated in the political process. He gave the impression that he was happily married to his wife, Sara, with whom he had two sons. However Fredric decided to engage in white-collar crime that was eventually detected by Sara. In the process of going through her husband's office, Sara discovered documents indicating Fredric's involvement in money laundering and tax evasion activities. In fact, Fredric used a booklet that detailed plans for money laundering drug money together with tax evasion advice. Sara did not realize that the information she uncovered could make her husband not merely a suspect, but a defendant in a federal investigation involving narcotics trafficking and fraud offenses. In fact, one of the prosecutors stated that Sara could have destroyed Fredric because of the fraud scheme she discovered and posed an even bigger threat by becoming a potential witness for the government. As one prosecutor later stated, "Sara was a ticking time bomb" for Fredric (McDonald, 1998, p. 414). After detecting that Sara was investigating his business affairs, Fredric told a woman with whom he was having an affair that Sara "knows too much…I'm going to have to have her taken care of" (McDonald, 1998, p. 176). Once he learned that Sara knew of his fraudulent business activities, in 1992 Fredric contracted with one of his criminal associates named Eddie Lawrence to have his wife killed for $25,000.

Eddie, however, did not have the courage to kill Sara, so he subcontracted the kill by hiring a street thug named Curtis Rower for $5,000. Eddie did mention to Fredric that his two boys would be without a mother, but Fredric responded stating, "They'll be all right…They're young, they'll get over it" (McDonald, 1998, p. 178). After coming home from a Thanksgiving vacation in Florida where Fredric still resided, Curtis, armed with a sawed-off shotgun, confronted Sara in her vehicle while the two boys were in the back seat. Curtis aimed the barrel of the shotgun at Sara's head and pulled the trigger. Afterwards, Curtis bragged to people in his neighborhood about the kill and they contacted the authorities disclosing what Curtis told them. What Fredric did not know was that Sara left the documents in the care of others that linked him to fraud and instructed them to bring the evidence to light should anything happen to her. Eventually the co-defendants Eddie and Curtis testified against Fredric at trial and he was found guilty of murdering his wife in a murder-for-hire scheme in April, 1994 (Tokars, 1996). While in prison, the psychiatrist assigned to Fredric observed: "Regarding his personality structure it seems apparent that he has been dealt many narcissistic blows. He has a long history of manipulating and coercing people. He did not talk of his crimes at all and he does not seem to have any remorse for his crimes" (Tokars, 2008).

Origin of Red Collar Crime

In 2005, the author of this book participated in a homicide trial as counsel to the accused who was charged with murdering his business partner (Perri, 2016). During the homicide investigation, a motive offered was that the murder resulted from fraud detection by the deceased partner who had learned that her business partner committed asset misappropriation from their business. To avoid detection and/or disclosure of the fraud, the accused silenced the partner by committing murder through blunt force trauma to the head with a hammer. After the trial and conviction of the accused, the author of this book explored via Internet searches whether the facts in this case reflected a statistical anomaly, or if violent white-collar offenders constitute an offender group researchers inadvertently overlooked. Through this method, the author located homicide cases with similar motives within legal documents, such as court decisions and homicide trials disclosed within various periodicals, where a white-collar offender was found guilty of homicide, or attempt murders. Moreover, the author discovered that academic research on violent white-collar offenders, their potential motive(s), and behavioral profile(s) was missing. The theory examining white-collar offenders becoming violent toward their victims is a phenomenon scholars and researchers have ignored for years (Brody & Kiehl, 2010). This void in research contributed to a widely-adopted viewpoint that white-collar offenders are non-violent. Unfortunately, a consequence of this scholarship gap is that offender profile misperceptions prevailed and have ultimately been reinforced by academia and the criminal justice system alike.

This has led to the previously-discussed topic of projection bias that was covered in chapter one. For example, consider the statement of a U.S. federal judge who illustrated offender profile misperceptions by stating, "White-collar criminals are not people who are threatening the lives of others; they are not violent people" (Wheeler et al., 1988, p. 63). These academicians believe, "white-collar offenders do not pose physical threats to others; the threat they pose consists of their ability to gain the confidence of a victim and then cheat him" (Kahan & Posner, 1999, p. 371). Other academicians stated, "There are some notable differences involved [with] white-collar criminals compared with…criminals on the lower rungs of the offense ladder. For one thing, white-collar criminals pose no physical danger...Violence is not their thing" (Hobbs & Wright, 2006, p. 79). According to another scholar, white-collar offenders, are "neither violent [nor] antisocial" (Mauer, 1974, p. 152). It appears that because white-collar crime is technically classified as non-violent, the offender is assumed to be non-violent by nature; assumptions repeated with enough regularity that they are accepted as fact (Perri, 2016). A review of the researched cases contained within this chapter revealed that violent white-collar criminals were not anomalous; they harbor behavioral risk factors that facilitate their use of violence as a solution to a perceived problem no differently than non-white-collar offenders that resort to violence, albeit for different motives. From his involvement with the above-mentioned homicide case, together with a review of the additional homicide and attempted homicide cases collected, this author coined the term "red-collar crime" to describe white-collar criminals who turn violent (Perri, 2016).

These offenders, however, should not be confused with white-collar criminals who have a mixed criminal history of white-collar and non-white-collar crime that might include violence. It is the motive behind the violence that determines the offender subgroup as a red-collar crime (Perri & Lichtenwald, 2007c). These offenders engage in violence to silence those who detect and/or disclose their fraud schemes: hence the name 'fraud detection homicide' describes the motive to classify the murder (Perri, 2016). Furthermore, the instrumental, planned nature of these disclosed homicides and attempted homicides, were derived from case facts in written judicial opinions, investigative and prosecutorial disclosures, and review of case facts that support conclusions as to the underlying motive. In reviewing the various classifications of crime and, in particular, homicide, the author of this book found that different types of homicides, such as sexual homicides, parricides, contract killings, and domestic homicides, to name a few, are counted, classified, and studied for behavioral patterns and offender characteristics which facilitates statistical analysis (Douglas et al., 1992). To date, fraud detection homicides are not tracked and studied in the same manner. Consequently, there are no longitudinal studies as to how many red-collar crimes have been committed to date which makes it difficult to come to absolute conclusions about this offender class.

As a result, there is limited availability of descriptive statistics, such as offender age, gender, and race, types of frauds that preceded the homicide, victimology, and behavioral make-up. It is the author's opinion, however, that it is more advantageous to begin the conversation by offering a template to refine and clarify an offender profile rather than ignore this lethal group simply because it has been missing from the narrative. Though only committed by a subgroup of white-collar criminals, a tendency towards violence is not surprising considering many white-collar criminals harbor the same deviant personality traits as conventional street-level criminals (Perri & Lichtenwald, 2007a). Moreover, although fraud and murder are two distinct offenses, offender behavioral traits may be a common driving force. For example, research suggests there is a relationship between narcissistic and psychopathic traits, when combined with criminal thinking patterns that creates a negative synergy that increases the risk of non-white-collar crime, white-collar crime, and eventually violence (Perri, 2016). Although violent white-collar offenders display narcissistic and psychopathic traits, these traits are not the cause of violence, rather, they are risk factors that have been empirically linked to violent aggression (Perri, 2016). Also, no different than non-white-collar offenders who kill, it is not necessary for violent white-collar offenders who kill to display a personality disorder (Alalehto & Azarian, 2018). However, the question becomes, can personality disorders facilitate the use of violence as a solution to a problem?

Within this chapter, we learn how violence permeates not only the workplace arena, but also unexpected venues such as families where one family member is exploiting relatives through fraud schemes that eventually lead to their murder, or attempted murder. In addition, we examine fraud detection violence on an international basis, murder-for-hire schemes, and the role of behavioral characteristics as risk factors that increase the probability that a fraud offender will resort to violence as a solution to a perceived problem. What is interesting about several of the international cases, especially those in the former Soviet Republics, is that although they are very much planned homicides, they also kill in a public manner with the intention of sending messages to others that may be tempted to disclose corruption. Moreover, we examine different types of murder-for-hire hitmen and how their different characteristics determine whether the person that hired them is actually apprehended. In relation to red-collar crime, it will become evident to the reader that, at least with the cases presented in this book and those red-collar crime cases in the United States, the hitmen can be characterized as non-professionl types who get caught due to the amount of evidence left behind that law enforcement uses to back-track to the the hitmen.

When White Collars Turn Red: Planned or Reactive Violence

Case facts overwhelmingly reveal that violent, white-collar offenders engage in violence in an instrumental (planned) manner. This observation appears to hold true whether we are considering American fraud detection violence cases or international cases. However, it is important to have an appropriate definitional apparatus to surgically classify how these offenders go about their crimes. The way they engage in violence is important. To classify the type of violence displayed in these cases, this author adopted a template offered by Woodworth and Porter (2002). For a homicide to be rated as instrumental, the offense must be goal-oriented in nature with no evidence of an immediate emotional or situational provocation. Instrumental violence is a means to an end; it is violence committed to further some other motive (Hart & Dempster, 1997). If there was "a cooling off period or a discernible gap in time between the provocation/frustration and the homicide" the homicide was classified as instrumental (Woodworth & Porter, 2002, p. 439). What this means in terms of fraud detection violence is the provocation and frustration may entail the offender first becoming aware that someone has detected their fraud schemes, and potentially disclosed them to the authorities.

The cooling off period means that there was a lag in time between when they became aware that their fraud was detected, and the act of silencing the person(s) who detected their fraud scheme. In contrast, for reactive violence to be present, there must be strong evidence for a high level of spontaneity and a lack of planning surrounding the commission of the offense. Thus, there is a rapid emotional reaction prior to and during the act with no apparent goal other than to harm the victim immediately following a provocation and/or conflict. Reactive violence can be characterized as emotional outbursts that are contemporaneous with a provocation triggering spontaneous violence (Woodworth & Porter, 2002). Reactive violence, immediately responding to a provocation, is the end in itself (Hart & Dempster, 1997). Reactive violence is more likely to occur between family members and acquaintances, while instrumental violence is more typical among strangers where the offender takes their time to plan an attack upon another (Woodworth & Porter, 2002). What is factually interesting in these fraud detection homicide cases is that the exact opposite holds true for most of them; the offender knew the victims, but instead the violence was very instrumental in nature. Specifically, many of the victims were individuals the offender knew for many years and may have been a close associate or spouse for that matter. It is not unreasonable to assume that even though these victims may have been aware of the fraudulent behavior of the offender, the ability to anticipate that they would also be capable of resorting to violence as a solution is almost negligible.

The author reviewed the available facts of red-collar crime cases listed in Table 1 which revealed that the offender did not display reactive violence, but rather planned the homicide once they believed the fraud scheme had been detected and/or disclosed to interested parties, including law enforcement. Case review revealed that there was a discernible time gap between the defendant's belief that his or her fraud scheme was detected and/or disclosed, and the execution of the homicide. If the facts were ambiguous as to the type of violence displayed, the case was coded as "unknown." As more cases surface, research can better identufy risk factors that make violence a solution for some fraud offenders together with studying the risk factors that put victims in harm's way. That being said, given the evidence that is surfacing, one can intelligently infer that red-collar offenders display predatory qualities no differently than violent non-white-collar offenders who might stalk their victims waiting for the opportune time to strike to satisfy a motive. In the event that the red-collar offender does not commit the homicide themselves, they are more than willing to pay for someone to stalk the victim and kill them.

Table 1   **Red Collar Crime Homicide Cases**

Offender Name	Fraud Scheme	Number of Victims	Murder Method	Type of Violence	Case Source
Ernesta Bernal	Mortgage	2	Gun	Instrumental	Cruz (2006)
Frank Marfo	Bank	1	Gun	Instrumental	Marfo (2014)
Jorge Cortes	Mortgage	1	Gun	Instrumental	Spencer (2005)
Rosie Baker	Benefits	1	Gun	Instrumental	Baker (2001)
Russell Moss	Check	1	Gun	Instrumental	DiGiacomo (2009)
Ronald Mikos	Benefits	1	Gun	Instrumental	Mikos (2008)
Robert Burke	Insurance	1	Gun	Instrumental	Smith (1991)
Ed Washington	Identity	1	Gun	Instrumental	Machen (2010)
Fred Tokars	Bank fraud	1	Gun	Instrumental	Tokars (1996)
Irwin Margolies	Accounting	2	Gun	Instrumental	Margolies (1987)
Santé Kimes	Mortgage	1	Gun	Instrumental	Kimes (2006)
Ken Kimes	Mortgage	1	Gun	Instrumental	Kimes (2006)
Dennis Gaede	Credit card	1	Gun	Instrumental	Gaede (2007)
Floyd Bogle	Credit card	1	Knife	Instrumental	Herman (2011)
Jon Broyhill	Accounting	2	Knife	Instrumental	Broyhill (2017)
Velma Barfield	Forgery	4	Poison	Instrumental	Barfield (1983)
Robert Petrick	Bank	1	Bludgeon	Instrumental	Petrick (2007)
Nancy Siegel	Credit card	1	Bludgeon	Instrumental	Siegel (2008)
Natavia Lowery	Credit card	1	Bludgeon	Instrumental	Martinez (2010)
Jose Alvarado	Check	1	Bludgeon	Instrumental	Parcher (2009)
John Lau	Mortgage	2	Bludgeon	Instrumental	Lau (2005)
Chris Porco	Bank	1	Bludgeon	Instrumental	Perri et al (2008)
Joe Collins	Bank	1	Bludgeon	Instrumental	Collins (2010)
Kathleen Nelson	Bank fraud	1	Bludgeon	Instrumental	Collins (2010)
Eric Hanson	Credit card	4	Bludgeon/gun	Instrumental	Hanson (2010)
Michael Howell	Insurance	1	Bludgeon	Unknown	Wright (2008)
Rosalba Contreras	Mortgage	2	Bludgeon	Unknown	KTLA (2009)

Behavioral Profile of Violent White-collar Offenders

It is a common belief among law enforcement and forensic professionals that people who commit violent incomprehensible crimes must be crazy, psychotic, or they 'just snapped' (Herve & Yuille, 2007). Although there are individuals who are mentally challenged and do engage in violence, research does not support the belief that incomprehensible violence, in general, is only perpetrated by those who are mentally challenged. Individuals who are rational and capable of engaging in their own risk assessments, such as weighing the cost versus the benefit of hurting others, do resort to violence as a solution to a perceived problem. The question becomes, how does one's personality facilitate whether they resort to violence, or not, especially if they are white-collar offenders? This is a rather important question since research on this issue is non-existent at least in its application to violent white-collar criminals. Personality traits may be a risk factor for someone to engage in fraud. Are fraud offenders who harbor narcissistic and psychopathic traits at risk for resorting to violence? If so, what are some of the traits and situations that can trigger a violent response? To better understand how these horrific homicides are possible, we examine fraud detection violence cases, but first we explore personality traits that could be interpreted as risk factors that increase the probability that a fraud offender would resort to violence.

Narcissism and Violence

Forensic psychological evaluations found narcissism to be a homicidal risk factor and a risk factor for white-collar criminals to commit murder (Perri, 2016). A narcissistic sense of entitlement can drive an individual to manipulate circumstances to satisfy their motives, whether the result is fraud, murder, or both (Ablow, 2008). Further, narcissism is linked to revenge which increases the risk of retaliation (Brown, 2004) by resorting to brutal forms of violence against those whom the offender perceives as interfering with their fraud schemes (Perri, 2016). Malignant, antisocial narcissists who display a history of interpersonal conflicts, criminal behavior, abuse, intense anger, blame externalization, entitlement, a lack of empathy, disdain for others, and arrogance are prone to violence (Russ et al., 2008). Narcissists often target those they perceive to be a threat to their sense of grandiosity and egocentricity (Baumeister et al., 2000). Moreover, aggression is used to support their highly favorable view of themselves, albeit perhaps a distorted sense of self, by aggressing against those that may threaten that self-view (Martinez et al., 2008). Furthermore, a toxic combination of entitlement and exploitive traits represent a high risk for aggression and violence (Reidy et al., 2008a).

Those narcissists who display traits of extreme entitlement and exploitation of others to satisfy their goals are more likely to resort to physical aggression against innocent people viewed as potential threats even when they are not provoked (Reidy et al., 2008b). Narcissists sometimes forego an escalation in aggression, such as verbal aggression, and resort to intense aggressive acts as their initial method to satisfy their sense of entitlement and to resolve perceived conflict with others (Perri, 2016). The perception of potential threats to their sense of entitlement creates uncertainty in the narcissist's mind and the discomfort caused by this perceived uncertainty needs to be removed. The unknown creates anxiety that must be neutralized by aggressing against those whom they perceive have or can hurt them in some way. Preemptive aggression may help them defend against future uncertainty or ambiguous conditions they may not be able to control; a preemptive strike reestablishes a sense of control, dominance, and superiority over others and situations (Martinez et al., 2008).

Psychopathy and Violence

Psychopathy appears to be one of the strongest predictors of unprovoked aggression and violence due to the distinct psychopathic traits of emotional detachment, lack of empathy and lack of remorse (Reidy et al., 2008a; b). Research suggests that psychopathy may be linked to violent white-collar offenders especially motives for psychopathic aggression which may include the need to control situations, persons or both (Babiak & Hare, 2019). Consider that aggressing against others in a violent manner is a form of control and killing someone is the ultimate form of controlling another person. Psychopaths can commit ruthless, cold blooded homicides for various motives. For example, one psychopathic offender admitted to the police that he decided to kill his ex-girlfriend because he felt she was interfering with his new relationship and he decided that murdering her would help resolve the issue (Woodworth & Porter, 2002). Another psychopathic offender killed his wife because he stood to gain financially from her insurance policy (Woodworth & Porter, 2002).

Taken together, the evidence suggests that psychopaths view both aggression and deception as useful tools with which to promote their own interests (Porter & Woodworth, 2007). Aggression may be caused by provocation; they retaliate in this manner if they believe they have been harmed in some way (Reidy et al., 2008a). The tendency toward aggression may reflect the fact that psychopaths see hostile intent in the action of others and are quick to react with a "preemptive strike" toward others be it family or non-family members (Hart & Dempster, 1997, p. 223). What they consider a provoking act is the victim actually catching them committing an act and then questioning them about their misconduct. In other words, they consider themselves the victim when their sense of entitlement and exploitative nature is challenged (Reidy et al., 2008a). What is ironic is that even though they perceive criticism, potential threats, and being confronted about their wrongdoing as a form of provocation worthy of retaliating against, often they were the ones that brought on the provocation by others in the first place (Reidy et al., 2008a).

They retaliate because their sense of entitlement makes them believe someone is trying to interfere with what they think is theirs regardless of how they may have provoked a reaction in others. Instead of asking for forgiveness, they interpret other people's behavior as a form of goal interference justifying retaliation. Currently, research debates exist as to whether psychopathy is more related to instrumental (planned) violence and the exact reasons for this association is not entirely clear despite numerous attempts to refine the link because they also engage in reactive violence (Blais et al., 2014). Thus, "there may be subtypes of psychopathic offenders who engage in more instrumental and severe violence than others" and this insight may apply to violent white-collar offenders (Laurell et al., 2014, p. 292). For example, some psychopaths are more impulsive, interpersonally hostile, anxious, aggressive, more apt to engage in reactive violence, while other variations of psychopathy display less anxiety, are more emotionally detached, and more instrumental in their violence, where their goal is to control and dominate (Skeem et al., 2007).

In addition, some psychopaths tend to be more immune to the thought of punishment as a deterrent to criminal engagement, as opposed to a non-psychopath who may experience fear or anxiety at the thought of engaging in a criminal act and subsequently refrain from acting upon impulses (Skeem et al., 2011). Moreover, narcissistic immunity may distort their risk assessment because their grandiosity makes them believe they are above apprehension due to their superior planning skills (Perri & Lichtenwald, 2008b). This observation makes sense in that if offenders are capable of successfully engaging in fraud schemes, then it is plausible that their narcissistic grandiosity leads them to believe they can superimpose their fraud scheme skills to successfully plan a homicide and avoid detection. Psychopathic white-collar offenders can approach violence in a methodical, planned, and strategic manner; they should not be labeled as being unstable and incapable of engaging in planned aggression (Perri, 2016). In one study, 93 percent of the convicted psychopathic killers committed the homicide in a predatory, instrumental manner, whereas only 48 percent of the non-psychopathic killers engaged in instrumental homicide, however they also engage in reactive violence (Woodworth & Porter, 2002). These observations may explain why psychopathic fraud offenders who commit fraud in a planned, calculated manner may apply the same deliberate, disciplined approach to planning their murders (Perri, 2016). How might this knowledge assist us in crime scene interpretation?

The mistake many in law enforcement make when they learn of a homicide that is between acquaintances is that the killer must have been angry which led to a violent, emotional outburst. Yet if the individual was psychopathic, then emotion may have had nothing to do with the kill because by definition they either cannot experience emotion or their emotions are blunted—murder was simply viewed as a solution to neutralize a problem (Perri, 2016). Psychopaths may consider violence as a means to an end; a useful tool to satisfy a motive where they consider planned violence no differently than any other planned activity (Porter & Woodworth, 2006). Psychopaths committing instrumental violence did not display a state of heightened emotional arousal at the time of the murder as contrasted to non-psychopaths whose reactive murders exhibited an emotional discharge such as jealousy, rage, or a heated argument during the offense (Woodworth & Porter, 2002). Thus the rage displayed by a psychopath should not be confused with the emotion-based rage that law enforcement erroneously concludes when they do not have insights into the behavioral profile of a suspect. Quite the opposite holds true, psychopathic display of rage in the context of instrumental violence represents a dispassionate expression of their devaluation of others where murder is a viable option to satisfy their motives (Perri, 2011a).

Psychopaths tend to approach violence dispassionately although the end may be the pleasure gained from the violent act itself coupled with the fact that the murder is not viewed as an unpleasant act that most people would find abhorrent (Perri, 2016). Moreover, their dispassion should not be interpreted to mean that they might not experience gratification, a smug satisfaction due to their belief that they have fulfilled their motive through dominance and control (Perri, 2016). It has been theorized that the absence of emotion actually assists them in planning the homicide because they can, with coolness, think through a plan as opposed to reacting impulsively where emotions dictate one's violent outburst that is contemporaneous with the provocation (Perri, 2016). By lacking empathy, not displaying the ability to anticipate remorse, and devaluing others, instrumental violence is possible especially given that their diverse motives to kill are not emotionally driven.

Moreover, the fact that psychopathic criminals are caught should not necessarily be interpreted as the result of a 'spur of the moment' decision to offend, lack of planning, or poor risk assessment due to an impulsive behavioral disposition. The result is an individual who appears "impulsive, rash, irrational, and/or reactive to an observer although in reality his or her plan came about in a calm, methodical, and instrumental fashion" (Herve & Yuille, 2007, p. 434). Furthermore, the displeasure caused by another person may be invisible to the person that allegedly caused the displeasure because it is disguised as silence or feigned indifference, however the thinking behind the calm, passive exterior may be shockingly sadistic, retaliating at a time least expected and in a manner totally unanticipated. It is this characteristic that becomes apparent in many of the fraud detection homicide cases where offenders do not display the behavioral indicators that would normally serve as a warning sign for potential victims to keep their guard up and remove themselves from the offender's presence.

Family, Fraud and Violence

Although family violence is unacceptable, it is common. When we speak of family violence that turns deadly, it tends to transcend certain sacred values that make people uncomfortable when discussing the topic, but it is necessary to understand. Within this section we explore what occurs when family members who are engaged in fraud either by taking advantage of relatives, or when they perpetrate fraud outside of the family, that is discovered by family members. What we observe within these cases is that family members are willing to use deadly force to silence other family members who discover or have the potential to disclose their misdeeds to interested parties. What is interesting in reviewing these case studies is that offenders display traits of narcissism and psychopathy previously reviewed especially in how they were willing to aggress against those who did not provoke them in any way but tried to help them in some manner. The family cases uncovered involved spouses killing another spouse. Here the murdered spouse discovered that their spouse was committing fraud against them or in other circumstances. There are also family cases where an adult child will kill a parent due to fraud detection; yet what is ironic is that the parents were actually supportive of their adult child.

The Robert Petrick Case

Janine Sutphen did not suspect that her husband, Robert Petrick, was capable of harming her financially and physically. When Janine became aware of Robert's fraudulent schemes affecting her bank accounts, Robert began to plan her murder. According to the prosecution, Robert killed his wife after she detected his fraud schemes and he subsequently reported her missing as a way to divert attention away from himself (Lewis, 2005a). Janine was found near her home, wrapped in a tarp, sleeping bag, blankets, and chains floating in a nearby lake. She died of asphyxiation. The prosecution offered evidence of a murder plan recovered from Petrick's computer searches where he searched under "22 ways to kill a man with your bare hands," and other Google searches included the words "neck, snap, and break" (Perri & Lichtenwald, 2008b, p. 28). It is interesting to note that according to the defendant, he was allegedly a computer consultant who should have known that searches are saved and retrievable. Petrick's response to the prosecution's use of this evidence was that his wife had martial arts training, and she could have been searching the Internet. There were other searches regarding the water level in the lake where Sutphen's body was found, however he gave no good explanation for those searches. Nor did he have any credible reasons for computer searches on the topic of "body decomposition" and "rigor mortis," or for visiting websites that explain how the human body deteriorates (Lewis, 2005c).

According to detectives, the computer searches occurred several weeks before Petrick reported his wife missing, but a cadaver dog detected odors of human remains in both the bedroom and the trunk of the defendant's car. Further evidence revealed that the defendant ordered a stun gun prior to his wife's disappearance. During the period that his wife allegedly went missing, one witness, a man befriended by Petrick recalled that when asked about his wife, he appeared upset claiming she died of cancer (Lewis, 2005a). The prosecution found another woman known to Petrick who claimed that he had fraudulently emptied her bank accounts to buy computer equipment. Another female witness testified that she and Petrick had been going through premarital counseling and had set a wedding date—even before he killed Janine (Lewis, 2005b). Mary Grigolia, a minister, testified that while visiting Petrick in jail, he was told that the police were searching a small lake near his home for Sutphen's body. She says he stated with "great disdain and arrogance, 'they'll never find her'" which reflects the antisocial trait of super optimism that was covered in chapter one (Lewis, 2005c). Petrick was convicted of murder while representing himself without the aid of counsel (Petrick, 2007).

The Eric Hanson Case

In 2008, Eric Hanson was found guilty of a quadruple homicide for murdering his mother, Mary Hanson, his father, Terrence Hanson, his sister, Katherine (Kate) Tsao, and his brother-in-law, James Tsao. Eric was also found guilty of identity theft where he stole his parents' identities to obtain credit cards. According to the prosecution, the defendant is responsible for the theft of more than $150,000 from his parents through forgery, mail fraud, credit card fraud, and identity theft schemes (Golz, 2008a). In fact, just hours before the killings on the night of September 28–29, 2005, because Eric lived with his parents, he was able to intercept a $13,800 check delivered to the family's home and deposit it into his personal bank account (Golz, 2008d). Although the father was shot in the back of the head and the mother was shot in the face while they were sleeping, the prosecution claims that he carried the bodies to his sister's home, where he had already killed both Kate and James by blunt force trauma (Gutowski, 2008c). Due to the blows to James, his face was not recognizable, and Kate's arms were broken as she tried to protect herself from the blows to her head (Gutowski, 2005).

Eric continued to use the parents' credit cards even after their murder (Gregory, 2008a). Family members told the police that Mary detected Eric's fraud scheme when she had trouble using one of her credit cards. Apparently, Eric opened multiple credit cards in 2004 using his mother's name and mailing address, but later Eric added himself as an authorized user and changed the mailing address from his parents' home address to a post office box (Golz, 2008e). Kate confronted Eric about the fraud and threatened to tell their father if he did not confess, but Eric threatened to kill Kate if she disclosed what she knew about his fraud schemes (Gregory, 2008b). Eric denied the threat, however, a letter he wrote to his cousin from jail confirmed the threat where he stated, "I called Kate and told her to stay out of my life...If she didn't, she would regret it. When she asked me if I was threatening her, I said, 'No, it's a promise'" (Golz, 2008c). According to Eric's other sister, Jennifer Williams, who lives in Minnesota, Kate told her that Eric threatened to kill her if she disclosed the fraud to their father (Gutowski, 2008d). Specifically, Kate told Jennifer that Eric threatened her by stating, "If you tell dad, I'll fucking kill you" (Hanson, 2010, p. 245).

Moreover, on the morning of September 29, after the murders, Eric went to Los Angeles to visit his ex-fiancée, Allison Beck. To give the impression that he had nothing to do with the murders, prior to leaving for his trip and after the murders had already been committed, Eric left a note which read: "Mom, dad, see you Sunday. Have fun in Galena" (Hanson, 2010, p. 243). Before meeting Allison in Los Angeles, he called her and told her of the murders of his parents, sister, and brother-in-law (Barnum, 2008b). At this point, because of Allison's apprehension of Eric, she did not meet with him because of a conversation she remembered having with Eric. Several weeks before the murders, Eric became livid with Allison when he suspected that Allison and Kate spoke about him and his fraud schemes. Allison denied the conversations, but Eric pressed her which led to the following dialogue concerning his anxiety at the thought of his fraud schemes being disclosed (Barnum, 2008b):
Eric: "If I ever find out, you're going to get it."
Allison: "What does that mean?"
Eric: "Wait and see."
Allison: "Is that a threat?"
Eric: "No, it's a fact."

When police wanted to talk to Eric about the murders, he initially declined, but then agreed. He told the police he was willing to talk to them about the murders, but that he was still in Los Angeles (Gutowski, 2008d). However law enforcement was able to discover through cell phone records that the call was traced to Wisconsin where Eric was on his way to Jennifer's residence (Gutowski, 2008d). After he was stopped in Wisconsin, he told the police that he was on his way to Minnesota to tell his sister Jennifer of his grisly discovery. Yet Jennifer received a call from Eric on September 28, 2005, where he asked if he could stay with her and her family because he wanted to attend a ball game (Gregory, 2008b). However, all the other times that he came to Minnesota, he would never spend time with Jennifer or her family (Gregory, 2008b). Practically, Eric was on his way to Minnesota to silence the last piece of the puzzle that he believed tied him to the murders because of his belief that Jennifer knew of his fraud through Kate's disclosures plus the threats he made on her life.

After the police stopped Eric, they found his father's Rolex watch, a glove stained his father's blood type, and his mother's diamond ring (Gutowski, 2008d). When questioned by the police, Eric denied any involvement in the murders (Hanson, 2010). Eric did acknowledge that he used his mother's and father's names to secure credit, and that his parents confronted him with credit reports where he admitted that he had been charging purchases to these credit cards without their permission (Hanson, 2010). According to Eric, he convinced his mother that he would stop using the falsely obtained credit cards and that he would pay her back. Eric also claimed that his father agreed to allow him to take out a consolidation loan in his father's name to pay off some of the credit card debt. At trial, the prosecutor advanced the motive for the murders stating, "Eric Hanson in a cold, calculated, and premeditated manner, committed the execution-style murders out of greed and fear of having his fraudulent scheme discovered" (Rozek, 2005). The motive reflects fraud detection violence where the offender silences those who discover and can reveal their fraud schemes that predate the murder. In this case, the homicides were overwhelmingly planned. The problems Eric had with his parents, his fraud schemes, his chronic lying, his deceitful ways, and violence towards others revealed a high probability that he displayed psychopathic traits.

Historically he had spent time in a youth home, went to prison for home invasion in Michigan, and former girlfriends disclosed how he lied, stole, and became violent with them (Gutowski, 2008c). He was known to watch videos of animals being tortured and killed, and a family friend told authorities that Eric had forcibly held his daughter's head under water (Perri et al., 2008c). Most disturbing of all was a 911 call from Kate in 1993, when she told the police that he held a knife at her throat. Kate stated, "He got very mad at me and grabbed the top of my hair and threw me down on the wooden floor. His face turned color because he was so angry, and he said, 'I might as well kill you because as soon as my probation officer finds out, I'll be sent away anyway…I can cover it up. No one will know'" (Gutowski, 2008c). Eric's aunt, Donna Hanson, stated that she observed "strange behavior over the years, but was told he was getting help, and so we wondered but did not get involved, figuring Terrence and Mary were trying their best to help him; this has been hell on the dynamics of the entire family" (Perri et al., 2008c, p. 48). In fact, Eric's lifestyle, chronic lying, flagrant spending, and constant freeloading caused family fights (Gutowski, 2008d). Yet Eric indicated that he had "zero money problems" (Perri et al., 2008c, p. 48). Eric's statement that he had "zero money problems" would seem reasonable given that he stated, "It just seemed like free money" to describe his fraud (Gutowski, 2008e). He spent more than $14,000 on a new motorcycle several months before the murders (Barnum, 2008c). One former co-worker, who chose to remain anonymous, stated the following:

> He told all of us at work that he had a day job selling insurance and that he played golf in college and was a pro but hurt his back. Then I found out he never graduated high school and never even went to college in Michigan or somewhere and he was in prison for home invasion. He also had a friend come into work and tell him his sister died in a car accident, so he could get the weekend off. We all chipped in some money, because he was going to miss work. He took the money and thanked everyone for understanding. Thing is, his sister never died in that car accident. Just an evil soul (Perri et al., 2008c, p. 48).

The evidence reveals that if Eric did kill, he did not kill because he had a mental illness, nor is there any evidence that he was abused. Psychologist Dr. Marva Dawkins evaluated Eric and concluded that he exhibited narcissistic personality disorder, attention deficit hyperactive disorder (ADHD), and learning disabilities, coupled with antisocial features with no evidence of psychotic disorders (Gutowski, 2008b). Dr. Dawkins described the narcissistic personality disorder Eric exhibited as "an element of self-love" and "believing they are superior or unique and deserve recognition by others" (Barnum, 2008a). As to his ADHD, Dr. Dawkins indicated that ADHD "doesn't tell us if a person will do good things or bad things" (Barnum, 2008a). Ironically, a psychologist who evaluated Eric a decade earlier indicated that he "wasn't a threat to commit more violence" (Gregory & Barnum, 2008). Dr. Dawkins further testified that Eric lacked the ability to form deep bonds or to feel much empathy for others (Gutowski, 2008c). However, we can observe the manipulative games Eric played when he attempted to inure an emotional quality to his relationship with his family when he told a reporter, "I think the older I got, the closer I got with my parents…I always looked at my family as kind of a rock, someone you could rely on no matter what" (Gutowski, 2008f).

Other psychopathic traits Eric exhibited that were disclosed by the prosecutor included "deceitfulness, lack of remorse, impulsivity, reckless disregard for the safety of others, irritability, and aggressiveness" (Golz, 2008b). Dr. Dawkins stated that Eric came from a loving, supportive home that one could characterize as affluent, or upper-middle class, but believed "He has the persona of presenting himself as a macho guy, someone who has it together…but from what we have learned, he's actually a very vulnerable, weak individual in terms of his own self-esteem" (Gutowski, 2008b). Though Eric's parents never turned their back on him, Jennifer Williams said that their mother was especially concerned with protecting the family image. In fact, the mother attempted to find a way to pay off Eric's fraudulently obtained money by taking out loans in the tens of thousands of dollars to pay off the credit card debt he had accumulated (Gutowski, 2008a). The mother wanted to cover for her son because she believed that he would try to hurt himself, even though Kate was livid and threatened to tell their father (Gutowski, 2008d). In the end, Eric was not capable of reciprocating family obligations despite his parents' effort to show, through example, what family support is as exemplified by Jennifer's victim impact statement to the court:

> My parents did so much for Eric…When he was in trouble at school, my parents would meet with the school officials. When Eric was in trouble at home, they would go to counseling with him to try and help him out. When he was in trouble with the police, my parents would get him a lawyer and attend court with him. They supported him when he wanted to go to golf school, when he wanted to be a CNA, or when he was trying to work as a mortgage officer. They let him live under their roof, helping him get on his feet… Eric murdered the only people in his life that loved him unconditionally (Williams, 2008).

The Christopher Porco Case

In the early morning hours of November 15, 2004, Christopher drove his yellow Jeep from the University of Rochester where he was a student, to upstate New York to murder his parents, Peter and Joan Porco, who lived in the town of Bethlehem, just outside of Albany. Christopher used a long-handled ax to cleave his father and mother while they were sleeping in bed. His father died, and his mother was left for dead. When the authorities found Joan, her brain was exposed, her jaw was dislodged, and she eventually lost one of her eyes. Interestingly, despite these injuries, she was able to indicate by nodding her head that Christopher was responsible for what happened when she was questioned by police (McNiff & Cuomo, 2006). To prove that Christopher was the killer, the evidence revealed video recordings from traffic cameras in Rochester, New York, which captured images of a yellow Jeep Wrangler as it headed in the direction of the New York State Thruway at 10:36 p.m. on November 14, 2004 toward his parents' house and headed back toward the campus at 8:30 a.m. on November 15, 2004. Witnesses stated that this yellow vehicle was of the same class and displayed characteristics unique to the defendant's Jeep. Forensic expert evidence revealed that the defendant was in the 0.39 percent of North Americans whose mitochondrial DNA profile matched the profile from a sample extracted from a toll ticket handed out at Thruway exit 46 in Rochester at 10:45 p.m. on November 14, 2004 and handed in at Thruway exit 24 in Albany at 1:51 a.m. on November 15, 2004.

Evidence also revealed that at 2:14 a.m. the burglary alarm system at the family home, located 9.3 miles from exit 24, was turned off by someone using a master code known only to the two victims, the defendant, and his brother who was stationed in the United States Navy in South Carolina at the time, and possibly defendant's uncle and a female family friend who were not in any way implicated. A neighbor testified that he observed a yellow Jeep Wrangler in the driveway of the family home around 3:45 or 4:00 a.m. on November 15, 2004, as he was driving from his residence on the same street on his way to work (Porco, 2011). Evidence also revealed that Christopher claimed on several occasions to have been planning to or to have slept in the lounge of his dormitory on November 14–15, 2004. Yet seven fellow students who were in the lounge for various extended and overlapping periods of time between 10:30 p.m. on November 14, 2004, and 3:30 a.m. on November 15, 2004, did not recall seeing him sleeping in the lounge. In fact, Christopher was first observed on campus running toward his dormitory on November 15, 2004 at 8:45 a.m., about one mile from where his Jeep was later found parked, and was seen in the lounge at 9:30 a.m. Christopher told several friends that he tried to contact his parents at home or at work by telephone on November 15, 2004, but the telephone records did not support this claim, and his father's secretary testified that she did not receive a telephone call from the defendant, although Christopher claimed to have told a friend that he had spoken with her.

There was a history of deceitful behavior on Christopher's part. He was known to have manipulated college transcripts from Hudson Valley Community College, located in upstate New York, reflecting false grades so he could be readmitted to the University of Rochester after he was forced to withdraw for poor grades (Karlin, 2006). While at the University of Rochester, there were reports from classmates that Christopher became a heavy drinker, threatened to kill a female classmate, and had to be pulled off another person during a fight at a party when it appeared that he would not stop choking him (McNiff & Cuomo, 2006). In addition, during the investigation, authorities determined that Christopher displayed a history of antisocial behavior. For example, during the night of November 18–19, 2002, while Christopher was home from college, he staged a burglary where two laptop computers were stolen. He ultimately sold one of the computers on eBay to a California resident 20 days later (Porco, 2011). The evidence of this staged burglary break-in is relevant in that it mirrored Christopher's argument that his parents were victimized again by a mythical stranger—but this time for murder. Interestingly, in 2004, one month before the murder, his parents froze their eBay accounts after Christopher failed to send the items that were sold to the eBay buyers. During the investigation, it was revealed that Christopher posed as his brother and sent e-mails to customers explaining that his brother died and was unable to send the purchased items (Lyons, 2006c). He was known to have broken into his former employer's workplace to steal cell phones, cameras, and computers (Lyons, 2006c). He fraudulently obtained loans using his parents as co-signers without their knowledge after obtaining his father's personal information.

Christopher told his parents that he only needed a cosigned $2,000 loan for school, yet he fraudulently took out a loan for more than $30,000 to pay for college expenses (McNiff & Cuomo, 2006). Moreover, to keep up with the appearance that he was from a wealthy family, he accumulated more than $40,000 in debt from lavish spending and Internet gambling (McNiff & Cuomo, 2006). There were several e-mails between Christopher and his parents that disclosed prior tension between the parties that accurately support research suggesting that conflicts and arguments are a catalyst for violence. The parents eventually confronted Porco about his fraudulent behavior. In one e-mail, the father wrote, "Did you forge my signature as a co-signer? What the hell are you doing? You should have called me to discuss it...I'm calling Citibank this morning to find out what you have done and am going to tell them I'm not to be on it as co-signer" (Perri & Lichtenwald, 2008b). The parents tried to contact Christopher, but he would not talk to them. In a follow-up e-mail, the father stated, "I want you to know that if you abuse my credit again, I will be forced to file forgery affidavits in order to disclaim liability, and that applies to the Citibank college loan if you attempt to reactivate it or use my credit to obtain any other loan" (McNiff & Cuomo, 2006). In the same e-mail, the father went on to say, "We may be disappointed with you, but your mother and I still love you and care about your future" (Perri et al., 2008c, p. 45). Amazingly, the next day, Citibank notified the father that Christopher again obtained a line of credit of more than $16,000 to purchase his Jeep Wrangler (McNiff & Cuomo, 2006).

Again, Christopher fraudulently used his father's name as co-signatory to secure the auto loan. Interestingly, Christopher indicated that he had committed fraud to "absolve my parents of the financial burden of college," but failed to mention the new Jeep he bought (Lyons, 2006a). There was no evidence that he took the money to pay off his earlier debts. Christopher's case supports the view that psychopaths are prisoners of the present in that they appear to display a diminished ability to reflect upon the past and learn from their mistakes. Additionally, they have a diminished ability to project into the future and determine how their behavior will impact others—including themselves. They appear to be masters of self-inflicted wounds due to their lack of insight about their own self-destructive behaviors. Furthermore, one can observe how the escalation in tensions in the case fits the research where many of these homicides are rooted in conflicts between family members (Heide & Petee, 2007). Despite the chaos Christopher brought into his parents' lives, they told him how much they loved him. Unfortunately, their love was irrelevant for what he planned to do next. Less than two weeks after his father warned Christopher that he would not hesitate to file forgery affidavits against him for fraudulent behavior, Christopher executed his plan to neutralize his father's threat. Research suggests that the victim's threat of exposing the fraud will force a shift in the psychopath's strategy from employing charm, cunning behavior, and manipulation on the victim, to employing violence to silence them (Perri et al., 2008c).

Several Albany, New York, area psychologists and mental health professionals familiar with the case stated that "Christopher Porco fits the profile of a psychopath" focusing on his continued pattern of deceitful behavior (Grondahl, 2006). Furthermore, these professionals also pointed to his pattern of grandiose perceptions as he presented himself to others as a member of a wealthy and influential family. Christopher was known to have lied to friends and acquaintances about a fictitious inheritance of millions of dollars from his grandmother. Even his father told a coworker that he believed Christopher was a sociopath (Lyons, 2006b). Many people found Christopher's behavior strange after he made bail on the murder charges and was released from custody. While awaiting trial, many found him to be strangely arrogant: drinking in bars, attending concerts, going out to entertainment establishments, and driving the yellow Jeep that witnesses state was the same vehicle used on the night of the murder. This behavior fits the traits of an individual in need of grandiosity and embellishment of his life (Grondahl, 2006). As forensic psychologist Edelgard Wulfert stated, "There's an overlap between psychopathic and narcissistic tendencies…He (Christopher) believes that the rules do not apply to him and he has a need to show off in front of people" (Grondahl, 2006).

The behavioral data from this case did not reveal a murder in which the adult child alleged that the murder was justified because his parents abused him as a youth or an adult, no history of mental illness was offered as a defense at his trial, nor did he fear for his life, which may have justified deadly force. What is instructive about the case is that Christopher displayed the traits of a psychopath when his parents attempted a variety of parenting techniques to both discipline and force him to adhere to their value system. Data from this study suggest that Peter and Joan did not understand that Christopher was capable of murdering them to prevent them from obstructing his wants and sense of entitlement. Additional research from the Porco case indicates that psychopaths who are raised in antisocial environments tend to develop into violent psychopaths, whereas those who are not raised in such environments, and have access to positive social and educational resources, are more likely to develop into non-violent white-collar criminals (Hare, 1999). The behavioral data yielded no indication that Christopher was raised in an antisocial environment, in fact the data reflects the opposite. He was highly intelligent and came from a solid, middle-class family. It is interesting to note that during an interview with CBS, while visiting his mother at the hospital, Christopher stated, "I saw her—she was swollen and covered in tubes and my reaction was I burst into tears. I fell on the floor right there" (Bell, 2007).

Yet a former youth leader minister named Joseph Catalano who went to the hospital to be with Christopher claimed to be "struck by Porco's odd behavior because he did not seem to exhibit any grief" (Bell, 2007). Psychopaths' use of the "chameleon strategy" is not surprising in that they attempt to read a situation and mimic the appropriate emotional response others want or expect to observe so they appear sympathetic to outsiders—in essence, they employ impression management to influence how they want outsiders to view them

(Perri et al., 2008c). Fortunately, his friend was present to capture Christopher's true behavioral response. Christopher was convicted of the murder of his father and the attempted murder of his mother.

Comparing the Porco and Hanson Case

There are certain types of activities that predate a murder that increase the risk of homicide. For example, many types of narcotics distribution involve death because violence is inherent in this activity. What is interesting about these two cases is that neither were raised as children in violent, antisocial environments where the probability of engaging in violence was high. Quite the opposite holds true. Both families appeared to be stable and offered a supportive environment. Yet, it is this outside appearance of family normality that makes understanding these homicides difficult to comprehend. One important aspect of Christopher and Eric's cases is that it did not appear as though their mothers posed a threat once becoming aware of their son's fraud schemes. In fact, the mothers appeared to be supportive of their sons. In fact Christopher's mother retracted her initial statement to the police who found her in her home that it was Christopher who committed the crime against her and her murdered husband. Christopher's mother appeared at his trial supporting him by being seen with him, walking into court with him, and being close to him. She wanted to give the impression that her son was not someone she feared desiring to give the impression that Christopher does not have the character to commit such a heinous act. Eric's mother actually tried to find ways to pay off the debt that Eric fraudulently accumulated. However, we do not see Christopher or Eric somehow sparing their mothers because they stood by their son's cause or attempted to bail them out. The mothers were not spared because their mothers' values and supportive nature were never important to Eric or Christopher to begin with; if these attributes had been important, they would not have taken advantage of them in the first place.

What is ironic is that for the psychopath, the "most serious damage to others is often largely through their concern for him [the offender] and their efforts to help him" (Cleckley, 1988, p. 262). This insight by Dr. Cleckley is most applicable to Eric and Christopher where the evidence is clear that their parents desperately tried to help their child even when they were harmed in the process. All too often, people who care about others believe that the person they are trying to help will see the err of their ways. Yet, by engaging in projection bias by believing that others will change their ways the way they would if they were in a similar situation is what puts them at risk for being harmed. Also, there was no evidence that Eric's father or brother-in-law were a threat to Eric's fraud schemes. Consider the previously-mentioned research appearing applicable to these cases that even in the absence of provocation, narcissism and a sense of entitlement drive them to aggress against innocent individuals whom they view as potential threats. Neither Christopher nor Eric engaged in a self-moral debate as to whether murder was an option—it was a solution to a perceived problem. Christopher and Eric perceived parental control as a form of provocation sufficient to trigger violence as a solution especially when their sense of entitlement and desire to control others and situations was infringed upon even though they instigated the provocation from family members in the first place because of the financial exploitation they experienced. Both Eric and Christopher tool advantage of their parents' good will instead of reciprocating the good will. Both interpreted the good will as a weakness to exploit.

In addition, their controlling, psychopathic nature may predispose them to seeing hostile intent in the action of others, which triggered a preemptive strike toward family members (Perri, 2016). Christopher and Eric's mothers were potential witnesses to their fraud schemes and to the murders of their husbands, thus in cold blood, they needed to be eliminated. Eric wanted to kill Kate, but also had to eliminate his brother-in-law James because he would have been a witness to Kate's murder even though there was no evidence that James was a threat to Eric. In both of these case, these men with cold ease were able to eliminate those closest to them. These offenders display the criminal thinking traits of power orientation and goal interference, which is the need to exert control over a person that appears to be interfering with their goal that, in both cases, was the perpetuation of fraud. Homicide, one can say, is the ultimate form of control over another. Table 2 explores case trait similarities and differences between these offenders.

Table 2 **Offender Profile Case Trait Comparison**

Case Trait	Christopher Porco	Eric Hanson
Race	White	White
Age at Time of Murder	22	29
Murder Weapon	ax	gun/blunt object
Psychopathic Traits	yes	yes
Narcissistic Traits	yes	yes
High Debt Held by Defendant	yes	yes
Time of Murder (Late Night)	yes	yes
Murder Location (Parent's Home)	yes	yes
Parents Killed in Their Bed	yes	yes
Location of Wounds (Head)	yes	yes
Fraud Perpetrated on Parents	yes	yes
Parental Confrontation about Fraud	yes	yes
Pre-Murder Family Violence	no	yes
Criminal Record	no	yes
Murder of Sibling	no	yes
Threats Prior to Murder	no	yes
Multiple Murder Locations	no	yes
Adult Child Lives with Parents	no	yes
Mother Murdered	no	yes
Post-offense Fraud	no	yes

Prevention and Protection of Family Members

Often, mental illness or abuse, common explanations used to rationalize these horrific situations, are helpful in protecting sacred values coupled with reducing our own anxiety. As the Porco and Hanson cases demonstrate, these explanations may not apply because it is the shear conscienceless behavior of these individuals rejecting those sacred family and societal values that makes murder an option. Family members who may be perpetrating fraud schemes against other family members display malignant narcissistic and psychopathic traits that propel them to use murder as a solution once their fraud schemes are detected. Despite the lack of a single definitive cause to explain the occurrence of this type of behavior, most would agree that encountering individuals displaying such behavior can be both frustrating and even dangerous. Together, the Porco and Hanson cases serve as a warning to family members who do not develop protective measures when they fail to acknowledge who their child really is in terms of displaying severe antisocial traits coupled with a disordered personality. We observe these traits during adolescence, continuing into adulthood, with wants being forced against family values coupled with no sense of remorse. Parents, by either ignoring or not interpreting their child's behaviors correctly, expose themselves and the rest of their families to psychopathic destruction, either emotionally, financially, or possibly even physically (Perri & Lichtenwald, 2007b). Also, there is often a pattern of conflict between the offender and family members that includes escalating verbal arguments coupled with threats and assaults; research reveals that family violence has its roots in arguments that predated the homicide (Heide & Petee, 2007).

It is not uncommon for psychopaths to lash out violently when they believe they are losing control over a situation—in essence they perceive their power orientation is being restricted. Consider that psychopaths have a strong need for psychological and/or physical control to reinforce their authority: for the psychopath, it's about winning (Perri & Lichtenwald, 2008c). In Christopher's case, the father indicated that he was willing to file forgery affidavits against him. Moreover, when psychopaths lash out violently, often society and those that investigate such crimes incorrectly assume that Christopher was angry at his parents and that his emotions got the better of him, thus his violence would be incorrectly interpreted as being reactive in nature. Somehow, under normal circumstances, it would not be his character to become violent. Again, societal projection bias incorrectly injects a non-psychopathic explanation to homicide by attempting to attach an emotion to the killing—the defendant's angry, emotional state was the impetus for the killings (Perri et al., 2008c).

For Christopher, the research suggests that the issue was neither about anger nor other unresolved emotions, but about his perception of murder as being an acceptable means of conflict resolution; eliminate others to maintain control and benefit however they may define a benefit. Many parents unaware of this mindset are probably ill-equipped to imagine that their child can harm them. Consequently, they do not perceive their parental behavior of imposing appropriate boundaries being interpreted as an obstacle to their child's sense of entitlement. Many parents of behaviorally-disordered children are in denial and underestimate their child's proclivity toward violence. Christopher's mother later retracted the statement she made to the police with her head nod that implicated her son even when the evidence overwhelmingly pointed to him as the assailant. She wrote a letter to the local newspaper, *The Times Union*, where she stated, "I implore the Bethlehem police and the District Attorney's Office to leave my son alone, and to search for Peter's killer or killers, so that he can rest in peace and my sons and I can live in safety" (Lyons, 2005b). She further stated,

> With every ounce of my being, I cannot accept that Christopher could have, or would have chosen to butcher us in any conceivable way, or for any conceivable reason…Please allow Christopher the opportunity to attain freedom in my lifetime. I believe him to be innocent with all my heart. Please give him a chance to use his talents to make a significant contribution to society (Lyons, 2006a).

Throughout the trial process, Christopher's mother was supportive and made sure she was present and featured alongside her son when photographs were taken. Unfortunately, she did not understand that her attempt to bond with her son did not mean that he would reciprocate the bonding—this is a common misperception that parents of psychopathic children harbor. What makes this case difficult to comprehend is the fact that Christopher's parents tried to do the right thing by being disciplinarians, while assuring him that he was loved. Despite all the parental goodwill bestowed upon Christopher, none of it influenced how he would treat his parents. They probably thought that he would one day see the error of his ways and thank them for using the "tough love" approach. For example, Christopher's destructive behavior did not decrease even after he was caught faking college transcripts at Hudson Valley Community College despite acknowledging, "I've learned my lesson, I really need this tough love" (Karlin, 2006). Parents have been known to exacerbate an already difficult family situation when dealing with psychopathic children and in this case, it was as if the parents were pouring gasoline on an already out-of-control fire where the result was an escalation of family turmoil (Perri et al., 2008c).

Ironically, Christopher's antisocial characteristics interpreted his parents' position of being caring and loving as a weakness to be exploited. Conversely, he did not view his parents' disciplinary, "tough love" approach as gestures of parental love; they were interpreted as goal interference due to Christopher's antisocial traits, as were explained in chapter one. The parents' actions were perceived as a form of provocation in their attempts to curtail his sense of entitlement. Most would also agree that managing individuals who display malignant narcissistic and psychopathic behaviors often becomes particularly problematic for family members and other personal associates. A large part of the difficulty stems from a lack of awareness that the family member may not have the capacity to experience empathy, they may lie frequently, steal from the family, and can readily provide ample verbal justifications for their antisocial behavior. Then the problem becomes how does the family cope with such individuals as they grow into adulthood, or if they become someone's spouse?

How parents, siblings, and spouses elect to interact with them is important because minimization of their antisocial behaviors exposes those closest to these individuals to serious harm. Just as a business implements internal controls to safeguard its assets from being misappropriated, so too should family members implement their own internal controls to protect their own tangible and intangible assets. First there needs to be some acknowledgment that their family member who is causing internal strife puts the entire family at risk for serious familial destruction and violence. Without this acknowledgement, denial of the problem will be the answer to the problem. For those who admit there is a problem, there are a couple of measures they can implement to protect themselves. First, financially-related documents, wallets, and purses, must not under any circumstances be accessible. For example, blank checks left around the home are a recipe for check fraud. Set up a lock box at a bank to store valuable items like jewelry, wills, and other items that could be stolen, manipulated, or forged (Perri & Lichtenwald, 2008c). Although such steps appear overly cautious, the amount of effort required to put these protective measures in place is minimal compared to the amount of effort required to reverse the damage of a poor credit record or the destructive impact of identity theft.

It is imperative that items such as utility bills, bank statements, social security cards, and records that have personal information be made inaccessible to the family member. In the Eric Hanson case, the police found credit card information traceable to the parents and his sister in his bedroom (Gutowski, 2005). Family should occasionally check credit history for unusual transactions they are not aware of in order to check the origins of such transactions, as there is a real possibility that one's family member may be the cause of the unusual transaction. For additional financial safety, fraud protection alerts that can be purchased should be considered. Contacting one's bank to be on alert can prevent the family member from using identity theft for fraudulent financial gains as we observed in the Porco and Hanson cases. In addition, computer access codes must remain within the control of the owner of the code. For example, Christopher used his parent's eBay account and abused this privilege as well as having access to his parents' personal information. Finally, communication between family members should be handled with care, especially if such communications could be interpreted as somehow threatening. This is not to imply that a family member should not be confronted about their wrongdoings, but if these individuals still live in the same residence, there could be a risk of retaliation.

So before confrontation, confronting parties should carefully weigh out the desired results and develop a strategic plan of action should things not go as intended. In addition, recall that family members may not get a reaction from the confrontation at all. A display of indifference on the part of the disordered individual should not be interpreted as a reason to not worry. Recall that the distress they feel caused by the confrontation may be invisible to the person(s) involved in the confrontation and may be disguised as silence or feigned indifference, yet the thinking behind the calm, accommodating exterior may be shockingly sadistic. They may retaliate at a time least expected and in a manner totally unanticipated. Even when they may not live in the same house, do family members have access to the residence by having electronic codes to enter the residence or a key? Are family members willing to call law enforcement on another family member if they sense danger? Are family members willing to separate themselves from such antisocial family members by removing them from their home? Answers to these questions are at the heart of understanding how family members define their relationships to each other.

Murder-for-Hire Considerations

Murder-for-hire, also known as contract killings, appeals to some criminals because of the belief that it offers an airtight alibi for the person, known as the solicitor, who takes out the contract on the person they want killed. By alibi this means that the solicitor who is buying the services of a contract killing try to physically distance themselves from the killing by relocating to another city or state so that they can argue that it is impossible that they were the ones who committed the murder. Contracts to kill typically begin in the mind of the solicitor as an insurmountable problem best solved by having someone else kill the victim, also known as the target. The time taken by the solicitor to arrive at the point where contract killing is acceptable to them can be within a few weeks, months, or even years, depending on how severe the solicitor perceives the circumstances to be. While murder-for-hire may appear to outsiders as an impulsive act, it is the product of considerable reflection (Black & Cravens, 2000). The killing is referred to as a "hit" and at the same time the person who actually commits the murder, the hitman, may have little or no direct connection to the victim.

This makes it more difficult for investigators to establish what happened because the victim-offender analysis can be considered non-existent; in other words, the ability to profile the killer becomes more difficult. We say hitman because the great majority of contract killers are male (Black & Cravens, 2000). Contract killings are usually associated with organized crime and while there is truth to this perception, it would be incorrect to believe that only organized crime figures engage in this behavior. However, organized crime contract killings and white-collar offenders who resort to contract killings have parallel motives. Both use the services of contract killers to silence the victim who detected their fraud schemes and may be or is able to testify against them in a court of law (Perri, 2016). Payment for the actual killing is usually divided by paying part of the total contract price prior to the killing and the balance after the successful completion of the hit. The actual amount for a hit may depend on the risks involved, whether the individual is a professional contract killer or not, whether law enforcement is involved, media attention in the case of a high-profile target, and the way the hit should occur.

Professor Donald Black, who has studied contract killings in the U.S., states that murder-for-hire is largely a white, middle-class phenomenon that commonly occurs in the suburbs and non-suburbs, and has been a practice since colonial times (Piper, 1999). In some respects, the ability to have someone killed has been democratized such that it is no longer the privileged who can afford to have someone silenced. Solicitors and hitmen are changing; there is a new demand for solving not only intimate, personal problems, but also a need for some to maintain a sense of self-preservation. For example, we see the sense of self-preservation that has little to do with personal, intimate matters between husband and wife, but about making sure fraud schemes are not disclosed to authorities so that they can avoid prosecution and continue to profit from white-collar crime. According to Professor Black, because murder-for-hire has not been viewed as an especially urgent topic in lethal violence, there has been little systematic research about it (Black & Cravens, 2000). Black's study of those who solicit murder and the hitmen they hire confirms some perceptions about the crime. According to Black, the primary motive for the hitman is material gain. For the solicitor the motives are varied, and may include: 1) to get rid of a spouse, 2) to get insurance money, or 3) to get out of a bad relationship. In addition, Black states, "Most solicitors do not see themselves as killers…They want to get rid of a problem and go on with their lives. They see themselves protecting a way of life or restoring a way of life" (Piper, 1999).

Once the decision is made to have the target silenced, the solicitor must convince another to accept the contract to kill. Trying to get someone to do the killing is usually accomplished through what is referred to as the "evoking context" (Black & Cravens, 2000). Evoking is the process of presenting the problem to a potential hitman with the goal of attaining participation. It is not uncommon for the solicitor to approach several individuals to find a hitman. How a solicitor approaches a potential hitman depends on who they are approaching. If the solicitor approaches a friend, relative, or acquaintance, this strategy is labeled the intimate track. Women tend to use the intimate approach (Black & Cravens, 2000). In the intimate track, the relative closeness of the interpersonal relationship between the solicitor and potential hitmen provides the structure for how to evoke participation in the killing. Sometimes the solicitor may use the intimate track to evoke participation through persuasion and sometimes through coercion and threats. There are times when the solicitor uses a degree of coercion to persuade a hitman by capitalizing on a weakness, for example a narcotics addiction, or by creating scenarios that force the hitman to kill. At times, solicitors who employ the intimate track will use humor to test the waters by making statements such as, "you know I am only joking" or "do you think I'm that crazy to think of such a thing?"

Humor allows the solicitor an exit strategy if the person they are trying to get to do the hit backs off. It is interesting that the intimate approach exposes the solicitor's state of mind and relationships, and therefore poses a greater risk of discovery by law enforcement. Solicitors often think that the people they approach will keep their discussions secret, yet in the end, what exposes the solicitor is that they talk too much. Therefore solicitors, fortunately, often fail to kill their target because people approached by the solicitor go to the police. In addition, if the solicitor succeeds, the person who does the killing typically is an amateur disclosing their murder(s) and the solicitor's identity to others. The second evoking approach, referred to as the staged track, involves solicitors seeking the help from experienced strangers or professional killers. The staged track is often used by undercover officers because the solicitor probably does not know the true status of the hitman. In the staged approach, research does not indicate that the solicitor approaches several potential hitmen. Usually the solicitor uses an intermediary to help find a hitman, especially if they are in jail and need outside help. In the staged approach, they negotiate fees and discuss strategies on how the kill should be carried out. Examples of murder-for-hire cases are illustrated below.

The Michael Burnett Case

For more than 40 years, Michael Burnett was a confidence man, stock swindler, and a suspected murderer. At times, he was the criminal, and other times he served as an informant for authorities and disclosed the names of corrupt elected officials and those who embezzled millions. In 1993 he and a female bank teller, Valleri Vassell, were co-conspirators in a bank fraud scheme. After the authorities detected the fraud scheme, Valleri agreed to testify as a witness against Michael (Fried, 1996). According to prosecutors, Michael planned a $100,000 murder-for-hire scheme to silence Valleri while he was imprisoned (Sexton, 1995). He used his attorney, Howard Krantz, as an intermediary to organize the contract killing (Sexton, 1995). On the evening of January 14, 1994, two of Howard's recruits forced their way into Valleri's apartment and shot her as she sat down to dinner with her family. In this case, Michael, Howard, and the other two co-conspirators were found guilty of murder. Other forensic evidence that was collected and used against these killers included shoeprint evidence, incriminating statements made by the defendant(s) or other witnesses, DNA, the murder weapon, fingerprints, blood spatter, and eye witness evidence.

The Edward Leak Case

Edward Leak, Jr. was a Chicago police officer who committed white-collar crimes that eventually escalated into violence. He worked part-time in the family funeral home business, where he embezzled more than $400,000 (Main, 2005). It was thought that the victim, Fred Hamilton, who worked at the business, was a co-conspirator. After the discovery of the fraud by the accountant, Fred's employment was terminated. The business apparently pursued fraud charges against Fred, but not Edward. To buy Fred's silence, Edward showered him with luxury vehicles, jewelry, and furs for Fred's girlfriend (Main, 2005). Fred, however, anonymously called the police and disclosed Edward's participation in the fraud. The police eventually discovered that it was Fred who made the call, and when Edward found out about the disclosure, he began to threaten Fred's life. Edward hired two hitmen, Alfred Marley and John Brown, to silence Hamilton. Eleven days before the murder, Edward used his police computer to run the license plate of Fred's Jeep.

Over a span of five weeks before the murder, Edward called John about 600 times on his cell phone. Initially, Edward denied knowing John until he was confronted with the phone records. In fact, cell phone tower records show that Edward's phone was in use near the shooting (Ahmed, 2007). Before killing Fred, John and Alfred went to Fred's home and punctured the tires of his Jeep so that he could not drive away. Outside of Fred's home, John chased him around the Jeep wearing a ski mask and shot him. Alfred then approached Fred as he lay on the ground and while standing over him, fired two more bullets. The two killers were apprehended, and the weapon, ski mask, and cell phone the killers used to coordinate the murder with Edward were recovered. Alfred pleaded guilty to the murder and testified against the other co-defendants in exchange for a reduced sentence. Interestingly, John and Alfred were not paid up front for the killing. In fact, they were not paid at all. It was not clear how much Alfred had been promised, but John was to receive $1,500 when the job was completed (Ataiyero, 2007). The reality is, life is cheap in the world of contract killing. The prosecution indicated Edward's motive was to prevent the disclosure of the fraud perpetrated on the family business (Parker, 2007).

Contract Person Characteristics

Hitmen have their own set of characteristics. Dr. Louis Schlesinger has written on the different types of hitmen and their characteristics such as those that are professional, semi-professional, and amateurs. Some professional killers may be members of an organized crime syndicate and perform their job out of obligation to the group, while others may be freelance agents and not connected to any criminal faction (Schlesinger, 2001). The semi-professional and amateur killers earn a living from other activities, legal and illegal, and engage in contract killing on a one or two-time basis. The semi-professional is more sophisticated than the amateur, but is less competent than the professional. They often reject conventional values and hard work believing that they can achieve success through criminal behavior. Semi-professionals are more characteristic of unstable but with less personality disturbance than street-level amateurs, but have displayed violence frequently in the past (Schlesinger,

2001). Amateur methods are usually poorly planned, in contrast to semi-professional and professional strategies which are highly planned. The amateur leaves evidence behind or talks to others about the kill, while the professional leave no evidence that is traceable to them or to the person who hired them.

Professionals may dispose of the body and effectively stage the murder to look like a suicide. Many amateurs have a criminal history and display more traits of lifestyle instability than professional killers (Schlesinger, 2001). These hitmen are usually someone down on their luck who can be pushed around and taken advantage of, especially those who are addicted to narcotics and willing to kill for just enough money to satisfy their addiction. Amateurs are often hired to murder intimate partners as observed in the Fredric Tokars case, while professional killers may be hired for business-related reasons. Consider Sammy "the Bull" Gravano, organized crime hitman and the prototypical professional killer who confessed to a minimum of 19 murders. Sammy described contract killings as a "logical means of achieving the goals of his group," meaning the organized crime group he belonged to (Schlesinger, 2001). Sammy further stated, "Everybody I killed was planned...I'm a hitman not a serial killer" (Wagner, 2017). During an interview at a restaurant, he told the reporter, "See that blonde over there? See that guy with her? I could go over there, pop him in the back of the head and come back here and finish my salmon. I know that it's supposed to bother me, but it don't" (Schwartzman, 1999). Reflecting on his life, Sammy could not explain why he became a killer, recalling:

> I had a good mother...I don't know how I got to be the way I am...No emotion. No feeling. Like [expletive] ice. I never killed in a fit of anger. I'm controlled, a professional. I kill because of my oath. It was part of the job. Like guys in the Army dropping bombs in Kosovo kill people as part of their job (Schwartzman, 1999).

The William Benbow Case

Tax preparer William Benbow was convicted of conspiring in a murder-for-hire scheme in which he planned to kill two company employees, their spouses, and a client, to prevent them from disclosing to the police information of the tax fraud schemes the business perpetrated (Geier, 2002). According to the facts, William's mother, Margaret, who was convicted of fraud, but not murder-for-hire, would charge $100 for fraudulently preparing tax returns by claiming itemized deductions that did not exist. William utilized an intermediary named Robert Taylorson to find a hitman. Robert introduced William to an individual named Kevin Pollard. William agreed to pay Kevin $5,000 to purchase guns, and conduct surveillance on the intended victims, and an additional $15,000 when the jobs were completed (Geier, 2002). Fortunately, several weeks after their meeting, Robert disclosed the murder-for-hire conspiracy to a relative who later told federal agents. When agents confronted William, he acknowledged that while at a bar drinking on a prior occasion, he asked friends if any of them knew where he might find a hitman. The day after the agents' visit, William told Kevin to take one of the employees and their spouse off the hit list because they were friends of Robert's cousin. William then told Kevin not to proceed against any of the intended targets because the police knew about the plot. Kevin told William he had spent about $600 on the weapon he planned to use, so William reimbursed Kevin with about $700 in cash and crack cocaine (Geier, 2002). When executing a state search warrant at Kevin's residence two days later, police recovered photographs and a handwritten hit-list bearing the names and addresses of the five intended targets, as well as a broken small-caliber pistol.

The Frank Marfo Case

From May 2009 through November 2011, Frank Marfo participated in a scheme to steal money orders and checks, and to defraud banks in Maryland and elsewhere. At first the scheme involved Frank stealing money orders and checks from rent deposit boxes located at apartment complexes in Maryland, Virginia, and Delaware. Co-conspirators Tavon Davis, Isaiah Callaway, and Bruce Byrd, at Frank's direction, recruited primarily homeless drug addicts to open fraudulent business checking, savings, and payroll accounts at banks in Maryland and New Jersey. They were directed to use their personal identification, in addition to documents provided by Frank and

Tavon, which purported to authenticate fraudulent businesses for new accounts opened in their names. Frank, Tavon, and other co-conspirators would alter the name of the stolen money orders and checks to correspond to the name of a fraudulent business account, then deposit and withdraw the stolen money. Tavon estimated that between $1 million and $1.5 million worth of stolen money orders were deposited and withdrawn from various banks in this manner.

On December 29, 2010, Isaiah was arrested by Baltimore County police while he was in the process of directing two individuals to open fraudulent business accounts at TD Bank and Bank of America. Isaiah was charged with possession of counterfeit documents and theft. Following his arrest, Isaiah was interviewed by detectives, during which Isaiah admitted his participation in the bank fraud scheme but did not identify others who were involved. After Tavon and Frank learned of Isaiah's arrest, Tavon met with Isaiah when he was released from custody waiting for his fraud case to be resolved. Between April 5-11, 2011, Tavon, Bruce, and Frank met several times to discuss the threat to the fraud scheme posed by the arrest and possible cooperation of Isaiah. They also discussed the murder-for-hire of Isaiah by Bruce to prevent Isaiah from disclosing to federal law enforcement officer's fraud scheme information (Marfo, 2014). On April 11, 2011, Isaiah was found dead in a car in Baltimore with multiple gunshot wounds to the head. In May, 2011, co-conspirator Michael Copeland, accompanied by his attorney, came forward with information about the murder of Isaiah by cooperating with law enforcement. Michael, who was also involved in the bank fraud scheme, explained that an unknown hitman, hired by Tavon and Frank, murdered Isaiah to prevent him from identifying Tavon and Frank to federal authorities in connection with the scheme. It was at this meeting with federal investigators that Michael agreed to allow his future meetings with Tavon to be videotaped and recorded.

During these recorded meetings between May 2011 and October 2011, Tavon made several statements incriminating himself in the bank fraud scheme and the murder. Tavon told Michael that if he were arrested, he would admit the bank fraud, but deny the murder stating he was not concerned that either the triggerman or Frank would testify against him because they were "just as involved as he was…It wouldn't behoove them at all" (Marfo, 2014). Tavon also described the scheme in detail, including an account of trips he and Frank made to steal money orders at apartment complexes in several states. Tavon was arrested on November 9, 2011, yet agreed to cooperate, and even admitted his role in Isaiah's murder. Tavon, in turn, implicated Frank in the murder and identified Bruce as the triggerman, stating that Bruce had been paid $2,000, to which Tavon and Frank contributed equally. Tavon arranged a recorded meeting with Bruce which eventually led to Bruce's arrest. From jail, and under the supervision of investigators, Tavon continued to have contact with Frank. During their recorded conversations, Frank revealed that he was still involved in the bank fraud scheme. Investigators directed Tavon to tell Frank that he had someone who could meet with Frank and deposit stolen money orders—that person was an undercover agent. The resulting operation led to Frank's arrest on February 13, 2012; he was eventually found guilty for murder-for-hire, bank fraud, conspiracy, and other offenses.

The Robert Burke Case

Robert Burke was a lawyer in Philadelphia. He was found guilty in a murder-for-hire scheme of victim Donna Willard, a mother of three. Donna was killed to prevent her from testifying about a fraudulent insurance scheme that Robert was involved in (Smith, 1991). Donna was shot twice in the head in March 1990. One of her sons, age 13, witnessed the shooting that took place at their home. Ironically, days before her testimony, she disclosed to friends that she was afraid she would end up "with two bullets in my head" (Caba, 1993). Donna was linked to Robert because she received $10,000 from a false insurance claim. Robert contracted James David Louie to hire a hitman, but Robert wanted someone cheap; they contracted Javier Lebron who was willing to kill Donna for $1,000 so he could buy drugs to support his addiction.

The Russell Moss Case

Disbarred attorney Russell Moss pleaded guilty to a murder-for-hire scheme pertaining to the killing of twenty-year-old Ellen Lewis in the 1980s. Russell contracted with Rodney Griffin to kill Ellen by paying him

$10,000, plus drugs. Russell ordered the killing after Ellen agreed to testify against Russell in a bank fraud scheme (DiGiacomo, 2009). Russell evaded authorities for nearly two decades during which time he earned a law degree and practiced law until Rodney, who was on death row, implicated him in the murder.

International Considerations

Until now, we have been studying cases that took place in the United States. Because fraud detection homicide cases are not tracked in the same manner as other types of homicides, the number of international cases illustrated are few, but worth noting. What we have observed, especially among cases from the former Soviet Union, is that for the most part, the homicides are surgical and non-traceable to any person(s) (Perri & Lichtenwald, 2008a). Victims were killed by professionals who left no evidence linking them to the murder. There are exceptions illustrated by the Andrei Kozlov case that typify how contract killings are detected when committed by amateurs.

The Andrei Kozlov Case

Andrei Kozlov was the Deputy Chairman of the Russian Central Bank back in the early 2000s playing a leading role in efforts to stamp out white-collar crime, such as fraud and money laundering in Russian banks that he shut down. As Andrei stated, without exaggeration in regards to his duties of rooting out fraud, "I am being observed very closely and very seriously right now" (Chazan, 2006). While playing soccer in one of Moscow's public areas with his colleagues, an unknown gunman shot both Andrei and his driver to death in 2006. Prosecutors solved the murder case with the arrest and conviction of Alexei Frenkel, the CEO of VIP Bank, which had been shut down by Andrei. Alexei was accused of hiring gunmen to kill Andrei to silence his fraud detection duties. According to investigators at the general prosecutor's office, because Alexei had no contacts within criminal circles, the banker asked an acquaintance, Liana Askerova, to organize a hit on Andrei. Lianam met Alexei when he patronized her restaurant is said to have mentioned her ties to prominent underworld figures in Alexei's presence more than once. Aiding Liana in organizing the murder was her business partner, a Ukrainian named Boris Shafray who found a middleman from the Ukraine named Bogdan Pogorzhevsky. Alexei paid a total of $310, 000 for the contract on Andrei. Liana received $90,000 and Pogorzhevsky received $200,000 and the remaining $20,000 went to those that carried out the murder. Liana's conspirators turned out to be a far cry from Godfather-style gangsters, and she failed to secure a professional killer for Alexei's job (Sergeev, 2007). For example, Bogdan recruited Ukrainian cab drivers Alexei Polovinkin, Maxim Proglyad, and Alexander Belokopytov to kill Andrei.

Detectives believe that hiring amateurs played a large role in the quick unraveling of the case. The killers drove into the parking lot of the Spartak sports complex where Andrei was playing soccer. Guards at the gate refused to let the three men through, and one of the guards wrote down the license plate number of the suspicious vehicle. One of the killers voluntarily contacted the police because they were being followed after he and the others who killed Andrei demanded payment. All three suspects cooperated with the investigation by describing their roles in the murder-for-hire explaining how they prepared to carry them out. Ultimately, Liana also gave herself away when upon learning of Boris's arrest. She became nervous and began searching for a lawyer to represent Boris, which brought her to the attention of the police. She was put under surveillance with her phone being tapped, and it became clear to investigators that she was the last intermediary and the one who could lead police to the contract solicitor. During questioning, Liana was told that her accomplice, Boris Shafray, betrayed her in a confession, a tactic that convinced her to give up Alexei Frenkel to the police. Alexei was eventually found guilty of ordering Andrei's murder and was sentenced to 19 years in prison. The co-defendants were also held accountable and went to prison.

The Paul Klebnikov Case

Paul Klebnikov was an American journalist who was known to expose fraud in government. At the time of his death, he was investigating a complex money laundering fraud scheme involving Chechen reconstruction projects. Paul's investigation had revealed that the fraud reached deep into the center of power in the Kremlin, with elements involving organized crime, and the former KGB, which is now known as the FSB. He was gunned down outside of his apartment. As stated by Russian prosecutors, the killing was "carefully planned," or, in other words, it was carried out by professional killers (Yasman, 2004). In addition to Klebnikov, there are additional international cases worth mentioning for illustrative purposes. Russian Vitaly Gamov, who had attempted to curb smuggling, was killed by arson. Dmitry Kholodov, a journalist who worked in the Russian Defense Ministry and specialized in anticorruption, was killed when his briefcase blew up in his office (Perri & Lichtenwald, 2007c). Shahen Hovasapian, head of Armenia's taxation division tasked with combating tax fraud, died after his government-owned car exploded near his apartment complex (Kalantarian, 2006).

The Zoran Radovanovic Case

In 2016, 52-year-old Zoran Radovanovic of Sweden, who was considered a respected member of the community with no previous criminal record, was found guilty of four cases of premeditated murder and 36 cases of serious fraud in the thousands of dollars (Alalehto & Azarian, 2018). The murdered victims were two married couples killed in their homes in March and May 2015, respectively. Prior to the murders, the offender functioned as the couples' private asset manager and had taken full control of their savings. The couples, one more than 70 years old, lacked the financial competence to manage their own investments, and left decisions to Zoran in return for a guaranteed revenue source. According to Zoran's confession, he made investments in his own name with the client's money and spent the revenues for personal consumption, including a luxury car and to cover gambling debts. Eventually the two couples, independently from one another, expressed their wishes to receive the revenues on their investments. Yet Zoran's attempts to put off the couples' demands failed, and his own financial problems made it impossible for him to deliver. At this point, he began to realize the risk of his scheme being detected and subsequently planned to kill the couples.

After beating the first couple to death in their home, he burned the house to destroy all evidence to create the illusion of a fatal accident. He tried to repeat the same method with the second couple, but failed at burning their house down. The police located the bodies of the couple and determined that they died from severe head injuries. Zoran's pre-trial psychiatric evaluation revealed no psychiatric disorder. The tests, however, did not assess personality disorders such as psychopathy and narcissism, but during the police interrogations and the trial, Zoran displayed signs of psychopathy (Alalehto & Azarian, 2018). For instance, throughout the entire court proceeding and in his meetings with the relatives and children of the murdered couples, he remained emotionally aloof and indifferent, and did not display anxiety, remorse, or sympathy. Even when repeatedly asked in the court to express his feelings towards the murdered victims and their children, he either neglected the question, or answered briefly "Ah…I killed them…I don't know why" (Alalehto & Azarian, 2018, p. 5).

The Wilhelm Rodius Case

On April 19, 1962, Swedish banking lawyer Wilhelm Rodius murdered a 68-year-old male retired dentist (Alalehto & Azarian, 2018). The killing took place at Wilhelm's home who first beat the dentist to death with a club and then cut his body into pieces and burned them in three stoves in his house. This brutal act was preceded by extensive embezzlement and forgery of the victim's bank assets to which Wilhelm had full access since he had been assigned as manager by the bank. The victim entrusted Wilhelm to manage the relatively large amount of money he inherited from his deceased sister. The money was placed in various bank accounts from which Rodius could draw any sum without restriction. Eventually, Wilhelm faced financial problems due to the unexpectedly high cost of renovating a country house he had purchased and the inability to maintain the standard of living that he and his family were used to. The management of the victim's assets came as an exploitable opportunity, and enabled Wilhelm to solve his financial problems by taking the victim's money. The scheme worked nicely for a while until one of the accounts started to run out of money, which would have alerted the victim and revealed the fraud. Wilhelm could see no other way out but to kill his victim and dispose of the body in the hope of making the problem vanish. According to a four-month, pre-trial psychiatric examination, experts did not discover any serious psychiatric disorder, yet his behavior displayed signs of psychopathy (Alalehto & Azarian, 2018). For instance, at no point after the murder did Wilhelm show any sign of remorse for killing and dismembering the dentist. In fact, directly after the homicide, Wilhelm went home to his family at their country house for dinner and socialized normally with his family for the rest of the evening.

The Lembit Kapanen Case

In 2015, 55-year-old Lembit Kapanen was found guilty in Finland for murdering an 84-year-old, relatively wealthy, physically disabled female who suffered from dementia (Alalehto & Azarian, 2018). The court records reveal that Lembit had, prior to the murder, forged a document confirming he was licensed to work professionally as a nurse. Appearing in the role of the victim's personal caretaker beginning in June 2013, Lembit had unrestricted access to her private residence where the homicide occurred. The victim formally authorized Kapanen to manage her assets through a firm he owned with his wife called Brome Care Services Ltd. The firm, however, begun experiencing financial difficulties in 2013. This is when the Kapanen couple began to embezzle thousands of dollars from the victim while, at the same time, Lembit had the victim alter her will, which upon her death would transfer Lembit additional money. As time passed, the stolen funds were not enough to save the firm. This is when Lembit planned the murder to obtain the willed money and save his firm from bankruptcy. Lembit's situation worsened, however, when the victim's granddaughter found out about the will and suspected irregularities concerning the way it had been rewritten and, in particular, the role Lembit played in the process. Her suspicions grew stronger when she realized that some of her grandmother's valuable personal items went missing without explanation and that the Kapanen's failed to deliver promised medical services. The murder was achieved when Kapanen obtained a fake prescription for and injected the victim with Digoxin, a drug developed for treating patients with a specific type of heart failure that is highly dangerous when used inadequately and when administered to people who do not have a heart condition. During the trial, Lembit argued that the victim committed suicide coupled with denying all charges of property thefts.

International Case Comparisons

In contrasting the U.S. fraud detection homicides with the former Soviet Republic murders, the majority of the U.S. homicides were committed by the person who perpetrated the fraud with a few that were contract killings. Except for the Andrei Kozlov case, the former Soviet Republic murderers appeared to be contract killings and some had the markings of skilled professionals who were capable of avoiding detection by executing a quality murder plan with surgical precision. It is not a coincidence that such murders go unsolved. Anecdotal evidence suggests that solicitors in the former Soviet Republics are willing to leave the killing to others so that there are enough buffers to shield them from being accused of murder. In addition, the former Soviet Republic murderers go beyond silencing the victim who detected their fraud. The murders were committed in a very public way to send a message to other potential people who can detect and reveal fraud to remain silent. Along with sending a message to others, in some cases offenders from the former Soviet Republic purposely left behind key forensic evidence to make it clear that the death was not an accident.

This trait is not evident in the U.S. murders, where killers silenced their victims in private settings. Moreover, no evidence discovered in the U.S. homicides indicated that the killers intended to leave threatening messages for others. Alternatively, U.S. offenders fortunately displayed traits of incompetence and carelessness in terms of how they performed the murders, and when they hired someone to do it for them. Several failed attempts where solicitors and hitmen were apprehended support the conclusions of Professor Black where 1) the solicitors lack discretion where they openly publicize their intentions 2) the solicitors hire amateur killers, and 3) the co-conspirators talked too much revealing their plans. Moreover, in the U.S. murders, forensic evidence and witness testimonials linked the amateur offender to the murder because the amateur offenders talk about their murders with people who then tell the authorities. U.S. solicitors' poor planning tends to produce an overconfident perception of their ability to avoid detection by not bothering to conceal incriminating evidence (Perri & Lichtenwald, 2007b; 2008b).

Keep in mind that evidence left behind is not just the physical evidence that is tangible to our senses, but also includes incriminating evidence of fraud that predates the murder. U.S. solicitors use the services of amateur contract killers who can testify against them in a court of law, as was the scenario in the Fredric Tokars and Edward Leak cases. Moreover, because U.S. solicitors displayed an intense need to control, they often hire someone they can micromanage, instead of professionals who would have produced a buffer between themselves and the murder. The amount of money U.S. solicitors paid for the contract is small, but it may be attractive to people who are down on their luck. For example, in the Leak case, John Brown was promised $1,500. What is interesting is that there was no upfront payment to these amateurs including the killers in the Michael Burnett case. Also, Fredric Tokars coerced the potential hit man Eddie Lawrence to accept the contract. Eddie Lawrence eventually agreed to do the hit for $25,000 but ended up subcontracting the hit to an amateur street criminal for $5,000. The hitman killed Sara, but never received payment, yet bragged to neighbors about how he killed someone; these acquaintances eventually went to the authorities (McDonald, 1998).

Not surprisingly, the investigation was able to be linked to the intermediary, Eddie Lawrence, and the solicitor, Fredric, from the hitman's inability to remain silent about the murder. Had Fredric not micromanaged the murder-for-hire and simply spent the money on a professional hitman, Fredric may have gotten away with Sara's murder given that he had a credible alibi of being in Florida at the time of her killing. Moreover, one observes the amount of forensic evidence collected and used against the U.S. amateur killers including, DNA, the murder weapon, fingerprints, blood-spatter, and eye-witness accounts. In many cases, the solicitor tries to control the hit while he is in jail and the hitman leaves an extraordinary amount of forensic evidence that would not been left by a professional. Their inability to think through a plan that would consider the potential risks of being caught and the evidence trail is another hallmark of an amateur's behavior.

Friends and Acquaintances

We would like to think that friendships entail the mutual reciprocity of affections and loyalty. Moreover, it is not unreasonable to expect that business associates and acquaintances behave in a professional manner. Unfortunately there are times when these reasonable interpersonal expectations are violated in the worst possible manner. We will examine several cases where at times violence among business associates appears to be foreseeable and expected and those cases where friendships are shattered by unspeakable violence. It is important to gleen important lessons from these cases.

The Albert Walker Case

This is a story about fraud, false identity, and murder. In 1990, Albert Walker left Canada with his daughter and flew to Britain after embezzling between $2.5 and $3.2 million from his investment clients, many of whom were friends and fellow church members. After fleeing to England, he was charged in Canada with eighteen counts of fraud, theft, and money laundering in 1993. However, in 1992 he took the identity of his English friend Ronald Platt, who spent time in Canada with Albert, but remained in Canada when Albert escaped. It seemed, for a while, that Albert disappeared with the money and would get away with it. However, Albert did not count on Ronald returning to England in 1995. Now there were two Ronald Platts in Britain and the real Ronald Platt decided to live near where Albert was living with his daughter, who posed as his wife. Albert had a personal problem to solve.

To escape detection, police allege that Albert invited Ronald to go sailing with him, knocked him unconscious, then threw his body overboard after weighing it down with an anchor effectively murdering Ronald to avoid detection of his fraudulent activity. Ronald's body was recovered after being caught in fishing nets. The police were able to identify the body because the serial number on the Rolex watch was linked to Ronald who was wearing it at the time of the murder. In the month between the time that Ronald's body was identified, and Albert was found, Albert bought over 67,000 pounds in gold bullion preparing to run again, but the police eventually caught him. In 1998, he was sentenced to life in prison although he maintained his innocence.

The Dennis Gaede Case

The story of Timothy Wicks is a story of friendship, betrayal, and murder. His friend, Dennis Gaede, worked in various jobs, including tax preparation. While preparing Timothy's tax return, Dennis stole Timothy's personal information, identity theft, for his own financial benefit (Perri & Lichtenwald, 2008b). Dennis then moved from Wisconsin to North Dakota with his wife and represented himself to his new employer as Timothy Wicks. Dennis stayed in contact with Timothy, and Timothy told Dennis that he believed someone was fraudulently using his credit card. As fraud detection closed in, Dennis persuaded Timothy to move to North Dakota with the promise that Timothy could play in a band with him. While Timothy was staying in Dennis's house, Dennis shot him. Dennis's wife testified against her husband stating that after Timothy was shot and still breathing, they put a garbage bag around his head to suffocate him. Subsequently, they decapitated Timothy and cut off his hands to prevent identification of the body. Dennis and his wife then dumped the naked body over the side of a bridge in Michigan and emptied Timothy's bank account to purchase a $17,000 vehicle. Dennis also stopped showing up for his job as a bookkeeper and office manager, and his employer discovered that money was missing. When the employer confronted him about the fraud, Gaede failed to explain the financial anomalies. The employer contacted the authorities about his bookkeeper, and referred to him as Timothy Wicks, but was informed by police that the real Timothy Wicks was dead. Eventually, Dennis was found guilty of murder and the prosecution argued that Timothy's fraud detection was the motive (Gaede, 2007).

The Jonathan Broyhill Case

In April 2010, Jamie Hahn hired Jonathan Broyhill at her political consulting firm, Sky Blue Strategies. Jonathan was considered a close and trusted friend to Jamie and Nation Hahn. Sky Blue provided clients with a variety of campaign services, including strategy, fundraising, and compliance. U.S. Congressman Brad Miller hired Sky Blue the following year for his re-election campaign. Jamie focused on fundraising and strategy, while Jonathan handled Federal Elections Commission (FEC) compliance, managed campaign donations, and disbursed funds for campaign expenses. Jonathan was a signatory on the campaign's bank account. In the Fall of 2011, Congressman Miller suspended his re-election campaign, leading Sky Blue to shift its focus from fundraising toward issuing refund checks to donors. Due to the change in circumstances, Jonathan became primarily responsible for the remaining work on the campaign. Unbeknownst to Jamie, Jonathan wrote checks to himself out of the campaign account from June 2011 to March 2013. The checks totaled more than $46,500. Near the end of his employment, Jonathan complained of various health issues. In August 2012, he told the Hahns he sought treatment for multiple sclerosis and claimed he scheduled surgery to remove gallstones.

In November or December 2012, Jonathan expressed to Jamie that, in light of his health problems, he would need to find a less stressful job. Jamie agreed to help Jonathan find a job elsewhere. Jamie soon discovered that certain Miller campaign expenses had not been paid. Although he was no longer employed by Sky Blue, Jonathan continued to manage campaign finances and FEC quarterly reports. In early 2013, Jamie received inquiries from campaign staffers concerning delays in refund check disbursements. Jonathan avoided Jamie's requests for information on the campaign finances, citing his preoccupation with the upcoming gallbladder surgery. Jonathan eventually agreed to meet with Jamie at the Hahns' home on April 8, 2013 to draft the quarterly report due the following week. When he failed to show, Jonathan claimed he was working late at his new job with LabCorp, a job he did not have. Jonathan agreed to reschedule their meeting for the next evening. Upon his arrival, Jonathan appeared physically weak He told Nation that doctors discovered a spot when they removed his gallstones, a spot which they believed was pancreatic cancer. Stunned by the news, the Hahns spent the evening comforting Jonathan rather than drafting the report. Two days later, the Hahns arranged to take Jonathan to Duke Cancer Hospital to confirm his diagnosis.

When Jonathan failed to meet at their home as planned, Nation and Jamie became concerned and drove to his house. He answered the door claiming he overslept. At this point, Jonathan realized he would miss the appointment. He pretended to call the hospital to reschedule for the next day and, at Jamie's suggestion, agreed to help with the quarterly report for the rest of the afternoon. Moments after arriving at the Hahns' home, Jonathan informed Jamie that he forgot to bring his computer. He left to retrieve it but never returned. Jamie made repeated attempts to contact Jonathan to no avail. When the Hahns finally heard from Jonathan the next morning, he told them he was at the beach. He said he had been fired from LabCorp, and with his presumed cancer diagnosis, he "just needed to get away." Jonathan apologized and assured Jamie that he would be back in time to prepare the quarterly report. Jamie asked Jonathan to reschedule his doctor's appointment for April 15, 2013, so that she and Nation could attend before leaving town. On Sunday, April 14, 2013, Jonathan purchased a large chef's knife before driving to the Hahns' residence to finalize the quarterly report with Jamie. During their meeting, Jamie received a message from Nation informing her that, according the FEC website, the Miller campaign's 2012 fourth quarter report had never been filed. Jonathan assured her that he filed the report and had received confirmation via facsimile from the FEC.

The next morning, Jamie and Jonathan met with Congressman Miller's campaign treasurer, John Wallace, to review the completed draft of the quarterly report. The report revealed a continuing indebtedness to Congressman Miller, a debt which Wallace believed had been retired. He requested that the draft be amended to reflect the debt as paid before the report was submitted to the FEC. At the time, a separate discrepancy in the draft report was overlooked. The report indicated that the campaign had $62,914.52 in cash at the end of the first quarter when, in fact, the campaign account had a negative balance of $3,587.06. After the meeting with Wallace, Nation and Jamie drove Jonathan to Duke Cancer Hospital for his appointment. Upon their arrival, the Hahns dropped Jonathan off at the entrance to check in while Nation and Jamie parked the car. When they reconvened inside, Jonathan said he had to go in for tests and the nurses would call the Hahns if needed. Nation and Jamie sat down in the lobby while Jonathan went through a set of double doors behind the reception desk. Jonathan did not have a doctor's appointment that day, instead he walked around the hospital for nearly two hours while the Hahns waited in the lobby. When he returned, Jonathan told them he did indeed have pancreatic cancer but the doctors were hopeful. The Hahns drove Jonathan back to Raleigh.

On the way out of town, Jamie received a call from Congressman Miller's office informing her that a check written from the campaign account had bounced. Based on the first quarter report, Jamie believed the campaign account had more than sufficient funds. She decided that the returned check must have been a mistake. On Wednesday, April 17, 2013, Wallace e-mailed Jamie and Jonathan about recent communications between the FEC and the Miller campaign. The FEC had requested additional information to address concerns over suspicious disbursements from the campaign account. The FEC had also informed the campaign that it had failed to timely file a report covering the last quarter of 2012. Jonathan responded on the e-mail thread: "Good afternoon, John. I am working on this now, and I will be in touch." In light of defendant's prior assurances and his e-mail response, Jamie assumed that Jonathan had the issues under control. Jonathan never followed up with Wallace. Jonathan, however, used Nation's credit card to purchase a one-way airline ticket from Charlotte to Las Vegas, departing Monday afternoon. He canceled his flight reservation one hour before take-off. Jonathan opted instead to purchase a one-way train ticket from Raleigh to Charlotte, departing Tuesday morning.

On Monday, April 22, 2013, Jonathan and Jamie met at the Hahns' home to finalize matters with Congressman Miller's campaign. In his backpack, Jonathan concealed the chef's knife he purchased. Nation arrived home around 5:00 p.m. Nation noticed Jamie on the phone in her office downstairs and Jonathan was walking through the kitchen. Nation greeted Jonathan with a hug and invited him to stay the night before another doctor's appointment in the morning. After a brief conversation, Nation went upstairs to change out of his work clothes. Shortly thereafter, Nation heard Jamie screaming from downstairs. He threw open the bedroom door and ran down the stairs shouting, "What's happening?" Jamie cried out, "He's trying to kill me." Nation rounded the corner of the staircase when he saw blood on the floor and Jonathan standing over Jamie with a knife. Nation shouted, "What the fuck are you doing?" Jonathan said nothing as he turned and came at Nation, raising the knife in the air as he moved closer. Nation grabbed the blade with one hand and started striking Jonathan in the face with the other. As the struggle continued, Nation yelled at Jamie to get out of the house. Jamie, covered in blood, ran out the side door and collapsed in a neighbor's yard. After gaining separation from Jonathan, Nation followed Jamie out of the house while shouting for someone to call 9-1-1.

Neighbors tended to Nation and Jamie until the ambulance arrived. Police surrounded the Hahns' home and Jonathan exited the house calmly with his hands in the air. Jamie died in the hospital two days later as a result of her injuries. An autopsy revealed multiple stab wounds, including one to her torso which penetrated her liver, and another to her chest which penetrated her lung and severed an artery. Nation survived the attack with injuries to his hands, including a deep laceration which transected an artery, tendons, and nerves in two fingers on his left hand. Jonathan admitted that he had embezzled money from the Miller campaign. At his last meeting with Jamie, Jonathan anticipated a conversation about the discrepancies in the campaign account. When asked to describe his memory of that night, Jonathan recalled stabbing Jamie, but did not recall attacking Nation or cutting himself. Jonathan was convicted of first-degree murder for the death of Jamie Hahn, and attempted first-degree murder against Nation Hahn. The trial court sentenced Jonathan to a term of life in prison without parole.

Workplace Violence and Fraud Detection

Common protocols of auditing, forensic accounting, and fraud examination professionals include understanding risk factors that increase the probability that fraud will occur, how fraud schemes are used to perpetuate criminality, and interviewing suspected or known white-collar criminals. In fact, it is widely taught by educational institutions that auditors and fraud examiners should maintain a healthy skepticism as to the fair presentation of financial statements and what individuals interviewed disclose by considering those risk factors and motives that increase the probability of fraud occurring. However little, if any, attention is devoted to the understanding of personal risks associated with the detection of workplace fraud, perhaps inadvertently, by an auditor or by a fraud examiner whose job it is to detect and unveil fraud (Perri, 2011c). Workplace violence is any physical assault, threatening behavior, or verbal abuse that occurs between employees of an organization that takes place within or outside of the workplace. According to the federal Occupational and Safety and Health Agency (OSHA), homicide is the fourth leading cause of fatal occupational injury in the U.S. Workplace violence can strike anywhere and none are immune. While workplace violence can occur in any setting, some employment situations may pose higher risks for violence. Environments that pose higher risk include mobile assignments, such as auditors and forensic accountants who may have to travel outside of their office, work alone at night or early in the morning, and/or work with unstable or volatile persons. Other risk factors include duties that involve carrying out financial inspection or enforcement duties such as a government auditor and seasonal job assignments during tax season. Consider the concerns of forensic accounting investigators and auditors as they relate some of their experiences; their safety concerns are not anomalies to ignore:

> A colleague of mine once continuously received threatening calls, at all times of the day and night....the police also were unable to do anything because the callers kept changing their SMS cards to avoid detection....but they felt that the calls were tied in with the investigation at the time, as the party concerned was a very powerful and influential person (Simha & Satyanarayan 2016, p. 38).

> When I go to remote places, small towns, I am a bit concerned about my security... in one small town, the people we were investigating arranged a strike so they gathered outside the office and we had to leave right away (Simha & Satyanarayan 2016, p. 37).

> My team has had to say no twice to a client...the reason being that the client wanted us to investigate matters which when we did some digging into, we found that it was tied in with the underworld....we had to refuse and tell the client that they needed to contact the governmental authorities to do that job (Simha & Satyanarayan 2016, p. 37).

The longstanding misperception that white-collar criminals are not violent may cloud antifraud professionals' judgment; that bias could affect their ability to accurately assess the risk involved. It should be noted that acts of violence against accountants, auditors, and fraud examiners occurs in other countries for the same reasons. In Russia, a top fraud investigator for the prosecution named Nazim Kaziakmedov was shot twice in the chest and once in the head by a man dressed in black while walking out of a restaurant in Moscow after it was learned that he was involved in a fraud investigation of the Finvest investment group (AFT, 2007). This murder illustrates a professional hit, a common technique used in Russia and the former Soviet Republics. As previously stated, many of these international murders purposely occur in public as a way of warning others that if they make any attempt to interfere with fraud schemes, they will also be targeted. Let us examine several cases of workplace violence tied to fraud detection.

The Sallie Rohrbach Case

North Carolina State insurance auditor Sallie Rohrbach was killed by Michael Howell, owner of the Dilworth Insurance Agency (Wright, 2008). Prosecutors indicated that Michael's motive for killing Rohrbach resulted from her investigation of his insurance agency and detecting evidence of insurance fraud (Boudin, 2009). Between March 2004 and May 2008, Michael embezzled more than $150,000 in insurance premiums from clients who were driving uninsured (Lowe, 2009). Sallie began her investigation after numerous clients began to question and complain about the insurance agency. Sallie e-mailed her supervisor indicating that "he [Howell] gave me 16 months of bank statements today…and there were issues in each month…No negative balances, but he is floating money" (Perri & Brody, 2011c, p. 96). According to Michael's wife, Michael displayed bizarre behavior such as snapping and arguing with Sallie as she questioned him about his finances eventually striking Sallie with a computer stand while she was at his agency (Perri & Brody, 2011c).

Her body was dumped in a wooded area near Fort Mill, South Carolina (Boudin, 2009). There does not appear to be any indication that Sallie let others know what was going on with the investigation that appeared out of character. As stated by the Department of Insurance spokesperson, Chrissy Pearson, "Sallie gave us no indication she was concerned about this case. It was a routine case. She was looking at some finances, looking at the books" (Coleman & Bowens, 2008). Furthermore, Pearson stated, "It's the last thing we expected…We just don't expect our people in the field to be put in this kind of danger" (Boudin, 2008). The comment by Pearson is partially accurate in that these cases appear to have a normal complexion until warning signs surface and it is when they surface that investigators, especially those in the field like Sallie, must give notice to others that a particular case may involve white-collar criminals who are willing to turn to violence as a solution to their problem of fraud detection by others.

Sallie's murder serves as a lesson for antifraud professionals to heed; do not become complacent. Sallie probably was involved in thousands of investigations, and the Howell investigation was no different. However, her guard was lowered by the routine nature of the work, and she ignored risk factors in Howell's case that should have warranted caution. She may not have been aware of the risk factors or may have been biased by the common misperception that white-collar criminals are not violent. The Rohrbach case could potentially be viewed as a mix of instrumental and reactive violence traits, although it is unclear if one trait is dominant. There is evidence of an escalation in Howell's emotional reaction to Rohrbach's questioning, as stated by his wife, which supports the argument that there was a reactive quality to the murder. However, it is plausible that he planned to kill Sallie depending on whether she was able to detect the fraud or not. Once he interpreted the questions she asked would lead to evidence that would expose his fraud, murder became a viable solution.

The Irwin Margolies Case

Irwin Margolies, head of bankrupt Candor Diamond Company, was found guilty of murder for the deaths of his controller, Margaret Barbera, and her co-worker, Jenny Chin, by murder-for-hire. According to Margaret, Irwin generated invoices that were fictitious to create the appearance of revenue in order to get advance cash payments from a financing company with fraud proceeds, estimated at almost $6 million, eventually sent to foreign countries. Margaret pleaded guilty to fraud and agreed to testify in a fraud inquiry involving the diamond company. According to the prosecutor, Irwin conceived the scheme to have Margaret and Jenny killed in order to "silence witnesses" who disclosed his fraud crimes (Perri & Lichtenwald, 2008b, p. 29). Irwin wanted to "get rid of two people" with Margaret killed first because she held the records that revealed his fraud (Perri & Lichtenwald, 2008b, p. 29). Irwin's attorney, Henry Oestricher, received prosecutorial immunity when he agreed to testify against Irwin stating that Irwin ordered the murders of Jenny and Margaret while he helped hire the hitman.

Irwin paid hitman Donald Nash $2,000 to kill Margaret. Prior to the murder, Nash stalked Margaret for four months to observe her day-to-day routine (Perri & Lichtenwald, 2008b). Margaret's brother indicated that Margaret feared for her safety the last three months of her life. Prior to the murder, Margaret was abducted and three civilians who came to her aid were killed. Margaret was later found dead in an alley in lower Manhattan with bullet wounds to the back of her head. On January 5, 1981, as Jenny was leaving Margaret's apartment, she was abducted by a man wearing a ski mask. Nine days later, Jenny's blood-stained station wagon with a .22-caliber shell casing in it was recovered (Brody & Kiehl, 2010). Her body was never found, but she is presumed to have been murdered. Fortunately, Donald left behind an extraordinary amount of evidence such as DNA as a result of blood retrieval, ballistic tests, telephone records, shell casings, tire tracks, license plates, and other incriminating evidence that eventually led to convictions for the murders of Margaret and Jenny.

The Michael Wansley Case

Michael Wansley was an Australian auditor who worked for Deloitte Touche Tohmatsu. During his auditing of Thailand sugar mills, Michael uncovered substantial fraud within the accounts of one company named Namtel Kaset Sugar Group. Upon discovering the fraud, he proposed countermeasures to strengthen the internal controls that may have been bypassed which increased the probability that fraud would occur. Upon discovering the fraud, Michael began receiving death threats to ignore the fraud, especially after he tried to resolve the matter. While driving to work, Michael was shot eight times and died on the scene. The murder was connected to Namtel's human resource manager and the owner of the company, Pradit Siriviriyakul. A company employee disclosed that Siriviriyakul stated, "This must be kept quiet—it's good that the foreigner is dead—so that nothing comes back to us" (Brody & Kiehl, 2010, p. 11). Although the gunman's phone records indicated that calls were made to Siriviriyakul's mobile phone and land line, the Thailand courts dropped the murder charges against Siriviriyakul for lack of sufficient evidence.

The Al Vondra Case

Employed as a forensic accountant by the U.S. Department of Justice, Al Vondra's job was to uncover the details of an illegal investment scheme devised by a group of businessmen (Brody & Kiehl, 2010). During his investigation, Al found that the owners of the fraudulent investment scheme were targeting heavily invested retirement funds and Amish investors. While commuting to work in Cleveland, Ohio, unexpectedly all four tires on his vehicle exploded while the gas tank was being dragged on the road. Fortunately, Al did not sustain any major injuries. The FBI was unable to link someone to the accident even though the incident was contemporaneous with Vondra's fraud investigation. Such investigations are exceptionally difficult when there may be little to no evidence left behind for the FBI to start an investigation in the first place.

Recognizing Warning Signs of Potential Violence

The first workplace violence myth that needs to be debunked is the idea that a person "just snaps" and commits workplace homicide (Burton & Stewart, 2008). For example, Sallie Rohrbach's husband, Tim, indicated that it was his belief that Howell "snapped" and did not plan to murder Sallie because he had no history of criminality (APA, 2008). It is erroneous to believe that a prior criminal record is an indication of whether someone had the intent to kill or not. It is not uncommon for these killers to rely on a lack of prior criminality as a strategy in the court of public opinion by projecting the image that they are not capable of such brutality. Yet research on these violent white-collar criminals reflects the exact opposite of what they attempt to portray and what they would like others to believe about their character (Perri et al., 2008a). It is important to note that workplace homicides seldom occur randomly; they are planned in advance and the perpetrator intentionally targets specific individual(s) (Burton & Stewart, 2008).

The fact that the perpetrator was sloppy in their planning to kill and is eventually caught is not an indication of an uncontrollable impulsive act of just "snapping." The behavior of violent white-collar criminals is often motivated by a clear goal, and void of emotional reactivity, rather than a powerful emotion of rage or despair associated with crimes of passion; murder is simply a solution to a perceived problem. An accounting and forensic professional's best protection is knowledge and an understanding of the warning signs of potentially violent individuals and situations. It is important to consider not only how a professional perceives an investigation, especially the interviewing of witnesses, but a professional must consider how the person they are investigating and possibly interviewing perceives the investigation. Consider the insights of one fraud investigator that supports this concern, "I was required to conduct certain interviews and during the interviews, they [interviewees] perceived it as a threat. It was in a remote area and people were making enquiries about where we were staying and what we were detecting and things like that" (Simha & Satyanarayan 2016, p. 38).

The warning signs listed in table 3 are not intended to cover all potential red flags, but they are a start for antifraud professionals to consider in reducing the personal risks attached to fraud detection. Just as it has been taught to auditing and fraud professionals to have a healthy skepticism about the reasonableness of financial statements by considering fraud risk factors, professionals must apply this mindset to the individual(s) they are investigating by considering the risk factors for workplace violence.

Table 3	**Warning Signs of Potential Physical Threats**
Physical Behaviors	Clenched jaw or fist, change in voice, pacing, a sense of desperation, scowling, violating personal space, destroying property, exaggerated or violent gestures, loud talking, glaring or avoiding eye contact, trembling or shaking, abusive language, and rapid breathing, shoving, and pushing.
Intimidating Behaviors	Argumentative, displays unwarranted anger, uncooperative, impulsive, easily frustrated, challenges authority figures, embarrassing statements, humiliation, and excessive phone calls. Have several people protested the fact that you are engaged in an investigation or audit?
Verbal Behaviors	Verbal threats, such as "What comes around, goes around," "I don't get mad, I get even," are signs that must be taken seriously. Some tend to ignore this behavior because they are perceived as jokes or clichés. Other signs involve swearing, insults, or condescending language.
Personality Traits	Blames others for his or her problems, displays a sense of entitlement, exploitative, egocentric, difficulty taking criticism, and feels victimized. These traits are reflective of the antisocial traits previously outlined.

Sallie Rohrbach experienced firsthand the physical, verbal, and intimidating behaviors of Michael Howell when she came closer to unveiling his fraud; his behavior changed as she questioned him about his finances. Moreover, we observe the inconsistency between Michael's true character and how others perceived him. One of Michael's acquaintances stated, "He's nice, normal, like a regular guy" (Coleman & Bowens, 2008). Another resident stated, "It's really out of character" (Boudin, 2008). Unfortunately, it is actually "in character" that these fraudsters are willing to resort to murder when a more complete picture of their personality is revealed. Too often individuals comment on what they perceive to be another's character have incomplete information to support their opinion, especially considering the fraud perpetrated and victims left behind. Antifraud professionals need to be trained on what to do when they find themselves in these difficult situations; such risks should not be viewed as rare situations to ignore.

The Randy Nowak Case

In December 2008, Randy Nowak was found guilty of attempted murder of Internal Revenue Service (IRS) Agent Christine Brandt (Smith, 2008). The prosecution argued that Nowak's motive for the murder revolved around the fact that he feared she would detect his tax fraud and money laundering schemes that amounted in the range of $3 to $4 million dollars in off-shore money laundering accounts (Geary, 2009). Nowak claimed to be in construction, but Scott Coulombe, President of the Polk County Builder's Association stated: "I never knew of one structure he built…he's a total stranger to us" (Pera & Geary, 2008). Nowak avoided paying $300,000 in taxes as a result of not filing corporate tax returns for four years (Pera & Geary, 2008). The most damaging evidence against the defendant was recorded conversations between Randy and one of the undercover FBI agents posing as a hitman that was to be paid $20,000 with a $10,000 down payment for eliminating Agent Brandt (Jones, 2008). Amazingly, Nowak was also prepared to burn down the local IRS office for another $10,000 so that any documents Agent Brandt possessed revealing his fraud would be destroyed (Geary, 2009). Interestingly, Nowak could have easily paid his tax liability by selling his custom home with an 11-car garage, 18 classic cars, and personal watercrafts. Ironically, an acquaintance of Nowak said, "He was a really nice guy. It didn't seem like he'd be that type of person" (Pera & Geary, 2008).

Strategies to Reduce the Risk of Workplace Violence

Although not a normal part of an accounting, auditing, or antifraud professional's training, it would behoove educational institutions and certification programs to instruct students and professionals on how to identify the negative personality traits and behavioral warning signs outlined in Table 3. Too often professionals naturally engage in projection bias believing that other professionals or people they are auditing and interviewing are not capable of engaging in violent acts. If these risk factors do surface during an interview, it is possible the subject perceives the line of questioning as a sign that their fraud could be revealed and disclosed to interested parties. In that case, it should serve as a warning to potentially terminate the interview and take life-saving precautions into account. No one wants to observe human behaviors escalate to the degree that someone is willing to hurt others, but it is a reality that certain personalities are willing to use violence as a solution to protect their fraud schemes from being detected.

Moreover, using common sense developed from years of experience may not be enough to protect us if we have adopted the myth that white-collar criminals are not capable of violence. Thus the common sense we think is correct and rely on can makes us engage in a flawed risk assessment of the potential harm we expose ourselves to when performing our duties. For example, many in our society tend to believe that because one is educated, gainfully employed, and appears to adhere to the norms of larger society that somehow they are not capable of resorting to violence. Consequently, one should not ignore risk factors associated with vulnerable situations and warning signs outlined in Table 3 at the expense of common sense that may be tainted by our biases. It is also imperative that management must be committed to setting a "tone at the top" where workplace violence is not tolerated. Management should conduct training on workplace violence as it relates to fraud detection homicide. Again, consider the insights of one auditor who spoke of conducting assignments abroad:

> [I]n some regions of the world, one has to be very careful about physical safety concerns…I remember when I was sent to [name of place deleted], there was no real law structure in place there…my company sent us there, but they thoughtfully provided us with security personnel to accompany us there…I think more organizations need to do that…it's almost like they do not anticipate anything happening to threaten the auditors (Simha & Satyanarayan, 2016, p. 38).

The tone at the top can take the form of, 1) written policies disclosing the warning signs previously discussed, 2) training employees on the issue of workplace violence, 3) encouraging employees to report incidents, 4) assuring employees who report incidents that there will be no retaliation against them, and 5) outlining the procedure for investigating incidents. Employees should not be made to feel that bringing concerns to management's attention is a form of personal weakness or unwarranted complaining where getting their assignments completed is more important than one's safety. Moreover, auditors, forensic accountants, and fraud investigators must routinely enter unfamiliar environments to complete audits or interviews. What realistic precautions can be taken to reduce their vulnerability when they enter unfamiliar environments?

- Let others know where you are going,
- Approach investigations as a team, if possible,
- Interview in public or at your office, if feasible,
- Disengage in arguments that appear to be escalating in tone,
- Consider an exit strategy if in another's office or home,
- Review an individual's criminal history, if available,
- Consider the location and remoteness of an assignment,
- Request security during audits and investigations when necessary,
- Consider time of day when interviewing, with risk being elevated late at night,
- Encourage employees to share information about suspicious behaviors,
- Consider contacting the authorities if you believe you are in danger,
- Plan in advance what the proper protocol will be if there is a safety concern,
- Does management show concern for employee safety,
- Determine if management has any policy regarding workplace violence, and
- If fraud is detected, how, when and where and to whom will a professional disclose the findings?

Attempted Fraud Detection Homicide Cases

Attempted murder is the incomplete, unsuccessful and unjustified act of killing someone. The cases listed in Table 4 reflect attempted red-collar crime homicides. Interestingly, some of these cases also reflect murder-for-hire schemes which displayed planned, instrumental violence. The offenders in these case appear to have relied on amateur hitmen to complete the homicide in addition to producing other evidence that connected them to the attempted murder. Consider the case of Paul Kruse and his brother as one example of attempted murder (USDOJ, 2013b). According to the evidence presented at trial, Paul and his brother conspired to recruit and defraud a number of clients to whom they provided financial advisory services. Although they were once licensed, at the time of the scheme they were unlicensed and created a sham investment called Yorkshire Financial Services. Paul and his brother told clients they were in the business for thirty years, and employed experienced traders, yet they took client money and bought themselves luxury goods which is often the practice of fraud offenders to satisfy their sense of entitlement.

In 2011, they hired an assistant who witnessed the Kruse's forging client signatures and not investing their money, but spending it on themselves. Eventually, the employee disclosed the securities fraud to the Federal Bureau of Investigations (FBI). Paul then hired a hitman to murder the former employee to prevent her from testifying for the government. Paul's brother, who was an accomplice, committed suicide prior to the resolution of the case which is not unheard of in fraud detection cases that are poised to go to trial or where the offender is to be sentenced by a judge (USDOJ, 2013b). Paul was eventually found guilty of attempted murder and various fraud crimes and sentenced to thirty years in prison. Consider also the case of Louisiana fire chief Donovan McMullen who pleaded guilty to a murder-for-hire scheme in 2007. In this case, the fire chief was involved in defrauding the federal government of medical equipment. Donovan wanted to have a particular government witness killed so that the fraud scheme would not be uncovered during a federal grand jury investigation into the case (Hill, 2007). Donovan's goal was to take the medical equipment worth thousands of dollars and sell it. Table 4 summarizes cases where attempts were made on the life of a victim, but the victim survived either from their wounds or the offenders were apprehended before they could harm the victim.

Table 4   **Attempted Red Collar Crime Cases**

Offender Name	Fraud Scheme	Murder-for-Hire	Type of Violence	Case Source
Christopher Porco	Bank	No	Instrumental	Perri (2016)
Randy Novak	Tax	Yes	Instrumental	Jones (2008)
William Benbow	Tax	Yes	Instrumental	Geier (2002)
Steven Martinez	Tax	Yes	Instrumental	USDOJ (2013a)
Paul Kruse	Securities	Yes	Instrumental	USDOJ (2013b)
James Buchan	Securities	Yes	Instrumental	Salzman (2009)
Aaron Hand	Mortgage	Yes	Instrumental	Rudolf (2012)
Paul Valkovich	Bank	Yes	Instrumental	ICE (2009)
David McMullen	Theft	Yes	Instrumental	USDOJ (2007)
Arnold Flowers	Bank	Yes	Instrumental	USDOJ (2002)
Sompang Khamsomphou	Bank	Yes	Instrumental	USDOJ (2002)

The Aaron Hand Case

Consider the conduct of Alan Hand, former president of AFG Financial Group, who orchestrated a $100 million mortgage fraud scheme. He personally wanted to kill the witnesses who disclosed the fraud scheme to authorities but could not because he was in jail (Perri, 2016). Aaron attempted to hire a contract killer while in jail but the person turned out to be an uncover law enforcement officer. He told the undercover officer, "I wish I was there to watch him suffer and kill the man's wife and children if they are home" (Perri, 2016, p. 64).

The Arnold Flowers and Sompang Khamsomphou Case

Convicted white-collar criminals Arnold Flowers and Sompong Khamsomphou attempted to have government witnesses who would testify about their bank fraud killed. The intended murder targets also included the U.S. District Judge and U.S. Attorney (USDOJ, 2002). According to the reports, Sompang hired an intermediary who was in charge of hiring the contract killer. Sompang and the intermediary traveled to a hotel to meet the contract killer and provided a down payment for four murder contracts. The defendants used telephones, that were traceable, to arrange the planned killings. Eventually the defendants were found guilty for the attempts they made on the lives of their targets.

The Pavel Valkovich Case

In 2008, the federal agency known as Immigration and Customs Enforcement (ICE), opened an investigation into Pavel Valkovich's involvement in a bank fraud scheme in which Pavel and others stole personal identifying information and used the information to transfer funds from the victims' bank accounts to PayPal accounts. Following his arrest and arraignment on the bank fraud charges, Pavel approached an individual and proposed that they kill the informant who provided the information that led to his arrest. Pavel wanted the hitman to use a silencer and kill the informant in a drive-by shooting. Pavel said all that was needed was a "pic and ten"— a picture of the informant and $10,000 to have the informant killed. Pavel also discussed coaching a witness to lie at his upcoming trial by claiming that the informant provided the witness with drugs, made improper sexual advances, and planted evidence (ICE, 2009). When authorities learned of Pavel's plot to kill the informant, he was charged for that offense and jailed. Once there, Pavel approached another individual and asked him to kill both the original informant and the individual Pavel approached to be a hitman regarding the original murder scheme. Pavel promised this man $40,000 in exchange for killing both men and provided information on the planned victims' appearance, residences, and cars. Pavel directed that one victim be shot and to have his head cut off. Pavel

110

eventually pleaded guilty to solicitation of murder, admitting that he was willing to pay a hitman to kill an informant working with federal investigators who were looking into a bank fraud scheme (ICE, 2009).

The Steven Martinez Case

Former IRS agent-turned-tax preparer Steven Martinez was sentenced to almost 24 years in prison for defrauding clients out of more than $11 million and then plotting their murders to prevent them from testifying about the tax fraud (USDOJ, 2013a). Steven admitted to presenting his clients with completed tax returns indicating that they owed a significant amount of tax. He requested that his clients write checks payable for the amount of taxes due and owing to an alleged client trust account instead of directly to the IRS or the California Franchise Tax Board. Steven also convinced these same clients to write checks during the tax year for estimated tax payments to the same alleged client trust accounts. Rather than deposit these checks into a true trust account, Steven took the checks and deposited them into several bank accounts. In an attempt to conceal his fraud, Steven filed a different set of false tax returns indicating that his clients owed little or no income tax. Steven converted approximately $11 million in stolen taxpayer funds to make home improvements, pay for the use of a private airplane, and to purchase real estate, including a beach home in Mexico.

Steven admitted that in late February 2012, he solicited a third party to murder four witnesses with the intent to prevent their testimony in his pending criminal tax case. The third party contacted the FBI to report the murder-for-hire plot by Steven and agreed to cooperate in the investigation. A subsequent meeting between the FBI's cooperating witness and Martinez was recorded and videotaped. In reference to two targets, Martinez told the would-be killer, who was the FBI's cooperating witness, that "he could make him rich for the rest of his life, $100,000 cash, if he eliminated the lady in Rancho Santa Fe and the lady in La Jolla" (USDOJ, 2013a). The cooperating witness said Steven "suggested that the former employee use two different pistols for the murders and that he acquire a silencer" (USDOJ, 2013a). Steven admitted he provided the third party with four written packets of detailed information about the former clients, including photos of the soon-to-be murder victims, their homes, and personal information. Steven confessed that once the murders took place, he would pay the killer $40,000 in cash, followed by the remaining $60,000 in cash within 72 hours of the murders.

Conclusion

Relying on inaccurate notions of what the face of criminality should look like could expose one to risks that are real and lethal, but often ignored. For decades, misperceptions prevailed about the white-collar offender profile based on projection bias due to the fact that academia failed to devote some of its energies to understand this offender class to produce a more refined and accurate behavioral profile of white-collar offenders, in general, and those who display violent tendencies, specifically. In the future, diverse disciplines should devote more of their talents to researching this understudied offender group so that offender profile misperceptions can be neutralized, behavioral risk factors can be refined, violence investigations can examine motives that are apparent but not necessarily considered, and a better understanding of this crime's victimology can be achieved. Violent white-collar offenders are not an anomaly to ignore; they harbor antisocial and behavioral traits the same way street-level homicide offenders do. People we would not normally suspect would harm others actually do, and sometimes their victims are their own family members. What makes this type of violence so deadly is that it is unexpected, and the risk factors are not obvious. Moreover, although not widespread, violence against antifraud professionals does exist. It is important for professionals to acquaint themselves with warning signs that often precede violence and have a plan in place to remove themselves from dangerous situations before they become victims.

Chapter 3

Predatory Fraud Offenders and Practices

Prior to becoming fraud victims, many said that Cambodian immigrant Seng Tan, together with her Canadian-Cambodian citizen husband, James Bunchan, impressed her fellow Cambodians who settled in Massachusetts with displays of wealth by the jewelry she wore and Mercedes Benz car she drove when she met them. Like them, Seng fled from the horrors of the Cambodian Pol Pot regime where she would pray, cry and laugh with them over their shared experiences. As a result of Pol Pot's policies, an estimated 1 to 3 million people out of a population of slightly over 8 million perished from the combined effects of executions, strenuous working conditions, malnutrition, and poor medical care. Many of the Cambodian fraud victims recall how they believed the couple, especially since they understood the community's suffering prior to relocating to the United States. Bunchan gave emotional speeches to the immigrants convincing them to invest with him and Seng because it was their turn to financially prosper. Fraud victim Tai Kim, believed that "God sent Seng here to help our community" (Abraham, 2006). Unknown to the immigrant families, who did not have enough cash to invest, they collected money from relatives, cashed out retirement accounts, and took out equity loans on their homes to facilitate a Ponzi scheme perpetrated by James and Seng who collected approximating $30 million from about 400 victims. Seng told them they would need to pay over twenty-six thousand dollars into a company called Worldwide Marketing Direct Selling, Inc., a vitamin and beauty-aid supplier. For that investment, the company would send them a $2,497 bonus, then $300 a month for life as well as money for their children.

For every five investors they recruited, payments would increase. Seng targeted longstanding, respected members of the community knowing that once they bought into the investment scheme, other Cambodians would follow. Some of the members of the community asked Seng why only Cambodians were investing and Seng replied, "We have to help all the Cambodian people first, before we go to another culture" (Abraham, 2006). James and Seng used their shared ethnic heritage to facilitate the infiltration and manipulation of the Cambodian community by, 1) speaking their language, 2) sharing the same religion, 3) exploiting the group's cultural propensity of maintaining a distant relationship with outsiders thereby reducing detection of their scheme, and 4) using the Cambodian group leaders to legitimize their reputation and alleged investments. Immediately the investments brought returns and checks arrived every month, as promised. However, after five years the Ponzi scheme collapsed, and the community lost all of its investment taking even Cambodian community leaders by surprise. Vong Ros, director of the Cambodian Mutual Assistance Association states, "The Cambodian community is very close-knit and very private…Seng knows the Cambodian populations don't trust anybody but their family and friends. That is why the wider non-Cambodian community didn't know about it" (Abraham, 2006). Seng, knowing the immigrant investors were wary of those outside their tight-knit community, succeeded in keeping word of their operation secret. It was only until one of the investors told someone at his place of work what occurred that the FBI became involved (Perri & Brody, 2013).

While in custody for his fraud charges, James planned to have the Cambodian fraud victims murdered so that the government could not prove the fraud charges against him. Erroneously, James believed that by eliminating the victims, the fraud case against him would be dismissed (Saltzman, 2009). He offered a hitman, who turned out to be an undercover FBI agent, $160,000 to eliminate the witnesses. James mailed the hitman a list of the people he wanted killed by grouping his targets in order of priority. The prices ranged from $10,000 to $20,000 per murder and price differences may have reflected the importance of the witness to his prosecution. James was found guilty of the murder-for-hire scheme in 2009 (Saltzman, 2009). The behaviors of James represent the classic fraud detection homicide cases together with methods used. James and Seng were found guilty of fraud in 2007 (Saltzman, 2009). The scenario described above occurs thousands of times throughout a year fleecing people out of billions of dollars. One would think that there would be safeguards in place to lessen the probability of such exploitation, yet the exact opposite appears to hold true. As we shall learn, the qualities that hold society together, namely trust to enable cooperation amongst people, is actually the quality that is exploited because fraud offender sees this quality not as a strength, but as a weakness (Perri, 2013a).

Consider the words of fraud offender CFO Samuel Antar where he stated that trust and our sense of humanity may make us a better person, but it is looked upon by criminals as weaknesses to be taken advantage of. The fact that one wants to extoll trust onto another does not mean that a person is obligated to reciprocate this trust and goodness. As we shall see, it is not just greed, gullibility, or excessive trust that grows from tight knit communities making investors fall prey to Ponzi schemes, it is a combination of a pattern of biases where individuals and groups tend to seek out information about other people they associate with that confirms their beliefs about them and not to look for or undervalue information that contradicts their beliefs (Bloise & Ryan, 2013). Then there is the influence of not challenging preconceived views because of the phenomena of belief perseverance which means that once people have formed an opinion, they cling to it tightly for very long times— unfortunately to their detriment (Lewis, 2015). Even if people were to be confronted with evidence that disproves their position, they treat it with excessive skepticism. Warning signs are simply ignored.

In this chapter, we analyze how predatory offenders go about exploiting people to satisfy their motives for financial gain. What we learn is that the essence of predatory offenses is the exploitation of trust. In order to illustrate how trust can be exploited, we examine the concept of affinity fraud and the ease with which it is perpetrated coupled with the skills predatory offenders use as well as the types of victims they prey upon. Furthermore, we outline the behavioral profile of these offenders as well as how group dynamics from a social psychological perspective actually facilitates the ease in which predators operate. Different examples will be used, but special attention is paid to how Ponzi schemer Bernard Madoff was able to exploit so many people and organizations causing irreparable damage both financially, emotionally and at times physical harms illustrated by the medical deterioration victims suffered. Lastly, we conclude as to the types of preventative steps that can be taken to reduce the incidence of exploitation.

At the Heart of Predatory Fraud Practices

Affinity generally refers to a sense of kinship or likeness based on characteristics common to a specific group. For that reason, affinity, the closeness between individuals based on similar traits such as race, religion, ethnicity, language, professional identity and age to name a few, is powerful because it allows individuals to lower inhibitions and feel safe because the other person is "like me" then I can trust him or her more than a person that does not share those similar traits mentioned above. The trust which naturally develops between members of a community with common interests can be exploited by a fraudster who is, or purports to be, a member of that community. Affinity frauds then, are in essence "investment scams that prey upon members of identifiable groups, such as racial, religious and ethnic communities, the elderly, professional groups, or other types of identifiable groups" (Perri & Brody, 2012, p. 305). At the core of such frauds "perpetrators take advantage of the well-known characteristic that it is human nature for people to tend to trust someone who is a member of their own group" (Lewis, 2012a, p. 8).

Consider that every day millions of individuals contribute their time, money, and goodwill to institutions that are established to benefit not only the members of the particular organization, but the wider community as well. These organizations are typically, but not exclusively, non-profit and religious organizations. In addition, there are for-profit organizations that attempt to utilize their shared characteristics by establishing bonds, an affinity, with customers based on race, ethnicity, age, professional designation, or other characteristics. They claim to be trustworthy and honest brokers of their services because they share some of the characteristics listed above. Often the fact that a person or organization shares similar characteristics to his or her target audience is enough to make them appear more credible. To date, securities regulators at the federal, state, and international level have expressed concern about the dramatic growth of affinity fraud, and since 1998 affinity fraud has been ranked one of the top five fraudulent investment practices (NASAA, 2011).

Historically speaking, one nationwide survey found that between 1984 and 1989, affinity fraud affected 13,000 investors out of $450 million and from 1998 to 2001, over 90,000 investors in 28 states lost more than $2.2 billion in affinity fraud schemes (Fairfax, 2002-2003). Recently, over the past several years, citizens of Utah alone who belong to faith-based organizations have been defrauded through the practice of affinity fraud of more than

$1.5 billion dollars (Morgan, 2011). In the United States, affinity fraud is conservatively estimated at $50 billion (Economist, 2012).

The Exploitable Concept of Trust

In discussing trust in a flexible manner, it is important to understand what trust actually consists of, why we desire it, and what influences our trust assessment of others since the exploitation of trust is at the heart of a predatory offender's strategy. Trust is one of the most important social forces within society; we literally could not function without the ability to trust. In fact, trust is so important that it has been described as "the crown jewel of personal ethics" and being trusted by someone is among the highest of individual achievements (McGinniss, 2013, p. 40). Studies on the topic of trust have provided varying definitions with no one approach existing to sufficiently account for all aspects of this concept known as trust. Trust is the willingness of a person(s) to be vulnerable to the actions of other people based on the expectation that other people will perform a particular action important to the person(s) relying on trust, regardless of the ability to monitor or control the other party (Christie & Geis, 1970). Another view of what trust consists of is where we can believe in and are willing to depend on another in that they will not harm us coupled with the belief that another is reliable, genuine, and whose behavior is predictable in given situations (McKnight et al., 1998).

Trust also reflects a reliance upon information received from another person about uncertain environmental states and their accompanying outcomes in a risky situation to reduce insecurity (Bierhoff & Vornefeld, 2004). Generally, people trust because we believe the other party we are dealing with is fair and willing to fulfill expectations (Brewer, 1999). Human nature is to trust others until they prove they are not trustworthy (Peltier, 2006). The honest person is trustworthy for its own sake regardless of whether there is a benefit to them or not and without regard to having to monitor his or her behavior. There are several factors that contribute to increasing trustworthiness in our relationships: 1) the other person has cooperated with others in the past, 2) the person has been involved in a conflict situation with the other person in the past, in which a cooperative solution was found, 3) the other person communicates that he or she has the intention to cooperate, and 4) one can assume that the other person has come to the insight that his or her own interests are best served by cooperating because mutual dependence is given (Bierhoff & Vornefeld, 2004).

Our source of trust is based in part on our past experiences, how we were raised, harboring a truth bias in that we expect others to be truthful, the reputation of others, on necessity, and how we perceive authoritative positions. We desire trusting relationships because we strive for predictability in our lives with the goal of achieving some semblance of stability; thus we strive to seek out others whose actions are predictably reliable. Through trusting relationships, we attempt to reduce the uncertainty inherent when meeting others (McKnight et al., 1998). Researchers have linked a wide variety of desirable outcomes to trust, including positive job attitudes, enhanced team processes, higher levels of cooperation, better task performance, leader-member exchange, and organizational justice (Christie & Geis, 1970). Trust contributes to economic growth and market efficiency, to social integration, cooperation and harmony, to personal life satisfaction, to democratic stability and development, and even to good health and longevity (Delhey & Newton, 2003). Trust is considered a social good that produces a positive synergy by removing barriers to interpersonal relationships (Delhey & Newton, 2003). For example, think of the societal benefits received from literacy. It would be difficult to imagine an industrialized society being able to function composed of illiterate people.

Analogously, relationships cannot thrive without some form of trust requiring a level of perceived competence, loyalty, openness, a sense of fair play, and conscientiousness contrasted to distrust entailing perceived threats, counterproductive behaviors, and a disregard for the safety of others (Brewer, 1999). Trust is highest when people have a social network of colleagues they rely on and the social conditions are marked by low conflict and a sense of personal and public security (Rothstein & Uslaner, 2005). When we extrapolate this research to affinity fraud, it is not surprising that exploitation of trust is so easy because people tend to lower their guard precisely because typically interpersonal conflict is low and personal safety is high such as in a religious setting. People attend religious settings, in part, to feel safe from the outside world and to be surrounded by people

114

they believe share the same belief systems and values. People benefit from a trusting culture and encourage the development of a trusting attitude through informal social networks such as family, community civic life and religious organizations.

As we shall see, this insight is one of the reasons why exploiting organizations is preferred by offenders; they have a readily built social network that is marked by shared sense of communal trust instead of strife that breeds distrust. When we trust, our sense of anxiety is lessened because of our belief that others can be relied upon to fulfill their social commitment, but the injury from the betrayal of trust in both material and emotional terms can be enormous. The inherent trust individuals who belong to specific groups with identifiable characteristics attach to others can be construed as strength because of the desire to reduce the amount of formality needed to attain personal and group goals. In essence trust saves a lot of time by allowing us to rely on other peoples' word that they will fulfill obligations (Lewis, 2015). In fact, trust emerges as a defining necessity for without trust some financial products may not be used at all especially when we rely on the advice of advisors to help us invest our money. Unless one is to spend every minute of the day monitoring for verification their investment decisions, there must be a reasonable belief that the trusted person will tell the truth and fulfill promises.

The qualities of trust and affinity groups use to advance the economic and social well-being of their members, regrettably, can be construed as a weakness to be exploited by those who may share these traits but harbor ulterior motives of how to use these shared traits against those who view them as a strength. Relying on group trust is often so powerful in overcoming people's skepticism that both the financially unsophisticated and the seemingly sophisticated fall victim to these scams. Affinity fraud poses a special danger since it undercuts the usual warnings about investment schemes promoted by strangers (Reed, 2007). All too often, "exploiting the trust that members within a specific group share is at the heart of affinity fraud" (Perri & Brody, 2012, p. 307). The predator gains the trust and confidence of his victims by exploiting the belief that those outside of the group would not have the victim's best interests in mind and would actually try to take advantage of them. Although these relationships may range from relatively superficial to deep personal relationships, trustworthiness in such relationships is based upon patterns of expected behaviors referred to as norms.

Norms very often are not explicit, nevertheless norms do convey what is considered unacceptable behavior and facilitate behavioral patterns which enable trust to evolve, so that members of a specific community trust each other with regard to certain categories of activity. This dynamic explains why victims of affinity fraud feel wronged because the predator exploited both the common shared bonds and the level of trust expected by individuals. If the victim of affinity fraud also belongs to a group that has historically been discriminated against, the victim may experience a particular shame and a deep sense of betrayal that the fraudster knows, appreciates, and preys upon. Moreover, trust overcomes risk and uncertainty in interpersonal relationships, therefore, people are especially sensitive to cues which indicate that others abuse trust and as a consequence are not trustworthy. Thus, situations that give rise to anxiety and insecurity are clearly powerful forces driving distrust. In addition, informal social networks are important for social trust. The more people believe that others are to be trusted, the more they will act in a trustworthy manner themselves, and the more they will reinforce the virtual circle of trust.

In this sense, trust is a social good that is fortified by constant use. Those that harbor a particularized trust tend to trust those in their in-group (Rothstein & Uslaner, 2005). Members of such groups, even if they were prepared to accept sharp practices such as deception and manipulations in other parts of their lives, would regard dishonesty and other socially manipulative behaviors within their relationships as unacceptable. Trust is found within these relationships because the people believe in each other's good faith, good intentions, and integrity. Within such relationships, it is expected that proper informal structures are in place to enable one party to anticipate successful transactions with another party because of this implied trust. Furthermore, this affinity people believe they have for each other increases group cohesion, group trust, and loyalty (Brewer, 1999). As a result, when trust is particularized to specific people, it can be referred to as displaying a deeper commitment to others that are perceived as being from a similar background, than those that are perceived as being outside of the group (Rothstein & Uslaner, 2005).

Affinity fraud thrives because an individual allows the trust they have for someone who seems to be "like them" serve as a substitute for paying attention to investment details because fraudsters know that individuals are looking for a shortcut way to judge character, and affinity settings offer that shortcut. In other words, trust becomes a substitute for due diligence blindly accepting predator representations about an investment opportunity as reliable with no need to verify the accuracy of such representations. As reviewed in chapter one, our weaknesses can be harbored by our attitudes and looking for short-cuts to make decisions is known to predatory offenders which is why they are so successful in their exploitation. In affinity fraud cases, fraudulent investments may come to one's attention as the result of a contact from a friend, colleague, or someone who inspires a bond of trust, "You can trust me because I'm like you…We share the same background and interests. And I can help you make money", the normal process of cautious skepticism is replaced by social banter (Perri & Brody, 2011a, p. 307). In many investment fraud schemes, the fraudster provides information, testimonials, and other documentation to overcome a potential investor's initial suspicion and apprehension to invest with the fraudster. One affinity fraud victim defrauded of $35,000 shared her experience:

> He told me that he had been guided by the spirit to people who are struggling financially and he had the revelation that he should come to me and he would be my financial rescue. These people who target and are doing affinity fraud, they know what they're doing and they're good at it and they just work you until you have their trust (Winslow, 2011).

Why Organizations are Preferred Targets for Predators

Why predators would choose to imbed themselves within a religious organization or other non-religious organizations is useful to know, but not always clear to us. Organizations give predators the opportunity to quick and easy access to an identifiable pool of individuals who become potential victims where they otherwise might not come into contact with them or they might have to spend a lot of time finding them (Navarro, 2014). In addition, because members typically trust one another due to sharing similar traits and motivations, this foundation allows an offender to accelerate overcoming the trust hurdle. Furthermore, the organization provides a convenient infrastructure for the offender to start targeting exploitable weaknesses displayed by people. Membership, especially in a legitimate institution, be it a branch of the military or a corporation, gives legitimacy to individuals coupled with deriving respect and trust forged from alliances formed within an organization. Organizations also serve as a convenient place to provide the predator information about others such as proprietary, personal, or sensitive data otherwise difficult to obtain. For example, some religious organizations require members to expose their faults, sins, or frailties in public by giving testimonials. Predators can use that information to better access or target their victims because information like that serves to provide all the exploitable weaknesses a predator needs; as one predator disclosed, "With that kind of information I know exactly who to target and when" (Navarro, 2014).

Within a religious organization, individuals of different social strata associate with one another with greater ease than in society, giving the predator of low social status access to people who often live and socialize within restricted or gated communities and who otherwise would be impossible for them to target. One can have access to those same socially higher-status people at a church gathering. This is a favored technique of con men, grifters, and swindlers facilitating the success of Ponzi schemes. Many religious organizations preach forgiveness, even for criminals which for these predators is ironically a blessing meaning that if they get caught, they ask for forgiveness and chances are it will be given in a pious but naïve effort to help the offender learn from his or her mistakes. Another advantage for the predator in a religious organization is that if caught, he or she can very conveniently say it was Satan's fault. Whether cheating, taking advantage of the elderly, conducting financial shenanigans, or even abusing children, for many religious entities the predator merely has to say that the devil tempted him or her and that is the end of the discussion of anyone being held accountable for the exploitation of others (Navarro, 2014). Predators know they can rely on a certain portion of the population to buy into this argument, and so they use it.

116

Consider that if the predator becomes a leader within the organization, or if lucky, becomes the head of a church or religious group, then he or she is immediately cloaked with power and moral authority coupled with access to many people and their money. Keep in mind that most people still have a high respect for their church leaders and are willing to give them greater latitude and the benefit of the doubt. To connive, or to con, the predator merely needs his victim(s) to have faith and trust in him or her, something that is often easily achieved within the confines of a legitimate religious organization. Predators soon realize that the ability to invoke God in their defense is a powerful position to hold that trumps all other arguments claiming that they were moved by the lord to do this or that. For victims that enjoy a faith life, a faith, emotionally-laden argument is difficult to challenge especially for believers that are already emotionally vested together with having spent time and money on an organization. Predators know or soon learn that society tends to revere and not question religious authority because to have faith is to believe in something that is more authoritative than mankind; in essence the word of God cannot be challenged even when invoked by criminals (Navarro, 2014).

Predatory Offender Skill Base Facilitating Exploitation

> Watch the guys who are nicer to you because, as a criminal, I was nicer to my victims than my friends. Just because someone appears to be likeable doesn't mean they're good people. You have to steal with a smile.
>
> CFO Samuel Antar (Gaetano, 2012)

Financial predators initiate committing crimes because the ethical foundation of our society is based on trust and our legal foundation is based on the presumption of innocence (Antar, 2005). The inclination to trust and the presumption of innocence gives the fraudster the initial benefit of any doubt while they are free to plan and execute their crimes. Therefore, trusting and decent law-abiding human beings are easier prey for fraudsters. However, people tend to ignore the fact that their trust, ethics, and good nature limit their behavior and create a fertile opportunity for white-collar criminals to seize the initiative and execute their crimes (Antar, 2005). Fraudsters are not deterred by society's moral constraints. In addition, the sensation of power over another individual(s) or a situation can be a strong motivating force for some fraud offenders to the point that it becomes an end in itself especially those that are considered predatory fraud offenders (Duffield & Grabosky, 2001). As one predatory offender put it, "For myself, I love to make people do what I want them to, I love command. I love to rule people. That's why I'm a con artist" (Duffield & Grabosky, 2001, p. 2).

Obviously one of the mistakes made by investors, especially in Ponzi schemes, was trusting the wrong person and to a large degree the reasons lay in the personalities of the offenders themselves and the nature of their schemes. Some of the characteristics exhibited is that they display traits of legitimate business people except in this case they are criminal entrepreneurs being creative in their schemes by tapping unique, exploitable niche markets (Lewis, 2015). Like legitimate entrepreneurs, they are optimistic, confident and self-assured which, in turn, evokes confidence in the people they are defrauding. These offenders have talents in inspiring trustworthiness by living in large homes, exclusive addresses and socialize with the well off. As a gesture of good will, they will offer their services for free, but at the same time appearing choosey in terms of who they associate with to give the aura of exclusivity and specialness. Their schemes signal respectability and safety by using words such as "backed by" or "secured by"; recall Charles Ponzi's company name was the Security Exchange Company.

Initially, in order to enhance trust between the offender and the investors, they tend to keep their commitments and actually pay investors what was promised until the scheme implodes or they close the scheme down disappearing with the money. Moreover, they prefer to operate by word of mouth so as to not draw attention to their schemes and use what are known as "song birds", people who become the predator's de facto spokesperson because they, like song birds, sing the predator's praises thus attracting more people to give the offender money. Predatory fraud offenders manifest their exploitation in a different form than conventional street-level offenders creating victims nonetheless (Perri & Brody, 2012). Such fraud offenders deceive, exploit and manipulate others in order to achieve personal gain (Barnard, 2008b). Furthermore, predatory fraud offenders seek out organizations and individuals to victimize, are pathological liars in that they are adept at lying without feeling uncomfortable about it, and may exhibit highly refined interpersonal skills where they are able to cajole, excite, and persuade their victims (Barnard, 2008a). These fraud offenders are skilled at reading their victims verbal and nonverbal behaviors and adjusting their own behavior to appear more credible.

They are adept at understanding the mindset of the ones they will defraud, feel no compassion for the weak they will exploit, and no empathy for the financial destruction they cause others. Predatory fraud offenders exhibit traits of extreme entitlement, callousness, lack conscience, have an inability to empathize with others, and show no remorse for their actions when violating the rights of others (Perri & Brody, 2011a). Trust is a hazard that can destroy one's livelihood and fraud predators rely on their victim's trust so that they will never have to be put in a position to verify their representations. However, even if a victim later seeks to verify the predator's representations, their skepticism may be substantially diminished by their increased comfort level due to the perceived trust they believe they share with the offender. In other words, the victim accepts the fraudster's deceptive answers as factual, even if they have some doubts (Antar, 2005). Their trust bias contributes to a distorted risk assessment of the person that seeks their money. A common mistake made by victims of fraud is called unexamined acceptance, yet, representations received from any source should not be taken for granted as being truthful and accurate without any critical analysis, investigation, and verification (Antar, 2005).

The Importance of Manipulation for Successful Victimization

Predatory fraud offenders, especially involved in face-to-face schemes, need an array of specific skills to be successful criminal entrepreneurs and some of these traits include as follows: inventiveness, an eye for scheming, ingenuity, practical knowledge of things, excellent language skills, street smarts, worldly-wiseness, social skills, business skills and the ability to be perceived as trustworthy. Successful con persons must be intellectually agile illustrated by being a capable speaker allowing for the construction of a plausible story, capable of communicating it with a sense of sincerity, and capable of keeping the story line straight in their head. Just as with many crimes, committing a fraud involves a sequence of actions known as a fraud script which includes: 1) preparation of target selection, 2) implement the fraud scheme, 3) completion of the fraud scheme, 4) exit from the setting, and 4) disposal of evidence. For example, a securities fraud offender must, at a minimum, include targeting the victim, building rapport, "setting the hook," extracting the cash, putting the cash out of reach, and taking steps to delay or avert detection. Elaborate frauds may also include the construction of a plausible business model, enlist people assisting the offender, negotiate with multiple investors, communicate sophisticated documentation in simple terms, transmission of funds outside the reach of authorities and their victims to recover, and sometimes relocation to avoid arrest.

Not only must the con person compose and deliver the fraud script, he must also be able to improvise by having the ability to shift ideas quickly in response to changing circumstances and a clever imagination to fill with details. All of these skills, of course, are the same skills required of any good salesperson selling a product or service, yet in the case of the predatory offender the scam is the product. Predatory offenders use a combination of persuasion and deceit to achieve their objectives to prey on the psychological vulnerabilities of their victims measuring their effectiveness by how likeable they are; the more their victims like them, the easier it is to exploit them (Gaetano, 2012). Predatory offenders purposely manipulate fear by trying to lower it, especially in circumstances where distrust might naturally exist. What is interesting about predatory fraud offenders is that their strategy is not to create fear in their targets, but to create trust so that they are open to being vulnerable psychologically to their exploiters. For example, someone who uses force or attempts to use force to control others also wants to rely on their fear to gain compliance. Thus, robbing someone entails creating the type of psychological response for compliance through fear to have him or her depart with their money. The exact opposite applies to financial predatory offenders. They want to create trust so that one departs with their money not out of force or fear, but with a happy heart—a voluntary act on the part of the victim.

How might a predatory offender create the appearance that they possess a trusting character? They might create trust by giving the appearance of straight talk, that is communicate clearly so that one cannot be misunderstood and to reduce the appearance of being evasive (Covey, 2006). They will inject into their discussion what their intentions are, so they leave no doubt about what they are thinking. These offenders want to neutralize suspicions they are withholding information, trying to use flattery and spin, distorting facts or leaving false impressions so that their targets internalize what they see and hear as truthful, straight talk. Another strategy is to demonstrate respect and this behavior is based on the principles of fairness, kindness, and civility. Other strategies include creating illusions of transparency and genuineness, displaying loyalty to those individuals by appearing to look after their interests and keeping commitments. There are also competence-based characteristics such as delivering results on what is expected. This is a way to convert cynics and establish trust in a new relationship. By establishing a track record, making the right things happen, being on time and on budget, and not making excuses for not delivering, one can enhance trust.

Another is to sprinkle a story with irrelevant or extraneous information, some of which the victim will know to be true and therefore make the story sound more convincing. Moreover, another technique is to anticipate and disarm the victim's skepticism or fear and defuse it by bringing their concerns up first. Still another technique conducive to believability has to do with listening; to be successful, a predatory offender must engage a prospective victim in enough conversation to reveal the victims' weaknesses and financial desires. Engaging the victim requires patience coupled with pretending to being empathetic. Stated another way, the offender must be willing to spend time listening to his victim's hopes, fears, aspirations, dreams, and desires, in order to determine the shape of the sales pitch. They will come across as the 'nice person' who listens to all of your problems which in reality is exaggerating his caring, his ability to love, and kills with kindness (Lewis, 2015). Then he must build a relationship, foster confidence, and know precisely when to ask for their money. One predatory fraud offender described the importance of listening to his victims stating: "I'm persuasive because I understand and listen to people. I study everything about a person. No detail is too small. People love to talk, and I love to listen. Listening to a person talk is the key to being able to outwit them" (Barnard, 2008a, p. 208).

A key factor in an offender's success for those involved in face-to-face schemes, is the ability to lie effectively over a sustained period of time. A good liar has to think of plausible answers, should not contradict him or herself, should tell a lie that is consistent with everything that the observer knows or might find out and should avoid making slips of the tongue. Moreover, they have to remember what they have said, so that they can say the same things when asked to repeat their story. Also, financial predators design their actions to shape the actions of others, persist in lying when they are challenged to tell the truth, do not feel uncomfortable when they lie, do not find lying complicated, view others cynically and display little concern for conventional morality. Plus, they must have highly refined interpersonal skills, the ability to persuade and continually refocus their victims on the ultimate goal of participating in their scheme during the course of the fraud. Among other skills, they must be acutely sensitive to their victim's state of mind because,

> [S]killed lying involves convincing the listener that the speaker believes what he or she is saying and has a truthful intention. A skilled liar also continuously "reads" the listener's nonverbal behavior and, in response to "feedback" from the listener, adjusts both verbal and nonverbal communications to be more credible. This skill markedly enhances one's capacity to manipulate other people's beliefs and behaviors (Barnard, 2008a, p. 203).

Lastly, predatory fraud offenders know that people live on the hope of a better financial future and it is their job to manipulate their aspirations by catering to people's hope for a better tomorrow. Predators understand that to be respected they have to exude confidence that are experts in what they are selling in addition to giving the impression that by engaging in altruistic behaviors such as giving to charity, they want their victims to interpret this behavior as someone who is honest and would not hurt them. Consider the insights of previously mentioned convicted CFO Samuel Antar that illustrate these manipulative tactics that served him well during his financial exploitations:

> We took advantage of investor's hopes, dreams, and aspirations for a better future. More importantly, we fully exploited investor's lack of skepticism that resulted from the wall of false integrity we built around ourselves. Hope is a fine human quality that motivates us to build a better future with Antar further stating. My cousin Crazy Eddie Antar taught me that "people live on hope". As white-collar criminals, we

preyed on your hopes and dreams by feeding you our spin and lies. Investors demand confident leadership and strong financial performance from company management. They want to hear management exuding confidence about their company's future business prospects. Eddie and I built an image of strong and confident leadership by promising investors a prosperous future backed up by our phony financial reports. We claimed that Crazy Eddie's accounting policies were "conservative." In addition, we gave huge sums of money to charity and were involved in many popular social causes in an effort to make investors comfortable with us. While we were in effect, "helping old ladies cross the street," we were heartlessly executing a massive fraud that wiped out the life savings of thousands of investors and ultimately caused a few thousand people to lose their jobs (Antar, 2010).

Direct and Indirect Persuasion Techniques

In addition, social psychology has identified alternative routes to persuasion that can be used in a manipulative manner. The two routes to persuasion used in this context revolved around the direct and indirect methods. This entails understanding the attitudes and beliefs influencing human interactions and techniques for persuasion that help establish emotional cues used for influencing fraud victims (Peltier, 2006). A direct, central route to persuasion depends on logical argument to stimulate a favorable response, prompting the listener or reader to think deeply about an issue and possibly reach consensus if that is required (Perri & Brody, 2012). Thus, the direct route, which depends on the responder's logical thinking toward the offered information from the offender, may not necessarily succeed as a strategy of persuasion because there may be statements that reveal symptoms of illegitimate, fraudulent activity. An indirect route to persuasion relies on mental shortcuts that serve as distractions to bypass logical argument and counterarguments seeking to trigger acceptance without deeply thinking of the matter (Perri & Brody, 2012).

Affinity fraud offenders typically utilize the indirect method of persuasion to make the intended victim more susceptible to persuasion by triggering an emotional response with the ultimate goal of having them participate in their fraud scheme. For example, recall James Bunchan giving emotional speeches to convince the immigrants to invest with him and Seng Tan. James would cry, recalling how his people had suffered under the Pol Pot Regime and explaining why it was their turn to prosper and the Cambodian fraud victims believed the couple especially since they understood the community's suffering prior to relocating to the United States. Gerald Payne, who ran Greater Ministries International, a Ponzi scheme that extracted nearly half a billion dollars from its victims in the 1990s, often quoted to congregations of Christian believers biblical verse, Luke 6:38, "Give, and it shall be given unto you" (Merling, 2013). Patrick Henry Talbert, one of the perpetrators of the Greater Ministries scheme, promised the congregation at the Indianapolis Baptist Temple, "You give a gift, we basically take it offshore — and we've been doing this for nine years, nobody's ever lost a dime — and we multiply it back through the body of Christ" (Melring, 2013).

The Ability to "Read" Victims

The key to a successful fraud scheme is the identification and manipulation of victims who are particularly vulnerable to a con person's persuasive skills especially offering hope, making us feel good about ourselves, exploiting personal weaknesses, and enhancing desires (Barnard, 2008a). The ability to sort out what a person desires or what their weakness entails is one factor that distinguishes a successful predatory offender from those that are not adept. In addition, successful offenders must have an ability to recognize, encourage, and exploit his or her victims' greed. With very little information, he must be able to distinguish between those victims likely to part with their money in response to an attractive investment opportunity and those who are too risk-averse to waste their time on. Victim selection is an intuitive art and a con person must identify the buttons to push to get the victim to actually make an investment decision. These offenders know that any lie custom-tailored to the victim's psychological makeup and biases, any lie that feeds vanity, jealousy, fear of rejection, or any other biases will be compelling in a way in which few other things are. One successful telemarketer knew who ached to be complimented through flattery, who desired to be abused through put-downs and belittlements even if subconsciously secure in the knowledge that the abused would do almost anything to turn things around to get into the offender's good grace (Barnard, 2008a). This offender was particularly adept at uncovering the loneliness of old people and how their desire to please him in order to get at least a few words and acts of kindness left out of him leaving them unprotected. In short, like most predatory offenders, they do not so much feel for others as they felt their way into them.

Displaying a Lack of Empathy for Victims

Predators do not have any attitude toward their victims except that they are a means to an end. Victims are the possessors of wealth desired thought of just like a fisherman thinks of a place to fish or a hunter of a place to hunt (Barnard, 2008a). Predators who deal with their victims face-to-face are perhaps the most seriously disturbed due to the requirement of intimate personal betrayal. The direct face-to-face deception of another individual involves utter ruthlessness and this may take such extreme forms as the person who takes a widow into his or her confidence and leaves her penniless. Offenders of this type may manifest a number of traits including lack of affection or empathy, lack of remorse, and a general lack of conventional conscience. Predators are not to be distracted by compassion or generosity toward his victims and the offender's empathy deficit, in fact, is one of the ironies of a successful fraud. Victims must sense an emotional connection with their defrauder and yet the defrauder must not feel any emotional connection with his victims. Sometimes offenders achieve the necessary distance from their victims by rationalizing to themselves that they are intellectually superior to their victims and they deserve to be exploited because of their weakness of relying on trust or that the victims are just as scheming, greedy, and dishonest as themselves.

Predator Fraud Scheme Strategy Indicators

Fraud schemes perpetuated by predators have identifiable strategies that facilitate their deceptions. Some of the tactics used include but are not limited to the following:
- They might offer high or unreasonably guaranteed rates of return that makes their investment offers attractive because there is no risk of losing money,
- Representations of the emotional desirability of holding a particular investment as the opportunity's principal attraction,
- Predators advertise their "expertise" in a given investment opportunity, but in fact they are not,
- There is a pressure to have victims invest all of their savings in a particular investment,
- Predators display wealth to others sending the message that their victims too can end up with such wealth if they listen to their advice and contribute money to the investments they are selling, and
- High pressure to buy investments before it is too late. The "once in a lifetime opportunity" sales pitch.

Predatory Fraud Offender Behavioral Profile

According to Dr. Robert Hare, those who are most adept at successfully perpetrating affinity fraud display psychopathic traits because they are able to target victims that establish emotional bonds with them even though they themselves are incapable of forming empathetic attachments with others (Carozza, 2008a). Dr. Hare further states, religious groups are extremely vulnerable; belief in the inherent goodness of others and the uncritical acceptance of professions of faith by others are tailor-made for the psychopath who views their inherent goodness not as a virtue, but rather as a weakness to be exploited (Carozza, 2008a). They appear to be generous, 'free-loving', 'free-and-easy' individuals, but in reality they are skilled in deception, feel no compassion for the weak they will exploit, and no remorse for the financial destruction they bring upon others (Perri, 2011a). Psychopaths often compartmentalize their behavior, enabling them to present themselves differently to various people; this can help them hide their manipulation and control over victims (Babiak & O'Toole, 2012).

Psychopaths are driven by what they perceive as their victims' vulnerabilities; they experience a perverted pleasure—a duping delight—from hurting and abusing their victims (Babiak & O'Toole, 2012). Their emotional poverty is visible in their shallow sentiment, yet they display emotions only to manipulate individuals around them by mimicking other people's emotional responses (Babiak & O'Toole, 2012). Psychopathic manipulation usually begins by creating a mask, known as psychopathic fiction, in the minds of those targeted. In interpersonal situations, this façade shows the psychopath as the ideal friend, advisor, and partner; these individuals excel at sizing up their prey. They appear to fulfill their victims' psychological needs, much like the grooming behavior of molesters (Babiak & O'Toole, 2012). Although they sometimes appear too good to be true, this persona typically is too grand to resist. They play into people's basic desire to meet the right person—someone who values them for themselves, wants to have a close relationship, and is different from others who have disappointed them. Belief in the realism of this personality can lead the individual to form a psychopathic bond with the perpetrator on intellectual, emotional, and physical levels. At this point, the target is hooked and now has become a psychopathic victim.

Moreover, psychopathic fraudsters use affinity groups to facilitate their schemes (Carozza, 2008a). They rely on the fact that members of an affinity group typically are very trusting of others who profess to share their values, beliefs, and interests. They gain entry into the group by developing an acquaintance with a group member who then introduces the fraudster as "one of us" (Carozza, 2009). Yet sadly, even after being victimized, many members of a group will refuse to face the truth, continuing to believe that the offender is basically good at heart or that there must be a reason why he or she took advantage of the group. Sherree DeCovny, a former investment broker, who has written on why Wall Street appears to be riddled with scandals such as the Madoff scheme believes that, in part, the people who work there display psychopathic traits stating:

> Sometimes these people turn out to be [serial killer] Jeffrey Dahmer and drill a hole through your skull. But if you send them to Harvard and dress them in a fine suit, they could become your boss, your CEO or your senator. They excel in any arena where aggressive behavior is rewarded and where grandiose levels of confidence can result in rousing applause. I have come to know many psychopaths, from Ponzi-schemers to book-cooking corporate executives. They are always charming and narcissistic. They display wonderfully glib senses of humor and spin the truth like a roulette wheel. It is often difficult to argue that these people are indeed sick until the day they have to exchange their Armani suit for an orange jumpsuit (Lewis, 2012a).

The Influence of Projection Bias in Facilitating Victimization

I am accepting that what I was experiencing was a projection of a person who wasn't there.

Carmen Dell'Orficie (Madoff Victim)

Recall from chapter one that projection bias is a psychological defense mechanism to reduce personal anxiety where an individual transfers his or her own attributes, thoughts, feelings and emotions, usually to other people, given a set of circumstances. It is the tendency to assume that others share similar values, beliefs or thoughts with their own. Thus it may be disturbing to observe those individuals, who may look like us in terms of being from the same faith, racial and ethnic background, behaving dishonestly especially in an altruistic faith-based setting. Projecting a value system to another because of a shared characteristic or affiliation can be problematic and the billions of dollars lost to fraud offenders is evidence of projection bias. Consider the statement of one victim that exemplifies the application of projection bias. A defrauded church member commented concerning another member to whom she had donated funds for a church project stated, "I trusted her as if she were a member of my family...we had the same values and beliefs" (Reed, 2007). This victim lost $100,000 by investing with a church member who was going to produce a film about the beliefs of the group. The film was not made and the scammer disappeared.

Another investor who was a victim of fraud commenting on the religious similarities between him and the pastor stated: "I trusted him implicitly due to [his] church position and [our] association" (Morgan, 2012). Again observe how victims project values on individuals by affiliations the offender claims to belong to implying that the person is trustworthy without any evidence to substantiate the offender's representations of who they are and what their true intentions are. In addition, character assessments made through projection bias and not facts accelerate the degree of trust individuals are willing to expend on another. People who know affinity fraud offenders often claim that their offense is "out of character" which may partially explain why victims of affinity fraud are unwilling to take action against such offenders because of the erroneous belief that they will see the error of their ways. Yet, there are criminal thinking patterns that predate the behavior at issue, and these thinking patterns express themselves at a moment of opportunity; the crime is very much within the character of the perpetrator.

Predatory Fraud Offender Case Studies

As stated in the beginning of the chapter, predatory offenders seek out their victims from a variety of venues be it religious based, professional organizations, those that are based on one's ethnicity or a combination of similar traits. For example, some churches may be populated by one particular race, ethnicity or have a common language. Thus the affinity is compounded by the fact that similar traits are not just based on one similar trait, but multiple similar traits. Also the intensity of the affinity is compounded by harboring the same faith, shared experiences, race and language traits all at the same time. In essence, when people harbor so many similar traits at once, people within a group are mirror images of each other. Defrauding investors in religious based settings is particularly effective because offenders can reach large groups of people when touting fraudulent investments to an entire congregation. However, perpetrators also use internet sites, ethnically affiliated media, conferences or other social gatherings of these groups to gain access to members of a specific group, designing their investment opportunities to appeal to them. The legitimacy of their investments is often based on religious references such as quoting certain verses from religious texts. For example, literature or presentations stress shared language or identity with other group members.

Religious-based Exploitation

Perpetrators use group religious affinity as a means of legitimizing themselves and their fraudulent investment programs. Consider the sales material convicted affinity fraud offender Vaughn Reeves, age 66, used to train church team members to sell securities to other church members urging them to fulfill their religious duties that is reflective of the indirect persuasion method previously discussed. Team training materials stated, "Never sell the facts, sell warm stewardship and the Lord" (AP, 2010). Consider the impact of Reeve's promotional material with the statement of a church member who lost over $40,000 in Reeve's Ponzi scheme: "It was a good place where Christians would be investing in the work of other Christians…We wanted to invest in something honest, doing the Lord's work and that just sucked us right in" (Wilson, 2010).

Church of Latter Day Saints

With almost one-quarter of Idaho's population belonging to The Church of Jesus Christ of Latter-day Saints, Idaho became a place where affinity fraud flourished. For example, between 2002 and 2008, Daren Palmer encouraged family and friends to invest over $78 million in Trigon Group—an investment company headed by Palmer promising twenty percent rates of return (Yardley, 2011). Although Palmer was not a bishop in the church, he used his membership in the church to facilitate access to his victims. As one commentator stated reflecting the risks of not keeping their projection bias in check, "A lot of people who invested [with Palmer] are active members of the LDS Church…They knew that Palmer was [a member], and that gave them comfort" (Yardley, 2011). In addition Palmer would spend lavishly on himself by building a multi-million dollar home. According to one observer, "He built the house so that people would see it and give him more money…he was making himself the 'Joneses' so that they would want to keep up with him" (Yardley, 2011). Yet even after he was arrested, victims who lost hundreds of thousands of dollars would shovel snow from his sidewalk and take meals to him. In 2005, Julius Blackwelder formed Friend's Investment Group recruiting investors with the lure that he was not only an experienced and successful commodities trader, but that he was investing their money in safe, long-term commodities futures contracts (Carson, 2013). Blackwelder perpetuated this fraud for years by

123

preparing and distributing promissory notes to the investors, providing updates on accounts, and writing memoranda describing the successes of his investments.

Blackwelder defrauded investors of almost $500,000 that he used to construct a 7,000 square-foot home, pay personal expenses and loans plus pay off earlier investors (Carson, 2013). One victim who was nearing retirement, took out a $100,000 home equity loan on his house and withdrew $130,000 from his 401k retirement plan to invest with Blackwelder.In 1994, Shawn Merriman, formed Mountain Springs Partners, along with other business entities and over the next fifteen years, represented to investors that he would use their money to buy and sell securities (Martino, 2012). Merriman fabricated financial statements to convince investors they were receiving returns on their investment. People already invested in the scheme provided credibility to the investment scam by the testimonials they gave of the money made by investing with Merriman. He did not use the money to purchase securities, but instead he defrauded hundreds of individuals totaling almost $21 million to fund the purchase of homes, collectible cars, artwork, firearms, and sports memorabilia earning him the infamous honor of being named "The Mormon Madoff" (Martino, 2012). LuElla Day, for example, lost $1.2 million by investing with Merriman, a fellow Mormon she had known for four years. According to Ms. Day who is eighty-one years old when she sold her farm, Merriman came to her and said their bishop had asked him to help me invest the proceeds of the sale by buying government debt. Ms. Day further stated, "I don't understand how anyone that could claim to be a good person, go to church every Sunday and then do the things that he did…it's just unbelievable" (Winslow, 2011).

African-American Dominated Churches

Another factor is the rise of prosperity theology, or the belief that God wants Christians to be rich as well as good and this idea has taken root fastest in black and Hispanic churches where networks of their church communities are being exploited. In a scheme in Arizona, members of a Baptist congregation were defrauded of $530 million when the perpetrators used the Baptist network to scam other Baptist churches (Fairfax, 2002-2003). In Alabama, Abraham Kennard was convicted of using a network of African-American churches, approximately 1,600 churches in over 41 states, to defraud investors of almost $9 million (Fairfax, 2002-2003). During his trial, where Kennard represented himself at trial, he attempted to appeal to the potential religious inclinations of jurors telling them "God is the biggest financial backer you can ever have…and that's who these people (the victims) put their trust in" (Reed, 2007). Known as "the black Bernie Madoff," Ephren Taylor focused his fraudulent efforts upon members of megachurches taking over $11 billion from mostly African-American Christians (Merling, 2013). Ephren Taylor delivered his "Wealth Live Tour" to more than fifty churches throughout the United States between 2008 and 2011, including 25,000 members of the New Birth Missionary Baptist church near Atlanta, Georgia, and Joel Osteen's Lakewood Church in Houston, Texas. Taylor boasted the fact that he had appeared on National Public Radio, CNN, The Montel Williams Show, 20/20, and being a speaker at the 2008 Democratic National Convention. Taylor used religion to "emphasize God, being a Christian and not being broke" (Merling, 2103). Moreover, he used kindness to encourage victims to invest with him, urging that his prosperity ministry sermon purported to offer low-risk investment with high performances chosen with guidance from God.

Seventh Day Adventists

Another notable affinity fraud case that exemplifies the pervasiveness of this scheme involves convicted white-collar criminal Winston Ross of Florida. Ross defrauded over 250 members of the Seventh-day Adventist Church by collecting more than $6.5 million to support a Ponzi scheme (Yang, 2005). During seminars to his target group, Ross encouraged attendees to incorporate themselves so they could avoid paying federal income taxes. For a fee of $600, Ross would assist in preparing paperwork to become incorporated. At his presentations, Ross told investors that one of his investment programs was completely risk-free and provided guaranteed returns of at least 10 percent a month for 15 months. Investors who deposited more than $100,000 would be paid 12 percent per month; those who invested more than $300,000 were guaranteed 15 percent per month. Ross encouraged victims to refinance their homes or take cash advances on their credit cards to invest in his programs.

The Amish Community

The Amish are known for their traditional, family, and community-based Christian values and austere lifestyle structured around plain clothes, simple lifestyles, and the rejection of many of modernity's offerings (Lewis, 2015). They form part of the Mennonite Church that migrated from Switzerland settling mostly in Pennsylvania, Ohio, and Indiana where there is an estimated population of about 250,000. Hard work, frugality, saving, and sharing are some of their core values—as is trust. Due to their financial success, the image of the honest, law-abiding Amish has been tarnished by members of the Amish community that exploited the inherent trust Amish share with each other. For example, in 2013, 61 year-old Mennonite John Sensenig lived in Lancaster, Pennsylvania. He advertised to the Mennonite and Amish community the sale of promissory notes reading, "We pay 6% on demand notes, 7% on 6-month notes, 8% on 3-year notes, 9% on 5-year notes…we ask only that our own people (Amish/Mennonite) invest" (Lewis, 2015, p. 108). Many who invested with Sensenig were impressed by his knowledge and confidence on the topic of financial investing, and that he spoke in their native tongue, Pennsylvania Dutch, creating an immediate bond.

Yet according to the SEC, Sensenig made material misstatements when he failed to disclose the use of the investor's money and the risks associated with the investment. Sensenig invested in amusement parks, land development, and a roofing firm to name a few of the ventures that did not produce a profit. In order to stay afloat, he needed new investors to pay off the older investors. When the scheme collapsed, investors lost millions of dollars. Only two of the hundred sued Sensensig, instead the "community closed ranks, resorted to long-standing traits: Trust your brethren. Resist outside influences. Be forgiving" (Lewis, 2015, p. 110). Between 1997-2009, about 1500 Amish investors incurred losses of up to $65 million. Consider the exploitation of Amish investors by Englishman Timothy Moffett. Moffett, although not an Amish person, professed being a devote Christian. He had Amish participate in a real estate development being promised a nine percent rate of return. Initially only a handful of Amish investors participated, but after these initial investors did well financially, others started to invest thousands of dollars with Moffett. Those who invested received regular interest payments together with his newsletter that reported the progress of the real estate development. Yet, upon further investigation, there was no real construction going on—it was all a ruse. Despite all the red-flags, none of the eighty-plus investors pulled out of Moffitt's scam. Given the aversion to government intervention, many of the victims of the scam resented law enforcement involvement.

One of the investors stated that he did not want to be seen as the person that ruined the investment by getting the law community involved. As stated by another one of the victim's "Tim had our word, to an Amish that commitment is sacred" (Lewis, 2015, p. 118). From 2009 to the present, about 80 Amish families incurred losses up to $20 million. In this example, we observe the application of the previous discussed concept of belief perseverance where once people have formed an opinion they tend to cling to the belief regardless of information that may contradict their beliefs. In June, 2012, 78 year-old Amish man named Monroe Beachy stood to be sentenced in court. He received over six years in prison. Beachy was convicted of running a Ponzi scheme with the money of the Amish community squandering over $16 million dollars between 1990-2010 (Lewis, 2015). Beachy told his investors that the money was invested in risk-free U.S. government securities, but in reality he invested in speculative investments such as high yield junk bonds, mutual funds and stocks. However, when he incurred losses, he accepted new money to pay off the older investors. When the investors were in court, they indicated that it is more important to forgive Beachy than to recover their money. In this example, we observe how religious beliefs may trump the harm caused to their group and the impact of their beliefs on holding a predator accountable for their crimes.

Exploiting the Elderly

Although affinity fraud often occurs in a religious-based environment, as illustrated above, there are those frauds that prey on other specific traits such as age. Elderly investors are natural targets in part because they may be more susceptible to fraud due to their diminished ability to detect deception coupled with the belief that because the advisor is a senior, they will better understand their needs. Consider the case of senior financial advisors, husband and wife team Thomas and Susan Cooper, ages 69 and 67 respectively who gained clients by the seminars they hosted. One couple who lost money stated, "We felt that the Coppers were close to our age, they would understand and would have dealt with a lot of the problems we face at our age: heath setbacks and that sort of thing…Isn't that supposed to be a plus—to get somebody who understands your problems" (Zweig & Pilon, 2010). Research suggests that the typical person's ability to make smart financial decisions peaks at about age 53, then wanes with each passing year while another study found that investing ability takes a steep drop after age 70 (Zweig, & Pilon, 2010). Older adults seek less data than younger people do when making complex decisions—and will go out of their way to avoid negative information or confrontations.

According to regulators and prosecutors, there has been a significant increase recently in the number of cases in which older investors have been taken advantage of by elderly scam artists. For example, convicted white-collar criminal and disbarred attorney Edward Digges, age 63, targeted senior citizens whom he located with newspaper ads (Pretty, 2010). Interestingly, Digges had already served time in federal prison for mail fraud which entailed an over-billing scheme. In the case in which he defrauded senior citizens, he collected at least $10 million for a Ponzi scheme by promising investors annual returns of 12 percent. Unscrupulous advisers tout their professional designations as further evidence of their expertise. Professional credentials have exploded in popularity among financial advisers in recent years and many of the newer ones can be gotten easily often with minimal study and just a few hundred dollars. One financial journal identified more than 200 financial service professional credentials, such as CFP which stands for Certified Financial Planner, including at least six with the word "senior" in their name: certified senior adviser; certified senior consultant; certified senior specialist; certified senior financial planner; and chartered senior financial planner (Zweig & Pilon, 2010). For example, in Louisiana, Judith Zabalaoui, 73, pleaded guilty to five counts of mail fraud and is now serving an eight-year prison sentence after persuading at least 35 clients, many of them elderly, to invest in two nonexistent companies that promised "safe" returns of 13% to 26% (Zweig & Pilon, 2010). She had clients sign a power of attorney, giving her access to their funds spending more than $3 million of their money on her own expenses, including clothing and vacations.

According to one defrauded senior couple who lost about $24,000 stated that they met Ms. Zabalaoui at a seminar and were impressed with her stating, "When you see the letters CFP after her name, you assume she has an enhanced position" (Zweig & Pilon, 2010). Referring back to the Cooper's case above, one retired factory worker who gave money to the Coopers felt more comfort with their professional credentials further stating: "Oh my goodness, yes, I was impressed by that" (Zweig & Pilon, 2010). The factory worker recalls how when he would have dinner with the Coopers, they would give very solid God-honoring prayers. As with many senior-on-senior fraud cases, a sense of loyalty kept the alleged victims from complaining. The factory worker in the Cooper case realized that something was wrong when the value of his investment were significantly dropping. He felt guilty about having the authorities involved and somehow believed that he and others should not have complained. Lastly, it is important for older investors to run financial decisions past a younger, and hopefully an insightful relative or someone who can resist the emotional pull of the situation. In some states, people are trained by securities regulators seek to attend any free lunch or dinner seminars hosted by financial advisers. If these people, referred to at times as "sentinels" see anything suspicious, they report it to state or federal investigators (Zweig & Pilon, 2010). According to regulatory and consumer advocates, younger relatives should periodically ask their older family members whether they have been pitched any products or services by financial advisers.

Charitable Exploitation

Thomas Petters, Founder of Petters Group Worldwide, operated a Ponzi scheme valued over $3.65 billion by appealing to religious and charitable organizations (Phelps & Tevlin, 2008). Affinity fraud offenders gain credibility of those they appeal to by engaging in philanthropic activities by supporting their causes and Petters donated millions of dollars to these organizations creating the appearance of legitimacy so that these organizations would invest in his alleged opportunities. Convicted of fraud, Petters stated to the sentencing court that he is a victim, yet the reality as demonstrated at trial is the defendant's life was a fraud, based on deceit and corruption.

By way of example, one victim wrote the following: "We had our entire savings including the full equity of the mortgage on our house invested with Petters. This was 57 years of savings! I knew Tom Petters personally and he knew we had our entire life's savings invested with him...He needs to be held responsible for the thousands of lives he has destroyed...Tom Petters also stole millions from Christian ministries, pastors and good non-profits" (Petters, 2010).

Petters refused to acknowledge how his actions impacted others and far from voicing remorse, the defendant displayed pride in the reality he believed he created with real companies with real employees (Petters, 2010). The evidence at trial, however, demonstrated that the defendant's companies were not operated as self-sustaining businesses, but were sustained with millions and millions of dollars in fraud proceeds. Salaries, bonuses, operating expenses were paid from the fraud schemes. Yet the defendant argued that he should be rewarded for his contributions making no effort to address the staggering and unprecedented size and impact of his fraud on victims and the community. The fact that so many people trusted Tom Petters because he portrayed himself to be a committed follower of God, and a supporter of charitable organizations is disturbing. As the sentencing judge went on to state:

Tom Petters has hurt and personally devastated so many, many lives – elderly people, nursing home residents, young families, retired people like myself...How could Tom Petters so blatantly lie to so many, many people, and then when apprehended continue to lie and refuse to take responsibility for his actions by trying to play on the sympathy of the jury. Lying while facing people and under oath, even when some of his close associates confessed to their parts in the scandal is almost inconceivable...Does this man not have a conscience? Does he not care for anyone else but only his own selfish, greedy motives? With a crime of this magnitude of $3.5 billion, and the personal devastation he has caused to so many, many people's lives, I believe that Tom Petters needs to be punished to the full extent of the law, especially when he takes no responsibility for his actions. Like Bernard Madoff, Tom Petters obviously does not care for anyone other than himself and his own extremely selfish, self-centered, greedy motives. Our society, unfortunately, is becoming plagued with too many people like this, and like Bernard Madoff. Tom Petters needs to learn that there are severe consequences for his incomprehensible behavior (Petters, 2010).

Other Types of Affinity Fraud

Consider the facts of accountant Allan McFarlane, who turned to perpetrating a Ponzi scheme in Australia defrauding many of whom were retirees from millions of dollars including very well-educated investors such as a CEO who lost all of his retirement savings (Lewis, 2015). To garner support, McFarlane fooled many people in the industry, one of whom described him as a "wonderful person" because his investments had a better rate of return than other similar securities in the market (Lewis, 2015, p. 92). According to reports, the scheme came to light only after his death when his car drove into the path of a truck. McFarlane ingratiated himself to his investors by attending their family birthdays, giving them expensive gifts, advising them on their financial plans which in turn helped gain their confidence by paying reasonable returns over time. One creditor observed that he connected with people on a personal level and worked his way in to their lives so they trusted him without question (Lewis, 2012b). McFarlane would stand in church and "declare that he could be trusted as he himself understood suffering as Christ did" (Lewis, 2015, p. 92). Although considered charming, he had a dark side where he was described as controlling especially for vulnerable individuals like the elderly where he would try to take over their lives by isolating them from their families to make the exploitation easier and more undetectable (Lewis, 2015). When confronted about his investment strategies, McFarlane would become confrontational and antagonistic like Madoff did when questioned about his operations by SEC auditors. Even after McFarlane's death, his lawyers still sent threatening letters to those who questioned his operations. Often there was little or no paperwork because of the trust he engendered issuing statements showing interest paid and balance, but short on detail (Lewis, 2012a, p. 202).

Living in a mansion, McFarlane became a generous contributor to charities and was heavily involved in disability causes. His property was left open to the public who were encouraged to come in and visit his extensive gardens. This openness encouraged the view that there was nothing secretive or unethical going on which is reflective of the strategy of transparency giving the impression of openness leading to more trust with his victims. These types of offenders typically display their wealth such as lavish homes, automobiles, dream vacations and expensive clothing for all to see sending the message that if you want what I have, then you need to listen to my advice and give me your money for my services. To gain the trust of his victims, Guy de Chimay operated a $7 million Ponzi scheme claiming a link to a Belgian royal family fortune enticing those connected to royalty to lend him money (Carter, 2011). He guaranteed their investments, falsely claiming control over more than $100 million associated with royal families. Marian Golemo, 60, a Polish immigrant, was convicted on securities fraud charges for defrauding fellow members of the Polish community out of hundreds of thousands of dollars in the 1990s (AP, 2011). Golemo operated a local market and travel agency when he borrowed money by targeting the Polish community with promises of repaying the loans with interest of 10-13 percent. The loans went unpaid and as one victim stated, "He destroyed dreams and hopes" (AP, 2011). Ponzi schemer Kenneth Starr, on the other hand, affiliated with several Hollywood celebrities defrauding them of over $30 million (Golding & Fermino, 2011).

The Exploitation by Ponzi Schemer Bernard Madoff

> My father and I had our life savings invested with him…We now have nothing... I told my father (89) he could not die because I didn't have enough to bury him (Lewis, 2010b).

Bernard Madoff Victim

For over a period of 16 years, Bernard Madoff operated a multi-billion dollar Ponzi scheme until the 2008 financial crisis accelerated its exposure. A Ponzi scheme is a fraudulent investment operation where the operator, an individual or organization, pays returns to its previous investors from new capital paid to the Ponzi operators by new investors, rather than from profit earned by the operator from a genuine business entity. Operators of Ponzi schemes usually entice new investors by offering higher returns than other investments, in the form of short-term returns that are either abnormally high or unusually consistent coupled with low risk from a business that does not actually exist or from an idea that does not work. The offender(s) help themselves to the investors' money to support their lavish lifestyles. When economies are doing well, it is less likely that the scheme will be discovered because money is available to keep the scheme alive. In order to keep the fraud active, the promoter needs an ever-increasing inflow of new deposits. Earlier investors often serve as references so new investors have reason to believe that the promised returns are legitimate. Ponzi schemes occasionally, but not always, begin as legitimate businesses, until the business fails to achieve the returns expected. However a Ponzi scheme does not always have to offer high returns. The Ponzi schemes that may be more difficult to detect, and more apt to escape regulator suspicion, are the ones that offer modest, but consist returns giving the impression of a safe, legitimate investment.

Ponzi schemes fail for several reasons and the most relevant reason is there is no money from new investors to pay established investors. When a Ponzi scheme is not stopped by the regulators, it sooner or later falls apart because the promoter vanishes, taking all the remaining investment money or since the scheme requires a continual stream of new cash inflow to fund returns, once investments slow down, the scheme collapses as the promoter starts having problems paying the promised returns. Moreover, the problem also starts to reveal itself when there are downturns in the economy, then it is difficult to give investors their money back because the cash is not available to satisfy everyone's demand to withdraw their money. Although exact figures vary from source to source, Madoff defrauded thousands of investors in his scheme in the multiple billions of dollars. Where Charles Ponzi promised massive investment returns, Madoff's seductive appeal lay not so much in his purported massive returns as in his consistency of reasonable, but above average returns that were immune to market downturns. The consistent, reasonable-sounding profits gave his operation an air of respectability enabling him to swindle wealthy people who prided themselves on their financial conservatism and sophistication.

Yet, Madoff created a problem for himself that is typical of Ponzi schemers. If Madoff was giving client returns of ten percent for example, but actually making five percent of the capital he invested, he would inevitably face an unslayable monster. He would simply have to keep getting more and more investors to keep covering the money he owed earlier investors with the hope that big day will come where the market will be in his favor and he could regain legitimacy. As Madoff stated, "I never wanted to think of what I was doing as stealing…Somewhere in my head I allowed myself to believe that I was going to make things work out, as crazy as that seems now" (Lewis, 2015, p. 144). Yet "when I realized I wasn't going to be able to get out of it, I don't know what the hell I was waiting for. I just didn't have the courage to unwind it…when you're in that deep and you realize what the potential problem is—you can't deal with it, you can't face it" (Soltes, 2016, p. 299). Madoff could not bring himself to tell others that he failed stating, "I was too afraid" (Fishman, 2011). In addition to not being able to accept the loss of status that would come from having failed he stated:

> Although I may not have intended any harm, I did a great deal of harm. I believed when I started this problem, this crime, that it would be something I would be able to work my way out of, but that would be impossible. As hard as I tried, the deeper I dug myself into a hole. I made a terrible mistake, but it wasn't the kind of mistake that I had made time and time again, which is a trading mistake. In my business when you make a trading error, you're expected to make a trading error, it's accepted. My error was more serious, I made an error of judgement. I refused to accept the fact, could not accept the fact, that for once in my life I failed. I couldn't admit that failure (Van Slyke et al., 2016, p. 28).

Madoff initially targeted those who shared his Jewish faith, gaining the trust and acceptance of the Jewish community by developing and exploiting contacts in Jewish schools, universities, synagogues, charities, and social circles (Henriques, 2008a). Madoff was known to those in the Jewish community simply as "Uncle Bernie" using his fatherly-like personality to provide the appearance that he would protect Jewish interests. Yet, what began as a quiet, coveted investment opportunity for the lucky few in the Jewish community became, in its final burst of growth, a thoroughly global financial product with global clientele and global financial institutions backing Madoff. Madoff enjoyed an impeccable reputation amongst his clients because he was considered a star of Wall Street together with the implied trust wealthy persons, charities, universities, government officials and other investment managers bestowed upon him (Rezaee & Riley, 2010). Although Madoff was considered a leader in the securities field, referred to as "a true global investment visionary", he emphasized secrecy and exclusivity (Jackson, 2012). Investors were more afraid of not being invited to invest than they were of the risk of losing money and as a result of their attitude towards him, his activities were never well scrutinized (Rezaee & Riley, 2010). Indeed when Madoff's scheme collapsed, many investors neither knew him personally nor were members of the Jewish community, but based their decision to invest in his funds purely because they trusted his reputation without due diligence.

Madoff's Manipulation

There's plenty of ways you can make money in the business doing the right thing…you don't have to look to do the wrong thing (Soltes, 2016).

Bernard Madoff

Forever dependent on a growing supply of fresh victims, Ponzi schemers cannot be fussy about their clients and are typically in a hurry to snare them in. Here, Madoff made his most audacious innovation where instead of openly courting investors, he pretended to fend them off to maintain an air of exclusivity and "specialness". As a rule, his fund was closed to new investors, requiring special introductions to the club. However, Madoff fostered a subtle climate of fear among investors where he grew agitated when quizzed about his methods and forbade investors from discussing their conversations with him. When one client dared to do just that in an e-mail to other clients, Madoff threatened to banish the man from his fund. A tacit understanding arose that Madoff would not discuss financial matters in social settings, preventing confrontations with inquisitive investors or encounters that might surprise him into unwanted revelations. Most of all, Madoff protected himself by being elusive and as one banker stated, "You couldn't meet Madoff...He was like a pop star" (Chernow, 2009). The aura of exclusivity was false, of course given that he ended up with almost five thousand client accounts. Madoff emphasized his extreme reluctance to accept new money. One acquaintance stated, "Bernie would tell me, 'Let them start small, and if they're happy the first year or two, they can put in more" (Lewis, 2012).

Madoff gave others, who wanted to investment through him, the impression that he was a man overwhelmed by his own generosity, taking on new clients as a favor to friends increasing the feeling of specialness his clients would experience because Madoff made an exception for them (Chernow, 2009). To understand Madoff, one has to understand how well he understood the mind of the victim and their need to feel related to—in essence a type of emotional seduction required for this type of fraud to be sustainable. He understood their need to feel unique, thus he made them believe that the "Madoff Club" was exclusive which increased their sense of excitement, but also their gullibility. The excitement of uniqueness and enjoyment of being part of a safe and exclusive protected group were crucial. Emotional seduction comes into play for fraud to work especially given the fact that some frauds require the cooperation of the victim. It is not unnatural for people to be drawn into relationship with others who can support their mental, emotional, financial and at times physical health. The Madoff scandal illustrates how the power of a promising relationship can be even when the relationship is new; "the reality as well as the fantasy of the relationship is powerful in fraud" (Ramamoorti et al., 2013, p. 90).

Also, a very large Ponzi scheme needs an active network of agents who pull people into the scheme. Madoff implemented his elaborate Ponzi scheme by building a network of well-compensated associates who in turn recruited others to invest in the scheme even though they may not have known that it was a scheme they were investing in (Palmer, 2012). As time went on, some of the associates and clients became suspicious of Madoff's funds' integrity, largely because the funds were not well documented yet they generated curiously consistent investment returns when compared to other similar investments even when the stock market was not doing well. In addition, his associates withheld their suspicions to curb investor concerns because they feared that if they questioned Madoff or allowed client concerns to surface that they would be expelled from Madoff's circle and his network—in essence the feeling that they would be professionally blacklisted from this professional circle. Furthermore, Madoff manipulated regulators for decades and it makes complete sense that Mr. Madoff would have courted regulators, even if he ran the risk of exposing his own actions by doing so. According to criminal psychologist Dr. Reid Meloy:

> In a scheme like this, it's very important to keep those who could threaten you very close to you...You want to develop them as allies and shape how they go about their business and their attitudes toward you...He spent one-third of his time in Washington...He was very involved with regulators. I think they used him as a sounding board and he looked to them like a white knight...He was smart in understanding very early on that the more involved you were with regulators, you could shape regulation...If you're very close with regulators, they're not going be looking over your shoulders that much. Very smart. (Creswell & Thomas, 2009).

Madoff's Behavioral Profile

In prison Madoff doesn't have to hide his lack of conscience. In fact he's a hero for it.

Steve Fishman (2010)

Predatory offenders like Madoff have contradictions in their mind and too often they appear like anyone else—kinder, more charming, yet, there is no sign announcing their intentions (Samenow, 2009). They can be very devious in how they work their way into people's lives and while they can do very kind things for people, no matter what the harm they inflict, no matter what charitable organization they are cheating, they see themselves as good people while professing the noblest of ideals. Recall from chapter one how such offenders are capable of harboring a dual mindset of contradictory characteristics referred to as doublethink. Here, Madoff-type offenders are capable of shutting off whatever elements of conscience they have left while claiming to be family men, officers of companies and pillars of the community yet inflicting devastating injury on those whom they say they love and who love them. In addition, according to Dr. Meloy, he was not surprised by Madoff's behavioral traits stating that people like Madoff, "typically…don't fear getting caught…They tend to be very narcissistic with a strong sense of entitlement…tend to strongly believe that they're special. They believe 'I'm above the law,' and they believe they cannot be caught…But the Achilles' heel…is his sense of impunity. That is, eventually, what will bring him down" (Creswell & Thomas, 2009).

Ironically, Madoff's sense of impunity was revealed when he made some telling comments to securities professionals: "By and large, in today's regulatory environment, it's virtually impossible to violate rules…It's impossible for a violation to go undetected" (Pressler, 2008). Recall from chapter one the concept of super optimism where the offender thinks they are so good at their crimes that they will not get caught. In Madoff's statement above, people will get caught committing crimes, except his own crimes. Gregg McCrary, who spent years constructing criminal behavioral profiles, cautions that although he has never met Madoff, Madoff appears to share many of the destructive traits typically seen in a psychopath. According to McCrary, because Madoff fooled regulators for decades, that would have been a "heady, intoxicating" experience and would have fueled his sense of entitlement and grandiosity feeding into his sense of superiority (Creswell & Thomas, 2009). McCrary posits that it is reasonable to compare white-collar criminals such as Madoff to non-white-collar criminals who engage in predatory violence stating: "With serial killers, they have control over the life or death of people, they're playing God. That's the grandiosity coming through, the sense of being superior. Madoff is getting the same thing. He's playing financial god, ruining these people and taking their money" (Creswell & Thomas, 2009).

With respect to Madoff, some criminal profilers see similarities between him and serial killers like Ted Bundy. Like Bundy who lulled women to the death, Madoff used his sharp mind and friendly demeanor to create a persona that did not exist, lulling his victims into a false sense of financial trustworthiness and emotional security while harboring no remorse. By lulling people in from the Jewish community, from charities, from public institutions and from prominent and relatively sophisticated investor networks worldwide, Madoff wreaked havoc on many lives (Foley, 2008). That is why, McCrary says, so many who came into contact with Madoff have been left reeling and in confusion about his motives. Again we observe the violation of societal norms people expect from others they interact with even at an arms-length transaction of obligatory reciprocity. This is due to the fact that the investors had a legal contract with Madoff, but also the personal betrayal they felt given that many of them knew him and trusted him implicitly because of the bonds they believed they forged with him. Consider the statement of a friend of Madoff: "There is no way to. I can't make it add up. It doesn't make sense…I cannot take the Bernie I knew and turn him into the Bernie we're hearing about 24/7. It doesn't compute" (Creswell & Thomas, 2009). According to Rabbi Mark Borovitz, "whether it's latino or black or Jewish or Christian, everybody wants to trust their own…Bernard Madoff took our trust and raped it, he took advantage of every vulnerability because he knew our vulnerable spots" (Seal, 2009). Individual Jewish investors were hit the hardest because many invested everything they had with Madoff (Carozza, 2009).

Commenting on the Madoff's exploitation of the Jewish community, Harry Markopolos, the Certified Fraud Examiner and whistleblower exposing Madoff observed: "Nobody thinks one of their own is going to cheat them, not when they can cheat so many others" (Markopolos, 2010, p. 114). Although labeling is of little use especially to victims, understanding disordered personalities helps us better understand how events happen instead of speculating how a person could resort to such ways. Understanding disordered personalities helps us construct a template on how behaviors play themselves out for the worse. Thus, perhaps when we try to be objective about a person's behavior, we can at least see how their personalities served as a risk factor for the event to occur especially when there are aggravating circumstances that may trigger disordered traits to come alive. For example, although Madoff was a very intelligent person, he was capable of displaying a lack of remorse, a failure to take full responsibility, an inability to plan ahead in a thoughtful manner with integrity, the duping delight he probably experienced when the regulators did not detect his fraud, his exploitation of others because he could exploit them, and pathological deceitfulness. Plus, consider his narcissistic qualities of grandiosity enjoying the attention and accolades he received from being in the public eye, celebrated by investors, respected by his peers, coupled with his entitled mindset of living a lavish lifestyle despite the fact that the lavish lifestyle was bought by fraudulent means.

In the end, his personal limitations enabled him to continue his fraud without remorse or guilt about the impact of his behavior on others, thus it is not surprising why he continued the Ponzi scheme for as long as he did. Madoff's dispassionate demeanor even about the most egregious facts of his behavior has called into question whether he may be displaying psychopathic traits. At least anecdotally, it is not unreasonable to make such a suggestion. Remember that Madoff and those like him display their weaknesses in their attitudes. Even though they might be able to take advantage of another's goodwill because they see it as a weakness to exploit, at some point, one cannot hide all of their traits from public view especially when it was Madoff's interpersonal strategy to try to avoid people that would reveal his fraud. That being said, his narcissistic need for attention, whether good or bad attention, propels him to accept interviews so that he can try to persuade others that he is not as bad as everyone says he is. Yet, in the meantime, he will expose his true personality traits because he cannot contain them forever. At some point his true colors will be on display. Consider the insights of academician Eugene Soltes who interviewed Madoff over several years and how Madoff's reaction about the death of his second son was found to be disturbing.

In September 2014, a colleague e-mailed me news that Madoff's second son, Andrew, had just died of cancer. As I was beginning to read the article, my office phone rang. I picked it up and was surprised to hear Madoff on the line. He had heard the news of his second son on the radio and asked if I could read the obituary to him…I turned my attention to describing the news in the most compassionate way I could…when I reached the end, I was at a loss to know what to say…I asked him how he was doing. Madoff responded, "I'm fine, I'm fine." After a brief pause, he said that he had a question for me. I thought he might want me to send a copy of the obituary to him or deliver a message on his behalf to someone. It wasn't that. Instead, he asked me whether I'd had the chance to look at the LIBOR rates we discussed in a prior conversation. This particular phone call with Madoff stuck with me more than any other. Shortly after finding out his son had died, Madoff wanted to talk about interest rates. He didn't lose a beat in the ensuing conversation, continuing to carry on an entirely fluent discussion on the arcane determinants of yields. It didn't seem as though he wanted to switch topics because he was struggling to compose himself. And it didn't seem as though he was avoiding expressing emotion because the news was so overwhelming. In some way, it almost seemed as though I was more personally moved by the death of Andrew in those moments than his father (Soltes, 2016, p. 307).

Madoff's fraud emerged from challenges that are not uncommon in business facing financial issues, but rather than restricting his operations to those areas that were viable and changing strategies, Madoff forged ahead as if there would be no consequences to his decision. In "decision after decision, he acted myopically without regard for the longer-term ramifications of his choice…He managed to create extraordinary suffering for his investors, his friends—even his family—while experiencing little emotional turmoil himself" (Soltes, 2016, p. 308). In some respects this observation of Madoff reminds us of previous insights where psychopaths are prisoners of the present; they display a diminished ability to project into the future of how their actions might impact others and display a diminished ability to reflect upon the past on how their behaviors did impact others—to learn from their mistakes. Madoff seems to be that prisoner even if we never know whether he is truly clinically psychopathic. He is incapable of reflecting on the past with a genuine sense of empathy and remorse, but instead blaming others for their own misfortune. While he was actually committing fraud, he either blocked it out of his mind by engaging in compartmentalization of his life or was simply incapable of understanding how his fraud would impact so many people. For example, Madoff viewed the less wealthy investors who were ruined by him as people who were simply foolish to put all their eggs in one basket by giving him all their money or that it was not his fault because it was other fund managers outside of the Madoff firm who took the victims money and transferred it to him (Carozza, 2017). His personality reflects that rigidity previously where in their world there are only a number of ways to react to a situation; there is not that wide variation of options on how we might react to a situation if we do not harbor a disordered personality. Personality rigidity produces reaction rigidity. Consider in Madoff's own words, the lack of insight into his own personality.

When I look back, it wasn't as if I couldn't have said no…It wasn't like I was being blackmailed into doing something…I know the rules and regulations better than most people because I drafted most of them…The bad news is if I violated them, I can't say I didn't know, I was ignorant, I know what the rules are…I really have not been able to figure out how I let myself do this…is there a flaw in me (Soltes, 2016, p. 287-289)?

For many fraud offenders, they may never see the victims they hurt, thus the harm is not readily in their face to deal with. The difference in timing between the crime and harm committed helps to facilitate fraud because the harm is not immediate and in the case of some of these offenders, they receive praise from the people that would later become their victims. In the case of Madoff, it was not as if the victims were distant and faceless investors. He intimately knew some his victims and even after the schemes exposure and the devastation became evident, the harm he caused simply does not resonate with him. Like "every Ponzi schemer, he was able to face his victims every day because they didn't look like victims…[and]…until the money runs out, people love the Ponzi schemer, they are grateful to him. In turn, Madoff did not see any "victims"; he only saw beneficiaries, reinforced every day by every thankful customer who says "Bless you, Bernie" (Lewis, 2015, p. 144). Consider the callousness, the coldness, and lack of empathy with how Madoff treated a widow.

The widow eventually went to see Mr. Madoff. He put his arm around her, as she describes it, and in a kindly manner told her not to worry, the money is safe with me. And not only did the widow leave the money with him, she eventually deposited more funds with him, her 401(k), her pension funds. Now all the money is gone (Lewis, 2010a, p. 446).

Yet, Madoff's weakness resulted from his compromised character, antisocial and disordered personality traits, and the circumstances giving rise to the fraud which in the end, created a negative synergy when all three elements aligned with each other facilitating the decision to go forward with a crime. In fact this is what gets many law-abiding people in trouble; it is the convergence of these factors that increase the probability they will engage in antisocial endeavors. It also parallels what Dr. Samenow stated in the first chapter that our actions are not "out of character", our actions reflect a set of circumstances that aligned for a decision to be made to go forward with an act or not. We may claim to be virtuous, but in the end virtue is acceptable as long as our self-interest is not sacrificed for virtues-sake. However, Madoff, like Marc Dreier, Walter Pavlo and the numerous other fraud offenders previously mentioned, continue their frauds because they have a misplaced optimism and confidence that someday they will be able to climb out of the hole they dug for themselves and be legitimate as they once were—at least in their eyes. Ponzi schemes are not always a result of sudden inspirations by criminal masterminds, although they can be, but as the gradual culmination of small moral compromises made by individuals who are not as smart as they think they are (Chernow, 2009).

Madoff's Rationalizations and Worldview

F--- my victims…I carried them for twenty years, and now I'm doing 150 years

Bernard Madoff (Fishman, 2010).

While the fraud was going on, Madoff rationalized to himself that his actions were harmless stating, "I sort of rationalized that what I was doing was okay—you know, that it wasn't going to hurt anybody" (Soltes, 2016, p. 302). Interestingly, Madoff saw his own behavior as exemplifying the pervasiveness of misconduct in the financial industry, thus there was nothing unique about his deceitfulness because so many others were doing it reflecting the previous rationalization of social comparison in chapter one where "everybody is doing it". As evidence of how widespread misconduct is, Madoff pointed to a study showing that more than a third of people making more than half-million dollars annually witness wrong-doing at their workplace (Soltes, 2016). For Madoff, his behavior simply reflected the norms of Wall Street and those of his clients and in some respects this touches on the concept discussed in chapter one on a person's worldview. In this case, Madoff disclosed how he views what occurs in the business world as basically displaying an amoral pulse where if you can get away with illegality then people will do so which is reflected in his opinion stating:

> Find me an owner in the manufacturing field that didn't cheat on his inventory counts or his taxes and I will be willing to change my opinion…Find me an individual who has not written off personal expenses on his tax returns as business expenses. Find me a person that has not padded or filed false insurance claims. I acknowledge there are different degrees of these activities and I am not suggesting they are acceptable. My point is simply to state that I believe this is the reality of life, and those that don't accept this are either delusional or less than honest. The same people are crying and whining to me now, these same people at every level, I'd say 80 percent of my clients…were involved in cheating in one form or another method that they could have gone to jail for if caught. I have never met an investor who cared whether his profit was made by questionable happenstance as long as he was not going to get in trouble (Soltes, 2016, p. 302-303).

What is fascinating about Madoff downplaying the victimology is that he believes much of the money investors lost was money that he earned for them, thus it was never money that they put into his investments in the first place. However, he fails to recognize that many lost everything including the money they initially invested with him. Madoff simply "denies causing the immense damage often depicted by his victims and the media" (Soltes, 2016, p. 304). According to academician Eugene Soltes who spent more than five years corresponding with Madoff, in those years he "never expressed a genuine sense of remorse or contrition for his fraud" (Soltes, 2016, p. 304). Madoff lacks the ability to relate emotionally to the havoc he created and even when presented with the victims harmed remaining callous to their situation. In fact, Madoff actually takes comfort in seeing his investors as the irresponsible party stating:

> All I did was make rich people richer and I made some rich people poorer, but not poor. This whole charade that's been going on with clients claiming that I wiped them out, I ruined them...there's not one client that I had that was not already a wealthy person by anyone's standard…when I was generating all these profits, a lot of these clients were throwing caution to the wind. It doesn't mean that what I did was correct—I'm not using this as a defense. But I sit here and look at these people sitting there like poor souls saying 'he wiped me out, he cheated. Yeah, I cheated them. I betrayed their trust—there's no question about that. But these are all people that signed statements that said they were all worth at least $2 million. They all had income of at least $250,000 net. These are wealthy people. A lot of them, their mothers, fathers, and grandparents, lived off the profits for years and then just left the money in accounts—and now that disappeared. Quite frankly, those monies weren't their money. It was money that was earned by me. If it wasn't for me, if their parents didn't have accounts with me over the years, they never would have lived so well (Soltes, 2016, p. 305).

Madoff displays a coldness, a callousness in how he views his behaviors, his impact on others and how he reflects on what he created especially since he defends himself by stating that he "earned" these people money when in fact nothing he did had any semblance of managing a bona fide business that earned legitimate profits. Somehow the investors should accept some of the responsibility for their naiveté for investing in something they did not fully understand. This view also parallels the legal concept of caveat emptor which is what is being reflected by Madoff. Caveat emptor is a Latin term used in legal circles meaning "buyer beware". Thus if you buy a defective product, it is your fault for not having it inspected before you buy it. The fact that the seller makes certain representations of the good quality of the product is not relevant if we are to interpret Madoff's view that everyone is willing to engage in unethical/illegal acts if it suits them and they believe they can get away with it. Thus, if someone that invested with Madoff was not willing to do their due diligence to determine the integrity of his securities, then they bear the risk of any loss incurred from his illegitimate investments.

Furthermore, Madoff seemed to not understand the impact on his own family and according academician Eugene Soltes, the manner in which he spoke of his son spoke volumes of his callousness. For example, Madoff stated that in hindsight he would have rather taken the case to trial, but he did not want to expose his family to the pressure stating in an emotionless, matter-of-fact manner, "The reality of it is my son couldn't stand up amongst the pressure anyhow, so he took his life" (Soltes, 2016, p. 306). It is not unreasonable to extrapolate that if this is his reaction to his son's death, then we could not expect him to display any more empathy to those investors he does not even know, except by their names on financial statements.

Madoff's Impression Management Strategy

It was more important to Bernie to keep up the façade, the image at all costs, no matter what the moral implications; it was about Bernie and who Bernie had to be to the world (Lewis, 2011b).

Sheryl Weinstein

As word spread that Madoff made money for investors, he acquired a social glow at the country clubs where he recruited his victims, solidified by his mansion in the Hamptons, his villa on the French Riviera, and yachts moored in various places. Dressed in charcoal-gray suits and fond of expensive watches, he took on the protective cloak of his status—a specialty of Ponzi schemers (Chernow, 2009). Madoff surrounded himself in establishment circles by being a trustee of Hofstra University, a nonexecutive chairman of the NASDAQ stock exchange, and a member of a government advisory panel on securities regulation such as the SEC. Like Charles Ponzi, he posed as a champion of small investors plus ingratiating himself with government regulators. His mystique led prominent personalities—including Steven Spielberg, Mortimer Zuckerman, Senator Frank Lautenberg, Elie Wiesel, Sandy Koufax, and Kevin Bacon—to invest with Madoff directly or through charities they established (Chernow, 2009). One individual who knew him, attorney Jerry Reisman, stated, "He moved in some of the best social circles in New York. He worked the best country clubs. He was utterly charming. He was a master at meeting people and creating this aura…People looked at him as a superhero" (Telegraph, 2008).

According to criminal psychologist Dr. Reid Meloy referencing Madoff, "People like him become sort of like chameleons. They are very good at impression management. They manage the impression you receive of them. They know what people want, and they give it to them" (Creswell & Thomas, 2009). Impression management is the social process, sometimes conscious and sometimes unconscious, by which individuals attempt to influence how others see and react to them by regulating and controlling information others receive of them (Lewis, 2011b). It is precisely because it is a natural part of social life that people do not think too much of the art of impression management in the course of daily social life (Lewis, 2011b). Specific impression management goals include trying to get others to believe that they have a pleasant, helpful disposition or perhaps giving the impression of intimidation which is a form of power orientation (Lewis, 2011b). However, when the impression of the person is tainted, it can evoke disappointment in people. One Madoff observer stated, "He was a hero to us. The head of NASDAQ. We were proud of everything he had accomplished…Now, the hero has vanished" (Creswell & Thomas, 2009). A former employee stated, "He appeared to believe in family, loyalty and honesty…Never in your wildest imagination would you think he was a fraudster" (Creswell & Thomas, 2009).

To manage their impression of being helpful and influential people, Madoff and his wife gave $238,200 to federal candidates, parties, and political committees between 1991 and 2008, almost ninety percent of it going to Democrats. Moreover, between 1999 and 2008, his firm spent between $400,000 and $590,000 for Washington lobbyists (Lewis, 2011b). Furthermore, perpetrators often incorporate some element of their charitable giving from the return on their investments to enhance their credibility by telling investors that a portion of their investment will enable them to give back to their community (Perri & Brody, 2011a). In the 1990s Madoff's wealth and reputation as a Wall Street star grew among market insiders coupled with being viewed as a generous philanthropist (Henriques, 2008b). For example, Madoff burnished his image by giving to the Center for Jewish History, Hillel Foundation for Jewish Campus Life, Jewish Federation of Palm Beach Type County, the American Liver Foundation, Lymphoma Research Foundation, Brandeis University, Pace University, Hofstra University and Queens College to name a few. In addition, Madoff exemplified the disciplined performer by fooling many people for a very long time by mastering the skills and goals of impression management which was evidenced by how he managed his Ponzi scheme so well for so long (Lewis, 2011b). The fact remains, Madoff-type offenders "must employ elaborate and meticulous personal fronts and often engineer meticulous social setting…The con man must carefully forestall the immediate impression that he might be what in fact he is" (Lewis, 2011b). Madoff was a master at friendliness and intimidation when required, a

> [D]isciplined performer, someone who remembers his part and does not commit unmeant gestures or faux pas in performing it. He is someone with discretion; he does not give the show away by involuntarily disclosing its secrets. He is someone with 'presence of mind' who can cover up on the spur of the moment for inappropriate behavior…And if a disruption of the performance cannot be avoided or concealed, the disciplined performer will be prepared to offer a plausible reason for discounting the disruptive event, a joking manner to remove its importance, or deep apology and self-abasement to reinstate those held responsible for it. The disciplined performer is also someone with 'self-control.' He can suppress his emotional response to his private problems (Lewis, 2011b).

Bernard Madoff's Escape from Regulatory Detection

On December 10, 2008, Bernard Madoff contacted the Securities and Exchange Commission (SEC) admitting that he victimized his clients in the largest Ponzi scheme in U.S. history only exceptional in terms of its size and longevity, but not in scheme complexity. According to Madoff, he began the scheme in the early 1990s due to suffering investment losses, and rather than admitting to his clients that they sustained losses which would impact his reputation, he generated false returns by engaging in Ponzi financing (Lewis, 2012). Furthermore, Irving Picard, the bankruptcy trustee overseeing Madoff's seized assets, found no evidence that any legitimate securities trading occurred for investors in the final thirteen years of the scheme's operation prior to Madoff's disclosure in 2008 (Lewis, 2012). Madoff stated that his intention was to resume legitimate investment activity once he was able to recover from investment losses, but it became too difficult to reconcile client accounts especially when the stock market collapsed in 2008 and investors wanted to withdraw their money (Lewis, 2012).

During this time, Madoff operated his Ponzi scheme in plain view of the Securities and Exchange Commission (SEC) and the SEC even investigated Madoff several times based on tips from people in the industry. On many occasions, Madoff gave SEC investigators conflicting and ridiculous explanations for his suspicious activity, but yet he escaped detection. In the words of Professor Robert Rhee, "the SEC and its lawyers were presented the proverbial "videotape" of the crime, and yet they were unable to comprehend what had occurred because they lacked the skills, knowledge, and education" (Rhee, 2009, p. 377). A consequence of the SEC's oversight is that numerous investors stated Madoff reinforced his credibility when he told them that he had been investigated on multiple occasions, but was ultimately cleared by the SEC. Investors relied on the SEC's conclusions of Madoff as evidence that his operation was legitimate which had the effect of encouraging additional individuals and entities to invest with him (OIG, 2009). A reasonable question often raised is how can a scheme of this magnitude occur, and in rather plain sight, when our regulatory agencies are in place to protect the public? Consider the testimonial of one of Madoff's victims referencing the SEC:

> I sit before you a broken man. Throughout my life I always believed the American system of capitalism was the best regulator in the world…But the Madoff scandal and the SEC's inability to detect it, despite repeated written and other warnings, have taught me this is not the case (Lewis, 2010a, p. 447).

The focus of this section is not to single out Ponzi schemes as somehow more important to comment on than other fraud schemes. However, the scholarly literature on investment scams is rife with examples of smaller and less well-known albeit, at least for the victims, equally destructive scams. In the years 2008 and 2009 alone, 190 Ponzi schemes collapsed in the United States alone, the majority of these costs fall on those who invested their money in the scheme (Reurink, 2016). Consider victims of Ponzi schemes also include financial institutions that have, perhaps unintentionally, facilitated the scheme by directing clients to these scheme's fraudulent investments. These schemes are used to illustrate how even simple fraud apparatuses can evade a large organization like the SEC when policies and organizational cultures may not set the proper antifraud tone and devote the necessary resources to train their staff to recognize fraud red-flags that pertain to the industries they are obligated to regulate. However, let us first understand the SEC's role. Currently the SEC regulates public companies and public offerings of securities under the Securities Act of 1933 and the Securities Exchange Act of 1934.

The 1933 Act regulates the disclosure of information in registration statements for new public offerings of securities, sometimes commonly referred to as initial public offerings (IPOs). Companies must file registration statements and prospectuses that contain financial statements audited by a CPA. In terms of the 1934 Act, this law regulates the ongoing reporting by companies whose securities are listed and traded on stock exchanges. This law requires the filing of quarterly 10-Q and annual 10-K reports and periodic filings of other types of reports when there are significant events that take place affecting the organization. The SEC regulates other participants in the financial industry, including securities exchanges, brokers and dealers, investment advisers, and mutual funds. Generally speaking, the SEC has several objectives. One of them is to prevent and deter violations of federal securities law alerting investors to possible wrongdoing, sanctioning wrongdoers, and returning funds to harmed investors. In addition, the SEC attempts to promote healthy capital markets through an effective and flexible regulatory environment that facilitates innovation, competition, and capital formation and improve investor confidence.

Furthermore, they encourage informed investment decision making by ensuring that investors receive complete, accurate, and transparent financial information and by implementing a variety of investor education initiatives. Also, the SEC attempts to maximize its resources through improvements in organizational internal controls effectiveness and sound investments in human capital and new technologies (Rezaee & Riley, 2010). Although examining a particular weakness within the SEC may not be the ultimate cause of some of their failures, cumulatively oversights and weaknesses addressed in the different sections of this chapter creates a negative synergy that increases the probability that an oversight will occur diminishing the ability to uphold its mission as the public watchdog. Furthermore, the Madoff case is particularly instructive because it amplified in a very public way the weaknesses of the SEC. The SEC's failures are symptomatic of a variety of interrelated weaknesses such as, 1) a culture that discourages examining frauds that appear complex when they in fact may not be complex, 2) attorneys who do not have securities industry knowledge to understand how the frauds they are charged to prevent and detect actually occur, and 3) the impression that the SEC's staff appears to be "captive" to private organizations on Wall Street because the people they intend to regulate are viewed as their future employers once they leave public service employment. Consequently, the requirement of regulatory independence, both in fact and appearance, seems compromised.

This section examines issues confronting the SEC involving unwritten policies that may encourage distorted incentivizing as to how it measures regulatory success by discouraging risk-taking to look into more complex fraud schemes. Moreover, we discuss whether former SEC staff now in private practice representing clients under investigation by the SEC appear to exert undue influence over current SEC staff when resolving disputes pertaining to securities law violations. Lastly, we observe the inadequate whistleblower protection apparatus for those who want to alert the SEC as to securities fraud that to date has not adequately been streamlined in terms of responding to tips. It is imperative the SEC not just acknowledge, but address some of the issues outlined below or else it stands to be viewed as incompetent, ineffective, and captive to special interests that work against the interests of honest investors.

Madoff: In the Beginning

Madoff founded his firm in 1960, but there is no agreement when he commenced his fraudulent activity. In court, Madoff said that the scheme began in the early 1990s, but the list of charges against him state that the fraud began at least by the 1980s (Sarna, 2010). Since the early 1990s, Madoff represented to his clients that he was investing their money in shares of common stock, options, and other securities of large, well-known corporations. Those representations were false, at least in relation to the Ponzi scheme that we are aware of, because Madoff never legitimately invested his victims' funds and instead paid false returns directly out of their contributions. To help conceal the fact that he was not actually trading, Madoff claimed he was making purchases in overseas markets and created account statements with falsified transactions and positions. Madoff was smart enough to address investors' fears by showing them a strategy that if the stock market ever crashed they would be protected from losses (Carozza, 2009). As an example, he created the illusion of an investment strategy that never hit home runs but instead earned a steady 1 percent a month; smart enough to show modest returns that did not seem overly high so as to avoid regulatory and investor suspicion (Goldstein, 2010).

Madoff admitted that he took client funds and instead of investing it in stocks and shares as the clients expected, deposited the money into a Chase Manhattan bank account. When clients wanted their money back Madoff stated, "I used the money in the Chase Manhattan bank account that belonged to them or other clients to pay the requested funds" (McCool & Graybow, 2009). Madoff was not alone in perpetrating the Ponzi scheme. Frank DiPascali, Madoff's confidant and financial officer fabricated the paperwork needed to maintain the appearance of trading, however they avoided talking about the scheme given that there was not anything they could do about stopping the perpetuation of the Ponzi scheme because they were in so deep (Soltes, 2016). Madoff originally recruited members of the Jewish community to invest with him, but over time his scheme drew funds in from additional multiple sources until the scheme grew into a thoroughly global financial product. Moreover, Madoff had to extend his client base beyond the Jewish community otherwise his scheme would have collapsed earlier since "Ponzi schemes usually have to attract new investments at an exponentially growing rate to sustain payments to existing investors" (Carvajal, 2009, p. 4).

For Madoff these additional sources included institutions with cash reserves, charities, and private individual investors. Indeed, when Madoff's scheme collapsed, many investors neither knew him personally nor were members of the Jewish community, but had based their decision to invest in his funds purely, without exercising due diligence, because they trusted his reputation. The attractive steady and consistent returns, false though they were, generated their own investment advertisement for potential investment (Fishman, 2011). For example, one Madoff fund averaged a 10.5 per cent annual return in the period 1991-2008 and, though the S&P 500 stock index fell by 38 per cent in 2008, the fund reported that it was up 5.6 per cent in the period January to November, 2008 (Appelbaum et al., 2008). In addition, the fees typically charged to investors like Madoff's included a management fee of one or two percent of the assets managed and for hedge funds, an incentive payment based on positive returns—at times as much as twenty percent (Schilit & Perler, 2010).

Interestingly, Madoff charged investors no such fees, but instead was content in receiving a few cents per share trading securities for clients (Schilit & Perler, 2010). The consistent returns and no fees that are normal in the industry should have alerted investors and the SEC that his business model raised red-flags that should not have been ignored. Yet, new money started pouring in as his scheme started to grow, but this was a different sort of money. It was the kind of money that came from bankers who would not have given Madoff the time of day earlier in his career. So Madoff took the money, placing it in treasuries, for example, earning perhaps 2 percent a year, while generating statements that maintained they were earning at times above 10 percent which is a very good rate of return in a slow market. Madoff expanded on the role of banks in facilitating his schemes stating:

> The chairman of Banco Santander came down to see me, the chairman of Credit Suisse came down, chairman of UBS came down; I had all of these major banks…entertaining me... It is a head trip. Those people sitting there, telling you, 'You can do this.' It feeds your ego. All of a sudden, these banks which wouldn't give you the time of day, they're willing to give you a billion dollars…It wasn't like I needed

the money. It was just that I thought it was a temporary thing, and all of a sudden, everybody is throwing billions of dollars at you (Fishman, 2011).

Potential Causes of the Regulatory Oversights

The SEC received more than ample information in the form of detailed and substantive complaints over the years to warrant a thorough and comprehensive investigation of Bernard Madoff for operating a Ponzi scheme; despite five investigation being conducted, a thorough and competent investigation was never performed (OIG, 2009). Between June 1992 and December 2008 when Madoff confessed, the SEC received six substantive complaints concerning Madoff's securities operations that should have led to questions about whether Madoff was actually engaged in securities trading (OIG, 2009). In addition, some of the most significant Ponzi scheme red-flags that surfaced, but were ignored included anonymous tips and insights by Harry Markopolos who approached the SEC on several occasions outlining how Madoff could not produce the rates of return he delivered to his investors without operating a Ponzi scheme. Reviewing the Markopolos disclosures illustrates what happens when regulators do not understand the industry they are purported to regulate and do not know how to synthesize information from whistleblowers, such as Markopolos, so that they can efficiently follow up on such tips. We examine specific reasons that lead to oversight in the Madoff case, but also with other lesser well-known cases that reveal deficiencies within the SEC. One of the biggest weaknesses we observe is the fact that SEC staff, in this case the attorneys whose job it is to regulate the securities market, may not have the necessary fraud scheme knowledge to recognize red-flags. The Madoff scandal provides the best documented case study of how the SEC operated mostly by lawyers, failed to understand the market they regulate and the non-legal business and financial complexities surrounding their work.

June, 1992

The first SEC investigation was conducted in 1992 after they received information leading it to suspect that Madoff associates were perpetrating a Ponzi scheme (OIG, 2009). Tips to the SEC reported that two Florida accountants named Avellino and Bienes were selling unregistered securities with written guarantees of being one hundred percent safe, with zero risk, coupled with guaranteed returns ranging from 13.5 percent to 20 percent. Not everyone could invest with Avellino and Bienes, as this was a "special" and exclusive club, with some special investors getting higher returns than others. Selling these securities for more than a decade, they collected $440 million from investors, but when the SEC investigated Avellino and Bienes seeking to recover investors' funds, they were told that all of the money had been invested with Madoff. As the SEC began investigating the matter, they learned that Madoff had complete control over all of Avellino and Bienes's customer funds and made all investment decisions for them. According to Avellino, Madoff achieved these consistent returns for them for numerous years without a single loss. The SEC suspected Avellino and Bienes were operating a Ponzi scheme and took action to ensure that all of Avellino and Bienes's investors were refunded their investments.

However, the SEC never considered the possibility Madoff could have taken the money used to pay back Avellino and Bienes's customers from other clients as part of a larger Ponzi scheme. Yet he created false records of accounts and a paper trail of trading records for seven of Avellino and Bienes accounts showing profitable securities trades prior to 1992 (Lewis, 2015). When SEC officials contacted Madoff and asked for help in returning the money due to a court order, he promptly turned over $440 million (Lewis, 2015). The SEC assembled an inexperienced examination team that conducted a brief and very limited examination of Madoff, making no effort to trace where the money that was used to repay Avellino and Bienes's investors came from. Although the SEC's lead examiner indicated the investment vehicle offered by Avellino and Bienes was suspicious, no effort was made to look at the questionable investment strategy and guaranteed returns. Consider it was Madoff who would have had to guarantee such returns if Avellino and Bienes were just the salespersons and not the ones actually doing the investing. The SEC's lead examiner said Madoff's reputation as a broker-dealer may have influenced the inexperienced team not to inquire into Madoff's operations and additional former SEC staff stated:

139

[W]hen Madoff was approached about liquidating the investments and returning the funds…he was able indeed to liquidate the investments and get the cash available within a very short period of time…which would suggest that the money was where we would expect it to be. [Another] former New York Enforcement Staff Attorney stated she did not recall any discussions at all that Madoff may have been running a Ponzi scheme. She was not aware of any analysis undertaken to determine how Madoff was able to achieve the returns he was promising for Avellino and Bienes' clients, although she acknowledged remembering that Avellino and Bienes had maintained that they never had a loss with their investment…There was no focus on Madoff in this investigation at all (OIG, 2009, p. 52).

In examining Madoff, the SEC did not seek verification of securities trades allegedly made by Madoff from the Depository Trust Company (DTC), an independent third-party that maintains securities trade records, but sought copies of such records from Madoff himself. Specifically, the DTC provides safekeeping through electronic recordkeeping of securities balances. It also acts like a clearinghouse to process and settle trades in corporate and municipal securities. The DTC holds trillions of dollars worth of securities in custody, including corporate stocks and bonds, municipal bonds, and money market instruments. The DTC is registered with the SEC and is a member of the Federal Reserve System and is owned by many companies in the financial industry, with the New York State Stock Exchange being one of its largest shareholders. Securities brokers, dealers, institutional investors, depository institutions, and banks use the DTC, but individual investors do not interact with it. Had the SEC sought records from DTC, there is an excellent chance that they would have uncovered Madoff's Ponzi scheme in 1992, 16 years before Madoff confessed (OIG, 2009). After the investigation, a *Wall Street Journal* article reassures investors that Madoff had nothing to do with the Avellino and Bienes issue and as a result much of the $400 million went back to Madoff as investors invested directly with him (Lewis, 2015).

May, 2001

Some ask why does Wall Street ignore signs of fraud when there are those who expose it, albeit partially, but enough to raise the curiosity of those it impacts and those charged with revealing fraud such as the SEC? Michael Ocrant, for example, a financial journalist who authored in May 2001 an article entitled, "*Madoff Tops Charts: Skeptics Ask How*", stated that he spoke to a former senior executive at one of the securities exchanges, who, in referring to Madoff told him, "everyone knows this isn't real", and "everybody knows he can't possibly be producing these kinds of returns" (OIG, 2009, p. 412). Even Madoff criticized other members of the financial markets who claimed they did not see any red flags with his operation pointing to their "willful blindness" and their failure to examine discrepancies between his regulatory filings and other information available to them stating, "They had to know…but the attitude was sort of, if you're doing something wrong, we don't want to know" (Henriques, 2011). When Madoff whistleblower Harry Markopolos was asked whether there was a culture of not exposing frauds on Wall Street, Markopolos stated "in Wall Street there is a code of silence" when it comes to how people make money (Pressler, 2009). Yet, there were industry professionals who suspected for many years that Madoff engaged in fraud with some on Wall Street remaining skeptical about how Madoff achieved such stunning double-digit rates of return on his investments (Rhee, 2009).

Two 2001 finance journal articles, one from *Barron's* and one from *MARHedge* raised significant questions about Madoff's unusually consistent returns that should have readily triggered some interest by the SEC to investigate a potential Ponzi scheme, but did not. The *Barron's* article, written by Erin Arvedlund entitled "*Don't Ask, Don't Tell: Bernie Madoff is so secretive, he even asks his investors to keep mum*", discussed how Madoff's operation was among the three largest hedge funds, and has "produced compound average annual returns of 15% for more than a decade" while the largest fund "never had a down year" (OIG, 2009, p. 28). The *Barron's* article further questioned whether Madoff's trading strategy could have achieved those remarkably consistent returns noting his "astonishing ability to time the market and move to cash in the underlying securities before market conditions turn negative and the related ability to buy and sell the underlying stocks without noticeably affecting the market" (OIG, 2009, p. 28). This article also described that "experts ask why no one has been able to duplicate similar returns using [Madoff's] strategy" (OIG, 2009, p. 28). The New York branch of the SEC, referred to as the Northeast Regional Office (NERO), was aware of the Barron's article when it was published in May 2001, but there is no evidence that it was reviewed. The second article in *MARHedge*, written by Michael Orcant that caters to hedge fund industry, disclosed the scale of Madoff's business, at the time to about $6 billion (Lewis, 2015). Madoff met with Orcant who question him about why no one else was able to duplicate similar returns using his investment strategy. No sufficient answer was given.

May, 2003

In May 2003, the SEC received a complaint from a respected hedge fund manager identifying numerous concerns about Madoff's strategy and purported returns. He questioned whether Madoff was actually trading securities in the volume noting that Madoff's strategy and purported returns were not duplicable by anyone else coupled with the fact that Madoff's strategy had no correlation to the overall equity markets in over 10 years. According to an SEC manager, the hedge fund manager's complaint laid out issues that were indicative of a Ponzi scheme. Yet when the SEC called Madoff to ask about his hedge funds, Madoff tells them that he does not operate a hedge fund, but just trades for them (Lewis, 2015).

April, 2005

Another complaint was part of a series of internal e-mails of another investor that the SEC discovered in April, 2005. The e-mails described red flags an investor's employees identified while performing due diligence on their own Madoff investment using publicly available information. The red flags identified included Madoff's incredible and highly unusual volume for equity trades, his misrepresentation of his securities trading and his unusually consistent, non-volatile returns over several years. One of the internal e-mails provided a step-by-step analysis of why Madoff must be misrepresenting his securities trading especially for the volume that Madoff was claiming to have been trading in. It was inconceivable that there would be counterparties to such a trade volume meaning buyers and/or sellers on the other side of the transaction Madoff claimed he was engaged in. The SEC examiners who initially discovered the emails viewed them as indicating "some suspicion as to whether Madoff is trading at all" (OIG, 2009, p. 22). Two SEC examiners spend several weeks examining Madoff's records, but they were only allowed to talk to Madoff. The SEC apparently was looking for front-running which is inserting one's own trade ahead of their client's order (Lewis, 2015). When the examiners could not prove front-running, the case closed in June, 2005. There is no evidence they were investigating for a potential Ponzi scheme such as verifying Madoff's disclosure of the counterparties to his sales transactions which as an investigation exercise is actually not complicated. Discovering that Madoff did not have counterparties that he said he had would have quickly unraveled his Ponzi scheme. Yet this non-complicated fraud investigation act was passed over and years went by where Madoff was never caught.

October, 2005

The SEC received a complaint in October, 2005 from an anonymous informant stating, "I know that the Madoff company is very secretive about their operations and they refuse to disclose anything. If my suspicions are true, then they are running a highly sophisticated scheme on a massive scale. And they have been doing it for a long time...After a short period of time, I decided to withdraw all my money (over $5 million)" (OIG, 2009, p. 37). There is no evidence that this tip was properly investigated.

December, 2006

Moreover, in December, 2006, another complaint was sent to the SEC by a "concerned citizen" advising the SEC to look into Madoff and his firm as follows: "Your attention is directed to a scandal of major proportion which was executed by the investment firm Bernard L. Madoff...Assets well in excess of $10 billion owned by the late investor, an ultra-wealthy long time client of the Madoff firm have been "co-mingled" with funds controlled by the Madoff company with gains thereon retained by Madoff" (OIG, 2009, p. 264). Instead of pursuing such leads that together with other evidence collected would have assisted the SEC into building a case against Madoff, the SEC rejected offers of additional evidence from the complainant.

The Multiple Disclosures by Harry Markopolos

May, 2000

Beginning in May, 2000, Harry Markopolos provided the SEC's Boston District Office (BDO) with an eight-page complaint questioning the legitimacy of Madoff's reported returns and encouraged BDO to investigate Madoff. The complaint stated the following two explanations for Madoff's unusually consistent returns: 1) that "the returns are real, but they are coming from some process other than the one being advertised, in which case an investigation is in order, or 2) the entire fund is nothing more than a Ponzi Scheme" (OIG, 2009, p. 61). Markopolos's complaint stated that Madoff's returns were unachievable using the securities trading strategy he claimed to employ, noting Madoff's "perfect market-timing ability" (OIG, 2009, p. 239). Markopolos also referenced the fact that Madoff did not allow outside performance audits to understand how he achieved such returns. According to Markopolos, when he first brought his concerns to the SEC in 2000, Grant Ward, the agency's New England regional director of enforcement, was woefully unprepared to handle the assignment stating, "As I explained this massive fraud to Ward, it very quickly became clear he didn't understand a single word I said after hello… if blank looks were dollar bills, I would have walked out of that room a rich man. He was coldly polite, but he didn't ask a single probing question. I never knew if that represented a lack of interest, a lack of comprehension or simply a desire to go to lunch" (Markopolos, 2010, p. 62).

March, 2001

In March, 2001, Markopolos prepares an updated report for the BDO and the report was sent to the New York Regional Office referred to as the Northeast Regional Enforcement Office (NERO) (Lewis, 2015). In April, 2001, after a one-day review of the submission, NERO decided to not investigate Madoff. This decision was not revisited despite the previously mentioned *MARHedge* and *Barron's* published articles in May 2001, raising some of the same questions regarding Madoff's claimed returns as Markopolos's March, 2001 submission to BDO and NERO. Markopolos was astounded when the SEC did not pursue the 2001 submission after these articles were published further stating, "[O]nce those articles hit in May, my team was convinced that Bernie Madoff would be shut down within days, that an SEC investigation team would be in there and shut him down" (OIG, 2009, p. 235).

October, 2005

In October, 2005, Markopolos submits his third, 19 page version of his complaint to BDO entitled "*The World's Largest Hedge Fund is a Fraud*", detailing approximately over two dozen red flags indicating that Madoff was "highly likely" operating a Ponzi scheme (OIG, 2009). The submission discussed an alternative possibility, that Madoff was front-running, but characterized this scenario as "unlikely." Some of the red flags indicating the presence of a fraud scheme was the fact that companies who invested with Madoff were not allowed to use his name in the investment opportunity written advertisements or that Madoff was the actual investment manager of the securities they were selling. The red flags identified by Markopolos fell into one of three categories, 1) Madoff's obsessive secrecy, 2) the impossibility of Madoff's returns, particularly the consistency of those returns, and 3) the unrealistic volume of options Madoff was supposedly trading to support his trading strategy (OIG, 2009, p. 35). The BDO took his complaint seriously, but believed it made more sense for NERO to conduct the investigation because Madoff was in New York and NERO had already conducted an examination of Madoff in the past. Moreover, Madoff did not allow independent outside performance audits to verify his incredible returns he claimed to be generating for his clients.

Markopolos also disclosed how securities professionals believed that Madoff's operation is an outright fraud and cannot possibly "achieve 12% average annual returns with only 7 down months during a 14½ year time

142

period" (OIG, 2009, p. 238). On January 24, 2006, NERO opened an investigation in response to Markopolos's memo, however, NERO staff investigating Madoff stated they did not believe Markopolos outlined sufficient facts thus lacking value to take him seriously "because he did not have firsthand knowledge of the fraud he was alleging" (OIG, 2009, p. 354). Also, the NERO enforcement staff, unlike the BDO, failed to appreciate the significance of the evidence in the 2005 Markopolos complaint and almost immediately expressed skepticism and disbelief about the information contained in the complaint claiming that Markopolos was not an insider or an investor, and thus, discounted his evidence (Perri & Brody, 2011b). One staff member expressed skepticism of the 2005 submission because she did not consider Markopolos a whistleblower further stating:

> I remember thinking that after I spoke to him that he wasn't technically a whistleblower because it wasn't inside information so that was, I think, a distinction that I'm sure I made, because I think – I think that, you know, when you hear "whistleblower" or "informant," there's an assumption that it's somebody who's inside an operation and has – and has nonpublic information to give you. And I remember realizing that he was not (OIG, 2009, p. 248).

In addition, Markopolos met with Meaghan Cheung, a NERO branch chief, who showed no interest in what he was saying coupled with lacking the basic financial and mathematical knowledge to understand the problem even though the BDO vouched for Markopolos's credibility (Langevoort, 2009). Instead, NERO staff questioned Markopolos's motives, indicating concerns that "he was a competitor of Madoffs" who "was looking for a bounty", meaning collecting a reward for exposing Madoff (OIG, 2009, p. 249). She further stated, "If the first thing I hear from someone is what's in it for me, then it raises my antenna a little bit" (OIG, 2009, p. 249). The staff member further stated in reference to Markopolos:

> I meant that I was concerned that – that he might have an agenda, that--that identifying himself as a fraud analyst, although he also appeared to have worked at least one investment advisory firm and one investment firm, I was concerned what his personal motivations might be, and I thought that was something – that was just a reaction that I had at the time (OIG, 2009, p. 250). The author's motives are to make money by uncovering the alleged fraud. I think he is on a fishing expedition and doesn't have the detailed understanding of Madoff's operations that we do which refutes most of his allegations (OIG, 2009, p. 256).

However, Markopolos himself noted in the 2005 submission that he would not be eligible for a money reward in the event the SEC discovered Madoff was operating a Ponzi scheme, the scenario Markopolos described as "highly likely" (OIG, 2009, p. 249). Another factor in NERO's skepticism of Markopolos' allegation that Madoff was operating a Ponzi scheme was their view that Madoff did not fit the profile of a fraud offender. As one NERO staff member stated, "It's certainly true that Madoff didn't fit the profile of a Ponzi schemer" (OIG, 2009, p. 261). The NERO branch chief believed that the Madoff investigation revealed there was "an inherent bias towards [the] sort of people who are seen as reputable members of society" (OIG, 2009, p. 262). We can observe the implicit credibility that the Madoff's of the world receive due to the bias that people harbor about people who are similar to themselves in terms of perceived economic status and position within society that Sutherland warned us about. Again, we can observe the projection bias that is taking place due to the belief that the Madoff's of the world could not be antisocial because they harbor presumably the same value system as the SEC regulators harbor.

June, 2007

In June, 2007, Markopolos once again notified the SEC by e-mail with attached documents proving that Madoff's scheme was becoming more brazen stating that "When Madoff finally blows up, it's going to be spectacular, and lead to massive selling by hedge funds…as they face investor redemptions" (OIG, 2009, p. 41) On November 21, 2007, NERO closed the investigation on the ground that "[t]he staff found no evidence of fraud" (Rhee, 2009, p. 366).

Deficiency in Fraud Detection Knowledge

It is difficult to conceive that the most important market regulatory agency and its attorneys could have missed exposing a fraud scheme that was spelled out in painstaking detail, especially Markopolos's 2005 submission. There are "two plausible, yet uncomfortable, explanations: either the SEC was influenced by Madoff's social and professional stature, a form of structural corruption in the agency, or its attorneys [were]...ignorant and the SEC agree that the most probable answer is a deficit in fraud detection competency" or both incompetence and Madoff's perceived influence on the SEC (Rhee, 2009, 366). Although incompetence is probably the more predominant reason why the SEC failed, there are also subtle hints that the SEC was uncomfortable about pushing an investigation on Madoff given his status and connections within the SEC. There were instances where SEC staffers voiced their concern about the power dynamic Madoff displayed during their interviews of him and concerns that were voiced between SEC staffers themselves. The failure of the SEC to detect the Ponzi scheme goes beyond the personal professional failure of the attorneys involved in the Madoff review.

Although it is of no surprise that accidents happen and oversights do occur in investigations, this scandal cannot be explained by stating that it was a simple oversight by the SEC staff involved in the Madoff investigation because we could conveniently avoid the larger causal connection between perpetrating fraud and failure to detect the fraud (Rhee, 2009). The multiple failures by the SEC review was conducted by many attorneys and other staff suggests a deeper problem that the SEC staff lacked the minimum level of knowledge and experience on the issues that the SEC is charged to regulate (Rhee, 2009). After the Madoff scandal surfaced, one of the major findings by the SEC in assessing its own oversight of the Madoff investigation was that its staff's failure to appreciate the red flags contained in Markopolos' 2005 submission was a lack of experience necessary for a fundamental understanding of securities trading. The SEC admitted they did not appreciate that Madoff was unable to provide a logical explanation for his incredibly consistent returns, but instead accepted as plausible Madoff's claim that his returns were due to his perfect "gut feel" for when the market would go up or down (OIG, 2009, p. 369).

If the SEC is committed to staffing attorneys as regulators, then at the very least these attorneys should receive training as to how securities fraud is perpetrated so they are better equipped to accomplish their mission. Consider the insights of Markopolos on his observations of SEC staff believing they suffered from "financial illiteracy," due to an "over-lawyering at the SEC," and "too many of the staff lawyers lack any financial industry experience or training in how to conduct investigations...The SEC is overmatched. They're too slow, they're too young, they're too undereducated" (Rhee, 2009, p. 377). Markopolos further observed, "Putting them (attorneys) in charge of supervising our capital markets has been an unmitigated disaster. Very few SEC lawyers understand the complex financial instruments of the 21st century and almost none of them have ever sat on a trading desk or worked in the industry other than in a legal capacity" (Issa, 2010, p. 22). In a general sense lawyers are fundamentally legal risk analysts, but the problem is that SEC lawyers in particular need to consider other disciplines and the risks they deal with that are outside of their legal frameworks such as those found in the accounting, business, criminology, psychology and the financial worlds to better accomplish their tasks especially those involved in field work where they are obligated to interview people who are suspected of engaging in securities fraud.

Legal risk in the business and financial worlds is only one of many different types of risks they will confront. Given that we live in an era of complexities evidenced by misbehaving corporations, and financial scandals such as Madoff, government lawyers will need to be more well-rounded by being literate in the relevant academic disciplines driving a modern economy to understand how they are incorporated into perpetrating fraud. For example, when we examine the responses Madoff gave regulators and the manner that he gave them, are we reminded of the antisocial traits and interpersonal strategies studied in chapter one that were in fact displayed by Madoff? Did regulators interpret Madoff's display of such traits as irrelevant or could they have interpreted his mannerism as a proxy for a fraud attitude? There may be obstacles impeding the SEC from obtaining the type of knowledge that would assist them in becoming better regulators. Often, SEC lawyers want to be viewed as successful by their peers outside of the SEC because these will be the same people they will one day work for once they leave the SEC (Perri & Brody, 2011b). SEC lawyers have an incentive in developing technical skills

144

and expertise in areas that will make them valuable to a Wall Street law firm and investment banks instead of being financial regulators (Macey, 2010).

Combating simple fraud and old-fashioned Ponzi schemes may help the capital markets and protect the small investors, but it does little to help SEC officials develop the skills and expertise that will make them valuable to Wall Street law firms, the clear focus of many SEC staffers today (Macey, 2010, p. 648). For example, the disclosure rules that require corporations and other regulated entities to publicly file certain disclosures ranging from lengthy annual reports on Form 10-K to disclosures of stock ownership by corporate insiders, have become so complex that these rules can only be understood by specialized lawyers who work for the SEC, private law firms and investment banks. Consequently, some "members of this elite group circulate back and forth between the SEC and the firms; maintaining the complexity of the system is in their personal financial interest" (Issa, 2010, p. 27). However setting aside these personal motivations, the investigations were conducted by inexperienced attorneys that lacked knowledge of the industry they were regulating, investigations that were not planned properly coupled with the fact that the investigations were limited in scope in terms of how far the SEC was willing to dig for evidence of fraud especially when red-flags surfaced (OIG, 2009).

While investigators discovered suspicious information and evidence catching Madoff in contradictions and inconsistencies when they questioned him, they either disregarded these concerns or inappropriately relied upon Madoff's representations as to how he was able to achieve consistent and above average market returns year after year without understanding his trading strategy which was nonsensical from a financial analysis perspective (Rhee, 2009). The SEC staff caught Madoff in multiple lies and misrepresentations, but failed to follow up on his inconsistent representations. When Madoff provided evasive or contradictory answers to important questions in testimony, they accepted his explanations even though privately they were suspicious of his answers. Although the SEC staff made attempts to seek information from independent third parties to determine if Madoff was actually engaged in buying and selling of securities, they failed to follow up on these requests such as asking for information on whether Madoff was engaged in securities trading on a specific date. For example, when they received a report that there were in fact no securities trading on that date, they did not take any further steps to confront Madoff about his representations. A SEC staff attorney made several attempts to obtain documentation from European counterparties, another independent third party that Madoff claimed he engaged in securities trading, and although a letter was drafted, the staff decided not to send it.

Had this effort alone been fully executed, it would have invariably led to the unveiling of a Ponzi scheme. Let us consider the interpersonal strategy Madoff displayed with the SEC examiners that even if the staff members did not understand Ponzi financing should have been a glaring fraud scheme red-flag that something was amiss with Madoff. The examiners discussed how Madoff executed and cleared securities trades and relied upon his verbal representations even though his representations were vague or misleading. One SEC investigator stated that "during the course of the exam, [Madoff] made a point to tell us…and emphasize that his family had a dramatic influence on the securities industry…I think…clearly he's a wonderful storyteller, very captivating speaker, and he has an incredible or had an incredible background of knowledge in the industry…I mean it became a little frustrating at times, though, because, you know, we obviously were there to conduct business, and so [he] can be sort of distracting" (OIG, 2009, p. 181). Madoff made efforts during the examination to impress and even intimidate junior examiners from the SEC (Perri & Brody, 2011b). SEC examiners described Madoff as "charismatic and charming, [e]xcept when he was angry with us" (OIG, 2009, p. 181). For example, Madoff's extreme anger was captured by one SEC investigator who disclosed in an e-mail:

[W]e were asking for documents… it was sort of disconcerting how angry he became. I mean his veins were popping out of his neck, and during that – it was a – I think his brother Peter might've been there, and he just repeatedly said, you know, "What are you looking for?" And his voice level got increasingly loud and the veins were popping out, and one of us – I may have said something, you know, "What do you want us to look for? What do you think we're looking for?" And then he – that's when he said something like, you know, "Frontrunning. Aren't you looking for front-running," or something –

something to that effect…I think he was frustrated because he couldn't figure out exactly why we were there, and I think at this point, we had asked him about all of his businesses and he had not revealed his investment advisory business. So I think we were hinting around things, trying to get him to admit or acknowledge he was conducting this business, and I think that frustrated him (OIG, 2009, p. 184).

Recall that front-running occurs when a broker derives a financial benefit by executing trades for his own account in front of the trades he executes for his clients, but at the client's disadvantage. Madoff stated that during the on-site examination at his firm, because he thought it was routine for the SEC to check with an independent third party that his Ponzi scheme would be exposed, however SEC examiners did not confirm the information Madoff provided with any third parties (OIG, 2009, p. 204). Madoff stated that the SEC "never really got into books and records as related to stock records or DTC records" coupled with being astonished that they did not ask for DTC records given only a regulator such as the SEC could get those records from the DTC. Madoff added the DTC does not have separate accounts for each customer, but rather provides a global report, but stating that if the SEC went to the DTC, it would have been easy for them to discover the Ponzi scheme (OIG, 2009, p. 207). Madoff went on to disparage the SEC investigation as a "fishing expedition," saying that "these girls", the SEC's lawyers, might not understand the strategy, plus "it's none of their business" how he managed his firm (Brander & Varchaver, 2009). Furthermore, when examiners began their on-site examination of Madoff, they learned he would be their primary contact and Madoff carefully controlled to whom they spoke at his firm.

On one occasion, when a Madoff employee was speaking to the NERO examiners at Madoff's office, after a couple of minutes, another Madoff employee rushed in to escort her from the conversation, claiming she was urgently needed (Sherter, 2009). When the examiners later asked Madoff the reason for the urgency, Madoff told them her lunch had just arrived (Sherter, 2009). It is apparent examiners intuitively recognized the antisocial interpersonal strategy Madoff used, but their supervisor discounted such behavior as a potential red-flag indicative of fraudulent behavior. Throughout the examination examiners experienced difficulty dealing with Madoff as he was described as growing increasingly agitated during the examination, and attempting to dictate to the examiners what to focus on in the examination, who they could talk to, and what documents they could review. In essence he displayed the antisocial trait of power orientation studied in chapter one where he wanted to control people and events. Yet, when the examiners reported back to their supervisor about the pushback they received from Madoff, they received no support and were actively discouraged from pursuing the issue.

Although the investigative staff was confused about certain critical and fundamental aspects of Madoff's operations, it should not be underestimated that the SEC staff was up against someone that was politically connected, noted for his philanthropy, had an excellent reputation at the time, and had relatives connected to the SEC's upper management (Gornall, 2010). It is not implausible to believe that an inexperienced staff would not want to attract Madoff's animosity by challenging his "evasive and contradictory answers" (Gornall, 2010, p. 5). For example, throughout the examination process he emphasized his role in the securities industry, would drop names of senior SEC staff, coupled with knowing who was going to be chairman of the SEC and that he was on the shortlist to be the next chairman (Katz, 2009). This is in no way a defense of these regulators oversight, however, when we have regulators who in the end may voice concerns that there may be a problem with Madoff's operations, but do not get the support they truly need from their superiors, Madoff's status and perceived power within Wall Street circles might dampen their motivation to continue their investigation. There also was the belief that because Madoff was so deeply tied to the Wall Street world in terms of business, family, personal wealth, and commitments that he would have no way to avoid them if he did engage in fraud thus concluding that he did not engage in fraud because the down side was too high (Langevoort, 2009).

Moreover, his clients were wealthy, sophisticated investors who were well positioned to do their own due diligence, making him vulnerable to having clients quickly withdraw their money if word spread that he was not to be trusted. Thus, a regulator might reason that there is no rational explanation for why, having built such a successful and apparently legitimate trading firm, he would ever take such a high risk by engaging in fraud (Langevoort, 2009). In other words, the risks associated of engaging fraud are so great that they are a deterrent to

Madoff engaging in fraud, consequently the extent of an investigation need not be in depth. At other points in their investigation, there were times when NERO examiners were planning to confront Madoff about the many contradictory positions he was taking, particularly as they related to Madoff's changing stories about how many clients he had. However, in 2004-2005, when the NERO examiners pushed Madoff for documents and information about his clients, it was Madoff who informed them that he already provided the information to the Washington, D.C. staff in accordance with their examination.

Astoundingly, both examinations were open at the same time in different offices without either knowing the other one was conducting an identical examination. The scope of the examination were in both cases too narrowly focused on the possibility of front-running, with no significant attempts made to analyze the numerous red flags about Madoff's trading and returns. The NERO examiners were taken aback, since they were unaware that the Washington, D.C. SEC office had been conducting a simultaneous examination of Madoff on the identical issues they were examining. One of the few points made in a conference call between the offices once NERO learned about the parallel investigation was a comment by a senior-level Washington D.C. examiner reminding the junior NERO examiners that "Madoff…is a very well-connected, powerful person" (OIG, 2009, p. 199). One of the NERO examiners interpreted this comment as a warning about pushing Madoff too hard without having substantial evidence revealing fraudulent behavior (Langevoort, 2009). Yet, during the course of both these examinations, the examination teams discovered suspicious information and evidence catching Madoff in contradictions and inconsistencies. Even when Madoff's answers were seemingly implausible, the SEC examiners accepted them at face value.

It is likely that Madoff's prominence played a role in the SEC's failure to uncover fraud in their examinations due to their disbelief that he operating a Ponzi scheme in the first place (OIG, 2009). Without compelling evidence of fraud as perceived by the SEC, Madoff is hardly an appealing investigation to pursue especially if one's intuition, albeit erroneous, tells them that the likelihood of finding fraud is very low and the risks of a Madoff backlash appear great especially with his ties to the SEC and Wall Street. Finding nothing of substance will have embarrassed and angered a powerful Wall Street figure and drained considerable resources in the process (Langevoort, 2009). Would Madoff try to get these SEC staffers blacklisted from ever finding Wall Street jobs that they might seek after getting the experience they need from the SEC? For example, Madoff disparaged the SEC's investigation stating that the SEC lawyers would not press too hard because they have ambitions to go into lucrative private practice and do not want to alienate the sort of legal and non-legal firms that might want to hire them (Bandler & Varchaver, 2009). Is Madoff wrong on this insight?

Turnover at the SEC has always been high because lawyers can earn much more working in the private sector. Empirical evidence also points to the fact that the turnover rate for SEC lawyers is twice that for all government lawyers giving the appearance that the "whole point of landing a job as the SEC's Director of Enforcement is to position oneself for a better paying one on Wall Street" (Macey, 2010, p. 649). John Freeman, a former SEC lawyer and professor of business ethics, indicated that eventually "the training and expertise gained at the SEC is put to use for the benefit of those working against the interests of investors" (McGinty, 2010b). For the most part, legal ethics experts see nothing wrong with the practice of going from public to the private sector, as long as lawyers follow ethical rules and err on the side of disclosure (McGinty, 2010a). There are times when the revolving door from public to the private sector employment creates impressions that public sector attorneys may be compromising a securities fraud investigation because of the perception that former SEC colleagues wield undue influence over current SEC staff. As one SEC staffer stated, if "you work for the enforcement division of the SEC you probably know in the back of your mind, and in the front too, that if you maintain good relations with Wall Street you might soon be paid huge sums of money to be employed by it" (Langevoort, 2009, p. 904). The revolving door appears to be a factor in not enforcing actions against violators and there is "indirect evidence to support the contention that post-agency employment at higher salaries may operate as a quid pro quo in return for favorable regulatory treatment" (Ramirez, 2016, p. 489).

This means that an SEC official may be lenient with counsel that represents the violator because the SEC official may need the assistance of the violator's representative for a future job. It is a way of doing favors for each other. The "reality is the revolving door between the private sector and the government undermines the effectiveness of both regulatory agencies and governmental departments, because self-interest interferes with effective oversight and enforcement, including criminal enforcement" (p. 490). Would such a staffer not be as diligent in the enforcement of the law because of the influence of someone outside of the SEC who might hire them one day? There is truth to the belief that an ambitious regulator would not want to alienate completely a future employer in the industry. There are some empirical studies that document the SEC's inclination to go easy on big Wall Street players in enforcement cases (Langevoort, 2009). Private sector clients know that bringing in a former senior enforcement division officer is almost expected in high-profile cases and it is hard for lower level staff members to compete with established reputations when arguing to bring a case, especially when former SEC staffers have longstanding ties with current SEC leadership (Henning, 2010a).

Will Madoff call the SEC chairman himself and demand SEC staffers be fired or demoted because of his perception that they pushed him too hard during the investigation? To lessen one's concern about a Madoff backlash, an SEC supervisor might have someone take a quick look at the front-running possibility, and when nothing turns up, feel better about letting the matter drop knowing that there was an effort made toward due diligence (Langevoort, 2009). In the end, SEC staff responded to complaints by focusing on whether Madoff was engaging in front-running because, and in their supervisor's words, "that was the area of expertise for my crew" and that a Ponzi scheme was "highly unlikely" (Issa, 2010, p. 6). While the Washington, D.C. examination team decided not to resume their examination, they sent their work papers to NERO examiners who reportedly conducted a scant review of the work papers and did not recall even reviewing the detailed complaints that prompted the examination in the first place. Furthermore, it does not appear that NERO discussed the D.C. examiners' open questions about Madoff's representations and trading, nor did they compare the list of clients Madoff produced for NERO with the list he produced for the D.C. team.

Unfortunately, the above oversight of not knowing there are multiple teams investigating Madoff illustrates one of the SEC's single weaknesses which is its unwieldy staff structure. The SEC is divided into five operating divisions with over a dozen independent offices; the fragmentation has resulted in devastating effects on collaboration, encourages uninformed rulemaking, generates bureaucratic rivalries, and prevents effective technological interconnectedness so that SEC staffs can share data (Perri & Brody, 2011b). Moreover, consider that on May 19, 2006, the SEC had a golden opportunity to detect Madoff's Ponzi scheme when the SEC brought Madoff in for a deposition asking him detailed questions about his business including where the securities supporting the investments were kept. Madoff voluntarily testified without counsel and answered their questions coupled with disclosing his Depository Trust Company (DTC) account number where he claimed housed the billions and billions of dollars of securities. After the deposition, Madoff thought that his scheme would be discovered given that in one account he had less than $24 million dollars of S&P 100 securities. In addition, according to SEC staff who interviewed Madoff, they stated that he provided evasive answers to important questions, coupled with some answers that contradicted his previous representations.

Furthermore, when the SEC staff asked the critical question of how he was able to achieve his consistently high returns, Madoff never answered the question but instead attacked those who questioned his returns, particularly the author of the previously mentioned 2001 *Barron's* article. Essentially, Madoff claimed his remarkable returns were due to his personal "feel" for when to get in and out of the market, stating, "Some people feel the market. Some people just understand how to analyze the numbers that they're looking at" (OIG, 2009, p. 39). Because of the staff's inexperience and lack of understanding of securities trading, they did not appreciate Madoff was unable to provide a logical explanation for his incredibly consistent returns. Each staff member accepted as plausible Madoff's claim that his returns were due to his perfect "gut feel" for when the market would go up or down. One staff member "didn't know what to think" about the magnitude of Madoff's claimed returns and she "did not have a view about how likely or unlikely it was that one person could achieve such consistent returns over 14 and-a-half years with only seven down months" (OIG, 2009, p. 311).

Other SEC staff stated that after Madoff's testimony, they "didn't know what to make of" Madoff's explanation for his returns (OIG, 2009, p. 311). Some staff members took Madoff's explanation at face value stating that "by not reaching for astronomically high returns," he could achieve such remarkable consistency, noting that Madoff's explanation, "while not 100 percent responsive, not a perfect answer, it did answer the question" (OIG, 2009, p. 369). Madoff testified at the deposition that the trades for all of his various client accounts were cleared through his account at DTC and that his different client accounts were segregated and not lumped into one client account, however, SEC staff caught Madoff lying about the number of investors and the identity of his investors (OIG, 2009, p. 319). When a SEC staff member subsequently spoke to a representative at DTC, she learned that Madoff's representation that his client's accounts were segregated was not true. However, instead of relying on professional skepticism and following up on the discrepancy between what Madoff stated and what the SEC learned, the SEC incorrectly concluded that the lack of segregation in Madoff's DTC account made it impractical to use DTC records to verify whether Madoff was placing any trades for his investors.

Madoff himself stated that they asked him about his DTC number and he gave the interviewers his DTC number which was 646. Madoff went on to state: "I thought it was the end game, over. Monday morning they'll call DTC and this will be over…and it never happened. Madoff stated that when nothing happened he thought, "After all this, I got away lucky" but he said he thought it was just "a matter of time…that was the nightmare I lived with" (OIG, 2009, 312). Madoff further stated, "everything the SEC did prior to 2006 was a waste of time" (OIG, 2009, p. 226). Even before Madoff's deposition, NERO learned that Madoff withheld client account information from the examination staff that could have been used to confront Madoff with during his deposition to expose his deception. For example on February 6, 2006, a SEC staffer e-mailed another SEC staff member about Madoff's deception appeared to understand the concept of verification of Madoff's representations when they stated, "We discovered…Bernard Madoff, mislead NERO examination staff earlier this year about the nature of his trading strategy…Additionally, Madoff did not disclose to the examination staff some of the accounts in which implemented this trading strategy. Because of these misrepresentations, and also because of the high amounts at issue, we would like to obtain some independent verification of the reported returns" (OIG, 2009, p. 319).

Yet ironically, when questioned about the importance of verification of Madoff's representations from independent sources to determine if a Ponzi scheme existed, one SEC staff member stated, "I don't think you can say it's essential. I think it would be a good thing to do but I don't think you can say it's essential" (OIG, 2009, p. 326) even after learning that Madoff lied about his securities trades when he testified in his deposition before the SEC (OIG, 2009, p. 330). No efforts were made by this SEC staff member to cross-reference the statements made by Madoff with the actual evidence from the DTC that would have revealed that he made no securities trades. For example, had the SEC cross checked the amount in the DTC with the amount he disclosed on a single fund investing with Madoff that reported $2.5 billion of the Standard & Poors (S&P) 100 stock on its statement, the variance in disclosures would have been a significant red-flag to justify further inquiry, but that never happened (Soltes, 2016). After Madoff confessed to operating a Ponzi scheme, NERO admitted that had they obtained DTC records for Madoff's account after his deposition testimony, they would have most likely had discovered his Ponzi scheme (OIG, 2009, p. 312). When Madoff's Ponzi scheme collapsed, SEC staff indicated that it took only "a few days" and "a phone call…to DTC" to confirm that Madoff had not placed any trades with his investors' funds" (OIG, 2009, p. 333). As if not exposing Madoff as a Ponzi schemer during his deposition was not enough to reveal the deficiency of fraud knowledge attached to the SEC staff, several SEC staff members actively involved in investigating Madoff were skeptical of the allegation that Madoff was running a Ponzi scheme.

Some believed this because Markopolos did not have any inside Madoff firm information to substantiate the allegation, thus they discounted his insights, but even when they received anonymous tips from people acquainted with Madoff, those tips were ignored. One SEC staff member testified that "often the only way the SEC can develop evidence…in a Ponzi scheme, is if we have somebody on the inside…It's very challenging to develop evidence about a Ponzi scheme until the thing actually falls apart" (OIG, 2009, p. 247). Yet, had NERO simply sought documents from DTC, Madoff's bank or his purported "Over the Counter" (OTC) option counterparties, they would have been able to uncover the fraud without any needed inside information (OIG, 2009, p. 368). The SEC's examiners' lack of securities fraud knowledge and experience not only contributed to their failure to understand that Madoff's returns could not be real, it also was a factor in their failure to conduct an effective investigation regarding how Madoff was creating those returns. According to a member of the National Securities Dealers, the SEC staff did not understand the basics about securities trading and even rejected Gene DeMaio's, Vice President and Deputy Director of the NASD Amex Regulation Division, suggestion to postpone Madoff's testimony "to do a little bit more homework," in addition to not accepting his offer of further assistance (OIG, 2009, p. 310).

Moreover, some NERO attorneys were offended when Markopolos questioned whether they understood securities trading enough to understand some of the red flags in his 2005 submission. NERO declined Markopolos's offer to help NERO staff understand the 2005 submission, his observations and analysis of Madoff, as he had done in his meeting with the Boston office (OIG, 2009, p. 369). Similarly, NERO did not seek help from the SEC's Office of International Affairs (OIA) regarding Madoff's purported trading activity in Europe. OIA may have been able to provide the necessary expertise that would have been helpful to understand Madoff's alleged overseas securities trading. If the SEC staff simply sought assistance from OIA on matters within their area of expertise, they would have discovered that Madoff was not purchasing equities from European counterparties. Yet, the SEC knew back in 2005 that Madoff was not trading with Barclays Capital Inc., when the requested information based on Madoff's representations revealed "no relevant transaction activity occurred during the period" requested (OIG, 2009, p. 315). Furthermore, several attempts to obtain documentation from European counterparties, and one of Madoff's purported counterparties was in the process of drafting a consent letter asking Madoff's permission to send the SEC the documents from its European account. However, the inexplicable decision was made not to send the letter and to abandon this effort. An SEC attorney working on the Madoff matter touched on that failure stated:

> I think people were too trusting. I don't mean this in a bad way. I think, you know, very often you hear these stories and the guy, you know, I didn't know his reputation, but he apparently did have a tremendous reputation. And I think people were trusting. I mean he gave testimony that was clearly, you know, a complete and utter fabrication…I mean why didn't they talk to the European options, you know, the people on the other side of the option trade, I don't know (OIG, 2009, p. 373).

Summary of the Madoff Regulatory Oversight

The 2005 Markopolos complaint is probably the best single documented analysis of the fraud revealing that Madoff's operation was a Ponzi scheme, and it provided the SEC a detailed roadmap for proving the fraud. The position here is not that the SEC could have uncovered Madoff's fraud on its own because detecting fraud without a complaining party or a whistleblower is very difficult. It is not surprising that Harry Markopolos, who had inside knowledge of the fraud that was occurring, is an industry specialist with an expertise in securities trading. Deep training and experience in accounting and finance are necessary to detect sophisticated market fraud. Markopolos also had the benefit of piecing together the puzzle because he had access to many sources of market information such as the Wall Street inside information and innuendo referenced in his memo, and access to information from several hedge funds that invested with Madoff (Rhee, 2009). Without this information, Markopolos could have made a persuasive case against Madoff.

However there is also a fundamental tension between the philosophy of securities regulation and the necessities of antifraud market enforcement since in securities law the predominant regulatory philosophy is disclosure of information and not assessment of the investment opportunity (Rhee, 2009). The assumption, of course, is that once honest disclosure is made, the investor should be free to choose and the government should not be a gatekeeper of investment quality and uncovering fraud schemes. However, if government does not have an obligation to be a gatekeeper of the investment's legitimacy, then it begs the question why does the SEC then have an enforcement division to make sure that fraud is not being committed? Taking the position to its ultimate conclusion would mean that each investor should conduct their own forensic analysis of an opportunity to determine whether fraud is behind the opportunity. In this case, it is apparent that the SEC did not seriously review the substance of the financial investment, the core of Markopolos's argument, but rather focused on process by initially finding that Madoff violated disclosure rules by failing to register as an investment adviser and not whether the investment was legitimate. The check-the-regulation box-mindset, consistent with a functional focus on disclosure, is clearly inadequate to the task of sophisticated financial analysis and market regulation. It is debatable whether the SEC can perform both market regulation and enforcement functions with a staff of mostly lawyers, many of whom lack even a basic education in finance and accounting, much less experience in financial markets.

Regulation means that there must be personnel who understand technical rules of law, but who also understand the industry the agency regulates. To the extent that the SEC is performing the dual functions of regulation and enforcement activities such as fraud detection, their lawyer regulators must have some capability to do investigative work, meaning that it must have a competent staff with substantial knowledge of business, finance, and markets and how they can be manipulated. Yet, in the end, the SEC did not understand Madoff's business, and therefore failed to realize what would have been clear to industry experts that his claimed strategy, transactions, and returns were misrepresentations. The "suggestion is not that lawyer regulators should have advanced degrees in the technical fields they regulate, but that they should have a level of knowledge and the capability to analyze the technical details of the transactions in question, or at least be aware enough to know what they do not know and to ask the relevant questions" (Rhee, 2009, p. 365). The Markopolos memo, although may appear intimidating to someone not familiar with this area of finance, is full of data and financial reasoning that reveal some simple, disturbing facts that anyone with some degree of financial training and knowledge should have appreciated. Markopolos showed the SEC that Madoff's strategy could not have yielded the type of returns he was claiming. A trained lawyer should recognize the important conceptual point regardless of the precise mathematical methodology, and this awareness should have driven the questioning.

Whether the stock market was up, down, or flat, the market's position on any given time was not relevant as Madoff's strategy always made profit because he stated that he was eliminating market-risk from the investments so that the investors did not have to worry about losing their money (Rhee, 2009). Yet, basic intuition suggests that if he was eliminating market risk, he could only earn the risk-free rate, net of any transaction cost, and yet he was purporting to earn relatively large, consistent, high-risk returns. If a lawyer regulator does not understand the significance of these contradictory representations in an investment document, or if he or she does not have even a sense of the market performance benchmarks and historical returns presented in Markopolos's memo, he or she simply does not understand how markets work and cannot properly perform his job function. Financial analysis requires a chain of reasoning and inferences, very much like the process that a lawyer would use to build a theory of the case. Markopolos did the heavy investigative work, and the SEC only had to understand what he was saying.

For a lawyer-regulator to comprehend the memo, they must have a basic literacy with these concepts: 1) fee structure and incentives, 2) securities transactions and their impact on market conditions, 3) options and trading strategies, 4) arbitrage, 5) principles of risk and return, and 6) historical and current market benchmarks (Rhee, 2009). The cause of the SEC's failure is fundamentally an inability of its attorneys to understand what a whistleblower such as Markopolos was saying; they were financially illiterate. They did not understand the workings of derivatives, options, arbitrage, pricing principles, historical and current market benchmarks, and generally the markets they regulate. Markopolos testified: "the SEC has so little investment management experience that they don't know what the industry standards for good performance are, and what the industry standards for unbelievable, fraudulent performance are" (Rhee, 2009, p. 380). If a lawyer-regulator does not instantly recognize the delivery of virtually risk-free 16 percent returns year-over-year as most unusual, he is incapable of investigating sophisticated market fraud. Madoff claiming that he was eliminating risk should have suggested that his strategy could not earn returns greater than the risk-free rate. As the Madoff Ponzi scheme shows, uncovering a fraud requires a substantive understanding of the investment and the financial logic.

The fact that the SEC takes years to solve Ponzi schemes is proof that they need to hire examiners with industry experience (Carozza, 2010). What may be the best way to reveal a securities Ponzi scheme? According to Markopolos, since a Ponzi scheme never really provides any underlying product or service, these types of frauds should not take more than a few hours to solve in most instances. One simply walks into the suspected Ponzi operator's headquarters unannounced and asks to be taken to the trading desk, which will not exist (Carozza, 2010). The trading desk is where there is the buying and selling of securities. According to Markopolos, if the fraudsters are fast on their feet, they will tell you their trading desk is located at a different, far more remote location to slow you down by a day or two until you can get teams to that location (Carozza, 2010). Moreover, if there is no trading desk at the firm's headquarters and the firm does not list any other offices in its marketing literature, then you can be sure it is a Ponzi scheme. Next an investigator would ask for the trading tickets showing those securities they traded and at which prices at what time—again, they probably will not have those either. If they do have trading tickets, then one would call the brokerage firms they purportedly traded through for verification and ask if the trades are real—most likely they will not. Alternatively, one can simply look at a "time & sales tick data feed" and attempt to locate these trades, but in the end they will not exist (Carozza, 2010).

In addition, another fraud red flag the SEC ignored was the role of Madoff's auditor Friehling & Horowitz, a little-known three-person accounting firm with only one certified public accountant on its payroll since 1991 to oversee Madoff's multi-billion dollar operation was ignored by the SEC (Reurink, 2016). Madoff claimed that Friehling conducted his audits and when asked to produce audited financial statements purportedly done by Friehling, the SEC learned that Friehling did not have the resources to conduct a competent audit of an operation as large as Madoffs. Friehling admitted that he never conducted audits that formed the basis of his audit opinions (Albrecht et al., 2012). Indeed, once Madoff was arrested, it took investigators visiting Friehling's office only a few hours to realize that no real audit work had ever been done. Moreover, one of the SEC's initial excuses for not exposing Madoff was that a severe lack of resources explains most of the SEC's problems pointing out that its regulatory task is immense, and that budgetary growth has not kept up with either the scope or complexity of the modem financial markets (Langevoort, 2009). In order to appeal to Congress and justify the SEC budget that tripled from 2000 to 2010 (Issa, 2010), the commission maximizes its appeal by showing that resources are being efficiently used and in particular uses the raw number of cases it brings and the size of the fines collected (Macey, 2010). These strategies brought the SEC a measure of success that has several advantages; it is simple and easy for those within and outside the agency to understand, however, this type of performance measure creates perverse incentives for regulators (Gornall, 2010).

This inclination to value only what can be easily measured has not served the SEC well and the SEC's narrow focus on such measurable indicia of success as the raw numbers of cases pursued explains, in part, the SEC's complete lack of interest in exposing Madoff's fraud that was constructed with a simple, well-known Ponzi scheme apparatus (Macey, 2010). Yet when criticized for failing to respond to the red flags in the Madoff case, the SEC responded by disclosing how many new investigations it opened as a metric of success. Even more evident, the SEC's 2008 Annual Report emphasized easily measureable criteria: "During 2008, the Enforcement Division also brought the highest number of insider trading cases in the agency's history…but in each of the last two years the Commission [SEC] set the record for the highest number of corporate penalty cases in the agency's history" (Macey, 2010, p. 645). In light of the method of measuring SEC success, it is not surprising it tackles simple violations, also known as picking low-hanging fruit, to increase their metric of success (Perri & Brody, 2011b).

In addition, Richard Sauer, Attorney and Assistant Director with the SEC's Division of Enforcement from 1990 to 2003 stated that "Ponzi and pyramid schemes…held low priority with the SEC top management who saw them as having to little press appeal and afflicting only small investors looking to make a quick buck" (Sauer, 2010, p. A13). Often, the SEC ignored evidence of fraud in well-known journals in corporate finance until it is made an issue by the media and the press thus forcing the SEC to look into an issue (Macey, 2010). A misperception harbored by the SEC is their belief that actually investigating fraud schemes requires the devotion of too many resources. Even beyond the Madoff investigation, investigating Ponzi schemes in general seems to have been regarded as a "burning of resources", further stating, "the most striking thing about the SEC Division of Enforcement's failure to conduct an adequate investigation into the Madoff scheme is that such an investigation would not have required much in the way of resources" (Macey, 2010, p. 656).

The SEC received six substantive complaints about Madoff but did not pursue these red flags, in part, because it did not want to devote the necessary resources. As one SEC official testified, such an investigation would be too expensive and time consuming, and because the SEC did not understand what the red flags represented even if it was aware of them (Markopolos, 2010). Attorney Sauer went on to state that, the "stat system" establishes perverse incentives creating biases in favor of quick-hit cases and against cases that appear novel or speculative (Perri & Brody, 2011b). In addition, the SEC takes on Wall Street far less aggressively especially the big investment banks; it cannot afford to litigate more than a tiny fraction of its cases (Langevoort, 2009). Furthermore, Bernard Madoff in an interview once stated "I'm very close with the regulators" (Fox, 2008). The full extent of whom, if anyone, at the SEC ever knew of Madoff's schemes or whether his close relationship with SEC regulators gave him the opportunity to escape detection for so many years will probably never be known. Arthur Levitt who served as SEC chairman from 1993 to early 2001, acknowledged he occasionally turned to Madoff for advice about how the market functioned, but denies that Madoff had undue influence at the SEC or that the agency's enforcement staff deferred to him. Levitt said he was unaware that Madoff even ran an investment management business, and that Madoff never had special access to him or other SEC officials. Yet Madoff was so respected at the SEC's inner circle that SEC commissioners sought him out for advice and commissioners appointed him to its advisory committee on market information.

Madoff also claimed that SEC Chairman Schapiro was a "dear friend" and SEC Commissioner Walter was a "dear friend", a "terrific lady" whom he knew "pretty well" – comments which imply he could achieve easy access to such influential people (Gendar, 2009). Harry Markopolos commented on the power Madoff wielded: "Mr. Madoff was one of the most powerful men on Wall Street. He owned a prestigious brokerage firm. He and his brother held numerous top-level positions on the most influential industry association boards. Clearly, the SEC was afraid of Mr. Madoff" (SCCMIGPE, 2009, p. 7). However, the Madoff scandal does illustrate the importance of implementing proper regulatory policy establishing expectations that former SEC staff, current staff, and other individuals in the private sector maintain a relationship that does not compromise independence in fact and appearance.

The Role of Social Influence in Facilitating Exploitation

People are motivated to achieve their goals in the most effective and rewarding manner possible. When examining decision making that exhibits a group-based quality to them, a person's desire to respond appropriately to a social situation demands an accurate perception of reality. In most of the examples examined, they reflect a group-based type of decision making quality to them where someone, in this case the offender, is trying to get others to go along with his or her scheme without their knowledge that it is a scheme. The offender is looking for compliance which refers to getting others to submit to a particular request. What are those factors that influence our desire to comply to another's request such as giving money to another person because of some perceived benefit in doing so? Frequently, people do not understand why they make decisions they do until after they may have been taken advantage of, and then still, it is not always clear that they can avoid the problem of being taken advantage of from occurring again. People can be seduced by offenders and drawn into Ponzi schemes, especially educated people who can be quite vulnerable, almost displaying blind obedience to the offender, coupled with displaying symptoms of naïve groupthink (Lewis, 2015).

In order to understand the process of seduction, both at the individual and group level, we need to understand the concept of social influence. Social influence is rooted in social psychology attempting to explain what occurs when a person's emotions, opinions, or behaviors are influenced by others, perhaps a group and how their behaviors in the converse influence others including those in a group. Understanding social influence directly impacts conformity referring to the act of changing one's behavior to match the responses of others and this is very important especially when offenders try to get individuals to conform to the way a group thinks. Thus, when individuals observe which direction a group is leaning towards, social influence factors that we shall examine increase the probability that an individual will succumb to conformity by following the direction the group is going. Moreover, individuals often engage in more conscious and deliberate attempts to gain the social approval of others which can have the direct effect of making them feel better about themselves because of group approval (Cialdini & Goldstein, 2004).

However, even when there is no group pressure to conform, there are social influence factors that increase an individual's desire to go along with the requests of another individual if there are, as we have studied, similar traits such as religion, race, ethnicity or language that increase the trust level of the individual even when they may not know the other person well. There is an emotional and intellectual aspect to the process of decision making and the emotional aspect is more important than expected (Lewis, 2015). The intellectual side may get so overwhelmed with detail that people look for shortcuts to make decisions by relying on the emotional seduction of trust as a substitute for due diligence. Furthermore Ponzi schemes evoke the emotion of making money quickly is definitely an allure where the desire is so strong that it may interfere with logical reasoning causing an individual(s) to display gullible-like behaviors. Yet greed is simply not enough to explain the seduction of people to hand over their money to an offender because at times the money promised is not that significant as is the promise of reasonable, but steady returns that Madoff offered as examples.

The non-volatile investment offered by Madoff offered an emotional security that made investors feel safe. Thus we must understand the social psychological process pertaining to social influence that gets people to behave a certain way to conform to the desires of an offender (Cialdini & Goldstein, 2004). Factors that contribute to effective persuasion techniques that overwhelmingly display themselves in affinity fraud cases are: 1) the desire to obey authority, 2) proclaiming scarcity of resources and opportunities, 3) uncovering similarities with others increasing the probability of being liked and trusted, 4) reciprocation of good will, 5) consistency in honoring commitments, and 6) social proof which is following the lead of others through vouching for the credibility of those we may not know personally (Luo et al., 2011). In some respects these factors parallel the antisocial interpersonal strategies offenders use discussed in chapter one especially those of being liked through altruism and charm and finding common ground in activities, same race, and ethnicity to name a few.

Authority

People pay attention to and obey authority figures and follow the lead of others in a position of authority (Lewis, 2015). Individuals are frequently rewarded for behaving in accordance with the opinion, advice and directives of authority figures in addition to being impressed by people who harness a sense of authority through business titles and education credentials. Giving the appearance of authority actually increases the likelihood that others will comply with requests even if their authority is illegitimate. For example, recall the tactic used by financial advisors who are seniors themselves touting their credentials as being "senior financial advisors" to increase the perceived authority and the sense of affinity due to age to get other seniors to pay them money. Authority plays a vital role since people are conditioned to respond to authority figures without diligently verifying their legitimacy (Cialdini, 2008). Social psychologists observe that unless there is strong evidence to the contrary, people have a natural tendency to think that authoritative statements reflect the true attitude of the person who made it (Rusch, 1999).

These observations are clearly illustrated in affinity fraud schemes because tactics of the offender is to target the leaders of a group, such as the religious leaders of an organization that represent an authority figure. Respected leaders are enlisted to spread the word that a fraudulent investment is legitimate and worthy of advancing the social and economic interests of the group. Moreover, leaders are usually the first to gain financially from the scheme which reinforces the belief that the offender and the financial opportunity is legitimate becoming the predator's "songbirds" because they sing the praises of the person they benefited from. Thus if the pastor of the church benefited, then his or her followers will benefit also. Psychology experiments have shown that for some people who tend not to scrutinize persuasive messages closely, their post-message attitudes were less dependent on scrutinizing the message when they perceived the source to be honest (Rusch, 1999). In this case if the authority figures endorse a salesperson as being legitimate, followers are more apt to accept the salesperson's opportunity as being legitimate (Rusch, 1999). Thus if the pastor trusts the predatory offender, there is no reason that the congregation cannot trust the offender; in such groups, news of success travels fast, thus word-by-mouth advertising works very efficiently.

Social Proof

Human beings rely heavily on the people around them for indications on how to think, feel, and act especially when people are uncertain about taking a given course of action (Cialdini, 2008). In many social situations one of the mental shortcuts relied upon, in determining what course of action is most appropriate, is to look to see what other people in the group are doing or saying. People tend to follow the lead of others they trust, thus social approval is important to them (Lewis, 2015). Often this is not an unreasonable way to behave since if others are doing it, it must be the right way. This phenomenon, known as social proof, can prompt one to take actions that may be against one's self-interest without taking the time to consider the decision they are making based on social proof more deeply. A common thread in many of these schemes is that new investors do little or no research into the investment opportunity being presented to them because of social proof.

This is why people give recommendations and testimonials especially to people who are similar to them based on religion, ethnicity, education, and professional status to name a few. It is a way of vouching for another stating that the person in question is reliable and trustworthy. All Ponzi schemers rely on this tactic to expand their scheme (Lewis, 2015). The mere fact that other members of their group are already investors is enough for them to write a check to these fraud offenders. Some academicians speculate that "the more affluent are more likely to be informed about the dangers of risky investments or products, employ independent financial advisors and spread their risks…they are more likely to read consumer journals and seek legal advice" (Croall, 2010). Yet this speculation does not fit the reality of what actually happens to the wealthy who are equally susceptible to being taken advantage of. Consider the insightful comments of Ronald Cass, Dean Emeritus of the Boston University School of Law, commenting on the Madoff case and how social proof can draw one into a scam:

> When my wife, who's a lawyer, and I were going to try to pick somebody to do health insurance for us, we asked the rabbi in our congregation, do you know anybody who does this? And he recommended another member of the congregation. We didn't go out and do due diligence, we didn't have to. The rabbi said this one's OK. And I think a lot of that is the sort of thing that was happening with the Madoff investments. Bernie Madoff was the chairman of NASDAQ, an advisor to the Securities and Exchange Commission (SEC), he was someone who had within his circle of clients enormously successful people. It was like he came pre-certified. You had every reason to trust the guy. He looked like and sounded like you and your friends. It is, in some ways, exactly that sort of set-up that makes sophisticated and successful people easy targets (Wertheimer, 2008).

Even those victims that, on the surface, would appear to be immune can be drawn into a fraud scam. Intelligence and education are not full-proof protection against deception, in fact there is evidence that highly educated people are easier at times to deceive because they do not expect to be deceived (Fenton-O'Creevy, 2005). For example, an educated friend of Madoff stated that when he asked Madoff about how he invests, Madoff stated, "I don't even know how to explain it…the system is doing it" (Kirtzman, 2009, p. 246). This friend lost millions of dollars that were invested on behalf of his family stating, "We just gave him everything…the betrayal was too horrible for him to even acknowledge" (Kirtzman, 2009, p. 246). Unfortunately, we are prone to believing that we have control over our motivations which may be to secure financial goals, but in fact our biases interfere with our ability to assess in a thoughtful manner the integrity of financial decisions (Fenton-O'Creevy, 2005). Many professional investors appear to have taken their due diligence enquiries no further than checking that the SEC was not flagging concerns about Madoff's operations.

They simply accepted the trust that existed because of Madoff's reputation. The comment above by Ronald Cass illustrates how well educated individuals are also capable of ignoring due diligence protocol for the sake of convenience established through trusting relationships. Consider Madoff's manipulation of Holocaust survivor and Nobel Prize laureate Elie Wiesel that mirrors the statements of Ronald Cass where the Elie Wiesel Foundation for Humanity, lost over $15 million and he and his wife lost their life savings of about $20 million. In an interview on National Public Radio, Wiesel met Madoff about 20 years previously through a friend, who, in turn, was a very close friend of Madoff, having known him for 50 years. The friend described Madoff as "so great and so good…And that's how we came to him" (Lewis, 2011b). Prior to investing with Madoff, Weisel stated, "We checked the people who have business with him, and they were among the best minds on Wall Street, the geniuses of finance…I am not a genius of finance, I teach philosophy and literature—and so it happened" (Strom, 2009).

What is interesting is that the concept of affinity fraud and the influence of social approval revealed itself with the financial institutions that were indirectly attached to Madoff that supported his securities. How do financial scams grow beyond the community that it originally began from? Madoff's fraud developed initially from the affinity and trust of the Jewish community, thus he was able to exploit this momentum of trust that occurred with those outside the Jewish community. There is a positive synergy that is created from these momentums of trust escalating Madoff's reputation as a financial advising "star". Their reputation for consistent or above average returns on investments acts attracts investors who demonstrate great trust in them by investing their money in the star's funds. Once an individual establishes a reputation as a star, then they can rapidly extend the range of their activities for, "if a person has a good reputation, one will quickly develop trusting beliefs about that individual, even without first-hand knowledge" (McKnight et al., 2006, p. 123). Indeed, even if a star has become less successful their reputation often remains undamaged, because "when many people perceive that an individual has a good reputation, it is harder for a negative event to significantly reduce a high level of trusting beliefs in that individual" (McKnight et al., 2006, p. 131).

Even when the SEC investigated Madoff, this fact was not enough of a red-flag for many to question his strategies. Madoff's demeanor and seemingly expert knowledge provided the perfect tool to manipulate his victims coupled with existing relationships with investigators while his spotless reputation allowed him to fly under the radar. In addition, modern financial markets are dependent on trust because markets are extremely complex and their products include significant reliance on trusting relationships to provide accurate information. For example, setting the share price for an initial public offering (IPO) is particularly difficult if, assessing the company's service quality is problematical or forecasting market conditions is recognized as being exceptionally challenging, so "parties that require this type of information therefore rely upon trusted intermediaries to provide it" (Morrison & Wilhelm, 2010, p. 3). Indeed a complete lack of trust would prevent a party from entering into any financial exchange because without it, endless safeguards would have to be sought. Consequently, even sophisticated investors often have to make assumptions about the security of investments they are making and to rely on the assessments and advice of others whose opinions they trust (Engel & McCoy, 2011, p. 59). The reality is trust requires one to be vulnerable in order to gain the benefits of trust—but it is not without its risks.

Likability through Similarities

One of the clearest indicators of whether we want to affiliate with others is that the more we like and approve of them, this in turn increases cultivating a closer relationship (Cialdini, 2008). People can be persuaded by people they like leading to complying with requests. They have a tendency to say yes rather than no especially to those whom are similar to themselves and make them feel good about themselves through charm and flattery (Lewis, 2015). Consider the offenders strategy of making people feel like they are the most important person in the world when they speak to them. It is difficult to not like and enjoy the company of someone that conjures up positive emotions in one due to feeling 'special'. People gravitate to and exhibit more pro-social behavior towards similar others (Baumeister, 1998), even others with incidental similarities, such as date of birth (Burger et al., 2004). Similar others are perceived as more persuasive (Perri & Brody, 2013). Recall the statements of offender Justin Paperny, when he was asked how he gained the trust of those that he would defraud. What tactics did you use to gain their trust? What seemed to work the best?

Paperny responded: "I never thought I was defrauding them...I was very polite, always leveraging off my vice president title, University of Southern California degree, and name dropping my baseball player clients did not hurt either. What I did best was find a way to identify with them. If they liked hockey, so did I. If they loved soccer, I did as well. I made it appear as if we had a lot in common" (Perri et al., 2014, p. 7). Our identification of a person as having characteristics identical or similar to our own such as other personal interests provides a strong incentive for people to adopt a mental shortcut in dealing with that person, to regard him or her more favorably merely because of that similarity. The optics of identifiable characteristics and affiliations creates the dynamic of inuring moral, trustworthy traits on an individual that may or may not exist. Again we can observe this factor illustrated by the Ronald Cass who commented on Madoff were he stated, "You had every reason to trust the guy. He looked like and sounded like you and your friends." The relationship between similarity, credibility, and compliance to a request is established; people are motivated to be attracted and influenced by similar others because it reinforces their own self-concept (Burgoon et al., 2002).

Scarcity and Exclusivity

In fundamental economic theory, scarcity relates to supply and demand. Typically the less there is of something in demand, the more it is valued; the more rare and uncommon an item is, access to a person, or service, the more people want it. Madoff was a master at creating the aura of exclusivity and scarcity. Madoff created a myth of exclusivity around his financial enterprise, giving his victims the impression that they belonged to a select group of people with access to his fund sending regular statements to them in which he detailed their holdings and their illusory high levels of profits (Reurink, 2016). Madoff's veil of exclusivity overcame victim's hesitancy to invest with him because he would tell them that he did not need their money due to having enough to manage (Carozza, 2009). Yet "he would say, because I like you I'll give you special access and allow you, and only you, to invest...Then he would give them a flattering reason why he considered them special and they'd fall for it hook, line and sinker" (Carozza, 2009, p. 61). Madoff made it known that he had, 1) turned away some investors, 2) refused future dealings with some existing investors, 3) insisted that investors he accepted should not talk to outsiders, and 4) returned funds to investors who asked penetrating questions.

Many Madoff investors bragged how Madoff had closed his funds to new investors, but they had special access because Madoff was willing to accepted new money from them. Madoff developed relationships by using his reputation to demand appropriate behavior from investors, shunned one-on-one meetings with most of his investors, wrapping himself in an "Oz-like aura" making him even more desirable to those seeking access (Chernow, 2009). Instead of openly courting investors, Madoff pretended to fend them off making it seem impossible to invest with him. Madoff also used the veil of exclusivity to overcome victims' hesitancy to invest. One of the reasons Madoff was able to perpetrate his fraud for so long was his preference for marketing his investment business by word of mouth (Brander & Varchaver, 2009). To invest with Madoff, new investors needed special introductions even though eventually they may never meet him personally. His seemingly random decisions not to accept some potential investors, while bewildering to those he rejected increased his reputation, making clients who had accounts with him feel special, part of a chosen fellowship.

What now appears to be his practiced indifference or disinterest in attracting new business became part of his mystique, part of his allure as one schoolmate of Madoff's described how this tactic ensnared him. The classmate claims he felt that Madoff was doing him a favor coupled with the fact that now he was connected to someone that was at the top of his field, immensely successful, connected with powerful friends, shared his Jewish faith, and Madoff has close ties to his family. Consider the effect on this classmate of the fear of not being part of the club when Madoff rejected him was offset by the excitement of now being accepted into the club coupled with the excitement of securing new wealth. After a 50 year hiatus, this friend called Madoff with some questions about where to invest the proceeds from his sold business and Madoff disclosed facts about his asset management fund, but when the friend asked about getting into his fund, Madoff declined stating:

'I can't, 'It's a closed fund.' At that, Bernie told him there was someone in the office who wanted to speak with him. He handed the phone to Ruth [his wife]." They chatted "excitedly," until she interrupted him in mid-sentence. "Bernie wants to talk to you again," she said and Bernie took the phone back. "You know what...we've known you a long time, and I'll open it up for you to come in...But can you meet the minimum?" Bernie cited $2 million. "I can meet that...Do you mind if I bring others in with me, some family?" Not at all, Madoff said (Lewis, 2011b, p. 71).

To further this issue of how Madoff was perceived, let us revisit the Elie Wiesel scenario. Elie thought quite highly of Madoff after they first had dinner together. One thing Elie remembered is that the topic of money never came up instead talking about ethics and education (Strom, 2009). Wiesel admitted that he bought into the Madoff mystique by being charmed and feeling that sense of specialness because of the exclusivity of being in Madoff's orbit creating the impression that he was making an exception by allowing Wiesel to invest with him. Madoff tried to persuade Wiesel to give up his academic position at Boston University and move to Queens College "Because his wife went to Queens College so they wanted to establish a chair, a special chair for me...We thought he was God, we trusted everything in his hand; everybody told us in the field of finances, you can do much more...because of Mr. Madoff, the saviour" (Lewis, 2011b, p. 75). Weisel further stated, "I remember that it was a myth that he created around him, that everything was so special, so unique, that it had to be secret. It was like a mystical mythology that nobody could understand...He gave the impression that maybe 100 people belonged to the club. Now we know thousands of them were cheated by him" (Nocera, 2009).

Fund managers, Avellino and Bienes, felt this sense of "specialness" being part of Madoff's select few who could benefit from his alleged investing genius. When Michael Bienes was interviewed, they asked him a series of questions such as whether Madoff intimidated Bienes and he responded "yes" (Lewis 2011b, p. 74). When they asked Bienes whether they thought he was up to no good, Bienes responded, "Up to no good? He was a god. He was my life" (Lewis, 2011b, p. 74). At a luncheon with Madoff, Bienes thanked him for being invited and Madoff said, "Hey, come on—we're family, aren't we." Bienes thought, "At that moment he had me. He had me. It really took me because he had a presence about him, an aura. He really captivated you" (Lewis, 2011b, p. 74). Bienes's insight provides us with information of how people bond to others even if they are confronted with evidence that someone like Madoff was involved in a multibillion dollar fraud scheme. We observe this same bonding by people who still think highly of their political leaders even when learning of the atrocities they ordered to be performed by their followers.

Reciprocity

A well-recognized rule of social interaction requires that if someone gives us or promises to give something, there is an inclination to reciprocate by providing something in return (Cialdini, 2008). The norm of reciprocation, ingrained in us through socialization, is one of the strongest and most pervasive social forces in all human cultures because it helps us to build trust with others (Cialdini & Goldstein, 2004). Reciprocation recognizes that people feel indebted to those who do something for them or give them something. For example, one can observe how affinity fraud offenders contribute to their target's cause by donating money in order to prove their allegiance to the group with the expectation that the target audience will feel obligated to listen to the offender's opportunity and/or participate in the opportunity. This dynamic is illustrated by offender Madoff and Petters donating millions to charities and religious organizations that invested with him. Recall how Madoff gave to the Center for Jewish History, the American Liver Foundation, Lymphoma Research Foundation, Brandeis University, Hofstra University and Queens College to name a few.

Consistency and Commitment

Generally speaking, people tend to align themselves more with others when they are clear as to commitments they are expected to fulfill (Cialdini, 2008). People do not like to back out of deals because people strive for consistency in their commitments, in other words, being true to their word. For example, once a step is taken, such as using a financial advisor, there is pressure to continue, be consistent and commit to the advisor unless there are red-flags to not commit (Lewis, 2015). People tend to continue a course of action once it is taken, even if their former decisions turn out to be poor or even blatantly wrong by escalating their commitment to a decision (Palazzo et al., 2012). The reason for this tendency lays in the fact that once people have invested time, money, or other resources in a decision, it creates sunk costs that should not be ignored, yet making it more difficult to consider a different path (Palazzo et al., 2012). The example of the Amish community previously mentioned above is an excellent example of the power of being consistent where even in the face of facts, they were unwilling to abandon their commitments to the people that defrauded them. Recall what one of the defrauded Amish previously stated about Timothy Moffett that illustrates this desire to not abandon their commitments even when there is ample evidence of deception, "Tim had our word, to an Amish that commitment is sacred" (Lewis, 2015, p. 118).

Challenges in Overcoming Predatory Offense Victimization

Affinity fraud is inherently difficult to overcome because group trust is so powerful in overcoming people's skepticism that the sophisticated and the unsophisticated, the educated and uneducated fall prey to such scams. Many such frauds receive little media attention because even if the losses involved are significant, many of the victims do not pursue or make their involvement public. Also, because of the unique relationship that the fraudster exploits in an affinity fraud scheme, many victims simply refuse to believe that an individual they trusted and that "seems like them" would actually steal money from them. It is not unusual for affinity fraud scams to last significantly longer than other frauds. This is because once the trust is established, not only are investors less likely to fully investigate the scam, but they also are less likely to believe they have been defrauded and, even when they do believe so, less likely to report the fraud outside of the group (Fairfax, 2010). Moreover, victims refuse to believe that someone from their own congregation would steal from them, especially when the perpetrators cloaked themselves in a religious value system to convince others that they were sent by a higher authority to make others wealthy (Perri & Brody, 2011a).

Furthermore, victims may be unable to face the truth because the fraudster was able to build emotional bonds with the victims based on the belief that their shared characteristics creates a special trust that only those within the group share and would not violate. Unfortunately, victims of affinity fraud believe that the fraudster would not lie to them and instead these victims choose to wait and hope for the big payoff they were originally promised or may attempt to work matters out within the group setting. Religious organizations embody non-judgmental principles, such as trust, honesty, and giving a person the benefit of the doubt. Recall from chapter one how goodwill and trust is perceived by the offender as weaknesses to exploit together with the projection bias that victims are willing to engage in believing that if they show goodwill, the offender will see the mistakes they have made and try to change their way. Overall, the exploitation of trust combined with projection bias is a recipe for disaster. Religious-based affinity fraud poses special problems for securities regulators because victims are reluctant to inform investigators that they have been scammed. Not only are victims of affinity fraud less likely to contact authorities or take legal action, affinity fraud is difficult for federal and state regulators or law enforcement officials to detect because of the tight-knit structure of many groups. At times the reluctance to involve securities regulators can be attributed to a negative impression of law enforcement and a desire to resolve the problem within a group rather than from outside help (Austin, 2004).

Recall with Seng Tan and James Buchan, the Cambodian victims did not go to the authorities. Affinity fraudsters mislead victims by convincing them that, by cooperating with the government to investigate the discovered fraud, they may be persecuted for their religious beliefs or their race. They also assert that reporting the fraud will prohibit any possible return on their investment (Austin, 2004). In addition, when these criminals are confronted by the authorities, they often attempt to persuade investors not to cooperate by referring to previously signed confidentiality agreements (Reed, 2007). Their reluctance may be attributable to a sense of embarrassment and the desire to not want to have a member of their organization prosecuted. In reality, these perpetrators never shared the goodwill and belief systems of the organization's membership to begin with. Organizations often try to handle negative news in-house to avoid bad publicity, so they are reluctant to report even gross criminal misconduct on the part of the predators in their midst, preferring to transfer them, fire them, or have them leave quietly. Victims may also believe that alerting the authorities may preclude the perpetrator from having a "change of heart" and returning the money although often there is no money left to return. Another reason that authorities are not alerted is because of the desire of the defrauded group to have the culprit "repent" for stealing from the church (Fairfax, 2002-2003).

Strategies to Reduce Predatory Fraud Victimization

Ironically, the qualities of trust and affinity that groups use to advance the economic and social well-being of their members are also their weakness. It is precisely because this type of fraud relies on people reducing formality as a result of their familiarity impulses that vigilance is in order to protect the goodwill of groups who want to engage in legitimate investment opportunities. Yet, Ponzi scheme victims are often labeled too greedy or too gullible feeding upon people's predictable behavior: self-interest and laziness (Baird & Rasmussen, 2002). Perhaps people can be too trusting or engage in misplaced trust where warning signs are ignored. However today, as contrasted in the past, we are required to look after our own financial security with more involvement which means looking for good investments to fund retirement as an example. In the past, a person could perhaps rely on a guaranteed pension from their place of work at least shaving down some of the anxiety associated with retirement. People, perhaps naively and not well versed in financial matters, do not have the ability to know how to navigate this area of life even if they are well educated. One can be educated but this does not necessarily mean they are educated in all areas of life.

Without trust in financial markets and relying on the advice of financial advisors, investors would have their investment options limited—the mistake they make is that they trusted the wrong person who exploited their confidence. In fact for so many victims, it was not greed that drove them to invest, but to gain some financial security to preserve their wealth. If there is one strategy that can be quickly implemented to protect oneself and a group from being victimized, it is to remind oneself that trust is not a substitute for due diligence. Although this strategy may appear to be a low-cost method to mitigate against victimization, it is probably the hardest obstacle to overcome especially when we are in the company of others that are encouraging participation in an alleged investment. That said, there are some steps one can implement to help them navigate opportunities that may appear too good to be true. Consider that one should implement professional skepticism previously discussed to assist in understanding the basis of people's representations. Although not an all-inclusive list, some steps to implement when evaluating opportunities and the accompanying red-flags include:

- Be wary of secrecy. If an investment is legitimate, there should be full disclosure.
- Do not ignore a business that is new in town and does not offer an adequate history of where the owners come from and where their operations were previously located.
- Be suspicious of investment success that is dependent on someone's "unique expertise" such as the uncanny ability to predict the timing of market fluctuations as to when to buy and when to sell.
- Inquire whether there is independence to avoid conflicts of interest and proper segregation of duties where a fund manager, for example, should not be broker or have custody of the money.
- Be wary of investments sold as once-in-a-lifetime opportunities, particularly when the promoter bases the recommendation on inside or confidential information.
- Find out who is auditing the firm in order to perform due diligence. If there is no auditor that is an immediate red-flag. Auditors should be familiar with the industry they are auditing.
- Avoid an investment if promoters that they do not have the time to reduce to writing the particulars about the investment or that they are unregulated because they are for religious institutions.
- Obtain in writing information detailing the risk in the investment, what the money is going to be invested in, who their attorneys and accountants are, financial statements, any conflicts of interests and procedures to get your money out.

- Investors should not let their guard down when someone attempts to appeal to their professional, cultural, racial or religious background. Consider the strategy that is being used to increase the emotional seduction by pointing out the common traits that one has with the group in general.
- Be careful not to be seduced by "star" advisors, celebratory activities they engage in such as throwing big parties and the celebrities and possibly politicians, they bring into their circle to convince others that they are legitimate and successful because of celebrity endorsement.
- Investors should be wary of opportunities that outperform competitors with similar investments. Typically, investments ought to move broadly in line with market trends. In addition, it is important for investors to understand how investment returns are actually generated.
- Be wary of investments that promise spectacular profits or guaranteed returns with little or no risk. If an opportunity has unbelievable returns, you are probably dealing with an amateur scam artist while opportunities that are reasonable and consistent is from an experienced scam artist.
- Ask for neutral professional advice from an outside expert not associated with the salesperson to evaluate the investment. When investors are told to keep the investment opportunity confidential and discourage independent professionals from evaluating an opportunity that is a red-flag increasing skepticism of the legitimacy of the opportunity.
- Find out how long the business has been in operation, where it is registered, and make sure it is registered to do business in your state. In addition, is the investment registered with the SEC or another other appropriate authority? Securities regulations tend to be high and any representation that the opportunity falls outside of regulation is an immediate red-flag.
- It is important to keep one's excitement and greed in check. Therefore, it is advised to take one's time in making a decision by not quickly participating in an opportunity and to consider the risks of participation. Consider that offenders want to increase your emotional commitment to their scam and not over think the risks attached by asking too many questions.
- What are the bases of the testimonials used that are pushing their product or service? Are the testimonials live testimonials or simple paper handouts? Are people that give testimonials allowed to be asked questions? Is their presence for a limited purpose and thus not allowed to be asked questions to verify the success they achieved through investing with a particular person(s)?
- Do not accept vague or evasive explanations to legitimate concerns and questions you have about an opportunity. The unwillingness to answer questions is an immediate red-flag as to its legitimacy. Any type of belittlement or public embarrassment projected to a person(s) who has questions such as making the person asking the question feel less than intelligent is an immediate fraud red-flag.

Conclusion

Affinity and the special trust we believe we share with someone is not a substitute for due diligence or not implementing safeguards by relying on representations that may or may not be genuine. Due diligence protocol should include seeking neutral, outside counsel who can serve as an objective voice in the evaluation of opportunities and being skeptical of those that appear to cater to one's emotional state by invoking that trust is inherent because of similar characteristics and affiliations. We cannot always know when predators will exploit us, but knowledge helps. If we are sensitized to how predators think and how they use legitimate organizations, we can better protect ourselves. It would behoove those that may be viewed as potential victims to implement due diligence protocol to minimize the risk of financial exploitation.

Chapter 4

Red and White Collar Crime Women Offenders

By all accounts Chalana McFarland appeared to represent the successful real estate attorney, yet she perpetrated a variety of fraud schemes including identity theft, fraudulent use of social security numbers, money laundering, and mortgage fraud devastating many families who bought homes and lending institutions who serviced these families. Chalana was sentenced to thirty years prison and ordered to pay $12 million even though she could have been sentenced to a life term for the fraud scheme she initiated and controlled with the assistance of her co-conspirators. The sentencing judge's comments in the case parallels current research on white-collar criminals who exhibit remorseless, exploitative behaviors when he stated that Chalana has "shown no remorse, she's done nothing but tell one lie after another. She's done everything possible to obstruct the investigation in this case. She continues to try to persuade everyone that somehow she just got involved in this thing and didn't know what was going on" (McFarland, n.d., p. 26).

Within the past 50 years, industrialized countries witnessed the rise of women holding positions traditionally held by men. At one time women, erroneously, were not thought of as capable of fulfilling such positions because of beliefs surrounding gender based on socio-cultural norms. Women were deemed less intelligent than men, thus the thought of a well-educated woman appeared foreign. Moreover, women were thought of as the weaker sex and the thought of women participating in the military or in law enforcement was not tolerated. Yet as we have observed throughout the decades, myths surrounding what women are and are not capable of has dissolved over time. While many areas of female progress are attributed to the empowerment of women, historically the study of female criminality, as opposed to the study of male criminality, has only recently been linked to female antisocial behaviors instead of relying on socio-cultural gender stereotypes. The topic of female criminality still adheres to myths accepted by some in society of what types of deviant behavior women are capable of which are not based on fact, but stereotype, yet perceptions have been changing.

Views have been changing because news about female criminality is widespread due to technological advancements that make what is occurring in one part of the country or the world known instantaneously. Thus what may have appeared to be isolated instances of female criminality only displayed in the past in local media outlets such as the local newspaper or the local television station, today we have the ability to observe more of the extent of female criminality through the use of the internet. Studies of women and white-collar crime are sparse and women's full participation in corporate and occupational crime remains in need of more research. There was a time when the idea that women could commit crimes in a similar manner to men, both white-collar and non-white-collar, was considered alien. Yet "women are no more honest, no more decent, and no more moral than men. The only reason they had lower crime rates, particularly white-collar crime, was because they had few opportunities to commit crime" (Dodge, 2016, p. 203). Moreover, they face the same pressures, incentives, motives, and exploitable opportunities that push men into committing white-collar crime for financial reasons is gender neutral (Dodge, 2016).

Within this chapter we learn what role female criminality plays in white-collar crime and those that engage in both fraud and violence. Consider the case of Natavia Lowery who was found guilty for the murder, by blunt trauma force to the head, of Linda Stein. Lowery was a personal assistant to Stein (Martinez, 2010). The prosecution argued that when Stein learned of and confronted Lowery about the identity theft, credit card and check fraud in excess of $30,000 that she perpetrated, Lowery planned the murder of Stein in Stein's apartment. The prosecution offered audio tapped evidence of Lowery pretending to be Linda Stein to obtain credit cards under Stein's name (Ross et.al, 2007). In addition, we explore female characteristics and case studies to illustrate the application of behavioral influences to their criminal profile. With more women in the workforce, additional research will be needed to construct precise female fraud offender profiles especially as they attain leadership positions. It will be interesting to observe if men's corrupt leadership traits exhibited are displayed by women in leadership positions or whether their style differs in order to facilitate misconduct.

Female White-collar Crime Characteristics

Although male sex role norms do not prescribe crime, risk-taking and defying social convention are qualities typically linked to men more than to women. Women are not less amenable to risk, rather, their risk-taking is less likely to violate the law and more likely to be rationalized as protective of valued relationships whereas men take greater risks to attain and protect status, power, monetary gain, or competitive advantage rationalizing their crimes as stemming from routine business practices (Steffenmeier et al., 2013). Research on work/occupations and business enterprise suggests women generally adhere to a different way of doing business that carries a sense of connectedness and brings a more ethical perspective to the workplace. It is suggested that corporate women, more than corporate men, use their organizational power to address issues of social responsibility and are more inclined to make people, not just profits, a priority (Steffenmeier et al., 2013). Female executives tend to score more positively on measures of socialization, self-control, empathy, and integrity with ethical orientations serving as a deterrent to corporate misconduct (Steffenmeier et al., 2013).

Gaining and protecting privileged status, economic power, and wealth may motivate men more than women to use illegal means. Furthermore, research on entrepreneurship and management styles finds that women are more risk-averse in business ventures, whereas men are more inclined toward strategic, proactive risk-taking and aggressive implementation of bold strategies in the face of uncertainty. Masculine traits emphasizing competition and achievement at all costs may propel more men than women who are in middle and managerial ranks to become involved in corporate crime. This is especially likely in male dominated environments and criminal coalitions where men's risk-taking propensities create a synergistic effect where the probability of engaging in misconduct increases. Consider research on stress and mental health finds that men are more focused on material goals, more vulnerable to financial strain and loss of status, and more likely to use criminal coping strategies in response to perceived pressures (Steffenmeier et al., 2013). Women as well as men adopt a rational approach to fraud meaning that when a criminal opportunity is attractive as a means of satisfying a motive, such as assisting family during financial difficulties or forestalling failure, rational actors will weigh the costs and benefits of the act and make a rational choice even if criminal. This does not mean that the offender's risk assessment to arrive at their cost-benefit analysis may not be flawed. The question is, does the risk assessment appear rational as interpreted in the mind of the offender.

Darleen Druyun, for example, began her career as a civilian contracting intern for the U.S. Air Force. As she moved up the bureaucratic hierarchy over the course of her 32 years, she earned a reputation as being dedicated and a no-nonsense administrator who saved the Air Force over $20 billion in procurement cost. Yet, by her own admission, she steered billions of dollars in contracts to Boeing Co., in appreciation for Boeing job offers to her daughter, future son-in-law, and ultimately herself (Palmer, 2012). The motivation underlying other female accounts aligns with a more traditional explanation of fraud. In one study, twice as many female offenders compared to men had a primary motivation of pleasing others (Goldstraw, 2005). Accounts of this nature included, a) not being able to refuse their families anything, b) wishing to appear as a perfect wife and mother, c) needing to contribute to the household finances, d) supporting children after the breakup of a relationship, and e) wishing to buy gifts for partners as a means of demonstrating affection (Goldstraw, 2005). Moreover, not all female offenders stated they committed their crimes due to greed, gambling or through duty to, or influence of, family or friends. Other motivations for the women related to ensuring the continuation of a business, whether this was their own, a family business or the organization for which they worked.

White-collar Crime Case Studies

Research on business crime and occupational misconduct suggests that even when similar on-the-job theft or fraud opportunities exist, women still are less likely to commit crime and, when they do, their crimes tend to yield lower gains (Steffenmeier et al., 2013). Along with differences in moral orientations and risk-taking, men and women may differ in how they view opportunities for corporate fraud because women who move into top management positions may be deterred by their unique placement and sense they are watched more carefully than men in those positions (Benson & Simpson, 2009). Statistics suggest women's opportunities to commit corporate crimes as executives remain limited, however, their opportunities for corporate crime as mid-level managers and supervisors have markedly increased (Steffenmeier et al., 2013). Crime statistics reveal that women are advancing through the corporate ranks to executive position and adopting a more traditional corporate mindset that can result in illegal activities especially because greater participation creates more opportunities to offend (Dodge, 2016). Women in management positions are more able to exploit opportunities or weaknesses in an organization's internal control systems because they know them, understand them, and have control over them.

Currently there does not appear to be precise personality differences between men and women that distinguish their participation in fraud, in fact "men and women may be more alike than unique in terms of the factors and circumstances that predict their involvement in white-collar crime, but they are likely to differ with regard to motivation and opportunity" (Van Herwaarden, 2018, p. 9). As more women enter professional status, further study will illuminate whether their motivations for fraud will change. That being said, "greed, fame, and power, however, are likely to impact both genders in a similar fashion, despite sociological and biological differences" (Dodge, 2007, p. 395). Moreover, as women move into higher executive positions, they too will be in a position to take advantage of opportunities to exploit whether legally or illegally driven by the same factors and motivations as men (Dodge, 2007). Time will tell to what extent female corporate executives will engage in fraud especially when they are exposed to the same financial pressures and opportunities to commit fraud as men coupled with having rationalizations available to rely on.

Enron Offenders

The first major corporate conspiracy of this century involved Enron. Top Enron executives were indicted for misrepresentation of financial statements or outright accounting fraud, such as falsely inflating sales, off-the-books partnerships and transactions, and concealment of expenses or bonuses to top executives. The three women, among the 34 employees charged in connection with Enron's illegal accounting practices, each occupied a strategically useful position for the conspiracy, but may have played a minor or no role in the fraud (Steffenmeier et al., 2013). Sheila Kahanek, an Enron accountant, was charged, but acquitted of helping push through Enron's false sale of power-generating barges to Merrill Lynch to inflate Enron's earnings. The false sale entailed Enron selling Merrill Lynch power-generating barges with the agreement that Merrill Lynch would at a later date resell them to Enron. Kahanek's trial testimony in her own defense revealed she was marginal to the conspiracy. Kahanek was left out of incriminating e-mails in which the main co-conspirators planned their actions, received no invitation to celebrate the deal because she protested the sale, and never earned a bonus on the barge deal, as did the executives, for meeting profit goals. However, Kahanek ignored multiple warnings about the impropriety of the fictitious sales eventually causing her to leave Enron in mid-2001 (Steffenmeier et al., 2013).

Paula Rieker, a board of director secretary and manager of investor relations, compiled information for investors and prepared revenue reports for the board. She had no role in the larger Enron conspiracy, but was charged with insider trading for selling stock upon learning of an upcoming report of a much larger than anticipated loss in Enron's broadband unit. In her testimony, she admitted to sometimes ignoring executives' aggressive bookkeeping techniques stating, "I fell into the role of being a good corporate citizen" (Steffenmeier et al., 2013, p. 466). However, when CEO Skilling directed her to falsify revenue reports in a news release, Rieker refused and e-mailed a top Enron official outlining the misrepresentation. Kahanek and Rieker became involved in the fraud because of their corporate positions involving financial or compliance transactions. Both women expressed objections to the actions deemed necessary to meet profit goals and neither woman was viewed by the men as part of the crime network. Their lack of illegal gain reflects their minor involvement.

Lea Fastow is one of a number of spouses who played a trivial role in the company's conspiracy, in contrast to the major roles played by their husbands. Her husband, CFO Andrew Fastow, was the main architect of the Enron conspiracy. Her main culpability was cosigning false joint income tax returns that failed to report ill-gotten gains from her husband's illegal dealings, making her complicit, but not proactively involved. She pled guilty to a misdemeanor tax crime and served a ten month prison term for her testimony against Enron officials and for encouraging her husband into pleading guilty and cooperating with the prosecution.

HealthSouth Offenders

When financial results failed to meet earnings expectations, senior executives held meetings with accounting staff who were directed to falsify HealthSouth's financial statements to meet Wall Street analysts' expectations. Ultimately, nineteen employees were indicted, including five women and all the women were in various accounting-related positions. These women were issued instructions by senior personnel to falsify financial records and create fictitious documents to conceal the massive accounting fraud. In contrast to senior officials who enriched themselves via bonuses, stock options, and loans, none of the five female defendants profited except through keeping their jobs or gaining a promotion. All five pled guilty and were sentenced to probation (Steffenmeier et al., 2013).

Theranos CEO Elizabeth Holmes

I don't think anyone disputes that Elizabeth and her team are visionaries.

Gary St. Hilaire, CEO of Capital BlueCross

This case and facts are partially provided by the Securities and Exchange Commission (SEC) involves the fraudulent offer and sale of securities by Theranos, Inc., a California company that aimed to improve medical diagnosis equipment (SEC 2018). The SEC and later criminal charges filed by the Department of Justice against Chief Executive Officer Elizabeth Holmes and Chief Operating Officer Ramesh Balwani, claim that they raised more than $700 million from late 2013 to 2015 through deception. They deceived investors by making it appear as if Theranos successfully developed a commercially-ready portable blood analyzer, referred to as a miniLab that could perform a full range of laboratory tests from a small sample of blood. They deceived investors by, 1) making false and misleading statements to the media, 2) hosting misleading technology demonstrations, 3) providing false and misleading financial information on its financial condition, and 4) overstating the extent of Theranos' relationships with commercial partners and government entities such the U.S. Department of Defense (DOD), and its regulatory status with the U.S. Food and Drug Administration (FDA).

Initially Elizabeth received positive media attention. Investors believed Theranos successfully developed a blood analyzer that was capable of conducting a comprehensive set of blood tests from a few drops of blood from a finger prick that was collected in a very small vial. Elizabeth interviewed and appeared in *Wall Street Journal* articles and additional articles written continued to raise Theranos' public profile and tout its technological capabilities. An April 2014 *Wired* article stated that "[i]nstead of vials of blood—one for every test needed—Theranos requires only a pinprick and a drop of blood. With that they can perform hundreds of tests, from standard cholesterol checks to sophisticated genetic analyses." Similarly a June, 2014 *Fortune* article noted that "[Theranos] currently offers more than 200 – and is ramping up to offer more than 1,000 – of the most commonly ordered blood diagnostic tests, all without the need for a syringe." *Fortune* also distinguished Theranos from other blood testing companies because "Theranos does not buy any analyzers from third parties." In contrast to the large traditional blood analyzers that occupied whole rooms, Theranos' miniLabs "look[ed] like large desktop computer towers."

By the end of 2014, *Forbes* declared that Elizabeth was "the youngest self-made woman billionaire" whose company could, "with a painless prick...quickly test a drop of blood at a fraction of the price of commercial labs which need more than one vial." In e-mail conversations with the *Fortune* reporter, Elizabeth stated that "it is ok to say the analytical systems are about the size of a desktop computer." Elizabeth also befriended well-regarded public figures to invest in Theranos and also to be board of director members. Former Secretary of State General James Mattis met Elizabeth around 2011 to 2012. He described Elizabeth as having "one of the most mature and well-honed sense of ethics—personal ethics, managerial ethics, business ethics, [and] medical ethics that I've ever heard articulated (Gitlin, 2018)." Other well-known public figures became involved with Theranos. Former U.S. Secretary of State, Henry Kissinger, was a Theranos Board of Directors member who invested $3 million of his own money into the company (Jackson, 2021a). Kissinger also introduced Elizabeth to the Walmart Walton family and De Vos family of Am-Way who invested money into Theranos. Other well-known citizens on the board where former Senator Sam Nunn and former Secretary of Defense William Perry under President Bill Clinton (Lopatto, 2021). William Perry is a mathematician, engineer and Stanford professor. He told *The New Yorker* magazine in 2014 that Ms. Holmes "has sometimes been called another Steve Jobs, but I think that's an inadequate comparison. She has a social consciousness that Steve never had. He was a genius; she's one with a big heart (Streitfeld, 2022)."

According to Elizabeth, Theranos' technology could provide blood testing that was faster, cheaper, and more accurate than existing competitor blood testing laboratories through its miniLab. Yet at all times Elizabeth was aware that in its clinical laboratory tests of their product, Theranos' miniLab performed only approximately 12 tests of the over 200 tests on Theranos' published clinical patient testing data used to attract investors. For the other clinical tests, Theranos used non-Theranos commercially available blood analyzers, some of which Theranos modified to analyze blood samples to process the remainder of its patient samples used to collect data. In early 2010, even though the miniLab was not commercially ready, Holmes pursued contracts with a large national pharmacy chain named Walgreens and a large national grocery chain named Safeway. The goal was to place miniLabs at designated "Patient Service Centers" in retail stores so that patients could get their diagnostic tests performed while shopping. Elizabeth approved and provided presentations and other written materials to Walgreen executives representing that Theranos had the ability to conduct a broad range of tests on its miniLab, including general chemistry tests, wellness tests, and some predictive and diagnostic health tests.

These presentation materials stated that Theranos would be ready to begin blood testing on its miniLab at Walgreens stores by the fourth quarter of 2010. Elizabeth also told Walgreens' executives that Theranos could conduct hundreds of blood tests through fingerstick or the puncture of a finger in less than one hour, and that it could be offered for less than Theranos' competitors. Based on these representations, Walgreens executives thought the miniLab was capable of performing a wide range of the tests offered by traditional laboratories. For example, Elizabeth told Walgreens that Theranos could perform approximately ninety percent of the tests that a large, traditional central lab could perform. Between 2010 and 2013, Theranos continued to work on developing its miniLab with an eye towards launching its services in Walgreens and Safeway stores. In July 2010, Walgreens entered into a contract with Theranos to service them. Elizabeth also told Safeway's then-CEO Steven Burd that Theranos successfully miniaturized the blood analysis laboratory in addition to the fact that the miniLab was used in the military. Based on these representations, in September 2010, Safeway contracted with Theranos to offer Theranos patient testing in Safeway stores.

CEO Burd who partnered and invested millions in the efforts to implement Theranos's technology, compared Elizabeth to four U.S. presidents he met in terms of her ability to command a room stating: "There are very few people that I've met in business that I would actually say were charismatic…she was clearly charismatic. She was very smart (O'Brien, 2021)." Burd further stated: "She would rise to the top of the pile in terms of vision, in terms of command of the information, clearly in terms of delivery. She was always decisive (Jackson, 2021b)." Interestingly, Burd stated that Elizabeth brought the Minilab to a board meeting and offered the board an opportunity to take the test. She ran a PSA or prostate antigen test that would serve as a indication of possible cancer; board members had their blood drawn, but were never told the results of the test (Siddiqui, 2021). Yet Safeway still signed a $400 million contract with Theranos, but Burd was disappointed due to launch delays, lost blood samples, nonsensical test results and poor patient experience together with the potential reputational risk.

As September, 2013 approached, the date for the launch of the first phase of the implementation of Theranos services in Walgreen stores, it became clear to Elizabeth that the miniLab would not be ready. Moreover, Elizabeth and Ramesh asked Theranos' engineers in July 2013 to modify non-Theranos blood analyzers so they could analyze blood samples as if the blood analysis came from their product. Elizabeth and Theranos never told Walgreens and Safeway about Theranos' technological challenges they experienced with the miniLab. For instance, in July and August 2013, Theranos coordinated technology demonstrations for various Walgreens executives in advance of the retail launch. Theranos collected finger pricked blood samples from

166

Walgreens executives. Instead of using Theranos machines to process the tests on these samples, unknown to the Walgreens executives, Theranos used the modified non-Theranos machines to process a portion of the tests. Elizabeth also instructed Theranos employees to place numerous miniLabs, which could only be used for research and development purposes and not for clinical testing, in a room in Theranos's clinical lab. This made it appear as if Theranos used its miniLab for clinical purposes.

Elizabeth then led a group of Walgreens executives on a tour of that room, and those Walgreens executives saw rows of miniLabs in Theranos' clinical lab. Based on Holmes' presentation, Walgreens executives understood that the blood from their demonstration samples would be tested on a Theranos miniLabs. In addition, Holmes invited Vice President Joseph Biden to visit Theranos' facility in Newark, California where she took him on a tour that turned out to be a fake automated laboratory. Elizabeth's deception parallels fraud offender and CEO Barry Minkow where he made a building look like he was renovating it by having auditors walk through it as verification that he had building restoration contracts. Recall another previous display of deception by Enron CEO Jeffrey Skilling when he tried to launch the broadband business claiming to be worth billions of dollars. To prove his claim, investors and Wall Street analyst were invited to Enron's headquarters where he opened the doors to the operations war room. Enron spent half a million dollars outfitting the war room to look like the hub of a thriving enterprise where computers were flashing up statistics and charts to make it appear like real transactions were occurring while secretaries were recruited from other floors to pretend that they were part of the business team.

In response to a question about a rumor that Theranos was facing technological challenges with its miniLabs, Elizabeth and Ramesh assured Safeway's General Counsel that there was no technological problems and that the miniLab was capable of performing ninety percent of the blood tests typically requested by doctors for their patients. From its retail launch in September, 2013 to the time it closed its clinical laboratories in 2016, Theranos never used its miniLab for patient testing in its clinical laboratory. Theranos conducted, at best, 12 tests using the earlier-generation miniLabs, and processed about 50 to 60 tests using the modified non-Theranos blood analyzers. Theranos processed the remaining 100-plus tests it offered at Walgreens using the same types of industry standard technology as other traditional laboratories, or sent tests out to third party laboratories. Furthermore, Holmes ordered Theranos employees to compile background material to be given to potential and actual investors in a binder. The typical investor binder included, 1) a cover letter drafted and signed by Elizabeth, 2) a company overview, 3) reports of clinical trials work Theranos performed with its pharmaceutical companies such as Pfizer, 4) financial projections, and 5) articles and profiles about Theranos, including the previously mentioned articles from *The Wall Street Journal*, *Wired*, and *Fortune*.

One section of the investor binders displayed work purportedly related to the clinical trials work Theranos performed with pharmaceutical companies. The reports prominently featured the company logos of well-known pharmaceutical companies, suggesting that the reports were drafted by these pharmaceutical companies. Pfizer denies giving Theranos permission to use its logo for Theranos's investor material claiming that their blood-testing technology had been comprehensively validated by ten of the 15 largest pharmaceutical companies. However, as Elizabeth knew, only one report in the investor binder was co-written by a pharmaceutical client. The other two reports were drafted by Theranos employees, deceptively displaying the logos of pharmaceutical companies that had no involvement with Theranos. Moreover, legal counsel to Elizabeth warned her that Theranos should not make claims that its technology was "more precise, faster and easier with the highest level of accuracy, that the company could provide results to you and your doctor faster than previously possible (De Chant, 2021b)." One attorney reviewing Theranos marketing materials stated: "I haven't quite worked my way through the whole website, but I'm worried. For example, every time you say 'better' without specifying what it is better than, you are making a comparative claim, at least to all market leaders. You must be able to substantiate these claims (Lopatto, 2021b)." Elizabeth ignored her lawyers' advice.

Yet "whenever anyone raised questions about her technology she fired them, tried to muzzle them with legal threats, or accused them of sexism (Belluz, 2018)." Elizabeth demanded unquestioned employee loyalty coupled with a corporate culture based on secrecy, paranoia and bullying (Thiruchelvam 2018). For example, when reporter John Carreyrou started to investigate Theranos claims which eventually lead to Theranos's downfall, Elizabeth appealed to owner of the Wall Street Journal and Theranos investor Rupert Murdoch to try to stay ahead of the Carryrou's reporting (Lopatto, 2021b). Elizabeth texted Ramesh about Carreyrou's reporting stating: "Need to get ahead of it all" and Ramesh trying to figuring out who Carreyrou's confidential sources at Theranos were responding: "Down to 5 people. We'll nail this motherfucker (Lopatto, 2021b)." One of Carreyrou's confidential sources that Theranos threatened with a lawsuit was Theranos employee and whistleblower Tyler Shultz, grandson to George Shultz who served at the cabinet level of several Republican presidents and also as Secretary of State; Shultz was also on Theranos's Board of Director (Lopatto, 2021b). Using an alias, Tyler contacted New York State's public health lab disclosing that Theranos manipulated lab results. Theranos accused him of violating confidentiality agreement and disclosing trade secrets. Tyler wanted to expose the problems at Theranos to protect the public, but also his grandfather's reputation. Theranos attorneys tried to pressure Tyler to change his story, but failed to do so because he would not allow himself to be intimidated and bullied, still Theranos hired private investigators to follow Tyler (Lopatto, 2021b).

Elizabeth made statements to investors about the status of Theranos' technology, historical contracts, commercial relationships, regulatory strategy, and financial performance that were consistent with the public image she was promoting of Theranos as a company revolutionizing the diagnostics industry. In terms of regulation, Elizabeth agreed to submit all components of Theranos' testing technology to the FDA for clearance or approval but told investors Theranos was seeking FDA approval voluntarily even though she knew FDA approval was necessary for Theranos' analyzer and tests. Elizabeth provided false or misleading statements concerning Theranos' historical business contracts with the DOD. In Elizabeth's cover letter, which she included in investor binders, she highlighted the company's historical work with military clients in order to boost Theranos' credibility in the eyes of investors. The company overview presentation introduces the company with the following statement, "[c]urrent and past clients include…U.S. and foreign government health and military organizations." Elizabeth mislead multiple investors by telling them that DOD used Theranos' technology in the battlefields of Afghanistan and on military medical helicopters known as medevacs in addition to claiming that Theranos' technology was used in a DOD burn study. Theranos earned limited revenues totally approximately $300,000 from three DOD contracts from 2011-2014.

Theranos included financial information in the investor binders projecting that Theranos would generate over $100 million in revenues and break even in 2014. In August 2015, Elizabeth met with a potential investor, during which she provided Theranos' financial results for fiscal year 2014. These financials showed 2014 net revenues of $108 million, and 2015 and 2016 net revenue projections of $240 million and $750 million, respectively. However, Theranos' actual financial performance bore no resemblance to the financial information Holmes shared with investors. Theranos recorded little more than $100,000 in revenue in 2014. Some of Theranos' projections provided to potential investors in October 2014, stated Theranos would earn $40 million from pharmaceutical services, $46 million from lab services provided to hospitals, and $9 million from lab services provided to physicians' offices, all by the end of 2014. In reality, Theranos had no revenues from any of those lines of business. Elizabeth also knew that the 2015 $1 billion revenue projections were unreasonable. Ultimately Elizabeth paid a $500,000 penalty, is barred from serving as an officer or director of a public company for 10 years, and returned 18.9 million shares she amassed during the fraud.

Elizabeth finally had her chance to convince the jury during her criminal prosecution that she was innocent of conspiracy to commit wire fraud. In part, Elizabeth's defense consisted of claiming that she was emotionally and physically abused by Ramesh. Yet text messages between these two were presented at her trial to counter her claim of abuse. For example in on exchange of text messages between the two she tells Ramesh: "I adore you, I love you so much…U have my heart and soul for a lifetime." Ramesh responds a few minutes later: "There is not a breath I take when I am not manifesting the best and the brightest and Lords Glory for you. You are my true north because you are Gods bright shining light (Rosenblatt, 2021a)." Ramesh further texted her: "U are God's tigress and warrior. You are extraordinary. Elizabeth responded: Coming from my tiger means the whole universe to me (Liedtke, 2021)." Moreover, Ramesh texted her stating: My heart is missing its heartbeat.

Love and prayers and all my energy for you in every breath. Elizabeth responded: Ditto (Somerville & Weaver, 2021)." Ramesh went on to text: "You live in my eyes. I see you everywhere. For me you are manifestation of love itself. Elizabeth responded: There is no love for you like mine (Somerville & Weaver, 2021)." There were hundreds of such text messages between the two.

Lynette Sawyer, Theranos' former lab director from 2014-2015, testified that she never was invited to the lab and never met Elizabeth stating that she grew uncomfortable with the way things were done and the lack of clarity from the lab even though she signed off on documents without reviewing the data collected by Theranos employees (Jackson, 2021a). Another former lab director Adam Rosendorff testified stating that both Elizabeth and Ramesh ignored his repeated warnings that the technology did not work, instead they were interested in the company's finances and public image (Khorram, 2021b). Daniel Edlin, a senior Theranos project manager testified that Theranos sometimes set up partitions to hide part of its labs before giving tours together displaying miniLabs that were never used for patient clinical testing (Jackson, 2021c). Elizabeth admitted that the statement made in 2014 *Fortune* magazine where the miniLab offers 200 diagnostic blood tests and will be capable of offering more than 1000 blood tests without a syringe was inaccurate, but still promoted the findings as accurate in order to appeal to investors (Khorram, 2021a). In company demonstrations, investors would have their finger pricked for testing in one of Theranos's devices, but the actual test would not be run in front on them, but somewhere away from their eyes (De Chant, 2021b). The machine shown to investors ran a "demo app" that would prevent error messages from displaying on device's screen or a "null protocol" that would not even analyze the blood sample (De Chant, 2021b).

In one demonstration, someone's blood was analyzed twice, once in New York and then again in California. The two different demonstrations produced two different results. Elizabeth wanted the discrepancy to be resolved and the solution was to change reference ranges so that the results would fall within an acceptable normal range of what one would expect to find even if there were discrepancies (De Chant, 2021b). At trial Pfizer denies giving Theranos permission to use its logo for Theranos's investor material claiming that their blood-testing technology had been comprehensively validated by ten of the 15 largest pharmaceutical companies. During her trial she did acknowledge that she had no evidence such as pharmaceutical contracts to back up her 2015 projected revenues of $40 million to entice investors (Khorram, 2021a). Elizabeth did not tell investors that she was using non-Theranos devices for the blood testing results that were presented to investors. Some investors claims that they did not independently verify Theranos's results because they did not want to upset Elizabeth and thus be uninvited to participate in Theranos investing (De Chant, 2021a).

General James Mattis testified at trial. Mattis described Elizabeth as "sharp, articulate, committed and confident…it was breathtaking what she was doing (CBS, 2021)." Mattis wanted to get Theranos technology in the Middle East due to the unrelenting number of U.S. casualties caused by the war stating, "I was interested in anything that would improve the care of causalities…I was taken by the idea that with one drop of blood and with remote capability you could basically test for a broad array of problems (ABC, 2021)." Mattis invested $85,000 of his own money into Theranos testified, "Looking back now I'm disappointed at the level of transparency from the company's technology…we were being deprived of fundamental issues. There came a point when I didn't know what to believe about Theranos anymore (Khorram, 2021b)." Elizabeth in a recorded 2013 conference call to investors stated that her technology was being adopted by the DOD (Rosenblatt, 2021b). Theranos claimed it had "something over $200 million in revenue from the DOD (Khorram, 2021b)." At trial Elizabeth testified that Theranos did not work with the DOD as previously claimed and promoted to investors (Lopatto, 2021a). Elizabeth was eventually found guilty of conspiracy to commit wire fraud and fraud against investors where she kept raising money on false claims concerning the miniLab.

In-Between Roles for Women

The $2.8 billion scheme by one of the nation's largest financing companies of healthcare-provider payrolls, National Century Financial Services (NCFS), defrauded investors by hiding, for example, massive cash. Eleven defendants were charged, including two women: Sherry Gibson, vice president of compliance, and

Rebecca Parrett, treasurer and co-founder together with her husband who was the chief operating officer (COO) Donald Ayers and CEO Lance Paulson (Steffenmeier et al., 2013). We focus on Gibson who was in-between a minor and major participant. Parrett, a ringleader with her spouse, played a central role rarely occupied by women in significant conspiracies. According to trial court testimony, Parrett, Ayers, and Paulson planned and implemented the scheme, directing Sherry Gibson and others to falsify reports and cover up the fraud by lying to auditors, investors, and rating agencies. Gibson, the key government witness, kept detailed records of actual versus falsely reported transactions. Testimony showed that Gibson, despite initial reluctance to carry out the directives, became actively engaged in manipulating accounting practices to make sure the books were in compliance. Gibson did not personally profit from her actions whereas Parrett and the male co-founders profited immensely. Gibson was convicted and received a four-year prison sentence. Parrett, Ayers, and Paulson were convicted and sentenced, respectively, to prison terms of 25, 15, and 30 years and ordered to jointly forfeit $1.7 billion of property from the conspiracy proceeds and pay restitution of $2.3 billion.

Government Fraud Offenders

Women employed in a government capacity have engaged in fraud. Betty Loren-Maltese, former town president of Cicero, Illinois, embezzled $12 million from the city in an elaborate insurance fraud scheme (Dodge, 2007). Consider the case of comptroller and treasurer of Dixon, Illinois named Rita Crundwell previously mentioned in chapter one. She worked in this capacity from 1983-2012 with an annual salary in 2012 of about $80 thousand. In the fall of 2011, while Crundwell was on an extended vacation, the city clerk discovered unusual city accounts with many checks written to the account. The city clerk contacted the Federal Bureau of Investigations (FBI) and the FBI allowed the fraud to continue for several more months in order to build a case against Crundwell. When Crundwell arrived to work, the FBI was waiting for her and eventually it was revealed that she embezzled over $53 million dollars over a period of 22 years to support her championship American Quarter Horse breeding operation (Carozza, 2018).

Crundwell used the stolen city money to buy hundreds of quarter horses and built a first class, horse farming business with an arena, an office and horse stalls. She used the money for credit card payments, jewelry, home remodeling, real estate and vehicles, including a luxury recreational vehicle bus (Carozza, 2018). To justify the payment of city funds to the secret bank account, Crundwell created almost 180 fake invoices over two decades to make it appear the State of Illinois was billing the city for work completed in Dixon (Jenco, 2013). External finance auditors for Dixon failed to notice Crundwell's fake invoices contained misspellings and were not even on State of Illinois letterhead plus not following standard practices of verifying the projects by calling the state or visually inspecting the projects. For at least two decades, the same auditors prepared Crundwell's personal tax returns, but were not alarmed by the hundreds of thousands of dollars she claimed in income a year on her returns even though she had no documentation. Due to the millions of dollars that Dixon's budget was off due to her fraud, Crundwell attempted to cut community services in order to cover up her fraud. She was sentenced to almost 20 years in prison.

White-collar Crime Female Ringleaders

A small 125-person telecommunications company, Network Technology Group's (NTG) financial problems began when a chief customer filed for bankruptcy owing close to $1 million. NTG officials failed to disclose the loss to the outside accounting firm preparing its year-end financial statements. Key participants were ringleader Michelle Tobin, co-founder and CEO, two male executives, CFO Thomas Bray and chief operating officer (COO) Victor Giordano, and female controller Beverly Baker. According to one employee, "[Tobin] was desperate…The company was her life" and she pressured Baker and other accounting staff to alter financial reports to conceal the loss, directives, at first, met with reluctance (Steffenmeier et al., 2013, p. 468). Typically, women ringleaders may have a harder time recruiting co-conspirators. Male executives Bray and Giordano were opposed to participating, but eventually played proactive or major roles facilitating the conspiracy. For example, they encouraged the unwilling Baker to make the entries Tobin demanded. Tobin, too, was persistent in rebuffing reservations stating "we're dead if we add up these year-end numbers…you'd better help us through this" (Steffenmeier et al., 2013, p. 468). Eventually, at Tobin's directive, Baker hid expenses and inflated accounts receivables so the company could continue borrowing money. Beverly's in-between role stemmed from her position dealing with financial matters, making her valuable for the scheme to work. Testimony indicated Baker raised numerous reservations but, vulnerable as the breadwinner for her disabled husband, believed her job was at stake.

Savings and Loan Scandal

The savings and loan crisis in the 1980s represents one of the most widespread examples of the abandonment of fiduciary duties of those in charge of overseeing the thrift banking industry and referred to as one of the worst financial disasters of the 20th century (Dodge, 2007). A savings and loan or "thrift" is a type of bank that accepts savings deposits and makes mortgage, car, and other personal loans to individual members who belong to the thrift. When deregulation occurred, these banks were allowed to engage in risky, speculative investments. The goal of the deregulation was to allow these thrifts to expand their business opportunities, however many of these speculative investments failed. Over a 1000 banks out of a total of about 3200 banks failed and the scandal is estimated to have cost the American taxpayer as much as $500 billion (Dodge, 2007). By October 1990, a total of 331 convictions had resulted in an average prison sentence of 3.5 years and included the involvement of at least 49 women. While only a small percentage of the crimes were committed by women, their behavior and seriousness parallel that of male counterparts. Based on fifteen cases, women involved in the scandal embezzled over $3 million and many of the convicted women held high-level executive positions no differently than men engaging in the same behavior.

Monica Iles: Ponzi Scheme

A business purportedly offering high-yield investments in international trading of bank financial instruments, FLP Capital, actually was a Ponzi scheme that raised more than $11 million from at least 30 investors. The defendants misappropriated almost all the funds for their own benefit. Six defendants were indicted, including one woman, Monica Iles, an expert in financial investment transactions who held a prior record for investment fraud and tax evasion (Steffenmeier et al., 2013).

Martha Stewart: Securities Fraud

Some portray Martha Stewart as the quintessential female corporate offender, others perceive her prosecution as a Department of Justice publicity stunt rooted in gender bias: a powerful businesswoman pursued for trivial offenses while male executives at Enron and WorldCom were indicted but never jailed, which as we know, is not true (Steffenmeier et al., 2013). Samuel Waksal, founder and CEO of pharmaceutical company ImClone Systems, gave advance notice based on an inside tip to family and friends that the Food and Drug Administration (FDA) would not approve the company's anti-cancer drug (Erbitux). Following Waksal's arrest, homemaking icon Martha Stewart was investigated for insider trading for selling ImClone stock just prior to the company's FDA announcement. Stewart played no role in the insider trading conspiracy orchestrated by Waksal. Rather, Stewart learned through her stockbroker that Waksal was selling all of his stock. Stewart ultimately was charged with making the false statement that her stockbroker had not informed her about Waksal's sudden stock sale. After her refusal to plead guilty and a highly publicized trial, Stewart was found guilty and sentenced to a five-month prison term for lying. "Given that Stewart saved just $46,000 on the trade, the sale of ImClone stock and subsequent cover-up surely ranks as one of the most ill-fated white-collar crimes" (Steffenmeier et al., 2013, p. 469).

Diane Hathaway: Bank Fraud

Convicted fraud offender Diane Hathaway, former justice of the Michigan Supreme Court, went to prison for engaging in bank fraud in 2013. Prior to becoming a lawyer and ultimately a judge in one of the highest judicial positions in the country, she participated in the real estate market as a broker and also taught real estate classes. Hathaway owned several properties that were initially under her name, but transferred them to family members under false pretenses in order to hide their assets from ING Direct Bank that held their Gross Pointe Park, Michigan residence mortgage. The debt owed by Hathaway and her husband to ING was estimated at $600,000 from a $1.5 million lakefront home. Hathaway tried to escape paying the debt claiming financial hardship even though her annual salary was over $160,000 a year (Livenhood, 2013).

Hathaway also transferred the ownership of her Windemere, Florida home to her step-daughter in 2010 while trying to qualify for a short sale on the home in Grosse Pointe Park, Michigan. After the short sale, the Florida home was transferred back into Hathaway's name in 2012. The short sale of the Grosse Pointe Park home allegedly allowed Hathaway to avoid foreclosure proceedings and walk away from $600,000 in mortgage debt (Livengood, 2013). In addition, prior to the short sale, Hathaway transferred another Grosse Pointe Park home to her stepson with no significant funds changing hands in 2010. Yet again, in a third Grosse Pointe Park home, purchased by Hathaway's stepdaughter for $195,000 with cash given to her by Hathaway, this residence was transferred back into Hathaway's name after the short sale previously mentioned (Livengood, 2013).

Societal Misperceptions of Female Aggression

Common and legitimate explanations used to rationalize violence committed by females include mental illness, coercion, prior abuse, and self-defense (Follingstad et al., 1989). Often women were perceived to be capable of committing only reactive or "expressive" violence, an uncontrollable release of pent-up rage or fear, killing unwillingly and without premeditation (Vronsky, 2007). Such explanations, however, ignore the possibility that motives for both genders may be steeped in antisocial behaviors where violence is not necessarily reactive, such as self-defense to a physically abusive situation, but planned in a cold-blooded manner. Violence may be facilitated by those who harbor narcissistic and psychopathic traits to satisfy diverse motives and those that may not display traits associated with these personality types, but still resort to violence as a solution to a problem (Perri, 2016). The myth that females are not aggressive is being challenged in scholarship as well as by statistical evidence that influences society's view relative to the existence of female aggression (Denfeld, 1997). However violent aggression is still considered the province of men, one of the most pervasive myths of our time (Pearson, 1997). Male dominance, expressed through aggression, was historically supported by a patriarchal society that viewed female aggression as unnatural and atypical (Jack, 1999).

Times have changed and women now participate in combat and the corporate world (Beckner, 2005). As for their criminal inclinations, "women hurt others…they abuse, kill, inflict harm on the human spirit, and dominate others through pain and intimidation…violence is not limited to men" (Jack, 1999). Some women resort to violence because they were abused, however, this explanation should not be used as a general explanation of all motives for female violence. As author and editor of the *New York Times Book Review*, Samuel Tanenhaus, stated, "female violence is stuck in a 'time warp' bound by themes of sexual and domestic trauma" (Wachter, 2010). Our belief in the intrinsic, non-threatening nature of the feminine is deceiving to both genders and actually exposes both to violence including homicidal risks that are ignored because of long-internalized myths about female criminality. When speaking of myths, what is being referred to is not necessarily the mythological stories of antiquity. Although these stories may be relevant, the reference to myths is the more common basis of some beliefs, which may or may not be accurate, that are extrapolated from fact or fiction and used to explain human behaviors and societal practices and ideals.

For example, some beliefs are based on fictional stories that convey a truism about human behavior, such as the Greek story of the character named Narcissus and the self-destructive behaviors of excessive pride—hence the personality trait narcissism. It is useful to understand myths because myths may facilitate explaining life lessons—the problem is that the use of myths lack completeness when applied to criminological elements. In essence, culturally we have forgotten how the ancients may have used myths to explain human behaviors in more complete terms that were gender neutral, such as the capability of depravity by both men and women. Moreover, we have cultural images such as Mother Earth, which evokes a nurturing image of the female gender. Conversely, the image of Mother Nature also evokes images of wrath in which innocents are not spared; it is this aspect of the completeness of the myth that tends to be ignored or denied when examining female aggression. Also, Sigmund Freud and psychoanalytic theory were influential in the evolution of ideas related to aggression; the influence of World War I shaped Freud's perception that the propensity for aggression was mostly male and instinctual (Jack, 1999). Women functioned as a calming effect on the aggressive drives that moved men to violent behavior (Beckner, 2005). Those women who did not repress their anger were considered masculine, thus perpetuating the belief that aggressiveness in women was an oddity.

Aggressive women were perceived as irrational (Beckner, 2005). Because of the historical position that women are passive, emotional, nurturing, and self-sacrificing, female criminals are viewed as psychiatrically unstable (Brown, 1996). Even from an evolutionary perspective, Charles Darwin's views influenced societal perceptions of his belief that the success of human evolution was due, in large part, to the differences between males and females (Jack 1999). For example, a female who displayed perceived masculine traits such as aggression or a male who had feminine characteristics was considered suggestive of a less developed species (Beckner, 2005). Considering the opinions of Freud and Darwin alone, then coupled with religious and cultural views of how females are perceived, it is not surprising myths of female aggression persist and have been perpetrated for as long as they have. From a societal perspective, this assumption that aggression is an inherent characteristic to males, as passivity is to females, perpetuated a patriarchal structure that was dominant until the feminist movement of the 1970s, but still influences certain aspects of society today.

In summary, the aggressive female is still considered for some segments of society to have an abnormal, unnatural quality even in the face of evidence illustrating criminal behavior that contradicts the myth of female passivity. They were essentially considered an anomaly and research pertaining to female aggression is underdeveloped. Almost all of what psychologists have thought about aggression has been shaped by a predominantly male perspective (Jack 1999). Some social and behavioral science communities were unwilling to accept that women could be violent to satisfy diverse motives, and men the victims, when researchers examined the evidence of female aggression (Beckner, 2005). Let us examine behavioral risk factors together with female cases in which both white-collar crime and violence take place.

Behavioral Risk Factors

There is no difference between men and women in terms of displaying basic criminal thought patterns when applied to white-collar crime. They can equally shut off their conscience and have little inclination to put themselves in the place of others and with more opportunity for women in society comes greater freedom to commit more crimes (Samenow, 2009). Yet according to Dr. Hare, there are many clinical accounts of female psychopaths, but relatively little empirical research (Carozza, 2008a). Available evidence suggests that male and female psychopaths share similar interpersonal and affective features, including egocentricity, deceptiveness, shallow emotions, and lack of empathy (Carozza, 2008a). Female psychopaths who not impulsive can be prolific criminals especially for non-violent crimes such as fraud while those that exhibit a more aggressive interpersonal style are apt to exhibit violent tendencies (Hicks et al., 2010). For example, female psychopaths are willing to resort to brutal violence to attain their needs; violence is simply a solution that is available to them as other methods to control someone such as deceit, manipulation, and charming someone (Perri, 2016). While most of us have strong inhibitions to injure others, violence is a solution psychopaths use when they are angered, frustrated that their narcissistic sense of entitlement is threatened, and give little thought to the pain and humiliation experienced by their victims.

Regardless of gender, their violence is callous and can be planned in order to satisfy a want, and psychopathic reaction to their actions are likely to be indifferent, possibly coupled with a sense of power, pleasure, and a smug satisfaction instead of remorse (Perri, 2016). Many of the personality and behavioral features associated with psychopathy in men are also found in women, and the more severe psychopathy in women has been linked to greater instances of violent and nonviolent offenses (Perri, 2016). What is certain is that although there may be differences on how psychopathy is expressed across gender or how it should be measured, the core traits of psychopathy such as exploiting others or institutions for self-servicing reasons, lack of empathy and remorse while blaming others for their behaviors is gender neutral (Perri, 2016). At their core, male and female psychopathic killers harbor a depravity that stands outside our moral universe (Wynn et al., 2012). Both male and female psychopaths are not affectionate, they do not value traditional social norms or close relationships, can be vengeful or physically violent, and victimize others for personal gain (O'Connor, 2002). Ratings of female psychopathy in youth reflected much less aggression than those of males (Salekin et al., 1997). Furthermore, physical cruelty to people and/or animals and bullying/threatening behaviors were prototypical of psychopaths (Cruise et al., 2003). Females displaying psychopathic traits might rely on different tactics than psychopathic males to achieve the same goals. For example, brute force in general is less likely to achieve the same results as men, thus women may resort to manipulation and flirtation as methods to achieve similar results (Nicholls & Petrila, 2005).

Psychopathic women who resort to physical aggression are willing to intentionally use violence as a way to control their victims or to extract compliance from them be it children or adults and also derive pleasure from inflicting violence coupled with no differences with the type of weapon used (Tuente et al., 2014). Psychopathic women start their criminal lifestyles earlier than non-psychopathic women and tend to exhibit more criminal versatility in their histories meaning that they may engage in different types of crimes such as fraud and violence related crimes (Warren et al., 2003). Psychopathic women are more apt to engage in violence, including homicide, for nefarious motives such as the need to be in control, to dominate as well as for financial or personal gain (Perri, 2016). Although there may be differences between male and female psychopaths perhaps in how their disorder is expressed, "what drives them both is power over others, the expectation of gain and the glorification of the self" (Tuente et al., 2014, p. 320). Violent psychopathic females tend to be similar in their behaviors to male psychopaths in that they are apt to commit violence against strangers as opposed to just close acquaintances or family members that is illustrative of violence committed by non-psychopathic women. It should not be interpreted to mean that psychopathic women committed more homicides than non-psychopathic women, however the reasons behind homicides are relevant and may be significant especially how these cases are investigated and how these offenders are approached during an interview.

Fraud Detection Homicide

Recall that fraud detection violence consists of white-collar offenders resorting to violence with the motive to silence those who are in a position to detect and/or disclose their fraud schemes. The violence tends to be planned and not the result of an emotional outburst that is contemporaneous with provocation. Consider the application of fraud detection homicide to female offenders.

The Sante Kimes Case

After the victim, David Kazdin, detected that his supposed friends Sante and Kenny Kimes committed mortgage fraud in which they obtained a $280,000 loan in his name, Kazdin began receiving threatening telephone calls from Sante demanding that he cooperate with the fraud scheme. Kenny indicated that it was his mother who made the decision to kill Kazdin after she stated to Kenny, "He knows too much and we got to do something about him, we're going to have to kill him" and as Kenny left Sante to kill David, Sante said to Kenny, "Good luck. Do a good job" (Perri & Lichtenwald, 2010a, p. 59). According to Kenny he went to Kazdin's home, followed Kazdin into the kitchen and shot him in the back of the head. After the killing, Kenny stated that he felt high from the killing and stopped by a florist shop to buy his mother flowers further stating, "In my mindset, I thought that I had completed a great duty for my mom. I felt that it was a significant completion and I wanted to celebrate" (Perri & Lichtenwald, 2010a, p. 59). In an attempt to control the impression others would form of her, during the homicide trial, Sante told the jury that she loved Kazdin stating, "God bless him wherever he is. I need his help. I wish he was here today" (Perri & Lichtenwald, 2010a, p. 59). As an interesting side note, in order to avoid the death penalty, Kenny testified against his mother in other homicides. For example, he disclosed that he and his mother drugged a 55-year-old banker by the name of Syed Ahmed. As Ahmed struggled against the sedative effects of the drugs, Sante and Kenny took turns holding his head under water in a bathtub (Perri & Lichtenwald, 2010a).

174

In another case Sante and Kenny murdered 80-year-old Irene Silverman with the motive of fraudulently obtaining her residence in Manhattan, New York (Perri & Lichtenwald, 2010a). The exploitation of the weak coupled with the super optimism exhibited by Sante given all the evidence the police collected to build a case against her is illustrated by the judge's statement, "It is clear that Ms. Kimes has spent virtually all her life plotting and scheming, exploiting and manipulating, and preying upon the vulnerable and the gullible at every opportunity…Sante Kimes had grossly overestimated her own cleverness. The stupidity of a criminal keeping a to-do list added one more extraordinary note to this bizarre case" (King, 2002, p. 263). Forensic psychologist Dr. Arthur Weider stated that "Sante Kimes demonstrate psychopathic personality features with no guilt, conscience, remorse or empathy," adding that Sante was "socially charming, arrogant, full of herself [and] egocentric coupled with a superiority complex, she feels everyone is stupid and will do her bidding, and everyone has their price and can be paid off" (King, 2002, p.250). Psychiatrist Dr. William O'Gorman stated that Sante displayed no "reflective judgment, "poor insight" and was "impulsive" (King, 2002, p. 252). There were other crimes Sante committed such as being one of several persons in the twentieth century to have been convicted of the crime of slavery (King, 2002).

The Nancy Siegel Case

Jack Watkins, a widower in his seventies, supported himself through social security benefits and annuity payments from New York Life Insurance. Before he met Nancy Siegel, Watkins had a few credit cards that he used sparingly, and owned his home outright, with no mortgage. Watkins, thirty years senior to Siegel ironically met in the fall of 1994, when she sold him a burial vault, and the relationship quickly became romantic. Within months after meeting Watkins, Siegel began using his personal information to open new credit card accounts. In May 1995, Siegel persuaded Watkins to buy her a new $44,000 BMW car. The financing, title, and insurance were under Watkins's name, but Siegel was the car's only driver. By August 1995, Siegel accumulated tens of thousands of dollars of debt on credit cards in Watkins' name. At Siegel's urging, Watkins obtained a $44,000 mortgage on his home in August, 1995. Siegel used the mortgage proceeds to pay off credit card debt, but then promptly began making new charges. Siegel apparently exerted as much control over Watkins' personal life as she did over his financial life. Before meeting Siegel, Watkins had breakfast several times a week with a group of friends, and regular contact with stepchildren from a prior marriage.

After he met Siegel, he began meeting his breakfast group less frequently and Siegel eventually drove him to one final breakfast where he said goodbye to his friends. Before losing contact, Watkins told his stepchildren, breakfast friends, and a neighbor about his relationship with Siegel and that they would be getting married. Telephone calls to Watkins from his stepchildren were forwarded to Siegel's telephone, but Watkins never knew about the calls. In February 1996, Siegel contacted a real estate company to inquire about the company buying Watkins's home. The company Siegel contacted bought Watkins' home in April, 1996. Watkins netted just over $3,800 from the sale of his home. Moreover, in the first week of April 1996, Siegel sold most of Watkins's personal possessions. After selling the house, Watkins and Siegel went to Atlantic City to celebrate their upcoming marriage. Watkins drank heavily in Atlantic City, and Siegel took him to the hospital when they returned to Maryland. Watkins was admitted to the hospital where he told hospital staff that Siegel was his fiancée, but Siegel told the staff that she was simply his caregiver, not his fiancée.

Although Watkins was oriented in time, place, and person, and appeared to hospital staff to be sensitive and responsive, he was diagnosed as suffering from dementia. Hospital records indicate that Siegel did not want Watkins to be discharged into her care and that she tried to have him placed in a long-term care facility. She was unable to find a facility with an immediate opening, so she took Watkins to her condominium when he was discharged on April 16, 1996. While still with Watkins, Nancy dated Eric Siegel, a wealthy commercial loan broker, for a time in 1992. The relationship resumed in May or June 1995, while Siegel was still involved with Watkins. As a side note, this case parallels the Robert Petrick case where Robert courted another woman to marry prior to killing his wife Janine. Eric's wealth made him a much more attractive target for Siegel's attentions, so she needed to find a way to end her relationship with Watkins that would not restrict her freedom or jeopardize her access to Eric's financial resources. If Siegel simply walked away from Watkins in order to pursue her relationship with Eric, Watkins, with no place to live, would have had little choice but to turn to his long-neglected friends or family for help. His family and friends would have discovered and explained to Watkins Siegel's financial exploitation which would have placed her at risk of being detected and prosecuted for fraud.

On May 14, 1996, Watkins's emaciated body was found near an access point to the Appalachian Trail in Loudoun, Virginia with the body stuffed inside two duffle bags and then stuffed into a footlocker. The cause of death was cervical compression with bruises and other marks on the body that were consistent with manual strangulation. A toxicology analysis revealed that Watkins' blood and liver contained toxic levels of an over-the-counter sedative medication, which suggested that Watkins had been ingesting extremely high levels of the medication for a period of weeks. Although Watkins' body was found within days after his death, the police were unable to identify the body. Siegel never reported him missing, and because Watkins lost contact with his friends and family, no one else even knew he disappeared. Siegel continued to use Watkins' identity well after his death. She stopped the direct deposit of his social security checks, and had the checks mailed to her post office box ultimately depositing them in her various bank accounts. Siegel continued to receive Watkins' insurance annuity payments, and she opened new credit card accounts in Watkins's name. After Watkins died, Nancy and Eric married in December 1998. Not surprisingly, Siegel did not spare Eric from her fraudulent schemes. She stole money directly from his financial accounts and incurred substantial debt in his name through credit accounts and loans about which Eric had no knowledge. When Nancy's actions came to light, Eric chose to make good on her debts, which amounted to about $300,000, rather than report Siegel to the police.

In January 2003, nearly seven years after Watkins was murdered, Virginia law enforcement officials identified his body through military fingerprint records. The Virginia officials sought help from investigators with the Social Security Administration, who quickly determined that Siegel received Watkins' social security checks since his death. After a few months of investigating and watching Siegel, postal inspectors and an FBI agent approached Siegel after she had retrieved Watkins's social security check from her post office box. She agreed to be interviewed. Siegel initially claimed that Watkins was alive and well, living in Pennsylvania with a woman named Ruth. She said that before moving to Pennsylvania some six years earlier, Watkins lived with her for about eight months after selling his house. Siegel said that she cashed Watkins's checks for him because he was a gambler and had financial problems that made it impossible for him to have a checking account. The investigators finally told Siegel that they knew what had happened to Watkins. While Siegel repeatedly told the investigators that she wanted to tell them everything, although she never provided them with any details about Watkins's death, except to say that "[i]t didn't happen the way you think" (Perri & Lichtenwald, 2010a, p. 58). Siegel said she came home one afternoon and found Watkins sprawled across the bed with a cord around his neck. The government proved not only that she killed Watkins, but did so for the purpose of preventing him from providing law enforcement with information about the fraud she had committed (Siegel, 2008).

Let us examine additional antisocial behaviors exhibited by Siegel to give a more holistic picture about her criminality. Siegel married Charles Kucharski in 1968, and the couple divorced in 1985. Sometime towards the end of the marriage, Siegel began gambling and to support her gambling habit, Siegel used Kucharski's name and personal information to obtain credit without Kucharski's knowledge. Siegel's actions left Kucharski more than $100,000 in debt, and he was forced to file for bankruptcy a few years after the couple divorced. Siegel then married Ted Giesendaffer in 1985 continuing to gamble by engaging in the same kind of fraudulent conduct she began in her first marriage. Siegel used Giesendaffer's personal information to obtain credit, and she stole money from him by altering mortgage payment checks to make them payable to her instead of the mortgage company. When Giesendaffer discovered Siegel's misconduct, he confronted her about it and threatened to go to the police. Siegel responded to that threat with such violence that Giesendaffer hid from her in a closet; not surprisingly they divorced in 1993. Moreover, Siegel took money that her daughter Jennifer had given her to make car payments and Jennifer's car eventually was repossessed because the payments were not appropriately applied.

Furthermore, Siegel used Jennifer's identity and that of her daughter Amanda to open credit accounts and then defaulted on those accounts, thus destroying her daughters' credit ratings. Siegel sometimes used her daughters' identities and bank accounts when cashing Watkins's Social Security checks and annuity payments in the years after his death. In 1992, Siegel convinced her friends John and Linda Mayberry to cosign a car loan and pay the required down payment. Not surprisingly, Siegel defaulted on the car loan, and the Mayberrys ended up repaying the loan. Siegel subsequently used John Mayberry's personal information to obtain a $3,000 loan in his name without consent. In December 1992, Siegel stole the wallet of Merle Beckman using the stolen credit cards until they were cancelled, yet she still managed to convince bank employees to give her the number of the account connected to Beckman's ATM card. In January 1993, Siegel stole the wallet of Burdell Dowdell. She wrote checks payable to "Charlene Townsend" on Dowdell's account and then posed as Townsend to cash the checks. In February 1993, Siegel stole the wallet of Leslie Wallace, whose daughter was in dance class with Siegel's daughter. Siegel immediately began draining the funds from Wallace's bank accounts. Wallace changed her account number twice, but Siegel managed to convince bank employees to give her the new account numbers over the telephone while withdrawing cash available to her at the drive-through window.

The Rosie Baker Case

Rosie Baker, the head of a $37 million home health care agency in New York, was found guilty for the murder of Dr. Daniel Hodge and sentenced to life in prison. Her son Vance Baker was also found guilty of the same charges. Initially, Rosie gave Vance the money to find someone to kill Dr. Hodge who was a medical doctor and a lawyer. However, Vance kept the money and killed Dr. Hodge himself (Baker, 2001). According to the prosecutors, the motive for the kill was that Dr. Hodge was going to go to the authorities to disclose the Medicaid fraud that Rosie Baker was perpetrating (Gearty, 1998). Dr. Hodge set up shame corporations where Rosie would receive payments from Medicaid funding. Dr. Hodge's kept copies of all the fraudulent documents prepared on behalf of Rosie and at times threatened Rosie that he would go to the police exposing the fraud. As an interesting parallel, like the Sante Kimes case, Rosie recruited her son to participate in the murder which is common in these types of murders.

The Ernestina Bernal Case

Ernestina Bernal pleaded guilty to the murder of James and Sherian Moller (Perri, 2016). Ernestina was employed by the Mollers at their real estate business. When the Mollers became suspicious that Ernestina funneled fraudulent mortgage loans through their business, they contacted the authorities. Ernestina believed that the Mollers detected her fraud with the assistance of law enforcement, thus she recruited her cousin Ernest Barajas to help her kill the Mollers. Both went to Moller's home killing them with a gun execution style.

Criminal Enterprise Homicide

Criminal enterprise homicide entails murder committed for material gain; in essence if we want the money we have to kill first (Douglas et al., 1992). The different types of criminal enterprise homicide include, 1) contract killings, 2) gang-motivated murder, 3) criminal competition homicide, 4) product tampering homicide, 5) drug murder, 6) insurance/inheritance-related death, 7) commercial profit murder and 3) felony murder (Douglas et al., 1992). For example, there are some people who take out life insurance on a person. They cannot collect life insurance money if the person that the insurance pertains to is alive, thus they kill the person to collect the money.

Helen Golay and Olga Rutterschmidt Case

I am evil…You have no idea how evil I am.

Helen Golay (Huck, 2008)

In April 2008, jurors found Olga Rutterschmidt, 75, and Helen Golay, 78, guilty of first degree murder for the deaths of homeless men Kenneth McDavid, 50, and Paul Vados, 73 (Deutsch, 2008). Prosecutors said the women recruited their prey from among the homeless of Hollywood and invested thousands of dollars in life insurance policies on them by enticing them with food and lodging (Keith, 2008). According to the prosecution, they took care of the men to the extent they needed them to stay alive for two years, the period in which insurers could not contest the policies for possible fraud (Rutterschmidt, 2009; 2012). For example, a homeless man named Jimmy Covington described Rutterschmidt approaching him on the street in 2005 offering to help. Although she seemed sincere at first providing shelter, food, and offering him $2,000 a month in benefits, Rutterschmidt started to ask for personal information from Covington and yelled at him when he would not provide such information. She started turning up in the early morning hours demanding that he fill out more of the insurance paperwork. Jimmy gave her his social security number, driver's license number, and medical history but escaped stating that it felt like a hustle who later learned that the two women requested an application for an $800,000 policy on his life. Golay and Rutterschmidt recruited Paul Vados and Kenneth McDavid under the same circumstance by providing lodging for a minimum of two years.

Ultimately Golay and Rutterschmidt drugged the men to sedate them, drove them to a secluded alley, laid them on the ground, and then ran them over until they were dead (Kim & Pringle, 2008). Golay collected more than $348,000 in life insurance proceeds from more than half a dozen insurance companies, while Rutterschmidt collected more than $246,000 from Vados' death. Moreover, Golay collected more than $1.5 million and Rutterschmidt more than $674,000 from McDavid's death (Perri & Lichtenwald, 2010a). According to court documents, while in custody, Golay and Rutterschmidt discussed the circumstances of their arrests without the knowledge that they were being videotaped which was disclosed to the jury during their murder trial. Rutterschmidt said, "That is very serious, everything dragged into Paul [Vados]…making all these extra insurances…You were greedy. That's the problem. That's why I get angry. We had no problem with the relationship. You pay me and be nice and don't make extra things. I was doing everything for you" (Perri & Lichtenwald, 2010a, p. 59). Still being recorded, Rutterschmidt continued to berate Golay, saying her actions in taking out 23 insurance policies raised a red flag when the men died. Rutterschmidt told Golay: "You cannot make that many insurances. It's on your name, only" (Perri & Lichtenwald, 2010a, p. 59).

Golay responded that she did not want to talk, but Rutterschmidt later told her, "[Y]ou did all the insurances extra. That's what raised the suspicion. You can't do that. Stupidity" Golay answered: "All they're after is mail fraud. It is no mail fraud involve." As the discussion continued, Golay reasserted that the insurance companies were complaining against them for "mail fraud—they have nothing else" (Perri & Lichtenwald, 2010a, p. 59). Ironically, they discussed suing the insurance companies to get the insurance benefits they had been denied. Interestingly, the defense attorney for Golay said, "This case is about the insurance industry retaliating against Helen Golay and Olga Rutterschmidt…They don't like the fact that two little old ladies are involved in an insurance scam…They are going to teach them a lesson…This is a nightmare for her…It's unfortunate that two men are dead" (Perri & Lichtenwald, 2010a, p. 59). The defendant's attorneys played into the myth of female aggression characterizing the women as grandmotherly types, two "little old ladies" not physically capable of this crime (Pringle, 2008).

Let us explore the callous mindset Golay displayed by her own statements. Golay stated to her hairdresser, "I am evil…You have no idea how evil I am" (Huck, 2008). She laid out a scenario where a woman marries an older man, ensures his life, and then uses Viagra to engineer a heart attack in addition to believing that homeless people were parasitic (Perri & Lichtenwald, 2010a). As for the people left homeless by Hurricane Katrina in 2005 with an estimate of over 1300 fatalities: "she said those people were nothing…They were just on welfare…they were useless to society" (Huck, 2008). Yet Golay, in attempting to control the impression others would form of her, said that McDavid "loved them and that he wanted to be part of our family" (Pringle & Kim, 2008). Neither of the women trusted each other and Golay tried to get Rutterschmidt's name removed from one of the policies. What is truly bizarre is that when Golay tried to change the fraudulently obtained insurance policies, Rutterschmidt called the insurance company stating, "I want to report a fraud…I'm the fiancée, she [Golay] is not the fiancée" referring to one of the homicide victims (Kim, 2008). Rutterschmidt began ranting that Golay committed fraud by listing herself as the beneficiary on the policies (Kim, 2008). Interestingly, Golay described Rutterschmidt as "crazy, very explosive, very loud…hard to deal with in public" (Pringle & So, 2006). Not surprisingly, Golay's daughter Kecia described her mother as exhibiting "thirty years of psychopathic behavior" (Perri & Lichtenwald, 2010a, p. 60).

Conclusion

It should be apparent after reading this chapter that engaging in crime is gender neutral. Although men may engage in crime at a higher rate that women, both genders engage in street-level offenses and fraud offenses. Furthermore, as we have studied, their offending behavior can be quite lethal. As women enter the work force in higher numbers not only nationally, but internationally, and the fact that they will attain higher executive positions, they too will be tempted to engage in fraud offenses. Research will be needed to assess female fraud offender personality traits no differently than those of men to determine if the manner in which women display antisocial traits, especially those in leadership positions, is similar to or different from the manner in which men behave. Traditionally, more research has focused on crimes committed by men, thus we need more researchers to focus their attention to female offenders so that we can construct a more well-rounded profile of the female offender.

Chapter 5

Terror Financing, Organized Crime and Fraud

When the FBI transported Ramzi Yousef by helicopter over Manhattan following his capture for the 1995 bombing of the World Trade Center's Twin Towers, an FBI agent pulled up Yousef's blindfold and pointed out that the lights of the World Trade Center were still glowing. "They're still standing," the FBI agent stated. Yousef responded, "They wouldn't be if I had enough money and explosives" (Perri & Lichtenwald, 2009).

Organized crime is generally considered a category of transnational, national, or local groupings of highly centralized enterprises operated by criminals who intend to engage in illegal activity, most commonly for money and profit, but some criminal organizations, such as terrorist groups, are also politically, religiously, and financially motivated. Terrorism is, in the broadest sense, the use of intentionally indiscriminate violence as a means to create terror, or fear, to achieve a political, religious or ideological aim. It is used in this regard primarily to refer to violence against peacetime targets or in war against non-combatants. A terrorist group typically is a collection of individuals belonging to a nonstate entity that uses terrorism to achieve its goals (Hesterman, 2013). The problems of organized crime and terrorism were often considered separate phenomena prior to the September 11th attacks in New York and elsewhere. Security studies, military, and law enforcement seminars discussed the emerging threat of transnational organized crime or terrorism, but the important links between the two were rarely made. Part of the reason for the lack of linkage may be due to the fact that organized crime and terrorism are usually viewed as two different forms of crime because organized crime's main focus is economic profit while terrorism is said to be motivated by ideological aims and a desire for political change (Bovenkerk & Chakra, 2005).

Yet since the end of the Cold War in the 1990s and the decline of state sponsorship for terrorism, terrorist groups have adopted organized crime tactics, such as white-collar crime, to raise money and in turn organized crime has adopted terrorist methods of violence to satisfy their agenda (Liang, 2011). Consequently, the 1990s can be described as the decade in which the crime-terror nexus consolidated and the two separate organizations identifiable by their distinct motives began to reveal operational and organizational similarities. In fact, organized crime and terrorist appear to be learning from one another and adapting to each other's successes and failures (Perri & Lichtenwald, 2009). Thus, when the two collaborate, terrorist organizations derive benefits from criminal activity such as smuggling illicit products with no loss of status as a perceived political movement that, at times, is simply a guise for their economic motives. Organized crime has forged an alliance, albeit an unclear one, with terrorists becoming more formidable and gaining in political clout. Both organizations operate on social network structures that at times intersect, such as using smuggling and other illicit means to raise cash, and then employ similar money laundering fraud schemes to move their funds though legitimate banking institutions.

Now, for several decades, terrorist and organized crime groups are sharing operational expertise and cooperating in kidnapping, arms, drug and human trafficking, smuggling, extortion, and fraud; the growing symbiosis of crime and terror is making both more powerful (Liang, 2011). The growing nexus of shared tactics and methods of terror and organized crime groups is due to several major developments: globalization, the communication revolution through the internet, the end of the Cold War, and the global war on terror. Both terror and organized crime groups are leveraging the internet for recruitment, planning, psychological operations, logistics, and fundraising. The internet has become the platform for both organized crime and terrorists to conduct cybercrimes ranging from video piracy, illegal use of encryption, industrial espionage, sending viruses, financial frauds, selling drugs, and money laundering to name a few (Crumbley et al., 2011). The growing nexus facilitates terrorists to access automatic weapons and explosive devices, empowering them to challenge police, land and naval forces with the latest sophisticated weaponry and intelligence (Liang, 2011). Although terrorism has become a top concern among policymakers, business executives, law enforcement officials, and scholars have virtually ignored how terrorist organizations are funded (Sullivan et al., 2014).

The majority of research on extremism and terrorism focuses on a small number of high profile violent incidents while failing to mention financial crimes, material support or preparatory crimes; attention to financial crimes and terrorism financing has been minimal (Sullivan et al., 2014). Today, many terrorists are engaged in some form of organized crime and a growing number of organized crime cartels engage in political violence (Wang, 2010). Trafficking drugs is the most common criminal act that is uniting organized criminals with terrorists. In some cases, criminal groups have adopted the ideology of terrorist groups or are highly supportive of their motives, especially in regions with ethnic and religious tensions. Today, "groups with dissimilar ideologies are working together to further their goals; they are also copying successful tactics, learning from each other's mistakes, and at the very least operating in the same physical space or virtual space" (Hesterman, 2013, p. 3). For example, in the 1980s, terrorist organizations in Latin America turned to narcotics trafficking to fund their activities, most notably the Colombian Revolutionary Armed Forces of Columbia (FARC), whose narcotic operations largely surpassed its terrorist ambitions in importance and scope. Consider in 1985, the Colombian Medellin drug cartel joined forces with the 19th of April Movement (M19) terrorists to help them in bomb making techniques.

In 1993, the Sicilian Mafia responded to a wave of criminal convictions of its top leaders by placing a bomb in the Uffizi Museum in Florence as a new strategy to intimidate the government and demonstrate its power (Perri & Lichtenwald, 2009). Moreover, globalization has meant that due to free trade flows and the reduction of trade barriers, as well as the ease of global travel, crime and terror can be conducted in all corners of the earth around-the-clock. The war on terror launched shortly after the September 11, 2001 attacks resulted in global cooperation to crack down on terrorist financing triggering a further decline in state sponsored terror and pushed terrorists toward closer cooperation with organized crime. While links between terrorists and organized crime cartels are not always clear and difficult to quantify, there is evidence that cooperation is growing mostly due to the use of cyberspace, global financial systems, and their more loosely knit social network structures used for recruitment purposes. Also, organized crime groups in the past where unwilling to cooperate with terrorists for many reasons, including an increased susceptibility to law enforcement or military action and a loss of public support, modern organized crime cartels appear more willing to do so.

Possessing no real loyalties to any government, these groups cooperate transnationally and conduct their criminal activities in fluid social network structures. They are able to offer their services to the highest bidder. In some cases younger, smaller, and more loosely organized groups have become ideologically radicalized and actively pursue business in the interest of politics as well as to support the goals of terrorist groups. Moreover, terror groups are involved in various types of fraud schemes to meet organizational goals and to finance their operations. The importance of funding is also made clear in the acknowledgement by the FBI's Terror Financing Operations Section that all terrorism cases involve some financial component, although the funding of terrorist organizations is a complex phenomenon to understand. The "financing of terrorism is a subterranean universe governed by secrecy, subterfuge, and criminal endeavors; but also a good measure of sophistication and an understanding of the global financial system. It is best described as an octopus with tentacles spreading across vast territories" (Sullivan et al., 2014, p. 3).

Complex terrorist networks must finance security, operations, support, intelligence, propaganda, material, recruitment, training, housing, food, communications, bribery, weapons, travel, forged documents and living expenses. Groups also must use funds to pay individuals to demonstrate in support of their cause and compensate families for family members killed (Sullivan et al., 2014). Terrorist organizations take advantage of lucrative market opportunities, with larger, more sophisticated operations utilizing multiple sources of funding, including the production and distribution of counterfeit products (Sullivan et al., 2014). Furthermore, although the perception may be that fraud is not linked to terrorism because white-collar crime issues are mostly thought of as the province of organized crime, the perception is misguided. Despite the fact that the nuances between these groups and their relationships may not be precisely defined, the war against terrorism cannot be separated from the fight against organized crime and fraud (Perri & Brody, 2011d). Fraud analysis must be central to understanding the patterns of terrorist behavior and cannot be viewed as a peripheral issue to consider when convenient.

Terrorists derive funding from a variety of criminal activities ranging in scale and sophistication from low-level crime, fraud, narcotics smuggling, from state sponsors, and activities in failed states and other safe havens. Some of the fraud schemes include but are not limited to, credit card fraud, mortgage fraud, charitable donation fraud, insurance fraud, identity theft, money laundering, immigration fraud, and tax evasion. Shell companies also have been used by terrorist groups to receive and distribute money. These companies display a legitimate complexion by appearing to engage in lawful activities to establish a positive reputation in the business community (Perri & Brody, 2011d). Consider that when we examine terrorist attacks in Europe, the vast majority of them did not require large sums of money or rely on the financing of established organized terror groups such as al-Qaeda or the Islamic State, also known as ISIS, ISIL, IS or Daesh (Basra et al., 2016). Whether small-scale or sophisticated, as part of a wider strategy, "jihadist groups are trying to keep financial barriers to entry low, making it possible for all their supporters—no matter how rich or poor—to participate" (Basra et al., 2016, p. 4).

Jihadism generally entails armed opposition to Western influence, to secular governments and institutions in Muslim countries or areas with Muslim populations when such opposition is perceived as fanatical or employing means that are immoderate or unlawful. Jihadists not only condone the use of street-level crimes such as robberies, drug dealing and white-collar crimes to raise funds, but they have argued that doing so is ideologically appropriate because the funds are used to support their cause. Consider that a large number of terrorists have a criminal background; engaging in crime does not trigger a moral dilemma for them to resolve. Terror financing will become more important as the number of former criminals in terror ranks increase, however their criminal acts are not merely financial in nature, but consist of a wide range of supporting activities including document fraud and illegal cross-border transport of people.

In this chapter, we examine the security implications of the nexus between terrorism and organized crime in addition to risk factors which make the organized crime and terror collaboration more likely. Furthermore, we look at the role product counterfeiting and fraud plays in financing terror activities. Moreover, we examine the rise of hybrid groups of crime and terror where in essence they are indistinguishable, as opposed to solely two distinct groups. This scenario is not unforeseeable when we apply the failed state concept which represents patterns of governmental collapse, especially to nations such as Afghanistan and Mexico illustrating the overlapping similarities between terror and organized crime groups.

The Nexus between Terrorism and Organized Crime

> Transnational organized crime has been linked to a cancer, spreading across the world. It can undermine democracy, disrupt free markets, drain national assets, and inhibit the development of stable societies. In doing so, national and international criminal groups threaten the security of nations (Hesterman, 2013, p. 23).

According to Robert Charles from the U.S. State Department on Narcotics, "transnational crime is converging with the terrorist world" (Kaplan, 2005, p. 22). Further illustrating the serious consequences of a convergence between organized transnational crime and terrorism, consider the insight of terrorist expert Louise Shelley, "Transnational crime will be a defining issue of the 21st century for policymakers—as defining as the Cold War was for the 20th century and colonialism was for the 19th" (Perri & Lichtenwald, 2009, p. 25). Transnational criminal groups "now have sophisticated business models that parallel legitimate corporations...feeding on globalization and advances in communications and logistics technology, modern transnational crime is more expansive, far deadlier, and extremely difficult to eradicate" (Hesterman, 2013, p. 3). Terrorists and transnational crime groups will proliferate because these crime groups are major beneficiaries of globalization. They take advantage of increased travel, trade, rapid money movements, telecommunications and computer links, and are well positioned for growth (Mooney et al., 2009). In addition, consider how terror groups think about their goals taking a long-term approach to destabilizing democratic societies.

Often called the "death by a thousand cuts strategy", those who want to turn democratic societies into an Islamic Republic hope to exhaust and overwhelm the people and their governments. For example, in 2004, al-Qaeda spokesman Osama bin Laden stated he "bled Russia for ten years until it went bankrupt and forced to withdraw in defeat...we are continuing in the same policy to make America bleed profusely to the point of bankruptcy" (Hesterman, 2013, p. 73). Moreover, the low cost to execute the 9/11 attacks in the United States and the resulting devastation to our economy from the airline industry, the many corporations suffering losses in the twin towers in New York, and our extensive military engagements overseas has not gone unnoticed by those desiring to hurt us. Dragging the United States into a "long slog" is not just a hope but an operational tactic" (Hesterman, 2013, p. 73). Although the connection between organized crime and terror groups is unclear, they both have a common enemy and that is the state in general and its law enforcement agencies in particular (Bovenkerk & Chakra, 2005). The development of these two entities resulted in the emergence of transnational organized crime and international networked terrorist groups as exemplified by al-Qaeda.

These types of groups create a state of heightened insecurity within the world of governments that are accustomed to military threats by known, identifiable state players who are now forced to react to economic, and social destruction perpetrated by unknown non-state players (Makarenko, 2004). Growing reliance on cross-border criminal activities, facilitated by open borders, weak states, immigration flows, financial technology, and an intricate and accessible global transportation system, coupled with an interest to establish political control, all have contributed to the rise of the crime-terror nexus. In essence international crime-terror groups are challenging legitimate governments, arguably for the first time in history, because they realize that first of all they have the power to do it now, and second they realize economic and political power enhance one another. Links between terrorism and organized crime groups is challenging international and national security by, 1) weakening democratic institutions, 2) compromising government institutions, 3) damaging the credibility of financial institutions, and 4) infiltrating the formal economy leading to increased crime and human security challenges (Liang, 2011).

While criminal activity and terrorism are security threats in their own right, the growing nexus of terrorism and organized crime is creating a dynamic which perpetuates conflict and war while emboldening and sustaining insurgencies. As criminal and terrorists' groups have grown into transnational entities contributing to the diversification of their enterprises and clientele, it is inevitable that they will come into direct contact (Roberts, 2016). They have no interest in bringing peace since they profit from government instability. The convergence of criminals and terrorists is facilitated by the proliferation of lawless enclaves which are referred to as "black holes", where government stability is almost non-existent making the rule of law irrelevant. Black holes thrive in chaos and we tend to observe them in nations or areas within nations where the government does not have strong institutions to bring law and order, thus the state has been taken over by crime-terror groups (Perri & Brody, 2011d). Furthermore, white-collar crime is one of the tools at the disposal of terrorists which also threaten a nation's financial institutions due to the fact that these institutions are used by terrorists to money launder their funds. Prior to the September 11th terrorist attacks, the tracking and interdiction of "terrorist financing was not a priority for either domestic or foreign intelligence" (Cliff & Desilets, 2014).

Since that day, it has become clear that understanding terrorist financing is a key, if not the key component, to combating terrorism. Although terrorist attacks alone may not seem expensive on the surface, the volume of monetary support needed to sustain terrorist training camps, control centers, and infrastructure is high especially for those terror groups that have extensive networks. Not only does the termination of terrorist financing rob terrorists of the ability to fund their activities, but "tracking the movement of funds among individuals in terrorist groups and their supporters provides verifiable indications of associations, relationships, and networks" (Cliff & Desilets, 2014). As previously stated, the link between these groups although evident is not always clear. The problem is due to the fact that there are different types of organized crime and terrorists groups. Thus, when there is reference to organized crime's link to terrorism, it is important to also consider what type of organized crime organization is being referenced. On the one hand, there are organized crime groups that use violence or the threat of violence to commit extortion or to enforce "business agreements" where the state fails completely or partially from enforcing contracts such as in Sicily and the former Soviet Republic (Bovenkerk & Chakra, 2005).

Then there is the type of organized crime preferring to operate in secret, such as in smuggling narcotics, people, and avoiding contact with the authorities. For example, consider that traditional organized crime syndicates need the state and the global economic system because they thrive on obtaining government contracts and the international financial system to retain its value and their wealth. These traditional organized crime groups have little in common with the newer organized transnational crime groups that often originate from conflict situations and thrive on chaos and who possess neither large resources nor loyalty to the state—their services are merely available to the highest bidder (Shelley, 2006). Most traditional "old school" criminal organizations reject association with terrorist organizations because they are typically not concerned with influencing public opinion; they are involved in crime to produce wealth for themselves (Weng, 2010).

On the other hand, terrorists are engaging in either terror activities or criminal activities in order to seek political ends, but this does not mean they are not hungry to gain financially if they can. Practically organized crime is likely to acquire in-house capabilities to guarantee their organizational security and operations without cooperation or assistance of terrorist groups. There is no evidence to prove that criminal and terrorist groups have converged into a single entity with similar ideologies, motives, and views of what constitutes success and failure (Weng, 2010). While different goals and ideological beliefs of these two entities are obvious and conflicts between them do exist, these realities make it extremely difficult to maintain long time cooperation or combine into one single entity (Weng, 2010). That said, terror and organized crime groups recruit from the same group of people because today members may not necessarily just belong exclusively to a terror group or an organized crime group (Basra et al., 2016). By recruiting from the same group of people, this may create synergies and overlaps that have consequences for how individuals become radicalized.

When we speak of radicalization, we are referring to the process causing someone to adopt an extreme position on political, religious or social issues consequently rejecting or undermining the status quo or undermining the contemporary ideas and expressions of the nation. The "terrorist-transnational crime relationship extends beyond a marriage of convenience that generates or provides logistics: it goes to the very heart of the relationship between crime groups and the state" (Weng, 2010, p. 13). Newer transnational criminal organizations are growing into hybrid organizations with in-house capability of employing mass, indiscriminate violence. These newer transnational crime groups, often originating in ungovernable regions, are now establishing links with terrorist groups because the criminal groups may not want neither stability nor strong states who can control them (Weng, 2010). Another significant reason is that new transnational groups likely take advantage of the chaos of war and dysfunctional state functions creating new and dangerous opportunities for collaboration between criminals, terrorists and social network extensions (Weng, 2010).

Moreover, newer organized crime groups have a different risk appetite compared to networks operating in established societies where law enforcement functions better and association with terrorists enhances risk of disrupting profitable and influence-enhancing operations (Shelley, 2006). In some instances, younger, smaller, and more loosely organized than traditionally hierarchical syndicates have become ideologically radicalized actively pursuing operations that will not only result in lucrative illicit profits but also further the goals of a terrorist group (Rollins & Wyler, 2010). The newer crime groups in ungovernable regions are now forging alliances with terrorist organizations; neither criminals nor terrorists fear the government because corrupt and ineffective law enforcement in conflict regions makes attempts at control almost futile. The newer crime groups may not share the ideological motivations of terrorists, but are willing to exploit weak states. In fact, these newer organized crime groups may promote chaos, similar to terrorist goals, because it is through the presence of conflict they enhance profits (Shelley, 2006).

The Interaction between Terrorism and Organized Crime

Similarities between organized crime and terror groups make it possible for the two entities to adopt each other's characteristics and tactics. In this case, terrorist groups begin to generate their own revenue through

184

engaging in a number of organized criminal activities, including but not limited to narcotics trafficking, intellectual property crime, credit card and financial fraud. Moreover, the similarities between the two entities is a factor contributing to the links between organized criminal organizations and terrorist groups (Skye, 2016). There are a number of reasons and opportunities that enable terrorist to embrace organized crime as a main source of funding. First and foremost, both organized criminal organizations and terrorist groups share numerous inherent organizational and operational similarities. Similarities between organized crime and terrorist groups include:

- Both are generally rational actors in that they are capable of engaging in risk assessments such as the risk of detection and a cost-benefit analysis,
- Both use extreme violence and the threat of violence to satisfy their motives,
- Both use kidnappings, fraud, assassinations, and extortion to fund their operations,
- Both operate secretly, though at times publicly in friendly territory,
- Both defy the state and the rule of law except when there is state sponsorship that enables these groups to thrive,
- For a member to leave either group can be fatal,
- Both present a threat to the United States and "friendly" nations,
- Both display "interchangeable" recruitment pools capable of having a supply of motivated followers to fulfill agendas,
- Both are highly innovative, resilient and adaptable to changing environmental conditions,
- Both have back-up leaders and foot soldiers to carry out their agendas, and
- Both have provided social services to communities they operate within, though this is much more frequently seen with terrorist groups (Weng, 2010).

In general, there appear to be three ways the crime-terror nexus interacts: 1) through shared tactics and methods, 2) through the process of transformation from one type of group to the other over time, and 3) through short or long-term transaction-based, service-for-hire activities between groups (Mullins, 2009). Organizations struggling to survive, wishing to expand their reach, seeking to develop more sophisticated skills and tactics, or simply requiring external assistance for a specific one-time service, may reach out to other entities for their support and expertise, even if such entities have different philosophical objectives (Rollins & Wyler, 2010). Common motivations for criminal and terrorist organizations to partner include financial viability, geographic growth, personnel protection, logistical support, support of mutually exclusive criminal activities, and the introduction of third parties to facilitate organizational goals, among others (Perri & Brody, 2011d). The worldwide antiterror campaign and an extremely broad approach of repressing terrorist funding makes cooperation a rational choice for both organized crime and terror groups. Moreover, the crime-terror nexus also take advantage of communication technology to minimize their risk getting caught. The linkages between organized criminal groups and terrorists occur in a combination of ways, both tactical and strategic alliances.

A tactical alliance means a one-time or a short time frame cooperation arrangement without any complementary enduring goals. In contrast, strategic alliances between organized crime groups and terrorists are based on their consistent interests aimed to achieve mutual expectations of long-term goals. Different aims and motivations of political and criminal groups lead organized crime groups and terrorists more likely to cooperate on a short-term basis (Basra et al., 2016). That being said, shared tactics have evolved into strategic alliances between organized crime and terrorist groups, especially if they are operating in the same territory. Most of the evidence of linkages between the two entities demonstrates a functional cooperation such as documents forging. Whether criminal organizations seek cooperation with terrorists or terror groups form alliances with criminal organizations, these linkages are based on a variety of reasons. Alliances are established in order to share expert knowledge such as bomb designing, money laundering, communication technologies or operational support such as access to trafficking routes.

While cooperating with terrorists could help organized crime groups gain significant profits through the prolonging of conflict, corruption, and undermining law enforcement, their alliances tend to be short-term in order to not draw attention to their operations. However, such collaborations are also fraught with great risk to both types of entities; partnering arrangements can, at times, lead to successful alliances, but they can also have the potential of sowing the seeds for distrust, competition, and opportunity for vulnerabilities to be exploited (Rollins & Wyler, 2010). In turn, these vulnerabilities could lead to improved detection and disruption of both the terrorist organization and criminal syndicates. Common disincentives for partnering may include 1) increased attention from government authorities, 2) fear of compromising internal security, 3) risk of infiltration by people whose intentions are unclear, 4) heightened vulnerability of leadership being captured, 5) ideological resistance to illicit endeavors such as drug trafficking, kidnapping, and fraud, and 6) sufficient sources of non-criminal funding from charities, large private donors, legal businesses, and state sponsors.

Several observers of the crime-terror nexus suggest that such disincentives are among the primary reasons why the core leadership of certain international terrorist groups such as Hezbollah and al-Qaeda, which have other lucrative funding sources, is not known to be significantly partnered with transnational criminal groups (Rollins & Wyler, 2010). There is concern that, over time, groups may become increasingly motivated by the lucrative nature of their illicit financing activities and transform from a group that is mainly ideological to one that is profit driven. Moreover, criminal groups already in control of lucrative revenue streams may not find the potential additional business with terrorist groups sufficient to outweigh the costs of potential exposure to government oversight. For example, those that study the Russian Mafia state that they are unwilling to ally with terror groups because to do so would bring a fierce response from the Russian authorities and huge political pressures from the United Nations; the doom of the Russian criminal groups would be inevitable (Weng, 2010). They tend to be satisfied with their steady and huge profits raised from their traditional and low risk business, such as private protection service, debt collection, extortion and legitimate business. Additionally, there remain cultural, operational, and practical differences between older criminal groups and terrorist groups, thus the different aims and motivations of the two entities also makes collaboration difficult if unlikely.

In practical and political terms, older criminal groups engaged in organized crime without attracting the public attention, while terror groups tend to draw unwelcome law enforcement attention (Weng, 2010). Criminal groups may opt to avoid collaboration with terrorist groups if such interactions would disrupt their relationships with corrupt government officials who are willing to facilitate criminal activities, but not terror-related ones. Given some of the incentives and disincentives to collaborate, what are some of conditions that assist in the collaboration process? Organized crime groups and terrorists thrive where the controls of the central state are least, and where there are porous borders and ineffective law enforcement. Research indicates that organized crime tends to flourish most when groups in society see their own interests as separate from that of the system of governance and the rules enacted from that system and where the standards of law enforcement and perceptions of legal authority are low (Shelley et al., 2005). They also flourish where local law enforcement, such as in many developed communities, cannot successfully police ethnic sub-communities within the larger community.

For example, many immigrant communities in Western Europe are outside the control of law enforcement and intelligence authorities. In these urban neighborhoods of major and secondary European cities, relationships can be established between terrorists and criminals in restaurants, cafes, businesses, and religious institutions. Crime-terror connections are more likely to occur in areas of the world where the state has the least presence and means of control, shadow economies, corruption, and regional conflicts (Shelley et al., 2005). In conflict zones and certain urban areas, for example, criminals are less constrained by respect for the political system and the rule of law, less intimidated by regulation and law enforcement, and often motivated by a desire to subvert or disregard the established order. It is also growing in many major cities or penal institutions in democratic societies where ethnic subgroups do not share the norms of the larger society. It is not just terrorists that benefit from adopting tactics from the organized crime play book. Cooperation with terrorists and adopting their tactics may have a significant benefit for organized crime by destabilizing the political structure, undermining law enforcement and limiting the possibilities for international cooperation so that they can maximize their profits (Makarenko, 2004).

Prison Facilitating Synergistic Interactions

Prisons provide another major area of interaction for criminals and terrorists; no longer merely schools of crime, prisons have become a de facto corporate headquarters of crime groups where relationships are formed and orders are entered for supplies of all varieties of illicit commodities. Terrorists commit criminal acts to survive, and are imprisoned for non-terrorist criminal offenses. Prisons are a place where terrorists recruit criminals to join them in their activities by radicalizing them so that they adopt the belief systems of terrorists. As one British terrorist recruiting propaganda poster referencing their desire to recruit criminals: "Sometimes people with the worst pasts create the best futures" (Basra et al., 2016, p. 7). Terrorists also recruit criminals with ties to organized crimes because of the expertise they have access to such as producing fraudulent documents through forging. In 2008 the French newspaper *Le Monde* interviewed prisoners inside Fleury-Mérogis about conditions within the infamous prison.

One inmate stated, "Prison is the best (expletive) school of crime. In the same walk, you can meet Corsicans, Basques, Muslims, robbers, small-time drug dealers, big traffickers, murderers…Over there, you learn from years of experience" (Basra et al., 2016, p. 44). That prisoner was Amedy Coulibaly, who was imprisoned for receiving stolen goods, drug trafficking, and robbery. Within Fleury-Mérogis, he began socializing with extremists and was mentored by Djamel Beghal, an al-Qaeda recruiter. He would also form a friendship with Chérif Kouachi, who he spent seven months alongside in the same prison section. Upon release from prison, Coulibaly continued to associate with both criminal and extremists, and was encouraged in doing so by his mentor Beghal who provided him with an ideological license to commit crimes to promote jihad. Jihad is a struggle or fight against the enemies of Islam. Coulibaly went on to carry out a series of terrorist attacks in January 2015 killing five people, culminating into a hostage crisis in a kosher supermarket in Paris; these attacks seemed to have been coordinated with the Kouachi brothers, Said and Cherif, who killed 12 people at the offices of Charlie Hebdo in Paris (Basra et al., 2016).

For those criminals that belonged previously in a gang, terror groups provide similar environments offering power, the excitement and mental "high" of the adventure, a sense of being antiestablishment and a sense of rebellion. Thus, it is not surprising that there is a cross-over appeal for criminals to engage in terrorists acts given that they do not reject violence as a solution. Yet terror propaganda, again, tries to give a different interpretation of their group as displayed in a recruiting video stating, "to all the…brothers who are asking for advice on how to leave that gangster life behind and join the life of jihad" (Basra et al., 2016). There are those criminals who are affiliated with gangs that may be susceptible to radicalization in prison especially if they are having a personal crisis where they reflect on their criminal behaviors and the impact such behaviors have had on others or some other personal crisis unrelated to criminal activity that makes them reflect on their life desiring change. As a result, because they may be at a weak point in their life, they might be open to breaking with their past and turning to religion, in this case a jihadist version of religion that endorses religious-based violence (Basra et al., 2016). The irony, of course, is that they might leave behind one type of criminal behavior and turn to another, albeit a more violent one.

However, recruiting criminals has its advantages because they may already be desensitized in the use of violence thus display a low psychological threshold for using violence as a terrorist. Thus the transition from being criminal to terrorist is not difficult. The terror group gives them a sense of belonging, a higher purpose that incorporates religion which enhances their sense of moral justification behind their acts, an identity that allows them to break from the past and a social network of support. In essence the terror group is another subculture a criminal can belong to with its own initiation rights, expectations of loyalty, secret codes and hand signs, ranking systems as well as cultural artifacts such as tattoos, and uniforms (Roberts, 2016). In fact, being a terrorist is deemed fashionable; countless recruiting on social media depicts a gangster lifestyle with members showing off military bravado, guns in the air, sitting in the back of trucks and on top of tanks. Some argue that jihadism reflects a global gang subculture where members are attracted to a sense of belonging, a sense of identity, and stability amid instability (Roberts, 2016).

Gangs harbor an "us versus them" mindset and this same mindset permeates many who join terror groups where their motives have not as much to do with religion, but rather the reason to participate was driven by an emotional response to injustices perpetrated by an outside group (Roberts, 2016). Yet in the end, shifting to terrorism may have nothing to do with religion, but it brings with it its own sense of pleasure and satisfaction as did their criminal lifestyle—it is aggression, a power orientation manifested in a different form, for different motives, relying on different rationalizations creating victims nonetheless. Many of the terrorists today had criminal histories prior to belonging to terror groups. For example, in August 2016 in Copenhagen, Denmark, a 25 year-old Danish-Bosnian named Mesa Hodzic was approached by two plain-clothed police officers. Hodzic pulled out a gun firing hitting a bystander and both police officers, but later died from his own gunshot wounds he received in the shootout—he was known as a drug dealer (Basra et al., 2016). After his death, ISIS claimed responsibility for Hodzic's actions also proclaiming him a soldier of the Caliphate. It became known that Hodzic was not just a prolific drug dealer, but also a member of the terrorist group known as Salafist's, where he expressed sympathies with ISIS while appearing in propaganda videos.

Consider that the Belgian Federal Prosecutor stated that at a minimum half of Belgium's jihadist that traveled to Syria to fight with ISIS had criminal records prior to traveling abroad. According to the German Federal Police, of the 669 German foreign fighters for whom they had sufficient information, about two thirds had criminal histories prior to leaving for Syria (Basra et al., 2016). A clear example of this crime-terror interaction is evident in Spanish prisons prior to the Madrid bombing in 2004, where terrorists recruited ordinary criminals to carry out the plot (Shelley, 2006). It is difficult to isolate terrorists from organized criminals when unrecognized terrorists are arrested on criminal charges. Prisons allow terrorists to recruit criminals, to help run their networks, especially in seeking specialists in fraudulent documents and cooperation in the trafficking of arms, drugs and humans. Prison authorities, lacking firm knowledge of who they have confined in their prisons, cannot isolate criminals from terrorists because they do not know that they have arrested terrorists. Unless they engage in undercover work in prisons such as introducing informants, monitoring conversations and visitors, they may be entirely ignorant as to the actual identity of those they have in their custody. The criminals targeted for recruitment transport illicit cargo, move people or provide false documents are likely to be aware of the true affiliations and motives of their new-found terror partners (Shelley, 2006).

Terror and Organized Crime Interaction Case Studies

In addition, terrorists are smuggled into Europe via the same logistics that are employed to traffic drugs, cigarettes and other contraband into Europe. For example, terrorists in Europe engage in human smuggling with and without the help of organized crime especially in Sicily. Authorities in Italy suspect that one gang of terrorists made over 30 landings in Sicily and moved thousands of people across the Mediterranean at some $4,000 per head (Kaplan et al., 2005). Consider the statement from a retired FBI official: "I am aware of a high-level Mafia figure, who was cooperating with authorities, being asked if the Mafia would assist terrorists in smuggling people into Europe through Italy…The retired agent is reported to have advised that he understood the high level Mafia boss to have said, 'The Mafia will help who ever can pay'" (Stuart, 2006). Matt Heron, of New York City's FBI Unit, voiced similar worries stating: "They [the mafia] will deal with anybody, if they can make a buck. They will sell to a terrorist just as easily as they would sell to an order of Franciscan monks. It's a business relationship to them. If the mob has explosives and a terrorist wants them and they have the money, they could become instant friends" (Perri & Lichtenwald, 2009, p. 17).

In 2006 during an undercover, FBI agents tracked a mafia member who was selling missiles to a person he thought was an al-Qaeda member who turned out to be an FBI informant (Hesterman, 2013). In fact, al-Qaeda uses the Naples-based Camorra Mafia for expertise in forging documents, extensive networks, and to move al-Qaeda operatives through Europe to safe houses (Chepesiuk, 2007). According to Italy's political crimes unit, the number of al-Qaeda operatives passing through Naples may have exceeded a thousand and if Camorra should experience any problems, they will send the operatives off on one of the many trains leaving the city or via speed boats that Camorra uses to traffic drugs, cigarettes and other contraband (Perri & Brody, 2011d). Others provide home bases for terrorist groups where a cooperative or even symbiotic relationship exists between the crime group and the terrorist group operating within the region. Traditional Mafia groups, for example, learned to use symbolic violence to reach a wider audience when in the early 1990s, the Sicilian Mafia carried out a series of car bombs in the Italian mainland, specifically Rome and Florence (Makarenko, 2004). Another example of short-lived cooperation between organized criminal groups and terrorists is the Italian Red Brigade formed an alliance with the Naples Camorra in the early 1980s (Weng, 2010).

Although, their motivations and views are extremely different from each other, the reasons the Red Brigade attempted to establish this alliance was because their organization and terrorism activities were seriously crippled by Italian authorities. As a result, the Camorra and Red Brigade exchanged services for a brief period of time and combated their common enemy—the Italian authorities. For instance, the police reported that the Red Brigade and the Camorra partnered with one another in order to kill or kidnap a number of police officers and senior politicians. The goal of course was to intimidate the public by openly challenging the political structure so that their Parliament would renounce the anti-Mafia legislation. Consider the interaction between the Provisional Irish Republican Army (IRA) and FARC from Colombia. The IRA was a militant organization whose aim was to remove Northern Ireland from the United Kingdom and set up a United Ireland through terrorist activities and guerilla warfare before its campaign of violence ended in 2005. Following the worldwide successful campaign of dismantling the IRA's financial system, the IRA was compelled to find alternative sources of funding. The IRA likely encouraged its members to engage in criminal activities in order to raise funds for organizational needs, rather than ally with any other organized criminal organizations.

The IRA is a classic example of a mutual terrorist group who stepped into organized crime, but the political aims and motivation of the groups were still paramount; they did not morph from a political group to solely an organized crime group. The IRA to some extent also acted like the Mafia, providing protection for citizens and in return generated plenty of money. Thus they successfully developed into an organization with in-house capability becoming a self-sufficient entity. Although the IRA seldom contacted with other criminal groups because of its self-sufficient financial system, a notable example indicated that its cooperation with other criminal groups did exist. Three members of the IRA engaged in cooperating with Colombian terror group FARC by sharing their expert knowledge of bomb-making (Weng, 2010). The linkage between the IRA and FARC can be regarded as a one-time cooperation designed for specific aims and operational needs. Patterns of criminal behavior generated overseas are transferred to the U.S. through U.S-based cells of foreign terror groups and tend to persist once transferred. For example, Hezbollah involvement in cigarette trafficking first observed in Latin America was subsequently prosecuted in North Carolina. Chechen terrorist's involvement in the sex trade industry in Russia has been noted by Los Angeles law enforcement.

In developing countries, criminals and terrorists tend to spawn more collaborative relationships that are closer knit, whereas in the developed world, organized crime is more likely to co-exist with terrorism through arm's length business transactions. For example, in Latin America, transnational organized crime has employed terrorist groups to guard their drug processing plants (Shelley et al., 2005). One of the newest crime-terror links is developing in the transit hub of West Africa where alleged Latin American traffickers are collaborating with al-Qaeda affiliates to smuggle cocaine to Europe (Rollins & Wyler, 2010). In addition, both crime groups and terrorists profit from the anonymity of the internet to diffuse propaganda, extort victims, and recruit new members. Both crime and terrorist groups can activate its many encryption devices to circumvent detection, and use widely available software tools to locate open ports and overcome password tools to facilitate hacking into banks and companies to steal identities, credit card information, copyrights, while extorting banks and companies for millions of dollars (Liang, 2011).

State Funded Terrorism

The Shia Islamist group Hezbollah was born into Lebanon's 1970s and 1980s narcotics boom and according to the Drug Enforcement Administration (DEA), Lebanese Colombians and Lebanese Shia in Lebanon established connections since the 1980s (Roberts, 2016). These ties expanded with Lebanese diaspora being kingpins of drug rings across South America funneling money back to Hezbollah. This elaborate business unfolded in the midst of receiving substantial state sponsorship from Iran where Iran funds Hezbollah to the tune of at least $100 million per year and analysts currently estimate that Iran bestows up to $200 million per year to Hezbollah (Roberts, 2016). The picture is clear—from its birth in the early 1980s to this day, Hezbollah was and is founded on supposedly ideological principles, but also on criminal entrepreneurialism to support its activities (Roberts, 2016). Hezbollah has been designated a terror group since 1995 and they have stated that one of its primary goals is to eliminate the state of Israel (Hesterman, 2013, p. 77). Today, however, state-sponsored terror is a dying concept as groups form around an ideology and leverage information technology and communication to form, train, fund and execute operations (Hesterman, 2013). In addition, the structure of terrorist groups is not always hierarchical where there is a distinct leader, chain of command, directors of training, logistics, directors of training, and a financial arm. The newer terror groups resemble super cells where their hierarchy is flatter, decentralized, and where there is no one leader that controls every terrorist movement; they are more fluid or rigid depending on the situation.

Terrorism and Smuggling

Just as organized crime is heavily involved in cigarette smuggling, it is not surprising that terrorist cells within the United States use cigarette smuggling as a method to fund their operations and it is considered one of the "top fund raising activities used by terrorists, along with illicit drug, weapon, and the diamond trade" (Shelley & Melzer, 2008, p. 10). Cigarette smuggling investigations have also been linked to Hamas, Hezbollah, al-Qaeda, the Taliban, and other designated foreign terrorist organizations such as the Irish Republican Army and its splinter groups in recent years (Wilson, 2009). Specifically, large quantities of cigarettes are sold on the black market at below retail cost by avoiding paying tobacco tax rates or paying lower tax rates in certain states. This was basically the business model of the Mohamad Hammoud and the Hassan Makki Terrorist Cell cases. From 1996 to 2002, Hassan Makki and his co-conspirators would obtain low-tax cigarettes from the Cattaraugus Indian Reservation in New York and North Carolina and sell them for a substantial profit in Michigan. Hassan admitted to trafficking between $36,000 and $72,000 of contraband cigarettes per month between 1997 and 1999 (Collins, 2003).

In September 2003, Hassan pleaded guilty to charges of cigarette smuggling, racketeering, and providing material support to a foreign terrorist organization. In the Mohamad Hammoud case, by avoiding Michigan's tobacco tax, it is estimated that these individuals were able to make anywhere from $3,000 to $10,000 on each trip (Lafaive et al., 2008). According to court documents, the conspiracy involved a quantity of cigarettes valued at roughly $7.5 million which translated into depriving the State of Michigan of $3 million in tax revenues (Shelley & Melzer, 2008). Interestingly, Mohamad applied for a fraudulent $1.6 million loan from the Small Business Administration to build a gasoline station that was to be used to distribute the contraband cigarettes and a way to launder illegal profits (Shelley & Melzer, 2008). Mohamad transferred funds generated by the cigarette trafficking scheme, as well as money raised from other sources, back to Lebanon to support Hezbollah (Horowitz, 2004). That support included cash and dual use equipment, such as night vision goggles, high-end computers, ultrasonic dog repellents, global positioning systems (GPS), drilling and blasting equipment, advanced aircraft analysis, and surveying equipment to name a few items (Lafaive et al, 2008).

Furthermore, according to terror expert Louise Shelley, terrorist financing through cigarette smuggling is "huge," stating, "Worldwide–it's no exaggeration...No one thinks cigarette smuggling is too serious, so law enforcement doesn't spend resources to go after it" (Wilson, 2009). In addition, David Cid, a Former FBI Counterterrorism Agent states, "cigarettes are easy to smuggle, easy to buy, and they have a pretty good return on the investment...Drug dogs don't alert on your car if it's full of Camels [cigarettes]" (Wilson, 2009). To end the flow of criminal money to terrorist groups and insurgencies, experts say, will mean cutting off the flow of contraband—whether narcotics or tobacco. Terrorism and criminal finance investigator Larry Johnson notes that it is much easier to crack down on the flow of legal products like tobacco: "You need to ensure that the products are being sold through legitimate channels through legitimate distributors—that they're not committing willful blindness. The contraband is fairly easy to deal with because it's in the power of the distributors and producers to control the process. This is actually one of those few problems that is fixable" (Wilson, 2009).

Furthermore, Mexican narcotics syndicates control access to transit routes into the United States. Hezbollah smuggles weapons, document traffickers, narcotics, alien and human contraband along routes used by drug cartels enlisting Lebanese Shiite expatriates to negotiate contracts with Mexican crime bosses. According to Michael Braun, retired Chief of Operations at the U.S. Drug Enforcement Administration, Hezbollah relies on "the same criminal weapons smugglers, document traffickers and transportation experts as the drug cartels...They work together, they rely on the same shadow facilitators. One way or another, they are all connected. They'll leverage those relationships to their benefit, to smuggle contraband and humans into the USA" (Carter, 2009). For example, U.S. and Colombian law enforcement agencies dismantled a Hezbollah drug trafficking ring that was funneling profits to markets in Europe, the U.S., and militias in Lebanon. In an operation in 2007, an undercover Drug Enforcement Administration (DEA) agent managed to gain the trust of the director of this crime ring named Shukri Mahmoud Harb and over a two year period, the agent collected intelligence on drug routes and recipients, while Harb alone laundered twenty million dollars during his operation. Harb's enterprise reportedly contributed 12 percent of Hezbollah's total income from narcotics (Roberts, 2016).

Harb was eventually arrested with 130 Hezbollah operatives (Sale, 2009). Although Hezbollah appears to view the U.S. primarily as a source of cash, there have been no confirmed Hezbollah attacks within the U.S. The group's growing ties with Mexican drug cartels are particularly worrisome at a time when a war against and among Mexican narco-traffickers has killed thousands of people and has destabilized Mexico along the U.S. border. Two U.S. law enforcement officers, familiar with counterterrorism operations in the U.S. and Latin America, said that it was no surprise that Hezbollah members have entered the U.S. border through drug cartel transit route. As a result, the "Mexican cartels have no loyalty to anyone...They will willingly or unknowingly aid other nefarious groups into the U.S. through the routes they control" (Gedalyahu, 2009). A senior U.S. defense official, who spoke on the condition of anonymity because of ongoing operations in Latin America, warned that al-Qaeda could use trafficking routes to infiltrate operatives into the U.S. stated, "If I have the money to do it...I want to get somebody across the border—that's a way to do it...Especially, foot soldiers...somebody who's willing to come and blow themselves up" (Carter, 2009).

Human Trafficking

Terror financing also relies on human trafficking that can take the form of slavery, migrant smuggling and exploitation towards its victims generating annual profits conservatively estimated at $150 billion annually (CTED, 2019). Trafficking in persons typically is defined as the recruitment, transportation, transfer, harboring or receipt of persons, by means of the threat or use of force or other forms of coercion, abduction, fraud, deception, of the abuse of power or of a position of vulnerability or of the giving or receiving of payments or benefits to achieve the consent of a person having control over another person, for the purpose of exploitation. Exploitation shall include, at a minimum, the prostitution of others or other forms of sexual exploitation, forced labor or services, slavery or practices similar to slavery, servitude or the removal of organs. According to the 2018 Global Slavery Index, around 89 million people have experienced some form of enslavement over the past several years. However, because human trafficking is both covert and illegal, it is difficult to gather accurate data, yet given the current absence of specific law enforcement case studies on the use of such exploitation for terrorism financing purposes, information on the human trafficking—terrorism financing nexus is limited (CTED, 2019).

Human trafficking constitutes one of the most serious human rights violations and one of the most profitable activities of organized crime including terrorists. It attracts a broad range of criminal enterprises, from small local groups to international networks that deal in large numbers of trafficked victims through connections in source, transit and destination countries. Sadly, people wishing to escape violence may turn to traffickers in the hope of finding a safe haven, but generally find themselves in an exploitative situation. Like other forms of illegal activities, human trafficking has become increasingly attractive to terrorist entities. Acts of violence associated with human trafficking have been central to the modus operandi of the Islamic State in Iraq also known as ISIS,

ISIL, IS, or Da'esh, Boko Haram, Al-Shabaab, and the Lord's Resistance Army (LRA). Human trafficking is not a new phenomenon, however, its use in the context of war and conflict has attracted increased attention. Despite the substantial military setbacks and territorial losses experienced by some terrorist entities, acts of exploitation and enslavement against women and girls and acts of forced recruitment and indoctrination against men and boys have continued for financial gain.

No country is immune to human trafficking or terrorism, however, the most affected countries continue to have little understanding of their vulnerability and to the potential links between them. In many cases, it is difficult to establish whether a person has been the victim of human trafficking, migrant smuggling, or kidnapping for ransom. Even though each crime has its own legal definition, the differences between them are often blurred. Furthermore, one crime may evolve and turn into another. This may occur if, for instance, a person is abducted, abused as a sexual slave, and then sold back to the family through the payment of a ransom, or when migrants who have begun their journeys by willingly placing themselves in the hands of smugglers to become victims of human trafficking along the way because of a debt bondage. For example, the sale of Yazidi women, who are members of a Kurdish religious minority, by ISIS are instances of human trafficking that may be associated with terrorism financing involving cash transactions, thus it is difficult to "follow the money" in order to identify financial patterns. Human trafficking also raises revenue for groups such as ISIS by holding people ransom. Migrant smuggling can be a stepping stone to human trafficking, notably in cases where the person cannot pay the smuggler or is forced into participating in crimes.

Consider that on March 27, 2017, Kenyan Police arrested Ali Hussein Ali, also known as "The Trusted One", a terrorist linked to ISIS, whom they described as a key link in terrorism financing through human trafficking. Ali was born in Mogadishu and entered Kenya in 2010 as a tourist, before moving to South Africa, Sudan and, finally, Tripoli, where he joined ISIS. He returned to Kenya in November 2016, becoming a key agent for the terrorist organization and the Magafe human smuggling/trafficking network in Libya. According to the police, he played a key role in the African terrorist network, known as Magafe, facilitated the travel of recruits from Kenya to Somalia to join ISIS in Libya, as well as the safe passage to Europe of irregular migrants via Libya. Ali facilitated the transfer of money linked to an ISIS network and travelled through several countries, including Libya, Somalia, South Sudan and Sudan. The money was transferred through various countries before reaching Libya, in order to conceal the transaction trail. At the time of his arrest, Ali was demanding $639,000 after safely delivering recruits and smuggled migrants to their destinations (CTED, 2019). Ali and his accomplices housed recruits and irregular migrants in lodges within Kenya and other areas before facilitating their travel to Libya, the Syrian Arab Republic, and Europe.

Upon their arrival in Libya, the recruits and smuggled migrants were detained by criminal gangs, notably Magafe, and would only be released upon payment of ransom of between $2500 and $7000 per person. The money was transferred to Mogadishu through hawalas, which are an informal method of transmitting funds, located in Kenya and then channeled to ISIS in Libya. Vulnerability to trafficking that creates the opportunity to profit from human trafficking by organized crime and terror groups should be broadly understood as the relationship between push factors: the conditions in the hosting and transit countries, people's access to entitlements, and their capacity to make migratory decisions. Women and girls, and those fleeing war and persecution, are most vulnerable to trafficking. All migrants make choices, but within divergent ranges of options for mobility, which can change over time on a migratory journey. A worst-case risk scenario is an already marginalized person, who is pushed into a country where terror trafficking gangs operate, and who has no access to resources or international protection.

Vulnerability is dictated not simply by exposure to risk, but by proximity to resources in social and political structures. For example, when war is looming, those with the most entitlements can choose to migrate early as an anticipatory decision, with a specific destination in mind. They procure travel documents through bribes or pay reliable smugglers for a full journey from country of origin to destination. Many migrants make the choice to move on a proactive basis as a result of poor life circumstances, rather than on a reactive basis such as the result of conflict or direct persecution, or, what is commonly called survival migration. People with fewer resources experience the same push factors, but have fewer choices. Thus traditionally marginalized groups, including women, minors, the poor, people with lower education, or ethnic minorities, are more vulnerable to trafficking. In situations that combine strong push factors with narrow regular migration channels, traffickers can trick or coerce migrants into abusive situations or offer to facilitate movement for later payment, resulting in situations of forced labor or prostitution. For example, people fleeing acute crises like civil conflict often have to move quickly and without a plan. The absence of international protection, or safe channels for migration, can render them more vulnerable to trafficking.

To take a prominent example, Syrian refugees who have fled the ongoing violence in their country appear to be particularly vulnerable to trafficking in neighboring countries, where they report a significant amount of indentured labor and among both adults and children, child marriages, and forced "temporary marriages" amounting to forced prostitution (CTED, 2019). Research shows that Syrian men and women are vulnerable to different forms of trafficking; while women and girls are open to more sexual abuse and men travelling alone are more vulnerable to forced labor. People escaping war and persecution are the most vulnerable to human trafficking. They are forced to make decisions within a short time frame and often flee to countries were the rule of law is weak coupled with preexisting displacement crises, a particularly worrisome trend given that most displaced people are hosted in the world's least developed countries. Within irregular migratory contexts, relying on smugglers means that interactions are often isolated to concealed markets that are characterized by the desire to avoid law enforcement. In the context of high levels of corruption and collusion between national authorities and criminal networks, migrant rights may be ignored and traffickers may act freely without risk of punishment. In crisis scenarios such as violent conflict, failed governments, or natural disasters, migrants face pressure to move in situations where they are effectively trapped.

Migrants thus have an even narrower range of choices in situations in which they are highly vulnerable because of subordinate social position, lack of legal status, exacerbated protection gaps, lack of assistance, and arbitrary detention. Women, unaccompanied minors, the poor, and the undocumented face even greater vulnerability. In crisis-affected countries, the issue of trafficking may be ignored, leading to more room for abusive situations. In the European context and elsewhere, crisis situations can cause refugees and asylum seekers, particularly unaccompanied minors, to be more vulnerable to trafficking, particularly for sex exploitation and forced labor. The connection between human trafficking and conflict is not new, however over the last five years, it appears to have grown significantly. Situations of armed conflict render people more vulnerable to trafficking by exacerbating instability, insecurity and economic desperation, eroding the rule of law and forcing individuals to flee for their safety. These factors also allow armed groups to engage in trafficking activities, notably to forcibly recruit new combatants, perpetrate sexual exploitation to generate revenues. Human trafficking in conflict thus encompasses a wide range of illicit conduct, including enslavement, child recruitment, sex slavery, organ trafficking, forced labor and fraudulent recruitment into an armed group resulting in illegal domestic servitude or military service.

In Libya, patterns of sexual exploitation against migrants, refugees and asylum seekers, perpetrated by smugglers, traffickers and hybrid criminal-terrorist networks, have been well documented (CTED, 2019). Moreover, human trafficking has become an opportunistic tactic to spread terror, control populations, and impede the restoration of peace and the possibility to conduct a normal life. Terrorists raid, pillage, abduct, extort, ransom, trade and traffic to supplement their personal micro-economies, while women suffer structural discrimination at the macroeconomic level, which reduces their resilience to financial and security shocks. Women have been victims of sexual violence face trauma, stigma, social marginalization, poor health and unwanted pregnancy. Children and minors who have been forcibly recruited and trained to combat alongside armed groups face detention for alleged affiliation. These alarming trends are common to a range of otherwise diverse conflicts, including in the Central African Republic, the Democratic Republic of the Congo, Iraq, Mali, Myanmar, Nigeria, Somalia and South Sudan. However, despite efforts to better ascertain the gravity of the issue, human trafficking in conflict, as well as in other crisis situations, remains largely overlooked and omitted from formulations of humanitarian and emergency response policies.

The systematic sale of Yazidi women by ISIS fighters represents the most significant known instance of the use of sexual slavery to generate revenue illustrating the human trafficking—terrorism financing nexus. As previously reported, following the August 2014 attack on the Yazidis on Mount Sinjar, ISIS forcibly transferred captive women and girls to holding sites in Iraq and the Syrian Arab Republic. Eighty percent of the slaves were made available to the fighters for individual purchase. The remainder were held as collective property of ISIS and distributed in groups to military bases throughout Iraq and the Syrian Arab Republic. In some instances, ISIS allowed its fighters to buy a group of Yazidi females in order to take them into rural areas without slave markets and sell them individually at a higher price. ISIS's slave trade was well organized and involved significant logistical investment: a network of warehouses in which to hold the victims, viewing rooms in which the victims were inspected and purchased, and a dedicated fleet of buses, used to transport them. In the Syrian Arab Republic, the bureaucracy of the Yazidi slave market was organized by a central body called the "Committee for the Buying and Selling of Slaves". Where this Committee authorized the opening of a slave market in a particular town, it devolved some of its functions to a local committee and commander.

According to an ISIS document, released online and considered to be authentic, fighters were required to pre-register if they wished to attend a slave market in Homs, Syria. In most cases, the sale was finalized through a bidding process. The offer was submitted in a sealed envelope at the time of purchase and the fighter who had won the bid was obliged to buy the slave. Women and girls were exposed, both at the slave markets and at the holding sites, as property. Interested buyers could check their hair or teeth and ask them to walk through the room, as if parading on a catwalk; their price was based on marital status, age, number of children and perceived beauty, and could range between $200 and $1,500 (CTED, 2019). According a Financial Action Task Force report on ISIS financing, the price paid for ISIS slaves was much lower, amounting, on average, to $13. Other sources report the following prices: a) $172 for those who are between 0-9 years old, b) $129 for those between 10-20 years old, c) $86 for those between 20-30 years old, and d) $75 for those between 30-40 years old (CTED, 2019). In addition, according to the United Nations Assistance Mission for Iraq, ISIS received between $35 million and $45 million in 2014 from ransom payments made by the families of hostages. It is believed that $850,000 was paid in January, 2015 for the release of 200 Iraqi Yazidi.

A further controversial issue is ISIS's alleged involvement in organ harvesting and trafficking. Again, the allegation is based on the verbal accounts of former prisoners and ISIS defectors. An ISIS document, released by the group's Research and Fatwa Department and retrieved by the U.S. Special Forces in eastern Syrian Arab Republic, sought to justify the harvesting of organs of infidels by stating: "the apostate's life and organs do not have to be respected and may be taken with impunity" (CTED, 2019). Even though this document offers no concrete evidence that ISIS engaged in organ harvesting and trafficking, it is not inconceivable that the group could have been profiting from trafficking in body parts. Interviews conducted by the International Center for the Study of Violent Extremism with former ISIS prisoners and defectors also shed light on the potential use of the practice, including for financial purposes. One of the interviewees, Abo Rida, a former ISIS surgeon, stated that ISIS surgeons removed kidneys and corneas from prisoners and had been told that "jihadists were more deserving of organs" (CTED, 2019). In December 2015, a former ISIS fighter stated, "from this point you do not kill the slaves. We need to use their bodies to make money, through organ trade; basically, they are saying that the slaves are already 'dead'. We need to make money off their bodies by selling body parts" (CTED, 2019).

According to media reports, in November, 2016, the Director General of the Syrian Coroner's Office disclosed that since 2011, more than 25,000 surgical operations had been performed in refugee camps of neighboring countries such as Turkey and ISIS controlled areas in Syria to remove the organs of 15,000 Syrians and sell them on the black market (CTED, 2019). A former intelligence officer from Kurdistan who coordinated the rescue of Yazidi captives claimed to have information relating to the sale of children for organ trafficking stating that part of the rescue network involved working with international law enforcement agencies to dismantle an organ smuggling ring believed to be based in Turkey. Additional information concerning the involvement of terrorist groups in the black market organ trade is provided by the analysis of financial patterns relating to kidney transplants, conducted by national security and money laundering experts at George Mason University.

Failed States Facilitating Terror Financing

Terrorists are happy to maintain the public façade that their goals are religious when the evidence no longer supports their statements (Ehrenfeld, 1990). No longer just driven by political and religious agendas, but by the quest for profit, groups that were solely terrorist use terror tactics for several reasons (Perri & Brody, 2011d). These groups evolved from being just a terrorist organization into a group that is primarily engaged in criminal activity such as Abu Sayyaf of the Islamic Movement of Uzbekistan. For example, in 2000 alone, Abu Sayyaf's kidnapping negotiations brought in about $20 million. There is little indication the group remains driven by its original political motive which was to establish an independent Islamic republic in the territory comprising Mindanao, surrounding islands and the Sulu Archipelago (Makarenko, 2004). The inability to distinguish the two groups, because of their hybrid complexion, may lead to what is referred to as the "black hole" syndrome (Makarenko, 2004).

The syndrome encompasses two situations; first, where the primary motivations of the group engaged in war evolves from a focus on the political and religious aims of a group to a focus on the criminal aims. Secondly it refers to the emergence of a black hole state which is a state, the government, that has been successfully taken over by a crime-terror group. Although this position reveals the extreme consequence of the crime-terror nexus ultimately blending into an indistinguishable entity, what is born is a scenario of constant civil or regional wars to secure economic and political power. These failed states, as defined by the patterns of governmental collapse within a nation, are considered incapable of sustaining themselves as a member of the international community and depends on steady streams of foreign assistance as witnessed in Afghanistan (Helman & Ratner, 2010). For example, Ciudad d'Este, the tri-border city between Brazil, Paraguay, and Argentina, is another region that is symptomatic of increasingly blurred lines between crime and war displaying black hole attributes (Robert, 2016).

Known as "Smuggler's Paradise", Ciudad d'Este is a virtually lawless zone absent of border and trade regulation and the triangle can arguably be considered the first trans-Atlantic safe haven for Islamist terrorist groups, notably for Hezbollah and al-Qaeda operatives (Roberts, 2016). In regions where Islamist terrorist groups operate, where organized crime and terrorism thrive and at times rely on each other, it is difficult to distinguish between ideologically and criminally motivated violence. Wars that were originally fought for ideological and religious reasons morphed into wars that are fought to advance criminal interests secured by terrorist tactics; today ideological, political, and religious rhetoric is the mask used to secure public legitimacy and as a recruiting tool (Roberts, 2016). The Afghanistan Taliban, once an organization of seminary students seeking to establish a caliphate, the Islamic form of government representing the Muslims, embraces Mafia-like activities that feed on insecurity for financial gain (Kunduz, 2009).

Together, with poor governance, ineffective policing and a weak justice system, which are characteristics of a failed state, the nexus between the Taliban and crime is becoming dangerously entrenched in Afghan society where it behaves like a broad network of criminal gangs (Phillips & Kamen, 2014). This enables the Taliban to utilize different sources of income where their main finances were generated from the cross-border smuggling of legal commodities, credit card fraud as well as robberies (Weng, 2010). The country of Afghanistan displays the characteristics of a black hole state. An obstacle in reversing Afghanistan's black hole condition is the fact that Afghanistan supplies the world's opium with the assistance of transnational organized crime groups facilitating its distribution (Makarenko, 2004). This is coupled with the assistance of terrorists within the country who facilitate the type of political destabilization that creates weak states; a perfect recipe for the birth of a black hole country. One could extrapolate the concept of the black hole syndrome to the current crime-terror war that is being waged in Northern Mexico on the border with the United States.

Although Mexico cannot be considered a failed state in technical terms, the narcotics war in Northern Mexico where thousands and thousands of people have died appears to display the qualities of an emerging black hole region similar to the region that occupies the area between Pakistan and Afghanistan known as Pakistan's Northwest Frontier Border. There is evidence that the war in Mexico is spilling over in the United States as evidence by recent murders of innocent individuals and those involved in the smuggling trade in the Southwest United States (Bricker, 2009). It is premature to conclude whether the Mexican government can restore a sense of order to this region of the country that borders the United States. Will the United States have its own black hole region referred to as the Southwest Frontier Province, an area that overlaps Northern Mexico and the Southwest region of the United States because of a porous border that facilitates illicit activity that is similar to the Pakistani-Afghanistan border in terms of its borderless characteristic? The diplomatic talks between the United States and Mexico on how to address this issue cannot have come soon enough due to the continued murder of innocent people, police officers, government personnel, where beheadings and torture appear to be favorite fear tactics organized drug cartels have borrowed from terrorist's tactics (Perri et al., 2009). Today there are killings on both sides of the Mexican-American Borders; these crime groups use the element of surprise and learn from failures and adapt accordingly. These groups have "announced their arrival in the United States—are we prepared" as they attempt to disrupt our societal fabric to satisfy their financial goals through the use of extreme violent tactics (Hesterman, 2013, p. 147)?

Terror Financing Schemes

The life-blood of any nefarious group is money and for criminal organizations money is the motivation with a side goal of corruption and influencing the political process in their favor to keep the money flowing (Hesterman, 2013). However for terrorist groups, the motivation, at least outwardly appears to be a religious ideology. Financing operations in the dark is critical especially since the cost to move and train people as well as buying material is expensive. For "all groups, earning, moving, storing, and laundering are critical, whether 'dirty' money that must be cleaned or "clean" money that will become dirty when funding a terror operation" (Hesterman, 2013, p. 4). Financing is required not just to fund specific terrorist operations, but to meet the broader organizational costs of developing and maintaining a terrorist organization and to create an enabling environment necessary to sustain their activities (Perri & Brody, 2011d). The direct costs of mounting individual attacks have been low relative to the damage they can yield; part of the problem is that it takes so little to finance an operation (Wilson, 2009). For example, the 2005 London bombings that killed over 50 people cost around $15,600 (FATF, 2008). The 2000 bombing of the USS Cole that killed many sailors is estimated to have cost between $5,000 and $10,000 (Farah, 2005).

Al-Qaeda's entire 9/11 operation that killed almost 3000 people cost between $400,000 and $500,000, according to the final report of the National Commission on Terrorist Attacks upon the U.S. (Farah, 2005). The terrorist attack at the Jakarta Marriot Hotel is estimated to have cost around $40,000 and the Bali Bombings in 2002 is estimated to have cost around $50,000 (Gomez, 2010). The November, 2015 Paris attacks were financed by a sum not exceeding $50,000 (Basra et al., 2016). One study found that three-quarters of European terror plots between 1994 and 2013 cost less than $20,000 (Basra et al., 2016). As we can see, terror financing does not require a dedicated terrorist fundraising operation giving individual terror cell autonomy as to how they want to carry out their terror plots because they can become self-funded through a variety of fraud and non-fraudulent means. However, organizations require significant funds to create and maintain an infrastructure of organizational support, to sustain an ideology of terrorism through propaganda, and to finance the ostensibly legitimate activities needed to provide a veil of legitimacy for terrorist organizations (FATF, 2008). Consider that some of the larger terror groups are viewed as de facto governments such as al-Qaeda, Hezbollah and al-Shabaab in Somalia paying for things such as schools and infrastructure which, in part explains why they have the support of the local populations who may not get support from anywhere else; in fact some of these terrorists are actually looked upon as heroes in their communities (Basra et al., 2016).

Prior to 9/11 and over a ten year period, al-Qaeda was estimated to receive between $300 million and $500 million in cash, averaging $30 to $50 million a year (Hesterman, 2013). These contributions are referred to as Zakat which is another fund-raising mechanism that has not received much attention, yet Zakat is singled out as one of the most important sources of terror financing coupled with the fact that the funds are moved through legal banking institutions (Hesterman, 2103). The literal definition of Zakat is cleansing and growth; it is a legitimate and some say an obligatory form of charitable giving for Muslims. The specific purposes of Zakat include but are not limited to 1) serving the poor, 2) helping those in debt, 3) paying those that are carrying the message of Islam and 4) those that collect Zakat must be compensated for collecting Zakat (Hesterman, 2103). The lack of record keeping makes the use of Zakat difficult if not impossible to trace. Approximately 10 percent of al-Qaeda's spending was on terrorists operations and attacks while 90 percent was used on the infrastructure of the network, including payments to other groups for support or to increase al-Qaeda's influence in the region (Hesterman, 2013).

Terrorist organizations need money not only to carry out operations but to recruit, train, travel, take care of everyday expenses, and to provide for the families of dead terrorists. However, one should not be tempted to believe that large organizations are needed to carry out attacks. Small semi-autonomous cells in many countries have discovered that they capable of conducting disruptive activities without extensive outside financial help by conducting smaller scale frauds (Rollins & Wyler, 2010). In addition, modern terrorists and organized crime engage in mortgage fraud, insurance fraud, charitable fraud, identity fraud and product counterfeiting. Almost all acts of terrorism enacted in the United States were facilitated by stolen identities. The 9/11 U.S. Commission Report maintains that many terrorists committed identity fraud, stating that access to travel documents is as important as weapons (Liang, 2011). Ramzi Yousef, the perpetrator of the first World Trade Center attack in 1993, committed immigration fraud (Liang, 2011). Let us examine the different fraud schemes they employ to raise funds for their nefarious goals.

Mortgage Fraud

Financial experts state that mortgage fraud has become one of the fastest growing type of white-collar crime and terrorist organizations have been quick to jump on the trend (Poole, 2007). It is the ease by which terrorists and their supporters can raise hundreds of thousands of dollars in a short period of time that makes mortgage fraud so attractive compared to the high risk world of drug distribution, or the low returns from other known petty crimes that have previously been used to finance terrorism. Fortunately, the mortgage industry, which has already taken action in response to the rapid rise of mortgage fraud, is becoming more aware of the involvement of terrorist organizations in some cases. Experts from the mortgage lending industry together with law enforcement and banking regulatory officials continue to educate us on how Hezbollah, Islamic Jihad, and the Taliban, established mortgage fraud rings in the United States (Poole, 2007). For example, in 2006, Nemr Ali Rahal from Michigan pleaded guilty to mortgage fraud in order to prevent being charged additionally with terrorist activities. At the time of his arrest, federal authorities found books, posters and recruitment videos for the Hezbollah terrorist organization inside his home. Rahal fraudulently obtained more than $500,000 by falsifying information on mortgage applications (Poole, 2007).

In another Michigan case, two men, Mohammed Krayem and Youssef Kourani transferred more than $200,000 obtained through real estate fraud and cigarette smuggling to the Hezbollah Chief of Military Security for Southern Lebanon (Poole, 2007). Tarik Hamdi was charged with mortgage loan fraud by U.S. investigators investigating an Islamic charity, the International Institute for Islamic Thought of Herndon, Virginia (Hesterman, 2013). Hamdi worked for the charity with links to terrorist financing. He delivered a satellite phone battery to al-Qaeda operatives for Osama bin Laden's personal phone, which he used to coordinate the 1998 U.S. embassy bombing in Kenya and Tanzania. In June 2005, Ahmad and Musa Jebril, were convicted of mortgage fraud charges after defrauding six banks of $250,000 and dozens of people of up to $400,000 (Poole, 2007). The Jebrils were active supporters of Hamas, and federal authorities said that Ahmad Jebril was training a cell of local men to wage jihad against the U.S. Subsequent to their conviction of mortgage fraud, the Jebrils' and one of their associates were additionally charged by the federal government with trying to bribe a juror during their fraud trial.

Charitable Fraud

Many thousands of legitimate charitable organizations exist all over the world serving the interests of all societies, and often transmit funds to and from highly distressed parts of the globe. They enjoy the public trust, have access to considerable sources of funds, and their activities are often cash-intensive. Furthermore, some charities have a global presence that provides a framework for national and international operations and financial transactions, often in or near areas most exposed to terrorist activity. Yet, charities or non-profit organizations possess characteristics that make them particularly attractive to terrorists or vulnerable to misuse for terrorist financing (Perri & Brody, 2011d). Terrorists use fraudulent charitable organizations claiming to support a particular cause, such as disaster relief or food services, in order to generate money for their cause. The sheer volume of funds and other assets held by the charitable sector means that the diversion of even a very small percentage of these funds to support terrorism constitutes a grave problem (FATF, 2008).

In developing key financial standards to combat terrorism, the misuse of nonprofit organizations for financing of terrorism is recognized as a crucial weak point in the global struggle to stop such funding at its source (FATF, 2008). Charities represent a perfect cover for collecting large amounts of money for terrorist activities and according to internationally recognized terrorist expert Steven Emerson, "charities played a key role in the September 11 attacks" (Emerson, 2002, p. 8). For contributors wishing to finance a terror group, their identities are virtually protected through charitable giving due to a lack of a paper trail and the charity's ability to hide within and be protected by a large, overarching religious organization (Hesterman, 2013). Charities are subject to significantly lighter regulatory requirements than financial institutions or publicly-held corporate entities for issues pertaining to starting capital, professional certification or background checks for staff and trustees at registration, or for ongoing record keeping, reporting and monitoring (Emerson, 2002).

In 2003, the U.S. Treasury Department revoked the tax exempt status of three Muslim charities accused of diverting contributions to help fund terror activities; they include the Benevolence International Foundation of Palos Hills, Illinois, the Global Relief Foundation of Bridgeview, Illinois, and the Holy Land Foundation of Richardson, Texas (Hesterman, 2013). Benevolence International had direct connections to Osama bin Laden and the leader of the foundation, Enaam Arnaout, pleaded guilty to aiding Islamic fighters in Chechnya. The foundation had branches in Bosnia, Chechnya, Pakistan, China, and Russia allowing money launderers to easily move and hide assets. Global Relief was a multimillion-dollar business, sending more than ninety percent of its donations oversees to Osama bin Laden and the Taliban. Foundation leaders consistently lied to investigators about the destination of their funds. Hamas still raises tens of millions of dollars per year using charitable fund raising as cover.

For example, in 2008, in the Northern District of Texas, all defendants in the *United States vs. Holy Land Foundation* case were found guilty of terrorist financing that involved money laundering and tax fraud. Holy Land Foundation raised millions of dollars for Hamas over a 13-year period (Emerson, 2002). The foundation had offices in three states and raised $13 million in 2000 alone; the money was allegedly used to support the Palestinian people, but it was mainly used to support the families of suicide bombers (Hesterman, 2013). These charities are able to disguise their true purpose and appear to be completely legitimate and functioning for the advertised purpose. However, donors must do their own research before donating because it becomes easy to be deceived by a convincing name and the affinity one might harbor for the charity's members because of shared religious beliefs. In the end it is incredibly difficult to determine with definitiveness how much of a charity's money is illegitimate and legitimate at least in terms of its relation to terror financing.

Identity Fraud

According to identity fraud expert Judith Collins from the Michigan State University Identity Theft Crime and Research Lab., "All acts of terrorism enacted against the United States have been facilitated with the use of a fake or stolen identity" (Koerner, 2005). Collins indicates that 5 percent of all identity thieves are connected to terrorism and 2 percent, specifically to al-Qaeda (Koerner, 2005). In fact, the al-Qaeda terrorist involved in the September 11, 2001 attacks opened 14 bank accounts using several different names, all of which were fake or stolen (Koerner, 2005). Terrorists use stolen or fabricated Social Security numbers and credit cards to create false identities to pay for their operations and passports are extensively used by terrorists moving between countries of interests (Scott, 2003). Identity theft is possibly one of the most lucrative enterprises which terrorists have engaged in and they get much more than money from this crime. Identity theft facilitates terrorist goals of avoiding watch lists, obscures their whereabouts, assist in terrorist funding activities and gaining unauthorized access to entry points such as airline gates, border crossings, or other facilities (Gartenstein & Dabruzzi, 2007). One critical aspect of identity theft, according to Denis Lormel, formerly of the FBI's Terrorism Review Group, is the "cloak of anonymity" that it provides (Lormel, 2002).

Identities are often stolen violating federal laws such as bank fraud, credit card fraud, wire fraud, mail fraud, bankruptcy fraud, and computer crimes. Moreover, this cloak of anonymity means that "[t]he use of a stolen identity enhances the chances of success in the commission of almost all financial crimes" which again enhances the importance of forensic examiners to unravel identity mysteries (Lormel, 2002). The 9/11 Commission Report established that terrorists commit identity fraud noting "travel documents are as important as weapons" (Commission Report, 2004). Terrorists must travel clandestinely to meet, train, plan, case targets, and gain access to attack (Poole, 2007). According to Lormel, "the ease with which these individuals can obtain false identification or assume the identity of someone else, and then open bank accounts and obtain credit cards, make these attractive ways to generate funds" (Hesterman, 2013, p. 182). Identity theft remains a crime that is fairly simple to commit and for which no easy prevention solution currently exists. Terrorists need to blend in when working the logistical aspects of the operation, such as obtaining clothing, components of weapons and, most importantly, fulfilling transportation needs such as rental vehicles and airline tickets.

Many people do not use cash for their purchases and terrorists would bring much unwanted attention if they were to do so, thus the need for credit cards. Credit card fraud allows a terrorist the opportunity to purchase goods, withdraw money until the fraud is detected and then the card is canceled. Credit card applications are solicited frequently, thus it is easy to open up multiple credit cards in other people's names. Al-Qaeda extensively used identity theft and credit card fraud. The 9/11 hijackers embarked on a scheme in Spain to raise money for the attacks and according to the authorities, "the pattern was very clear within the North African contingent of al-Qaeda members operating in Europe…every time you arrest one of them he has twenty different identities and twenty different credit cards" (Hesterman, 2013, p. 182).

Consider the case of Ahmed Ressam of the Armed Islamic Group, with ties to Osama bin Laden, who was caught in 1999 at the U.S. and Canadian border with about one hundred pounds of explosive stored in his rental car. He assumed the name of Benni Norris to obtain a passport, a false birth certificate, a student ID as well as opening several bank accounts to deflect suspicion. Once captured he told the authorities that he relied on public aid and petty crime to support himself including credit card fraud, and trafficking in false identity documents. He was also involved in a theft ring stealing credit cards, passports, cellular phones to name a few items to support Muslim extremist groups (Hesterman, 2013). The theft ring also plotted to buy gas stations and use the business to obtain credit card numbers and place a camera in locations where it would be possible to watch people punch in their personal identification number (PIN) when paying for items or extracting cash.

In addition, consider that one month before the November 2015 attacks in Paris, Belgian police were conducting an investigation into a large-scale forgery ring in Brussels. Inside an apartment in the district of Saint Gilles, investigators discovered a sophisticated factory that created hundreds of fake identification cards, drivers' licenses, and social security cards (Basra et al., 2016). The apartment was complete with a hot press, computers, and ID card printers, as well as hundreds of printing rolls and negatives of fake IDs. Among those negatives were IDs that had been produced for the terror cell that perpetrated the attacks in Paris in November, 2015 and Brussels in March, 2016. It was only in the immediate aftermath of the Paris attacks when one of its organizers, Salah Abdeslam, was on the run from police that investigators revisited the forgery operation and discovered its connection to terrorism. As it turned out, the network used fraudulent documents throughout their attack planning in order to wire money, travel between countries, rent cars, and importantly, acquire safe houses. For example, one of the Paris terror operatives, Khalid el-Bakraoui, used fake identification, adopting the name 'Ibrahim Maaroufi' to rent an apartment in Charleroi, which was used by at least two of the Paris attackers.

Another apartment in Schaerbeek, rented under the pseudonym Fernando Castillo, was used as a bomb factory to manufacture homemade bombs known as TATP explosives and suicide vests for the Paris attacks. Even after those attacks, the network maintained the same methods, again renting an apartment in Schaerbeek, which served as a bomb factory for their TATP suitcase bombs to be detonated. Khalid's brother, Ibrahim el-Bakraoui, used a fake Belgian ID, adopting the pseudonym of a Portuguese 'Miguel Dos Santos', complete with a wig and glasses. Rather than becoming forgers themselves, the Paris-Brussels network used their contacts within the criminal social network to reach out to forgers that supplied human smuggling traffickers. This is how they came across Djamal Eddine Ouali, an Algerian who ran the forgery operation in Saint Gilles. The supposed 'profit vs. ideology' dichotomy, which is frequently debated in the academic literature, was no barrier to this. In fact, there is no evidence that Ouali knew of their true intentions, or was even interested in them. Instead, it is likely that they appeared as ordinary customers from a criminal social network. As the Belgian investigator in charge of Ouali's case said, "[He] was a professional document falsifier whose main goal was to make as much money as possible" (Basra et al., 2016, p. 37).

Insurance Fraud

Other examples of terrorists using a variety of fraud schemes to raise funds include insurance and benefits fraud. A 2006 case in the United States involved Karim Koubriti and his co-defendant Ahmed Hannon, who were found guilty of mail fraud, insurance fraud, and material support of terrorism in connection with his "economic jihad" scheme to defraud the Titan Insurance Company (O'Neil, 2007). In this case, Koubriti and Hannon falsely claimed to have been injured in a car accident and then filed a false insurance claim with Titan. Koubriti and Hannon provided fictitious invoices for medical bills, lost wages as well as mileage and services accrued due to the purported injuries. Koubriti's motivation was twofold: to commit fraud in order to both support terrorist activities and to cause economic harm to U.S. businesses. In another case, according to media reports, a pair of jihadists in Germany hoped to fund a suicide mission to Iraq by taking out nearly $1 million in life insurance and staging the death of one in a faked traffic accident (O'Neil, 2007).

Immigration Fraud

For many terrorists, immigration fraud is one of the first acts taken in a long line of criminal activities. Individuals who have planned acts of terror against the U.S. or raised money for terrorist organizations have engaged in immigration violations such as Ramzi Yousef, the mastermind of the first World Trade Center attack in 1993, used an altered passport and fraudulent documents (Elderidge, 2004). Immigration fraud facilitates the entry of terrorists into a country. Terrorist, including some of those involved in the 9/11 attacks, continue to take advantage of weaknesses in the U.S. immigration system not only to enter, but to remain indefinitely until their nefarious acts are fulfilled. Several kinds of document fraud can occur during the immigration process through forgery, lying, false statements, or the misuse of visas. Former counsel to the 9/11 Commission authored a report titled Immigration and Terrorism that examines the histories of 94 foreign born terrorists who operated in the U.S. between the early 1990s and 2004, concluded that 59 terrorists committed immigration fraud prior to or in conjunction with taking part in terrorist activity (Kephart, 2005). Michael Cutler from the Center for Immigration Studies, states that when aliens acquire immigration benefits through fraud and deception, the security of the system is breached leaving the door open for terrorists to game the system and to teach others how to game the system (Cutler, 2006).

Product Counterfeiting

Terrorists commit a variety of financially related, nonviolent offenses, including tax fraud, money laundering, identity theft and product counterfeiting (Sullivan et al., 2014). Counterfeiting is an intellectual property crime. Intellectual property refers to the legal rights corresponding to intellectual activity in the industrial, scientific and artistic fields. These legal rights pertain most commonly in the "form of patents, trademarks, and copyright, protect not only the moral and economic entitlement of the creators, but also the creativity and dissemination of their work" (Hesterman, 2013, p. 175). Intellectual property crime therefore refers to counterfeited and pirated goods, manufactured and sold at a profit without the consent of the patent or trademark holder. This type of crime is black market activity operating parallel to the formal market and includes the manufacturing, transporting, storing and sale of counterfeit or pirated goods. Product counterfeiting has been termed by the FBI and others as a 21st century crime and consumer markets for counterfeit and pirated goods consists of consumers either purchasing goods they believe to be legitimate, or knowingly searching for bargains with the understanding that many will be fraudulent. Terrorists use product counterfeiting because of the financial incentives involved, with proceeds fulfilling multiple purposes including personal enrichment, support to individual criminal enterprises, and broader terrorist missions and operations.

Terrorist and organized crime groups imitate each other's successful practices and reports indicate that groups such as al-Qaeda, Hezbollah, the Irish Republican Army (IRA), Hamas, Armenian, Russian, Italian, Japanese and the Chinese Mafia participate in counterfeiting (Sullivan et al., 2014). Product counterfeiting may pertain to clothing, food, chemicals, designer goods, luxury items, automobile parts, pharmaceuticals, electronics, purses, the illegal duplication of software, movies, music and other products to name a few. Counterfeit products not only result in financial losses to consumers, businesses, tax revenue for governments, and investors, but can pose health and safety risks to those who manufacture and purchase them because of a lack of regulatory oversight as to what their product is actually made of. Counterfeit goods also undermine economies by denying income to legitimate businesses and creating an elusive underground economy funding criminal enterprises. Although quantifying the impact and scope of product counterfeiting on the global economy is fraught with challenges, conservative estimates consistently place the losses in the hundreds of billions of dollars annually. The Counterfeiting Intelligence Bureau of the International Chamber of Commerce conservatively estimates that product counterfeiting consists annually of 5–7 percent of all global commerce representing about $450 billion (Sullivan et al., 2014). In the U.S. alone, losses to counterfeiting are estimated at $200 to $250 billion annually (Hesterman, 2013).

Unique qualities facilitate the production and distribution of counterfeit goods, including ties to other types of illegal behavior such as terrorism and organized crime. Technological advances, outsourcing, globalization, and information sharing have provided opportunities for individuals and groups to become involved in counterfeiting by increasing the quality of counterfeits while enhancing the efficiency of counterfeit manufacturing. Counterfeiting operations are difficult to uncover due to the secrecy surrounding this illicit activity and the use of various production and distribution methods, including the internet and existing criminal trafficking distribution networks. Over half of the purchases of counterfeit products occur over the internet, creating problems for tracking and intercepting the numerous manufacturing and distribution chains (Sullivan et al., 2014). Internet sales are attractive to sellers who perceive a low risk of detection, as consumers are unable to validate products and have little knowledge or recourses when defrauded by a counterfeit purchase. Terrorist groups are directly involved in the counterfeiting business in that they identify market niches, acquire the necessary production materials, produce and then sell goods if this is the business model they desire.

In addition, sympathizers, supporters, militants, and profit-motivated collaborators are involved in counterfeiting in a variety of different ways, from small to large scale operations, often sending a portion of their profits to a terrorist organization. Whether a terrorist group is directly involved or benefits indirectly from counterfeiting products, the profits are used to fund groups in ways that allow them to accomplish their ideological objectives. Terrorists and organized crime syndicates realize there are few barriers to entry into the counterfeiting product business, with minimum financial and technical expertise needed to counterfeit most products. Trafficking in counterfeit goods is relatively easy because a terrorist can make a profit from the sale of such goods without having to be involved in its actual production. Thus there is a low cost of entry with the potential to make a substantial profit especially from those terror groups that may not belong to a sophisticated organization that raises funds through more complex means that require a sophisticated organized crime network. Consider the previously mentioned Kouachi brothers. The Kouachi brothers initially received the equivalent of less than $20,000 from the al-Qaeda Arabian Peninsula (AQAP) after a 2011 trip to Yemen, although this money is likely to have been spent by the time of the Charlie Hebdo attack (Basra et al., 2016).

Potentially more significant is the fact that Said Kouachi was involved in running a counterfeiting operation whereby he was importing fake Nike shoes from China. The proceeds from this trade are reported to have been used for buying the weapons that were used in the January 2015 attacks. French Customs discovered the operation in 2013, resulting in a fine for Kouachi. His wider connections, and the ultimate purpose of his trade, were never discovered because repeated requests for support from France's domestic intelligence service were never considered despite counterfeiting being a well-established funding method of terrorist groups across the world. Amedy Coulibaly, on the other hand, was selling drugs only a month before the attacks, in addition to being owed street debts worth thousands of dollars. Notably, he and his wife raised funds via two consumer loans from Cofidis in December 2014, and from Financo in September 2014 totaling under $50,000. The Financo loan was used to purchase a car, which was then exchanged for weapons. Though Coulibaly provided genuine identification for the Cofidis loan, he used a fraudulent pay slip listing a monthly income of under $4000 at a company called Naxos. Even a brief check could have raised suspicion because public records revealed that Naxos had no employees and that the phone number provided was not in use.

Around the same time as the Cofidis loan, Coulibaly also tried to obtain credit from Crédipar, again by listing Naxos as his employer. On that occasion, Naxos's parent company Telcité was contacted and confirmed that Coulibaly was not an employee. The principal difficulty in detecting crime as a means of terrorist financing is that it does not involve a change of behavior, but merely one of purpose. Individuals with criminal pasts often continue what they were doing in their earlier lives, except that the profits are used to finance terrorist attacks or trips to the Middle East. As a result, it can be difficult to separate funds that were raised for terrorism from money that is spent on other, often entirely mundane purposes. Saïd Kouachi, for example, sold counterfeit goods, received money from AQAP, engaged in bank fraud, and was involved in theft. Not all of his money went into the funding of the Charlie Hebdo attack, but some of it did. How is it possible to distinguish one from the other? Did Kouachi, in his own mind, separate the different streams of income? The merging of criminal and terrorist environments, together with the self-financing of attacks, makes it hard to maintain traditional notions of terrorist financing. Rather than just tying particular transactions and streams of income to terrorism, it might be fruitful to concentrate on individuals, their backgrounds and financial histories.

This is borne out by the individuals whose terrorist fundraising methods often mirrored their criminal pasts. Even before becoming a terrorist, Kouachi traded in counterfeit products and continued doing so to finance his attacks. The same logic applied to the British jihadist Choukri Ellekhlifi, who had criminal convictions for several robberies, and financed his trip to Syria by doing more of them. Similarly, a group of would-be foreign fighters from Germany worked in construction and funded their journey by selling copper they stole from a building site. In all of these cases, the common thread was not any particular source of funding, be it counterfeit, copper, or robberies, but individual fund raising method consistency. If today's jihadists are former criminals, we should not be surprised if this is how they finance their 'jihad'. Law enforcement attention to product counterfeiting is limited and penalties are lax, resulting in the potential loss of income due to counterfeit merchandise as merely a cost of doing business. Although the potential scope of harm is extensive, there is a limited understanding of how terrorist groups and/or organized crime networks are involved in product counterfeiting while the media and the intelligence and enforcement communities have speculated about the connections between product counterfeiting and terrorism (Sullivan et al., 2014).

Product counterfeiting schemes are unpredictable and constantly evolving, making these crimes difficult to study ultimately complicating the development of anticounterfeiting strategies. If there is seizure of such goods, there is no further investigation on the money trail which is typically untraceable cash transactions without reliable recording keeping to identify the parties involved. Moreover, at least with respect to counterfeited goods, local law enforcement finds it difficult to treat counterfeiting a high priority crime worthy of devoting resources to their investigation. Furthermore they may not have the personnel who can devote their time investigating these crimes, thus terror groups have found this activity a low risk, lucrative source of funding (Hesterman, 2013). Also, terrorists know that if caught and prosecuted, the sanctions are minimal if it cannot be proven that their operations are tied to terrorism. Interestingly, al-Qaeda provides a training manual not only on forgery, but counterfeiting (Roberts, 2016). Ultimately document general patterns of counterfeiters and the offending capacities of organized counterfeiters of terrorists, organized and criminal networks.

Financing through Legitimate Corporations

In 2007 Chiquita Brands International, Inc. (Chiquita) pleaded guilty in the District of Columbia to the felony charge of engaging in transactions with a specially designated global terrorist (CFTP, 2008). On September 17, 2007, Chiquita was sentenced to a criminal fine of $25 million and five years of probation. From 1997 through early 2004, Chiquita paid the Colombian terrorist organization Autodefensas Unidas de Colombia (AUC), a designated global terrorist organization a total of over $1.7 million in over 100 installments. The investigation into the company's conduct revealed that Chiquita violated the books and records provision of the Foreign Corrupt Practices Act. In connection with the guilty plea, the Company admitted that its corporate records never reflected that the intended recipient of these funds was the AUC.

Miscellaneous Fraud Schemes

In addition, terror expert Matthew Levitt believes a substantial portion of the estimated millions of dollars raised by middle eastern terrorist groups comes from the $20 million to $30 million annually brought in by the illicit scam industry in America (O'Neil, 2007). According to Levitt, some of these illicit scams include credit card fraud, welfare fraud, coupon fraud, stealing and reselling baby formula, and food stamps fraud (Levitt, 2005). Other fraud scams include Nigerian scams conducted through the internet e-mail such as "you have won the lottery", inheritance notifications, or people who are in need of emergency funds because of an illness. Unfortunately in the U.S. alone, citizens, typically the elderly fall prey to these schemes costing them between $1 to $2 billion annually.

The Movement of Terrorist Funds

Once terror organizations have acquired financing through some of the schemes outlined above, how do they move their money about so that it can support their nefarious goals of terrorizing societies? Terror groups such as al-Qaeda use various methods to transfer funds with the aim of avoiding detection by the authorities. Among them are informal systems of money transfers such as hawala, cash couriers, money laundering, and the use of legitimate financial systems (Gomez, 2010). However, other mechanisms such as international trade and new methods of payment allowing anonymity have emerged. Let us exam in detail some of these methods.

Money Laundering

Money laundering is a term used to describe a scheme in which criminals try to disguise the identity, original ownership, and destination of money that they have obtained through criminal conduct. The laundering is done with the intention of making it seem that the proceeds have come from legitimate sources. Criminals want their illegal funds laundered because they can then move their money through society freely, without fear that the funds will be traced to their criminal deeds. In addition, laundering prevents the funds from being confiscated by the police. Predicate crimes are the underlying crimes that that give rise to money laundering in the first place (Kyriakos-Saad, 2016). Traditionally, the most important of these crimes was considered to be narcotics trafficking. As the 1990s progressed, however, the increasing recognition of the significance of the proceeds generated by non-drug-related crimes led to the designation of such crimes as predicates to money laundering. Such categories of offenses as predicate offenses to money laundering including terrorist financing refer to crimes such as trafficking in human beings and migrant smuggling, sale of human organs, illicit arms trafficking, illicit trafficking in stolen and other goods, corruption and bribery, fraud, counterfeiting currency, counterfeiting and piracy of products, environmental crime, violent crimes, kidnapping, illegal restraint and hostage-taking, robbery or theft, smuggling, tax crimes extortion, piracy, and insider trading.

Activities constituting money laundering process, generally develops in three phases. The first phase, called placement, consists of introducing the funds gained from criminal activities into the banking and financial system; this phase has become more and more fraught with risk due to the heightened attention now given these movements of cash by law enforcement, and the now widespread requirement that banks report suspicious transactions. Placement can take many forms such as moving money out of one country in s suitcase to another country. Another method is to deposit the money in an offshore bank or break up the amount of money into smaller amounts and deposit it into bank accounts or purchase cashier's checks, traveler's checks, or money orders. The process of breaking money into smaller denominations to evade reporting requirements is known as smurfing. A sophisticated smurfing operation might involve hundreds of accounts in dozens of cities. The second phase, called layering, consists of putting funds into the legitimate financial system, the purpose of which is to mislead potential investigators and to give these funds the appearance of having a legal origin. This is the money laundering phase that most often uses offshore mechanisms.

Numerous comings and goings between financial havens and the launderers' banks, punctuated by false invoices, false loans, or other devices, ultimately mislead investigators regarding the origin of the money. In addition, smurfing is difficult to detect and it becomes easier than wiring money to other countries because there is no evidence of suspicious activity to report. Finally, the third phase in money laundering known as integration, involves giving the money the appearance of having a legitimate origin, then reintroducing the funds into the legal economy to buy hard assets through consumption of luxury items and to pay for other items that may have a criminal intent. Consider another goal of profitable criminal activity is to be able to use the ill-gotten funds through investments in common place assets such as shares in companies and real estate. This includes investments in economic entities that are themselves susceptible of becoming money laundering machines including casinos, hotels, and restaurants as well as in companies in which payments are made in cash and where dirty money can easily be comingled with legitimate money.

Money and High-Value Goods Couriers

The physical movement of money across borders is predominant in countries where bank transfers are rarely used by common people. Couriers carrying money are also used where financial institutions have increased the efficiency of due diligence practices with clients. It is also one of the methods used by terrorist organizations such as al-Qaeda to move funds while avoiding antimoney laundering and counterterrorism financing measures implemented by national and international financial institutions (Gomez, 2010). The 9/11 investigation provided a good example of how al-Qaeda used human couriers to move money. One of the financial backers of the attack, Khalid Sheikh Mohamed, passed a large amount of money, possibly as much as $200,000, to Abdul Aziz Ali in Dubai, who subsequently transferred it to the hijackers in the U.S. Various counterterrorism operations have demonstrated that money couriers moved funds between Middle Eastern and South Asian countries. They often did so by using indirect flights between origin and destination, with large numbers of couriers and frequent exchanges of money. Moving money by using couriers can be more expensive than a simple transaction, but it leaves no trace even if the courier is detained, since the origin and final destination of the money might be unknown to him or her. Some terrorists have converted the money into high-value goods where the source is difficult to trace, such as gold and precious stones, moving smuggling activities away from formal financial systems (Gomez, 2010). For example, in 2003, six al-Qaeda members were arrested in Germany for plotting attacks; their operation was to be funded from smuggling gold from Dubai to be resold at a profit of $7.5 million (Hesterman, 2013).

The Ancient Tradition of Hawala

Hawala, meaning "in trust" or "to transfer", is a paperless financial dealing system operating on the basis of trust among money brokers; it is an informal system to transfer money without physically moving money across countries, for example, that eliminates or reduces its traceability (Brisard, 2002). Hawala can be used by migrants to send money back to their home country where there is no terror intent. Most clients are immigrants who use the system, which often transfers money faster than regular banks, for the legitimate purpose of sending money to relatives and friends abroad. Hawala is widely used in the Middle East, the Indian subcontinent, in South East Asia and parts of Africa, particularly in rural areas where people have no access to the formal financial system (Gomez, 2010). While not limited to Muslims, it has come to be identified with Islamic Banking. It is also prevalent in countries populated by émigrés and refugees, who use this system to send money to families in their countries of origin in order to avoid paying excessive bank charges.

Hawala is based on a short term, discountable, negotiable, promissory note or bill of exchange that is agreed upon by the parties. Hawala is also used in isolated localities, such as the tribal areas of Pakistan and Afghanistan. Originally they mainly served those who did not have a bank account, particularly in remote areas without a functioning normal financial system. The transferring of money goes through money changers, called hawaladars, receiving cash in one nation with no questions asked (Chugani, 2009). Correspondent hawaladars in another country dispense an identical amount to a recipient or, less often, to a bank account. Hundi, which act as negotiable promissory notes, are emailed between hawaladars in differing nations. The sender will provide the recipient with code words or agreed signals like a head nod or a handshake to retrieve money leaving no paper or electronic trail (Chugani, 2009). Understandably, such systems have almost no chance of being detected due to lack of paper work and the ancient and ethnic cultural relationship based on trust (Chugani, 2009). The hawaladars are left to regulate themselves and are reluctant to disrupt the ancient practice.

What distinguishes hawala from other informal systems is a strong sense of honor as these often exist in extensive family networks based on regional and tribal connections of those who use it (Gomez, 2010). Hawala brokers advancing funds often operate from a back of a store or, in remote areas, may not even have an office from which to conduct transactions. Brokers are known to use telephones to communicate. Furthermore, hawala's generations of existence throughout South Asia and the Middle East make it difficult for foreign authorities to eradicate the arcane system. Hawala is traceable in the United States since the 1980s (Brisard, 2002). Some users, however, exploit the system to launder money obtained or intended for illegal activity. Since hawala lacks formal record keeping, it serves as a delivery system for terrorist financing just as drug and arms dealers rely on hawala to send profits abroad. The hawala system is basically an "end user" tool for terrorists on the ground, used to transfer money for operational purposes; it has never been a primary tool or instrument for moving money (Brisard, 2002).

For example, Indian authorities have found Kashmiri militants making extensive use of the hawala system to finance terrorist operations there. Many hawala transactions originate in, or are destined for, Dubai or Yemen, or pass through these places (Gomez, 2010). Some Middle Eastern countries have tried to regulate hawala operations and require users to register and provide information about the identity of senders and receivers. There are also requirements to report suspicious transactions. Currently in Afghanistan, all businesses offering hawala must obtain a license, and report transactions to a financial intelligence agency of the Central Bank. Other countries pay little attention to informal money transfer systems, or attempts to regulate them.

The Formal Financial System

Government regulated financial institutions constitute the formal financial system. It is the world's principal gateway for financial transactions across borders. Al-Qaeda uses the formal financial system as a means of moving money to support its own cells and affiliated terrorist groups to finance their actions. The speed and ease with which money can be moved via the international financial system enables terrorists to move funds efficiently, unfortunately still with relatively small risk of detection (Gomez, 2010). One of those involved in the July 7, 2005 bombings in London financed the operation with his own funds, which were deposited in various accounts; these movements did not attract the attention of bank employees (Gomez, 2010). Combined with other mechanisms such as offshore companies, the formal financial system can still provide terrorists with sufficient cover to carry out operations and launder crime money. The sheer volume and speed with which sums of money rush through the computer-linked international financial system make watertight counter-measures impossible.

Money remittance companies, which are companies that offer payment for goods and services, are particularly attractive to terrorist groups, which has used branches of such companies, which often operate globally, to send and receive money (Gomez, 2010). These companies are in principle obliged to register identification details of the individual who has sent the money from one country and of the person who is meant to receive it in another. This should enable the authorities to track individual transactions by means of the logged details of every transaction. However, the lack of a consistent and worldwide application of due diligence procedures involving identification, record keeping and reporting of suspicious transactions are an obstacle for investigators when trying to track specific financial transactions.

International Trade

International trade has a range of characteristics which make it vulnerable to abuse by terrorist groups because the enormous volume of international commercial transactions obscures individual transactions. International trade is characterized by the complexity of its transactions and payment methods. The mixture of funds from a variety of sources together with the limited resources available to customs agencies in tracing them makes it very difficult to detect illegal transactions without case-specific additional intelligence. Various techniques are used for this such as the over-valuing or under-valuing of goods and services. Laundering through over-valuing and under-valuing of goods and services is a method of fraudulently transferring currency across borders. It involves setting prices to goods and services that differs from the actual market price. By selling goods and services at a price lower than the market, the exporter transfers currency to the importer, since the ultimate value will be lower than the amount the importer receives in selling them on the market.

On the other hand, selling at an amount higher than the market price, the exporter receives currency from the importer since the price of the goods and services will be higher than their value. In order for such operations to succeed, it is necessary that the exporter and importer agree on manipulating prices. For example, if Company "A" exports 1,000 units of an item whose value is $2 per unit but sells to Company "B" at $1 per unit, it would lose $1,000 in the operation. This makes no sense unless both exporter and importer agreed to carry out such a rigged transaction. Another possibility would be for the two companies to be controlled by the same organization. Banks play a fundamental but no longer unique role in making international transactions possible. They sometimes act as simple intermediaries to enable the movement of funds from one country to another, while in other cases they carry out a dual function of intermediary and guarantor to ensure that the conditions in the buying and selling contract are met.

Bank payment methods that can be used in international trade vary in terms of the guarantees offered and the costs involved personal and bank checks, transfers, payment orders, banking remittances and credits. The participation of various parties in these operations and the complexity of payment methods can make the process of observing due diligence complicated. In addition, international trade is vulnerable to the use of falsified documents for the purposes of money laundering, terrorist financing and the avoidance of sanctions to breach international embargos. The use of front companies in high-risk jurisdictions can make it all the more difficult to track these operations. In other cases, international trade in services or commodities is used as part of more complex money laundering and hawala fraud scheme (Gomez, 2010). What is not always considered as part of the analysis is the extent to which deregulation by governments serves as a force-multiplier to use international trade as a method to avoid detection of terror financing.

Alternative Payment Methods

Alternative money transfer systems are a cheap and rapid way of sending funds and making transactions. As an alternative to cash transfers and the use of bank accounts, various payment methods have evolved which are generally used by legitimate customers who lack access to regular banking services; they also are convenient for terrorist groups (Gomez, 2010). Among these methods are prepaid phone cards, online payment services, virtual money that is exchanged in the form of gold, silver and other metals and, most recently, mobile phone payments. Prepaid phone cards are a much-used alternative to cash and they can often be obtained with complete anonymity and are easily transported, making them particularly attractive. One such type of card can be used to withdraw money from various ATM cash-point networks throughout the world and they do not require a bank account nor do they require the user to deal with a bank employee who would verify the identity of the client. They can also be used to buy items in shops. In some countries, these cards have become very popular amongst immigrants who wish to send money to their families overseas. A reasonable issue that is raised is what do families overseas do with these cards. They can easily be used to barter in trade negotiations for hard assets such a weapons.

From the point of view of counterterror financing, these cards present a risk, since they can be used by a member of a terrorist organization in any country, allowing other members of the organization access to money from cash-points. The vulnerability of these cards lies principally in the way they can be obtained and traceability of these cards may be impossible due to the nominal amounts they represent and that are not apt to raise suspicion. Terrorists can buy cards on the Internet, by fax and in those shops which do not require identification from customers or apply any system for tracing suspicious transactions. They can move money through massive scale purchase of such cards and their subsequent sale. Online payment services are often a service used by people without bank accounts or credit cards when they wish to make purchases over the Internet. People who use this service can first use their bank accounts, credit cards, electronic transfers or prepaid cards or, in some cases, simply cash to open an account with an online intermediary which will then carry out payments (Gomez, 2010).

One of these online services is PayPal, which enables anybody or any business with email to send and receive money quickly over the Internet. It is more difficult to know the client's identity if the service provider does not insist on sufficient proof of identity or is willing to accept cash to open the account. Other payment systems such as E-gold are based on virtual money which is exchanged via ounces of gold and other precious metals. One of the characteristics of such business transactions is that the funds which are transferred to them are automatically converted into a specific metal such as gold. At any time, the client can see the value of the gold in various monetary denominations such as dollars, euros, etc, and can make a payment of a specific amount of dollars (Gomez, 2010). These systems can be used to pay for articles exchanged for specific items through commercial websites. The risks associated arise from registration of the online user with a limited amount of information, the lack of identification details, the speed of business transactions, access to items of any value whose price is difficult to establish, and fictitious transactions whereby companies do not guarantee delivery (Gomez, 2010).

All this can enable the transfer of money between members of a terrorist organization pretending to pay for business transactions while the price of items is manipulated or the goods are simply not delivered. Payments via mobile telephones are another alternative to the use of cash and the formal financial system, principally in countries where it is difficult to find a reliable banking network. Technology enables the users of mobile telephones to pass funds between individuals in anonymity and the money sender buys a prepaid phone card which is can be reloaded anonymously with funds which are subsequently transferred to the other person's card (Gomez, 2010). This person can withdraw money from a cash-point using the prepaid card, thus, both the sender and receiver remain anonymous—another method used by terrorist to transfer money.

Al-Qaeda's Reliance on Terror Financing

Apart from the operational level, one must not confuse the requirements of al-Qaeda in terms of daily logistics and the super-structure level, which is the real innovation introduced by Osama bin Laden. Al-Qaeda is not only a combatant organization, it is also and most of all a confederation of militant organizations around the world. The first purpose of money for al-Qaeda at this level is to support the broad international terror network of organizations, to fund them, to stabilize and leverage their support, and to develop their reach to deliver destruction to their targets (Brisard, 2002). Over the years, al-Qaeda financially supported several entities, from Libya to the Philippines, from Indonesia to Somalia. The second purpose of money at the super-structure level has been to pay for protection and asylum of its members. The magnitude of terrorist attacks attributed to al-Qaeda in multiple countries implies that the network continues to have access to substantial financial resources to support its activities.

Funding for terrorist training camps, travel expenses, payment of operatives, weapons, technologies, and housing is funded by a combination of Osama bin Laden's purported inheritance, individual contributions, Zakat manipulation, and charitable organizations. The international community has so far not succeeded in cutting off many of al-Qaeda's sources of financing; the organization continues to access funding from wealthy benefactors, legitimate business and criminal activities (Gomez, 2010). It is currently very difficult to make a reliable estimate of the operating cost of al-Qaeda, as it now acts through a large number of cells and satellite terror groups which are more or less autonomous. The means terrorist groups use to perpetrate attacks such as vehicles, components of explosives, and surveillance material are of relatively low cost compared to the damage they cause. Moreover, Al-Qaeda operational cells rely on hawala networks and did so even before the 9/11 attacks. After al Qaeda's leadership moved to Afghanistan in 1996, there was no practical alternative as the Afghan national banking system was antiquated and insecure.

Later, hawala became again al-Qaeda's system of choice when the government-regulated official financial systems stepped up controls on bank-based money transfers across national borders. In addition to the rather modest funds needed to conduct colossal attacks such as 9/11, al-Qaeda and other terrorist organizations must locate finances to fund their overall infrastructure. However, terrorist organizations have to defray both the costs of carrying out an attack and the more substantial structural costs of maintaining the organization and disseminating its ideology (Gomez, 2010). Moreover, to purchasing weapons, vehicles, explosive material and detonators to be used in attacks, terrorist groups need to anticipate other needs, such as subsistence living costs for its members and sometimes also their families. These expenses are considerable, despite the terrorists' generally frugal lifestyles. Costs vary according to the proximity of terrorists to their targets. The costs of activities in Western Europe will be considerably higher than those in African or Asian countries. A terrorist cell also needs for its members reliable channels of communication, including highly secret channels to its leadership, from which it receives its instructions.

Although communications costs have been reduced considerably through the use of mobile telephones, prepaid cards and e-mail often sent from Internet cafés, the procurement and use of communication tools can entail significant expenses (Gomez, 2010). Training new recruits constitutes a large investment for terrorist groups, both in terms of ideological indoctrination as well as the procurement of practical items to prepare for attacks. Although part of the general preparation can be carried out in terrorist training camps, some specific operations may require specialist skills such as piloting planes which can only be achieved with expensive training. Travel costs for group members in preparation of an attack and acquiring false documentation papers, which may also involve travel. Further travel is required to meet other members of the network, to meet senior members of the hierarchy or to meet individuals able to provide material or financial support. Al-Qaeda spent between $400,000-500,000 for the 9/11 attack. Evidence shows that the nineteen airline hijackers collectively received a monetary reward of $300,000 from al-Qaeda through wire transfers, physical transportation of cash, and use of debit or credit cards to access funds from foreign financial institutions. The 9/11 terrorists used official financial institutions both within and outside the U.S. to deposit, transfer and withdraw money.

None of the terrorists or their backers were experts in using the international financial system. The money was deposited in U.S. banks, generally via transactions, cash deposits and travelers' checks bought overseas. Some of them kept funds in overseas bank accounts to which they had access through cash-point machines (ATMs) and credit cards. The money laundering controls at the time were primarily designed to detect drugs trafficking and large-scale financial fraud, not necessarily terror financing. Therefore bank employees at that time were not suspicious of apparently routine transactions as those carried out by the 19 hijackers (Gomez, 2010). According to plot leader Khalid Sheikh Muhammad, the Hamburg, Germany cell members each received $5,000 to pay for their return from Afghanistan to Germany in late 1999 or early 2000 (Chugani, 2009). Once the non-pilot hijackers received their training, each received $10,000 to fund travel to the United States. The hijackers' primary expenditures included flight school, living expenses, and travel. All hijackers utilized the U.S. banking regime to store their funds and facilitate transactions. The plotters spent money in ordinary ways, making detection of criminal behavior difficult while easily bypassing the detection mechanisms in place prior to 9/11.

The Manipulation of Zakat

Moreover, an unresolved dilemma involves the comingling of religious practices and finance in Saudi Arabia and other countries that acknowledge Zakat. By mixing religious beliefs and interpretations with financial purposes, without proper regulations and controls, Saudi Arabia opened an avenue for terrorism financing through the traditional Zakat, a legal almsgiving conceived as a practice for religious purification that turned into a financial tool for terrorists. Currently, al-Qaeda and other groups continues to take advantage of Islam's call for Zakat. Zakat is the most important source of financial support for the al-Qaeda network, especially because it is the most usual and unregulated way to raise donations in Saudi Arabia. Abusing this pillar of Islam and benefiting from the Saudi Arabian regulatory vacuum, al-Qaeda was able to receive between $300 million and $500 million prior to 9/11 from wealthy businessmen and bankers through a web of charities and companies acting as fronts, with the notable use of Islamic banking institutions (Brisard, 2002).

The Use of Charitable Organizations

In several cases, money originating from Islamic banks and charities in the Middle East was moved and laundered through Western and specifically U.S. correspondents, whether banks or charities, before reaching their recipients (Brisard, 2002). This transfer of money has occurred through a network of charities and companies acting as fronts with the notable use of legitimate Islamic banking institutions. Charities have certain characteristics that make some of them particularly vulnerable to exploitation for the financing of terrorism (Gomez, 2010). They generally enjoy the confidence of the public and have access to significant resources, in many cases in the form of cash. In addition, many of these organizations have a transnational presence which provides them with the necessary infrastructure to enable national and international transactions. In certain countries they are subject to only limited or no regulation at all in terms of registration, accountability, transparency and audits of their accounts (Gomez, 2010). They are also often easy to establish where there is no need for initial capital and where no background checks on employees are made; since its inception, al-Qaeda has made attempts to use charitable organizations to finance some of its activities (Gomez, 2010). Charities enable a number of terrorist organizations to collect, transfer and distribute the necessary funds for the purposes of indoctrination, recruitment and training. Prior evidence shows al-Qaeda had funding of approximately $30 million per year by diversions of money from Islamic charities and other financial facilitators and gathering money from generous donors.

According to a Central Intelligence Agency (CIA) report, al-Qaeda's financial requirements before the September 11, 2001 attacks amounted to $30 million annually; this money was earmarked for carrying out attacks, for the maintenance of its quasi-military apparatus, for training and indoctrination of its members, for contributions to the Taliban regime in Afghanistan, but also for the occasional support of associated terrorist organizations. Many of these well-to-do individuals utilize Islamic charities to satisfy this desire to support al-Qaeda. An article appearing shortly after the 9/11 attacks in the United States quoted a Pakistani cleric who claimed that al-Qaeda had "hundreds of well-to-do people almost everywhere in the world" eager to financially contribute to the cause (Chugani, 2009). Al-Qaeda takes two approaches to using charities for fundraising. The first is to rely on al-Qaeda sympathizers who work in foreign branch offices of large, international charities where the employees secretly siphon money from charitable funds to al-Qaeda. They also collect money through charity by convincing entire charitable organizations to willingly participate in funneling money to them. Al-Qaeda has mechanisms abroad to retain charitable contributions to support their activities through a strategy of placing employees in charities to divert money from the charities' legitimate humanitarian or social programs towards its own illicit activities (Gomez, 2010). The current situation of many of these charities is unclear and despite the freezing of their assets, in many cases financial activities have continued in the same locations, using bank accounts and resources in the name of third parties.

Offshore Entities and Companies

Al-Qaeda uses commercial companies to finance itself as well as to transfer funds. One example is Barakaat, a network of companies which in 2001 had a foothold in 40 countries operating its telecommunications, construction, money remittance and cash exchange services from the United States and Somalia (Gomez, 2010). For Osama Bin Laden, Barakaat was a suitable instrument for making cash transfers; he invested in its telecommunications network and Barakaat acted as a source of financing and arranged cash transfers for him. Its owners channeled millions of dollars every year from the United States to al-Qaeda or its associates. Barakaat also managed, invested and distributed funds for al-Qaeda and most of Bin Laden's transactions were carried out between Mogadishu (Ethiopia) and Dubai, Mombassa (Kenya) and Nairobi (Egypt). In general, these funds were interlinked with transfers made in the name of non-governmental organizations such as al-Haramain and the International Islamic Relief Organization. Al-Qaeda also uses shell companies and front operations to launder their money. Osama bin Laden made extensive use of bakeries in Yemen to store and move his money prior to 9/11 (Hesterman, 2013).

Another case is the one of the Somalian group al-Itihaad al-Islamiya which, according to United Nations officials, led terrorist training centers and collected money from followers in Europe and the Middle East. Al-Itihaad al-Islamiya financed its activities with distinct commercial operations. Among these activities was the exporting of coal to the Middle East, telecommunications, commercial centers, operating hawalas and other financial services, agricultural and hotel companies and was even involved in the distribution of fishing rights (Gomez, 2010). The use of fictitious and offshore companies to shield the identity of individuals or entities taking part in terrorist financing poses difficult problems for those trying to regulate business transactions (Gomez, 2010). These are companies, funds, entities or businesses that are registered in an extra-territorial financial location. One example are International Business Corporations (IBC) that are used to create complex financial structures. They can be established using bearer shares and do not have to publish accounts. Residents of these financial locations can act as fictitious directors or shareholders in order to disguise the true identity of directors or owners.

These entities are attractive to investors who seek anonymity or wish to carry out their activities beyond the official scrutiny of their national government. For example, according to Spanish investigators, the former Salafist Group for Preaching and Combat (GSPC), now integrated into al-Qaeda in the Islamic Maghreb (AQIM), obtained funds that its front men and couriers transported to Algeria and Syria (Gomez, 2010). In order to do this, they used inactive companies or companies in the process of liquidation in tax havens such as the Bahamas and Delaware. The investigators followed the trail of an Algerian citizen in Spain with bank accounts in Palma de Mallorca in the name of an American company formed in Delaware. He transmitted funds totaling $200,000 with the supposed purpose of paying for the services of an information technology company with bases in the Netherlands and Germany (Gomez, 2010). The company denied having issued these invoices that turned out to be false. This led investigators to believe that this money left Spain for other purposes.

Drugs Trafficking and other Common Crimes

Al-Qaeda and its associated groups have greatly diversified their methods of raising money to finance jihad; they finance themselves to varying extents, like the Taliban, through common crime, according to the conditions and opportunities in the locations in which they operate (Gomez, 2010). The Afghan Taliban is an insurgent and terrorist organization that makes extensive use of taxing proceeds from drugs to finance itself. In Afghanistan, the links between both pro-government and anti-government elements and drugs trafficking is well-established. Unlike the al-Qaeda network, the Afghan Taliban is an insurgent group whose activities and range is so far limited to Afghanistan and Pakistan. Although the Taliban receives or received support from al-Qaeda and private donors from the Middle East, a large part of its revenue in Afghanistan and Pakistan is derived from collections in Mosques, contributions from sympathizers and taxes on opium.

The Taliban practices extortion at several points in the heroin business in Afghanistan: taxing poppy farmers, laboratories where the drugs are processed and traffickers who transport precursors into the country and heroin out of it. Currently, many of those involved in the destabilization of Afghanistan are directly or indirectly involved in illicit drug production, processing or procurement (Gomez, 2010). In addition, the Taliban also raises taxes on legitimate business seeking to operate in Afghanistan. It is more than likely that part of the money that these activities generate leaves the country and enters the international financial system. It is therefore often difficult to distinguish between terrorist groups, insurgents and organized crime groups since these categories often overlap. Their methods and sources of financing are similar if not the same; there is also an emerging relationship between Islamic terrorist groups and the commission of cybercrimes.

According to investigations led by the United Kingdom police, three members of a terrorist cell that planned to carry out attacks in the U.S., Europe, and the Middle East used several stolen credit cards to buy items such as GPS systems, night vision goggles, sleeping bags, telephones, knives and tents from hundreds of websites. These were meant to be sent to jihadists in Iraq (Gomez, 2010). Among their purchases were hundreds of prepaid mobile telephones and more than 250 airline tickets. These were bought with 110 different credit cards from 46 different airline companies and travel agencies. The three men involved also laundered money plundered from bank accounts with the help of on-line gambling sites. Numerous stolen credit cards and hacked bank accounts were also used to buy web-based services in the United States and Europe with the apparent aim of creating an online network to be used by jihadist cells throughout the world to exchange information, recruit members and plan attacks. The three cell members involved spent $3.5 million from credit cards stolen by phishing on hundreds of websites coupled with distributing spyware contained in emails or websites which enabled them to gain control of infected computers.

Pakistani extremists based in Spain developed operating methods of their own. These groups have close relations with radical cells in the United Kingdom that specialize in stealing credit cards. Such cards are cloned and sent to Spain, where hundreds to thousands of euros in charges are made by a certain business owner who then transfers the money to radical organizations, asking a commission of 10 percent for himself (Gomez, 2010). Radical Pakistani groups obtain funds by collecting a revolutionary tax from fellow countrymen based in Spain. On occasions they engage in kidnappings which end once family members pay a ransom in Pakistan. According to Interpol, which is an intergovernmental organization that facilitates cooperation between criminal police forces, there are also important links between intellectual property crimes and the financing of Islamic terrorist networks. Some terrorist groups participate directly in the production and sale of fake items and divert part of the profits to finance attacks. Also profits from the sale of items such as illegally copied CDs go to religious networks and are eventually sent to terrorist groups via informal money transfers such as hawala.

Challenges in Confronting the Lack of State Oversight

The United States and other nations will continue to encounter obstacles when attempting to persuade other nations to alter their economic surroundings under U.S. based guidelines; governments within numerous Middle Eastern nations appear to have an interest in preventing terrorist financing, but such efforts could cause social upheaval and threaten to further radicalize the Middle East (Chugani, 2009). Saudi Arabia and other nations that participate in Zakat and charities find themselves in this situation. How can a nation risk upheaval from its citizens on the basis of strictly adhering to U.S. based policies that expect restrictions on Muslim charities and benevolent individuals? This political reality causes the Saudi government to take a nearly contradictory position: it is forced to appear to be confronting terrorism and terrorist financing by writing laws, but must turn its back if these laws are broken in order to appease radical clerics, its citizenry, and al-Qaeda (Chugani, 2009). The politics seen in Saudi Arabia are echoed throughout the entire Middle East, as well as in other Muslim nations throughout the world. The thin line between regulating religion and avoiding social upheaval forces the government to loosen their grasp on those exploiting Zakat for terror.

Since Zakat is viewed as religious responsibilities, governments are reluctant to scrutinize their usage. For example, both companies and individuals in Saudi Arabia have a legal and religious obligation to pay Zakat. Their contribution is calculated on earnings, profits, capital and all other property and monetary acquisitions. Saudi banks pay Zakat on financial transaction fees. These voluntary contributions leave no paper trail, providing little opportunity for government oversight. Zakat contributed by companies is controlled by the Department of Zakat and Income of the Saudi Ministry of Finance and National Economy, which has developed guidelines on who shall pay Zakat and how these funds shall be received. The Saudi government claims it has strict guidelines on how to transfer these funds to charities, however the al-Qaeda organization defies the common understandings of traditional terrorism by being able to hide terror behind a visible, mostly legitimate, business cover using and abusing tools and methods that constitute the basis of Islamic banking, religious donations, charities, and modern economic globalization to move and raise money, recruit and train operatives, buy arms and entertain local operational cells able to carry out terrorist attacks around the world (Brisard, 2002).

Moreover, there may be obvious opinions of how Middle Eastern countries look at how Islamic charities should be viewed that enhances the suspicion of those that try to mitigate against terror financing on the sincerity of these countries that harbor Islamic charities. For example, in November 2002, Saudi Prince Salman bin Abdul Aziz said the country was not responsible if "some change the work of charity into work of evil...if there are those who change some work of charity into evil activities, then it is not the kingdom's responsibility, nor its people, which helps its Arab and Muslim brothers around the world" (Brisard, 2002, p. 17). Through these various unsuccessful attempts to regulate or control the recipients of Zakat or donations through charities, one must question the real ability and willingness of Saudi Arabia to exercise any control over the use of religious money in and outside the country (Brisard, 2002). The result of that weak policy toward donations made for so-called charitable purposes and the unwillingness of the Saudi government to consider its responsibility in that regard is a major setback in the war against terrorism financing.

The Saudi cooperation in the war against terrorism financing is largely insufficient, if not inconsistent. Saudi Arabia has been mostly negligent, and to some extent, irresponsible in letting suspected organizations to receive funds and continue their operations while being fully aware of their links to terrorists (Brisard, 2002). Without clear and enforced regulations, several instruments used by the Saudi financial system morphed into being perfect tools for terrorists. Saudi Arabia must also face its history and errors in acknowledging it has supported or at least facilitated by negligence the funding of the al-Qaeda terrorist network, along with funding those who were giving them refuge (Brisard, 2002). To that extent, Saudi Arabia faces growing responsibility if it remains unable to control the overlap between religious principles and financial regulations.

Recommendations to Reduce Terrorism Financing

Banks and other financial institutions continue to ask the authorities what more they should be looking for to detect possible transactions associated with terrorism. Many of the mechanisms available to financial institutions to detect money laundering activities are not directly applicable to detecting terrorism (Gomez, 2010). For example, the nineteen September 11, 2001 airline hijackers formed a simple plan to disguise their transactions without revealing their intentions. Although the U.S. authorities had information that several of the hijackers might be members of al-Qaeda, the banking personnel where they held accounts never suspected that their clients were potential terrorists. Financial institutions and governments have made a considerable effort to create a profile of "the terrorist". The FBI examined financial transactions made by the 9/11 hijackers focused on the following: they visited the banks in groups, identified themselves as students, spent a large proportion of their income on pilot training schools and were financed to a large extent from money transferred from the United Arab Emirates (Gomez, 2010).

Yet other terrorist cells such as the London attackers used the legal income of one of their members deposited in various bank accounts to finance the attacks. In other words, profiles may be of some help to detect more or less identical types of attacks, but do not help much to warn of attacks developed in a different way. Analogously terrorism financing does not always follow a clearly recognizable profile. This is especially true in cases of local terror cells whose members save or collect money to finance their own activities. These cells can use their own legally obtained funds, but can then carry out illegal operations. In many cases it is difficult to detect a terrorist motive or a purely criminal one or a combination of both. It is not an easy task to create a general profile of financing and using funds for terrorist purposes. For example, when an Islamic charity receives money from donations and then makes money transfers to areas such as Afghanistan or Chechnya, this might be to finance terrorist operations or might constitute humanitarian aid to a very needy population.

Intelligence services and governments can hold information that may distinguish one use of funds from another, but it is unlikely that financial institutions are capable by themselves of determining the difference. The international community has so far failed to discover or block many of the sources of financing of al-Qaeda; the organization formerly headed by Osama Bin Laden continues to have access to money through various channels at the margins of the formal financial system. Al-Qaeda succeeds in moving a part of its financial activities through its associated groups to areas in Africa, the Middle East and South-East Asia where authorities often lack effective counterterrorism institutions and where individuals can continue their financing activities by using companies and fictitious businesses to conceal transactions. Al-Qaeda, the Taliban and the network's associates are in a position to seek, obtain, gather, transmit and distribute considerable sums of money to support their ideological, logistical and operational activities. Financial information alone is not sufficient to detect the financing of al-Qaeda and its affiliates, however, when combined with other types of information held by intelligence services, it may help a financial institution to detect signs of possible suspicious activity.

Terrorists use an assortment of alternative financing mechanisms to earn, move, and store their assets; to earn assets, they focus on profitable crimes or scams involving commodities such as stolen cigarettes, counterfeit goods, and illicit drugs and the use of systems such as charitable organizations that collect large sums of money, not to mention precious jewels (Johnson & Jensen, 2010). To follow the money trail is a solid counterterrorist tactic in that the flow of money can help to identify donor's middleperson's and even recipient cells and their members, but there is no evidence that lack of money puts terrorist groups out of business (Johnson & Jensen, 2010). However shutting the flow of money to terrorist organizations requires international cooperation at all levels. The international efforts to combat terror financing and money laundering since the beginning of the 1990s are built on strategies aimed at attacking criminal organizations through their financial operations, firstly to deprive them of the means to act, and secondly, by unraveling the web of their financial networks and financing methods; to gain knowledge of how better to combat them. A range of international organizations such as the World Bank, the International Monetary Fund (IMF), the United Nations and the International Financial Action Group are involved in combating the financing of terrorism.

The World Bank and the IMF provide technical assistance to countries where the counterterrorist financing system is weak and where this can present a risk to governance and development (Gomez, 2010). Technical assistance from the World Bank and IMF is based on the introduction of new regulations based on best international practices, their application by authorities in the financial sector, the establishment of legal frameworks by financial intelligence bodies, the development of tax programs and awareness-raising to address the concerns of the private and public sectors as well as cooperation with other organizations under multinational programs and the development of training material (Gomez, 2010). Moreover, the goal of the Financial Action Task Force (FATF) is to set standards and promote effective implementation of legal, regulatory and operational measures for combating money laundering, terrorist financing and the financing of proliferation, and other related threats to the integrity of the international financial system.

In collaboration with other international stakeholders, the FATF also works to identify national-level vulnerabilities with the aim of protecting the international financial system from exploitation. The recommendations set out below are a framework of measures which countries should consider implementing in order to combat money laundering and terrorist financing, as well as the financing of proliferation of weapons of mass destruction (FATF, 2018). Even with a common objective, countries have diverse legal, administrative and operational frameworks and different financial systems, thus countries cannot all take identical measures to counter these threats especially over matters of detail. The recommendations, therefore, set an international standard countries should strive toward. Some of the recommendations set out essential measures countries should have in place in order to approach antiterror financing objectives in a unified manner.

Adopting International Standards

Each country should criminalize the financing of terrorism, terrorist acts and terrorist organizations. In recent years, the FATF has noted increasingly sophisticated combinations of techniques, such as the increased use of legal persons to disguise the true ownership and control of illegal proceeds, and an increased use of professionals to provide advice and assistance in laundering criminal funds. The FATF now calls upon all countries to take the necessary steps to bring their national systems for combating money laundering and terrorist financing into compliance with the FATF recommendations, and to effectively implement these measures. Recommendations on terrorist financing provide an enhanced, comprehensive and consistent framework of measures for combating money laundering and terrorist financing. The recommendations set minimum standards for action for countries to implement the detail according to their particular circumstances and constitutional frameworks. The recommendations cover measures that national systems should have in place within their criminal justice and regulatory systems coupled with the preventive measures to be taken by financial institutions and certain other businesses, professions and international cooperation. An element in the fight against terror financing is the need for country systems to be monitored and evaluated relative to these international standards.

Reporting Suspicious Transactions

If financial institutions, or other businesses or entities subject to antimoney laundering obligations, suspect or have reasonable grounds to suspect that funds are linked or related to, or are to be used for terrorism, terrorist acts or by terrorist organizations, they should be required to promptly report their suspicions to the appropriate authorities (FATF, 2018). Financial institutions, their directors, officers and employees should be protected by legal immunity from criminal and civil liability for breach of any restriction on disclosure of information imposed by contract or by any legislative, regulatory or administrative provision, if they report their suspicions in good faith to the financial investigation unit (FIU), even if they did not know precisely what the underlying criminal activity was, and regardless of whether illegal activity actually occurred. Prohibited by law from disclosing the fact that a suspicious transaction report (STR) or related information is being reported to the FIU. Financial institutions should develop programs against money laundering and terrorist financing which include the development of internal policies, procedures and controls, including appropriate compliance management arrangements, and adequate screening procedures to ensure high standards when hiring employees.

An ongoing employee training program and an audit function to test the system should be in place in order to intelligently respond to STRs. Countries are strongly encouraged to extend the reporting requirement to the rest of the professional activities of accountants, including auditing. Dealers in precious metals and precious stones should be required to report suspicious transactions when they engage in any cash transaction with a customer equal to or above the applicable designated threshold. The basic principles for combating terrorist financing have developed in a form essentially parallel to those regarding antimoney laundering measures, but there are some differences between the two issues. In money laundering, criminal elements generally need to deposit money into the financial system, and transactions relating to terrorism, the amount of money used is considerably less and is usually consistent with the client's stated profile, which makes them look harmless. Thus, financial institutions may not be able to separate suspicious transactions from those which are not.

Yet authorities often consider the financial sector to be in an ideal position to detect money laundering and terrorist financing activities. Reports of suspicious activities sent by financial institutions to national financial intelligence units form the basis of this preventative system. However, it is not easy for financial entities to detect suspicious terrorist financing operations. To qualify as a suspicious transaction, deviations from the client's profile and usual practices must be taken into account, which implies the application of a policy based on "know your customer" (Gomez, 2010). It is not enough to identify clients; it is necessary to know their usual practices and sources of income. When business relations are established, it is necessary to obtain information from the client about the nature of his professional or company business and establish beyond reasonable doubt the truthfulness of the information provided. In particular, it is necessary to pay particular attention to any operation that is complex, unusual or lacks an apparent financial or lawful purpose. In order that financial institution personnel or similar entities may detect suspicious operations when assessing transactions, it is the norm to use a number of indicators according to the sector of activities in which the client is involved.

These indicators come from experience compiled by various government agencies, international organizations, and financial intelligence units in various countries that take a coordinated approach when detecting suspicious transactions. The financial sector uses various information technology programs aimed at detecting suspicious operations to evaluate transactions made by customers. Each client is given a specific profile that describes the expected usual practice of the said client. In general, this includes the number of transactions and the amounts involved which are expected to take place over a particular period of time with an acceptable margin of deviation from the norm. When the client's transactions go beyond this margin, information technology programs issue an alert. Yet when submitted to closer scrutiny, many of these transactions result in false positives. False positive, in this case, would mean that the alert should not have been issued. Given that there is no single effective set of indicators to detect suspicious transactions for countering terrorist financing, it is necessary to evaluate a high number of activities to come to responsible conclusions as to whether something significant is going on or not (FATF, 2018). This is an inconvenience, since submitting a high number of false positives to further investigation takes up time and resources to investigate.

In order to avoid an excessive number of false positives without adversely affecting the control of operations, it is necessary to maintain a current profile of clients, establish an adequate frequency for review according to the risk presented, and take into account the conditions of the time and the market which may affect the operations being carried out. There is currently a general concern within financial institutions that most of the indications they receive are orientated towards money laundering rather than terrorist financing. It is a common complaint that they receive little or no information about high-quality indicators that enable the detection of financing for terrorism purposes. Consequently, many of the reports of suspicious transactions are valuable only if these actually trigger an investigation by the authorities. There is a significant imbalance between the high volume of reports on suspicious activities generated by financial institutions throughout the world and the scant value of terrorist assets located or frozen as a result of these reports (Gomez, 2010). In many cases, reports are clearly defensive to protect the institution against possible sanctions from the authorities and focus on the type of client rather than the nature of the transaction, which makes them of little use to investigators. The large volume of suspicious transactions filed by financial institutions tends to overburden the financial intelligence units tasked to analyze them. Backlogs are common which reduces the amount of actionable intelligence gained from monitoring suspicious transactions.

International Extradition Cooperation

Countries should rapidly, constructively, and effectively provide the widest possible range of mutual legal assistance in relation to money laundering and terrorist financing investigations, prosecutions, and related proceedings (FATF, 2018). In particular, countries should not prohibit or place unreasonable or unduly restrictive conditions on the provision of mutual legal assistance coupled with ensuring that they have clear and efficient processes for the execution of mutual legal assistance requests. Countries should not refuse to execute a request for mutual legal assistance on the sole ground that the offense is also considered to involve fiscal matters nor refuse to execute a request on the grounds that laws require financial institutions to maintain secrecy or confidentiality. To avoid conflicts of jurisdiction, consideration should be given to devising and applying mechanisms for determining the best venue for prosecution of defendants in the interests of justice in cases that are subject to prosecution in more than one country. Countries should, to the greatest extent possible, provide mutual legal assistance regardless of the absence of dual criminality meaning conduct may be illegal in one country but not another. Where dual criminality is required for mutual legal assistance or extradition, that requirement should be deemed to be satisfied regardless of whether both countries place the offense within the same category of offenses or satisfy the offense by the same terminology, provided that both countries criminalize the conduct underlying the offense (FATF, 2018).

Countries should recognize money laundering as an extraditable offense. Extradition means handing over a person who is accused of or has committed a crime from one country where the person is situated in another country for prosecution. Each country should either extradite its own nationals, or where a country does not do so solely on the grounds of nationality, that country should, at the request of the country seeking extradition, submit the case without undue delay to its appropriate authorities for the purpose of prosecution of the offenses set forth in the request (FATF, 2018). Those authorities should take their decision and conduct their proceedings in the same manner as in the case of any other offense of a serious nature under the domestic law of that country. The countries concerned should cooperate with each other, in particular on procedural and evidentiary aspects, to ensure the efficiency of such prosecutions. Subject to their legal frameworks, countries may consider simplifying extraditions to allow direct transmission of extradition requests between ministries, extraditing persons based only on warrants of arrests or judgements, and/or introducing a simplified extradition of consenting persons waiving extradition proceedings.

Freezing and Confiscating Terror Assets

Each country should afford another country, on the basis of a treaty, arrangement or other mechanism for mutual legal assistance or information exchange, the greatest possible measure of assistance in connection with criminal, civil enforcement, and administrative investigations, inquiries and proceedings relating to the financing of terrorism, terrorist acts and terrorist organizations (FATF, 2018). Countries should also take all possible measures to ensure that they do not provide safe havens for individuals charged with the financing of terrorism, terrorist acts or terrorist organizations, and should have procedures in place to extradite, where possible, such individuals. Each country should implement measures to freeze without delay funds or other assets of terrorists, those who finance terrorism and terrorist organizations in accordance with United Nations resolutions relating to the prevention and suppression of the financing of terrorist acts. Each country should also adopt and implement measures, including legislative ones, which would enable the authorities to seize and confiscate property that is the proceeds of, or used in, or intended or allocated for use in, the financing of terrorism, terrorist acts or terrorist organizations (FATF, 2018). There should be authority to take expeditious action in response to requests by foreign countries to identify, freeze, seize and confiscate property laundered, proceeds from money laundering or predicate offenses, instrumentalities used in or intended for use in the commission of these offenses, or property of corresponding value. There should also be arrangements for coordinating seizure and confiscation proceedings, which may include the sharing of confiscated assets.

Wire Transfers and Alternative Remittance

Countries should take measures to require financial institutions, including money remitters, to include accurate and meaningful originator information such as name, address and account number on funds transfers and related messages that are sent, and the information should remain with the transfer or related message through the payment chain (FATF, 2018). Moreover, they should take measures to ensure that financial institutions, including money remitters, conduct enhanced scrutiny of and monitor for suspicious activity funds transfers which do not contain complete originator information such as name, address and account number. Furthermore, they should take measures to ensure that persons or legal entities, including agents, that provide a service for the transmission of money or value, including transmission through an informal money or value transfer system or network, should be licensed or registered and subject to the recommendations that apply to banks and non-bank financial institutions. Each country should ensure that persons or legal entities that carry out this service illegally are subject to administrative, civil or criminal sanctions for without corrective action being taken for infractions, the recommendations are simply in place to give the impression of serious intention without any true follow-up to suspicious transactions.

Non-Profit Organizations

Countries should review the adequacy of laws and regulations that relate to entities that can be abused for the financing of terrorism (FATF, 2018). Non-profit organizations are particularly vulnerable, and countries should ensure that they cannot be misused by, a) terrorist organizations posing as legitimate entities, b) to exploit legitimate entities as conduits for terrorist financing, including for the purpose of escaping asset freezing measures, and c) to conceal or obscure the clandestine diversion of funds intended for legitimate purposes to terrorist organizations (Chugani, 2009). Islamic charities seek to provide basic goods and services to communities, both local and abroad, in a manner consistent with the values and teachings of Islam. The U.S. government is not easily able to discern whether Islamic charities that collect funds for a particular humanitarian cause are actually being utilized for that purpose, or, as many government agents fear, for monetary support of terrorism. Described as "reverse money laundering," charity-based financing of terrorism is concerned with using legal assets for an illegal activity, namely terrorist attacks. Charitable organizations are also attractive targets for terrorist entities because of the reluctance of many outside nations to rigorously monitor and scrutinize their activities (FATF, 2018). Especially prevalent, authorities are faced with discerning between legitimate charities and those that are unknowingly or knowingly being used to divert funds to terrorists.

Cash Couriers

Countries should have measures in place to detect the physical cross-border transportation of currency and bearer negotiable instruments, including a declaration system or other disclosure obligation together with ensuring that their competent authorities have the legal authority to stop or restrain currency or bearer negotiable instruments that are suspected to be related to terrorist financing or money laundering, or that are falsely declared or disclosed (Chugani, 2009). Countries should ensure that effective, proportionate and deterrent sanctions are available to deal with persons who make false declarations or disclosures. In cases where the currency or bearer negotiable instruments are related to terrorist financing or money laundering, countries should also adopt measures which would enable the confiscation of such currency or instruments.

Customer Due Diligence and Record Keeping

Financial institutions should not keep anonymous accounts in obviously fictitious names and they should undertake customer due diligence measures, including identifying and verifying the identity of their customers, when a) establishing business relations, b) when there is a suspicion of money laundering or terrorist financing, c) when the financial institution has doubts about the truthfulness or adequacy of previously obtained customer identification data. The customer due diligence (CDD) measures to be taken are as follows:

- Identifying the customer and verifying that customer's identity using reliable, independent source documents, data or information.
- Identifying the beneficiary, and taking reasonable measures to verify the identity of the beneficiary such that the financial institution is satisfied that it knows who they are. For legal persons and arrangements, this should include financial institutions taking reasonable measures to understand the ownership and control structure of the customer.
- Obtaining information on the purpose and intended nature of the business relationship.
- Conducting ongoing due diligence on the business relationship and scrutiny of transactions undertaken throughout the course of that relationship to ensure that the transactions being conducted are consistent with the institution's knowledge of the customer, their business and risk profile, including, where necessary, the source of funds (FATF, 2018).

Financial institutions should apply each of the CDD measures above, but may determine the extent of such measures on a risk sensitive basis depending on the type of customer, business relationship or transaction. The measures that are taken should be consistent with any guidelines issued by competent authorities. For higher risk categories, financial institutions should perform enhanced due diligence. In certain circumstances, where there are low risks, countries may decide that financial institutions can apply reduced or simplified measures. Financial institutions should verify the identity of the customer and beneficial owner before or during the course of establishing a business relationship or conducting transactions for occasional customers. Countries may permit financial institutions to complete the verification as soon as reasonably practicable following the establishment of the relationship, where the money laundering risks are effectively managed and where this is essential not to interrupt the normal conduct of business (FATF, 2018).

Where the financial institution is unable to comply with CDD, the institution should not open the account, commence business relations or perform the transaction and should terminate the business relationship coupled with consider making a suspicious transactions report in relation to the customer. These requirements should apply to all new customers, though financial institutions should also apply this recommendation to existing customers on the basis of materiality and risk, and should conduct due diligence on such existing relationships at appropriate times. Financial institutions should, in relation to politically exposed persons, in addition to performing normal due diligence measures have appropriate risk management systems to determine whether the customer is a politically exposed person. Obtain senior management approval for establishing business relationships with such customers. Take reasonable measures to establish the source of wealth and source of funds. Conduct enhanced ongoing monitoring of the business relationship (FATF, 2018). Financial institutions should, in relation to cross-border correspondent banking and other similar relationships, in addition to performing normal due diligence measures gather sufficient and competent information about a respondent institution to understand fully the nature of the respondent's business.

In addition, institutions should determine from publicly available information the reputation of the institution and the quality of supervision, including whether it has been subject to a money laundering or terrorist financing investigation or regulatory action. Moreover, assess an institution's antimoney laundering and terrorist financing controls coupled with obtaining approval from senior management before establishing new correspondent relationships. Document the respective responsibilities of each institution with respect to "payable-through accounts" and be satisfied that the respondent bank has verified the identity of and performed on-going due diligence on the customers having direct access to accounts of the correspondent and that it is able to provide relevant customer identification data upon request to the correspondent bank (FATF, 2018). Financial institutions should pay special attention to any money laundering threats that may arise from new or developing technologies that might favor anonymity, and take measures to prevent their use in laundering schemes.

In particular, financial institutions should have policies and procedures in place to address any specific risks associated with non-face to face business relationships or transactions. Countries may permit financial institutions to rely on intermediaries or other third parties to perform CDD processes or to introduce business, provided that the criteria set out below are met. Where such reliance is permitted, the ultimate responsibility for customer identification and verification remains with the financial institution relying on the third party. Financial institutions should take adequate steps to satisfy themselves that copies of identification data and other relevant documentation relating to the CDD requirements will be made available from the third party upon request without delay. It is left to each country to determine in which countries the third party that meets the conditions can be based, having regard to information available on countries that do not or do not adequately apply the recommendations. Financial institutions should maintain, for at least five years, all necessary records on transactions, both domestic and international, to enable them to comply swiftly with information requests from the competent authorities.

Such records must be sufficient to permit reconstruction of individual transactions including the amounts and types of currency involved if any so as to provide, if necessary, evidence for prosecution of criminal activity. Financial institutions should keep records on the identification data obtained through the customer due diligence process such as copies or records of official identification documents like passports, identity cards, driving licenses or similar documents, account files and business correspondence for at least five years after the business relationship is ended. The identification data and transaction records should be available to domestic authorities. Financial institutions should pay special attention to all complex, unusual large transactions, and all unusual patterns of transactions, which have no apparent economic or visible lawful purpose. The background and purpose of such transactions should, as much as possible, be examined, the findings established in writing, and made available to help competent authorities and auditors. The customer due diligence and record keeping requirements applies to designated non-financial businesses and professions in the following situations,

- Casinos: when customers engage in transactions equal to or above the applicable designated threshold.
- Real estate agents: when agents transact for their client concerning the buying and selling of real estate.
- Dealers in precious metals and dealers in precious stones: when they engage in any cash transaction with a customer equal to or above the applicable designated threshold (FATF, 2018).

218

- Lawyers, notaries, other independent legal professionals and accountants when they prepare for or carry out transactions for their client concerning the following activities: a) buying and selling of real estate, b) managing of client money, securities or other assets, c) management of bank or securities accounts, d) organization of contributions for the creation, operation or management of companies, and e) management of legal persons or arrangements, and buying and selling of business entities.

Adequate Regulation of Antiterrorism Financing

Countries should ensure that financial institutions are subject to adequate regulation and supervision and are effectively implementing FATF recommendations. Competent authorities should take the necessary legal or regulatory measures to prevent criminals or their associates from holding or being the beneficial owner of a significant or controlling interest or holding a management function in a financial institution. For financial institutions, the regulatory and supervisory measures that apply for legitimate purposes and which are relevant to money laundering, should apply in a similar manner for antimoney laundering and terrorist financing purposes. Other financial institutions should be licensed or registered and appropriately regulated, and subject to supervision or oversight for antimoney laundering purposes, having regard to the risk of money laundering or terrorist financing. At a minimum, businesses providing a service of money or value transfer, or of money or currency changing should be licensed or registered, and subject to effective systems for monitoring and ensuring compliance with national requirements to combat money laundering and terrorist financing.

Designated non-financial businesses and professions should be subject to regulatory and supervisory measures as set out for casinos that should be subject to a comprehensive regulatory and supervisory oversight that ensures that they have effectively implemented the necessary antimoney laundering and terrorist financing measures. At a minimum a) casinos should be licensed, b) competent authorities should take the necessary legal or regulatory measures to prevent criminals or their associates from holding or being the beneficial owner of a significant or controlling interest, holding a management function in, or being an operator of a casino, and c) authorities should ensure that casinos are effectively supervised for compliance with requirements to combat money laundering and terrorist financing. Countries should ensure that other categories of designated non-financial businesses and professions are subject to effective systems for monitoring and ensuring their compliance with requirements to combat money laundering and terrorist financing. This should be performed on a risk-sensitive basis by a government authority or by an appropriate self-regulatory organization, provided that such an organization can ensure that its members comply with their obligations to combat money laundering and terrorist financing. The authorities should establish guidelines and provide feedback which will assist financial institutions and designated non-financial businesses and professions in applying national measures to combat money laundering and terrorist financing, and in particular, in detecting and reporting suspicious transactions.

Investigative Considerations

Countries should establish a financial investigation unit (FIU) that serves as a national center or clearing house for the receiving and, as permitted, requesting, analysis and dissemination of a suspicious activity transaction (STR) and other information regarding potential money laundering or terrorist financing (FATF, 2018). The FIU should have access, directly or indirectly, on a timely basis to the financial, administrative and law enforcement information that it requires to properly undertake its functions, including the analysis of STRs. Countries should ensure that designated law enforcement authorities have responsibility for money laundering and terrorist financing investigations. Countries are encouraged to support and develop special investigative techniques suitable for the investigation of money laundering, such as controlled delivery, undercover operations and other relevant techniques. Countries are also encouraged to use other effective mechanisms such as the use of permanent or temporary groups specialized in asset investigation, and cooperative investigations with appropriate authorities in other countries (FATF, 2018).

When conducting investigations of money laundering and underlying predicate offenses, authorities should be able to obtain documents and information for use in those investigations, and in prosecutions and related actions. Predicate offenses are those crimes that raised money for terrorists such as credit card fraud as an example before they actually laundered the money. This should include powers to use compulsory measures for the production of records held by financial institutions and other persons, for the search of persons and premises, and for the seizure and obtaining of evidence. Supervisors should have adequate powers to monitor and ensure compliance by financial institutions with requirements to combat money laundering and terrorist financing, including the authority to conduct inspections. They should be authorized to compel production of information from financial institutions that is relevant to monitoring such compliance, and to impose adequate administrative sanctions for failure to comply with such requirements. Countries should provide their authorities combating money laundering and terrorist financing adequate financial, human, and technical resources.

Countries should have in place processes to ensure that the staff of those authorities are of high integrity together with ensuring that policy makers, the FIU, law enforcement and supervisors have effective mechanisms in place which enable them to cooperate, and where appropriate coordinate domestically with each other concerning the development and implementation of policies and activities to combat money laundering and terrorist financing. Countries should ensure that their authorities can review the effectiveness of their systems to combat money laundering and terrorist financing systems by maintaining comprehensive statistics on matters relevant to the effectiveness and efficiency of such systems. This should include statistics on STRs received and disseminated, on money laundering and terrorist financing investigations, prosecutions and convictions, on property frozen, seized and confiscated and on mutual legal assistance or other international requests for cooperation.

Conclusion

Although terrorism and organized crime are different phenomena, the important fact is that terrorists and criminal networks overlap and cooperate in some circumstances. Unfortunately, the synergy of terrorism and organized crime is growing because similar conditions give rise to both and because terrorists and organized criminals use similar approaches to promote and finance their agendas. Moreover, their adaptation of incorporating fraud into their larger criminal goals is lethal and the examples used in this chapter represent the proverbial tip of the iceberg. Just as terrorists pool their abilities and resources to achieve synergistic outcomes, government agencies and all those who are directly or indirectly involved in the fight against fraud and its link to terror must pool their talents to counter their inhumane goals.

Chapter 6

The Corporate Fraud Offender Behavioral Profile

Convicted chief executive officer (CEO) Joseph Nacchio of telecommunications company Qwest from 1997 to 2002 was "considered a visionary for his dogged pursuit of Internet opportunities" (CRN, 2000). However, Nacchio engaged in fraudulent revenue recognition of $3 billion resulting in a personal gain of $52 million from insider stock trading. While at Qwest, Nacchio displayed a tyrannical management style by creating a culture of fear where one subordinate stated, "people were just afraid of the man…He created such a culture of fear that Qwest employees thought it was better to comply with his demands rather than question them and face his wrath" (Bucy et al., 2008, p. 414). Upon release from prison, while still remaining unapologetic about his misconduct and regardless of the damage he caused investors, Nacchio stated, "I can't wait for the first person to come up to me and say something to me about the conviction, I'm going to look them in the eye and say, you must be confusing me with someone who gives a f— about your opinion" (Searcy, 2013).

In the early 1990s, CEO Garth Drabinsky, a well-known theatrical producer cofounded Livent, a Canadian firm that produced successful Broadway musicals. However, as his success diminished, Drabinsky resorted to committing financial statement fraud by understating expenses to appear more profitable than he was. Acting with the goal of self-enrichment, he cost investors and creditors $7.5 million (Anderson & Tirrell, 2004). Described as tyrannical, Drabinsky bullied and abused subordinates, especially the accountants, where "[T]hey were told on a very regular basis that they are paid to keep their [expletive] mouths shut and do as they are [expletive] told. They are not paid to think…berating them when they failed to live up to his perfectionist standards or questioned his decisions" (Knapp, 2009, p. 391). One auditor, named Robert Webster, refused to succumb to Drabinsky's bullying tactics stating that he "never experienced anyone with Drabinsky's abusive and profane management style" (Knapp, 2009, p. 390). Drabinsky "accused Webster of attempting to tear the company apart with his persistent inquiries" and told Webster "that he was there to service his [Drabinsky's] requirements" (Knapp, 2009, p. 391).

To facilitate its massive collusive fraud, Drabinsky relied on Livent's top executives who "screamed and swore at the company accountants" while engaging in "coercion and intimidation to browbeat their accountants…displaying a contemptuous attitude toward outside auditors" believing that it was "no one's business how they ran their company" (Knapp, 2009, p. 394). Drabinsky, his executive team, and the accountants held meetings on how to commit financial statement fraud so that it would go undetected. In order to facilitate the financial statement fraud, management maintained two sets of accounts: the real and the fictitious. As the executive who maintained the two sets of books stated, "I have to keep all the lies straight. I have to know what lies I'm telling these people [outsides auditors]. I've told so many lies to different people I have to make sure they all make sense" (Knapp, 2009, p. 394). When one of the accountants asked which documents should be revealed to the auditor, the executive responded, "[Expletive] you and your auditors…I don't care what they see or don't see" (Knapp, 2009, p. 395). Many of the accountants that participated in the financial statement fraud were known to be terrified of management and at times emotionally broke down and pled guilty to criminal charges when the fraud was unveiled.

One might prefer to think that corrupt CEO leadership described above, but also those affiliated with the upper-echelons of management, represent the exception and not the rule. Unfortunately, top management fraud is a worldwide problem that cuts across ideological and cultural divides (Zahra et al., 2005). The reality is, "serious white-collar crimes are not necessarily committed by those who own corporations, but rather by those who have access and control over organizational resources, for instance CEOs and CFOs or even upper-level line managers and supervisors" (Shover & Wright, 2001, p. 165). The accounting and financial services firm KPMG supports the above observation; they found that in a 2011 global survey, CEOs were involved in 26 percent of organizational fraud cases, up 11 percent from a similar 2007 survey (Helm & Mietzite, 2011). Furthermore, in the wake of corporate scandals, such as Enron, Adelphia, and WorldCom in 2001 and 2002, the U.S. Department of Justice

(DOJ) created the Corporate Fraud Task Force. In their report, the department indicated that since the task force's inception, it obtained convictions or guilty pleas from at least 214 former CEOs and presidents, 53 CFOs, and 129 vice presidents (DOJ, 2007).

In another study examining CEO and/or CFO involvement in fraud for the period 1998-2007, the SEC named the CEO and/or the CFO involvement in 89 percent of its fraud cases; within 2 years of completing their investigation, over 20 percent of these executives were indicted for some type of fraud and of this amount, 60 percent were convicted of a fraud crime (Perri, 2011a). Consider the comprehensive study of the criminal backgrounds of CEOs named in accounting frauds that were facing sanctions by the SEC. In the study, 11 percent of the CEOs had previous prior criminal conduct including "felony possession of narcotics, domestic violence, and reckless endangerment" (Soltes, 2016, p. 55). Also, instructive are the results of a global survey examining CFO conduct where 3 percent would be prepared to misstate financial performance, 7 percent would prematurely book revenues before they were earned, 9 percent would be prepared to backdate contracts, 13 percent would offer cash payments to win or retain business, and 36 percent could rationalize unethical conduct to improve financial performance (Stulb, 2016). Reflect upon the fact that these are the results of CFOs who were willing to admit to engaging in misconduct. In the same survey, when over 2,800 executives were asked whether they could justify unethical behavior to meet financial targets, 42 percent said they could (Stulb, 2016). It is not surprising that white-collar crime is a central reason why approval and trust of America's businesses and its leaders have eroded over the past three decades (Eaton & Korach, 2016).

Ironically, many of the executives who topped the charts in terms of unethical and criminal practices had been exalted as corporate visionaries (Perri, 2013b). Visionaries create a mental image portraying an idealized future state of where they want to be in terms of fulfilling agendas (Conger, 1990). Yet these fraud offenders labeled visionaries strove to make their visions a reality not by careful contemplation, but by disregarding laws, regulations, and social norms that ultimately culminated into criminal misconduct (Cleff et al., 2013). We witnessed the "dramatic fall of leaders once held in high esteem considering that the same people spoke at university commencements, graced the covers of *Fortune* magazine, and donated generously to charities while taking pride in being role models for employees and aspiring business school students alike" (Soltes, 2016, p. 2). For example, *Fortune* magazine described Enron's CEO Kenneth Lay as a "revolutionary" (Tourish & Vatcha, 2005, p. 462), who offered "visionary leadership...unafraid to redefine the status quo by being bold and innovative" (Georgiou, 2010), and "a caring community leader and philosopher" (McLean & Elkind, 2003, p. 85). CEO Jeffrey Skilling, considered another one of Enron's visionaries (Zellner, 2002), was hailed as "the No. 1 CEO in the entire country" (Knapp, 2009, p. 7). According to Paul Koppel, chairman of ImClone's audit committee, "I regarded [convicted CEO] Sam Waksal as a visionary who started the company" (Bloomberg News, 2002).

The *New York Times* praised convicted WorldCom CEO Bernard Ebbers as "a long-distance visionary; he was blunt, folksy, the entrepreneurial stepchild of the telecommunications revolution" (Lohr, 1997). Convicted CEO of CA Inc. Sanjay Kumar, considered a visionary in the software industry (Lyer, 1999), also had the honor of contributing a chapter on his leadership insights in the book *Leadership Secrets of the World's Most Successful CEOs* before being sentenced to prison for orchestrating a $2.2 billion scheme involving fraudulent revenue recognition, securities fraud, and obstruction of justice (Yaverbaum, 2004). Cal Turner, convicted CEO of Dollar General, was considered a "marketing genius", Jeffrey Citron, convicted CEO of Datek Online, was referred to as a "technology wizard" and ousted Sunbeam CEO Al Dunlap was known as "a miracle worker" (Cohen et al., 2010, p. 169). Convicted WorldCom CFO Scott Sullivan received the 1998 CFO Excellence Award in mergers and acquisitions by *CFO Magazine* (Yang & Grow, 2005). Convicted Tyco CFO Mark Swartz received the 2000 CFO Excellence Award in mergers and acquisitions from *CFO Magazine* in the midst of their misconduct. Enron's convicted CFO Andrew Fastow, one of the architects of the company's fraud, received the 1999 Excellence Award in capital management structure by the same magazine (Perri, 2013b). After numerous CFO convictions, *CFO Magazine* decided to scrap the award entirely (Soltes, 2016).

The revelation of organizational misconduct does not always result in personnel change or prosecution. D.J. Krumm, CEO and chairman of the board of Maytag, retained his position despite a settlement of charges that the firm secretly reconditioned defective microwave ovens, changed their serial numbers, and sold them as new (Agrawal et al., 1999). In another example, although Hertz Corporation pleaded guilty to charges that it overbilled customers for repairs to automobiles damaged in collisions, the company paid over $20 million in fines and restitution, while the CEO Frank Olson kept his job (Agrawal et al., 1999). Interestingly, Olson received praise for his advocacy of business ethics and legislation to limit deceptive practices in the car rental business. The evidence is rather blatant that, "there exists exceptionally smart people in the business environment who are unethical and there is little that will deter their willingness to engage in fraud to achieve their goals" (Finn, 2015, p. 40). Consequently, it is normal to observe organizational misconduct, but when speaking of normality, it should not be interpreted as acceptable.

Consider the findings by the accounting firm KPMG in a 2013 integrity survey on misconduct (KPMG, 2013). Misconduct was defined as behaviors that could undermine the organization's reputation for integrity. Some of the categories of misconduct included financial statement fraud such as manipulating or falsifying financial reporting information, engaging in conflict of interest activities, asset misappropriation, insider trading, violating company values and principles, violating environmental standards, making misleading public statements, bribery and kickbacks, violating intellectual property rights, discrimination against persons, and sexual harassment. The 2013 survey included government, real estate, energy, media, pharmaceuticals, chemicals, healthcare, banking, and automotive industries, to name a few. Seventy-three percent of those surveyed stated that they observed misconduct in the prior 12 months before the survey was administered, and 56 percent reported that what they observed could cause "a significant loss of public trust if discovered" (KPMG, 2013, p. 1).

These results represent a significant increase from the 2009 integrity survey that reported 46 percent observing conduct that would cause a significant loss in public trust if discovered. According to the survey, the most commonly cited drivers of misconduct continue to be attributed to pressure to do "whatever it takes" to meet business goals. Other reasons include rewards that favor the ends and not the means of how ends are achieved, the fear of losing one's job if goals are not met, and that employees are more apt to look the other way when they observe misconduct than report it for fear of retaliation. Additional drivers of misconduct included lack of resources to get the job done, bending the rules for personal gain, and believing that the company's code of conduct is not taken seriously. While organizations are larger than any one person, individuals are ultimately entrusted with the task of maintaining the organization's integrity and trustworthiness (Javor & Jancsics, 2013). Moreover, consider many organizational frauds are a result of months of scheming, endorsed by senior management; they are not the result of one criminal act on one particular day, which may be more characteristic of a street-level offense.

Unlike street crimes, which disproportionately victimize those of the lower socioeconomic strata, top management fraud is more pervasive and wide-reaching in its impact (Zahra et al., 2005). Moreover, unlike street-level offenses where the impact of criminality is readily observable, damage caused from white-collar crimes may not be noticed until the fraud scheme is no longer sustainable. In many cases, there is a time lag between the actual act of committing fraud and the resulting harm that may not be observable until months or years later which reinforces the perception that fraud is a victimless crime. In reality, corruption at the executive level has destroyed hundreds of companies, drained shareholders of their investments, impacts communities and leaves innocent employees without work (Mahadeo, 2006). Employees of companies that commit management fraud are often the hardest hit, even though they are often unaware of management's illegal activities which cause employees to lose retirement savings, which are often tied up in company stock, and their reputations. Corporate fraud can also damage managers' reputations, end their careers, and cause their imprisonment. Fraud can lead to a general lack of faith in the integrity of senior managers, depress the moral climate in a society, erode confidence in a free market system, including its political institutions and leaders, and greater societal cynicism (Zahra et al., 2005).

The most corrosive consequence of an environment in which individuals do not trust the leading institutions of society, such as large corporations and their leadership, is the destruction of social capital. Social capital is a form of economic and cultural capital in which social networks are central to facilitating transactions marked by reciprocity, trust, and cooperation aimed for a common good. Edwin Sutherland recognized early on the corrosive impact of white-collar crime on social capital stating white-collar offenders "are by far the most dangerous to society of any type of criminals from the point of view of effects on private property and social institutions" (Sutherland, 1934, p. 32). Some commentators argue that the success of capitalist societies relies on a level of trust necessary to foster cooperative behavior (Zahra et al., 2005). In addition, corporate scandals demonstrate that misconduct is directly correlated to ineffective boards of directors, ineffective corporate governance, ineffective internal controls, accounting irregularities, failure of external auditors to follow-up on potential fraud red flags, domineering CEOs, greed, a desire for power, and the lack of a sound, ethical tone at the top (Soltani, 2014). Even well-meaning CEOs, who engage in what can be characterized as small frauds in the belief that it will not lead to long-term harm, get caught up in cycles of increasing misconduct, and find it difficult to disengage from unethical and/or illegal behavior once they start (Chen, 2010).

If we want to understand why organizations do the things they do, or why they perform the way they do, we must consider the dispositions of their most powerful actors—their top management leaders. Unfortunately the leadership qualities most admired in many CEOs such as drive, confidence, charisma, and being visionaries, while sometimes capable of producing exceptional results for the organizations, can also in the wrong set of circumstances lead to their downfall. When we observe offenders who had been highly successful and, at times, revered in their fields, it begs the question that U.S. District Judge Richard Sullivan asked himself when sentencing a white-collar criminal, "It's hard to understand why someone who has reached the pinnacle of success would risk all that for more" (Soltes, 2016, p. 1). In some respects, this chapter attempts to answer the insight Judge Sullivan offered by applying criminological and behavioral risk factors that increase the probability that executives will engage in fraud. Furthermore, another goal is to answer the question of whether there is a common pattern of personality traits corrupt leadership harbor and the manner in which those traits are displayed. This is important to understand, especially in terms of how corrupt leaders interact with others because they facilitate subordinate misconduct by establishing the tone at the top. Through examples, we illustrate how leadership may display criminal thinking patterns discussed in chapter one together with how distinct personality traits serve as risk factors that increase the probability of engaging in corrupt corporate fraud.

Leadership, Fraud and the Tone at the Top

Corrupt corporate leadership is considered a reciprocal relationship between the leader and followers, where the leader uses social influence to persuade people to set aside individual pursuits in order to attain organizational goals. Leadership is usually coupled with the ability to alter or influence the actions, behaviors, and mindset of followers through communication, inspiration, and setting the organizational example (Jones & Jones, 2014). Leadership, by their words, actions, and inaction, sets the proverbial "tone at the top" which represents the type of culture, values, and expectations deemed relevant to the organization influencing the consciousness of the employees. The vast majority of literature over the past five decades has focused on determining the characteristics of effective leadership which led to it being romanticized through Lincolnesque images of goodness and self-sacrifice—void of personal flaws. Consequently, leaders are often perceived as heroic or saviors of organizations in crisis. This perception ignores the possibility of a darker side in which leadership is not necessarily good or constructive to organizational purposes. It also overlooks personality behaviors which steer organizations, and potentially countries, to a position of decline and ultimately non-existence.

Leader traits can be defined as consistent, relatively predictable patterns of personal characteristics that reflect individual personality differences, motives, values, worldviews, and thinking patterns that result in coherent leadership effectiveness or ineffectiveness (Regnaud, 2011). Authentic, responsible, and ethical leaders engage in constructive behaviors while those that harbor destructive qualities display bully, hubristic, Machiavellian, and narcissistic dispositions (Jones & Jones, 2014). Experts agree that corporate leadership, top management, and, in particular, the CEO sets the corporate ethical tone (Barnard, 1999). The tone set by top management within which financial reporting occurs is the most important factor contributing to the integrity of the financial reporting process. An organization's tone at the top influences, 1) the integrity, ethical values, and competence of its employees, 2) management's philosophy, 3) the manner in which management assigns authority and responsibility, 4) how they organize and develop personnel, and 5) the attention and direction provided by the board of directors. This concept, although not exclusively applicable to for-profit organizations, is mostly used in the context of financial reporting and auditing emphasizing its importance in preventing fraudulent financial reporting. The tone at the top also applies to organizations that are religion-based, not-for-profit, government agencies, and the military, to name a few.

Moreover, leadership values, actions, and beliefs shape corporate culture, affect the attitudes and behavior of other members of the organization, influence perceptions of an ethical climate, and determine the behavioral patterns considered acceptable in the organization. These executives may set a high standard for ethical and professional behavior or they alternatively create an atmosphere in which unethical or unlawful conduct is overlooked, implicitly condoned, or even overtly encouraged. Whether positive or negative, the values of, and the role played by the CEO, are important in determining a corporation's receptiveness to deviant, unethical, or criminal behavior. When analyzing the underlying causes of various types of corporate misconduct, one will observe time and time again how top management and corporate culture did not deter the practice of business misconduct. Top management often places undue performance pressure that, in turn, motivates less than ethical behavior by those who are "under the gun" to perform (Barnard, 1999). Ultimately top management cannot escape blame for sustaining a corporate culture encouraging subordinate misconduct and rewarding performance at all costs; yet sadly top management is more than willing to engage in rationalizations to morally distance themselves from their corrupt decisions.

Positive Tone at the Top Characteristics

Research in moral development suggests that honesty can be reinforced when a proper example is set, also known as modeling and in the case of management, it is known as the tone at the top (Albrecht et al., 2012). Leaders who exercise open-door policies and who allow subordinates the right to speak honestly and openly without fear of punishment, cultivate confidence, security, steadiness, and trust among team members. By aligning words with behavior, displaying integrity, and remaining consistent with authentic behaviors, leadership credibility is enhanced (Jones & Jones, 2014). Organizational management cannot act one way and expect others to behave differently; they must reinforce to employees, through their actions and words that dishonest, questionable, or unethical behavior will not be tolerated (Albrecht et al., 2012). In addition, effective leadership is not the same as ethical or responsible leadership given that goals can be met through misconduct which can give the impression that leaders are also ethical.

Responsible leaders exhibit the character trait of virtuousness where they set the organizational example regarding ethical and moral standards, and act in the best interest of stakeholders, be it internal or external stakeholders such as shareholders, employees, and the general public (Jones & Jones, 2014). They take into account the long-term consequences of their decisions, while promoting an organizational culture of stewardship, and motivate followers to recognize the value of working for the common good of each other, the organization, and society. They protect the reputation of the organization by maintaining legitimacy and public trust, create value for shareholders and stakeholders, and engage in moral self-regulation. Accountable leaders do not compromise their moral principles or violate organizational policies when faced with difficult decisions by putting the organization at risk for financial goals that require rule-breaking (Jones & Jones, 2014). They are proactive in addressing ethical issues, treat ethics as a priority, learns the legal and ethical aspects of business, and does not plead ignorance when asked a question (Sims & Brinkmann, 2002). Such leadership is essential for organizational legitimacy, it earns the confidence and loyalty of followers, elevates an organizations moral climate, and may display personal sacrifice (Chandler, 2009).

Leaders displaying ethical awareness demonstrate the capacity to perceive and express sensitivity to relevant moral issues that deserve consideration when making choices that have a significant impact on others.

Responsible leadership implies high morals, integrity, and principled behaviors coupled with the intent to promote ethical behaviors in followers (Jones & Jones, 2014). Furthermore, responsible leadership entails steadiness in decision making, authenticity when communicating and interacting with others, and a sense of self-awareness of one's strength and weaknesses (Jones & Jones, 2014). They also facilitate open communication with followers, share knowledge with colleagues, possess a tolerance for criticism, genuineness with interactions with others, and trust from followers. These leaders align verbal communications with appropriate actions, deliver on promises, and remain true to convictions that are authentic behaviors.

Negative Tone at the Top Characteristics

Some CEOs, especially those with tyrannical management styles, are more likely than others to inspire their subordinates to adopt the kinds of behaviors they value. In companies headed by such CEOs, employees may come not only to embrace officially illegal and/or unethical procedures once frowned upon, but also copy the speech patterns, or even the manner of dress of the CEO while internalizing the competitive values and behavioral practices embraced by the CEO. As a consequence, the most powerful CEOs often play a significant role in a corporation's movement toward criminality, sometimes doing so to the point that misconduct becomes normalized and routinized. If the CEO is obsessed with profits, for example, profit-seeking behavior by lower-level employees may ultimately trump honest business practices. If the CEO is protective of employees who are caught breaking the rules, or resists sanctioning wrongdoers out of a misguided sense of loyalty, his or her mid-level managers are far less likely to manage "by the book" or to enforce the company's ethical guidelines (Barnard, 1999). If leaders focus only short-term financial results, employees internalize the message and adjust their behavior to accommodate this agenda. The consequences of pushing ethical boundaries are not immediately realized and this philosophy typically ignores taking into account long-term legal ramifications.

A bottom-line mentality being the only goal may promote short-term solutions that appear financially sound despite the problems it may expose the organization and its employees to, including criminal prosecutions. Such a tone from the top promotes an unrealistic belief that everything boils down to a monetary game and rules of morality are obstacles to the end-goal of profit realization. This is a risk factor to consider in that profits have to be immediately gained at any cost regardless of potential ethical compromises to achieve such profits. For example, when Lockheed President Carl Kotchian admitted to paying millions of dollars in bribes to foreign dignitaries, payments that would eventually lead to the imprisonment of Japan's foreign minister, he expressed little remorse because, in his mind, these payments were simply a cost of doing business. Kotchian stated, "Some call it gratuities. Some call them questionable payments. Some call it extortion. Some call it grease. Some call it bribery. I look at these payments as necessary to sell a product. I never felt I was doing anything wrong" (Soltes, 2016, p. 124).

Even organizations that express zero tolerance for unethical behaviors can slide into weak environments through executive action or inaction. CEOs whose cultural message is to 'win at all costs' are often found presiding over tragically compromised institutions (Barnard, 1999). Consider the views of John Rangos, founder of Chambers Development Company (CDC), a waste management firm that demanded bottom-line profits. When his subordinates reported that his 1990 profits would fall short of projections, Rangos responded, "go find the rest of it" (Sims & Brinkmann, 2002, p. 328). The subordinates created false profits until their fraud was discovered during a 1992 audit. Former Rangos subordinates stated that in pursuit of growth, numbers were manipulated and that the manipulation was tolerated and even encouraged. A former CDC employee stated, "this is how the game is played" (Sims & Brinkmann, 2002, p. 328). Leaders communicate their priorities and values through themes that emerge from what they focus on and if leaders are consistent in what they pay attention to, measure, and control, employees receive clear signals about what is important in an organization.

Therefore the organization's tone at the top is displayed by the "people it promotes, dismisses or allows to stagnate" (Sims & Brinkmann, 2002, p. 335). For example, consider the impact on an organization's tone at the top when we examine the opinion of a CEO upon learning that his subordinates had been criminally convicted in a price-fixing scandal. The CEO did not plan to take punitive action against them and, in fact, would retain their former positions because "[T]hese men did not act for personal gain, but in the belief that they were furthering the company's interest...each of these individuals is in every sense a reputable citizen, a respected and valuable member of the community, and of high moral character" (Soltes, 2016, p. 30). The reality is some leaders have the ability to lead, but not the values to set a proper tone at the top to ensure the welfare of the organization.

Consider that Salomon Brothers CEO John Gutfreund selected employees who "shared his aggressive, win-at-all cost mentality which preserved his short-term view, but prevented him from seeing what the long-term consequences could be on an organization as a whole" (Sims & Brinkmann, 2002, p. 335). He only looked at the most recent bottom line, expecting immediate results from employees, and disregarded long-term implications of how they had generated the revenue, covered up legal transgressions, and tolerated unethical behavior by promoting those who were like him, especially any that were not committed to ethical principles. This 'win at all costs' culture led to unethical and illegal acts at Salomon. Gutfreund's behavior communicated messages to others about what was expected and what would be tolerated as acceptable business behavior.

Significant corruption at the bottom is typically invisible to higher level managers and conversely, low-level employees do not necessarily see either the "big organizational games" or the nature of illegal deals higher up in the organization either; however, through gossip, they assume the existence of corruption at higher levels of their organization (Javor & Jancsics, 2013). There are cases when senior management becomes aware of corruption in the middle and lower levels, but do not intervene because it is less expensive than intervening. One CEO of a technology company pays kickbacks in return for government contracts, gave the following cynical opinion about corruption at the bottom: "Who cares what they are doing there...they can probably steal some package of printer paper and that is it (p. 15). However, the typical reason for this indifferent passivity is often the realization of higher-level organizational financial interests. For example, a middle manager in a sales department disclosing his embezzlement stated, "I think my boss knows about this but he just does not care because I bring much more money in for the company. I can let my people in the department deliver the numbers...and this is what matters" (p. 3). Moreover, sanctioning or disrupting illegal activities at the middle may cause a power imbalance and/or a threat to cooperation at the top.

Consider the example of a senior executive who has knowledge that another senior executive's assistant he works with is embezzling from the business. This executive who had knowledge of the embezzlement went on to state: "I get on well with him [the other senior executive]. We have been managing the firm together for 10 years. I know that his assistant is stealing...but I will not go after him because it is not worth it...I do not need a conflict with my fellow CEO, we just run the firm too smoothly together to bother, this relationship with petty cases" (p. 20). Moreover, middle level actors do not always cooperate because of threats to their employment, many also engage in senior management corruption because they count on some reward; sometimes rewards for illegal activities are perceived as unethical but not illegal. One senior executive observed: "managers always need subordinates to conduct corruption. There are always people who assist their bosses in the dirty business. This is the part of their career strategy...They want to get higher in the hierarchy and will do anything for it...or also possible that they do dubious bookkeeping for their chiefs because this is the secret of the sheltered life in the organization. They think: I do what my boss told me and I do not care anything else" (p. 15). Other finance managers were rewarded for their passive cooperation in not reporting fraudulent cases. As one manager stated:

Do not tell me that if you are a manager in the financial department and see that totally irrational numbers on the contract that you have to put your signature on and you do not understand why those numbers are there. Of course, you will sign it because they [top leaders] grabbed your balls. They know that you know. But it is also true that you can expect something extra in return. Nobody has to tell a word about anything. I have already seen many 'in return' things people got for closing their eyes, like brand new company cars, weekends in resorts or paid internships for children (p. 16).

Also, senior management can deploy sophisticated techniques to cover up corrupt practices than at lower levels. One of the most important practices in successful corruption is to intentionally "turn off" all crucial organizational control mechanisms facilitating collusion. Typically, different forms of control mechanisms should detect corruption in organizations such as focusing on personal behaviors or through administrative or social network channels. Organizational controls might consist of compliance management, internal auditors, board of directors, controllers, quality assurance, and trade unions and external controls such as external auditors, regulatory agencies, police, court, and public prosecutors. Corrupt senior management is able to deactivate internal control systems inside or outside the organization by building relationships or by building informal ties to control points through informal networks who are open to being corrupted and are willing to deactivate control mechanisms such as documenting truthful financial transactions. Thus, middle level employees legitimize corrupt transactions by falsifying records or approving improper transactions. Also, changing divisions of labor, rules, processes, and information routes into less transparent structures is a form of control deactivation. In such cases, the elite intentionally creates structural secrecy by finding those subordinates who are willing to carry out his or her agenda. A public company chief financial officer disclosed facts about a new director who reduced organizational controls relating to verifying financial protocol:

> Previously serious paperwork was needed to verify financial procedures. There was a protocol list that must be filled out by the director, the accountant, the engineers, and project managers to prove that the project was necessary. It was a one-page check list attached to each receipt with many signatures. Now, this item is totally missing. The new director just cancelled it. The reason for reorganizing these processes was not to create a transparent, straightforward, and regulated system. The story was about reducing control. Now, he can pump money from the firm (p. 21).

Another executive explaining the role of middle management in facilitating fraud stated: "Of course they need the middle level because the elite simply do not have access to certain procedures and forms"; direct access to organizational documents and enough discretion to falsify them (p. 15). A manager offered this narrative where the corrupt CFO wanted a maid in his house to be paid by the company:

> We [the department] hired the maid as a normal employee, so she was on our headcount. But this was totally against the company's policy. She could not appear on the headcount reports we quarterly sent to the mother company. She was in our inside records, but did not show up anywhere else. As with any other employee, she was originally on the bonus list, but the HR director told me to get rid of her from there. We had to cut these connection points, so that many people were told not to give her things that are automatically given when it is a new hire…for example, meal vouchers, company phone, computer, username and password, employee ID and access to the building…She was our virtual colleague…she was the boss' maid (p. 17).

The Importance of Understanding Leaderships' Darker Traits

A behavioral framework will improve our understanding of why individuals such as Enron's CEO Jeffrey Skilling, HealthSouth's CEO Richard Scrushy, and Tyco's CEO Dennis Kozlowski are more at risk for committing white-collar crimes and how they increase their organizations' propensity toward unethical or criminal behavior. Even though Sutherland's prototypical high-status offenders, such as CEOs and CFOs, represent only a fraction of the actual number of fraud offenders, their isolation for study is warranted given the financial and emotional destruction they are capable of inflicting on individuals, organizations, and society in general, due to their positions of authority (Perri, 2013b). Thus, it is important to examine in a more extensive manner how the behavioral traits of leadership may contribute to organizational misconduct, specifically fraud. What has been missing in understanding the link between corporate leadership and misconduct is the application of individual personality traits. How are personality traits risk factors that increase the probability that someone will engage in criminal, or at a minimum unethical acts?

Interestingly, little is understood about the relationship between individual behavioral traits and white-collar crime because most criminological research on white-collar crime does not consider the personality traits of these offenders (Listwan et al., 2010). Consequently, this lack of research created a void where academic and non-academic circles resorted to making highly erroneous character assumptions about this offender group. As a result, society is at greater risk of being financially exploited by this offender class and, at times, becoming victims of their violence (Perri, 2016). The author cautions that harboring behavioral traits discussed below should not be interpreted as being the cause of criminal behavior, but their correlation to fraud is considered a fraud offender risk factor (Perri, 2013b). However, the notion that individual traits and characteristics affect one's propensity for engaging in crime is not new to the field of criminology. For example, as early as the turn of the twentieth century, scholar Edward Ross argued that the white-collar criminals of his day, whom he called criminaloids, were morally insensitive, lacking consideration of the rights and well-being of others and are simply not bothered by the harm that they inflict on them stating, "They want nothing more than we all want—money, power, and consideration—in a word, success; but they are in a hurry and they are not particular as to the means" (Ross, 1977, p. 31).

Fraud offender Steve Comisar, who exploited investors through get-rich-quick schemes, appears to support the insights Ross observed well over a hundred years ago when Comisar stated, "I know I wanted to make a lot of money…and I figured I am going to take a short cut" (Wells, 2012, p. 55). Throughout most of the study on white-collar crime, assumptions have been made that these offenders are free of psychological pathologies we normally equate with street-level offenders who are not well-integrated into society (Van Slyke et al., 2016). A partial explanation for a lack of application of psychological scholarship to white-collar crime is that Edwin Sutherland held a rather negative opinion of psychological and psychiatric positions on explaining any criminal behavior (Perri et al., 2014). Scholars, in turn, adopted Sutherland's position and for many decades erroneously assumed that personality traits had nothing to do with committing crime, including white-collar crime, because Sutherland advocated for a reorientation away from an emphasis on individual personality characteristics to explain criminality in whole or in part (Perri et al., 2014). Sutherland emphasized a strict sociological framework focusing solely on the socialization or learning process within close personal and/or social groups to explain the acquisition of criminal attitudes and thinking patterns producing unique rationalizations, and motives attributable to different crime classifications (Boduszek & Hyland, 2011a). Yet white-collar crime is a human endeavor, and it is important to understand the behavioral factors that might influence an offender's actions to construct a better offender profile (Ramamoorti, 2008).

In essence, "when presented with seemingly identical opportunities and motives, why does one person or organization(s) turn to fraud and another does not" (Murphy, 2012, p. 242)? Unlike Sutherland's approach, which put little emphasis on the behavioral makeup of white-collar offenders, the modern approach to studying white-collar crime incorporates the offender's behavioral traits as important risk factors in the decision to commit crime even though there are legitimate debates on how important behavioral traits may be and which specific traits are common among offenders (Perri et al., 2014). Although not a comprehensive explanation for these offenders, if individuals harbor personality traits that increase the risk of offending, in general, "we should not be particularly surprised" when they commit white-collar crime (Benson & Simpson, 2009, p. 51). Contemporary research suggests that personality traits should not be ignored as anomalies because they may at times be symptomatic of potential white-collar criminal behavior especially when combined with criminal thinking traits outlined in chapter one. Although fraud offenders may not generally manifest their criminality in ways that are easily recognized by the general public, such as property or violent crimes, it does not mean that they do not harbor personality traits that facilitate the decision to consider white-collar crimes as a solution to satisfy a motive (Perri et al., 2014). What is problematic is when individual characteristics are ignored and important offender risk factors may be overlooked.

Specifically, according to internationally renowned criminal psychologist Dr. Robert Hare, white-collar criminal's fraudulent activities may reflect "a virulent mix of criminal thinking and behavioral traits, including a sense of entitlement, a propensity to deceive, cheat, and manipulate, a lack of empathy and remorse, and the view that others are merely resources to be exploited—callously and without regret" (Carozza, 2008, p. 38). Research confirms that there is a relationship between personality traits such as antisocial dispositions, evidence of narcissism, and/or psychopathy which creates a negative synergy when combined with criminal thinking patterns increasing the risk of white-collar crime together and violence (Perri et al., 2014). Moreover, testimonies from leadership who facilitated fraud and subordinates who carried out the fraud shed light on personality traits that make up a general profile of a white-collar crime offender and how they interact at the organizational level (Eaton & Korach, 2016).

Auditors, fraud examiners, and law enforcement consequently must place an emphasis on understanding and evaluating organizational culture because management personalities and their attitudes shape that culture (Cohen et al., 2011). They should evaluate the fairness of the work climate such as are employees overworked, are ethical behaviors rewarded, and are employees fairly compensated? Such conditions could lead to resentment and an incentive to commit fraud (Cohen et al., 2011). Also, the behavioral aspects of managers coupled with the opportunity to commit fraud serve as a deadly mix that increases the risk that fraud will occur (Cohen et al., 2011). For example, do fraud offenders exhibit a controlling personality, do they avoid transparency when dealing with clients, do they exhibit revengeful attitudes to others, and is there a hunger for power, aggressiveness, financial success, and a display of intellectual superiority (Goldstein, 2011b)?

We will explore the application of personality disorders such as narcissism and psychopathy to help explain why these disorders are risk factors for white-collar criminality just as they are risk factors for violent crime or any other crime classification (Perri, 2011a). In addition, recently scholars in the accounting, business, and financial fields who write about white-collar crime have begun to incorporate behavioral scholarship into their disciplines, thereby creating a more holistic picture of white-collar crime and its offenders. Not only are scholars beginning to explore white-collar crime from a multidisciplinary approach, but practitioners such as fraud examiners, auditors, and forensic accountants are incorporating findings from researchers into their practice area so they too can become more refined in their prevention and detection of white-collar crime (COSO, 2010). Currently, the Federal Bureau of Investigations (FBI) participates in the behavioral profiling in order to make investigations more productive by looking at white-collar offender behavioral traits (Perri et al., 2014). Using criminological concepts as a foundation, law enforcement is constructing an overarching offender profile by integrating their personality and the psychology, and sociology of white-collar crime to better engage in fraud investigations.

Studying the personalities of past offenders can be extremely useful for law enforcement, auditors, accountants, and fraud examiners because the personality traits fraud offenders display can act as a guide that connects behavior patterns to characteristics which would describe an offender (Eaton & Korach, 2016). When partnered with conventional investigative and forensic approaches, understanding risks associated with certain personality traits can add tremendous value when narrowing the field as far as the type of person(s) who might be more apt to commit organizational fraud. The application of the behavioral sciences to understanding white-collar crime is finally catching up to the present day even though it has been neglected for decades relative to its application to conventional, non-white-collar street-level crimes (Perri et al., 2014). What is becoming more evident is that even though personality traits are not a cause of criminality, when they start to combine with criminal attitudes that may be encouraged within an organizational setting, the risks of fraud in general, are apt to increase. Greater understanding of these factors will assist scholars, white-collar investigations, and those in related fields who encounter these offenders such as auditors.

In this section we will learn what the traits of destructive leadership entail, the application of antisocial/criminal thinking traits to leadership and other fraud offenders, and the role that personality plays in increasing the risk of fraud from occurring. Without understanding the behavioral risk factors that contribute to destructive leadership, we are apt to put these individuals in positions of power where they can satisfy their motives through fraudulent practices at the expense of numerous stakeholders. Practically, it will take all hands from multiple disciplines pulling together on the proverbial ship oars to gather information on this type of offender to create a profile that is more accurate and not based on speculation facilitated by projection bias.

230

Destructive Leadership Traits: An Overview

As recent high-profile fraud offender cases highlight, destructive leadership is often at the heart of many organizations' immense economic and social losses, such as loss of retirements, employment, and some facing serious criminal liabilities. Most scholars do not have an explicit definition of destructive leadership, but treat it as a "you know it when you see it" phenomenon (Padilla et al., 2007, p. 177). A problem with many existing definitions of the dark side of leadership is that they do not necessarily consider the multidimensional aspects of leadership that incorporate follower and environmental dynamics. Leadership performance cannot exist without followership and much of the literature does not take into account the impact of followers on the perpetuation of organizational misconduct. Destructive leaders, like leaders in general, do not operate in a vacuum. They require followers and an environment that allows the seeds of destructive leadership to grow. Consider, however, leaders who behave destructively toward subordinates may not necessarily be destructive in other interpersonal relationships, be it with customers, business partners or upper management (Einarsen et al., 2007).

However, organizational success and failure are seldom due to a single factor or enlightened individual who adopts a holistic approach by acknowledging the interactional process among destructive leaders, susceptible followers, the influence of group dynamics, favorable environments, and the situations they encounter. Conducive work environments enable corrupt behaviors to flourish and may be linked to a company's board of directors who are not independent and/or competent, weak organizational internal controls, a compromised organizational culture, or peer and external pressures such as competition and market forces. With these characteristics in mind, destructive leadership has been viewed as the "repeated behavior by a leader, supervisor, or manager that violates the legitimate interest of the organization by undermining and/or sabotaging the organization's goals, tasks, resources, and effectiveness and/or the motivation, well-being, or job satisfaction of subordinates" (Tourish & Vatcha, 2005, p. 208). Terms such as 'dark leadership,' 'toxic leadership,' 'destructive leadership,' and 'deviant leadership' have been used to describe unethical leadership behavior. For purposes of flexibility, some of these terms will be used interchangeably to describe the same observations.

Leaders might display a dark side due to a range of factors and there is little empirical evidence pointing to one definite causation, but in some instances, situational factors and personality traits combine to cause destructive behaviors (Maccoby, 2004). Whatever the terminology used, destructive leadership has resulted in a number of negative outcomes including, poor productivity, employee resistance, poor job satisfaction, high turnover, counterproductive work behaviors, and poor organizational performance. Are there observable patterns that destructive leaders rely maintaining their authority to advance their agendas? First, it is important to consider that destructive leadership is seldom entirely or absolutely destructive (Padilla et al., 2007). Leaders, with followers and the environment, contribute to outcomes distributed along a destructive–constructive continuum, with outcomes related to destructive leadership primarily falling at the negative end of this spectrum. Secondly, those who display destructive leadership traits have a desire to control and dominate; they exhibit power orientation qualities that were previously discussed, such as coercion and intimidation, rather than leading by persuasion or commitment. Power is the most important ingredient in the leadership process.

In the context of destructive leadership behavior, it is a tool uses to control subordinates in order to achieve personal agendas (Chandler, 2009). Destructive leadership behaviors are recognizable because they are often characterized by interpersonal dynamics, such as undermining and demeaning others (Chatterjee & Hambrick, 2007). Leaders who manage by fear aim to control people by using threats in direct and indirect ways, thus a manager might threaten an employee with termination or a low performance rating if they do not engage in misconduct. In interpersonal relations, such leaders often reflect bullying dynamics by targeting individual(s) who may be in submissive or powerless positions. Not surprisingly, they may leave followers worse off, stifle respectful dissent, encourage destructive competition amongst followers, display reckless disregard for risks associated with their decisions, fail to understand issues they are asked to make decisions about, and/or exhibit insatiable ambitions, greed, or a lack of integrity (Chatterjee & Hambrick, 2007). Unethical leaders compromise standards depending on the situation, use the company's resources and reputation for self-gain, downplay the importance of ethics until there is an obvious and significant problem, ignore legal advice or use legal advice to

231

get around rules by stretching their potential application. Moreover, corrupt leadership avoids taking action on ethical issues in favor of expediency and efficiencies misconduct offers.

They rationalize away unethical behaviors while demonstrating an unwillingness to confront ethical issues unless they are safe, uncomplicated, and lack risk by dealing with them behind the scenes (Sims & Brinkmann, 2002). Whatever the cause of destructive leadership behavior consists of, the long-term impact on organizations is negative, and often result in bullying, harassment, decreased productivity, conflict, theft, and unethical behavior (Chandler, 2009). One of the primary objectives of destructive leadership in maintaining its power is the control of others, and such control is achieved through methods that create fear and intimidation (Einarsen et al., 2007). Such leaders typically possess formal organizational power such as being appointed to their position by a board of directors. They may frequently engage in a range of behaviors including self-aggrandizement, belittling of followers, lack of consideration for others, a forceful style of conflict resolution, punishment for no apparent reason, discouraging initiative, undermining organizational goals, and ignoring or worsening the well-being of followers. Bully leaders lack personable communication skills, hold low regard for others, and promote a chaotic organizational culture (Jones & Jones, 2014). In order to force compliance, bullying tactics include being overly argumentative, excessive rudeness, unwarranted public criticism, public humiliation, verbal abuse, and yelling with the goal of taking advantage of their power status by overwhelming subordinates (Jones & Jones, 2014).

Coercive, counterproductive, and threatening behaviors by an organizational leader set a negative example and send implicit and explicit authorization to lower-level managers to engage in similar destructive behaviors. Moreover, destructive leadership is inherently selfish in nature; it stresses the leader's own goals and objectives over the needs of constituents and the broader social organization. They display behaviors aimed at obtaining personal rather than organizational goals by abuse of power, inflicting damage on others, and breaking rules to satisfy personal needs. Such leaders behave without integrity by engaging in misconduct such as "corruption, hypocrisy, sabotage, and manipulation, as well as other assorted unethical, illegal, and criminal acts" and put their self-interest ahead of the organization's legitimate interest (Lipman-Blumen, 2005, p. 18).

Antisocial and Criminal Thinking Traits of Corrupt Leadership

Recall from chapter one that antisocial and criminal thinking are conceptualized as distorted thought patterns or thinking errors coupled with one's attitudes and values that support a mindset that rationalizes and justifies law-breaking behavior. In other words, thinking patterns that support the belief that it is alright to violate others and/or the property of others (Perri et al., 2014). Criminal thinking posits that those who are involved in a criminal lifestyle engage in certain modes of thought facilitate antisocial behavior ultimately leading to bad life choices and the prediction of future criminal behavior (Taxman et al., 2011). Those who harbor antisocial thinking patterns are comfortable using deceit, manipulation, and violence to satisfy a motive together with a sense of ownership; people are things or objects to be possessed. It is through the application of concepts that readers of this book can experience a tangible and perhaps, an emotional reaction to how white-collar offenders exhibit criminal traits even though they do not exhibit an overall criminal lifestyle because they engage in prosocial activities. Consider that all traits may not be observable at the same time or with equal intensity or pervasiveness, but it would be difficult for someone to engage in antisocial without displaying some of the traits below. Some of the traits covered include, 1) weakness exploitation, 2) a disregard for rules and norms, 3) a victim mindset, 4) a desire for excitement or gratification, 5) harboring a super optimistic attitude; the belief that one is immune from getting caught for wrong-doing, 6) a person's sense of social identification, 7) power orientation and goal interference, 8) sentimentality, 9) exhibiting a lack of responsibility and accountability for one's actions, and 10) a sense of entitlement.

Weakness Exploitation

White-collar criminals often share the same exploitative traits with non-white-collar criminals; criminal classifications are typically distinguished by the victims they create (Perri & Brody, 2011). Weakness exploitation entails taking advantage of vulnerability in others and/or situations in order to satisfy a motive. Recall that weakness exploitation is not limited to taking advantage of the vulnerabilities of a person, but it can also mean taking advantage of the weaknesses of an organization's internal controls or lack of internal controls. Consider how fraud offender Jerry Schneider, whose motive was to see, as if playing a game, whether he could commit the perfect crime by engaging in asset misappropriation of nearly $1 million from his employer Pacific Telephone Company. At his trial he revealed how much he despised his employer, his drive to prove his own superiority, and how much he believed in exploiting weaknesses. Observe how he imputes to himself the character of integrity despite admitting during an interview that he would seize an opportunity to commit fraud,

> When he was asked whether he considered himself an honest man, Schneider responded with a firm, "yes". When he was asked whether, if he saw a wallet on the sidewalk, he would pocket it or try to return it to the owner, his answer was that he was like everyone else—he'd try to return it if it was at all possible. However, when he was asked whether, if he saw $10,000 lying in an open cash box in a supermarket and no one was watching him, if he would take it, he answered, "Sure, I would. If the company was careless enough to leave the money there, it deserved to have the money taken" (Albrecht et al., 2012, p. 52).

Moreover, weakness is displayed by our attitudes and beliefs that interfere with our ability to engage in quality risk assessments (Druckman, 1994). For example, weakness exploitation tactics can involve creating seemingly genuine bonds with victims enhancing the offender's ability to proverbially "lower the victim's guard," thus exploiting their trust, and thereby gaining access to victim information and resources they normally would not disclose in order to facilitate financial exploitation. White-collar offenders relish the sense of superiority over the victim that comes when an offense is successfully executed (Stotland, 1977). The feeling of power and superiority that arise from the offense is psychologically rewarding to the offender and becomes a source of motivation for continued offending (Benson & Manchak, 2014). Consider the strategies often employed by chronic fraud offender Barry Webne.

Once Webne left prison for committing fraud at his place of work, he established a consultancy to teach other businesses where their organization's controls where weak. While at these businesses, he defrauded them, which led to his prosecution and ultimately returning to prison. The businesses that hired Webne trusted him with access to the organization's assets; Webne exploited weaknesses in their internal controls to misappropriate assets. Thus Webne exploited the trust the businesses had in him where he stated "if you put me in a position of trust again, chances are that I am going to violate that trust" (Perri, 2016, p. 64). Consider that fraud offenders like Webne may be knowledgeable in the fraud they committed, but it does not mean they are experts in so many other fraud schemes that are available, thus competent to set up a consultancy to advise others. Consider the statement of securities fraud offender Justin Paperny when he was asked how he gained the trust of those whom he would ultimately defraud. What tactics/strategies did he use to gain their trust? What seemed to work best? Paperny responded:

> I never thought I was defrauding them…I was very polite, always leveraging off my vice president title, University of Southern California degree, and name dropping my baseball player clients did not hurt either. What I did best was find a way to identify with them. If they liked hockey, so did I. If they loved soccer, I did as well. I made it appear as if we had a lot in common (Perri et al., 2014, p. 7).

Again, we observe how Paperny found a weakness to exploit: the perceived trust the victim believes is shared with his aggressor. Paperny knew his victims' weaknesses created their false sense of security that mutual trust and confidence existed. In fact, the term "con man" derives from the phrase "confidence men." These offenders gain victims' confidence, which motivates victims to lower their guard and believe the offenders can be trusted with their money. He built walls of false integrity around himself by supposedly espousing the same value system as his victims and then gauged this technique's effectiveness according to his victims' increasing level of comfort with him. In many instances, regardless of the scope and category of the fraud, offenders use the same

233

strategies: gain trust that others view as a strength with others, and eventually exploit the trust offenders perceive as a weakness.

Ignoring Rules, Laws, and Codes of Conduct

White-collar criminals, like non-white-collar criminals, engage in antisocial behaviors of rule-breaking, disregarding appropriate social boundaries and ignoring laws and ethical standards (Croall, 2007b), believing "they don't have to follow the rules because they made them" (Swartz, 2003, p. 302). Accordingly, consider the insights of previously mentioned CFO Samuel Antar, "It's not uncommon, you know, in a small business, that people are paid off the books…nobody is denying its illegal. It is more like a casual thing, like an entitlement. There was never a morality issue that I can recall…committing fraud was just like another part of life" (Wells, 2012, p. 56). Antar further stated, "People like to ask me if I am redeemed, I like to say that I'm possibly retired. The only reason I stopped was because I got caught" (Goldstein, 2011b). Consider that WorldCom engaged in financial statement fraud by understating operating expenses by capitalizing them instead of including operating expenses on the income statement for the period they were incurred. There was a time when WorldCom executives proposed a Code of Ethics or also referred to as Codes of Conduct. Codes are formal statements that describe how organizations expect their employees to treat each other. They define behavior that is and is not acceptable, and outline rules for respect, fairness, and civility that employees are expected to follow (Ferrell et al., 2013). Codes can help guide employees when they are not sure what is and is not acceptable.

They help to communicate expectations, enhance employee morale, minimize inconsistent managerial standards, and help promote constructive social interaction by raising awareness of the needs of all stakeholders, including employers, fellow employees, shareholders, boards of directors, and customers. Codes may also put employees on notice of the punishment that can expect to receive if they violate codes of conduct. Research suggests that organizations with codes that are actually followed tend to be less tolerant of employee or other stakeholder unethical behavior than companies that do not have a code, or that do not take their code seriously (Ferrell et al., 2013). Bernard Ebbers, for example, was the CEO who went to prison for his participation in WorldCom's corruption. When Ebbers considered the idea of establishing a code, he reportedly described the effort as a "colossal waste of time" (SEC, 2003, p. 18). Perhaps WorldCom might have avoided bankruptcy, thousands of employees could have retained their jobs, shareholders would not have lost value, and Ebbers could have avoided going to prison for decades had he considered the importance of a code.

Power Orientation

Power orientation entails the display of aggression by controlling others and situations. The desire to control is a trait linked to white-collar offenders that are employees and executives (Van Slyke et al., 2016). Control may be gained through the conventional criminal strategy of overpowering someone physically, but it may also entail manifesting the desire to control through interpersonal tactics such as manipulation, intimidation, and punishment—behaviors often observable when criminogenic organizations perpetuate fraud by sending the message to others that they should not interfere with their agenda. The desire to control is a need to exercise dominance over interpersonal situations to minimize the extent to which others have power. They inject themselves into the lives of others by looking for exploitable vulnerabilities, concealing their motives without announcing their intentions, and finally preying upon them. Offenders with high levels of desire for control are assertive, decisive, and seek to influence others for personal advantage (Van Slyke et al., 2016). As we shall observe when studying predatory fraud offenders, they also seek control over others. As one predatory fraud offender stated, "For myself, I love to make people do what I want them to do, I love command. I love to rule people. That's why I'm a con artist" (Duffield & Grabosky, 2001, p. 2). Such individuals may attain positions of considerable power within an organization by treating others as they would pawns on a chessboard while their faults are overlooked. Colleagues and peers endure their exploitative and abusive conduct which only serves to reinforce the offender's sense of invulnerability.

These people may not be perceived accurately for who they really are until they have done irreparable damage. Time and again, an analysis of people whose crimes appear out of character will reveal their unrelenting determination to control others (Samenow, 2012b). Consider bankrupt computer disk drive maker MiniScribe's and its former CEO Quentin Wiles. In 1988, MiniScribe Corporation was described as the most well-managed personal computer disk drive company in the industry increasing sales from $113.9 million in 1985 to $603 million in 1988; unfortunately the increase represented fictitious sales. As a result, in May 1989, MiniScribe announced that the financial statements from 1986 through 1988 were inaccurate due to artificially inflated income. What we see is that MiniScribe's performance was not consistent with industry averages especially given how intensely competitive the industry was, severe price cutting was the norm, and companies were reporting losses. Yet for MiniScribe, their sales were exploding, which was a red flag for fraud. Other red flags consisted of money owed on sales that was never collected in addition to the fact that even though sales were increasing, their inventory was not increasing proportionately to meet the increasing demand for their product.

CEO Quentin Wiles displayed a management style that was strict, autocratic, and overbearing, coupled with not tolerating executive failure to meet goals by telling subordinates "to force the numbers if they needed to" (Albrecht et al., 2012, p. 146). Described as a tyrant that instilled fear in the hearts of employees, he would have employees stand up in front of everyone to be fired. When asked why he chose this method of management, he answered, "That's just to show everyone I'm in control of the company" (Jennings, 2006, p. 67). As a result of the unethical tone at the top Wiles set, subordinates engaged in the following fraud schemes including, 1) packing bricks and shipping and recording them as disk drive sales, 2) shipping disk drivers to warehouses and recording them as sales, 3) shipping defective disk drives and recording them as sales, 4) secretly changed auditors' working papers without the auditors' knowledge to reflect better company financial health, and 5) changing shipping dates on shipments to customers so that revenues were recognized before sales were made. Wiles profited from the fraud, but eventually went to prison for his role.

Power orientation by management may reflect a management style characterized by governing people based on fear (Warigon & Bowers, 2006). The center of their managing philosophy is based on unchecked power and discourages employees from communicating openly and frankly about their views on organizational matters. They manipulate communication channels to ensure that employees only say and write positive things about the organization to external parties. Supervisors who subscribe to this management style routinely reprimand employees who express unfavorable opinions about working conditions. There is no commitment to truth in that leaders censor or sanitize communications to board of director members, fraud examiners, external auditors, and regulators to conceal the real organizational climate and culture. Personal agendas are disguised as organizational agendas and such leaders use their power to routinely eliminate employees who challenge their authority or question them even if for valid concerns. Such individuals are the least accountable people in organizations, yet quick to take credit for successful initiatives and blame others for their failures while meticulously scapegoating or building cases against dispensable employees.

These leaders treat fraud examiners, internal auditors, external auditors, and other independent reviewers with open disdain. They do not want anyone to review and criticize their activities or the activities of their employees preferring to operate under the illusion that their actions are not questionable and are not subject to audit from anyone. Consider the previously mentioned executives at Livent where to facilitate its massive collusive fraud, CEO Drabinsky relied on Livent's top executives who exercised "coercion and intimidation to browbeat their accountants…displaying a contemptuous attitude toward outside auditors" and believing that it was "no one's business how they ran their company" (Knapp, 2009, p. 394). Power can also be used by government officials in an exploitative manner. Consider the case of Colonial Pipeline Company's secret payments to New Jersey Public officials in return for a favor, which involved obtaining building permits and the right to build storage tanks on the property of the City of Woodridge (Palmer, 2012). Colonial executives first declined the official's request, but eventually paid the extortion in order to get the permits. When the scheme was uncovered, the executives were arrested and went to trial. Although, technically, they were guilty even though they were not the ones who initiated the payments, it is important to note how power dynamics exerted by public officials influenced their behavior for the worse; this case should not be thought of as an isolated incident.

Entitlement

Entitlement refers to the belief that one is privileged and deserves special access to resources regardless of the consequences to others (Benson & Simpson, 2009). White-collar criminals possess this sense of entitlement (Walters, 2002). Securities fraud offender Justin Paperny illustrated the entitled state of mind when he said, "cheating became easy to rationalize as I felt entitled to more" (Paperny, 2009, p. 104). Further elaborating, Paperny stated, "I felt entitled to oversee hundreds of millions of dollars, I felt entitled to my country club memberships, I felt entitled to flashy Rolex watches, to sport designer suits, to drive high-end BMW sedans" (Paperny, 2010, p. 195). Paperny later on cooperated with the authorities stating, "I only cooperated because I thought it might keep me out of jail…I didn't really feel bad. I told the SEC everything they wanted to hear—the truth" (Wells, 2012, p. 55). Another example involved a controller at a small business who began to embezzle by writing checks to himself justifying his actions by believing he was entitled to the money as a high-ranking employee who thought he was underpaid (Wells, 2012). Interestingly, this controller lost his position, was prosecuted, and received probation. However, when he was hired at another company, he again began to write himself checks because he did not receive the raise he believed he deserved. He stated, "I got upset so I started cutting checks to myself again to the level I should be compensated for" (Wells, 2012, p. 54).

This controller was caught, re-prosecuted, and spent time in jail. This narrative is not unusual in that studies indicate people higher in the organizational ladder are more likely to behave unethically because their elevated wealth status makes them desire more wealth—they are motivated to break rules to accumulate wealth (Wells, 2012). Consider the case of Mark Whitacre, an informant and fraud offender who was a corporate vice president at Archer Daniels Midland Corporation (ADM). Whitacre tape recorded conversations of other ADM executives and ADM competitors when they were colluding to engage in price-fixing of lysine, a widely-used food additive. Initially, he received whistleblower immunity in that he was not going to be prosecuted as long as he cooperated fully with law enforcement, however he eventually lost his immunity status. While Whitacre was working with the Federal Bureau of Investigation (FBI) to gather evidence that ADM was participating in price-fixing, he misappropriated an estimated $9 million dollars from ADM by funneling money through a shell company he created. Whitacre eventually acknowledged his misconduct, but relied on the antisocial trait of entitlement and the rationalization of social comparison to justify his actions. He believed his wrong-doing was not as severe as the fraud being committed by ADM stating:

> I thought I was bullet-proof—being able to stay at the company, be made the CEO…I had a sense of entitlement and felt like anything I took was mine; the company owed it to me because I worked hard enough. I wasn't worried about them firing me when I was taking money, because I knew if they ever came to me and said, "Look, Mark, you took $9 million," I'd say, "Wait a minute, you guys are stealing hundreds of millions on the price-fixing scheme every month." So I wasn't worried about the company turning me in (Abkowitz, 2009).

Lack of Accountability

Despite the difference in their offenses, white-collar and non-white-collar offenders will do their utmost to dispel responsibility by implicating or blaming others. For example, regardless of the industry, Enron, WorldCom, and other large organizations display bureaucratic characteristics and hierarchical structures. Thus, it is not surprising to hear white-collar offenders use rationalizations and excuses to distance themselves from their financial crime by downplaying the power they hold. Yet ironically, when it is to their benefit, they exalt themselves as being the best and brightest executives taking credit for the successes, but are conveniently unaware of the fraud within the organization they exerted tight control over (Perri, 2013b). A key criminogenic trait of organizational structures is the diffusion of responsibility. Numerous hierarchical levels can be used by executive officers to deny knowledge and therefore to deny responsibility of illegal practices occurring at work to meet the ambitious goals set by the same executives. Likewise, management at a parent company might claim not to be responsible for the actions of autonomous subsidiaries. Subcontracting partners might even be used to designate a scapegoat. Vice versa, lower-ranking employees may use hierarchical complexity or subunit autonomy to escape oversight, to claim they were just following orders, or to claim that they are just a cog in the machine and missed the bigger picture of the organization's illegal practices.

As one scholar observed, bureaucracy is "rule by nobody" (Arendt, 1969, p. 81). Because of the nature of bureaucratic hierarchy, subordinates blame their superiors and these superiors, in turn, insist that their subordinates acted independently without their knowledge (Perri, 2013b). With corporate crime, it is seldom the case that any one individual is clearly responsible for all of the misconduct because it typically takes the cooperation of others to successfully execute misconduct. Thus, when a crime is committed, everyone can with some degree of plausibility, point the finger at someone else (Heath, 2008). The person who carried out the action can blame the person who made the decision; the person who made the decision can blame the person who vetted the decision and so on. Interestingly, a federal prosecutor echoed the insights of previously mentioned scholar's on how bureaucracy can diffuse responsibility and make it difficult to identify the true wrongdoers:

> There are…many substantial challenges unique to pursuing individuals for corporate misdeeds. In large corporations, where responsibility can be diffuse and decisions are made at various levels, it can be difficult to determine if someone possessed the knowledge and criminal intent necessary to establish their guilt beyond a reasonable doubt. This is true in determining the culpability of high-level executives (Yates, 2015).

For example, convicted CEO Walter Forbes illustrates this lack of accountability stating, "the accounting fraud was a terrible blow, I simply had no idea this had been going on…I was no less outraged, and no less affected…I knew these charges against me were false" (Taubman, 2007, p. 148). Consider the lack of accountability demonstrated by convicted WorldCom CEO Bernard Ebbers. Ebbers maintained WorldCom CFO Scott Sullivan and subordinates kept him in the dark about financial statement fraud that occurred over several years. Ebbers stated, "Shocked…I couldn't believe it. I never thought anything like that would have gone on. I put those people in place. I trusted them" (Belson, 2005). Yet, Sullivan testified that Ebbers knew of the fraud because Ebbers told him not to issue an earnings warning to Wall Street and authorized Sullivan to create false profits (Yang & Grow, 2005). The same dynamic holds true for Enron CEO Kenneth Lay blaming subordinates, including CFO Andrew Fastow, for orchestrating the fraud scandal. Fastow indicated that he received permission to engage in financial statement fraud from his superiors convicted CEOs Kenneth Lay and Jeffrey Skilling (Perri, 2013b). In turn, Lay and Skilling claimed ignorance about Fastow's fraud that went on for years. Consider the diesel emission fraud scandal at Volkswagen. When the fraud was uncovered, the Chief Executive Officer, Martin Winterkorn, denied knowing anything and blamed the fraud on a handful of "rogue engineers" (Rorie, 2020, p. 145).

Gratification and Excitement

Regardless of socioeconomic status, some criminals experience a sense of pleasure, gratification, and excitement from their acts (Clinard & Meier, 2010). In manipulating victims, some fraud perpetrators seem to take a contemptuous delight in the act itself rather than simply the outcome. Executives are particularly likely to offend when there is a direct benefit to them such as career advancement and this is true especially if they receive a thrill from engaging in misconduct that usually is associated with street-level offenders (Paternoster & Tibbetts, 2016). Thrill-seeking can be enhanced by the fact that organizations may reward excessive risk-taking that brings with it a certain amount of psychological pleasure in attaining a goal, albeit unethically or illegally (Paternoster & Tibbetts, 2016). An individual's motivation for crime may have originally been characterized as experiencing some type of pressure such as financial problems, greed, revenge for believing they are being treated unfairly, and so forth.

Yet, "as they found themselves successful at this crime, they began to gain some secondary delight in the knowledge that they are fooling the world, that they are showing their superiority to others" (Duffield & Grabosky, 2001, p. 2). They enjoy what is referred to at times as a duping delight, knowing that they were able to take advantage of another person and/or situation without being caught (Hare, 1999). Similar to the sense of superiority over others is the gratification and pride obtained from mastery of a situation being particularly prevalent in more complex, long-term frauds. The following quotation illustrates the thrill of engaging in fraud as stated by a fraud offender, "When I score, I get more kick out of that than anything; to score is the biggest kick of my whole life" (Duffield & Grabosky, 2001, p. 3). Consider the similarity in the statement made by William Sutton, a bank robber, explaining his motivations that illustrates how the application of antisocial traits to offenders can be crime classification neutral. In expressing his reason for engaging in bank robbery he stated: "Because I enjoy it. I love it. I was more alive when I was inside a bank robbing it, than any other time in my life. I enjoyed everything about it so much that one or two weeks later I'd be out looking for the next job. But to me the money was the chips, that's all" (Ramamoorti et al., 2014, p. 66).

Thrill-seeking attracts all types of offenders regardless of socioeconomic status. Research has found that thrill-seeking desires predict corporate offending intentions amongst corporate managers (Simpson, 2013). Furthermore, those in leadership positions often need to be in the spotlight, relish attention, feel an overwhelming desire to maintain the level of excitement, and may artificially maintain the level of excitement by engaging in excessive risk-taking and fraudulent behavior. Chronic white-collar offender Barry Webne, who, after spending time in prison, established an anti-fraud consultancy that was used as a ruse to establish additional fraud schemes with business organizations that hired him to assist with antifraud controls. Webne described how his thrill-seeking behavior served as a motivator when he said, "One side was looking over my shoulder worried about getting caught; the other side was concerned about getting the next rush" (Patterson, 2011). David Levine, a former inside trader, characterized the gratification and excitement upon seizing fraud opportunities like this: "Something deep inside of me forced me to try to catch up to the pack of the wheeler-dealers who always raced in front of me…I was addicted to the excitement, the sense of victory" (Levine, 1991, p. 390). Several of Levine's participants also described their insider trading schemes as "exhilarating" (Palmer, 2012, p. 54). Michael Rapp, a high-level executive convicted of fraud during the 1980s savings and loan crisis, also experienced gratification when committing fraud, as Palmer notes:

> Rapp loved to spend his days figuring out schemes. A brilliant man, he could have been successful as a legitimate businessman, but the excitement of swindles held too powerful an allure for him, as did the vast sums of quick and easy money they produced. From the days of thrifts were deregulated, it was inevitable that Rapp would loot them. Opportunities of that magnitude could not possibly go unnoticed by swindlers like Rapp (Palmer, 2012, p. 54).

Super Optimism, Embellished Abilities and Immunity

Most people don't prepare for failure. Like people don't plan to go bankrupt, criminals also don't prepare to get caught.

CFO Samuel Antar (2013)

Embellished abilities pertain to harboring a super-optimism of being able to engage in crime without detection. The white-collar offender's sense of superiority is accompanied by arrogance that further motivates offending (Shover & Hochstetler, 2006). If there is a trait that stands out in criminals of all persuasions, it is their super optimism from either the bank robber or the bank embezzler—they have convinced themselves they cannot get caught. When insider trader David Levine conspired to commit his offenses, he reassured himself and his co-conspirators that they would not get apprehended for their activities because the Securities and Exchange Commission (SEC) investigators were not as smart as he. If the SEC investigators were as smart as he was, "the investigators would be working on Wall Street and pulling down large salaries and bonuses, rather than policing Wall Street and earning a relative pittance" (Palmer, 2012, p. 119). When comparing himself to auditors and his ability to deceive them, fraud offender Barry Webne stated: "I'll have them for lunch" (Patterson, 2011). It is this type of criminal thinking that is often their downfall because their excessive confidence leads to a lapse in judgement leading to carelessness that exposes their misdeeds (Wells, 2012). Securities offender Jordan Belfort, known as the Wolf of Wall Street, never worried about the SEC, occasionally worried about the FBI and laughed at the thought of being questioned by the National Association of Securities Dealers (Rubin, 2014). Fraud offender Mark Whitacre from Archer Daniels Midland Co. who created fraudulent invoices for expense reimbursements stated: "I wasn't worried about the internal auditors catching the fraudulent activity that myself or some of my co-workers were involved with…all they would do if they caught a fraud like that would be to go to management. I didn't have any cover-up when I submitted these invoices, I simply signed them and it got processed" (Wells, 2012, p. 54).

Sentimentality

Sentimentality is the trait of doing good deeds to make up for bad acts; a way to mitigate the negative byproduct of criminal, antisocial acts. How is this trait displayed in the context of white-collar offenders? The answer revealed itself well over a hundred years ago by previously mentioned Edward A. Ross in his book *Sin and Society* (1907) who wrote of the methods used by white-collar offenders then, especially those occupying the upper echelons of society and corporate management, to deflect attention away from their misconduct. Ross wrote of how they cloak themselves in "patriotism", "puts on the whole armor of good…with the breastplate of respectability", displays their "religiosity" at the "assemblies of the faithful", and engages in showy, "ostentatious philanthropy" (Ross, 1907). The strategies used then still hold true today. As Ross went on to observe, the white-collar offender straddles the "camps of good and evil" by convincing others of their goodness while engaging in the misconduct (Ross, 1907). One way that executives lessen the guilt of their fraud and to appear good to the public is in their belief that their actions helped other people and/or organizations through their charitable causes.

Philanthropic contributions are one popular method of constructing false integrity, however, the presence of philanthropic contributions is no guarantee that the company's reporting processes are honest or in compliance with accounting standards.By giving the appearance of virtue, the desired interpretation is to deflect any suspicion of fraud at their organization; in essence the virtuous one cannot be capable of criminal activity (Perri, 2013b). To answer this question is to again invoke the words of previously mentioned CFO Samuel Antar, who stated that white-collar criminals build 'walls of false integrity' around themselves such that they give the appearance of virtue while displaying traits of success through charitable giving. Samuel gave huge sums of money to charity to enhance public image stating:

> Fraudsters like myself, we build a whole world of respectability around ourselves. I gave money to a lot of charities while I was committing my fraud. My cousin Eddie, he gave a lot of money with his stolen money to a lot of charities. He gave a lot of money to politicians. He built wings on to hospitals and built a big aura of respectability around him and people were in awe of him. This is what fraudsters do (Antar, 2005).

These companies and their officers use the metaphor of the ledger rationalization in that the good they do should shave off some of the punishment they will receive for their fraud. So long as they were good at the impression management strategy that reflected they were good to the environment, strong on diversity, involved in the community and generous with charitable donations, their schemes and frauds were not a problem. Yet, do not equate social responsibility with virtue ethics. The fact that they are generous should not be extrapolated to mean they are above committing fraud because doing well is the distraction they create to deter suspicion, thus, "be very cynical about corporate generosity and social responsibility" (Jennings, 2007, p. 25). Many of the collapsed companies studied within this book were universally admired for their social responsibility; benign behaviors such as these create smokescreens to advance fraudulent and/or unethical corporate agendas (Jennings, 2006). Remember their actions may be altruistic, but their motives are self-interest. Convicted CEOs Ken Lay of Enron, Bernard Ebbers of WorldCom, and John Rigas of Aldephia, for example, controlled their image by engaging in the 'optics of virtue' by their associations with philanthropic causes, some publicly displaying their piety, and participating in civic organizations.

Attorneys for convicted former McKinsey & Company CEO Rajat Gupta, attempted to introduce evidence to the jury of the philanthropic work he had been involved with in order to convince them to not find him guilty of securities fraud (Antilla, 2012). John Rigas, founder and former CEO of Adelphia Corporation, was convicted for concealing $2.3 billion in liabilities from shareholders and making personal use of corporate funds. Although many of Rigases donations were made with Adelphia funds, at his sentencing Rigas pleaded for leniency and highlighted his charity work. The sentencing judge responded by stating, "To be a great philanthropist with other persons' money is not very persuasive" (Reh, 2005, p. 5). Convicted fraud offender Charles Wang of the company Computer Associates was reported to be a caring executive reportedly ended every meeting with his staff by talking about the charities he was working on (Cohen et al., 2010). A white-collar defendant's record of charitable works can be a powerful factor supporting a lenient punishment, even if the works were performed after being arrested, and are not particularly exceptional (Newcomer, 2010). For example, Bill Tomko pleaded guilty to one count of tax evasion for using his construction business to avoid paying over $200,000 of taxes on the construction of his multimillion-dollar home.

Although his offense carried between 12 to 18 months imprisonment, the judge sentenced him to one year of home confinement in his new mansion, plus probation and a large fine. One of the principal factors cited in the court's analysis was Tomko's involvement in exceptional charitable work and community activity such as Habitat for Humanity and helping needy families during holidays (Newcomer, 2010). William Thurston, vice president of Damon Clinical Laboratories, was found guilty of defrauding Medicare of more than five million dollars. Thurston was to be sent to prison, but the court sentenced him to three months incarceration and 24 months supervised release. The judge cited only two factors to justify his punishment, and one was Thurston's "exceptional" good works. Factually, the record showed that Thurston was a member of a church, gave 10 percent of his income, and devoted time every week to unpaid service with the church in a variety of positions. He was also helpful to his neighbors and at times had temporarily taken extended family members and others into his home. Nevertheless, the sentencing judge was later instructed to impose a harsher sentence of no less than 36 months imprisonment (Newcomer, 2010).

Fannie Mae was named the most ethical company in America in 2004 by *Business Ethics* magazine and yet by the end of 2005, its CEO was removed for what was called earnings manipulation crafted in an arrogant corporate culture (Jennings, 2009). AIG paid a billion dollar fine for earnings manipulation, but the former CEO Hank Greenburg ran in the best New York philanthropic circles elevating his perceived status as a benefactor (Jennings, 2006). Convicted Enron CFO Andrew Fastow gave away over $60,000 to charities in the Houston, Texas area alone (Bernstein, 2002). Furthermore, many men and women who engage in a lifetime of criminal behavior profess to be devout adherents to a religion, attend a church, mosque, or synagogue, read religious writings, quote scripture, and observe holidays; they also send their children to schools that are religiously affiliated (Samenow, 2016). Consider the case of convicted CEO of General Reinsurance Corporation, Ronald Ferguson, who faced a potential life sentence for helping American International Group deceive its shareholders.

Ronald told the judge that he wanted to get back to his seminary education to live his purpose which was "to serve others" (Antilla, 2012). Many criminals adorn their bodies with jewelry of a religious nature, while compartmentalizing their religious practices and beliefs from how they conduct themselves in their daily lives. For example, members of organized crime erect elaborate religious shrines in their homes, give generously to their churches, and participate in parish activities. Yet, this does not deter them from executing their adversaries or engaging in various criminal activities such as theft, fraud and murder to fund their nefarious lifestyles. How is it that these individuals commit brutal crimes while continuing to regard themselves as religious? Concrete in their thinking about religion, they do not develop a conceptual understanding of how religious principles apply to living day to day. Criminals are likely to be sincere while espousing religious teachings and engaging in specific practices, such as attending church, lighting candles, and observing religious holidays, but their "religiosity" is not translated into how they treat other people (Samenow, 2016).

Some criminals turn to religion during periods of sentimentality especially when they are imprisoned due to having time on their hands, or when attending religious gatherings. Religion, like sentimentality, does not consistently deter criminal thinking or actions, but supports their self-image as a good and decent person (Samenow, 2016). Whatever forms a criminal's religiosity takes, it provides a boost to his view that, overall, he is truly a good person while begging God to get them out of trouble they have created for themselves or pleading to a sentencing judge for leniency (Samenow, 2016). A criminal may be sincere when being pious and espousing noble intentions, but their sincerity is superficial as it is overcome by their desire for power and control over others to satisfy a motive. Good intentions evaporate as they devise new schemes and maneuvers toward self-serving objectives. Convicted WorldCom CEO Bernard Ebbers donated more than $100 million to various charities, though approximately $35 million was related to his WorldCom stock, which had appreciated due to financial statement fraud (Perri, 2013b). Ebbers raised record sums of money for Mississippi College, arranged scholarships for local children, aided local businesses, and gave to churches. WorldCom and Ebbers were revered by the community for their generosity to colleagues and charities in Mississippi (Jennings, 2004) while Ebbers considered himself an ethical leader and a religious Baptist man (Palmer, 2016, p. 275). Ebbers would start each board meeting with a prayer, "a tradition that especially endeared older Mississippians, many of whom had invested their life savings in WorldCom stock" (Jeter, 2003, p. 91). We will observe the use of religion by other fraud offenders throughout this and other chapters to come as a reflection of sentimentality.

Social Identification

Consider how people may identify with others who display antisocial personalities to the point of wanting to be like them (Boduszek & Hyland, 2011a). What is considered positive, constructive, and valued in society is rejected while the antisocial traits are considered desirable. In other words, personal values begin to reflect an adopted identity which mirrors the antisocial traits of others or groups that a person hopes to emulate, whether it is at home or at work. This is how organized crime, for example, is able to recruit people who support their organization; belonging to the group is a form of social identity. People who identify with terrorists will behave like terrorists by adopting terrorist attitudes, beliefs, emotional displays, and value systems (Boduszek & Hyland, 2011a). Criminal identification establishes mutual agreement among members who have similarly agreed, as a group, to reject conventional models of social norms. The criminal self-image/identity derives from the process of rejecting individual(s) who are not associated with their antisocial norms. They define themselves by what they represent, and by what they reject, which are norms valued by society. Thus, once the antisocial identity is adopted, members socialize with other in-group members to express their conformity.

It may not take much persuasion to have someone become antisocial because the process of identification will lead someone to adopt those attitudes and voluntarily commit acts without coercion. That sense of belonging and encouragement from the group will be an impetus to engage in crimes the group approves of. However, how one behaves in a group setting does not mean that they will behave in that manner in all situations or in different group settings. Thus, the way one might behave within an organized crime setting may not be the same when they are at home. They may engage in notorious acts when carrying out the expectations of the group, but display love and affection with their families. This is why we see the compartmentalization of people's lives by how they identify themselves in each given setting. They may be moral and honest at home, but when placed in a work environment, what they believe is expected of them changes who they are because they now identify with the values and attitudes of the group. One day they might contribute to a church fund raising effort because they identify with the goodness represented by the church and the next day they might go to work and engage in financial statement fraud, bribery, or kickbacks. Again, they display a different identity for different realities. The application of virtue is not always constant, but situational depending on what is at stake and what trade-offs people are willing to make. We will examine this issue of self-identification more in depth in upcoming chapters.

Finding examples of social identification to antisocial personalities is challenging, but it can be illustrated. Consider that in the 1987 Oliver Stone film *Wall Street*, Stone portrayed Michael Douglas as the financial "Master of the Universe" character Gordon Gekko. As an unapologetic corporate raider and inside securities trader, Gekko delivered a famous, frequently-quoted monologue at a stakeholders meeting where he described the philosophy now equated to the financial industry: "Greed, for lack of a better word, is good. Greed is right, greed works. Greed clarifies, cuts through, and captures the essence of the evolutionary spirit. Greed, in all of its forms, greed for life, for money, for love, knowledge, has marked the upward surge of mankind." Michael Douglas expressed his astonishment at the many Wall Street employees who have sought him out in public places just to say—"Man, I want to tell you, you are the biggest reason I got into the business. I watched Wall Street, and I wanted to be Gordon Gekko" (Lewis, 2010, p. 126). Consider the statement by convicted hedge fund manager Seth Tobias, "I remember when I saw the movie in 1987. I recall saying, that's what I want to be. I want to start out as Bud Fox and end up as Gordon Gekko" (Lewis, 2010, p. 126). The film's equally perplexed screenwriter, Stanley Weiser, has made the same point, in a different way, "We wanted to capture the hyper-materialism of the culture…That was always the intent of the movie not to make Gordon Gekko a hero" (Lewis, 2010, p. 126).

Previously-mentioned CEO Michael Monus of Phar-Mor from chapter two encouraged a form of hero worship. Patrick Finn, for example, the CFO who collaborated with Monus, called Monus "his god" resulting in a blind loyalty to Monus whose orders were followed without any real checks or balances (Cohen et al., 2010, p. 285). According to CFO Samuel Antar of Crazy Eddies commenting on his cousin and CEO Eddie Antar, "Eddie was a godlike figure to me. We all looked up to him like a leader. He worked out with weights; he carried himself like a prince or something; he was just charismatic" (Tschakert, 2017, p. 711). When one understands that offenders come from different walks of life, criminals socially identify with similar others they want to emulate regardless of the crime classification or the criminal's socioeconomic background: they could be Mafia bosses, gang leaders, corrupt management or the Gordon Gekko's of the world (Perri, 2013b).

The Case of ImClone CEO Sam Waksal

One of the first fraud offenders to be convicted during the major fraud scandals of the early 2000s, in addition to Enron and WorldCom executives, was Sam Waksal, founder and CEO of ImClone. Dr. Waksal was convicted and sent to prison for the same insider trading scandal that involved celebrity Martha Stewart. As the CEO of ImClone, he sold an interest in a new cancer drug to Bristol-Meyer for $2 billion, but it was contingent on the Food and Drug Administration's (FDA) approval of the sale (Albrecht et al., 2012). When the FDA did not approve the sale because clinical data on its risks were questionable, Waksal feared that ImClone's stock price would go down once the news became public. Based on insider knowledge, Waksal could not sell his shares, but attempted to transfer seventy-nine thousand ImClone shares that belonged to him to his daughter in order to avoid the appearance of insider trading. The daughter would then sell the shares and it was Waksal's belief that he did nothing wrong because he did not conduct the sale. He said, "I could sit there at the same time thinking I was the most honest CEO that ever lived. And at the same time, I could glibly do something and rationalize it because I cut a corner, because I didn't think I was going to get caught (Albrecht et al., 2012, p. 51).

The day before the FDA's negative news was released, Waksal's father and daughter sold substantial numbers of ImClone stock based on Waksal's tip to them. In addition, the SEC discovered that the day Waksal was trying to unload his shares, he bought a series of 'put options' on his own stock through a Swiss intermediary. In other words, Waksal placed bets against ImClone; the worse ImClone stock did, the more money he made from the put-options. The put-options were a hedge, or insurance policy so that even if Waksal could not sell his ImClone Stock to avoid a loss, he could avoid a bigger loss by off-setting declines in ImClone stock value with gains from put-options (Farrell, 2006). With respect to a psychological tendency, known as moral equilibrium, people tend to keep a running scorecard on their ethical self-image (Prentice, 2014). Thus, when they perceive they have a moral deficit, they try to make up for it by accumulating 'moral compensation,' and if they believe they have a moral surplus, they might give themselves permission to deviate, or moral license (Anand et al., 2004). Moral equilibrium parallels the metaphor of the ledger rationalization. The moral rationalization process helps explain why people are willing to engage in moral deviations through flexible moral reasoning while still being able to maintain a sense of their own morality.

Consider the statement Waksal made during a television interview on the news program *60 Minutes* where he suggests that he had done so much good with his drug company, there might have been a degree of moral license for him to benefit from illegal insider trading (Leung, 2003). Waksal stated, "The day I was arrested was a horrible day in my life...It is very difficult for someone who thinks about himself as someone who does good things for society to be led away, in handcuffs, and thought about as a common criminal" (Leung, 2003). We may perceive the law or the provisions of a code of ethics as being vague, complex, inconsistent, rarely enforced, or merely politically-motivated, thus we can rationalize that there is nothing wrong or unethical when we contravene it. For this rationalization, the offender believes that they really did nothing seriously wrong and are being singled out unfairly by those who are charging them with acting improperly, especially when no one else is being punished for doing the same thing (Heath, 2008). In the same *60 Minutes* interview, Waksal displays this rationalization by stating he was unfairly targeted by the U.S. government due to the simplicity of his case, along with his profile and association with Martha Stewart stating, "I know that I would have, at another point in time, gone to court...And I doubt that the U.S. attorney, absent other situations, would have ever taken that case to court. This was done because the U.S. attorney was trying to make an example out of me" (Leung, 2003).

In other cases, we might rationalize that a certain prohibition only applies to other people and not to ourselves, especially when we are well connected, wealthy, or powerful. This is known as the entitlement rationalization. Waksal appears to believe that he deserved special treatment permitting him to engage in insider trading so that he could live in extravagance which is reflective of the antisocial trait of entitlement (Farrell, 2006). Waksal states, "what difference does it make that I do a couple of things that aren't exactly kosher?...I think, in that way, there may have been an arrogance where I didn't have to deal with details—that these details were meant for other people, not for me" (Leung, 2003). Waksal went on to state, "Did I know that I had committed an illegal act? Yeah, I knew. I tried to rationalize beyond rationality that I hadn't...It was sort of playing with linguistics. But I knew" (Leung, 2003). As Waksal's former colleague observed, "Cutting corners for Sam was like substance abuse. He did it in every aspect of his life, throughout his entire life" (Albrecht et al., 2012, p. 51).

Behavioral Traits of Corrupt Leadership

> Until society learns about the psychology of white-collar crime and the tactics used by criminals to defraud their victims, society is doomed to be victimized over and over again by ruthless thugs like I was, as the criminal CFO of Crazy Eddie.
>
> CFO Samuel Antar (2010).

In Sutherland's research on white-collar crime, he did not study the individual offender per se, but instead focused on corporate wrongdoing (Van Slyke et al., 2016). However, Sutherland "repeatedly used the belief in the psychological normality of the white-collar criminal as an argument against the psychological explanation of crime" rejecting the notion that individual personality traits served as a risk factor as to whether someone decided to engage in crime or not regardless of the crime classification (Coleman, 2002, p. 184). Sutherland further believed "the assumption that an offender must have some pathological distortion of the intellect or the emotions seems to be absurd, and if it is absurd regarding the crimes of businessmen, it is equally absurd regarding the crimes of persons of the lower classes" (Cohen et al., 1956, p. 96). In Sutherland's view, individual involvement in white-collar crime resulted from exposure to the cultural values of the worlds of business and finance (Benson & Manchak, 2014). Through the processes of learning from others on how to behave, business people come to accept and adopt behaviors that are favorable to violations of the law in the form of white-collar crimes. Thus, in Sutherland's view, white collar crime is primarily the product of a deviant culture and not the result of deviant individuals (Benson & Manchak, 2014).

Sutherland initially supported a multidisciplinary approach to explain criminal behavior, including psychology and psychiatry, but in his later years he became increasingly rigid in that he rejected any explanation that was outside his own discipline (Laub & Sampson, 1991). Since sociological crime theory focused on organizational causation while ignoring individual differences, Sutherland adhered to the belief that individual psychological differences are inadequate to explain criminality (Lesha & Lesha, 2012). The majority of white-collar crime scholarship followed Sutherland's anti-psychological position (Perri et al., 2014). As a result of this tradition, little research explored the psychological traits of white-collar criminality despite the fact that it dwarfs street-level crime in terms of financial costs (Lesha & Lesha, 2012). For example, most sociologists have a long-standing aversion to individual behavioral explanations for white-collar crime in that "they are either ignored or ridiculed" (Rowe & Osgood, 1984, p. 526).

We observe this sentiment in how scholars phrase their questions about this offender class: "Why do psychologically normal individuals, who share the conventional value-consensus of the society in which they live, sometimes take advantage of opportunities to engage in criminal conduct?" (Heath, 2008, p. 602). Indeed, white-collar offenders have long been assumed to not harbor personal pathologies that seem so common in street-level offenders, thus the psychological makeup of these offenders was not thought to be an important dimension of white-collar crime scholarship (Benson, 2015). As a result, "the psychology of white-collar offenders is not a subject on which researchers have invested much effort" (Simpson & Weisburd, 2012, p. 177). Consequently, the sparse empirical scholarship by the behavioral sciences has failed to examine the potential implications of personality's role as a white-collar offender behavioral risk factor giving rise to misperceptions about this offender class. Although white-collar offenders, as a whole, appear not to display symptoms of major psychiatric disorders such as hallucinations, delusions, or neurotic compulsions, it does not mean that they do not harbor personality traits that facilitate an offender's decision to commit fraud (Coleman, 2002). Yet, Sutherland's view dominated theory and research on white-collar crime for decades and as with most theories of criminal behavior, his belief that all criminality is a learned behavior simply does not provide a comprehensive understanding of the potential risk factors relating to white-collar offending (Benson & Manchak, 2014).

In particular, the theory falls short because it implicitly assumes that everyone responds in the same way to cultural and situational influences and ignores evidence that people differ in their susceptibility to such forces (Benson & Manchak, 2014). Moreover, it gives no guidance as to who is most likely to be susceptible to criminogenic environments or to seek out such contexts simply because they afford opportunities for offending (Benson & Manchak, 2014). The assumptions that white-collar offenders are psychologically normal and that individual differences have little or nothing to do with white-collar crime is misguided. Sutherland's rejection of psychological factors was premature and more recent research suggests that an increased focus on the behavioral aspects of white-collar offenders is essential to better understand, predict, and control white-collar offending (Perri et al., 2014). Insights of criminal psychiatrist Dr. Walter Bromberg dampen interdisciplinary squabbles as to who should be in charge of understanding criminality. Dr. Bromberg, a contemporary of Sutherland, believed that debates should not revolve around which discipline, behavioral science or sociology, has the complete answer to explaining criminal behavior, but what contribution each discipline can make in the explanation of such behavior that the other discipline may not be able to explain (Bromberg, 1948). His book *Crime and the Mind*, in which he referenced both Edwin Sutherland and psychiatrist Dr. Hervey Cleckley who pioneered work in psychopathy, displayed the type of spirit encouraged toward this understudied crime classification and its offenders:

> The psychological approach to crime does not minimize the extensive and valuable contributions from related fields of investigation in the evaluation of factors in crime. Sociology has not only traced and described the influence of unfavorable environmental and cultural factors in producing crime; it has as well supplied a mighty stimulus for the development of prevention and treatment techniques.

> The sociologist will continue to demonstrate these potent environmental factors and to bring about further amelioration of situations which society cannot afford to neglect. It is the responsibility of the psychiatric criminologist, however, to describe and delineate the emotional mechanisms which play a specific role in the criminal reactions of maladjusted individuals to their social background (Bromberg, 1948, p. 4).

In addition, the past several decades has revealed white-collar crime scandals both within organizations and those committed by individuals targeting victims cause enormous damage, both financially and emotionally. Scholars have offered opinions on what offender personalities may consist of especially those that ended up achieving notoriety from extensive media coverage due to their socioeconomic status and the senior management positions they held in organizations. Yet, behavioral scientists have not offered an in-depth, well-defined, and well-understood psychological characteristic or a set of characteristics that are diagnostic about fraud offender propensity (Ramamoorti, 2008). That being said, while research investigating the relationship between offender personalities and fraud has been scarce, there has been thoughtful research clarifying the key role of executive personality traits in the likelihood of financial statement fraud which we will explore (Rijsenbilt & Commandeur, 2013). Empirical data that would help formulate and drive scholarship toward explaining their behavioral traits is virtually negligible when compared to non-white-collar offenders (Perri, 2011a). For various reasons, it is difficult to get access to white-collar offenders while in prison to study their personalities (Benson & Manchak, 2014).

Of course, corporations are unlikely to be open to having their employees' personality and thinking scrutinized, and smart individuals are quick to pick up on the unspoken goals of a research study and may thus be less willing to report honestly on traits that are generally perceived as negative (Benson & Manchak, 2014). Researchers will need to develop new and innovative strategies to improve access to white-collar offenders and increase the accuracy with which they can describe them from a psychological perspective, perhaps by visiting them while in prison. The attention to individual behavioral traits and thinking patterns must also be at the forefront of understanding the risk factors facilitating white-collar crime. Fortunately, over the past several decades, criminology has taken a decisive turn toward individual differences, especially in regard to their psychological and criminal thinking traits, as important explanatory risk factors in understanding antisocial behavior. Furthermore, we find both intriguing and concerning the possibility that certain personality traits may promote both occupational success in organizations and criminal tendencies at the same time. Of course, this does not mean that leaders of corporate America are all corrupt, but it does suggest that being corrupt may not necessarily disqualify one from entering the higher ranks of the corporate world—harboring criminal thinking traits and displaying the appearance of operating as a productive citizen do coexist (Benson & Manchak, 2014).

Research suggests that personality traits play a key role in the likelihood of financial statement fraud (Cohen et al., 2010). Personality traits are correlated to white-collar offenders reoffending behaviors especially their inability to control their urges or delay their gratification (Van Slyke et al., 2016). Research indicates not only that personality and thinking processes are important to understanding the psychology of white-collar offending, but also that they may be differentially expressed across white-collar offenders (Benson & Manchak, 2014). Moreover, trivializing individual behavioral pathologies and perceiving them as normal disturbances is detrimental in an organization that is already displaying bullying, toxic behaviors, aggression, and undiagnosed or misdiagnosed pathologies in leaders and their followers—all precursors to ever-escalating organizational dysfunction including white-collar crime (Gudmundsson & Southey, 2011).

Understanding Personality

Before defining personality disorder, it may be helpful to consider what is meant by the term personality. Although there is not yet a consensus about the definitive structure of what personality consist of, most modern explanations of personality suggest that it comprises a number of broad characteristics that could be used to describe an individual. For example, are they friendly or antagonistic, empathetic or exploitative, deceitful or trustworthy (NOMS, 2015)? Personality defines us as individuals and provides a framework for how we relate to others and our environment; how we perceive, think, experience, and express emotions. Personality is the relatively stable and enduring aspect of individuals which distinguishes them from others and forms the foundation for predictions concerning their future behavior—it remains fairly consistent over a lifetime. While personality defines how we react and interact with others, it is important not to confuse personality with behavior. Personality is who we are, and behavior is what we do, yet personality does influence how we behave.

245

For someone's personality to be considered disordered, it must be problematic, persistent, and pervasive (NOMS, 2015). For a personality disorder to be present, the individual's personality characteristics need to be outside the norm for the society in which they live; that is they are problematic not only for the person who exhibits the disorder, but also for those who interact with them. Personality disorder symptoms usually emerge in adolescence or early adulthood, are inflexible and relatively stable and persist into later life. Those who have personality disorders display a rigidity or inflexibility in their thinking, feeling, and behaviors that impairs them from functioning with others in a larger societal context. A disordered personality causes a pervasive disturbance in a person's ability to manage his or her emotions, maintain a stable sense of self and identity, and prevents them from maintaining healthy relationships at work, with family, and friends (Webster, 2016). Symptoms that might indicate the presence of a personality disorder, for example, would be if the individual is callous, lacks emotions, has a difficult time controlling their behavior, is hostile toward others, displays an attitude of superiority, and/or acts highly suspicious. While these symptoms could be present in the general population, a disordered personality is unusual or extreme to the point where it deviates from societal expectations of appropriateness. They self-sabotage their own well-being or that of others while hindering healthy interpersonal functioning (NOMS, 2015).

In contrast to personality disorders, mental illness is characterized by a probability of a biochemical imbalance that may act as a catalyst for the individual to behave in an inexplicable, erratic way that has no connection to logic, such as cause and effect. While we all possess a range of both adaptive and maladaptive personality traits to varying degrees, individuals displaying personality disorders are likely to possess higher numbers of problematic personality traits and experience them to more extreme degrees (NOMS, 2015). For example, an individual with a narcissistic personality disorder may be unusually grandiose and entitled, while an individual with an antisocial personality disorder may be deceitful, exploitative, and prone to rule-breaking (NOMS, 2015). It may therefore be helpful to think of disordered personalities, and the difficulties encountered due to their rigidity in how they interact with others, as existing along a continuum, with adaptive personality functioning at one end and personality disorder at the other end.

One way to understand and contextualize disordered personalities is to observe how they function in everyday life, since personality is reflected by how a person copes with stressful situations, personal concerns, motives, and consequences of particular traits (Livesley & Jang, 2005). An individual can infer much about another's personality by how they react to criticism; can they react in a way that is not aggressive and insulting? In reality, there can be harmful outcomes to some personality traits; are they capable of adapting to life expectations in a way that is not harmful to oneself and others? How do they react to life tasks and situations for others and themselves? In addition, is there a capacity for intimacy? Can they establish quality, cooperative, and stable interpersonal relationships? Do they engage in prosocial behaviors? Those with disorders are more readily recognizable because their behaviors are more predictable due to personality rigidity and this may be observable by corrupt corporate leadership that harbors a particular type of personality such as narcissism.

Disordered personalities can be predictable because they cannot undue their rigid styles of reacting to specific triggers. For example, while leadership should encourage feedback, a leader who has a personality disorder may avoid seeking input from subordinates if they are hypersensitive to feedback in general because they cannot fathom being wrong about a particular decision (Livesley & Jang, 2005). They are simply not flexible enough to display diverse reaction patterns to provocation triggers, or capable of mitigating their harmful behaviors to others and themselves. Thus, they may punish those who express opinions that are true and that could be helpful to others. As we observe, personality disorders among white-collar offenders parallel those found with street-level offenders (Van Slyke et al., 2016).

The Dark Triad, White-collar Crime and Leadership

The dominant historical focus of leadership theory has been on the identification of the factors contributing to leader effectiveness, not behavior that would otherwise be considered inappropriate. The very notion that the behavior of business leaders could be linked to the traits inherent in the psychological profile of individuals displaying antisocial dispositions has received limited attention in white-collar crime literature

(Gudmundsson & Southey, 2011). However, research in the area of destructive personalities has identified at least three dark disordered personalities that are relevant to business-related outcomes. Thus, the attitudes and behaviors of such individuals, especially those in leadership positions, may be the most difficult to realign with company or societal goals because of the potential for misconduct (Jones & Hare, 2015). The destructive leadership stream includes research examining the personalities of Machiavellianism, narcissism, and psychopathy that constitute what are known as the 'dark triad' (Paulhus & Williams 2002). The dark triad personality traits linked to fraud offender personalities include Machiavellianism, narcissism, self-centeredness, egoism, disagreeableness, competitiveness, manipulativeness, antagonism, and hostility (Lesha & Lesha, 2012).

As noted, the literature suggests that certain personality traits found among white-collar offenders facilitate both white-collar offending and success in some types of organizational settings that financially reward dark triad traits such a competitiveness and manipulativeness that many find problematic. If it exists, this sort of interaction between personality traits and the environmental context of white-collar crime is a potentially very important facet of the white-collar crime phenomenon (Benson & Manchak, 2014). The general weakness of the research on white-collar offenders is that they are often studied in isolation from the organizational context in which so many of them are situated. As a result, while there is a large body of research on organizational behavior and a growing body of research on the psychological characteristics of white-collar offenders, to date research that systematically explores the interaction between organizational characteristics and white-collar offending by individual organizational participants is scant (Benson & Manchak, 2014).

The problem currently experienced is that it is unclear within an organizational setting to what extent are unethical or illegal behaviors accomplished through coercive and manipulative techniques are the result of the influence of psychopathy, narcissism, Machiavellianism, or a combination thereof. Consider that manipulation is viewed in the dark triad concept as an unemotional means to an end; in essence being callously manipulative. Manipulation can also be viewed as the deliberate act of attempting to create a favorable outcome through the calculated use of actions and words. Manipulation often requires an awareness of another's values or weaknesses to facilitate exploitation. Thus manipulation does require the ability to interpret another's emotional state. The overlapping traits shared by Machiavellianism, narcissism, and psychopathy are callousness and selfishness (Furnham et al., 2013). All three traits contain a degree of malevolency that directly influences the type of interpersonal behavior (O'Boyle et al., 2012). Although dark triad traits may help people to get ahead, they do not necessarily help people get along with others—key to life success for these individuals is manipulation of others for self-advancement. Dark triad personalities are considered toxic and antagonistic as they share an exploitive behavioral style, striving for self-beneficial goals at the expense of or at least without regard for communal welfare and others (Rauthmann, 2011).

Hence, dark personalities' demeanor in social situations is often marked by coldhearted, self-beneficial, antagonistic, and manipulative behaviors coupled with the fact that narcissism, Machiavellianism, and psychopathy have been linked to financial misbehaviors in business, counter-productive work place behaviors, and white-collar crime (Jones, 2014). These traits are linked to making selfish financial decisions with other people's money and are likely to risk those assets for personal gain (Jones, 2014). Although these personalities traits exist among corrupt leaders who engage in corporate fraud, it is not always clear what personality category is more predominate than others to explain offender behavior given that there is overlap among categories (Perri et al., 2014). For example, narcissists' inflated view of self, coupled with delusions of grandeur, creates a desire to self-promote and engage in attention-seeking behaviors. For those high in psychopathy, a disregard for societal norms, rules, and laws leads to antisocial behavior, while Machiavellians' beliefs about the gullibility of and lack of concern for others' rights facilitates manipulative behaviors as a desired interpersonal strategy (O'Boyle et al., 2012).

Dark triad individuals may temper their aggression to allow for less overtly antagonistic strategies to work (Jones & Neria, 2015). Yet, dark traits may emerge during periods of stress where they lack the mental resilience necessary to control impulsive behaviors or adhere to social norms, rules, and expectations (Harms & Spain, 2015). Individuals that possess dark triad traits are often preoccupied with dominance and power, and will

247

use aggressive tactics such as manipulation to get whatever they think they are entitled to. Dark triad leaders are not able to relate well with others; they lack empathy, fail to conform, display reckless disregard for the needs of others, and use people to gain personal advantage while harboring a lack of accountability. Dark triad characteristics and behaviors have been normalized, tolerated, and even valued among corporate offenders because the traits these individuals display are desired by this type of leader who sets the tone at the top. If corporations reflect their flawed leaderships' personalities, it is not surprising if they are not concerned with the morality of harmful decisions. Instead, they focus on creating a socially-desirable appearance, and projecting an image that portrays them as concerned, caring, and responsible organizations (Pardue et al., 2013b).

Maintaining a good reputation and presenting the appearance of virtue, ethics, and morality is advantageous for corporations, while actual social responsibility compromises profit maximization (Pardue, et al., 2013b). Moreover, they rely on public relations firms and business-sponsored policy institutions to produce misleading facts, opinion pieces, expert analysis, opinion polls, and mail and phone solicitations to generate public advocacy and image-building campaigns (Pardue, et al., 2013b). Dark triad personalities can interfere with relationships and judgement where such individuals can have good social skills but conceal a counterproductive nature, such as using intimidation and aggression to discourage disagreement (Kaiser et al., 2015). They may attempt to break rules cautiously, while being hostile to others due to a cynical worldview: a dog-eat-dog view where someone has to win and someone has to lose (Jones & Neria, 2015). Some individuals solve problems through prosocial means, such as striving to uphold the public good and displaying conscientious behaviors, while others, especially those displaying dark triad traits, use antisocial interpersonal strategies to satisfy their motives (O'Boyle et al., 2012).

Within this section, each personality type is applied to fraud offenders as a risk factor, especially in leadership positions, in order to provide a more thorough template to explain potential destructive leadership leading to misconduct should it become evident. The author cautions that much more research is needed in refining the dark triad concept, however, its importance cannot be overstated given the behavioral patterns that start to reveal themselves when we exam leadership and its relation to organizational dysfunction ultimately leading to corporate fraud. It is fair to say that the evidence that starts to develop cannot simply be considered an anomaly to ignore just because more research is needed.

Machiavellianism: An Overview

The concept of Machiavellianism is named after the author of the book, *The Prince* (1513), Niccolo Machiavelli, in which the medieval author outlined governance principles to maintain power, observing that the "ends justify the means." Machiavellianism has been equated, perhaps erroneously, to the belief that it is necessary to practice an amoral quality to decision making in that what is important is the end goal and not how the end goal is attained. Yet, it is overly simplistic to look at the ethics of Machiavelli and state that they are always amoral in nature, however he did believe that applying one's morality to decision making could be dogmatic, impractical and irresponsible (Harris, 2010). Machiavelli did not advocate for brutal or indeed devious actions as the norm, because virtue was important to Machiavelli, but not to the point that one is to be taken advantage of by those that are not virtuous. At times private morality must be sacrificed to maintain authority, thus in instances such as defending a country under attack, Machiavelli entertained an amoral approach to decision making in order to survive (Harris, 2010). The application of the Machiavellian concept drew the attention of researchers in psychology and management based on Machiavelli's principles as they relate to everyday life circumstances and their application in a corporate setting (Christie & Geis, 1970).

The Machiavellian concept is defined by three sets of interrelated values: a) an avowed belief in the effectiveness of manipulative tactics in dealing with other people, b) endorsing a cynical worldview and untrustworthy view of human nature, and c) an amoral outlook that puts expediency and self-interest above virtue. By amoral we mean being unconcerned with the rightness or wrongness about a given scenario. A Machiavellian personality describes an amoral attitude or a viewpoint where the ends justify the means regardless of whether the means to achieve the ends were ethical or legal (Ray, 2007). Machiavellianism is a manipulative personality characterized by a lack of empathy, possessing an unconventional view of morality, a willingness to manipulate, lie to, and exploit others. Exploitation of others is especially enticing when it involves the weak and gullible while taking a certain pleasure from successfully deceiving others (Spain et al., 2013). In addition, Machiavellianism is a strategy of social interaction that involves manipulating others for personal gain while, at times, displaying ethical behaviors even though they privately hold fewer moral beliefs due to harboring an unethical and deceitful value system. They have little trust in others and believe that others do not trust them (Den Hartog & Belschak, 2012). Whereas they clearly seek to manipulate situations, Machiavellians perceive that others are doing the same as well (Christie & Geis, 1970).

Machiavellians also view others unfavorably where in their cynical and misanthropic worldview, people are weak and fallible. Indeed, their cool detachment and pragmatic tough-mindedness entails a cynical worldview where one must manipulate others before others have a chance to manipulate them (Rauthmann, 2011). Machiavellians think of themselves as skillful manipulators of others, however a willingness to manipulate does not necessarily coincide with the ability to manipulate. They are likely driven to pursue goals such as wealth, power, and status, while displaying a lack of affection, general distrust, and control of others in interpersonal relationships (Dahling et al., 2009). In addition, they see the reliance on ethics, rules, and morality as being naïve, impractical and quite frankly irresponsible behavior if being ethical does not benefit them. Their true self is not always obvious to others because Machiavellians are able to show both ethical behaviors and unethical behaviors at the same time to achieve their goals; they do not always engage in unethical, deceptive practices. They are adaptable and willing to exercise ethical behaviors if it gets them closer to their goals, thus if the means necessary to achieve the ends need to be ethical, then so be it (Den Hartog & Belschak, 2012).

Machiavellians have an amoral manipulative quality in that they are adaptive and if they perceive that doing so will accelerate their goals and interests, they may engage in pro-organizational, good citizenship behavior in a friendly and cooperative manner that is visible to supervisors (Sendjaya et al., 2014). Machiavellians may respond positively and appropriately to the realignment of personal with organizational goals using long-term deception and cautious planning when executing their selfish goals (Mathieu, et al., 2012). Such individuals are bottom-line focused and their deception is difficult to detect because these individuals remain dormant with respect to antisocial activity as long as their personal interests coincide with those of the organization (Mathieu et al., 2012).

Machiavellianism and Corporate Fraud

In Niccolo Machiavelli's view, to be a leader, it is not necessary to own all virtues such as goodness, integrity, a belief in fairness, and goodwill, but they must appear to outsiders as if they own them all. Thus, when it is useful to them, Machiavellian leaders appear merciful, trustworthy, humanitarian, faultless, and religious, but only up to a certain degree. They are always prepared, if required, to act exactly the opposite way suggesting that even a morally-righteous leader must make deliberate use of ruthless, amoral, and deceptive methods when dealing with unscrupulous people (Perri, 2013b). Understanding the application of Machiavellianism to management is based on studies of political and religious extremist groups, ultimately focusing on how the leaders of these groups manipulated subordinates to serve their needs (Christie & Geis, 1970). Although much more research is needed in this area, it seems that Machiavellianism does influence leadership behaviors, yielding a more directive style with less genuine interpersonal consideration (Dahling et al., 2009). Reputations for ethical leadership derive from acting both as a moral person and a moral manager.

The traits and behaviors associated with being a moral person and a moral manger, such as integrity, trustworthiness, showing concern for people, being open, and following ethical decision rules, are contradictory with the traits and behaviors associated with Machiavellianism. Ethical leadership is suppressed when they harbor Machiavellian qualities where they are unlikely to place much value on ethical behavior if it stands in the way of personal rewards (Den Hartog & Belschak, 2012). Machiavellians are emotionally detached from their decisions and engage in impression management to convince others of their goodness and friendliness or employ a coercive strategy to satisfy their motives (Den Hartog & Belschak, 2012). The reality is that ethical leadership is not always an authentic expression of truly held values because Machiavellians are able to simulate behaviors expected by non-Machiavellians (Den Hartog & Belschak, 2012). Machiavellian-type leaders will exhibit a high level of ethics if actions are helpful to the attainment of self-interest goals disguising their true identities, beliefs, and values to portray a public image that best serves their personal ambition.

Machiavellians are more likely to financially misrepresent information than non-Machiavellians, especially when opportunity and motive are present. They express less guilt than others who misrepresent financial information, and are inclined to rationalize misrepresentations and ultimately fraudulent behaviors (Murphy, 2012). Some of the most consistent research on Machiavellians suggests they are prone to engaging in a variety of behaviors that would be categorized as counter-productive work behaviors that harm the well-being of organizations such as white-collar crime (Furnham et al., 2013). Interestingly, convicted Enron CEO Jeffrey Skilling was known as "The Prince" and subordinates to Skilling were "instructed to read *The Prince* from beginning to end" (Tourish & Vatcha, 2005, p. 462). One former Enron executive read the book, which "helped in understanding better how to deal with Mr. Skilling [because] when Jeff started to take over, I felt like I was being eaten alive" (Schwartz, 2002b). Another former Enron vice president, in describing Enron's Machiavellian tone from the top where the ends justify the means stated, "You can break the rules, you can cheat, you can lie, but as long as you make money, it's alright" (Sims & Brinkmann, 2003, p. 250).

According to one study, business ethics professor Scott Reynolds examined why some managers recognize a situation as involving moral issues while others do not. His research suggests that when facing ethical dilemmas, managers either focus on the ends such as whether profit levels are attained or the means or methods as to how profits are attained (Reynolds, 2006). Although Reynold's research was not focused on understanding the link between Machiavellianism and management focus, the research does shed some light on how Machiavellian characteristics are displayed by management. Reynolds found that people who focus primarily on the ends acknowledge ethical issues when harm caused by their decisions is blatant, but are much less sensitive to ethical issues that seem to only involve a violation of the means such as someone lied, broke a promise, or violated a policy. As Reynolds went on to state, "ends-based decision-makers might be very surprised to know what others call or treat as ethical issues…You could say that ends-based decision-makers are 'blind' to those kinds of ethical issues" (Reynolds, 2006). When it appears that no harm is done, ends-based decision-makers are much less inclined to see an ethical issue within a decision.

Means-focused people, however, recognize potential harmful outcomes associated with the means used to achieve an end that should not be ignored (Reynolds, 2006). The results suggest means-based or process-based decision makers are affected by a much broader range of what they consider to be ethical issues. The findings suggest that when attempting to improve moral awareness in organizations, leaders should take the initiative to better educate managers about the moral value of rules, principles, and guidelines when considering how goals are to be achieved (Reynolds, 2006). Improving managers' appreciation for such guides increases their ability to access moral frameworks in the face of not just harmful situations, but also seemingly inconsequential violations of rules. This point is relevant because many financial scandals began with simple violations of professional norms such the application of inappropriate accounting standards and consulting practices, but the harm did not emerge until much later (Reynolds, 2006). With increased awareness, hopefully the ability to foresee how one's decisions unfold will be triggered impacting how one's behaviors play themselves out in the future.

Narcissism, Leadership and White-collar Crime

Narcissism is a broad personality construct displaying a pervasive pattern that defines an individual's view of self and the environment they interact with in terms of an exaggerated sense of self-importance, fantasies of unlimited success or power, need for admiration, entitlement, lack of empathy, exploitation of others, a belief that one is superior and unique, and prone to exaggerations such as inflated views of one's accomplishments and abilities. Understanding this personality type is important especially when considering how narcissism impacts leadership decisions on whether to engage in fraud or not. Narcissism should be viewed as a continuum where at one end is a healthy self-confidence and at the other is a pathological interference with one's ability to function normally and maintain meaningful relationships (Grant & McGhee, 2012). The dysfunction is related to how their narcissism causes friction in relationships due to their inability to empathize with others when needed. Narcissistic entitlement reflects the assumption that those who interfere with their narcissistic sense of preferential treatment can expect to be attacked in some form (Exline et al, 2004). Being attacked can range from verbal to physical abuse (Perri, 2011b).

Grandiosity has been described as central to narcissism, which is characterized by an excessive need for admiration, embellished abilities, arrogance, and exploitative tendencies toward others (Pardue et al., 2013b). Consider the statement of convicted CFO Samuel Antar who displayed the narcissistic trait of grandiosity by boasting about his criminal abilities stating, "If I were out of retirement today, I'd be bigger than Bernie Madoff" (McCartney, 2011). Narcissists, especially for those in management positions, have a high need for power and a low need for intimacy which explains why they tend to value status more than interpersonal relationships. Moreover, narcissism is related to viewing interpersonal relationships in a zero-sum manner where relationships are valued for status and not closeness (Miller et al., 2009). They tend to display a lack of concern for the welfare of others while viewing others as opportunities to control and exploit for self-gratification (Miller et al., 2009). Narcissists are likely to rationalize their unacceptable behaviors and attitudes, blame others for their mistakes, display self-absorption, and exhibit a sense of entitlement—they believe they have the right to exploit others (Grant & McGhee, 2012). They are more apt to respond to rewards and excitement and are prone to being insensitive to signs of punishment. Most individuals display some degree of narcissistic traits, but someone who is pathologically narcissistic is hypersensitive when faced with critical feedback that may actually be helpful.

Narcissistic people display higher rates of aggressive behavior against people who threaten their self-esteem because they are preoccupied with defending an image of themselves that may not be accurate (McCullough et al., 2003). They are likely to rely on unhealthy coping mechanisms to manage their behaviors, thus they may display an aggressive and antagonistic interpersonal style when responding to feedback (Pincus & Lukowitsky, 2009). Narcissists aggress because they are more prone to attribute hostile intent to the behavior of others when in fact there is no hostile intent. Criticism provokes them to unjustifiably lash out at others for not agreeing with them (Cleff et al., 2013). Predictably, we may observe a vicious cycle in that they respond to others' innocent statements in an antagonistic manner because they view such statements as a personal attack. This, in turn, prompts a negative reaction from the person making the innocent statement, which reinforces the narcissist's belief that they are a threat, thus innocents become targets (Miller et al., 2009). As a result of this heightened sensitivity, narcissists ruminate where they brood about their perceived injury and how to punish others for what they perceive to be a personal attack (McCullough et al., 2003).

Narcissism and Leadership

From a leadership perspective, narcissism can be useful, even necessary for leadership to occur and some scholars believe that the difference between good and bad leaders comes down to the distinction between healthy and unhealthy narcissism (Maccoby, 2000). There is strong evidence suggesting that people who are narcissistic are more likely to emerge as leaders precisely because of their desire for dominance, admiration, and grandiosity (O'Reilly, 2014). Partly as a reflection of this, studies of leader emergence as opposed to leader effectiveness, have shown that narcissists are more likely to be chosen as leaders than are non-narcissists. The narcissists, especially those in power prefer to dominate the space in which they participate—both on an individual and group level which explains why we find them in positions of power. Indeed, it is only to be "expected that many narcissistic people, with their need for power, prestige, and glamour, eventually end up in leadership positions" (Kets de Vries, 2003, p. 23). Healthy or productive, or what some call constructive narcissistic leaders, have a drive and vision for organizational success and work collectively with others to achieve goals and are confident in their ability to succeed (Regnaud, 2011).

Effective corporate leadership may be enhanced by individuals who exhibit productive narcissistic traits since they may be more willing to take risks that other executives in the same position might avoid, but that might be needed in a time of crisis (Maccoby, 2000). Narcissistic leaders help shape our "public and personal agendas", they can be visionaries in that they see the big picture leaving the detail to others, and when they do not like the rules, they might ignore, or even change them (Maccoby, 2000, p. 69). At times their visions are grand because they are inspired by a personal need for power, glory, and a legacy; through these grand visions, coupled with great charisma, they gain devoted followers. In turn followers fulfill the narcissistic leader's need for admiration further bolstering their confidence and conviction in their visions. Narcissistic leaders will make personal sacrifices in order to succeed coupled with being charismatic and skilled speakers (Dattner, 2004). According to Harry Levinson, a psychologist who directs the Levinson Institute that studies managers states, "A healthy narcissist knows what he's good at and knows to take advice about what he's not so good at…Their self-confidence is the basis of their charisma"…by contrast, unhealthy narcissists combine an almost grandiose sense of certainty with a disdain for subordinates (Coleman, 1990). Problems occur when the leader's level of narcissism leans more toward the pathological side versus the healthy, constructive side (Maccoby, 2000). Dr. Robert Hogan, a psychologist at the Tulsa Institute of Behavioral Sciences who has studied thousands of managers, believes that there is a dark side to some executives where they look good to their peers and their bosses, but turn out to be terrible for their companies observing,

> They are particularly good at ingratiating themselves with their seniors but brutalize their juniors…They act as though normal rules don't apply to them…they climb the corporate ladder quickly, they're outstanding at self-promotion. These are flawed managers, whose glittering image masks a dark destructive side…They end up being costly by creating poor morale, excessive turnover, and reducing productivity. Sometimes they can ruin a company altogether. Trouble occurs when charismatic leaders rise to the top, only to reveal personality flaws that mattered relatively little when they had less power (Coleman, 1990).

Narcissistic corporate leaders have a strong need for power, high self-confidence, and strong convictions, yet they tend to be overly sensitive to criticism, can be poor listeners, and lack empathy (Maccoby, 2000). Such leaders may find themselves prone to displaying embellished abilities, making exaggerated claims for a corporate vision, portraying images of uniqueness to manipulate audiences, suppressing negative information, and maximizing positive information (Tourish & Vatcha, 2005). As a result, "the vision in essence becomes so much a part of the leader's personality that they are unwilling or unable to consider information to the contrary" which can lead to suboptimal decision making (Kramer, 2003, p. 219). Furthermore, according to Dr. Hogan, good managers are easy to spot because "they have charisma, intelligence and a knack for strategic planning, [and] they have enormous charm and energy" (Coleman, 1990). However, because of their need for recognition, narcissists are more likely than others to self-promote to employ their skills in deception, manipulation, and intimidation in order to secure leadership positions, even those for which they are underqualified (Rosenthal & Pittinsky, 2006). They may be adept at gaining leadership positions, but this should not translate into exceptional leadership due to the risks involved. According to Dr. Maccoby:

> The danger is that narcissism can turn unproductive when, lacking restraining anchors and self-knowledge, narcissists become unrealistic dreamers. They nurture grand schemes and harbor the illusion that only circumstances or enemies block their success. This tendency toward grandiosity and distrust is their Achilles' heel. Because of it, even brilliant narcissists can come under suspicion for self-involvement, unpredictability, and – in extreme cases – paranoia (Maccoby, 2004, p. 94).

The narcissist's worldview is built largely on unrealistic fantasies of omnipotence illustrated by statements made by convicted Enron's CEO Jeffrey Skilling confirming this pattern: "We were doing something special. Magical. It wasn't a job—it was a mission. We were changing the world. We were doing God's work" (Perri, 2013, p. 335). Others have noted similar motivations by narcissistic leaders to maintain or enhance their standing in the organization include a personalized need for power (Padilla, Hogan, & Kaiser, 2007), a win-at-all-costs competitiveness that does not contemplate the possibility of defeat (Feeley 2006), and a view of competition as a zero-sum game where the narcissist can prevail only if competitors lose (Blair et al., 2008). Highly narcissistic CEOs make decisions in order to "maintain a positive sense of self, engage in ego-defensive behavior, and preserve their self-esteem" (Brown, 1997, p. 645). The published financial statements of their organizations are an ideal mechanism for narcissistic CEOs to satisfy their "intense need to have [their] superiority continually reaffirmed" (Chatterjee & Hambrick 2007, p. 354). This line of reasoning concurs with other scholars who state that finance has "greater narcissistic possibilities than other management functions" (Schwartz, 1991, p. 262). Financial accounting reports are "a mirror of the self" to serve the narcissistic needs of the CEO. In addition: "there is a preoccupation with fantasies involving unrealistic goals.

These goals may include achieving unlimited power or fame. The fantasies frequently substitute for realistic activity in pursuit of success…but even when the goals are satisfied, it is usually not enough; there is a driven "pleasureless" quality to the ambitions that cannot be satisfied" (Post, 1997, p. 200). Moreover, wide variation of narcissism exists among leaders, and while it can facilitate effective leadership, it can also manifest itself destructively (Rijsenbilt, 2011). Narcissism is correlated with destructive leadership (Padilla et al., 2007). Narcissists are strongly motivated to strive for external self-affirmation achieved by obtaining a steady stream of self-image reinforcement such as frequent praise and admiration (Buss & Chiodo, 1991). In order to obtain frequent praise and admiration, narcissistic CEOs must undertake challenging or bold actions which the audience can easily observe. They use their organizations as tools to satisfy their need for attention and are more likely to undertake bold actions without adequate reflection or risk assessment that may have beneficial or detrimental consequences for the organization. These offenders proclaim to have a strong sense of morality and ethics, but their actions reveal a different mindset. Given sufficient opportunity, narcissistic offenders will likely consolidate their power and authority to create an organizational culture that is not only supportive of unethical behavior but whose adherents share the leader's corrupt vision.

This organizational phenomenon is referred to as normalized corruption where senior management is obsessed with enhancing power and control; they are motivated by "a sense of entitlement to special privileges and resources" (Bucy et al., 2008, p. 416). Their need for power and control pushes them to the outer limits of ethical behavior, making them indifferent to conventional rules of conduct and more apt to take risks. These individuals lack the ability to put themselves in the place of others or envision that the consequences of their actions may fall on the shoulders of numerous other people including subordinates, shareholders and consumers as examples (Ablow, 2008). At times, even when they are caught and shown evidence of their wrong doing, narcissistic executives assume a defensive posture since they are so insulated from criticism, feedback, and reality checks that they remain defiant and detached from the excesses of their conduct until the end (Jennings, 2006). Their conduct was unchecked for so long they are incapable of introspection and no one can rein them back into reality. Furthermore, given their ability to manipulate others, they also have "a knack for establishing quick, superficial relationships that serves them well in organizational life" (Kets de Vries, 2003, p. 23).

It has also been shown that dimensions associated with narcissism were positively correlated with poor leadership performance (Regnaud, 2011). Narcissism has also been associated with poor manager ratings of interpersonal skills such as team building, sensitivity, confrontation effectiveness, and integrity. Narcissistic leaders can create a toxic work environment due to cold, distant social interactions and an inability to empathize with workers. Social praise is positively correlated with a CEO's level of risk-taking and as the level of narcissism increased, so did the level of risk-taking. This is consistent with an earlier study conducted by the same researchers which confirmed narcissistic CEOs favored making bold decisions that were visible and resulted in either extreme wins or extreme losses reflecting the consequences being erratic organizational performance (Chatterjee & Hambrick, 2007). They are more apt to make difficult decisions without being distracted by empathy, sadness, or guilt. While they may be gifted at encouraging dedication, it does not mean that there are bonds between the narcissist and the follower (Dattner, 2004). It may be that the bonding goes in one direction— from the follower to the narcissistic leader.

What is ironic is that narcissists are suspicious of very people they seek approval from which explains why they display paranoiac tendencies (Grant & McGhee, 2012). In addition, the threat of self-righteous and out of control rage in a leader is possible. They may exhibit vengeful hostility, or display disproportionate reactions to perceived provocations which, in turn, stimulate a desire for retaliation for the leader's aggression (Horowitz & Arthur, 1988). Whatever virtues narcissistic leaders bring to an organization, their traits of being exploitative and entitled need to be tempered (Rosenthal & Pittinsky, 2006). Although desirous of empathy from others, productive narcissists are not known for being particularly empathetic themselves. Indeed, lack of empathy is a characteristic shortcoming of some of the most charismatic and successful narcissists because empathy is not a required trait to communicate and inspire (Maccoby, 2000). In fact, in times of radical change, some consider a lack of empathy a strength because it is easier for them to make decisions that inevitably make many people angry, however such leaders typically have few regrets for their decisions (Maccoby, 2000). However, pathological narcissism occurs when one is unable to integrate the idealized beliefs one has about oneself with the realities of one's inadequacies. Narcissistic leaders resist advisers' suggestions, take more credit for successes than they are due, and blame others for their own failures and shortcomings (Rosenthal & Pittinsky, 2006). They are highly prone to lapses in professional judgment and personal conduct.

Moreover, because of their drive, narcissists make poor judgments and decisions with greater certainty and confidence. They lose sight of their goals when they become increasingly self-absorbed and defensive (Duchon & Drake, 2009). Research suggests narcissistic leaders, typically characterized by dominance, self-confidence, a sense of entitlement, grandiosity, and low empathy, can both positively and negatively influence organizations (O'Reilly et al., 2014). On the positive side, narcissists are more likely to be seen as inspirational, succeed in situations that call for change, and be a force for creativity. On the negative side, narcissistic leaders have been shown to be more likely to violate integrity standards, have unhappy employees, create destructive workplaces, and inhibit the exchange of information within organizations (O'Reilly, 2014). Narcissistic leaders can turn on followers when they inevitably do not get everything they ask for deciding their followers have forfeited the right to exist (Glad, 2002). Narcissistic leaders may succeed in the short-term, but over time, they destroy the systems that they and others depend on to survive and thrive. Contrasting narcissistic leadership with Machiavellianism, Machiavellian leaders are more rational actors capable of flexibility in their thinking and behavior while avoiding carelessness born of overconfidence (Glad, 2002). Narcissists' fantasies, grounded by desires, fears, and the need to maintain power, provide poor guides to action living under the illusion that others are obligated to serve them. Their own wishes take precedence; they believe they have the right to control, possess, and exploit others without remorse.

Consequently, centering on a leader's inclination towards disproportionate concern with their own glorification, or a naïve assumption that they can impose their will on others without consequence, can help us differentiate between leaders who are focused on themselves or others (Sheard, et al., 2013). The existence of narcissism at this level is no coincidence because successful managers typically exhibit narcissistic personality traits throughout their business careers (Barnard, 2008b). Thus, narcissistic CEOs sometimes lead their companies to initiate high-risk ventures and deliver volatile performance for their organizations. When those initiatives do not succeed, narcissistic CEOs are likely to be slow to recognize failure as attributable to their mistakes. Rather, they minimize them as controllable and seek to correct them through an increase in persistence and aggression which compounds the risk of throwing good money after bad (Barnard, 2008b). Even when they do not undertake high-risk initiatives or fail to end unsuccessful initiatives, narcissistic CEOs can still have a debilitating influence on their organizations due to their self-serving behavior (Rosenthal, n.d.).

This leads to frustration from senior managers whose views cannot get a fair hearing, development of an atmosphere of resentment and mistrust, cynicism among subordinates about their role in the organization, and diversion of resources from desirable uses to those that enhance the CEO's personal goals. A narcissistic CEO often blames others for his or her own failures while claiming credit for the good ideas of others (Hogan, 1994). They hire people like themselves who tell them what they want to hear and silence dissenting opinions that do not reflect their own (Miller et al., 2009). Above all, pathological narcissistic CEOs avoid criticism, advice, and negative feedback by surrounding themselves with lawyers, public relations people and subordinates who become their "yes-people." In addition narcissistic leadership,

254

Often test the limits of what is permissible because they are so confident of success. They take more credit for success than is warranted or fair, and they refuse to acknowledge failure, errors, or mistakes. When things go right, it is because of their efforts; when things go wrong, it is someone else's fault. This leads to some problems with truth-telling because they spin tales compulsively, and quickly reinterpret their failures and mistakes, usually by blaming them on others. At their best, these people are energetic, charismatic, leader-like, and willing to take the initiative to get projects moving. At their worst, however, they are arrogant, vain, overbearing, demanding, self-deceived, and pompous" (Hogan & Hogan, 2001, p. 49).

In terms of how they relate to subordinates, healthy leadership tries to bring out the best in people, their creativity, and energies using persuasion and empowerment to convince subordinates to accept a leader's vision. Good leadership encourages dialogue and incorporates dissent into decision making when possible. Destructive narcissistic leadership is the opposite relying on suppressing dissent, intimidation, and bullying to maintain control; the control is not necessarily for the betterment of the organization, it is to make sure that their self-concept is not damaged by anyone. Outbursts of temper may demoralize those who witness them, cause subordinates to withhold information that might evoke further outbursts, and, over time, breed resentment and disobedience among employees. Even those who remain in their jobs experience "a decline in work and life satisfaction, reduced commitment to their employer, and heightened depression, anxiety, and burn out…In other words, mean-spirited people do massive damage to victims, to bystanders who suffer the ripple effects, to organizational performance, and to themselves" (Barnard, 2008b, p. 425). Studies of CEO charisma also show that career success and leadership effectiveness stem from different characteristics (Kaiser et al., 2008).

One study of Fortune 500 firms found that CEO charisma predicted level of pay, but not firm performance (Kaiser et al., 2008). Although boards of directors and compensation committees may believe that charismatic CEOs add disproportionate value, research suggests that this is not usually the case. Non-charismatic CEOs shared two characteristics. First, they were modest and humble, as opposed to charismatic, and secondly, they were extraordinarily persistent in their pursuit of the organizational agenda. Thus, although charismatic CEOs transform their personal wealth, modest and persistent CEOs who possess a talent for leadership transform lackluster organizations into effective competitors (Kaiser et al., 2008). The lesson is, do not confuse narcissism and charisma with leadership competence.

Narcissism and White-collar Crime

Narcissism has been linked to low personal integrity, traits of entitlement, and the exploitation of others. Narcissists believe there is no need to follow rules; others are there to satisfy his or her motives regardless of the impact their actions have on others (Blair et al., 2008), coupled with deviant workplace behavior (Judge et al., 2006). Thus, a narcissist who cannot achieve the desired success through ordinary levels of performance may turn to fraud as the only way to maintain the illusion of invincibility (Naso, 2012). Narcissism has been identified as a fraud offender risk factor (Ham et al., 2017). Their sense of entitlement may also signal a higher propensity to commit fraud since they believe they are deserving of greater rewards than can be obtained through nonfraudulent means (Perri, 2011a). Narcissistic white-collar offenders are more hedonistic and place a higher value on material success than non-narcissistic white-collar offenders which increases the risk that they will engage in white-collar crime to satisfy their motivations (Van Slyke et al., 2016).

Narcissistic leaders' inflated sense of self-worth, coupled with their need to be respected and admired, appeared to increase the risk that they would engage in white-collar crime without feeling guilt (Van Slyke et al., 2016). A high level of narcissism becomes problematic if leaders lose contact with reality, start living in their own world, and cultivate hubris with an obsession to satisfy greed. Narcissistic CEOs are prone to engaging in unethical and or criminal conduct by playing "loose with the company's reported financial position…and live in a fantasy world of delusion about the company's financial strength" (Amernic & Craig 2010, p. 80). They may set goals unrealistically high because they need a constant stream of self-affirmation and "so desire profit or reputation that they will behave unethically to obtain these goals" (Duchon & Drake 2009, p. 306). A CEO who sets unrealistic goals coupled with irrational risk-taking whose company falls short of achieving goals is likely to take steps to mask failure by manipulating information which increases the company's risk for fraudulent behaviors. The greater the CEO fears failure, the more likely they are to succumb to temptation and commit fraud (Barnard, 2008b). Research on chief financial officer (CFO) narcissism suggests that these executives are more apt to engage in financial statement fraud such as not recognizing expenses in the period they are incurred consequently artificially inflating income (Ham et al., 2017).

In addition, income statements may have to be restated to reflect correct information and weaker internal controls are associated with narcissistic CFOs resulting with more potential for intentional financial statement fraud (Ham et al., 2017). By restatement we mean having to revise previously disclosed financial information to reflect accurate information. For example, if it was disclosed that the company made $1 million, a restatement might entail taking into account expenses that were not previously recognized. Thus, true income might be $800 thousand and the income statement would have to be restated disclosing this income. The narcissist who believes the world is made up of winners and losers is willing to do more than the average person to get ahead especially in highly competitive work environments that encourage ruthless behaviors (Webster, 2016). Narcissistic personalities who believe they are justified in resorting to criminal behaviors do so without guilt since they believe they have permission to follow a corrupt road (Naso, 2012).

Offenders exhibiting narcissistic traits of extreme entitlement may not be deterred from committing fraud because they may not "fear being caught or what punishments may come their way", nor does such entitlement create a moral dilemma for them to resolve (Bucy et al., 2008, p. 417). In one study of incarcerated white-collar criminals, subjects were significantly more narcissistic when compared to a group of non-criminal, white-collar professionals (Blickle et al., 2006). CEOs exhibiting extreme forms of narcissism are more inclined to commit white-collar crimes to keep up appearances, retain their status, and silence dissent through intimidation and other antisocial interpersonal methods previously discussed in chapter one (Rijsenbilt, 2011). As a result, their intimidations and anger make others uncomfortable. It is their method of controlling others so that their own sense of self is preserved even when they have not actually been questioned in a way that could be interpreted as a criticism; others may have simply been asking legitimate questions. Misappropriation of corporate assets by senior management is linked to a constellation of narcissistic factors, namely, extreme ambition to the point of obsession (Duffield & Grabosky, 2001).

General attributes of senior corporate fraud offenders are described as "extremely ambitious, obsessed with enhancing power and control, having a sense of superiority bordering on narcissism, which is fed by admiration and attention and which encourages a sense of entitlement to special privileges and resources" (Bucy et al., 2008, p. 416). This negative side can lead to the victimization of others when the focus of the leader is not on the higher purpose of the organization, but rather on satisfying one's sense of entitlement and egocentricity by committing unethical or criminal acts coupled with being prone to being exceedingly manipulative and ruthless (Steinberger, 2004). Consider insights by criminal psychiatrist Dr. Walter Bromberg who, while observing the narcissistic tendencies of fraud offender and former president of the New York Stock Exchange Richard Whitney at Bellevue Psychiatric Hospital, stated: "Whitney impressed the examiners as a realist…yet unaware of his rather strong tendency towards recklessness…Egocentricity and…feeling of omnipotence shone through Whitney's character structure…stating that at no time during his five or six years of financial difficulty did he imagine that he could run afoul of the law" (Bromberg, 1965, p. 388).

Dr. Bromberg went on to state that even though there are variations of white-collar crime and its perpetrators, "on examination [they] present a personality image startling like that of Whitney" (Bromberg, 1965, p. 388). Moreover, Dr. Bromberg's clinical observations of white-collar offenders he examined parallel observations made by other scholars in regard to the role of narcissism as a fraud-risk factor, further stating, "White-collar offenders examined by this author, and his associates display little guilt; their consciences have become identified with the common business ideal of success at any price…On the basis of a narcissistic character structure…self-advancement through fraud [and] white-collar crime occurs with ease" (Bromberg, 1965, p. 389). Senior management who display high-levels of narcissism are at risk of committing fraud because such executives believe that company procedures, rules, and values do not apply to them (Lodder, 2012). A "combination of a narcissistic and dishonest CEO in conjunction with financial pressures can easily lead to self-propelling, increasing cycles of financial misreporting" (Chen, 2010, p. 48). Believing to be invincible, they listen even less to words of caution and advice. Rather than trying to persuade those who disagree with them, they believe they are justified to ignore dissenters, and take risks that can lead to catastrophic decision making (Maccoby, 2000).

The Narcissism of Fraud Offender Barry Minkow

In the mid-1980s, ZZZZ Best Inc., through its founder Barry Minkow, perpetrated financial statement fraud that fooled auditors of one of the, then, largest international public accounting firms along with ZZZZ Best's investors who lost a reported $100 million which later was determined to be a Ponzi scheme. Minkow started a carpet cleaning business at age 15. By age 21 he was personally worth, at least on paper, $100 million and when he went public in 1986, ZZZZ Best reached a market capitalization of over $200 million (Rezaee & Riley, 2010). Most of the fraud involved recording fictitious revenues though fictitious accounts receivables to artificially inflate stock price when the company went public five years after its inception. Recall Minkow's previous statement, "Receivables are a wonderful thing…you create a receivable and you have revenue" (Albrecht et al., 2012, p. 401). While Minkow admitted to manipulating the company's stock, he claimed he was forced to turn the company into a Ponzi scheme under pressure from organized crime figures who secretly controlled his company—a story he later admitted was false. With the help of fraud schemes, Minkow's business grew into a fictitious building restoration enterprise where he was able to obtain financing on the false representations of non-existent restoration jobs, and then took the money to repay investors from prior phony projects.

While most Ponzi schemes are based on non-existent businesses, ZZZZ Best's carpet-cleaning division was real, however, its building restoration division, which eventually accounted for the majority of company's alleged revenues, was nonexistent. The company claimed to earn most of its revenues through lucrative insurance restoration jobs which involved cleaning and repairing buildings damaged by floods, fires, and other major catastrophes. Minkow set up Appraisal Services, a fake company that allegedly verified ZZZZ Best's business dealings. One of his vice presidents forged the documents and contracts necessary to support alleged restoration jobs. Minkow relied on his employees to pull off the ZZZZ Best fraud by offering them salaries that were much larger than they could earn elsewhere and promising larger bonuses if they participated in the fraud. When auditors insisted on physically inspecting one multimillion dollar building restoration site, ZZZZ Best management found a large building under construction. They were able to persuade the construction foreman to provide them with keys to the building for a weekend on false representations that they were with a property management firm and were going to provide a tour to a prospective tenant. Before the auditor's visit, they placed signs throughout the building indicating that ZZZZ Best was the contractor for the building's restoration. This building had not been damaged, instead, it was under construction, but the plan succeeded and the auditors were fooled (Mintz & Morris, 2017). On another similar occasion, when the auditors insisted on visiting another multi-million dollar restoration site, ZZZZ Best had to rent some floors of a new building quickly.

For the floors that were not completed, ZZZZ Best spent approximately $1 million to make the space look realistic by hiring subcontractors to make the floors look like they were being restored. Minkow and his co-conspirators entered the high rise on a Sunday when work crews were not there and placed ZZZZ Best signs, t-shirts, and other paraphernalia throughout the building prior to the tour. Minkow entertained auditors at his residence, but he also had them sign confidentiality agreements that effectively precluded them from verifying Minkow's representations that restoration contracts existed. The stipulation stated, "We will not make any follow-up calls to any contractors, insurance companies, the building owner, or other individuals involved in the restoration work" (Knapp, 2009, p. 115). Moreover, if the auditors asked too many questions, Minkow would threaten to take his business to other auditors and given that Minkow gave the appearance of a growing business, they did not engage in much professional skepticism (Mintz & Morris, 2017). Later, Minkow took the investors on a tour of the building to back up representations that he had won the contract (Palmer, 2012).

In 1989, Minkow was sentenced to 25 years in prison for his fraud and in sentencing him, the judge stated, "you are dangerous…you don't have a conscience" (AP, 1989). Minkow served less than seven and a half years and while imprisoned, he became involved in Christian ministry claiming to have experienced a religious conversion. Upon release from prison in 1997, Minkow became pastor of Community Bible Church in California and spoke at schools on the importance of ethics. Yet, again in 2014, he went to prison for five years after he pleaded guilty to conspiracy to commit bank fraud, wire fraud, mail fraud, and to defraud the federal government. He opened unauthorized bank accounts purportedly on behalf of the church, forged signatures on church checks, diverted money from legitimate church accounts for his personal use, and charged unauthorized personal expenses on church credit cards. He concealed $890,000 of income and $250,000 in taxes from the IRS. In total he admitted to embezzling over $3 million in donations from the Community Bible Church from 2001 to 2011 (Mintz & Morris, 2017). Among his victims was a widower who gave $75,000 to the church to fund a hospital in Sudan to honor his wife who had died of cancer (Mintz & Morris, 2017). However, there was no hospital because Minkow pocketed the money. He eventually resigned as pastor of the church believing he "was no longer qualified to be a pastor" (Mintz & Morris, 2017, p. 318). Prior to being sent to prison, he was evaluated and found to have exhibited antisocial and narcissistic personality features (Brinkmann, 2011).

Leadership Hubris Facilitating Tyrannical Behaviors

It is not new to suggest that business executives, particularly CEOs, often display overconfidence—referred to at times as executive ego, hubris, or arrogance (Paredes, 2005). While the concept of hubris is typically studied in the realm of politics, it has also been applied in business settings. Some equate leadership hubris as being synonymous with an extreme case of pathological narcissism, but this is not necessarily the case. Even though hubris overlaps considerably with narcissism, they are not interchangeable definitions (Petit & Bollaert, 2012). Hubris is an acquired condition triggered by accession to a position of power resulting in a lack of constraints on the individual's behavior (Petit & Bollaert, 2012). The narcissistic aspect of hubris is linked to destructive characteristics, such as manipulating subordinates (Hogan, et al., 2008), setting unrealistic corporate goals, suppressing negative information when the goals are not met (Conger, 1990), engaging in self-serving abuses of power (Maccoby, 2000), and intimidating subordinates through irrational anger (Blickle et al., 2006).

Hubris is characterized as the vice of the leader where a leader ceases to be a leader and transforms into a tyrant. Authentic leadership relies on virtue, empathy, and trust to lead while the tyrant relies on fear as a tool to rule others. A by-product of a hubristic mindset includes being potentially reckless with organizational resources, taking credit for successes but blaming subordinates for failures, reacting aggressively, and exhibiting irrational behaviors when criticized. Hubristic, tyrannical leaders possess an exaggerated sense of self, unjustifiable self-importance, and typically a flawed opinion of personal expertise and insights. Those in positions of power who are infected with hubris, 1) display contempt for authorities, 2) manage through fear, 3) refuse to listen to advice or criticism, 4) silence critical voices, 5) may use violence or intimidation as an interpersonal strategy, 6) are willing to manipulate rules and laws to satisfy their motives, 7) engage in fraud, and 8) tend to display a grandiose style of language when communicating (Petit & Bollaert, 2012). Such behaviors demoralize subordinates, lead to inappropriate organizational risk-taking, and often result in the overestimation of the probability of success (Jones & Jones, 2014). Top executive hubris is displayed by beliefs and behaviors revolving around three different aspects: how they view themselves, how they view others, and their interaction with the world.

First in how they view themselves, hubris implies the narcissistic grandiose sense of self—a belief in their invincibility and sense of entitlement. In their relationships with others, hubristic executives consider themselves to be above the community of humans, which makes them disrespect people and harm others without remorse in order to achieve goals. They may exhibit a recklessness when making decisions that do not examine the costs and risks of their actions, but which impact others and/or situations: all to satisfy their desire to achieve a vision engrained in their mind (Petit & Bollaert, 2012). Leadership occurs when there is virtue and when virtue is absent, tyrannicism fills the void by bringing fear to others in order to maintain power (Petit & Bollaert, 2012). Hubris takes on a tyrannical form in that they are unwilling to listen to reason in order to mitigate against such risks to others. Thus, tyrants at the head of corporations "may behave in accordance with the goals, tasks, missions and strategies of the organization, but they typically obtain results not through, but at the cost of subordinates" (Jones & Jones, 2012, p. 212). Tyrannical or autocratic personalities do not foster a collective healthy culture in a firm making it difficult to promote honest dialogue between all levels of an organizational hierarchy.

Corporate managers and employees feel obligated and committed to act in conformity with corporate pressure and policies even when they are questionable or unethical—this leads to rationalizations (Petit & Bollaert, 2012). Tyrannical leaders may humiliate, belittle, and manipulate their subordinates in order to get the proverbial job done (Aasland et al., 2010). Tyrannical leaders may appear as though they are trying to achieve goals, but to subordinates they appear as bullies; their leadership methods undermine employee motivation, well-being, and job satisfaction (Aasland et al., 2010). Subordinates, in essence, do not believe that the upper management is looking after their well-being (Aasland et al., 2010). Several behaviors apt to be displayed include personal insults, invading one's 'personal space, both verbal and nonverbal threats and intimidation, intimidating e-mails, public shaming or 'status degradation' rituals, rude interruptions, and dirty looks (Barnard, 2008b). For example, Network Associates' CEO Bill Larson displayed tyrannical, bullying behavior. Larson gave subordinates unreachable targets to meet, and then berated and belittled them if they failed, and reminded managers that "suicide was sometimes an appropriate response to failure" (Cohen et al., 2010, p. 169). Convicted CEO Martin Grass of Rite Aid Corporation displayed tyrannical traits pressuring subordinates to endorse fake documents and bragged that cover-ups would never be discovered (Cohen et al., 2010). Grass threatened KPMG accountants with retaliation if Rite-Aid suffered due to an audit.

Leadership Over-Optimism and Misguided Risk Assessments

CEO over-optimism is evident in many corporate fraud scandals (Barnard, 2008b). Visionary managers can frequently be narcissistic in their behavior which increases the risk of failure when business conditions change. Moreover, when faced with a crisis, narcissistic leaders isolate themselves from the advice of others, ignore words of caution, interpret criticisms as a threat, and frequently become myopic in their views (Maccoby, 2000). Exaggerated pride fosters a hubristic attitude, inflated self-confidence, and arrogance which lead them to make impulsive decisions and to take unnecessary risks (Jackson et al., 2002). CEOs must be, or at least must appear to be, optimistic by articulating a future that inspires employees and customers to want to follow them while constructing a message which investors can be enthusiastic about (Barnard, 2008b). There is a difference between well-grounded optimism and delusional or over-optimism which is disconnected from business reality.

Over-optimism can be characterized by a selective interpretation of information which leads to reality distortion (Sheard et al., 2013). Over-optimists fail to recognize the limits of human control and therefore exhibit a lack of judgment. In the worst cases, over-optimism may simply be a distraction that allows a CEO to fend off critics and keep moving forward with a fruitless or misguided plan. The consequences of CEO over-optimism are similar to those of CEO narcissism where CEOs may lead their companies into ill-considered ventures. Second, they may fail to recognize when corporate strategies are failing and set expectations so high that employees engage in fraud to achieve them. Over-optimistic CEOs may stifle the delivery of bad news or even routine results (Barnard, 2008b). For example, having initiated an ambitious project, over-optimistic CEOs often fail to acknowledge that it is time to turn back or regroup. Georgetown's Donald Langevoort labeled this scenario the optimism-commitment stating:

> When forecasting the outcomes of [these] projects, executives [often] fall victim to what psychologists call the planning fallacy. In its grip, managers make decisions based on delusional optimism rather than on a rational weighing of gains, losses, and probabilities. They overestimate benefits and underestimate costs. They spin scenarios of success while overlooking the potential for mistakes and miscalculations. As a result, managers pursue initiatives that are unlikely to come in on budget or on time—or to ever deliver the expected returns (Barnard, 2008b, p. 423).

Consequently, overconfident executives are more likely to commit fraud because of their unrealistic beliefs in positive future financial performances which, they believe will in turn, compensate for any earnings management and avoid fraud detection. Possessing over-confidence may become a liability because of irrational risk-taking with organizational resources. It can damage corporate culture, demoralize workers, and negatively affect financial performance, including increasing the risk of fraud (Jones & Jones, 2014). Over-optimistic CEOs may infect their organizations with aspirations that employees cannot achieve, which drives others to make foolish decisions because they wanted to ensure that their companies achieved ambitious earnings estimates by generating fraudulent financial statements or otherwise engaging in some form of fraud; these fraudulent behaviors can go on for years before they are revealed if in fact they do get revealed (Barnard, 2008b).

Competent professionals commit some type of fraud in the mistaken and over-optimistic belief that failure to meet those estimates was just a temporary problem that could be solved in the future (Barnard, 2008b). The problem with this view is that the temporary problem takes on a life of its own and becomes permanent and non-fixable. When CEOs promote over-optimistic expectations, subordinates may get the clear message that they should distort or conceal bad news (Barnard, 2008b). This problem is exacerbated when the CEO has a volatile temper or when, narcissistically, he or she personalizes corporate performance and views every setback as a personal failure. In short, CEO over-optimism, like CEO narcissism, can lead a company to ruin through reckless decision making when reality is not taken into consideration. Consequently,

[CEOs] drive so hard for perfection that they are incapable of acknowledging either failures or weaknesses. When confronted with their failures, they try to cover them up…Often they look for scapegoats on whom to blame their problems, either within their organization or outside. Through the combination of power, charisma, and communications skills, they convince others to accept these distortions, causing entire organizations to lose touch with reality. In the end, it is their organizations that suffer (Barnard, 2008b, p. 424).

In addition, such leaders may engage in a distorted risk assessment. Narcissistic individuals exhibit an over-confident form of impulsivity where they have a tendency to disregard important information from others. With distorted risk assessments, they are likely to make poor decisions (Mathieu et al., 2012). Why do narcissists engage in self-defeating behaviors that undermine their urgent goals of power and recognition?..."the answer may be very simple: Because they can't help it" (Vazire & Funder, 2006, p. 162). Narcissistic behavior appears to have a self-defeating quality in that they undermine themselves because of the rigidity of their personality structure (Miller et al., 2009). This inherent rigidity makes them more apt to disregard risks associated with decision making, where a more balanced person would be more reflective and weigh the risks associated with decisions before moving forward. Narcissism is not linked to a lack of premeditation or disregard for cost-benefit analyses; they simply have difficulty weighing the cost and benefits of their actions in a deliberate, thoughtful manner (Miller et al., 2009). They display a tendency to miscalculate risks when they make decisions because they ignore facts that would lead to a more balanced analysis of the risk involved (Sheard, et al., 2013).

Instead they pursue their goals in an immediate and forceful manner, but to an outsider their decision making appears to be distorted since the costs of a decision are ignored. Their self-defeating behaviors are also linked to a tendency to process feedback in a hostile, biased manner which will likely lead to an aggressive interpersonal response to those that offered their feedback (Miller et al., 2009). Narcissists' self-sabotaging behavior appears to be triggered by different factors, such as a lack of empathy and a low regard for life. Although they have the ability to assess risk, their decisions can be at the expense of risk to themselves, organizations, and others (Miller et al., 2009). What appears irrational or rash does not mean that they exhibit a lack of self-control, it means that they are unwilling to take empathetic issues into account. Without the ability to empathize, insensitive fraud offenders will make rash decisions without considering the potentially painful impact such decisions will have on others; the needs of others do not matter to them and therefore irrelevant to their decision making process (Gottfredson & Hirschi, 1990).

260

Leadership Reaction to Criticism

Pathological or destructive narcissistic leaders also have drive and vision, but their focus is on obtaining personal power, status, and success. When faced with challenges or potential failures, these leaders turn to abusive and unethical behaviors which become toxic and detrimental to the organization. Some of the components of such leadership include the need for self-enhancement, intolerance of dissent from subordinates, removing subordinates that do not display unquestioned loyalty, the use of deceptions to motivate subordinates, and the exploitation of employees in order to meet personal needs (Regnaud, 2011). They perceive others who may innocently provide feed-back as a rival and threat and will discount their advice, especially from subordinates (Mathieu et al., 2012). Pride also prevents some managers from taking advice and according to Dr. Larry Hirschhorn, a psychologist at the Wharton Center for Applied Research, "While any leader needs an inspiring vision, there's trouble if he starts ignoring data about the limits of his ideas...Such a manager only wants to hear what confirms his own ideas; he turns against anyone who challenges him" (Coleman, 1990).

Dr. Hirschhorn believes ineffective, narcissistic leaders bring out several forms of behavior in their subordinates such as where workers cannot be themselves due to believing they must censor what they say in meetings because it is too dangerous to criticize the supervisor. In addition, the supervisor expects loyalty from subordinates above what is best for the organization, thus subordinates distort the truth because they experience a strong impulse to twist facts in order to be pleasing or agree with whatever the supervisor says. Narcissistic leaders are threatened by others who might shine more brightly than they do for fear they could displace them. In an effort to discredit someone they believe is a threat, they will engage in character assassination, dispense disinformation, and block access to funding and other resources (Morf & Rhodewalt 2001). Narcissistic leaders destroy the organizational culture and inevitably leave a trail of damaged relationships and systems. Although particular strengths of narcissistic leaders may exist, weaknesses are noticeable, such as being hypersensitive to criticism, unable to listen, lacking empathy, unwilling or unable to mentor or be mentored, and intensely competitive (Maccoby, 2000). Some risks of narcissistic leadership are that they may be the kind of person who,

> Does not listen to anyone else when he believes in doing something...often exhibit an insatiable need to be admired...they cultivate what passes for people skills and use those skills to manipulate others. They see themselves as leaders whom others should naturally follow. [They] cannot tolerate what they perceive as disrespect. They are oversensitive to criticism...have a tendency to exaggerate to the point of lying, are quick to anger at putdowns, are isolated, paranoid, and grandiose. (Barnard, 2008b).

One serious consequence of this oversensitivity to criticism is that narcissistic leaders often do not listen when they feel threatened or attacked. As one CEO bluntly put it, "I didn't get here by listening to people" (Maccoby, 2000). Indeed, on one occasion, when this CEO proposed a daring strategy, none of his subordinates believed it would work; his subsequent success strengthened his conviction that he had nothing to learn about strategy from his subordinates (Maccoby, 2000). Obsessed with maintaining an attractive stock price, CEO Dean Buntrock of Waste Management "stifled debate" amongst employees in order to continue the strategy of misreporting revenue numbers" (Carlsson, 2001, p. 118). Although narcissism can be a positive in a top-level executive, narcissistic executives can also drain the life out of an organization with Dr. Michael Maccoby stating:

> No matter what their strengths, productive narcissists are incredibly difficult to work for. They don't learn easily from others. They are oversensitive to any kind of criticism, which they take personally. They bully subordinates and dominate meetings. They don't want to hear about anyone else's feelings. They are distrustful and paranoid. They can become grandiose, especially when they start to succeed. Perhaps their most frustrating quality is that they almost never listen to anyone (Barnard, 2008b, p. 410).

For example, Australian white-collar offender Christopher Skase, CEO of Qintex, is said to have "had a ferocious faith in the rightness of whatever he was doing" and that he was "very impatient with criticism" (Perri,

2011a). They also avoid criticism simply by failing to hear it and Dr. Maccoby vividly described this self-destructive scenario of one case study:

> As a narcissistic CEO takes charge and initiates change, he boasts…that all his top executives support his moves. I hear from a key vice president that he doesn't listen when they disagree with him. He becomes cramped with paranoia. He tries desperately to control everything because no one can be trusted. He starts to see enemies everywhere. He can't slow down or stop, continuing on his path of expansion and debt even though his colleagues counsel against it. No one can talk to him. He thinks his critics are just protecting themselves or jealous and out to get him…No one can reach him, and he is fired three years after he took the position (Barnard, 2008b).

Leadership Expectation of Unquestioned Loyalty

Narcissistic leaders are acutely aware of whether or not subordinates are with them wholeheartedly in advancing their agenda, whether legal or illegal. The risk, of course, is that the narcissist finds enemies that are not there—even among their colleagues. The narcissistic CEO wants all subordinates to think the way they do about the business (Maccoby, 2000). Narcissists eliminate dissent and promote a homogeneous and insular group mentality, with the accumulation of power at the center; they frequently fail to sufficiently consider alternative courses of action (Tourish & Vatcha, 2005). Thus, it is not surprising to observe criminal narcissistic leaders displaying a tendency to surround themselves with organizational conformists, sycophants, or otherwise referred to as "yes-men", who are accomplices to the fraud crime (Bucy et al., 2008). The term "yes-men" refers to a situation in which members of the group continuously agree to the decisions of a leader with little to no objections, ethical, technical, or feasibility issues being raised for fear of becoming group outcastes which would interfere with their own personal agendas. Narcissistic leaders expect unquestioned loyalty and to be given whatever they want regardless of the imposition placed on others, leaving them incredulous, infuriated, and likely to respond angrily when those expectations are not met. They are at times unwilling to seek out or accept feedback and may throw tantrums if they are questioned or criticized—they do not want to know what people think of them and cannot tolerate dissent (Dattner, 2004). They interpret dissent, criticism, or feedback as a threat or lack of confidence in their visions making them distrustful and paranoid of others (Dattner, 2004).

In one study where subordinates were asked to disclose toxic behaviors by management, one of the interviewees stated that one manager would get rid of any employees who he thought may prove to be a threat stating, "If he didn't think he had complete, 100 percent loyalty within the juniors in his team, then he would basically lean on them to make them want to leave and hand in their resignation" (Boddy et al., 2015, p. 537). As a result, they can be abrasive with employees by publicly humiliating them which is an antisocial form of power orientation previously discussed in chapter one. Although narcissistic leaders say they want teamwork, in practice the more independent-minded subordinates who could competently critique the leader either leave, are pushed out and eventually replaced by 'yes-people' (Maccoby, 2000). Therefore, any opportunity for debate or constructive criticism is prevented. The risk of harboring narcissistic traits as a leader is that individuals who harbor unrealistic impressions of their capabilities, when reinforced by yes-people, lack a reality check and may be more likely to engage in fraudulent behavior than more grounded executives (Sheard et al., 2013). For example, executive director John Friedrich, who defrauded the National Safety Council of Australia, was said to surround himself with loyal workers and "demanded unquestioned loyalty" (Sykes, 1994, p. 240). Theranos founder and CEO Elizabeth Holmes demanded unquestioned loyalty from employees and dissent, however well-intentioned, was punished with dismissal (Thiruchelvam, 2018). Holmes falsely claimed that a vile of blood could diagnosis a person's medical risk factors better than competitors. Michael Milken, nicknamed the "junk bond king," worked at Drexel Burnham for over 20 years. Milken was prosecuted for violating U.S. securities laws in 1989, but eventually pleaded guilty to securities reporting violations. Milken had an obsession with a follower's unquestioned loyalty even though he instigated a perfect storm of illegal insider trading, stock manipulation, and tax evasion ending in his 1990 guilty plea (Chandler, 2009).

Leadership Strategies to Secure Follower Loyalty

How do fraud offenders in leadership positions instill a sense of loyalty to employees and upper management? Researchers have distilled a process that appears to reflect the strategy leaders use to gain the loyalty of subordinates in order to carry out misconduct. The process includes, 1) first generate excitement among subordinates by showering them with unexpected money that may be above and beyond their own expectations of what they deserve, 2) corrupt leaders instill a sense of nobility and specialness to their organization in order to decrease individual fears associated with the risks they undertake when committing fraud, 3) they use explicit or implicit threats to instill fear if the leader perceives a disruption to the special relationships he or she has created, and 4) shaming and engaging in bullying tactics when a powerful person is disappointed should a subordinate question the ethics of a given situation (Ramamoorti et al., 2013). For example, Enron CEO Jeffrey Skilling's philosophy appears to support such research when he stated, "You buy loyalty with money. This touchy-feely stuff isn't as important as cash. That's what drives performance" (McLean & Elkind, 2003, p. 55).

The Case of WorldCom CEO Bernie Ebbers

In the late 1990s, WorldCom became one of the largest telecommunications companies in the world, with annual revenue topping $30 billion. In 1996, the *Wall Street Journal* ranked the firm as having the "best ten-year performance out of thousands of companies surveyed" (Soltes, 2016, p. 127). By the late 1990s, executives faced declining profits and consequently engaged in financial statement fraud by not including all line expenses on their income statement that they should have which in the end fraudulently inflated income (Schilit, 2010). Their line costs represented fees WorldCom paid for the right to use other providers' telecommunication line networks. Thus a WorldCom customer might have to use the network line of a company in Germany to make a connection and WorldCom had to pay the German company a line fee to be able to make the connection. Initially WorldCom expensed these costs in the period they incurred. However with declining revenue, investors starting paying more attention to the company's operating expenses such as line costs. In mid-2000, WorldCom failed to record the line costs as expenses, but treated them as capital expenditures and placed them on the balance sheet as assets to be expensed little by little over time. This had the impact of not recording the full expense of the line costs in the period they were incurred, but instead spreading out the expenses over time to lessen the impact on income in the current period by artificially inflating it (Rezaee & Riley, 2010).

The line costs were capitalized as long-term investments to the tune of $3.8 billion. In addition, WorldCom used money ear-marked to cover its liabilities by reclassifying it as revenue to the tune of about $2.8 billion (Rezaee & Riley, 2010). David Myers, WorldCom's controller who oversaw the preparation of the firm's financial statements recalls how the fraud began: "We closed the books and the results were nowhere near where expectations were…we thought there was an error that we were going to fix…once you fixed it you'd be understating expenses in one quarter and you'd overstate it in the next quarter and get it all back to zero…No harm, no foul" (Soltes, 2016, p. 127). Myers recalled spending much of his time "thinking that you're helping people and doing the right thing" instead of thinking about the eventual consequences of his actions further stating; "it was just shortsighted by not trying to understand what the true outcome was going to be" (Soltes, 2016, p. 127). What makes white-collar crime, at times, distinct from other crimes is that the results of fraud are not readily apparent to the perpetrator. It may take months, perhaps years before the negative consequences unfold for one to observe.

In the case of WorldCom, it took several years before the actual impact of the fraud became apparent because it was no longer sustainable. When the fraud was revealed, the stock price dropped from $90 a share in the Fall of 1999 to less than a $1 a share in the summer of 2002 resulting in thousands of employees losing their jobs and pensions (Soltes, 2016). Referencing WorldCom CEO Ebbers and CFO Sullivan again, they engaged in very questionable dealings with their employees to harness their subordinates' loyalty by purchasing it. For example, over an 18-month period ending in 2002, Ebbers gave Ron Beaumont, WorldCom's ex-Chief Operating Officer, a total of $650,000, whereas Sullivan engaged in questionable dealings with subordinates (SEC, 2003). CFO Sullivan wrote personal checks to seven of his managers giving them $20,000 each and another check for

$10,000 to one of the employee's spouse (Scharff, 2005). Sullivan rationalized these payoffs as company bonuses even though they were written on his personal checking account, and they were not authorized by the board of directors (Scharff, 2005). There were "also a select number of employees who were compensated above WorldCom's salary guidelines to promote loyalty to the company" (Scharff, 2005, p. 113).

Investigations into the WorldCom fraud uncovered a culture of fear and intimidation where employees were pressured to follow management because they were terminated when they did not follow orders (Blumenstein & Pullman, 2003). Convicted WorldCom CEO Bernard Ebbers and CFO Scott Sullivan established a culture where decisions were unchallenged; they exercised unquestioned authority and demanded unquestioned loyalty from employees (Rosenbush, 2005). Ebbers demanded automatic compliance from the Board of Directors; it was known as "Bernie's Board" because few members would ever disagree with him (Jennings, 2006, p. 152). In fact, WorldCom bankruptcy court examiner, Dick Thornburgh, referred to WorldCom's boardroom as an environment in which "critical questioning was discouraged and the board did not appear to evaluate proposed transactions in appropriate depth" (Hoyk & Hersey, 2011, p. 45).

The Case of Charles Keating of Lincoln Savings and Loan

Consider how convicted bank offender Charles Keating, best known for his role in the savings and loan scandal of the late 1980s, ran the Lincoln Savings and Loan Association. Keating was known as 'Mr. Clean' for being an Eagle Scout, his overt religious piety, and his antipornography campaign (Mueller, 2019, 384). The bank that he led was losing money in very high risk real estate development schemes in addition to raising money in what is referred to as the 'junk bond' market; this activity eventually cost the taxpayer $3.4 billion in a government bailout in 1989 when Lincoln went bankrupt (Mueller, 2019). Keating hired very young people with little experience, and gave them huge salaries and impressive titles knowing that they would advance his agenda without question. He also conveyed a fundamental message to his employees of their superiority, in that they were smarter, braver, and more moral than others, especially the government regulators; anyone with a contrary view was considered an enemy (Pontell & Shichor, 2001). This trait reflects how corrupt leaders instill a sense of nobility and specialness to their organization by accentuating an "us versus them" mentality in order to decrease individual fears associated with the risks of committing fraud. Moreover, Keating told his salesforce, "Always remember, the weak, meek and ignorant are always good sales targets" (Mueller, 2019, p. 384).

Keating intentionally targeted elderly widows by sending his team of impeccably groomed young salesmen who played the role of the ideal grandson to persuade the victims to transfer their savings into his high-risk investments which became worthless after Lincoln went bankrupt. Yet there were federal bank regulators, such as Bill Black, who realized that Keating was engaged in corporate fraud, but experienced resistance from Keating's colleagues who were politically connected. For example, former Federal Reserve Chairman, Alan Greenspan and former federal judge Richard Posner vouched for Keating's savings and loan as being 'sound' and 'safer than comparable thrifts' (p. 385). Keating also went after Black with a vengeance telling his lobbyist, Jim Grogan, in a written memorandum "GET BLACK…KILL HIM DEAD" (p. 385). In 1987, Keating was also able to persuade five United States senators, known as the Keating Five: John McCain, Dennis DeConcini, Donald Riegle, John Glenn, and Alan Cranston to meet with Black and several other bank regulators to ease their oversight on savings and loan banks and to halt their investigation into Keating's affairs. The decision to suspend the investigation into Keating allowed Keating to continue his fraud for an additional two years which ultimately translated into a larger taxpayer bailout; it is more often the case that corporate fraud will be paid for by taxpaying citizens who expected more from corporate leaders.

How did Keating deal with those who disclosed their concerns of organizational misconduct to him? When an accountant at Lincoln Savings notified Keating of accounting irregularities after the bank's CFO did not take her concerns seriously, Keating wrote her a thank you note and notice of termination (Jennings, 2006). According to those who knew Keating and the practices at their organization, the "best way to get fired was to ask difficult questions" (Pontell & Schichor, 2001, p. 75). Keating also relied on impression management to generate feelings of sentimentality to deflect suspicion from his criminal behavior by making charitable donations to

264

Mother Theresa (Lilly et al., 2011). Eventually Keating pled guilty to wire and bankruptcy fraud and received credit for time he spent in prison towards his punishment. Typically, when employees bring issues of importance to management's attention, we would like to think that they would be acknowledged for their integrity and loyalty to the organization, but this simply is not always the case when management is the culprit behind the corruption.

The Case of Tyco CEO Dennis Kozlowski

Tyco manufactured a variety of products from electronic components to health care products employing roughly two hundred and forty thousand people. The list of Tyco's worst practices included, 1) poor documentation and lack of disclosures, 2) inadequate policies and procedures to prevent misconduct by senior executives, 3) a lack of oversight by senior management at the corporate level, and 4) a pattern of aggressive accounting (Rezaee & Riley, 2010). The case of Tyco's CEO Dennis Kozlowski and CFO Mark Swartz reflects self-serving, secretive misconduct embezzling millions of dollars through unauthorized and improper low-interest loans or interest free loans and compensation not disclosed to shareholders. In addition, they engaged in many profitable related party transactions without disclosure to shareholders. Yet CEO Kozlowski indicated "nothing was hidden behind the scenes" and Tyco's disclosures were "exceptional" because Tyco "prided itself on having a sharp focus with creating shareholder value" while CFO Swartz told investors that "Tyco's disclosure practice remains second to none" (Albrecht et al., 2012, p. 514). Tyco's chief corporate counsel from 1998 to 2002 received approximately $14 million in interest-free loans to buy and renovate a $4 million apartment in Manhattan and to buy a $10 million ski resort in Utah. They later pocketed millions of dollars by causing Tyco to forgive repayment of their improper loans. These loans and their forgiveness were never disclosed to the board of directors; eventually Swartz and Kozlowski went to prison.

Tyco's convicted CEO Dennis Kozlowski was named a top-25 executive in the country by *Business Week* for his daring nonstop acquisition strategy (Lipman-Blumen, 2005), called corporate "America's most aggressive CEO" (Sweeney, 2002, p. 22) and referred to "as a second Jack Welch" (Perri, 2013b, p. 332). In 2005, Kozlowski spent over six years in prison for grand larceny, securities fraud, other crimes, and for taking unauthorized bonuses of more than $120 million as well as selling $575 million in inflated stock (Mintz & Morris, 2017). Considering he robbed Tyco's coffers for close to a decade, Kozlowski remains adamant about his innocence in an interview with journalist Morley Safer from *60 Minutes*. Kozlowski claimed that jealous jurors convicted him out of spite, not because he had done anything wrong (Lipman-Blumen, 2005). Kozlowski used Tyco money to buy his New Hampshire home for $4.5 million even though it was valued at $1.5 million with Tyco incurring a $3 million loss (Farrell, 2006). From 1997-2000, Kozlowski rented a Manhattan apartment on Fifth Avenue for $264,000 per year, all paid for by Tyco. Again, using Tyco funds, he paid $16.8 million for an apartment in Manhattan, spent $3 million for improvements, and $11 million to have the place furnished by a decorator who was a personal friend to his wife.

He had Tyco pay for his daughter's summer apartment in Madrid, Spain while she was there for a semester (Farrell, 2006). In addition, he donated approximately $106 million of Tyco funds to various charities, including some $43 million to his alma mater, Seton Hall and Berwick Academy, with the goal of having a building named in his honor (Farrell, 2006). In one case he donated $1.3 million to a charity to preserve a swamp in Nantucket, Massachusetts. Interestingly the swamp was next to Kozlowski's own estate; the donation was used to prevent new developments that would encroach on his property (Rezaee & Riley, 2010). Kozlowski even hired a public relations professional to tout his philanthropy though millions of dollars of his donations were made with Tyco's money (Jennings, 2006). Moreover, prior to his arrest and imprisonment, Kozlowski delivered a commencement address at St. Anselm College, a small Catholic college in New Hampshire, to which Tyco had given $1 million in which he told the students, "As you go forward in life you will be confronted with questions every day that test your morals...The questions will get tougher, and the consequences will become more severe. Think carefully, and for your sake, do the right thing, not the easy thing" (Bianco et al., 2002).

Several weeks after delivery of this commencement speech, Kozlowski was arrested for tax fraud and eventually resigned from Tyco. Kozlowski was described as a "supreme narcissist who was also highly skilled in accumulating power…whose actions were motivated by a sense of entitlement" (Bucy et al., 2008, p. 410). According to his value system, he deplored the thought that CEOs abused their positions for hedonistic lifestyles stating, "We've been made out to be freewheeling jet-setters, playboys reliving our adolescent years…For me, and for most CEOs, that irresponsible image really rankles" (Jennings, 2006, p. 107). Moreover he stated that, "We don't believe in perks, not even executive parking spots" (Jennings, 2006, p. 108). However, the evidence revealed behaviors that contradicted the above statements where he had no problem charging Tyco for $2,900 coat hangers, a $6,000 shower curtain, $6,300 sewing basket, $15,000 dog umbrella stand, and $17,100 travelling toilet box (Jennings, 2006). He did claim, however, that the $6000 shower curtain was not for him because it was in the maid's room (Farrell, 2006).

Abraham Zeleznik of the Harvard Business School, suggests that Kozlowski was undone by an intense sense of entitlement stating, "By entitlement I mean an aspect of a narcissistic personality who comes to believe that he and the institution are one" and thus "that he can take what he wants when he wants it" (Bianco et al., 2002). Ironically, while in prison Kozlowski stated that, upon reflection, he was living in a "CEO-type bubble…I knew I was doing something wrong at some level…My conscience told me one thing, but my sense of entitlement allowed me to rationalize what I did" (Jones, 2012). Yet despite this insight, to this day Kozlowski believes he was wrongly convicted and claims to have no regrets over his behavior (Boostrom, 2011). Kozlowski had a philosophy as to who he wanted on his staff, stating, "I choose managers from the same model as myself: smart, poor, and wants to be rich" reflecting that desire to achieve the American Dream of unlimited monetary success (Jennings, 2004, p. 15).

Kozlowski hired young people so that once they received all the trappings of financial success, they would be reluctant to speak up about ethical and legal issues for fear of losing their expensive homes, boats, and cars and the prestige that comes with financial success at a young age (Mintz & Morris, 2017, p. 119). They were selected by him for their positions based on their inexperience, possible conflicts of interests, and the unlikelihood that they would question his decisions (Mintz & Morris, 2017). Yet, within Tyco's method of performance review, salaries were set low and each manager could earn a bonus pegged to the earnings of the profit center they managed, but they could also be fired. To emphasize the importance of performance, Kozlowski held a banquet at which he presented awards not only to the best warehouse manager, but also to the worst one. The recipients had to walk up through the banquet hall, surrounded by colleagues, to receive their awards. As one former executive stated, "It was kind of embarrassing watching a guy go up…It was like his death sentence" (Bianco et al., 2002).

Such a tactic represents the power orientation traits previously discussed; the desire to control others and situations, and to influence group dynamics of conformity. Kozlowski used his position to demand loyalty from his subordinates by threatening and intimidating them in order to obtain conformity. For example Tyco's attorney, Mark Belnick, brought to Kozlowski's attention Tyco products that were not working. In 2000, when the U.S. Consumer Product Safety Commission tentatively approved a recall plan of defective sprinkler systems manufactured by a Tyco subsidiary, Belnick wisely recommended that Tyco offer consumers replacements for faulty sprinkler heads. Yet to Belnick's surprise, Kozlowski accused Belnick of intentionally siding with the government, "Do you work for the government or Tyco?" (Kim, 2005, p. 1019). In ridiculing Belnick, Kozlowski questioned Belnick's loyalty to the corporate team and his fitness as a corporate citizen believing that serving the company meant not conceding to government's wishes, even if doing so would be good and fair to consumers and the long-term interest of Tyco.

In addition to obedience and group pressures, Belnick was subject to considerable conformity pressures that arise from personal relationships with colleagues and peers. Generally speaking, conformity is usually a change in one's belief or behavior in response to real or imagined group pressure when there may or may not be a direct request to comply with the group's goals (Kim, 2005). Although Kozlowski's demand for "take no prisoners" loyalty was rather explicit, he implicitly appealed to Belnick's social identity with a particular group— the corporate team at Tyco. At Tyco, Kozlowski's questioning of Belnick's loyalty in a discussion about the recall of the faulty sprinklers triggered an outpouring of frustration by Belnick. When Belnick threatened to leave, Kozlowski warned that Belnick "would leave with nothing; no severance, no bonus" (Kim, 2005, p. 1019). Consider how Kozlowski rewarded loyalty. Patricia Prue, vice president of human resources, obtained a loan from Tyco for $748, 309 and Tyco paid the $521, 087 taxes that were due on the forgiven loan (Jennings, 2006). She received a bonus of $13,534,525 and Tyco paid the tax on the bonus equal to $9,424,815.

In addition, CEO pay is the most significant validation and form of recognition a chief executive receives, perhaps more important than other possible measures of a CEO's success, value to the firm, and a form of feedback on performance (Paredes, 2005). Compensation has repeatedly been characterized as an important scorecard by which CEOs rate themselves (Paredes, 2005). For example, in 1997 Kozlowski stated, "If it's a system that's truly gauged toward incentivization or success for shareholders, compensation is your scorecard. It's a way of keeping score at what you're doing" (Paredes, 2005, p. 717). Many people erroneously believe that the personal financial benefit is the primary incentive for economic crimes. While personal financial benefit can be one of many motivations to commit white-collar crimes, in many cases it is not the primary reason; many white-collar criminals commit fraud for ego, status, and sheer arrogance (Antar, 2007). Now that Kozlowski is out of prison, he is back at work consulting on mergers and acquisitions (Fins, 2017).

The Case of HealthSouth CEO Richard Scrushy

Consider the case of HealthSouth CEO Richard Scrushy who was found not criminally, but civilly liable for fraud at HealthSouth, a medical services provider that became the first national chain of orthopedic hospitals and rehabilitation centers. Scrushy did eventually go to prison not for the fraud committed at HealthSouth, but for bribery of former Alabama governor Donald Siegelman (Rezaee & Riley, 2010). From 1996 to 2002, HealthSouth committed financial statement fraud by fictitiously overstating revenue by $2.5 billion (Rezaee & Riley, 2010). In terms of the financial statement fraud, Scrushy instructed his senior executives, such as HealthSouth co-founder and CFO Aaron Beam, to overstate revenue in the billions of dollars. As CEO, Scrushy fit the prototype of the narcissistic leader in that he "had no tolerance for criticism or contrary opinions while being exquisitely sensitive to any hint of a personal slight" yet demanded constant approval and adulation from those around him (Perri, 2013b, p. 337). Interviews with associates of Scrushy, government officials, and former employees, as well as a review of the litigation history of HealthSouth, paint a picture of an executive who ruled by top down by creating a culture of fear, threatened critics with reprisals, and paid his loyal subordinates well (Abelson & Freudenheim, 2003).

Scrushy "hired young people, paid them more than they ever thought they would make, promoted them faster than they thought they would be promoted" in order to gain their loyalty (Beenen & Pinto, 2009, p. 278). When Scrushy held meetings on a Monday, they were referred to as "Monday morning beatings" because the main purpose of the meeting was for Scrushy to call attention to some failure. By relying on the antisocial trait of power orientation, he would publicly berate the person(s) he deemed to be responsible for the perceived failure (Abelson & Freudenheim, 2003). Moreover, Scrushy would "publicly berate financial analysts who dared to challenge his forecasts of continued growth" (Haddad et al., 2003, p. 70). The meetings were just one way Scrushy exerted control while taking pride in exposing any manager who was not performing as he stated in an interview, "Shine a light on someone—it's funny how numbers improve" (Abelson & Freudenheim, 2003). Scrushy, too, engaged in the rationalization of comparison to other companies engaging in financial statement fraud claiming, "I am convinced that there are 8000 companies out there right now that have shit on their balance sheets. Everyone I've been involved with, everyone I know, everybody docs" (Farrell, 2006, p. 134).

Yet over the years he became increasingly paranoid and hired body guards to escort him to his headquarters with a separate entrance for him and those he picked to use the special entrance and elevator. His accountant, William Massey who engaged in fraud, committed suicide (Heylar, 2003). Eventually all five of the company's CFOs pled guilty as well as other subordinates to financial statement fraud and other charges. As one former HealthSouth executive stated, "the corporate culture created the fraud and the fraud created the corporate culture" (Heylar, 2003). Scrushy's response to those CFOs and others who stated that he too was involved in financial statement fraud relied on the antisocial trait of being a victim stating, "I've been mistreated, so lied to, it's just massive" (Heylar, 2003). Several former CFOs at HealthSouth testified that Scrushy, their boss, managed by immense fear and intimidation, and would not accept financial statements unless they met forecasts.

Consider the statement of a former subordinate to Scrushy who stated to the sentencing judge after pleading guilty to fraud that he felt "coerced to participate in the fraud...[and] how relieved he was after the company was raided by federal agents thinking it provided him the opportunity to finally get out of this mess" (Wolfe & Hermanson, 2004, p. 40). CFO Aaron Beam's perspective revealed there was the emotional seduction of money because he invested a few thousand dollars of his own money into HealthSouth, but now made millions. His relationship with Scrushy was not one of friendliness, but of intimidation and fear. Beam knew that creating fictitious revenue to increase the company's stock price was wrong, but he did not feel comfortable challenging Scrushy, stating, "I didn't really talk to Richard or challenge him...I had learned from working with him for four years that he didn't like to be told he couldn't do something; he made it very unpleasant when you challenged him" (Wells, 2012, p. 55). Eventually Beam left HealthSouth assisting in the prosecution of Scrushy, further stating:

> In 1996 we didn't make our numbers, we had a bad quarter. Richard Scrushy, in essence, asked Bill Owens and me to cook the books. And because I was intimidated by Richard—he had begun carrying a gun, he had body guards...and I wanted to keep the dream alive, too. I'm not going to say that Richard literally held a gun to my head and made me commit fraud, but he is very persuasive with what he can get you to do. And I was proud of the company. I wanted to keep the dream going. I didn't want to disappoint Wall Street, either, and I went along. Bill Owens, the chief accountant, made entries on the books. Literally credits to revenue that didn't exist (Ramamoorti et al., 2013, p. 68).

Powerful people use shame tactics as a distraction from their misconduct which reflects the antisocial trait of power orientation by trying to control others and situations. They may also exercise the antisocial interpersonal strategy of threatening others, either blatantly or veiled. Consider Scrushy's response to a staff member who told a story, as told by CFO Beam, about a fishing trip revealing what happens when Scrushy was not the center of attention:

> Richard managed by intimidation. It's tough to put into words just how brutally nasty Richard could be...Richard used his facial expressions, his voice and his demeanor to intimidate others...During our regular Monday morning meeting, one of the accountants who reported to me started talking about how he had gone fishing over the weekend, and like Richard, had caught a big fish. He described the fish and how it was huge. Richard did not like this. He had to be the center of attention—it always had to be about him and no one else. Richard jumped all over the poor guy. Veins popped out of his neck and his forehead. He was irate. He aggressively admonished the guy. "Shut up! Nobody wants to hear about your damn fish!" Richard yelled, shaking his fist at the fellow. The guy became silent. Richard continued with his barrage, "if you keep that up you'll find yourself doing accounting in the basement" (Ramamoorti et al., 2013, p. 106)! As brilliant as Richard was in his business dealings, he was equally diabolical, callous and cruel in his justifications for achieving success. Unbeknownst to me from the onset was the fact that Richard was an egotist of the highest order, a consummate narcissist, likely a sociopath, and one of the biggest liars and fraudsters to ever lead a Fortune 500 company (Ramamoorti et al., 2013, p. 152).

Power orientation can be displayed as a form of punishment especially when there is the perception that someone is interfering with their goals, albeit fraudulent goals. In an organizational setting, retribution may take the form of punishment without legitimate cause for interfering with one's criminal activities. One of the clearest signs of punishment without cause is through demotions and terminations at an organization perpetrating fraud. Subordinates are treated inequitably depending on whether or not they participated in the fraud. HealthSouth CFO William Owens also exercised intimidation as a form of power orientation. For example, HealthSouth Vice President of Finance, Diana Henze, refused to sign off on financial statements due to her suspicions that they were fraudulent. Henze even lodged a complaint with the compliance department, but her complaint drew no reaction.

After being passed over for a promotion to a lesser qualified candidate, she confronted Owens who told her: "You made it clear that you would not do what we asked" (Jennings, 2007, p. 23). This response referred to her refusal to sign off on the financial statements that were in fact fraudulent. Recall that this behavior reflects the antisocial trait of goal interference where someone is punished if their actions are perceived as getting in the way of one's agenda. In this case, Henze was getting in the way of Owens' goal of providing Scrushy with the fraudulent financial statements he needed to perpetuate the fraud scheme.

Scrushy not only lacked a sense of humility about his success, he had his own version of the American dream. In 2003, CBS journalist Mike Wallace interviewed him for the program *60 Minutes* that gave Scrushy a platform on which to display his sense of narcissistic entitlement. When Wallace brought up the subject of the 2002 stock sales that led to the SEC's allegations of insider trading, Scrushy explained that he was forced to exercise his stock options because they were about to expire. Not content to leave the matter alone, he went on to say, "When you build something from nothing, you should have the right at some point to have some liquidity…That's what every young MBA in America is working toward. So what I did was, you know, the American dream" (Solieri et al., 2008, p. 349). Yet, for Scrushy, the American dream went far beyond mere financial security for himself and his family, it meant making more money than anyone else and enjoying perks that were reserved for only the richest men (Solieri et al., 2008). Scrushy satisfied his desire for grandiosity by building a museum as a tribute to himself on HealthSouth's headquarters campus located Birmingham, Alabama which depicted how he turned his small hospital into an empire (Haddad et al., 2003). His community college alma mater also boasted a Richard M. Scrushy campus (Heylar, 2003).

Scrushy also donated money to schools such as the University of Alabama and community centers who, in turn, glorified his name on signage which granted him celebrity status in the local community (Romero, 2003). Consider the insights from those who observed Scrushy's need for attention: "Scrushy needed applause the way he needed oxygen" in that he would pay celebrities to spend time with him and expected his employees to watch him play in his band (Helyar, 2003, p. 79). In fact, he made videos of his band and required them to be played at HealthSouth's annual meetings and brought the band on tours with expenses paid by HealthSouth (Farrell, 2006). At his home outside of Birmingham, Scrushy would welcome visitors by ushering them to the 'media room' where on the wall hung a massive painting of himself cruising along the highway on a Harley-Davidson motorcycle, wearing a bandana to look like actor Dennis Hooper in the movie *Easy Rider* (Farrell, 2006). Once visitors had time to absorb the painting, Scrushy insisted they watch him sing with celebrities, in videos that he claimed ranked number one on Australian popular music charts during his 'Down Under' Tour.

In the past, Scrushy attended an all-white church in an affluent Birmingham suburb, but after his legal problems began, he joined a predominantly black church and preached at several black churches around the city. Several pastors and congregants from the black churches appeared each day in court with him (Rezaee & Riley, 2010). Citing a religious conversion, Scrushy and his wife founded the Grace and Purpose Church that hosted a bible show airing five days a week (Antilla, 2012). Scrushy stated, "All of us turn to God first thing when we go through the fire…I have been called as a soldier for the end times and the age of grace…I would like to be free to continue helping people" (Reuters, 2007).

Psychopathy, Leadership and White-collar Crime

Most people acquainted with the concept of psychopathy think they know what a psychopath is, what they look like, and how they behave, yet few psychological concepts evoke such fascination and misunderstanding at the same time. Even within academic circles, disagreement persists about what psychopathy consists of, coupled with contemporary academic descriptions containing puzzling contradictions. Among the general public, psychopathy remains a poorly understood concept reflecting some combination of our childhood fears of the bogeyman, our adult fascination with human evil, and perhaps envy of people who appear to go through life unencumbered by feelings of guilt, anguish, and insecurity (Skeem et al., 2012). On one level psychopathy seems to connote predatory violence where these individuals use their intelligence and social friendliness to lure victims to their death; traits demonstrated by notorious serial killers such as Ted Bundy, Jeffrey Dahmer, and John Wayne

269

Gacy. However, the concept of psychopathy is not synonymous with violence despite media descriptions where the words psychopathic and killer are used interchangeably. Psychopathy can and does exist in the absence of official criminal convictions, and many psychopathic individuals have no histories of violence (Warren, 2009).

An alternate image of psychopathy, commonly referred to as the corporate psychopath, evokes images of the manipulative, bullying, yet charming boss. Such individuals are capable of rising through the ranks to leadership positions, and in some cases, achieve wealth and fame (Babiak & Hare, 2006). They are viewed as capable of elaborate white-collar crime scheming and masterful manipulations with calmness. Bernard Madoff, the Wall Street money manager who was convicted for swindling investors out of billions of dollars over many years in a massive Ponzi scheme, comes to mind as the prototypical corporate psychopath (Perri & Brody, 2012). Modern descriptions of psychopathy derive most directly from the observations of American psychiatrist Hervey Cleckley who wrote, *The Mask of Sanity* (1941). Cleckley drew from his experience with psychiatric patients and existing scholarship that spanned over one hundred years to clarify the major traits of psychopathy.

As a psychiatrist, Cleckley noticed a troubling pattern of behavioral traits in some of his clients that stood notably in contrast to those observed among his patients undergoing psychiatric treatment (Benson & Manchak, 2014). For example, Cleckley would have interacted with those who are psychotic. Psychotic individuals hear voices, experience hallucinations, and perceive an altered sense of reality, whereas psychopaths recognize reality, but display deficits in moral emotions that in turn affect their moral decision making and behavior. The people Cleckley referred to as psychopathic were not psychotic or from the criminal population even though it is clear in his writings that they displayed antisocial behaviors, albeit in a different form. However, consider the fact that an individual may have a mental illness does not mean that they cannot also be psychopathic (Murphy & Vess, 2003). Yet many psychopaths are capable of fooling professionals who observe abnormal behavior and equate it to a mental illness issue when the same professionals ignore the calculating, manipulating, and planning beneath their schemes that are not the symptoms of someone who is mentally ill (Hakkanen-Nyholm & Hare, 2009).

Psychopaths he encountered were not disoriented or out of touch with reality, nor did they experience the delusions, or intense subjective distress that characterizes most other mental disorders. They were rational and aware of what they were doing and why plus their behavior was the result of free choice (Perri & Lichtenwald, 2007a). Typically, psychopathy is referred to as a personality disorder, but is not considered to be as functionally disabling as a more commonly known mental illness such as a psychotic disorder where irrational and disorganized thinking makes the afflicted unaware of the consequences of their actions (Perri, 2011a). Psychopaths differ from people with other mental disorders in that they have rational decision making processes, but lack an emotional sense of right and wrong (Walker & Jackson, 2016). Presently scholarship has identified different types of psychopaths and this distinction is important because it impacts the type of psychopath we are more apt to encounter at work and those that are at risk to engage in organizational misconduct that entails illegal and unethical practices.

First of all, there are those psychopaths that display an emotionless quality about them where they do not experience anxiety that others would; in essence they appear to be immune from anxiety attributed to disturbing circumstances and appear to represent the ones that Cleckley would have encountered in his practice (Cleckley, 1988). The psychopaths Cleckley encountered exhibited low anxiety while displaying an emotional flatness that we equate with their demeanor reflecting that remorseless quality where they do not internalize the pain and distress they may cause others. These psychopaths at times are referred to as Cleckleyan psychopaths because they were the ones that Cleckley observed and wrote about and the ones we are most apt to encounter at work because they outwardly appear to be socially well-adjusted although they are capable of harboring and eventually displaying antisocial traits—hence a mask of normalcy. They have a tendency to make a positive first impression, yet are less prone to experience embarrassment (Spain et al., 2013). On the other hand, there are psychopaths who display higher levels of anxiety exemplified by an emotional instability, frustrations due to not being able to satisfy their needs, and meanness, referring to as sense of cruelty and callousness, as observed by those in the prison system. The probability of encountering the unstable criminal psychopath with no work history and an extensive criminal history at work is lower.

Cleckley's *Mask of Sanity* suggests that the essence of psychopathy entails a mystery where these individuals appear normal on the outside, but not on the inside. As described by Cleckley, psychopaths, at least those that he studied and treated as contrasted to unstable criminal psychopaths, are marked by an outward appearance of positive social adjustment, including friendliness, however these features occur hand in hand with persistent, antisocial behaviors (Cleckley, 1941; 1988). Cleckley describes a psychopath as someone who, in terms of initial appearances, comes across in conversation as sound in judgement, ethics, morals, values, and reasoning (Cleckley, 1941; 1988). Psychopaths can be effective at presenting themselves well and can be very likeable and charming (Hare, 1999). They appear to wear as Cleckley vividly put it, a "mask of sanity" referring to the tendency of psychopaths to present themselves as confident, personable, and well-adjusted in comparison with most psychiatric patients he encountered (Skeem et al., 2012). Yet they harbor an underlying pathology through their antisocial behaviors and attitudes, but over time their true selves are revealed (Skeem et al., 2012). Moreover, several skills make it difficult to see psychopaths for who they really are:

> First, they are motivated to, and have a talent for, "reading people" and for sizing them up quickly…many psychopaths come across as having excellent oral communication skills…their insight into the psyche of others combined with a superficial—but convincing—verbal fluency allows them to change their personas skillfully as it suits the situation and their game plan…Like chameleons, psychopaths can hide who they really are and mask their true intentions from their victims for extended periods. The psychopath is a near-perfect invisible human predator (Babiak & Hare, 2006, p. 37–39).

According to Dr. Robert Hare, international psychopathy expert from the University of British Colombia, the concept of psychopathy refers to a specific cluster of traits and behaviors used to describe an individual (Gunn & Wells, 1999). Psychopathy is a personality disorder characterized by behavioral, emotional, and interpersonal deficits including, but not limited to, pathological lying, impulsivity, being interpersonally manipulative, reduced concern for social norms and rules, and lack of guilt or conscience, remorse, and empathy. They share overlapping traits with an antisocial personality, but is yet quite distinct (Benson & Manchak, 2014). It is estimated that clinical psychopathy is present in about one percent of the population and about ten percent are in the "gray zone" displaying "sufficient psychopathic features to be of concern to others" (Babiak & Hare, 2019, p. 175). Since personality traits are the result of genetic-environmental interactions, recent research in behavioral genetics indicates that callous, unemotional traits and antisocial tendencies, likely precursors to the dimensions of psychopathy, are highly heritable. Presently there is no evidence psychopathy results solely from environmental influences although environment influences might enhance and trigger the display of psychopathic traits (Carozza, 2008a). However, just as one symptom does not make a disease, nor does being narcissistic, lacking empathy, being callous, make someone a psychopath; they may be difficult people to deal with perhaps, but they are not necessarily psychopathic (Carozza, 2008a). Let us examine some of the traits characterizing this disorder.

Pathological lying is characterized by a history of frequent and repeated lying, often for no apparent purpose (Hare, 1991). Manipulativeness is characterized by charm, deceit, reckless risk-taking, and a cavalier attitude about rules and social norms (Pardue et al., 2013b). Thrill or sensation-seeking refers to the tendency to seek out thrilling and exciting activities, to take risks, and to avoid boredom (Pardue, et al., 2013b). Other signature traits of psychopaths are chronic self-centeredness, a parasitic lifestyle, egocentrism, and narcissism that places their own interests and the pursuit of their desires above all others in a way that disregards the rights or feelings of others. Psychopaths already are aware of their own motivations, see little wrong with them, and do not believe they need to change (Carozza, 2008a). Psychopaths experience difficulty attributing guilt to themselves or shame because of their low concern for social norms, but they are willing to display concern for social norms when it is to their benefit (Walker & Jackson, 2016).

Guilt refers to the private feelings of a troubled conscience caused by a personal wrongdoing or by exploiting a valued other (Pardue et al., 2013b). These individuals also engage in antisocial behavior with "little or no evidence of the conscious conflict or the subsequent regret" (Cleckley, 1988, p. 344). As serial killer Ted Bundy stated displaying a lack of conscience, "I don't feel guilty for anything, I feel sorry for people who feel guilt" (Walker & Jackson, 2016). What might a lack of conscience look like? Consider the case of Dr. Farid Fata who was sentenced to 45 years in federal prison for violating more than 550 patients' trust and making more than $17 million from fraudulent billings, money laundering, and kickbacks (Allen, 2015). Dr. Fata told his patients that they had cancer and then would administer chemotherapy, when in fact they did not have cancer. Moreover, consider the conscienceless behavior of Dr. Michael Swango who poisoned to death as many as 60 hospital patients under his care. Swango described in his diary the pleasure he experienced from killing stating he loved the "sweet, husky, close smell of indoor homicide" reminding him that he was "still alive" (Kocsis, 2008, p. 8).

If there is an absence of emotion, conscience, empathy, and the ability to form attachments to others, what replaces these human qualities? What replaces empathy and one's inability to authentically harbor emotions to guide and regulate behavior is a desire for power, dominance, control, and exploitation over others and situations for selfish reasons (Perri, 2016). For example, according to Dr. Liane Leedom, the inability to have emotions is replaced by the motivation for dominance, control, or power; to them, having power over another is the pleasure (Leedom, 2006). Another way to think about what replaces these human qualities is to consider Dr. Martha Stout's assessment when she states that life, in essence, is reduced to a contest and human beings are nothing more than game pieces to be moved about, used as shields, or destroyed—it's about winning to satisfy an intrapsychic need (Stout, 2005). Dr. Reiber stated it another way, "[f]or psychopaths, power can be experienced only in the context of victimization: If they are to be strong, someone else must pay. There is no such thing, in the psychopath's universe, as the merely weak; whoever is weak is also a sucker that is someone who demands to be exploited" (Reiber, 1997, p. 47).

Empathy is the understanding of another person's point of view or the ability to detect accurately the emotional information transmitted by another person. The capacity for empathy is considered a necessity for the development of moral emotions such as guilt and compassion and to promote prosocial behaviors while inhibiting antisocial ones. Dr. Hare further states, "[I]t is possible to have people who are so emotionally disconnected that they can function as if other people are objects to be manipulated and destroyed without any concern" (Chivers, 2014). Lacking in feelings for others, they take what they want and do as they please, violating social norms and expectations without the slightest sense of guilt or regret (Hare, 1999). Harboring an emotional deficit can be viewed as a risk factor that increases the probability of engaging in antisocial and criminal acts (Lingnau et al., 2017). Although all of the traits are important, there are certain traits that stand out more than others in terms of identifying psychopaths. This trait most closely relates to a psychopath's lack of remorse for their actions because the psychopath is not capable of emotionally internalizing how their behavior impacts another person. For example, one homicidal offender was asked whether he had any remorse for his heinous, homicidal crimes. The offender stated, "Remorse, what for? I didn't even know them" (Odell & Donnelly, 2016).

Another example of what a display of a lack of remorse might entail is the answer given by a rapist when he was asked about whether he felt bad for hurting someone. The offender answered, "Do I feel bad if I hurt someone? Yeah, sometimes. But mostly it's like...uh...[laughs]...How do you feel the last time you squashed a bug?" (Hare, 1999, p. 33). It is understandable that people differ in their capacity to empathize and display emotions, yet most people are attuned to the basic feelings and emotions of others. Empathetic feelings help people understand what values facilitate socialization and the bonding that occurs between people (Soltes, 2016). Yet the reality is that some people have a much weaker capacity to appreciate the emotional state of others and how their actions may impact another's emotional state. In fact, not being able to understand how one's actions impact another's emotional state helps explain why some are capable of committing crimes; they either cannot envision how their behavior impacts others, or they do not care. For example, one female homicidal offender who was known to have killed multiple elderly individuals expressed an opinion on her crimes stating, "Most of the people I killed were old enough to die anyway or else had some disease that might cause death. I never killed children. I love them" (Vronsky, 2007, p. 133).

They do not internalize remorse, instead they deny responsibility for their own poor behavior and blame others for failures and harms they claim they never caused (Boddy, 2016). By being emotionally shallow, they can demonstrate a show or display of emotion, but without any true feeling. They are unresponsive to personal interactions in a normal sense such as not responding to kindness or trust in the ordinary manner or express an appreciation for what others have done for them. They may not display anxiety even in upsetting circumstances which would disturb or upset most other people, for example, when discovered in bizarre or immoral situations (Boddy, 2016). Psychopaths intellectually understand emotions, but do not experience the physiological reaction associated with them (Warren, 2009). Usually when people feel remorse for hurting someone, there is an unsettling physical reaction that accompanies these feelings. This quality does not apply to psychopaths but for appearance purposes and impression management, they are capable of fooling people with outward signs of emotions. They understand another's point of view, but lack sufficient emotional capability or concern to alter their actions appropriately to take those concerns to heart. Psychopaths cognitively understand that people have emotions, but they never "lose themselves" in another's emotional experience (Engelbert, 2019, p. 877). Consider the egocentric statement of a psychopathic rapist when asked about the impact of his crime on his victims:

> What do you want me to say? That won't change anything for them. Maybe it did hurt them, but how do you expect that to change things for me?...What I think now won't change anything about their situation or mine; I can well understand when other people want to express their feelings, but it's got nothing to do with me. What other people feel isn't important to me (Engelbert, 2019, p. 878).

They understand the moral context to a situation, but their lack of emotions impacts how they react to moral issues. Moreover, they have the intellectual ability, but lack the emotional capability of understanding what others are experiencing which explains why they seem shallow and do not bond in a sincere manner (Mullins et al., 2006). Yet what is paradoxical is how can they read other peoples' emotional state and exploit their vulnerabilities when they themselves do not experience emotions in the same manner? Psychopaths, especially those that are intellectually bright, will practice associating certain types of responses with a given situation, thus their outward but false display of emotions were learned by watching others and how they behave in a given set of circumstances (Meloy, 2002). For example, consider psychopathic white-collar offender Norman Sjonberg who killed his clients and took their money. Norman spoke about this "emotional void, an inability to feel things like anybody else; to know when to cry, when to feel joy" (Hare, 1999, p. 54). Norman would read self-help psychology books to learn the appropriate responses to everyday life events in order to give others the appearance of normality.

In essence they know emotions through words by watching how others react to situations, but not through normal physiological reactions people experience naturally that words can trigger within us. As homicidal offender and author Jack Abbott stated in his book *In the Belly of the Beast*, "These are emotions—a whole spectrum of them—that I know only through words, through reading and my immature imagination. I can imagine I feel those emotions...but I cannot" (Abbott, 1981, p. 13). They may experience frustration and duping delight, but the deep-rooted complex emotions such as love, empathy, remorse, and guilt are absent (Herve, 2003). Psychopaths and non-psychopathic individuals experience emotions differently as far as the kind, degree, and manner in which they are displayed. As a result, there is a disconnect between what they say and the message conveyed that can appear illogical because the message does not have an emotional context to make the message sound appropriate. For example, consider the previous statements of the offenders who stated not having remorse for victims because one does not know them or claiming not to kill children because one loves them, but killing older people is deemed acceptable.

Emotions are required to control basic human impulses either by providing alternative courses of action or by signaling their inappropriateness through a future anticipation of regret, remorse, or guilt if one were to carry through with a course of action harmful to others (Herve, 2003). As a result, lacking complex social emotions in their day-to-day activities may lead psychopaths to act upon their shallow emotions, impulses, and urges without thoughtful reflection. Moreover, most psychopaths are mentally capable of appreciating the criminality of their actions and can be rather methodical and strategic regarding their crimes even though they may display an impulsive lifestyle (Hanlon, 2010). One of the most obvious expressions of psychopathy involves the flagrant criminal violation of society's rules (Mathieu et al., 2015). However, antisocial behavior is not always criminal in nature, but can mean unethical behaviors such as sabotaging relationships or attempting to control others emotionally.

While psychopathy has similarities to antisocial personality disorder, which is characterized by a disregard for societal rules including criminal behavior, it is not synonymous with nor should it be confused with criminality or violence, in general. We observe psychopathic individuals with antisocial dispositions in financial positions and they appear to be more unresponsive to potential punishment and do not learn from their mistakes (Jones, 2014). This quality may explain why psychopaths "remain prisoners of the present, unable to project into the future and foresee the consequences of their actions, and lacking a capacity to reflect upon the past in any meaningful way" so that they can learn from their mistakes and avoid repeating them (Gacono & Meloy, 2012, p. 49). They are more apt to ignore or not even consider the risks inherent in certain decisions and miscalculate the risk of being caught and punished. They can be self-destructive in that for psychopaths even when the threat of punishment is clear, they still are willing to take the risks associated with financial misconduct. Even when psychopaths engage in fraud, they will jeopardize much in order to seek what is trivial; at times their crimes are incomprehensible and are not done for any material gain at all (Cleckley, 1988).

Psychopaths can make the same kinds of moral distinctions as non-psychopaths when it comes to evaluating moral dilemmas. They understand the distinction between right and wrong, but are not concerned about the understanding of the rightfulness or wrongfulness of the dilemma, or appreciate the consequences resulting from morally inappropriate behavior (Cima et al., 2010). Emotional processing in evaluating the appropriateness of a given moral scenario is not a necessary condition for its evaluation or to form judgements about dilemmas (Cima et al., 2010). Yet emotions do assist with how we should respond to moral dilemmas; normal emotional processing is likely to be the most important trait in generating a response to the moral question (Cima et al., 2010). Where psychopaths deviate is that what is morally forbidden is not relevant to them nor does it inhibit morally inappropriate behavior. Psychopaths are not as apt to engage in the kinds of motivational systems that inspire appropriate behavior (Cima et al., 2010). Psychopaths can be highly impulsive and irresponsible often acting on a whim to fulfill immediate needs with little if any thought to the consequences of their actions (Warren, 2009). Unlike Machiavellianism and narcissism, individuals high in psychopathy are likely to engage in short-term gratification and high-stakes risks, even when they clearly face the possibility of future punishment (Mathieu et al., 2012). In some respects, this research reflects the previous statement that psychopaths reflect the description of being "prisoners of the present".

Machiavellians tend to plan ahead, are more strategic, display more self-control, and do not display the dysfunctional impulsivity more aligned with psychopaths who may engage in self-sabotaging behaviors. Fearfulness that is otherwise uncomfortable and acts as a constraint for a non-psychopath does not apply in the same manner to psychopaths. The psychopaths' lack of anticipatory fear diminishes their ability to foresee the negative consequences of a behavior. Lack of fearfulness also diminishes their ability to thoughtfully assess risk and plan accordingly and once caught for their misdeeds, they are likely to blame others for their misfortunes (Warren, 2009). Psychopaths are intrinsically self-interested so they are unlikely to direct positive emotions in support of others, but are comfortable directing negative emotions toward others, such as intimidations, bullying, anger, and aggression (Walker & Jackson, 2016). The limited research suggests that psychopaths are not affected by directing such negative emotions, because they are not concerned about what other people think of them, apart from individuals who have access to desired resources and capabilities they want for themselves (Walter & Jackson, 2016).

Also, it is not uncommon for the terms psychopathy and sociopathy to be incorrectly assumed to be synonymous with each other; they are related but not identical conditions. Sociopathy refers to a pattern of attitudes, values, and behaviors that are considered antisocial and criminal by society at large, but seen as normal or necessary by the subculture or social environment in which it developed. Sociopaths may have a well-developed conscience and a normal capacity for empathy, guilt, and loyalty to those in their inner-circle, but their sense of right and wrong is based on the norms and expectations of their subculture or group (Carozza, 2009). For example, individuals who belong to organized crime, terrorist groups, and gang-related associations display sociopathic qualities and some within these groups may and probably are psychopathic. One final note before we look at the links between fraud and psychopathy. What is debated is to what extent does how people are socialized produce psychopathic characteristic byproducts namely, cold, remorseless, without guilt viewpoints. Let us consider the opinion of journalist L. Frank Baum, known for his *Wizard of Oz* books. Baum was not seen as a "moral monster" but as a man of goodwill who expressed an understanding of race shared by millions of people during his lifetime. His opinion of indigenous peoples is rightly considered barbaric, but during his lifetime, his views represented the views of many others. He stated:

> The nobility of the Redskin is extinguished, and what few are left are a pack of whining curs who lick the hand that smites them…The Whites, by law of conquest, by justice of civilization, are masters of the American continent and the best safety of the frontier settlements will be secured by the total annihilation of the few remaining Indians. Why not annihilation? Their glory has fled, their spirit broken, their manhood effaced; better that they should die than live like the miserable wretches that they are (Koonz, 2003, p. 7).

Also, consider the experience that philosopher Karl Jaspers had with a German youth illustrating how displays of cold, brutal, conscienceless, remorseless behavior may have not be a result of psychopathic disposition, but potentially cultural socialization. Jaspers tells the story that after World War II he was in the hospital with an injured German youth who had been a guard in a concentration camp. The youth was deeply upset about something and Jaspers asked him questions about what was so troubling to him. Jaspers learned that the youth would guard a line of Jewish prisoners waiting to be led into the gas chambers and noticed that a small Jewish boy was sneaking away to escape. The youth pretended that he did not notice and let the Jewish boy escape. Jaspers ultimately learned that what was upsetting and gnawing away at the youth was that he could find "no peace because he let the boy get away" and that he failed in his duties (Duska et al, 2011, p. 126).

The youth's conscience was bothering him. This is not an individual that could not experience emotions like a true psychopath. One perhaps would rather want to believe that the youth was expressing remorse for even participating in this barbarous behavior, but that is not the emotional display he experienced. This youth's conscience was not bothered by what he did, but by what he did not do. If we assume that the majority of humans are equipped to have a conscience, this does not mean that we are co-equally programmed to be bothered by the same behaviors. What may be ghastly and unconscionable to one group of people may be totally acceptable to another group of people due to how they are socialized, what beliefs they hold which ultimately impacts how they make decisions that may impact the lives of others. The story provides a clear case of a badly-formed conscience that was more likely than not a product of corrupt socialization into a Nazi ideology and adopting the behaviors of those around him that did not have any problem expressing cold brutality.

Corporate Fraud and Psychopathy

Not all psychopaths are in prison. Some are in the Boardroom.

Babiak & Hare (2006)

Initially Edwin Sutherland acknowledged psychopathy as a risk factor that increased the probability of engaging in antisocial behavior. He expressed the usefulness of the concept in his first textbook published in 1924 which was seventeen years before Cleckley's 1941 publication of the *Mask of Sanity*. In examining a potential correlation between crime and behavioral science, Sutherland initially acknowledged that the concept of psychopathy was not well defined but nonetheless important stated:

> One type of personality that seems to be closely connected with criminality…is the psychopathic personality…the concept has not been clearly defined, methods of diagnosis have not been standardized, and the classification of types of psychopathic personalities is not satisfactory, [yet] there is good reason to believe that the psychopathic personalities…will get into difficulty with other people more frequently

that the average individual...[W]hen the term psychopathic personality is considered...[It] is apt to include criminality... (Sutherland, 1924, p. 124).

However, later on Sutherland rejected his previous belief that behavioral differences between people might be a risk factor that increased the probability of engaging in crime. For example, Sutherland wrote in a 1940 article on white-collar crime that white-collar offenders "are not feebleminded or psychopathic" (Sutherland, 1940, p. 10). Although individually Sutherland authored four textbooks, his views continued in subsequent textbooks that bore his name. Consider that in Sutherland and Cressey (1966), *Principles of Criminology, Seventh Edition*, the authors did not consider psychopathy as a risk factor for criminal behavior. Instead, Sutherland and Cressey state, "Because it is difficult to define or identify a psychopath, the label psychopathic personality can be applied to almost anyone...The concept is often designated a waste-basket category into which not-otherwise-explicable criminal behavior is tossed" (Sutherland & Cressey, 1966, p. 169). Times have changed and today the concept of psychopathy is better understood even if more research is needed to understand the links between psychopathy and antisocial behavior. Currently, however, the majority of the literature on psychopathy has focused on the relationship between psychopathy and what is commonly referred to as street-level offenses, such as violence. If psychopathy is linked to street crimes, it is not unreasonable to make extrapolations that it is probably linked to white-collar crime.

In the face of large-scale Ponzi schemes, embezzlement, insider trading, mortgage fraud, and internet frauds and schemes, it was inevitable that psychopathy would become one explanation for such callous and socially devastating behavior (Babiak, Neumann & Hare, 2010). Yet even though psychopathy has become a highly researched personality disorder predicting criminal behavior, "there is little understanding as yet how psychopathy contributes causally and under what circumstances" to criminal behavior (Skeem et al., 2011, p. 126). While several experts in the field allude to the idea of psychopathy in the corporate world, very little empirical research is available to understand white-collar crime psychopaths and the role of psychopathy in fraud, corruption, and other egregious violations of the public trust (Lesha & Lesha, 2012). Its application to white-collar criminality cannot simply be based on anecdotal evidence of an expression of psychopathy (Smith & Lilienfeld, 2013). Even as far back as 1948, criminal psychiatrist Dr. Bromberg recognized before Dr. Cleckley and Edwin Sutherland that psychopathic behavior as a social problem cannot be ignored especially its link to white-collar offenders stating, "as Cleckley has pointed out, the disregard of reality...has been seen to exist in men otherwise successful as professionals or business executives, who sooner or later betray themselves through some crass action" without experiencing remorse (Bromberg, 1948, p. 104).

Unfortunately, the impetus for conducting extensive research on the behavioral profile of these offenders is lacking (Ragatz et al., 2010). The information gained from such investigations would provide valuable clues about corporate psychopathy and would establish an empirical base for conducting and evaluating research on the more high-profile offenders who have wreaked financial and emotional havoc in the lives of so many people on an individual and organizational level. Furthermore, we know little about psychopathic individuals committing fraud, or about the ways in which they manage to avoid prosecution, termination, or formal censure, perhaps with the help of organizations that strive to keep problems in-house. However, according to industrial psychologist Dr. Babiak and forensic psychologist Dr. Hare, sounding the proverbial alarm to accelerate research examining the links between psychopathy and white-collar crime, state that psychopathic white-collar offenders often are "heavily involved in obscenely lucrative scams of every sort where they lead lavish lifestyles while their victims lose their life savings, their dignity, and their health—a financial death penalty" (Carozza, 2008a, p. 38). This is because psychopaths see empathy and a sense of responsibility—qualities usually considered as the epitome of goodness and humanity—as signs of weakness to be exploited, and laws and social rules as inconvenient restrictions on their freedom (Hare, 1999).

Their insights parallel the previous statement of CFO Samuel Antar who stated, "White-collar criminals consider your humanity, ethics, and good intentions as weaknesses to be exploited in the execution of their crimes" (Antar, 2010). Furthermore, what exactly does research reveal about white-collar offenders, their potential links to psychopathic traits, and the influence of psychopathy in the workplace, its subordinates, and leadership? Scholarship is beginning to emerge, albeit sparse, examining links between the criminal personality, psychopathic traits, and white-collar offenders. Several key findings have emerged suggesting psychopathy is a fraud offender risk factor (Perri, 2013b). In one study, a relationship exists with psychopathy and attitudes justifying intentions to commit white-collar crime where offenders displayed self-centered and Machiavellian personalities (Ray, 2007). In another study, white-collar offenders differ from non-white-collar offenders on criminal thinking and lifestyle criminality in addition to psychopathic traits (Ragatz et al., 2012). The study sample included 39 white-collar crime only offenders, 88 white-collar versatile offenders representing offenders who also previously committed white-collar and non-white-collar crimes, and 86 non-white-collar crime only offenders incarcerated in a U.S. federal prison.

White-collar only offenders were found to score lower, overall, for having engaged in criminality as a lifestyle choice, but higher on some measures of psychopathic traits than non-white-collar offenders. White-collar versatile offenders, however, scored highest in criminal thinking traits that were covered in chapter one of this book. Research also suggests a significant positive association between psychopathy, egocentricity, Machiavellianism, and a cavalier, non-planning attitude toward engaging in white-collar crime, all leading toward the intention to commit white-collar crime (Ray & Jones, 2011). White-collar offenders are fundamentally driven by narcissism, lack of humility, lack of integrity, self-centeredness, and an egocentric sense of entitlement (Ray & Jones, 2011). They are likely to endorse workplace antisocial and manipulative behaviors—such as blaming others for their own mistakes—and disregard organizational norms (Ray & Jones, 2011). When compared to non-white-collar offenders, they are more likely to employ charm, pathological lying, and other manipulative strategies to exploit those who have something they want or need (Ragatz et al., 2012). Not surprisingly, many psychopaths are criminals, but many others use their chameleon-like abilities to appear normal while harming others (Boddy, 2015). Such white-collar criminals are capable of living double lives and evading capture for long periods of time (Yildirim & Derksen, 2015).

In addition, research is beginning to suggest that the concept of psychopathy may not necessarily reflect a homogenous construct, but rather one with a similar core, but different expressions of the traits (Skeem et al., 2011). In other words, psychopathic traits may be displayed differently by white-collar versus non-white-collar classes of criminals. Where violent psychopathic offenders may be interpersonally aggressive, such traits are not useful to white-collar criminals who are attempting to financially exploit someone, which requires voluntary trust so that assets can be taken surreptitiously by deceit, not fear. As a result, not all psychopaths are violent and incarcerated criminals; some are unethical and predatory business associates (Walsh & Hemmens, 2008). Psychopathic offenders high in conscientiousness prefer planned rather than spontaneous behavior to effectively regulate their impulses by keeping their behavior in check, controlling their destructive impulses, and preventing detection (Burkley, 2010). Some of the traits consistent with psychopathy are shared among white-collar offenders and non-offending individuals who are situated in white-collar type occupations (Babiak et al., 2010).

Furthermore, given that thrill-seeking appears to be one of the traits that some psychopaths express, excitement seeking business individuals are willing to take excessive risks in order to achieve financial success and status through white-collar crime (Lesha & Lesha, 2012). In addition, white-collar offenders appear to exhibit selected personality traits that are consistent with the construct of psychopathy, especially traits of being egocentric and domineering, yet they can be selectively sociable when interacting with others (Benson & Manchak, 2014). These seemingly contradictory personality traits are not necessarily mutually exclusive and their co-existence makes sense if one considers that being social is necessary for exploitation of others in a fraud scheme. White-collar criminals tend to be more outgoing, assertive, and engaged in self-promotion and social networking to impress powerful individuals who can position them near opportunities to engage in white-collar crime. Indeed, their somewhat more desirable personality traits allow white-collar offenders to gain access to and "win over" or "dupe" vulnerable people and companies, and their egocentrism, coupled with a lack of empathy, allows them to do so with little concern for how their behavior impacts others (Babiak & Hare, 2006).

Leadership and Psychopathy

Leaders with psychopathic personalities are found in the military, industrial, academic, and non-profit circles (Gao & Raine, 2010). Their ability to thrive in corporate settings presents the most significant global threat to ethical leadership, and begs for an important new direction in leadership research and corporate fraud examination (Gudmundsson & Southey, 2011). The existence of white-collar and professional psychopaths has been acknowledged since Cleckley's *The Mask of Sanity*. Yet, it was not until the final decades of the last century that psychopathy among managers of corporations was discussed in a series of papers from academics in psychology and management. Psychopathy is not necessarily an impediment to success in an organization and in fact psychopathic individuals are found in positions of authority because risk-taking, low fear, and lack of concern for consequences are associated with ambition and strong leadership styles (Babiak et al., 2010). Most of the research on dark personalities and leadership has focused on narcissism and Machiavellianism, not psychopathy, but research suggests that individuals with such personalities rise to the top of organizations with the potential of adversely impacting the lives of many individuals (Walker & Jackson, 2016). However, the link between psychopathy and leadership is weak and more work is needed to understand how they actually reach levels of leadership and their potential downfall (Boddy, 2015).

Current research suggests that psychopathy may be associated with leadership emergence, but not with effectiveness. Such individuals may display strategic thinking, creativity, and good communication skills, but they may not be effective team players with a track record of accomplishments (Mathieu et al., 2015). Corporate psychopaths manipulate power holders so they can also acquire power. They are unreliable, not supportive, fail to protect subordinates, and rely on intimidation despite being initially charming and engaging in the short-term. Over time, their true colors may be revealed through recklessness and broken commitments (Mathieu et al., 2015). Psychopaths are behaviorally antisocial by nature which leads to antisocial interpersonal strategies, abusive tactics, and attitudes that may be the most difficult to re-align with company or societal goals (Mathieu et al., 2012). Consider the insights of one who interviewed a CEO who displayed an inability to express a sense of regret for his financial crime during his parole hearing:

> During one discussion, a CEO casually described…the hours he had spent with his attorney rehearsing how to express contrition in preparation for his parole hearing. While he felt little reason to repent, his attorney advised him that he needed to effectively convey penance to improve his chances of parole. After much practice, the former CEO was soon able to present a convincing, albeit, false, display of remorse (Soltes, 2016, p. 5).

Leadership displaying psychopathic traits is heavily weighted in narcissism and Machiavellianism because they are rewarded for manipulative, deceptive, and callous behavior (Schouten & Silver, 2012). Managers and executives with such traits display a "self-centered manipulation and lack integrity that can bring down an entire corporation, causing financial and emotional damage to thousands or tens of thousands—think Enron" (Schouten & Silver, 2012, p. 147). These leaders may list short-term achievements, but in the long-term have the potential to destroy the internal culture and spirit of an organization (Hakkanen-Nyholm & Nyholm, 2012). Moreover, the links between psychopathy and white-collar crime will lead to the "deterioration of an ethical climate in the corporate context, thus facilitating criminal actions within corporations" (Lingnau et al., 2017, p. 1213). Furthermore, according to Dr. Hare, there are more people in the business world who would score high in the psychopathic dimension than in the general population, and that are located in organizations where, by the nature of their position, have power and control over other people and the opportunity to satisfy personal agendas (Deutschman, 2005).

It may be necessary to block the rise of corporate psychopaths by developing policies that target them in order to prevent financial accounting fraud (Lingnau et al., 2017). Supporting Dr. Hare's observation, "serious white-collar crimes are not necessarily committed by those who own corporations but rather by those that have access and control over organizational resources, for instance chief executive officers (CEOs) and chief financial officers (CFOs) or even upper-level line managers and supervisors" (Shover & Wright, 2001, p. 165).

278

Psychopathic leadership has been linked, albeit through anecdotal, qualitative studies, to white-collar crime (Boddy et al., 2016). In business contexts, psychopathy is related to irresponsible leadership and increased incidences of white-collar crime (Babiak et al., 2010). Clinical psychologist Dr. Ellsworth Fersch from Harvard University commenting on Enron's convicted CEO Jeffrey Skilling's personality traits believed:

> Skilling displayed the traits of a corporate psychopath. He was manipulative, glib, superficial, egocentric, shallow, and impulsive, and he lacked guilt, remorse and empathy. Skilling had the nerve to ruin thousands of people's lives by committing insider trading and fraud. Billions of dollars were lost overnight including retirement and life savings. Furthermore, Skilling claimed to be innocent and said he was the victim. Since Skilling was a high-level executive at Enron, he knew that illegal business practices were going on and could have easily stopped or reported them. Instead, he became so carried that he could not stop his illegal activities, in court skilling told lie after lie. Convicted nonetheless, he faced decades in prison (Fersch, 2006, p. 107).

Although exposing the psychopathic traits of business leaders is important given the positions of authority they hold with the potential for destruction, there does not appear to be a discipline-wide impetus by researchers to verify anecdotal evidence of traits that are an expression of psychopathy even though empirical tools are available and a control group exists in prisons who might agree to being assessed for psychopathy. One of the reasons we know little about corporate psychopathy, its link to corporate fraud, and its implications is because of the difficulty in obtaining the active cooperation of business organizations and their personnel for research purposes (Babiak et al., 2010). Drs. Babiak and Hare conducted the only study this author could find on measuring psychopathy and its implications within an organization. The study assessed 203 managers and executives identified for participation in the management development program of their respective companies. The subjects were administered the Hare Psychopathic Checklist Revised (Hare PCL-R) which is a tool to measure the extent of a subject's psychopathy relative to a prototypical psychopath. The PCL-R consists of interviewing subjects as well as reviewing a subject's past such as whether a criminal record exists. There are twenty different psychopathic traits to be measured and the assessment has a top score of 40; many of the most remorseless psychopathic criminals come close to this score.

In this case, the participants were highly educated, with one percent possessing a two-year degree, 77.8 percent had four-year degrees, and 21.2 percent possessed Ph.D., legal, or medical degrees. The vast majority of scores, about 80 percent, were between 0 and 3. However nine of the participants (4.4 percent) scored 25 or higher and eight of these nine participants (3.9 percent) scored 30 or higher—which is the common research threshold for psychopathy (Babiak et al., 2010). Also, two of these nine participants scored a 33, and one scored a 34 (Babiak et al., 2010). It is important to note that, out of nine participants with a PCL-R score of 25 or higher, two were vice presidents, two were directors, and three were managers or supervisors. There appears to be a bias within the research community to focus on non-white-collar offenders to the exclusion of other types of offenders. No compelling reason has been offered by researchers as to why they cannot go into prisons to conduct research on these offenders as they do with violent offenders, but also those who are convicted white-collar offenders out in the general population.

Yet consider interest in measuring the degree of psychopathy present in killers. Female serial killer Aileen Wournos, who was administered the PCL-R, received a score of 32 out of a possible score of 40 (Myers et al., 2005). Double homicide offender Brian Dugan received a PCL-R score of 37 out of a possible score of 40 (Gregory & Barnum, 2009). Consider the PCL-R scores of these serialists: Ted Bundy scored a 34, John Wayne Gacy scored a 27, Edmund Kemper scored a 26, Jeffrey Dahmer scored a 23, and Gary Ridgeway scored a 19 (Brooks et al., 2020). Although Dr. Fersch's observations of Jeffrey Skilling above are anecdotally accurate, we need to start applying the PCL-R or other reliable psychopathic measures to the Jeffrey Skillings and Bernard Madoffs of the world who are capable of destroying lives, albeit in a different manner. Do we believe that it is necessary to measure the psychopathy of some of these offenders given the damage they cause?

Corporate Psychopathy and Fraud in the Workplace

The business world is a perfect feeding ground for those psychopathic individuals to commit white-collar crime due to perceptions of mild legal punishments coupled a risk assessment of low detection makes these factors make white-collar crime attractive for the psychopathic leader (Palmen et al., 2020). Undiagnosed or misdiagnosed employee pathologies in the workplace are a precursor to ever-escalating organizational dysfunction. Trivializing such pathologies by perceiving them as normal disturbances or characterizing them as "personality quirks" is potentially detrimental in a workplace that is already embroiled in bullying, toxic, and aggressive behaviors coupled with participation in white-collar crime (Gudmundsson & Southey, 2011). Consequently, some commentators suggest that "one way to respond to the potential financial havoc resulting from unethical decisions within an organization is through a deeper understanding of the individuals" who are referred to as successful psychopaths (Babiak et al., 2010, p. 175). The terms corporate, organizational, and industrial psychopaths are used interchangeably with the term successful psychopath (Smith & Lilienfeld, 2012). Today's corporate psychopath may be highly educated with doctorate, medical, and legal degrees who are capable of circumventing financial controls and successfully passing corporate audits even though they committed fraud (Babiak & O'Toole, 2012).

Successful psychopaths are members of the general population who usually possess some degree of psychopathic traits potentially attaining success in certain domains of life; they are capable of engaging in work considered high paying by being functionally adaptive in their work life (Howe et al., 2014). Research suggests that psychopathy can be advantageous for individuals who seek personal rewards within a corporate setting—it can help them succeed (Walker & Jackson, 2016). Yet caution warrants that while some individuals in the corporate world, as well as the general population, may display features of psychopathy, such as being manipulative, cold, callous, and irresponsible, those traits alone do not reflect psychopathy because they can also be reflective of other dark triad personalities notably Machiavellianism, and narcissism (Jones & Hare, 2015). Moreover, the literature has not been able to decide on a common definition for success in this context but most conceptualizations define successful psychopathic individuals as those high in psychopathy that are better at evading incarceration. Dr. Cynthia Mathieu offers her insights on defining what 'success' means:

> If success is defined by the accomplishment of one's goal, then psychopathic individuals, by definition, are often successful. That is, they are successful at manipulating others into getting what they want, whatever the cost might be to others. Their ability to charm, manipulate and lie to others, coupled with the fact that their lack of empathy and guilt and failure to accept responsibility for their actions, gives psychopathic individuals the upper hand to attain their goals, by any means possible (Mathieu, 2016).

Successful behavior in this context can be defined best by considering the outcomes that increase positive consequences for an individual or reduce negative consequences for the individual. These outcomes can then be calculated into net gain meaning the positive consequences relative to negative consequences. Through such a conceptualization of success in the context of psychopathy, one can define success in any specific situation by considering the meaning of success in that specific context. Successful psychopathy also represents an expression of core psychopathic traits in ways conducive to attaining prominence in the general community, while avoiding serious adverse consequences such as social ostracism and loss of freedom (Benning et al., 2018). Successful psychopathy does not necessarily mean achieving a successful life by attaining status and wealth or that they are able to sustain fulfilling interpersonal relationships; it typically means that they may have avoided the criminal justice system (Ulrich et al., 2008). Their interpersonal style is correlated with an ability to advance in life, but there is not enough evidence to suggest that harboring psychopathic traits in and of itself leads to material success (Howe et al., 2014). A successful psychopath might get along in a corporate setting using charm and manipulation tactics, but this should not be extrapolated to mean that they do not produce broken relationships with family, friends, and coworkers. Psychopathic traits may appear useful in corporate manipulation, but those same traits can ultimately lead to their downfall.

In fact, a lack of empathy, antisocial behaviors, callousness, and a lack of remorse can be counterproductive for the accumulation of status, wealth, and maintaining successful interpersonal relationships (Ulrich et al., 2008). There has been an interest in identifying and studying successful psychopaths, but it is doubtful that the most likely candidates would volunteer to have their personality structure dissected for a study on psychopathy (Mullins-Sweat et al., 2010). Would someone who may recognize their own psychopathy want it to be exposed when they have spent their life hiding behind a façade of who they really are? One qualitative study attempted to exam psychopathy in highly educated professions, specifically those who would qualify for the term successful psychopath. Study participants were asked if they were moderately to highly familiar with the psychopathy construct, and whether or not they knew anyone who fit the description of a successful psychopath (Mullins-Sweat et al., 2010). The study revealed that individuals who were considered professionals, such as attorneys, were identified as having traits of dishonesty, exploitation, low remorse, minimizing self-blame, arrogance, callousness, and shallow affect; all considered to be among the core features of psychopathy.

The results suggest a consistent description across professions and convergence with descriptions of traditional psychopathy, though the successful psychopathy profile had higher scores on conscientiousness. Case studies of successful psychopaths who display psychopathic characteristics in business or working environments do not display the typical progression of increasing antisocial behavior and deviant lifestyles seen in incarcerated psychopaths, paralleling Dr. Cleckley's observations that psychopaths are not limited to those in mental health facilities or prisons (Mullins-Sweat et al., 2010). Successful psychopaths were rated high in aggressiveness, excitement-seeking activity, achievement orientation, self-discipline, and low in traits such as altruism, compliance, and modesty. Moreover, they have been characterized as self-serving, opportunistic, egocentric, ruthless, minimize self-blame, low remorse, callous, and shameless, but they can also be charming, manipulative, and ambitious. Some corporate psychopaths play mind games with a strong desire to win (Babiak & O'Toole, 2012). While expecting corporate psychopaths to be similar to criminal psychopaths in how they are influenced by not experiencing moral emotions, corporate psychopaths may be smarter, have more social skills, and be less prone to aggression than street-level psychopaths (Walker & Jackson, 2016).

In addition, successful psychopaths may understand interpersonal dynamics well enough to respond appropriately to others even though they have difficulty understanding experienced emotions, display low empathy for others, but are capable of managing their stress levels during interpersonal conflicts (Fix & Fix, 2015). However, these psychopaths are not exempt from instrumental, lethal violence under certain circumstances where they perceive their fraud schemes are detected; these fraud offenders are referred to 'red-collar criminals' (Babiak & Hare, 2019, p. 65). The successful psychopath displays a more responsible, less chaotic approach to life, as opposed to the erratic and impulsive nature of those who lead a criminal, violent, and parasitic lifestyle (Mullins-Sweat et al., 2010). It has been hypothesized that successful psychopaths may have enhanced neurobiological functioning, which could enable normal social interaction and superior thinking abilities (Gao & Raine, 2010).

Successful psychopaths are likely to be low on moral emotion by any definition, thus they may be aware of social norms of right and wrong, but they do not care because the understanding does not stem from experiencing moral emotions. They may articulate what they believe to be socially appropriate responses to moral issues, and may be able to fake such responses, but they are unlikely to feel emotions that are associated with morality (Walker & Jackson, 2016). While they do not feel such emotions, they may express them in order to gain advantage if they get caught stealing company funds and an expression of remorse may encourage the company to deal with the matter internally rather than seek police intervention. Any behavior is simply a means to satisfy their agenda, thus they are unconcerned if their corporate fraud steals a client's life savings rendering them destitute, or if their hostile interpersonal behavior, such as bullying, makes subordinates miserable in the workplace (Walker & Jackson, 2016). Corporate psychopathy has emerged as a lens to understand unethical behavior in organizations contributing to workplace deviance (Walker & Jackson, 2016). Emerging studies have found a highly significant correlation between corporate psychopaths and an organization's cultural acceptance of white-collar crime to financially exploit organizations and people (Lingnau et al., 2017).

They are more likely to respond unethically to ethical dilemmas, due to their unique constellation of manipulative tendencies, blunted emotions toward the concerns of others, and a proclivity toward violating social norms; they morally disengage from dilemmas by reframing how they think about moral scenarios facilitated by rationalizations (Perri, 2013b). Successful psychopaths may be more apt to engage in white-collar crimes due to their intelligence, education, less unstable lifestyle choices, more conscientiousness, and better behavioral controls (Gao & Raine, 2010). Corporate psychopathic offenders are partially responsible for organizational white-collar crime because they search for weakness and vulnerability in other people and/or organizations to exploit, such as an organization's weak internal controls (Hakkanen-Nyholm & Nyholm, 2012). Although Dr. Cleckley did not refer to corporate psychopathy, consider his observations that professionals who work in organizational settings and operate within mainstream society possess traits that compromise their ability to successfully function on an ethical level (Cleckley, 1988). Dr. Cleckley noted that such traits can go undetected until corporate relationships had been damaged, which are costly to repair, as illustrated by his example below.

A bright and attractive young man who for some years now has shown typical features of the psychopath obtained a new job. As so often in the past, he began almost at once to succeed and to excel his fellow salesmen. Soon he was regarded by the company as the best man in his line, full of promise for much greater tasks and opportunities in the near future. He regularly earned a good deal more than any of the other salesman, had an ample income for his family, and seemed on the sure road to high success. His sales record, already surpassing all competitors, soon began to increase still more, finally becoming almost unbelievable. A short time later it became evident that something was wrong. His apparent straightforwardness and his confident explanations kept the company confused for a while longer…It was eventually established that he had been selling the commodities with which he dealt at below cost. Thus he had sold widely and on a vast scale, and his commission had increased proportionally. By intricate and exceedingly well-planned tactics, both in the field and at the central office, he had covered up all discrepancies until the company had to sustain heavy losses in setting matters right (Cleckley, 1988, p. 263).

There has been little empirical research conducted on the interaction of successful corporate psychopaths and their environment, thus relatively few insights are available from clinical psychopathy studies to suggest how they may behave in specific business situations (Gudmundsson & Southey, 2011). Initially they may be friendly and charming; management may be fooled until considerable damage has been inflicted both at the individual level through directionless leadership, and at the corporate level through misuse of resources. Some psychopathic individuals prosper in corporate settings, particularly if their work thrives on an emotionless style with a consistent focus on achievement. In fact, some business cultures value profit above all regardless of how it is attained, thus a psychopath's moral deficits may be regarded as beneficial to the organization. As a result, psychopathic traits do not necessarily impede progress and advancement in corporate organizations. It is difficult to detect and avoid psychopaths in business or in any other type of organization such as the government or the military, no matter how educated or astute one is until their traits display themselves (Gao & Raine, 2010). They use the ability to hide their true selves in plain sight and display desirable personality traits to the business world (Babiak & O'Toole, 2012).

Ironically the very skills that make the corporate psychopath so unpleasant and sometimes abusive in society can facilitate a career in business even in the face of negative performance ratings (Babiak & Hare, 2006). What this means is that organizational cultures favoring a manipulative and self-centered managerial style, as long as corporate objectives are met, ignore psychopathic tendencies because their qualities are viewed as a desired asset—in essence their negative qualities are overlooked because the good they bring to the table outweighs the bad. Organizational cultures that have no issues with unethical and improper practices reward ruthless conduct and create the ideal environment for corporate psychopaths to thrive and take advantage of compromised ethical climates. In a corrupt organization, for example, the emotionless, power-oriented, aggressive psychopath may be viewed as a good corporate citizen, provided these qualities are displayed toward targets outside the organization rather than the membership and leadership of the organization itself. Furthermore, consider the insights of this psychopathy expert:

> Organizations want to see the candidate's aggressiveness, remorselessness and "bending the rules" attitude being used against their competition, not towards their own organization…They are only after one thing: their own benefit and they will not feel any remorse for defrauding their own company…Still, some label individuals who defraud organizations and clients and who are abusive towards others in the workplace "successful psychopaths." While the end result may be associated with success for the individual, who may obtain hierarchical status, money and power, success needs to be also related to the process through which individuals achieve these goals…While it may be tempting to hire candidates with psychopathic traits, these "bad boys" will not act faithfully and honestly towards the organizations, regardless of how well the organization is treating them (Mathieu, 2016).

Yet psychopaths are just as likely to engage in corporate misbehavior within the firm as they are with the firm's clients. What organizations that employ psychopaths fail to understand is that these employees, who they probably do not know are psychopathic, are not only making money at the expense of others outside of the organization, they are also out to exploit their employers through fraud. The reality is, it is a human tendency to see more of the positive attributes of an individual and fail to recognize negative qualities that may be real but hidden from observation especially when there is the perception that a person is benefiting us (Schouten & Silver, 2012). Psychopathic behaviors that have been normalized, tolerated, and even valued within organizations and organizational chaos provides sufficient cover for their psychopathic manipulation and abuse of power (Pardue et al., 2013, a, b). Consequently as Drs. Babiak and Hare observe, the psychopathic white-collar offender is the kind of individual that can give others a good impression, have a charming facade, and look and sound like the ideal corporate leader (Steinberger, 2004). However, behind this mask, they have a dark side that is deceitful, promotes fraud in the organization, and steals the company's money; this behavior has left many businesses bankrupt (Steinberger, 2004).

Individuals displaying psychopathic traits successfully enter the mainstream workforce and enjoy profitable careers in organizations by lying, manipulating, and discrediting their coworkers. There motivations and behaviors are not always aligned with the long-term success of the organization. They use divide and conquer tactics to maintain control over employees, destroy organizations from within by causing good employees to leave, abandon good business plans, and destroy organizational reputations (Boddy et al., 2015). Psychopaths are less likely to find value in indirect rewards, such as social regard and coworker acceptance. In fact, they are apt to instigate interpersonal divisions among team members which makes them easier to control (Gao & Raine, 2010). Evidence suggests that when participating in teams, corporate psychopathic behavior can wreak havoc and in departments managed by psychopaths, their conduct decreases productivity and morale plus increasing the risk of financial fraud (Babiak & O'Toole, 2012). Also, consider the insights of a expert on psychopathic leadership outcomes:

> Because psychopathic individuals do present some of the features that are viewed as associated with leadership or the "business world", many are of the opinion that to be a successful leader within organizations, one needs to possess psychopathic traits. It is crucial to understand that although psychopathic individuals may share some of the characteristics of great leaders, they do not make great leaders…corporate psychopathy in managers is associated with increased psychological distress in employees, increased employee turnover and job neglect, and lower employee job satisfaction and work motivation. Managers who score higher on corporate psychopathy also score higher on negative leadership style and lower on positive leadership styles. In fact…psychopathic traits in leaders are better predictors of employees' lowered job satisfaction, job neglect, lowered work motivation and intention to quit their job than the manager's leadership style (Mathieu, 2016).

They are unconcerned with meeting social obligations and compliance with the norm of reciprocity. Their low affectivity means that they are less likely to be concerned for other people or to feel a sense of loyalty to their employer although they display loyalty for appearance purposes and self-interest. Furthermore, while a particular mix of psychopathic features might be compatible with good performance in some corporate settings, it is likely that the influence of many psychopathic features generally relates more to good impression management and style than with good job performance and substance (Babiak & Hare, 2006). The ability to present well can hide or override subpar performance and behaviors damaging to the organization. Although very little is known about the "prevalence, strategies, and consequences of psychopathy in the corporate world" (Babiak et al. 2010, p. 175), successful corporate psychopaths display tendencies toward fraud and irresponsible leadership (Gudmundsson & Southey, 2011). Corporate psychopathic leadership abilities are usually associated with poor outcomes (Walker & Jackson, 2016). From a leadership perspective, those who display a self-centered orientation rely on manipulation, and lack of integrity can bring down an entire corporation, causing financial and emotional damage to thousands of people (Perri, 2013b). They display traits such as ambitiousness, shrewdness, and moral flexibility fostering both upward mobility in organizational hierarchies and a willingness to put the achievement of organizational goals ahead of ethical principles and legal mandates (Benson & Manchak, 2014). Leadership displaying psychopathic traits set a tone that suppresses subordinate discussion that is contrary to their own positions, they provide poor personnel management and mismanage resources while participating in fraudulent activities (Boddy et al., 2015).

Moreover, compensation structures that value profits and stock price above all enable the deviant behavior of corporate psychopaths by giving them the latitude for destructive leadership behavior especially in the absence of institutionalized rules or formal limits on leader prerogatives, delegated authority, and reward systems (Gudmundsson & Southey, 2011). In exploring why organizations promote such leaders, organizations tolerate unethical practices because they favor manipulative, egotistical, and self-centered managerial behavior that probably reflects the behaviors acceptable to other executives and the board of directors. Corporate psychopaths maintain multiple identities at length such as the façade they establish with coworkers and management of being the ideal employee and future leader which can prove effective, particularly in organizations experiencing turmoil and seeking a "knight in shining armor" to fix the company (Babiak & O'Toole, 2012). Recall the previously mentioned case study with how organizations viewed individuals displaying psychopathic traits where out of 203 participants, nine scored 25 or higher on the Hare PCL-R, eight scored 30 or higher, two scored 33, and one scored 34 (Babiak et al., 2010). Individuals scoring high on a measure of psychopathy held senior managerial positions or were identified as high potentials for leadership positions. Most of the participants with high psychopathy scores held high-ranking executive positions, and they were invited to participate in management development programs. Ironically, opinion suggests that psychopathic managers rise rapidly through organizational ranks into positions of power because traits of charm and grandiosity are mistaken for leadership potential (Babiak et al., 2010).

High psychopathy total scores were associated with perceptions of good communication skills, strategic thinking, plus creative and innovative abilities. At the same time, scores were associated with poor management style, failure to act as a team player, and poor performance appraisals. Some companies viewed psychopathic executives as having leadership potential, despite having negative performance reviews and low ratings on leadership and management by subordinates; this is evidence of their ability to manipulate decision makers within an organization (Babiak & Hare, 2006). It is easy to mistake psychopathic traits for specific leadership traits and a successful corporate psychopath's attributes such as grandiosity, confidence, good presentation skills, persuasiveness, and courage, can be mistaken with the behaviors of effective charismatic leaders (Gudmundsson & Southey, 2011). For example, their lack of realistic goal setting combined with grandiose statements is erroneously interpreted as displaying visionary and strategic thinking ability. To organization, these individuals' irresponsibility is interpreted as giving the appearance of a risk-taking, entrepreneurial spirit—highly prized in today's business environment. Their thrill-seeking behavior is mistaken for high energy, enthusiasm, and the ability to multitask (Babiak & O'Toole, 2012). Again, consider this expert insight:

Most would argue that the ideal CEO profile is an extraverted charismatic individual who shows no sign of emotion under stressful circumstances, who is goal-oriented, aggressive with the competition, able to sell anything to anyone and who will be able to take drastic actions when needed. Coupled with the nice clothes, the charming smile, the expensive watch and the promises of bringing more money or wealth to the company, who can blame anyone for wanting to hire such individuals? However, will these characteristics bring success to the organization? If success is defined as getting new contracts or making risky business investments and decisions, and bringing profits for the organization, then they might be able to bring short-term success. However, in the long-run, their risk-taking behaviors, their lack of respect for rules and abusive attitude towards others will leave a negative mark on the organization, especially on their colleagues and employees (Mathieu, 2016).

An inability to feel emotions due to not being able to experience empathy and human feelings is extrapolated to mean one has the ability to make hard and unpopular decisions (Babiak & O'Toole, 2012). Manipulation skills are mistaken for good persuasion skills (Babiak et al., 2010). The visual of the high potential or ideal leader is difficult to define, and executives tend to rely on their intuition to judge who they consider to be ideal leaders. Unfortunately, once decision makers believe that an individual has future leader potential, even bad performance reviews or poor evaluations from subordinates and peers do not shake their belief since they are too vested in their own opinion coupled with the all too human trait of the difficulty of having to admit that one made a hiring decision mistake (Babiak & Hare, 2006). Employees displaying excellent communication and convincing lying skills, which together would have made them attractive hiring candidates in the first place, apparently continued to serve them well in furthering their careers. In this sense, better vetting procedures and the use of instruments designed to assess psychopathic and other problematical traits may help prevent those who excel at manipulation from sliding into management ranks (Perri, 2011a).

The Case of Robert Maxwell

Potential psychopathic CEOs include Robert Maxwell, a twentieth century United Kingdom (UK) competitor to publisher Rupert Murdoch and at one time a rival purchaser of the UK newspaper *The News of the World* (Boddy, 2016). Maxwell was the disgraced British media tycoon found to have stolen billions of dollars from his company's pension fund. Dr. Robert Hare reportedly said "I'm not saying Maxwell was a psychopath…but he sure had psychopathic tendencies" (Boddy, 2016, p. 79). Yet Maxwell's antisocial behaviors started well before his media empire imploded in the 1990s. For example, an inquiry into a business transaction where Maxwell reportedly lied about the profitability of a publishing company he was trying to sell led a UK Department of Trade and Industry (DTI) investigation to conclude in 1969 that Maxwell was "not in our opinion a person who can be relied on to exercise proper stewardship of a publicly quoted company" (Boddy, 2016). This investigation proved to predict future misconduct regarding Maxwell's fraudulent management of other businesses.

At one stage, Maxwell owned numerous companies including *The Daily Mirror* in the UK and *The New York Daily News* in the United States, in addition to the publishing group Macmillan and the market research group AGB. His empire crashed in 1991 when subsequent examinations found millions of dollars were missing from *The Daily Mirror*'s pension fund. It was estimated that thirty thousand pensioners were affected by Maxwell's behavior (Spalek, 2001). Largely due to the lack of legislation governing pension fund oversight, Maxwell was able to use his position of influence and power as an employer to use pension fund assets as collateral for bank loans. In turn, he used the hundreds of millions of dollars of loan money to fund his other businesses (Spalek, 2001). Moreover, the need for close personal control of organizations and their boards appears to be common among corporate psychopaths; Maxwell was reported to subjugate boards to his will in something "analogous to a master-slave relationship" (Boddy, 2016). At the time it was not illegal to use pension money as collateral, but failure to replace it was illegal. Maxwell convinced more than 25 banks and investment firms that his network of around 400 companies was solvent, rather than being billions in debt and largely unprofitable.

Untruthful and insincere, Maxwell lied to his accountants in an effort to persuade them that his businesses were solvent and financially viable. This deception eventually got his accountants into trouble. Maxwell used a web of private and public companies to artificially inflate profits in core companies while embezzling millions of dollars from his employee's pension funds (Boddy, 2016). Maxwell denied accountability for plundering *The Daily Mirror's* pension fund for his other businesses which demonstrated no regard for the rights of pensioners. In business he overwhelmed critics and investigators with lawsuits to delay and silence them while writing about people he admired, such as Romanian dictator Ceausescu who had been executed in an uprising against his authoritarian and brutal regime. With a reportedly autocratic management style, Maxwell harbored a colossal opinion of his own importance, displayed reckless behaviors, and was determined to win at all costs, which Dr. Hare reports are qualities that are typical of corporate psychopaths. Maxwell enjoyed humiliating people and applying a casual and careless approach to business and financial record keeping. He was found to be single-minded in his devotion to his own cause, described as cheerful but intimidating, abrasive, inauthentic, would fire people on the spot, created a culture of fear, and bullied subordinates while flattering those he deemed useful to his agenda; all characteristics of a corporate psychopath doing what they have to in order to fulfill their agendas.

His organizations were marked by his personal aggression and a climate of fear, a common interpersonal strategy for corporate psychopaths. Similarly, Maxwell was reported to leave a trail of resignations behind him particularly among newly acquired companies whose staff were not used to his intimidating style of aggressive management. Moreover, he was "reported to be physically and verbally intimidating to his staff…He ruled via a culture of fear" (Boddy, 2015, p. 2415). An outcome of the presence of corporate psychopaths is reduced job satisfaction, high staff turnover, and withdrawal. Maxwell behaved like a corporate psychopath and may have been one. He was callous, dishonest, fraudulent, ruthless, and he belittled and bullied people in public. Commentators on business ethics have noted that organizational members need to possess levels of moral courage if they are to promote ethical actions and refrain from unethical actions when faced with temptations or pressures. However, when faced with the aggressive bullying and intimidation of a corporate psychopath, such moral courage is difficult to display, even for human resource professionals who are exposed to such aggressive interpersonal tactics.

Corporate Psychopathic Interpersonal Strategies

How are workplace psychopaths able to manipulate people within an organization to achieve upward mobility? A typical workplace psychopath climbs to and maintains power by following a five-phase model consisting of, 1) entry, 2) assessment, 3) manipulation, 4) confrontation, and 5) ascension (Babiak & Hare, 2006). The entry phase is where psychopaths use highly developed social skills and charm to obtain employment within an organization. At this stage it will be difficult to spot anything which is indicative of psychopathic behavior, and as a new employee, one might perceive the psychopath to be helpful and even benevolent. The second phase is assessment and here psychopaths analyze others according to their usefulness. One is either recognized as a pawn, which is a person with some informal influence yet is easily manipulated, or a patron, those who possesses formal power and will be used by the psychopath to shield against attacks by others when situations become uncomfortable.

Junior employees are typically the first to notice psychopathic manipulation since they are less useful to a psychopath than patrons (Mullins-Sweat et al., 2010). The psychopath views as patrons those with power, status, or access to desired resources. Patrons are like mentors who can assist psychopaths through an organization's political minefield on their way to the top. Patrons will be used until their usefulness is depleted, and then dispensed with or even sacrificed with the goal of replacing them. When they seek to deepen relationships with a pawn or a patron, they first convince their target that they are more similar than different in character and interests. Moreover, they convince the target that they fully understand and accept the target's own true, private, and inner personality, the one with all of its secrets, and therefore because of this acceptance, they can be trusted. Finally, they convince the target that they are the ideal friend, partner, coworker, and so forth; this forms the psychopathic bond. This bond is quite seductive, but it is not based on genuine interpersonal affection. Once this bond is formed, it is very difficult for the target to see the truth about the psychopath as he or she continues to be manipulated.

Psychopaths often come across as good psychologists, but in reality they are just more observant of others and motivated to take advantage of the personal situations of those around them (Carozza, 2008a). The third phase is manipulation where the psychopath will create a scenario referred to as "psychopathic fiction." At this phase, we can expect them to generate positive information about themselves and negative disinformation about others. Each pawn and patron will be utilized and groomed to accept the psychopath's agenda. Psychopaths use negative emotions and deceitful strategies to manipulate others in order to maximize individual gain (Walker & Jackson, 2016). Patrons are those in the higher echelons of management who could be an immediate supervisor or someone several levels higher in the chain of command; without a powerful patron, one's advancement prospects are very poor (Jackall, 2010). Patrons are very important to psychopaths because they provide opportunities and visibility to showcase abilities and make connections with those of high status so they can advance. A patron also provides information on crucial political developments in the corporation so the psychopath can navigate and manipulate interpersonal relationships more skillfully.

Some negative emotions directed toward others include anger, indignation, contempt, disgust, resentment, and scorn. It is not uncommon for psychopaths to: 1) steal another coworkers work product and claim it as their own, 2) blame others for mistakes or for incomplete work, 3) emotionally manipulate people to cause high anxiety, 4) intentionally isolate people from organizational resources, and 5) encourage coworkers to torment, alienate, harass and/or humiliate their peers, especially in front of others. Those who are on the receiving end may feel as though they have behaved inappropriately, even if their behavior was suitable (Walker & Jackson, 2016). When these emotions are stimulated, the person under attack is likely to change their behavior in a way that supports the psychopath's agenda. A corporate psychopath may also use these emotional tools for flattery, which is another way that corporate psychopaths may climb the corporate ladder. Management high in psychopathy and in the trait of meanness, that is tendencies toward excitement seeking, callousness, and cruelty display a predatory aggressive orientation toward others, especially those they might perceive as competitors, when activated by prospects for upward mobility and the prospects for income increases (Blickle et al, 2018).

The fourth stage is confrontation where the psychopath will use techniques of character assassination to maintain their agenda. Although the following individual behaviors are not exclusive to the psychopath, those who are quick to resort to such tactics are likely to fit the psychopath's characteristic profile: 1) public humiliation of others, 2) malicious spreading of lies, 3) deceit to advance agenda, 4) sets unrealistic or unachievable job expectations to set employees up for failure, 5) refuses to provide adequate training or instructions to single out employees for bullying, and 6) threatens others perceived as adversaries with job loss and/or disciplinary action. The fifth and last phase is ascension. In the psychopath's quest for power, the pawns and patrons will be discarded and the psychopath will take for themselves a position of power from anyone who once supported them (Carozza, 2008a). In some cases, corporate psychopaths see opportunities to move up within the power hierarchies by unseating those who have mentored or protected them and their patrons, representing the ultimate act of betrayal.

The abandonment phase that accompanies ascension is difficult to manage since the psychopath cannot move forward without confronting former pawns and patrons who, justifiably, feel that they have been taken advantage of. However, by then the psychopath has already neutralized complaints spreading disparaging information about these individuals. By "poisoning the water," leadership is unlikely to take the complaints of abused pawns or patrons seriously. Consider the case of "Dave", representing the pseudonym of a real person, illustrating how successful psychopaths maneuver within organizations. The case of Dave is documented by Dr. Paul Babiak in the paper titled *When Psychopaths Go to Work: A Case Study of an Industrial Psychopath* (Babiak, 1995). Dr. Babiak provides a detailed analysis of Dave, a newly employed individual who created conflict and division amongst co-workers. The initial description at the time of his employment was as follows displaying qualities of the desired employee:

Dave was in his mid-thirties, a good looking well-spoken professional, married for the third time with four children. He had a degree from a large university and had been hired into a newly created position during a hiring surge. Dave interviewed well, impressing his prospective boss as well as the department director with his creative mind, high energy level, and technical expertise. Routine reference checks seemed positive as did a security check (p. 177–178).

Having started out positively, Dave was quick to create problems in the organization, critical of his co-workers, demanding staff were fired, engaging in verbal tirades towards colleagues, leaving during the middle of meeting, plagiarizing work material and failing to meet deadlines. After three months, his supervisor Frank called a meeting with Dave, outlining his concerns, particularly his inability to get along with co-workers, unwillingness to complete work and displaying emotions inappropriately. Dave was surprised by Frank's comments, denying that here was a problem and suggesting that some aggression was necessary to achieve outcomes. Frank continued to monitor Dave's performance and despite many co-workers being troubled by Dave, others found him humorous, entertaining, flirtatious, creative and bright. Dave formed unusual friendships within the business, finding allies in different hierarchical levels and positions that included a middle-aged staff assistant, a secretary, a number of executives and a young female security guard. However, Frank's concern about Dave came to a culmination when he discovered evidence of misconduct that violated company policies and had to be addressed. The account of this is as follows:

Frank discovered that Dave had been using company time and materials to start his own business. After collecting enough physical evidence to undertake disciplinary action, Frank went to his own boss, the director, for support, only to find out that Dave had been complaining to him about Frank since he joined the company. After hearing the other side of a lot of stories, the director realized that Dave was distorting the truth to make Frank look bad and gain sympathy for himself. Convinced that Dave was a liar and possible thief, the executive went to the president and vice president only to discover that Dave was well regarded by them and considered a high potential employee. They told him to leave Dave alone! Within a couple of weeks, a reorganization took place; Frank ended up in a new function and Dave was promoted (p. 180–181).

Upon becoming involved in the matter, Dr. Babiak assessed Dave with the Hare PCL-R previously mentioned. Dave scored a 29.4 out of a possible top score of 40, suggesting Dave displayed a psychopathic personality. In Dr. Babiak's analysis, he determined that Dave's ability to advance in corporate life and successfully achieve an advantage over his coworkers was due to a series of factors: 1) establishing a network of useful and powerful relationships that would eventually help him; 2) avoiding situations and meetings where maintaining multiple façades was difficult; 3) creating conflicts which led to distraction and prevented co-workers from sharing information about him because these co-workers were pitted against each other; 4) abandoning co-workers who were no longer useful once he had established a level of power and agendas had been satisfied; and 5) neutralizing critics and detractors by raising doubts regarding their competence and loyalty. Dr. Babiak also believed that inadequate management, unstable cultural factors and the changing nature of the organization further served to provide cover for Dave's psychopathic behavior.

Corrupt Corporate Psychopathic Leadership Profile Insights

The difference between psychopathy in the business world and general psychopathy is the suit. In essence, the crimes are the same but it all comes in a more expensive and well-spoken package. Make no mistake, the long-term results are just as devasting.

Dr. Cynthia Mathieu (2016)

Corporate psychopathic leadership is a form of successful psychopathy; however, success should not necessarily be equated with successful life outcomes, professional or leadership success. Even though they present a profile of leadership that appears antagonistic to traits of authentic leadership, somehow, they are capable of navigating hierarchical structures to achieve their quest for power. Overall research suggests that if corporate leadership is in fact representative of successful psychopathy, they appear to reflect a controlled primary psychopathic subtype that is attracted to leadership positions due to a desire to exercise dominion over others and situations. They represent a contrary profile from the unstable, criminal psychopath who is not as apt to engage in thoughtful risk assessments, however this does not mean that their risk assessments especially as they relate to corporate fraud is flawless and above detection by fraud examiners. Moreover, these psychopathic leaders are more likely to have better interpersonal skills navigating conflict more skillfully due to their ability to assess the emotional state of those they are interacting with.

Also, as to psychopathic impulsivity, they appear to reflect a functional, sensation seeking type of impulsivity where they are attracted to new experiences that may trigger thrill seeking, but approach new experiences with more thoughtful planning. These successful psychopaths may be well-educated, charismatic, and adept at strategic planning. At the same time, successful psychopathy is associated with poor management style, failure to act as a team player, and poor performance appraisals while manipulation skills are mistaken for good persuasion skills. Corrupt psychopathic leaderships' authority has the ability, thus is at risk of encouraging an organizational culture where rule-breaking is expected and rewarded especially since such leadership will need the assistance of subordinates to actualize fraud schemes to satisfy motives. Regrettably, it is easy to mistake psychopathic traits for specific leadership traits and a successful corporate psychopath's attributes such as grandiosity, confidence, good presentation skills, persuasiveness, and courage, can be mistaken with the behaviors of effective charismatic leaders.

Moreover, these psychopathic individuals have a template to navigate and ascend hierarchical structures that may be facilitated especially if an organization is embroiled in chaos, unethical behaviors, and high employee turnover. However, in their ascension, when the prospects for upward corporate mobility and increased pay are available, this can trigger a callousness, aggressive predatory tone with others but without diminishment to their self-control. Chaos also provides a perfect environment to exploitive weaknesses within an organization not to mention if corporate governance controls have been relaxed. Moreover, we should not lose sight of the fact that they are willing to engage in antisocial and criminal behavior no differently than criminal psychopaths who are more apt to engage in aggression that is violent in nature. In contrast, psychopathic fraud offenders display an exploitative, remorseless aggression against others, albeit in a different form, to satisfy their agendas that still brings financial destruction and emotional trauma upon peoples' lives.

Their proclivity for antisocial behaviors means that they are at risk to exploit weaknesses in corporate governance structures or find ways to weaken and or circumvent corporate governance that can detect fraudulent activity. Given that when addressing psychopathic leadership, there is the implicit assumption that such an individual interacts with others in an environment that has hierarchical structures. If the psychopathic leader is engaging in white-collar crime, subordinate participation is needed coupled with the expectation of unquestioned subordinate loyalty; leadership will find ways to remove those that do not unequivocally embrace their agendas and hire those that will. They may, when necessary, engage in aggressive interpersonal tactics such as bullying and veiled threats as a way to motivate subordinates. This is not to argue that all subordinates participate in corporate fraud against their will because there are subordinates who will gladly support corrupt leadership agendas out of self-interest such as the perception of being rewarded with promotions and money.

Overall, the visual of the high potential or ideal leader is difficult to define, and executives tend to rely on their intuition to judge who they consider to be ideal leaders. Unfortunately, once decision makers believe that an individual has future leader potential, even bad performance reviews or poor evaluations from subordinates and peers do not shake their belief since they are too vested in their own opinion. Employees displaying excellent communication and convincing lying skills, which together would have made them attractive hiring candidates in the first place, apparently continued to serve them well in furthering their careers. In this sense, better vetting procedures and the use of instruments designed to assess psychopathic and other problematical traits may help prevent those who excel at manipulation from sliding into management ranks. In the end, the "successful psychopath's greatest success may be making everyone believe that he or she is successful; psychopathic success only benefits psychopathic individuals and comes at a high price for others and organizations who are merely seen and treated as means to an end" (Mathieu, 2016).

Conclusion

In summary, this chapter should have given readers a better understanding of how personality can be viewed as a risk factor that increases the probability that someone will engage in crime in general, and in this case, fraud. However, it is important to remember that one's personality is not the cause of misconduct, but rather as a risk factor that may facilitate the motivation and decision to engage in misconduct. Often the issue of personality is ignored to our detriment. People exhibiting disordered personalities reach leadership positions where they, with ease, are willing to exploit subordinates and organizational resources to satisfy their motives. Regardless of whether one is involved in fraud examination or not, in general, working in an organization almost requires one to understand how to identify different personalities for their own protection. We have observed how personality affects human interaction and, unfortunately, not in a professional manner, but to take advantage of others, sabotage relationships, and, at times, ruin careers through deceitful, antisocial tactics. Furthermore, by being able to recognize leadership personality traits that are linked to those who may consider fraud as a viable option, one is better prepared to navigate their career more effectively.

Chapter 7

Organizational Misconduct Enabling Corporate Fraud

There are no conditions of life to which man cannot get accustomed to especially if he sees them accepted by everyone around him.

Leo Tolstoy

The Misconduct of Wells Fargo Bank

For many years, Wells Fargo bank employees created sham credit card accounts by registering customers for banking services without their knowledge (Corkery, 2016). In many cases, customers took notice only when they received a letter in the mail congratulating them on opening a new account while accumulating unexpected fees. Customers were harmed in numerous ways by Wells Fargo's misconduct such as, a) customers lost money to monthly service fees charged for unauthorized accounts, b) customer accounts were placed into collection forcing customers to fight with debt collection agencies for fees charged by Wells Fargo on unauthorized accounts, c) customer credit reports were affected, impacting job applications, loans for automobiles, and mortgage applications, and d) customers were forced to purchase identity theft protection services to ensure against further fraudulent activities (Levine, 2016). Federal banking regulators found their unethical sales practices reflected serious flaws in their organizational culture relating to sales practices and lack of corporate governance oversight at Wells Fargo. One former bank manager stated that, "It's all manipulation. We were taught exactly how to sell multiple accounts…it sounds good, but in reality it doesn't benefit most customers" (Reckard, 2013).

For example, in order to fulfill sales quotas, bankers created unauthorized accounts by moving a small amount of money from the customer's current account to open new ones. Shortly after opening the accounts, employees would close them and move the money back into the customer's account. Other methods included employees opening accounts with forged customer signatures and some bankers opened fraudulent accounts with their own money (Wells Fargo, 2017). To open unauthorized accounts, bankers would impersonate customers and "input false generic email addresses such as noname@wellsfargo.com or none@wellsfargo.com to ensure the transaction is completed" (Egan, 2016b). Friends and family accounts referred to employees opening accounts for family and friends to meet sales goals and one branch manager's teenage daughter held 24 accounts, an adult daughter held 18 accounts, the husband held 21 accounts, a brother held 14 accounts and the father held 4 accounts (Wells Fargo, 2017). Bankers also engaged in the unethical practice called pinning where the bank issued ATM cards and assigned PIN numbers without customer authorization. Despite the unethical sales practices, employees received credit for fraudulently opening accounts to meet sales quotas.

Employees were ranked against each other on their performance relative to goals. Their compensation, promotional opportunities, and potential termination were based on whether or not sales quotas were satisfied. To many employees, the route to success was to out-sell your peers which created pressures to engage in unethical sales practices (Wells Fargo, 2017). Major friction developed between employees who were ethical and those who were promoted due to achieving sales quotas unethically. According to a Columbia University professor, "If the managers are saying, 'We want growth, we don't care how you get there,' what do you expect those employees to do" (Corkery, 2016)? Unethical behavior was rewarded with large bonuses while ethical employees who did not meet quotas because they would not engage in unethical sales practices were punished and bullied. Managers berated, demeaned, and threatened employees to meet these unreachable quotas by telling employees to do whatever it takes to achieve them. Employees who did not reach their quotas were often required to work hours beyond their typical work schedule, without compensation or risk termination.

Some of them traumatized by the berating stated, "When I worked at Wells Fargo, I faced the threat of being fired if I didn't meet their unreasonable sales quotas every day" (Levine, 2016). Another employee stated, "we were constantly told we would end up working at McDonald's if we did not make sales quotas, we had to stay for what felt like after-school detention or report to a call session on Saturdays" (Reckard, 2013). Fulfilling quotas was the end goal of sales employees and one employee stated that his supervisor told him, "I don't care how you do it—but do it, or else you're not going home" (Reckard, 2013). One former banker tried to balance the

291

bank's aggressive sales quotas without doing something illegal, but sacrificing her morals pushed her into deep depression stating, "every day you went to work you wondered...am I a good employee today or a worthless one" (Egan, 2016a)? Other bankers experienced "bullying, punishment and intimidation" impacting their physical and mental health due to the pressure for meeting quotas" (Egan, 2016a). One banker experienced superiors yelling in her face because they wanted her "to open up dual checking accounts for people that couldn't even manage their original checking account...The sales pressure from management was unbearable" (Egan, 2016b).

Poor performance also led to "shaming or worse" (Wells Fargo, 2017, p. 30). Thus, it was not just private bullying, but public humiliation occurred as described by one bank manager: "if you did not make your goal, you are severely chastised and embarrassed in front of 60-plus managers in your area by the community banking president" (Reckard, 2013). How can misconduct of this nature occur for so many years without action being taken to end such behavior? One analyst observed, "It is way out of character for one of the cleanest banks around...It's a head-scratcher why so many employees felt comfortable crossing the line" from ethical to unethical conduct (Corkery, 2016). Where was Wells Fargo's leadership, which includes the board of directors, during this period when misconduct was rampant? CEO John Stumpf oversaw Wells Fargo's four main business groups: the Community Bank, Consumer Lending, Wealth & Investment Management, and Wholesale Banking. Stumpf, referred to as the "Mr. Clean of banking", stated at a congressional hearing on the company's sales practices that had been carried out for years that, "I do want to make very clear that there was no orchestrated effort, or scheme as some have called it, by the company" to exploit consumers (Egan & Isidore, 2016).

Stumpf refused to believe that the sales practice culture could be flawed which resulted in minimizing the obvious problems (Wells Fargo, 2017). Although the scandal did not become publicized in a noticeable manner until 2016, the misconduct flourished for over a decade and the leadership, including the board of directors, were put on notice of the problem, but they did not address the misconduct with enough intensity to end its pervasiveness that was deeply engrained in its organizational culture. Stumpf knew for years that there were issues concerning questionable sales practices under the leadership of Carrie Tolstedt, the head of Wells Fargo's Community Bank division where the fake accounts originated (Wells Fargo, 2017). In 2002, the Community Bank took steps to address the increasing number of sales practice violations through training and utilization of audit programs to identify suspicious activity. In a 2004 email to Stumpf, Tolstedt acknowledged the importance of setting compensation plans that incentivized appropriate sales practice behaviors. However, even though there was a plan to reduce the number of violations, as one employee indicated, in truth, "there was no appetite to change the model" of how sales practices were conducted under Tolstedt especially since she did not allow for scrutiny or criticism of how she ran her division (Wells Fargo, 2017, p. 31).

Even when the corrupt sales practices were published in major newspapers across the country in 2013, Stumpf still did not take the initiative to lead an investigation to identify and address the injuries the customers suffered which ultimately also impacted Wells Fargo's reputation. Moreover, Wells Fargo's decentralized organizational structure and the deference paid to the lines of business where they were told to "run it like you own it" contributed to the longevity of the misconduct especially to the division headed by Tolstedt (Wells Fargo, 2017, p. 19). Tolstedt and her inner circle became defensive when others challenged their decisions on sales practices with no desire to hear feedback, while some senior leaders within the Community Bank were afraid of or discouraged from airing contrary views to Tolstedts. Tolstedt challenged and resisted audits both from within and outside the Community Bank where she and her subordinates failed to escalate problematic issues outside the bank, but she also worked to impede escalation which included keeping away from the board of directors' information regarding sales practice violations. In essence, Tolstedt was empowered to suppress the unethical sales practice information and insulate herself and her subordinates from oversight of her division to expose the misconduct (Jackson, 2017).

Moreover, Stumpf provided her another layer of protection from being exposed to scrutiny of her practices. When CFO Timothy Sloan was asked about the impact of sales practices on employees he stated, "I'm not aware of any overbearing sales culture" (Reckard, 2013). Eventually Sloan acknowledged the sales practice scandal stating, "Despite our ongoing efforts to combat these unacceptable bad practices and bad behaviors, they persisted, because we either minimized the problem or we failed to see the problem for what it really was—something bigger than we originally imagined (Wells Fargo, 2017, p. 59). Yet he acknowledged that Tolstedt displayed a controlling personality were others did not work well with her expressing his opinion that she should not lead the Community Bank (Wells Fargo, 2017). Chief Administrative Officer Patricia Callahan believed Tolstedt could manage the Community Bank, but her concern was that Tolstedt was "obsessed with control" and slow to make changes especially the ones pertaining to unethical sales practices (Wells Fargo, 2017, p. 86). However, Tolstedt had the support of Stumpf who acknowledged to the board of directors that she displayed a controlling personality, but still called her the best banker in America because she delivered results. In fact, Stumpf stated on her 2009 performance review that the management structure Tolstedt devised was nothing short of a "stroke of genius" (Wells Fargo, 2017, p. 57).

Moreover, Stumpf was advised in December, 2015 to terminate Tolstedt due to the enormity of the unethical sales practice concerns evident in her division that were not properly addressed (Wells Fargo, 2017). The board of directors began to take notice of the unethical sales practices in the Community Bank shortly after a December 21, 2013 *Los Angeles Times* article on the subject surfaced (Jackson, 2017). The board stated that the sales practices were not identified as a noteworthy risk until 2014 because they considered the issue to be minor or "victimless" (Wells Fargo, 2017, p. 14). The board claimed to only learn of the pervasiveness of the misconduct when about 5,300 employees had been terminated for sales practices violations in the Fall of 2016 (Jackson, 2017). Yet as earlier as the Spring of 2016, the board knew that 2,000 to 3,000 firings, roughly one percent of the workforce, were due to sales practice violations (Jackson, 2017). Furthermore, by early 2015, management reported to the board that corrective action addressing the unethical sales practices was working, however the board later claimed that management reports did not accurately convey the scope or pervasiveness of the problem to them (Wells Fargo, 2017). Moreover, the board claimed to have failed to find the right personnel prior to 2016 to get a realistic assessment of the cause of the employee turnover rates (Jackson, 2017).

In retrospect, the board simply took note of the reported firings and corrective actions without digging further to disclose the full scope of the problem. With respect to Tolstedt, in advance of an April, 2014 board meeting, directors apparently indicated that they "wanted to hear from Tolstedt whether the pressure of cross-sell goals cause bad behavior," but "Tolstedt's presentation was removed from the agenda when she was summoned to jury duty" (Wells Fargo, p. 68). Apparently it was a long trial because Tolstedt did not report back to the Risk Committee on this issue until a year later in April, 2015 (Jackson, 2017). The Risk Committee members found her presentation "too superficial and optimistic" (Wells Fargo, 2017, p. 103). Once the City of Los Angeles filed a lawsuit against Wells Fargo that alleged illegal sales practices, the board further accelerated its attention to the problem of unethical sales practices, resulting in another Tolstedt presentation of which the directors were "highly critical" (Wells Fargo, 2017, p. 105). More meetings followed later in the year with outside experts disclosing mounting evidence related to misconduct to the point where directors "felt blindsided" by management representatives, and by December, 2015, came to the "view that Tolstedt could no longer effectively lead the Community Bank" (p. 105-107).

Yet, on February 23, 2016, when the Board's Human Resources Committee met to determine compensation for top executives, including Tolstedts, it turns out "the reaction of the board members to Tolstedt is a complicated one" (Jackson, 2017) despite the fact "that Tolstedt was not changing her management practices" (Wells Fargo, 2017, p. 59). Most of the directors, while believing that she had been overly optimistic and minimized problems were not critical, allowed her to remain in her position at least several more months while her performance could be assessed (Jackson, 2017). In the Spring of 2016, as the board received detailed accounts of thousands of sales force firings in Tolstedt's division, Wells Fargo shareholders were informed that Carrie Tolstedt would be the third highest paid employee at the firm (Jackson, 2017). Ultimately CEO Stumpf and Tolstedt resigned due to the scandal, but received severance packages worth millions of dollars. These illegal banking practices cost Wells Fargo $185 million in federal government fines, including a $100 million penalty from the Consumer Financial Protection Bureau. State governments will recover $575 million in fines.

The Predictability of Organizational Misconduct

Whether it is Enron, Wells Fargo, or Arthur Andersen to name a few examples, why do these scenarios, perhaps different in substance, severity, and outcome, repeat themselves time and again within organizations causing damage to investors, employees, and consumers? Recall the findings by the accounting firm KPMG in a 2013 integrity survey on organization misconduct that included categories such as financial statement fraud (KPMG, 2013). According to the survey, the most commonly cited drivers of organizational misconduct continue to be attributed to 1) pressure to do "whatever it takes" to meet business goals coupled with rewards that favor the ends and not the means of how the ends are achieved, 2) the fear of losing one's job if goals are not met, and 3) employees are more apt to ignore misconduct than report it for fear of retaliation. The question is not if organizational misconduct will occur, but when.

An enduring legacy of Edwin Sutherland's approach to white-collar crime is to sensitize us to how organizational culture within a legitimate company is transmitted to workers ultimately leading to misconduct either in the form of unethical acts or those exposing an organization and its employees to civil and criminal liabilities (Lilly et al., 2011). When norms regulating legitimate methods to achieve goals are weakened or considered ineffective, people resort to fraud to achieve their ends especially if there are perceptions of business pressures such as companies suffering from financial problems. Consequently, the ends become more important than the means to achieve those ends especially when the ends are financial survival. As previously studied, pressures occur throughout all levels of society whether we are speaking of those of the lower socioeconomic levels experience frustration that they cannot achieve financial success through legitimate means to those that are well-off, but feel some type of pressure motivating them to resort to fraud to maintain a certain lifestyle. However, there are pressures that may not directly be attributable to a particular person's needs, but to the wants and needs of an organization that are difficult to attain thus driving individuals to internalize the pressure an organization experiences and engage in misconduct on behalf of an organization.

Research suggests that failing and marginal organizations, firms with low or declining profits, firms in depressed industries, firms suffering from competition, as well as those confronting resource scarcities, are at a higher risk to engage in misconduct (Greeve et al., 2010). Loss of or the potential to lose existing status, the inability to achieve status, declines in social standing, and retaliation for perceived injustices may also promote organizational misconduct. Yet, misconduct can also arise from the pressures of success, power, and status. This may explain why some studies suggest that high growth firms are also likely to engage in misconduct than their less successful peers, and that moderate to very good performance is also closely associated with misconduct than just poor performance (Greeve et al., 2010). Consequently, because competition is widespread, all organizations are vulnerable, regardless of organizational condition; the weak are tempted to engage in misconduct to gain position and the strong are tempted to maintain their position. Research into financial statement fraud suggests that nearly all these crimes are perpetrated by multiple players within the organization working together, thus it is necessary to understand the relationship that takes place between the initial perpetrator of a fraudulent act and any additional participants (Albrecht et al., 2015). Given that this chapter is about organizational misconduct, organizations in general refer to social systems with a number of similar characteristics such as, but not limited to, individuals expending a significant time commitment on behalf of an organization and the socialization of newcomers.

In addition, organizations display their own organizational culture consisting of expectations and values, and organizational hierarchies including leadership with formal authority that controls rewards such as salary, promotions, and imposes punishments such as termination on subordinates (Greeve et al., 2010). Thus, for purposes of definitional consistency, when we speak of organizational misconduct or corrupt acts, which are terms used interchangeably within this book, we are broadly referring to acts in the workplace that are committed with a deliberate purpose resulting in a violation of rules pertaining to such acts (Vardi & Weitz, 2004). Some of the most widely observed types of misconduct management and employees are likely to observe or engage in include but not limited to, 1) asset misappropriation, 2) intentional misrepresentations about particular facts, 3) cheating or taking advantage of a situation, 4) breaking organizational rules and laws, 5) conflicts of interests and influences

294

such as bribes, payoffs, and kickbacks, 6) organizational abuse of power and inequitable compensation, 7) fraud and deceit pertaining to creating and perpetuating false impressions such as financial statement fraud, 8) hiding versus disclosing information that another party has a right to know or failing to protect personal and proprietary information, and 9) interpersonal abuse such as workplace bullying or sexual harassment (Sims, 2003).

Also, consider that even if acts are not committed with a deliberate mindset, this does not mean that the acts do not reflect misconduct simply because people rely on collective, group rationalizations to reduce the culpability of their misconduct. Regrettably, an individual's values and sense of morality can be weakened within corporate settings where employees are expected to replace their own values and morals in exchange for corporate expectations and norms (Pardue et al., 2013b). As a result, the risk of white-collar crime increases because there is an organizational culture that provides rationalizations for illegal acts to flourish and a structure of financial incentives to reward misconduct coupled with punishments for not participating in a group's collective unethical and criminal acts (Apel & Paternoster, 2009). Unfortunately thoughtful, ethical people can turn into criminal offenders due to participating in collective acts that can be criminal in nature. Consequently, one of the enduring puzzles for white-collar crime scholars is to explain why people who are generally law abiding, upstanding members of the community and the business world engage in misconduct resulting in financial and frequently physical damage to others such as selling the public products that are defective and dangerous (Apel & Paternoster, 2009)?

The answer typically given, and not without merit, is that the organizational climate or culture of businesses turned normally good people into unethical people. Yet this answer begs the question, why are people so susceptible to being influenced by organizational culture that apparently facilitates their engagement in misconduct if they claim to be ethical individuals? This chapter and chapter five expose some of the risk factors that facilitate misconduct at the organizational level. While the fraud triangle, as discussed in chapter one, explains why an individual becomes involved in financial statement fraud due to pressures/incentives, available opportunities to commit fraud, and rationalizations, the fraud triangle does not enlighten us as to how large groups of individuals engage in misconduct. The unethical behavior of leadership, subordinates, legal counsel to the leadership, board of director memberships, and corporate advisors such as accountants who are reluctant to challenge corporate misbehavior, points to a disturbing group dynamic reality that has been overlooked in the discussion. More often than not corporate scandals usually involve multiple offenders, thus a group dynamic that binds members together also blinds them to their failings and abuses (Frankel, 2008-2009). As we observe, people involved in groups are capable and willing to adopt an amoral and immoral perspective towards unethical practices when they are accepted by those around them.

Thus, the corruption of morality, due to the corruption of practices, virtues, values, and customs leads to the corruption of the decision making process to the point where it becomes less and less possible to identify the morality attached to risk-taking. Virtues can include honesty, courage, compassion, generosity, fidelity, loyalty, fairness, self-control and prudence; such traits assist us to understand the ethical dimensions of our decisions. When we remove virtue from our moral compass, it is predictable that individuals, groups, and ultimately organizations rationalize antisocial behaviors facilitating the normalization of corruption. The void created by ignoring virtues is filled by greed and rule-breaking which is facilitated by the antisocial interpersonal strategies displayed by leadership such as intimidation, unwarranted punishments, public humiliations, rewarding misconduct through increases in financial rewards and status, and suppressing differing opinions that may have actually enhanced the efficiency of an organization. The many studies documenting incidents of embezzlement, antitrust violations, securities fraud, and other such activities suggest that rule breaking is not uncommon in organizations with members violating organizational rules, and often the law, both on behalf of and at the expense of the organization (Maclean, 2001).

Collective corruption displayed within organizations represents a dark blight on society where corporate misdeeds tear the social fabric more so than street crime because they corrode trust in authorities and institutions (Sutherland, 1949). Corruption is likely to cause tremendous damage to the organization because the entire organization is blamed for the corrupt acts of its members and may face dire consequences in terms of financial, legal, and reputational loss (Aguilera & Vadera, 2008). A troubling trend in white-collar crime is that these crimes appear increasingly to be perpetrated through the actions of numerous employees as opposed to the actions of a single misguided individual. A corporate climate perceived to encourage or at least permit offending by ignoring misconduct increases the intention to offend (Paternoster & Tibbetts, 2016). When multiple individuals are involved in perpetrating a crime, this is broadly viewed as co-offending. Specifically, co-offending refers to the perpetration of criminal or unethical conduct by more than one person, including cooperation in different times and places, where individuals pool their talents and resources in the pursuit of shared, but at worse, illegal goals (Free & Murphy, 2015). Consider that so many of the large scandals such as Wells Fargo, Enron, and WorldCom cannot be enacted by one person, but requires the cooperation of others to make misconduct successful, thus giving rise to conspiracy which is a common prosecutorial charge in co-offending behaviors.

This trend may be partially due to the fact that for many people, work is the center of their lives and not only do they spend more waking hours at work than anywhere else, but they do most of their socializing there as well. As a result, many personal interactions that would traditionally have occurred outside the workplace now occur within the workplace increasing the risk for misconduct. A potentially significant unintended consequence of this trend is that it leaves employees increasingly cut off from any contact with the broader community, and in many cases, even from their own families. Such arrangements are troublesome because they leave individuals isolated from contact with those who might challenge the company line on illegal practices, or reject the rationalizations conventionally offered within the firm. Groups can often support corrupt beliefs that individuals cannot justify for themselves if acting alone. If the beliefs are not subject to a reality check, perhaps by a neutral, independent party, the group-fed confidence can spiral into arrogance, leading to group ignorance and ultimately face criminal liability. As Sutherland argued about group dynamics, corrupt "corporate behavior is like the behavior of a mob", where business enterprises can be organized to engage in criminal activities (Sutherland, 1983, p. 235).

The majority of organizational frauds occur with the participation of the CEO, CFO, and multiple subordinates (Free & Murphy, 2015). Often organizational misconduct begins when management experiences financial pressures coupled with the concern that not meeting publicly available earnings forecasts would result in significant declines in the market value of the stock or basic survival of the organization. In one study, while the initial encouragement to commit fraud came from the CEO and the chief operating officer (COO), the CFO was the primary manipulator of the financial statements motivated to maintain high stock prices by meeting Wall Street earnings expectations every quarter so that their stock options did not lose value (Albrecht et al., 2015). At first management used acceptable, but aggressive accounting methods to reach the desired numbers. When aggressive accounting methods no longer achieved the desired targets, the top management team pressured the CFO to do whatever was necessary to meet the published numbers relying on false revenue recognition, and understating liabilities and expenses to perpetrate the fraud (Albrecht et al., 2015).

Many people were involved in preparing the financial statements of this large corporation. When the need to involve others in the fraud became necessary, the CFO recruited the controller, the vice-president of accounting, the vice president of financial reporting, and the director of financial reporting. Several individuals, especially those at the executive level, became involved because they were promoted and received higher salaries coupled with valuable stock options. This inner circle of perpetrators recognized the fraud scheme and further recruited others to manipulate individual fraudulent transactions including various controllers at the company's subsidiaries who, in turn, recruited others within their own organizations to help perpetrate the fraud (Albrecht et al., 2015). Though the number of people involved in the fraud expanded over the years, the detailed knowledge of the overall fraudulent scheme was generally limited to the persons in higher level positions. Yet, even upper management who initiated the fraud did not know how many people were actually involved. Other individuals participated because of fear of dismissal or punishment while other participants removed from the inner circles of upper management usually had little knowledge of the overall scheme, and did not understand exactly what was going on. Within the inner circle, individuals participated because they trusted their colleagues and because, at first, the fraudulent amounts were small, thus inconsequential in their mind.

296

As a whole, the group justified their actions as acceptable by relying on rationalizations and before the fraud was discovered, more than 30 identifiable employees participated in the fraud (Albrecht et al., 2015). Many of these individuals had different levels of knowledge regarding the fraud and while some of the perpetrators had complete knowledge of the criminal acts that were occurring, others performed tasks simply because they were asked to participate. Those with full knowledge of the fraud rationalized their acts as acceptable believing that accounting manipulations were necessary for a limited time, yet when regulators discovered the fraudulent financial statements, the scheme occurred for over four years (Albrecht et al., 2015). Research suggests that when corruption infiltrates an organization to the point of becoming an institution-wide force, it displays a momentum and life of its own while being thrust into a negative direction where there is no returning to an ethical climate unless there is an organizational meltdown prompting a change in leadership and subordinates (Buchard, 2011). Even then it may be difficult because there are still the remnants of a corrupt culture with those remaining with an organization who may not have participated in the misconduct, but who did not necessarily disapprove of it either because of the benefits that flowed from the misconduct.

The reality is once a corrupt system is in place, it tends to stay there unless there are drastic actions taken to disrupt it such as removing current leadership and subordinates (Rothstein & Uslaner, 2005). Unfortunately, corrupt activity can become routine within an organizational culture infiltrating the corporate decision making process that enables otherwise law-abiding individuals to commit otherwise unethical acts. Members will continue to remain in this cycle until either the organization itself finally implodes, or the individual reevaluates his or her value, perceives a lack of fit, and chooses to exit the organization (Buchard, 2011). Over time this normalization of corruption becomes rationalized so that it is deemed more acceptable to the people involved (Einarsen et al., 2007). Consider the statements of a college graduate who initially refused to participate in misconduct at several other organizations and quit because of the demands to participate, but in the end succumbed to its participation stating, "I sometimes felt disgusted and wanted to quit, but I argued that I did not have a chance to find a legitimate firm. I knew the game was rotten, but it had to be played—the law of the jungle and that sort of thing" (Sutherland, 1983, p. 241).

If there is a major lesson to take away from the research on human behavior, it is not so much the kind of person an individual perceives themselves to be as is the kind of situation a person finds themselves in that determines how he or she will act; in essence our character is revealed by how we react to a given situation (Mayhew & Murphy, 2014). People are willing to morally disengage when faced with sufficient inducement to behave unethically by reconstructing the act itself as ethical, by minimizing the consequences of the act, or by shifting responsibility elsewhere. In the end, a display of one's morality and ethics is situationally determined and people who consider themselves moral in their private lives may "leave their consciences at home when they enter the portals of the firm" (Kailemia, 2016, p. 80). As convicted fraud offender CFO Steven Garfinkel stated, "What we all think is, when the big moral challenges comes, I will rise to the occasion...there's not actually that many of us that will actually rise to the occasion" (Soltes, 2016, p. 31). For example, if people are asked what qualities they like about themselves, many would typically state that they like their sense of honesty, dependability, a solid foundation in maintaining an ethical lifestyle, and being law abiding.

Such opinions are truly believed at heart by those proclaiming them. Yet consider for example the Panalba case, involving the pharmaceutical company Upjohn to tell us a little about how one's "outstanding character" aligns with how we behave when faced with making decisions that squarely pit the situation to our character within an organizational context. Does one's sense of right and wrong predominately influence how a decision will be made or does the situation dictate one's course of action? After strong medical evidence emerged that a drug Upjohn produced caused serious side effects, including unnecessary deaths, and that it offered no medical benefits beyond those that could be obtained by other products on the market, the board of directors of the firm decided not only to continue marketing and selling the drug, but also arranged to have a judge issue an injunction to stop the U.S. Food and Drug Administration (FDA) from taking regulatory action to prevent the drug's sale (Heath, 2008). When the FDA finally succeeded in having the drug banned in the United States, the firm continued to sell it in foreign markets. When this story is presented as a case study to consider the ethical

297

issues raised, respondents are almost unanimous in their conviction that the actions of the Upjohn board were "socially irresponsible" (Heath, 2008, p. 598).

Attitude surveys also show that respondents in the United States regard executives who allow their firm to sell a drug with undisclosed harmful side effects as having committed a serious criminal offense, second only to murder and rape in severity. However, when management and executive training students were put in a role-playing scenario as members of a corporate board, faced with the same decision that confronted Upjohn, 79 percent chose the "highly irresponsible" option, of not only continuing with sales of the drug, but also taking action to prevent government regulation (Heath, 2008, p. 598). The other 21 percent chose to continue selling the drug for as long as possible, but without trying to interfere with the regulatory process. Thus, the range of behavior extended from "highly" to "moderately" irresponsible (Heath, 2008, p. 598). Not one group chose the "socially responsible" action of voluntarily withdrawing the drug from the market. These results were obtained from 91 different trials of the experiment in 10 different countries.

It is worth noting that Scott Armstrong, the investigator who conducted these studies, initiated them because he was puzzled by the Upjohn case, and believed that his own students at the University of Pennsylvania's Wharton School of Management would not possibly make such decisions. Yet it was his own students who became the first group to challenge his belief. The reality is a situation exerts pressure on the individual; it is not so much the kind of person one believes they are as the kind of situation they find themselves in that exposes their character and the type of conduct they are willing to participate in especially within an organizational context (Kim, 2005). Perfectly ordinary people are able to commit serious crimes or moral offenses when put in the right situation reflecting the insight that virtue is situational. Research suggests "that situational factors far outweigh the effects of character when it comes to determining behavior" (Heath, 2008, p. 599). Fraud offender Steven Hoffenberg stated reflecting this insight, "when responsibility is there and you have to meet budgetary numbers, you can forget about morals. Circumstances over-rule morals" (Soltes, 2016, p. 272). In some respects, our values are sacrificed for some other agenda after engaging in a cost-benefit analysis. Unfortunately, short-term agendas turn into long-term agendas and it is difficult if not impossible to return to a routine where ethics mattered.

When one becomes immersed in the norms of their group, one can lose their sense of responsibility, their sense of individuality, and their sense of who they are that contributes to the ease in which they are capable of engaging in misconduct. Thus, humans will redefine their sense of who they are, their self-identity, and adapt to a situation by fulfilling expected roles within an organization, which are opposite to their value systems, and disregard rational thinking to evaluate the risks of their conduct. They are capable of being controlled without much provocation because there are people who can blindly follow those in power. The evidence suggests that individuals tend to do what they are told, even if they believe it may not be the right thing to do. There are conditions people are likely to ignore especially the unethical behavior of others when they become an integral part of day to day activities. The reason why unethical behaviors are ignored is because individuals may not even be able to see the inappropriateness of their behaviors when institutionalized corruption occurs in part "due to repetitive cycles of routinized activity" (Gino & Bazerman, 2009, p. 709).

In this chapter we learn about how corruption can become an organization-wide phenomena or at times referred to as systematic corruption. Often, we think that there are only one or two individuals that are responsible, but as we shall see, organizational corruption can become widespread which means that there are a number of people, not just a few, that actually must contribute to the misconduct. In addition, we study the impact of how organizational environments shape one's identity of how they perceive themselves, organizational values they are willing to adopt as their own facilitating organizational misconduct, and the role organizational culture plays in influencing the type of conduct expected from an employee. Lastly, Enron's misconduct and eventual downfall is examined. Analyzing Enron is like participating in a behavioral forensic accounting autopsy. Once the beautiful veneer of Enron cracked, we had the opportunity to analyze its corporate cavity to see what a cancerous organization looks like coupled with backing into the risk factors that gave rise to such a cancer ultimately leading to its death by bankruptcy.

The Process of Normalizing Organizational Misconduct

Scholars observe that the rational nature of corporations, which includes making a profit, might encourage the amoral selection of illegal practices that can be done secretly regardless of the harm to others. For many, business is not simply to achieve efficiencies, but also to manipulate people through advertising, propaganda, and lobbyists leading companies to adopt "a truly Machiavellian ideology and policy" where violations of law are deliberate and analogous to organized, criminal entities (Lilly et al., 2011, p. 276). The practice of promoting misconduct encourages an infiltration in the ranks of leadership unethical management who have either engaged in rule breaking as a way of doing business or are aware of and tolerate rule breaking as a means of achieving financial goals. This infiltration is the foundation for the processes that allow rule breaking to persist, proliferate, and eventually become routinized between managers, their superiors, and their subordinates. Senior managers routinely attempt to blame corruption on a few bad apples, however, the intertwined processes of institutionalization, rationalization, and socialization converge to normalize and perpetuate corrupt practices so that the corrupt system trumps any one individual's misconduct.

Management participation in misconduct plays a significant role in creating shared understandings between coworkers of what is expected. Infiltration of the management ranks by those willing to tolerate, ignore, or participate in rule breaking assists in creating a common understanding that the ends justify the means, and that productivity is critical even at the expense of the law (Maclean, 2001). If this caliber of individuals infiltrate management, they are now in a position to create and guide shared understandings around what rule breaking entails. Shared meanings that justify or normalize rule breaking in service to productivity create a climate that supports more acts of individual rule breaking, thus bringing the cycle of persistence and proliferation of misconduct full circle. What is missing for those who want to understand how organizational misconduct through such management described above actually takes root is a template to begin the analysis of how organizational misconduct eventually becomes normalized for participants. Normalization refers to a process by which actions come to be taken for granted, where they are viewed as unremarkable and unquestioned over time.

When we combine someone harboring antisocial thinking traits and the individual personality traits studied in the previous chapters coupled with the normalization of misconduct process characteristics outlined below, it is not surprising that organizational misconduct actually thrives. Moreover normalization reflects the institutionalization of misconduct within organizational cultures, such that sayings like "if you're not cheating, you're not trying" take on a legitimate quality (Greeve et al., 2010). When misconduct is normalized, the standards against which future deviations are evaluated are loosened, and with each successive loosening of standards, the system becomes increasingly vulnerable to misconduct and potentially to ultimate failure such as bankruptcy. The three risk factors that contribute to the normalization of organizational corruption include: 1) institutionalization, which is the process by which corrupt practices are enacted as a routine matter, 2) collective and individual rationalization which is the process by which individuals legitimize both past, present, and future misconduct, and 3) socialization which is the process by which people are taught to perform and accept corrupt practices (Ashforth & Anand, 2003). Let us examine factors that facilitate organizational misconduct.

Institutionalization of Misconduct

Institutions usually strive to pursue a particular type of behavior by creating belief systems with the expectation that organizational members follow established practices. The benefit of institutionalized norms and practices is that they reduce uncertainty because they embed the interaction between individuals and organizations in a shared context of stable mutual expectations. As a result, institutionalized behaviors have been viewed as stable, repetitive and enduring activities that are enacted by multiple organizational members without significant thought about the appropriateness or usefulness of such behavior (Palazzo et al., 2012). Institutionalization is about embedding practices into organizational processes such that they can survive the turnover of generations of employees. The concept of institutionalization is not in and of itself exclusively tied to misconduct because there can be legitimate reasons to rely on institutionalization. However, the concept does help explain, in part, the question previously posed as to why otherwise law-abiding people are susceptible to engaging in corrupt acts when their behaviors may be contrary to their self-proclaimed ethical value system.

Generally speaking, institutionalization makes corrupt acts appear routine and not out of the ordinary. In the institutionalization stage that normalizes misconduct, misconduct becomes embedded in organizational memory and solidified in routines such that how things were done before legitimize current behavior. Misconduct becomes understood as "the way things are done," and thus a *de facto* rule of acceptable behavior (Greeve et al., 2010). As institutionalization sets in, individuals perform corrupt acts without giving significant thought to the reasons for those actions; indeed the actions may come to seem like the right and only course to take. Consider that institutionalization relies on socialization where employees, for example, experience common indoctrination practices under the direction of veteran members that teach newer members how things are done. The use of institutionalized socialization increases employee acceptance of organizational activities, leading to common interpretations and potential solutions to a given situation and less questioning of the status quo. Institutionalization also relies on collective rationalizations masquerading as rational arguments. The persistence of misconduct supported by rationalizations reinforce certain behavioral standards as normal when in fact they are not normal, but the misconduct feels like normal behavior.

Because we depend on legal institutions and non-legal norms to develop a societal consensus to convey what is right and wrong, a consequence of normalized misconduct is that what society as a whole deems to be right or wrong may not be reflected by those within the organization who instead relies on rationalizations to neutralize those societal norms that may disapprove of a given organizational behavior. Once misconduct has begun to spread to lower levels of the organization, it can proliferate through interaction among employees that learn from one another on how to engage in misconduct (Greeve et al., 2010). When practices become routinized habits, they tend to become taken-for-granted and enacted mindlessly, that is, with little or no real problem solving or even conscious awareness or reflection on the nature of one's actions (Milgram, 1974). Their routinized nature blunts the perceived need to reexamine the premises that gave rise to the practices in the first place or the outcomes they produce, creating a certain bureaucratic momentum. The mindlessness induced by institutionalization may cause individuals to not even notice what might arouse outrage under other circumstances (Javor & Jancsics, 2013). Moreover, there are factors that contribute to the cyclical nature of corruption that creates this perception of institutionalization.

Corrupt organizations encourage employees through their culture on what is expected of them. This culture at times involves harboring contempt for government and regulators to neutralize one's moral conscience and any feelings of shame, and rationalizations designed to redefine illegal and unethical behaviors as not truly criminal or unethical. In addition, the corporate veil allows perpetrators of white-collar crime to remain hidden and for criminal responsibility to be spread out across diverse officials in the organization. As a result, attributing criminal liability to any one person is difficult. Furthermore, institutionalization becomes normalized when organizations create both the opportunity and the pressures that drive individual acts of rule breaking and rule breaking is more likely to occur if it is linked to increased productivity when the organization financially rewards employees for this productivity. In this particular case, productivity is by far the most important measure of one's success, the primary driver of compensation and advancement. Close alignment of rule breaking and productivity make it more likely that rule breaking will occur in an organization, especially if the negative consequences appear relatively minor (Maclean, 2001).

When organizations promote high-producing individuals with disregard for their operating practices, they essentially promote bad behavior in two ways: 1) by advancing rule breakers into the ranks of management and 2) by implicitly advertising that rule breaking is a rewarded manner of achieving high levels of production (Maclean, 2001). Among the most important organizational structures that facilitate institutionalization are those that enable the selection of employees who are receptive to engaging in misconduct. Moreover, there are people susceptible to the types of influences that draw them into misconduct such as those who have internalized the norm of obedience to authority regardless of what is asked by authority to be performed (Greeve et al., 2010). As a result, management can explicitly or implicitly direct employees further down the hierarchy by encouraging misconduct by fostering a culture that endorses, permits, or creates conditions conducive to misconduct, and can also use formal authority to direct subordinates to engage in misconduct (Simpson & Piquero, 2002). Individuals become subjected to a process that normalizes corrupt behaviors whether they include white-collar crime type behaviors or in some of the worst scenarios they engage in atrocities of epic proportions such as those observed throughout history.

In institutionalized corruption, the driving force is not identifiable to just any one person; corruption is a property of the collective because there is a collective act behind it. Collective corruption has a slippery slope quality where initial, idiosyncratic corrupt practices become institutionalized over time and thus normalized as business as usual. As a result, corruption results from either the lack of formalized procedures or from the violation of existing formal procedures. In other words when employees at all or some levels of the organization do not follow or are not mandated to follow ethical procedures of business conduct, the corrupt outcome is defined as procedural corruption. Organizational processes can become faulty by developing routines to handle repeated tasks more efficiently, however the routines can reflect misconduct but are overlooked as misconduct because of the perception that all is well due to the organization operating smoothly (Greeve et. al., 2010).

In essence, routines create a false sense of security that the organization is operating legally when it is not. Habitual, routinized, or taken-for-granted pursuit of organizational goals can motivate employees with strong attachments to their organization to act unethically on behalf of their organization (Umphress & Bingham, 2011). Routinization can be looked at as transforming actions into mechanical, highly programmed operations neutralizing the impact of corruption in our minds, in addition to creating a momentum that sustains action without the necessity for thought. As an antitrust violator put it in reducing competition through collusion, "It was a way of doing business before we even got into the business. So it was like why do you brush your teeth in the morning or something…It was part of the everyday" routine (Benson, 1985, p. 591). Let us recall the example of Walter Pavlo and MCI from chapter two. MCI's fraudulent bookkeeping in the face of the failure of corporate customers to pay their bills might provide an example of this kind of routinized misconduct. Because one of MCI's biggest customers, WorldCom, was habitually late in making its payments, MCI executives responsible for collecting customer bills began sending a subordinate to WorldCom's headquarters on the last day of the payment period to accept the check and immediately fax a copy of it back to MCI headquarters.

Then the firm recorded the bill as paid, even though the check had not even been deposited in the firm's bank account. Over time, MCI extended this practice to other customers and routinized the process, to the point that the faxed-check entries were widely referred to as "the-check's-in-the-mail" deposits. The routinization of this unacceptable accounting practice set the standard against which other more egregious accounting manipulations were evaluated. Moreover, to increase efficiency, routinizing tends to break down corrupt acts into specialized tasks that are assigned to separate individuals. The result is that individuals may perform their tasks without knowing how their individual actions, in conjunction with the actions of others, contribute to the enactment of a corrupt practice. Thus, specialization not only fosters a diffusion of responsibility, it makes it difficult for any individual to comprehend and easy to deny the knowledge of the overall fraud scheme. Recall how segregation of duties may lead to rationalizations where an individual participates in only one aspect of an overall fraud, but claims innocence because they did not commit the entire misconduct that lead to fraud.

White-collar crimes tend to proliferate when the routines unremarkableness of everyday actions slip through the perpetrators' moral filters not pausing to think about the potential consequences due to their decisions (Olejarez, 2016). As one fraud offender stated reflecting the lack of moral reflection on making a decision: "I never once thought about the costs versus the rewards" (Olejarez, 2016, p. 110). Thus as a deviant culture becomes institutionalized within an organization tolerating repeated, collective misconduct, this reduces or eliminates the need for thoughtful reflection on one's behavior. Sometimes top management can cause subordinates to resort to corruption by setting unrealistic financial goals that are not achievable legally, and then just ignore the illicit means by which subordinates achieve them (Javor & Jancsics, 2013). Routinizing blunts awareness that a moral issue is present and if a moral issue is not recognized, moral decision making processes becomes minimized or outright irrelevant. Typical is the statement by one General Electric executive that price-fixing "had become so common and gone on for so many years that we lost sight of the fact that it was illegal" (Shover & Wright, 2001, p. 353). Reflect on the attitudes of employees of a drug company who concealed tests showing the dangerous side effects produced by their drug, "No one involved expressed any strong repugnance or even opposition to selling the unsafe drug...Rather, they all seemed to drift into the activity without thinking a great deal about it" (Shover & Wright, 2001, p. 353).

In considering corporate fraud as a collective act, group norms about theft become so entrenched that to steal is normal and prosocial in the eyes of the group and not to steal is considered deviant, antisocial behavior, thus institutionalization enhances legitimacy of the corruption. Moreover, routinization leads to the desensitization of ethical considerations behind decisions, thus one becomes accustomed to the riskiness of corruption that leads to engaging in a distorted risk assessment of the foreseeable consequences of their behavior. In essences, their distorted risk assessment downplays in their mind the potential dangers of engaging in misconduct such as the risk of facing a criminal prosecution. For example, the head of a Wall Street investment bank commented on insider trading in the 1980s that displayed this desensitization: "You definitely saw the abuses growing but you also saw the absence of people getting caught, so the atmosphere grew relaxed...There really was a deterioration of caution" (Sims & Brinkmann, 2002).

If upper management appears unconcerned with ethics and focuses solely on the bottom line, employees will be more prone to commit fraud and believe that ethical conduct is not a priority, thus employees will follow the examples of their bosses (Mahadeo, 2006). Leniency also facilitates the spread of amoral practices and where industry governing bodies may themselves become part of an institutionalized system of amorality. Given a permissive ethical climate, an emphasis on financial goals coupled with rewards for success, and an opportunity to act amorally or immorally, the ends may soon come to justify the means leading to a decision to engage in misconduct (Mahadeo, 2006). Furthermore, the leniency and low frequency of formal sanctioning by governments and professional associations often makes corruption economically rational; it appears that crime often does pay with groups providing self-serving accounts to neutralize ethical standards (Mahadeo, 2006). Amoral or immoral calculation is the most common route, in part because such a calculation is often necessary for acts of corruption to continue and become institutionalized, regardless of its origin.

The lack of ethical standards allows unethical behavior to become normalized and in such environments, "ethical concerns can be reframed as legal, economic, or public relations issues, leaving employees who perceive strong connections to their organization free to engage in amoral reasoning" (Ashforth & Anand 2003, p. 6). Leadership plays a huge role in the institutionalization process even though they may not actually engage in corruption, but serve as role models of what is expected by subordinates. In addition, leadership establishes expectations by rewarding, condoning, ignoring, or otherwise facilitating corruption, whether intentional or not, explicit or not, that sends a clear signal to employees. An emphasis on the ends rather than means, supported by high standards and strong rewards or punishments for attaining or not attaining them, creates a permissive ethical climate. For example, the bond trading scandal at Salomon Brothers during the 1990s can be traced to its corporate culture. Salomon Brothers' CEO, John Gutfreund institutionalized an unethical climate by focusing on, a) rewarding short-term results, b) displayed aggressive and Machiavellian behavior himself, c) failing to punish employees who broke laws in the pursuit of those short-term results, d) lying about and covering up ethical and legal lapses, e) promoting like-minded employees, and f) randomly and without cause firing others with the goal of sending the message that conformity to organizational goals and methods of pursing those goals are not to be criticized (Sims & Brinkmann, 2002).

Salomon was characterized as a company rewarding clever evasion of rules, silenced anyone standing in the way of profit, coupled with a company governed by "a culture of greed, contempt for government regulations, and a sneering attitude toward ethics or any other impediment to earning a buck" (Sims & Brinkeman, 2002, p. 334). Those that wanted to succeed followed the corporate culture and adherence to a code of ethics would only get in the way of getting ahead at Salomon; those who were like CEO Gutfreund did not hesitate to manipulate a situation to their advantage regardless of the ethical consequences. Gutfreund rewarded aggressiveness stating "I'm addicted to this business" (Sims and Brinkeman, 2002, p. 334). Yet, Gutfreund reaction to the unethical and illegal behavior was to cover it up sending the message to subordinates that wrongdoing was to be hidden from the authorities at any cost. In reference to Gutfreund's collusion and price fixing, he displayed a lack of accountability for his role in the scandal stating, "I'm not apologizing for anything to anybody...Apologies don't mean [expletive]" (Sims, 1992, p. 658).

Collective Rationalizations at the Organizational Level

Further, acts of corruption tend to gain a certain institutional momentum as the organization comes to count on the rewards of such acts. Rationalization is a process by which the moral or ethical considerations associated with an act are masked, overlooked, or dismissed. Collective rationalizations can pertain to white-collar crimes involving money laundering, wire fraud, bank fraud, financial statement fraud, asset misappropriation and insider trading (Free & Murphy, 2015). Through collective rationalizations, groups like individuals justify their misconduct and protect their self-image from self-blame, thereby make immoral behavior seem less distasteful in order to pursue their agendas. Rationalizations can be invoked prospectively meaning before the misconduct is carried out to forestall guilt, anxiety, stress and resistance by those who are uneasy about participating in misconduct or retrospectively meaning after the misconduct take place to ease regrets about one's behavior. Moreover, groups engaging in corrupt actions may not see themselves as corrupt and may continue to espouse a strong value system, even as they commit unscrupulous deeds (Ashforth & Anand, 2003).

As the ethical implications of decisions are removed, unethical acts become business decisions, not ethical dilemmas (Umphress & Bingham, 2011). Because rationalizations remove the ethical content from unethical behaviors, rationalizations are ironically related to and viewed as pro-organizational behaviors (Umphress & Bingham, 2011). As a result, group offenders adopt "a set of values and ideologies that can be used to define illegal behavior in favorable terms...the availability of these norms and customs enables white-collar offenders to interpret their criminal intentions and behavior in non-criminal terms" (Lilly et al., 2011, p. 287). At times organizational members who engage in misconduct compare their misconduct to other organizational behavior to show that their misconduct is less blameworthy. For example, misreporting a thousand dollars is not that bad when one considers that another company misreported one hundred thousand dollars. Thus, the fraud triangle often applied to the single offender can be applied to the organization to explain motivations, opportunity, and rationalizations that group members rely on (Free & Murphy, 2015).

Former HealthSouth CEO Richard Scrushy instructed his subordinates to engage in financial statement fraud in order to meet Wall Street analyst forecasts justifying such behavior by claiming that other companies engage in fraud. Managers may not be aware that a culture created through a reckless and overly aggressive leadership style can lead to individuals rationalizing actions while ignoring even state-of-the-art management controls (Free et al., 2007). Once invoked, rationalizations not only facilitate future wrongdoing, but dull awareness that the act is in fact wrong. Indeed, if rationalizations are perceived as a positive, shared resource in the organization's or industry's culture, they may pave the way toward defining the practice as business as usual—the way things are done. Some corporate cultures encourage antisocial behaviors to meet financial goals with a 'whatever it takes attitude" giving employees the permission they need to reduce their sense of guilt about their behaviors (Naso, 2012). Some of the most significant rationalizations encountered at the organizational level include, appealing to higher loyalties, perceiving acts as non-criminal in nature, and denying there is a victim.

Taken together, rationalizations coupled with socialization allow perpetrators of unethical activities to believe they are moral and ethical individuals, thereby allowing them to continue engaging in these practices without feeling pangs of conscience. Positive relationships facilitate rationalization, which in turn creates favorable conditions for unethical behaviors. Rather than focusing on the ethicality of the actual deed, employees with positive social exchange relationships may view the action in terms of a specific employment role or situation. Individuals with positive relationships, therefore, may focus on their duty to engage in the act and the possible beneficial consequences to the organization rather than on the moral implications associated with the unethical act. If employees look to situational factors such as role expectations to explain their unethical behavior, employees are able to accept less personal responsibility and distance themselves from the unethical act rather than internalize blame (Umphress & Bingham, 2011).

Yet their rationalizations may be different with co-offending as opposed to when a fraud offender acts alone (Free & Murphy, 2015). Consider, however, that multiple rationalizations can co-exist from those participating in co-offending in addition to individual rationalizations while participating in co-offending. For example, someone may co-offend because of their loyalty to the organization, but also rationalize the behavior for their own personal reasons such as believing that they are underpaid. The question that often arises is what was the primary motivation for co-offending that may transcend individual motivations? For example, someone may co-offend when they may not have any individual basis to offend and under different circumstances they might not even consider offending. Positive relationships may create a higher sense of loyalty that may encourage rationalization. Employees with positive social exchange relationships might view their unethical behavior as being good citizens. For instance, highly committed employees exhibiting positive reciprocity of norms are more likely to reciprocate through working harder and performing duties outside their job titles.

Similarly, highly committed employees may also perform unethical pro-organizational behavior when seeking to reciprocate favorable treatment. Positive relationships may cause employees to lose sight of what they actually do at work, and organizational goals can be placed above individual or societal standards for ethical behavior (Umphress & Bingham, 2011). This may prompt employees to view unethical pro-organizational behaviors as a way of simply carrying out their duty for the organization because contributions to the goals of the organization trump one's moral obligations to themselves and when applicable, the law. In addition, co-offending has an emotional quality attached to it due to the bonds that are formed through friendships and personal confidences built up through interpersonal exchanges which can be enhanced especially when they have a common motive. Common motives for co-offending can be varied such as engaging in fraud because the company does not pay us enough. Another reason for co-offending is the moral justification rationale which is to help the organization succeed or to save the company from bankruptcy. Consider the mindset of a fraud offender who engaged in financial statement fraud:

> We all believed in the company. We were part of an overall scheme of making the company successful….We were the darlings of the community. We were very good corporate citizens…there was an us versus the world mentality. We had a chip on our shoulder…people tend to think of us as less progressive, as less sophisticated, and we wanted to prove that we could be the biggest company in the field (Free & Murphy, 2015, p. 37).

There are times that the individual who co-offends does so not out of greed or some personal rationalization. The decision to co-offend is rooted in the concept of social identity, meaning what group do we identify with, where group expectations of loyalty, trust and distrust, and even antagonism towards other groups, can cement a group together while providing easy rationalizations for perpetrating fraud (Free & Murphy, 2015). Employees go along with co-offending because of the bonds they have created with others that may trigger a loyalty bias. Practically, "criminal behavior raises questions of loyalty to levels that are rarely glimpsed in other domains of life…That is probably the reason why trustworthiness or loyalty seems to be the most important trait that adult offenders look for in one another" (Free & Murphy, 2015, p. 34). Consider CFO Samuel Antar's insight into the impact of loyalty on co-offending:

> In the family business type of organized fraud, the members of the criminal group share family, religious, ethnic, racial and cultural ties, such as in the Mafia and other organized crime groups. The criminal participants are not just bound together by money, but by their sociology. I was in a group like this. We felt intense family loyalty. This loyalty and quest for status within our tight-knit group was part of my incentive to act criminally (Antar, 2013).

The Beech-Nut Corporation Case

The case of Beech-Nut Corporation illustrates how corruption becomes institutionalized and rationalized, but offenders ultimately being held accountable for their misconduct. Jerome LiCari was director of research and development for Beech-Nut, the second-largest U.S. baby food manufacturer and a subsidiary of Swiss food giant Nestle (Welles, 1988). For several years LiCari believed Beech-Nut's apple juice products were adulterated chemical drinks, yet they were labeled as 100 percent fruit juice. During LiCari's time at the firm, Beech-Nut was under great financial pressure, and using cheap, fake concentrate from a supplier at a 20 percent below market value saved the company millions of dollars. Even though LiCari voiced his opinion about the adulterated juice being sold as 100 percent fruit juice, employees justified their actions by relying on the rationalization of social comparison exemplified by statements such as "many other companies were selling fake juice" and that their fake juice was safe to consume (Welles, 1988). Another executive relied on the rationalization that there were no victims stating, "So suppose the stuff was all water and flavor and sugar, why get so upset about it? Who were we hurting" (Welles, 1988)?

When the Food and Drug Administration (FDA) identified a specific apple juice lot as tainted, Beech-Nut would quickly destroy it before the FDA could seize it. According to one executive, some Beech-Nut employees wanted the entire inventory destroyed or relabeled, but President Neils Hoyvald ordered it distributed at deep discounts. When Beech-Nut's actions were finally exposed by the New York State authorities, rather than acknowledge their illegal practices, they moved their entire adulterated stock to New Jersey at night, eventually to be sold in other than U.S. markets. Even during the investigation, Beech-Nut managed to unload thousands of cases of juice from its warehouse to Puerto Rico, despite the fact that the Puerto Rican distributor was already overstocked (Traub, 1988) and to other Caribbean destinations such as the Dominican Republic (Welles, 1988). The most revealing insight of LiCari and his relationship with Beech-Nut was his 1981 performance review which lauded his loyalty and technical ability, but said his professional judgment was "colored by naiveté and impractical ideals" especially his concern over the adulterated juice (Kelley, 1988, p. 6).

Asked during the trial if he had been naive, LiCari said, "I guess I was. I thought apple juice should be made from apples" (Kelley, 1988, p. 6). Is LiCari a good employee? Well not to his dishonest supervisors, but he is certainly the kind of employee most companies want to have: loyal, honest, candid with his superiors, and thoroughly credible. In an ethical company, this kind of employee can head off embarrassment and litigation by being skeptical of questionable practices. In 1987, the company pleaded guilty to selling adulterated and misbranded juice and CEO Hoyvald pleaded guilty to ten counts of mislabeling. The total cost to the company, including fines, legal expenses, and lost sales, was an estimated $25 million (Paine, 1994).

The Socialization Process Facilitating Misconduct

How does an otherwise ethically sound person become steeped in corruption? In part, the answer lies in the dynamics of socialization where people come to embrace an organization's cultural content, regardless of whether the content is right or wrong (Palmer, 2012). It is through socialization that newcomers and current employees learn what is expected of them. To be sure, some newcomers are presocialized into corruption through, for instance, previous experience in corrupt occupations, workgroups, organizations, and industries, and through recruitment via personal or social networks. However, given that most newcomers prefer to think of themselves as ethically sound, socialization into corruption tends to consist of pressures for change. Socialization is the mechanism for insuring that employees function effectively in a corrupt work environment (Greeve et al., 2010). The socialization processes produce a self-fulfilling prophecy whereby a group's intent on corruption produce a workforce that is receptive to corruption. In the socialization stage, new organizational participants are exposed to the techniques and attitudes that support the wrongful course of behavior.

The socialization process is composed of three phases: unfreezing, change, and refreezing (Greeve et al., 2010). In the unfreezing stage, through socialization the goal is to get the employee to abandon their old identity and at times this is usually accomplished by the humiliation of the old identity, isolation from others that support the old identity, and motivation to change away from the old identity. In the change phase, organizational participants incorporate their new identities through exposure to role models with whom they can identify and to situations that facilitate internalization. In the refreezing stage, once the old identity is sidelined, the new identity is to be embraced and internalized with role models whom mentor the newcomers into the organization so that they can internalize and reflect the organizations, norms, values, assumptions and beliefs. Criminal values, motives, beliefs, behaviors, and techniques are learned through interactions within intimate personal groups and in the case of corruption, groups often create a psychologically, if not physically, encapsulated social cocoon where,

- Veterans model the corrupt behavior, through example, for others to adopt as their own,
- Newcomers are encouraged to affiliate and bond with veterans, fostering desires to identify with, emulate, and please them,
- Newcomers are subjected to consistent statements that the ambiguity of one's action are resolved in clear black and white terms by the organization's expectations,
- Newcomers are encouraged to attribute any misgivings they may have as their own shortcomings, particularly naiveté, rather than to what is being asked of them,
- Newcomers receive frequent reinforcement for displaying corrupt behaviors, especially through rewarding such behavior, and
- Newcomers are discouraged and possibly punished for displaying doubt, hesitancy, or a tendency to backslide into non-corrupt behavior (Sutherland, 1949).

Co-optation facilitates socialization. Through co-optation, newcomers are induced by rewards to skew their attitudes if not their self-identities toward certain corrupt behavior. Socialization via co-optation is often subtle because the individuals themselves may not realize how the rewards have induced them to resolve the ambiguity that often pervades business issues in a manner that suits their self-interest. In co-optation, rewards are used to induce attitude change toward unethical behaviors. Finally, when individuals are forced into compromised situations, the rewards associated with an unethical course of action may induce them to choose it over the ethical course of action. There is an escalation of commitment where small, seemingly innocent, and routine decisions, can lead one down a road that one would not have taken if the destination had been clear at the outset. Coercion is not typically part of the socialization process because the goal is to have others voluntarily accept the socialization process so that there is no anxiety in accepting a different way of thinking that one would normally reject under other circumstances. Indeed, blatant coercion may provoke resentment against the source of coercion inducing a greater likelihood of grudging compliance, whistleblowing, and voluntary turnover and thus, risk of exposure. For these reasons, blatant coercion tends to be an ineffective means of socialization to sustain corruption even though this is not to argue that coercion and bullying is not used to get employees to comply with their demands. Aggressive, interpersonal tactics are used especially during employee performance reviews with the goal of influencing people's behaviors to support corrupt means and ends.

In terms of corruption, newcomers are initially induced to engage in small acts that seem relatively harmless and voluntary. The acts, although small, can create anxieties, but newcomers can reduce the anxiety by invoking collective rationalizing ideologies thereby realigning their attitudes with the acts as not being that harmful. The realigned attitudes then facilitate an escalation of the behavior and the process continues. It is often the seemingly small steps of incrementalism that lead newcomers to become more easily co-opted and compromised. Newcomers may be inadvertently seduced into corruption and not realize that their actions could be construed as illegal or unethical, at least by outsiders, until they are sliding down the slippery slope of corruption. By the time such a realization occurs, it may be very difficult to halt the behavior and remove oneself from the situation without suffering stiff psychological, social, financial, and legal costs from guilt, social isolation, shame, job loss, and so on. The temptation to simply continue and cover up one's misdeeds, aided by the rationalizing ideologies, is present, thus what may have been a one-time inadvertent act now becomes deliberate and ongoing and ultimately those same individuals become guilty participants. As one manager commented: "My ethical standards changed so gradually over the first five years of work that I hardly noticed it, but it was a great shock to suddenly realize what my feelings had been five years ago and how much they had changed (Ashforth & Anand, 2003, p. 31)."

When socialization takes place on the job facilitating reinforcement of attitudes that support misconduct, this consists of taking the new member from a rightful reference point to a wrongful one. Consider how the training and development of new trainees at Salomon Brothers illustrates the socialization process expecting exploitation at the expense of their clients. Trainees were initially humiliated by senior staff when the trainee could not answer their questions coupled with being isolated from others by the all-consuming nature of the training program that would go into the late evening hours. Trainees were punished for expressing assumptions, values, and beliefs that were perceived to be contrary to Salomon's and rewarded when they abandoned their old identities. Supervisors were displeased when trainees asked questions about ethics and social responsibility because the trainees did not understand yet that money was the most valued commodity. Salomon's socialization strategy demanded that their employees think of themselves as superior and view customers as stupid and that stupid people deserve to be exploited thus providing a rationale for pursing the firm's interests at the expense of the client (Palmer, 2012).

Other Salomon employees referred to clients as victims, fools or "ducks that were trained to fly repeatedly over the same field of hunters until shot dead" (Hoyk & Hersey, 2008, p. 83). An offender can believe that those harmed by their wrongdoing deserve their fate due to their inferior status—there is an implied or expressed expectation that those who are perceived as weaker deserve to be taken advantage of (Palmer, 2012). Thus, "the more we dehumanize others, the easier it is to harm them, and the more we harm them, the more we dehumanize them" (Hoyk & Hersey, 2008, p. 84). In many respects, their socialization methods resemble the antisocial trait of weakness exploitation studied in chapter one. The socialization strategy of teaching trainees to dehumanize Salomon clients made the "policy of screwing investors" easier to do with less guilt, thus reinforcing the practice of unethical behavior (Hoyk & Hersey, 2008, p. 83). When these members are driven by collectivistic motives and justifying their behaviors through socialization, they are more likely to engage in corruption that involves the entire organizational fabric (Aguilera & Vadera, 2008).

Acme Corporation: A Case Study of Normalized Corruption

This case study explored widespread rule breaking at Acme Insurance Company by interviewing former life insurance agents and sales managers who spoke freely because they were no longer employed at Acme (Maclean, 2001). At one time, being over a century old, Acme was one of the largest life insurers in the United States and during the 1990s, it employed between 15,000 and 20,000 sales agents and sales managers at any given time. Acme was chosen as a study because it is a publicly documented and highly visible example of widespread rule breaking at an organization being the subject of a national regulatory investigation of its widespread sales practice of churning. Churning is defined as a strategy to encourage repeated sales to generate commissions where sales agents improperly induce policyholders to apply the cash value and dividends from their life insurance policies to purchase new or additional life insurance products (Maclean, 2001). Churning is essentially a violation of what are known as replacement regulations of existing policies and although all replacements are not a violation of state law, replacements based on misleading or inaccurate information are in violation of state regulations. A churner convinces customers who had long-standing policies with built-up cash value to take out new, bigger policies on the false promise that the added coverage would not cost them anything (Van Slyke et al., 2016). Customers often did not realize that they had purchased additional insurance or were unaware that they had taken out loans on older policies to purchase additional coverage. Customers in this position, if unable to pay unexpected premiums due, can have their insurance policies canceled for nonpayment.

Let us look at an example. A policy holder buys a life insurance policy valued at $10,000 ten years later. A sales agent would then convince the policy holder to buy new or additional insurance with the accumulated money in the policy which in this case is $10,000. When that money is used to buy more insurance, the sales agent then makes another commission because it is recorded as a new sale and of course management would benefit from the churning because they too received bonuses for how much revenue is generated by the number of new policies opened. The policy holder may never have needed new or additional insurance. In fact, the new policy may end up costing the policy holder more money because the new insurance may be more expensive than what the policy holder originally bought. The Acme study illustrates how normalized corruption enabled churning to become widespread among sales agents and supported by senior management because they rose through the ranks of Acme at one time as a sales agent that engaged in churning.

Former employees suggested the importance of learning churning techniques and how to persuade clients to get additional insurance from one's supervisor. They disclosed the importance of being connected to someone who could shield them from the consequences of churning as stated by one former employee, "I saw guys getting promoted or getting choice agencies because they were in favor with the vice president, even after they had run their previous agency into the ground. They'd move them somewhere else and let someone else clean up the mess" (Maclean, 2001, p. 167). When rule breaking is profitable and rewarded by the organization with promotions into management, it drives changes in the overall composition of management in that sales management is dominated by those who have advanced by virtue of rule breaking and a shared understanding of rule breaking as acceptable behavior encouraged in the organization. The evidence suggests that it would be difficult for any sales manager not to be aware of deceptive sales practices and that in fact, many managers encouraged churning or knew about churning, but kept silent by not objecting to the practice because it would disrupt the way business was conducted and the way in which they earned a living.

The infiltration by such managers created an organizational foundation supporting the institutionalization of churning at Acme. At Acme there were family analogies supporting the spread of organizational rule breaking with accounts of the social nature being like "one big happy family" with a "frat-house" atmosphere. Social relationships repeatedly described as family-like imply an exceptional degree of closeness and intimacy as well as alluding to the obligations and loyalty inherent in family relationships. For instance, one interviewee stated, "They took very good care of myself and my family, but by the same token, I think I took pretty good care of Acme" (Maclean, 2001, p. 181). Another former agent states that agents with long tenure with the organization often referred to it as Mother Acme. These close relationships were considered one of the benefits of working for Acme: "When I started…there was a family sense. The agents and managers did a lot of socializing together, and that was one of your selling points if you were trying to recruit new agents" (Maclean, 2001, p. 181). Positive relationships were important to personal success at this organization which required a willingness to break the rules and the unwillingness to break the rules could result in demotion, termination or loss of favor and connections that were key to advancement at Acme. Being connected with the right people and being in favor with the right managers and executives was critical to success at Acme, as demonstrated in the following insight by one of its employees:

> I look at it as if it were [the movie] *The Godfather*. If you were in good graces with the godfather, then you were fine. As soon as you fell out of grace with the godfather, you were screwed. And that came from the top. And it's that old network, you know? It's a little network of good boys. OK, well this guy comes up the ranks with this guy and that one came up with that one. I went to this college. And this one idiot couldn't say enough times that he went to Notre Dame. You had some maybe political connections. I think it's a safe bet that if a VP didn't like you, for whatever reason, even though you produced, you wouldn't get promoted (Maclean, 2001, p. 181).

Agents also learned how to churn from other experienced agents. All agents in a given district office gathered at least once weekly for a mandatory sales meeting at the agency. This gathering provided a forum for informal sharing of sales ideas and techniques with each other for "beating the system":

> You'd know day to day what everyone was doing. You'd hear about different sales, and it all—it doesn't take long. Everything just kind of shakes out. But you could always have conversations on how to do it [churning], how to get the job done one way or the other. "Well, how do I do this? I've got this guy, he wants to cancel his policy…I don't want to lose commissions." And somebody else is sitting three seats down, usually an agent, who learned it from another agent, and he says, "Pay it in cash out of your own

pocket; wouldn't you trade an apple for an orchard?" Older reps would tell stories in the bullpen and laugh about the way they wrote business (Maclean, 2001, p. 185).

The Benefits of Churning

Churning results in increased sales productivity via misrepresentation of the product and Acme promoted agents into sales management primarily on the basis of their sales productivity. The following quote from an interview participant highlight both the opportunities to break rules offered and pressure to achieve results triggered churning as a solution:

> It's tough…Very early on in your career, you're absolutely going to be tempted. You're absolutely going to have the opportunity to screw somebody and make a lot of money. It all happened because everyone was making money off it. I mean, there was a direct correlation between an agent's production and the manager's income. And between the manager's income and the vice president's income. Was there a great deal of pressure working for Acme? Well, a lot of the agents who couldn't take the pressure went out to get jobs like air traffic controllers. So, the focus was always to sell more policies. More policies, more policies, more policies, so every week, or every month, there'd be a new sales push week, sell as many policies as we possibly can (Maclean, 2001, p. 181).

Organizations generally have formal rules and guidelines that prohibit unwanted or illegal activities in the workplace. Rules are enforced by systems of monitoring and sanctioning and sending explicit messages regarding what is acceptable behavior. Acme had a formal set of rules that forbid churning in accordance with SEC regulations, but was simultaneously sending implicit, yet clear messages regarding sales practices that contradicted formal rules via the practice of promoting successful sales agents into management positions. Thus successful sales people were promoted into sales management positions, successful sales managers into district manager slots, and successful district managers into regional vice president of sales positions. The following quote from an interviewee demonstrates the clarity with which Acme agents received the implicit message that what was important was the sale and not how the sale was achieved:

> The real thing, you know, is if you wanted to be somebody, you made the sales. And then you rose up in the system, regardless of whether or not all your sales were on the up and up. [Promotions] were commission based. Solely on commissions. Not based on anything else. Not based on how your lapse rates were, not based on the rapport you have with people, it was based strictly on the cash flow. Not over 5 years, or 3 years, but over the last 12 months. So if you were able to come in and get the job done and force people into situations, then you were promoted! Getting the job done was paramount. No one would come out and say that it was OK to do the wrong thing, or to make all your sales by dividends…but you watched who got ahead, you watched who was doing it (Maclean, 2001, p. 183).

The Role of Leadership in Facilitating Corruption

Churning involves an ability to circumvent a number of rules, which means outwitting a variety of checks and balances built into the administrative and monitoring systems at Acme. As one person explained, "There are rules against it, but if you knew the reporting systems, you could get around it" (Maclean, 2001, p. 183). Firsthand experience in sales gave Acme leadership the knowledge of the types of deceptive practices agents engaged in to sell life insurance, including churning because it was ignored, tolerated, or encouraged resulting in financial rewards for all. The promotion-from-within norm at Acme virtually guaranteed that members of management at all levels of the sales channel were at least aware of the existence of churning and most likely participated in churning themselves. As one former executive stated, "This is what's being done. It's wrong. It shouldn't be done. With documentation, with all kinds of stuff. And it was—it was just ignored. It was totally ignored"

(Maclean, 2001, p. 187). Interview participants describe such managers at all levels of sales management as stated by one former employee:

> I can't believe that the higher ups [regional executives] weren't fully aware of this [the use of churning as a sales technique]. Just as your sales managers were. Just as your district managers were. So what happened…is that the people a couple levels up made their money that way [churning]. So now, all of a sudden, you have a hierarchy of say three levels up and down, this is how they all sold insurance [by churning]. Well, sales managers grew out of the ranks. They did what someone had taught them or what they had figured out on their own, and I suppose the general manager grew out of the ranks as well, had seen all of this, was exposed to it and knew what was happening (Maclean, 2001, p. 183).

The management-sales agent relationship at Acme was one of exceptional closeness, especially in the first few months of a new agent's career. Sales managers were almost solely responsible for the training an agent received. The training was primarily composed of assisting agents in making appointments, constructing proposals out of existing client information, taking agents out on sales appointments, modeling presentations, and guiding them in filling out the appropriate paperwork. A former sales manager describes the relationship: "If you were assigned to my staff…your success would depend on my abilities and willingness to work with you…so it was a love/hate relationship. Everything we tried to do was for the good of the agent" (Maclean, 2001, p. 184). Throughout these processes associated with making a sale are multiple opportunities for rule breaking associated with churning, and sales managers taught new agents how to take advantage of these opportunities. The following participant describes the importance of mentoring relationships in the diffusion of rule breaking practices:

> The agent is out there churning, and he doesn't come into the business knowing how to do that. It has to be learned, it has to be taught…they're learning it from the people who are training them. Most of the time, as the manager would go out with a new agent, the manager would sell that way, and then the agent would pick it up. But they're being taught by their sales managers, who in turn were previously taught by general managers. (Maclean, 2001, p. 184).

The likelihood of being caught and punished by leadership for violating rules and regulations that forbid churning seemed to be minimal at Acme. For example, high-producing agents and managers violating company rules would be transferred, promoted, or shielded from serious consequences when it appeared that they might be caught and punished. These shared understandings helped create the climate in which churning was viewed as an acceptable business practice, thus facilitating its spread in the organization. Shared understandings or cultural norms existed among sales agents and management regarding the way business was done at Acme, what was valued, and important. The data clearly demonstrated that interviewees shared a belief that management was far more concerned with the sale than with sales practices. According to one interviewee, their attitude was:

> Don't tell me about the labor pains, show me the baby! Management cared about the business, period, the end. That was it. From what I saw, that was it. It was a win at all costs mentality. But a sale was a sale was a sale. "Just tell me about the results. Okay? Don't tell me the facts, unless it's a problem—and then tell me later, you know? We'll take the sale today." The culture was, you know, "How many sales did you have this week?" This was what you had to strive for. This was the top level. To be in the top 500 agents. And management didn't really seem to care how you got there (Maclean, 2001, p. 188).

The Role of Social Identification Facilitating Misconduct

Social identity typically refers to that part of an individual's self-concept derived from membership with a social group; in essence what group(s) does one identify with. There are conditions that give rise to group loyalty and the bases is assumed to be lodged in human needs to be affiliated with one another. Just as we may adopt a national identity to a country, we also develop a group identity as it relates to belonging to an organization and as an example belonging to a particular military branch. Consistent with social identity research, people's sense of who they are, their self-identity, is partly shaped by the social groups they belong to. When people identify highly with their group, they see themselves primarily as group members. In contrast, when group identification is weak or absent, people view themselves primarily as individuals. Studies found that social identity is particularly noticeable when people perceive a threat to the status of the group they belong to (Van Vugt & Hart, 2004). There may be multiple identities a person harbors such as the social identity of the organization they work for or the social identity of the professional or religious organization they belong to.

Thus, the way they display their identity within a religious setting may be different than the way they engage within their work environment. Some persons maintain a highly integrated idea of who they are in that how they behave in a religious setting is similar to how the behave at home which is the same as how they behave at work, while others have a looser definition of who they are increasing the contradictory set of behaviors they exhibit depending on what environment they find themselves in (Shover & Wright, 2001). Thus, in one sense they are part of a group at work that engages in crime while at the same time, they participate in church activities with integrity and perhaps for the betterment of others. Some will not cross the line and engage in misconduct while others do so with ease. Assumptions, values, and beliefs evolve in organizations to rationalize corrupt practices in ways that neutralize the stigma of corruption. Yet, how can a group hold a worldview so at odds with the wider culture and not appear to be greatly conflicted by it? Consider that an individual develops social identities specific to the social domains, groups and roles that he or she occupies such as manager, a parishioner belonging to a religious organization, and for others the political party they belong to.

Given the diversity of social domains and groups and roles one typically occupies, one's social identities tend to be correspondingly quite diverse. In the case of corruption, an otherwise ethically-minded employee may forsake societal norms about ethical behavior and ignore the law in favor of particular behaviors on behalf of his or her group because their self-interest is tied to the perceived benefits of belonging to a group. This tendency to always put the in-group above others clearly paves the way for collective corruption. Unfortunately there is a false sense of security in the belief that groups provide cover from the consequences of their misconduct. Extreme examples include organized crime, the Mafia, terrorists, and street gangs where members of these groups tend not to see themselves as corrupt, but as faithfully serving themselves, their in-group and perhaps their neighborhood. The wider society exists as a counterpoint to be exploited. Thus, the individual may bend their commitment to ethics under the pressure of a particular situation explaining why people are virtuous at the abstract level, but are willing to sacrifice virtue for the immediate situation that needs to be addressed.

Think of one's acceptance of different identities as a form of compartmentalization in which they psychologically divide their life into different compartments. For example, when an individual goes to work, they automatically slip into their work roles while adhering to cultural expectations, rationalizing decisions, and respond to pressures in a predictable manner. When they exit the workplace, they slip into their other roles such as parent, spouse, or parishioner, along with the norms and expectations of those roles. It is not that individuals forget their other selves, it is that they tend to defer to whatever identity is expected at the time. In order not to compromise the usefulness of identities tailored to particular situations, individuals mentally compartmentalize their identities. In other words people have different identities for different realities and engage in those realities in a different manner. Consider the insights of a CEO who went to prison for securities fraud illustrating this concept of compartmentalizing one's life choices by creating different identities to cope with the fraud:

> When you're CEO…you have to put your life into different boxes. You don't have a choice. You have to put your family life into one box, your business in a box, and your emotions in another. You've got no choice. That's the way it had to work or you can't function. If you put things in boxes, you'll be able to slide through and pull it off (Soltes, 2016, p. 272).

Let us be clear; compartmentalization does not just apply to fraud offenders as a way to cope with their wrongdoings. Other offenders too compartmentalize their emotions—their activities. As stated in chapter one, issues of criminality and antisocial behaviors that may not be criminal in nature are socioeconomic and educationally neutral. Terrorists that commit horrific crimes compartmentalize their lives by being loving family members, supportive friends, and devoted to their faith. Well-educated Nazi doctors performed diabolical experiments on the innocent and yet saw themselves as honorable physicians. Organized crime hitmen who kill for a living otherwise lead ordinary family lives. Serial killers are gainfully employed, have families, support their neighbors and are unmercifully cruel in their treatment of strangers (Kocsis, 2008). For example, Hillside Strangler Kenneth Bianchi clearly divided the world into two camps. The individuals toward whom he had no feelings including the twelve women he brutally tortured and killed.

Ken's inner circle consisted of his mother, his common-law wife, and his son, as well as his cousin Angelo Buono, with whom he teamed up for the killings. Bianchi's wife Kelli Boyd once told investigators: "The Ken I knew couldn't ever have hurt anybody or killed anybody. He wasn't the kind of person who could have killed somebody" (Kocsis, 2008, p. 7). Indeed, the killer relies on the normalcy of compartmentalization, when he interacts with those in his inner circle. For example, despite his conviction on 33 counts of murder, John Wayne Gacy was seen by those in his community as a rather decent and caring man. Lillian Grexa, who lived next door to Gacy while he was burying victims in the crawl space underneath his house, remained supportive, even writing to him on death row. "I know they say he killed 33 young men," explained Grexa, "but I only knew him as a good neighbor—the best I ever had" (p. 7). In contrast an "executive might be a heartless "son of a bitch" to all his employees at work, but a loving and devoted family man at home" (p. 7). This being said, people define, in part, their identity by the organization they belong to and acquire such an identity through the organization itself (Schaef & Fassel, 1988).

Moreover, as traditional sources of social cohesion, the family, the church, and civic societies, lose their centrality in one's life due to being replaced by the workplace, the workplace becomes the central source for daily social interaction which in turn contributes to the sense of who they are (Hulsted, 2010). Consequently, corporate involvement influence who and what workers' commitments and priorities are to the point where, despite their best intentions, they are driven to commit more to the corporation than to other external occupational social ties and loyalties (Hulsted, 2010). For some individuals, the organization exists to make their aspirations a reality such as striving for upward social mobility and they will not tolerate others who might interfere with that aspiration for financial gain, power, and status (Schaef & Fassel, 1988). The promise that their future will be better is a strong inducement to make others displace one social identification for another, thus the organization remains central in their lives. This is especially true when wealth disparities within an organization send the message that to obtain more wealth means to adhere to the norms, values, and expectations of the organization. When membership in a group is highly prized, employees are more likely to adopt the norms of the group and are unlikely to challenge ethical lapses or compromised leadership.

However, the downside to building such a strong sense of identity is that it increases the likelihood of blind acceptance of the organization's norms. The organization can control what they represent by the promises they make of future benefits and the power of the promise keeps people loyal, thus the benefits of loyalty are strategies organizations use to keep people focused and loyalty is what keeps the organization afloat (Schaef & Fassel, 1988). From an organizational misconduct perspective, social identity can influence a person to adopt a group's rationalization to engage in corrupt practices even though from their perspective they do not believe they are engaging in any corrupt behaviors (Umphress & Bingham, 2011). One offender engaged in the rationalization of the condemnation of the victim which in this case is the government stating, "I guess I was involved in a group of people that thought that the government just kept printing dollars…they rob, steal and cheat us" (Free & Murphy, 2015, p. 136). Consider these observations of the emotional bonds formed by the language used and the desire to keep the organization successful through fraud:

A colleague started to refer to the group involved in the fraud as "the family." The question is what made the family hang together?...These were all people who liked the people they worked for...to be a team player they went along...Why did I do it? I was very proud of the company. We had gone from nothing to billions of dollars in a matter of a few years. Our reputation was superb. Unlike Enron, our business wasn't phony. I wanted to keep the dream going, to keep the stockholders happy (Free & Murphy, 2015, p. 36).

Organizational identification, a form of social identity, is an employee's perception of belonging and membership to their employing organization. Organizational identification enables individuals to embody and support their organization. As organizational identification strengthens, organizational values and related worker practices become important. Employees who strongly identify with their organization internalize the organization's successes and failures as their own and behave in ways that are consistent with organizational expectations and ways that benefit the organization, such as through higher loyalty, working outside their assigned job roles, job performance, and decreased employee turnover (Umphress & Bingham, 2011). Employees with high organizational identification may be willing to engage in unethical pro-organizational behavior within organizations displaying amoral cultures especially when the duty to obey trumps personal preferences in rigid, hierarchical organizations. Employees who identify positively with an organization are more likely to commit unethical acts intended to benefit the organization when ethical norms seem unclear.

Similarly, employees who strongly identify with the organization may simply choose to conduct unethical pro-organizational behaviors given that such behavior would fit within a culture dominated by amoral norms and practices. Such an identity may also compel employees to disregard their own ethical standards, even at the expense of their own clients, in favor of misconduct that supposedly helps the organization (Ashforth & Anand, 2003). When one's social identity within the organization is increasingly important to the individual, employees may modify their own sense of what morality entails to coincide with the morality of their social in-group. Through a desire to protect the group's identity, individuals may place the interests of the group above the interests of those harmed by an unethical act such as shareholders. Thus, organizational identification could allow employees to perceive unethical pro-organizational behaviors as dutiful acts that serve their group or organization (Ashforth & Anand, 2003). High levels of organizational identification cause employees to conduct unethical acts such as lying to protect the organization or covering up evidence that could harm the organization.

Moreover, employees are more likely to engage in unethical pro-organizational behavior to satisfy their agendas will also engage in denial of misconduct coupled with failing to admit the need to move on and leave the organization (Hayes, 2009). People are willing to reduce the conflicts between their private beliefs and their public expression in social life in favor of conformity in order to maintain a peaceful, predictable life even if that entails making choices that do not reflect their true preferences (Hayes, 2009). Employees can neutralize unethical acts through organization identification by 1) ignoring the plight of the victims to protect the identity of the organization, and 2) maintaining a higher loyalty to the organization than to the morals or norms within society and the law (Umphress & Bingham, 2011). If a highly identified employee lies for the organization to protect it from external auditors as an example, it might be difficult to recognize any personal harm caused by the unethical act, especially when the benefits to the organization may seem obvious.

Second, employees may also engage in rationalization by focusing on the wrongs committed by their victims. If employees perceive that the organization has been wronged, they may interpret disrespect as a threat justifying retaliation such as alienating or bullying a whistleblower who discloses corporate misconduct. Employees perpetrating unethical acts preserve the group's identity and are likely to view themselves as heroes by carrying out seemingly justifiable actions against disreputable victims. Because one's social identity influences how individuals construct and interpret an issue, ethical compromise is likely to occur if the goals of the organization are seen as relevant or vital to one's self-interest than society's moral values or the potential negative outcomes resulting from the unethical acts. Thus "an otherwise ethically-minded individual may forsake universalistic or dominant norms about ethical behavior in favor of particularistic behaviors that favor his or her group at the expense of outsiders" (Ashforth & Anand 2003, p. 10). Thus, role of one's identity in relation to their group is more important than upholding a certain ethicality.

The Impact of Misplaced Loyalty

Misplaced loyalty lies at the heart of virtually every recent scandal in corporate governance. Corporate officers and directors, who should have known better, put loyalty to a dynamic Chief Executive Officer above duty to shareholders and obedience to the law. The officers and directors of Enron…and almost every other allegedly misgoverned firm could have asked questions, demanded answers, and blown whistles, but did not. Ultimately they sacrificed their whole careers and reputations on the pyres of their CEOs (Forbes & Watson, n.d.).

One important psychological force contributing to group stability is a member's loyalty to the group—that desire to forgo alternatives for group membership (Van Vugt & Hart, 2004). Loyalty and identification to a group become tied to one's sense of self where the individual and the group become one and what the group stands for is adopted by the individual as their own. Once people start to identify with their group, their welfare becomes intertwined with the welfare of the group and are willing to make personal sacrifices for the benefit of the group (Van Vugt & Hart, 2004). At times loyalty creates an "us versus them" mentality which is evidenced by how group members dislike when regulators and auditors come to inspect whether compliance has been met (Druckman, 1994). What increases our loyalty to others is when we have similar traits to them and actually like the people we interact with coupled with a sense of commitment to look after the interests of others that can ultimately lead to organizational misconduct (Palmer, 2012). For example the experience of strong, positive emotions such as empathy associated with group membership may enhance that sense of loyalty and generally the stronger the identification to a group is the stronger the loyalty to the group. Yet a loyalty bias can blind us in such a way that interferes with quality decision making.

A misplaced, dysfunctional form of loyalty can develop when individuals within a group expect others to commit antisocial acts, such as fraud, to benefit an organization because of loyalty to the group. For example, the position of CEO grants this person immense authority, control over resources, and over the careers of his or her subordinates; in short, the CEO has power that could potentially be used to override safeguards to protect the organization (Forbes & Watson, n.d.). Such individuals frequently abuse their authority to cultivate susceptible followers by financially rewarding them for their loyalty. We often see this misplaced loyalty in the context of power within an organization where management directs subordinates to engage in misconduct out of a sense of loyalty to their superiors. People seem prepared to obey orders from authority figures that are clearly in conflict with their personal moral codes and legal responsibilities because of their sense of loyalty to the group and leadership. Even individuals such as independent board of directors that can disregard the requests of an authority figure such as the CEO are not more immune to this desire to obey due to a loyalty bias.

Consider the case of Michael Cohen. Michael Cohen was a confidant and one of President Trump's attorneys. Cohen pleaded guilty to obstruction when he lied under oath to Congress. Regardless of one's political preferences, the reality is Cohen committed a crime and will spend time in prison for his crime. Yet his statements illustrate how someone can become so immersed in the activities of their colleagues and superiors that they lose sight of the fact that their loyalty does not diminish their criminal behaviors. According to Cohen, "My loyalty to Mr. Trump has cost me everything…My family's happiness, my law license, my company, my livelihood, my honor, my reputation and soon my freedom…I am ashamed of my weakness and misplaced loyalty—of the things I did for Mr. Trump in an effort to protect and promote him. I am ashamed that I chose to take part in concealing Mr. Trump's illicit acts rather than listening to my own conscience" (Cohen, 2019).

The Influence of Culture on Organizational Misconduct

The paradox of "why good people do dirty work" is partially resolved by understanding that some organizations disregard ethical and legal consequences if it benefits the firm due to a culture encouraging, or at a minimum, ignoring rule breaking which is learned just as any other business practice is learned (Simpson & Weisburd, 2008). Risk factors for white-collar crime to flourish include organizations that exhibit distinctive cultures which are more or less tolerant of law violations for the benefit of the firm. Cultures play a significant role in determining ethical behavior because it influences organizational members' focus of attention, interpretations of events, attitudes, and behaviors (Simpson & Weisburd, 2008). Culture provides collective norms about ethical conduct and the foundation for employees' determinations about what is and what is not appropriate behavior within the organization. Culture reflects aspects of workplace life whether communication is confrontational or collaborative, whether morality is considered or not, whether emotional expression is encouraged or discouraged, and whether disappointing news is perceived as a threat or as an opportunity.

Consider some of the scenarios that commonly arise in corporate life whose responses are shaped by workplace culture. Would a salesperson be willing to provide a kickback to the person they are trying to sell a product or service to? When sales targets are not met, are managers willing to recognize sales contracts that have not been performed yet as a bona fide sale to reach a sales revenue target? When the results of a new product are disappointing and potentially harmful, does the engineer describe the issues fairly and openly or are they hidden in the fine print? What are the expectations these employees harbor and how does the culture they navigate within impact how they perform their duties? What do we mean by culture? By culture we mean a set of important understandings that members of a community share in common such as 1) customs and traditions, habits, norms, implied understandings of conduct, values, and shared assumptions, 2) common meanings that are understood by and guide group members toward a particular set of attitudes and beliefs and away from other attitudes and beliefs as well as 3) written and unwritten expectations of behavior that influence members of the organization (Grant & McGhee, 2012).

Culture creates cohesiveness among individuals and people rely on culture to figure out how to think about and act in a given situation and how to respond appropriately when problems arise while values and beliefs tend to refer to our concept of what is right and wrong (Palmer, 2012). Culture includes knowledge, beliefs, morals, law, and any other capabilities and habits acquired by people as members of a society (Van Slyke et al., 2016). Culture assists us in terms of how to interpret and make sense of our environment, how to respond to situations or how to refrain from responding in a given way in addition to reinforcing values (Sims, 2003). Organizational culture includes the shared social knowledge within an organization regarding the rules, norms and values that shapes the attitudes and behaviors of its employees and generally speaking most people desire to behave according to the expectations that respected others have for them. Moreover, organizational culture refers to the shared moral beliefs of organizational members where on the one side are corporations that on the whole subscribe to be ethical and on the other side are corporations supporting antisocial behaviors.

Organizational culture facilitates the framework of a standardized, routine manner to solve problems, reduces uncertainty in decision making coupled with helping employees adopt programmed patterns of expected conduct at their disposal that dictate how they should perceive and design their own course of action when reacting to specific situations (Van Slyke et al., 2016). Individuals tend to be socialized into environments that provide them with behavioral indicators of what behavior is acceptable and unacceptable, even providing rationalizations for neutralizing any reservations about the ethicality or legality of certain questionable behaviors (Van Slyke et al., 2016). Organizational culture guides people on how to think, reason, and make decisions and if cultures can therefore be developed and controlled by those at the top, the overall impact on people is likely to be enormous. Cultural explanations assume that people will engage in misconduct when they think the misconduct is consistent with their organization's norms, values, and beliefs. This explanation purports to account, at least as a partial explanation, for why educated and seemingly conventional persons can commit crime when they are employed in white-collar occupations.

Corporate culture can fill in the social need of identity, the personal need of belonging to a group, as well as the financial need of earning a living. People want to socialize, participate and engage in activities with other individuals however an individual's motivation, judgements and perceptions are influenced by organizational culture. Organizational culture also facilitates distributing power and status and allocating rewards and punishment. Culture even regulates how people dress, language considered appropriate, and employee interactions that are approved and not approved. Culture can act as a form of social control and this should not necessarily be interpreted in a negative manner simply because social control is used. Imagine what would happen within

315

organizations if there were no expectations of how to behave in order to coordinate activities—chaos would rule. Consider, however, there may not only be one culture within an organization, but several subcultures that are contradictory to each other that exist within a larger organizational context especially for those multinational organizations with facilities throughout the world. For example, it is not unreasonable to observe that the culture at an organization's headquarters where the CEO is located may be different from a satellite office located in Asia where the leadership there might set a different tone at the top.

Organizations are typically populated by people who share the same ideas about the appropriate ways of thinking and acting about a given situation to help them decide which course of action to take whether ethical or unethical, legal or illegal. In this view, organizational misconduct arises when an organization's culture becomes perverted and deems wrongdoing as appropriate. In fact subordinates do not see themselves as co-offenders, but as morally righteous especially if they perceive themselves as having little or no control over the conditions that led to misconduct in the first place due to circumstances such as intense peer pressure, financial, and management pressures. Organizational cultures can also convey messages that create and reinforce rationalizations. For example, some cultures contain subtle messages that encourage misconduct if the harm is minimal, outright deny that there is a victim altogether, or that the apparent victim deserved the harm they incurred (Palmer, 2012). Furthermore, some cultures convey messages that their misconduct is acceptable especially if it is less harmful than another's misconduct. For example, some believe that their "small" misconduct in terms of embezzling money from their employer is nothing compared, in their mind, to the embezzlement that is perpetrated by those at the top who have access to funds to take.

Organizational culture transfers their values to members and at times the individual is expected to replace their own values with those of the organization even when they are contrary to their personal beliefs (Grant & McGhee, 2012). At times this explains why someone that does not conform to the groups expectations because they may reject a value that the organization expects to be adopted, are retaliated against by others who expect conformity (Grant & McGhee, 2012). Perhaps employees may see an issue, but they remain silent, and if they do share their concerns, they are either terminated or alienated within the organization (Jennings, 2007). Culture can be used to control people desiring to voice their opinions because he or she may disagree with another's opinion. Thus, organizational cultures, whether explicitly or implicitly, send the message that dissent will not be tolerated, that loyalty is expected, and if these expectations are not observed, punishment in the form of demotions or outright dismissal can be expected. Believing that organizational culture is ethical, when in fact it is not, employees may engage in unethical behaviors even though what they believe is for the benefit of an organization actually ends up harming the organization (Umphress & Bingham, 2011).

To an outsider, these practices are obviously wrong, but insiders who have internalized the culture's logic cannot see anything wrong, perceiving themselves and the behavior of the organizations they work for as good and right. Ultimately, to question the appropriateness of organizational culture is to threaten the collective identity, which cannot be tolerated. Conformity is critical and only a tightly regulated communication of beliefs and behaviors is permitted. It is not surprising to observe members replace their preexisting beliefs and values with those of the group, experiencing social punishments such as isolation by other members if they deviate from carefully prescribed cultural norms of an organization (Langone, 1995). The culture of the organization reflects leaderships tone at the top, which in turn is reinforced by rewarding and hiring those that best reflect the organization's tone at the top (Duchon & Burns, 2008). Leaders may encourage a culture void of ethical standards by supporting amoral initiatives, such as rewarding questionable practices, holding employees accountable for performance goals, but not for the manner in which those goals were achieved, or implicitly condoning corrupt practices (Umphress & Bingham, 2011).

For instance, a leader may instill a certain level of trust and identification among his or her subordinates, making employees less likely to question methods for carrying out work. In this way, a subordinate identifying with the organization may rationalize what appears to be seemingly authorized unethical acts as "business as usual," and such justifications may trump personal ethical values (Ashforth & Anand 2003). Early socialization into an organization's culture is especially important in shaping an individual's vision of acceptable behavior as part of their reality. Unethical behavior certainly can yield beneficial outcomes, and although these outcomes are perhaps not sustainable, they are appealing enough that mechanisms such as socialization and incremental exposure to corruption can be used to normalize opportunistic corruption in organizations (Ashforth & Anand, 2003). Even more explicitly, a culture can convey acceptance and appreciation of actions that break rules and violate norms, particularly those that value risk-taking or innovativeness.

For instance, the culture of investment bank Salomon Brothers assumed that their clients were stupid and that stupid people deserved to be exploited thus endorsing a cultural content that could be used to justify counseling clients to purchase investments that earned the firm superior commissions, but earned its clients inferior returns (Greeve et al., 2010). At Archer Daniels Midland (ADM), the organizational culture included the assumption that the firm's competition were natural allies and its customers were naturally antagonistic to the interests of ADM. Employees were familiar with the ADM motto that "competitors are our friends and our customers are our enemies" (Palmer, 2012, p. 68). This assumption may have provided the ideal rationale needed to engage in collusive behavior with competitors through price-fixing agreements for a food ingredient called lysine at the expense of customers. Participants in the price-fixing scheme were ultimately prosecuted and fined (Greeve et al., 2010).

Cultural Amorality within Organizations

Organizational cultures can give rise to conditions that facilitate misconduct and this is observable where cultures place a high value on achieving extraordinary performance especially when the methods to achieve performance are not as relevant as simply achieving the performance. A culture can focus members on the ends without simultaneously providing guidance about the means with which ends should be achieved. More explicitly, a culture can focus members on achieving the ends while simultaneously conveying, sometimes subtly, a lack of concern about the moral character of the means with which ends should be achieved. A more concerning ethical implication is the potential of cultural amorality to spread and take root in an organization reflecting opportunistic, unethical behavior consistent with a Machiavellian attitude becoming socialized, reinforced, and eventually ingrained into a corporate mindset (Ashforth & Anand, 2003). This is true for unethical leadership whose deceit encourages acceptance and rationalized support for misconduct among others in the organization. Some suggest that organizational culture can reflect a Machiavellian disposition where: "Amorality is a theme corporations often find themselves described by, unlike immorality, it is not a pathological desire to commit sadistic abuse of others due to a lack of empathy. Neither is it the need to function morally due to values one is raised with, it is simply calculating which action brings the most overall value" (Kailemia, 2016, p. 78).

Corrupt behavior is fostered when an organization's culture favors highly ambiguous ethical norms and instills notions of amorality to facilitate misconduct (Umphress & Bingham, 2011). Thus, if it is to their benefit to engage ethical behavior to satisfy their agendas then they will behave ethically. Conversely, if engaging in unethical and perhaps an illegal behavior satisfies an agenda, then they will behave accordingly. Within amoral cultures, employees with high organizational identification are likely to rationalize away the ethicality associated with their own actions when those actions benefit the organization. Employees within amoral cultures also are likely to engage in higher levels of unethical pro-organizational behavior than are those within more ethical organizational cultures. Organizational goals influence unethical activity within amoral organizational cultures. Goals are frequently tied to financial success and resource acquisition which facilitates immoral pursuits in the interest of meeting organizational objectives (Ashforth & Anand 2003). Most companies and organizations have goals and feel the pressure to meet the numbers that produce profits, yet a company with an amoral culture dives into a zone of perversity where they start with the number they want to report and work backwards by relying on accounting interpretations to reach the predetermined number (Jennings, 2007).

Rather than actively encouraging members into advancing organizational goals through unethical means, amoral organizations indirectly encourage unethical practices (Umphress & Bingham, 2011). Amorality may be encouraged by leaders who implicitly, and not through words, authorize unethical behavior even if they do not engage in unethical behaviors themselves. Within amoral cultures organizational leaders emphasize less-than-ethical means to do business, and those high in organizational identification are likely to internalize and behave consistently with this message. Deviant behavior within the organization may not merely be the result of individual choice, it may be driven and controlled by rules, policies, procedures and goals within the corporate culture which govern the behavior of its members (Hulsted, 2010). Some of the strongest evidence for the impact of organizational amorality comes from those white-collar offenders who have come around to acknowledge that they broke the law, but at the time they did not believe so (Shover & Wright, 2001).

In some instances, cultural endorsement of specific types of misconduct can be explicit such as when TAP pharmaceuticals contained cultural norms that convey expectations of actually engaging in misconduct such as giving doctors kickbacks if they prescribed TAP drugs, and encouraging doctors to falsely bill Medicaid for drug samples they received for free. Moreover, TAP did not have an in-house legal counsel and according to one executive, "legal counsel was considered a sales-prevention department" (Palmer, 2012, p. 68). When the company held a sales meeting to launch its ulcer drug called Prevacid in 1995, TAP devoted little concern to discussing the scientific data as to the legitimacy of what the drug is supposed to do. Instead the sales teams had a party in which they featured a large mechanical stomach called "Tummy" that belched fire conveying in a subtle manner that scientific validation is not as important as the optics of the goal which is to increase sales.

Moreover, the studies of the allocation of contracts among heavy electrical equipment operators in the 1950s illustrates how cultural values and beliefs can guide misconduct and make it appear normal. Bid rigging was wide-spread during this period especially because the production and transmission of electricity involved government. Several of the sales persons that worked for these equipment operators testified at public hearings that it was their belief that allocating and spreading out business among competitors was good not just for the different operators, but also for the industry and the economy as a whole (Geis, 1995). In addition, they reasoned that by establishing in advance which company would get the contract would smooth out sales among all the firms in the industry, thus avoiding instability that firms might experience had they had to be competitive with their prices. In this case, as soon as sales persons were hired, they would meet with sales persons from other firms for the purpose of determining who would win a particular contract. Several sales persons testified that they agreed to participate in the meeting because they believed their superiors expected them to participate in the meetings and that if they did not participate, then someone else takes their place agreeing to participate.

Misconduct Facilitated by Social Networks

Individual-level theories of misconduct tend to assume that organizational participants embark on wrongdoing as independent actors. A culture of misconduct may provide a good explanation of the average propensity of organizational participants to commit misconduct, but it cannot explain variation in participation across organizational participants—this is where social network theory comes in. Social networking is the practice of expanding the number of professional and social contacts by making connections through individuals by a variety of methods such as face to face interactions or via one's computer as examples. Many misconduct cases involve multiple individuals linked by social ties. Indeed, many cases are examples of collective efforts intentionally orchestrated by a number of interconnected individuals striving to achieve the same unethical and illegal goals. For example the falsification of test reports in the B.F. Goodrich brake scandal previously discussed in chapter one were approved by multiple managers overseeing and instructing the engineers in charge of conducting and reporting the tests. There are even cases of coordination among firms involved in joint misconduct, as in the price fixing in the heavy electrical equipment industry, where three of the social networks involved between 21 and 33 individuals spread across many companies (Greeve et al., 2010).

Enron and an Organizational Culture Endorsing Misconduct

Enron's initial success was in natural gas marketing, however in order to accelerate growth, Enron attempted to expand by entering new markets (Ferrell et al., 2013). The core of Enron's business was relatively straight forward in that it tried to do a better job at matching buyers and sellers of energy products whether it was electricity, coal and metals in addition to creating markets in areas such as Internet bandwidth, weather, and even air quality. For example, Enron operated a thirty-two thousand mile gas pipeline, was the largest manufacture of wind turbines, and managed dozens of power plants in places such as India, Poland, and Turkey. It was during the 1990s and beyond that the media, including finance journalists, began to heap praises onto the company making statements such as, "in contrast to the boringly predictable regulated utilities of old, which were safe havens for widows and orphans, the newcomers hold the promise of skyrocketing returns…celebrating Jeff Skilling's vision of Enron as a cutting-edge company" (Rosoff, 2007, p. 514). Other journalists covering Enron stated, "Forget about Microsoft, America's most successful, revered, feared—even hated—company is no longer a band of millionaire geeks from Redmond, Washington, but a cabal of cowboy traders from Houston: Enron" (Rosoff, 2007, p. 514).

Enron was named "America's most innovative company" six times in a row with an admired management team (McLean & Elkind, 2003). Starting in January, 2001, nine months before its collapse, Enron was celebrating how successful it was with massive parties, distributing bonuses worth millions while touting accolades received from the media for its successes. The New York Times called Enron a "model for the new American workplace" labeling Enron founder and CEO Kenneth Lay "an idea man" (Rosoff, 2007, p. 514). Enron was cited as a role model by the market's leading experts, including stock analysts, investment analysts, journalists, consultants and business schools professors—its success story was required reading at Harvard's Business School (Di Miceli da Silveira, 2013). In fact, faculty at this school produced 11 case studies uniformly praising Enron's successes and recommending its business model to others (Tourish & Vatcha, 2005). When MIT's Sloan School of Management sought to determine "which firm to name eBusiness of the Year in April 2001, an award for the company that best demonstrates innovation, leadership, and social responsibility over the past year," it did not have to look any further than Enron (Soltes, 2016, p. 232).

The company also displayed its power and political influence where it was estimated that three quarters of U.S. lawmakers received campaign donations from Enron and since 1989, a total of $5.7 million of the company's money found its way to Washington, D.C. (Sims, 2003, p. 206). In 1999, its lobbyists in Washington included people like Henry Kissinger and James Baker, both former U.S. Secretaries of State and Enron managers gave George Bush, who was running for governor of Texas $774,000, and Enron as a company gave $312,000 to his campaign (O'Connor, 2003, p. 1272). Enron's Chairman and founder, Ken Lay, was affectionately called Kenny Boy by his then friend George Bush (McLean & Elkind 2003). President George W. Bush's campaigns alone received $623,000 over the course of his political career (Sims, 2003, p. 206). Republican John McCain admitted to receiving $9,500 from Enron in two campaigns, but he publicly stated that "We're all tainted by the millions and millions of dollars that were contributed by Enron executives" (Sims, 2003, p. 206). Prior to Enron's collapse, Nelson Mandela and Alan Greenspan traveled to Enron's headquarters in Houston to receive the prestigious "Enron Prize". Eventually, Enron became known for a large number of business mistakes, overpriced acquisitions, and disastrous overseas investments.

Their business strategy created much risk for Enron because undertaking these projects put pressure on their performance and eventually its financial statements since cash inflows lagged cash outflows creating the need for Enron to turn to elaborate fraud schemes to keep it financially afloat to give the appearance of success (Rezaee & Riley, 2010). Enron's innovations accelerated the problem because these projects required large initial capital outlays that were not expected to generate cash flow until much later. Even with all the revenue it claimed to be making, it was hemorrhaging cash; in other words, they did not have the cash to prove they were making money (Rezaee & Riley, 2010). Yet Enron's revenues grew from less than $10 billion in 1995 to over $100 billion in 2000 (Soltes, 2016). In September 2001, a month before the eruption of the scandal, Enron was on the list of the 50 fastest growing U.S. companies, being by far the largest company on the list (Di Miceli da Silveira, 2013). Even though Enron's "sales was increasing, income never grew proportionally to sales; for example in 2000, sales grew by more than 150 percent, but its income increased by less than 10 percent (Schilit & Perler, 2010). Suspicions started to surface when many believed it was virtually impossible for a company to achieve this type of growth without acquiring other companies to assist in its growth in such a short period.

For example, consider the fact that ExxonMobil first reached $10 billion in 1963 and it did not reach the $100 billion mark until 1980 and General Motors reached $10 billion in 1955 and did not reach the $100 billion mark until the mid-1980s (Schilit & Perler, 2010). Walmart was one of the few corporations that was able to hit the $100 billion mark, but it took Walmart 10 years (Schilit & Perler, 2010). Yet during 2001, Lay sold millions of dollars of his Enron stock while falsely assuring the public that there was no problem at Enron (Hueston, 2007) and encouraged Enron employees to invest their retirement money into Enron (Rosoff, 2007). Fewer than four months before Enron filed for bankruptcy, when Enron's demise was accelerating, Lay remained highly positive about the company's financial health (Ferrell & Ferrell, 2010). In August 2001, after Kenneth Lay took over as CEO again after CEO Jeffrey Skilling resigned, CEO Lay declared, "I have never felt better about the prospects for the company" (Cruver, 2003, p. 91). On August 15, 2001, CEO Lay addressed investors stating:

If anything, there seems to be even a little acceleration in the company's financial performance and operational performance. There are no accounting issues, no trading issues, no reserve issues, and no previously unknown problem issues. I think I can honestly say that the company is probably in the strongest and best shape that it has probably ever been in (McLean & Elkind, 2003, p. 347).

As to the issue of cash flow, Lay proclaimed, "Our liquidity is fine…As a matter of fact, it's better than fine. It's strong" (Pelley, 2005). Lay further stated on August 20, 2001, "Investors don't like uncertainty, when there's uncertainty they always think there's another shoe to fall. There is no other shoe to fall" (Hueston, 2007, p. 210), because "the balance sheet is strong…third quarter is looking great," and "Enron stock is an incredible bargain at current prices" (Ferrell & Ferrell, 2010). In late September, 2001, Lay encouraged employees to "talk up the stock" because "the company is fundamentally sound" (Johnson, 2003, p. 48). Throughout October 2001, Lay insisted that Enron had access to cash and that the company was "performing very well" (Sims, 2003, p. 166). Lay maintained his innocence stating he was not purposely lying to employees and the investor community, but trying to save the company that he loved (Ferrell & Ferrell, 2010). In October, 2001, Enron finally incorporated all of the liabilities hidden in its special purpose entities (SPEs) into its own financial statements and restated its earnings, which resulted in a $500 million accounting loss and a $1.2 billion reduction in shareholder equity. With Enron declaring bankruptcy by the end of 2001, more than twenty thousand employees lost their jobs and over $60 billion in market value vanished; the workers who invested their pensions in Enron saw their retirement savings literally evaporate (McLean & Elkind, 2003). It is estimated that of the $2.1 billion in Enron's employee pension fund, $1.3 billion was in Enron stock in late 2000 (Van Slyke et al., 2016). Moreover, a bankruptcy examiner reported that Enron claimed a net income of $979 million in 2000, yet it actually earned just $42 million (Ferrell et al., 2013). Although Enron claimed $3 billion in cash flow for the same year, they had a negative cash flow of $154 million (Ferrell et al., 2013).

In the end, Enron become the ultimate symbol of corporate misconduct synonymous with words such as greed, ethical disaster, corporate corruption, dishonesty, accounting fraud, and corporate governance failure. Twenty-two former Enron employees were indicted and convicted, however, there were 130 unindicted co-conspirators which included most top managers that worked with Kenneth Lay and Jeffrey Skilling (Ferrell & Ferrell, 2010). The reality is the "Enron scandal grew out of a steady accumulation of habits and values and actions that began years before and finally spiraled out of control" (McLean & Elkind, 2003, p. 132). It was "the sum of incremental transgressions that produced the business catastrophe" where Enron's leadership would "reinforce a culture that was flexible, opening the doors to ethics degeneration, lying, cheating, and stealing" (Sims & Brinkmann, 2003, p. 247). When corporate leaders encourage rule breaking and institute a culture where intimidation of employees is acceptable to satisfy a motive, it is not surprising that ethical boundaries erode as they did within Enron. Information released from Enron's leadership was distorted in substance and the vast majority of employees did not know things such as where the money went or how overall strategic decisions were made.

Enron tightly controlled how and what information was released to the public. The intended effect was to reinforce the authority of Enron's leaders and people assumed that at least the leaders knew what was happening, and that they had the employees overall best interests at heart (Tourish & Vatcha, 2005). Yet Enron's leadership was concerned about its own personal financial rewards thus, if the stock price began to drop, they sold their shares while regular, non-executive employees were not allowed to sell theirs. Management never communicated to the employees the true financial position of Enron, thus thousands of employees lost tremendous amounts of money that was in part ear-marked for retirement. Moreover, "there was misrepresentation of hard data, that is, concealment of debt, lying about accounting results, as well as about the stream of earnings, and the distortion of the company's future prospects" (Cohan, 2002, p. 280). Enron went from the personification of economic superiority, to abruptly becoming the personification of greed and a source of national outrage (Howard, 2011).

In this case study we examine the impact of Enron's leadership on its tone at the top, how leadership influenced Enron's culture, and the financial statement fraud scheme that Enron relied on to maintain the appearance of success. Moreover we review the role CFO Andrew Fastow played to perpetuate the fraud together with factors that influenced how Enron allocated rewards and punishments influencing subordinate behaviors to participate in the fraud. Finally, we explore how Enron interacted with parties outside of Enron such as investment banks influencing their decision to, even if indirectly, encourage misconduct that lead to Enron's downfall by recommendations made by their stock analysts.

Enron's Financial Statement Fraud Schemes

The new businesses Enron participated in caused Enron to experience large earnings fluctuations from quarter to quarter potentially affecting the credit rating it received, and its credit rating was important because it affected their ability to obtain low-cost financing and attract investment. Enron pursued questionable accounting and finance practices while Wall Street harbored unrealistically high growth expectations for the firm partly because it perceived that Enron had the capability of dramatic expansion when in fact it was a public utility entity where traditionally it was an industry that experienced low, single digit growth (Palmer, 2012). As a result, management was preoccupied with doing deals such as building electric generating plants, buying and selling natural gas and developing water distribution networks because doing deals helped the firm meet Wall Street expectations and to maintain and increase its stock price. However, management was concerned about failed deals that would eventually be reflected in its financial statements as not producing expected income and underperforming assets that would not be valued favorably on its balance sheet. Moreover, there was a concern that too much debt would discourage future deal making because of the inherent risk in carrying debt that needs to be paid off eventually.

Enron executives performed a variety of questionable accounting maneuvers and completed an assortment of dubious financial transactions, later determined to be fraudulent, in an attempt to remove debt from its balance sheet and add fictitious revenue to its income statement. In order to ensure an investment-grade credit rating, Enron's financial statement fraud emphasized increased cash flow, lower debt, and smoothing its earnings to meet the criteria set by credit rating agencies like Moody's and Standard & Poor's. By keeping debt off of its balance sheets, Enron was able to report ever increasing revenues which artificially increased the value of its stock; for example Enron's stock increased from $19 a share on November 5, 1997 to $82 on January 25, 2001 (Van Slyke et al., 2016). In addition, consider that for the fraud to materialize, a host of parties including Enron's management, lawyers, and accountants devised schemes to defraud the investing public by, 1) making Enron appear more financially successful than it actually was, 2) artificially inflated Enron's stock price, 3) avoided government regulations to escape proper financial reporting, 4) engaged in fraudulent transactions using special purpose entities (SPEs) with the aid of its external auditor Arthur Andersen and legal counsel, 5) concealed debt and underperforming assets, and 6) filed false and misleading financial statements with the SEC to name a few of its infractions (CGASS, 2002a, b; Batson, 2003).

Let us look at a few of the examples of how Enron artificially boosted income through revenue and equity fraud schemes, and through the use of special purpose entities that were used to hide Enron's loses and debt from its income and balance sheet. In one revenue-based scheme, Enron developed a partnership with BlockBuster where BlockBuster was to provide movies to homes directly over phone lines. Just a few months after this partnership was formed, Enron recorded over $110 million in profits even though nothing had actually been earned yet by Enron (Keller, 2002). In fact there was never any profit because the partnership failed after only a 1,000-home pilot study. Including improperly accounted for revenue on its income statement was one of Enron's fraud strategies, but others included utilizing mark-to-market accounting treatment when valuing its commodities contracts to create artificial revenue and equity schemes such as treating the sale of company stock as revenue (Rezaee & Riley, 2010). For example, in terms of equity schemes, when Enron exchanged its common stock for notes receivables, then it should have, but did not, decrease its stockholder's equity to reflect the amount converted into notes receivable. As to creating artificial revenue through its commodities contracts, Enron became creative with its accounting methodology by conveniently forgetting that it was primarily a utility company, but instead pretended to be a financial institution (Schilit & Perler, 2010).

As a utility, Enron entered into long-term commodity delivery contracts with customers pertaining to the future delivery of natural gas. Accounting principles tell us that Enron as a utility company must record revenue on these long-term service contracts when the delivery of the natural gas took place. Yet, Enron would take these long-term contracts and immediately recognize anticipated revenue instead of recognizing revenue when it was earned (Mintz & Morris, 2017). Moreover, Enron did not treat these contracts as service contracts, but instead classified them as the sale of financial trading securities or more specifically, the sale of commodity futures contracts (Schilit & Perler, 2010). Using this interpretation of their contracts, Enron relied on an accounting methodology, known as mark-to-market, intended to be used by financial institutions that trade securities. Under this method, the service contract would be viewed the same way as any other tradeable security which meant that all expected profits under the contract would be recorded immediately. As estimates of contract profitability changed over time due to market fluctuations, the value would be adjusted as well.

Because there was no actual market for many of the contracts Enron was selling, this allowed Enron to use its own aggressive assumptions in determining the fair value of the contracts and any future mark-ups or mark-downs depending on what Enron was trying to financially achieve. Essentially, Enron used an accounting treatment that was not meant for the utility industry. Moreover, the problem with Enron's method was that if the contracts were not fulfilled, it was Enron that bore the risk of losing money because Enron generated money from the difference between the buying and selling price (Sims, 2003). In addition to recognizing revenue immediately, Enron accelerated its growth by recognizing the entire amount of what the asset in the contract sold at which is unheard of. For example, when a brokerage company sells stock, it is basically acting as a middle-person or agent of the transaction getting a commission on the sale, but what is recorded is the commission as revenue, not the entire amount of the value of the stock that was sold. Yet, this was the practice Enron engaged in or else it could not have accelerated its revenue the way it had achieving such astronomical growth. Envision what the revenue of a brokerage house would be if it recorded the entire amount of the sale as revenue.

To encourage the sale of commodities contracts, Skilling came up with the idea of a gas bank where Enron could benefit on the fluctuation of gas prices by acting as a middleman by creating a futures market for buyers and sellers to buy and sell gas to be used tomorrow at a stable price today (Albrecht et al., 2012). The problem Enron encountered in marketing stable, long-term custom-made contracts to its customers was that many of the gas producers were not comfortable with this arrangement because it required estimates to value what future gas contracts would be worth today. As a result, Enron's solution was to entice gas producers by offering money up front for the contracts, but the problem then became, where does Enron get enough cash to pay the gas producers when it simply did not have sufficient cash on hand (Albrecht et al., 2012)? To come up with the money, CFO Andrew Fastow used special purpose entities (SPEs) to raise cash from banks to pay the gas producers. SPE's are freestanding enterprises created by a parent company, such as Enron, and jointly owned by them with outside investors.

They are similar to subsidiaries in that they are independent from the parent company in terms of having their own financial statements, but they differ from subsidiaries because they carry out specialized purposes for a limited time period. SPEs are a popular tool that helps firms isolate risk. SPEs are legal, but in certain circumstances they have to be included as part of the larger parent company's financial statements instead of being reported as independent entities and not consolidated with the parent company which in this case is Enron (Albrecht et al., 2012). The general partner of the SPEs had to be independent of Enron and the general partner of the SPE cannot be a related party, an Enron employee, a board member or a family member. If there was no independence, then the SPE's assets and liabilities had to be consolidated onto Enron's balance sheet for the benefit of the investing public to get a true representation of Enron's financial health and the risk that Enron was exposed to through these SPEs. With the approval of the board of directors, CFO Andrew Fastow became one of the investors in some of the SPEs, thus creating a related party issue triggering the obligation to consolidate the assets and liabilities of the SPEs into Enron's financial statements, but they did not.

Fastow used the SPEs to hide losses, increase its cash inflow (liquidity), hide bad investment results, sell under-performing assets at a gain, increase its revenues, and hide its debts all with the goal of not having to disclose the SPEs to the public through consolidation on Enron's financial statements (Albrecht et al., 2012). In addition, these SPEs accelerated gains from sales, and delayed the recognition of losses. For example, Enron's profit was overstated by $405 million and debt understated by $2.6 billion on its balance sheet by the use of an SPE (Mintz & Morris, 2017). Enron became dependent on SPEs to finance its energy business and keeping debt off Enron's balance sheet which allowed it to maintain a high credit rating so that it would not have to post tangible assets as collateral to borrow against (Sims & Brinkmann, 2003). If Enron made bad business decisions, SPEs were used to clean up the mess so that the bad decisions would not be reflected on Enron's balance sheet and income statement. Enron would increase cash inflow by selling their undervalued assets to the SPE for a gain and then Enron would show a gain on their financial statements reflecting fraudulently inflated earnings. Let us take an example to illustrate the point. Enron would sell an asset they paid $15, but is now worth $10, to the SPE for $20 and record a gain.

Had they sold the asset in the open market, it would be sold for less than the $15 they paid for it. When institutions were not comfortable in lending to the SPEs because of their concern of not being able to collect on the loans and the interest due, the SPEs started to offer Enron shares as collateral, however, it was the lenders that requested Enron stock be used as collateral (Ferrell et al., 2013). When Enron began to lose money on its energy contracts, this was unacceptable because if revenues declined, then Enron's stock price would decline and a stock devaluation would trigger a debt repayment that Enron could not meet (Van Slyke et al., 2016). This again would mean that senior management such as Lay, Fastow and Skilling were under pressure to keep the stock price high so that lenders would not be dissuaded from lending (Ferrell et al., 2013). Since Enron assumed and further put itself at risk because its shares were used as collateral, the SPE's assets and liabilities should have been consolidated into Enron's financial statements which Enron did not want to do. When Enron finally collapsed, its off-balance sheet financing stood at $17 billion (Mintz & Morris, 2017).

Leadership's Influence on Organizational Culture

Just as "the destiny of individuals is determined by personal character, the destiny of an organization is determined by the character of its leadership…and when individuals are derailed because of lack of character, the organization will also be harmed" (Sims & Brinkmann, 2003, p. 250). Leaders are responsible for communicating culture in their organizations, and the ethical dimension of organizational culture is no exception (Trevino & Brown, 2004). There are several strategies a leader can use to influence an organization's culture including, 1) role modeling, mentoring, teaching and coaching, 2) reward, status and punishment allocation, 3) criteria to be recruited, hired and promoted and 4) how leadership reacts and deals with problems and crisis (Sims & Brinkmann, 2003). Role modeling reflects the values that leaders convey through the examples they set for subordinates. Once a new and possibly corrosive value system emerges, employees are vulnerable to manipulation by organizational leaders to whom they have entrusted many of their vital interests (Free et al., 2007). For example, leaders encourage innovation, but they can display an aggressive tone that values unethical behavior to reach goals coupled with discouraging others from questioning behaviors that appear unethical.

The Enron demise points to numerous risks associated with a compromised leadership and degenerate cultures including, 1) the risk that a culture motivating and rewarding creative entrepreneurial deal making provides strong incentives to take additional risks, thereby pushing legal and ethical boundaries, 2) ignoring bad news impacting the health of an organization, and 3) internal competition for bonuses and promotion leading to hoarding information to bolster individual short-term performance (Free et al., 2007). The destructive practices of Enron's leadership remained unchallenged even by the board of directors, while a destructive corporate culture took deeper root that encouraged conformity and penalized dissent. A survey of Enron employees found that many were uncomfortable about voicing their opinions and "telling it like it is at Enron" (Swartz & Watkins, 2003, p. 76). Overall, Enron inculcated a powerful set of cultural norms in its employees by displaying its belief that human nature is driven by self-interest and that innovation and exceptional performance was driven by unfettered competition. Enron's goal was all on profit and not how profit was earned, where making money became a game without boundaries with the end goal of improving its stock price to support the SPEs.

Enron's focus on stock price at their headquarters was reinforced with elevators equipped with televisions allowing employees to know what the stock price was at all times (O'Connor, 2003). It is not surprising that "the company's stock price goes deeply to its executives sense of identity and self-worth" in order to retain their status by hyping their way to stock market stardom by manipulating accounting rules to create paper profits and not profits based on real economic value offered to customers (O'Connor, 2003, p. 1254). In describing Enron's Machiavellian culture of focusing on the ends and not the means, one executive stated, "You can break the rules, you can cheat, you can lie, but as long as you make money, it's all right" (O'Connor, 2003, p. 1273). Another employee stated, "the only thing that mattered was adding value and it was an atmosphere of deliberately breaking the rules" (Sims, 2003, p. 148). Enron was populated with people who displayed disrespect for the law, ethics, and social responsibility, especially executives who created and encouraged the breeding ground for misconduct.

Enron rewarded cleverness over integrity conveying the message that misconduct will be tolerated, even appreciated as long as the end goals were met (Palmer, 2012). When "corporate leaders who encouraged rule-breaking foster an intimidating, aggressive environment, it is not surprising that the ethical boundaries at Enron eroded away to nothing" (Sims, 2003, p. 163). An atmosphere of corporate arrogance, the constant media portrayal as a success story, and its highly valued stock enhanced the internal atmosphere of hubris and intellectual superiority shown by Enron executives especially with regard to its competitors leading to the reinforcement of unethical practices without relevant internal challenge to blatant corruption. Enron's Chief of Staff described Enron's culture as "a near mercenary culture that encourages organizations to hide problems, discourages cooperation and teamwork, and drives off people who demand at least a modicum of civility in their work environment" (Batson, 2003, p. 90). In addition Skilling promoted fierce competition among subordinates and he expected others to adopt this philosophy (McLean & Elkind, 2003). His worldview shaped the organization's culture more than any other executive as one commentator observed:

> Skilling sought to shape Enron into something akin to a pure state of nature where individuals could advance themselves—and the company stock—unencumbered by the typical restraints found in corporate civilization…Vicious competition among employees was a natural outgrowth of the Skilling approach…Skilling encouraged the dog-eat-dog culture, and it reflected his own survival-of-the fittest mentality (Callahan, 2004, p. 129).

In addition, the culture at Enron reflected unchecked behaviors all in the spirit of making money, performance reviews that fired those that allegedly underperformed, unrealistic goal expectations that pushed ethical and legal boundaries by adopting a "whatever it takes" mindset to meet those goals, unchecked ambitions, and a sense of entitlement (Sims & Brinkmann, 2003). Employees would state, 1) you were expected to perform to a standard that was continually being raised 2) the only thing that mattered was adding value, and 3) it was all about an atmosphere of deliberately breaking the rules (Sims & Brinkmann, 2003, p. 244). Obsessed with its stock price, Enron leadership avoided rules because the rules did not apply to them; the message was they were entitled to success and riches because Enron was changing the world. Jeffrey Skilling created a culture where boasting and bragging became institutionalized and his subordinates liked to show off, being known as the best and the brightest by indulging themselves with flashy, sleek offices that were meant to symbolize the smart, gifted people they believed themselves to be. Others did not shy away from exhibitionism such as using private jets and hosting expensive parties that were considered part of the Enron identity of endorsing excessive lifestyles. Enron rewarded oil and gas traders who reaped massive bonuses as well as those that developed financial schemes creating the appearance of financial strength (Van Slyke et al., 2016). Enron was famous for minting millionaires where the lavish compensation system clearly oriented employees toward focusing on appearing to be a successful company when in reality the day-to-day management was incompetent at best (Van Slyke et al., 2016). Many of the energy traders were generously rewarded, but Enron's policies created perverse incentives such as over-pricing contracts so that traders would receive bigger commissions. Moreover, contracts lacked financial integrity which placed more responsibility on Enron's risk assessment department, but traders pressured the risk assessment department to approve contracts that were too risky (Van Slyke et al., 2016).

The Role of Enron's CFO Andrew Fastow

We're going to do the right thing and make money without having to do anything but the right thing.

Andrew Fastow (Streitfeld & Romney, 2002)

The story of convicted CFO Andrew Fastow is a good example of how power and misconduct evolve over time. Recall that as one of the architects of the company's fraud, he received the 1999 Excellence Award in capital management structure by *CFO Magazine* (Perri, 2013b). Commenting on his abilities, Fastow stated, "I ought to be CFO of the year…Do you realize what a great job I've done at this company" (Ham et al., 2017, p. 1090). Fastow's job was to lessen Enron risk exposure so that Enron could meet Wall Street expectations, sustain its stock price, and generate badly needed cash. He further stated, "There was an overarching theme at Enron since its founding, you could use as much money as you wanted as long as you didn't use Enron's balance sheet" (Soltes, 2016, p. 233). Such a philosophy was adopted by Fastow, thus it was his job to find ways to remove the debt off Enron's principle financial statements. Fastow moved the debt into SPEs to eventually sell to investors, plus remove poor performing assets from Enron's balance sheet to prevent the appearance that Enron was not as financially healthy as it appeared.

CEO Skilling became dependent on Fastow and when he was warned about what Fastow was doing by one of his associates, he stated, "Well, those are the people I depend on. Those are the people who got me where I am"…Skilling saw Fastow as a problem solver (Palmer, 2012, p. 201). Skilling did not question Fastow's use of Enron stock as collateral to secure loans whose proceeds from investors were used to offset Enron's failing investments. Despite "persistent failure, Skilling approved one far-fetched business plan after another, believing that each would be what he called the big enchilada—the successful investment that would pay off the firm's escalating debt" (Langbert, 2010, p. 2). He "believed himself, Fastow, and other Enron senior executives to be geniuses—'guys with spikes'—who were capable of coming up with major breakthroughs even though literally hundreds of their ideas failed and occasionally involved criminality" (Langbert, 2010, p. 2). In turn Fastow worshiped Skilling and even named his first-born after him, working hard to emulate the values that Skilling advocated (Raghavan et al., 2002).

Consider how Fastow naming his child after Skilling parallels the trait of social identification studied in chapter one where people look up to others they respect and want to emulate because they reflect their own value system. Interestingly, it was CEO Lay who replaced CFO James Alexander with Fastow because Alexander refused to certify the financial statements due to his belief that they were not accurate (Jennings, 2006). One of the problems with the use of SPEs is that Fastow attached himself to these SPEs making millions of dollars at the expense of Enron (Albrecht et al., 2012). With one SPE, Fastow also funneled payments to his wife in the amount of $54,000 and other financial gifts, in amounts under $10,000 to avoid paying gift tax (Albrecht et al., 2012). There was a conflict of interest because Fastow was in essence negotiating against the interest of Enron for the benefit of the SPEs while still Enron's CFO where he owed fiduciary duties to Enron and its shareholders. Fastow believed that the firm's conflict of interest provisions in its code of ethics should not apply towards his own self-enriching activities (Abelson, 2002).

Moreover, for Fastow to construct SPEs for his benefit and Enrons, he needed the cooperation of a number of people, the authorization of his superiors, the backing of outside investors, the approval of Enron's external auditors, the approval of outside legal counsel, the approval of the board of directors and his subordinates who carried out his orders. Recall the concept of social networking previously discussed and its application in this scenario where Fastow used the social networking both within Enron and with people and organizations outside of Enron to facilitate his financial statement fraud. To avoid the appearance of a conflict of interest, Fastow found individuals he believed who could not be considered related parties to be the general partners of the SPEs, thus believing they were complying with the legal requirement of avoiding conflict of interests. Michael Kopper was one of Fastow's assistants and he became involved in the SPEs when Fastow was trying to get outsiders to be the owners of the SPEs.

Fastow used Kopper's domestic partner because Kopper was gay and gay marriage was not recognized in Texas at the time, thus there would be no related party issues according to Fastow (Soltes, 2016). Thus, to mitigate the specter of a conflict of interest that Kopper might be seen as controlling an SPE, Kopper transferred his interest in one of the SPEs to his domestic partner William Dodson (Sims, 2003). Kopper invested $115,000 and Dodson invested $10,000 for an investment return of $10.5 million (Sims, 2003). Kopper, in addition to his Enron salary, was paid about $2 million in questionable management fees related to the SPE from 1997 to 2000. Fastow also used his position to staff the chain of command below him with subordinates who were likely to support his agenda. People within his finance unit who were qualified to be promoted, but would not commit to Fastow's agenda, were transferred to other departments within Enron or they were fired. For example, Fastow fired treasurer Bill Gatham after Gatham supplied Moody's Investors Services with accurate accounting numbers that nearly provoked Moody's into downgrading Enron's bond ratings.

Then Gatham's replacement, Jeff McMahon, resigned when he opposed Fastow's SPEs and Fastow finally replaced McMahon with Ben Glissan who delivered what Fastow wanted. Furthermore, if executives and accountants are breaking the law, it is highly probable that part of the problem is that the lawyers who are involved are not doing their jobs. The truth of the matter is executives and accountants do not work alone, and anybody who works in the corporate world knows that wherever you see corporate executives and accountants working, lawyers are virtually always there looking over their shoulder. Fastow invited in-house attorney Kristina Morduant to work on his special projects because he knew her willingness to "work in the grey areas" (Palmer, 2012, p. 200). Mordaunt not only facilitated some of the more controversial transactions, but also greatly profited from her personal investments in one of Enron's special purpose entities. Mordaunt "reportedly received over $1 million in return for a $5800 investment without obtaining the consent of Enron's Chairman and CEO, in violation of Enron's Code of Conduct" (Maclean, 2005, p. 1006).

In addition, Enron's attorneys from the law firm Vinson & Elkins (V&E), "wrote opinion letters vouching for the legality of some of the deals"…playing "a creative role in structuring and managing some of the company's controversial special purpose partnerships" by downplaying their risks (Sims, 2003, p. 200). According to one former Enron employee, "the company might not have been able to pull off many of its transactions…without V&E opinion letters…The company opinion-shopped for what it needed [and] if it hadn't gotten the opinion letters, it couldn't have done the deals" (Sims, 2003, p. 203). Consider that Enron management were friends with the lawyers at V&E going back decades before Enron's collapse coupled with being intertwined with the Houston corporate community, political scene, and giving to similar charities. Also, Enron was V&E's biggest client earning them $35.6 million in 2001 which was about 7.8 percent of its total revenue (Sims, 2003).

Arthur Andersen's audit teams faced coercion from Enron as to Fastow's related party transactions when they rated the risk of business transactions as being high; at Enron's request, an Andersen audit team member faced reassignment because he was asking too many questions (O'Connor, 2003, p. 1292). Moreover, commenting on Enron's ability to exert pressure on Andersen, one Enron in-house attorney expressed in an e-mail to another attorney the displeasure he felt when an Arthur Andersen employee questioned the appropriateness of Fastow's transactions from an accounting perspective. The attorneys expressed their opinion about this accountant's future: "A very junior person at AA in London said no, that will not work…We will see if the junior person who has made this trouble is employed with AA…very few people around here are betting on that" (Batson, 2003, p. 102). In the end, Fastow admitted that his role was structuring finance transactions that intentionally created a false appearance for Enron. However, even though he admits misconduct, Fastow still tries to rationalize away his behavior even when he clearly knows that benefiting at the expense of Enron created a conflict of interest. Fastow states:

> What does accounting fraud mean and where does it come from?…It starts with the fact that accounting rules and regulations, and securities laws and regulations are vague, they're complex, they're sometimes nonexistent, so people have to make judgments. Now how do you treat situations when you have to make judgments like that? What I did at Enron and what we tended to do as a company is to view that complexity, that vagueness, that lack of existence of rules and regulations not as a problem, but as an opportunity. When judgment is allowed and it's vague what the rules are, it gives you vague latitude to make decisions. The trap I fell into is, if the filter you're using is the rules allow it or may be interpreted to allow it, where do you stop? And I didn't stop. All of you talk about controls and systems, and we thought about that too. I thought about that. What do you do if the rules are complex, vague or nonexistent? Well, you do four things, from where I was standing. You get management and board approvals, you get legal opinions, you get an accounting opinion from outside auditors to make sure it's OK, and then you make disclosures in your financial statements. Here's what's not widely reported. We did that in every deal at Enron, and still it's considered the largest accounting fraud in history. How can that be? You're getting approvals for deals. The attorneys and accountants are telling you it's OK. The board is approving it, and it's still fraud (Cohn, 2013).

Yet Fastow fails to mention that he got rid of the people who refused to do what he wanted because they told him the truth about the inappropriateness of SPEs. Fastow knew that he purchased sham professional opinions so that he could depend on the denial of responsibility rationalization by claiming that he was simply relying on their expertise to justify the legality of the SPEs. Fastow eventually pleaded guilty to conspiracy to commit securities fraud and wire fraud and was sentenced to 6 years prison with the expectation of testifying against Kenneth Lay and Jeffrey Skilling. Fastow further stated "I think I'm guilty, and the most egregious reason that I'm guilty is that I engaged in transactions that caused a misrepresentation and caused Enron to appear different to the outside world than it really was" (Cohn, 2013). After being released from prison, Fastow gives speeches on corporate misconduct and in one interview Fastow stated:

> My intentions were good. I was trying to do what was best for Enron, but the way we as a company defined success was incorrect. We defined success by reported earnings and the stock price. There may have been a belief at points that we were doing both, both I think as time passed we deceived ourselves into confusing reported financial results with economic substance. We tried to do it by technically following the rules…couldn't you say that if all transactions and accounts are technically correct, then whatever the outcome, they are not misleading? I was doing what I was incentivized to do…We were finding ways to get around the rules but going through a complex process to find the loopholes to allow us to do it. I cheated fair and square. People always asked me whether the transactions followed the law. No one ever asked me about the intent of what I was doing. It was precisely the innovative and aggressive structuring that I was getting awards for. People thought this stuff was frickin brilliant (Soltes, 2016, p. 242). If I had the character I should have had, I would have said time out… but I didn't. But the reality is, if at any point in my career I said 'time out, this is bullshit, I can't do it'…they would have just found another CFO, but that doesn't excuse it. It would be like saying it's OK to murder someone because it I don't do it someone else would have…guys who find loopholes are sometimes celebrated (Soltes, 2016, p. 255).

Fastow's insights parallel a sentiment held by many executives in that what might be morally disapproved in one community might actually be applauded in another. Without any immediate consequence to misconduct, executives end up feeling a sense of pride in their actions and even be exalted by members of their insular business community (Soltes, 2016). This mindset is easy to create given that they receive accolades and signs of approval that may dilute the appearance and the emotional unease that fraud is actually occurring. In addition, as opposed to in the past where communities may have expected that certain behaviors would be looked down upon, that may not be the case today where business relationships span the globe creating opportunities, but also dismantling social norms that expect accountability (Soltes, 2016). Down-playing the expectation of accountability enhances the probability of relying on rationalizations to justify decisions.

Allocation of Rewards and Punishments

The organizational factor most likely to influence the perceived benefits of white-collar crime is the reward system, especially when there is pressure to achieve goals at any cost (Van Slyke et al., 2016). The allocation of rewards and punishments refers to how leaders reward the behaviors they want to see displayed by their subordinates and the consequences of not seeing subordinates carry out their agendas. Corporate leaders are able to persuade their subordinates to engage in misconduct often without ordering them to do so because of the rewards and punishments that are important to them (Shover & Wright, 2001). The process of goal attainment through rewards and punishments should be monitored to ensure that unethical means are not chosen as a solution. Organizational leaders should create a formal, comprehensive ethics program beyond the mere presence of a code of ethics by conducting ethics training, enforcement mechanisms, and top management support (Van Slyke et al., 2016). If the reward system is not managed correctly, it can actually induce more favorable attitudes toward unethical behavior.

For example, if employees are rewarded for how much in sales they produce, they might oversell unnecessary products or services to a customer or engage in bribery and kickbacks to obtain contracts. Poorly specified reward systems tend to, even if inadvertent, reward undesirable behaviors and fail to generate desired behaviors. Research suggests that individuals tend to make more unethical choices when the reward system rewards unethical behaviors and punishes ethical behaviors (Van Slyke et al., 2016). The reward system conveys what is valued and expected within an organization and in the case of Enron, they rewarded aggressive business and accounting tactics that encouraged fraudulent behavior (Moorh, 2003). Lack of controls, combined with an intense, competitive, results-driven culture made it easier to ignore the company's code of ethics. Moreover, Enron's "aggressive business tactics were embraced by the rank and file...even if many suspected it was a house of cards" as long as in the end they are financially rewarded (Sims & Brinkmann, 2003, p. 253). To be rewarded "employees were focused on the bottom line and promoted short-term solutions that were immediately financially sound despite the fact that they would cause problems for the organization as a whole...rules of ethical conduct were merely barriers to success" (Sims & Brinkmann, 2003, p. 253).

In addition, corporate leaders tend to live in extraordinary wealth, a disparity which is used to reinforce the impression that such people have exceptional abilities and wealth certainly characterized the lifestyle enjoyed by Enron's top executives. The desired message to be sent was that others could someday hope to acquire wealth for themselves providing they embraced the value system and vision articulated by the leaders, copied their behaviors, and suppressed whatever critical internal voices that might be contrary to the value system of the organization (Gilbert et al., 2012). The display of wealth became a means of enforcing conformity with the vision of the leader and obtaining enthusiastic demonstrations of support for whatever the direction the organization proclaimed to go in. Compensation plans, a powerful shaper and emblem of Enron culture, had one purpose in mind and that was to influence subordinate behavior to carry out CEOs Lay, Skilling, and CFO Fastow's agendas. For stock option incentives, Enron added the condition that if profits increased sufficiently, vesting schedules could be accelerated, meaning executives could get their hands on the stock and cash-out more quickly (Free et al., 2007).

Skilling handed out extremely large salaries, bonuses and stock options to traders who met their earnings targets; in 1999, Enron granted 93.5 million stock options compared with 25.4 million in 1996. John Arnold, a gas trader, booked $700 million in 2001, took his $15 million bonus and left Enron, and Lou Pai cashed out over $250 million in Enron stock over three years. On bonus day, upscale car dealers set up shop around the Enron headquarters building showing the latest most expensive Mercedes, BMWs, Aston Martins, and Alpha Romeos (Free et al., 2007). Enron's performance review process was called "rank and yank" in which the bottom 10–15 percent performers knew they were at risk of losing their jobs. Enron's rank and yank system consisted of a performance evaluation system where employees were required to rank their peers on a 1-5 scale based on four values: communication, respect, integrity, and excellence. This method of review where peers graded each other caused great distrust and paranoia because it pit employees against each other which diminished the possibility of cooperative efforts required for the company to succeed both financially and from an ethical perspective.

The performance evaluation guaranteed that only employees in the upper 85th percentile would be retained creating an "anything goes environment" where the "ends justify the means" (Palmer, 2012, p. 71). Those employees ranked in the lowest category had a short period of time to find another position in the company or be let go (Cruver, 2002). Overall, Enron's performance review system rewarded individuals who embraced Enron's aggressive, individualistic culture of short-term profits at the expense of integrity establishing a "win-at-all costs" mentality with a willingness to cross ethical lines (Sims & Brinkmann, 2003). In practice, the evaluation process was a sham because the only real measure of performance was the profit generated and in the pursuit of good evaluations, many executives began producing artificial revenue coupled with working out agreements with their peers based on personal relationships in order to secure good evaluations (McLean & Elkind, 2003). When employees worked on creative, aggressive, fraudulent structures, they received positive performance reviews (Beenen & Pinto, 2008). Performance reviews were public events and poor performers were ridiculed while extremely high bonuses were given to executives who behaved in ways that were unethical which in turn encouraged executives to do whatever they had to in order to keep stock prices up because that goal was a major requirement by management.

In addition, because the rank and yank system was both arbitrary and subjective, it was easily used by managers to reward blind loyalty and suppress brewing dissent. As a former employee expressed their opinion about the byproduct of the performance system, Enron's 'rank and yank' protocol created "an environment where employees were afraid to express their opinions or to question unethical and potentially illegal business practices" (Free et al., 2007). The rank and yank system created a work environment where employees were unable to express opinions or valid concerns for fear of a low-ranking score by their superiors (Albrecht et al., 2012). These disincentives led to compliance as executives avoided encounters that could negatively affect their evaluation. Enron's performance review committee (PRC) was a powerful mechanism for preventing the emergence of any subcultures that might run counter to the mercenary organizational tone set by Skilling's leadership (Free et al., 2007). As a member of the PRC, Fastow used the PRC to reward supporters and punish opposition to his SPEs. For example, Clifford Baxter was a Fastow subordinate who opposed his SPEs. Fastow warned Baxter that he would punish his subordinates during their evaluation and once Baxter heard that his subordinates would be punished, he backed off from his opposition to the SPEs (Palmer, 2012). Baxter told Skilling, that "we are headed for a train wreck and it's your job to get out in front of the train and try to stop it", but his warning fell on deaf ears (Sims, 2003, p. 175).

Employees described Fastow as a "vindictive man, prone to attacking those he didn't like...further stating that Fastow was such a cut-throat bastard that he would use it against you if you did not agree with him" (O'Connor, 2003, p. 1291). Fastow sent indirect messages to others as to what they would face if they disagreed with him where on his desk he had a cube laying out Enron's values. One of the inscriptions on the cube was the word "communication", and the inscription defined what that meant: "When Enron says it's going to rip your face off, it will rip your face off" (Raghavan et al., 2002). Fastow was known to display a terrible temper where, "One minute he wore his pleasant smile...then something would set him off. He'd twist his head, stretch his neck and jut his chin like a boxer warming up in the ring. The torrent of curses followed" (Swartz & Watkins, 2003, p. 74).

Moreover, how a leader decides who to recruit or dismiss signals a leader's values to all of his employees and it also reinforces the organizational culture. Leaders look for people similar to current members in terms of values and assumptions of how to behave (Sims & Brinkmann, 2003).

When Enron recruited executives, it "placed no priority on integrity, only an ability to fit in and win", as a result managers were focused on achieving earnings no matter what (Farrell, 2006, p. 45). Lay hired candidates who thrived in competitive environments while Skilling "hired Ivy League graduates with a hunger for money that matched his" and who considered themselves to be the best and brightest motivated to advance their own agendas (Sims, 2003, p. 170). Skilling perpetuated a focus on short-term transactional goals and "did everything he could to surround himself with individuals who had similar values," by hiring employees that "embodied his beliefs that he was trying to instill: aggressiveness, greed, a will to win at all costs, and an appreciation for circumventing the rules" (Sims & Brinkmann, 2003, p. 251). In addition, Skilling "hired people who were very young, because very young people did not insist on coming in at nine or leaving at five, or on keeping things as they had always been, or, for that matter, on questioning authority once they had signed on with him" (Swartz & Watkins, 2003, p. 58). At Enron, employees who tried to blow the whistle or voiced their concerns over accounting methods were punished by career set-backs and hostility, yet those who closed their eyes were rewarded (Sims, 2003).

For example, consider the reaction from chief accounting officer Richard Causey. According to former Enron executives, at a top-level Enron management meeting as late as September 2001, Causey, "pounded the table after hearing his colleagues labeled the company's accounting practices as aggressive…Causey fumed that he considered such criticism a personal affront, adding that he would stake his career on the propriety of Enron's accounting" (Eichenwald, 2005). Several years later, Causey went to prison for securities fraud. Consequences of unethical or illegal actions are not usually realized until much later than when the act is committed which explains why some individuals may not realize that they actually engaged in misconduct, but only believing they are living up to what Enron expects of them. For example, the culture at Enron eroded little by little ethical boundaries allowing for more questionable behavior to slip through the cracks. Employees were loyal because they wanted to be seen as part of a team, but as one former Enron employee stated, "loyalty required a sort of groupthink. You had to keep drinking the Enron water" (Sims & Brinkmann, 2003, p. 252).

Enron's culture displayed groupthink traits where employees felt real pressure to behave a certain way without questioning anyone's behavior and where conformity was expected even when there is the belief that being an individual is valued (Sims & Brinkmann, 2003). One former Enron senior manager's summary of the internal culture stated, "There was an unwritten rule…a rule of 'no bad news. If I came to them with bad news, it would only hurt my career" (Cruver, 2003, p. 176). Another employee was concerned about the appropriateness of the company's business transactions stated, "I continued to ask questions and seek answers…[but] I never heard reassuring answers. I was not comfortable confronting either Mr. Skilling or Mr. Fastow with my concerns. To do so would have been a job terminating move" (Sims & Brinkmann, 2003, p. 249). What is ironic is that Skilling stated that he wanted others to voice their concerns stating, "People have an obligation to dissent in this company…and if you don't speak up, that's not good" (Jenning, 2006, p. 59). Yet Enron whistleblower Sherron Watkins commented on Skilling's interpersonal style stated, "If you were going to ask a bunch of questions, he would intimidate you and make you feel you were not smart enough to get it" (Stachowicz-Stanusch, 2011, p. 119).

Such insight stands in sharp contrast to Enron's code of ethics on importance of communication stating, "We have an obligation to communicate. Here, we take the time to talk with one another…and to listen. We believe that information is meant to move and that information moves people" (Free et al., 2007). It is interesting how Skilling's interpersonal strategy stands in sharp contrast Enron's code of ethics stating, "We treat others as we would like to be treated ourselves. We do not tolerate abusive or disrespectful treatment. Ruthlessness, callousness and arrogance do not belong here" (Free et al., 2007). Consider the case of Vince Kaminski who was head of Enron's risk assessment group, responsible for conducting due diligence on the firm's proposed deals (Beenen & Pinto, 2009). Kaminski examined one of Fastow's SPEs, but believed it reflected flawed accounting methodologies. Before Kaminski could complete his analysis, Fastow quickly went to get Enron's Board of Directors' approval.

Yet Kaminski's supervisor, Rick Buy, went to the board outlining how the SPE was flawed, containing conflicts of interest and a payout structure that was disadvantageous to Enron's shareholders, but the board still approved Fastow's request that was against Enron's Code of Ethics. Kaminski stated that Skilling told him that "there have been some complaints, Vince, that you're not helping people to do transactions. Instead, you're spending all your time acting like cops. We don't need cops Vince" (Palmer, 2012, p. 202). Skilling notified Kaminski that he was being transferred out of the risk assessment group to a research unit which was considered a dead end job; the message was sent to others who may have wished to protest Fastow's accounting approach of what will happen to them (Beenen & Pinto, 2008). As risk manager named Glenn Dickson stated, "the pressure was—you just didn't have a choice but to approve the deals once everyone had their heart set on that deal closing" (Sims & Brinkmann, 2003, p. 252). Skilled displayed the antisocial trait of power orientation where he desired to control both the individual, in this case Kaminski and the situation, in this case perpetuating the fraud scheme.

Enron's Treatment of External Parties

Through the use of Enron's economic leverage due to its massive size, executives not only created an aggressive culture within Enron, but displayed an aggressive demeanor when interacting with outside financial groups that lent money to Enron or covered Enron's performance as outsiders commonly known as stock analysts and journalists. Moreover, a good relationship with Enron's senior management was essential for investment banks to secure access to business opportunities. Enron paid millions of dollars in fees to investment banks for advisory services—approximately $238 million in 1999 alone (McLean & Elkind, 2003). Enron executives had a "we're smarter than you guys' attitude toward analysts who covered Enron's performance, while becoming offended when they asked questions about their operations. Enron held an inflated sense of its members' moral and intellectual superiority while viewing outsiders as inferior. Executives believed that any outsider who did not understand their business model or accounting practices was ignorant and "just didn't get it" (Howard, 2011, p. 442). For example, Enron had a reputation for publicly humiliating those that asked too many questions about Enron's financial health. We can observe the antisocial trait of power orientation and an antisocial interpersonal trait displayed by Skilling where he attempts to control the person and the surrounding circumstances through public humiliation.

Skilling labeled reporters who questioned how Enron made any money as unethical and even called one analyst an asshole when the reporter questioned the company's performance during a conference call (Johnson, 2003, p. 48); "no one asked any more questions after that exchange" (O'Connor, 2003, p. 1285). As one analyst summed up the interaction, "Enron had Wall Street beaten into submission" (p. 1285). It is important to observe that Skilling is making sure that no one questions him in order to suppress any dissenting voices that might influence how others perceive him and what he is trying to accomplish which in the end means avoiding exposure of his fraud schemes. Again in referencing Skilling, business and financial analysts who covered the company stated that he "spoke often of the optics," that is, how issues confronting Enron appeared to outsiders (Schwartz, 2002b). Organizations want to control how they are perceived by others, which is a form of impression management, by dictating topics they want discussed. The right impression is part of the desire to appear credible to other organizations and the public in order to get others to interact with them because if the public saw the misconduct they engaged in, people probably would not deal with them (Schaef & Fassel, 1988). For example, when Skilling was confronted with questions that placed Enron in a potentially negative light, it was imperative for him to maintain control by intimidation and belittlement of those who questioned him.

Consider the comments of investment analyst and writer for *Fortune* magazine Bethany McLean, who interviewed Skilling about accounting and financial irregularities that she observed at Enron. She reported that "Skilling became irate, calling her ignorant and unethical for asking such questions [about Enron's practices]" (Fersch, 2006, p. 119). When McLean first broke the story about Enron's questionable financial practices, she was referred to as someone who "doesn't know anything," and attorney Loretta Lynch, in questioning Enron's practices, was referred to as "an idiot" (Sims & Brinkmann, 2003, p. 248). Thus, it is not surprising Skilling used an aggressive impression management strategy with McLean by attempting to intimidate her from asking any further questions on topics that would reveal his and other Enron employees' misconduct. Skilling also engaged in deceptive interpersonal strategies with outside parties. Consider that when he tried to launch the broadband business, he claimed that it would be worth billions of dollars and to prove it to the public, investors and Wall Street analyst were invited to Enron's headquarters in Texas (Farrell, 2006).

Skilling opened the doors to the operations war room located on the sixth floor of the company's fifty story building. When Skilling walked alongside stock analysts through the war room in January, 1998, the room was filled with employees frantic with excitement of all the business that was occurring; they worked the telephones, typed orders into their computers, and appeared to be negotiating with clients (Farrell, 2006). Enron spent half a million dollars outfitting the war room to look like the center of a thriving enterprise where employees painted the phones black, computers were flashing up statistics and charts to make it appear like real transactions were occurring, while secretaries were recruited from other floors to pretend that they were part of the business team (Farrell, 2006). Skilling even had a rehearsal the day before to make sure that all went smoothly. As employees were staging a mock event, they even decorated their trading desks with family photos. As one employee stated, "It was absurd that we were doing this. But to me the most absurd part was that it worked" (Klein, 2016, p. 138).

In addition, it was made clear to financial institutions that when their stock analysts were not supportive of Enron's stock, they were either terminated or given a clear message that their recommendation should take into account the business relationship between the financial institution and Enron even though this produced conflict of interests of not being able to report objectively about the desirability of a given stock. Consider that Fastow needed stock analysts to give positive reviews of Enron stock because the stock was used as collateral to support the SPEs and it was important that Enron's stock price was as high as possible in order to attract outside investors to invest in the SPEs. Fastow exerted his power over external parties, such as their external auditor Arthur Andersen, where Enron was a lucrative client for Andersen. Thus, Fastow used his power to make sure that Andersen gave him the types of auditing opinions that validated his SPEs as appropriate. As for the banks that serviced Enron, Fastow kept a list of those that questioned his SPEs, reminding them that future business with Enron would be at risk. Fastow punished those banks that reported their concerns about Enron's stock valuation, thus if their recommendation was not favorable, he would not include them in future deals.

Fastow denied Merrill Lynch's role in a public offering of Enron stock by letting it be known that he was unhappy with the stock recommendations of a highly regarded Merrill analyst named John Olson who Merrill eventually fired because of Fastow's and Lay's complaint. In fact, Lay sent a note to Olson's boss, Donald Sanders, stating "Don—John Olson has been wrong about Enron for over 10 years and is still wrong" (Schwartz, 2002a). According to Olson, "There was a strong mandate, unwritten, unspoken, at Enron that if you the investment banking house ever wanted to do business with Enron, your analyst had to have a strong buy rating on the stock" (Schwartz, 2002a). Fastow also denied Salomon Smith Barney a significant role in another public offering letting it be known that he was unhappy with the recommendation of well-respected analyst Don Dufresne who was later fired. Both firms subsequently found analysts who would give great buy recommendations for Enron's stock. The problem with these arrangements was that many of the analysts worked for firms that sold Enron's debt and equities.

This created a conflict of interest where these firms had an interest in making sure that Enron received favorable coverage from their analysts because negative analyst reviews could jeopardize their investment in Enron especially if the stock price dropped (Sims, 2003). Yet, what these intertwined relationships show is how the Enron scandal was not simply an Enron matter, but took into account external institutions that fed into Enron's corruption. Enron depended on banks lending it money to make the fraud scheme viable (Farrell, 2006). As one Chase banker stated, "We are making disguised loans, usually buried in commodities and equities derivatives and I'm sure in other areas. With a few exceptions, they are understood to be disguised loans and approved as such" (Farrell, 2006, p. 52). As another Enron observer stated:

One of the most sordid aspects of the Enron scandal is the complicity of so many highly regarded Wall Street firms—a complicity that is stunningly documented in internal presentations and e-mails…They show banks helping Enron mask debt as cash flow from operations and create phony profits at the end of a quarter. They also show how almost all of them put money into Fastow's partnerships because of—not in spite of—their potential for abuse. Most of all, the documents show that the banks weren't merely enablers; they were truly Enron's partners in crime (Di Miceli da Silveira, 2013, p. 14).

To illustrate how institutions and journalists contributed to creating a false impression of Enron's financial health, just prior to the exposure of the Enron scandal, 16 out of the 17 stock analysts covering the company continued to post "buy" or "strong buy" recommendations and no bank warned their investors about the problems at Enron (McLean & Elkind, 2003, p. 230). A *Forbes* magazine article noted that even as late as November 8, 2001, the date of Enron's disclosure that nearly five years of earnings would have to recalculated, 11 out of 15 stock analysts covering Enron recommended buying the stock (Albrecht et al., 2012, p. 363). In October, 2001 when Enron shares were trading at about one-third of their peak value one year before due to the eruption of its dismal accounting, a Goldman Sachs report called Enron: "Still the best of the best, indicating a target price for its shares about 45% superior than its market price, praising the company with sentences such as "We expect Enron shares to recover dramatically in the coming months…our confidence level is high…Misconceptions abound and perceptions are far below reality, in our view…We believe Enron's fundamentals are still strong" (Di Micela da Silveira, 2013, p. 14).

Moreover, the three major credit rating agencies, Moody's, Standard & Poor's, and Fitch-IBC, who received substantial fees from Enron, failed to alert investors of the pending problems (Albrecht et al., 2012). Furthermore, when Enron's financial manipulations became public and the stock collapsed in November 2001, executives from J.P. Morgan, Chase and Citigroup pressured Moody's to keep Enron's credit rating in place until the banks arranged a bailout of Enron in order to avoid bankruptcy and delay an investigation into the company's dealings (Maeda, 2010, p. 184). In fact, just weeks prior to Enron's bankruptcy filing of December 12, 2001, all three agencies gave investment grade rating to Enron's debt (Albrecht et al., 2012). Even journalists covering Enron after exposure of the scandal wrote that "it's still a company with innovative people who have shown they can turn ideas into profitable businesses. That's why the current problems will blow over" (Rosoff, 2007, p. 515).

Enron's Reflection of Organizational Narcissism

An organization's identity shapes its decision making processes and management practices by establishing what is normal, acceptable, and desirable. Organizations, like people, are motivated to protect their identities by rewarding behaviors that will sustain a positive sense of self and reduce collective anxieties (Duchon & Burns, 2008). However, entire organizations can become self-absorbed and focus on protecting an identity that has taken on narcissistic qualities resulting in losing sight of the reality of its purpose in the marketplace. In addition, such organizations employ denial, acceptable justifications of unethical behavior through rationalizations, engage in self-aggrandizement, and display a sense of entitlement to prop up its damaged sense of identity (Duchon & Burns, 2008). A narcissistic organizational identity seeks to justify and legitimize itself at all costs, with scant reference to accountability, civic responsibility, or ethical concerns coupled with institutionalizing dominance, control, entitlement, and exploitation to reinforce its maladaptive identity even at the expense of sacrificing its integrity (Duchon & Drake, 2009). Such an identity makes cynicism, exploitation, and a lack of empathy acceptable creating a morally flawed identity neutralizing the inclination to act virtuously. In turn, the organizational identity and ultimately its culture reflects the narcissism of its leaders such as Skilling who was described as being "smart, ruthless and arrogant…[he] fit most of the characteristics of a narcissistic leader" (Maccoby, 2004). Consider that ultimately,

[N]arcissistic organizational cultures are excessively egocentric and exploitive; they will obsessively employ a sense of entitlement, self-aggrandizement, denial, and rationalizations to justify their behavior in order to protect the collective identity. Such organizations cannot behave ethically because they do not have a moral identity, that is, a self-concept organized around a set of moral traits. For example, they may have formal ethics programs but devise rules that feed and exaggerate the culture's preoccupation of themselves by enabling excuses and wishful thinking. They give the appearance or image of practicing virtue (Arjoon, 2010, p. 62).

Enron presented an image that was almost completely contrary to its internal reality, by offering the appearance that virtue was important and by considering its code of ethics as the gold standard (Arjoon, 2010). For example, Lay stated, "Values are incredibly important to the fiber of this company" (McLean & Elkind, 2003, p. 353), and "Enron's reputation depends on its people, on you and me...Let's keep that reputation high" (Barth, 2003, p. 120). A section of its code of ethics states, *Employees of Enron Corporation* are charged with conducting their business affairs in accordance with the highest ethical standards. Furthermore, "An employee shall not conduct himself or herself in a manner which directly or indirectly would be detrimental to the best interests of the Company or in a manner which would bring to the employee financial gain...Moral as well as legal obligations will be fulfilled openly, promptly, and in a manner which will reflect pride on the Company's name" (Barth, 2003, p. 125). Narcissistic organizations deny facts about themselves using propaganda campaigns, annual reports and public relations specialists to rationalize their actions with the goal of manipulating the media who inquiries about an organization's financial status (Grant & McGhee, 2012). They display an exaggerated sense of pride and embellished abilities to justify the types of risks they take when engaging in business ventures. When confronted with accusations of misconduct, the narcissistic organization will attempt to suppress information through cover-ups all in the effort to protect the organizations collective identity (Grant & McGhee, 2012). Enron was an example of a narcissistic organization where:

> Crime was just one ingredient in a toxic stew of shocking incompetence, unjustified arrogance [and] compromised ethics. Ultimately, it was Enron's tragedy to be filled with people smart enough to maneuver around the rules, but not wise enough to understand why the rules had been written in the first place. They avoided conventional accounting practices wherever it wanted to. Leadership believed that they were entitled to a healthy-looking balance sheet. Enron viewed itself as omnipotent, changing the world for the better in a Godlike manner. The executives often spoke in messianic tones and viewed themselves as the best of the best...Finally, when everything came to its inevitable conclusion in 2002, Enron and its executives went into denial mode...ignoring the evidence of fraud and insider trading for years. Indeed, this had become standard practice in the company desperate to protect its identity (Grant & McGhee, 2012, p. 10).

After the Fall

Among central figures in white-collar crime scandals that had a distinguished record of philanthropy was Enron founder Ken Lay. Lay donated over $2.5 million to more than 250 organizations through his family's foundation, and he had Enron give one percent of profits to mostly Houston-based charities (Green, 2004). Lay considered himself a value-based leader and spoke often about the importance of moral issues when making business decisions claiming, too, of being a religious man because his father was a Christian minister and he began many of Enron's business meetings with a prayer (Palmer, 2016, p. 275). Lay "spoke openly about how his own religious beliefs motivated him to make Enron a place where people were encouraged to fulfill their spiritual potentials" (Beenen & Pinto, 2009, p. 286). Lay's devout Christianity added to the impression of Enron as an ethically run company stating, "I spend much of time on philanthropy and on charitable works. I love to speak about corporate values. Everyone knows that I personally have a very strict personal code of conduct that I live by. This code is based on Christian values" (McLean & Elkind, 2003, p. 3).

Despite Lay's representation of being a moral man, he was comfortable with compromised ethics; consider his reaction when he learned of unethical behaviors exhibited by his employees. When employees from the oil trading division were caught embezzling funds after an internal audit in 1987, they evaded punishment on

334

the condition, in a memo written by Lay, that they "keep making us millions" (Di Miceli da Silveira, 2013, p. 9). When Lay was indicted for fraud, he denied any knowledge of the fraud, but blamed subordinates Jeffrey Skilling, Andrew Fastow and accountant Richard Causey for Enron's demise (Behr, 2004). Insisting he was a victim, in an interview with 60 Minutes before his trial, Lay said, "I don't think I'm a fool, but I think I was fooled…I can't take responsibility for the criminal conduct of someone inside the company" (Leung, 2009). During the trial Lay "appeared arrogant, resentful of the government's investigation, remained unapologetic and indignant to the end" (Bucy et al., 2008, p. 410). Lay acknowledged that Enron took excessive risk and internal controls failed, but believed that aggressive employees pushed the boundaries of acceptable conduct for financial rewards (Ferrell & Ferrell, 2010).

Lay denied knowledge of corruption, yet relied on the board of directors, lawyers, accountants, and senior executives to keep him informed of issues such as misconduct and to approve all decisions related to SPEs denying knowledge of Fastow's schemes until it became general knowledge (Ferrell & Ferrell, 2010). He believed there were only three or four individuals engaged in major misconduct that created the negative news events and assumption of widespread corruption. Most of the damage, according to Lay came from the negative press that destroyed investor confidence. A denial of a crisis is how corrupt leaders cope with problems by claiming it was someone else's fault (Sims & Brinkmann, 2003). Yet, while Lay claimed not to know about any misconduct, internal reports told a different story especially when it came from whistleblower's reports. Although he did not remember ever seeing the reports in question, internal whistleblower reports had increased three hundred percent between the time when Lay was CEO and when Skilling took over as CEO.

Interestingly Skilling insisted that he too was a victim, claiming he is not versed in accounting well enough to know that fraud occurred even though he is responsible for the company's financial statement and by the fact that he earned his MBA from the Harvard Business School where accounting is an important part of their curriculum—it is difficult envisioning Skilling claiming accounting ignorance overseeing a multibillion dollar company. However the evidence revealed that "Skilling exercised control over almost all facets of the organization, particularly regarding its accounting procedures, which were designed to "massage" reported earnings in order to meet analysts' expectations" (Free et al., 2007). Skilling denied all knowledge of fraud at Enron or that there was anything wrong at the time he resigned in 2001 for personal reasons stating, "I had no idea the company was in anything but excellent shape" (Schwartz, 2002b). Skilling further stated referencing his prosecution that "I am innocent of every one of these charges" (Barrionuevo, 2006a). As to their reaction, when problems at Enron surfaced, the solution was not to correct the problem, but to double-down on the way they made money. Skilling claimed that he did not understand all of the complex factors in the operations of Enron that contributed to its downfall until the bankruptcy even though he claims that if "he knew then what he knows now—he still would not do anything differently" (Sims, 2003, p. 166).

Yet even though he publicly denied that anything was wrong with the company, he was willing to resign in 2001 after only six months as CEO while selling an estimated $60 million in stock. Skilling later admitted that Enron's demise was a result of a "severe liquidity (cash flow) crisis" (Barrionuevo, 2006a). The reality is the criminal charges eventually took a personal toll on Skilling. For example after Skilling was indicted for fraud, one evening while spending time with friends in Manhattan, he accused them of being undercover FBI agents (Farrell, 2006). In addition, he would try to remove the license plates off of their cars because of his belief that they were federal agents together with grabbing the blouse of the woman who owned the car suspicious that she was wearing a recording device (Farrell, 2006). When the police responded to the incident, they observed Skilling wandering the streets gazing up at the sky and talking to an imagined satellite camera believing that it was tracking his every movement. Consider the impression management strategy Skilling wished he had engaged in. When interviewed in prison, Skilling stated that prior to his trial he wished he had developed a media strategy to influence public opinion of the reputation of himself and his firm (Georgiou, 2010). CFO Fastow, in turn, who actually structured the financial statement fraud, testified at trial that he was encouraged by his superiors, Lay and Skilling, to make the financial health of the company look as positive as possible and to avoid public disclosure (Flood, 2006).

Fastow revealed his inability to stop his behavior stating, "Did I know it was wrong? Absolutely. I knew I was doing something wrong, but at the time I didn't know it was illegal. Once you start doing these types of transactions, when do you stop? I just didn't stop" (Pavlo, 2013). Fastow's remarks of how he could not stop his fraudulent behavior parallel previously mentioned Steven Hoffenberg's reason why he could not stop his Ponzi financing scheme to keep his business alive when he stated, "You couldn't stop because you would wreck everything. Morals go out the window when the pressure is on" (Soltes, 2016, p. 272). Often fraud offenders, especially executives, see themselves as others see them, as some type of heroic figure, perhaps a form of negative heroism brought on to continue their desire for more admiration from others, more success, and higher social status (Arnulf & Gottschalk, 2013). Corporate offenders share the stature of belonging to a celebrated group of individuals what are publicly acknowledged for their virtues before being discovered for their crimes; in essence their social and professional status is an effective distraction from their antisocial trait intentions (Arnulf & Gottschalk, 2013). Illustrating this point, Fastow reflected on how he viewed himself stating: "A significant number of senior management participated in this activity to misrepresent our company...and all benefited financially from this at the expense of others...Yet, within the culture of corruption that Enron had, that valued financial reporting rather than economic value, I believed I was being a hero" (Barrionuevo, 2006b).

At Enron, everything was done with a set purpose in mind and that was to make the deal at any cost, to line one's pock with ill-gotten gains, and to deceive shareholders, employees, the public and those that it transacted business with by giving the impression that it was doing better than it really was. The "Enron affair illustrates just how quickly a company can go from good to bad when those at the top respect only nonethical values, such as power, wealth, and fame, rather than the ethical values of honesty, integrity and responsibility" (Mintz & Morris, 2017, p. 451). A company that employed intelligent people squandered its potential as a viable business and value system for illicit gains. Within organizations, the impact of culture and leadership on even the most sophisticated management control system cannot be overlooked or minimized. First, it underlines the vital role of top management leadership in fostering organizational culture. Jeffrey Skilling's influence is blatant in all accounts of Enron's organizational culture as he set the tone at the top making it rather clear to all that making profit at all costs to support a growing stock price was what was valued. Enron's plight also highlights the vulnerability of rank-and-file employees to prevailing cultural norms, morals and sanctions (Free et al., 2007). Particularly in the absence of dissenting opinions, increased identification with an organization's cultural values is likely as is the fraud they participate in due to this identification. Enron whistleblower Sherron Watkins commented on importance of leadership and its role in whether misconduct occurs:

> One thing I learned through all of this is that individual leadership matters more than I would have ever thought. I think if you take Skilling out of the picture, Enron would not have happened. Even if you leave Skilling in the picture, but you have Rich Kinder, Enron's former [chief operating officer] COO, never leaving the company, the Enron fraud would not have happened. Kinder was an amazing COO, not charismatic in anyway. Incredibly sharp. He knew the right questions to ask to expose any potential wrongdoing. He is an ethical person. I think he would have not allowed Fastow to do what he did. But without Skilling in the picture, I think it would have never happened, even with Fastow there. So I think Skilling's leadership was key, and the whole mess probably boils down to the leadership of one or two people (Stachowicz-Stanusch, 2011, p. 119).

Conclusion

Corruption can become normalized in an organization. Corruption takes on a routinized complexion reinforced by risk factors consisting of institutionalization, collective rationalizations and socialization. The mindlessness produced by routinization blunts moral and legal considerations behind decisions. Consequently, routinization is interpreted as being efficient and thus legitimate. Unfortunately, when corruption is widespread, it is difficult to overcome such a corrupt attitude until there is a significant change in leadership. Even with a change in leadership, it is not always guaranteed that a different mindset can overcome entrenched views that have been in place for years and people's identities have been molded to the old ways of doing things.

Yet we have seen what happens to organizations that do not reverse course and try to mitigate against corruption. Enron provides a perfect example of what happens when corruption is entrenched and where the only outcome is complete collapse. Enron further taught us how thousands of peoples' livelihoods can be destroyed because of the acts of a few at the top of the organizational hierarchy—namely its leadership. It is important that employees do the best they can to evaluate their environments to determine what types of values they display in order to determine whether their own values can blend with those of the organization. Equally important is to consider if one's moral values are changing and being replaced, slowly and over a period of time, by those of a corrupt organization. Moreover, observe what behaviors an organization rewards and punishes and consider how their culture impacts how we react to instances of misconduct. Do we blindly adopt organizational culture as our own or do we question the implications of how they may impact our reputations and future employability?

Chapter 8

Challenges in Overcoming Corporate Fraud

By all accounts, certified public accountant and WorldCom employee Betty Vinson represented the law-abiding, hardworking citizen we admire in others. Yet in 2005, she went to prison for participating in financial statement fraud with other WorldCom employees in order to make WorldCom's income look better than it was. From the first quarter of 2000 through the first quarter of 2001, Vinson, together with colleagues, assisted with taking operating expenses that should have been included in the income statement, and capitalized them on the balance sheet so that they would gradually, and over time, be included on future income statements. Recall that financial statement fraud accomplished through capitalization reduces the impact of claiming relevant expenses on the income statement in the period incurred in order to artificially inflate income. During this period, WorldCom overstated earnings by $3.8 billion dollars. Consider the supervisor-subordinate dynamics contributing to WorldCom's fraud. In court, CFO Scott Sullivan testified that CEO Bernie Ebbers, his boss, told him, "We have to hit the numbers," when discussing the financial statements so that WorldCom would meet Wall Street expectations and maintain a growing stock price (Perri & Mieczkowska, 2015). In turn, accounting managers Betty Vinson and Troy Normand initially reacted negatively when their supervisor, Sullivan, requested that they manipulate the financial statements in order to meet Wall Street earnings expectations. When Vinson and Normand attempted to resign because of the request, Sullivan discouraged it assuring Vinson and Normand that reporting false accounting entries represented a one-time request and he appealed to them with this analogy:

> This is a situation where you have an aircraft carrier out in the middle of the ocean and its planes are circling up in the air…and what you want to do, if you would, is stick with the company long enough to get the planes landed to get the situation fixed…Then if you still want to leave the company, then that's fine, but let's stick with it and see if we can't change this (Cooper, 2008, p. 7).

Normand wondered if maybe he was making too much out of this request given that Sullivan was a "financial wizard…he must know what he is doing" (Cohen et al., 2010, p. 172), coupled with the fact that he had been awarded the CFO Excellence Award in 1998 and his reputation represented impeccable integrity (Howard, 2011). As a result of the impression he made on others, many employees aware of the accounting irregularities rationalized them by assuming Sullivan knew best perhaps because he found a new accounting methodology or loophole to support the accounting entries he directed others to make. Moreover, the numerous awards Sullivan received probably reinforced these beliefs as well as the clean audit opinions from their external auditor Arthur Anderson. Also, with the consistent buy recommendations from Wall Street financial analysts, subordinates were assured by Sullivan, who appealed to their sense of loyalty, that they were doing nothing illegal and that he would take full responsibility for their actions (Murphy & Dacin, 2011). However, the request to manipulate the financial statements was followed by additional requests over several quarters even though Vinson and Normand were promised that the accounting adjustments would occur only once in order to get through the first quarter of 2000.

Although their emotional reaction to Sullivan's request made them uncomfortable, they accommodated his request, in part, due to Sullivan's authoritative position relative to theirs. However there were probably other motives explaining why Vinson accommodated Sullivan's request. When asked why she participated in the fraud, she stated, "I felt like if I didn't make the [fraudulent] entries, I wouldn't be working there" (McClam, 2005). Consider the other factors that may have influenced Vinson to participate in financial statement fraud. She was her family's principal breadwinner, and there were few jobs in the small town of Jackson, Mississippi where WorldCom's headquarters was located, that offered an equivalent salary (Palmer, 2012). Thus from a self-interested perspective, she may not have had the alternatives to find another job to avoid participating in the fraud that she would have had if she lived near a large city with more plentiful employment opportunities.

Vinson depended on her superiors for her family's livelihood even though they never brought this issue up as to what would happen to her if she refused to participate in the fraud, indirectly, she felt the power they had over her. Did Vinson also go along with the request because of the group pressure she may have felt at WorldCom in that Sullivan's request cannot be wrong if others are going along with it? Is it possible that she may have clung to a false sense of security found when one belongs to a group where members support each other even though collectively they engaged in misconduct with criminal implications? If leaders such as CFO Sullivan rationalize their misconduct as contributing to the betterment of the organization, they are more likely to engage in corruption that implicates the entire organization. Thus subordinates too are frequently rewarded by leaders for behaving in accordance with the opinions, advice, and directives of authority figures even when these individuals know they are engaging in misconduct. Consequently, the rewards make it more difficult to dissociate themselves from the organization because of the perceived benefits received from their misconduct.

Ethical behavior and legal compliance may not appear to benefit employee careers in the short-term when unethical behavior is expected and financially rewarded which further encourages employee retention (Pierce & Synder, 2015). Ironically unethical demands are perceived as pro-social behavior looked upon as a legitimate benefit to the organization. Such views facilitate rule breaking where employees violate rules for the benefit of the organization, coworkers, customers, and themselves (Pierce & Synder, 2015). Additionally, subordinate's needs, attitudes, and behaviors are likely to influence the unethical behaviors of leaders, thus blaming the decline of many institutions on bad leadership alone is to oversimplify the complex relationship between leaders and followers. Followers and subordinates play an instrumental role in the unethical behavior of leaders by passive or active participation which reinforces leaders' objectives, goals, and values; for example, is bribery as a sales tactic to bring in business acceptable to the leader. If leaders are sliding down the slippery slope of unethical behavior, followers may unintentionally contribute to unethical leader behavior by remaining silent and fearful to disclose misconduct (Chandler, 2009).

Alternatively followers may intentionally, and with enthusiasm, collaborate with leadership's unethical behavior to protect their self-identities, out of self-interest to fulfill financial agendas, and because they share the leader's value system of how goals are met regardless of the means by which they are achieved (Chandler, 2009). Unethical behavior is more likely to occur in organizations with high pressure for increased productivity, including the desire to beat the competition and dominate within a particular industry. When employees perpetrate financial statement fraud, more often than not they commit it at the direction of senior management. Even though the people who committed fraud may not have been explicitly told to commit it, there can be direct and indirect pressure by management, such as setting unachievable profit goals, threats of termination or other reprimands, or personal pressures associated with making a living (Smith, 2015b). For example, Hisoa Tanaka stepped down as Toshiba's CEO due to an accounting scandal when it was discovered that Toshiba artificially inflated profits in the billions of dollars by fraudulently misrepresenting the true costs incurred to operate the business (Smith, 2015b).

There existed a corporate culture at Toshiba, supported by the CEO and upper management, where it was impossible to question management's goals and rationalizations together with employees being pressured into engaging in inappropriate accounting to achieve profit goals (Ueda et al., 2015b). Yet, did all of these employees feel "pressured" to commit fraud, or did some willingly participate, without feeling pressured, believe that participation was the path toward upward mobility at Toshiba? Is it accurate to believe that all Toshiba employees perceived their misconduct as an ethical or legal violation, especially if their value system paralleled Tanaka's? Some subordinates have a vested interest in preserving the status quo even if it requires them to engage in misconduct. In order to protect their interests, they will engage in self-promotion and cronyism, and are willing to become a leader's "yes-person" (Gilbert et al., 2012). As a result, it is important to consider the different types of subordinates that exist to understand how organizational misconduct can occur on a widespread basis given that it might be initiated at the top, but still requires the participation of subordinates to actually implement the fraud scheme.

In this chapter, we consider the challenges in overcoming organizational misconduct. For example, what are the different types of followers who are typically the subordinates within an organization, that participate in misconduct due to their willingness to go along with requests by those in authority? Moreover, research suggests that certain group dynamics arise within organizations, even at times without an organization being consciously aware of them. For example, the influence of groupthink may distort decision making and increase the risk of engaging in misconduct because of the reluctance to consider alternative solutions to problems. What risk factors contribute to the rise of groupthink? In addition, we explore the impact of workplace bullying on perpetrating organizational misconduct together with the role that obedience to authority plays in influencing subordinates to carry out orders to engage in misconduct or at a minimum to be silent about its existence. Furthermore, we examine how the concept of ethical blindness and ethical fading can lead leadership and subordinates down the slippery slope toward misconduct that is only apparent when it may be too late. Like Betty Vinson, they may go to prison for fraud that could have been prevented, had they been aware of the dilution of their own ethical awareness brought about by ethical fading as an example.

Lastly, the moral ambiguity of organizational misconduct is explored in order to determine whether white-collar crime can realistically be addressed in a similar manner and no differently than non-white-collar crimes. Does society however, through its political system, accommodate a certain amount of organizational misconduct in order to not interfere with the benefits that society and governments appear to enjoy from corporations overall? Are high-level executives who engage in financial statement fraud held accountable for their crimes or does the political system that includes law enforcement and regulatory agencies tolerate a certain amount of their criminal behavior because they also create economic value for society and tax revenue for governments?

The Influence of Groupthink on Organizational Misconduct

Yale research psychologist Irving Janis developed the theory of groupthink to help explain how U.S. decision makers led the country into major political and military fiascos. Some examples include: 1) the Cuban Bay of Pigs invasion during President Kennedy's administration in the 1960s where the U.S. almost engaged in a nuclear conflict with Russia, 2) the failure to anticipate the 1941 attack by Japan on Pearl Harbor, 3) the Korean War stalemate of 1952, and 4) the escalation of the Vietnam War during the 1960s. Eventually, the groupthink concept was applied to business settings given that the business community had to answer for some of the largest financial meltdowns in modern times. Groupthink helps to partially explain how and why intelligent people can make terrible decisions leading to organizational collapse. For example, at its height, Enron was considered one of the biggest American success stories and viewed as a beacon of capitalism, but even Enron succumbed to fraud, and groupthink played a role in the crimes committed by its leaders and subordinates (Howard, 2011).

Janis embarked on understanding how group dynamics can lead to a type of interaction explaining how intelligent people can go down a road that results in suboptimal decision making as noted in the above disasters, be it political, military, or business. Groupthink is a social psychological phenomenon that occurs within a group of people when the desire for group harmony or conformity leads to an irrational or dysfunctional decision making process leading to undesirable outcomes. However, it should not be assumed that all poor decisions made by groups are the result of groupthink behaviors. Groupthink research was not based on empirical testing, but on qualitative observations of how decision making becomes distorted, and the forces that converge to make groupthink observable. Groupthink is a mode of thinking that people engage in when they are deeply involved in a cohesive group where members strive for unanimity in decision making which overrides their motivation to realistically appraise alternative courses of action that may be more appropriate for the occasion (Janis, 1982). Groupthink can also be characterized by group self-deception, a forced manufacture of consent, and conformity to group values and ethics.

In the process, critical thinking and decision making become distorted because the decision making process might ignore evidence contrary to the group's beliefs, and lean increasingly toward reaching a decision which pleases group members. Groupthink can be motivated by group members who attempt to maintain a shared, positive view when faced with a challenge. Although groupthink does not assure the failure of a decision, its presence increases the chances of low-quality, potentially unethical, decision making in an organization especially among those who share the same organizational identity, values, motivations, and goals. Groupthink can reduce opportunities for employees to raise concerns about a certain course of action, specific practices, or their influence

340

with group leaders. Consider that cohesive groups should not necessarily be linked to groupthink because cohesive groups may help with team performance through better decision making, a sense of loyalty among group members, and enhanced group identity (Choi & Kim, 1999). Cohesive groups facilitate the ability to help subordinates learn, improve skills, and foster team work that could lead to greater productivity and efficiency.

Positive group cohesion inspires employees to achieve organizational goals and professional fulfillment (Hodges & Hodges, 2013). However, group member characteristics may assist one in determining whether they are at risk for the rise of groupthink especially in light of what the group's goals consist of. Do groups display ethical goals or do they contain antisocial motivations? The characteristics of groupthink include, 1) a feeling of invulnerability, 2) the ability to rationalize events and decisions, 3) moral superiority within the group, 4) group pressure on dissenters to conform to the group's wishes, 5) the use of stereotypes to characterize others, whether they are from outside or inside the group, as being inferior or characterizing them as adversaries, 6) self-censorship within the group, and 7) unanimity in decision making (Scharff, 2005). Other indicators of groupthink include the presence of group members who display arrogance and excessive or blind loyalty to the group and its leaders (Sims, 1992), and who believe, at times, they are above having to comply with the law and regulations (Scharff, 2005). For example, media reports noted the cult-like atmosphere at Enron; specifically, Enron employees reported being 'fanatically loyal' to CEOs Jeffrey Skilling and Kenneth Lay. One Enron employee stated, "Every time Skilling spoke, I'd believe everything he'd say" while another former Enron executive went as far as to analogize Enron to the Taliban (O'Connor, 2003, p. 1264).

We are apt to observe groupthink that involves unethical practices driven by "aggression, greed, and hate" (Morgan, 1997, p. 246). Ironically, Skilling hired employees that "embodied his beliefs that he was trying to instill: aggressiveness, greed, and a will to win at all costs" (Sims & Brinkmann, 2003, p. 251). Ultimately, groupthink is a defensive mechanism for coping with stressful decisions within a group. Group members under stress may develop certain defenses including, 1) misjudging relevant warnings, 2) inventing new arguments to support a chosen policy, 3) failing to explore dangerous implications of uncertain events, 4) forgetting information that would enable a challenging event to be interpreted correctly, and 5) misperceiving signs of the onset of actual danger (Sims, 1992, p. 653). When confronted with difficult moral decisions, group members discount contrarian opinions and move toward group consensus as a form of social support to lower anxiety since maintaining group cohesiveness is more important than a realistic appraisal of the facts at hand (Howard, 2011). Some have equated the concept of groupthink to individuals who unconsciously see illusions or distortions of reality even when faced with the truth that their reality was flawed.

They resist change to the point of punishing the individual(s) attempting to persuade them that their version of reality is flawed and not based on facts (Scharff, 2005). For example, most executives believed Enron's convicted CEO Ken Lay's position on the status of Enron's financial health included an "unhealthy capacity for self-delusion; he tended to deceive himself about harsh truths he didn't want to face…He invents his own reality" (McLean & Elkind, 2003, p. 90). Recall what Lay claimed in addressing investors stating, "There are no accounting issues, no trading issues, no reserve issues, and no previously unknown problem issues. I think I can honestly say that the company is probably in the strongest and best shape that it has probably ever been in" (McLean & Elkind, 2003, p. 347) proclaiming, "Our liquidity is fine…As a matter of fact, it's better than fine. It's strong" (Pelley, 2005). In terms of corporate social responsibility, the ability of employees to raise doubts or concerns about the ethics of a practice, and the potential harm of a product or practice is crucial to the organization being held accountable internally to its employees and externally to shareholders and the broader public.

When groups display most of the characteristics of groupthink, they are less likely to examine alternate courses of action and will purposely avoid thoughtful examination of the risks involved when selecting a course of action. Once a decision has been made, there is strong commitment from the group to see it through, regardless of any new evidence that questions the practicality, efficiency, and ethics of the decision(s). Where there is an acute failure of the group to incorporate new information into the decision making processes, the group becomes highly guarded against outside criticism which could be from within the organization itself. Also, groupthink suggests that in an effort to maintain the approval of their leader, members are likely to adopt a solution without critical evaluation. In fact, the type of leadership displayed may be one of the preconditions that increase the likelihood of groupthink, especially if the leader displays destructive or disordered personality traits. As a result, subordinates do not question upper management decisions due to their fear of being retaliated against, losing their job, and covering up for one another (Hodges & Hodges, 2013).

When groups are highly cohesive, members might have a tendency to censor their own and fellow group members' contributions to collective decisions as an act of loyalty to the group in the interest of preserving group unity, especially if the group is under stress (Palmer, 2012). Pressures to censor opinion can sometimes be beneficial to make group decisions more efficient instead of wallowing in discussion points that are irrelevant and inefficient from a time management perspective. Yet, at the same time, quickly making decisions without discussion can lead to a preferred, but flawed decision. Coming to quick decisions can result in the group avoiding a thorough and realistic examination of the preferred choice and its alternatives. Further, quick decisions can cause a group to focus on information that confirms their preference and avoid the search for information that may discredit the information that was relied upon to make the decision. This approach can cause decision making errors both in practical terms and in moral judgements (Palmer, 2012). There are characteristics that one can consider to start the process of identifying whether groupthink symptoms are present within one's organization (Choi & Kim, 1999). Some symptoms or red flags which indicate the presence of groupthink include, but are not limited to:

- Does the group leader discourage open communication or dominate group discussion? If so, are group members reluctant to communicate relevant information? Is there even the desire to hear about relevant information?

- Do group members criticize others who raise questions concerning a selected solution? Is there a desire to examine the risks attached to a decision?

- Are warnings ignored? Misjudged? Is there evidence that relevant information is misinterpreted about a desired course of action?

- When new information is contrary to a decision, do group members engage in rationalization, of the group's earlier decision?

- Do group members refrain from raising objections in order to maintain group unity?

- Do group members fail to survey as many alternatives as possible to solve the problem? Is there a failure to explore implications of unclear, unsubstantiated, and ambiguous information that is used to make a decision?

- Do group members fail to reevaluate a solution for unforeseen risks after adoption of a particular course of action?

- Do group members fail to obtain or reject expert advice or qualified information from outside the group?

- Do group members fail to consider the advice of others even when it is contrary to the group's preferred solution?

- Do group members fail to develop contingency plans in case the first solution does not work? If there are contingency plans, are they improper or inaccurate (Sims, 1992)?

Preconditions to Groupthink

Consider that it is not necessary for all of the groupthink characteristics to emerge for it to be present, however the probability of observing groupthink increases if, 1) there is a high level of group cohesiveness, 2) there are structural problems such as decision makers are insulated from outside influences, 3) there is no history of objective leadership, 4) a lack of procedural norms or failure to follow procedural norms when making decisions, and 5) a provocative situational context, including high-stress within a group, recent group failures, and moral dilemmas that need to be resolved. Let us explore some of these preconditions.

Group Cohesiveness

Groupthink often displays itself and "occurs in organizations that knowingly commit unethical acts when the group is cohesive, a leader promotes solutions or ideas even if they are unethical, and the group has no internal rules or control mechanisms to continually prescribe ethical behavior" (Sims, 1992, p. 654). Cohesiveness involves inclusive feelings that typically promote well-being and happiness within a group, however, cohesiveness which displays strong relationships among members involving an emotional tie may cause a group to avoid facing hard questions and avoid conflict (Sims, 2003). Group cohesion may still occur if group members do not like each other if they share a common goal or strong ties to one leader. When a group is overly-cohesive, it can have a detrimental impact on decision making because of the priority of not upsetting the group's sense of harmony and conformity as opposed to making quality decisions the priority (Palmer, 2012). Interestingly, overly-cohesive groups tend to believe they have reached a fail-safe conclusion when consensus is achieved; in other words, agreement among like-thinking members of a group can lead to overconfidence among group members believing their decision cannot fail (Glover & Prawitt, 2012). Also, group cohesiveness can take different forms and it is no surprise that the board of directors of Fortune 500 companies exhibit high levels of cohesiveness. Boards are typically considered an elite group of people with an abundance of power that enjoys associating with other successful people while having access to prestigious social networks.

Boards of directors tend to be homogenous meaning members share similar ideologies, and come from similar social and cultural backgrounds which increase cohesiveness. These factors foster a sense of belonging to a powerful and protective group. This level of cohesiveness among independent board members, and the board at large, puts them at risk of succumbing to the pitfalls of groupthink. A recent survey of board of director members who participated on their audit committees indicated that they believe unhealthy groupthink tendencies influence their meetings (KPMG, 2011b). For example, one Enron director indicated that "personally, I believe while we may have initially just been a collection of individuals, we have now evolved into a very cohesive and collegial group...specifically, the Enron directors indicated they had possessed great respect for senior Enron officers, trusting their integrity and competence" (O'Connor, 2003, p. 1263). Yet to fully understand this cohesiveness, we need to understand why it existed within Enron's board of directors. Cohesiveness existed because, 1) there was a high degree of homogeneity among board members, 2) they had similar educational and career backgrounds representing the power elite of corporate America, 3) financial incentives bound them together given that Enron board members were among the highest paid in the world at that time, and they were also Enron shareholders worth millions of dollars, and 4) a corporate culture promoted loyalty to the senior executives which applied to the board (O'Connor, 2003, p. 1263).

Problems within the Organization

Another precondition is an organization's failure to have proper protocol in place or ignoring proper protocol for decision making within the group to deal with organizational issues (Howard, 2011). When there is a lack of protocol, group decision makers can be insulated from outsiders who are not permitted to know about the new policies being discussed until the decision has already been made. In addition, when the leader strongly states his or her views to the group at the onset of meetings and discourages debate and dissent within the group, it is unlikely that discussion will reflect a balanced, thoughtful quality. A cohesive group working in isolation under an authoritarian-type leader under stressful conditions may lead to poor decision making through the incomplete surveying of alternatives and objectives, information, and risk assessment. As a result, the group is not apt to have or if they do have methodical procedures for gathering information and evaluating different resolutions, they may actually ignore gathering information that is contrary to a group or leader's preferences. Last of all, if there is a lack of diversity within a group in terms of different ideas and perspectives represented, risks associated with unchallenged viewpoints and poor decision making outcomes are elevated.

Provocative Situational Context

The final groupthink precondition focuses on the group's need to make significant policy decisions during a provocative situational context (Sims, 2003). These types of contexts can be broken down into two categories: external and internal threats. The most vulnerable context a decision making group can encounter is when threats from outside the organization increase stress to high levels; examples may include when a group is under investigation by regulators, if they struggle to meet Wall Street expectations, or if there are adverse business conditions. When a group with a strong leader experiences this high stress, the tendency will be for members to quickly agree with whatever solution the leader proposes because they are desperate for a solution to alleviate the stress. This tendency results in little debate and analysis during the decision making process, which again leads to poor decisions. Thus, in the example where there is stress from an external investigation, instead of cooperating with regulators, the leader may propose to continue with the misconduct and double-down on not cooperating with the regulators which further draws suspicion as to their misconduct. Recall the case of Beech-Nut where the CEO continued to have the tainted apple juice sold to off-shore destinations while also destroying inventory at the company's manufacturing base. Internal threats might include a problem or decision that is highly complex and surpasses the competence of the decision maker(s) within a group, or when a necessary decision poses a moral dilemma for the group (Howard, 2011).

An example might include how to deal with a whistleblower that exposed some type of organizational fraud. How is senior management to deal with this person? Will they approach the whistleblower in an ethical and humane manner by attempting to investigate the alleged misconduct? Or does the group demonize and make the person's life at the organization as difficult as possible so that they voluntarily leave? When such perceived threats surface, decision makers consciously or unconsciously strive to avoid negative thoughts, social condemnation, and self-disapproval by turning to others for rationalizations. To promote this rationalization process, members turn to group consensus to ease worry or doubt that stem from breaking ethical standards. By relying on the mechanism of group consensus, each member is able to believe that he or she and the group made the correct and moral decision. This is how a member avoids raising ethical concerns that imply their group could, in fact, be making an incorrect, immoral decision, casting doubt on the entire group's ethics and morals.

Groupthink Symptoms

Although groupthink is not inherent in most group decisions, special care must be made when a group is highly cohesive to recognize symptoms of groupthink that may appear if the preconditions are apparent. Such groupthink symptoms include, 1) the illusion of group invulnerability, 2) collective rationalization, 3) the illusion of group morality, 4) excessive stereotyping of outsiders, 5) pressure for group conformity, 6) individual self-censorship, 7) the illusion of group unanimity, and 8) the presence of group mind guards where some members appoint themselves to protect the group from outside information that is perceived to potentially influence the group's decision making (Sims, 2003). Consider that the symptoms above do not have to appear in the order outlined above for groupthink to be present or experienced with equal intensity.

Illusion of Invulnerability

The first symptom is the illusion of group invulnerability. This illusion typically leads intelligent and sensible individuals to become overly confident, overly optimistic, take extraordinary risks, and ignore clear warning signs that may indicate a certain decision may be faulty (Howard, 2011). Overconfidence is the tendency for decision makers to overestimate their own abilities to perform tasks, or to make accurate assessments of risks, judgments, and decisions. When under this illusion, group decision makers may begin to believe that they are infallible and will ultimately always make the best decision (Sims, 2003). This symptom increases as the power level of the group increases, as well as when the group has achieved success in the past. Even if the plan is high risk, the group will move forward with the decision based on past success and the perception that group members and the leader are competent. The tendency to be more confident than is justified is likely to affect individuals even when they are doing their best to be objective.

344

Research indicates that many people, including experienced professionals, are consistently overconfident when estimating outcomes or probabilities (Glover & Prawitt, 2012). So what is the potential problem with overconfidence? Some argue that being confident is a necessary attribute of successful business professionals. Although it is true that confidence is an important trait, overconfidence can lead to faulty judgments because it can result in taking on too many projects, missed deadlines, budget overruns, shutting down potentially useful discussions, reaching ill-considered snap judgments, considering too few alternatives, misinterpreting risks through poor risk assessments, cutting short or skipping an information search, or solving the wrong problem (Glover & Prawitt, 2012). Overconfidence can result in underestimating the likelihood or potential magnitude of risks, ignoring certain stakeholder perspectives, or neglecting to plan for the possibility of events with potentially adverse outcomes. In terms of assessing the possibility of fraud in the organization, overconfidence can lead to an insufficient level of skepticism and questioning. Overconfidence on the part of business executives can lead to an optimistic bias in financial reporting and, in turn, "leads them down a slippery slope of intentional misstatements" (Glover & Prawitt, 2012). Hubris leads managers to rationalize and adopt aggressive tactics believing they could handle such risk without danger (O'Connor, 2003).

When financial incentives and pressures are coupled with excessive risk-taking, it is not surprising that organizations can go down the slippery slope of fraud which ultimately leads to organizational implosion. For example WorldCom perpetrated one of the largest accounting frauds in U.S. history. In hindsight many of the senior executives at WorldCom were extremely optimistic and more than willing to assume extraordinary risks up to and including fraud. To illustrate this sense of invulnerability at WorldCom, during the time when the fraudulent activities were occurring, one manager wrote an email to her employees referring to accounting irregularities on the financial statement. The email stated, "[t]hese documents are sensitive and confidential and should not be distributed outside of the department without advising [her] or myself first" (SEC, 2003, p. 69). One of her subordinates replied: "Oops! I sent it to AA [Arthur Andersen]. IT'S A JOKE. I fully agree with your concerns"; the manager then replied, "smart ass. Just trying to be dramatic and liven things up a bit" (SEC, 2003, p. 69). While most of the thousands of WorldCom employees had no knowledge of the fraud, it was not limited to only a handful of top executives. Yet the email string displays a certain level of audacity and bravado from lower level employees that fooling the external auditors was considered appropriate.

Belief in Inherent Morality of the Group

The belief in a group's inherent morality causes decision makers to ignore the ethical or moral consequences of their decisions because they perceive that they control the moral compass, know what everyone's best interests are, and are acting for the benefit of all (Howard, 2011). Highly cohesive groups might display self-righteousness where "members consider loyalty to the group the highest form of morality" (Janis, 1982, p. 11). Some groups do not believe they need to have policies and procedures to assist them in making quality decisions that have a moral underpinning because the group decides what is ethical. For example, WorldCom CEO Bernard Ebbers scoffed at the idea of a code of conduct, calling it a "colossal waste of time" (Howard, 2011, p. 438). Some displays of inherent morality touch on religious overtones such as the statement by Enron's CEO Jeffrey Skilling, "We're the good guys, we're on the side of angels" where one journalist described Enron as an "evangelical cult," with Kenneth Lay as its "messiah" and Skilling as a "religious zealot" (O'Connor, 2003, p. 1275). Yet this issue of a cult-like description is not just assigned to Enron. Employees who worked at HealthSouth, previously mentioned, stated it "was like being in a cult" where employees were overly obedient and eager to please (Abelson & Freudenheim, 2003). The problem becomes for those employees who do not want to belong to this "cult-like" atmosphere are ostracized and considered outsiders not to be trusted. These individuals may be subjected to bullying by co-workers which can impact the mental and emotional health of employees.

Collective Rationalization

Another symptom is the group's rationalization of ignoring warning signs that would lead members to second-guess, if not completely change their positions (Sims, 2003). Collective rationalization explains how individuals can claim to perceive nothing wrong within their group while making very risky decisions. This is a convenient way to ignore warning signs indicating the need for change because people are predisposed to preserve the status quo under the illusion of normalcy. Thus, groups can rationalize and interpret negative information in a way that supports the preservation of previously agreed-upon decisions. In order to avoid facing the situation and save face, groups not only stay the course, but increase their invested resources to convince themselves that they are making the right decision (Howard, 2011).

Out-Group Stereotypes

The fourth symptom is the group's stereotyping of adversaries both outside and within the group itself (Sims, 2003). Strong distinctions between an "us" versus "them" mentality are typical for cohesive teams, and important elements of groupthink, that is, a mode of thinking that may ultimately lead to biased group decision making (Palazzo et al., 2012). Groupthink engages in stereotyping, even those within the organization itself, by fostering a philosophy of either being with us or against us. If you are against us, one is perceived as a threat to aggress against leaving no middle ground for contrarian views that actually help the group make better decisions. Through negative stereotyping, the group views all of those who oppose its decision, from outside and within, as weak-minded and unenlightened (Howard, 2011). These negative views are not necessarily against members of competing companies, in many instances, they are negative opinions of anyone deemed not a member of the inner circle or group within the larger organization.

To support the view of stereotypes, groupthink organizations view any external group as generally inept, incompetent, and incapable of effectively countering any action by the group, no matter how risky the decision or how high the odds are against the plan succeeding. For example, Enron had a reputation for publicly humiliating those from outside and inside the organization who asked too many questions about their financial circumstances, such as the financial community, journalists, stock analysts, and employees who questioned the validity of how they presented financial statements to outsiders, such as investors, auditors, and government regulators (O'Connor, 2003). Internally, it was imperative that an employee appeared to be towing the company line and as Enron employees stated, "you either got with the system or you were out the door" (O'Connor, 2003, p. 1285). Another employee stated, "One day, you are viewed with favor, and the next day you are not. You know who is in the in-crowd and who is not. You want to continue to be liked in that organization. You do everything you can do to keep that" (O'Connor, 2003, p. 1285).

Illusion of Unanimity

The fifth symptom is the illusion of unanimous group consensus that pressures members to conform and accept decisions (Sims, 2003). When a group member believes a sufficient number of other members favor a proposal, that member wants to avoid being the last to adopt the consensus view (Howard, 2011). For example, when at a meeting the CEO states "it appears that the group has reached a consensus" even though the CEO never asked for anyone's opinion, silence is interpreted as being in agreement with the decision. Such a comment by a CEO would probably silence those who wish to speak up, but will not for fear of appearing to sabotage organizational goals and perhaps the fear that they will be perceived as challenging the CEO thus risk being replaced by someone who is perceived as being more compliant. Again, in referencing Enron and the belief that there was only one way and that was top managements way, an Enron executive stated, "You have to keep drinking the Enron water"...or as another put it, "drink the Kool-Aid" (O'Connor, 2003, p. 1288). With groupthink, employees may feel so loyal to the group that they do not raise objections or reservations to the decisions being made and simply seek unanimous decisions.

For example, WorldCom decision makers too suffered from the illusion of unanimity where management interpreted employee silence in response to the accounting fraud as agreement, thereby mistakenly believing that there was unanimous support within the organization to continue the fraud. As time passed, and the accounting irregularities grew, a greater number of WorldCom employees became aware of the accounting improprieties, yet no one raised an objection. Ron Beaumont, WorldCom's ex-chief operating officer (COO), at one point asked

346

Sullivan for an explanation of the differences between what he was seeing and what was publicly reported; Beaumont never received a reply and dropped the inquiry (Scharff, 2005).

Self-Censorship

The sixth major symptom is self-censorship where group members avoid deviating from what appears to be group consensus (Sims, 2003). Building consensus may be a function of many healthy organizations, and not all attempts to gain agreement should be misconstrued as groupthink. However, managers at all levels should be aware of the risks involved with agreement since one study found that 37 percent of group participants felt pressure to express an opinion consistent with the group's opinion even though they did not agree with the group's opinion (Howard, 2011). Another study found that 64 percent of group participants surveyed gave unanimous answers to questions notwithstanding instructions to participants to ignore the group's prior discussions and that the final reports from participants need not be unanimous (Howard, 2011). These studies highlight the difficulty management has in receiving constructive feedback, even in healthy organizations. Furthermore, consider these quotes from Enron employees that displayed a self-censorship culture, "you don't object to anything, the whole culture at the vice-president level and above just became a yes-man culture" and "people went from being geniuses to idiots overnight if they questioned superiors" (Howard, 2011, p. 443). By standing out as the sole objector and being perceived as a road block for the rest of the group, a member believes he or she will suffer embarrassment and upset his or her fellow group members. It is difficult to be a part of a group if everyone else in the group is against you, and most members would rather censor their own concerns than turn the group against themselves.

In essence no one wants to be the lone objector so they "go along to get along" (O'Connor, 2003, p. 1288). Therefore, members publicly agree or remain silent during group decision making, even though they privately disagree. When groupthink is present, the opportunities to dissent are far fewer and this is especially true when a leader has already expressed a strong opinion on the matter at hand before any group discussion takes place. For example, WorldCom investigators found individuals in the finance and accounting departments were aware, to varying degrees, of the fraudulent activities of their senior executives, yet no one came forward to voice their dissent. The SEC Report on WorldCom noted that knowledge of the irregularities was not limited to a few high level executives (SEC, 2003). Many lower level employees were aware that the accounting entries being posted were not supportable and that the prepared financial reports were false or, at a minimum, very misleading. The report went on to state, "remarkably, these employees frequently did not raise any objections despite their awareness or suspicions that the accounting was wrong, and simply followed directions or even enlisted the assistance of others" (SEC, 2003, p. 7). Almost all employees that could have done something chose not to because they did not want to break the consensus within the company. The SEC concluded on the issue of resisting engaging in misconduct that:

> The answer seems to lie partly in a culture emanating from corporate headquarters that emphasized making the numbers above all else; kept financial information hidden from those who needed to know; blindly trusted senior officers even in the face of evidence that they were acting improperly; discouraged dissent; and left few, if any, outlets through which employees believed they could safely raise their objections (SEC, 2003, p. 18).

Yet there is an ironic twist to management's perspective on how they perceive a lack of input from subordinates and how subordinates perceive not sharing their opinions. The irony may stem from the fact, as previously discussed, where narcissistic management does not want to hear opinions that are different from their own because they perceive debate as being disloyal. Such management may even provoke discussion and ask for opinions to find out who they want to eliminate from their team by focusing on who actually voices their opinion. Thus, employees are not apt to believe management really is sincere in wanting to hear dissenting opinions and, in fact, voicing one's opinion might result in receiving a diminished role within an organization. Subordinates who personally disagree with the group remain quiet and either internally play down or withhold their disagreement when the group appears to favor a decision (Howard, 2011).

Direct Pressure on Dissenters

The seventh symptom involves group members' use of common forms of social pressure against members who actually stand up and question the group's judgment (Sims, 2003). Pressure is put on others to conform in order to reduce their own doubts about the questionable decision the group made. This pressure may be reflected in the comment that the employee, for example, is not a good team player. The more extreme the pressure a member puts on dissenters, the quicker a culture of fear is created within the group, which transforms the lower level, less powerful members into "yes men or yes women." It is not surprising to find the classic yes-men or women in these groups that attempt to subdue dissention using whatever methods available to send the message that dissention is not approved of. For example, when one of Enron's board members, Brent Scowcroft, questioned the veracity of the financial statements and confronted Lay, Lay displayed the classic groupthink mindset when he told Scowcroft, "How could you be right and men of this caliber [referring to Fastow and Skilling] be wrong" (Perri, 2013b, p. 337). After this exchange with Lay, Scowcroft was brought back into the line of strict compliance that consumed the Enron culture.

One of the most obvious symptoms of groupthink occurred within WorldCom when pressure was put on dissenters within the management and accounting teams who should have served as a check on accounting fraud by detecting, preventing, and disclosing it. Regulators concluded that, "Ebbers created the pressure that led to the fraud. He demanded the results he had promised, and he appeared to scorn the procedures (and people) that should have been a check on misreporting" (Howard, 2011, p. 438). WorldCom CFO Sullivan and Director of General Accounting Buford Yates claimed they felt intense pressure to make incorrect accounting entries and too were afraid of the repercussions of stopping the fraud. This pressure trickled down through them to other lower level accountants who feared losing their jobs if they questioned their superiors. In many situations, the group leader or manager, by stating their opinion up front before soliciting feedback, can build pressure leading the organization toward groupthink. In the case of WorldCom, CEO Bernie Ebbers and CFO Sullivan exercised unquestioned authority and demanded unquestioned loyalty from employees (Rosenbush, 2005).

Ebbers continued to feed Wall Street's expectations of achieving double-digit growth by demanding that his subordinates meet those expectations, but he did not provide the leadership or managerial attention that would enable WorldCom to meet those expectations legitimately (SEC, 2003). Due to WorldCom's culture, and their perception of CEO Ebbers, employees were "scared and intimidated by him," and constantly under intense pressure to follow management orders, with many reporting they feared they would lose their jobs if they disagreed with or did not follow policies or executive orders (Jeter, 2003, p. 61). When asked specifically if Ebbers pressured him to make the incorrect accounting entries, Yates response was "you know Bernie, he could put pressure on you indirectly" (SEC, 2003, p. 127).

Self-Appointed Mind Guards

The final symptom is the emergence of self-appointed "mind guards." These are individual group members who, on their own initiative, decide to protect the group from any adverse information that could influence the group's decisions (Howard, 2011). The mind guard performs many self-assigned tasks, which include informing others in the group that the leader is not open to criticism and notifying the leader any time there are indications of dissent from a group member. Consider the scenario when an Enron executive tried to share his concerns about fraudulent behavior with CEO Kenneth Lay. Within minutes, this executive was ushered out the door by Lay's subordinates ultimately with no action by Lay to investigate this executive's concerns (Duchon & Burns, 2008). Interestingly, Lay stated that he wanted Enron "to be a highly moral and ethical culture and that he tried to ensure that people honored the values of respect, integrity and excellence…on his desk was an Enron paperweight with the slogan "Vision and Values" (Ferrell et al., 2013, p. 396). Despite good intentions, ethical behavior was pushed aside for different agendas.

Summary Insights on Groupthink

The reality is "groups bring out the worst as well as the best" in organizations and ultimately people (Hodges & Hodges, 2013, p. 13). It is important that organizations be on the lookout for symptoms of groupthink and encourage opinion sharing to mitigate the risks attached to decision making. However, if management is populated with those who display narcissistic tendencies, groupthink may be a byproduct of such leadership where subordinates become "yes-people" and simply confirm the values and decisions of leadership resulting potentially in suboptimal decisions. Unfortunately, following this approach can expose one to criminal liabilities when unethical and illegal decisions are followed blindly by subordinates.

Workplace Bullying and Corporate Fraud

Workplace bullying, particularly among managers who tolerate it and the potential participation of their subordinates who abuse authority, is a social issue that impacts workers and businesses in every country. The key to understanding why bullying exists is to study the interactions and relationships between three core players: the environment (organization), the bully, and the target (victim). Researchers have confirmed the prevalence of bullying is higher among organizations whose culture endorses and may actively encourage such conduct, together with management's failure to protect employees from bullying (Regnaud, 2011). Within organizations that are focused on self-interest or are highly competitive, bullying may not only be accepted but may be rewarded as well, both of which result in the perpetuation of the problem. The degree of workplace bullying is a reflection of management's tone at the top, not just management neglect. Work places that have high workloads and place pressure on workers to perform are more likely to accept such bullying behavior and actually normalize it as part of the organizational culture (Braithwaite et al., 2008). Bullying in the workplace has been an ethical issue for as long as there have been formal organizations and there is no reason to believe that the intensity of this deviant behavior will diminish (Harvey et al., 2008). If bullying is accepted in the workplace, it is likely to continue due to the practice being passed down from one employee to another by learning from others eventually becoming normalized (Harvey et al., 2008).

It has been estimated that workplace bullying costs U.S. businesses more than $23 billion each year; one national survey reported that 8.8 percent of U.S. workers are currently victims of workplace bullying, 25.7 percent had previously been victims of bullying, 22.4 percent are currently witnesses to bullying, and 19.6 percent had previously been witnesses to bullying (Regnaud, 2011). Despite the significant costs and negative consequences associated with workplace bullying, many employers seem uninterested or unwilling to effectively deal with the problem and, in fact, often condone bullying after being made aware of its existence if it advances corporate agendas. This is supported by results of one study which discovered that when bullying was reported, 44 percent of employers failed to do anything about it, 18 percent made conditions worse for the victim, and only 32 percent successfully ended bullying (Regnaud, 2011). Findings from another study are even more alarming where after participants reported to their employer about being bullied, 71 percent were retaliated against and of that group 24 percent were terminated; only 6 percent reported the employer punished the bully while merely 2 percent reported their employer completely resolved the situation satisfactorily (Regnaud, 2011). For organizations with human resources departments, the results are just as dismal because these departments tell people who report bullying to work it out with the person(s) who bullies them (Ferrell et al., 2013).

Workplace Bullying Characteristics

Workplace bullying is characterized as workplace incivility, which is behaving in a disrespectful and offensive manner with a complete lack of regard for others. There is a general consensus among researchers that bullying is characterized by several features, 1) frequent and repeated unwanted negative acts, 2) acts occur over an extended period of time, 3) a power disparity between the parties exists, and 4) there is intent to cause harm or distress (Regnaud, 2011). Furthermore, workplace bullying has been equated with emotional abuse with the intent to cause the victim to feel incompetent. The goal of bullying is to get others to lose their sense of identity of who they are, so the targets of bullying are easier to manipulate and control becoming the proverbial puppets on a string. Interestingly, "corporate bullies often target employees who excel at their jobs and are popular with their coworkers" (Ferrell et al., 2013, p. 67). This incivility is displayed by humiliating others, intimidations, or abusive supervision, which is the continued use of aggressive and antagonistic verbal and nonverbal behaviors on the part of the supervisor. Such negative behaviors are designed to disgrace, embarrass, and invoke shame on another with the intent of isolating them from a group.

Workplace bullying is also illustrated by exposure to frequent hostile behaviors, such as excessive criticism of work, withholding information that impacts performance, belittling remarks, questioning people's loyalty, questioning their competences, harassments, spreading rumors, social isolation, scapegoating, physical abuse, insults, false accusations, public humiliations and belittlements, threatening employees with the loss of employment, and purposefully creating conflict among group members, to name a few (Pilch & Turska, 2015). Work-related behaviors linked to bullying include, 1) work-load, which includes work overload, removing responsibilities, assigning meaningless tasks, and setting unrealistic goals, 2) work-process, which includes overruling decisions, controlling resources, flaunting power, and 3) evaluation, which includes micromanaging, judging work inaccurately, and blocking promotions (Regnaud, 2011). Overt bullying might include rude or dismissive behavior, particularly in front of other employees or customers, persistent criticism and derogatory comments which undermine employees' credibility, lack of trust for no apparent reason, and unreasonable demands that make it difficult for employees to succeed (McGeehan, 2010).

Impact of Workplace Bullying on Subordinates

The consequences of bullying are startling and begin with the impact on victims in terms of both psychological and physical harm. Those who witness bullying can also be affected, and influence the organization in terms of poor performance and high financial costs (Regnaud, 2011). Psychological harms include higher levels of anger and fear, reduced levels of self-esteem, increased levels of stress, reduced self-confidence, damaged personal relationships, reports of depression and anxiety, symptoms of post-traumatic stress disorder, and in the most serious cases, thoughts of suicide. Victims also experience work-related consequences such as job burnout, increased absenteeism, loss of organizational commitment, lower job satisfaction, preoccupation with thoughts of quitting, poor morale, decreased performance, increased time off, and income loss due to medical expenses or job loss. Witnesses and observers of bullying often suffer consequences similar to those targeted, and have reported increased anxiety and stress, preoccupation with thoughts of quitting, decreased job satisfaction, and increased health problems.

Such behaviors leave the target feeling threatened, and stressed. Bullying leads to impaired job performance, high employee turnover, and depression (Pilch & Turska, 2015). Additionally, organizations are negatively impacted by bullying through loss of productivity, decreased organizational citizenship behaviors, increased workers' compensation and medical insurance costs, higher levels of absenteeism, decreased work quality, increased employee counter-productive behaviors, weaker customer relationships, lower creativity, increased legal costs, and more incidents of employee theft (Regnaud, 2011). Recall the experiences of Wells Fargo employees who were pressured to meet sales quotas that reflect, in a very real sense, what bullying looks like, and how it affected their lives. Fulfilling quotas was the end goal of sales employees and one employee stated that his supervisor told him, "I don't care how you do it—but do it, or else you're not going home" (Reckard, 2013). Other bankers experienced "bullying, punishment and intimidation" which impacted their physical and mental health due to the pressure for meeting quotas (Egan, 2016a).

One personal banker stated that she "had managers in my face yelling at me…They wanted you to open up dual checking accounts for people that couldn't even manage their original checking account…The sales pressure from management was unbearable" (Egan, 2016b). Poor performance also led to "shaming or worse" (Wells Fargo, 2017, p. 30). Thus, it was not just private bullying that occurred, but public bullying as one Wells Fargo bank manager described that "if you did not make your goal, you are severely chastised and embarrassed in front of 60-plus managers in your area by the community banking president" (Reckard, 2013). Bullying might be so subtle that employees find it difficult to articulate exactly what is happening and how it makes them feel (McGeehan, 2010). Subtle bullying might lead employees to feel isolated when excluded from meetings, lunches, or other social gatherings in which information is traded creating an environment in where employees do not feel valued. Most bullies are supervisors or managers and are split evenly between men and women.

Bullying might be ingrained in their management styles because they do not know any other equally effective way to motivate employee performance or enhance their positions. Bullies might decisively pick their targets because they perceive them as threats—real or imagined. For instance, a bully might be competing with a targeted employee for a promotion or recognition. By targeting them, the bully can negatively impact their performance, thereby supporting the bully's goals; they might undermine their target's work, make them miserable so they will resign, or simply make them change their behavior. Among organizational factors that influence the frequency of bullying acts are a chaotic and unpredictable work environment, work pressures, interpersonal conflicts, and a destructive management style and organizational culture, to name a few (Pilch & Turska, 2015). Bullying in the workplace can also affect employees' willingness to report suspicions of fraud.

The fact that the majority of employers fail to effectively address bullying when it is reported indicates it may be an accepted practice that is imbedded within the organization's culture (Regnaud, 2011). Consider a recent poll conducted by the Workplace Bullying Institute which revealed that HR representatives typically fail to resolve the problem. Of those polled, 11.5 percent chose not to report the bullying to HR, 30.9 percent indicated HR had not taken action, and 37.3 percent stated HR was not helpful and retaliation occurred, 18.2 percent reported HR was not helpful, that job loss occurred, and only 1.9 percent indicated HR was helpful resulting in justice and complete satisfaction (Regnaud, 2011). One reason HR often fails is because HR representatives are not in a position to help victims since their allegianceis to the organization, which makes it difficult for them to be neutral and objective.

Leadership, the Dark Triad and Workplace Bullying

Workplace bullying illustrates unfair victimization of a subordinate by a leader through intimidation. Intimidation might be for the purpose of forced compliance, retaliation, or exploitation of formal power. Such leaders employ an authoritative, exploitative leadership style and lack civil communication skills. Coercive and threatening behaviors displayed by the leaders set negative examples while sending permissive signals to subordinates to engage in similar behaviors to achieve organizational goals (Jones & Jones, 2014). Such leaders have no qualms about sudden outbursts of anger, are willing to insult others, and will question employee competence and loyalty in public. Consider the interpersonal relationship tactics of Joseph Cassano, head of the financial products division at insurance giant AIG. A subordinate described him as follows,

> His temper…it was brutal and indiscriminate—terrifying when unleashed …sometimes he could seem uncontrollable. Cassano would rage at traders who were making the company a fortune and traders who were on a losing streak. He would go out of his way to embarrass executives in front of their peers and blow up over inconsequential things. Talking to him was like walking on egg shells…you were always worried about what was going to set him off. Once a new hire corrected his statement about some figures and "Cassano erupted, 'How dare you do the math on me?' He was a bully. It was his fatal flaw (Ramamoorti, 2013, p. 110).

One explanation for organizations' failure to stop bullying is because the culture is created by the top leader such as the president or CEO. Thus, when leaders accept bullying as part of the organizational culture, they are essentially showing a lack of consideration for their workers and therefore may be a possible contributor to workplace bullying. It has also been established that managers and supervisors who are exposed to bullying are more likely to become a bully themselves. In addition, many organizations are so focused on achieving financial goals that they are willing to overlook negative behaviors and may embrace such behaviors if they contribute to high performance. The literature pertaining to the topic of workplace bullying provides support for the argument that organizational culture and leadership are both important contributors to the existence and perpetuation of the problem (Padilla et al., 2007). Highly competitive environments are often controlled by abusive, intimidating, and sometimes violent management behaviors (Regnaud, 2011). The root of the problem is not only that bullying happens, but that employers allow it to continue pointing to top leadership as a highly influential force in the development and sustainability of bullying.

However, it is important to consider that it is possible leadership may not be aware bullying is present because lower level managers are in a position to hide the problem, especially if there are multiple work sites that are removed from where leadership resides. For example, a corporation's headquarters and leadership may reside in one country with multiple satellite offices and manufacturing plants in other countries. Thus, what happens in one country may never reach the ears of a CEO in another country who actually has an antibullying policy in place. It has been argued that any one of the dark triad personalities can facilitate workplace bullying because such individuals are concerned with the fulfillment of personal needs over the needs of others. Some of the apparent traits of destructive leadership within the body of current research include bullying, hubris, and certain individual personality traits such as narcissism and Machiavellianism (Jones & Jones, 2014). Psychopathy, narcissism, and Machiavellianism are linked to bulling with psychopathy showing the strongest link (Baughman et al., 2012). Workplace bullying may be one of the negative consequences associated with destructive leadership, as was suggested by research which looked at the behaviors exhibited by destructive leaders.

Participants were asked if they had ever witnessed their leader act in a harmful manner and, if so, were then asked to explain the behavior. Based on data collected, eight behaviors displayed include, 1) attacking follower's self-esteem, 2) pitting group members against each other, 3) alienating and excluding individuals, 4) showing favoritism or promoting inequalities, 5) angry outbursts and yelling at workers, 6) threats to job security, 7) taking credit for others' work, and 8) a sense of indifference or failure to make decisions and behaviors associated with bullies (Regnaud, 2011). For example, former UBS and Citigroup securities trader Tom Hayes was sentenced to fourteen years in prison after being found guilty of conspiracy to manipulate the benchmark Libor exchange rate. As the ringmaster of a global network, Hayes would bully, bribe, and reward other traders and brokers for their help in manipulating the Libor rate which is among the most commonly used interest rate benchmark indexes. Libor is used to price more than $350 trillion of financial contracts from credit cards to mortgages (Finch &Vaughan, 2015). Bullying is about control of others and situations by gaining compliance through coercion, threats, and other aggressive acts to maintain organizational power and control to satisfy an agenda that may or may not be public. Observe how bullying parallels the antisocial trait of power orientation studied in chapter one. Employees who raise concerns may be terminated or demoted. Consider the statement of this subordinate:

> In the IPO (Initial Public Offering) process, we were coerced by the investment bankers to agree to a 25 percent growth rate. We wanted to agree to a 15 percent growth rate, but the CEO still agreed to commit to a 25 percent growth rate in the IPO process. In the first quarter, initial financial statements indicated we missed our earnings. By only tens of thousands of dollars, but we missed our earnings. The CEO screamed and yelled and said that we didn't know what we were doing. I took the weekend off to look at the numbers. I had to be a little more aggressive with the valuation of our accounts receivable. The CEO told me, "I had to fix the numbers and help us." The next quarter rolled around and the numbers were a little worse. I got the same speech from the CEO and I agreed to do it again. In the third quarter, I said this is not getting any better, in fact it is getting worse. The CEO's response was to shame me into continuing the process. He said, "What are you going to do now, quit?" (Freeman & Murphy, 2015, p. 39).

Machiavellianism and Workplace Bullying

Machiavellians tend to have an egocentric motivation coupled with a pragmatic morality; it is linked to bullying behaviors when it is to their benefit to bully. Machiavellianism is linked to counterproductive work behaviors, which include harmful interpersonal acts akin to abuse such as workplace bullying and intimidation. (Dahling et al., 2009). Consider that bullying for the Machiavellian is an interpersonal influencing strategy due to their negative views of others. According to their worldview, they may feel the need to preemptively bully before they are bullied. In addition, organizational cultures that favor bullying may trigger bullying behaviors in Machiavellians. Their interpersonal methods of intimidation, demanding loyalty, exploitation, and fear are how stability and control are obtained; they cannot maintain control without exploitation through bullying tactics.

Psychopathy and Workplace Bullying

Research supports the existence of psychopathic traits among non-prison community members who display them in a non-criminal fashion (Warren, 2009). Non-criminal psychopaths encountered on a daily basis may be unknown to us as psychopaths; while they may behave differently than criminals, their core traits are the same. Such individuals have been found to function well in business environments due to their ruthless, manipulative nature, no differently than psychopathic criminal offenders who pursue nefarious agendas. Their harmful interpersonal strategies may include indirect aggression, since they understand that direct aggression is riskier. It would disrupt their lives to serve jail time and a criminal record would affect employment prospects. Increased, intentional indirect aggression relates back to their lack of empathy and attachment to others. They manifest aggression, perhaps not as antisocial in the criminal sense but differently, in a more indirect manner, albeit still antisocial in complexion. Recall that antisocial behaviors do not always have to be criminal in nature; they can display themselves by violating social norms of civility and we observe violating norms of civility in the workplace.

For example, indirect aggression can take the form of bullying displayed as verbal assaults under the guise of feedback and advice, malicious humor intended to harm others, socially excluding others through isolation, and withholding information from others. Additional examples include emotional blackmail by trying to make others feel guilty, pressuring others to conform, shaming to get conformity, sabotaging relationships, attacking reputations, and manipulating social environments (Warren, 2009). This behavior is in line with the expectations from bullying literature where there is a clear correlation between bullying and employee withdrawal as observed by this subordinate who had to work with a corporate psychopath, "Typically, three or four times a day, everybody went through a humiliating dressing down to an extent which was quite public. The whole atmosphere was very hostile and unpleasant" (Boddy et al., 2015, p. 540). When corporate psychopaths are present, the incidents of bullying are significantly higher than when they are not present (Regnaud, 2011). Corporate psychopaths use bullying as a tactic to control and humiliate others because they may enjoy and be stimulated by hurting people or it is used as a tactic to confuse and disorient those who may be a threat to their activities, especially those who crave the power that management hierarchy brings so that they can be in a position to control others and/or events (Boddy, 2006). Psychopathic bullying is used as a tactic to demand obedience and sow confusion.

The corporate psychopath who resorts to fraud uses bullying to intimidate staff and keep them from questioning their agendas as observed by one individual who had to work with such a person, "I think his bullying tactic was the bit about him that was so unpredictable…you never knew what he was going to do" (Boddy et al., 2015). How is a chaotic behavioral disposition used to control others? Most people desire predictability in others' behaviors so that they can adjust their behavior accordingly. Yet when there is a lack of predictability, it causes a feeling of uncertainty, which ultimately makes people unsettled and fearful. The psychopaths goal is to maintain control over the an individual. The literature on corporate psychopaths characterizes them as bullies where instilling fear and public humiliations were reportedly both frequent and regular (Boddy et al., 2015). In one case study, management orders were issued via shouts or screams, and normal everyday pleasantries were reportedly absent. The atmosphere was described as extremely hostile to the extent that in one study, an employee just walked out and never came back after being humiliated (Boddy et al., 2015). As described by a subordinate, one manager who displayed psychopathic traits created an atmosphere of fear where: "Amongst a very senior population there was a huge amount of fear around dealing with the individual. So everybody was trying to develop strategies to cope with what might come their way. It was never balanced and reasonable. It was provocative, it was undermining people, it was making a fool of them in public" (Boddy et al., 2015, p. 540).

Narcissism and Workplace Bullying

With the strong link between destructive leadership and bullying incidents, along with the proven relationship between narcissism and destructive leadership, it is plausible that narcissistic behaviors exhibited by leaders may be the reason the problem of workplace bullying remains unsolved because it is a tactic used to fulfill their needs. Research suggests a positive relationship exists between leaders who exhibit narcissistic behaviors and their personal participation in bullying, along with others in the organization who bully each other (Regnaud, 2011). The abusive narcissist in power asserts their superiority by relying on contempt to make others feel inadequate, belittle their work output, ridicule them at meetings, and make them doubt their competence and value to the organization (Burgo, 2015). As the level of leadership narcissism moves toward the pathological, behaviors become more pronounced and detrimental to the organization. The leader is desperate to fulfill personal needs of power, prestige, and superiority, and will take whatever steps are necessary to make it happen. While it is possible to coexist with a bullying narcissist, provided one does not pose too obvious a threat, once one becomes the target of a vindictive narcissist they will try to destroy the person emotionally and financially (Burgo, 2015).

When a subordinate expresses concern, for example, about potential financial statement fraud, narcissistic authority resorts to destroying them through character assassination, or by withholding crucial information in order to sabotage their work; they will pursue such destruction without regard to truth or fairness (Burgo, 2015). The presence of character assassination is one way of detecting the presence of narcissism. In one study, bullies were more competitive, assertive, concerned with their own success, and aggressive than non-bullies; all characteristics associated with narcissism (Regnaud, 2011). Workplace bullying is much more prevalent in organizations with cultures that are not supportive or concerned with the well-being of workers; this illustrates the characteristics associated with narcissistic leaders. Workplace bullying can be institutionalized and begins with the bully's narcissistic need for recognition and success, and ends with a toxic and demoralizing work environment. Positive correlation between narcissism and bullying with indirect bullying tactics include, taking credit for work, withholding information, feeding misinformation, and sabotage being the most common tactics (Regnaud, 2011).

The Case of Lance Armstrong

Consider the narcissism and bullying together with the rationalizations of Lance Armstrong, the seven-time winner of the Tour de France when his titles were stripped after it was learned that he took performance enhancing drugs—also known as doping (Burgo, 2013). Armstrong believed he was singled out because he fought back so aggressively against those who accused him of doping (ESPN, 2013). Armstrong indicated that if he had to do the Tour de France cycling race over again, he would still dope stating "everyone else in cycling was doping too….I knew what my competitors were doing. We [his U.S. Postal Service team] were doing less" (ESPN, 2013). Here we can observe the rationalization of social comparison were he states that his team was doping less than the competitors. Armstrong rationalized his actions as not taking advantage of anyone and thus he did not believe he was cheating since the use of banned drugs was pervasive in professional cycling. He stated, "I…looked up the definition of cheat and the definition of cheat is to gain an advantage on a rival or foe that they don't have. I didn't view it that way. I viewed it as a level playing field" (Telegraph Sport, 2013).

In addition, Armstrong carefully cultivated his impression management to craft his public image through philanthropy. Armstrong believed that the positive impact he had on the sport of cycling and the tremendous good his Livestrong cancer foundation was doing for society by raising significant funds for cancer research made it easier for him to rationalize taking performance enhancing drugs. Again, we observe the use of the metaphor of the ledger rationalization where the good that one does offsets their misconduct. Armstrong indicated that he did not regret the impact his career had on the sport or on his cancer foundation when he stated, "I know what happened to the sport, I saw its growth. I know what happened to Trek Bicycles [his bike supplier]--$100 million in sales to $1billion in sales. And I know what happened to my foundation, from raising no money to raising $500-million, serving three million people. Do we want to take it away? I don't think anybody says 'yes'" (Cary, 2015). Armstrong's desire to be perceived as special through the admiration of others drove him to engage in unethical behavior, and winning brought the admiration he craved.

For an individual, like Armstrong, to lose means that he is no longer that unique, special person worthy of admiration. Admiration is what keeps a narcissist's sense of self stable; it is very important for them to craft an image of who they want others to think they are to support their self-identity. While being investigated, Armstrong repeatedly lashed out against critics, former teammates whom he believed betrayed him, and the U.S. Department of Justice, which he believed was out to persecute him. When narcissists feel their idealized self-image is threatened, they will lash out and seek revenge to right what they perceive is a personal attack. Consider his reaction when teammate Tyler Hamilton released his book on doping in the cycling world. Armstrong accosted him in public, stating, "When you're on the witness stand, we are going to fucking tear you apart. You are going to look like a fucking idiot, I'm going to make your life a living fucking hell" (Burgo, 2013). Even when Armstrong apologized, it rang hollow—devoid of genuine empathy for how he hurt others.

Yet, Armstrong made a statement that gives insight into the narcissist's distortion of reality when he stated, "The truth isn't what I said. And now it's gone...the story was perfect for so long...You won the disease...it was this mythic perfect story, and it just wasn't true" (Burgo, 2013). In an interview, when Armstrong was asked whether he was a bully toward others including his teammates he stated, "Yeah, yeah, I was a bully. In the sense I tried to control the narrative and if I didn't like what someone said...I tried to control that...a guy who expected to get everything he wanted and to control everything" (Burgo, 2013). Interestingly, Armstrong said his comeback to cycling was a tactical mistake that triggered the investigation which eventually unraveled the deception. In the interview he further stated, "We wouldn't be sitting here if I didn't come back" implying that he would have gotten away with his previous doping scandal that earned him the Tour de France titles (Burgo, 2013).

Antibullying Policies and the Tone at the Top

Unfortunately, there is limited research in the field of workplace bullying regarding the impact of antibullying policies. However, studies conducted in the field of school bullying show a relationship between antibullying policies and the reduction of bullying incidents. Moreover, when it comes to workplace bullying, many businesses appear to be void of antibullying organizational policies and one sign an organization may condone bullying is the absence of antibullying policies (Regnaud, 2011). Policies define the rules of conduct and outline unacceptable behaviors which are core elements of the culture and directly influence employee behavior. The presence of an antibullying policy is one way a company can show its intolerance, and opens the door for employees to raise issues regarding such behavior. Without such policy, it is unclear if bullying behaviors are unacceptable and managers have no foundation to intervene on behalf of employees. While having an antibullying policy does not guarantee that it will be minimized, failure to have one is a direct reflection of a cultural norm that is likely to accept the behavior.

Regardless of how much we understand why bullies bully and what organizational factors are likely to result in bullying, the problem will not be solved until top business leaders take a stand and refuse to tolerate bullying within their organization. The solution would be much simpler if all business leaders believed bullying was an undesirable behavior, but some leaders' innate personality may drive them to exhibit bullying behaviors themselves which, in turn, results in bullying being an acceptable organizational norm. Leadership influences behaviors that allow bullying to exist and it is their example which can stop it. Moreover, now that we know there is a relationship between the dark triad behaviors exhibited by the top leader and the prevalence of bullying in the workplace, HR professionals and managers can conduct personality assessments when hiring or promoting new top leaders. The answer to workplace bullying is to put a leadership team in place that strongly opposes it and exhibits it by implementing antibullying policies, processes which quickly address bullying when it is reported, and constructive training programs.

Obedience to Authority Facilitating Misconduct

There are several different foundations upon which cultures or groups establish their definition of morality, including their sense of what fairness and justice means to them, the importance of loyalty to the group, the role of authority, and the significance of respect and obedience (Haidt et al., 2009). Hence, an individual may be in a situation where an authority figure instructs them to participate in some type of fraud, be it corruption, producing fraudulent financial statements, or covering up even when such an order is contrary to that person's value system. The individual may simply do what they are told, and perceive that they are being a loyal subordinate without consideration of the legality or ethicality of the conduct. However, even if the person ordered to carry out misconduct disapproves of the order, they may not perceive their actions as blameworthy; since an authority figure ordered them to commit fraud, they personally did nothing wrong. While authority is a valuable and necessary tool that permits managers to discharge their duties, too much emphasis on obedience to authority can have dangerous consequences where there may be considerable pressure on a subordinate to obey managerial directives even if such orders diverge from what the employee knows to be appropriate (Tomlinson & Pozzuto, 2016).

Fraudulent behavior becomes normalized within organizations when unethical management instructs subordinates to perpetrate fraud and, over time, such behavior becomes acceptable and common. Generally, obedience is the initial mechanism for perpetrating fraud, followed eventually by an organizational climate of obvious fraudulent behavior (Murphy & Dacin, 2011). For example, consider the case of a chief accountant who was instructed by the CFO to fraudulently increase earnings by $100 million. The accountant was suspicious about the purpose of the instruction, but did not challenge the CFO to give an explanation for the increase. The accountant created a spreadsheet containing several pages of improper journal entries in order to carry out the CFO's instructions, freely and doing so quietly (Albrecht et al., 2012). The reflexive impulse to obey authority figures illustrates that the habits of obedience are so strong and pervasive that most people have a difficult time actively defying orders that they do not condone. Further, the relative sense of powerlessness often associated with subordination may induce individuals to abdicate responsibility for moral issues.

In essence, a widely-held view among those who hold lower-echelon corporate positions is to allow those earning high salaries to tackle difficult ethical decisions. Also, many people who commit fraud may feel an uncomfortable tension between being loyal and the thought of engaging in misconduct. It is important to think about how one views authority, their relationship to authority figures, and how loyalty influences their behavior when given orders. Are we easily swayed by authority to the point we are willing to engage in fraud in order to be viewed positively by those with power? For example, employees follow the orders of superiors who possess legitimate authority without considering the merits of the orders themselves. They may also copy the behavior of coworkers without considering the rationale for that behavior (Greve et al., 2010). The fact that a superior has issued an order is sufficient to cause an employee to follow the order and engage in misconduct (Greve et al., 2010). The norm of obedience to authority dictates that subordinates comply with their superior's commands, regardless of whether they agree or disagree with their orders, because their very survival, or the organization's, is at stake. Authority can facilitate wrongdoing explicitly by causing those subject to it to comply with specific misconduct demands.

When it does, it can lead to unquestioning or grudging compliance when subordinates view themselves as powerless typically because resistance is seen as futile (Palmer, 2012). Obedience to authority can be characterized as an "impulse overriding training in ethics, sympathy, and moral conduct" (Hoyk & Hersey, 2008, p. 20). In fact, this is where many people who normally would not be deviant get into trouble with the law. Even though they did not come up with the fraud scheme, they did participate in making the scheme functional because of their compliance with authority. This is why employees who just grudgingly go along with the scheme become criminally liable. It is plausible that the obedience tendency might have blinded these individuals to the fact that they were committing fraud. This step within a fraud context is critical because it leads directly to fraudulent behavior without reasoning. This obedience bias would be especially strong if individuals subscribed to the following moral foundation—the importance of respect and obedience toward authority figures (Murphy & Dacin, 2011). Moral foundations are "psychological systems that enable people to perceive actions and agents as praiseworthy or blameworthy" (Haidt et al., 2009, p. 112). The individuals may follow the moral foundation that views obedience as an important moral compass, perhaps more impactful than the discomfort of the participation in fraud itself (Murphy & Dacin, 2011).

Even when there is a perception that authority is legitimate, subordinates may engage in misconduct in a grudging manner, however this should not be interpreted to mean that all do so in such a manner. There are those who happily engage in misconduct, and believe that doing so will yield benefits when they foster approval from leaders who relies on them to do what they must in order to get the job done. Let us examine a study that simulated a business environment to illustrate how authority impacts our compliance with misconduct. Participants were surveyed about their superiors' commands to discriminate against black job candidates. The study found that a superior's instruction to discriminate significantly increased a subject's propensity to discriminate, even among subjects who did not hold biased views towards blacks (Brief et al., 2000). People can mindlessly follow orders without reflecting on the consequences of their behavior, especially when those who are in power are viewed by subordinates as being legitimate. There are certain organizational situational factors that can overwhelm one's disapproval against fraud, which, ironically, can lead to fraud, such as silence and obedience to authority, an organization's ethical climate, and forecasts to achieve certain goals. Each of these situations can overpower the recognition against committing accounting fraud, or they may interact with one another to create a negative synergy which enhances the risk of fraud.

It is possible these individuals are aware that they are doing something wrong, but believe it is more important to be loyal to their boss (Murphy & Dacin, 2011). Thus we observe both Troy Normand and Betty Vinson display their loyalty to CFO Sullivan even though they knew there was something wrong with his request. Moreover, although authority and misconduct may not necessarily be intertwined, they do develop interdependently over time, thus a person's position in the chain of command determines the resources over which they exercise control over. As a result, advancement up the chain of command typically improves a person's access to resources and increases their power within the organization especially getting others to do what they want because they control resources others want (Palmer, 2012). The more power people have, the better able they are to manipulate rewards and punishment which are important to employees which increases their perceived legitimacy. Authority places them in a better position to manipulate others into engaging in misconduct. Recall how CFO Andrew Fastow served on the performance review committee (PRC) and exploited this power to reward supporters and to punish opposition to his SPEs. Clifford Baxter was subordinate to Fastow and opposed the SPEs. Fastow let Baxter know that he would punish his subordinates when their turn came up for evaluation. Once Baxter heard this, he backed off from opposing the SPEs knowing they were fraudulent (Palmer, 2012).

The Fen-Phen Drug Case Study

Authority can serve as a short-cut or altogether reduce the thought process relating to a decision whether or not to follow orders that might harm others. Thus, a superior can use authority to compel a subordinate to engage in misconduct by explicitly issuing an order that may be communicated in subtle ways (Palmer, 2012). Consider the case of an employee named Amy Myers who was a Safety Surveillance Officer at Wyeth-Ayers Pharmaceutical Company. She was responsible for maintaining the company's Adverse Drug Event (ADE) database. At the time, a drug named Pondimen was prescribed with another drug named Phentermine, where together they were commonly referred to as Fen-Phen. Fen-Phen was used as an appetite-suppressant drug that unfortunately contributed to heart valve disease and primary pulmonary hypertension, which is a condition where fluid accumulates in a person's lungs and is almost always fatal. Myers, as required by the company and the Federal Drug Administration (FDA), filed the report of these incidences she received into the company's database. However, Myers removed the report from the company's database because Wyeth-Ayers feared that news of the drug's serious side effects might jeopardize the firm's efforts to obtain FDA approval of another, closely-related drug.

Myers was ordered to remove those reports stating that "her immediate supervisor questioned the necessity of entering those reports so quickly in the ADE database…and that her boss asked her if she was certain the Fargo patients had really taken Wyeth's diet drugs suggesting that if she wasn't 100 percent sure…it was premature to record them [who] posed the question, couldn't the reports be cancelled" (Palmer, 2012, p. 184). Moreover, scientist Dr. Leo Lutwak wanted to voice his opinion about Fen-Phen, but his superior discouraged him. Lutwak was a researcher who joined the FDA after a stellar career at Cornell University as a professor of pharmacology. Lutwak recognized the dangers early on, and worked to prevent patients from taking the combination of drugs. Lutwak's supervisor Jim Bilstad instructed him to curb his criticisms, thus Lutwak felt obliged to assume a subdued posture at a meeting where the drugs were discussed. Lutwak never came forward with all he knew about the public's exposure to a dangerous drug. According to researcher Alicia Mundy who commented on the Fen-Phen debacle:

> Leo sat next to Dr. Jim Bilstad, a director of the FDA office supervising endocrine and metabolic drugs. Leo was already on notice from Bilstad that he must not advocate approval or disapproval in his testimony or when answering questions. Bilstad had snapped at Leo after the session with Wyeth and Interneuron reps, "You cannot take sides, that's not our role!" "If our role isn't to take sides on whether a drug is safe or not, what is our role? He snapped back. "We cannot speak so bluntly to the industry," Bilstad told him, echoing the FDA line. "They are our customers. And you are rude to them," added Bilstad, warning Leo, "They've complained about you." With that earlier exchange in mind, Leo sat still and listened (Mundy, 2001, p. 64).

Organizational Followership Facilitating Misconduct

People gravitate toward leaders who they believe can provide clarity, direction, a sense of community and belonging, and instill in them a clear sense of self. In turn, people's personal identification with leaders increases their desire to emulate them. Their strong affection, devotion, and idealization of the leader results in dependence and vulnerability to manipulation. Some followers are inclined to obey unethical orders given their loyalty to the leader and desire for his or her approval of who they are; they will tailor their behavior to garner leadership approval (Thoroughgood et al., 2012). By offering a sense of community and a group with which to belong, as well as acting as a source of financial gain, people will sacrifice their autonomy and obey unethical orders to please their leaders (Padilla et al., 2007). Yet, personal identification with leaders creates the potential for blind obedience. Once people over-align themselves with an organization, and invest excessive faith in the wisdom of its leaders, they are liable to lose their original sense of who they are, what virtues they claim to believe in, and their sense of identity. Moreover, they tolerate ethical lapses they would have previously rejected, which allows a new and possibly corrosive value system to take root. Throughout history, human beings appear to gravitate toward believing in something, but are frequently naive when it comes to where they invest their belief, and are vulnerable to manipulations designed to intensify their loyalty to beliefs and leaders.

Yet, as much as we may believe that misconduct always starts at the top, it can occur at the lower levels of an organization and become known to leadership who endorse the misconduct (Palmer, 2012). WorldCom vice president of internal auditing and whistleblower Cynthia Cooper observed, "Most of the people who participated in the WorldCom fraud were ordinary, middle-class Americans. They were mothers and fathers who went to work to support their families. They had no prior criminal records and never imagined they would be confronted with such life-altering choices" (Rezaee & Riley, 2010, p. 212). Even though Ms. Cooper's initial observations may be accurate, what views do these people align themselves with as pertaining to those who were subordinates to CEO Ebbers and CFO Sullivan in order to go along with the misconduct? Did they engage in fraud as a form of upward mobility at WorldCom or because they believe in the leader no matter what they are requested to do? Recall previously-mentioned Phar-Mor CFO Patrick Finn who collaborated with CEO Michael Monus's fraud scheme referred to Monus as "his god" resulting in a blind loyalty to Monus whose orders were followed without any real checks or balances (Cohen et al., 2010, p. 285). Consider the cult-like atmosphere at Enron where Enron employees reported being 'fanatically loyal' to CEOs Jeffrey Skilling and Ken Lay where one Enron employee stated, "Every time Skilling spoke, I'd believe everything he'd say" (O'Connor, 2003, p. 1264). Would these followers to these CEOs feel like they were being "pressured" into engaging in misconduct or perhaps would they be willing to engage in illegal acts to please their leader with a happy heart even knowing that what they were doing was wrong?

Organization hierarchies create dilemmas for followers who react to managerial misconduct. Early socialization into hierarchical thinking stresses obedience to authority together with promoting silence and passivity in the face of unethical leader behavior (Uhl-Bien & Carsten, 2007). In fact, certain people construct their follower roles around passivity, deference, and obedience, rather than constructive questioning of leaders (Carsten et al., 2010). Certain follower's passive dispositions make a leader's destructive behaviors more prevalent and readily accepted. Leaders tend to instill their own value system to followers who are similar to them. In fact, value similarity between leaders and followers forges increased follower motivation, commitment, and satisfaction (Sharonpande & Srivastava, 2013). Followers have found to experience career success if their values are aligned with the leader, however it should be understood that many followers become "yes-people" in order to gain favor with the leader to obtain desired benefits (Sharonpande & Srivastava, 2013). Followers can contribute to negative organizational outcomes through compliance with unethical behaviors or active undermining of the leader (Padilla et al., 2007). Thus, the interaction of leader and followership makes a potent mix, and if supported by a conducive environment, can lead to organizational decline or destruction (Padilla et al., 2007). Those who participate in fraud by following the directives of a corrupt leader have been described as "less confident, less aggressive, less ambitious, passive subservient, gullible, less likely to accept responsibility for their own actions, and view themselves as less culpable" (Bucy et al., 2008, p. 411).

Different themes emerge as to the motives of such followers, including, 1) they are convinced in the righteousness of their cause even if it involves fraud because they are following the leader whom they trust, albeit naively, 2) they engage in fraud for financial reasons, and 3) they feared losing their job or physical harm (Bucy et al., 2008, p. 409). It is foreseeable that many of these people may have regretted their decision of going along with the fraud scheme after they were held accountable, but the display of collective regret does not mean that there was unanimity amongst group members as to the reason why they initially participated in the fraud scheme especially in terms of how the reacted to requests from those who had power over them. As we shall see, we need to break down the types of followers even further to understand the thinking behind their motivations to understand how and why they obey authority. Ask yourself, in what category would Betty Vinson place herself in? What category would Troy Norman, Betty's colleague, put himself in? Did their views on how they perceive authority influence their decision to participate in fraud? Do not lose sight of the fact that there will always be followers who are opportunists, careerists-types, bureaucrats and technocrats who are morally flexible enough, lack or disregard reflection of their contributions to an agenda that they will be with us for long time regardless of whether we get rid of corrupt leadership or not.

Authoritarian Followers

Some followers are referred to as authoritarians where their propensity to follow stems from a deeply-ingrained authoritarian ideology (Padilla et al., 2007). Authoritarians possess rigid, hierarchical attitudes that prescribe leaders' legitimate right to exert power over them and their inclination to unconditionally accept such influence. It has been suggested that people who unconditionally accept legitimate authorities are characterized by an intolerance for ambiguity and a preference for a simple, well-defined, and unambiguous world (Padilla et al., 2007). Authoritarianism is linked to a high need for closure, which refers to a preference for order and structure and a desire for firm answers and knowledge rather than confusion and ambiguity. These individuals might be less motivated to process information and tolerate uncertainty, and inherently more likely to submit and support authorities and social institutions that serve the need for stability, clarity, and order. As such, authoritarians do not necessarily obey because they seek approval or fear retribution, but because the leader holds a higher rank in the organization which brings with it power to make decisions for others.

It encompasses uncritical deferment to authority based on a leader's legitimate power, position, and status within an organization or society, in general (Thoroughgood et al., 2012). Furthermore, authoritarians strictly adhere and conform to in-group norms and rules and display a general intolerance toward perceived out-group members. Authoritarians are also more likely to display unconditional respect for and trust in legitimate authorities, engage in hostility towards others in the name of authority, volunteer in the persecution of out-groups, and are less likely to hold accountable those who punish norm violators (Thoroughgood et al., 2012). There is an inclination to comply based on the belief that job requirements, position power, organizational culture, and normative roles in the organization align with the leader's requests. Thus, a corrupt leader's power is a powerful influence on the authoritarian's engagement in crimes of obedience. Authoritarians may become submissive followers and even perpetrators of corrupt acts under leaders, such as an order to commit financial statement fraud. Thus, authoritarians' blind obedience can change to active collusion in unethical leader-directed plots and initiatives with ease.

Opportunistic Followers

Opportunistic followers base their loyalty to leaders on the potential for personal rewards. A key aspect of opportunists is their focus on achieving external indicators of success. Given their ambition and willingness to conspire with those who can reward them for their services, they are apt to promote the leader's corrupt agenda to get ahead (Thoroughgood et al., 2012). Opportunists are more likely to violate ethical codes of conduct, sabotage coworker relationships, follow coercive policies to further their interests, and engage in corruption. While additional research is needed, opportunists possess personal ambition, and unsocialized characteristics, such as Machiavellianism and greed. Opportunistic followers are prototypical "yes" people, who flatter their leaders and withhold criticism with the primary motivation of personal rewards they expect from their leader instead of an altruistic desire to help the organization. In addition, opportunists are willing to overlook morally-bankrupt leaders if there is something the leader can offer that satisfies their agendas.

Bystander Followers

Some followers are simply bystanders—passive and motivated primarily by fear of the loss of position, property, and status and, at the extreme, their life. Thus, the bystander's fear-based motivations are inherently planned in nature; they exchange conformity and compliance for a safe haven from potential punishments (Thoroughgood et al., 2012). In contrast to the other conformers, they tend to be independent, with their feelings toward destructive leaders ranging from anger and disapproval, to indifference and apathy. These followers may hold negative opinions of such leaders in private, but will often do their bidding and even publicly endorse them to be seen as "good" followers. Given that they do not tend to personally support destructive leaders, but act out of fear, their behavior may range from disengagement to obedience, depending on the degree to which they are coerced into compliance. Because bystanders are inclined to comply with destructive orders given, they believe a failure to obey will result in negative consequences and manipulative triggers such as fear reflecting the essence of their susceptibility. Bystanders interpret leadership orders as threats and believe they can impose punishments, no matter whether they intend to send such a message, or not. When leaders resort to manipulative triggers in bystanders, the stronger the link to tangible outcomes such as rewards and punishments, the greater the chance such tactics result in compliance.

Values-driven Followers

Values-driven followers comply because they share similar values and goals with the leader (Thoroughgood et al., 2012). Thus they actually align their participation with the leaders because they share the same value system. These followers have a clear sense of who they are and seek expression of their values and beliefs through the leader's vision. Thus, their motivations for following leaders are rooted primarily in their personal values.

The Influence of Bias on Decision Making

Generally speaking, judgment is the process of reaching a decision or drawing a conclusion after considering possible alternative solutions; an effective judgment process will be logical, flexible, unbiased, objective, and consistent (Glover & Prawitt, 2012). Effective judgment utilizes an appropriate amount of relevant information, and reaching a judgement requires a balance of experience, knowledge, intuition, and emotion. Ironically, despite the fact that we constantly make decisions that demand good judgment, most people receive very little formal training in what good judgment consists of or are made aware of the human tendencies and biases that compromise good judgment. Consider that much of our decision making relies on intuitive thinking which depends on emotions, impressions, and feelings which prepare our actions to flow effortlessly. For example, we can walk and think about multiple things at the same time to help us interpret what is going on around us. How we interpret a situation may not take into account alternative interpretations of the same situation. This is where the concept of bias comes into play making us aware of how we might erroneously interpret a situation without considering alternative interpretations that actually improves decision making.

A straightforward explanation of what bias consists of is when we have an attitude, preference, position, or belief and are inclined to favor or be against something or someone or harbor a preconceived notion about something or someone. Yet biases should not always be interpreted as negative. There may be a constructive role for bias since people harbor preferences that may be useful to accelerate decision making when time is of the essence. However, bias may impact our ability to be rational because we might draw conclusions about our preferences in an illogical manner even though we may not be aware of our own illogic. Individuals rely on their version of reality that ultimately drives decision making that at times is not based on objectivity, but on some distortion of reality, illogical interpretation, or inaccurate judgement which, broadly speaking, some refer to as irrational thinking. As an example, for decades women were not part of the professions because of the belief that they were not capable of engaging in male dominated jobs. The gap between our beliefs and what the evidence tells us is the bias gap. This distorted way of looking at women is not based on evidence, but on some preconceived, erroneous notion of female competencies.

Also known as confirmation bias, this is the tendency for people to selectively search for and consider information that confirms already held preferences, opinions, and beliefs while rejecting evidence that contradicts their opinions. Bias can interfere with the ability to look at a situation in a more realistic manner because we intentionally seek facts that support our belief system; in other words, bias facilitates our need to hear what we want to hear. Confirmation bias can lead to potentially weighing one piece of evidence too heavily at the expense of other quality information that would actually improve decision making. Biases facilitate mental shortcuts to more complex issues of how we think and eventually approach solutions to an issue. Yet these shortcuts can lead to poor judgments which, on trivial tasks are of little consequence, but on critical, high stakes judgments, they can be devastating (Glover & Prawitt, 2012). Bias can result in overconfidence and unwarranted optimism that can result in flawed risk assessments. Previously discussed groupthink can exacerbate bias leading to suboptimal decision making. Bias can influence decision makers, such as business executives, to seek confirmatory evidence rather than conducting an objective search that includes looking for information that might be inconsistent with their initial views and preferences (Glover & Prawitt, 2012).

Bias-inducing tendencies can lead even the brightest people to make suboptimal judgments due to overconfidence. Thus, confirmation bias may explain why highly intelligent, conscientious people might not always effectively assess risk management processes or why they might fail to recognize indicators that management is perpetuating fraud (Glover & Prawitt, 2012). The more confirmatory evidence that they are able to accumulate, the more confident decision makers become, however in many cases, we cannot know something to be true unless we explicitly consider how and why it may be false (Glover & Prawitt, 2012). Let us look at an example of how bias might impact the application of professional skepticism that auditors are supposed to exhibit. An auditor might harbor a bias toward people they have audited for years, thus they may attribute an implied credibility to management representations which potentially reduces their professional skepticism. In other words, because they trust what others tell them, they are more apt to accept their explanations to questions that are asked of them. This trust bias may manifest itself through an auditor's willingness to accept management representations about a given issue while ignoring stronger types of evidence that suggest one's belief is inaccurate.

The problem with this bias is that it can impact an auditor's ability to make good assessments about fraud symptom red flags that could be evident had an auditor relied on professional skepticism with more intensity

(Knapp & Knapp, 2012). Thus, if management records on their financial statements that they have a certain amount of inventory on hand, but the visual inspection of the inventory does not appear to support their representation, does our bias interfere with our professional skepticism, especially if they had been truthful in the past? Are we willing to overlook this discrepancy? Trust bias in this example would expedite the auditor's decision to accept management's representation as truthful and dilute the necessary professional skepticism to engage in due diligence and confirm representations through verification (Knapp & Knapp, 2012). Auditors might be lulled into a false sense of security and apply the "same as last year" conclusion without really looking at the facts that might disprove their conclusion especially if management offers an explanation that is not confirmed (Tsahuridu & Vandekerckhove, 2008).

In addition, auditors need to be aware of the fact that people tend to be truth biased which means there is tendency to judge messages as honest independent of the actual truthfulness of the message. Consider the insight of offender Vernon Beck, a former Director at Texas Petrochemicals, who embezzled $14 million from a $1.6 billion annual revenue petrochemical company. Vernon stated: "Anyone knows that when you do something wrong over and over, it gets easier. You become numb to the affects. We started out stealing a small amount of money each week, and it grew to over $160,000 each week, getting easier over time. The same can be said for cheating—it gets easier and more comfortable. You have to ask yourself, "where does it all end" (Crumbley & Beck, 2020, p. 448)? Moreover, consider the statement of an offender referencing an auditor's due diligence failure which also illustrates the impact of trust bias on professional skepticism:

> Initially, I wasn't surprised that we got away with it. Because it wasn't many entries and we were very careful. But by the end, I couldn't see how they couldn't detect anything. I spoke to the CFO and he said that if they, the auditors, did detect anything, he would say that we would get back to them. And he couldn't believe how they would accept even the flimsiest of possible excuse. A note was sufficient (Free & Murphy, 2015, p. 45).

In conclusion, bias makes us deviate from a norm or from a sense of rationality in our decision making whereby we make inferences about other people and situations that are irrational even though they may appear rational to us. Biases, however, may not even be obvious to the person or groups that harbor the bias which is why relying on biases can get people, groups, and ultimately organizations into trouble with the law because they end up creating their own sense of reality that may not be based on available facts or thoughtful analysis. Thus, we may think that we engaged in a rational choice, but our rational choice is distorted by bias which applies to both organizational and individual decision making. This is why different perspectives and interpretations are needed to shave down the negative consequences of bias.

Ethical Blindness Facilitating Misconduct

Ethical decisions are not always simple, they can be complex by nature. The notion that "it's easy to be ethical" assumes that individuals automatically know they are facing an ethical dilemma and that they should simply choose to do the right thing (Trevino & Brown, 2004). Moral judgment focuses on deciding what is right, not necessarily doing what is right. Even when people make the right decision, they may find it difficult to follow through and do what is right because they will be influenced by the words and actions of peers and leaders more than the consequences of their decision. This aspect of understanding the ethical impact of a decision appears to be absent from financial crimes, especially among people who are criminally liable for acts they believe they are innocent of in their own minds. Financial crime, at times, lacks the instantaneous feedback pertaining to the harmful consequences that may take months, even years, to manifest after the initial act (Soltes, 2016). Thus it is possible for those perpetrating the crime to not know that they are involved in a crime even though they may have an unsettling feeling that what they are doing is at a minimum unethical. In contrast, with street-level crimes, such as narcotics peddling or a robbery, it is more apparent that the person committing the crime immediately knows that they are committing a criminal act given that they behave in ways to avoid detection; there is no ambiguity as to the rightfulness or wrongfulness of the decision. Due to the delay between the act and the consequences, some have argued that white-collar crime lacks an emotional quality that would otherwise trigger a physiological response to criminal acts that would serve as a warning that the act is unacceptable (Soltes, 2016).

Let us look at some examples in which the harm of misconduct is not necessarily obvious nor is the gravity of the harm apparent to wrongdoers. Consider in 2015, regulators revealed that Volkswagen car makers illegally installed software in numerous diesel car models causing them to report artificially low emissions readings. In reality, the cars produced dangerous emissions closely linked to lung disease at levels up to forty times above emissions standards (Soltes, 2016). When researchers from the Massachusetts Institute of Technology (MIT) and Harvard teamed up to measure the effects of this additional pollution on public health, they estimated that the extra emissions were responsible for 59 early deaths. However, for those individuals who installed this deceptive software and for the executives who knew about its existence, the "true effects of this malfeasance are hidden: they will never know, or even be able to identify, the 59 people they killed" (p. 127). Moreover, in the case of Betty Vinson and her colleagues at WorldCom, the actual act of committing financial statement fraud appeared to them as a wrongful act, but at the same time they were not able to think in a holistic manner about the consequences, including how their actions would impact their lives and the lives of thousands of WorldCom employees and other stakeholders. People who are aware of their misconduct may even convince themselves that they are doing the right thing if they rely on rationalizations to support their behaviors, especially if rationalizations point to a higher moral purpose, such as supporting colleagues or helping their organization through a difficult time.

Furthermore, and especially in white-collar crime cases, there are many available rationalizations that allow one to morally distance themselves from their misconduct. Rationalizations are convenient for fraud offenders because so often their misconduct is commingled with legal activities that allow them to justify their behavior. It may be only later that fraud offenders fully realize the unethical and consequential dimension of their decision. This inability to fully appreciate that misconduct is taking place and its potential consequence is referred to ethical blindness. Ethical blindness is the decision maker's inability, perhaps temporarily, to see the ethical dimension at stake where people make decisions that are counter to their own values and without being aware of it where decent "people behave in pathological ways that are alien to their nature" (Palazzo et al., 2012, p. 325). People who have been sent to prison for fraud, such as Betty Vinson, realize later on that they strayed from their original value system to the point that they committed not just an unethical, but an illegal act.

People who are ethically blind may not be aware of the extent they deviate from their values or they cannot and do not access those ethical values when making a decision. What this means is that there is no deep thought as to weighing the potential moral, legal, and ethical implications of a decision because one's mind does not even access this aspect of decision making. For example, if Betty Vinson and Troy Normand felt uncomfortable from engaging in fraud, how much thought did they give to how far they would be willing deviate from their value system and for how long? In this case they were told by CFO Sullivan that it was a one-time accounting adjustment to help WorldCom. Did they imagine that they might be breaking the law and the consequences to themselves? Perhaps had they had a more complete understanding of the actual consequences of their actions, it is not unreasonable to believe that they may have made a better decision as to their participation in the fraud by not succumbing to CFO Sullivan's request (Palmer, 2012). People have difficulties seeing or imagining consequences that reveal themselves in the future impacting their well-being.

Some argue that ethical blindness thrives because people exhibit the lack of a moral imagination of the consequences of their decision (Arendt, 1963). Moral imagination involves whether a person has a sense of the variety of possibilities and moral consequences of their decisions, as well as the ability to imagine a set of possible solutions (Werhane, 1998). Yet for some, if they try imagining these consequences, they are so speculative and abstract that people cannot emotionally connect to them (Palazzo et al., 2012). Ethical blindness becomes even more of a problem due to the amount of time between the decision, acting on the decision, and the consequences of the decision. Although they may have the intellectual ability to understand what a crime is, they lack the ability to understand how their actions play themselves out to the point that their actions are criminal. Some acts are simply clear-cut for most people, such as the crime of sexual assault of children. It is a crime that resonates with most people, but fraud cases may take on a different complexion because offenders may not realize what specific acts that may feel unethical are actually illegal. Thus even doing a cost-benefit analysis is distorted because one may think they are unethical but not criminal, thus the ability to predict consequences of a decision is flawed. Another example illustrating ethical blindness and its relation to power and authority involves the famous 1971 Stanford Prison Experiment relating to the human response of power dynamics in a make-believe prison made up of guards and prisoners. Those assigned to play the role of guard were given sticks and sunglasses. Those assigned to play the prisoner role were forced to wear chains and prison garments, and transported to the basement of the Stanford psychology department, which had been converted into a makeshift jail.

Several of the guards became progressively more sadistic, particularly at night, but the experiment quickly got out of hand due to a riot breaking out on day two. After only six days out of a planned two weeks, the experiment was shut down, for fear that one of the prisoners would be seriously hurt. Although the intent of the experiment was to examine captivity, its results suggest how people react when placed in positions of authority and view their own conduct, perhaps imperfectly, illustrating this concept of ethical blindness. One of the guards taking part in the prison experiment later reported how he felt by the manner he treated the prisoners stating, "While I was doing it, I didn't feel any regret, I didn't feel any guilt. It was only afterwards, when I began to reflect on what I had done, that this behavior began to dawn on me" (Palazzo et al., 2012, p. 324). We observe these same reactions for those who are involved in atrocities. Consider the insights of a German policeman participating in genocide in Poland and Russia in the early 1940s who stated: "Truthfully I must say that at the time we didn't reflect about it at all…Only years later did any of us become truly conscious of what had happened then…Only later did it first occur to me that [it] had not been right" (Palazzo et al., 2012, p. 325). Thus, it is with hindsight they see that their decision was criminal or unethical, perhaps grudgingly recognizing their rationalizations were not valid to rely on such as "we were only following orders" to commit the atrocities. In addition, how people frame an issue contributes to ethical blindness. Framing is a way of defining and explaining a problem or an issue which influences how we evaluate and respond to it. The underlying analogy behind framing is that different perspectives are visible through different window frames even though it may be the same building (Glover & Prawitt, 2012).

Moreover, different views or frames can trigger how we respond to a perceived issue. Framing helps to communicate information and assists how individuals, groups, and societies organize, and communicate how they perceive reality. People use frames to help them make decisions, but how an individual or group frames an issue is important to how an issue and potential biases are resolved (Palmer, 2012). Different frames can lead to significantly different understandings or interpretations of a situation, and these different understandings and interpretations will affect behavior and decisions (Glover & Prawitt, 2012). Although framing is an important part of the process of resolving issues, framing can also facilitate the formation of rationalizations, reduce the range of legitimate arguments, and undermine the sensitivity to the moral values that could have been relevant to the decision in the first place (Palazzo et al., 2012). Note that ethical blindness may contribute to the perpetuation of misconduct, but it is not exclusively linked to framing; it is using a frame in a rigid manner that increases the risk of ethical blindness (Palazzo et al., 2012). Decision makers are likely to pursue unethical choices when they frame decision options in terms of loss avoidance (Palmer, 2012). When we craft an issue and frame it in our minds in terms of how can we avoid the problem of loss, such as making sure that profit targets are not jeopardized, people start to think of how to use misconduct to prevent the problem of profit loss from actually occurring. Consider an example where a CEO states that all that matters is meeting Wall Street expectations so that the company's stock price does not fall. There is great pressure to meet such expectations and the CEO tells employees they must do whatever it takes to meet these expectations. The way the CEO frames the problem can be interpreted as the means to justify the ends—whether ethical or not, it is the end result that matters not how we achieve the goal.

Consequently, it is irrelevant whether we are breaking the law, or not. The issue that needs to be resolved is did we meet Wall Street expectations at all costs. When we frame issues in such a narrow manner, we become blind to the additional responsibilities we have to others, the community, shareholders, employees, and clients thus creating a false picture of obligations we owe others but ignore (Duska et al., 2011). Ethical blindness can be enhanced by organizational routines. As a result of framing, doubtful business practices become normalized and habitualized through routinizations. For example, the importance of earnings forecasts places significant pressure on top management to engage in financial statement fraud. Management's focus on meeting earnings forecasts can blind them to the possibility that they could commit fraud (Murphy & Dacin, 2011). These initial processes appear to relate more directly to our work environment and lead to a lack of moral awareness. In other words, if we are situated in a work environment which tends to ignore ethical considerations in its decision making or consistently prioritizes the bottom line over ethical concerns, then we would likely be less inclined to be morally aware when facing a dilemma. This situation becomes more likely when amoral language is used during business operations and decision making. Managers tend to ignore moral language and frame morally-defined objectives in terms of 'organizational interests' and 'economic good sense.'

Consider the statement of convicted Qwest CEO Joseph Nacchio that exemplifies the above insights when a challenge is narrowly framed in financial terms: "The most important thing we do is meet our numbers. It's more important than any individual product, it's more important than any individual philosophy, it's more important than any individual cultural change we're making. We stop everything else when we don't make the numbers" (Thibodeau & Freier, 2014, p. 12). Former Enron CEO Jeffrey Skilling would reportedly say, "all that matters is money…Profits at all costs" (Sims & Brinkmann, 2003, p. 247). The bottom line emphasis at Enron contributed to each of these processes taking place including ethical fading, ethical blindness, and non-moral decision frames. This all led to a lack of moral awareness at Enron and, ultimately, misconduct at all levels of the organization. Competition between groups or teams over scarce resources, such as wealth or recognition, have repeatedly shown to give rise to unethical behavior that includes hostility toward other members and groups. Similar behaviors can be observed in the corporate world.

Organizations that promote aggressive competition are likely to support rigid world perceptions among their members by reinforcing the dominant use of a frame that divides the world into an "us versus them" scenario (Palazzo et al., 2012). As a result, organizations are willing to resort to fraud to "beat out the competition." Finally, time pressure is another powerful situational factor that affects decision making strategies. Given that decisions are often time sensitive, managers normally favor speed over accuracy when making sense of the world, which, in turn, might foster the use of more rigid frames because all that matters is that the deadline is met regardless the manner in which we meet the deadline (Palazzo et al., 2012). Thus it is not surprising that employees may overlook legal and compliance obligations to satisfy agendas. Powerful ideological beliefs, such as the virtue of the free market and related institutional practices, for example specific industry standards, can provide support for the rigid economic framing of a decision facilitating the rise of ethical blindness. Since there is a strong tendency to defend, protect, and apply the accepted norms and practices of one's society, actors living in a free market system, especially those who strive for a career in business, tend to perceive common business practices and market-driven procedures and outcomes as fair, legitimate, and morally just (Palazzo et al., 2012).

A strong anti-government and anti-regulation ideology can provide the frame and ultimately the justification for significant rule-breaking. As a result of the belief in the dominance of free market ideology, other ways of reasoning and other values are unlikely to be considered, even if they would be preferable on moral grounds; we end up suppressing alternative frames which emphasize a more balanced view. A key assumption of free market ideology is the strict separation of market activities from other social forms of interaction (Palazzo et al., 2012). They believe the market directs the behavior of free and self-interested individuals that automatically transforms their self-interest into a common good. It is thus unnecessary and even counterproductive, to apply criteria other than economic ones when making decisions in corporations. As a result, managers tend to amoralize even genuinely ethical topics, such as the sustainability practices of their corporation which may be corrupt because no one should tell them how to run their business (Palazzo et al., 2012). Recall the comments of Livent's executives as to their view of having outsiders, such as auditors, point out issues that relate to the company's financial statement that illustrates this view of sustainability practices. To facilitate its massive financial statement fraud, CEO Drabinsky and Livent's top executives displayed "a contemptuous attitude toward outside auditors" believing that it was "no one's business how they ran their company" (Knapp, 2009, p. 394).

Another concept related to a lack of moral awareness facilitating ethical blindness is the use of non-moral decision frames or what otherwise might be referred to as incomplete framing. This takes place when one focuses only on the economic implications of an issue rather than on the moral considerations, which can increase our chances of engaging in unethical behavior. The process of framing an issue in a non-moral manner leading to a lack of moral awareness can result in insufficient or biased information gathering, or constructing facts in a particular manner to suit our needs. For example, moral awareness can result from "moral attentiveness," which has been defined as the extent to which a person persistently perceives and considers morality and moral elements in their experiences (Reynolds, 2008, p. 1027). Similar to the notion of moral attentiveness, others have linked moral awareness to the concept of mindfulness, which is described as the awareness of an individual both internally, 1) awareness of their own thoughts, and externally, 2) awareness of what is happening in their environment. If rigid framing is a factor behind ethical blindness, flexible framing may be part of the solution. Decision making can be improved by considering the problem from the vantage point of multiple frames (Glover & Prawitt, 2012). Flexible framing reduces the risk of ethical blindness because it challenges mindless routines and promotes moral imagination that is an ability to imaginatively discern various possibilities for acting within a given situation. Through flexible framing, we envision the potential help and harm that are likely to result from a given action and understand that they cannot see certain aspects because of the frame(s) they use. The most effective cure for ethical blindness is an atmosphere of open and critical deliberation.

Ethical Fading and the Inevitable Slippery Slope

> We descend into hell by tiny steps.
>
> Charles Baudelaire

Corruption can be a slow process occurring over time and people who engage in fraudulent behavior ultimately find it is difficult to stop once the start (Beenen & Pinto, 2009). When people engage in questionable conduct that may be unethical, illegal, or socially irresponsible, the conduct can become normalized and, over time, people become desensitized to their behavior making it more likely that they will repeat it in the future. The perpetuation of these behaviors loosens those emotional constraints that stop the behavior from beginning in the first place or serve as a break to stop the behavior from continuing. However, when we engage in misconduct time and again, what we consider our morally acceptable benchmark triggers the rise of the proverbial "slippery slope" ultimately leading to ethical fading. What we considered wrong yesterday we redefine in our mind as acceptable conduct today, and if it is acceptable today, it is acceptable tomorrow. In other words, the reference point for today's decision is yesterday's decision; if today's misconduct just goes a bit further than yesterday's decision, the ethical compromise remains acceptable.

The overall progression toward a more unethical course of action goes unnoticed (Palazzo et al., 2012). People might view small steps of misconduct as insignificant ethical infractions, but acceptable because those steps seem to deviate only very little from what they perceive as the right thing to do. Ultimately this dynamic may lead into an escalation process where small transgressions spiral into more severe ones because the consequences of yesterday's actions become the preconditions of tomorrow's behaviors. This development takes place step-by-step, gradually over time where an individual cannot see the overall magnitude of the change that takes place. Especially within organizations, ethical fading may occur when decisions become more and more routinized and rigid until the organization is locked into a situation where only a considerably reduced range of decision making options is perceived as possible (Palazzo et al., 2012). As a result, options for doing the right thing become increasingly difficult because misconduct may require additional misconduct to keep the organization afloat. Moreover, people fail to notice minor infractions, especially when they occur gradually and with a negligible difference because minor infractions are interpreted as being insignificant.

Such a process of slow and incremental change can be understood as a sequence of small transgressions, as illustrated by a former Enron executive stated, "You did it once, it smelled bad...you did it again, it didn't smell as bad" (McLean & Elkind 2003, p. 128). Consider the statement of one fraud offender who embezzled more than $500,000 from a consulting firm through credit card fraud exemplifying ethical fading: "It wasn't a check for $500,000…it was a little bit here, a little bit there…It was an incremental descent into destruction" (Ramamoorti et al., 2013, p. 56). Recall the statement of one General Electric executive engaged in price-fixing with competitors stating that "it had become so common and gone on for so many years that I think we lost sight of the fact that it was illegal" (Gobert & Punch, 2007, p. 101). As another manager commented, "My ethical standards changed so gradually over the first five years of work that I hardly noticed it, but it was a great shock to suddenly realize what my feelings had been five years ago and how much they had changed (Ashforth & Anand, 2003, p. 31). It is precisely these linked decisions of misconduct and the consequences of such decisions that creep up on us that give rise to ethical fading and ultimately to unethical and potential illegal outcomes. Often those who step on to the slippery slope are management who oversee financial reporting and decide to violate an accounting principle or rule. The initial violation is small compared to the overall size of the fraud that is eventually detected.

Rationalizations surface when management and their accountants believe they are simply using their knowledge to manage earnings in a way that is helpful to the organization; they may label their accounting methodology as aggressive and not fraudulent. These mindsets are accompanied by expectations that their actions are a one-time event that will eventually be corrected when the economy or performance improves. The result is small fraudulent adjustments that may not appear to be problematic thus easier to rationalize, but several years later, the cumulative impact of small adjustments is simply not sustainable and ultimately leads to organizational meltdowns. Recall WorldCom accountants Betty Vinson and Troy Normand who initially reacted negatively when requested by their boss, CFO Scott Sullivan, to manipulate the financial statements in order to meet Wall Street earnings expectations. When Vinson and Normand attempted to resign, Sullivan discouraged resigning assuring them reporting false capitalizations entries were "one-time adjustments", however those one-time adjustments occurred over several years illustrating how the slippery slope becomes difficult to navigate and difficult, if not impossible, to reverse. Also, because wrongdoing often leads to small deviations from prior behavior, such evaluations are unlikely to cause as much anxiety for some people (Palmer, 2012).

In order for ethical fading to take place, people engage in self-deception through the use of euphemistic language such as aggressive accounting practices as opposed to being deceptive, borrowing company funds with the possible intention to return them rather than asset misappropriation, and other rationalizing techniques to protect themselves from their own unethical behavior. In addition, the rationalizations that accompany misconduct help people maintain their ethical identities and reduce the discomfort that some people feel when making unethical decisions. It may be difficult for wrongdoers, especially when they belong to a group, to acknowledge their own ethical fading because there are so many decisions they were able to rationalize away over a period of time, that collectively the decisions appear ethical. Also, ethical fading explains the gradual erosion of ethical standards because people are more likely to accept small deviations from ethical behavior that develop slowly over time than if ethical deviations are considered very significant and occur abruptly (Gino & Bazerman, 2009).

The consequence of misconduct may be the same whether it is achieved gradually over time through small ethical deviations or by fewer, but larger ethical deviations occurring more abruptly. Moreover, if an individual perceives the behavior of others as ethical, then a slight deviation of that perception by committing an unethical act does not alter one's perception that the person is still ethical. People can rationalize away such behaviors together with unconscious biases in how people view others which is that they are moral and good, especially if they know them. They also have a need to feel accepted by others and this need leads to conformity issues in that people may care less about the content of the decision, whether it is ethical versus unethical, than about the potential acceptance of the decision. People offer opinions that are likely to gain the favor of those to whom they believe they are accountable to despite the influence of ethical fading (Gino & Bazerman, 2009).

In addition, a deviant organizational culture might first reluctantly accept the wrongdoing, but then gradually, over time, internalize and even embrace the values and beliefs linked to the wrongdoing becoming numb to the fact that they engaged in misconduct. Eventually, the probability that people see ethical colors in their decision decreases and the risk of ethical fading increases. Employees must perceive formal policies going beyond mere window dressing to represent the real ethical culture of the organization; one that rewards ethical conduct and punishes unethical conduct (Trevino & Brown, 2004). Employees who believe top management acts ethically are much less likely to commit fraud versus those who believe that management only talks about ethics without exhibiting actions to support their words. Important ways to reduce the risk of ethical fading include, 1) schedule time to talk about the importance of ethics and inform them of ethics policies, 2) follow through with proper rewards and punishments as they relate to appropriate conduct, and 3) model ethical behavior from the top down (Mahadeo, 2006). Moreover, employees who observe peers acting ethically are more likely to act ethically, and those who observe peers engaging in misconduct are more prone to engage in misconduct themselves increasing the risk of falling prey to ethical fading and relying on rationalizations to justify their behaviors.

The Moral Ambiguity of Organizational Misconduct

In "the present moment, when the largest multinational corporations can be ranked in economic size alongside entire national economies, and where as in the U.S., they have been granted such rights as citizenship as to expand their influence on elections and public policy, both their potential for great public harm and the difficulties of controlling them have grown substantially" over time especially given the march towards globalization (Yeager, 2016, p. 643). We have observed this phenomenon especially in connection with the 2008 financial crisis associated with the mortgage lending industry and their lending practice abuses. While some corporations were assessed civil fines in the millions of dollars, the government did not pursue criminal penalties against large companies and their top executives. Some reasons offered included that their misconduct was too difficult and too costly to prove, while others argued that they were "too big to jail" (Yeager, 2016, p. 644). Whatever the source of a perceived selective non-enforcement, the consequence ranged from reduced deterrence to wide public perceptions of compromised justice and a reduced perceived legitimacy of the law. For some, the corporation and its agents were untouchable because they are proverbially, "above the law."

White-collar crime is "inextricably linked to legitimate economic activity and opportunities for white-collar crime expand or contract depending on the evolution of political-legal arrangements and the pendulum-like swings in cultural orientations that oscillate between belief in the efficacy of government regulation versus faith in the invisible hand of the free market" (Van Slyke et al., 2016, p. 13). Typically, there is a political element in terms of how much misconduct leading to white-collar crime political administrations are willing to tolerate as long as it does not stop economic progress that propels the system forward. What appears to drive this contradiction between what we ought to expect from corporations and how we react when they engage in misconduct? The practical challenges of controlling corporate misconduct are rooted in societal, cultural, and political beliefs; norms and values that eventually influence views about the relative role of economic markets and government in organizing and imposing rules on civil society. How much should government leave society to its own devices, including businesses? At the heart of regulation is the balancing of the above question.

For example, there was a time that children worked under dangerous conditions for centuries and in some countries this still occurs because it is deemed acceptable by local standards. At some point, at least to a certain degree in industrialized countries, there was a view that children should not be working in the same conditions that adults worked, thus there was a changing view that government intervention should prohibit and enforce child labor laws. In addition, there was a time when dumping toxins into water that people drank was considered a lawful business practice, and yet it was only a few decades ago that this activity was first criminalized in the 1970s. However, when there are laws to criminalize certain behaviors, ideological views on the proper boundaries between government and the private sector relating to the issue of corporate misconduct have trumped the enforcement of laws. Consider that while the public was supportive of new environmental laws demanded from the United States Congress, the outlawing of environmentally-detrimental practices was contested by companies since it would put their businesses at risk for closing, laying off employees, and government intrusion into the prerogatives of business and the free market.

Yet, important in the conversation about the relationship between government and business, when we speak of the "government" or the "state", how do we conceptualize these terms? The state is not a "thing" that possesses or concentrates power but a collection of institutions and processes that provide a basis for the organization of social forces (Rorie, 2020, p. 131). For example, schools, churches, and business organizations, as well as police forces and armies, are part of the ensemble that projects state power by providing leadership and guidance in the dominant morals and political ideas, or they contribute to the institutional ordering of a society. Generally speaking, one of the reasons for the constitutional separation of powers in liberal democracies is to ensure that the political system is not corrupted by particular interests and to make sure that private interests are not used to wield political power to expand their private agendas. Thus, the political sphere is supposed to represent the will of the people, whereas the private sphere is where individuals and institutions are supposed to pursue their own private interests. Although in principle the idea is admirable, liberal democracies do not operate according to those principles in practice at all times.

This is an observation that is not particular to Western liberal democracies or capitalist societies more generally; we can find these symbiotic relationships in China or the former Soviet Union. Regulatory collusions and failures occur where this constitutional segregation expected is compromised, for example when regulators fail to uphold the law because their close relationship with a company has weakened their enforcement strategy. Moreover, when we analyze state facilitated corporate misconduct, we are looking for a flaw in the system of regulation. In other words, we are compelled to look for a breakdown in the relationship between two, potentially antagonistic, parties, the state and the corporation. Yet, often there is no clear antagonism or opposition of interest in those relationships, since misconduct may occur as a result of commonly shared or mutual goals, but potentially for different motives. The corporation may engage in misconduct to maximize profits while the state needs to collect taxes and maintain social order, thus ignoring the misconduct that may harm others for what they perceive to be more pressing concerns. In some cases, state facilitated corporate crimes are the result of negligence or inactivity on the part of the states or their regulatory agencies in ways that collusively facilitate corporation misconduct that benefits the corporate and the state (Rorie, 2020, p. 133).

The ways that governments and private corporations interact raises the possibility that particular groups and institutions that are normally regarded as existing "outside" of the government can be used to enhance government power. Indeed, we can question the extent to which an institution or group can be considered to exist outside the state if there exists a symbiotic relationship between "public" and "private" sectors. The distinction between the private sector and a public sector is one that is defined in law. It is the formal definitions and powers prescribed in law, as well as custom, that decide which institutions are regarded as public and which are regarded as private. The state then mediates power relationships in society through key institutions such as the workplace, economic markets, and so on, and as such the state can be more usefully thought of as a complex of mechanisms and apparatuses that mediate and organize social relations of power. Corporations play a crucial role in this process. To say that private institutions are part of the state ensemble is not to say that they are under the autocratic control of governments or that their interests always coincide with those of the state because there can be real tension in terms of what regulators expect and what private business expects in terms of enforcement.

That being said, what do we really do when corporate misconduct is discovered given that corporations are also independent from the state? Are we actually going to hold organizations accountable by applying the law as it was intended which was to protect the public, or are we going to negotiate with corporate offenders by basically imposing a fine, which is essentially a tax on their misconduct, because corporations are a necessary component that supports the type of governmental system we have? In other words, modern day governments cannot exist without the benefits that corporations produce, thus will we have to put up with their misconduct as it arises if we want to receive their benefits? Corporate fraud is not absolutely disfavored given the number of rationalizations available that facilitates its existence; this is why white-collar crime for some is morally ambiguous. The ambiguity does not exist to the same extent with conventional, non-white-collar crimes, such as terrorism and sexual assault, where there is public condemnation with no exceptions for moral hesitation or equivocation. There are behaviors society views as evil refusing to tolerate rationalizations regardless of the offender's benefit to society. This type of behavior is discouraged with draconian punishments, such as sentencing homicide and terrorist offenders to many years in prison.

In terms of white-collar crime, although changing, the mindset is still one in which we are willing to engage in a cost-benefit analysis of whether the perceived benefits we received from the corporate offender justifies a criminal liability response to their misconduct. If criminal liability applies, what should the punishment be? We can rationalize their behaviors toward a higher good, such as producing jobs, even though they engaged in financial statement fraud that misled shareholders and investors, for example. Even the opinions of those in the judiciary reflect a double standard in punishment as it applies to white-collar offenders due to the perceived benefits the offenders bring to society which accentuates this moral ambiguity we have toward white-collar crime when compared to non-white-collar crime. Judges might "empathize with white-collar offenders at times" which explains why they receive lenient sentences (Wang & Cheng, 2016, p. 545). This further supports the perception that the criminal justice system and regulating agencies that could impose financial punishments are ineffective since people who are regulated are not punished in proportion to their misconduct in comparison to non-white-collar offenders.

Recall from chapter one that in 2013 a judge sentenced CEO Michael Peppel to seven days in jail for fraudulent financial statements, money laundering, and securities fraud that had caused his business to collapse, 1,300 employees to lose their jobs, and investors to lose eighteen million dollars. Yet, despite the damage Peppel had done, the judge stated that he was "not just a man, but a remarkable good man" (Gnau, 2013). The judge further noted that Peppel's lenient sentence was warranted given that he was now "involved in a business venture that is apparently a growing success and provides a very much needed service to a large number of people…[is a] talented business man, entrepreneur…that it would be wasteful for the government to spend taxpayers' money to incarcerate someone that has the ability to create for his country and economy" (Moore et al., 2013, p. 16). Could we envision a judge making such a statement and imposing a light prison sentence on rapists or terrorists because of the type of life they led before committing their nefarious acts? Yet, when it comes to white-collar crime, some in the judiciary are morally flexible in how punishment is imposed regardless of the harm suffered by innocent parties because of the perceived benefits these offenders somehow bestow upon society. Some people want government to regulate corporate behavior and some do not. Thus, when new administrations descend upon Washington D.C., their political ideology dictates whether or not laws will be vigorously enforced since they now represent the financial supporters who put them in office; they may not want government telling them what they can and cannot do.

Unless society vigorously denounces a particular behavior through outright public condemnation, then what is considered acceptable antisocial behavior worthy of tolerance will fluctuate with the political winds. Problems in protecting society from corporate harm have been with us since corporations were allowed to exist by governments. These problems stem from the power held by large companies while their organizational complexity and political might that comes from their resources are central to the functioning of modern governments. In the face of such power, law often proceeds cautiously, if at all, because the enforcers of the law fear the wrath of their political superiors who rely on the support of these corporations. Unfortunately, the consequences of not enforcing the law is a reduction in the legitimacy of the law, a reduction of faith in our institutions, and repeated waves of corporate offending. Because economic efficiency is king and corporate offenses that are committed in pursuit of larger goals that offer a competitive advantage, corporate penalties tend to be mild because government does not have to expend huge amounts of investigative and prosecutorial resources to impose some type of accountability. In some respect, it resembles the metaphor of the ledger rationalization discussed in chapter one. The corporation does produce a benefit for society and part of the cost of having that benefit is that we have to tolerate their misconduct to some degree. Imposing fines are not a sign of public condemnation, but reflect the cost-benefit analysis that governments made in having to impose some type of punishment to discourage misconduct, but not so punitive that it prevents governments from attaining the benefits of corporations.

The Political Accommodation of Corporate Misconduct

The corporation, on balance, is generally perceived as a positive social actor, and the interests of the corporate elite are projected as being beneficial to larger society; this common understanding, however, needs to be reconsidered with a more accurate interpretation of how corporate behaviors impact society. If the "endless list of high-profile corporate disasters shows us anything, it is that corporations can cause serious harm and will rationally choose to do harm if it means securing profits if the benefits outweigh the perceived risks" (Rorie, 2020, p. 497). Corporations and their executives can produce harm with relatively little fear of criminal justice scrutiny, and thus, evade accountability. The reality is, certain legal, political, economic conditions are only possible through government intervention, making corporate crime more probable. Close linkages between government and the corporate sector share mutual interest in maximizing economic productivity; the government-corporate symbiosis is an essential element of understanding the limits of controlling corporate crime (Rorie, 2020). The purpose of acknowledging this symbiotic relationship is not to dismiss current forms of corporate regulation, but to acknowledge their limitations.

We must moderate the notion that government polices corporations as traditionally understood as an independent body that enforces the law and instead focus on the ways that government intervenes in traditional market economies to ensure both of their mutual survival and what this means in terms of government's unwillingness or inability to properly regulate the modern corporation. Consider "states must always intervene in formally private institutions to guarantee their smooth functioning, in ways that seek to stabilize the social order, the state is therefore first and foremost a capitalist state with a vested interest in maximizing economic activity" (Rorie, 2020, p. 496). Ironically, the instinct is to protect key actors even when those being protected pose threats to our safety, and well-being. Thus, it is not surprising that scholar Edwin Sutherland observed decades ago that white-collar offenders from the upper-echelons of society were "segregated administratively from other criminals" in terms of how accountability applies to them versus non-white-collar crimes (Sutherland, 1940, p.8). It is this offender high social status and the respectability linked to it, often difficult to reconcile with their criminality that makes the white-collar crime concept so meaningful: the tension the concept radiates fits quite well for the corporate offender.

The "harmful actions committed by these 'respectable' people and/or organizations are bound to contradict and, even more, betray the social trust that is so vital…for the very fabric of society" (Rorie, 2020, p. 65). This is especially true when trust is placed upon people enjoying elite status, and upon the major political, corporate, and financial institutions they manage. The potential for harm is even more probable considering how the elite customarily express a "contempt for law, for government, and for governmental personnel," growing out of the fact that law is seen as a hindrance to their practices even though their misconduct is met without punishment (Sutherland 1983, p. 229). These characteristics, besides being essential features of white-collar and corporate crime, should also be deemed relevant in assessing their peculiar harmfulness, consisting in a damage to social relations and financial damage to which they lead. Actually, white-collar crimes, unlike most conventional crimes, whose effects on social institutions and social organization are generally negligible, "violate trust and therefore create distrust, which lowers social morale and produces social disorganization on a large scale" (Sutherland 1940, p. 5).

That being said, the government is highly dependent on the financial health of its economy to produce both tax revenue that runs the engines of government and the creation of employment that is necessary for political stability. Consequently, government is highly sensitive to signals from business as to the regulatory costs it will bear that impact economic growth and employment. If costs are too high, it forces industries to relocate to more relaxed regulatory environments, which leads to job and tax revenues lost, and ultimately impacts who retains political power. As a result, an environment exists where misconduct is not vigorously condemned coupled with a strained understanding and an uneasy tension existing between government and business. We observe government's willingness to tolerate a certain amount of corporate misconduct as long as the efficiency of the marketplace that has become the foundation of modern day, corporate democracy is not compromised. Yet government and business do not enjoy a frictionless relationship, especially when governments are charged with protecting the public. Tensions and inevitable collisions arise when harmful business behaviors are rejected by the public and government is asked to regulate or prohibit certain practices which impacts corporate profits (Ramirez, 2016).

However, even if the public is able to influence the political process in such a way that regulates corporate behavior to reduce the incidences of misconduct, a legal victory does not necessarily translate into an effective regulatory enforcement. The enforcement apparatus necessary to hold people and organizations accountable can be weakened by political forces that do not fund enforcement. Regulations can be tedious and expensive to enforce. The enforcement of such complexity is no small task because it requires government to support a criminal and civil justice system made up of an army of investigators, prosecutors, and judges who are capable of imposing the rule of law when necessary. Laws prohibiting corporate misconduct become impotent when white-collar crime law enforcement resources are reduced and regulations are diluted in the name of efficiency and regulatory relief to promote economic growth (Antar, 2008). Ironically, at times regulated organizations may be in a better position to understand the complexity of the regulations than the law makers who put them in place since they have the resources to acquire and employ a legion of lawyers and lobbyists to challenge the regulatory maze on the enforcers own turf.

Consider that regulatory agencies in place to monitor corporate behavior are subject to the will of the political party in power that controls their budgets. Thus, if the political party in power harbors an ideology that disfavors regulations, then regulations meant to curtail corporate misconduct becomes nothing more than a moral victory. The assertions of the public interest and moral force of the law are diluted when budgets that were earmarked for enforcement are reduced, and corporate misconduct is handled through quiet, behind closed door negotiations (Ramirez, 2016). The rigor of regulatory enforcement is also controlled by shifting political ideologies regardless of which political party has the dominant influence at any particular time. This dynamic signals the type of enforcement inconsistency in the law's purpose that undermines its moral force and deterrent effect. For example, in one large-scale study of corporate offenses, researchers found that government tends to be harsher on corporate misconduct such as securities fraud and antitrust violations as opposed to violations of labor, product, safety, and environmental infractions (Clinard et al., 1979). Large American corporations were not as apt to violate antitrust or securities laws as opposed to the other infractions listed above because of the harshness of the penalties. This pattern indicates that government is more sensitive to corporate misconduct that blatantly impacts the smooth function of corporate capitalism, namely competition and violations of trust that are necessary for a securities market to operate smoothly. It is less concerned about misconduct that does not blatantly undermine the immediate needs of the economy such as a labor violation.

For example, a significant investigative report found that between 2004 and 2009, business facilities, such as chemical factories and manufacturing plants, violated the nation's water pollution laws more than half a million times (Duhigg, 2009). According to the report, state and federal agency enforcement was routinely relaxed and, as a result, the nation's water did not meet public health and other clean water goals nearly forty years after the passage of major federal water pollution control laws (Duhigg, 2009). Consequently, consider the Flint, Michigan water contamination scandal which began in 2014 when the public water source was switched from treated Detroit water sourced from Lake Huron and the Detroit River to the Flint River. Officials failed to apply corrosion inhibitors to the water and, as a result, there was a series of problems that culminated with lead contamination. The Flint River water was treated improperly causing lead and elevated levels of heavy metal neurotoxins to seep into the water supply. In Flint, thousands of children were exposed to drinking water with high levels of lead and are experiencing a wide range of medical issues linked to lead poisoning. Over a dozen defendants have been charged with crimes ranging from involuntary manslaughter, water treatment violations, conspiracy, lying to law enforcement, tampering with evidence to official misconduct to name a few of the charges. Regardless of the political party, political ideologies impact the intensity of enforcement and thus the potential deterrence of corporate misconduct.

Both major political parties are involved in their own version of relaxing regulations for their political constituents in order to limit the enforcement of deterring corporate misconduct (Ramirez, 2016). For example, both the Reagan Republican administration and the Clinton Democratic administration views on financial institution deregulation contributed to the wave of financial fraud from the 1980s to the 2008 economic crisis (Ramirez, 2016). In one study of antitrust violations, between 1927 and 1981 companies were more likely to violate antitrust laws during Republican administrations in Washington D.C. as compared to Democratic ones (Simpson, 1986; 1987). Similarly, the high rates of water pollution offenses in the 2000s correlated with the particularly lax enforcement of environmental laws during the Republican administration of President George W. Bush from 2001 to 2008 (Duhigg, 2009). One water enforcement government manager stated, "There is now always attention that we did not have in the past to what are the political ramifications [of our cases]?, while an anonymous [Environmental Protection Attorney] EPA attorney said that, "[The Administration] is pro-energy and pro-industry...Every time they think they can weaken the regulations they do so. They are trying to relax everything in sight" (Yeager, 2016, p. 649).

In contrast, President Barrack Obama's Democratic administration had one of the lowest federal white-collar crime prosecutions in twenty years (Sirota, 2015). Intuitively one would think that a Democratic administration would lean more toward white-collar prosecutions given their philosophy toward equity in prosecution meaning it should not be just non-white-collar offenders that are prosecuted (Sirota, 2015). Consider how President Obama's Attorney General Eric Holder viewed white-collar prosecutions (Holder, 2014). First, Holder wrote a memo during President Clinton's Democratic administration where he voiced his concern and recommended that prosecutors consider the "collateral consequences, including disproportionate harm to shareholders and employees not proven to be personally culpable" before attempting to convict corporations for wrongdoing (Sirota, 2015). In a statement given in 2013 to the Senate Judiciary Committee about the adverse effects of convicting a corporation of a crime, Holder stated, "I am concerned that the size of some of these institutions becomes so large that it does become difficult for us to prosecute them when we are hit with indications that if we do prosecute—if we do bring a criminal charge—it will have a negative impact on the national economy, perhaps even the world economy" (Henning, 2014).

Does Holder's opinion reflect the preservation of the moral ambiguity of white-collar crimes mentioned in the preface of the book where a cost-benefit analysis is applied to this crime classification that is not observed in non-white-collar offenses? Observe how the prosecution can unintentionally mask a political advantage by not pursuing corrupt corporations by advancing an economic explanation that has a certain amount of appeal because the focus is on the collateral damage that a prosecution would have on the employees, shareholders, and other stakeholders and not on the underlying misconduct. This is not to state Holder does not believe that collateral damage is not real. However, when we hear prosecutors speak of collateral damage, consider a wide-horizons perspective of what they mean so that we have a more sober understanding of why corporations are not held accountable even though the evidence is available for a successful prosecution (Watch, 2014). Such damage might reflect a potential loss in jobs, economic growth, lower tax revenue to fill government coffers, and potential political implications for an administration in office, be it national or local.

These administrations are at risk for being voted out by the voices who were hurt by the prosecution of the organization they worked for, but for many who had nothing to do with the corruption in the first place. The reality is, there is a political component to prosecution that may not be apparent to the overall public. Behind the scenes, decisions have to be made about whether to hold financially powerful people and their organizations accountable no differently than street-level offenders. However, the factors that go into the decision to prosecute are different and some would say unfair because of the perception that some are "above the law" because of who they are. Is this perception wrong? Holder also complained that "the buck stops nowhere" when a corporation violates the law because "responsibility remains so diffuse, and top executives so insulated, that any misconduct could, again, be considered more a symptom of the institution's culture than a result of the willful action of any single individual" (Henning, 2014). In some respect, Holder's views parallel those of Hannah Arendt who stated, bureaucracy is "rule by no one" where pinpointing the exact culprit is not easy (Perri, 2013b, p. 338). Given Holder's view on individual prosecution of white-collar offenders, how many corporations, executives, CFOs, CEOs, and others can we think of who were held criminally liable for the financial crisis of 2008 resulting from the banking scandals that facilitated the mortgage fraud schemes originating from Wall Street?

What message did Holder send to those organizations about the risk of being caught and prosecuted for the misconduct? Now with Republican President Donald Trump in office, perhaps a different tone may be set, although it is too early to assess. According to his former deputy attorney general Rod Rosenstein: "Corporations, of course, don't go to prison. They do pay fines. The issue is: can you effectively deter corporate crime by prosecuting corporations or do you, in some circumstances, need to prosecute individuals? [Mr. Rosenstein answered]—I think you do" (Lynch, 2017). It is not surprising that like other regulatory agencies, they tend to focus on the amount of money they collect in fines from organizations to show how successful their prosecutions are even though corporations are rarely prosecuted and people are not necessarily held accountable. Although such achievements are laudable and should be pursued, does taxing misconduct through fines actually achieve any deterrent effect when the amount of fines relative to the billions these corporation collect in revenue is a negligible amount? Thus, under Holder's tenure, JP Morgan Chase paid $13 billion and Bank of America paid $16.65 billion in fines for their roles in issuing mortgage-backed securities tied to faulty subprime loans (Henning, 2014). BNP Paribus paid close to $9 billion fine for violating economic sanctions laws, however in a rare event, they were required to enter a plea of guilty for a criminal charge (Henning, 2014). No individual at BNP was prosecuted for any wrongdoing.

Consider the London-based banking group HSBC with 4,000 offices in 70 countries and some 40 million customers. In the summer of 2012, the U.S. Senate released a report following an investigation of HSBC. According to the report, the bank laundered billions of dollars for Mexican drug cartels and violated sanctions by covertly doing business with corrupt governments (Keefe, 2017). Specifically, Mexico's Sinaloa organized crime cartel, which is responsible for tens of thousands of murders, deposited so much drug money in the bank that the cartel designed special cash boxes to fit HSBC's teller windows. On a law enforcement wiretap, one drug lord raved about the bank as "the place to launder money" (Keefe, 2017). In addition, HSBC helped a Saudi Arabian bank with links to al-Qaeda transfer money into the United States. Some officials in the U.S. Department of Justice wanted to criminally charge HSBC, however according to e-mails found by a congressional investigation, Britain's Chancellor of the Exchequer George Osborne warned U.S. authorities that a prosecution could lead to "very serious implications for financial and economic stability" (Keefe, 2017). HSBC was granted a deferred prosecution agreement due to the fears of the collateral consequences of prosecuting HSBC for money laundering.

A deferred prosecution agreement (DPA) is a voluntary alternative to a full-blown prosecution that could result in criminal accountability in which a prosecutor agrees not to pursue a criminal conviction in exchange for the defendant agreeing to fulfill certain requirements such as restructuring their internal controls to prevent and detect fraud coupled with a change with the 'tone at the top' and a more rigorous compliance program. Thus, deferred prosecutions are the threat of criminal liability and as long as agreements are upheld, the people and the corporation are not prosecuted. A case of corporate fraud, for instance, might be settled by means of a deferred prosecution agreement in which the defendant agrees to pay fines, implement corporate reforms, and fully cooperate with the investigation. Fulfillment of the specified requirements will then result in dismissal of the charges. HSBC executives were summoned to Washington, D.C., and the bank's CEO, Stuart Gulliver, said that he was "profoundly sorry" (Keefe, 2017). It is one argument to state that the collateral consequences of prosecuting corporations affect parties such as employees who may be innocent of wrongdoing, but is that enough of a reason not to prosecute corporations?

However, U.S. District Court Judge Jed Rakoff questioned the fairness of having corporations get the benefit of not having to admit wrongdoing as long as they pay a fine with no one being held criminally liable (Carozza, 2016). Many organizations receive lenient sentences by paying fines as stated by Judge Rakoff, "it's management buying its way off cheap, from the pockets of their victims" (Taibbi, 2011). In addition, Judge Rakoff found no proof that prosecuting individuals who facilitated crimes triggers an economic fallout creating undeserved collateral damage and, in many of these deferred prosecutions, no one is held criminally liable and punished for their misconduct. Judge Rakoff points to the successful prosecutions of high level executives from Enron and WorldCom as examples of the importance of holding individuals criminally liable for behaviors that do, in fact, impact the lives of employees, shareholders, and communities (Taibbi, 2011). It is true that the prosecution of these individuals may be time consuming, but there is also the issue of how inequitable the criminal justice system is perceived when people from lower socioeconomic levels of society are prosecuted and punished for street-level offenses. In contrast, offenders who occupy powerful positions in society somehow are able to escape accountability because their prosecutions are more time consuming and expensive.

In the end, no political administration is clean because misconduct is accommodated for the perceived greater good of economic growth, employment opportunities, and political stability. The reality is governments need to promote economic development may, to some extent, override their responsibility for protecting the public. Some question the fairness of this approach in that corporations avoid the stigma of a criminal conviction and whether there is any real deterrence when in the end all they do is pay a fine that is negligible in comparison to their revenues. There are few prosecutions of corporations such as Arthur Andersen. In order to save time and money, civil and criminal prosecutors will resort to these types of accommodations to resolve misconduct. Prosecutors may believe they are able to achieve the same if not better results through this manner of prosecution where there is less resistance from corporations, a smaller impact on the innocent parties within a corporation, financial costs in the form of fines due to misconduct, and those who may deserve criminal prosecution are held accountable in less draconian ways. For example, Goldman Sachs agreed to pay $550 million to settle federal charges that it misled investors regarding their subprime mortgage product. This fine amounted to a fraction of the previous year's profit of $13.39 billion and its stock price rose 5 percent after the settlement was disclosed (Yeager, 2016, p. 655). Similarly, when the pharmaceutical giant Glaxo-Smith-Kline settled a federal prosecution in 2011 for a $3 billion fine, its stock price rose 3 percent (Yeager, 2016, p. 655). Was there any reputational penalty imposed or a stigma that accompanies a criminal sanction? Was there real deterrence to future misconduct? Can we name one executive who was personally held criminally accountable?

Furthermore, the political apparatus accommodates misconduct by underfunding or understaffing regulatory agencies further undermining their effectiveness (Ramirez, 2016). Legislators can effectively prevent the oversight of financial markets by withholding the funding necessary to effectuate the mission of regulatory agencies. This change may result from lobbyist pressures who desire to see a certain regulation removed or not vigorously enforced. For example, as early as 2004, the Federal Bureau of Investigations (FBI) requested additional funds to investigate the burgeoning number of mortgage-fraud related complaints. However, FBI personnel were shifted from white-collar crime investigations to national security investigations after the September 11, 2001 terrorist attacks which practically means offenders are free to do what they want more often. The "revolving door—and the support of powerful members of both political parties with financial favors—creates a sympathetic cartel of actors eager to distract the general public from the misconduct for the few by redirecting the focus for the American public to external risks" such as shifting resources from investigating fraud to protecting our physical security from terrorism which is also important (Ramirez, 2016, p. 493). From 2001 through 2007, the number of cases against financial institutions decreased 48 percent, from 2,435 cases during that period to 1,257 cases, while the number of FBI investigators working on white-collar crime cases decreased by 35 percent (Ramirez, 2016, p. 489).

Moreover, in the wake of Enron and other corporate scandals, the Department of Justice (DOJ) created the Corporate Fraud Task Force to address the massive accounting frauds, but the task force lacked its own prosecutorial staff or budget, and no additional staff or money was given to the U.S. Attorney's Office to pursue corporate crime. Consider, that even with budgetary issues, the department obtained convictions or guilty pleas from at least 214 former CEOs and presidents, 53 CFOs, and 129 vice presidents (DOJ, 2007). Yet, with the increase in successful prosecutions that followed holding CEOs, CFOs, and other executives criminally accountable, the White House and the Treasury Department "expressed concern that the pursuit of corporate criminality demonstrated an antibusiness attitude that could chill corporate risk-taking; major fraud cases dropped significantly after 2005" (Ramirez, 2016, p. 491). For example, in relation to the Securities and Exchange Commission (SEC), from 2005 through 2012, their budget was flat or declining and its failure to investigate credible reports of fraud in the securities industry together with its failure to provide effective market oversight contributed to the financial markets collapse in 2008 (Ramirez, 2016). What was observable in relation to the SEC was that they were, 1) resolving fraud civilly without requiring admission of wrongdoing or with fines substantially below reasonable amounts based upon the seriousness of the violations, 2) failing to refer cases of known criminal conduct for criminal prosecution to the U.S. Department of Justice, and 3) accepting plea deals that grossly understate the criminal responsibility and harm, which created the appearance that government superficially and selectively enforces the rule of law (Ramirez, 2016).

Judge Rakoff criticized the SEC's practice of agreeing to plea arrangements because the wrongdoers did not have to admit that they violated securities law especially when the SEC found them in violation multiple times in the past (Ramirez, 2016). The SEC states that they must resolve cases in this manner because they do not have the resources to bring fraud cases to trial, however some courts have accepted agreements only if the wrongdoer admits to accepting responsibility for their violation. Others have argued that the criminal justice system favors those who make the rules and this observation is not entirely without merit. In regard to white-collar crime, credible oversight means that potential offenders are aware that there is significant probability illegal behavior will be detected by regulators, law enforcement, or employees. A "widely accepted rationale for conducting oversight of white-collar crime, in general, is that oversight ensures that rules and regulations regarding white-collar crime are appropriately, effectively, and efficiently developed and implemented to prevent, detect, punish, and deter such crime" (Wang & Cheng, 2016, p. 544). The credibility of oversight can be defined as the degree to which the oversight commitments are implemented. Credibility means that the law and the operations of oversight agents dealing with white-collar crime are competent, trustworthy, appropriate, and effective. Therefore, oversight credibility must be understood in relation to public confidence which requires that the public perceive the law as being effective. When the public does not perceive that those who are put in charge of protecting the nation's wealth are treated differently, simply because of their socioeconomic status, the public looses faith in the belief that people are treated equally in society regardless of their socioeconomic position.

Organizational Culture Facilitating Moral Ambiguity

Organizational cultures can also contribute to the lack of moral clarity in relation to misconduct. For example, organizational cultures in which discussion of ethical problems is explicitly and implicitly discouraged often occurs when top management places high performance expectations on subordinates who believe that they cannot communicate back to management any difficulties they may experience in attaining such goals for fear they will be viewed as incompetent (Van Slyke et al., 2016). Where this dynamic exists, the moral imperative of the law and perceived risks of punishment are diluted to the extent that those involved no longer believe they are responsible for the offenses and ultimately rely on rationalizations that were discussed in chapters one and four. When top management claims ignorance to misconduct and subordinates believe they had no choice but to obey authority and carry out misconduct if they want to survive, it becomes difficult for regulators to squarely pinpoint who the responsible parties are. There are many buffers between top management who ordered the misconduct and those subordinates who carried out the misconduct. As a result, for both top management and the subordinates, deterrence of the law and restraints of conscience are diluted which further facilitates the rise of moral ambiguity (Yeager, 2016). It is not surprising that such crimes are considered victimless when multiple parties with their own antisocial attitudes and rationalizations contribute, perhaps in a small but culpable way, to a larger misdeed.

Additionally, there is often a time-lag between when a misdeed occurs and when others suffer the consequences further contributing to the moral ambiguity of white-collar crime. In other words, because the harm is not instantaneous with the offending act, the harm is not as apparent to others which further reinforces the attractiveness of rationalizations. In this sense, offenses take on the character of victimless offenses which further neutralizes the moral force of law. Consider the insights of one researcher that illustrates this moral ambiguity commenting on the 2008 economic crisis that resulted from the buying and selling of financial instruments where many people in the industry, including the leaders of the firms that bought and sold these instruments, did not understand the implications of their actions: "The victimization was abstract in the sense that corporate officials, dealing long distances with intangible investment vehicles and absentee customers rather than local customers purchasing tangible products, could not easily perceive real victims and moral harm. These characteristics of the market facilitated the crimes by reducing the role of conscience in them (Yeager, 2016, p. 652).

Conclusion

There are many challenges present in overcoming organizational misconduct and the ones presented within this chapter represent some of them. Groupthink is a phenomenon to be aware of especially when specific symptoms start to surface. Some of the symptoms include illusions of invulnerability, individual self-censorship where one does not voice their opinion that may be contrary to the group's position, pressure for group conformity, and collective rationalizations. Understanding group dynamics is crucial because the negative by-product includes making poor decisions that expose groups and its members to criminal prosecutions. Moreover, if we lack the courage to speak up about wrongdoing, it is possible that groupthink is present. A lack of courage may be the red flag that prompts us to consider that fraud may be the by-product of not wanting to discuss sensitive issues that involve organizational misconduct. Is there evidence of group dynamics rejecting relevant information, do group members criticize others for wanting to engage in thoughtful discussions about risks attached to a decision, are alternative approaches to a problem considered, and is a group willing to consider contingency plans in the event the first alternative approach to problem solving fails?

In addition, it is important to understand how one views authority since people who would normally not engage in misconduct often do so because of their relationship to authority. Understanding one's relationship to authoritative figures is important because many people have been found criminally liable for fraud due to obeying management's orders to commit an illegal act. Furthermore, it is not uncommon for people to be exposed to workplace bullying that can facilitate fraudulent behavior. Often this type of behavior is tied to peoples' disordered personalities, thus it is important to not dismiss destructive traits as personality quirks. They must be taken seriously especially when inappropriate behaviors are displayed. Also, studies on organization misconduct focus on leadership and authoritative figures and not as much as the people leaders rely on to carry out the misconduct they ordered.

Yet equally important are the subordinates who participate in misconduct given that organizational misconduct in particular usually entails co-offending. What kind of followers are they? Are they authoritarians who believe that the one who has legitimate power makes them right in terms of what they ask of subordinates? Do they represent opportunists who obey orders because they see something in it for them whether what is being asked of them is legitimate or not? Corruption can be a slow process occurring over time, thus we must be aware of the potential for ethical fading. Often changes are so slow that we cannot notice how our own reaction to a situation changes over time. The proverbial "slippery slope" does exist and it gets people into trouble. Perhaps one should ask themselves if they have compromised their integrity in small ways over time. Do decisions that were acceptable in the past appear acceptable today? If so why? What has changed to make moral compromises acceptable? Did we rely on rationalizations unacceptable to us in the past?

Lastly, we need to recognize that there is a political element to crime in that as much as we would like to believe that all who are caught engaging in criminal behavior will be prosecuted equally, it is simply not the case. Although no citizens are supposed to be above the law, there are some who are more privileged and do escape criminal liability. This prompts the question, is government willing to devote resources to the prosecution of white-collar offenders, or do we engage in a cost-benefit analysis and determine that white-collar offenders' contributions to society off-set the corruption they engage in?

Chapter 9

Mitigation of Corporate Fraud

Bunatine Greenhouse rose to become the highest ranking civilian at the U.S. Army Corps of Engineers (Corps). In 1997 the Corps' commander, Lieutenant General Joe Ballard, hired Greenhouse to be the principal assistant responsible for overseeing $23 billion worth of contracting coupled with addressing an entrenched "good old boys" corrupt contracting culture in the government (Carozza, 2006). Improper contracting practices were the norm and her job was to bring fairness and integrity into the Corps' contracting process. Greenhouse encountered opposition from those within the Corps and bidders who wanted the contracts, but she still enjoyed Ballard's support and for three years received the highest possible performance reviews. Contracting oversight for Greenhouse became strained as the build-up to the Iraq War led to the improper awarding of billions of dollars of no-bid, no-compete contracts to Halliburton Corporation that were in conflict with contracting guidelines.

Greenhouse protested that the Corps gave Halliburton a no-bid, sole-source emergency contract to provide services in Iraq for two and possibly five years. She believed that the contract should be limited to one year in addition to her observations of unjustified overcharges by Halliburton. When Ballard retired in 2000, Greenhouse stated, "the new command was poised to return to the good old days when contracts were awarded based on relationships commanders had with the industrial community" (Carozza, 2006). The new commander replacing Ballard indicated that Greenhouse's performance was exceptional and gave her a Level 1 rating, the highest rating a civilian senior executive service employee could achieve, but the next performance review proposed a Level 5, a failing rating. Eventually the new commander gave her a letter stating she would be removed from her position and demoted even though she believed that government business must be conducted in a manner that is impartial, nonpreferential, and above reproach (Carozza, 2006). Greenhouse was never accused of having engaged in any act of impropriety to deserve such a low performance review where she further stated:

> Let there be no mistake, I was downgraded in performance and removed because I did my job too well. Indeed, at the point in time I was removed from my position and demoted. My removal from office continues to have a chilling effect on the government contracting community. I voiced strong objections to the contract abuse I witnessed in the ramp-up to the Iraq War and questioned the award of billions of dollars in no-bid, cost-plus contracts….publicly testifying about the contract abuse I witnessed cost me my career…because I failed to support the cronyism and the good old boys' mentality that remains a considerable force in Army contracting. I thought of myself as just someone who was trying to do my job to the best of my ability, giving every fiber of my being to protect the public trust and making sure that at all times that the nation and our war fighters were getting the best value for the goods and services that would get them to the battlefield and provide them the facility to fight and to win. That's a contribution that I was able to make as a civilian leader in the business of contracting and that made me proud that I had the privilege to serve in a way that truly made a difference…Regardless of the consequences, I am proud to be called a whistle-blower and I am proud to have the courage to be loyal to the truth. Integrity in government is not an option, it is an imperative (Carozza, 2006).

What happens to those dissenting voices who actually want to confront misconduct? Do we embrace people who are whistleblowers when they are, unfortunately, demonized by the very organizations that should exalt their integrity? This chapter will address the issue of whistleblowing because when used properly and whistleblowers are treated fairly without fear of retaliation, it can mitigate the risk of organizational misconduct. The problem is that as we can see from Greenhouse's experience and others that we will read about in this chapter, being a whistleblower is not a pleasant experience and it can take years for someone that is a whistleblower to satisfy their sense of justice, if at all. The irony is whistleblowers are trying to do the right thing, yet corporate leadership turns against them. At times we harbor misperceptions about how integrity is viewed by those at the top of the organizational hierarchy. We erroneously believe that by coming forward and exposing misconduct, the whistleblower will be thanked for its exposure. Unfortunately this is not always the case because the misconduct may have originated at the top or perhaps condoned by top management even though the misconduct originated at the subordinate level. We examine factors a professional should consider as to whether to blow the whistle or not once they detect misconduct. Moreover an area that has garnered support to mitigate against misconduct is for organizations to engage in better hiring practices.

Too often employers, which includes the personnel in charge of hiring, attach character attributes to candidates they prefer that may not be accurate. We hear hiring personnel claim to have a "gut feeling" about a candidate that tells them that they would be a good fit. However that gut feeling may be inaccurate and we may end up missing detecting antisocial character traits hidden within a person. By having employee candidates complete integrity or also called honesty assessments, such assessments can help identify candidates that may harbor antisocial thinking tendencies studied in chapter one and disordered personalities. Hiring honest people is not fool proof, but we can reduce the risk of hiring people with low integrity. For example, even if we could verify all information on an applicant's resume, train management to conduct skillful interviews, and require applicants to affirm the truth as to the matters contained on their resume, an organization can still hire individuals prone to engaging in white-collar crimes. We need more than just background checks and interviews to find the right people to employ. Consider the example of what occurs when we engage in poor screening of an employee, especially one that has access to information facilitating fraud:

A controller defrauded his company of several million dollars and when he was investigated, it was discovered that he had been fired from three of his previous five jobs all within eight years. The offender was discovered when the CEO came to the office one night and found a stranger working in the accounting area. The nocturnal stranger turned out to be the phantom controller who was actually doing the work of the hired "corporate controller", who wasn't even trained in accounting (Albrecht et al., 2012, p. 106).

Furthermore, it is important to understand the legal concept of 'state of mind' as it applies to fraud offenders because so often students learning about fraud issues and antifraud professionals have an incomplete understanding of the concept potentially impacting how they eventually perform their job duties. State of mind refers to a person's awareness of the fact that his or her actions or inactions are criminal. Thus it is not just what they do or do not do that is criminal, but that their mental state also has to be guilty of the act. As an example, was the act an accident or was it intentional. Did we get into a car crash by accident or were we trying to deliberately hurt someone by running into them with a car? Proving state of mind by the surrounding facts of a case is a necessary element of a successful prosecution in order to hold someone criminally accountable for their actions or inaction. Frequently people who engage in fraud distort the legal definition of state of mind in order to enhance the credibility of their rationalizations to neutralize their mental state. For example, we often hear offenders talk about how they never intended to commit fraud because they were going to put the money back in the future or we hear corporate executives claim that they never intended to commit financial statement fraud because they were just trying to save the company from a slow economic period. On its surface, these explanations sound appealing until we more fully understand the legal principles that can be used to hold someone accountable for fraud. Part of the problem of why the concept of state of mind is narrowly understood lies in how fraud is typically presented in textbooks.

Fraud is commonly defined as the intentional misrepresentation to deceive another for monetary gain through providing false information or through omission which is withholding information. Fraud in this definition revolves around the word 'intentional' or 'intent' to deceive for financial gain. Intent from a legal perspective generally refers to acting in a purposeful manner to accomplish a goal which in this case is fraud. This definition of fraud is not incorrect, but it is not complete neither from a legal perspective nor instructive for those that study fraud issues and its offenders from an accounting, investigative, or academic perspective. How we understand the legal concept of state of mind not only influences how we interpret the rationalizations offenders offer, but it can impact us both personally and professionally. From a personal perspective, if we hold an incomplete understanding of the state of mind concept, we can expose ourselves to criminal liability. For example, some offenders who may be merely office workers with no criminal histories state that they were just following orders from management to commit financial statement fraud—it was never their intent to engage in it but for being ordered to. What this subordinate does not understand is that the prosecution has other states of mind available in their prosecutorial arsenal to hold them accountable and not just the state of mind of intent. Also, not understanding the legal concept can influence how we conduct investigations especially interviewing potential fraud offenders.

Are we not as thorough in our interviewing because we accepted the offender's explanation that they never intended to steal from their employer, thus ending the interview of how they actually went about taking the money? The law constructed different states of mind in order to accommodate the many different factual scenarios prosecutors will face when attempting to hold an offender accountable for their fraud crimes. If the law did not have different types of states of mind, the logical conclusion would be that fraud offenders could escape prosecution simply by stating that they never had the intent to commit fraud because they had valid rationalizations for committing the acts in the first place. We will learn to understand this concept in a more holistic manner by bringing the different types of states of mind into the conversation which have the effect of neutralizing fraud offender rationalizations. Moreover examining the importance of improving our decision making processes and promoting ethical awareness within an organizational setting can assist in reducing the risk of misconduct. First of all, people would like to believe that they engage in rational, ethical decision making, yet there is substantial literature based on empirical research that suggests otherwise. Individuals may lack the awareness to engage in moral judgment and actually make decisions that are counter to their values and principles (Chugh et al., 2005). In other words, peoples' ethical mindset comes with limits regardless of one's desire to be ethical due to impediments to decision making such as biases, groupthink, obedience to authority, ethical blindness, and ethical fading (Prentice, 2014).

Biased judgment or obedience to authority, as examples, does not justify or excuse criminal or unethical conduct, but it may explain why the deterrence model of criminal law of imposing punishments does not always deter future criminal conduct especially when people do not even know that they are committing a criminal act. It is not until later on when problems surface due to their behavior that criminal liability becomes a reality for people to deal with and it is no defense to state that there was no time to think of the consequences of a decision because the business world operates on such a fast pace today than in the past or that one is simply following orders. Decisions are more complex today which further necessitates being more surgical in our decision making approach. Unfortunately when the realization takes root that misconduct actually took place, the overconfident person may, albeit erroneously, decide to continue the self-deception in the hope that the crisis will pass which only further exposes a guilty state of mind (Moorh, 2003). We examine how to approach better decision making that can reduce misconduct and also lead to a more ethical organizational environment. Yet the question becomes, can we become better decision makers if corporate leadership has no interest in listening to what other senior executives and subordinates who do want to do the right thing think because their personality structure does not allow for dissenting opinions to be tolerated? Can we promote ethical awareness if ethical leadership is not promoted to influence the tone at the top?

Moreover, qualities of what constitutes ethical leadership are outlined in addition to the value of instituting ethics programs and the role that an individual's moral identity plays in reducing the temptation to engage in misconduct. Also, it is important to understand how the possibility of holding the organization criminally liable can act as a deterrent to engaging in misconduct. Pivotal is examining some of the factors prosecutors consider to determine whether to hold the organization itself liable for the actions of the individuals who caused the crime to occur in the first place. Too often people do not think that corporations can be held legally liable because it does not have the characteristics of a natural, living person. However this perception is incorrect. The impact of holding a corporation criminally and civilly liable can have massive implications for the corporation's employees who can lose their livelihoods if there organization is prosecuted. One only has to observe the impact of prosecuting Arthur Andersen had on its employees who were permanently terminated by the thousands. How does the prosecution of a corporation qualify as a way to mitigate misconduct?

Consider the corporation employs millions of people and these same people may have devoted their lives to building the business and its reputation will have an incentive to make sure that the corporation maintains its integrity. Consequently, prosecutors do look at the role the corporation played in fraudulent misconduct to determine whether the corporation shall too be prosecuted together with those fraud offenders who actually perpetrated the fraud. Understanding what factors prosecutors use can make corporate employees more vigilant in making sure that if personnel strive for an organization that is virtuous through its tone at the top and its antifraud policies are taken seriously, the likelihood their organization will face a prosecution, both civil and criminal in nature, will hopefully decline.

Whistleblowing: Public Heroes and Organizational Villains

Our lives begin to end when we become silent about things that matter.

Martin Luther King, Jr.

When we speak of whistleblowing, there is usually not one definitive definition of what it entails although it characterizes the practice as disclosing to others inside or outside an organization an act that violates organizational norms or the law. One broad definition states that whistleblowing is the "disclosure by organization members, former or current, of illegal, immoral, or illegitimate practices under the control of their employers to persons or organizations that may be able to effect action" (Mintz & Morris, 2017, p. 154). The definition includes those that blow the whistle internally and those that are external whistleblowers who report misconduct to a regulatory agency such as the Securities and Exchange Commission (SEC). The method of disclosure used can include using a hotline or to an actual person within an organization or external to the organization. More often than not, scandals occur in corporations because an inner circle of those at the top of the management hierarchy perpetrated and benefited from the fraud were reluctant to object to the fraud while whistleblowers that cared about the corporation did not fare well (Frankel, 2008-2009). Employees who whistleblow are loyal to the organization and would rather have misconduct resolved internally than go outside the organization (Miceli et al., 2009).

Whistleblowers are routinely punished by their employers even as they are lauded by the general public— hence they are villains and heroes all at the same time. Organizations are apt to retaliate against whistleblowers when top management is under financial pressure and management themselves are involved in the misconduct (Lee & Fargher, 2014). Management retaliates by eliminating the whistleblower's position, making it difficult for them to do their job, and setting them up for termination or demotions ultimately with the goal of making sure they do not work in the industry again (Devine & Maassarani, 2012). Interestingly higher level employees who may be close to the misconduct are apt to report the misconduct especially since they are more exposed to the information that gave rise to the misconduct in the first place (Gao et al., 2015). There are nonfinancial disincentives and the predominant disincentive to whistleblowing is psychological pressure. Retaliation by the organization and even fellow employees can be indirect and subtle, thus harassments are very difficult to successfully prove.

The psychological pressures on the whistleblower has been described as not necessarily firing the person outright for their disclosure, but the usual practice is to demoralize and humiliate them so that it becomes more difficult to do their job and the whistleblower leaves voluntarily because the work environment has become so uncomfortable. The pressure typically starts immediately after fellow employees find out about the whistleblower's disclosures and the pressure increases from them resembling what could be described as "silent social ostracism"—a form of social rejection with the intention of isolating one from others (Lipman, 2012, p. 59). This ostracism might be displayed as excluding the person from social events, e-mails, and giving them the overall silent treatment. Recall that an organization can contribute to a person's self-identity and once ostracism occurs, this can directly challenge their sense of who they are within a group setting. Ostracism threatens the basic human motivation to avoid exclusion from important social groups; whistleblowers can face full blown social rejection. As one psychologist stated, "no more fiendish punishment could be devised" than social ostracism (Lipman, 2012, p. 59). Other nuances of ostracism is transferring the whistleblower to other locations such as giving him or her a closet for an office, spreading false rumors, and increased scrutiny of his or her personal background.

On occasion, employers will isolate whistleblowers from the evidence through a long standing tradition by physically locking them out so that they do not have access to evidence or they make it virtually impossible for an employee to get access because of the bureaucratic red tape that the employee has to cut through but for which may never happen. Similarly, revoking an employee's security clearance is both a tactic of retaliation and a technique for hiding damaging information from those workers who would otherwise have access to it (Devine & Maassarani, 2012). Retaliation can occur at different levels of an organization and amongst coworkers because misconduct need not start at the top of an organization, but can be initiated by middle managers and lower-level employees eventually being endorsed by senior management (Lee & Fargher, 2014). Coworkers are known to alienate whistleblowers by not socializing with them in an employment setting in addition to pressuring them to stop complaining about the misconduct. Some whistleblowers are concerned for their safety. Consider the fear felt by Bernard Madoff whistleblower Harry Markopolos and what he would do if Madoff approached him:

> [I]f he contacted me and threatened me, I was going to drive down to New York and take him out. At that point it would have come down to him or me; it was as simple as that. The government would have forced me into it by failing to do its job, and failing to protect me. In that situation I felt I had no other options. I was going to kill him (Markopolos, 2010, p. 145).

Moreover we observe tighter oversight from management by withholding information from these employees to do their job, denial of promotions, suspensions from work, unjustified poor performance appraisals, reassigning them to different geographic locations, denial of opportunity to receive training, verbal abuse, harassment, intimidation, character assassination, and relocation of desk or work area within the office (Near et al., 2004). According to a study of eighty-four whistleblowers conducted in the 1990s, "82% experienced harassment after blowing the whistle, 60% were fired, 17% lost their homes, and 10% admitted to attempted suicide" (Maclean, 2005, p. 1025). For example, Home Depot employee and whistleblower Francis Leonard was bullied into continuing a fraudulent billing practice where vendors were falsely billed for lost, stolen or damaged goods. After Francis quit his job in February 2009, a month later he was found hanging from an electric tower with a suicide message for his attorney urging him to "pursue Home Depot for what has been done and to take care of his relatives" (Devine & Maassarani, 2011, p. 61). In the end, as one observer summed up how these people are viewed, "a corporate employee who blows the whistle is as about as welcome as a skunk at a picnic" (Brickey, 2003, p. 363).

Ironically, the display of ethical behavior that should be viewed as routine behavior is categorized as exceptional; choosing morality, ethics, and adherence to corporate governance to guide decision making is tied to personal fates, not as an organizational goal to encourage. Corrupt leadership conflates the whistleblower's moral courage to disclose the truth as synonymous with being treasonous. In other words, a blatant indication that the whistleblower is disloyal and causing harm, both financial and reputational, to the organization and co-workers. Authority will vigorously attempt to discredit whistleblowers by characterizing the disclosure of truth as an act motivated by greed and revenge coupled with encouraging a work culture where truth tellers are to be viewed as a plague worthy of distancing oneself from and making their personal lives purposely uncomfortable so that they will give up the fight only to be discarded as refuse.

Whistleblowing Efficacy

One way to prevent white-collar crime from within the organization is through whistleblowers because staff and workers in corporations have much better knowledge of wrongdoing than external regulators (Rorie, 2020). Major legislation has provided an impetus to stimulate whistleblowers to come forward. The United States is again a good example. Since the 1986 False Claims Act (FCA), several major federal laws, including the 2002 Sarbanes–Oxley Act (SOX) and the 2012 Dodd–Frank Wall Street Reform and Consumer Protection Act (Dodd–Frank), provide protections for whistleblowers, for instance against retaliation by their employers. Some of these laws such as Dodd–Frank also incentivize employees to come forward by offering bounty rewards for bringing information to the Securities and Exchange Commission (SEC) that results in successful enforcement action. The question remains, do these whistleblowing policies actually work? Studies inform us about two questions: first, whether whistleblowers actually come forward to speak out, and second, when they do, whether this helps correct and prevent corporate wrongdoing.

Unfortunately, there is more research on why employees do or do not speak out against their employers than there is on what speaking out may actually accomplish (Rorie, 2020). A common finding in the whistleblower studies is that potential whistleblowers face tremendous obstacles and risks. Regardless of all the legal protections, many whistleblowers get fired or quit under duress. If they continue at their job, many are demoted and come to work with much less satisfaction, often in a hostile environment. Employees who stay on face the risk of retaliation. For example, in one case, a nuclear physicist whistleblower office was first moved to a broom closet, then lost his computer, and finally was put to work in the mailroom (Rorie, 2020). When whistleblowers remain with their employer, they can suffer an endless chain of abasement and some employers retaliate by requiring whistleblowers to undergo psychiatric fitness-for-work examinations. Those employees forced to leave their job, or quit voluntarily, often find their whistleblowing hurts their chances in the job market. In fact, studies show that potential employers may see whistleblowers as disloyal and less attractive to hire (Rorie, 2020). Studies also find that whistleblowers can incur large financial, social, and personal costs. While their claims are investigated, whistleblowers incur expensive legal fees; they need lawyers to protect them especially if their employer sues them. The whole process produces tremendous stress and anxiety, which can affect their personal relations at home often resulting in divorce and/or substance abuse. Clearly, whistleblower legal protections are not sufficient to protect those speaking out and do not offer enough guarantees for those considering whether to come forth.

How does whistleblowing impact corporate wrongdoing? Here we have far less literature to rely upon, as few studies have sought to link whistleblowing to corporate misconduct. The few studies available cast doubt on the actual effect of whistleblowing on compliance. A method to study the effects of whistleblowing is to look at changes in corporate misconduct and wrongdoing that have occurred after the whistleblower protection laws came in place. One researcher examined whether the whistleblower protections of SOX that were installed in 2002 had much effect in motivating the early disclosure of major fraud in subsequent years (Rorie, 2020). His conclusion is that whistleblowers did not significantly help to uncover the massive corporate fraud that resulted in the 2008 financial crisis. He relates how major financial institutions simply failed to respond when their employees disclosed instances of major and systemic fraud. Rather than addressing the fraud, firms often would retaliate against whistleblowers; one problem that surfaced due to internal codes of ethics procedures, is that employees would first have to report to their supervisors, who had great power to block and filter the reports. Moreover, whistleblowers were powerless against the pervasive fraudulent corporate culture. All of these statistics and evidence suggest that Sarbanes–Oxley, above all else, failed to change corporate culture sufficiently to address misconduct when employees report it (Rorie, 2020).

Another way to understand whistleblowing would be to measure whether individual firms with strong whistleblower protections have a better compliance record than those without. One study of 999 large Australian firms concluded that, unfortunately, organizations with such whistleblower protection policies do not have better compliance behavior than those without. However, they do find that a clearly defined system to handle external complaints by clients/customers positively affects compliance behavior; it seems that companies may respond more to their clients than to their employees (Rorie, 2020). Thus, the few studies about the effects of whistleblowing do not clearly show that it enhances compliance behavior; in fact, whistleblower programs may have negative effects. For example, one study observed Canadian workers who were granted the right to speak out about work safety violations and become responsible for reporting misconduct. However, often the right to speak out is not matched with the actual ability to speak out and might go against an engrained corporate culture of misconduct and vested hierarchies in the workplace. When there is a major accident, employees will be blamed for not using their right to speak out, even though they never truly had the ability to do so.

Finally, whistleblowers only alter corporate conduct under specific conditions. Studies find that whistleblowing will be more effective the greater the credibility and power of both the whistleblower and the recipient of the complaint, and the lesser the credibility and power of the actual wrongdoer the complaint addresses (Rorie, 2020). In other words, whistleblowing fails when a weak whistleblower forwards a complaint to a weak complaint manager about a powerful wrongdoer above both of them hierarchically. They also find that the level of criminal behavior involved and the extent to which the behavior is of vital importance to the organization matters. In other words, if the complaint is about major criminal misconduct, likely a felony, and about behavior that is not part of the core business model of the company, the whistleblower is more likely to succeed in getting the company to address it. They find that whistleblowing works best in organizations open to outside influence and pressure have a culture supporting compliance. Whistleblowing, by its very nature, often entails lower-level employees, with lesser power and credibility, reporting on higher-level staff and management. Consequently, whistleblowing has a low chance of successfully achieving internal changes and ending wrongdoing, while the risks to whistleblowers are great. When wrongdoing is culturally deeply engrained, studies show that whistleblowing will be less likely to succeed in ending misconduct (Rorie, 2020).

Executive Whistleblowers

At times we believe it is top management that punishes whistleblowers, but this is not always the case. Often top management is close enough to misconduct to obtain the evidence to prove misconduct to actually try to stop it or else they too become enmeshed in the web of normalized corruption. This is not meant to exempt individuals from personal responsibility for corruption, particularly senior managers with their relatively greater power and fiduciary responsibility to the organization. The point is that when bad apples produce a bad barrel through pervasive institutionalization, the barrel itself must be repaired. Practically, only a bold response by removing those at the top and subordinates that condoned and participated in misconduct can attempt to reverse systemic normalization of corruption. Let us examine some executives that tried to do the right thing by becoming whistleblowers.

Michael Woodford of Olympus

The Olympus scandal was exposed in 2011 when Olympus CEO Michael Woodford believed he was obligated to investigate the issue of accounting irregularities and suspicious transactions. His questioning eventually exposed Olympus's $1.7 billion accounting scandal where the company engaged in fraud schemes to hide their losses for years. When Woodford first became suspicious of the fraud, he notified the Olympus board of directors (Carozza, 2012). Woodford, a native of Great Britain who had been appointed Olympus's chief executive officer (CEO) just two weeks earlier, expected that the meeting would be eventful. Why? Because the day before, Woodford sent a letter to Tsuyoshi Kikukawa, Olympus's former CEO, demanding that he resign his position as the chairman of the company's board of directors (Knapp & Knapp, 2014). Subsequently, Kikukawa called a special 15 member board meeting for October 14, 2011. Instead of tendering his resignation, Kikukawa began the October 14th board meeting by making a motion to have Woodford dismissed as Olympus's CEO.

The meeting began at 9:07 a.m. at which time Woodford was fired, with the meeting ending at 9:15 a.m. Woodford was told to vacate his apartment and take the bus, not his company car, to the airport flying back to London. Woodford believed that *yakuza*, Japan's notorious organized crime organization, was linked to the suspicious transactions he uncovered, thus he feared for his life. The board also ratified a second motion which reappointed Kikukawa as CEO of Olympus. At a news conference Kikukawa stated, "We hoped that he could do things that would be difficult for a Japanese executive to do...but he was unable to understand that we need to reflect a management style we have built up in our 92 years as a company, as well as Japanese culture" (Carozza, 2012). The board indicated that he was fired because Woodford engaged in an aggressive Western management style (Mintz & Morris, 2017). Olympus warned other employees not to talk to Woodford or else their own careers would be in danger. The Olympus case illustrates how once misconduct becomes entrenched, dismantling an organizational culture that normalizes misconduct, due to institutionalizations, collective rationalizations and socializations, is very difficult. What lead up to this meltdown?

In his early 30s, Woodford became friends with Kikukawa and Kikukawa became Olympus's CEO in 2001. Seven years later he chose Woodford to oversee Olympus's foreign operations and in early 2011, Kikukawa promoted Woodford to chief operating officer (COO). At the time, Olympus was struggling financially and Woodford immediately transferred to Olympus's Tokyo headquarters and began an intensive study of Olympus's financial affairs as a prelude to developing a comprehensive turnaround plan to revitalize the company's operations (Knapp & Knapp, 2014). However, Woodford soon uncovered a series of large and unusual transactions that included several acquisitions unrelated to the company's two primary lines of business. Among those acquisitions were the purchase of a mail-order cosmetics company and a manufacturer of microwave ovens. Woodford could not understand why Olympus would purchase companies that had no connection to the company's other lines of business. More troubling to Woodford was the fact that by any conventional standard Olympus had paid grossly more than the companies were worth, which was readily confirmed by the two companies' extremely weak operating results subsequent to their acquisition (Knapp & Knapp, 2014). The gross overpayments for the companies suggested to Woodford that Olympus management was covertly conveying corporate assets to third parties, a serious violation of their fiduciary responsibilities to company stockholders.

Woodford also discovered that Olympus had purchased a well-known British medical equipment manufacturer. While investigating that acquisition, Woodford was shocked when he learned that Olympus had paid a nearly $700 million fee to an obscure investment advisory firm that had supposedly helped arrange the deal (Knapp & Knapp, 2014). That amount represented one-third of the total cost of the acquisition. Woodford realized that investment advisory firms typically receive a fee of approximately one percent of the value of a merger and acquisition (M&A) transaction that they help arrange, which meant that the Cayman Islands firm had been paid a fee thirty times greater than normal. After discovering the series of questionable business deals, Woodford arranged a meeting with Kikukawa, his longtime friend and mentor. During a meeting with Kikukawa, Woodford confronted him about allegations of fraud occurring at Olympus but Kikukawa would not answer his questions. Yet, Woodford and Kikukawa argued for months over a series of suspicious transactions that Woodford had discovered in Olympus's accounting records believing that the transactions were intentionally recorded improperly and that they might involve criminal activity. When Woodford continued to pressure him to discuss them, Kikukawa suggested that Woodford's responsibility was to focus on the future of the company's operations while ignoring any less than optimal decisions that the company had made in the past. Woodford told Kikukawa that it was impossible for him to overlook more than $1.5 billion of bad investments and suspicious third-party payments when Olympus's total profit the previous year had been only $350 million; at the time, Olympus had total assets of approximately $10 billion. Woodford came up with an even more pragmatic reason why he needed to have a complete understanding of the questionable transactions telling Kikukawa that he had to be fully knowledgeable of the transactions because, "I'm the one who signs the letter of representations with the auditors" (Knapp & Knapp, 2014).

After Kikukawa refused to discuss the series of questionable transactions, Woodford retained accounting firm PricewaterhouseCoopers (PwC) to investigate them. The report that PwC subsequently provided to Woodford convinced him that he had stumbled upon a fraudulent scheme being engineered by company insiders. PwC indicated that the given transactions appeared to have been recorded improperly and that they may have involved unlawful activity. While he pursued the suspicious transactions, Woodford wrote six letters to the members of Olympus's board, including Kikukawa, in which he documented his concerns. On October 17, 2011, three days after he was fired, Woodford told a *New York Times* reporter that Olympus needed a thorough forensic accounting investigation because he believed that there was something sinister about the company's recent corporate acquisitions. An Olympus spokesperson responded to Woodford's allegations by insisting that "all our mergers and acquisitions have been carried out with proper accounting and through appropriate procedures and processes"

(Knapp & Knapp, 2014). Another company representative suggested that Woodford had made the false allegations to retaliate against Olympus after he was dismissed. Although the Japanese press downplayed Woodford's claims, reporters of international news organizations pressured the company to investigate those claims. As the pressure mounted on Olympus, Kikukawa resigned as the chairman of the company's board of directors. The company's board then organized an independent panel, chaired by a former Japan Supreme Court Justice, to investigate Woodford's allegations. In early November 2011, less than one month after Woodford was dismissed as Olympus's CEO, a company spokesperson publicly admitted that Olympus engaged in a fraudulent accounting scheme that would prove to be one of the largest in Japan's history.

Although Kikukawa was not one of the original participants in the long-running fraud, he became aware of it in 2000, shortly before he was initially appointed Olympus's CEO. Over the next decade, he closely monitored the elaborate efforts of company insiders to conceal the fraud from the investment community, regulatory authorities, and other parties. On December 6, 2011, the six-member panel appointed by Olympus to investigate Woodford's allegations released a report of its findings. The forty-page report provided a chronological summary of the company's accounting fraud; the series of events that sparked the fraud actually began in the mid-1980s. To compensate for an earnings shortfall, Olympus's top management decided to implement what is known in the Japanese business culture as a zaiteku strategy. This strategy involves liquidating underperforming corporate assets and investing the proceeds in high-risk but potentially lucrative investments. Olympus's senior management created a secretive team consisting of three executives that would be responsible for deciding how to invest the cash resources devoted to the new zaiteku strategy. Collectively, this team was referred to within the company as the "few and proud group." Hideo Yamada, an accountant by training who previously had been assigned to one of Olympus's finance divisions, was placed in charge of this team. Initially, the zaiteku strategy proved successful. Yamada and his subordinates produced sizable gains that bolstered the company's reported operating results. But then, in the early 1990s, the speculative bubble in Japan's securities markets burst. Over the two-year period 1991-1992 alone, major Japanese stock indices declined by more than 50 percent. When the market values of Japanese securities collapsed, Yamada's team suffered large losses on its investment portfolio. As the losses continued to mount, Yamada's team made increasingly speculative investments, which, in turn, produced even larger losses.

By the late 1990s, the zaiteku strategy had piled up cumulative losses exceeding $1.7 billion, losses that were concealed from the users of Olympus's periodic financial statements. When Woodford blew the whistle on the Olympus accounting fraud in mid-October 2011, many parties immediately questioned how such a large-scale and long-running fraud could go undetected by the company's auditors. The most vocal critic of Olympus's auditors was arguably Woodford himself. A few months after the details of the fraud were revealed, Woodford told a reporter, "I still find it hard to fathom how the auditors missed the fraudulent nature of these bizarre and sizeable transactions" (Knapp & Knapp, 2014). Throughout the nearly two decades that the Olympic accounting fraud was taking place, the company received an unqualified audit opinion each year from a series of three accounting firms. Those firms included the Japanese affiliates of Arthur Andersen, KPMG, and Ernst & Young. Woodford had earlier characterized the audits performed by Olympus's independent auditors and the series of unqualified opinions they issued on the company's financial statements as "hollow, shallow and completely meaningless" (Knapp & Knapp, 2014). While criticizing Olympus's auditors, Woodford suggested that their failure to uncover the accounting fraud was linked to systemic weaknesses in Japan's independent audit function. Among those systemic weaknesses, Woodford singled out the modest audit fees paid by Japanese companies.

Those fees, which are typically less than one-half those paid by comparable U.S. companies, limit the scope and rigor of independent audits performed by Japanese accounting firms. Even more problematic for independent auditing in Japan is a deferential culture that pervades the nation's business community, a culture that places an emphasis on relationships and harmonious working practices (Knapp & Knapp, 2014). This cultural norm allegedly spawns cordial relationships between auditors and their clients and causes auditors to routinely subordinate their judgment to the wishes and demands of client executives. Even when corporate clients ask the auditors to do something that is not allowed under the law, they just do it (Knapp & Knapp, 2014). The close ties between Japanese auditors and their clients are also manifested by Japanese companies rarely changing their audit firms and by individual auditors often remaining on client engagement teams for decades. Eventually the Olympus board and those responsible for the massive fraud were held accountable.

More than one dozen Olympus executives faced criminal charges as a result of their roles in the accounting fraud. Woodford felt vindicated when Kikukawa admitted that Olympus intentionally misrepresented its operating results and financial condition for two decades (Knapp & Knapp, 2014). Tsuyoshi Kikukawa and Hideo Yamada pled guilty in July, 2012 to violating Japanese securities laws. On September 25, 2012, three other former executives pleaded guilty to accounting fraud (Mintz & Morris, 2017). That vindication convinced Woodford to launch a campaign to regain the CEO position at Olympus. His campaign ended after a few weeks when Olympus's major stockholders, which were primarily other large Japanese corporations, refused to support him. Olympus's major stockholders reportedly viewed Woodford as an outsider who did not understand that the most important trait of Japanese corporate executives is absolute loyalty to their companies. In their view, Woodford should have resolved the concerns he had privately rather than sharing them with the media and law enforcement authorities. Two months later, a Japanese judge gave each of them a three-year suspended prison sentence, meaning that neither of them would spend time in jail (Knapp & Knapp, 2014).

Interestingly, a spate of high-profile scandals at leading Japanese companies show reforms and rhetoric aimed at improving the country's corporate governance do not go far enough to unwind the culture of secrecy and hierarchy that plagues some companies in Japan (Hass et al., 2018). As one observer noted about how business is conducted in Japan, "It is a cultural issue—they have to give up hierarchical obedience…They have to do this because if they cannot be more alert and agile as companies, they will not succeed in the modern world" (Hass et al. 2018, p. 269). Woodford stated that, "What is Japanese is the culture of deference and obedience. These qualities make hiding corrupt transactions much easier. You have people blindly following leadership" (Hass et al. 2018, p. 269). Prior to the Olympus scandal, the highest profile accounting fraud in Japan involved Kanebo a large conglomerate. In August 2006, three of Kanebo's former independent auditors were convicted of helping conceal material errors in the company's financial statements; one of those auditors had served for more than 30 years on the Kanebo audit engagement team (Knapp & Knapp, 2014). Critics of Japan's independent audit function point out that the systemic weaknesses in that function have been perpetuated by ineffective regulatory and judicial oversight of the nation's public accounting profession. As an example, for a period of more than twenty years, the regulatory body overseeing Japan's public accounting profession did not revoke a single CPA license or otherwise severely sanction a CPA. Likewise, Japanese courts have been extremely reluctant to hand down punitive sentences to auditors who abrogate their professional responsibilities. Consider the three auditors convicted of participating in the Kanebo accounting fraud actually recommended methods to help conceal the company's deteriorating financial condition received suspended prison sentences; the same punishment given the former Kanebo executives who were the masterminds behind the fraud (Knapp & Knapp, 2014).

Elin Baklid-Kunz of Halifax Hospital

Elin Baklid-Kunz was the finance department's director of Physicians Services, at Halifax Hospital located in Daytona Beach, Florida where she specialized in medical compliance issues. She filed a whistleblower lawsuit against the hospital when the hospital fraudulently overbilled Medicare, engaged in fraudulent medical coding of procedures, paid kickbacks to doctors, wrongfully admitted patients for inpatient service that were unnecessary coupled with various other forms of misconduct (Mueller, 2019). Halifax's "revenue-above-all philosophy was widely espoused by managers and doctors alike" (p. 147). For example, Halifax earned more money by admitting patients for inpatient services than by admitting them for outpatient services where they would be released after being observed by a doctor. However, some doctors would not even see patients that came to the hospital for observation as opposed to being admitted as an inpatient; in fact, they would "leave the patient in the emergency room" (p. 147). As one hospital employee who was well aware of the fraudulent practices stated that referring patients to Halifax was like "sending lambs to slaughter, because they were almost invariably operated on" (p. 148).

When Elin transferred to the compliance department, she began to notice irregularities such as doctors being paid bonuses based on how much profit the hospital made—a practice she believed to be illegal, but was reassured from her supervisor, George Rousis that Halifax's practices were legal. However, she subsequently learned from an attorney at a compliance conference that such a practice violated the Stark Law. The Stark Law prohibits doctors from referring Medicare patients to hospitals they have a financial relationship with because such arrangements create a conflict of interest and can induce doctors to recommend testing, surgery, or other medical procedures that earn them money, but that may not be in the best interest of the patient. When she spoke to George about her concerns again, he indicated that if the government finds out about the hospital's arrangement with doctors, that would create a "firestorm" (p. 144). A Halifax attorney wrote a memo stating that Halifax practices violated the Stark Law and should self-report the misconduct to the government, but senior management was comfortable with outside counsel who opined that the hospital's practices did not violate any law. Senior management did not self-report the misconduct to the government as is required, nor did they change their contractual arrangements with their doctors—they decided to roll the dice and take their chances.

In terms of fraudulent billing, Elin observed how in one case a patient had been hospitalized for brain cancer and eventually died. The Medicare claim form showed that the neurosurgeon billed for critical care everyday of the patient's hospital stay, yet the patient's medical record showed that the doctor provided no critical care at all. According to Elin, "we had billed the insurance company, Medicare, and the patient's family for the co-pay, and we didn't even perform the service, because the office manager had automatically entered charges for every day the patient was in the hospital, without looking at the physician's documentation...the family had lost their relative, and now they're stuck with this bill" (p. 145). Elin realized that every form she submitted that was false carried with it a potential criminal prosecution that included fines and imprisonment. Elin further had a well-respected, outside medical consultancy group made up of four board certified neurosurgeons peer review medical procedures performed by Halifax neurosurgeons.The consultancy found numerous examples of improperly performed surgeries and surgeries that were not properly coded that could have harmed the patient. In one case, the consultancy found that a neurosurgeon, during a time period, performed nine out of ten surgeries that were medically unnecessary, but which earned Halifax desired revenue. Elin consulted the hospital's general counsel sharing with him her concerns to which he said that it was not necessary to worry because Halifax is a public hospital and could not be hurt by the False Claims Act. Moreover, he said that "he had friends high up in DOJ (Department of Justice) and would know if there was any investigation going on" (p. 149).

Yet, Elin also brought her concerns to various other legal, management and compliance professionals at Halifax. In "one particular heated exchange, George Rousis told her that her loyalty was to the Halifax Hospital, not to the government, and that if she ever thought about becoming a whistleblower, she should leave right away (p. 150). Elin recalled how she would give speeches to new hires proclaiming Halifax's compliance and high level of integrity coupled with referring to a letter from CEO Jeff Feasel who stressed the hospital's tradition of strong moral, ethical and legal standards of conduct. The letter also included Halifax's core values of respect, honesty, integrity, compassion and trust. These values she presented to others were the ones that Halifax violated and at some point Elin felt like she harbored two personalities that were in conflict with each other—the honest Elin and the lying Elin. Due to the stress, Elin would experience frequent nausea and sleep related problems in addition to weight gain. What is common amongst whistleblowers is that they do not want to be whistleblowers, they just want someone to correct the problem—someone that will take their concerns seriously. Elin stated:

> I never wanted to become a whistleblower...I gave the information to so many people, in compliance, in legal, because I thought they'd have to do something with it once they knew. I never imagined people in their position could just walk away. I was in shambles over all these things that were wrong. I was devastated that they hadn't self-disclosed, that nothing had changed. I would have given anything to get them to listen, but it was like we were speaking different languages. It must be like having a child that's a drug addict. You did everything you can to fix the problem, and then one day you realize that it doesn't matter what you do. It's beyond your scope. I spent a great deal of time thinking if I could walk away

from this and not do anything. I wanted to do that so bad, to just get another job and forget that this happened. When defenseless people are getting hurt, you can't turn your back (p. 150-151).

In the end she was motivated to do the right thing because she was "scared for the patients" and that the hospital knew that they had broken the law but did nothing about it; "I kept hoping that someone else would do it, but sometimes you have to be that someone" (TAF, 2014). Eventually Elin retained an attorney to help her navigate the whistleblowing process and to help her interface with the civil division of the department of justice, however she still worked at Halifax. At work, once co-workers learned of the whistleblowing lawsuit, they refused to sit next to her at meetings and her performance reviews which were in the past stellar plummeted as well as receiving a score of zero on leadership. One "longtime colleague stopped her at the entrance to the hospital and said loudly, in front of patients, 'How dare you come back here...You should be ashamed of yourself'" (Meuller, 2019, p. 160). When she reported this incident to the hospital's legal department, the associate legal counsel dismissed it with a shrug: 'What else can you expect, after what you've done?" (p. 161). Again, we see how group dynamics influence how people see those that appear to be outside of the group's position on issues and where behaviors outside of the group's norms is interpreted as disloyalty.

Moreover, a company has an informal culture whose norms, signals and pressures influence employee behavior for more than any formal compliance and ethics program ever will. A culture is not necessarily publicly pronounced in official declarations, but is passed along informally among employees teaching what the company really expects which in Halifax's case is profits, not necessarily how profits are earned such as through integrity. Elin's office was eventually moved to a small unpainted room at the end of a long hallway where her computer access credentials also changed. During the litigation process, Elin's colleagues denied having conversations with her about the misconduct they observed at Halifax. Halifax hired a public relations firm to attack Elin's credibility by attacking her character. Halifax CEO Feasel spoke of the unwarranted attack on the hospital, how they take care of everyone in the community, and as for the physicians, "These physicians that were raked over the coals and made to feel like they criminally did something wrong" (p. 169). Moreover, he stressed that the hospital did nothing wrong even though his statements were in direct contradiction to the documents submitted to Medicare for services not rendered. Halifax also focused on the big financial payoff that Elin would receive and that her whistleblower lawsuit was motivated by pure greed, of course ignoring their own greed satisfied by fraudulent behavior. Moreover, during the investigation into Halifax's practices, it was learned that there were periods where documents that referred to the improper patient services were destroyed.

Yet, a retired accounts payable clerk called Elin's behavior "beyond morally obscene" (p. 169). Also, even those colleagues that wanted to stay friends with Elin were retaliated against and there is no law to protect Elin's colleagues from retaliation, thus her friends were pressured to disassociate themselves. Eventually Halifax settled the case with the government by admitting no wrongdoing and Elin was financially rewarded as a whistleblower. Yet interestingly, many of the people that participated in the fraud, including physicians, were not held accountable and in many cases were promoted. Eric Peburn, the CFO who had ultimate responsibility for certifying that its cost reports were truthful, correct, complete, and did not violate any laws, was recognized by a major healthcare trade publication as an outstanding financial manager and CEO Feasel still retained his position. Elin tried to find new employment, yet, it has been difficult. In one scenario, a senior vice president of a healthcare firm invited Elin for an interview and promptly offered her a position. However, a short time later the vice president sent Elin an apologetic email stating that the firm's board of directors and the general counsel objected to hiring a whistleblower. The vice president stated, "I did all I could to make the argument for why it makes sense to hire you, the concern is how our large clients will handle knowing that we're employing a whistleblower and that they could drop us as a client" (p. 172). Interestingly, shortly thereafter, this vice president resigned for unknown reasons.

What is fascinating is that even some compliance professionals appear uncomfortable associating and being in the presence of Elin. For example, when Elin's attorney, Marlan Wilbanks, discussed her case at a major compliance conference, the organizers declined to invite her to the conference let alone include her on the panel to discuss the case even though whistleblowing and anonymous and non-anonymous inside tips are a major fraud detection tool that prosecutors rely on to build their civil and criminal cases. Elin, on her own, paid $1,500 to attend the conference, yet she noticed that people were avoiding her. One of Elin's friend who attended the conference told her why they were avoiding her stated: "A lot of people here are thinking, 'What are you doing here? You got your money. Just move on.'" (p. 173). Elin disagrees with this mindset stating, "A lot of people look at whistleblowers like bounty hunters, they look at the reward as blood money. But people don't understand that most whistleblowers are motivated to act by something more than money, because there's really no guarantee of any reward at all. So many things could go wrong, and you can end up with nothing: no job, no future" (p. 171). Although Elin is pleased to win her case, she still "doesn't feel successful when the people doing the wrongdoing are still doing it…that's the part that is so hard to deal with" (DeGregorio, 2019).

Douglas Durand of TAP Pharmaceuticals

Douglas Durand left his job at Merck Pharmaceuticals to join TAP Pharmaceuticals as their Vice President for Sales. Within a few months of joining TAP, Durand became extremely concerned about certain practices at TAP such as, 1) giving doctors a 2 percent administration fee for prescribing TAP's prostate cancer drug, Lupron, 2) encouraging doctors to bill Medicaid for the cost of drugs that had been provided to them as free samples, and 3) providing doctors with lavish discounts, gifts, and trips (Brody, 2007). Durand's efforts to stop these practices were futile, both at the senior management level above his own title and those that were his subordinates who were out in the field selling TAP products even when he tried to offer financial rewards to be more ethical. Durand was told that he did not understand TAP's culture and was kept out of key sales and marketing meetings. His requests for information about unethical practices were routinely ignored. He was concerned that TAP did not have an in-house legal counsel, but found out that TAP employees referred to such individuals as sales prevention departments. Finally, after several frustrating years, he informed the government. Durand left the company and filed a lawsuit on behalf of the federal government, contending that TAP engaged in a broad range of illegal marketing activities. Confronted with the overwhelming documentation of its rampant corruption, Durand's reward of the $875 million settlement against TAP was $126 million.

Sherron Watkins of Enron

Former Enron vice president of accounting, Sherron Watkins, was the ideal person to describe the complex dynamics that led to Enron's demise because she was close enough to top management, but not necessarily in their inner circle, to critique operations (Beenen & Pinto, 2008). Enron was under extreme pressure from Wall Street to achieve earnings goals, thus, according to Watkins, there was "a firm culture in place that emphasized making earnings targets no matter what, and I don't think any one person could have changed that culture" (Beenen & Pinto, 2008). According to Watkins, there was a "culture of intimidation at Enron where there was widespread knowledge of the company's shaky finances" (Maclean, 2005, p. 1025). Watkins also commented on Enron's "rank and yank" performance review process which she believed created extreme performance pressure, including an "ends justify the means" approach, whereby perpetrators and innovators of corrupt practices were rewarded with large bonuses regardless of how goals were achieved. In addition, the rank and yank performance management system provided an impetus for managers to be in continual fear of losing their jobs, thus even if they personally objected to the corrupt practices, they did not raise their concerns to upper management. At Enron, fear appears to have been an emotion that generated and sustained corrupt practices and some Enron employees may have been too afraid of senior executives, such as CEO Jeffrey Skilling's intimidating leadership style, to raise questions. To illustrate this point:

> According to Watkins, Skilling was charismatic and intimidating. He was very hypnotic, and convincing. He is sharp and could sell anything. If you were going to ask a bunch of questions, he would intimidate you and make you feel you were not smart enough to get it. You are either in our smart guy club or not.

That is how he suckered people in. 'Ah! You are smart like me.' That was the message (Beenen & Pinto, 2008, p. 279).

Sherron eventually sent the late Enron CEO Kenneth Lay a memo outlining Enron's corrupt accounting stating in part, "I am incredibly nervous that we will implode in a wave of accounting scandals" (Brickey, 2003, p. 360). Shortly after sending the first memo, Watkins met with Lay providing five new memos that both detailed problems with Enron's off-book partnerships, special purpose entities, and suggested a strategy for disclosing the accounting irregularities, restating third quarter earnings, and rebuilding investor confidence. Sherron encouraged Lay to engage an independent law firm to conduct a preliminary investigation into the accounting problems and urged him not to retain law firm Vinson & Elkins (V&E) because they helped structure some of the questionable deals in the first place. Lay agreed to investigate her concerns, but V&E conducted a brief and limited investigation into her allegations and, to no one's surprise, reported that the special purpose entity transactions were not problematic.

Within days of Watkins' meeting with Lay disclosing the accounting irregularities, Lay wanted to terminate her (Beenen & Pinto, 2008). A V&E lawyer discouraged terminating Watkins due to the "possible risks associated with discharging employees who report allegations of improper accounting practices," including a report on the status of the Texas law covering whistleblower protection (Maclean, 2005, p. 1024). CFO Andrew Fastow was furious that Watkins talked to Lay and upon learning that she had, he wanted her removed from her position and seized the laptop computer from her desk. Despite Fastow's wishes to see her terminated, Watkins remained an Enron Vice-President, but she was reassigned from her executive suite to a starkly furnished office at the bottom of the Enron building performing make-work tasks. Watkins wrote a colleague a note stating that "I haven't had a real job since my first meeting with Ken" (Brickey, 2003, p. 363). Eventually Watkins was lauded as a whistleblower testifying before Congress explaining the corruption at Enron. Those at the top, such as Jeffrey Skilling, Andrew Fastow, Ken Lay and many others were eventually found to be criminally liable for their misconduct either by pleading guilty or by being found guilty at trial.

Government Whistleblowers

Whistleblowing issues are not particularized to only private industry, these issues occur within government too. For example, regulatory agencies are created by Congress in order to control some powerful forces in society such as corporations, which benefit society but which are prone to abuse their power (Carozza, 2008b). In order to do this, Congress gives administrators of regulatory agencies broad discretionary power to write regulations for industries for which they are responsible. Thus, any discretionary authority given to a regulatory agency administrator is, in fact, given to the President of the United States to be used as the President sees fit, and the administrator is no more than a White House staffer. The Food and Drug Administration, the Nuclear Regulatory Commission (NRC), the National Highway Traffic Safety Administration (NHTSA), and EPA, among many others, regulate giant corporations. Big corporations have big power, money, and influence helping to elect governors, congressmen, senators, and presidents (Carozza, 2008b). For example, the threat of a corporation's withdrawal from a state causes governors to hesitate to enforce the state's laws as they may relate to environmental and financial matters; again the issue of political accommodation of misconduct surfaces.

The EPA, for instance, cannot write regulations governing the petroleum industry without the oil companies going to the White House claiming an "energy crisis!" (Carozza, 2008b). When the FDA wants to thoroughly evaluate a new drug, the pharmaceutical company resorts to a public relations attack about how the bureaucratic delays are costing lives. Regulatory agency employees learn that drafting and implementing rules for corporations means making enemies of powerful and influential people. Government whistleblowers do not necessarily get fired, but they do not advance either; their responsibilities are transferred to others, and they often leave the agency in disgust (Carozza, 2008b). Employees who are cynical of their agency believe that nothing would be done if they came forward and reported misconduct. Those who see but do not report misconduct fear that if they were to come forward with a report, their identities would be revealed. Not surprisingly, these groups of employees also believe that if their identities were exposed, they would suffer retaliation from their superiors (Mahadeo, 2006). However, let us examine the status of some government whistleblowers who believed in doing the right thing regardless of the consequences to their employment status, but not ignoring the fact that they too pay a price for their desire for truthfulness.

David Graham of the Food and Drug Administration

David Graham, a scientist at the Food and Drug Administration (FDA) for over 20 years, stated that many U.S. citizens died from the effects of the arthritis drug Vioxx. According to Graham, "between 1999 and 2004, an estimated 20 million Americans took Vioxx, 80 million worldwide…We've estimated that up to 140,000 patients, who took Vioxx, suffered heart attacks…Of this number, 60,000 died (Carozza, 2008b). In November, 2004, Graham testified before the U.S. Congress that the FDA silenced him and his colleagues from reporting on the risks of Vioxx and other drugs. Graham stated that because the FDA is unduly influenced by the drug industry, it is "incapable of protecting Americans against another Vioxx. We are virtually defenseless" (Carozza, 2008b). Merck eventually pulled Vioxx from the marketplace. According to Graham:

> If I failed to speak the truth…I would become part of the problem, and all these deaths would, in part, be my responsibility. The decision to speak the truth wasn't difficult. My conscience guided me in the way I should go…Graham said the personal costs have been high. Internal criticism, threats and ostracism, coupled with an orchestrated campaign of slander and innuendo initiated and carried out by FDA managers, took a great toll on my family…Human life is worth far more than a little difficulty at the office…Being able to look my children in the eye and for them to know that I have acted with integrity is priceless…Plus, I'm able to sleep at night (Carozza, 2008b).

William Sanjour of the Environmental Protection Agency

When William Sanjour is asked how he was able to stand up to injustices at the Environmental Protection Agency (EPA) for more than 30 years, he simply says, "It's in my genes. I come from a long line of people who would not be cowed when they are right" (Carozza, 2008b). Sanjour further stated that it is not easy being a whistleblower anywhere, "but it's often toughest in a governmental regulatory agency" (Carozza, 2008b). According to Sanjour, employees often feel pressure to obey unwritten rules of conformity and as branch chief in the Hazardous Waste Management Division, Sanjour supervised studies of hazardous waste damages and treatment technologies (Carozza, 2008b). What began as an effort to do his job by developing regulations for the treatment, storage, and disposal of hazardous waste became a long, drawn-out battle with the EPA, multiple presidential administrations, and several government agencies as he fought to implement the true spirit of the hazardous waste legislation (Carozza, 2007). In 1995, Sanjour won a landmark suit against the U.S. federal government, which established the First Amendment right of federal employees to whistleblow on their employers. Until his retirement in 2001, Sanjour faced retaliation, reassignments, and demotions—all the while stubbornly continuing his government service and assisting grassroots environmentalists (Carozza, 2008b). At no time did William compromise his ethics to accommodate the agency's misconduct, but the process of having to uphold the truth is not without challenges.

Employee Whistleblowers

Employees who are not technically considered management too face push back from their superiors when they are simply trying to do their jobs with integrity regardless of whether they work in government or the private sector. Let us consider cases illustrating how employees face retaliation for doing the right thing and what the outcome was for these whistleblowers.

Amy Stroupe of Branch Banking & Trust Company

In 2007 Certified Fraud Examiner, Amy Stroupe, believed her former employer Branch Banking & Trust Co. (BB&T) in North Carolina, fired her because she exposed a $100 million North Carolina real estate development scam (Carozza, 2010). In February of 2007, a BB&T retail service officer came to Stroupe with concerns about a series of suspicious loans made by a BB&T financial center manager for a real estate development project. Investigators later found the venture was a Ponzi scheme where there was no evidence that homes were being built and that the bank was aiding the fraud by making loans to these investors. In March, 2007, Stroupe contacted the FBI asking if they might be interested in investigating a possible fraud case, however she was discouraged from her supervisors to work on such investigation projects. Stroupe, at trial, testified that in the termination meeting on June 20, 2007, her boss said, "Amy, it's become obvious that you cannot conform to a corporate setting, therefore, we are terminating your employment" (Carozza, 2010). Stroupe testified that prior to her termination, she did not receive any disciplinary actions or written warnings when she worked for BB&T and was unaware that anyone recorded that she was at risk of losing her job. Stroupe said that during the two years she worked for BB&T, she received five positive performance evaluations and several with high performance marks. However, four months after receiving a positive performance evaluation and after supervisor assurance that they supported her 100 percent, she was terminated for no other reason but that she was doing her job professionally. Yet, according to Judge Tureck:

> I find it virtually unfathomable that BB&T would fire an employee as highly regarded as Stroupe, and who had recently provided invaluable service to BB&T. Stroupe received excellent performance evaluations throughout her employment with BB&T. Amy is an asset to the BB&T Corporate Investigations team," her supervisor wrote in her 90-day review report. Amy has established herself as a consistent contributor to the investigative team." In her second annual review report, her supervisor wrote, "Amy's future with BB&T is very bright. Amy is always willing and open to learn new ways to complete her job assignments in the most professional and timely manner. Stroupe's credibility is of utmost importance in this case. I had the opportunity to observe her over the more than two full days that she testified, and I found her to be a very credible witness. In particular, her candor, energy and strong sense of doing what is right were apparent. She displayed a strong work ethic and a desire to perform her job well. She did not resort to self-serving testimony, admitting mistakes and uncertainty. She was also cooperative and non-confrontational on cross-examination. Finally, she displayed remarkably little animosity toward anyone at BB&T. I give the greatest weight to her testimony (Carozza, 2010).

Marta Andreasen of the European Commission

In 2002, Marta Andreasen, the European Commission's (EC) chief accounting officer at the time, reported that the EC budget was "massively open to fraud" (Carozza, 2008b). Andreasen found serious and glaring shortcomings with the accounting computer system, such as no double-entry bookkeeping, and software that allowed any EC staff to change entries without leaving evidence of who made the changes or leaving an audit history. She was asked to sign off on the EC's 2001 accounts but would not do it because she believed she had evidence that the accounts did not accurately reflect the EC's financial position. The EC hierarchy threatened her with dismissal if she did not comply, but she eventually reported the accounting system problems to her supervisors and EC's president and vice presidents. Upper management continued to pressure her even after she reported the inaccuracies. The reward for her forthrightness was suspension from her duties and forced residence into professional limbo eventually being removed from her position.

Andreasen said at the time she discovered the misconduct, there was a complete lack of understanding of the basic control principle of separation of duties for those that were in charge of accounting and finance. Andreasen said she has paid both professionally and personally for being a whistleblower, but she has "always tried to ensure I fight until the end to defend my integrity" (Carozza, 2008b). Andreasen displayed the ethical mindset her organization should have exalted and held up as an example for others to follow. Andreasen took her case to the Tribunal for the European Civil Service in June 2005, but it was not until November, 2007 that the tribunal rejected her lawyer's arguments and judged against her. Andreasen said she gave up "the illusion that the EU will become the shining example of financial probity" (Carozza, 2008b).

Dinesh Thakur of Ranbaxy

In 2004 Dinesh Thakur, a research executive at the Indian generic drug company, Ranbaxy Laboratories, investigated the extent to which the firm provided false data to the World Health Organization (WHO) (Carozza, 2014). The regulatory agencies in India, equivalent of the U.S. Food and Drug Administration (FDA), were corrupt and colluded with the local manufacturers who were negligent in discharging their duty to protect public health in their country putting profits before people. Ranbaxy sought prequalification which enables pharmaceutical companies to sell their products to WHO member countries for drugs used by AIDS patients in South Africa. Thakur, an American-trained engineer and a naturalized U.S. citizen, discovered a company culture that not only tolerated fraud, but apparently encouraged, celebrated, and rewarded misconduct among its employees. This created a business environment where companies like Ranbaxy exploited gaps in oversight, and this led to years of finding innovative ways to circumvent regulations. Ranbaxy took shortcuts on testing their products before being released to the market, and fabricated data in its clinics to prove they were effective on patients (Carozza, 2014).

Thakur gave the findings of his investigation to his supervisor, who presented it to Ranbaxy's board of directors. The board did nothing to correct the problems and Kumar and Thakur eventually resigned rather than participate and perpetuate the misconduct. Three months after Thakur's presentation to the board and after his resignation, Ranbaxy's internal auditors went after Thakur's character in order to reduce his credibility to the authorities. They conducted a 10-week audit of Thakur's department, accused him of browsing pornography sites from his office computer, but in the end found nothing. Eventually in 2013, Ranbaxy USA Inc., a subsidiary of Ranbaxy Laboratories, pleaded guilty to seven federal criminal counts of selling adulterated drugs with intent to defraud, failing to report that its drugs did not meet specifications, and making false statements to the government.

Conditions and Guidelines for Effective Whistleblowing

A whistleblower is one whose loyalty is to the truth. A whistleblower is one who exposes government and corporate misconduct, actions violating the law, and threats to the public safety.

Bunatine Greenhouse (Carozza, 2006)

Most whistleblowers would rather have misconduct resolved internally, however, there are times that an internal whistleblower will go outside an organization if they do not see their disclosure on misconduct internally resolved. For example, Sherron Watkins of Enron preferred to have the accounting misconduct she discovered handled internally which is why she initially went to CEO Kenneth Lay to let him know of what she had found and how Enron could resolve the problem. Studies have shown that whistleblowers divulge their concerns outside the organization and the reasons include but are not limited to, 1) they anticipate that the internal reporting is futile, 2) the organization shows no interest in resolving the misconduct by their unresponsiveness to the problem, and 3) the whistleblower wants support from regulators such as the Securities and Exchange Commission (Klein, 2016). To successfully engage an external regulatory agency, the whistleblower must find the appropriate agency and person within a maze of bureaucracy (Devine & Maassarani, 2011). Potential whistleblowers must understand that outside agencies can be rather direct in their questioning of their claims because a successful prosecution of misconduct relies on solid evidence of misconduct plus what violation of actual law or regulation occurred. Typically there needs to be a link between the disclosed misconduct and a violation of some law. For example, a company dumps toxic waste in a lake used to draw drinking water. It is safe to assume that there are strict laws prohibiting this conduct. Thus the question, becomes what is the evidence that ties the company to the toxic waste in the water.

Regulators have only so many resources to put into whistleblower claims, thus there has to be significant legal and public policy implications to warrant an investigation together with solid evidence of misconduct. As one whistleblower stated, "blowing the whistle isn't about telling the truth, it's about proving the truth" (Klein, 2016, p. 253). One academician supports this position stating, "unfortunately, most whistleblowers are naïve about the precautions they must take, the amount of evidence they must bring forth, and about the fact that virtually no one will be on their side when the case gets underway" (Klein, 2016, p. 253). As we have seen, many of the successful whistleblowers were higher level executives who were close to the evidence that proves misconduct. Yet even with evidence, their lives and that of their families were put under incredible stress because of the retaliation they faced which typically takes the form of character assassination. Moreover, informants are painted as a disgruntled employee who is trying to get even with the organization for a variety of reasons such as being passed over for a promotion. When we observe misconduct, typical protocol requires one to go to their supervisor to report, but this may be a problem when one's supervisor may be contributing to the misconduct.

Usually the misconduct should be the type that causes unnecessary harm, violate human rights, are illegal, run against the purpose of the organization, or are otherwise unethical that requires one to inform superiors or some governmental agency of those activities (Duska et al., 2011). A question that often arises is when is it permissible and an ethical obligation to blow the whistle especially when there appears to be a cultural aversion to exposing another's misconduct. For example, some people are taught to never 'tattle tale' on another, the importance of being a 'team player', or do not 'rat' on another for fear of being called a 'rat'. Setting aside some of these cultural norms, there are times when misconduct disclosure becomes an obligation especially if auditors detect and disclose fraud that is material to senior management and the board of directors and they do nothing to address the problem. Under certain time requirements, auditors auditing publicly traded companies will have to disclose what they know to the Securities and Exchange Commission.

In addition, it is highly recommended that a potential whistleblower consult with multiple attorneys who specializes in whistleblower cases until they find the right one to represent them (Kohn, 2011). Legal counsel is indispensable for such an important decision and it is *not recommended* that an individual go to an attorney who has no specialization in this area. The reason is because reporting misconduct may have statute of limitations as to holding an entity responsible for their misconduct and the type of protections a whistleblower may forfeit because of time sensitive issues. Counsel can advise a whistleblower of these time requirements so that they do not forfeit their right to being protected from retaliation and collecting compensation. In fact many whistleblowers have lost their case because the strict legal requirements as it relates to statute of limitations were not followed. Some other guideline to consider when considering whether to whistleblow include:

- Has the person actually observed organizational misconduct?
- Is there some law or regulation that is being violated by the misconduct?
- How serious is the misconduct that one is willing to report it internally or externally?
- Are there financial rewards available to give one the incentive to report misconduct?
- Does the whistleblower qualify for any protections under the law as it relates to a particular type of whistleblowing?
- Does the misconduct produce an actual harm to others including harm to the organization?
- Consult an attorney as soon as possible to put together a strategy to deal with a whistleblower case. What does one's attorney recommend and is one willing to listen to their attorney?
- What are the risks of retaliation by coworkers and management and is the whistleblower willing to adjust to such retaliation?
- Is one's family prepared for a potentially long legal battle that may take place to prove misconduct and retaliation for its exposure?
- Does the whistleblower have solid, relevant evidence, such as a paper trail, to prove that misconduct actually occurred? Are there other people who can support one's assertion that misconduct and retaliation took place? Without a paper trail, management knows it is more difficult to prove a case because the case becomes one's word against another (Klein, 2016).

Anticipating Offender Misconduct with Integrity Assessments

Hiring honest employees is helpful in creating a culture of organizational integrity. Yet, not all people are equally honest or have equally well-developed personal codes of ethics. Research suggests that many people when faced with significant pressure and opportunity to engage in misconduct will behave dishonestly rather than face the negative consequences of honest behavior such as failing to meet quotas, inability to pay debts, and inadequate job performance (Albrecht et al., 2012). If an organization is to be successful in mitigating against fraud, it must have hiring practices that can discriminate between those who are marginally honest and those who are highly ethical persons. Proactive hiring procedures include conducting background checks, checking references, and learning how to interpret responses to inquiries asked about candidates and testing for honesty. Consider how hiring the wrong person by not conducting a background check and using integrity assessments proves harmful to an organization:

> Philip Crosby was the name of an entrepreneur who started a business advocating for the production of error-free products named Philip Crosby Associates (PCA). Philip hired an individual by the name of John Nelson who appeared to have an understanding of international marketing. The vice president of human resources said, that John "seemed like the kind of honest individual we'd want to hire". John Nelson was not who he said he was; his real name was Robert Liszewski. Robert decorated his office with an Illinois CPA license that he forged, a CPA certificate that he created from his home computer, and a reference letter by his previous job that detailed his excellent qualifications. Yet the reference letter was written by Robert's wife who worked at the company where the letter originated from. Robert was unable to produce the work expected of a CPA and told the CFO that the reason he was falling behind was because he had cancer and had three months to live. Over time the CFO was unable to transfer company funds due to there not being sufficient funds to transfer. The CFO found thousands of dollars being transferred to a dummy company to the hometown where Robert was from. The dummy company was named Allied Exports and according to the Indiana Secretary of State, Robert's wife was the president named Patricia Fox. Robert's wife was arrested when she tried to withdraw several hundred thousand dollars from the dummy company's account. Police spotted Robert driving in a white Porche but were unable to catch him until later on. It was later discovered that Robert had been fired from a bank in Indiana where he embezzled more than $400,000 and spent eighteen months in prison (Albrecht et al., 2012, p. 74).

How is it possible for fraud offenders to fool executives and employers? They often use manipulation skills during interviews to convince hiring managers that they have the knowledge, skills, and abilities to do an outstanding job. Interviewers must avoid the temptation of being impressed with a candidate's credentials until they have been confirmed because by using their deception skills, they create phony resumes, diplomas, and fictitious work experience to further their claims coupled with manipulating others to act as references (Babiak & O'Toole, 2012). In this sense, better evaluation procedures and the use of integrity instruments designed to assess antisocial and other problematical personality traits may help prevent those who excel at manipulation from sliding into management ranks (Perri, 2011a). Faced with a competitive environment and business failures due to fraud, employers are turning to employment testing, specifically honesty/integrity assessments, as a way to protect themselves and as a useful supplement to the standard background check. Such assessments are also being used more extensively on upper level management hires given that they have enormous control over the corporate governance of a business.

Integrity assessments measure factors such as a person's beliefs as they relate to whether they are at risk to disregard rules while endorsing unethical behaviors, blaming others for their mistakes, and making rash decisions without considering the consequences of those decisions (Brody et al., 2015). Since at least the middle of the last century many employers, including the military, have utilized these assessments to assist in the hiring process. As opposed to a background check, which only looks into a person's past, integrity assessments are more predictive of future behaviors. Furthermore, legally organizations face liability for the actions of their employees, thus they may want to know in advance who is at risk to engage in antisocial behaviors. The fact that an organization has a robust compliance program in place does not shield an organization from civil or criminal liability for the actions of their employees. As a matter of law, illegal and unethical employee behavior is frequently imputed back to the corporation, thus shareholders have a financial and reputational interest in employee integrity.

Hiring managers, human resources, and other individuals involved in the employee selection process "all have a stake in preventing their organization from becoming victims of unethical behavior, be it white-collar or other" (Martin & Austin, 2010, p. 437). Under the legal doctrine of *respondeat superior*, also referred to as the master–servant doctrine, organizations are legally responsible for the actions of their employees when, 1) employees are acting on behalf of the organization and are within the scope of their employment-related duties, 2) the employee's action benefit the organization, and 3) the employee's actions are imputed back to the organization (Plimpton & Walsh, 2010).

Limitations of Background Checks

Typically an organization relies on background checks to determine the acceptability of a candidate. A background check may include, among other things, an educational and professional credentials check, employment history, a media check, a credit check, a reference check, and a criminal record check (Brody et al., 2015). However, a background check cannot predict how likely it is that a prospective employee will engage in misconduct. The majority of companies rely on background checks to screen job applicants. Background checks are a standard practice among companies for screening potential employees, but they do not always uncover the truth as there are several limitations associated with these searches (Brody, 2010). Fraud with respect to academic success is common because, "in the business world, these fictitious achievements are memorialized in a resume filled with lies, self-generated letters of commendation, and even fake wall plaques and awards" (Babiak & Hare, 2006, p. 57). Many companies added criminal background checks to their employee screening process, but criminal information is not easily obtainable for various reasons. For example, information is not always updated in a timely manner, such as cases that are not entered into public records for months or years after the case has been resolved.

In addition, there is no national system in place to provide all of the information that should be reviewed and a criminal record will not always be found especially if someone has lived in several states. Moreover, when a company conducts criminal background checks, typically only those offenses in which the applicant was prosecuted and convicted will be uncovered. Therefore, if an individual commits fraud but is not prosecuted, that crime will not be revealed on a criminal background check when they attempt to get a job elsewhere (Brody et al., 2015). Also, locating an applicant's criminal history is not simple because a master criminal record database which compiles an instant criminal record on the individual, including details of every offense ever committed, alias names, and a recent picture from their driver's license may not be accessible (Jones, 2011). The National Criminal Information Center (NCIC) database, operated by the FBI, is the real-life version of a criminal record database, and it has its share of problems. For example, it is a federal offense in most cases for employers or screening agencies to even access the NCIC database (Jones, 2011).

There are also issues with conducting employee reference checks because reference checks frequently fail to provide employers with meaningful information. Prior employers are hesitant to reveal negative information about their departing employees for fear of defamation lawsuits and many employers either refuse to give any reference, or they provide neutral information such as the dates of employment and job titles (Stabile, 2002). Thus, it is difficult for the hiring employer to get an honest appraisal of an applicant's job history from past employers. Companies routinely verify a potential new hire's resume to ensure that any information presented is not fictitious in nature or an embellishment of some sort. In particular, companies verify past employment and any degrees or professional credentials listed on an applicant's resume (Brody et al., 2015). Unfortunately, people exaggerate titles or responsibilities in previous positions, yet companies think background checks are enough, but they should be using other assessments in addition to background checks to ensure their hiring due diligence is as thorough as possible.

The Value of Integrity Assessments

Organizational misconduct plaguing companies typically refers "to a broad set of illegal, immoral, and/or deviant employee behaviors that include serious offenses such as employee theft, fraud, and drug use" (Fine et al., 2010, p. 73). Such misconduct is responsible for "as much as 30% of all business failures," and they "are becoming increasingly prevalent, with a 10% increase from 2003 to 2007 in the percentage of employees who observe violations in company ethics standards, policy or the law" (Fine et al., 2010, p. 73). Since so many deviant behaviors go undetected, the actual frequency of employees engaging in misconduct may be even higher. Given the prevalence of misconduct, it is in the best interest of companies to find a way to predict how a job applicant might act given certain scenarios. Fortunately for companies, there is a tool to gauge an employee's likelihood to engage in misconduct. Currently, "the most widely used personal assessment tools to predict misconduct among job applicants and employees are integrity tests" (Fine et al., 2010, p. 74).

Psychologists have developed integrity assessments that can be used to help measure a job candidate's risk level for engaging in undesirable work activities (Oliver et al., 2012). Being utilized for decades, according to the U.S. Office of Personnel Management, an integrity test is a specific type of personality test designed to assess an applicant's tendency to be honest, trustworthy, and dependable (Brody et al., 2015). Further, integrity testing saw a surge in popularity after the Federal Employee Polygraph Protection Act of 1988 banned the use of preemployment lie detector tests for all but a select few jobs due to their lack of reliability in detecting deception (Roberts, 2011). After preemployment lie detector tests were banned, "employers began to want and vendors began to offer, more broad-based personality tests, which are also valid and shed light on many character traits, including integrity" (Roberts, 2011). Other settings where recruiters have a tendency to use integrity tests are the military, nuclear plants, law enforcement agencies, and child care facilities (Roberts, 2011).

In addition, the American Management Association reports that a majority of the Fortune 500 companies now use testing as part of their hiring process (Brody et al., 2015). Integrity and other personality assessments were specifically designed to predict the predisposition of job applicants to engage in counter-productive work behaviors such as on-the-job theft, absenteeism, substance abuse, and insubordination using composite measures of personality dimensions, such as reliability, conscientiousness, trustworthiness, and sociability (USDL, 2000). In relation to theft-related issues, they measure attitudes related to one or more of the following psychological constructs: 1) tolerance of others who steal, 2) acceptance of rationalizations for theft, 3) inter-thief loyalty or also known as collusion, 4) antisocial beliefs and behaviors, and 5) admissions of theft-related activities (Brody et al., 2015). Currently, it is estimated that anywhere from 33 to 75 percent of employees have engaged in some form of deviant behavior which translates in to company losses (Fine et al., 2010).

Collective damages from employee theft and fraud are estimated to be as high as $400 billion dollars a year, and this is just in the United States (Fine et al., 2010). According to estimates made in the early 1990's, up to 5 million integrity tests are administered annually in the U.S. alone and, in particular, it is estimated that 10-15 percent of all U.S. retailers, banking and food service organizations use integrity tests for personnel selection (Fine et al., 2010). The growth of testing in the workplace reflects a broad consensus in the business world that hiring the wrong person, particularly the wrong senior level executive who may be in a position to commit fraud, can negatively impact the tone at the top, morale and productivity. Concerns about high level management committing fraudulent acts are not an anomaly to ignore (Brody et al., 2015).

The Effectiveness of Integrity Assessments

Organizations benefit when they select employees that are less likely to engage in misconduct and in particular, companies that use integrity tests for hiring have reported reduced thefts and inventory shrinkage rates (Fine et al., 2010). Large U.S. retailers and banks already administer integrity assessments to their job applicants. For example, when the company Payless Shoes first started using honesty tests, "losses totaled nearly $21 million per year among its 4,700 stores. Within only one year of implementing its screening program, inventory shrinkage fell by 20 percent to less than 1 percent of sales" (Bohlander & Snell, 2007, p. 258). In another study, a group of convenience stores using an integrity assessment to select employees experienced a 50 percent reduction in inventory shrinkage due to theft over an 18-month period (Shaffer & Schmidt, 1999). Moreover, a large North American retailer participated in a study to determine whether the implementation of preemployment assessing at many of its store locations would impact the number of thefts per store and the dollar amount stolen per store. After the first nine months of implementation, the average number of employee theft apprehensions in locations where the program was implemented was 5.72 versus 7.89 in non-participating locations, and the average dollar amount stolen per store in the assessed locations was $10,743 versus $15,829 in non-participating locations (Fisher & Nobile, n.d.).

Another major North American retailer began using an integrity test in about 600 of its 1,900 locations (Votaw, 2011). In one year, the sites using integrity testing saw an inventory shrink drop by 35 percent as compared to a 10 percent increase by those that did not use the integrity testing. Moreover employee turnover decreased by 13 percent for those that used the integrity assessment and those that did not saw employee turnover increase by 14 percent (Votaw, 2011). In another instance, Cornell University reported on a hospitality company that screened its job applicants for integrity (Sturman & Sherwyn, 2007). As part of the study, workers' compensation claims for new employees who had been screened for integrity were compared with those of current employees who had not been screened for integrity. Interestingly, "the data showed that the average annual cost per employee for workers' compensation was more than three times higher for unscreened existing employees than for the new hires who had been screened for integrity"; overall, the amount of savings that companies realize "by screening out potentially expensive hiring mistakes, theft and fraud more than make up for the typically reasonable cost of conducting integrity tests" (Sturman & Sherwyn, 2007).

The Legality of Integrity Assessments

Overall, regardless of how rigorous an organization's attempts are to use integrity assessments in their workplaces, these tools should still be used as only part of the hiring process. It is equally important that employers use traditional hiring practices including conducting a background check, reviewing the candidate's resume, and participating in the interview process before making a decision to hire or not hire a candidate (USDL, 2000). To use these tools properly, employers must be aware of the legal issues involved in assessments. Although there are legal reasons for exercising caution in using integrity and other personality assessments for employment purposes, there are also trends that argue strongly for the most extensive use of such assessments (Brody et al., 2015). Well-designed and well-implemented assessment programs may actually assist companies in demonstrating due diligence in hiring, thereby reducing the company's exposure to negligent hiring liability claims (Shaffer & Schmidt, 1999). Where these assessments can be shown to be scientifically sound, legally defensible, and predictive of an individual's job performance, it is understandable that they are being used more and more often as part of the hiring and promotion process.

The good news for employers wishing to use integrity assessments is that few, if any, assessment performance differences are found between men and women or applicants of different races or ethnicities (Brody et al., 2015). Furthermore, "integrity tests have been shown to not adversely discriminate against minority groups for race, gender, or age to any significant degree, as well as not to elicit negative reactions from applicants in terms of their invasiveness or job relevance as sometimes believed to be the case" (Fine, et al., 2010). In addition, leading integrity assessment publishers provide statistical evidence demonstrating the validity of their instruments at predicting theft and job-relevant counterproductive behavior that would satisfy the employer's legal burden (Eisenbraun, 2006). Using assessment instruments that are valid is critical to effectively assess candidates and reduce legal risk. According to the United States Department of Labor, validity is an important issue in selecting assessment instruments (USDL, 2000). Validity refers to the trait the assessment instrument measures and how well the instrument measures the trait. Basically does the instrument predict the trait it purports to measure such as predispositions towards theft?

399

Integrity assessments should be validated before they are used to select people into jobs by showing that scores on these assessments correlate with employees engaging in counterproductive work behavior. Assessment manuals usually provide the validity coefficient where the higher the coefficient, the more confidence we are that the instrument used for measurement of a specific trait is predictive for a specific purpose under specific circumstances. Interestingly, among all types of methods used in the employee selection process, including background screening, integrity assessments display the highest validity for predicting counterproductive workplace behaviors (Roberts, 2011). With any test, a common area of legal concern is whether the test is reliable or in other words, are the results of the test consistently repeatable so we have confidence in the results? If a person takes the same test again, will he or she get a similar score, or a very different score? A reliable instrument will provide accurate and consistent scores. To meaningfully interpret test scores and make useful career or employment-related decisions, use only reliable tools. Test manuals will usually provide a statistic, known as the reliability coefficient, giving one an indication of a test's reliability. The higher the reliability coefficient, the more confidence one has that the assessment score is accurate in its predictive ability. Over the years, integrity assessments have not been devoid of criticism. Some opponents believe that integrity tests weed out too many candidates, others express concerns over false positives, and still others

believe that there is a susceptibility to faking during the taking of the assessment meaning people do not put down answers of what they truly believe. Indeed, "evidence in experimental conditions has shown that faking can artificially improve integrity test scores" (Fine et al., 2010). One method companies use to control for faking is to ask the same question, worded differently, at different points throughout the assessment. In the instance of a false positive, an integrity test may label an honest person as dishonest. Supporters of integrity testing argue that "all assessments—interviews, resume screenings, other tests—used for employment purposes have false positives and false negatives" (Roberts, 2011). They contend that the best way to combat the issue of false positives is to make integrity tests highly valid because the higher the test's validity, the lower the error rate (Roberts, 2011). As for the issue of weeding out too many candidates, supporters argue that all misconduct is positively correlated, "so, if an employer is concerned about many behaviors—rates of employee theft, sabotage, unexcused absences, aggression toward coworkers and so forth—the number of applicants filtered out might be high" (Roberts, 2011).

Assessment instruments, like other tools, are helpful when used properly, but they can be useless, harmful, or illegal when used inappropriately (Brody et al., 2015). Often, inappropriate use results from not having a clear understanding of what is to be measured and why it needs to be measured. Thus, employers must first be clear about what they want to accomplish with an assessment program in order to select the proper instrument to achieve those goals. Assessment strategies should be based on both an understanding of the kind of employment decisions to be made and the population to be assessed. Once a strategy has been developed, selecting appropriate assessment instruments becomes more efficient. It is recommended to only use assessments that are appropriate for a particular purpose. Although assessments provide important employment-related information about an individual, no assessment tool is 100 percent reliable or valid; all are subject to errors, both in measuring job-relevant characteristics and in predicting job performance (USDL, 2000).

Moreover, a single assessment instrument provides a limited view of a person's qualifications. Using a variety of tools to measure skills, abilities, and other job-relevant characteristics provides a more solid basis upon which to make important career and employment-related decisions and minimizes adverse impact (Brody et al., 2015). Using unbiased and fair tests will help select a qualified and diverse workforce. Review the fairness evidence associated with assessment instruments before selecting tools by examining the test manual reviews. An assessment tool is usually developed for use with a specific group; it may not be valid for other groups. For example, an assessment designed to predict the performance of office managers may not be valid for clerical workers. The skills and abilities required for the two positions may be different, or the reading level of the assessment may not be suitable for one type of employee over another. Assessments should be appropriate for the individuals desired to be tested, that is, one's target population and manuals should indicate the group or groups the assessment is designed to assess (Brody et al., 2015). The target population should be similar to the group on which the assessment was developed.

In determining the appropriateness of an instrument for a target group, also consider such factors as reading levels, cultural backgrounds, and language barriers; the perception of fairness must be in fact and in appearance. Thus socioeconomic concerns should not be ignored. It is fair to say that increased use of any kind of testing of employees or applicants means an increase in the potential for litigation, however, an employer can take special precautions in order to minimize the risk of litigation (Seegull & Caputo, 2006). Deciding whether to implement psychological testing with applicants and employees does not need to be an anxiety-riddened experience. With careful planning and execution, an employer should be able to use psychological assessments as a way of efficient hiring and promotion without violating federal and state employment laws. For example, 1) do not use assessments as the sole criterion for hiring or promotion decisions, 2) administer the test in a standardized fashion that ensures that all job applicants or employees are assessed in the same way, and 3) take active steps to ensure the confidentiality of assessment responses (Brody et al., 2015). In addition, assessments need to be administered by people who are properly trained in this area or else we increase the risk of incorrectly interpreting results. According to one industrial organizational psychologist, "people are out there putting on amateur psychologist hats and using personal opinions, memory, and other unscientific types of processes" to administer and interpret assessments (Daniel, 2005). Assessments are used to make inferences about people's characteristics, capabilities, and future performance and inferences should be reasonable, well-founded, and not based upon stereotypes.

If assessment scores are not interpreted properly, the conclusions drawn from them are likely to be invalid, thus leading to poor hiring decision making. Moreover, ensure that there is solid evidence to justify assessments score interpretations and the employment decisions made on those scores. In addition, "a test should be based on some theory of job performance; it should have integrity and reliability, and it should accurately predict what it's supposed to predict and be backed up by studies" (Daniel, 2005). Furthermore, every test should come with a technical manual that proves the rigors it went through in development and should have studies to vouch for its validity (Brody et al., 2015). At times vendors refuse to provide evidence of validity and claim that the information was proprietary. However, such a denial of information should be a red flag to employers to avoid using their product because vendors should stand by their product by providing their validity studies. Legal experts also caution against an overreliance on representations made by test manufacturers regarding test validity for a particular job and encourage conducting periodic audits of employment selection testing procedures to monitor for possible adverse impact, significant changes in jobs, outdated validity studies, and other potential problems (Vann, 2007). Furthermore, concerns about invading a person's privacy can be alleviated if the potential employee gives informed consent to taking the assessment. Informed consent is typically a signed document so that there are no misunderstanding that all parties are comfortable with participation in the assessment.

Lastly, integrity assessments are more defensible if the employer is open with the applicant concerning the purpose of the assessment, how the results of the assessment will be used, and the relative importance of the assessment compared to the other selection criteria that will be used in the hiring process. The applicants should be given reasonable notice that they will be asked to take an assessment. If an employer decides to use some form of assessment either to hire new employees or to award internal positions, the assessment must also be administered fairly and accommodations may have to be made for someone that has a disability (Brody et al., 2015). The assessment should be administered by a trained individual in a manner that is consistent for all of the people taking the assessment.

Screening for Potentially Corrupt Leadership

According to forensic psychologist Dr. Robert Hare and those that study criminal behaviors, the risk of corporate scandals that have plagued society could have been mitigated if high-level executives were screened for antisocial behaviors, especially given the billions of dollars they are asked to manage (MacDonald, 2002). The growth of testing in the workplace reflects a broad consensus in the business world that hiring the wrong person, particularly the wrong senior level executive who may be in a position to commit fraud, can negatively impact morale, income, and reputation (Deutschman, 2005). Research has shown that individuals who perform poorly on these assessments are more likely to demonstrate counterproductive work behaviors, such as theft, and are ultimately terminated or possibly prosecuted. Screening out candidates for antisocial traits during a job interview and background check process can be extremely hard because candidates may exhibit all the right qualities when companies are evaluating them for jobs (Carozza, 2008a). Such candidates display effective interviewing skills, so relying on employment interviews and background checks alone when making hiring decisions can lead an organization to make the wrong choice (Steinberger, 2004). The screening process for the assessment of a potential CEO can play a very important role in the prevention of fraud (Anderson & Tirrell, 2004). Though a strong-willed candidate may appear initially desirable, potential problems may be lurking behind such a choice. Self-deception is difficult to detect because the individual believes his or her own self-aggrandizing lies, yet it is a powerful tool for making a good first impression especially in job interviews (Mathieu et al., 2012). Such candidates can look and sound like the ideal leader, but behind this mask exists a dark side that lies, is deceitful, promotes fraud in the organization, and steals the company's money (Steinberger, 2004).

Moreover, some CEOs believe they can accomplish goals by the strength of their personality such as Al Dunlap of Sunbeam stating "We will be successful because I say we will be…Whenever we decide to make a move, we'd announce what we were going to do, set a time frame and paint ourselves into a corner we never let ourselves out" (Anderson & Tirrell, 2004, p. 37). It was Dunlap's goal of 20 percent growth and 20 percent return on equity within a year. However, unable to achieve such a goal, Dunlap engaged in financial manipulation to give the appearance of a turnaround because he was brought in at Sunbeam to revive a stagnant company. Sunbeam artificially inflated income by prematurely recognizing revenue. This was done by recording revenue on products that were ordered by not delivered to customers. Moreover, Dunlap would take expenses that would come due in 1997 and incur them in 1996 thus making it look like he was in fact turning Sunbeam around in 1997 because there were not as many expenses to offset revenue with thus artificially inflating income (Anderson & Tirrell, 2004). Dunlap neglected to mention during his interview process that he was fired from Nitec, a paper mill company in New York, and Max Philips and Son, a waste company in Wisconsin, on his resume. Search firms verified his employment history as part of a background check, but failed to uncover those two dismissals.

After Dunlap was ousted as CEO of Sunbeam in 1998 for engineering a massive accounting fraud, it was uncovered that he behaved in a similar manner during his time at Nitec. There is a common tendency among people who rise to the top of an organization that find it difficult to report poor results that suggests any sort of failure on their part. Executives whose self-identity is tied to the success of an organization or whose performance fails to live up to their job title is a recipe for misconduct; unfortunately fraud is their answer in many instances to preserve their pride (Anderson & Tirrell, 2004). Fraudulent reporting can be viewed as an attempt to protect themselves from public humiliation and prevent damage to their self-esteem. Careful selection processes can delve into the candidates' attitudes about risk-taking, how they view themselves, how they deal with failures, and to give examples of failures. Another technique is to give situational examples and ask the candidate to make decisions based on the situation presented (Anderson & Tirrell, 2004). For example, would the candidate disclose unfavorable information, such as losses, that would impact the profitability of the company?

The goal can no longer be to make a profit without questioning how the results were attained; quality financial reporting has to be part of the goal. There are professionals who can administer such interviews and report their findings to a hiring committee. Although there are costs attached to such prehiring protocols, they would probably be dwarfed by an organization involved in a fraud scandal especially the legal fees to represent such an organization if brought to court by investors and the government (Anderson & Tirrell, 2004). Pathologically challenged corporate leaders may neglect the functional requirements of leadership, the human needs and constraints involved in the work, and the value systems that constitute one of the important measures against which to judge administrative and technical responsibilities (Hayes, 2009). Organizational controls such as corporate governance, weak board of directors and ethics structures are insufficient in preventing unscrupulous behaviors and actions carried out by psychologically flawed organization members. Employers can assess individual integrity, especially within the scope of a hiring criteria platform, coupled with background checks to identify troublesome candidates before they become part of an organization triggering unnecessary misconduct.

Also important is the obligation where organizations should investigate before promoting someone for whom there is a large disparity between a person's self-ratings and colleague and subordinate ratings of that person (Walker & Jackson, 2016). Staff surveys that include feedback from colleagues and subordinates can assist in determining who to promote by using a 360-degree appraisal to ensure they are assessing and promoting individuals with a consistent track record for integrity (Walker & Jackson, 2016). 360-degree appraisals provide those who have to promote someone to positions of leadership valuable insights into their professional strengths and weaknesses by soliciting feedback from people that work with them regularly and those that are their superiors. Is there a consistent pattern displaying differences between how those that work with a candidate directly on a day to day basis from how senior level people view them? Recall how corporate psychopaths operate in that they might bully and manipulate those below them and ingratiate themselves to those above them. This is an example of how perceptional differences between how superiors view a candidate and how subordinates view a candidate can reveal hidden traits about a person's true character and ultimately negative consequences such as corporate fraud could have been avoided; unfortunately the damage to an organization might not be reversible when certain employees reach leadership positions.

The problem of promoting this person to senior management is these employees can potentially create an extreme workplace environment. This can include not only the individual-level problems such as abusive supervision, but also the corporate-level problems such as large-scale fraud that leads to corporate collapse (Walker & Jackson, 2016). These assessments are important because even "trained industrial/organizational psychologists, if not made aware of the problematic evaluations or profiles, may think certain individuals are good fits for the organizations when, if fact, they are potentially toxic" (Mathieu et al., 2012, p. 5). In fact, "some executives tend to rely on their 'gut feeling' to judge candidates and that unfortunately, once decision makers believe that an individual has future leader potential, even bad performance reviews or evaluations from subordinates and peers do not seem to be able to shake their belief" (Mathieu et al., 2012, p. 5). It is clear that background checks have many limitations associated with them. Given the damage that a dishonest employee can cause an organization, the use of integrity assessments are an appropriate countermeasure that should be used as part of the pre-screening process. While there are individuals and organizations with concerns associated with the use of assessments, if done properly, there is no legal reason to exclude their use. In fact these assessments are beneficial as part of the screening process as they are expected to identify applicants who are likely to engage in behavior that is counterproductive to the organization. Given the time, expense, and importance associated with the hiring process, it is strongly recommended that organizations consider the use of integrity assessments to help them hire the right individuals and avoid hiring the wrong ones that can causes irreparable harm.

Improving Decision Making to Reduce Misconduct

There are obstacles that influence our ability to engage in rational decision making that is ethical and law abiding. People often respond to ethical dilemmas in an instinctive and emotional manner by also using the proverbial "gut-feel" or intuition, meaning they experience a physiological influence to decision making. Research suggests that people rely on their intuition to determine if there is something wrong with how a decision is being made in that if there is an uncomfortable physiological reaction to a particular scenario, that should encourage one to become more deliberative before a course of action is taken (Palmer, 2016). It is understandable that at times there is missing information that would guide one to make a more thoughtful decision, thus their intuition is all they have to rely on. However, the problem is that even when we have access to information to help guide us make better decisions, it is not considered, perhaps even rejected due to biases and we still rely on our gut-feel to help guide us to erroneous decisions. Not taking the time to be more deliberative and thoughtful in acknowledging our biases influences how we frame an issue to determine how we proceed to think about an issue can lead individuals to make suboptimal decisions that ultimately can inadvertently turn into misconduct even though they believe that their gut-feel is correct. People might even acknowledge that their decision is unethical, but not illegal because the path of how they arrived at a decision did not take into account other factors that would have revealed to them that the decision is more complex than originally thought. Moreover, gut instincts can only take one so far in life, and anyone who operates outside of a sound decision making framework will eventually fall prey to poor decision making because of bias, misinformation, groupthink, misunderstanding, manipulation, impulsivity or some other negative influencing factor.

In addition, distorted decision making may display itself with people who would normally not be accustomed to misconduct because these same people have to deal with formal authority structures and group dynamics. As a result, the type of thinking behind a decision tends to reflect a more emotional, reflexive, quick to the point approach, and not a reflective quality. Yet, the type of thinking we should be engaging in should be more deliberate and reflective which takes time, requires more mental energy, thus not as apt to take place as often when important decisions have to be made, especially those exposing one to legal liabilities. Although not a comprehensive list, areas where there is a tendency to not engage in rigorous reflective thinking include, 1) not questioning management representations about their operations and financial statements, 2) not questioning their strategic plans, financial forecasts, estimates, and assessing the potential impact of legislation or investigations, and 3) the impact of regulations on decisions. We may make assumptions about management's representations, for example at an audit, based on our biases of how we may personally feel about them instead of relying on good old-fashioned due diligence such as gathering evidence to confirm their representations.

It will often prove difficult to shut off personal feelings such as loyalties to others and the temptation to want to be accepted by the group one encounters on a daily basis as opposed to being alienated by the group that one has generated affection for over time. Also, consider the difficulty of removing oneself from misconduct once pressures to rationalize have been adopted to continue that interferes with quality decision making. Even the most law-abiding organizational participants are at risk for engaging in misconduct and not even know it by how they participate in decision making especially when misconduct is normalized. People may understand at an intuitional level that something may not feel right in how decisions are being made, but to extrapolate that insight into knowing that they engaged in misconduct that rises to potential criminality reflects a different level of comprehension. Thus, although people may be acting in a rational manner at a given point in time, it is a limited type of rationality because they are not dealing with or understand the full set of facts that leads them to better anticipate the consequences of their decisions.

In other words how they might engage in a cost-benefit analysis is skewed—it resembles a distorted analysis that may appear mindless to those on the outside observing how they approached an issue to resolve (Palmer, 2012). It appears mindless because our reactions to issues that may be ladened with ethical concerns are mechanical and routinized attaching ourselves automatically to innate personal biases, learned organizational social norms, and rules and protocol that dampen our natural reaction which is to be suspicious of such behaviors. Not engaging in misconduct is a constant, ongoing, active, conscious exercise of our will to train ourselves to understand what can lead us astray and how to avoid those traps that may get us into trouble when making a decision. For example, do we rationalize small misconducts and not see the larger cumulative impact of these small misconducts? Although talent and experience are clearly important components of effective professional judgment, researchers have discovered key insights in judgment and decision making over the last few decades that have the potential to enhance the professional judgment skills of people (Kahneman et al., 2011).

Making sound decisions is a skill set that needs to be developed like any other skill. Just as people rely on templates in their lives to help them navigate other aspects of their behavior through acknowledging laws, social norms, rules and regulations, actually encouraging them on how to engage in better decision making at an organizational level is not a theoretical idea. People need to be taught how to determine what they do not know so that they can better approach situations with a better set of decision making skills especially when it comes to tackling ethical and legal issues that invariably arise within an organizational setting. By becoming better decision makers, we can avoid misconduct by not having to confront an ethical dilemma in the first place. We become better at decision making by recognizing potential ethical issues before they arise allowing us to engage in that "moral imagination" referred to before where we can better foresee the consequences of our decisions.

Many executives today realize how biases can distort reasoning in business, but just awareness of the effects of biases has done little to improve the quality of business decisions at either the individual or the organizational level, but it is possible to take steps to counteract biases. Over time, by using these tools, they will build decision processes that reduce the effect of biases in their organizations, and in doing so, they will help upgrade the quality of those decisions.

Companies that effectively consider multiple perspectives when faced with important judgments are able to develop a more precise issue definition and devise more effective strategies to deal with issues as they arise. We need to be sensitive to the forces that give rise to misconduct so that we can blunt their influence and avoid engaging in wrongdoing ourselves. Furthermore, the complexity of the current business landscape, combined with ever increasing expectations of performance, and the speed at which decisions must be made, are a potential recipe for disaster for today's executive unless a defined methodology for decision making is put into place. Understanding how to make good decisions is learning how to synthesize the overwhelming amount of incoming information we must deal with on a daily basis, while making the best decisions possible in a timely fashion. Also, is there any reason to suspect thinking errors that are motivated by self-interest (Kahneman et al., 2011)? The issue here is not intentional deception as much as it is about what motivates us to make a decision and what rationalizations are used to justify our thinking to support a course of action. For example, might a doctor prescribe more of a medication if he makes more money in prescribing the medication?

Recall the whistleblower case of TAP Pharmaceutical's Vice President Douglas Durand where he found doctors receiving a 2 percent administration fee for prescribing TAP's prostate cancer drug, Lupron. Can a doctor separate out the self-interest bias in prescribing Lupron in making the decision to prescribe the medication or not versus what is in the best interest of the patient? There is also the self-interest that goes beyond monetary gain, such as the self-interest of acquiring organizational power, reputation and career options. Moreover we must ask ourselves if we have become so emotionally attached to a course of action that we tend to minimize the costs and exaggerate the benefits. In addition, what are some of the issues that arise which can interfere with implementing a quality decision making apparatus especially since decisions are made within team environments? When making a decision, especially in a group environment, were alternative solutions to a problem explored? Were others in the group able to voice their concerns in a supportive environment or does groupthink creep into the scenario (Kahneman et al., 2011)? When there is no room for dissent, this should sound an alarm. When this work environment takes root, red-flag situations are not addressed. A red flag situation is when a decision or strategy is known to be false, illegal or technically not feasible and no objection or criticism is raised because of the environment of fear. Individuals who would normally speak out do not, out of fear of being reprimanded or they simply have psychologically distanced themselves from the situation ultimately engaging in self-censorship.

When this distancing occurs, the responsibility for the decision is placed squarely onto the shoulders of another, and it becomes a situation of "I was only following orders", without any second or critical thought to the meaning and outcome of those orders (Hulsted, 2010). The culture of critical and open thinking starts at the top and it is this tone of open communication that assists in becoming better decision makers especially since it is critical discussion that helps to shave down the influence of biases, groupthink, and dysfunctional loyalty that does not discriminate between good conduct and misconduct. Management must cultivate an organizational culture in which employees openly share ideas, possible solutions and methods of implementing those solutions. Without that creative dynamic of being able to openly and constructively criticize, an environment of fear, antipathy, and stagnation sets in leading to suboptimal decision making that can lead, even inadvertently, to misconduct. By consistently following a sound judgment process by acknowledging our vulnerabilities to bias which is inherent in decision making, we can improve the oversight and monitoring of an organization's strategies and risks, including the risk of fraud (Glover & Prawitt, 2012). Unfortunately, people try to disavow and dismiss information that contradicts their worldview, thus continuing as if nothing is wrong. Discounting information may continue eventually until "they come across a piece of evidence too fascinating to ignore, too clear to misperceive, too painful to deny...forcing them to alter and surrender the worldview they have so meticulously constructed" (Soltes, 2016, p. 321).

As uncomfortable as it is to have our beliefs questioned, the process of having to defend a viewpoint can lead us to reevaluate and improve our judgements especially if some of the symptoms of groupthink are present. When our judgements are unchallenged because they are shared among like-minded individuals, decisions can reflect naïve or unsubstantiated intuitions resulting in suboptimal decision making. Fostering healthy debate and avoiding early consensus is key to avoiding unhealthy tendencies toward suppression of views or early, potentially premature consensus. Instead, group interactions should be designed and conducted to stimulate and encourage the expression of different perspectives. Most of the time, decision makers do not even realize when they have fallen into the "rush to solve" trap (Glover & Prawitt, 2012). This tendency is a trap because people fall into it unaware and unknowingly develop a limited view of the problem that they are addressing, the objectives they are trying to achieve, and the available alternatives. In other words, if we rush to get to a solution, we are likely to underinvest in the vital early steps of a good judgment process because we go with one of the first workable alternatives offered. Although it is likely that tendencies and related biases will never disappear from our judgment processes, the first step in mitigating biases is to be aware of possible sources of what we are basing our decision on and to recognize situations where we might be vulnerable to poor decision making. Groups tend to produce better judgments when diversity of thought is not only tolerated but explicitly encouraged.

Illustrating this point is Alfred Sloan, former chairman of the Board of General Motors, who saw the lack of debate as a sign the group did not appreciate the underlying problems of an objective, stated the following at the end of a meeting with the company's board of directors: I take it we are all in complete agreement on the decision here...Then I propose we postpone further discussion of this matter until our next meeting to give ourselves time to develop disagreement and perhaps gain some understanding of what the decision is all about (Glover & Prawitt, 2011, p. 5). It is critically important to rigorously question management's assertions and conscientiously consider potentially opposing views and information (Glover & Prawitt, 2012). As a result, making judgments in groups has the potential to greatly improve judgment quality, but poorly structured group interaction can actually exacerbate the traps and biases previously discussed when we studied groupthink. Groups facing difficult judgments can typically boost the quality of their decision making by having individual members carefully and conscientiously prepare before the meeting and then, in the meeting, by having each individual share his or her initial views openly without critique from others. Such an approach can increase the effort and participation of fellow group members, encourage a broader and more complete set of perspectives and alternatives, and enhance the quality of final decisions.

Leadership and Decision Making

At the heart of this discussion of better decision making is how leadership responds to criticism assuming subordinates are not afraid to voice their opinions. Unfortunately moral superiority, fear, and distrust of people outside of a group immerge from insular groups; this process is at times exacerbated by leadership manipulating subordinates to enhance control over the group's decision making process (Brewer, 1999). Generally, leaders should not only tolerate, but explicitly and genuinely encourage diversity of thoughts, opinions and open sharing with full consideration of ideas and perspectives, especially those that go against the flow of the group's predominant views. For example, when evaluating a project are we willing to insert checks and balances in the deliberative process that slows down what often seems like a rush to say "yes" to senior management (Paredes, 2005)? Studies show that considering arguments against a course of action, such as by asking probing questions, challenging key assumptions, considering conflicting evidence, or developing other options can reduce overconfidence (Paredes, 2005).

By incorporating the following questions into leaderships' decision making framework, they can work towards minimizing the chances of making a bad decision. Some additional questions directed toward leadership should include, 1) what is motivating the need for a decision and what would happen if no decision is made?, 2) who will the decision impact both directly and indirectly?, 3) what data, analytics, research, or supporting information is available to validate the inclinations driving a decision? and 4) if a decision was publicized, would that influence one's decision to follow through with it or would there be concerns about the ethics of the decision that would meet with disapproval? (Myatt, 2012). Other questions to consider are, how would shareholders and employees perceive the decision and has leadership sought counsel and feedback before making a decision? Moreover, insightful leaders understand that the best thought out decision may fail; it is important to have a contingency plan knowing circumstances can fall beyond the boundaries of one's control. Contingency plans can help mitigate against initial plans not being fulfilled.

A number of features of post-Enron corporate governance, such as more independent directors and investors, is to challenge a CEO to consider why he or she might be wrong, or to at least explain himself more fully and to consider alternatives more carefully. It may simply take asking the CEO, what are the top five reasons why we should reject your proposal? One technique that has been used to challenge senior management is to employ what is known as the "devil's advocate" approach or the contrarian approach (Hodges & Hodges, 2013). The devil's advocate technique involves someone in the group being assigned the role to critique and identify the risks involved in a proposed course of action. This type of critique is intended to foster a more in-depth review of the issues surrounding the proposal, ensure all alternatives are equally reviewed, and identify any underlying pitfalls or unethical practices. For example, what are the uncertainties and risks inherent in the different alternatives? Are we being overly optimistic about a decision especially if we have been right in the past thus believing we will be right in the future?

A benefit of taking on the proverbial devil's advocate approach is to challenge the chief executive, as well as to put pressure on deferential members of the management team and the board of directors who are silent, is that it normalizes debate within the organization. Formalizing the advocate role, when appropriate, frees the CEO from the obligation of asking for assistance and input from others if he wants opposing viewpoints when others may be unwilling to voice their opinion that may be contrary to the leaders views (Paredes, 2005). Individuals filling the advocate role should have stature and should be well-regarded so that their views are respected and heeded. Advocates should be independent of the CEO and otherwise unconcerned about the potential costs of expressing an opposing view, yet not to block projects, but to ensure that project risks are more evenly appraised. Second, advocates need access to good information in order to bring their independent judgment to bear effectively in pressing the CEO, as well as other senior managers and directors, with probing questions and in developing alternative strategies and courses of action to achieve optimal decision making with available information.

Among other things, this might mean giving advocates more direct access to personnel throughout the firm, as well as to the firm's outside lawyers and bankers, so that the CEO and other senior officers are not the sole source of information for an advocate to rely on (Paredes, 2005). The purpose of the advocate's role is to ensure that arguments against some proposal are heard, risks are adequately considered, assumptions are challenged, and flawed logic is exposed—in short, to ensure proposals are fully aired but, without being too disruptive, grinding decisions to a halt, or usurping the CEO's role (Paredes, 2005). Good leaders seek the counsel of others, but maintain control over the final decision. Leaders who openly invite dissent are more likely to challenge rigid framing of issues and foster sense-making activities characterized by flexible framing in order to reduce the risks associated with overconfidence that may lead to poor decision making and potential financial disaster (Palazzo et al., 2012).

For example, some areas to challenge leadership include, 1) how accounting estimates were derived, 2) how to achieve a more balanced and thoughtful decision, 3) consult with others that do not have a stake in the decision to get their objective input, 4) consider alternative explanations for that which is observed, 5) consider different opinions and objective data that may disagree leadership's position, 6) be aware of common threats to judgment such as biases, overconfidence, and the rush to solve a problem tendency, and 7) consider the reliability, validity, and accuracy of information used in decision making (Palazzo et al., 2012). Moreover, effective leaders can reduce the symptoms of groupthink by seeking outside expert advice when needed, and remove top leadership from subordinate group discussions to reduce the influence of authority so that people are free to discuss their problem solving ideas (Hodges & Hodges, 2013). In addition, effective leaders diversify groups so that they are not always homogenous in how they think about issues in order to encourage open and honest dialogue without the fear of backlash for sharing opinions that are contrary to senior managements that is often an indication of groupthink (Hodges & Hodges, 2013). A few suggestions for defending against groupthink include: 1) establishing multiple groups to study the same issue, 2) training all employees in proper ethical conduct, 3) initiating programs organization-wide to clarify and communicate ethical conduct, 4) increasing the staff and scope of internal audit departments, 5) displaying impartiality by not stating preferences at the onset of a project, and 6) rotating new members into a group in order to bring fresh perspectives into their discussions.

Promoting Organizational Ethical Awareness

When we see people of virtue, we should think of equaling them; when we see people of a contrary character, we should examine ourselves.

Confucius

Ethics in all forms is concerned with right and wrong, good or bad and what is our moral duty and obligations; typically ethics is either a set of principles held by an individual or group or the discipline that studies those ethical principles (Sims, 2003). Systems of beliefs that affect what the individual defines as right, good, and fair are referred to as values and ethics reflects the way values are displayed. For the individual this typically means acting in ways consistent with one's personal, organizational and commonly held societal values. People, generally speaking, have an ethical set of beliefs such as cheating and stealing is wrong, unjustified violence is wrong, promises ought to be kept, and so on. Harboring personal ethical standards involves, 1) understanding the difference between right and wrong, 2) respecting appropriate boundaries, be it personal and property, 3) having a sense of fair play, 4) learning to care for and empathize with others, 5) acknowledging the importance of the principles of integrity, and 6) behaving in an ethical manner on a consistent basis (Albrecht et al., 2012). Each of these opinions constitute our moral beliefs that reflects our ethics and our ethics helps us to evaluate situations, others, organizations and their practices, social, political and economic systems (Duska et al., 2011).

For example, someone might believe that a government system that punishes dissenting opinion is unethical, but also illegal. The study of ethics is important because without a foundation to understand our own ethical framework, it would be rather difficult to implement organizational awareness on the topic of ethics. The fact is that we do have foundations of what we deem to be ethical and unethical and to deny this would mean that anyone's way of living life and how they conduct themselves is co-equal to anyone elses and that opinions are just opinions not subject to challenge. The ultimate conclusion to this position would mean we could not have criminal laws that define behaviors as criminal and worthy of punishment because the collective body politic is passing laws that are criminal based on subjective opinion of right and wrong. That being said, it is proper to subject our beliefs to ethical analysis because we might hold beliefs that are not adequate and not worth holding on to. Understanding ethical principles also assists us in determining what should be done and why when we are faced with a difficult situation that needs to be addressed.

It is helpful to have a template to guide us to make a decision such as asking questions of the impact of a decision on others, is the decision fair or just, does the decision harm others, what are the foreseeable consequences of a decision, and so on. We would think that how one behaves in a private setting, which may reflect the qualities discussed above, will be applied in a work setting, but that is not always the case. This is why it is important to understand how a person truly thinks about different environments that produce different situations to deal with. Many fraud offenders consider themselves to be honest, ethical people, but when faced with the choice to be ethical, they failed. They acknowledge that what they did was wrong, but did not have the courage to apply their personal code of ethics in a work environment. Just as individuals face ethical issues on a personal level, the same dynamic holds true at the organizational level. At the personal level, one might decide whether to cheat on a tax return or whether to notify their bank that they credited their account with more money than was deposited. Within an organization, we may encounter ethical issues that impact not only employees, but also the organization's reputation and success.

An organizational ethical issue might be whether to, 1) offer bribes to attract business, 2) should a product be made safer even though there is compliance with the law, but the legal standard is out of date and there is a safer way to make the product, and 3) should unethical and/or illegal acts be committed to make the company look more profitable than it is given the financial difficulties the company is facing? These are but a few of the countless examples one can come up with given the complexities and pressures people face every day at their place of work. In most organizations, what we observe is a small group of employees who have a well-defined personal code of ethical conduct and are able to easily apply those ethical standards in a work setting while other employees who lack a personal ethical code will be dishonest if it benefits them on a consistent basis (Albrecht et al., 2012). Moreover, there is a group of employees who are situationally ethical which means they are ethical depending on the situation they find themselves in.

They know the difference between right and wrong and at times have the courage to do the right thing, but there are situations in which they will not do the right thing. These situationally ethical employees are influenced by organizational culture, the tone at the top, and are more apt to do the right thing if the tone at the top projects an expectation of ethical conduct (Albrecht et al., 2012). However, the reverse also holds true in that if the tone at the top projects a corrupt message, it is not unreasonable to foresee how this large situationally ethical group can be swayed to engage in misconduct. Many wrongdoer's behaviors are influenced by organizational structures that facilitate and encourage wrongdoing no differently than organizational structures that facilitate and encourage doing the right thing (Palmer, 2012). Thus everyone, including those that believe they are above wrongdoing, need to understand those forces that can influence a person's decision to engage in misconduct and this is where promoting ethical awareness comes into play. There needs to be active, explicit organizational ethical awareness that we are capable of engaging in misconduct approaching situations, at times, in an almost lazy manner where we rely on routinized behaviors to guide our decisions.

This is why at times and as previously stated, misconduct has a mechanical, robot-like feel to it where there is no decision making; one is simply reacting to a situation without thinking of the consequences or even becoming aware that their actions have an ethical and potentially a criminal component. The temptations to cut ethical corners and to continue questionable practices encouraged by others are strong indeed especially since businesses today are under extreme pressure to produce quarterly results, increase productivity, decrease costs, and fend off competition (Ferrell & Ferrell, 2010). Moreover, given the ambiguity, complexity, and the fast-paced nature that displays itself in contemporary environments, there is ample room to rationalize transgressions as unavoidable, commonplace, and even rewarded. People tend to create their own standards in a constantly changing environment, consequently the high pressure and speed of change occurring in many professions leads corporate leaders to make up their own rationale for what is acceptable behavior (Hayes, 2009). Management, at times, find themselves in environments where corrupt activities are being justified by rationalizations need to question these practices rather than meekly acquiesce. What also is observable is a lack of moral awareness, also referred to as unintentional amoral awareness where amoral managers do not think about business activity in ethical terms (Tenbrunsel & Smith-Crowe, 2008).

They are simply casual and careless about, or inattentive to the fact that their decisions and actions may have negative impact on others. These managers lack ethical perception, that is, they cavalierly go through their organizational lives not thinking that what they are doing has an ethical dimension to it. They may be well intentioned, but are either too insensitive or egocentric to consider the impact of their behavior on others (Carrroll, 1987). Most ethics experts believe that we will never be able to create enough laws to prevent schemes designed to inflate earnings and engage in other forms of misconduct. To prevent future Enron-type failures, the corporate ethical culture, corporate governance, and reward systems will have to change in many organizations. For example past practice, even if fraudulent, is erroneously interpreted not only as being efficient, but because it is efficient it is also an ethical practice. Yet past practice should not guide executives in their judgments about the appropriateness of such activities coupled with the fact that rationalizations can endure over a long period of time and can be collectively practiced in organizations and industries. Furthermore, managers would be mistaken to regard legal compliance as an adequate means for addressing the full range of ethical issues that arise every day; "If it's legal, it's ethical" is a frequently heard slogan (Aguilera & Vadera, 2008).

Even in the best case scenarios, legal compliance is unlikely to unleash much moral imagination or commitment. Those managers who define ethics as legal compliance are implicitly endorsing a code of moral mediocrity for their organizations; it is no guide for exemplary behavior or even good practice. As Richard Breeden, former chairman of the Securities and Exchange Commission (SEC) noted, "It is not an adequate ethical standard to aspire to get through the day without being indicted" (Paine, 1994). While compliance is rooted in avoiding legal sanctions, organizational integrity is based on the concept of self-governance in accordance with a set of guiding ethical principles that go beyond the minimal requirements to fulfill legal compliance. From the perspective of integrity, the task of ethics management is to define and give life to an organization's guiding values, create an environment that supports ethically sound behavior, and instill a sense of shared accountability among employees. Ethical values shape the decision making process used by individuals and groups providing a common frame of reference serving as a unifying force across different functions, lines of business, and employee groups.

Many integrity initiatives have structural features common to compliance-based initiatives: a code of conduct, training in relevant areas of law, mechanisms for reporting and investigating potential misconduct, audits, and internal controls to ensure that laws and company standards are being upheld. Moreover although a CEO acting alone cannot "sink the ship", weak corporate governance conditions facilitated the collapse of large public companies because they did not serve as a check on the authority of leadership and this problem still pervades corporate life today which explains why we still witness corporate scandals. The lessons learned from these cases discussed within this book are many especially since ethics and compliance starts with top management who make it known that unethical and illegal behaviors will or will not be tolerated. If the senior officers and board of directors do not develop an effective compliance program, they invariably expose themselves to the increased risk of misconduct disasters that can destroy a business (Ferrell & Ferrell, 2010).

In the end management and the board of directors are responsible and accountable for enhancing the intangible resource of integrity such as decreasing the risk to behave unethically (Ferrell & Ferrell, 2010). Although ethics training tends to focus on employees, training management on communicating the importance of ethics and reinforcing ethical behavior by displaying it themselves, there is a greater likelihood the impact on ethical leadership will trickle down to subordinates (Mayer et al., 2009). Ethics, however, is more than the character of a few individuals, it requires resources and proactive management associated with understanding and preventing misconduct. Leaders play a crucial role in developing and maintaining organizational culture. Yet, even when the tone at the top is one espousing ethical behavior, subordinates do not always adopt the tone from the top, but ignore it because they harbor antisocial inclinations (Greeve et al., 2010). Surveys indicate that leadership behavior is the factor that most strongly influences individuals' willingness to engage in misconduct and even if not explicitly engaging in corruption, by allowing, rewarding, or ignoring it (Greeve et al., 2010).

Installing top managers who, 1) approach their work in an ethical manner, 2) respond to crises in the proper way, 3) setting proper examples, 4) reward proper and punish improper behaviors, and 5) hire ethical people and dismiss those that engage in illegal and unethical practices can transform a corrupt culture into a rightful one. How should we interpret the above quote by Confucius who said, "When we see people of virtue, we should think of equaling them; when we see people of a contrary character, we should examine ourselves"? Although quotes are subject to multiple interpretations, one interpretation of his quote is, are we aware of the impact that other peoples' values have on our reaction to their behavior? Recall the example of accountant Betty Vinson of WorldCom who went to prison for assisting in the misrepresentation of WorldCom's financial statement. Initially her intuition told her that there was something wrong with CFO Scott Sullivan's request that made her uncomfortable enough to react to such a request by resigning, but she did not. Sullivan's value system endorsed engaging not only in an unethical, but in an illegal act, and he recruited others to help him in the process because he could not participate in fraud alone to fulfill his agenda. He recruited Betty and others to engage in the financial statement fraud persuading them that they would have to make the fraudulent adjustment one time and that he would take full responsibility for their actions.

Betty may not have changed the way Scott reacted to the financial pressures he felt as CFO, but Betty could have controlled how she reacted to someone who had a value system that was, at least in this situation, contrary to her own. She was close to doing the right thing and resigning, having control over her destiny and not having to face the specter of prison, but in the end, she succumbed to Sullivan's request. As Confucius states, Betty should have more carefully examined her own reaction and controlled her destiny instead of having someone else, like CFO Sullivan and his value system, dictate the trajectory of her life which meant going to prison. The Betty Vinson matter also reveals how being in a group environment can lead to a false sense of security in that if there is a general consensus amongst group members to go along with an act coupled with their particular rationalizations, then it must be the right thing to do under the circumstances. Moreover, consider the statement of offender Vernon Beck, a former Director at Texas Petrochemicals, who embezzled $14 million from a $1.6 billion annual revenue petrochemical company that parallels the insight of Chinese philosopher Confucius "When we see people of virtue, we should think of equaling them; when we see people of a contrary character, we should examine ourselves." Beck stated: "My advice would be to question yourself closely, and often" (Crumbley & Beck, 2020, p. 448).

Just as misconduct can be institutionalized within an organization, it is possible to institutionalize ethical awareness within an organization by agreeing that there are certain behaviors that are not acceptable. Recall that when speaking of institutionalization, we are referring to specific acts that persist over time and exist as part of the daily functioning of an organization. It should be clear that these specific acts do not have to be present in every situation because they can vary within an organization as to their degree and how wide-spread it is. Institutionalizing ethics may be more important than ever before to counteract the increasingly blatant, unethical, and often illegal behavior within organizations, whether business, religious, educational, governmental and so on, that are often highly regarded until their misconduct is exposed (Sims, 2003). There are a variety of ways that organizations can institutionalize ethics and one way is through encouragement of its culture that ethics is valued and rewarded. Management can set the tone at the top by explicitly and publicly explaining ethical concerns that arise when decisions have to be made that may have an ethical component. Management can also institutionalize ethics by supporting people who are whistleblowers when they observe misconduct instead of punishing them for looking after the interests of the organization.

Organizations have begun to implement ethics programs, including seminars or workshops to reinforce good ethics with the hope of preempting misconduct from occurring in the first place. Some downplay the importance of these training programs believing that they are irrelevant, but the question becomes, is it important to counteract those forces that increase the risk of misconduct? For example, part of ethics training must include neutralizing the rationalizations that people use to justify fraudulent behavior; at a minimum employees learn that they cannot lean on rationalizations to mitigate in their mind their crimes or unethical conduct (Heath, 2008). There are factors that assist in making institutionalization of ethics a reality. First of all there needs to be a real sense of commitment to ethics meaning peoples' sense of organizational identity has to be linked to a strong belief in the organization's commitment to an ethical environment. To increase people's sense of commitment to ethical standards, there needs to be a sense of visibility of ethical values on display. Unobserved behaviors are unlikely to have a committed force behind them because we cannot link ethical behavior to a specific person (Sims, 2003).

Visibility can also be increased by the presence of a code of ethics and a corporate ethics committee which in turn will increase the visibility of expected ethical behavior and the institutionalization of ethics within an organization (Sims, 2003). It is important that expected behaviors are made explicit in terms of what is expected in order to reduce the ambiguity of the message, thus lessening the ability to deny their existence. Explicitness can be accomplished by having management and employees acknowledge in writing by signing a letter confirming their understanding of an organization's ethical policies coupled with an understanding that they will report misconduct. Employees should agree that ethical standards are not just standards to be applied when convenient. In addition, we can have the best policies in place, but without an organizational culture that supports such commitments to ethical behavior and a tone from the top that addresses violations of ethical standards, ethical training and programs designed to facilitate the institutionalization of ethics will fall flat. Organizations must constantly find ways to ensure that unethical cultural characteristics are identified and eliminated before they become so embedded in an organization's culture that it spreads like a cancer.

Like a cancer, it must be removed as quickly as possible before ethical fading sets in and misconduct becomes normalized. For example, one unhealthy trait that can contribute to unethical behaviors is a "politicized internal environment that allows influential managers to operate as autonomous fiefdoms and resist staying true to the organization's accepted values, principles and practices" (Sims, 2003, p. 248). In politically dominated cultures, issues and decisions get resolved by power plays as to who is perceived as having the most influence and power to guide the most benefits to that person and their sphere of influence; it is not based on what is best for the organization. Recall in the Enron case how their executives lost sight of what is in the best interest of Enron because they were in a politically powerful position to guide the decision making process in a way that financially benefited them first. Enron also adopted principles that were publicized to all in the organization and they defined "respect" to mean, "We treat others as we would like to be treated ourselves. We do not tolerate abusive or disrespectful treatment. Ruthlessness, callousness and arrogance don't belong here". Yet the reality was that the code of ethics was not practiced, but it made a positive impression on paper. Employees were in fact bullied to fit into their culture of aggression and anything goes as long as money is made or one could leave.

Consider how CFO Fastow sent indirect messages to others as to what they would face if they disagreed with him where on his desk he had a cube supposedly laying out the company's values. One of the values was on communication, and the cube's inscription explained what communication meant: "When Enron says it's going to rip your face off, it will rip your face off" (Raghavan et al., 2002). This message hardly seems to parallel the values exemplified by their code of conduct above on mutual respect—it is a message permitting aggression when convenient. In contrast to how Enron operated, consider how different the tone from the top is from an organization that understands leaders must stress the importance of integrity and morality as crucial components of the organization's culture because an organization needs to advocate for a climate of "moral consciousness" (Sims, 2003, p. 252). In this organization, senior management practices include, 1) clear and concise policies that define the company's business ethics and conduct, 2) select people for employment that aligns with the values of the organization, 3) promote people on the basis of performance, but also their ethical conduct, and 4) company employees must feel safe in being able to voice their concerns about perceived irregularities in ethics and accounting transactions.

The Value of Ethics Training Programs

Generally, there is no one right integrity strategy to implement because we need to consider multiple factors such as company history, culture, lines of business, and industry when shaping an appropriate set of values and designing an ethics program (Paine, 1994). Yet the guiding values and commitments should make sense and clearly communicate important organizational obligations and widely shared aspirations that appeal to the organization's members. The value of ethics training is that it provides a template to help guide decision making regardless of the changing environment. Constantly changing conditions are the very reason why morals, ideals and principles are needed so that there are standards in place to follow regardless of an environment that is always changing. Having a formal ethics program continues to make a positive difference as there is a strong correlation between ethics and compliance programs and perceptions of what constitutes appropriate behavior (KPMG, 2013). Ethics training support the ethical climate that is driven and perpetuated by formal organizational mission, vision and value goals. Employees at all levels should take them seriously, feel comfortable discussing them, and have a concrete understanding of their practical importance while displaying a willingness to seek solutions compatible with the framework of values. Exemplary conduct usually reflects an organizational culture and philosophy that is infused with a sense of responsibility displaying ethical awareness. There is ample evidence that many public companies approach ethics from a compliance perspective, without bothering to build up an ethical organizational culture, which address more of the underlying causes of the risks of ethical lapses.

This signals a lack of support for organization-wide compliance with ethical codes and policies. Academic research continues to point to the importance of an ethical culture to support integrity to avoid major misconduct, which includes extreme risk-taking that can damage many stakeholders (Ferrell & Ferrell, 2010). Managers can attempt to create a more ethical culture by developing a formal ethics program characterized by several components including, 1) a formal code of ethics that outlines standards ethical behavior, 2) ethics training to communicate these standards to employees, 3) enforcement mechanisms to detect and punish unethical behavior such a confidential hotlines, 4) mechanism to reward ethical behavior, and 5) top management support (Tomlinson & Pozzuto, 2016, p. 376). An ethics training program assists in disseminating the code of ethics and providing organizational members guidance pertaining to its application in their day-to-day duties. Business codes, which are another form of ethicality, is a distinct formal document that is developed by and for a company to guide present and future behavior on multiple issues of at least its managers and employees toward one another, the company, external stakeholders and/or society in general (Kaptein & Schwartz, 2007). When codes are supported by training, there is a positive effect on employee perceptions. Codes that are simply window dressing do not make the intended impact on their behavior because of the perception that the code states the behavior favored, but management does the exact opposite thus reducing the credibility of the code (Kaptein & Schwartz, 2007). Although codes of ethics may not affect individual employee behavior directly, they do appear to have value in prompting employees to consult other employees about the appropriateness of a given behavior.

Moreover codes give employees a shield to refuse requests for unethical behavior, provide employees with a tool to deter others from unethical employees, and lastly they encourage employees to report unethical behavior (Tomlinson & Pozzuto, 2016). Research suggests that the existence of an ethics training program lowers the extent to which employees perceived that they had to do unethical things to get ahead in their organization making them more sensitive to moral issues (Tomlinson & Pozzuto, 2016). Moreover the presence of an ethics program reinforces an ethical culture by explicitly recognizing that employees will encounter moral dilemmas and the organization is committed to supporting employees who want to make moral and ethical decisions. However be cautious of the fact that although ethics training has its place, sometimes we avoid doing the right thing in real time, but do great in being ethical when presented with case scenarios in ethics training (Soltes, 2016). One of the reasons we do well in ethics training is because there is debate about what the right course of action should be and develop some optimal, ethical answer to a scenario, yet in real time we may not have the debates necessary to reveal and address potential ethical issues in a thoughtful manner (Soltes, 2016).

A glossy code of conduct, a high-ranking ethics officer, a training program, an annual ethics audit, represent optical trappings of an ethics program, but they do not necessarily add up to a responsible organization whose espoused values match its actions. Consequently, be aware that a formal ethics program can serve as a catalyst and a support system, but organizational integrity depends on the integration of ethics training into practical workplace action. Ethics training is broader than mere legal compliance in that it seeks to enable responsible conduct whether there is a legal component or not. Ethics training ultimately must target what the organization truly stands for when it comes to issues of integrity in that its ethical values provide guidance for its values and patterns of thoughts and actions. The drive towards ethics is more demanding than just legal compliance in that it requires an active effort to define the responsibilities that constitute an organization's ethical compass. In many cases when employees use rationalization tactics to justify inappropriate behaviors, awareness of the dangers of those tactics reduces the likelihood of employees using them.

Clearly, training employees to be familiar with rationalizing and socialization tactics can go a long way toward reducing the likelihood of misconduct. For example, rationalizations often sound suspect to outsiders precisely because they are not members of the group that encourages them. Thus, training employees to at least periodically think about a decision from the perspective of customers, shareholders, and other constituents might help to puncture the rationalization balloon. Note also that if employees have rationalized their corrupt acts and have been performing them for some time, those acts can become highly routine and be interpreted as legitimate. It is crucial that part of ethics training is to neutralize the rationalizations used before they are considered by employees (Heath, 2008). They need to be told upfront that the use of the common rationalizations previously studied in chapter one will not be accepted by the organization. Organizations need to have periodic events where employees look at all the acts they perform and examine them for ethical implications. Through ethics training, awareness must be inculcated and institutionalized at all levels of an organization and incorporated into everyday decision making and action; in fact we want to observe a routinization of ethical awareness.

Ethical training, based on a code of ethics that is grounded in specific role-based situations and dilemmas, can foster awareness of ethical issues and reject amoral calculations and expose the dangers of rationalizations. Individuals at all levels of analysis must know they will be held accountable for the means as well as ends of how goals are attained, and real sanctions should be promulgated to encourage ethical behavior and discourage misconduct. Employees need clear and consistent messages from the executive team that ethics is essential to their business model (Trevino & Brown, 2004). Most businesses send countless messages about competition and financial performance, and these easily drown out other messages. In order to compete with this message about the importance of the bottom line, which is not without merit, leadership might consider tying ethics to business success by providing examples from their own experience or the experiences of other successful employees. Train employees to recognize the kinds of ethical issues that are likely to arise in their work by expecting discussion of ethics and values as part of the routine business decision making process. When making important decisions, ask, "Are we doing the right, ethical thing? Who could be hurt by this decision? How could this affect our relationships with stakeholders and our long-term reputation?" Share those deliberations with employees.

Finally, be sure to let employees know about exemplary ethical conduct. For example, the famous story about Arthur Andersen losing the railway business because he refused to alter the books was recounted over and over again in the firm and made it absolutely clear that "think straight, talk straight" actually meant something in the firm (Trevino & Brown, 2008). To have value, ethics training needs to be part of a virtuous practice, part of the essential character of the organization's identity. An ethics program helps to maintain a moral course when situations are tense, but these programs can also help avoid criminal acts whether they are actual acts or omissions which is not doing what is legally required. By having ethics training programs to follow up on detected misconduct, we can address these issues early on avoiding larger consequences in the future. Moreover, ethical programs help employees face reality, both the good, the stressful and the bad increasing their confidence when having to confront various situations. In addition, there is not only legal expectations between employers and employees, but a social contract of how to interact with one another. Ethics training might address some of these issues including but not limited to:

- Assist employees in identifying the ethical dimensions of a decision,
- Discuss what misconduct actually entails to reduce the need to speculate as to their definitions,
- Provide employees with rationales and vocabulary to participate in ethical decision making,
- Make employees aware that their decisions and actions ultimately expose the company's moral compass both internally and externally,
- Enhance employee conscientiousness and sensitivity to ethical issues and ethical solutions,
- Improve the ethical climate of organizations by creating ethical codes of conduct,
- Explain to employees how unethical acts impact an organization's reputation but also the financial costs such as the legal costs associated with fraud and misconduct,
- Encourage disclosures of misconduct and the importance of not retaliating against whistleblowers,
- Eliminate the belief that unethical behavior is ever acceptable coupled with neutralizing rationalizations as acceptable reasons justifying misconduct (Sims, 2003).

Encouraging Ethical Leadership

Typically, lack of ethical awareness explains, in part, the self-sustaining nature of normalized corruption. When unethical acts are uncovered in organizations, there is often strong resistance to accepting the facts facilitating misconduct, no matter how strong the evidence because the misconduct became normalized over time due to not being proactive in removing the risk factors that increase the probability of it from occurring in the first place. Furthermore, even when wrongdoing is acknowledged, senior executives tend to blame rogue individuals or isolated groups, arguing that they do not represent their otherwise pristine organization. In cases of collective corruption, such excuses miss the point that individuals and systems are mutually reinforcing. As our discussion of rationalization and socialization suggests, bad apples can be the product of bad barrels. Indeed, one of the chilling lessons of the many cases of corporate corruption is that otherwise good people can be induced to do bad things. Accepting wrongdoing and moving quickly to address it is critical if a company is to overcome enduring fraud of the kind supported by rationalization and socialization. When socialization and rationalization underlie corruption, insiders are often so embedded in the organization that they may lack the ability, will, and credibility to effect the needed changes.

Having been part of the system, they continue to be susceptible to the rationalizations associated with corrupt actions and are a visible reminder to stakeholders of the old way of doing things. In many cases, calling in an outsider to clean house is the only viable option at reversing corruption for a variety of reasons. First, their appointment signals a break from the past and sends a clear message to employees and other stakeholders of the organization's intention to make the necessary changes that will definitely include a signal that ethics matter. Consequently, employees and stakeholders are more likely to cooperate with the change efforts and provide needed resources. Second, outsiders come to the organization with a fresh and different perspective. They are much more likely to question organizational culture and practices long held to be sacred within the organization. Third, while outsiders may know the business less intimately than insiders, they are also likely to possess social networks diverse from those held by employees within the firm. This allows them to seek advice from individuals and entities that are not linked to the organization, further emphasizing their ability to question existing organizational practices.

Consider the case of Waste Management in which Maurice Myers did not work in Waste Management's industry prior to becoming CEO of the firm. In 1998, Waste Management participated in a massive accounting fraud scheme that contributed to artificially inflating earnings and disbursing almost $30 million in illegal bonuses to top management. Myers who was hired to take over the firm in the wake of the scandal, acted quickly. He acknowledged the corrupt practices prevalent in the company and launched an in-house newspaper that discussed and described questionable actions and the impact on the company. He also created an anonymous hotline to enable employees to report any unethical practices that they came across. Acceptance of wrongdoing, coupled with quick action, resulted in a significant turnaround; Waste Management moved out of the shadow of its corrupt past. Ethical leadership refers to verbal and nonverbal behaviors and examples displayed to others which consist of appropriate norms demonstrated through personal actions, interpersonal relationships, and the promotion of such conduct to followers through communication and decision making emphasizing integrity (Demirtas, 2015).

Ethical leaders not only speak of the importance of ethics, but explicitly display ethical behaviors to reinforce their importance. Leadership combining ethical behaviors while aspiring to high performance display the lowest level of organizational deviance, by rewarding ethical and punishing unethical behaviors (Neeves & Story, 2015). When leaders establish that positive behaviors are valued and unethical behaviors are not, subordinates are more likely to exhibit ethical behaviors and refrain from unethical ones. Moreover, ethical leaders motivate their followers to do the right thing and that goes beyond defining compliance as simply following the law and regulations; consequently such organizations reduce the incidence of misconduct (Neves & Story, 2015). Ethical leaders also pay attention and focus on the horizon of business opportunities and ethical challenges that could create the temptations for misconduct. Middle-level leaders too need to display integrity because they are often stuck in the middle of the organizational hierarchy and frequently face conflict that entails how to deal with misconduct.

For example, middle-level managers need to carry out the vision of upper management, but often there are conflicting realities with those below them and their peers who may interpret the way to achieve the vision as unethical (Gentry et al., 2012). It is the rare executive who understands the ethical culture in an organization because the higher up in the organization one goes, the rosier the perception of an ethical culture is likely to be. The reason is because information often gets stuck at lower organizational levels, and ethical executives are often insulated from bad news especially if employees perceive that the organization "shoots the messenger" who is trying to warn management of misconduct. Executives need anonymous surveys, focus groups, and reporting lines, and people need to believe that the senior leaders really want to know if they are to report honestly on the current state of the ethical culture (Trevino & Brown, 2008). In addition, a true test of whether management is committed to institutionalizing ethical awareness is how they respond to people who dissent to policies and practices that might trigger misconduct and those that disclose misconduct.

Management must be committed to ethical training stressing that whistleblowers will not be retaliated against for doing the right thing and in fact ethical training must stress whistleblowers who are retaliated against will face consequences for such behaviors. Whistleblowing should be encouraged by having procedures in place that give an individual a place of safety to voice their concerns. Management should be pleased that misconduct is reported because it can save the company bigger problems in the future in addition to safeguarding the company's reputation. Furthermore, given that organizations are by their nature susceptible to corruption, it is extremely important for leadership to assess the risk factors associated with their particular organization and industry that may facilitate misconduct. For instance, industries in ill-defined or dynamic environments tend to have fewer clear examples for what constitutes ethical acts to mitigate against managerial fraud thus allowing greater leeway for leadership to define it for themselves. Management fraud can be thought of as a perversion of effective management behavior where environments display entrenched modes of operating and sense-making that can institutionalize unethical practices in the pursuit of money. As one academician observed:

> Nobody would deny that our system of economic incentives rewards imagination applied in the pursuit of profit, and that it rewards managers who exploit profit opportunities. Nobody would deny that this should be so. Yet this often has the effect of encouraging managers to operate as closely as possible to the borderline between legality and illegality—the borderline between what is ethical and what is unethical...And it follows, in turn, that for any of a variety of reasons, an individual manager or management group may cross over the line (Ramamoorti et al., 2013, p. 15).

Employees who work in organizations exposed to an ethical tone at the top report fewer observations of misconduct, less toxic pressure to hit performance targets, and higher levels of confidence in management's commitment to integrity (KPMG, 2013). Thus, ethical leaders influence their subordinates specifically by serving as a model of behavior to subordinates (Mayer et al., 2009). In order to achieve effective and successful working environments over the long-term, leadership ought to have an ethical framework and leadership must display the highest moral behavior in their actions (Demirtas, 2015). Providing ethical leadership means making ethical values visible, communicating about not just the bottom-line goals, but also the acceptable and unacceptable means of getting there. At the heart of integrity is being consistent, honest, moral, and trustworthy. Leaders with integrity are consistent in the face of adversity, show consistency in their words and actions, and are unfailing with who they are and what they stand for. They act with authenticity and honesty by speaking the truth, presenting themselves in a genuine way with sincerity, showing no pretense, and taking responsibility for their own feelings and actions. Being an ethical leader also means asking how important decisions will affect multiple stakeholders such as shareholders, employees, customers, society and making transparent the struggles about how to balance competing interests. It means using the reward system to communicate what is expected and what is accepted plus rewarding ethical conduct and disciplining unethical conduct, even if the rule violator is a senior person or a top producer. Ethical leaders are personally committed, credible, and willing to take action on the values they display and scrutinize their own decisions.

Consistency on the part of leadership is key and sending mixed messages on values will lead to employee cynicism and a rejection of the tone at the top that gave the impression that ethics mattered. At the same time, managers must assume responsibility for making tough calls when ethical obligations conflict. The espoused values are integrated into the normal channels of management decision making and are reflected in the organization's critical activities: the development of plans, the setting of goals, the search for opportunities, the allocation of resources, the gathering and communication of information, the measurement of performance, and the promotion and advancement of personnel. Integrity is also important for middle-level managers who must relate well with people in order to build and maintain strong social networks and relationships with others across the organization as well as above and below them in the organizational hierarchy. Integrity makes it easier for others to trust a manager, which is likely important as middle-level managers fulfill their duties in networking, consensus-building, and relationship management.

Leadership that displays beneficial behaviors for fellow colleagues pave the way for positive exchanges. One of the listed traits that others admire in leaders is their sense of bravery to do the right thing. Bravery is defined as acting with valor by not shrinking from threat, challenge, difficulty, nor pain and speaking up for what is right despite facing an unpopular environment. Brave executives are more likely to take the lead on unpopular but necessary actions because of their moral courage (Gentry et al., 2012). This is an important character strength that leadership needs to display to do their job effectively. Leaders who are viewed as brave are evaluated as capable of producing long-term sustained success. Moreover, ethical leadership supports enforcement mechanisms as a tool to shape the ethicality of an organization's culture. For example, confidential reporting hotlines provide one specific example whereby misconduct can be reported and handled by organizational officials and the enforcement mechanism reinforces the value placed on ethical behavior signaling that infractions will be detected and punished (Tomlinson & Pozzuto, 2016).

Lastly, ethical leadership understands that ethics code enforcement is effective to the extent that it is performed consistently and fairly and that misconduct is dealt with regardless of the status of the perpetrator and in a manner that is proportional to the violation (Tomlinson & Pozzuto, 2016). Leadership support refers to creating the perception among employees that those in position of authority throughout the organization are committed to ethical behavior. This support entails leadership setting a good example for their employees to follow rather than merely instituting ethical standards with no example to follow. Employees look to managers as a source of information regarding the norms, standards, and practices that are expected in organizations. Indeed, research suggests that antisocial, deviant behaviors among employees is lowest when managers provide both ethical guidance and actually practice what they expect of others (Tomlinson & Pozzuto, 2016). In contrast, antisocial behavior is highest when managers do not practice what they ethically expect of others.

In summary, many "managers think of ethics as a question of personal scruples, a confidential matter between individuals and their consciences; these executives are quick to describe any wrongdoing as an isolated incident, the work of a rogue employee. Rarely do the character flaws of a lone actor fully explain corporate misconduct" (Paine, 1994). More typically, unethical business practice involves the silent, if not explicit, cooperation of others and reflects the values, attitudes, beliefs, language, and behavioral patterns that define an organization's operating culture. Ethics, then, is as much an organizational as a personal issue where executives who ignore ethics run the risk of personal and corporate liability in today's increasingly tough legal environment. An integrity-based approach to ethics management combines a respect for the law with an emphasis on managerial responsibility for ethical behavior (Paine, 1994). Though integrity strategies may vary in design and scope, all strive to define companies' guiding values, aspirations, and patterns of thought and conduct. When integrated into the day-to-day operations of an organization, such strategies can help prevent damaging ethical lapses while tapping into powerful human impulses for moral thought and action (Paine, 1994). Then an ethical framework becomes no longer a burdensome constraint within which companies must operate, but the governing ethos of an organization.

A strategy based on integrity holds organizations to a more robust standard. While compliance is rooted in avoiding legal sanctions, organizational integrity is based on the concept of self-governance in accordance with a set of guiding principles. From the perspective of integrity, the task of ethics management is to define and give life to an organization's guiding values, to create an environment that supports ethically sound behavior, and to instill a sense of shared accountability among employees. The need to obey the law is viewed as a positive aspect of organizational life, rather than an unwelcome constraint imposed by external authorities. An integrity strategy is characterized by a conception of ethics as a driving force of an enterprise. Ethical values shape the search for opportunities, the design of organizational systems, and the decision-making process used by individuals and groups (Paine, 1994). They provide a common frame of reference and serve as a unifying force across different functions, lines of business, and employee groups. Organizational ethics helps define what a company stands for. Many integrity initiatives have structural features common to compliance-based initiatives: a code of conduct, training in relevant areas of law, mechanisms for reporting and investigating potential misconduct, and audits and controls to ensure that laws and company standards are being met. In addition, if suitably designed, an integrity-based initiative can establish a foundation for seeking the legal benefits that are available under the sentencing guidelines should criminal wrongdoing occur. There is no one right integrity strategy. Factors such as management personality, company history, culture, lines of business, and industry regulations are taken into account when shaping an appropriate set of values and designing an implementation program. Several features are common to efforts achieving some success:

- *The guiding values and commitments make sense and are clearly communicated.* They reflect important organizational obligations and widely shared aspirations that appeal to the organization's members. Employees at all levels take them seriously, feel comfortable discussing them, and have a concrete understanding of their practical importance. This does not signal the absence of ambiguity and conflict but a willingness to seek solutions compatible with the framework of values.
- *Company leaders are personally committed, credible, and willing to take action on the values they espouse.* They are not mere mouthpieces, but are willing to scrutinize their own decisions. Consistency on the part of leadership is key and waffling on values will lead to employee cynicism and a rejection of the program. At the same time, managers must assume responsibility for making tough calls when ethical obligations conflict.
- *The espoused values are integrated into the normal channels of management decision making and are reflected in the organization's critical activities:* the development of plans, the setting of goals, the search for opportunities, the allocation of resources, the communication of information, the measurement of performance, and the promotion and advancement of personnel.
- *The company's systems and structures support and reinforce its values.* Information systems are designed to provide timely and accurate information. Reporting relationships demand checks and balances to promote objective judgment. Performance appraisal is sensitive to how we achieve our goals, the means, the ends.
- *Managers throughout the company have the decision-making skills, knowledge, and competencies needed to make ethically sound decisions on a day-to-day basis.* Ethical thinking and awareness must be part of every managers' mental equipment. Ethics education is usually part of the process (Paine, 1994).

Success in "creating a climate for responsible and ethically sound behavior requires continuing effort and a considerable investment of time and resources. A glossy code of conduct, a high-ranking ethics officer, a training program, an annual ethics audit—these trappings of an ethics program do not necessarily add up to a responsible, law-abiding organization whose espoused values match its actions" (Paine, 1994). A formal ethics program can serve as a catalyst and a support system, but organizational integrity depends on the integration of the company's values into its driving systems. Yet, an integrity strategy is broader, deeper, and more demanding than a legal compliance initiative. Broader in that it seeks to enable responsible conduct. Deeper in that it cuts to the ethos and operating systems of the organization and its members, their guiding values and patterns of thought and action. And more demanding in that it requires an active effort to define the responsibilities and aspirations that constitute an organization's ethical compass. Above all, organizational ethics is seen as the work of management. Corporate counsel may play a role in the design and implementation of integrity strategies, but managers at all levels and across all functions are involved in the process.

The Significance of One's Moral and Professional Identity

For some individuals, being successful is more important than being honest by engaging in misconduct to achieve that success. Although susceptibility to engaging in misconduct applies to most people in general,

418

research indicates that people displaying high integrity need a great deal more pressure to engage in misconduct than a low integrity individual who does not need much encouragement (Albrecht et al., 2012). Moral identity reflects the importance of moral values to defining one's self-identity and how they believe they will behave when confronted with a moral issue; moral identity plays an important role in refusing to engage in dishonest behavior (Xu & Ma, 2015). Having a moral identity allows one the opportunity to construct a template to interpret and respond to social events and for individuals high in moral identity, moral considerations are abundant in everyday living because morality is rooted at the core of who they are. Although the expectations of perfect honesty is not realistic, a moral identity in terms of self-control helps one to lessen an internal battle with temptation as to whether they should commit the act or not.

In essence people can rely on their moral identity to make the decision for them as opposed to relying on resisting temptation because good people do fall prey to temptation (Xu & Ma, 2015). For example, if one is asked to commit homicide for no justifiable reason, the typical quick, unequivocal, and expected response is no. There is no hesitation reflecting on the cost-benefit of committing the homicide or whether one is going to get away with the homicide. Our moral identity as to harming someone in such a manner does not rely on temptation or an internal debate as to whether to kill someone without justification. It simply is a wrong behavior, both morally and legally to engage in. Moral templates assist in defining who were are which facilitates confronting ethical and legal decisions with more precision without regard to temptations. When confronted with misconduct, do we disavow such behaviors and requests to engage in it with a quick response of 'no' as we answered with the homicide hypothetical, or do we submit to temptations and actually engage in a cost-benefit analysis to influence our decision one way or the other?

Let us add money to the example; would we kill someone for $500 or $10,000? Does our moral identity still immediately disavow entertaining such barbaric thoughts or do we engage in a cost-benefit analysis now tempted by the thought of a financial gain. Do we engage in a risk assessment based on the probability of getting caught murdering another person for money? Although the dynamics of the example changed because we added the element of money, it would be fair to say that most people still would immediately shut down such a thought without being influenced by temptation and actually having to talk ourselves out of the decision of whether to kill or not. This is not to say that there is never any individual who would not be tempted and will carry out such an act for a price they deem appropriate. Yet, what we can intuitively sense when we have a strong moral identity between what is right and wrong is that it helps shave down the amount of mental energy needed to make an ethical decision even when temptations trigger the desire to do otherwise especially when money is involved. When relying on resisting temptation, one uses more mental energy to maintain self-control to assist them in resisting unethical acts.

People who rely on their moral identity do not have to use up as much mental energy to resist temptation and as a result their behavior is more consistent with their moral identity (Xu & Ma, 2015). Thus individuals with high moral identity display honesty without active resistance to temptation. Moreover, people tapping into their moral compass for guidance tend to reduce temptation to engage in misconduct regardless of whether punishments exist or not (Paternoster & Tibbetts, 2016). Individuals with low moral identity rely on their willpower to resist temptation to reject dishonest gain, but they tend to fail resisting temptation more than succeeding (Xu & Ma, 2015). Thus it is important to remove temptations in making opportunity for unethical acts a reality, but it is important to have reminders that activate the moral identity within us coupled with reminders of why moral identity is important (Xu & Ma, 2015). Leadership should encourage the enhancement of one's moral identity by rewarding those behaviors that display one's moral disposition through their work product and how they react to observed misconduct. Ethical training helps to activate and remind us of our moral identities instead of them becoming stale.

Lastly, professional identity is a form of social identity representing the strength of the association between one's identity and the profession (Taylor & Curtis, 2010). In fact moral identity can be enhanced by our commitment to professional identity. For example, auditors are more likely to report management misconduct when they have a strong sense of commitment and identity to the integrity of their profession. This identity aligns with their commitment to the organization and when they perceive an act to be of great moral intensity in that the act is of a serious nature, then there is an obligation to report such an act (Taylor & Curtis, 2010). One way in which accounting professionals demonstrate professional identity is through guidelines, observing integrity displayed by other professionals, and acknowledging standards and practices of their profession regarding what is acceptable behavior to maintain reputational integrity. Professional identity reflects a commitment to the organization displaying a sense of reliability, responsibility, and readiness to support colleagues within an organization when confronted with ethical dilemmas (Taylor & Curtis, 2010).

Debunking the Myth of the Accidental Fraud Offender

It is not uncommon to hear fraud offenders proclaim that they never intended to fraudulently take any money because it was only, in their mind, perceived as a temporary loan. In other circumstances, fraudulent financial statement schemes are devised to artificially inflate an organization's income while management proclaims there was no intent to deceive anyone because it was a temporary measure to get an organization through a difficult economic period. Because of this reliance on the word "intent", those that comment on fraud offenders' motives and rationalizations erroneously classify offenders as a way to distinguish them from the predictable street-level offenders as accidental fraud offenders (Dorminey et al., 2010). Unfortunately confusion exists as to what a guilty state of mind means in antifraud circles, be it academic or from antifraud practitioners, and this section is an attempt to clarify some misperceptions that exist which can potentially impact, as an example, professional skepticism in audits.

Understanding the definitions and application of the different but acceptable legal states of mind necessary to be held criminally liable is at the heart of neutralizing fraud offenders who attempt to distance themselves from their crimes by claiming they never intended to commit fraud. By familiarizing oneself with the various states of mind, antifraud professionals will improve their own skill base by understanding how these offenders rely upon manipulating legal concepts as legitimate rationalizations especially during interviews. To facilitate the understanding of this important but understudied antifraud concept, this section illustrates through fraud and non-fraud examples the different types of criminal states of mind that are acceptable in order to hold fraud offenders accountable. Lastly, state of mind is commonly confused with the concept of one's motive and rationalizations to commit a crime. We address the issue of motive and its relation to state of mind, however legally one's state of mind is not equivalent to one's motive or rationalization to engage in criminal acts.

White-collar Crime and the Guilty State of Mind

State of mind plays a crucial role in fraud prosecutions because it is a key element that must be proven by the prosecution for charged fraud and non-fraud offenses. In order to be guilty of most crimes, a person must exhibit what is referred to in criminal law as *mens rea* which in English can be translated from Latin to a guilty mind or a culpable mind. Different types of state of mind exist in order to accommodate different factual scenarios so that individuals cannot avoid being held accountable, and it also impacts the severity of punishment an offender faces. Generally the three common, but different states of mind consist of, 1) intent, 2) knowledge, and 3) recklessness or reckless conduct. We define and apply these states of mind because they are the most common antifraud professionals encounter and applied in white-collar crime prosecutions and one that fraud investigators in particular should be aware of especially since potential suspects will try to persuade interviewers that they did not have the one state of mind most citizens are aware of and that is the state of mind of intent.

In many cases, white-collar offenders acting in a business context are purposeful, deliberate, and rational, however there are organizational pressures that can make individuals engage in behaviors that may be contrary to their preferred course of conduct (Van Slyke et al., 2016). Moreover, white-collar offending at times may not "feel" like a crime especially with the variety of rationalizations available to rely on that may not be as plentiful with street-level offenses. However, the fact that one's actions may not personally feel like a crime in the traditional sense or that someone would have preferred an alternative way to solve financial problems than having to engage in fraud does not neutralize the presence of a guilty mind. In addition, white-collar crime may not feel like crime because within an organization, its members may not be even aware that they are breaking the law because, 1) they may be unaware of its existence, 2) they are aware, but do not know how to comply with it, and 3) they may not have the resources to comply with the law (Van Slyke et al., 2016). However these reasons, as innocent as they may seem, does not mean the law cannot hold them criminally accountable.

White-collar crime can also be due to omissions where corporations violate rules because they did not take a prescribed action that may be attributable to incompetence and not a deliberate choice of refusing to comply. Thus, even when we actually do not do something required by law, that can contribute to the formation of a guilty state of mind. The problem is that many offenders do not understand that omissions can be a basis for criminal liability. In addition, ignorance of the law is not a defense to escaping criminal liability or neutralizing the state of mind prosecutors rely upon. It is not always clear whether offending is the result of an individual's decision making or whether there are organizational factors that facilitate the individual's decision to engage in wrongdoing. Thus, state of mind is inferred from organizational failure where corporate managers fail to oversee subordinates adequately, to assess risk intelligently, to implement quality internal controls to prevent and detect misconduct, and mechanisms to address regulations that impacts them (Van Slyke et al., 2016, p. 440).

The Application of Intent

Fraud offenders, like non-fraud offenders, have their own rationalizations to morally distance themselves from their criminal acts and one of them is to neutralize the *mens rea*, which is necessary for the law to find them accountable for their fraud. Fraud offenders rationalize that if one had no intent to commit fraud, one is not guilty of fraud. Confusion revolves around how the concept of state of mind is interpreted which stems from the fact that antifraud professionals who are not thoroughly acquainted with criminal law equate the word intent as being synonymous with the only type of state of mind that exists and as such the one needed to hold fraud offenders accountable. Thus, many antifraud professionals erroneously believe that if intent cannot be shown, then an offender cannot be criminally liable. When referring to having the intent to commit a crime, we are referring to a person acting with a deliberate, purposeful resolve—a desire to bring about a particular result (Perri & Mieczkowska, 2015). The problem with just referring to a guilty mind as one that requires a showing of intent is that it potentially leaves the defining of whether one is criminally liable up to the offender to determine what their state of mind consists of at the time of the crime.

Practically all a fraudster would have to say to avoid prosecution is that they never had the intent to keep the money because their intention was to always put the money back. Realistically few offenders of any crime classification would admit that they had any guilty state of mind given the number of rationalizations that are readily available to them to rely upon. Legally intent, that sense of deliberativeness, may be inferred from the amount of planning that went into committing a criminal act. For example, an individual may admit that they wanted to murder revealing his or her thoughts that also may reveal how they went about planning the homicide in a methodical manner thus revealing one's state of mind that death was not an accident, but a purposeful plan to bring about a particular result. From a fraud offender's perspective, intent may be inferred from the surrounding factual circumstance such as the length of time an offender engaged in a planning a fraud scheme, statements made that prove the desire to commit fraud or, again, admissions by the fraudster that they intended to commit fraud within an organization for whatever motives and rationalizations were revealed by exploiting weak internal controls for financial gain.

The Application of Knowledge

However not all criminal acts represent such a deliberative purpose to bring about a certain outcome with a state of mind that is intentional. The law needs to accommodate the different factual scenarios with different states of mind that represent something other than intent. Thus, let us turn to another equally applicable state of mind referred to as acting with "knowledge" or sometimes referred to as "knowingly" that takes on a different complexion of what one's state of mind can consist of. A person acts with knowledge refers to a scenario where one's acts are practically certain to create a risk that results in an outcome that is deemed criminal due to a deliberate indifference to the consequences of one's behavior (Perri & Mieczkowska, 2015). The offender is aware of the nature of his conduct, and did not act through ignorance, mistake, or accident. The focus is on the consequences of the person's behavior that can harm another to determine whether the necessary state of mind exists for someone to be held criminally liable. For example, someone that shoots into a crowd may kill someone because there is a practical certainty that others will be put at risk of great bodily harm.

The offender may not have wanted to kill anyone by shooting into the crowd, but the risk of such behavior is one that cannot be excused simply because the offender did not "intend" someone to die. In such an instance, an individual could be charged with murder because the consequence of such behavior created the risk that someone would suffer great bodily harm resulting in death. Thus whether someone had the "intent" to murder becomes less relevant in deciding whether to charge someone with homicide because the law recognizes that an offender's behavior can create outcomes that are harmful regardless of whether one had the desire for a certain outcome. In terms of fraud, a person who commits asset misappropriation may claim to not have the intent to commit fraud because of their personal belief that they were going to put the money back. The focus, however, is not on how the fraud offender interprets their own behavior or whether the act was committed with a purposeful or deliberative manner, but on the consequences of their behavior which is to deprive an organization of their property without authority to take such property.

For example, an offender's state of mind is exposed when they act with knowledge that with practical certainty exploiting weak internal controls for financial gain causes financial harm to an organization regardless of the fact that their acts were in the offender's mind a non-criminal matter because it was perceived as a loan. Consider the SEC complaint against Enron CEO Jeffrey Skilling and accountant Richard Causey stating that "Skilling and Causey knowingly and substantially caused Enron to file materially false and misleading annual reports" (Perri & Mieczkowska, 2015). Whether Skilling or Causey were to argue that they never had the intent to mislead any users of the financial statements is not relevant. Even if their motive was one of good intent in their mind, their motive is not relevant. What is relevant is the impact of their fraudulent actions on the users of financial statements and the harm caused to investors by relying on their misrepresentations.

The Application of Recklessness

Recklessness, at times referred to as gross negligence, means a gross deviation of an expected practice of reasonable conduct exposing others to unjustifiable risk. For example most states attach criminal liability to deaths that are a result of someone driving under the influence of alcohol. These acts might be classified as reckless homicides. In terms of fraud, criminal liability may attach when we go beyond just innocent, careless mistakes and show a pattern of mistakes that are being ignored that in the end cause harm to others. For example, to establish one of many different securities fraud claims, the prosecution must show that the person making statements involving the sale of securities, had either or both the intent and knowledge or engaged in reckless conduct that resulted in deceiving, manipulating, or defrauding investors. Thus, the SEC's complaint against WorldCom's Bernard Ebbers stated that "Ebbers knew, or was reckless in not knowing, that WorldCom's true method of accounting for line costs was not disclosed to WorldCom's auditors" (Perri & Mieczkowska, 2015).

Courts explaining the requirement agree that a showing of recklessness satisfies the requirement, which is defined as misstatements or omissions that are not just careless or inexcusable, but reflect an extreme departure from the standards of ordinary care. For example, consider a CEO who continues to use on multiple occasions a standard investor presentation over a period of time without getting regular updates to ensure information accuracy prior to making public statements. This CEO's lack of due diligence and care-free disclosure of financial information could be subject to a claim of recklessness if investor presentations contain material inaccuracies. When the CEO keeps making public statements that are not true, but for which the public relies on the statements to make decisions, this exposes the CEO to criminal liability with recklessness being a potential state of mind used by the prosecution. Thus, the reckless state of mind focuses on the risk of harm an offender's action or inaction exposing others to that is unjustified representing a gross deviation from standard practice regardless of the fact the CEO never intended to deliberately deceive any investor.

Evidence Relied Upon to Prove State of Mind

There are erroneous assumptions about the type of evidence necessary to prove state of mind. Some antifraud professionals consider intent to be proven by direct evidence only such as offender statements disclosing that it was their plan and desire to engage in fraud. Direct evidence usually entails the type of evidence where someone has personal knowledge about the facts of a case. For example, if a person saw the offender actually commit the crime, that is considered direct evidence because the witness has personal knowledge of the crime facts. In terms of fraud, if a witness saw a fraud offender manipulate internal controls to misappropriate assets, that would be considered direct evidence. If the fraud offender confessed to committing fraud, that would be considered direct evidence. Proving state of mind also can be inferred by the surrounding circumstances of the facts and this is referred to as circumstantial evidence. This type of evidence does not require offender admissions of guilt which may be helpful, but is not required. Consider few fraud offenders would be prosecuted if only those offenders who confessed could be held accountable, thus the law has to accommodate the different types of evidence available for someone to be held accountable.

Circumstantial evidence is evidence that tends to prove a fact by proving other events or circumstances which offers a basis for a reasonable inference to draw a conclusion. Some have explained it in less legalistic terms as coming to a conclusion about what is known, but without having the personal knowledge to back it up. Consider an example of circumstantial evidence. If one were to wake up one morning and see snow on the ground, one would infer that it snowed during the night because before they went to sleep they looked out the window and it was not snowing. The fact that we did not see the snow actually falling does not change the undisputed fact that there is snow on the ground; we can infer that it did snow during the night. Forensic evidence such as fingerprint evidence is a form of circumstantial evidence in that the evidence suggests that the fingerprints are in fact the persons we believe is the culprit. Let us apply this concept in a fraud case scenario. If an employee takes vacation and a fraud examiner found that fraud was perpetrated at the time the employee was present and from his or her personal work area, but there was no evidence of fraud during the period that the employee was on vacation, such circumstantial evidence could be used as a basis to single out the employee as a potential suspect even though no one saw him or her committing the fraud. This inference would serve as a basis to further question this employee to determine if they have any involvement in fraudulent activity. The law does not consider one type of evidence to be "stronger" than another type of evidence meaning the law does not consider direct evidence to be superior to circumstantial evidence or vice versa.

Some people erroneously believe that if someone saw the crime, that means that it is better than having to make inferences about evidence such as how do we look at fingerprint evidence. The law leaves it up to the fact finder, be it a jury or a judge, to determine what significance they want to attach to a given piece of evidence be it direct or circumstantial evidence. Consider that many types of direct evidence such as eye witness testimony is fraught with reliability issues and some confessions have been deemed false confessions, thus unreliable. A number of CEOs have been found guilty of some form of fraud such as Jeffrey Skilling of Enron and Bernard Ebbers of WorldCom who represented cases where their state of mind can be inferred from the surrounding factual circumstances and direct evidence regardless of their defense strategy of claiming ignorance of any wrongdoing at their organizations. Fact finders, such as juries or a judge, are allowed to consider the entirety of the circumstances to determine whether offenders had knowledge of wrongdoing and to what extent they may have participated to infer whether the required state of mind for fraud exists. Recall that it is not just what one does that is evidence, but what one does not do that can also be considered evidence to infer state of mind such as ignoring blatant fraud and doing nothing about it as a CEO. Let us revisit the WorldCom offenders. Consider the position that WorldCom CEO Bernard Ebbers took when it became obvious that WorldCom was involved in a massive financial statement fraud scandal.

Beginning in 1999, WorldCom commenced making large offsetting accounting entries after the quarter closed in order to achieve the aggressive revenue targets established by the company and expected from the financial community. The SEC Report (2003) found written documentation at WorldCom that recalculated the difference between the actual results, found on the monthly revenue or as it was internally called at WorldCom the

MonRev report, and the target or needed numbers. Once the variance was calculated, accounting entries were made to cover the shortfall so that financial targets would be met. Yet CEO Bernie Ebbers, known as a micromanager who poured over financial statements, denied any knowledge of fraud claiming not to know enough about accounting to be aware of any fraud. He maintained his CFO Scott Sullivan and his subordinates kept him in the dark. Ebbers stated, "Shocked...I couldn't believe it. I never thought anything like that would have gone on. I put those people in place. I trusted them" (Belson, 2005).

In turn, Sullivan testified that Ebbers knew of the fraud when Ebbers told Sullivan not to issue an earnings warning to Wall Street giving Sullivan the green light to create false profits (Yang & Grow, 2005). While Ebbers memorialized very little of his intentions in written form, one memo revealed Ebbers discussing his rationalization of "those one-time events that had to happen in order for us to have a chance to make our numbers" (Economist, 2004). In this case, the testimony of CFO Scott Sullivan would be considered direct evidence because he had personal knowledge of Ebbers' involvement in the fraud and Ebbers put pressure on Sullivan to "make the numbers". Whether or not the factfinder, in this case the jury or a judge, wants to accept the direct evidence as proof that Ebbers too is guilty is another issue. The prosecution would present the memo above in order to contradict Ebbers' position he had no knowledge of the fraud. Furthermore, the SEC investigation uncovered a voicemail message from Sullivan to Ebbers recorded on June 19, 2001 to confirm initial findings (SEC, 2003, p. 15):

> Hey Bernie, it's Scott. This MonRev just keeps getting worse and worse. The copy, um the latest copy that you and I have already has accounting fluff in it...all one time stuff or junk that's already in the numbers. With the numbers being, you know, off as far as they were, I didn't think that this stuff was already in there...We are going to dig ourselves into a huge hole because year to date it's disguising what is going on (SEC, 2003, p. 15).

The Role of Motive in Proving State of Mind

Motive is our reason for doing something. Many employees state that they never had the motive to commit fraud, but the prosecution does not have to prove what one's motive is or is not in order to hold an offender accountable for fraud. Motive is not interchangeable with state of mind, thus motive is not the same as one of the available states of mind such as intent. Motive may be helpful to expose and better explain one's state of mind, but it is not necessary. For example, if someone unjustifiably kills another, the prosecution may never know the real reason behind the homicide. Think of how easy it would be for homicide offenders to be held unaccountable because the prosecution could not get inside their head to determine why they committed the homicide. The same rationale can be used for fraud. In terms of fraud, we may never know the real reason why someone exploited an internal control especially if they refuse to speak about their involvement. Did they do so for their own financial gain? Did they do it to give the money to someone else? It may help the prosecution to know the offender's motive to better expose a criminal state of mind, but it is not necessary. Recall that the offender's own personal motivations for engaging in risky behavior may not be relevant as it relates to accountability because it is the consequence of their behavior that is being questioned which is taking property from another without permission. In addition, personal motivations may be relevant to the severity of punishment imposed by a court when considering what the personal reasons that someone committed fraud were: was it to pay off debts, struggles with personal addictions, or tries to sustain an unaffordable lifestyle.

The Prosecution of Organizations as a Deterrent to Misconduct

Up to now, we have addressed issues related to people, however we should not forget that organizations can face criminal liabilities just as people can because under the law corporations are entities that take on the identity of a person. Under our corporate legal structure corporations are considered legal persons that are, 1) capable of suing and being sued, 2) capable of committing crimes, and 3) being prosecuted and punished. As a result, organizations themselves may be deterred from engaging in misconduct even though in the end it is people who run the organization. The deterrent effect of prosecuting organizations takes on a different complexion making it especially difficult when criminal behavior spans a whole organization because in such cases it may be difficult to determine exactly where the fault lies. Those high up on the organizational chart, who bear the most responsibility for the company, may know little about its day-to-day activities and quite frankly not all corporate misconduct starts at the top; it is plausible that lower level employees encouraged misconduct that exposed the organization to criminal liabilities. For example, lower level employees may have illegally dumped toxic waste exposing individuals including the organization itself to criminal liabilities. There may be those reading this section that may not understand how the prosecution of an organization relates to them personally, however there is a personal connection. Many students in addition to those that are in the working world may someday be exposed to an investigation by government officials who are deciding whether to hold both corporate employees and the corporation criminally liable. Consequently, it is important to know the factors government officials consider when making the determination of whether to criminally prosecute the corporation.

Even if one did not engage in misconduct, thus removing the fear of being personally prosecuted, there is the organization that may be exposed to prosecution which directly impacts one's livelihood. As a result, understanding the factors that the prosecution considers in deciding whether to prosecute an organization or not may place employees in a position where individual persons may be held accountable, but at least the organization itself can avoid total demise and hopefully avoid the fate experienced by Arthur Andersen and its employees as an example. Thus, it is important that management, employees, and auditors who advise management know the factors that prosecutors consider important in their decision to prosecute a corporation or not so that they become organizational priorities before misconduct becomes an issue. In other words, plan ahead for the proverbial rainy day. Research suggests that if people perceive their organization would suffer from their misconduct, for some individuals, such a threat does act as a deterrent to engaging in misconduct especially since they know it will directly impact their livelihood (Paternoster & Tibbetts, 2016). Deterrence has to be looked upon as a continuum where some will be deterred more than others and some may be more willing to come forward to disclose misconduct in order to preserve their livelihoods, but the goal being that deterrence overall does mitigate some of the temptations to engage in misconduct.

Punishing a large company, through massive fines or by sending its most senior leaders to prison can destroy the company, which trigger serious economic ripples impacting innocent employees, customers, and communities. Recall in 2002, a federal jury in Houston, Texas convicted the major accounting firm of Arthur Andersen of obstruction of justice in connection with its destruction of documents relating to its accounting work for Enron Corporation. The firm agreed to stop auditing public companies which in effect meant closing its auditing business where over twenty thousand employees lost their jobs. The Andersen firm was subsequently ordered to pay a $500 thousand fine and sentenced to five years probation. There was a clear, causal connection between Andersen's negligence in auditing public companies besides Enron and the decision to prosecute Andersen leading to its ultimate demise. The question is, how do we determine whether organizations such as Andersen should be prosecuted in addition to its individual employees? Such a decision is not to be treated lightly given the number of people that are innocent in an organization's misconduct and whose reputations and livelihoods are at stake depending on what a prosecutor's decision is.

Some people may deem it unfair that their livelihoods should be in jeopardy for the acts of a few, but the legal reality is that the prosecution does not have to show that many of a firm's employees engaged in misconduct to prosecute the organization—just one is enough regardless of where they are in the hierarchical structure of an organization. Under the legal doctrine of respondeat superior, a corporation may be held criminally liable for the illegal acts of its directors, officers, employees—commonly referred to as agents of the employer. In other words the corporation is liable for the acts of its employees just as a regular employer, who is a person and not a corporation, can be held liable for the acts of its employees. For example, in the case of Arthur Andersen, the prosecution's only burden was to prove obstruction of justice, beyond a reasonable doubt, that any one of Andersen's thousands of employees "acted knowingly and with intent to cause or induce another person or persons to, a) withhold a record or document from an official proceeding, or b) alter, destroy, mutilate or conceal an object with intent to impair the object's availability for use in an official proceeding." Recall Arthur Andersen CPA David Duncan destroyed documents related to the Enron prosecution.

The government was not required to prove that the Andersen employee in question acted solely for an improper purpose, so long as the action was taken at least in part, with the improper purpose of impeding an official proceeding which in this case was the prosecution of Enron employees. As long as an employee was acting within the scope of his or her employment, the fact that the employee's act was illegal and contrary to Andersen's policies does not relieve the corporation of its responsibility for an employee's behavior. Furthermore, corporations should not be treated leniently because of their artificial nature nor should they be subject to harsher treatment (CFPF, 2008). Indicting corporations for wrongdoing enables the government to address changes in corporate culture, alter corporate behavior, and discover, prevent, and punish offenders. An indictment is the formal written statement crafted by the prosecution that accuses an individual or a corporation of a crime the prosecution believes they have committed. Corporations are likely to take immediate remedial steps when they are indicted for criminal conduct that is pervasive throughout a particular industry, and thus an indictment often provides a unique opportunity for deterrence on a massive scale especially those crimes that pose a risk to the public such as environmental and financial crimes that are more likely to be committed by businesses (Dervan & Podgor, 2016).

Moreover, prosecution of a corporation is not a substitute for the prosecution of criminally culpable individuals such as officers, directors, or employees that are within or outside of the corporation. In addition, a corporate compliance program, even one specifically prohibiting the very conduct in question, does not absolve the corporation from criminal liability under the doctrine of respondeat superior. A compliance program, generally, is defined as a formal program specifying an organization's policies, procedures, and actions within a process to help develop effective internal controls to prevent and detect violations of laws and regulations by its employees, officers, and board of directors. Compliance programs are established by management as part of its corporate governance protocol to ensure that corporate activities are conducted in accordance with all applicable criminal and civil laws, regulations, and rules. A corporation may be held criminally responsible for acts committed by its employees if they were acting within the scope of their authority, or apparent authority which means a third party reasonably believes that an agent has authority to act on behalf of an employer.

The employer is still responsible for the agent's actions even if such acts were against a corporation's express instructions not to engage in a particular act. To hold a corporation liable for these actions, prosecutors must establish that the agent's actions were within the scope of his or her duties and were intended, at least in part, to benefit the corporation. For example in one case, the court upheld the corporation's conviction for the actions of a subsidiary's employee despite the corporation's claim that the employee was acting for his own benefit, namely his "ambitious nature and his desire to ascend the corporate ladder" (AML, 1985). Moreover, the court stated that the substantial personal benefit reaped by the employee meant the fraudulent scheme required money to pass through the corporation's treasury and the fraudulently obtained goods were resold to the corporation's customers in the corporation's name (AML, 1985). Prosecutors typically apply similar factors in determining whether to charge a corporation as they do with respect to individuals.

Thus, the prosecutor should weigh all of the factors normally considered in the sound exercise of prosecutorial judgment including, 1) the sufficiency of the evidence, 2) the likelihood of success at trial, 3) the probable deterrent, rehabilitative, and other consequences of conviction, and 4) the adequacy of noncriminal case resolution approaches. The prosecutor generally has wide latitude in determining when, whom, how, and even whether to prosecute for violations of law and in exercising that discretion, prosecutors should consider the following principles in discharging their prosecutorial responsibilities. In doing so, prosecutors should ensure that the general principles of criminal law are met such as the assurance of appropriate punishment and restitution for victims and affected communities are adequately met by taking into account the special nature of the corporate person. It is entirely proper in many investigations for a prosecutor to consider the corporation's pre-charging conduct such as voluntary disclosure, cooperation, and restitution made to victims in advance of prosecution, in determining whether to seek an indictment (CFPF, 2008).

Consider since 1990, officials used sophisticated prevention standards for assessing corporate criminal liability. Under these standards, "the scope of corporate efforts to prevent offenses, usually as reflected by the presence of substantial corporate law compliance programs, is considered in determining whether corporations should be charged with offenses undertaken by employees for corporate gain and, if they are so charged and convicted, in determining what sorts of penalties and compelled reforms the corporations should bear (Gruner, 2007, p. 279). What do we mean by organizational, corporate culpability? In terms of how prosecutors look at this issue, it is typically defined as those individuals, organizational practices, policies and procedures that increase the risk of criminal activities by employees. Hopefully corporate compliance programs increase the probability that misconduct will be detected even though we should be clear that not every corporate activity increases the risk of criminal activity. At times, prosecutors will enter into what is known as a deferred prosecution agreement with the corporation. Under these agreements, corporate criminal charges are filed against a firm based on misconduct in the firm's activities, but prosecutors agree not to pursue a conviction on the charges and eventually will dismiss the charges against the firm as long as the corporation institutes the proper reforms discouraging future misconduct (Gruner, 2007).

In essence deferred prosecutions give corporations the incentive to get their act together so that they can avoid criminal liabilities, avoid the stigma of a criminal conviction, poor media and press coverage, and avoid not being able to participate in bidding for government contracts. As a result, corporations turn into self-policing entities that should be interested in preventing corporate crimes and internal misconduct that can invariably impact investors, consumers, and the public at large. In addition, the aura of self-policing may act as a deterrent because potential offenders may realize that they will not be able to count on internal corporate shelters to protect them from their involvement because the corporation has much to gain from self-policing and disclosure to the prosecution the identity of the wrong doers. In some respect, the prosecution is telling corporations choose what side you want to belong to—the wrong doers or the prosecutions that holds immense power over your operation's viability. Self-policing demands place the burden on management in exchange for the privilege of operating their business through the corporate form that is in the end a government created private business entity. Operating a business in often social isolation, an organization tends to shield internal misconduct from external detection due to their corporate form.

Thus, is not unreasonable to expect parties operating through this business form, who receive the legal protection and benefits of being a corporation, to undertake the extra steps to counteract the relative isolation of corporate activities from scrutiny by traditional law enforcement (Gruner, 2007). This is especially true given that there are few institutions other than traditional law enforcement that discourage illegal conduct. The impetus is on the organization to assist in their own protection from misconduct that occurs from within so that they do not become victims from the hands of their own employees. In essence they are in the best position to know of and report misconduct. Furthermore, the growing complexity and isolation of large corporate organizations from other portions of society partially explains increasing public demands for regulatory oversight and criminal investigations of corporate activities. The public with little to no access to corporate operations have no basis to evaluate the social responsibility of corporate actors, yet the pressure for profits may be at the expense of public interests (Gruner, 2007). Coupled with this pressure is the perception that misconduct will eventually occur inside a firm where there is a tendency towards corporate secrecy and a desire to protect coworkers by encouraging concealment rather than disclosure to public authorities. Thus the public looks to regulators to provide the necessary oversight especially when there are suspicions of misconduct from isolated corporate bureaucracies (Gruner, 2007).

This is not to argue that all those within an organization will have a cooperative relationship with prosecutors because there will be those that will not cooperate especially if they were involved in misconduct and will do whatever they can to avoid accountability. The question that cannot be ignored is whether prosecution will, in and of itself, deter corporate crime and violations. Unfortunately, existing research does not provide strong evidence that prosecution and subsequent punishment consistently and effectively deters corporate wrongdoing. One rigorous, systematic review of all available studies about corporate deterrence of corporate crime found that:

"The evidence fails to show a consistent deterrent effect of punitive sanctions on individual offending, company level offending, geographic-level offending" or offending among studies using other measurements of analysis" (Rorie, 2020, p. 229). There are several explanations for why corporate deterrence of corporate crime and at a minimum unethical conduct is difficult.

First of all, just like for individual crime, certainty of punishment matters more than severity of punishment; stronger sanctions will have an effect if a tipping point of certainty of accountability is more probable (Rorie, 2020). However, because of the complexity of corporate organizations and processes, detecting corporate violations in the first place is quite challenging. In fact, stronger punishment threats can actually lead to more investment to prevent getting caught and ultimately result in a cat-and-mouse game (Rorie, 2020). For instance, when automobile maker Volkswagen discovered that California and U.S. regulators knew about their cheating on emissions testing, their initial response was to improve the software and hide their cheating through a recall (Rorie, 2020). Further, when wrongdoing is actually detected, it remains difficult to prosecute and even when it is successfully prosecuted, penalty fines often remain uncollected.

A second reason is how deterrence is perceived is subjective; oftentimes, corporate executives who are supposed to be deterred simply are not aware of the certainty and severity of punishment and thus engage in a flawed risk assessment of whether to engage in corporate misconduct. For some companies, the expected penalties are seen as the price of business and made part of the budget. For example, since 2006 Volkswagen's high-level engineers and executives received penalties in other misconduct cases besides the one on emissions, but in the words of former New York Attorney General Eric Schneiderman: "They had concluded we can survive this type of penalty", in essence the benefits of misconduct outweighed the costs (Rorie, 2020, p. 230). Indeed, even with the massive damages and penalties Volkswagen had to pay after it finally admitted to its cheating, setting aside $25 billion, in 2017 it had its highest sales ever and retained its number one ranking in car sales, and in 2018 it further extended its lead over Toyota. These findings do not mean that corporate wrongdoing should not be punished; however, these findings do mean that punishment is not enough to prevent future violations and harm.

Nevertheless, let us specifically examine some of the factors the prosecution considers in its assessment of whether to agree to a deferred prosecution or whether to prosecute with the goal of achieving a conviction which means the corporation would have a criminal record in addition to being punished. Some or all of these factors may or may not apply to specific cases, and in some cases, one factor may override all others. The nature and seriousness of the offense may be such as to warrant prosecution regardless of the other factors. Furthermore, national law enforcement policies in various enforcement areas may require that more or less weight be given to certain factors more than to others. Prosecutors consider the following factors that will be examined in more detail, in reaching a decision as to the proper treatment of a corporate prosecution:

- The nature and seriousness of the offense including the risk of harm to the public and applicable policies and priorities, if any, governing the prosecution of corporations for particular crimes;
- The pervasiveness of wrongdoing within the corporation, including the involvement in or encouragement of the wrongdoing by corporate management;
- The corporation's history of similar conduct, prior criminal, civil, and regulatory actions against it;
- The corporation's timely and voluntary disclosure of wrongdoing and its willingness to cooperate in the investigation of its agents, including, if necessary, the waiver of the corporate attorney-client and work-product protection;
- The existence and adequacy of the corporation's compliance program;
- The corporation's remedial actions, including efforts to implement effective corporate compliance programs or to improve an existing one, to put in place responsible management, to discipline or terminate wrongdoers, to pay restitution, and to cooperate with the relevant government agencies;
- Collateral consequences, including disproportionate harm to the public, shareholders, pension holders, and employees not proven to be personally culpable; and
- The adequacy of the prosecution of individuals responsible for the corporation's misconduct and the adequacy of remedies, such as civil or regulatory enforcement actions (CFPT, 2008).

Pervasiveness of Wrongdoing within the Corporation

Charging a corporation for minor misconduct may be appropriate where misconduct was pervasive and committed by a large number of employees in a particular role within the corporation especially if the misconduct is condoned by upper management. Even if management did not condone the employees' misconduct, the corporation is held responsible for failing to fulfill its duties of making sure their employees do the right thing. In other words, criminal liability is imposed on a firm due to its failure to adequately serve as a public trust for law enforcement within the firm (Gruner, 2007). Although acts of even low-level employees may result in criminal liability, a corporation is directed by its management and they are responsible for a corporate culture in which criminal conduct is either discouraged or explicitly or implicitly encouraged. Thus the role of management and the pervasiveness of misconduct is a very important factor. Specifically,

> [P]ervasiveness is case specific and will depend on the number, and degree of responsibility, of individuals with substantial authority...who participated in condoned, or were willfully ignorant of the offense. Fewer individuals need to be involved for a finding of pervasiveness if those individuals exercised a relatively high degree of authority. Pervasiveness can occur either within an organization as a whole or within a unit of an organization (CFPT, 2008).

In addition, pervasiveness is determined by actions that promote corporate offenses including managerial policies or practices that are themselves illegal because they authorize or compel criminal behavior by subordinates. Defective management responses, such as not doing anything to respond to detected offenses, may signal management support for similar conduct in the future where there may be systematic blindness toward illegal conduct (Gruner, 2007). Another type of culpability is present where management fails to monitor the impact of their incentive systems to determine if those systems encourage illegal behavior by employees. Once managers create strong financial incentives encouraging their employees to increase profits and minimize compliance cost, firms have a corresponding duty to monitor whether the incentives have gone too far and created a heightened risk for criminal behavior to thrive (Gruner, 2007). When an employee commits financial crimes to increase the profits of the firm, they also enrich themselves due to the incentive programs offered by the firm, thus the firm bears some responsibility for that employee's actions due to its failure to balance its incentives with compliance checks and balances.

Even if the specific behavior may not have been encouraged by the organization, corporate management may indirectly promote such behaviors leading to criminality that reward profit-making and cost-savings performance that they would otherwise not be able to achieve but for their specific misconduct. Employees know management will ignore misconduct as long as goals are met. Prosecutors pay particular attention to the role of the board of director's in the conduct of the organization's affairs to assess pervasiveness such as, 1) whether the directors exercise independent judgment rather than unquestioning approval of management's recommendations, also known as rubber-stamping management's decisions, 2) whether they are provided with information sufficient to enable them to exercise independent judgment, and 3) whether established information and reporting systems such as whistleblower protocol enabled them to reach informed decisions regarding compliance with the law (CFPT, 2008).

The Corporation's Past History

Like natural persons, prosecutors may consider a corporation's history of similar conduct, including prior criminal, civil, and regulatory enforcement actions against it in determining whether to bring criminal charges. A corporation, like a natural person, is expected to learn from its mistakes and a history of similar conduct may be evidence of a corporate culture that encouraged, or at least condoned misconduct regardless of any compliance programs in place to discourage it. Criminal prosecution of a corporation may be particularly appropriate where the corporation previously had been subject to non-criminal guidance, warnings, or sanctions, or previous criminal charges, and yet it either had not taken adequate action to prevent future unlawful conduct or had continued to engage in the misconduct in spite of the warnings or enforcement actions taken against it (Dervan & Podgor, 2016). Consider the numerous times that Arthur Andersen was warned by regulators for its lack of due diligence related to numerous failed audit engagements prior to Enron such as those at Sunbeam and Waste Management that ultimately led the prosecution to conclude that Andersen was not serious about improving its audit obligations.

Cooperation and Voluntary Disclosure

In determining whether to charge a corporation, a corporation's timely and voluntary disclosure of wrongdoing and its willingness to cooperate with the government's investigation may be relevant factors in deciding whether to hold the corporation responsible together with individuals (Gruner, 2007). In gauging the extent of the cooperation, the prosecutor may consider, 1) the corporation's willingness to identify the responsible person(s) within the corporation, including senior executives, 2) making witnesses available to law enforcement for interviewing such as employees, board of directorship members, and management as an example, 3) disclosing the complete results of its internal investigation and, 4) waiving the attorney-client and work-product privileges protection (CFPT, 2008). The attorney-client privilege means that an attorney is obligated not to disclose the contents of conversations with their client. Thus when there is a waiver, the client is giving the attorney the right to talk to law enforcement about information that typically would not be disclosed to law enforcement. In investigating wrongdoing by or within a corporation, a prosecutor is likely to encounter several obstacles resulting from the nature of the corporation itself.

For example, lines of authority and responsibility may be shared among operating divisions or departments, and records and personnel may be spread throughout the United States or even among several countries. Where the criminal conduct continues over an extended period of time, the culpable or knowledgeable personnel may have been promoted, transferred, or fired, or they may have quit or retired. Moreover, a corporation's cooperation may be critical in identifying the responsible person(s) and locating relevant evidence. In some circumstances, therefore, granting a corporation immunity which means that regardless of whether there is evidence justifying being criminally charged, the corporation will not be held accountable. Immunity may be considered in the course of the government's investigation because it is in the public's best interest to grant immunity so that the prosecution can hold specific individuals responsible for their misconduct. In addition prosecutors, together with regulatory agencies, encourage corporations as part of their compliance programs to conduct internal investigations and to disclose their findings to the appropriate authorities (Sharma et al., 2009).

Some agencies, such as the Securities and Exchange Commission (SEC) and the Environmental Protection Agency (EPA), have formal voluntary disclosure programs in which self-reporting coupled with resolving issues that lead to the misconduct, may qualify the corporation for immunity or reduced punishments (Gruner, 2007). Even in the absence of a formal compliance program, prosecutors may consider a corporation's timely and voluntary disclosure in evaluating the adequacy and management's commitment to the program or whether it looks good on paper, but for which there is no real application in practice (Dervan & Podgor, 2016). However, prosecution and economic policies specific to the industry may require prosecution regardless of a corporation's willingness to cooperate. For example, prosecutors offer immunity or leniency as to potential punishments when corporations agree to cooperate creating an incentive to participate in anticompetitive conduct, such as price-fixing, to disclose information of their misconduct and the others involved.

Furthermore immunity or reduced sanctions may not be appropriate where the corporation's business is participating in multiple crimes such as price fixing, bribery and financial statement fraud. Another factor to be weighed by the prosecutor is whether the corporation appears to be protecting its guilty employees and agents whether inside or outside the organization. Thus, while cases will differ depending on the circumstances, a corporation's promise of support to guilty employees, either through the advancing of attorney's fees to defend them, through retaining the employees without punishment for their misconduct, or through providing information to employees about the government's investigation, may be considered by the prosecutor in weighing the extent and value of a corporation's cooperation. A corporation's offer of cooperation does not automatically entitle it to immunity from prosecution because a corporation should not be able to escape liability merely by offering up its directors, officers, employees, or agents in lieu of its own prosecution.

One of the most effective ways to combat misconduct is by seeking accountability from those perpetrating the wrongdoing. Accountability is important for several reasons: 1) it deters future illegal activity, 2) it incentivizes changes in corporate behavior, 3) it ensures that the proper parties are held responsible for their actions, and 4) it promotes the public's confidence in our justice system (Yates, 2015). In order for a company to receive consideration for cooperation, the company must completely disclose all relevant facts about individual misconduct. Companies cannot pick and choose what facts to disclose, thus the company must identify all individuals involved in the misconduct at issue, regardless of their position, status or seniority, and provide all facts relating to that misconduct. Moreover, individual accountability cannot be avoided simply because the company as a whole is cooperating; deterrence of future misconduct is necessary (Yates, 2015).

Obstruction of Justice

Prosecutors are directed to examine whether a corporation engaged in conduct, inconsistent with their effort to cooperate. For example, is the corporation willing to implicate culpable employees including senior management? While stating they intend to cooperate, is the corporation engaged in conduct that gets in the way of the investigation which could be viewed as obstructionist? Has the corporation engaged in conduct that makes the investigation difficult or inefficient? Examples of such conduct include, 1) encouragement not to cooperate openly and fully with the investigation including, 2) making the decision to refuse to be interviewed, 3) making representations that contain intentionally misleading statements or not disclosing information, 4) incomplete or delayed production of records, and 5) failure to promptly disclose illegal conduct known to the corporation (CFPT, 2008). For example, in the Arthur Andersen case, one of its employee's shredded documents related to the Enron investigation which is equivalent to destroying evidence. All told, these factors reflect an increased focus not merely on the conduct of corporate officers and employees during the course of a criminal investigation, but on the conduct of corporate counsel in representing the corporation in its dealings with prosecutors. Corporate counsel's vigorous representation of corporate clients may be interpreted by prosecutors as an effort to impede investigations rather than to resolve them favorably for their clients. At the same time, prosecutors should avoid using this provision as an excuse to undermine a company's right to be represented responsibly by counsel even if in the end the organization pleads guilty (Lilien, 2017).

Corporate Compliance Programs

Another factor is whether the corporation has an effective corporate compliance program to prevent and detect wrongdoing; in essence does the corporation make earnest efforts to mitigate against the risk of misconduct (Dervan & Podgor, 2016). Yet, even if a corporation has a compliance program, the corporation may nevertheless face prosecution if the prosecutor determines that the program is not sufficiently meaningful because it was implemented to give the appearance of compliance and there was no true interest in preventing corporate wrongdoing. The decision whether to charge a corporation may turn on a prosecutor's judgment about the quality of a corporation's internal governance mechanisms. Indeed, the fact that a crime was committed by an employee may be enough to lead a prosecutor to conclude that a compliance program was flawed, no matter how individually motivated the employee's behavior for self-profit. A compliance program must satisfy several criteria, listed below, for prosecutors to consider in their deferred prosecution programs, however the weight to be given to a particular criteria is left up to the discretion of the prosecution.

Due Diligence	An effective compliance program must reflect an organization's due diligence to prevent and detect criminal conduct and efforts to otherwise promote an organizational culture that encourages ethical conduct and commitment to compliance with the law. Such a program must be reasonably designed, implemented, and enforced so that the program is effective in preventing and detecting criminal conduct.

431

Target Principles	The design of a compliance program must take into account such factors as the organization's size, the nature of the organization's business, types of offenses likely to be undertaken by corporate employees and the prior offense history of the organization.
Disqualifying Characteristics	A compliance program may not be appropriate if the organization continues to engage in misconduct, the pervasiveness of the misconduct, who actually is involved in the misconduct such as senior management or senior management failing to report misconduct in a timely manner.
Required Features	In order for a compliance program to be effective, such programs must be implemented with the aim of preventing future misconduct, incentives to promote compliance, high level management will implement such programs, and enforcement actions addressing misconduct that promotes compliance.
Ongoing Risk Assessments	A compliance program must include ongoing efforts by an organization to periodically assess the risks of criminal misconduct and to adjust those compliance procedures to reduce the risk of misconduct. Such assessments must include evaluations of both the nature and seriousness of potential corporate offenses (Gruner, 2007).

Keep in mind that agreeing to a compliance program should not be a substitute for creating an organizational culture which respects why we should comply with the law and it should not be promoted as being all that is required from employees when it comes to ethical behavior. Compliance, at times, is interpreted to mean that an organization is being ethical in all its endeavors and this is simply not the case. Legality deals with what one must do and ethics typically means what we should do even if not required by law. Do we engage our moral imagination to think about foreseeable consequences to our decisions that might result in misconduct that is not necessarily illegal, but carries with it complexions of unethical behavior? Thus we need to convey expectations through messaging that go beyond just compliance and again this should be set by management's tone at the top. Corporations are expected to serve as agents of the public in carrying out misconduct prevention functions which entails duties to assist public authorities, such as the SEC, in preventing crimes and to aid them in investigations when necessary especially since they are isolated and have access to information that law enforcement does not.

Corporate managers can use their insights to interpret data gathered on possible misconduct and information from employees especially since employees have obligations to work on behalf of their employers due to the fiduciary duties they owe employers (Gruner, 2007). Hopefully prosecutors will give greater weight to the overall effectiveness of a compliance program and not automatically conclude that it was defective just because it failed to prevent the particular crime in question. Prosecutors encourage corporate self-policing, including voluntary disclosures to the prosecution of any problems that a corporation discovers on its own. Furthermore the nature of some crimes, for example antitrust violations, may be such that national law enforcement policies mandate prosecution of corporations regardless of the existence of a compliance program. No compliance program can ever prevent all criminal activity by a corporation's employees, however, critical factors in evaluating any program are whether the program is adequately designed for maximum effectiveness in preventing and detecting wrongdoing by employees.

In addition, other factors include whether corporate management is enforcing the program or is tacitly encouraging or pressuring employees to engage in misconduct to achieve business objectives and ignore compliance. The fundamental questions any prosecutor should ask is whether the corporation's compliance program is well designed and does the corporation's compliance program work? In answering these questions, the prosecutor should consider, 1) the comprehensiveness of the compliance program, 2) the extent and pervasiveness of the criminal conduct, 3) the number and level of the corporate employees involved, 4) the seriousness, duration, and frequency of the misconduct, and 5) and any remedial actions taken by the corporation, including restitution, disciplinary action, and revisions to corporate compliance programs (CFPT, 2008). Prosecutors attempt to determine whether a corporation's compliance program is merely a "paper program" or whether it was designed

432

and implemented in an effective manner. In addition, prosecutors determine whether the corporation has provided for a staff sufficient to audit, document, analyze, and utilize the results of the corporation's compliance efforts.

Prosecutors also determine whether the corporation's employees are adequately informed about the compliance program and are convinced of the corporation's commitment to it. This will enable the prosecutor to make an informed decision as to whether the corporation has adopted and implemented a truly effective compliance program that, when consistent with other federal law enforcement policies, may result in a decision to charge only the corporation's employees. Compliance programs should be designed to detect the particular types of misconduct most likely to occur in a particular corporation's line of business. Many corporations operate in complex regulatory environments outside the normal experience of criminal prosecutors, thus prosecutors should consult with relevant regulatory agencies with the expertise to evaluate the adequacy of a program's design and implementation. For instance, the SEC and EPA have experience with compliance programs and can be helpful to a prosecutor in evaluating the effectiveness of such compliance programs especially if there is a systemic culture of organizational corruption. At times, even the best intentioned compliance programs may not overcome a culture of corruption.

Restitution and Remediation

Although neither a corporation nor an individual suspect may avoid prosecution merely by paying a sum of money, a prosecutor may consider the corporation's willingness to make restitution which means to pay back victims money lost due to misconduct and steps already taken to do so (Dervan & Podgor, 2016). A prosecutor may consider other remedial actions, such as implementing an effective corporate compliance program, improving an existing compliance program, and disciplining wrongdoers, in determining whether to criminally charge the corporation (CFPT, 2008). Among the factors prosecutors consider and weigh are whether the corporation appropriately disciplined the wrongdoers regardless of their position within an organization and whether the corporation disclosed information concerning their illegal conduct to the government. It would appear suspicious if prosecutors did not expect cooperation in exchange for equity and cooperation in terms of how the charges against corporation and its officers are eventually resolved. The public needs to be assured that there is an expectation that those engaged in wrongdoing are held accountable under the law or else the impression given is that those in the upper-echelons of society are able to side-step responsibility even though this unfortunately happens where executives are not held accountable at all for their fraudulent behavior.

The public looses confidence in government institutions when those that are consider the societal elite are able to avoid accountability due to their socioeconomic status. A corporation acknowledging the seriousness of their misconduct and accepting responsibility for it should take steps to implement the personnel, operational, and organizational changes necessary to establish an awareness among employees that criminal conduct will not be tolerated. Employee discipline is a difficult task for many corporations because of the human element involved and sometimes because of the seniority of the employees concerned. While corporations need to be fair to their employees, they must also be unequivocally committed at all levels of the corporation to the highest standards of legal and ethical behavior. Effective internal discipline can be a powerful deterrent against improper behavior by a corporation's employees. A corporation's efforts to pay restitution in advance of any court order is evidence of its acceptance of responsibility may be considered in determining whether to bring charges. However, corporations should not presume that they can commit fraud, pay restitution, and avoid the consequences of corruption believing that the case has been concluded. If this were the case, there would be no real incentive to be ethical and law abiding because the strategy is to simply determine whether the benefit of misconduct still outweighs the cost of misconduct especially if there is no personal accountability and all that we end up with is a corporation paying a fine on its misconduct.

Collateral Consequences

Practically corporate convictions, like natural person convictions, will have an impact on innocent third parties, thus prosecutors may consider the collateral consequences of a corporate criminal conviction in determining whether to charge the corporation with a criminal offense (Dervan & Podgor, 2016). One of the factors in determining whether to charge a natural person or a corporation is whether the likely punishment is appropriate given the nature and seriousness of the crime. In the corporate context, prosecutors may take into account the possible substantial consequences to a corporation's officers, directors, employees, and shareholders, many of whom may, depending on the size and nature of the corporation and their role in its operations, have played no role in criminal conduct, due to being completely unaware of it, or were wholly unable to prevent it (CFPT, 2008). Prosecutors should consider, when applicable and in accordance with any other regulation or policy, non-criminal punishments that may accompany a criminal charge, such as potential suspension or permanent revocation from eligibility for government contracts or government funded programs such as health care (CFPT, 2008). For instance, the balance may tip in favor of prosecuting corporations in situations where the scope of the misconduct in a case is widespread and sustained within a corporate division or spread throughout pockets of the corporate organization. In such cases, the perceived unfairness of punishment for the corporation's crimes upon shareholders may be of much less concern where those shareholders have substantially profited, even unknowingly, from widespread criminal activity.

Thus, in other cases, accountability may be satisfied without the necessity of instituting criminal proceedings and prosecutors may consider whether sanctions would adequately deter, punish, and rehabilitate a corporation that engaged in wrongful conduct. In evaluating the adequacy of non-criminal alternatives to criminal prosecution, such as civil or regulatory enforcement actions, the prosecutor may consider all relevant factors, including alternative sanctions available as means of case resolution, the likelihood effective sanctions will be imposed, and the effect of a non-criminal disposition on deterrence of future misconduct (CFPT, 2008). Non-criminal sanctions may not be an appropriate response to serious violations, a pattern of wrongdoing, or a history of non-criminal sanctions that were ignored by the corporation. In determining whether criminal charges are appropriate or whether to seek non-criminal alternatives to prosecution, other factors to consider include, 1) the strength of the regulatory authority's interest, 2) the regulatory authority's ability and willingness to take effective enforcement action, and 3) the probable sanction if a regulatory enforcement action is upheld.

Compliance Programs: A Cautionary Note

In the past several decades, there has been rapid growth in corporations adopting compliance management programs and one of the driving forces is that the law actually incentivizes these practices. For example, U.S. law offers lenient treatment for companies that have an effective compliance and ethics program. Consequently, it is unsurprising that we see many companies adopt compliance management systems in the wake of major scandals and prosecutorial investigations. Siemens Corporation employees, a German electronics giant, bribed governments worldwide to get favorable contracts overseas, funneling an estimated total of $1.4 billion to officials in Asia, Africa, and Latin America. Once the massive bribery scheme was uncovered, Siemens became part of a major U.S. criminal investigation. As the investigation proceeded and Siemens began negotiations with the U.S. Department of Justice (DOJ), it developed new anticorruption compliance policies, including a handbook, web-based complaints channels, improved financial controls, and an anti-corruption tool kit operated by 150 dedicated staff members. These efforts cost Siemens over $150 million while expanding its compliance operation to 500 staff members. This helped Siemens get more lenient treatment, as the DOJ asked the court to impose a more lenient sentence.

As the DOJ sentencing memo stated: "The reorganization and remediation efforts of Siemens have been extraordinary and have a set a high standard for multinational companies to follow. These measures, in conjunction with Siemens' agreement to retain a Monitor...for a term of four years, highlight the serious commitment of Siemens that it operates in a transparent, honest, and responsible manner going forward" (Rorie, 2020, p. 231). We may see this as a typical case where a major multinational company got caught in criminal activities that were endemic to the organization, and then got off lightly given no major executives were actually sent to prison and the company simply had to pay a fine. Siemens' compliance reforms effectively reduced the company's criminal liability and enabled it to receive favorable treatment from the DOJ. Alternatively, we can see

Siemens as a complex organization that needed to initiate a broader compliance management reform to prevent bribery throughout its worldwide operations.

Bribery became a major part of the Siemens practices and was well ingrained throughout its business practices across many countries. Punishing top executives probably would not in and of itself automatically change the culture of a large organization with several hundred thousand employees. Altering the behavior of such an organization is very different from doing so on an individual level. It requires knowing what happens in the organization, what the organizational processes are, and the incentives and values that sustained the bribery for so long. The official rationale for adopting compliance systems is that they help organizations install mechanisms that prevent misconduct and crimes. If misconduct does occur, they help deal with those infractions at the earliest possible moments. The question is whether corporate compliance management systems, such as the one adopted by Siemens, actually do deter corporate crime and wrongdoing. The body of literature does not provide a simple answer; some studies directly question whether compliance management can be effective.

For example, several scholars studied whether ethical compliance programs consisting of ethical codes, ethics communication, ethics training, and the incorporation of ethics into human resource management practices could reduce occupational health and safety violations. They studied 108 large American firms and found no positive effect associated with the programs and further found that these programs failed to support a commonly held assumption that the types of corporate ethical compliance programs advocated by DOJ will result in less organizational illegality (Rorie, 2020). On this basis, they concluded that ethical compliance management may be more about window-dressing or at least a marketing ploy to differentiate firms from competitors than actually improving corporate behavior and reducing violations. The authors also concluded that if meaningful ethics programs are to be developed, they must be supported by top management; this factor is more important than external controls such as the sentencing guidelines. Institutionalizing ethics involves more than codes and training; it must be supported by a culture change and examples of ethical leadership from top management. In sum, they found that on its own, compliance management is not enough.

Other scholars agree that compliance management is mere window-dressing. One study finds that "a growing body of evidence indicates that internal compliance structures do not deter prohibited conduct within firms and may largely serve a window-dressing function that provides both market legitimacy and reduced legal liability". She concludes that this not only fails to improve corporate behavior, but also comes at a high cost for corporations adopting these programs. Similarly, scholars looked at whether the top 1000 American industrial and service firms in the mid-1990s actually implemented the ethical compliance management practices that they so widely adopted. They found that "the vast majority of firms have committed to the low cost, possibly symbolic side of ethics management such as adoption of ethics codes and policies. Yet, firms differ substantially in their efforts to see that those policies or codes actually are put into practice". It seems that for these top firms in the 1990s, compliance management was more about checking-the-boxes" show of compliance management efforts than actually changing operations and improving corporate behavior.

Compliance management systems may have actually made matters worse. The more firms incorporated ethical compliance into their operations, the *more* likely they were to have "willful and repeat" violations. Moreover, employees get mixed messages. On the one hand, they see that their firm has publicly adopted a lofty ethics and compliance system. On the other hand, they see in everyday working practices that the firm does not "follow through." What results is a form of corporate dissonance that harms future compliance inside the company as employees will learn not to believe lofty messages from their leaders. Some scholars argue that such a mismatch may damage employee expectations of procedural justice; procedural justice are thought to be strong motivators of compliance. Part of the problem is that it is remarkably difficult to determine what a good, effective compliance program is. Yet, according to law, corporations with a compliance management program get treated with much more leniency than those without. As scholars argue, the indicia of an effective compliance system are easily copied and true effectiveness is difficult for courts and regulators to determine; for this reason, there will be more window-dressing (Rorie, 2020).

Firms engaged in legally prohibited, but potentially profitable, conduct can reduce or eliminate firm-level liability by mimicking an effective compliance system, without reducing the incidence of prohibited conduct within the firm. There is ambiguity not just about which compliance programs may work, but also in what the law actually requires corporations to do. For example, employment discrimination compliance programs, shows that organizations often create so-called symbolic structures, such as special affirmative action officers and antidiscrimination codes. Organizations are often caught in a dilemma, as they must appear to care about the law, while also keeping costs at a minimum. Because the law is often unclear about what it exactly requires, organizations can overcome the dilemma by having compliance management processes. These then "serve as visible efforts to comply with law," without actually achieving the substantive goals of the law, such as reducing actual employment discrimination. Thus, compliance management is about the optics of serving the often vague letter of the law rather than its original intent. Other scholars are less negative finding that there might be some evidence that corporations with compliance programs do perform better than those without.

Some scholars studied how government-mandated compliance management programs, which they call management-based regulation, performed in improving food and worker safety, and pollution prevention in the United States. They find that while significant noncompliance with the management program standards still existed, the programs did help to reduce risk, especially when independent monitoring and oversight is in place (Rorie, 2020). Yet, compliance systems can make a difference, albeit only under certain conditions. One of the most comprehensive to date and the study surveyed 999 large Australian firms about 21 elements of their compliance management systems and compliance with competition and consumer protection law. They found that of the 21 components of a compliance management system, only six played a positive role in enhancing compliance behavior as reported on the survey. The six were a) having a written compliance policy, b) a dedicated compliance function, c) a clearly defined system for handling complaints from customers/clients, d) a clearly defined system for handling compliance failures, e) induction for new employees that includes compliance training, and f) having an external consultant review the compliance system (Rorie, 2020).

Findings show that a few elements of compliance management systems can make a difference in curbing corporate misconduct. However, the studies also shows that the majority of compliance management system elements play no role. These included having a hotline for complaints about compliance, using a compliance manual, using a computer-based training program for compliance, written policies to protect internal whistleblowers, requiring managers to frequently report on compliance, compliance performance indicators for employees, and internal employee discipline for noncompliance. Yet there are mixed conclusions. It shows that we must look carefully at the actual elements of compliance management systems. Even elements we intuitively might think will work, such as whistleblower protection programs, having internal indicators and discipline to promote employee compliance might not actually work, but are encouraged by DOJ. More importantly, compliance management systems on their own are not enough to improve organizational behavior. Such systems work if they can operate in the right organizational system that has sufficient leadership support and values. Others in the field have come to similar conclusions wondering whether compliance management systems can implement a compliance culture.

Indeed, we cannot be sure that it is not the other way around that better compliance culture leads to greater implementation of compliance systems. Studies of corporate ethics codes reveal mixed conclusions about their ability to help reduce unethical behavior. Scholars reviewed the existing body of research on whether instituting an ethics code, which is a core part of most compliance programs, reduces unethical behavior. They found very mixed results: 35 percent of the studies found that such codes are effective, while 16 percent found only a weak relationship, 33 percent found no effect, 14 percent found mixed results, and one study in the sample found negative effects (Rorie, 2020). Overall, we see that the simple adoption of a code in and of itself does not directly reduce unethical behavior. As the scholar notes, a code of ethics cannot make people or companies ethical, they are necessary tools which need intelligent design and use. In a follow-up study, scholars sought to understand what conditions then made these ethics codes more effective in reducing unethical behavior. The author found that what counts most is whether workers perceive that their management sufficiently support and internalize these ethics codes. Also, ethics codes will work better if their content addresses a broad set of ethics issues and if the organization properly communicates them to the employees.

The body of scientific work on the effectiveness of compliance management programs is not conclusive. At worst, compliance management programs serve as window-dressing that allow corporations to maintain legitimacy and to receive lenient treatment from regulators, while undermining the internal legitimacy of the law and internal rules. At best, these programs are able to help prevent unethical and illegal conduct, but even in the most positive studies, there is hesitation. Corporate compliance management systems may sometimes, but not always, improve corporate behavior. What is found, then, is that installing a corporate compliance management system is not enough. Studies show that corporate leadership must be committed to compliance as well as ethics for compliance and ethics management programs to be effective (Rorie, 2020). Many studies also stress the importance of a favorable corporate culture in which the programs can successfully operate. Furthermore, some argue that compliance management can only function well if there is some form of independent oversight. These are troubling findings given the main reason to have compliance management programs is that some or all of these conditions are missing. We have moved toward internal compliance management because independent oversight, often in the form of governmental enforcement, simply lacks the capacity to unearth illegal behavior hidden inside the corporation. Also, we have developed compliance management systems because they may be able to change an unethical and criminal corporate culture, and we have compliance management systems to keep unethical leaders in check. What we see here is that the law, most notably in the United States' Federal Sentencing Guidelines, has incentivized companies to adopt systems for which there is very little evidence that they actually work.

In the Siemens case, we see how much belief the DOJ places in these practices, without actually acknowledging the existing studies that question their effect. Apart from installing compliance management programs, corporate crime and wrongdoing can also be addressed by protecting workers who want to speak out against illegal behavior in the company. For example, some Volkswagen employees must have known about the fraudulent emissions software the German carmaker had been using to evade California pollution standards for its "clean diesel" engines, or consider the "tell-alls" that many Siemens employees could have written about whom the company bribed and where, long before the scandals became public. While corporations may be able to hide illegal behavior from external inspectors, and even from internal compliance managers, employees often directly observe misconduct and crimes. If employees speak out about misconduct and crime in their organizations, they can help initiate action within and outside the company toward compliance. The question is will they or are the forces encouraging silence too strong to overcome?

Conclusion

Mitigating organizational misconduct is not easy, but it is not impossible. The belief that because misconduct cannot be totally eliminated is not a reason to not implement policies that encourage ethical decision making, improve hiring of personnel through the use of integrity assessments, and encourage leaderships' tone at the top to be proactive in setting the example for ethical behavior. Also, in reviewing the research and the real-life examples contained within this chapter, the facts that appear to surface time and again is the need to encourage people to voice their concerns about misconduct. Yet without senior management setting the tone that misconduct will not be tolerated coupled with encouraging people to voice their opinions, it is unlikely that fraud can be mitigated even with the best of intentions whether they are management themselves or subordinates that want to do the right thing. Leadership must set the example and make clear that whistleblowers will not be retaliated against for being courageous and doing what is expected of all employees.

Moreover, it is important to consider the different states of mind that exist in the law so that we are not manipulated by fraud offender explanations that because they never had the intent to commit fraud, they really are not responsible for the fraud they perpetrated. In these situations it is crucial to recognize the different states of mind the law relies on to hold people accountable for their fraud crimes. Be aware of the state of mind of recklessness and knowledge together with the state of mind of intent.

Lastly, making the decision to prosecute an organization is not to be taken lightly especially since the impact of a corporate conviction can end the careers of thousands of honest employees who may be blameless for the misconduct that lead to the prosecution in the first place. Yet corporations should not operate believing they are above the rule of law due to not displaying natural person attributes. When appropriate they need to be held accountable no differently than a natural person for their misconduct. As a result, employees at all levels should understand what is at stake if corporate governance is not taken seriously especially when a review of corporate compliance is replete with weaknesses that cannot prevent or detect misconduct it is trying to mitigate. It should be in all corporate officers and employees self-interest to implement a compliance program that serves the interests of all stakeholders while protecting the reputation of the organization.

Chapter 10

Corporate Governance's Link to Corporate Fraud

Don Dixon's saving and loan bank, known as Vernon Savings, was considered a very conservative bank with a religious board of directors prior to Dixon's acquisition of the bank. In order for Dixon to commit fraud, he needed the board of director's approval of his schemes. To accomplish this goal, Dixon provided them and Texas' top state saving and loan regulator with prostitutes (Lilly et al., 2011, p. 76). In retrospect, it is apparent that the board did not fulfill its fiduciary duty of looking after the interests of the shareholders in addition to being a check on Dixon's fraudulent behaviors as well as their own. Although we would like to believe that these cases are not widespread, there have been instances in which board of directors have failed in their duties in different ways resulting, at worst, in organizations imploding into bankruptcy most notably Enron and WorldCom to name a few. At a minimum these behaviors may provoke criminal investigations resulting in convictions of its top management while damaging the reputation of the organization, whether the organization is for-profit or not-for-profit, religious institutions, charitable organizations or any other entity that may have a corporate governance structure that includes a board of directorship.

In addition to negligence on the part of boards, there is a plethora of instances in which external auditors have failed in their duties in overseeing the accuracy of financial statements that the public relies on to make investment decisions. An especially prominent and long-standing concern in this regard has been the lack of independence, conflict of interests, and accountability for external auditors (Reurink, 2016). Consider the case of now defunct accounting and consultant firm Arthur Andersen. In this case Andersen CPA David Duncan was one of the external auditors charged with making sure that Enron's financial statements fairly and accurately represented the financial condition of Enron. Yet when it became known that Enron was involved in fraudulent behaviors, Duncan began shredding documents that could have been used by federal prosecutors proving Andersen was complicit in perpetrating fraud. Duncan, as well as Arthur Andersen, was prosecuted and eventually Andersen closed its auditing function doors forever while thousands of employees lost their job. Immediately destroyed was the reputation that built Andersen into a powerful business from its inception, maintaining the highest level of integrity while performing their duty. Did corporate governance fail if it existed at all? Generally speaking, corporate governance is defined as a process of managing, directing, and monitoring a corporation's business to create shareholder value.

Moreover, corporate governance includes protecting the interests of other stakeholders such as creditors, the government, and the community by focusing on the combination of, 1) applicable laws and regulations to facilitate and monitor entities in attracting investors, and 2) being efficient to create shareholder value (Rezaee & Riley, 2010). Some of the parties that make up corporate governance include the board of directors, external and internal auditors, and management. Corporate governance is needed to avoid the concentration of power by acting as a checks and balance on management to make sure financial reports, as an example, are constructed with integrity. In addition, corporate governance should monitor the interests of investors by assessing the risks of the investments undertaken by the entity. Corporate governance best practices center around concepts namely of, 1) accountability, 2) efficient and effective use of corporate resources, 3) legal and regulatory compliance, 4) integrity with the financial reporting process, 5) improvements in business decisions, and 6) creating trust and confidence in corporate activities by promoting quality and fair relationships with the company, shareholders and society at large (Rezaee & Riley, 2010).

In this chapter we exam the role corporate governance is supposed to play in the checks and balances of an organization in addition to that of the internal and external auditor. Moreover, we explore what factors influence how auditors perform their duties to the benefit, and at times, to the detriment of the organizations they are obligated to oversee. In addition we study solutions that can assist auditors become more competent in their duties, plus the criminal liability accountants and auditors exposes themselves to when they ignore principle-based accounting as a guide to resolve accounting issues. Lastly, the dynamics that led to the fall of accounting firm giant Arthur Andersen, how Enron's board of directors facilitated Enron's demise, and how an organization manages fraud risk factors are explored.

The Role of the Board of Directors

Typically, the board of directors sits at the top of a company's governing structure where their duties include, 1) reviewing the company's overall business strategy, 2) selecting and compensating the company's senior executives, 3) evaluating the company's outside auditor, 4) overseeing the company's financial statements and 5) monitoring the overall company performance. The challenge for board members is to effectively analyze the judgments of corporate officers, monitor their actions, and protect the interests of the shareholders (Glover & Prawitt, 2012). As part of this, they must be prepared to challenge and hold accountable the CEO and remove them if there is a failure to discharge their duties adequately (Hamilton, 2008). One of the corporate boards most important function include monitoring firm performance to prevent managerial self-dealing and abandonment of their fiduciary duties by providing guidance to senior management in making major policy decisions (O'Connor, 2003). The board also serves a relational function whereby board membership provides links to various stakeholders such as the community where they are physically located, customers, and shareholders to name a few (O'Connor, 2003).

In most states, directors operate under a legal doctrine called the business judgment rule, which generally provides directors with broad discretion, absent evidence of fraud, gross negligence or other misconduct, to make good faith business decisions. The business judgment rule helps directors meet the challenging role of strategic decision making without undue fear of liability by granting immunity to directors and officers for losses incurred in corporate transactions within their authority so long as the transactions are made in good faith, with reasonable skill, prudence, and in the best interest of the corporation and its shareholders (Glover & Prawitt, 2012). The duty of care and duty of loyalty are traditional hallmarks of a fiduciary who endeavors to act in the service of a corporation and its shareholders. The duty of care requires a director to act in good faith with the diligence that an ordinary prudent person in a similar position would exercise under similar circumstances (CGAUSS, 2002b). The duty of loyalty requires a director to be independent and objective, and to put the interests of the corporation before others, including his or her own. Among the most important of board duties is to work with management and auditors to ensure that the financial statements provided by the company to its shareholders and the investing public fairly present the financial condition of the company (Rezaee & Riley, 2010).

Another significant function is the directors' responsibility to sign the company's annual report to signal to investors that the directors have reviewed and approve of its contents (CGAUSS, 2002b). Directors must be independent and financially literate, at least one of who has an accounting and finance background. In addition, directors must evaluate the objectivity and independence of the company auditor coupled with discussing the auditor's judgements about the quality of the financial statements. This means not just the acceptability of the company's accounting principles as applied in its financial reporting, but including the clarity of the company's financial disclosures and degree of aggressiveness or conservatism of the company's accounting principles applied to its financial reporting. Moreover, directors must determine whether the company's financial statements are fairly presented in conformity with generally accepted accounting principles in all material respects which entails discussing with the auditor, 1) significant accounting adjustments, management judgement and accounting estimates, 2) significant new accounting policies, and 3) disagreements with management (CGAUSS, 2002b).

In essence corporate governance is enhanced when directors improve their ability to exercise an appropriate level of skepticism and actively engage with management meaning effectively challenge management's judgments, explicitly consider alternative perspectives, and engage management in frank, open discussions (Glover & Prawitt, 2012). An effective board must act as a brake on poor decision making because lack of scrutiny may allow the board to negligently accept management financial statements without serious question (Hamilton, 2008). A competent board must ensure that sound internal controls, risk assessment, and management are in place, and that the organization's accounts give a true and fair view of the company's affairs. The board should encourage compensation packages that focus on long-term achievement, penalize poor performance, and reduce the incentive to increase short-term earnings at the expense of the long-term health of the company (Hamilton, 2008). Corporations that are unsupervised appear to invite dysfunctional corporate governance whereby power liberates unethical and criminal temptations in people. This tendency involves acting on one's own desires in a social context without considering the effects of one's actions on others (Frankel, 2008-2009).

In relation to management, the board must understand the fraud risks the company faces and especially those inherent in the business itself ensuring that fraud risk has been considered as part of the organization's risk assessment and strategic plans (Crumbley et al., 2011). Moreover, the board is to monitor management's reports on fraud risks, policies and control activities which includes obtaining assurance that the internal controls are effective (Moran & Kral, 2013). Monitoring management in this aspect includes establishing a process to ensure the board receives accurate and timely information from management, employees, internal and external auditors and other stakeholders regarding potential fraud occurrences. Lastly, the board must oversee the internal controls established by management, have the ability to retain and pay outside experts when needed and provide external auditors with evidence regarding the board's active involvement and concern about fraud risk management (Crumbley et al., 2011).

Board of Director Oversight Challenges

According to Stewart Hamilton, professor of accounting and finance, ineffective boards are one of the main culprits of organizational collapse such as Enron and WorldCom (Hamilton, 2008). Among the mistakes that actually lead a company to fail are fear of top executive management by subordinates, the lust for acquisitions, a dysfunctional board of directors, ignoring risks and being beholden to Wall Street expectations (Frankel, 2008-2009). At the industry level, scholars have scrutinized the facilitating roles played by boards of directors, external auditors, attorneys, and credit rating agencies in many financial statement frauds. It is argued that these gatekeepers or reputational intermediaries, such as the board of directors, failed in their tasks of certifying the soundness of financial information provided by corporate insiders to investors; instead they are said to have colluded with those they were supposed to oversee (Reurink, 2016). Research on fraudulent financial reporting found that even boards and their audit committees are sometimes misled by management who have fraudulently distorted the organization's financial statements (Glover & Prawitt, 2012). Briefly, the primary purpose of an audit committee is to provide oversight of the financial reporting process, the audit process, the system of internal controls and compliance with laws and regulations. The audit committee can expect to review significant accounting and reporting issues and recent professional and regulatory pronouncements to understand the potential impact on financial statements.

The committee reviews the results of the audit with management and external auditors, including matters to be communicated to the committee under generally accepted auditing standards. Audit committees will consider internal controls and review their effectiveness. In addition, controls over financial reporting, information technology security and operational matters fall under the functions of the audit committee. Furthermore, the audit committee establishes procedures for accepting confidential, anonymous concerns relative to financial reporting and internal control matters. Often referred to as a whistleblower policy, the procedures allow individuals to bring questions and issues to light without fear of retaliation. The audit committee is responsible for the appointment, compensation and oversight of the work of the auditor, thus the auditor reports directly to the audit committee, not management. Audit committees should meet separately with external auditors to discuss matters that the committee or auditors believe should be discussed privately. The committee reviews the proposed audit approach and handle coordination of the audit effort with internal audit staff, if applicable. Directors are required to exhibit sound judgment in fulfilling their fiduciary responsibilities of corporate governance and oversight, including overseeing the entity's efforts to prevent fraud and effectively manage enterprise risks.

Yet, directors often do not have valuable information or, in the alternative, are sent so much information that they become overloaded and are unable to distinguish what is important (Paredes, 2005). Board members may not have enough time to fully consider the information they do have, and they lack the requisite knowledge and insight into the company to evaluate critically matters before them. Moreover, outside directors have limited access to various personnel, such as junior officers, office heads, plant managers, and managers of business units, who might help them understand issues coupled with no appreciable contact with suppliers, customers, creditors, or employees (Paredes, 2005). Boards must receive sufficient and adequate information: not too little but also not so much as to drown board members in the details (Frankel, 2008-2009).

Boards are not supposed to run a corporation's day-to-day operations, that is the job of the fulltime management, and they are not supposed to work full-time in their capacity as board members. However, boards have been criticized as being too deferential to the CEO, perhaps due to the fact that they often lack the time, information, and expertise needed to challenge the CEO on business matters, let alone to block a course of action the CEO supports, and may see little reason to doubt a CEO who can point to a track record of success. Further, CEOs have control over the board's agenda and, therefore, can set what the board considers at its meetings. Many directors complain that they have relatively little say over what is brought before them and that scripted management presentations consume most of the time allotted to an agenda item, affording directors little opportunity to ask to discuss the matter during formal meetings (Paredes, 2005). A weak board often, after a period of seemingly successful management, effectively surrender oversight duties and power to a CEO whose drive, charisma and ruthlessness have contributed to earlier successes (Hamilton, 2008).

Lulled into a false sense of security by rising share prices and earnings, the board becomes reluctant to challenge the CEO's judgement and falls into the habit of rubber-stamping his or her decisions (Hamilton, 2008). When viewed in a similar light, it is understandable how intelligent, experienced directors who monitor firms and are responsible for risk assessment on a part-time basis may be hesitant to, or completely refrain from, challenging management's business expertise (Howard, 2011). Furthermore, independent professionals, particularly, do not want to risk public embarrassment by displaying their ignorance in front of the group. They pretend to understand the complicated issues at hand, but in reality they are relying on the judgment of their fellow directors. This can result in independent directors not asking questions or speaking their mind because they fear appearing unintelligent or misinformed when it comes to discussing complex financial matters in front of management. At the same time, as his or her power base expands, the dominant CEO begins to behave as though the company is his own creation, believing his own invincibility and no longer distinguishes between personal ambitions and those of the company (Hamilton, 2008).

Senior management becomes packed with like-minded executives who owe their position to the CEO, and who are unlikely to challenge him. This compounds the lack of scrutiny and debate. The problem is exacerbated if the CEO role is combined with that of chairman of the board, removing another check and balance. An ineffective board increases the likelihood of poor strategic thinking and decision making. The board is there to "stress test" strategic proposals and ensure through considerable debate that they are based on proper research and commercial sense together with considering risk assessments. In one study, 150 directors surveyed who serve on the boards of more than 300 public companies, reported that approximately 56 percent of the directors polled said they only moderately know what is going on at the companies they serve, while 14 percent of the directors polled responded that they really know what is going on at their companies (Paredes, 2005). Of the directors surveyed, 76 percent said that the CEO largely controls and shapes what directors learn about the company. Accordingly, the rational choice for members of the board often is to go along with the insiders who have the best information and insight into the business.

The CEO may be particularly convincing about his decision to pursue some course of action if he exudes confidence and, if the CEO has a track record of achievement, the board may be more inclined to defer to the CEO and to give him additional leeway in running the company. When misconduct surfaces, the board either did not know, but should have known of the manipulations and misappropriations, or they knew of the wrongful acts and did nothing to prevent them. At times, it is only after the discoveries and indictments of these frauds when the regulators, investigators, and prosecutors entered the scene, that boards take action and remove or force the resignation of their CEOs. Furthermore, the mere fact that a CEO decisively makes a bold and risky move might persuade others to go along with him especially if people interpret prior achievement as a sign of ability. High

CEO compensation too, may be a source of power because of the assumption that pay is relevant to perceptions of leader ability. Since effective performance of the figurehead role depends on creating an aura of legitimacy, and if legitimacy is enhanced by the salary paid to an incumbent CEO, then it is reasonable that higher paid executives command greater respect and are perceived as having superior credibility.

Lack of Independence and Conflict of Interests

It is difficult to get a man to understand something when his salary depends on his not understanding it.

Upton Sinclaire

An essential characteristic of a director must be independence of mind, which needs to be coupled with a willingness to walk away if they are unable to exercise an independent mindset (Hamilton, 2008). The accommodating stance boards historically have taken toward their CEOs is more often attributed to a lack of director independence coupled with conflicts of interests than a lack of director competence. An inside director may be beholden to the CEO because his job may be at risk if he expresses disagreement with the CEO. An outside director may also be beholden, compromising his independence, because the director's renomination may be similarly jeopardized if he opposes the CEO, although the conflict may be less severe than for directors that come from inside the organization who are subject to the scrutiny of the CEO. Even if the prestige and director fees that accompany sitting on a board do not suppress dissent and lead to relative appeasement of the CEO, an outside director may be conflicted because of lucrative consulting arrangements or other business dealings he has with the company he or she serves. Still other independence problems arise when the company, if not the CEO personally, makes significant contributions to charities or other organizations important to the outside director. As a result, social and personal relationships between a director and the CEO can undermine a director's independence (Paredes, 2005). At Tyco, for example, some of the independent directors depended directly on the company for the bulk of their income. The majority of Tyco members had served for ten years or more, and they were familiar with CEO Dennis Kozlowski's management style. As directors, they were responsible for protecting Tyco's shareholders through disclosure of questionable situations or issues that might seem unethical or inappropriate. Despite this, after the arrests of CEO Kozlowski and CFO Swartz, investigations uncovered the following troubling relationships among the board's members:

- Richard Bodman invested $5 million for Kozlowski in a private stock fund managed by Bodman,
- Stephen Foss received $751,101 for supplying a Cessna Citation aircraft and pilot services,
- Michael Ashcroft used $2.5 million in Tyco funds to purchase a home, and
- Frank E. Walsh, Jr. received $20 million for helping to arrange Tyco's acquisition of CIT Group without the other board members' knowledge. Walsh also held controlling interest in two firms that received more than $3.5 million for leasing an aircraft and providing pilot services to Tyco between 1996 and 2002 (Boostrom, 2011).

The Display of Potential Groupthink Symptoms

At the board level the well-known groupthink bias, "many heads, one mind" should be guarded against. When there is an active tendency to ignore bad news due to either indifference, not wanting to upset the CEO, or sheer laziness, board members may miss important signals indicative of fraud. Moreover, senior executives, as a result of having successfully climbed the corporate ladder, will tend to overestimate their capabilities, "perhaps as cream rises to the top, hubris does too" (Paredes, 2005, p. 720). For example, large executive compensation packages are paid to chief executives against the backdrop of a corporate governance system that is characterized by deference to the CEO and his business judgment. CEO overconfidence is also a likely product of corporate governance in that CEOs receive little criticism and too much affirmation from the individuals, such as the board who should challenge the CEO when necessary; especially when there is evidence of misconduct that goes beyond unethical acts.

Although control is also dispersed to other senior officers, the board of directors, and shareholders, these individuals and groups generally defer to the CEO and allow the CEO a great deal of latitude in how the business is managed. The concentration of control in the hands of the CEO and their relatively unbridled exercise of power can actually embolden them and in turn contribute to CEO overconfidence (Paredes, 2005). Executives enamored with risk-taking who display an unbridled confidence in their own abilities frequently exceed the legal limits of their own corporate executive action (Frankel, 2008-2009). Group dynamics, such as those that govern the boardroom, can bind group members together and blind them to their failings and excesses, thus groupthink in decision making is one predictable consequence of this process. A conventional explanation for why boards exist is that groups often make better decisions than an individual actor, yet the benefits of group decision making, though, depend on open and frank group deliberation. In terms of boards, this requires that directors, at the very least, consider a wide range of information and possibilities, develop competing ideas, and challenge each other as well as management.

In other words, effective group decision making requires constructive tension within the group and the willingness of individuals to share information and to express their independent views. When boards instead defer to the CEO without real questioning of his or her decisions, the deliberative process of the board is compromised as the CEO's views go unchallenged and as a result groupthink neutralizes the benefits of deliberation and group decision making (Paredes, 2005). Groupthink facilitates directors convincing themselves that they are right to avoid the stress and discomfort of disagreeing with the company's executives, as well as with other members of the board. Aside from its implications for chief executive confidence, board deference to the CEO undercuts the purpose of group corporate decision making. For example, former convicted Tyco CEO Dennis Kozlowski, described how infrequently he experienced any challenge to his position stating:

> When the CEO is in the room, directors—even independent directors—tend to want to try and please him…The board would give me anything I wanted. Anything. We believed our own press…with myself and others—even the board—you become consumed a little bit by your own arrogance and you really think you can do anything (Soltes, 2016, p. 315).

There is a concern of groupthink with those involved in board of directors, especially those involved in audit committees, that there has not been enough professional skepticism within the audit committees in challenging management on auditing issues (KPMG, 2011b). Common backgrounds and social ties among group members can lead to in-group bias and stifle the willingness for board members to dissent especially when loyalty may be questioned for simply asking questions that are uncomfortable to ask (O'Connor, 2003). Groupthink symptoms display themselves when director criticism of the CEO signals disloyalty or "no confidence" in the CEO thus this may jeopardize the renomination to the board which means they need to conform to the "cult of politeness" (O'Connor, 2003, p. 1249). This symptom seems very relevant when analyzed in the context of the pressures of a boardroom. Boards function in a hierarchical structure, which serves as an easy avenue for this pressure to permeate the relationships between directors and CEOs.

Because of self-censorship, it is difficult to know whether an individual director is complying with a decision as a form of obedience to his or her appointer, or that the director truly agrees and supports the decision. As a result, "the norms of polite boardroom behavior discourage directors from openly questioning or challenging the CEO's performance or proposals" (Hoyk & Hersey, 2011, p. 44). The great emphasis on politeness and courtesy at the expense of truth and frankness in boardrooms is both a symptom and cause of failure in corporate governance. Yet, the reality is healthy decisions are made by debate and critical analysis and when this dynamic is not present, the pressures for conformity where dissent is viewed as detrimental or unneeded facilitate the creation of a false sense of security through group consensus (Hoyk & Hersey, 2011). As another consultant stated, "Many directors simply don't want to rock the boat. No one likes to be the skunk at the garden party. One does not make friends and influence people in the boardroom or elsewhere by raising hard questions that create embarrassment or discomfort for management" (Sims, 2003, p. 119).

Board of Director Bias Considerations

Whatever the relationship might be at the start of a directorship, the very process of working closely for a number of years can create affinities and biases over time that can cloud a director's independent judgment. Furthermore, an outside director, who himself is a CEO at another company, might be biased toward going along with the CEO on whose board he sits, identifying with and deferring to the chief executive, just as he hopes his board will defer to him. The director might simply believe that CEOs generally know what is best for the business and should be afforded wide discretion. In addition, an outsider may feel indebted to the CEO who put him on the board and might therefore give the chief executive the benefit of the doubt. As a background point, directors may be biased toward preserving the status quo, seeking to avoid the dissension associated with CEO criticism and especially CEO turnover (Paredes, 2005). Indeed, the mere fact that management has a recommendation may bias the board toward approving it making it difficult as a practical matter for a board to stop a transaction that has considerable momentum, such as when senior management, the lawyers, the accountants, and the investment bankers also approve of the transaction.

Directors understandably bask in the reflected light of a successful CEO, happy to take credit when their CEO is a winner. Having selected the CEO through some form of competition, directors become highly invested in their selection in that they want their CEO to do well and that he or she will do well. Often they cannot bear the thought that their CEO will fail. Failure impairs the board's own reputational capital meaning it undermines their strongly-held sense of competence and control. As a result of the pervasive nature of the confirmation bias, boards may have a tendency to rely on management's assertions and unknowingly or unintentionally be biased toward considering and seeking only confirmatory evidence at the expense of ignoring contradictory evidence that may actually improve decision making (Glover & Prawitt, 2012). A sign that the board might be falling prey to the confirmation tendency is if meetings with the board and management tend to be overly comfortable or agreeable (Glover & Prawitt, 2012). As one observer of board of director bias reflects on how this dynamic may play out:

> [A] streak of good fortune for the firm-which may be managerial skill, but may be just as much the state of the economy—creates a psychological dynamic that works to the CEO's favor. First, the CEO has ample opportunity and resources to expand the board's external influence, thereby making ingratiation tactics more effective. The social ties grow, which makes the inclination to monitor diminish. Not far under the surface here…a related set of commitment biases: the longer a streak of positive information flows, the more board members attribute that success to the person they've put in place and hence develop mental schemata that credit the CEO with skill…Any negative information that subsequently appears tends to be dismissed until the threat is undeniable, partly because of simple cognitive conservatism, partly because the board having committed itself to the CEO by virtue of both selection and generous compensation, is averse to acknowledging that it may have made an error (Barnard, 2008b, p. 427).

Interacting with Disordered Personalities

Boards need to pay attention to personality traits when evaluating the risk of management committing fraud (Cohen et al., 2011). In previous chapters, we examined evidence of CEO pathologies, observing both what pathology looks like and how it may shape the decision making process ending in fraudulent practices. Boards often fail to grapple with CEO pathologies because boards are made up primarily of CEOs, former CEOs and people who aspire to be CEOs failing to recognize CEO pathologies because they share them. Second, these directors may recognize pathologies, but fail to act on them because of their self-serving belief that these pathologies reflect healthy, competitive, and successful behavior. Third, these directors may recognize pathologies and also their harmful potential, yet are unwilling to correct the pathological behavior, at least so long as it seems to generate profits. Fourth, these directors may be fooled by CEOs who willfully mask their pathologies through charm or manipulation. The very same pathologies that can distort CEO performance can also distort the board's oversight role. A narcissistic CEO who is mistrustful and controlling of others may become even more so when acting from a position of fear or paranoia.

Pathologies, in short, can align in different combinations creating negative synergies such as an overly optimistic CEO who systematically discounts risk may compound that error if he or she narcissistically rejects criticism—especially from the board of directors (Barnard, 2008b). The board of directors, as a by-product of their success, may be oblivious to the failings of others because they share a professional affinity with them. Moreover, they may fail to recognize signs the CEO and other senior executives with whom they do business are behaving pathologically to the detriment of the firm. In other words, directors themselves are sometimes subject to narcissism and over-optimism. The very same pathologies that can distort CEO performance can also distort the board's oversight role. What should be done to correct a harmful pattern of behavior? A board must consider if it should engage in senior executive "pathology audit." What might a pathology audit look like? Leadership pathologies can be mitigated by conscious effort such as having executive candidates evaluated for dark triad traits. Directors should take the pulse of their executives, conduct a performance evaluation designed to tease out behavioral problems, and squarely address the issue of CEO pathology.

Self-awareness and a serious discussion of CEO pathologies, including their own, may improve directors' own leadership and decision making skills. The appropriate locus for a mitigation process is, ultimately, the board of directors (Barnard, 2008b). Step one in the mitigation process is to know what pathologies are, how they are displayed and how they may influence CEO behavior. Step two is to recognize whether a particular CEO is behaving pathologically, and if so, to assess whether that behavior is having a negative effect on the organization. Step three is to determine an appropriate course of action for dealing with the effects of the pathology. Is the CEO displaying the traits of a narcissist and, if so, is that a subject that needs to be addressed through executive coaching or other intervention? Is the CEO displaying temper tantrums or unrealistic expectations are driving good people away especially if there are signs of abusive behaviors? They should familiarize themselves with the signs of antisocial behavior, making it clear that such behaviors are unacceptable and will not be rewarded.

The Board of Directors and Risk Management

Just months after David Brooks, the former CEO of DHB Industries, was convicted of defrauding the government contractor of more than $185 million, the SEC filed civil charges against three of the company's outside board of directors, alleging that they willfully and repeatedly "turned a blind eye to numerous, significant, and compounding" warning signs of a massive financial statement fraud and asset misappropriation scheme perpetrated by executive management (McNeal, 2011, p.1). The SEC further asserts that the fraud "was facilitated by the egregious, wholesale failure of the company's board to act in the face of mounting red flags" (McNeal, 2011, p.1). The DHB case is not the first of its kind, nor is it likely to be the last, but the SEC made clear its intentions to continue to hold directors accountable for lack of appropriate fraud risk oversight. At the very least, the SEC action can be taken as a warning to all directors that being unaware of or turning a blind eye to warning signs and red flags is not acceptable; fraud is not on its own an excuse that grants legal immunity. More important, the DHB scandal casts a spotlight on the role of the board in addressing fraud risk, and provides an opportunity to emphasize the critical need for directors to require, oversee, support, and consistently evaluate their organization's fraud risk management programs.

By requiring a proactive fraud risk management plan, directors will meet their fiduciary responsibilities, while helping to secure a financially and ethically sound future for their organization. The business case for managing fraud risk should be a priority of every director when considering the cost-benefit of fraud detection and prevention efforts. Thus, how much money does the organization stand to lose if it fails to implement an effective fraud risk management plan? How successful will any plan be without oversight from the board and frequent reporting from management? The indirect costs that result from fraud are demonstrated by a loss in the confidence of employees, vendors, and customers of victim organizations. Dramatic decreases in shareholder value can destroy a public company before efforts at damage control are even implemented coupled with facing increased scrutiny from regulators for the foreseeable future. Good governance principles demand that an organization's board of directors, or equivalent oversight body, ensure overall high ethical behavior in the organization, regardless of its status as public, private, government, or not-for-profit, its relative size, or industry.

The board is responsible for the legacy of the organization while being accountable to multiple stakeholders, thus it should evaluate its performance regularly with respect to reputation risks and ensure that consideration of reputation risk is part of the organization's risk assessment process. The board's role is important because historically most major frauds are perpetrated by senior management in collusion with other employees. In addition, research suggests that firms with poor corporate governance is linked to organizations manipulating their financial statements. Specifically fraud firms have, 1) fewer numbers of board members who are outside the firm, 2) fewer audit committee meetings, 3) fewer financial experts on the audit committee, 4) a smaller number of large accounting firms performing audits, and 5) a higher percentage of CEOs who are also chairpersons of the board of directors (Farber, 2005, p. 560). Dedicated and observable fraud risk oversight activities by the board not only set the stage for establishing an internal antifraud culture, but serves to increase confidence amongst stakeholders by enhancing the ethical reputation of the organization.

Moreover, directors' proactive involvement in fraud risk management initiatives has the added benefit of serving as a strong deterrent to management fraud by heightening the perception of detection. Increasing the perception that potential offenders will be caught is among the most effective deterrence mechanisms available given that employees in management positions generally cause the greatest fraud losses because of the authority they have over internal controls (McNeal, 2011). Accordingly, directors must be educated on fraud's red flags and willing to ask hard questions of management whether they are of a general nature or specific to potential fraud risks. The best director is inclined to think like an investigator when details do not make sense or explanations do not add up. Answers should not be accepted at face value as necessarily accurate or even, in some cases, honest. The board should be willing to employ the assistance of an expert to questions that go behind their knowledge base. Being involved in the fraud risk management process also includes gaining a full understanding of what management is doing to engage in fraud risk assessments, prevention and detect fraud—not just on paper, but in action. Management's report on which antifraud controls are in place tells us little if management does not lead by example. For example, managers who set unrealistic expectations or who visibly operate in gray ethical areas themselves can derail even effectively designed antifraud program. Given that management override of controls is a significant and common risk for all organizations and that fraud by high-level employees is potentially catastrophic, directors must consider the character and leadership style of the individuals responsible for setting the organization's ethical tone, enacting the fraud risk management program components, and reporting its results to the board (McNeal, 2011).

Engaging in candid conversations with employees, reviewing tips and complaints made through the company hotline, and observing interactions between management and staff members can all assist directors with obtaining a critical view of the company's leaders and their commitment to fraud risk management. Fraud risk oversight also means knowing how internal and external audit strategies address fraud risk. The board should, 1) engage in regular consultation with internal audit staff regarding their ongoing assessment of the organization's fraud risks, 2) review external auditors' assessment of the effectiveness of the organization's antifraud programs and controls, and 3) inquire specifically about any frauds identified by internal or external auditors (McNeal, 2011). To make the most of these conversations, however, directors must have at least a foundational understanding of fraud risks and their underlying factors. For example, board members should be aware of the three primary factors when combined, create conditions ripe for fraud such as indicators of opportunity, incentives/pressure, and rationalizations. However, as we have reviewed in previous chapters, the board should be aware of what antisocial traits look like as well as antisocial interpersonal behaviors. What may appear to the board as simply a personality quirk can actually be reflective of much more. It is best to not ignore personality traits because they can be interpreted as proxies for a fraud attitude. Vigilant handling of fraud cases within an organization sends clear signals to the public, stakeholders, and regulators about the board and management's attitude toward fraud risks and about the organization's fraud risk tolerance.

Particularly, they are expected to explain how, 1) the organization responds to regulations, as well as public and stakeholder scrutiny, 2) what form of fraud risk management program the organization has in place, 3) how it identifies fraud risks, 4) what is it doing to prevent fraud, or at least detect it sooner, and 5) what process exists to investigate fraud and take corrective action (McNeal, 2011). To ensure a proper foundation for the organization's fraud risk management activities, the board should work closely with management to clearly define and formally record the following in the organization's antifraud policy or fraud risk management policy: 1) the board's expectations of management in managing fraud risks, 2) the specific responsibilities of both the board and management for fraud risk management, 3) the ownership of risks at the executive, senior manager, and business-unit manager levels, and 4) the overarching objectives of the fraud risk management program (McNeal, 2011). Once the objectives of the program are articulated and agreed upon, the board must evaluate management's underlying strategy to manage fraud risks, including how fraud risk management program components, both independently and together, support the program objectives.

The board should be involved in determining the organization's risk tolerance for the identified fraud risks, ensuring that the established level of acceptable risk is aligned with the entity's business strategy. Without an adequate understanding and articulation of how much risk those charged with governance are willing to accept, the stated objectives of the fraud risk management program will be incomplete and possibly inaccurate. Once established and clearly documented, the program objectives, risk assessment results, and determined risk tolerance together form the lens through which the board must oversee the design and implementation of the fraud risk management activities and controls (McNeal, 2011). As part of this oversight, one significant issue that should be addressed concerns access to details of the fraud detection methods and controls. Information regarding the design and operation of such activities must remain closely guarded to ensure their effectiveness. The board should approve a list of individuals who are permitted access to such information, as well as define its own level of information access related to these mechanisms (McNeal, 2011). Many companies struggle to determine who will be responsible for managing fraud examinations and fraud risks. Typically, a company designates one person to handle its antifraud program responsibility such as the chief financial or compliance officer or its general counsel.

However, often a company might not designate one person as the "owner" of its antifraud efforts and as a result confusion can ensue causing, 1) a lack of trust in the proactive antifraud program for management and employees, 2) a dangerous deficiency in sharing of knowledge, and 3) inefficient responses to fraud (Torpey & Sherrod, 2011). Furthermore, corporate culture needs to be cultivated and maintained, beginning with basic steps to ensure the board itself is governed properly and does not fall captive to condoning unethical behaviors because it is convenient to do so. This encompasses all aspects of board governance, including independent minded board members who exercise control over board information, access to management and outside advisers, and who independently carry out the responsibilities of compensation, audit, and other committees. The board also has the responsibility to ensure that management designs effective fraud risk management documentation to encourage ethical behavior and empowering employees, customers, and vendors to insist those standards are met every day. The board must understand fraud risks and maintain oversight of the fraud risk assessment by ensuring that fraud risk has been considered as part of the organization's risk assessment and strategic plans.

This responsibility is addressed as an agenda item at board meetings when general organizational risks are considered together with management's reports on fraud risks, policies, and control activities, which include obtaining assurance that the controls are effective (McNeal, 2011). The board establishes mechanisms ensuring it receives timely information from management, employees, internal and external auditors and other stakeholders regarding fraud occurrences. In addition the board should, 1) oversee the internal controls established by management, 2) set the appropriate tone at the top through the CEO job description, hiring, evaluation, and succession-planning processes, 3) have the ability to retain and pay outside experts when needed and, 4) provide external auditors with evidence regarding the board's active involvement and concern about fraud risk management (McNeal, 2011). The board needs to work proactively with management to encourage a corporate culture that rewards ethics, honesty, accountability, and integrity, while also reinforcing a strong antifraud stance. The following are some measures the board should take to help set a proper ethical tone:

- Establish a thorough code of conduct for employees.
- Ensure that financial incentives for management and other key employees are not linked too closely to short-term financial results, which can breed motivation for fraud.

448

- Examine how the incentive program might affect employees' behavior when conducting business or applying professional judgment, for example, determining accounting estimates or appropriate revenue recognition procedures.
- Examine reasonableness of financial results in light of specific current business, industry, and economic considerations. For example, is profit very high when other competitors are struggling and there is an economic downturn?
- Analyze key fraud risk areas, such as revenues, reserves, and estimates on a regular basis, for example on a quarterly basis. Are there any red-flags for financial statement fraud especially for revenue and expense accounts?
- Assess and monitor the true tone used by executives and middle management to communicate to and motivate employees. Perhaps, if financially feasible, engage an outside industrial psychologist to administer feedback assessments from colleagues to gauge who engages in bullying tactics.
- Assess how its own processes might contribute to the organization's fraud risk. For example, does the organization encourage financial incentives that may tempt employees to engage in fraud to achieve them? Does management set revenue goals too high such that they encourage subordinates to engage in fraud to meet such goals? Set goals that are aggressive, but not unrealistic, so as to not reduce management to the choice between failure and falsification.
- As part of establishing a proper tone at the top of the organization, the board of directors should provide an open letter to employees in which they stress the importance of fraud risk mitigation, acknowledge the organization's vulnerability to fraud, and establish the responsibility for each person within the organization to support fraud risk management. The letter should be endorsed or authored by a senior executive or board member, provided to employees as part of their orientation process, and reissued periodically. The letter could serve as the foundation for, and may be the executive summary of a fraud control policy (McNeal, 2011).

The board should approve protocols to ensure reported fraud-related issues are timely reported to appropriate parties, such as the compliance team, HR, the board and the audit committee, the legal and security department. Distributing reports to these parties in their respective areas of responsibility ensures that no single person or functional area controls this highly sensitive information and increases accountability. Charged with the responsibility for having documented procedures for receiving, retaining, and investigating complaints or tips alleging the possibility of misconduct or possible fraud, many boards have turned to independent service providers to operate hotlines and notify the organization of any reported accusations. The board must also approve and oversee the established protocols to ensure reported fraud-related issues are given to the appropriate parties in a timely manner. Depending on the organization's structure and operations, as well as the specifics of the tip received, such reports might be referred to the compliance team, internal audit team, human resources department, legal department, and security personnel. In serious circumstances, such as potential management fraud, the tip should be referred directly to the audit committee. The board should clearly outline which reports will be sent directly to the audit committee, and then ensure that the audit committee monitors and follows up on those reports (McNeal, 2011). Likewise, the board's oversight should encompass all areas—from the implementation of a fraud risk management policy, investigations, and oversight of the resolution of reported cases.

Specifically, the board should ensure a system exists for timely, competent, and confidential evaluation, investigation, and resolution of allegations involving potential fraud. The protocol for this system that is formally documented includes, 1) who should conduct the investigation—internal personnel or external experts, 2) the board's expected involvement in investigations, 3) mechanisms to report results to those charged with governance, 4) legal considerations, such as rules of evidence and chains of custody, and 5) regulatory requirements (McNeal, 2011). Some of these factors will vary based upon the specifics of the investigation. For example, the protocol for investigating senior management differs from those involving an entry-level staff member. Nonetheless directors should review and assess the effectiveness of the organization's documented investigation process. Additionally, in their oversight of fraud response activities, directors should, 1) ensure that the same rules are applied objectively to employees at all levels of the organization, including senior management, 2) receive regular reports on the status of any investigations into reported or alleged fraud, 3) select outside legal counsel to direct investigations when necessary, keeping the selection process independent of management to ensure investigation is free from bias, 4) be actively involved in any investigations involving senior management, and 5) together with management and legal counsel, determine whether, when, and to whom voluntary disclosure of fraud incidents is necessary (McNeal, 2011).

Furthermore, the board should have a zero-tolerance policy for retaliation against whistleblowers with protocol in place to investigate any complaints of bullying. The ultimate goal of a reporting mechanism is to provide anyone with information about potential wrongdoing the means to come forward. Empowering and educating employees to report concerns can help ensure that such issues are brought forth and addressed internally, rather than referred to law enforcement or the media as a first step. For example, corporate compliance might be more cosmetic than real, thus serving a public relations function by keeping up with appearance, but when compliance officers actually have clout in implementation, then their effectiveness is more apt to be realized (Van Slyke et al., 2016). However, compliance may be compromised when individuals have to report to the CEO than the board of directors and their employment depends on how they implement compliance. For example, how hard is a compliance officer willing to push management to acknowledge the importance of compliance if the tone at the top is one of avoiding compliance? Consider the senior compliance officer responsible for Barclay bank's whistleblower program, Jonathan Cox, who left Barclays, located in England, after there was a settlement between Cox and Barclay (Colchester, 2017). CEO Jes Staley employed the bank's internal investigation unit to unmask the whistleblower who criticized the CEO's hiring of a longtime associate for a top position. The CEO apologized for his treatment of whistleblowers and the board of directors reduced his pay due to his conduct.

Risk Management through Hiring and Promotion of Leadership

Many individuals display a dysfunctional approach to risk that leads them to engage in self-destructive conduct ultimately impacting the organization they serve. A non-trivial number of individuals with problematic personality traits occupy leadership positions in corporations where they have the capacity to cause significant harm especially those that approach risk in an irrational manner (Jones, 2017). There is value in identifying personality traits among CEOs and senior executives that correlate with fraud and board members should familiarize themselves with these personality traits so that they do not dismiss them as mere personality quirks. This kind of information could be helpful to not only auditors who have to determine the scope and depth of audits when they observe behaviors that are correlated to fraudulent behavior such as narcissism, but also boards of directors who incorporate this research in their oversight of corporations and their management (Jones, 2017).

Such information could be useful when hiring and supervising managers and in designing compensation structures that consider the type of risks a person will take to reach a compensation level and the potential for circumvention of internal controls to satisfy one's risk appetite. For example, one potential danger is that incentive policies promote the pursuit of self-interest facilitating the effect of tempting individuals with reckless risk-taking to exploit organizational internal control weaknesses and sales policies. Such policies emphasizing self-interest may trigger antisocial tendencies among corporate employees, facilitating unethical and criminal corporate conduct. A first step toward protecting corporations from employees with propensities toward reckless risk taking would be consistent hiring practices for all employees. Firms should adhere to strict hiring protocols including resume verification and reference checks. Following "consistent procedures for hiring and promoting executives should spare firms from the embarrassment and reputational damage that occur when high-level executives are exposed for resume fraud" (Jones, 2017, p. 754). However, integrity assessments should be considered as part of the hiring process to disclose attributes about a person that a traditional background check cannot uncover.

Furthermore, comprehensive performance evaluations can help prevent bad apples who manage to slip through the cracks from advancing in the organization. Experts recommend performance assessments also focus on ethical, interpersonal, and citizenship-oriented behaviors (Jones, 2017). Anecdotal evidence suggests that monitoring antisocial tendencies and attitudes toward risk is of paramount importance at the highest executive levels because a corporation's CEO and CFO make important strategic decisions and control a corporation's financial reporting apparatus coupled with setting the ethical tone for the entire corporate enterprise. Unfortunately, research on CEO personality suggests the very qualities that can propel a person to the top of an enterprise may also threaten organizational long-term success (Jones, 2017). Thus, directors who make key hiring and promotion decisions must remain watchful for behavior that correlates with a dysfunctional approach to risk which can impede organizational functioning through its association with increased unethical behavior.

For example, examining allegations of CEO misbehavior, one study conducted an extensive review of the news media between 2000 and 2015 in which the authors identified 38 incidents where a CEO's misbehavior garnered a meaningful level of media coverage defined as more than 10 unique news references (Larcker & Tayan, 2016). These incidents can be categorized as follows, a) 34 percent involve reports of a CEO lying to the board or shareholders over personal matters—such as a drunken driving offense, prior undisclosed criminal record, falsification of credentials, or other behavior or actions, b) 21 percent involve intimate relations with a subordinate, contractor, or consultant, c) 16 percent involve CEOs making use of corporate funds in a manner that is questionable, but not strictly illegal, d) 16 percent involve CEOs engaging in objectionable personal behavior or using abusive language, e) 13 percent involve CEOs making controversial statements to the public that were offensive to customers or social groups (Larcker & Tayan, 2016).

Most importantly, directors must remain focused on reaffirming the personal integrity of CEOs and CFOs to ensure that senior executives establish high standards for conduct throughout the organization. Directors and corporate managers should remain alert to behavioral problems among executives that suggest a struggle with impulsive decision making where there is no thoughtfulness embedded in decision making to understand as best as possible the true risks of engaging in a decision (Jones, 2017). When faced with reports of misconduct by senior executives, board directors should evaluate all available information and take steps to affirm their confidence in the personal integrity of the officer and to ascertain if there are symptoms of groupthink within the organization itself. Board members, if they have a desire for self-awareness, should have a frank discussion if groupthink symptoms that permeate the board in any respect. That being said, depending on what directors learn, termination of employment for those in leadership positions may be the only appropriate step if remedial action is not available. Reports from recent corporate scandals point to broad categories of problematic executive conduct that often becomes evident to employees, directors, and outside observers before fraud or mismanagement is publicly revealed.

Problematic executive behaviors correlate with fraud include substance abuse, improper workplace relationships, illegal and unethical conduct, and a gambling problem (Jones, 2017). When executives commit unethical acts, crimes or engage in other legal transgressions, there may be more misconduct that remains uncovered. For example, former Tyco CEO Dennis Kozlowski was brought down by what started out as New York Attorney General Robert Morgenthau's investigation of sales tax evasion. Kozlowski shipped art from New York to New Hampshire in an effort to avoid paying sales tax on purchased artwork. After these charges became public and Tyco dismissed Kozlowski, the scope of his fraud and embezzlement at Tyco became clear. As another example, a documentary film titled *Inside Job* illustrated how prosecutors had evidence of solicitation of prostitutes and accounting fraud by high-level Wall Street executives (Jones, 2017). How should directors respond when a senior corporate executive has a brush with the law? At a minimum, the issue deserves the board's attention as an executive's prior contact with the law may constitute a fraud risk factor.

Reports of the behavior of CEOs of firms embroiled in legal troubles support the view that directors should not ignore reports of personal misconduct by corporate leaders. The point of examining personal conduct is that corporate executives should expect to be held to the highest standards of professionalism. When information comes to light that calls into question the personal integrity of a senior executive, directors should take note and treat the situation as an impetus to consider whether the trust they have shown to the individual in question is deserved. For example, gambling problems correlate with impaired decision making and mental health experts believe that many Wall Street securities traders resemble gambling addicts. According to neuroscience studies, the anticipation of financial gains produces the same "high" as addictive drugs like cocaine and motivates risky financial decisions (Jones, 2017). As one expert observed, "the personality traits between the two groups are quite similar: risk-taking, sensation seeking, and action driven" (Jones, 2017, p. 760). In the absence of careful monitoring of their trading activities, gambling addicts with access to corporate resources are capable of harming an organization to the point of ruination.

Stories of securities traders who destroyed some of the world's most prestigious financial firms offer sobering examples of these dangers. If it is possible to become addicted to stock trading, then policies based on the assumption that decisions of traders or corporate managers are guided by rational self-interest are potentially destructive. Consequently, incentive compensation schemes that replicate the reward structure of gambling could induce managers to compulsively pursue irrational financial risks. This dynamic would run counter to the predictions of rational choice theory, which argues that incentive compensation motivates the kinds of decisions that shareholders and society prefer where we try to match the interests of shareholders with those who run the organization. Thus when the firm does well, so do the shareholders and management. In addition, problem gamblers and other antisocial risk takers are more likely to have impaired decision making skills meaning they have trouble making rational decisions regarding risk. Antisocial risk takers tend to make excessively risky decisions, and show a preference for small short-term gains at the expense of large long-term losses. Substance abusers and gambling addicts also prefer immediate gains to long-term rewards.

Moreover, in the public mind, substance abuse is associated with crime and social failure, however, substance abuse problems also plague elite professions such as those in business, medicine and law to name a few. Professional associations and licensing authorities have found that substance abuse contributes to professional malpractice, creating a risk of serious physical or financial harm for the addict's patients or clients. Journalists' investigations and a few public trials reveal that some of the senior executives of firms were brought down by scandal used illegal drugs. Reports have documented the prevalence of cocaine and other forms of substance abuse among Wall Street traders and executives. Despite widespread reports of drug use on Wall Street, neither Wall Street firms nor their regulators seem to have focused much attention on the problem. For example, convicted WorldCom CFO Scott Sullivan admitted that he used cocaine on numerous occasions with fellow WorldCom employees coupled with being convicted of drunk driving in 1984 (Jones, 2017). This lack of attention to substance abuse in the financial industry is troubling given that financial managers have fiduciary responsibilities for large sums of other peoples' money.

Extramarital affairs with subordinates represent another form of high risk conduct by executives. Corporate policies toward workplace relationships vary, but most firms impose limits on consensual relationships between managers and their subordinates, as such relationships create conflicts of interest, raise perceptions of unfairness, and create potential legal liability for employers. Despite such policies, a number of CEOs involved in fraud engaged in inappropriate personal relationships at work before their firms failed, but did not face professional consequences for their behavior. Although in some cases the corporation's directors were aware of these improprieties, they failed to address the policy violations or take steps to mitigate obvious conflicts of interest. Some of the men abused their authority to promote their mistresses to corporate positions where they could help facilitate asset misappropriation and financial statement fraud. For example, Tyco CEO Dennis Kozlowski, had extra-marital affairs with employees at Tyco such as lavishing his mistresses with large bonuses and luxury housing coupled with placing them in positions at Tyco where they helped to facilitate his unauthorized spending sprees (Jones, 2017). Enron's CEO Jeffrey Skilling had an open affair with manager Rebecca Carter. Skilling promoted Carter from a management position to a $600,000 a year post as Corporate Secretary managing the executive team's communication with the board (Jones, 2017). There did not appear to be any evidence that the Board questioned this arrangement.

The Case of Tony Menendez: Where was the Board of Directors?

Just as it is important for management to not retaliate against whistleblowers, the board of directors must be stead-fast in their position that people who come forward disclosing misconduct should not be demonized, marginalized or punished, but protected. Unfortunately this is not always the case as we examine the Menendez case. In 2005, Tony Menendez, a former Ernst & Young auditor and director of technical accounting and training for Halliburton, blew the whistle on their accounting practices and external auditors KPMG for filing materially misleading financial statements (Mintz & Morris, 2017). Tony discovered that Halliburton's bill and hold policies were violated and that revenue was recognized before it was earned. Typically, the risk of ownership has to pass to the customer for the revenue to be recognized. In this case, some of the goods were not even assembled and ready for use by the customer, but unearned sales revenue was recorded as earned. Tony also contacted Halliburton's CFO Mark McCollum about the questionable revenue recognition, yet within hours of the disclosure, McCollum distributed the information that was to remain confidential to other parties. The disclosure was followed by retaliatory actions, specifically: "Halliburton management stripped Menendez of teaching and research responsibilities, ordered subordinates to monitor and report on his activity, excluded from a meeting handling the case that KPMG had insisted that Menendez be excluded from meeting concerning the accounting for a potential joint venture arrangement called "RTA". Halliburton indicated that it acceded to KPMG's demand and excluded Menendez from the meeting" (Mintz & Morris, 2017, p. 188).

Tony also provided a confidential report to Halliburton's board of director's audit committee, but according to the committee, his concerns lacked merit nor did the committee address Halliburton's bill and hold policy violation. Tony also contacted the SEC in Fort Worth, Texas, but they never levied any penalty against Halliburton. Many Halliburton and KPMG personnel involved in the misconduct continued to prosper and were promoted. If corporate governance is to be relevant and not simply used for public relations motivations, all the talk about its importance means nothing unless both management and the board take them seriously. In the end, Tony was exposed and retaliated against—corporate governance failed because the misconduct did not represent the behaviors of a few individuals, but approval by its leadership. Eventually Tony left Halliburton and went to Detroit to meet Nick Cypress, GM's chief accounting officer and comptroller. Tony disclosed what happened at Halliburton believing that Cypress would find out anyways and asked him.

"Does this bother you?"... "Hell no!" Cypress stated. Cypress was asked about the disclosure stating, "I was moved by it, it takes a lot of courage to stand tall like that, and I needed that in the work we were doing. I needed people with high integrity who would work hard and who I could trust to bring problems directly to senior management" (Mintz & Morris, 2017, p. 191)   .

The Enron Board of Directors: A Story of Willful Blindness

What should a CEO expect from the board? A lot of really good advice, but not too much of it.

Enron CEO Kenneth Lay

On December 2, 2001, Enron Corporation, together with its subsidiaries, referred to as Enron, filed for bankruptcy protection, making it at the time the largest company to declare bankruptcy in the nation's history (CGAUSS, 2002b). At this time, Enron's Board of Directors consisted of 15 members, several of whom had 20 years or more experience on the board of Enron. Some of the Enron board members, both past and those present at the time of Enron's collapse could be viewed as being accomplished. Consider some of their backgrounds:

Norman P. Blake (1994–2002)	Interim Chairman of the Enron board has extensive corporate, and investment experience, including past service on the board of General Electric and Owens Corning;
John H. Duncan (1985–2001)	Former Chairman of the Enron Executive Committee, has extensive corporate and board experience, including helping to found and manage Gulf and Western Industries;
Herbert S. Winokur (1985–2002)	Held two advanced degrees from Harvard University and has extensive corporate, board, and investment experience;

Robert K. Jaedicke (1985–2001)   Former Chairman of the Enron Audit and Compliance Committee, Dean Emeritus of the Stanford Business School, and a former accounting professor.

Board member John Duncan described his fellow board members as well educated, experienced, successful businessmen and women and experts in areas of finance and accounting together with having a good working relationship with Enron management. Several had close personal relationships with Board Chairman and CEO Kenneth Lay with all members indicating they possessed great respect for senior Enron officers, and trusted the integrity and competence of management. The total cash and equity compensation of Enron board members in 2000 was valued by Enron at about $350,000 or more than twice the national average for board compensation at a U.S. publicly traded corporation meeting about six to eight times a year (Beenen & Pinto, 2009). Yet, board members failed to protect Enron shareholders and contributed to the collapse by allowing Enron to engage in inappropriate conflict of interest transactions. The board knowingly allowed Enron to conduct billions of dollars in off-the-books activity to make its financial condition appear better than it was and failed to ensure adequate public disclosure of material off-the-books liabilities that contributed to Enron's collapse (CGAUSS, 2002a). Enron created more than two thousand separate business entities, many of which were special purpose entities (SPEs) intended to absorb Enron's liabilities, but which were not included in Enron's financial statements.

Although Enron's economic collapse triggering bankruptcy near the end of 2001 came as a surprise to many, there were warning signs of financial problems to come that were not concealed from the board. Enron directors indicated they were as surprised as anyone by the company's collapse, but more than a dozen incidents over several years should have raised board concerns about the activities of the company. The board failed to safeguard Enron shareholders by allowing Enron to engage in high risk accounting practices, inappropriate conflict of interest transactions, excessive executive compensation, and failed to monitor the cumulative cash drain from Enron (CGAUSS, 2002a). The board knew that Enron's accountant, Arthur Andersen, classified Enron as a maximum risk client because it used the most aggressive permissible accounting principles that ultimately crossed the line to the illegal (Howard, 2011). In fact the board was alerted as early as 1999 when Andersen told them that Enron employed accounting strategies that "push the limit" to what may be acceptable practices (Sims, 2003, p. 183). Enron's directors protest that they cannot be held accountable for misconduct that was concealed from them, but much that was wrong with Enron was known to the board. In too many instances, by going along with questionable practices and relying on management and auditor representations, the Enron board failed to provide the prudent oversight and checks and balances that its fiduciary obligations required and that a company like Enron needed. By failing to provide sufficient oversight and restraint to stop management excess, the Enron board contributed to the company's collapse and bears a share of the responsibility for it.

Inappropriate Conflicts of Interests

The independence of the Enron Board of Directors was compromised by financial ties between the company and certain board members. Despite clear conflicts of interest, directors approved an unprecedented arrangement allowing Enron's CFO Andrew Fastow to establish and operate SPEs which transacted business with Enron and profited at Enron's expense. The board exercised inadequate oversight over these SPEs which Fastow was compensated for ultimately failing to protect Enron shareholders from unfair dealing (CGAUSS, 2002a). Expert witnesses testified that the independence and objectivity of the Enron board had been weakened by financial ties between Enron and certain directors creating conflict of interests that too many were obvious, but ignored. These financial ties, which affected a majority of the outside board members, included the following:

John Urqhart   A board member since 1991, in 2000 Enron paid him $493,914 for his consulting work alone.

Lord John Wakeham   Since 1996, in addition to his board compensation, Enron paid a

	monthly retainer of $6,000 for consulting services compensation. In 2000, Enron paid him $72,000 for his consulting work alone.
Herbert Winokur	In addition to serving on Enron's Board, Winokur served on the Board of the National Tank Company. From 1997 to 2000, National recorded revenues in the millions from sales to Enron subsidiaries.
Dr. Charles LeMaistre	Enron and Ken Lay donated nearly $600,000 to the Anderson Cancer Center. In 1993, the Enron Foundation pledged $1.5 million to the Cancer Center where Dr. LeMaistre served as president.
Dr. Wendy Gramm	Since 1996, Enron and the Lay Foundation donated more than $50,000 to the George Mason University and its Mercatus Center in Virginia where Dr. Gramm is employed by the Mercatus Center.
Robert Belfer	Since 1996, Enron and Belco Oil and Gas engaged in hedging arrangements worth tens of millions of dollars. In 1997, Belco bought Enron affiliate Coda Energy and Enron Board member Robert Belfer was the former Chairman of the Board and CEO of Belco.
Charles Walker	An board member from 1985 until 1999. From 1993–1994, Enron paid more than $70,000 to two firms that were partly owned by Walker for governmental relations and tax consulting services.

A number of corporate governance experts identified these financial ties as contributing to the board's lack of independence and reluctance to challenge Enron management. Robert Campbell, retired Chairman and CEO of Sunoco, Inc., who sat on the boards of several large corporations, testified before Congress that "consulting arrangements with directors is absolutely incorrect, absolutely wrong" because directors are already paid a substantial fee to be available to management and provide their perspective on company issues (CGAUSS, 2002b). Enron's high risk accounting practices, for example, were not hidden from the board because the auditor, Arthur Andersen warned the board of Enron's high risk accounting, but the board took no action to prevent Enron from using them. Mr. Campbell further stated that he could not, "Imagine...sitting down with the auditors and being told that we are using high-risk auditing practices and just agreeing with that.

Campbell called going forward with that kind of an environment equivalent to going down a slippery slope, and said board approval of high risk practices is unlike any board that I have ever seen or heard of" (CGAUSS, 2002b). Charles Elson, Director of the Center for Corporate Governance at the University of Delaware, testified that public company directors should have "no financial connection to the company whatsoever other than their board compensation, but the Enron board was problematic because a number of directors were service providers or recipients of corporate largess in some way, shape, or form" (CGAUSS, 2002b). Mr. Elson testified that being told of high risk activities by the company's outside auditor "is a giant red flag" that should have caused board members to ask "an awful lot of questions" and might have necessitated bringing in a third party to evaluate the company's accounting practices (CGAUSS, 2002b). Mr. Elson further stated:

> By taking those fees, you are effectively becoming part of the management team, and I think there is a real problem with exercising independent judgment vis-a-vis what the management has done if you feel part of that team, either through participating in the development of management plans and strategies or the fear that if one objects too strenuously, those consulting fees may disappear...You may take what they are telling you at face value without being more probative because of the relationship...[I]f a director's role is as a consultant, hire the director as a consultant. If the director's role is to be a director, hire them as a director. You cannot blend the two (CGAUSS, 2002b).

For example, the company waived Enron's Code of Ethics three times to allow CFO Fastow to serve as general partner of the entities Enron used as conduits for much of its highly complicated and controversial financial maneuvering. Three times, from 1999 to 2000, the board was asked to and approved an unprecedented arrangement allowing Enron's CFO Andrew Fastow to set up SPEs to do business with Enron for the purpose of improving Enron's financial statements by removing liability and underperforming assets off its balance sheet. While the evidence indicates that, in some instances, board members were misinformed or misled, overall the board received substantial information about Enron's plans and activities and explicitly authorized or allowed many of the questionable Enron strategies, policies, and transactions without oversight of how they were being managed. The waivers were unusual events and several experts on corporate governance stated that such conflict of interest proposals should never have been approved. One former CEO commenting on the waivers stated, "In my wildest dreams, I can't imagine how a director can sit there and approve that" further stating that if he were on such a board and it was approved he would resign the next day (O'Connor, 2003, p. 1269). When Enron board members testified before Congress after Enron's collapse, they indicated they waived the code of ethics because the benefits outweighed the cost, plus they believed Fastow had the expertise to handle the SPEs and the foreseeable related party issues.

Yet they acknowledged the risk of public criticism of such related party transactions and conflict of issue that would arise. Moreover, despite clear conflicts of interest, the board approved an unprecedented arrangement allowing CFO Fastow to establish SPEs which transacted business with Enron and profited at Enron's expense, but the board failed to protect shareholders from unfair self-dealing by Fastow who profited at the expense of Enron. The board's decision to waive the company's code of conduct was highly unusual and disturbing because this arrangement allowed inappropriate conflict of interest transactions as well as accounting and related party disclosure problems, due to the dual role of Fastow as a senior officer at Enron and an equity holder and general manager of the SPEs. Nevertheless, with little debate or independent inquiry, the board approved three code of conduct waivers. The board knew that controls would be needed to ensure that transactions and Fastow's compensation were fair to Enron, but they failed to follow through on any controls to monitor Fastow. The result was that the SPEs realized hundreds of millions of dollars in profits at Enron's expense even though Enron's code of conduct expressly prohibited Enron employees from obtaining personal financial gain from a company doing business with Enron. Enron's Code of Ethics states: "Employees of Enron Corp…An employee shall not conduct himself or herself in a manner which directly or indirectly would be detrimental to the best interests of the Company or in a manner which would bring to the employee financial gain separately derived as a direct consequence of his or her employment with the Company."

In addition, the Code of Ethics position on Conflicts of Interest, Investments, and Outside Business Interests of Officers and Employees stated: [N]o full-time officer or employee should…[o]wn an interest in or participate, directly or indirectly, in the profits of any other entity which does business with or is a competitor of the Company, unless such ownership or participation has been previously disclosed in writing to the Chairman of the Board and Chief Executive Officer of Enron Corp. and such officer has determined that such interest or participation does not adversely affect the best interests of the Company. At the congressional hearing, Mr. Winokur and Dr. Jaedicke argued that the board did not actually "waive" the company's code of conduct, but "applied" it, however management explicitly requested board approval of a code of conduct waiver. This prohibition could be waived, however, by the CEO upon a finding that a proposed arrangement would "not adversely affect the best interests of the Company."

In the case of the partnerships, CEO Lay approved waiving the code of conduct prohibition for Fastow, but also asked the Enron Board to ratify his decision, even though board approval was not explicitly required by company rules. Despite these highly unusual features, the board ratified the code of conduct waiver and approved Fastow's proposal with little study or debate (CGAUSS, 2002b). In addition, the board knowingly allowed Enron to conduct billions of dollars in off-the-books activity to make its financial condition appear better than it was and failed to ensure adequate public disclosure of material off-the-books liabilities that contributed to Enron's collapse. Evidence introduced in the Andersen criminal trial indicates that the idea for board ratification may have originated with Andersen. Apparently, a number of senior Andersen personnel, including auditor David Duncan, had serious concerns about the partnership proposals and was reluctant to support it. Benjamin Neuhausen, a member of Andersen's Professional Standard Group, wrote in an email to David Duncan in 1999:

> Setting aside the accounting idea of a venture entity managed by a CFO is terrible from a business point of view. Conflicts galore. Why would any director in his or her right mind ever approve such a scheme? Mr. Duncan responded in a 6/1/99 email as follows: "[O]n your point 1 (i.e., the whole thing is a bad idea), I really couldn't agree more. Rest assured that I have already communicated and it has been agreed to by Andy that CEO, General Counsel, and Board discussion and approval will be a requirement, on our part, for acceptance of a venture similar to what we have been discussing" (CGAUSS, 2002b).

For example, Enron's board that did not belong to the audit committee did not challenge those audit committee members to inquire why they did not press Andrew Fastow as to how much money Fastow and other executives made from the related party transactions. One of the board members did ask why the information was not gathered and the answer was that they wanted to "avoid office gossip" (O'Connor, 2003, p. 1289). In addition, after several attempts to get the compensation information, the matter was dropped, but the board learned of his compensation that was acquired at the expense of Enron by reading the newspapers that Fastow received $30 million from the related party transactions, yet the actual amount was $45 million according to Fastow (O'Connor, 2003, p. 1289). At congressional hearings, when pressed about why they did not engage in due diligence to find out in advance Fastow's compensation, board members stated that it was "inappropriate or intrusive" to ask such questions which appears to reflect a contradiction in the above facts where they made attempts to inquire without follow-up (O'Connor, 2003, p. 1289). Furthermore, illustrating inconsistencies in the board's answers to why they did not pressure Fastow to disclose his SPE compensation, the above mentioned board member, Charles LeMaistre, stated in his testimony before Congress, "I do not believe that the Board of Directors would ever have approved Mr. Fastow's participation in the partnerships if we had known he would be generating such compensation" (Sims, 2003, p. 183).

Lack of Independence

The board also failed to ensure the independence of the company's auditor, allowing Andersen to provide internal audit and consulting services while serving as Enron's external auditor (CGAUSS, 2002a). Board members indicated they believed Andersen and Enron had a good working relationship, and took comfort in knowing that Andersen was more than Enron's outside auditor, but also provided Enron with extensive internal auditing and consulting services, combining its roles into what Enron called an integrated audit. Dr. Jaedicke maintained that it was a significant benefit to Enron for Andersen to be involved with Enron's activities on a day-to-day basis and to help the company design its most complex transactions from the start. Although one board member, Lord Wakeham, displayed concern that this high level of involvement meant Andersen might be too close to Enron management, most board members indicated the issue had not been a concern (CGAUSS, 2002b). The board was criticized for inadequate oversight to ensure the independence and objectivity of Andersen in its role as the company's outside auditor. Board members rarely had any contact with Andersen outside of an official board meeting and none ever contacted anyone from Andersen regarding Enron outside of an official meeting; none had ever telephoned Andersen directly (CGAUSS, 2002b).

No board member expressed any concern Andersen might be auditing its own work, or that Andersen auditors might be reluctant to criticize Andersen consultants for Fastow's partnerships that Andersen had been paid millions of dollars to help design. In contrast, the accounting and corporate governance experts condemn the very concept of an integrated audit, not only for diluting the outside auditor's independence, but also for reducing the effectiveness of an outside audit by allowing the auditor to audit its own work at the company. The board members observed they had given Andersen regular opportunities outside the presence of Enron management to communicate any concerns about the company, including whether company officials were pressuring Andersen accountants who raised objections to company proposals. The interviewed board members indicated they did not consider whether Andersen might be reluctant to express concerns about accounting practices out of an unwillingness to upset Enron management or endanger Andersen's fees (CGAUSS, 2002b). A number of the interviewed directors discounted the importance of Andersen's fees, even though Enron was one of Andersen's largest clients and, during 2000, paid Andersen about $52 million or $1 million per week for its work (CGAUSS, 2002b).

McKinsey & Company, where CEO Jeffrey Skilling came from, received $10 million a year (Beenen & Pinto, 2009). Andersen's consulting fees at Enron exceeded its auditing fees for the first time in 1999, and, in 2000, totaled about $27 million compared to auditing fees of about $25 million. When asked by Senator Susan Collins at the hearing if Dr. Jaedicke had "ever known an auditor to come in and say, we are not independent." Dr. Jaedicke responded "they would not last very long if they did that." Senator Collins responded: "Exactly my point…When you are making over $40 million a year, the auditor is not likely to come to the Audit Committee and say anything other than that they are independent. Is it not the job of the Audit Committee to make sure that the auditor truly is giving full, accurate, and appropriate advice to the Board" (CGAUSS, 2002b)? Reflecting on the answer by Dr. Jaedicke, it becomes apparent that if someone of his apparent caliber cannot see the error in his opinion, it is not surprising board failures occur as frequently as they do. Is it not the obligation of auditors to maintain independence? It becomes less difficult to imagine why corporate scandals are prevalent when individuals. like Dr. Jaedicke, exist in enough numbers to dilute the purpose of auditing which is to protect the public.

Summary Insight of Enron's Collapse

American culture portrayed the CEOs of Enron, Lay and Skilling, as modern day heroes, larger than life leaders because they were the engines of social change that society periodically goes through. Financial and popular press exalted Enron executives and Lay received iconic corporate royalty status viewing themselves as revolutionaries with "some executives described themselves as being like Gandhi and Martin Luther King" (O'Connor, 2003, p. 1277). It is not implausible that the board did not want to interfere or stifle the hero-like reputation that Lay and Skilling acquired. Moreover, they may have experienced feelings of intimidation from Skilling, even at a subconscious level, to explain why they did not questions Enron's business deals in addition to not wanting to be rejected from serving on the board for being too critical of management's decisions. Let us not forget the above-average compensation they received for their board membership and "almost every vote by Enron's board of directors was unanimous" (Hoyk & Hersey, 2011, p. 45). The board succumbed to Enron due to the "perception of invincibility, superiority and gamesmanship in manipulating Enron's financial statements to keep the Enron stock price soaring" with CEO Skilling boasting that "Enron has reported 20 straight quarters of increasing income…there's not a trading company in the world that has that kind of consistency" (O'Connor, 2003, p. 1271).

This sense of invincibility permeated the Enron board hailed as one of the best boards in the country at the time, but as watch-dogs, the board ignored fraud red-flags in order to maintain a positive image of Enron (O'Connor, 2003). Anyone who questioned suspect deals quickly learned to accept assurances of outside lawyers and high risk deals approved by Andersen. Former SEC Chairman Arthur Levitt, in a now famous speech called the "Numbers Game," spoke about gaps in the system of gatekeepers more than three years before Enron imploded. In that speech, then-Chairman Levitt expressed deep concern about earnings management, the manipulation of accounting in order to meet Wall Street's earnings expectation. Levitt stated, "Too many corporate managers, auditors and analysts are participating in a game of nods and winks…I fear that we are witnessing an erosion in the quality of earnings, and therefore, the quality of financial reporting. Managing may be giving way to manipulation; integrity may be losing out to illusion" (CGAUSS, 2002b, p. 3). Sadly, the Enron debacle coupled with the failure of all of those charged with protecting against such fraud appear to have left many investors with doubts about whether they can rely on any of the financial information in the marketplace (p. 3). Levitt later commented on the failure of corporate governance to ensure integrity in corporate life stating:

Enron's collapse did not occur in a vacuum. Its backdrop is an obsessive zeal by too many American companies to project greater earnings from year to year. When I was at the SEC, I referred to this as a 'culture of gamesmanship'—a gamesmanship that says it is okay to bend the rules, to tweak the numbers, and let obvious and important discrepancies slide; a gamesmanship where companies bend to the desires and pressures of Wall Street analysts rather than to the reality of the numbers; where analysts more often overlook dubious accounting practices and too often are selling potentially lucrative investment banking deals; where auditors are more occupied with selling other services and making clients happy than detecting potential problems; and where directors are more concerned about not offending management than with protecting shareholders. What emerged was a story of systemic and arguably catastrophic failure, a failure of all the watchdogs to properly discharge their appointed roles. Despite the magnitude of Enron's implosion and the apparent pervasiveness of its fraudulent conduct, virtually no one in the multilayered system of controls devised to protect the public detected Enron's problems, or, if they did, they did nothing to correct them or alert investors.

Not one of the watchdogs was there to prevent or warn of the impending disaster: Not Enron's Board of Directors, which asked few, if any, probing questions of Enron's management and which authorized various related-party transactions that facilitated many of Enron's fraudulent practices; not Enron's auditor, Arthur Andersen, which certified the apparently fraudulent financial statements; not the investment banking firms, which structured and sold securities and other financial products that appear to have allowed Enron to obfuscate its financial position; Not the attorneys, whose opinions and work were critical to certain transactions that may have been central to Enron's collapse; not the Wall Street securities analysts, many of whom continued to recommend Enron as a "buy" up until the bitter end; not the credit rating agencies, who rated Enron's debt as investment grade up until 4 days before the company filed for bankruptcy; and not the SEC, which did not begin to seriously investigate Enron's practices until after the company's demise became all but inevitable (CGAUSS, 2002b).

In the end, the board simply became a rubber stamp for Enron's auditors and lawyers even when they were aware of the riskiness of their accounting practices (Sims, 2003). Whether they were negligent because they did not have the knowledge to understand what Enron was actually doing to ask pertinent questions, whether they felt intimidated by Skilling and Lay's personality to have the courage to ask questions, or they were negligent because they did not take the time to evaluate what Enron was actually doing by employing their own expert to help them in their evaluation of Enron's practices, in the end they were still negligent in their duties. Yet board members failed to take any responsibility for their role in Enron's collapse believing that information was concealed from them and as one board member stated reflecting the sentiments of the other board members, "I do not believe that Enron's fall would have been avoided" if the directors asked more questions (Sims, 2003, p. 183)

The Role of the External Auditor

The Securities and Exchange Commission (SEC) and accounting firm Ernst & Young LLP entered into an agreement where Ernst & Young paid more than $11.8 million to settle charges related to failed audits of an oil services company named Weatherford that used deceptive income tax accounting to inflate earnings due to auditor negligence where they disregarded significant fraud symptom red flags during their audits (SEC, 2016). Ernst & Young's audit team repeatedly failed to detect the company's fraud until it was more than four years ongoing. The audit team was aware of Weatherford's financial statement fraud impacting their income tax when it relied on Weatherford's unsubstantiated explanations to questions concerning their income instead of performing the required audit procedures to scrutinize the company's accounting methodology. The SEC found that the firm took no effective measures to minimize recurring problems auditors experienced when auditing tax accounting stating, "Audit and national office professionals must appropriately address known deficiencies in their auditing of high-risk areas, and auditors must have the fortitude to refuse to sign off on an audit if important issues remain unresolved…Ernst & Young failed to ensure that material post-closing accounting adjustments were justified by appropriate audit evidence, leading to a significant audit failure" (SEC, 2016).

Audit failures occur frequently and it is important to understand where the problem lies. What is often forgotten, but which deserves attention, is that the Federal government gave the accounting profession the valuable private franchise to audit firms after the stock market crash of 1929, but in return, auditors are expected to do their best to make sure investors can trust corporate financial markets (Sims, 2003). The external auditor was tasked with assessing the effectiveness of client internal controls and rendering a report, either separately or as part of an integrated audit report, referencing the financial and internal control audits. Yet even though there is closer regulatory scrutiny for financial statement fraud, there seems to be little improvement in identifying fraud among those who seek to uncover it; a mere 4 percent of financial statement fraud is identified by the external auditor and 15 percent by the internal auditor (Kleinman et. al, 2020).

Accountants can learn how to better detect financial statement fraud by understanding the mistakes others made in cases where the SEC imposed sanctions on auditors for their association with fraudulently misstated financial statements (Beasley et al., 2001). In an important study, the SEC examined the most prevalent reasons that contributed to audit failures by examining 81 audit failures that contributed to auditors being sanctioned like Ernst & Young over the period 1998–2010 coupled with instances of alleged fraudulent financial reporting by U.S. publicly traded companies. The study found the top reasons for audit failures in order of pervasiveness as: 1) failure to gather sufficient, competent audit evidence in 73 percent of cases, 2) failure to exercise due professional care in 67 percent of cases, 3) insufficient level of professional skepticism in 60 percent of cases, 4) failure to obtain adequate evidence related to management representations in 54 percent of cases, and 5) failure to express an appropriate audit opinion in 47 percent of cases (Beasley et al., 2013).

We will examine in more detail these reasons and how auditors can mitigate against audit failures from occurring in the first place. Moreover, part of the problem of why there are so many audit failures is because auditing today as we know it no longer advocates that an auditor is responsible for fraud detection—it is not considered a job function (Smith, 2015a). Yet consider the classic text, *Auditing: A Practical Manual for Auditors* which states, "The detection of fraud is the most important portion of the Auditor's duty, and there will be no disputing the contention that the auditor who is able to detect fraud is—other things being equal—a better man than the Auditor who cannot…Auditors should therefore assiduously cultivate this branch of their functions" (Dicksee, 1928, p. 8). Presently, in the standard audit reports that accompany corporate financial statements, the auditor's responsibility for detecting fraud is not discussed, in fact the word fraud is not mentioned at all. Yet, whenever an accounting deception is uncovered, one of the first questions investors ask is, "Where were the auditors?" The auditing profession calls the discrepancy between what investors expect and what auditors do an "expectations gap".

The Center for Audit Quality (CAQ) states, "because auditors do not examine every transaction and event, there is no guarantee that all material misstatements, whether caused by error or fraud, will be detected" (Smith, 2015). This insight is not invalid, yet the issue is rather auditors, at times, are not willing to follow up on fraud symptom red-flags when they become apparent and even when fraud is discovered, they do nothing about it and in many cases exacerbate the problem by implicitly condoning it to continue receiving their audit fees. The reasons delineated by the SEC have to do with basic due diligence professionalism expected of auditors that is overlooked, but for which contributes to the facilitation of fraud because due diligence may have revealed fraud symptom red-flags to investigate and which may have unveiled fraud. Thus, it is not explicitly looking for fraud that is the issue, it is not engaging in the due diligence in the first place that could have detected fraud symptom red flags that is the problem. However, the accountant relies on a false sense of security in their belief that it is not their duty to detect whether fraud is present because if their belief was accurate, then they would not be liable for civil fines by the SEC and potential criminal liability for approving fraudulent financial reports. In essence they would be immune from these liabilities which is simply not the case.

This false sense of security is further perpetuated by senior executives who are in charge of auditing in their respective countries where mixed messages are offered adding to the unnecessary confusion as to what an auditor's duty is when in fact it is clear. For example, these senior executives shared their opinion on whether fraud detection was considered part of their duties. United Kingdom KPMG Chairman Bill Michael, "We are not responsible for the material detection of fraud" and United Kingdom Grant Thornton CEO David Dunckley disclosed his opinion on the purpose of an audit stating, "We are not looking for fraud. We are not looking at the future. We are not giving a statement that the accounts are correct. We are saying they are reasonable. We are looking in the past, and we are not set up to look for fraud" (Hodgson, 2019). Later, Dunckley clarified his position after realizing the error of his initial position stating: "When you sign off the audit, you are not signing off to say there has not been a fraud. If there is a fraud that affects the materiality of the accounts, you will want to find it…the nature of an audit itself is not designed to target fraud necessarily, and there is an expectation from the public that it is" (Hodgson, 2019).

However, Scott Knight, head of audit at BDO in the United Kingdom, believes that "If they [frauds] are sizeable and material then I think you do have to look for them. In a large organization there will be petty frauds and that is not something an audit is designed to wheedle out. But if they are material to the financial statements and of relevance to the shareholders, then you should be expected to find them" (Hodgson, 2019). Even though financial statements are the responsibility of management, the primary responsibility of an external auditor is to express an opinion on a client's financial statements after conducting an audit to obtain reasonable assurance that the client's financial statements are free of material misstatements (Sawayda, 2011). The objective of an independent audit of a client's financial statements is the expression of an opinion on the fairness with which the financial statements present, in all material respects, financial position, results of operations, and its cash flows that are in conformity with generally accepted accounting principles (Sawayda, 2011). Organizational misconduct due to financial statement frauds provide vivid examples of how internal controls breakdown, flawed and dishonest management, and auditing can result in misstated financial statements that ultimately harms a national economy. Audit failures endanger the relevance of the profession and its development in the long run when there is a serious distortion in the financial statements that is not reflected in the audit report, and the auditor made a serious error in conducting the audit (Zhang & Zhang, 2009).

Another common issue is the failure to express an appropriate audit opinion. Examples of audit failures include situations where the auditor issued an unqualified opinion even though the auditor has knowledge that does not support an unqualified opinion. The unqualified opinion is the best possible audit outcome. An unqualified opinion is an independent auditor's judgment that a company's financial records and statements are fairly and appropriately represented, and in accordance with Generally Accepted Accounting Principles (GAAP)—in essence, the company's financial statements are sound. When do problems arise? For example an auditor fails to modify the audit report even though there are material scope restrictions whereby the auditor failed to verify written representations by management and the auditor knew that a material portion of the accounts receivables, for example, did not have any supporting documentation (Beasley et al., 2001; 2013). Thus, audit failure cannot occur unless there is serious auditor error or misjudgment and the nature of auditor error has four systematic causes (Zhang & Zhang, 2009). First of all, the auditor can blunder by misapplying or misinterpreting accounting principles. Such unintentional blunders could be caused by fatigue or human error.

Secondly, the auditor can commit fraud by knowingly issuing a more favorable audit report than is warranted. This may occur when the auditor accepts a bribe or bows to client pressure or threats. Moreover, the auditor can be unduly influenced by having a direct or indirect financial interest in the client. Also, the auditor can be unduly influenced because of having some personal relationship with the client beyond what is expected in a normal audit between independent parties. Based on the deficiencies, the SEC found there are a number of areas that warrant specific attention from CPA firms performing audits and from individual auditors themselves (Beasley et al., 2001; 2013). In many of the fraud cases, it appeared auditors simply chose not to pursue identified audit issues, perhaps fearing the time spent investigating those issues would hinder career advancement or result in penalties during salary and bonus reviews because they ran overtime budgets or missed client-imposed deadlines.

Solutions to Reduce the Risk of Audit Failures

White-collar crime is present in both good and bad economic times, but such crimes are either less noticed during a good economic climate or more noticed during a bad economic climate. In a relatively good economy, white-collar crime is easier to execute and harder to uncover and in a relatively bad economy, many white-collar crimes in progress implode upon themselves because they become unsustainable (Antar, 2012). It is unfortunate that many white-collar crimes are uncovered because they implode upon themselves, instead of the result of effective work by internal auditors, external auditors, and audit committees (Antar, 2012). Yet there are solutions to help mitigate against criminal mindsets faced by auditors. It is important to acknowledge there is no audit devoid of risk where certain incentives/pressures, opportunities, or inappropriate attitudes or rationalizations may exist enhancing the likelihood of fraud being present. Also, those standards recognize the risk of management override of internal controls is present in all audits. However, in many cases, the best remedy for such problems is for auditors to develop a properly designed and executed quality control system to perform audits. Such a system creates a culture encouraging all members of an audit team to maintain a baseline acceptable level of performance, regardless of perceived day-to-day engagement and accounting firm pressures.

CPA firms should evaluate their own quality control systems to ensure policies and procedures emphasize the importance of proper audit planning, supervision and review, including timely involvement by engagement partners. Additionally, firms should reexamine existing quality control procedures to make sure they are detailed enough to assure firm leaders that audit teams are examining appropriate documentation and that teams complete all audit program steps. Those procedures emphasize that auditors verify management representations with additional evidence and not over rely on managements' representations as a form of audit evidence. The accounting firm's system of quality control should include policies and procedures addressing each of the following elements: 1) leadership responsibilities for quality control within the accounting firm, 2) ethical requirements, 3) acceptance and continuance of client relationships and specific engagements, 4) human resources, 5) engagement performance, 6) documentation, and 7) monitoring. Quality control policies and procedures should be implemented at the audit firm level and on individual audits; these policies should be implemented on a consistent basis (Zhang & Zhang, 2009).

Within this section, we examine the deficiency issues auditors encountered in the SEC study that can actually be the solutions auditors need to rely upon such as exercising due professional care, gathering competent evidence, maintaining auditor independence, improving professional skepticism and consider a more principles-based approach when applying accounting standards and not just a rules-based approach.

Exercise Due Professional Care

Some of the deficiencies cited suggest a failure on the part of the auditor to discharge responsibilities with competence and diligence to the best of the auditor's ability, including the performance of procedures generally expected to be performed in an audit. There is a belief that auditors fail in their due diligence because they do not devote enough hours to their engagement in order to keep the cost of the audit as low as possible. Toby Bishop, former president of the Association of Certified Fraud Examiners (ACFE), believes competitive bidding for auditing business places tremendous pressure on audit firms to limit the number of hours in an audit engagement which inadvertently discourages auditors to look for fraud during an audit (Chui & Pike, 2013). Also, there may be opportunities for additional analysis to better understand causes that led to failures in a particular audit engagement, so as to strengthen the competence and diligence of the performance of the audit. Some examples of a failure to exercise due diligence might reflect:

- The audit firm failed to adjust its audit procedures in light of noted and documented risk concerns on client accounting practices that are deemed highly aggressive or unusual.
- The audit firm failed to plan and properly supervise the audit, and the firm failed to consider the underlying audit risk.

- While the firm requested the client to present documentation to support a material amount in the financial statements, the audit firm failed to conduct further audit procedures when management claimed the documentation was unavailable.
- The audit firm failed to act with due diligence when multiple pieces of documentation suggested the client's accounting records were held open beyond the fiscal year end, and the audit firm ignored the client's failure to record depreciation expense (Beasley et al., 2001; 2013).

In some of the cases reviewed, audit deficiency involved auditors who failed to perform procedures generally accepted as appropriate and expected in most audits. In many of those instances, the deficiency did not appear to involve overly complex audit decisions as to what Generally Accepted Accounting Principles (GAAP) might require in the circumstances. Rather, the deficiency was sometimes linked to a failure to perform procedures generally understood to be core and expected to any audit. In essence, the auditor failed to do what a prudent auditor should know is expected in an audit. For example, auditors were cited for audit deficiencies because they failed to obtain evidence about estimates used to value an account, failed to obtain documentation supporting reconciliations, did not supervise the engagement team or did so remotely, accepted documentation they knew was unreliable, and failed to confirm receivables as examples (Beasley et al., 2001; 2013). Failures such as these may be due to a lack of understanding the underlying requirements contained in GAAP, which can be addressed through education, training, hiring, and performance evaluation assessments. However, it is possible deficiencies were triggered by an execution failure whereby the auditor may have had knowledge of what is expected to be done in the audit, but failed to ensure the required procedures were carried out in an effective manner. The latter challenge may be the result of several causes, such as time pressure concerns in completing the audit, multi-tasking across a number of audit engagements, or inadequate quality control review procedures at the engagement level.

To address the concern related to a failure to exercise due professional care, audit firms and the profession may benefit from conducting an analyses of instances detected within the firm's own quality control reviews or peer reviews where generally understood audit procedures are not being performed to determine the root-cause issue leading to a failure to perform required audit procedures (Beasley et al., 2001; 2013). Such an analysis may identify areas where education and training are warranted, or it may identify areas where firm culture or personnel-related issues are causing members of the engagement team to not perform procedures generally understood as core to any audit engagement. In the spirit of continual efforts to improve audit quality, firms may benefit from surveys of current employees and exit interviews of former employees who may shed insight into issues affecting the exercise of due professional care. Addressing concerns related to exercising due professional care helps to strengthen one of the front-line defenses against audit failure. Here is an overview of several considerations noted for external auditors to consider.

- Based on the fraud risk assessment developed in planning the audit, proactively suggest questions that the board and audit committee may want to ask management.
- Regularly evaluate the audit firm's internal communications and training programs to confirm that they adequately address the exercise of professional skepticism and the assessment of fraud risk.
- Reinforce the importance of interviewing and inquiry skills in the audit process, including consideration of verbal communications.
- Emphasize the value of verifying as a means of obtaining sufficient audit evidence, and provide guidance on mechanisms and methodologies such as company communications for obtaining verifiable information.
- Consider including in the brainstorming sessions individuals outside of the engagement team with industry expertise and experience with situations involving financial reporting fraud.
- Consider face-to-face meetings to obtain information, in order to encourage open discussion and assess the credibility of such communications.

- Encourage the academic community to strengthen the auditing curriculum's focus on professional skepticism and techniques for fraud detection (Beasley et al., 2001; 2013).

Gather Sufficient and Competent Evidence

A common deficiency involves overreliance on management representations as a form of audit evidence. Auditors fail to verify managements' explanations or to challenge explanations that were inconsistent or refuted by other evidence the auditor previously gathered. Yet, auditors may actually gather less sufficient evidence to avoid unpleasant interactions with management (Hobson et al., 2017). This is due to the fact that collecting additional evidence means expanding audit procedures causing tensions in audit budget overruns especially given the declining trend in audit fees. Auditors fail to gather verifying evidence and to challenge managements' assumptions and methods underlying the development of estimates as an example. In some cases, the auditor fails to adjust audit procedures to gather sufficient, competent evidence in light of risks identified and documented by the audit team. It may also be triggered by failing to adequately link audit procedures to underlying risks. For example, the auditor may identify conditions that either change or support a position regarding the assessment of risks such as discrepancies in the accounting records, unsupported transactions, conflicting or missing evidence such as missing or altered documents.

Other considerations that either change or support a given position regarding risk assessments include unexplained transactions and problematic or unusual relationship issues between the auditor and management such as denial to access records, personnel, customers or unusual delays in providing information or an unwillingness to add or revise disclosure. For example, were analytical procedures during the audit that may result in identifying unusual or unexpected relationships considered in assessing the risk of material misstatements due to fraud? At times, analytical procedures can be performed before an audit with the objective of identifying the existence of unusual transactions, events, ratios, and trends that might influence financial statements and audit planning implications. If the result of these procedures yield unusual or unexpected relationships, the audit should consider the results in identifying the risks of material misstatement due to fraud. Determining whether a particular trend or relationship is a fraud risk of requires professional judgment. Unusual relationships involving revenue often are particularly relevant especially at the end of a reporting period. Analytical procedures are useful because management or employees are unable to manipulate all the information necessary to produce expected relationships.

For example, the relationship between net income and cash flow from operations may appear unusual because the manipulation of revenue does not always extend to being able to cleanly manipulate cash although manipulation of cash as we learned from chapter two is possible. After gathering the information in light of conditions such as incentives, pressures, opportunities and rationalizations, the auditor should consider the type of risk that exists in terms of whether it reflects financial statement fraud or misappropriation of assets. Moreover, the auditor should, 1) consider the significance of the risk, 2) the likelihood that the risk will result in a material misstatement, 3) how wide-spread is the risk, and 4) its potential to impact financial statements as a whole and to a specific class of transactions. Furthermore we determine whether to adjust the nature, timing, and extent of audit procedures. Thus in terms of the nature of audit procedures, do we consult independent sources or conduct physical inspections as opposed to just accepting management representations. The timing of the audit involves whether we do the audit at the end of an accounting period. The extent of the procedures reflects the assessment of the risk of fraud by increasing the sample size or performing analytical procedures at a more detailed level.

Detailed review of the underlying audit deficiencies suggests a concern that the auditor's lack of exercising due professional care and failure to maintain an overall level of appropriate professional skepticism results in an auditor failing to obtain sufficient competent evidence to support amounts in the financial statements. Some examples of failure to gather sufficient, competent audit evidence reflects a lack of verification of management representations such as is the amount of inventory management claims to have true. In this case we would need to verify inventory amounts instead of just taking management's word as to the amount of inventory available. Another ripe area for fraudulent misrepresentations is in estimates that were used to establish financial statement balances. In these cases, research shows that auditors failed to obtain additional evidence about estimates used when concerns were noted about potential bias in those estimates by management. Thus, are the estimates used by management, realistic? Are they overly aggressive? What evidence does management have to support their conclusions on appropriate estimates?

Lastly, auditors failed to perform additional procedures when information requested contained ambiguous information. For example, if we are trying to verify revenue and the customers that bought the seller's product cannot be verified, auditors do not go that extra step to actually confirm whether such a buyer exists or whether management is creating fictitious revenue through fictitious accounts receivables. Related to inadequate audit evidence is inadequate preparation and maintenance of audit documentation. Audit documentation failed to identify what audit procedures were performed and what conclusions were reached, and the documentation failed to show that accounting records reconciled with the financial statements.

Audit Planning and Design

Planning the audit engagement is crucial to its success and the SEC study found that auditors who over rely on internal controls typically fail to expand testing in light of identified weaknesses in the client's internal controls. The study found that auditors implicitly assume the presence of a baseline level of internal controls, even though the auditors documented that the client essentially have no controls in place. Auditors can best remedy audit planning deficiencies by promoting more extensive and timely involvement by audit partners and managers in planning the engagement. Such involvement increases the likelihood the auditor will correctly assess risks, both inherent and control, and modify the firm's audit approach as to the nature, timing and extent of those tests, as appropriate. Involving the audit team partner and manager during the planning phase helps to ensure that audit plans emphasize careful scrutiny of nonroutine transactions, particularly those recorded near year end when management sometimes records inappropriate transactions (Beasley et al., 2001; 2013). Deficiencies in audit planning were cited in 44 percent of the cases; specifically, the auditor failed to properly assess inherent risk and adjust the audit program accordingly.

In addition, auditors failed to recognize the heightened risk associated with non-routine transactions or in some cases inappropriately reused the audit plan from prior years. Other examples of deficiencies related to this issue include, 1) the audit partner failed to supervise the person performing the audit, and that person was not an accountant and had no audit experience, 2) a different manager was asked to review the audit work when that manager had never worked on the engagement and had no knowledge of the client's operations or audit issues, and 3) certain work papers prepared by senior staff, including planning areas and high risk accounts, were not reviewed. Let us as an example briefly examine the external auditors' discussions during the planning and design phase as they relate to detecting and addressing material misstatements of the financial statements resulting from fraud. First of all, as an auditor, it is important to understand the concept of materiality. Information is considered material if they could, individually or collectively, influence the economic decisions that user's make on the basis of the financial statements. Materiality depends on the size and nature of the omission or misstatement judged by the surrounding circumstances or a combination of both.

The magnitude of an omission or misstatement of accounting information, in light of the surrounding circumstances, makes it probable that the judgement of a reasonable person relying on the information would have been changed or influenced by the omission or misstatement (Sharma et al., 2009). For example, undisclosed news that a product defect caused serious injury with millions to be paid in damages to the injured is information that should be disclosed because it impacts the financial health of the entity. Not disclosing it may give a false impression that the entity is not facing risks that impacts its profitability or survival as a business. What is material may have a subjective quality inherent in its application, however there are some circumstances that might assist in determining whether information should be classified as material. Other examples include, 1) does the misstatement involve concealment of an unlawful transaction, 2) does the misstatement impact management's compensation, 3) does the misstatement change a loss on the income statement into income or vice versa, 4) whether the misstatement impact a borrower's obligation under loan terms, and 5) whether the misstatement arises from an item capable of precise measurement or whether it arises from an estimate and if so, the degree of imprecision expected in the estimate (Sharma et al., 2009). Some factors auditors should take into account during the planning and design phase include:

- Auditors should conduct a financial statement audit with an attitude of professional skepticism, recognizing the possibility that a material misstatement may exist.
- Audit engagement teams should conduct discussions as part of the planning stage of the audit to consider how the financial statements might be vulnerable to a material misstatement due to fraud.
- Auditors should accumulate the information necessary to determine the risks of fraud, including interviewing management, and consider the results of analytical procedures.
- The audit team should identify the appropriate fraud risk factors which may be based on the size, complexity, and ownership of the client or the incentives, pressures, opportunities, attitudes and rationalizations to commit fraud.
- The auditor should consider the internal controls the organization has in place to identify risks of material misstatements and programs appropriately address the identified fraud risk factors.
- When necessary, the auditor should adjust the nature, timing, and extent of the audit procedures to respond to the identified risks of material misstatement due to fraud.
- In the event a material misstatement due to fraud is identified, the auditor should communicate the issue to the appropriate level of management or to the board of directors, especially the audit committee (Sharma et al., 2009).

Confirming Management Assertions

At a minimum, auditors need to carefully review the underlying data, assumptions and methods a company's management used to develop financial statement estimates. An adequate review hinges on auditors with an appropriate level of both general and industry-specific expertise being involved. In cases of particularly complex or unusual estimates, specialists may be needed. The SEC cited numerous deficiencies in confirming accounts receivable present in 29 percent of the cases. These deficiencies included, 1) failure to confirm enough receivables, 2) failure to perform alternative procedures when confirmations were not returned or were returned with material exceptions, 3) problems with sending and receiving confirmation requests for example, failing to corroborate confirmations received via fax, e-mail, or allowing the client to mail confirmation requests. CPA firms need to ensure their audit teams are effectively handling the confirmation process. Firms should remind team members to confirm an adequate portion of the accounts receivable unless confirmations would not be effective. Employ alternative procedures when confirmations are not returned or exceptions exist.

Let us examine an example where management's assertion of the amount of inventory they claimed they had was not properly verified. In the 1960s, an entrepreneur named Anthony DeAngelis rented petroleum tanks in New Jersey and filled them with seawater, however one of the tanks has some oil in it while underneath the oil was seawater (Skalak et al., 2011). DeAngelis was able to persuade auditors that the tanks contained more than $100 million of oil because when the auditors looked in the tanks, they saw oil not knowing that just below the surface of the oil was seawater. The auditors did not get a good sample of what DeAngelis was asserting as the existence of oil. Because of the auditors' inspection, DeAngelis was able to get loans of $170 million and used the alleged oil as collateral for the loan. Although it is reasonable to assume that it would be difficult to physically inspect what is in the tanks, that is where auditors can confirm assertions by bringing in an expert on this issue to assist them in the confirmation.

Accounting for Related Party Transactions

Studies also reveal that the auditor is either unaware of related parties or appeared to cooperate in the client's decision to conceal related party transactions (Beasley et al., 2001; 2013). To increase the likelihood of detecting related party transactions, the auditor should prepare a list of related parties, continually updating it throughout the engagement and distribute it to all audit team members. Auditors should make inquiries of management regarding the existence of related party transactions. Confirm with the counterparty the nature and existence of material or unusual client transactions, including whether a relationship exists between the counterparty and the client or its management. Once the auditor uncovers a related party transaction, he or she has two additional responsibilities: 1) closely examine the transaction to make sure that it occurred and is correctly valued and 2) ensure the GAAP requirements are satisfied especially disclosure as to its nature.

Respecting the Role of Independence

The auditor's independence from his client is at the heart of our financial reporting system. Auditor independence has come to mean an absence of any and all relationships that could jeopardize—either in fact or in appearance—the validity of the audit, and therefore, of the client's financial statements; the auditor is the guardian of financial integrity (Duska et al., 2011, p. 123). The value of auditing depends heavily on the public's perception on the independence of auditors and its importance is reflected by the fact that the concept of independence is one of the first subjects addressed in the rules of professional conduct. Independence is a crucial concept that sets auditors apart from the accountancy profession, as their core mission is to certify public reports describing a company's financial status. By expressing an opinion, the independent auditor assumes a public duty. The function of the "public watchdog" demands that the auditor subordinates responsibility towards the client in order to maintain complete faithfulness to the public trust. The peril in the lack of independence is that the shareholders as a class who reads and relies on the financial statements upon which the auditor has rendered an opinion to its detriment has a cause of action against the auditor as previously discussed above in the liabilities accountants and auditors expose themselves to. Although auditing the financial statements of publicly traded companies is not the only role of auditors and accountant, it is very important. Investors need to be able to rely on the independence of auditors in order to believe in the integrity of the financial statements and if that integrity is under suspicion, then capital markets will suffer if investors believe they cannot rely on the integrity of those statements. Consider the insights of John Vogle, founder of The Vanguard Group, illustrating the importance of independence in the type of economic system we have:

> The integrity of financial markets—markets that are active, liquid, and honest, with participants who are fully and fairly informed—is absolutely central to the sound functioning of any system of democratic capitalism worth its salt. Sound securities markets require sound financial information. Investors—and have a right to require…information that fairly and honestly represents every significant fact and figure needed to evaluate the worth of corporation. For more than a century, the responsibility for the independent oversight of corporate financial statements has fallen to [the] public accounting profession. It is the auditor's stamp on a financial statement that gives it its validity, its respect, and its acceptability by investors. And only if the auditor's work is comprehensive, skeptical, inquisitive, and rigorous, can we have confidence that financial statements speak the truth (Duska et al., 2011, p. 114).

Just as there is no absolute assurance that an auditor can attest to, but instead give reasonable but not absolute assurance, absolute independence is probably not attainable. It is debatable whether total independence can be achieved because there are biases that can subconsciously interfere with the concept of independence, but that being said, the goal is to be aware of biases and to try to mitigate against them as best as possible to avoid even the appearance of compromised independence between the auditor and the paying client. Auditors should be aware of potential threats that can compromise their duty of independence and avoid situations that may lead outsiders to doubt their independence and the value of their function. Threats to auditor independence refer to "sources of potential bias that may compromise, or may reasonably be expected to compromise, an auditor's ability to make unbiased audit decision" (Duska et al., 2011, p. 125). To serve such a class of persons, an auditor needs to display an unbiased viewpoint when performing audit tests, evaluating the results, and issuing an audit report and opinion with respect to financial statements. Additionally, increased restrictions on auditor-client consulting should reduce the likelihood of audit failure. For example, can a CPA firm be objective in evaluating a client's financial statements when that same firm helped to create the information system they are judging?

Moreover, the revenues generated from consulting may be sufficiently large to influence the auditor's judgment regarding questionable accounting policies (Zhang & Zhang, 2009). Recall the multi-million dollar fees Arthur Andersen received from Enron that probably compromised their ability to be truly independent coupled with the many former Andersen employees who went to work for Enron. It was very probable that employees from Andersen had to work directly with their former colleagues from Andersen who now would be working at Enron. Although the auditor's clients are the ones who pay the auditor's fees, the auditor's primary responsibility is to safeguard the interests of the public; the auditor's fiduciary responsibility is to the public trust and independence from the client (Duska et al., 2011). However, there is an inclination auditors may believe they face divided loyalties because of their belief that their loyalties are to the paying client. The key requirement is that the auditor is an independent auditor which is why they fulfill that special role as the public watchdog that is independent of their paying client. The reality is the auditor's relationship to their client is different from relationships other professions have to their client. As United States Supreme Court Justice Warren Burger stated in his classic statement on auditor responsibility:

> The auditor does not have the same relationship to his client that a private attorney does….who has a role as a….confidential advisor and advocate, a loyal representative whose duty it is to present the client's case in the most favorable light. An independent CPA performs a different role. By certifying the public reports that collectively depict a corporation's financial status, the independent auditor assumes a public responsibility transcending any employment relationship with the client. The independent public accountant performing this special function owes ultimate allegiance to the corporation's creditors and stockholders, as well as to the investing public. This 'public watchdog' function demands that the accountant maintain total independence from the client at all times and requires fidelity to the public trust. To insulate from disclosure a CPA's interpretation of the client's financial statements would be to ignore the significance of the accountant's role as a disinterested analyst charged with public obligations (Duska et al., 2011, p. 116).

Maintaining Professional Skepticism

The auditor should engage in their duties with a mindset that recognizes the possibility that fraud can be present regardless of any past experience with an organization and regardless of the auditor's belief about management's honesty and integrity (Sharma et al., 2009). In the professional arena, critical thinking requires a disciplined approach to problem solving by being intellectually committed to the use of thought processes to guide behavior and in this sense, this includes professional skepticism (Rezaee & Riley, 2010). Due professional care requires the auditor to exercise professional skepticism, but exercising professional skepticism requires auditor independence (Duska et al., 2011). In addition:

> [A]n audit of financial statements in accordance with generally accepted auditing standards should be planned and performed with an attitude of professional skepticism. The auditor neither assumes that management is dishonest nor assumes unquestioned honesty. In exercising professional skepticism, the auditor should not be satisfied with less than persuasive evidence because of a belief that management is honest (Duska et al., 2011, p. 133).

Critical, strategic thinking is necessary for professional skepticism which includes a neutral but disciplined approach to detection and investigation displaying, 1) a recognition that fraud may be present and that the perpetrator(s) intentionally conceal the organization's true financial performance, 2) an attitude that includes a questioning mindset that incorporates some doubt as to the evidence and representation being made, 3) a critical assessment of information, data, and analysis, and 4) a commitment to persuasive evidence for decision making including making sure that one pays attention to details with a desire to verify management statements with sufficient evidence (Rezaee & Riley, 2010). Other characteristics of professional skepticism is withholding judgment until appropriate evidence is obtained, displaying a sense of moral independence, self-direction, and a conviction to decide for oneself rather than accepting the representations of others at face value. This includes an understanding of people's motivations and perceptions which can lead them to provide biased and misleading information. The challenging issue for auditors and the audit profession as a whole is that the concept of professional skepticism has been a fundamental aspect of auditing standards for decades.

Therefore the question becomes, despite the recognition that professional skepticism has been fundamental to the audit process for decades, what leads to problems in exercising sufficient levels of professional skepticism on a day-to-day basis during an audit? Unfortunately, a stream of research suggests that auditors face disincentives to exercise skepticism to detect fraud such as supervisors penalizing junior auditors who act on the skepticism (Hobson et al., 2017). Conversely, auditors may not desire to engage in skepticism, but instead are willing to endorse management's desire to engage in aggressive accounting methodologies. Moreover, evidence suggests that auditors who maintain a skeptical mindset and investigate fraud related risks receive lower performance evaluations (Hobson et al., 2017). Furthermore, research suggests that an inherently trusting disposition may help an auditor build quality client relations, but make them less effective auditors than those with less trusting dispositions providing them with the professional skepticism tools to better detect fraud (Rose et al; 2010). In turn the excellent client relationships built by some auditors may help them secure career advancements because of the self-interest bias of maintaining the survival of the firm (Rose et al., 2010).

A trusting disposition may be the factor marking an auditor as a future accounting partner, and the significance of trust can have profound implications for the ability of audit firms to detect financial statement fraud (Rose et al., 2010). Thus, trust may advance one's career at the expense of implementing professional skepticism. Some auditors may be overly optimistic about the likelihood that a client is not engaging in fraud, and an auditors' lack of experience in seeing actual cases of fraud may cause them to underestimate the likelihood that material misstatements due to fraud may be present. In addition, a partial explanation to this question is that auditors rely too much on management representations because they harbor a trust bias. The trusted relationships that exists between external auditors and their clients sometimes make auditors let their guard down which in turn means a diminished role for professional skepticism. This in turn results in relying on our bias to confirm our beliefs about a person and/or situation and not the strength of audit evidence. Auditors may benefit from reminders of the importance of exercising appropriate levels of professional skepticism, and those reminders may need to be made multiple times in multiple ways during an engagement. Moreover, professional skepticism does not occur in a vacuum, but relies on the character of the auditor and the firm's organizational culture that is set by leadership's tone at the top (Mintz & Morris, 2017).

Does leadership set the example of making the application of professional skepticism an important trait to apply at an audit or is it glossed over so that client's do not threaten to leave if the auditor asked too many questions? Does leadership train new auditors what professional skepticism might look like or is it just thought of as an abstract idea? For example, some issues that should give rise to professional skepticism include, 1) unexplained accounting anomalies, 2) internal controls weaknesses that have been exploited, 3) observed extravagant lifestyles, 4) observed unusual behaviors such as excessive kindness or veiled threats, and 5) complaints and tips that point to potential fraudulent behavior (Rezaee & Riley, 2010). Even when internal controls and checks and balances are present, they are often circumvented by criminals taking advantage of the lack of professional skepticism of those persons responsible for compliance and oversight (Antar, 2012). Further elaboration by convicted CFO and CPA Samuel Antar of Crazy Eddies explains why displaying an attitude of professional skepticism is warranted:

The white-collar criminal hopes that you will never verify and even if you do verify, your skepticism of the criminal's deceptive answers may be corroded by your comfort level—in other words, you will accept the criminal's deceptive answers as factual. All white-collar criminals require an opportunity to commit their crimes, unfortunately, our society creates that opportunity. Society's belief in the presumption of innocence until proven guilty, trust and then verify, and giving people the benefit of the doubt limits society's behavior while providing the white-collar criminal with the freedom of action to take advantage of society and commit their crimes. In addition, lack of internal controls, lack of effective oversight, questioning irregularities, and a general lack of professional skepticism creates a fertile opportunity for white-collar criminals to commit their crimes (Antar, 2010).

Samuel further remarked that as a general practice, "most large accounting firms use relatively inexperienced kids right out of college to do basic audit leg work. They are supervised by slightly more experienced senior auditors who unfortunately depend on feedback from these inexperienced kids in making informed decision" (Chui & Pike, 2013, p. 205). For example, the auditors of Crazy Eddie routinely left their documents overnight in a locked file cabinet at Crazy Eddie's offices (Tschakert, 2017). Samuel including his cousin and CEO and founder of Crazy Eddies, Eddie Antar, observed that the auditors would hide the key to the cabinet in a paper clip box on their work desk at Crazy Eddie. Every night after the auditors had left, Eddie and his cousin Samuel accessed the auditor's cabinet and altered audit records, specifically inventory counts to inflate inventory. By reviewing the auditor's records, Eddie was able to foresee the auditor's travelling route as it relates to inventory inspection and counting. Eddie would then, overnight, ship inventory from stores that had already been counted to stores that have yet to be counted in order to inflate the value of inventory they claimed they possessed. Samuel further explained how he was able to corrode the auditors' professional skepticism because the auditors "did not want to believe we were crooks.

They believed whatever we told them without verifying the truth" (Chui & Pike, 2013, p. 205). The fraudster focuses their concerns not just on obstruction such as not providing desired documents, which raises immediate red flags, but on misdirection meaning leading auditors down paths that act as distractions from where they want to focus on. A CPA may realize that some of management's numbers do not check out, but may miss the significance if they are unprepared for the psychological games a white-collar criminal will play. Thus, Antar states, "They're looking at the numbers, at the documentation, looking to check this against this…and that's all fine and dandy, but I'm a criminal and I know how to manipulate that situation…The most important thing we don't teach is how to handle the lies, the liars" (Gaetano, 2013). Antar noted that he became adept enough at manipulating the accountants in his own company to "make them into enablers," through aggressive likability and familiarity with the relevant actors; "The more I'm with you, the more I can get you to like me as a criminal—without even knowing I'm a criminal. I'll know your tastes, your politics, what you like, what you dislike" (Gaetano, 2013). Consider the statements of Justin Paperny that parallel the strategy of exploiting the weakness of the people he would manipulate: "I never thought I was defrauding them…I was very polite, always leveraging off my vice president title, University of Southern California degree, and name dropping my baseball player clients did not hurt either. What I did best was find a way to identify with them. If they liked hockey, so did I. If they loved soccer, I did as well. I made it appear as if we had a lot in common" (Perri et al., 2014, p. 7).

A lack of an appropriate questioning mindset and a failure to critically evaluate audit evidence create opportunities for a number of audit deficiencies to be present across all aspects of an audit. While the SEC tends to include this general deficiency in most of its sanctions against auditors, it is helpful to consider concerns noted by the SEC about the lack of sufficient professional skepticism to see if there are additional insights that might contribute to the profession's continual efforts to improve auditor skepticism. The critical nature of professional skepticism is a core theme in the Center for Audit Quality's (CAQ), Deterring *and Detecting Financial Reporting Fraud: A Platform for Action* (CAQ, 2010). The report noted that skepticism is:

An essential element of the professional objectivity required of all participants in the financial reporting supply chain. Skepticism throughout the supply chain increases not only the likelihood that fraud will be detected, but also the perception that fraud will be detected, which reduces the risk that fraud will be attempted…For both internal and external auditors, skepticism is an integral part of the conduct of their professional duties, including the consideration of the risk of management override of internal controls (CAQ, 2010).

Within the CAQ report, a chapter titled *Skepticism: An Enemy of Fraud* provides a valuable discussion of the critical role of exercising appropriate professional skepticism and highlights the realities of how biases impact all individuals as they make judgments and decisions. The chapter highlights the natural tendency that all players in the financial reporting process, including auditors, tend to believe that the organizations they serve and leaders with whom they are aligned have integrity. That belief predisposes auditors and boards of directors to trust other players in the financial reporting process. This trust bias may lead to a lack of asking probing questions and a failure to critically assess audit evidence. To help address this tendency, auditing standards, including the standards related to auditor consideration of fraud in the financial statement audit, emphasize the importance of all members of the engagement team recognizing the reality that the risk of fraud is present in every audit. In addition, encourage all personnel to maintain an attitude of professional skepticism that focuses on the importance of the auditor's role in protecting the public interest and maintaining strong capital markets. A firm can accomplish this by conducting periodic engagement-wide team meetings to discuss concerns about management integrity issues and by highlighting for staff members the risks of not being skeptical (Beasley et al., 2001; 2013). An attitude of professional skepticism means the auditor makes an assessment, with a questioning mind, of the validity of audit evidence obtained and is alert to audit evidence that contradicts or brings into question the reliability of documents and information obtained from management and those charged with governance.

Auditors are often civil and criminally liable when they are presented with information indicating a problem that they fail to recognize or if they do recognize a problem, they fail to explore the issue further. Auditors should plan and perform an audit with an attitude of professional skepticism recognizing circumstances may exist that cause the financial statements to be materially misstated (Zhang & Zhang, 2009). This challenge has implications for training and helps to motivate analyses to understand root causes of failures in applying professional skepticism consistently. Additional research, however, is needed to determine if these challenges may be exacerbated by differences in cultural norms that will be increasingly realized as the audit process continues to be affected by globalization or as new generations of audit professionals emerge who may apply professional skepticism differently than today's audit professionals (Beasley et al., 2013). Examples of a failure to maintain a sufficient level of professional skepticism include: 1) the auditor failed to assess documents he suspected might have been fabricated by the client and did not question the authenticity of those documents, 2) despite being confronted with a number of factors that should have heightened the auditor's professional skepticism in regards to a number of risks of material misstatement, the auditor's procedures did not appear to be modified in light of these risk concerns, 3) the auditor failed to respond to information that suggested account valuations were overstated, 4) the auditor failed to verify certain representations made by management, 5) the audit firm failed to respond to numerous red flags and inconsistencies, and 6) ignored a number of specific audit program steps.

Professional skepticism plays an important role in the audit by facilitating professional judgment especially on several key decision making areas such the nature, timing and extent of audit procedures performed to reduce the risk of material misstatements. Recall that audit procedures are specific acts performed by the auditor to gather evidence about whether a specific management representation is being met. For example, management states that available inventory is worth $1000. Does the auditor accept management's representation or does he rely on a physical count? As previously stated, auditors need to be aware that people tend to be truth biased which means there is tendency to judge messages as honest independent of the actual truthfulness of the message. Other decisions that play into the issue of professional skepticism is whether there is sufficient, competent, and relevant evidence has been gathered to support management representations or do we simply accept answers without verification as to the reliability of the answers given. Unfortunately, all too often answers are accepted without verification which explains why there are audit failures leading to auditor negligence lawsuits. Recall the example from chapter five of the statement of a fraud offender referencing the auditor not fulfilling their due diligence but also illustrating the impact of bias on professional skepticism:

Initially, I wasn't surprised that we got away with it. Because it wasn't many entries and we were very careful. But by the end, I couldn't see how they couldn't detect anything. I spoke to the CFO and he said that if they, the auditors, did detect anything, he would say that we would get back to them. And he couldn't believe how they would accept even the flimsiest of possible excuse. A note was sufficient (Free & Murphy, 2015, p. 45).

Consider the insight of offender Vernon Beck, a former Director at Texas Petrochemicals, who embezzled $14 million from a $1.6 billion annual revenue petrochemical company commenting on how his manipulation strategy of external auditors to hide the fraud scheme:

I chose a category within the transportation budget to embezzle money, which was an area most people simply do not understand. Any time an auditor would begin asking questions, I would baffle them with shipping terms and double-speak. Sometimes I would almost embarrass them by showing their ignorance on the subject. They would quickly move on to the next topic. After all, who wants to be shown their ignorance? I would not say that I actually tricked them. I would characterize it more as trying to cause confusion or confound the issue we were discussing during the audit in order to make it harder to understand any one concept... Most auditors had little real experience in our business...Audit firms must not be afraid to spend the money to hire those experts where needed (Crumbley & Beck, 2020, p. 449).

Moreover, because professional skepticism is a reflection of one's state of mind, auditors should document their thought processes, alternative view points, and how decisions were made. Also important is to document disagreements with management and the reliability of documents used by management. Professional skepticism is important because audits often have a routinized quality meaning financial statement auditors use predictable audit procedures allowing fraud offenders to plan in advance how to conceal their schemes (Albrecht et al., 2012). Auditors should be self-aware of their own diminishment of professional skepticism that accompanies routine assignments especially during the planning of an audit. Professional skepticism must take into account the several methods fraud offenders use to conceal their deception from auditors that auditors need to be aware of including but not limited to:

- Collusion by insiders or outsiders that may be difficult to unveil.
- Forgery of documents where auditors may not be trained to detect.
- Fictitious documents created by management to support the fraud.
- Fictitious transactions that use normal-looking amounts rather than rounded numbers.
- Small frauds relative to the overall financial balances or large frauds that are spread out over several subsidiaries that have their own set of financial statements.
- Silence by individuals that know about the fraud but remain silent.
- Blatant lying by management and other key people.

In addition, experts agree that without proper and adequate forensic training, it would be difficult, if not impossible, for auditors to uncover fraud in a financial statement audit (Chui & Pike, 2013). Thus, there is a mismatch between auditors' training and skills and what is required of them in their responsibilities as auditors. This perhaps helps to explain why the ACFE has found a deteriorating trend in external auditors' abilities in detecting fraud despite the emphasis and focus on fraud detection, the ACFE found the majority of fraud cases were detected by tips rather than through external audit (Chui & Pike, 2013). Auditors have been reluctant to take on additional responsibility for detecting and providing assurance regarding the presence of fraud (Chui & Pike, 2013). Contrary to what many think, typical audits of financial statements do entail certain responsibility for the detection of fraud; it is the duty of all auditors to be on the lookout for fraud and in fact they are to put procedures in place that may detect fraudulent activities (Carmichael, 2018). When auditors fail to detect a misstatement of financial statements caused by fraud, the defensive refrain is often that an audit of financial statements is not a fraud audit. This comparison improperly implies that an auditor of financial statements has no responsibility to detect fraud which erodes the public's confidence in the quality and usefulness of independent audits (Carmichael, 2018). The greater significance involves the integrity of the audit process; if auditors view detecting fraud is not really an auditor's job, then compliance with the requirements of auditing standards on fraud detection becomes a rote, meaningless exercise (Carmichael, 2018).

To improve auditors' fraud detection abilities, it is necessary to integrate forensic procedures and fraud examiners in audit engagements (Chui et al., 2012). That is audit engagement should consider there to be at least one individual on the audit team who can be classified as a fraud examiner. Moreover, this individual needs to be present during the entire audit engagement, rather than either providing limited input or being called into the engagement once fraud is detected. Although this proposal might be ignored as a result of the additional cost burden related to such a requirement, then at the very minimum, it is of paramount importance to train financial statement auditors in the areas of forensic accounting and fraud examination to heighten their senses and sharpen a fraud detection mindset as well as make professional skepticism not just an abstract requirement (Chui & Pike, 2013). With such training, auditors' propensities to correctly identify and investigate fraud-related red flags should increase, resulting in a greater probability that more fraud will be detected by external audits as well as more confidence in auditors' abilities to protect the interests of stakeholders (Chui & Pike, 2013). Yet, without proper training, invariably we will be reading year after year accounts of corporations that were able to avoid fraud detection due to the corporation's ability to outsmart even well-educated auditors.

Improving the Identification and Assessment of Risks

The failure to exercise due professional care and the failure to maintain sufficient levels of professional skepticism are natural preconditions to an inadequate identification and assessment of risks of material misstatement in the audit, including the risk of fraud. Any improvement in risk assessment skills that can be identified will help enhance audit quality and improve the recognition of fraud risk. Another common deficiency is the failure to adequately address audit risk and materiality. Typical deficiencies included:

- The audit firm failed to implement appropriate follow-up procedures to ensure that planned audit responses were performed to address certain audit risk areas and that reviewing audit partners functioned effectively for the high risk client.
- The auditor did not understand the client's internal controls, did not competently identify audit risks, and followed a generic audit program obtained off the internet.
- Management made certain representations about discrepancies between inventory on the books and actual physical balances, but the auditor failed to request evidence supporting the reconciliation.
- The auditor relied on management representations about certain key estimates and relied on oral representations about accruals on unbilled receivable balances (Beasley et al., 2013).

In some of the cases, the audit firm failed to conduct required audit risk assessment procedures, such as procedures to perform fraud risk assessments. In other cases, the auditor failed to respond to risk conditions previously identified by the auditor. The situations examined illustrate how the lack of due professional care and insufficient levels of professional skepticism can lead to inadequate risk assessments or responses to noted risks. Thus, addressing those underlying causes will have a direct impact on an auditor's identification and assessment of risks, however, there are likely other causes that help to explain why deficiencies are noted in the auditor's risk assessment process. While auditing standards have been risk-based for years, some may oversimplify the risk assessment process due to a number of pitfalls, such as groupthink and confirmation bias previously discussed which can impact the quality of our decisions, including decisions related to risk identification and assessment.

Understanding Disordered Personalities as Fraud Risk Factors

The accounting profession extrapolates personality traits to the attitudes, character, and values of management as risk factors when considering asset misappropriation and fraudulent financial statement, however there is no actual definition of what "attitude" means for the accounting profession (Cohen et al., 2011). Observable narcissistic traits, those that were studied, are a proxy for harboring a fraud attitude defined as displaying an entitled mindset or rationalization that justifies the commission of fraud (Johnson et al., 2013). Those with lower levels of personal integrity are prone to satisfying their motivation by exploiting opportunities, therefore perceptions of management personal integrity are fundamental to evaluating the risk of fraud. Auditors are encouraged, for example, to look for narcissistic traits to determine whether it exists for it will impact the scope of their audit and potential for fraud risk assessments (Johnson et al., 2013). In fact, auditors expand their audit scope when they observed narcissistic traits which serves as a proxy for a fraud attitude. Moreover, does management exhibit an antisocial interpersonal strategy? For example, fraud red flags include management displaying interpersonal mannerisms that are dismissive of auditor requests, argumentative, exhibit bullying behaviors such as veiled threats and being overly sensitive to auditor feedback.

Arthur Andersen: The Fall of an Accounting Firm Giant

Arthur Andersen once exemplified the integrity that characterized the accounting profession, and stories about the founder's ethics became part of the firm's lore (Sawayda, 2011). At the age of 28, Andersen faced down a railway executive who demanded that his books be approved—or else. Andersen displayed the previously discussed concept of professional and moral identity when he said, "There's not enough money in the city of Chicago to induce me to change that report" (Trevino & Brown, 2004). Andersen lost the business, but later the railway company filed for bankruptcy and Arthur Andersen became known as a firm one could trust. Andersen talked about the special responsibility of accountants to the public and the importance of their independence of judgment and the ethical culture continued for many years. Andersen was considered a stable and prestigious place to work where people did not expect to become wealthy, but rather desired a good career at a firm with an excellent reputation. Employees displayed commitment to the overall philosophy of reaching financial goals without questioning the ethics of achieving such goals (Toffler & Reingold, 2003). However, starting in the 1970s, problems began to surface between the auditors and those providing consulting services that generated a substantial amount of revenue for Andersen. The chairman of Andersen during the 1970s, named Harvey Kapnick, foresaw potential conflicts of interests that could surface between the consultants and the auditors who would be in a position to audit their consultants' work.

Kapnick sought to split its auditing and consulting arms into separate firms believing that the dilution of standards at Andersen could be traced to the rise of the auditor-salesmen and the poisoning effect its drive for profits had on Andersen's famous independence for auditing work (McRoberts, 2002d). Eventually, leadership's earlier commitment to ethics were marginalized by the firm's increasing laser-like focus on revenues. The Securities and Exchange Commission (SEC) was concerned how consulting was becoming the main growth business of auditing firms, especially Andersens, and according to SEC chairman Harold Williams from 1977 to 1981, "I was uncomfortable and concerned that the level of non-audit services could compromise the independence of the audit" (McRoberts, 2002a). As a result of this concern, the SEC proposed the requirement that when a company went to its shareholders each year to approve the choice of auditors, it would have to disclose the amount and percentage of the auditor's fees that came from consulting (McRoberts, 2002a). By 1979, 42 percent of Andersen's $645 million in worldwide fees came from consulting and tax work, as opposed to accounting and auditing and in the U.S., the proportion was greater: more than half its income came from non-audit services. According to Kapnick, Andersen's consulting division "was worth a ton of money...it was almost too successful" (McRoberts, 2002a). Andersen's consulting business became recognized as one of the fastest growing and most profitable consulting networks in the world with revenues from consulting surpassed the auditing unit for the first time in 1984.

Kapnick believed that it would be best to separate the two services into two different firms before the SEC demanded Andersen to break up. When Kapnick brought his proposal to other Andersen partners, he was forced out of his position because they did not want to give up the wealth consulting brought in; Kapnick's departure sank any thought of splitting the auditing and consulting divisions and the foundation was laid for the eventual downfall of the firm (McRoberts, 2002a). The ethical culture eventually began to unravel and it was attributable to the fact that the firm's profits increasingly came from consulting rather than auditing (Trevino & Brown, 2004). A firm founded on the principle that auditors were not mere businessmen but gatekeepers of a public trust and that high standards were more important than high fees, was paying the price for a legacy of tarnished audits and ethical lapses such as those at Enron, WorldCom, and Sunbeam to name a few (McRoberts, 2002d). Auditing and consulting are very different, and the cultural standards that worked so well in auditing did not fit the needs of the consulting side of the business.

This mismatch was never addressed, and the resulting mixed signals helped precipitate a downward spiral into unethical practices. Serving the client began to be defined as keeping the client happy and getting return business, and tradition became translated into unquestioning obedience to the partner, no matter what one was asked to do. For example, managers and partners were expected to pad their prices and reasonable estimates for consulting work were simply doubled or more as consultants were told to back into the numbers. The training also began falling apart as consulting took over. New employees were once required to attend a three day session designed to indoctrinate them into the culture of the firm, but new consultants were told not to forego lucrative client work to attend—ethics was not discussed. One Andersen consultant expressed her thoughts about excessive billing of clients by rationalizing as follows:

> The client, a bank that had been required by regulators to use this specific consulting service, was desperate. So we billed our brains out, charging more than one million for what should have been about a $500,000 job. We billed time on the subway, we billed time rewriting notes…I rationalized what we were doing by telling myself that they were paying a premium for the short time frame and intensity of the work (Anand et al., 2004, p. 42) .

According to former employees, the corporate culture became highly competitive during the 1980s and into the 1990s where it was made clear that the goal was to maximize revenues and an auditor who thought something was wrong was discouraged from raising uncomfortable questions. At Andersen, growth became the highest priority with an emphasis on recruiting and retaining big clients came at the expense of quality, independent audits, coupled with removing accountants who failed to adapt to the firm's new direction and culture. Andersen promoted a new accounting breed who could turn modestly profitable auditing assignments into "consulting gold mines" (McRoberts, 2002a). There was a belief that Andersen could be driven by a profit-seeking culture without compromising its integrity (McRoberts, 2002b). Yet this new direction led Andersen to become a key player in financial scandals that cost thousands of employees their jobs, eroded the pensions of millions while contributing to billions of dollars in losses for the general public. This philosophy destroyed the firm's reputation by building up a record of sliding standards of excellence, bad audits and financial scandals while rewarding salesmanship over technical skill to pursue higher profits even if it meant compromising a legacy of defiant independence.

Throughout the 1990s, Andersen reaped huge profits selling consulting services to clients whose financial statements it audited, but would later pose an ethical conflict of interest dilemma for some partners who had to decide how to treat questionable accounting practices discovered at some of its largest clients (Sawayda, 2011). As the details of these investigations into accounting irregularities and fraud surfaced, it became apparent that Andersen was more concerned about its own revenue growth rather than where the revenue came from or whether its independence as an auditor had been compromised (Sawayda, 2011). The firm's focus on growth also generated a fundamental change in its corporate culture in that those individuals who could deliver the big accounts were promoted before those people who were concerned with conducting quality audits. Andersen expected everyone to protect the firm and its clients at all costs punishing those who dissented while encouraging an "up or out" philosophy, in which employees either moved up the ranks or were moved out of the firm (Kinsler, 2008). Andersen promoted a sales culture and unloaded experienced, old-line auditors that resulted in botched audit after botched audit that will be discussed (Greisling, 2002).

According to Kapnick, even when he was no longer employed at Andersen observed, "The culture changed where the auditor was no longer the guy people respected in the '80s and '90s…If you were an auditor, you were relegated to second-class status…If you were a consultant, you were the top of the heap" (McRoberts, 2002a). Another executive observing Andersen's downfall stated, "The '90s were a go-go period in which the mentality was if you weren't getting rich, you were stupid…I think that permeated Andersen" (McRoberts, 2002b). Even as many partners and staff continued to uphold a high standard, others compromised the quality of their work in the interest of generating fees. One Andersen executive commenting on the culture at Andersen during the 1990s stated, "It came down to doing the job as quickly as possible and making the most money…They pushed the edge of the envelope—pushed it too far…I just think it got out of control. What it ended up being is greed. Total greed" (McRoberts, 2002a). Former partner, David Walker, made the following observation:

> The Andersen story illustrates how a few people can do the wrong thing with catastrophic consequences for many innocent parties. It was not long ago that Arthur Andersen was viewed as the premier professional service firm in the world. For years, Andersen had the reputation of "thinking straight and talking straight" and doing what it felt was right in connection with challenging accounting and reporting issues—even if the client didn't like the answer (Ramamoorti et al., 2013, p. 19).

In her book *Final Accounting*, Barbara Toffler describes how Arthur Andersen employees billed clients excessively as a matter of routine. When she asked a partner who had overbilled a client, she was told: "Relax. We're Arthur Andersen. They need us. They'll pay" further observing, "The prestigious name was being used to justify behavior that never would have been tolerated in the past" (Toffler et al., 2004, p. 3). Andersen employees were generally inclined to violate legal and ethical principles if asked to do so by a partner, thus it was not surprising that Andersen employees were frequently referred to as "Androids," since for an "Android the idea of challenging a partner was downright unthinkable" (Kinsler, 2008, p. 130). The lack of regard for law and ethics was not limited to the business side of Andersen because the lawyers also had a tendency to look the other way. For example, when Andersen's general counsel was confronted with an obvious case of overbilling, he said "[n]othing. He just stood there" (Kinsler, 2008). Such universal disregard for ethical and legal standards can occur in an environment where dissent was quashed:

> For most of [Andersen's] existence, this was not a place where independent activities were tolerated or encouraged. It was a culture in which everyone followed the rules and the leader. When the rules and leaders stood for decency and integrity, the lockstep culture was the key to competence and respectability. But when the game and the leaders changed direction, the culture of conformity led to disaster…This was a culture so strong that most individuals were helpless to change things (Kinsler, 2008, p. 130).

Enron's Control of Andersen's Employees

Arthur Andersen had a history of problems with the SEC and over the years, many of Andersen's clients were forced to rework and reissue their financial statements because of failed audits (Sawayda, 2011). The Waste Management and Sunbeam accounting scandals at the end of the 1990s left Andersen executives concerned about the potential legal ramifications of some of Andersen's accounting practices (Argenti & Tait, 2001). With such a history, Andersen did not appear to be an unwitting victim of a single corporate bankruptcy that highlighted industry-wide accounting problems, but rather a firm that had known for years that its accounting practices violated SEC regulations. Andersen was the audit firm retained by Enron uninterruptedly since the company's founding in 1985 until its collapse in 2001. In addition to the external audit services, Andersen rendered consulting and internal audit services for Enron and by late 2000, Enron was Andersen's second largest client worldwide. During this year, Andersen received $52 million from Enron—about $1 million per week generated mostly from consulting services.

Andersen occupied an entire floor with about 100 auditors at Enron's headquarter throughout the year (McLean & Elkind, 2003). Over the years, it became common practice for Enron to employ people from Andersen especially in the position of controllers and chief accounting officers. At Andersen, displeasing "Crown Jewel" clients was a cardinal sin, and Enron was the Crown Jewel; the Enron account had become so lucrative for Andersen that the firm was unwilling to step away, even when it determined the engagement was one of its most risky (McRoberts, 2002c). During the late 1990s, the way for Andersen employees to move up the ranks was to keep both their bosses and the people at Enron happy by approving every transaction. By the fall of 2000, the two business giants were so entangled that dozens of the Chicago accounting firm's most ambitious auditors reported to work each day at Enron. Short-circuiting their system of checks and balances and overriding their own technical staff, Andersen's lead Enron auditors signed off on questionable deals instead of telling their client "no", until it was too late (McRoberts, 2002c). Andersen was so willing to accommodate Enron's executives that it sometimes allowed them to influence who at Andersen would audit the client. For example, the sure way for Andersen employees to move out of the firm was to dissent to an Enron transaction. One of their least favorite people at the firm was Carl Bass (McRoberts, 2002c).

The experience of Andersen partner Carl Bass located in Houston, Texas exemplifies the "yes-man" culture at Andersen. He served on the prestigious Professional Standards Group (PSG), an internal team of accounting experts that reviewed troublesome accounting issues confronting local offices (McRoberts, 2002c). For decades, the PSG's word was accepted as the final word at Andersen. Enron was considered one of Andersen's highest risk clients. In February 2001, Bass, who had been assigned to monitor…high-risk audit[s], strongly objected to Enron's accounting, especially Enron's use of special purpose entities (SPEs) and, not surprisingly, tensions grew between Bass and Enron. In one memo to his Andersen colleagues describing one of Fastow's partnerships, Bass wrote "this whole deal looks like there is no substance" (McRoberts, 2002c). Enron insisted that Bass be excluded from its account because they "considered him a roadblock to their rapid fire deal-making" according to insights by several Andersen partners (Kinsler, 2008, p. 132). Eventually Bass was removed from the Enron accounting and demoted for being "too rules-oriented" and the demotion was no small matter because it was approved by then Andersen CEO Joe Bernardino. At least two other Andersen accountants were removed from the Enron engagement for challenging Enron's use of SPEs. The message was clear: "Keep the client happy, no matter what the consequences" (Kinsler, 2008, p. 132).

According to Bass, he stated, "I was upset, that we had a client that was telling the firm, basically, who they would or would not have the engagement team consult with on their transactions" (McRoberts, 2002c). Bass did request to be part of the team that audited Enron, but that request was denied. The idea that Enron could dismiss someone from the standards group made a tremendous impression on Andersen's Houston auditors as one auditor stated, "I felt like that if you didn't act a certain way sometimes or give certain answers in certain circumstances, that it could jeopardize your existence on the Enron engagement" (McRoberts, 2002c). There was no indication that senior level executives defended their own auditors against Enron's aggression. Key employees inside both firms believe the closeness between Andersen and Enron depleted the auditor of its independence and ultimately its good judgment (McRoberts, 2002c). Employees were rewarded for the amount of money they brought into the company rather than for working with integrity.

In October 2001, the SEC announced that it was launching an investigation into Enron's accounting, however, on November 8, 2001, Enron was forced to restate five years worth of financial statements that Andersen signed off on, amounting to over $580 million in losses (Sawayda, 2011). The U.S. Justice Department began a criminal investigation into Andersen in January 2002, where the firm eventually admitted to destroying a number of documents concerning its auditing of Enron, which led to an indictment for obstruction of justice on March 14, 2002. On June 15, 2002, the jury found Andersen guilty of obstruction of justice. The company agreed to stop auditing public companies by August 31, 2002, essentially shutting down the business (Sawayda, 2011). Let us examine some of Andersen's other failed audits that contributed to the decision to prosecute Andersen. As we will learn, there were a series of failed audits that led up to Andersen being prosecuted.

Baptist Foundation of Arizona Ponzi Scheme

While the Baptist Foundation of Arizona (BFA) did not have the same media coverage as Enron, it served to remind the American public that Enron was not an isolated incident for Arthur Andersen (Argenti & Tait, 2001). In what would become the largest bankruptcy of a nonprofit charity, BFA, which Andersen served as auditor, lost $570 million of donor funds (Sawayda, 2011). BFA was founded in 1948 to raise and manage endowments for church work in Arizona by investing heavily in real estate, at times speculative investments, where profits from investments were supposed to be used to fund the churches' ministries and numerous charitable causes. Problems began when the real estate market in Arizona suffered a downturn, and BFA's management came under pressure to show a profit. In what court documents would later dub a Ponzi scheme, foundation officials allegedly took money from new investors to pay off existing investors in order to maintain cash inflow (Sawayda, 2011). The investor lawsuit against Andersen accused the auditing firm of issuing false and misleading approvals of BFA's financial statements, which allowed the foundation to perpetuate the fraud. Serving as BFA's auditor, Andersen failed to realize the company was running a Ponzi investment scheme. Such a scheme involved pooling the individual retirement account balances of over 10,000 elderly people into a fraudulent scheme (Miller, 2004). Andersen blamed BFA management for the collapse arguing that it was given misleading information on which to conduct the audits. However, during nearly two years of investigation, reports surfaced that Andersen had been warned of possible fraudulent activity, and the firm eventually agreed to pay $217 million to settle the shareholder lawsuit in 2002.

Sunbeam's Collusion with Andersen

Andersen's troubles over Sunbeam Corporation began when its audits failed to address serious accounting errors that eventually led to a class action lawsuit by Sunbeam investors and the removal of CEO Albert Dunlap in 1998. Sunbeam artificially inflated earnings through fraudulent accounting strategies namely improper revenue recognition such as booking sales revenue months ahead of actual product shipment artificially boosting quarterly net income. In 2002, Sunbeam paid $110 million to settle claims brought by shareholders for accounting irregularities without admitting fault or liability while losses to shareholders amounted to about $4.4 billion, with job losses of about 1,700 employees (Sawayda, 2011). This example of accounting fraud and reissuance of financial statements to reflect accurate earnings was so egregious that the SEC had to step in and end the partnership of CEO Dunlap and Andersen (Miller, 2004). Together they misappropriated funds and misstated accounting books to make it seem like the appliance manufacturer was rebounding after a few bad years. Going beyond its negligent role in the BFA scandal, Andersen now readily took part in the accounting fraud for the sake of its own increased revenues by shredding documents that would have incriminated both Andersen and Sunbeam executives. This was only after Andersen helped the company fraudulently misstate $189 million (Miller, 2004).

Waste Management's Lack of Disclosure

Waste Management, a U.S. trash hauler, had an internal accounting team populated by former Andersen auditors and until 1997 every chief financial officer and every chief accounting officer at Waste Management previously worked for Andersen (Rezaee & Riley, 2010). Andersen had been Waste Management's auditors for three decades without legal troubles until the 1990s. The story begins in 1992 when Andersen found evidence that Waste Management misstated taxes, insurance and expenses, but Waste Management was unwilling to make changes to restate their prior financial statements so that the corrected information would be included in the most current financial statements. At first, Andersen identified improper accounting practices and presented them to Waste Management officials in a report called "*Proposed Adjusting Journal Entries*," outlining entries that needed to be corrected to avoid understating Waste Management's expenses and overstating its earnings. However, Waste officials refused to make the corrections but instead allegedly entered into a closed-door agreement with Andersen to write off the accumulated errors over a 10-year period and change its underlying accounting practices, but only in future periods. The SEC viewed this agreement as an attempt to cover up past frauds and to commit future frauds. Andersen auditors knew Waste Management's financial statements were inaccurate and tried to get the company to mend its ways (McRoberts, 2002b).

However, when Waste Management ignored Andersen's recommendations, the accounting firm went along with its client's wishes rather than resign especially since between 1991 and 1997, Waste Management paid Andersen $7.5 million in audit fees and $11.8 million for consulting and other services. Unfortunately, Andersen displayed a short-sighted incentive to collude with their client because they consider Waste Management a crown jewel client, thus unwilling to stand up to management to disclose the above information to the public for their use. Andersen auditors were under pressure to retain their clients at the expense of compromising their ethical conduct and professional responsibilities. Waste Management and four Andersen partners colluded to perpetuate the fraud (Rezaee & Riley, 2010). According to SEC documents, Waste Management capped the amount of fees it would pay for Andersen's auditing services, but it advised Andersen that it could earn additional fees through "special work." For example, in 1993, Andersen documented a $128 million misstatement and in 1995 documented a $160 million misstatement, but Andersen concluded that it was not necessary to disclose this information because it was not considered to be material, but the SEC finally stepped in to stop the corruption (Miller, 2004).

The SEC began examining Waste Management in November, 1997, when the company announced that a change in accounting methods would result in a $1.2 billion loss. A complaint filed by the SEC charged Waste Management with perpetrating a massive financial fraud over a period of more than five years. The accounting scandal at Waste Management exposed the fact that they were changing the depreciation time length on their property, plant and equipment to make it stretch out over a longer period of time so that the amount of depreciation expense would be lower, thus artificially inflating income (Rezaee & Riley, 2010). Furthermore, Waste Management improperly capitalized a variety of expenses that should have been fully expensed on the income statement and failed to record expenses for decreases in the value of landfills as they were filled with waste. Andersen was named in the case with Waste Management as having assisted in the fraud by repeatedly issuing unqualified audit opinions on Waste Management's materially misleading financial statements (Sawayda, 2011).

Andersen found itself in court over questionable accounting practices with regard over a $1 billion of overstated earnings at Waste Management from 1992 to 1996 (McRoberts, 2002b). Another failure that would ultimately come to haunt Andersen due to the accumulations of other failures. In addition, senior management helped others violate antifraud reporting and record keeping provisions of federal securities laws, resulting in a loss to investors of more than $6 billion. The result of these cases was that Andersen paid some $220 million to Waste Management shareholders and $7 million to the SEC. Four Andersen partners were sanctioned, and an injunction was obtained against the firm. Andersen, as part of its consent decree, was forced to promise not to sign off on spurious financial statements in the future or it would face disbarment from practicing before the SEC—a promise that it would later break with Enron. After the dust settled, Waste Management shareholders lost about $20.5 billion and about 11,000 employees were laid off; as we can see, fraud is not victimless.

WorldCom's Fraudulent Financial Reporting

WorldCom "prove[d] to be the final nail in the coffin," for its auditor Arthur Andersen (Miller, 2004). WorldCom filed for bankruptcy in 2002, making it the largest U.S. filing in history—dwarfing that of Enron. Andersen withheld crucial financial statements for years leading up to the bankruptcy. After WorldCom admitted to misstating $3.85 billion, the SEC investigation revealed over a $408 million debt cover-up where Andersen, knew of this debt, together with artificially inflated assets due to improperly capitalizing expenses (Miller, 2004). In addition, Andersen withheld crucial accounting figures to increase the revenues it gained from consulting and started to shred documents once again before it was caught (Miller, 2004). The destruction ended in August 2002 when Andersen lost its license to perform audits. Decades of building a world-class reputation was destroyed within a short period of time over the desire for more profit.

Summary Insights on Arthur Andersen

The Chicago-based accounting firm closed its doors in 2002, after 90 years of business (Sawayda, 2011). Andersen seemed utterly incapable of recognizing that it had seriously failed in its core mission of protecting investors against fraudulent financial reporting and the consequences of that failure. One observer, commented on the force that led to Andersen's destruction stating:

> Hubris dictated Andersen's decision in the 1980s to assume it could turn auditors into salespeople and not undermine auditor independence. Hubris caused the firm to deny or minimize errors in failed audit after failed audit, and particularly in the Enron disaster. Hubris ultimately caused Andersen to gravely underestimate the threat it faced in Department of Justice prosecutor Michael Chertoff, or the outrage of an investing public who felt scammed by Andersen's poor work…The firm seemed utterly incapable of recognizing that it had seriously failed in its core mission of protecting investors against fraudulent financial reporting—and the consequences of that failure. A firm that made its name auditing the performance of others in the end faced the ultimate accounting for its own failings (Greisling, 2002).

The Role of the Internal Auditor

Internal auditors interact with top management and should assist them to fulfill their role in developing accurate and reliable financial statements, ensure the effectiveness of internal control systems, and monitor compliance with laws and regulations (Mintz & Morris, 2017). Specific obligations include, 1) monitor corporate governance activities and compliance with organization policies, 2) review the effectiveness of the organization's whistleblowing provisions, 3) assess audit committee effectiveness and compliance with regulations, and 4) oversee internal controls and risk management processes. Internal auditing is an independent, objective assurance activity designed to add value and improve an organization's operations. It helps an organization accomplish its objectives by bringing a systematic, disciplined approach to evaluate and improve the effectiveness of risk management, control, and governance processes. Despite their important duties, they do not assume the responsibility of management, instead they must remain objective in their assessment of evidence in order to provide an opinion or conclusion regarding a process, system or other subject matter; it is management's duty to implement internal controls (Sharma et al., 2009). Internal auditor's independence from company management is reinforced by a direct reporting line to the board of director's audit committee or the general counsel that allows them the opportunity to express any concern about management's attention to internal controls or report suspicious fraud involving management. The internal audit function is motivated by a "sense of mission, due to 1) its commitment to the organization and management and 2) its commitment to independence in allegiance to the board and the organization's stakeholders" (Sharma et al., 2009, p. 117).

If an internal auditor detects suspicious events or an indication of fraud, they are ethically bound to investigate to determine if there is fraud and to report fraud in a timely manner to management and if management does not respond, then they are obligated to tell the audit committee or the board of directors if there is no audit committee. Any fraud committed by senior management must be reported directly to either the audit committee or the board of directors. Internal auditors are part of the organization's culture and should operate in accordance with the ethical values embedded in that culture; they can serve as outlets for employees who face ethical dilemmas in the workplace, but are not sure how best to handle them (Mintz & Morris, 2017). They can support employees in conflict situations and enable them to voice their concerns. In relation to fraud, this means that internal auditing provides assurance that the controls they have in place are appropriate given the organization's risk tolerance. Internal auditing should provide objective assurance that fraud controls are sufficient for identified fraud risks and ensure that the controls are functioning effectively. Internal auditors review the comprehensiveness and adequacy of the risks identified by management especially when management overrides its risk tolerance and the antifraud controls in place that target such risks. However internal auditors are not under the same requirements as external auditors to detect material fraud because they are not all experts in fraud detection and investigation (Sharma et al., 2009).

Consider, like external auditors, internal auditors may have to report fraudulent behavior that is not addressed by management to the SEC because there is a regulation violation (Mintz & Morris, 2017). Internal auditors should consider the organization's assessment of fraud risk when developing their internal audit plan and periodically review management's fraud management capabilities. They should interview and communicate regularly with those conducting the organization's risk assessments, as well as others in key positions throughout the organization, to help them ensure that all fraud risks have been appropriately considered. When performing engagements, internal auditors should spend adequate time and attention to evaluating the design and operation of internal controls related to fraud risk management. They should exercise professional skepticism when reviewing activities and be on guard for signs of fraud. Potential frauds uncovered during an engagement should be treated in accordance with a well-defined response plan consistent with professional and legal standards. Internal auditing should also take an active role in support of the organization's ethical culture.

The importance an organization attaches to its internal audit function is an indication of the organization's commitment to effective internal controls and following the law especially if it's a public corporation. The internal audit charter, which is approved by the board of directors or designated committee, should include internal auditing roles and responsibilities related to antifraud controls. Specific internal audit roles in relation to fraud risk management could include initial or full investigation of suspected fraud, underlying cause analysis and control improvement recommendations, monitoring of a reporting whistleblower hotline, and providing ethics training sessions. If assigned such duties, internal auditing has a responsibility to obtain sufficient skills and competencies, such as knowledge of fraud schemes, investigation techniques, and laws. Effective internal audit functions are adequately funded, staffed, and trained, with appropriate specialized skills given the nature, size, and complexity of the organization and its operating environment.

Internal auditing should be independent, have independent authority and reporting relationships, coupled with adequate access to the board of directors, the audit committee, and adhere to professional standards. Although the above professional duties of an internal auditor appear reasonable and straight forward, what is often overlooked in the technical duties is the human element. Often internal auditors have to communicate information that is unpopular potentially facing the displeasure of senior management who may perceive these employees as obstacles to their goals: be it legitimate or illegitimate goals. Internal auditors may come under significant pressure to compromise their professional and ethical obligations so that management can satisfy their motives regardless of the means they use. Unfortunately, at times, and in this case accountants such as Betty Vinson from WorldCom, relax their ethical standards in order to comply with authority. However, in the end, they engage in collusion to perpetrate fraud which ultimately put them in a prison. Internal auditor will face an ethical dilemma or difficult situation at some point in their career and among the toughest scenarios is when the CEO or other senior executive exerts pressures to suppress or change the results of an audit finding because it reflects poorly on management or some other aspect of the business. An internal auditor must ask themselves whether they are willing to risk criminal prosecution given that they would be seen as colluding with management if there was evidence of fraud that was facilitated by the internal auditing department.

One study by the Institute of Internal Auditors, finds that 25 percent of the internal auditors at North American organizations surveyed said they have been pressured to "suppress or significantly modify a valid internal audit finding or report" during their career (McCafferty, 2016). Chief audit executives (CAE), 29 percent, were the most likely to face pressure, while 20 percent of staff internal auditors reported pressure to change audit findings. The source of the pressure to suppress or change findings, when it occurred, was surprisingly varied and depended on largely on the rank of the internal auditor reporting the pressure. CAEs, 38 percent, faced pressure most often from the CEO, 25 percent from the operations management, and 24 percent from the CFO. Staff internal auditors, 21 percent, more often faced pressure from operations management and 44 percent from the internal audit department itself, presumably from the CAE (McCafferty, 2016). Perhaps the most troubling results of the survey are that CAEs even face pressure from the board. Of those who reported being pressured, 12 percent said it came from the board and 6 percent said it came directly from the audit committee (McCafferty, 2016).

The overwhelming reason for the pressure to change results was that the operational audit would reflect badly on key operational management. In addition, the study revealed that at large internal audit departments, that was the case in 77 percent of instances where there was pressure to change findings and in 70 percent of cases for small-to-medium-sized internal audit functions (McCafferty, 2016). Again we can see the probable financial strain that organizations experience and the desire to survive. Other reasons for large department auditors who faced pressure were executive misuse of corporate funds (9 percent), and financial reporting issue at odds with the external auditor or the CFO (4 percent). The study found that when internal auditors stood up to the pressure to suppress or change findings, they often faced consequences. Indeed, 33 percent of internal auditors said they were excluded from meetings for standing their ground on an audit issue. Another 18 percent said they lost out on job opportunities, and 4 percent said they faced budget cuts as a result of resisting pressure to alter findings. In some rare instances, internal auditors said they faced job elimination, pay cuts, or hostile work conditions after resisting pressure. Let us examine the conduct of WorldCom internal auditor Cynthia Cooper that illustrates how doing the right thing, albeit uncomfortable at times, can in the end benefit a person and those impacted by their perseverance.

The Story of Cynthia Cooper of WorldCom

The WorldCom fraud was the largest in U.S. history, beginning modestly during mid-year 1999 and continuing at an accelerated pace through May 2002, resulting in an $11 billion dollar earnings overstatement where investors collectively lost an estimated $30 billion (Mintz & Morris, 2017). The fraud was accomplished by improperly capitalizing expenses rather than classifying them as operating expenses which would have meant the WorldCom would have had to include them in their current income statement coupled with fraudulently inflated revenue with fake accounts. During 2002 Cynthia Cooper, vice president of internal auditing, responded to an internal company tip indicating WorldCom engaged in fraudulent accounting especially on the issue of improperly capitalized accounts that should have been immediately expensed. Her team worked often at night and in secret, to detect the $3.8 billion fraud (Mintz & Morris, 2017). Her job proved challenging because the internal audit department was supposed to have "full, free, and unrestricted access to all company functions, records, property and personnel" according to the internal audit charter, but few had full system access to the company's reporting system and the company's general ledger" (Thibodeau & Freier, 2014, p. 218). Moreover, management dodged or refused to answer their questions or delayed providing information in a timely manner.

Cooper eventually notified the board of directors and their initial response was to do nothing, but to look to CFO Sullivan for explanations. When Cooper questioned CFO Scott Sullivan about various accounting issues, including artificial earnings, Sullivan became hostile and condescending (Cooper, 2009). Sullivan screamed at her in a way that she has never been spoken to before (Kaplan & Kiron, 2004). Cooper was asked about her role as an internal auditor and how she knew that something was wrong at WorldCom. She stated that "It was a process. My feelings changed from curiosity to discomfort to suspicion based on some of the accounting entries my team and I had identified, and also on the odd reactions I was getting from some of the finance executives" (Mintz & Morris, 2017, p. 108). As a result of her insights, Cooper did what a competent internal auditor should do which included approaching the investigation of the improper capitalization of expenses with a healthy dose of professional skepticism while maintaining her integrity despite being bullied by CFO Sullivan into having her drop her investigation. According to Cooper, she blamed the corporate culture on CEO Ebbers for his reckless risk-taking approach that led WorldCom to incur up to $40 billion of debt to fund one acquisition after another by using WorldCom stock as collateral (Mintz & Morris, 2017).

As a result, the price of stock became the only metric of success that mattered because that was the asset that supported the collateral, thus it was no surprise that financial statement fraud occurred to prop up the stock price to meet Wall Street expectations. Moreover, Cooper more likely than not knew accountant Betty Vinson, but in the end, Vinson went to prison for her role while Cooper was exalted for her courage. Cooper continues to encourage fraud examiners and auditors to listen to their instincts stating, "If something doesn't feel or see or seem quite right, it might not be…Continue to ask for support and dig until you are satisfied that you've gotten it right.

Don't allow yourself to be intimidated by superiors" (Carozza, 2006). Cooper further stated, "strive to be persons of honor and integrity. Do not allow yourself to be pressured. If your company tells employees to do whatever it takes, push the envelope, look the other way, and be sure that we make our numbers, you have three choices: go along with the policy, try to change things, or leave. If your personal integrity is part of the equation, you're probably down to the last two choices" (Hermanson & Rama, 2016, p.428).

Managing the Risk of Organizational Misconduct

Effective corporate governance processes are the foundation of fraud risk management and a lack of effective governance seriously undermines any fraud risk management program (McNeal, 2011). As previously stated, corporate governance generally refers to a system by which companies are directed and controlled in which management and those charged with oversight accountability, such as the board of directors, meet their obligations and fiduciary duties to various stakeholders such as government entities, shareholders, employees, communities and vendors to name a few. Corporate governance raises awareness and expectations of what is acceptable corporate behavior, and as part of an organization's corporate governance structure, a fraud risk management program should be in place, including written policies to convey the expectations of the board of directors and senior management regarding managing fraud risk. Risk management can refer to an organization's overall enterprise risk that takes into account the identification, prioritization, treatment, and monitoring of risks that threaten an organization's ability to provide value to its stakeholders, be it for-profit, not-for-profit or a governmental agency as examples. Risk management balances risk tolerance levels that are unique to organizations in terms of how much risk they are willing to accept with the ability to meet organizational goals such as operational and compliance goals. Effective and well-run organizations exist because management takes proactive steps to anticipate issues before they occur and to take action to prevent undesired results. It should be recognized that the dynamics of any organization require an ongoing reassessment of fraud exposures and responses in light of the changing environment the organization encounters overtime.

Companies that have built antifraud programs, which include setting the proper tone at the top, forming proactive and reactive measures, and clearly defining roles and responsibilities, will stand the best chance of mitigating risks and effectively addressing fraud (Torpey & Sherrod, 2011). In other words, a well-conceived antifraud program helps place a greater emphasis on the company's oversight by providing a framework for responding when issues arise instead of just reacting in a chaotic fashion when misconduct is exposed. Although managing the risk of organizational misconduct is absolutely necessary as a countermeasure to corporate wrongdoings, corporate wrongdoings are tricky problems because they occur in organizations that are powerful, internally complex, and able to both hide misconduct and resist change (Rorie, 2020). A deterrence strategy, on its own, is not sufficient to create a sustained form of compliance. Punishment is necessary, especially to end impunity and reassure those who are in compliance, but for corporate compliance problems, a broader organizational change is needed. Legislators and regulators, including those in the United States, have introduced a number of approaches such as incentivizing firms to develop compliance management and ethics programs, offering protection and incentives for whistleblowers, and imposing independent monitoring on companies caught breaking the law. Ironically enough, the available evidence indicates that these initiatives work best where they are needed the least. As we saw, compliance management and whistleblower protection work in situations where the wrongdoing is neither supported by powerful leaders nor systemic within the organization's ranks or business operations (Rorie, 2020).

While programs may curb minor wrongdoing at lower corporate levels, they do not work for the systemic culture of deviant behavior at the root of many cases, such as the years of fraudulent sales practices at Wells Fargo, the decades of emissions cheating at Volkswagen, and the repeated safety and environmental catastrophes by British Petroleum (Rorie, 2020). Yet, despite the research warning of harboring an unshakeable faith on the efficacy of compliance programs, the law continues to favor compliance management, whistleblower protection, and monitoring arrangements as best practices to reduce corporate misconduct. The law is not alone here in supporting these unproven internal approaches to deal with corporate wrongdoing (Rorie, 2020). For businesses, internal compliance management, whistleblower protection, and monitoring, while costly, are strategies to alleviate legal sanctions or reduce liability. In many cases, these strategies even provide an opportunity to restore their reputation—sometimes, and ideally, like Siemens, going from fraud villain to compliance hero (Rorie, 2020). Meanwhile, the people whose job it is to regulate or prosecute corporate misconduct often fail to publicly express strong concerns about the effectiveness of these internal systems. Prosecutors and regulators appear continually pressed to show that they take corporate wrongdoing seriously, while being structurally challenged to create actual deterrence. The best they can hope for after a scandal is the proud press release of another multibillion-dollar settlement, with the installation of compliance management and monitoring to signal their commitment to future risk prevention, and maybe, if fortunate, a successful verdict against individual executives (Rorie, 2020). For most regulators, and especially prosecutors, achieving sustained behavioral change is simply not their most pressing concern. So, what about compliance professionals?

These are the individuals who work in the emerging compliance industry, staffing compliance and ethics programs and developing whistleblower, complaint, and independent monitoring systems. Certainly, these professionals have difficult jobs. They are officially responsible for generating compliance, often where few would believe it possible. They do so from a position of limited power, with the immense risk that if they fail, they may be held individually liable. Moreover, many of them, especially lawyers, simply do not have adequate training in how to achieve behavioral and organizational change. All the while, they operate either as employee or hired consultant of a business that ultimately has its own interests that may not always align with compliance management. So how would a compliance manager, manage these expectations and risks? Would one focus on behavioral change and tie one's own fate to successfully is to focus on managing corporate liability, ensuring that there are systems in place that, at least on paper, meet the requirements of regulators. The company gets what it wants, namely managed liability and the ability to shift blame downwards toward lower-level employees should things go awry.

Regulators can show success as the company has installed the systems they demanded, while compliance managers can build ever-expanding systems that they alone know how to manage and operate at a lower personal risk. At present, empirical knowledge about how to make these systems more effective is limited. This means that practitioners have very little to go on and often must design systems using anecdotal evidence or "common sense." It also means that we do not really know how to define quality here. How do we know whether a compliance and ethics system is robust and worthy of the leniency by the Department of Justice? How do we know what type of whistleblower scheme will actually enhance compliance and what makes a good monitor? Now that we have had decades of leniency for corporate compliance systems, over a decade of whistleblower protection in federal law, and also a decade of increased imposed monitoring, we should have sufficient data points for a rigorous empirical analysis. Yet we simply have too little good research that systematically shows what works and what does not. There is an overarching lesson here. We need to redefine how we approach corporate crime and misconduct. Rather than always discussing the need for stricter punishment or merely complaining about the costs of compliance management, we need to become pragmatic. What matters when corporations break the law is that we effectively prevent future violations. This means, first of all, using every available insight about how punishment, social and personal norms, capacity, opportunity, and unconscious influences can be employed in these particular situations.

We need to change the training of compliance professionals, with less focus on studying legislation, court cases, and legal procedures, and more on the criminology, psychology, sociology, and organizational science of how humans actually respond to rules. These insights must be translated to fit corporate organizational settings. That being said, typically, the management of fraud focuses on three categories previously studied: fraudulent financial statements, misappropriation of assets, and corruption. In addition to understanding the role of management, this section explores some of the major components of fraud risk management organizations focus on when dealing with these different types of misconduct listed above which include, 1) fraud risk assessments, 2) fraud prevention, 3) fraud detection, 4) investigative protocol, 5) corrective actions, and 6) monitoring risk management. Moreover we examine how the board of directors assist in the management of fraud risk. The issue of fraud risk management is an immense topic in compliance circles, thus consider that what is presented within this section is a template to begin the process of understanding what organizational fraud risk management typically entails.

The Role of Management

Typically management may be reluctant to support a fraud risk management program for several reasons. First, management concerns are not on fraud issues because they do not understand that fraud is often the quiet crime that is hidden with losses going unnoticed. Moreover, they do not believe that fraud is actually occurring in their organization, but reflects misconduct occurring at other organizations. Also, because of the hidden nature of fraud, managers are reluctant to believe that it may be an organization-wide problem, but rather an isolated incident not worthy of devoting time and resources to. Unfortunately displaying such a reaction is erroneous because misconduct can be wide-spread and by the time management acknowledges the problem, it may be too late. Furthermore, management may believe that bringing up fraud issues may alienate their work force because it may come across as accusatory in nature. Often the best way to convince management of the importance of a fraud risk management program is to actually present them with data proving to them how much fraud actually costs an organization and its impact on the bottom line. In addition, executives may be sensitive to adverse publicity where even small fraudulent acts can be devastating to their bottom line.

Also, fraud is not a subject that any organization wants to deal with, yet the reality is most organizations experience fraud to some degree. A proactive approach to managing fraud risk is one of the best steps organizations can take to mitigate exposure to fraudulent activities. Although complete elimination of all fraud risk is realistically unachievable or uneconomical to eradicate, organizations can take positive and constructive steps to reduce their exposure. The combination of effective fraud risk governance, a thorough fraud risk assessment, strong fraud prevention and detection as well as coordinated and timely investigations and corrective actions, can significantly mitigate fraud risks. Furthermore, fraud risk management design and implementation is the initial responsibility of management, even though in the end, strong controls against fraud are the responsibility of everyone in the organization where all staff should have a basic understanding of what constitutes fraud behavior red-flags, and the detection, prevention and corrective action when fraud is unveiled (Sharma et al., 2009). In essence fraud risk management starts with management, but a risk management program requires a team approach.

Management must ensure that the organization has specific and effective internal controls in place to prevent and detect fraud, set the proper tone at the top ensuring that a culture of integrity is encouraged, clearly communicate through words and action that fraud is not tolerated, while also discussing expectations of integrity with new hires as well as current staff. Moreover, management must take seriously reports of fraud and undertake investigations when necessary coupled with appropriate corrective action which sends a message that reinforces the commitment to a culture of ethics. Companies realize that fraud challenges need to be addressed, but they may not be able to overcome inconsistencies, duplicative efforts, and a lack of communication because those responsible for antifraud efforts often operate independent of each other and not in a coordinated way. Depending on the corporate structure and overall corporate governance model in place, fraud is more likely to go undetected when the responsibilities for education, monitoring and risk management are spread out across reporting lines so no one individual or group can truly get a handle on the fraud risks facing an organization and, unfortunately, because responsibilities are spread out, people are more likely to believe that their small part in the total fraud detection model is unimportant thus not worth expending time and effort.

Consequently, everyone must craft and share a vision on how fraud can best be prevented; for example, internal auditors may not coordinate with the legal department and employees who do not know who they can turn to when they observe fraud as an example (Torpey & Sherrod, 2011). Management needs to create a culture through words and actions where it is clear that fraud is not tolerated, that any such behavior is dealt with swiftly and decisively, and that whistleblowers will not suffer unwarranted punishment (Sharma et al., 2009). Staff members must understand how their jobs are designed to manage fraud risks even when it is not obvious that they have a role in fraud risk management and when noncompliance may create an opportunity for fraud to occur or go undetected. In addition, they must read and understand policies and procedures relating to antifraud policy, behaviors that are expected as outlined in a code of conduct, whistleblower policy, and reporting and assisting in a fraud investigation. Although it is apparent that fraud risk management is not without its costs to support, it is recommended that the ownership of antifraud efforts should be shared by a select group of individuals who each have, as part of their responsibilities, a role in addressing fraud proactively and reactively.

The shared responsibilities of the overall fraud risk management program would ensure that the roles of the team members would be more effective to the overall group and each individual would then have a specific goal and greater accountability to the group (Torpey & Sherrod, 2011). This approach gives comfort to the board of directors and executive management within the company that an antifraud program is effective and efficient in its approach to fraud risk management. An antifraud mindset among staff should clearly define its overall ownership and responsibility of the implementation and continued oversight of its fraud management program. Team members must possess diverse skill sets to address the complexities of fraud cases and proactive fraud risk initiatives. If applicable, the team should include representation from executive management, the audit committee, the investigations group, the compliance department, the controllers' group, the internal audit department, information technology, security, the general counsel's office and the human resources department.

For example the legal and compliance personnel will identify risks that give rise to potential criminal, civil, and regulatory liability if fraud were to occur (Sharma et al., 2009). The internal audit personnel will be familiar with an organization's internal controls and monitoring functions, thus integral in developing and executing responses to significant risks. These risks cannot be mitigated practically by preventive and detective controls alone, but together with accounting and finance personnel who are familiar with the financial reporting process and internal controls (Sharma et al., 2009). Nonfinancial business unit and operations personnel leverage their knowledge of day-to-day operations such as customer and vendor interactions and a general awareness of issues within the industry. If internal expertise is not available, external consultants with expertise in applicable standards, key risk indicators, antifraud methodology, control activities, and detection procedures should be considered to be part of the team. The team must clearly articulate each member's role and responsibilities to avoid duplication of effort and ensure that the process will achieve the desired outcomes, but one that is also efficiently conducted and cost effective.

Fraud Risk Assessment

Fraud risk assessment is a process aimed at proactively identifying and addressing an organization's vulnerabilities that are both internal and external fraud risk factors (Sharma et al., 2009). If management is aware of it vulnerabilities, it can put in place plans to mitigate against such risks because they are ultimately accountable for the effectiveness of the organization's fraud risk management efforts. By vulnerabilities we mean fraudulent financial statements, asset misappropriation, and corruption and whether such exposure could result in a material misstatement of the financial statements. The extent of activities required for the evaluation of fraud risks is commensurate with the size and complexity of the company's operations and financial reporting environment. Management should recognize that the risk of material misstatement due to fraud exists in organizations regardless of the size or type and effective fraud assessments require thoughtful judgments that reflect a company's individual facts and circumstances (Sharma et al., 2009). When engaging in a fraud risk assessment, it is important for the organization to define what fraud means to them.

Management's assessment of the significance of an identifiable risk should not only refer to the financial statement and monetary significance, but also to an organization's operations and reputation, as well as exposure to criminal, civil, and regulatory liability. Assessing those areas that are at higher risk for fraud to occur does not mean that fraud is actually taking place, but it does mean that it is an area to investigate in the event that misconduct does occur; in other words we are more attune to those areas that are prone to being exploited. The process evolves over time as the results of the identification of the risk factors begin to dictate how to respond to them because we are better able to identify them, where they are most likely to occur, and how to respond to such risks. A quality fraud risk assessment is one that fits within the culture of the organization, is supported by the proper people that encourages all to participate, and is supported throughout the organization as an important and valuable process.

For example, if the organizational culture and the tone at the top is dominated by leaders that display antisocial traits previously studied, candid communication is likely to be fruitless. However, if there is a genuine concern about fraud, then fraud risk assessments are a good way for an organization to begin the communication process to raise awareness about fraud. When we have a discussion about this sensitive topic, we begin to reduce the stigma attached to this topic with the hope that it becomes part of the general discussion of organization topics no differently than other topics be it improving sales, reducing costs, or human resource issues (Sharma et al., 2009). People have to get into the habit of talking about fraud so that it becomes second nature to them. Moreover the synergy that comes from open discussion helps tap into the knowledge employees have about an organization's weakness that we otherwise would not know had the discussion not taken place. It is up to the organization to determine how it wants to communicate the desire to start such a discussion, but some of the ways include through one on one interviews, focus groups, surveys, and anonymous feedback through an easy to use mechanism.

Employees are reminded that the organization does take fraud issues seriously and it may potentially deter potential fraud offenders from engaging in such conduct because they realize others are watching their behaviors who refuse to provide cover for them in the event they are engaging in fraud. Furthermore, consider the fraud risk assessment process is, 1) an ongoing process that is revisited on a regular basis, 2) tailored to the particular entity and its specific fraud risk factors, 3) appropriately diversified among the organization's geographical locations, business functions, or divisions, and 4) used to properly communicate the entity's risks to external auditors (McNeal, 2011). Organizations by nature are different, thus the process usually requires the creativity of those involved in the process to understand how to tailor a risk management program to a particular organization. There is no one-size-fits-all approach that works because organizations are involved in different businesses reflecting different risk factors and risk tolerances. For the organization to be effectively managed, their unique risks must be identified using a formal risk assessment and if performed properly, an assessment can be an excellent proactive tool in the fight against fraud (McNeal, 2011).

Management's assessment of the likelihood of a fraud risk occurring is informed by instances of that particular fraud occurring in the past at the organization and the prevalence of the fraud risk in the organization's industry. Assessments can categorize the likelihood of potential frauds occurring in as many categories as deemed reasonable, but three categories that seems to work well are: 1) remote possibility, 2) reasonably possible, and 3) probable. Moreover, financial incentive programs should be evaluated as to how they may affect employees' behavior when conducting business or applying professional judgment. Incentives and the metrics on which they are based can provide guidance to where fraud is most likely to occur. Also important, and often harder to quantify, are the pressures on individuals to achieve performance or other targets. Some organizations are transparent, setting specific targets and metrics on which personnel will be measured while other organizations are more indirect and subtle, relying on corporate culture to influence behavior. Individuals may not have any personal financial incentive to engage in fraud, but there may be ample pressure, real or perceived, for an employee to act fraudulently.

Meanwhile, opportunities to commit fraud exist throughout organizations and may be reason enough to commit fraud. These opportunities are greatest in areas with weak internal controls and a lack of segregation of duties. For example, a skeptical mindset in the assessment process could ask the following questions, 1) how could a fraud offender exploit the organization's internal controls? 2) are there opportunities for collusion that make internal controls ineffective? 3) are there internal controls that are irrelevant given organizational changes? and 4) how could an offender conceal their fraud? However some frauds, especially those committed by management, may be difficult to detect because of the limitations internal controls offer revealing their inherent risks where management can often override the controls and issues of collusion. Such opportunities are why appropriate monitoring of senior management by a strong board of directors, supported by internal and external auditing is critical to fraud risk management (McNeal, 2011).

However, consider honest employees and management may not truly understand how weak internal controls impact fraud risk, which is why having a relationship with an auditor can assist in the assessment because they tend to know from their training and experience where vulnerabilities exist and what internal controls might address such vulnerabilities (Sharma et al., 2009). Consequently, fraud risk assessment is most effective when management and auditors share ownership of the process coupled with accountability. Outside auditors can bring a sense of independence and objectivity to the process mitigating against management bias. Moreover, because organizational cultures can be strong and entrenched, an outside auditor can have a frank discussion with management of how organizational culture can too be a fraud risk factor if fraud risk factors are cast aside as irrelevant because of the view that all that matters is revenue growth regardless of how the revenue is obtained. However, the relationship has to be based on integrity and the desire to do the right thing. This observation makes sense when we consider what happens when auditors and management do not do their jobs correctly resulting in corporate meltdowns. Let us identify some of the more common risks to consider.

a. Tolerance for and Identification of Risk

Being efficient in the assessment process is important or else an ineffective fraud risk assessment approach can result in spending organizational resources on insignificant risks while remaining ignorant of risks that are likely and potentially devastating (CIMA, 2008). One of the first steps in a fraud risk assessment involves identifying potential fraud risks inherent to the organization and this can be accomplished by brainstorming to identify the fraud risks that could apply to the organization (CIMA, 2008). Through brainstorming we consider how the fraud triangle warns us of the risk factors pertaining to the opportunity, rationalization and pressure/incentives that can tempt a person to commit fraud (Sharma et al., 2009). The vulnerability that an organization faces when exposed to these factors can be considered the starting point of a fraud risk assessment. Assessing the likelihood and significance of each potential fraud risk is a subjective process coupled with the fact that all fraud risks are not equally likely to occur, nor will all frauds have a significant impact on every organization (CIMA, 2008).

Assessing the likelihood and significance of identified risks allows the organization to manage its fraud risks and apply preventive and detective procedures rationally. Considering the inherent fraud risks that apply to organizations without consideration of known controls, management will be better able to take into account all relevant fraud risks and design controls to address the risks. When we state inherent risk regardless of whether there are controls in place to mitigate fraud risk, what we mean are those types of inherent risks internal controls may not be able to control for such as collusion or management override of such controls. We can have some of the best controls in place for an organization, but realistically there are ways to circumvent controls and those are the inherent risks that must be taken into account. Management must evaluate the potential significance of inherent risks and decide on the nature and extent of the fraud preventive and detective controls and procedures to address such risks (Sharma et al., 2009).

An organization's risk tolerance level provides management support on how to respond to fraud risk. Risk tolerance varies from organization to organization and at the highest level, senior management and the board of directors sets the organization's risk tolerance level, taking into consideration its responsibilities to all shareholders, capital providers, and stakeholders. While some organizations want only to address fraud risks that could have a material financial statement impact, other organizations want to have a more robust fraud response program. Many organizations display a zero-tolerance policy with respect to fraud. However, there may be certain fraud risks that an organization considers too expensive and time consuming to address by implementing more internal controls. Consequently, the organization may decide not to put controls in place to address such risks. Fraud risks can be addressed by accepting the risk of a fraud based on the perceived level of likelihood and significance, increasing the controls over the area to mitigate the risk, or designing internal audit procedures to address specific fraud risks (CIMA, 2008).

The board of directors should ensure management has implemented the right level of controls based on the risk tolerance it has established for the organization. In effect, one should look at an organization's financial statements and operations and ask "What can be wrong in this picture?", and then design appropriate controls. The key is to be selective and efficient because there are probably thousands of potential controls that could be put in place. The goal is a targeted and structured approach, not a haphazard approach, and efficient controls that deliver the most benefit for the cost of resources. The overall objective is to have the benefit of controls exceed their cost. In addressing fraud risks, one should be careful to ensure that antifraud controls are operating effectively and have been designed to include appropriate steps to deal with the relevant risks. Therefore, antifraud controls should be designed appropriately and executed by competent and objective individuals. Management's documentation of antifraud controls should include the description of what the control is designed to do, who is to perform the control, who is to monitor and assess the effectiveness of the control, and the related segregation of duties (Richards et al., n.d.).

Assessing the likelihood and significance of each potential fraud risk is a subjective process that should consider not only monetary significance, but also the significance to an organization's financial reporting, operations, and reputation, as well as legal and regulatory compliance requirements. Fraud risk identification may include gathering external information from regulatory bodies such as the Securities and Exchange Commission (SEC), industry, and other sources such as law societies. Other key guidance setting groups on internal controls include, 1) the Committee of Sponsoring Organizations of the Treadway Commission, and professional organizations such as 2) the Institute of Internal Auditors, 3) the American Institute of Certified Public Accountants, and 4) the Association of Certified Fraud Examiners (Sharma et al., 2009). Internal sources for identifying fraud risks should include interviews and brainstorming with personnel representing a broad spectrum of activities within the organization, review of whistleblower complaints, and analytical procedures. Employee incentive programs and the metrics on which they are based can provide a map to where fraud is most likely to occur.

b. Risk of Management's Override of Controls

The speed, functionality, and accessibility that created the enormous benefits of the information age have also increased an organization's exposure to fraud. Consequently, any fraud risk assessment should consider management access and override of system controls as well as internal and external threats to data integrity, system security, and theft of financial and sensitive business information (CIMA, 2008). Personnel within the organization generally know the controls and standard operating procedures that are in place to prevent fraud. However it is reasonable to assume that individuals who are intent on committing fraud will use their knowledge of the organization's controls to do it in a manner that will conceal their actions. For example, a manager who has the authority to approve new vendors may create and approve a fictitious vendor and then submit invoices for payment, rather than just submit false invoices for payment. Hence, it is also important to keep the risk of management's override of controls in mind when evaluating the effectiveness of controls; an antifraud control is not effective if it can be overridden easily (Sharma et al., 2009).

c. Risk of Fraudulent Financial Reporting

When we are thinking about fraudulent financial reporting, what are the risks that increase this type of fraud to occur? Acceleration of revenue recognition can be achieved via numerous schemes such as recognizing revenue on product not shipped. For example, starting with the revenue recognition component of fraudulent financial reporting, the assessment should consider the following questions: 1) What are the main drivers of revenue at the organization? 3) Are revenues primarily from volume sales of relatively homogeneous products, or are they driven by a relatively few individual transactions? 3) What are the incentives and pressures present as they related to revenue? 4) Are there any revenue recognition fraud risks specific to the organization's industry? 5) What controls are in place to monitor internal reporting of these disclosures? 6) Does someone monitor the organization's disclosures in relation to other organizations and ask questions about whether the disclosures are adequate or could be improved (CIMA, 2008)?

d. Risk of Misappropriation of Assets

An organization's assets, both tangible such as cash or inventory, and intangible assets such as proprietary or customer information, can be misappropriated by employees, customers, or vendors; the organization should ensure that controls are in place to protect such assets (Sharma et al., 2009). Considerations made in the fraud risk assessment process include gaining an understanding of what assets are subject to misappropriation, the locations where the assets are maintained, and which personnel have control over or access to tangible or intangible assets. Protecting against these risks requires not only physical safeguarding controls, but also periodic detective controls such as physical counts of inventory. Remember, an offender is thinking about such controls and designing the fraud to circumvent those controls. Those conducting risk assessments should keep this in mind when thinking about fraud schemes and their impact to the organization. Individuals who have access to tangible assets such as cash, inventory, and fixed assets and to the accounting systems that track and record activity related to those assets can use information technology (IT) to conceal their theft of assets. For example, an individual may establish a fictitious vendor in the vendor master file to facilitate the payment of false invoices, or someone may steal inventory and charge the cost of sales account for the stolen items, thus removing the asset from the balance sheet. Given the transition to a services-based knowledge economy, valuable assets of organizations are intangibles such as customer lists, business practices, patents, and copyrighted material. Examples of intangible asset theft include piracy of software or other copyrighted material by individuals either inside or outside of the organization.

e. Risk of Corruption

Corruption is typically defined as the misuse of entrusted power for private gain either directly or indirectly, to obtain or retain business. Organizations that have operations outside their home countries need to consider other relevant anticorruption laws when establishing a fraud risk management program. Transparency International, a multinational organization focused on anticorruption and transparency in business and government, issues an annual Corruption Perception Index (CPI), which ranks countries on their perceived levels of corruption. The CPI can assist organizations in prioritizing their anticorruption efforts in areas of the world at greatest risk. Consider that corruption can also occur in an organization's home country.

f. Information Technology Risk

IT is an important component of any risk assessment, especially when considering fraud risks (CGMA, 2012). IT risks include threats to data integrity, threats from hackers to system security, and theft of financial and sensitive business information. Whether in the form of hacking, economic espionage, Web defacement, sabotage of data, viruses, or unauthorized access to data, IT fraud risks affects everyone (Kroll, 2015/2016). Keep in mind, fraudsters who use the internet do not even have to leave their homes to commit fraud, as they can route communications through local phone companies, long-distance carriers, internet service providers, and satellite networks. They may go through computers located in several countries before attacking targeted systems around the globe. What is important is that any information, not just financial, is at risk, and the stakes are high and rising as technology continues to evolve. To manage the ever-growing risks of operating in the information age, an organization should know its vulnerabilities and be able to mitigate risk in a cost-effective manner. Therefore, IT risk should be incorporated into an organization's overall fraud risk assessment. Organizations rely on IT to conduct business, communicate, and process financial information, thus a poorly designed or inadequately controlled IT environment can expose an organization to fraud (Kroll, 2016/2107). Today's computer systems, linked by national and global networks, face an ongoing threat of cyber fraud and a variety of threats that can result in significant financial and information losses.

Fraud Prevention

Because of the entrenchment of normalized corruption, misconduct is best handled through prevention and through proactive means of forestalling corruption rather than a reactive means of removing it (CIMA, 2008). Prevention techniques to avoid potential key fraud risk events should be established, where feasible, to mitigate possible impacts on the organization, but despite the best efforts of those responsible for preventing fraud, one inevitable reality remains and that is fraud does occur more frequently than we care to believe. While prevention encompasses policies, procedures, and training that stop fraud from occurring, detection focuses on activities and techniques that recognize whether fraud has occurred or is occurring (CIMA, 2008). Preventive measures cannot ensure that fraud will not be committed, but they are the first line of defense in minimizing fraud risk. One key to prevention is making personnel throughout the organization aware of the fraud risk management program, including the types of fraud and misconduct that may occur. This awareness should enforce the idea that all the techniques established in the program are real and will be enforced. The ongoing communication efforts provides information on the potential disciplinary, criminal, and civil actions that the organization could take against the individual. If effective preventive controls are in place, working, and well-known to potential fraud perpetrators, they serve as strong deterrents to those who might otherwise be tempted to commit fraud (Sharma et al., 2009). Fear of getting caught is always a deterrent, thus effective preventive controls. Let us examine fraud prevention ideas that are commonly addressed.

a. Tone at the top

One of the best antifraud strategies is creating a culture of integrity that is determined by the leader's attitudes and choices and a culture that promotes following processes ensuring compliance. When setting the proper tone, management must go beyond stating that "we hire good people," or "we operate our company with integrity;" it must demonstrate how these principles are actually embedded into the company's daily operations to create a culture of constant integrity (Torpey & Sherrod, 2011). The tone is also set by a code of conduct or code of ethics establishing the guiding principles of a company. Among other things, it should promote honest and ethical conduct, compliance with applicable laws and regulations, and prompt reporting of violations of the code. Clearly establishing fraud policies and procedures helps employees understand acceptable conduct and how to report suspected violations. Fraud awareness training, another significant and often overlooked aspect of an antifraud program, is a key element in setting the proper tone within an organization because it sends a message that management takes an antifraud mindset seriously (Sharma et al., 2009).

b. Antifraud Training

An organization can hire or promote competent individuals who, having undergone appropriate background checks, represent low fraud risk. Yet this does not mean that there should be any exemption from receiving an initial orientation and ongoing education on the fraud risk management program in place, regardless of the individual's position in the organization (Sharma et al., 2009). Such education serves to reinforce the tone from the top regarding individual responsibility and the process to deal with suspected fraud. All employees should receive fraud awareness training as part of the hiring orientation process and as a component of the integration process for newly acquired companies, joint ventures or subsidiaries. Antifraud training lets employees know the organization will not accept rationalizations as legitimate explanations to justify their behavior. Many companies take antifraud training programs a step further by educating their top executives and then evaluating them on their character development. Organizations are increasingly hiring outside firms to help evaluate executives' leadership abilities and train them in understanding integrity issues (Torpey & Sherrod, 2011).

An organization's human resources (HR) group is often responsible for developing and providing the necessary training on the purpose of the fraud risk management program, including the codes of conduct and ethics, what constitutes fraud, how to identify it, and what to do when fraud is suspected. It is important that employees understand why the training is relevant and that they comprehend the information presented. Moreover, almost every time a major fraud occurs, people who were unwittingly close to it are shocked claiming they had no idea it was going on, therefore, it is important to raise awareness through education and training.

491

Particular attention should be paid to employees working in high risk areas, such as procurement and finance, and to those with a role in the prevention and detection of fraud. Training methods include: 1) formal training sessions, 2) group meetings and, 3) posters, employee newsletters and internet content. Communication should be ongoing and a combination of methods is usually most successful. Spending money on preventing fraud brings many benefits, but there can be downsides, for example, excessive and expensive controls may be created which reduce efficiency and demotivate staff because of the number of steps one has to go through to get their job done.

In addition, companies that have antifraud training often spend too much time focusing on occupational fraud, such as stealing assets from the company, because participants can easily visualize and understand these crimes. However, they often overlook other important areas such as corruption, financial statement fraud, vendor due diligence when dealing with third parties, and theft of intellectual property and sensitive data (Torpey & Sherrod, 2011). Some companies are creating fraud awareness training programs for all employees on a general level and then providing more specific, comprehensive training dealing with relevant risks for different groups or business areas. Sophisticated training includes modules taught by the company's internal audit, technology, compliance, and security professionals. Additional emphasis should be on detecting schemes involving revenue recognition, bribery, and corruption issues. Employees, vendors, customers, and other stakeholders who do not learn a company's antifraud policies and procedures, compliance and ethics programs, reporting protocols, and fraud risks will not know what the organization's acceptable behavior consist of. As a result, this may expose the company to major problems because they do not know how to identify and effectively respond to suspected fraudulent activities. Thus, it is actually more cost effective to understand procedures than trying to back into them once a major problem has surfaced that can cost an organization millions of dollars in legal and other related fees.

c. Establishment of an Effective Whistleblower Hotline

It has been reported that approximately two-thirds of companies in the U.S. are affected by fraud, losing an estimated 1.2 percent of revenue each year to such activity and indirect costs linked to fraud, such as reputational damage and costs associated with investigations (Kastiel, 2014). When and where implemented, an internal whistleblower hotline is a critical component of a company's compliance and antifraud program, as tips are consistently the most common method of detecting fraud (Sharma et al., 2009). It is essential that companies implement an effective whistleblower hotline and incentivize employees to use the hotline, at times also referred to as a helpline. Whistleblowing provides a company with the opportunity to address and remedy misconduct before it becomes unlawful or the company is required to report it to regulators. Research reveals that internal employee hotlines facilitate the detection of unethical and unlawful conduct, as tips are the most common detection method for suspected wrongdoing in companies with or without hotlines (Kastiel, 2014). In companies with an internal hotline, tips account for over half of all fraud detection versus only one-third of detections in companies with no internal hotline.

To the extent hotlines are currently in place, companies need to evaluate them to ensure they operate as intended and are effective in preventing and identifying unethical or potentially unlawful activity, including corporate fraud, securities violations, and employment discrimination or harassment (Kastiel, 2014). It is up to company directors, along with senior management under the oversight of the board, to set the all-important 'tone at the top' for the entire company. Setting the standard in the boardroom that good corporate governance and rigorous compliance are essential helps establish a strong corporate culture throughout a company. Creating a culture in which internal reporting is valued and where whistleblowers are protected is essential to preventing and detecting suspected unethical or unlawful conduct. A positive tone may ease the stigma of utilizing a company hotline, making employees feel less intimidated when they decide whether to report to the internal hotline in the future. Also, a board's and management's effective and expeditious response to hotline calls facilitates communicating a proper message to employees so they do not lose faith in the board or management and believe their only option is to report suspected wrongdoing to regulators or not disclose anything at all.

Consider that the higher executives climb in their organization, often the less likely they are to know what is and is not working at their companies coupled with issues of misconduct due to being surrounded by yes people who filter information they will hear. Others might dismiss or ignore messengers of bad news, yet whistleblowers can help break through the communication barriers and provide the information executives need to respond to misconduct (Miceli et al., 2009). As a result, senior management should praise whistleblowers who first report suspected unethical or unlawful conduct internally to reinforce the commitment that such action is encouraged and supported. Yet, whistleblowing systems at times fail in their attempt to detect misconduct for a variety of reasons. An effective whistleblowing system must conceal the identity of the whistleblower and there may be the perception, real or imagined, of a lack of anonymity where people believe that if they report misconduct, they will be exposed as the whistleblower (Albrecht et al., 2012).

There are a number of other reasons employees avoid hotlines, such as the fear of retaliation including dismissal, loss of career advancement opportunities, or being labeled a snitch or rat. Further, employees may perceive that they do not have shared values with the company or that the tone at the top among the board of directors and management is not one that promotes or rewards ethical behavior. Moreover, employees simply may not be aware of the hotline, how it works, the procedures involved, the ramifications of calling and making a report, or the various hotline-related protections provided to them, including the confidentiality of calls. Trust in a company's whistleblower processes, including making hotline reports without fear of retaliation, is essential to motivate employees to report suspected unethical or unlawful conduct internally. Many whistleblowers are uncomfortable revealing misconduct and believe they do not have sufficient power to make a difference coupled with the fact that they want to report misconduct, but not at their personal expense. Moreover, the fact that employee dissent is stigmatized is confirmed by a growing body of organizational behavior literature that explores the causes of employee silence as a collective phenomenon within organizations especially the negative characteristics of groupthink.

In one study, researchers analyzed the reasons for employee silence, based on interviews with employee subjects (Maclean, 2005). The study found that being silent about issues and problems at work is a very common experience among employees. Furthermore, a large number of respondents believe that ethical or fairness issues were "undiscussable", not to be raised with superiors coupled with the fear of retaliation in the form of punishments such as losing one's job, demotions or not getting a promotion (Maclean, 2005). Another reason reported in the study was the desire to avoid stigma which is the fear of being labeled or being viewed as a troublemaker, complainer, or tattletale. This is coupled with the fear that speaking up about issues would damage their relationships with colleagues and people they rely on either for information or to do their job. Silence is a product of forces within the organization stemming from management and systematically reinforced by other employees (Maclean, 2005). Employees who are silent note that they are not alone in withholding sensitive information. Indeed, many employees in the study suggested that knowledge of a problem may be widely known among peers, but not necessarily conveyed to senior management given that they may be at the heart of the problem in the first place (Maclean, 2005).

Even in the face of unethical conduct, conformity pressures that are common to all organizational settings can lead inside employees to remain silent and not risk the consequences of whistleblowing. Although not impossible to resist, the desire to avoid stigma and maintain good social relations, as displayed by remaining a team player, are powerful self-preserving influences (Maclean, 2005). Moreover, if policies in relation to what is misconduct is not clear, employees may not know what to report if they sense that there is something wrong assuming they are aware that a hotline exists to voice their concerns. Employees are more apt to use a fraud hotline when there is an independent third party that monitors the hotline so that it is not connected internally to management (Gao et al., 2015). Furthermore it is important to have several methods of communication available to report misconduct such as telephone, e-mail, and the mails as examples. Also, incidents reported must be followed up and corrective action taken when necessary demonstrating the benefit of reporting misconduct. If misconduct is confirmed, it is important that corrective action be taken against those engaged in misconduct to send a message to the rest of the organization that misconduct will not be tolerated.

Companies should ensure that their compliance and ethics program includes regularly educating employees on and publicizing the who-what-when-where-why-how of reporting suspected unethical or unlawful activity via the company's whistleblower hotline (Kastiel, 2014). A portion of the compliance department's budget should be dedicated to educating on what types of activities or observations are appropriate for reporting and those that are not and promoting the company's hotline. Certain compliance experts note that keeping a positive hotline message, for example, using words such as accountability, transparency, responsibility and citizenship as opposed to fraud, corruption, embezzlement, bribery and crime may help alleviate psychological barriers that prevent or discourage tipsters from using the hotline because of the negative connotation of such words (Kastiel, 2014). The hotline should be promoted with educational materials provided to shareholders, employees, customers, and vendors, all of whom can provide valuable information from a variety of reliable sources. Hotlines ideally support a multilingual capability and provide access to a trained interviewer 24 hours a day, 365 days a year and staffed by individuals trained in dealing and eliciting sensitive information as well as recognizing fake reports (Kastiel, 2014).

Employees may feel more comfortable reporting suspected wrongdoing outside of normal work hours to preserve anonymity. Employees should be able to make whistleblower tips anonymously or, at the very least, confidentially, as research indicates that employees are more comfortable reporting suspected wrongdoing when such options are available. Anonymous and confidential reporting mechanisms help foster a climate where employees are more likely to report or seek guidance regarding potential or actual wrongdoing without fear of retaliation (Kastiel, 2014). The hotline should be well-publicized through employee training, posters in break rooms and other common areas, and in newsletters. Companies must emphasize when publicizing hotline reporting procedures that they will not and are prohibited by law from retaliating against employees who make whistleblower reports. Assessing the effectiveness of an internal whistleblower hotline should address reasons why employees choose to avoid reporting tips in favor of reporting to regulators. Companies should offer financial as well as non-financial reporting incentives, such as cash rewards or extra vacation days, for whistleblower reports that lead the company to identify suspected unethical or unlawful activity (Kastiel, 2014).

The Whistleblower Program established by the Securities and Exchange Commission (SEC) for example, like certain other federal government whistleblower programs, provides monetary incentives for individuals, including employees, to come forward and report possible violations of the federal securities laws to the SEC. A company can train its employees to be aware of areas that are at risk for misconduct, emphasizing confidentiality and non-retaliation, simplify reporting procedures and attempt to make related policies more accessible and easier to understand. A company's hotline policy should be a clear, well-communicated written policy allowing for a reward system to compensate internal whistleblowers for tips that identify unethical conduct, fraud and waste and those that save the company resources, for example, through workplace safety and process improvements. Companies should expand the reasons an employee may contemplate calling the hotline, such as having the hotline also serve as a helpline, as this may alter the perception or negativity associated with hotlines and facilitate reducing the fear of calling and the associated stigma (Kastiel, 2014).

For example, a company can encourage employees to use the hotline/helpline to receive interpretative guidance on provisions of the company's code of ethics, make efficiency and process improvement suggestions which could potentially save the company resources through innovative employee ideas or report quality control or workplace safety concerns (Kastiel, 2014). Further, board and management actions help change the perception of using the company hotline may reduce the discomfort and barriers an employee feels before reporting his or her first tip and, after such tip, the employee may be more readily inclined to report future suspected wrongdoing. Also, information or data a company receives in connection with its whistleblower hotline should be reviewed by management with board oversight to monitor, together with other metrics that measure, 1) the rate of employee hotline use, 2) the company's record of following up on tips, 3) whether claims are substantiated, and 4) the departments that are most frequently implicated in the reports (Kastiel, 2014).

Company data is often available by way of its internal or third party hotline database, while peer and industry hotline data may be purchased from third party providers. Measuring hotline data to that of its peers and industry should also be part of a company's compliance program evaluation and may provide valuable insight into the effectiveness of a company's whistleblower hotline. Hotline data metrics provide companies with comparative information to determine reporting patterns that are higher than, lower than or in line with peers and their industry, which information may suggest mistrust or misuse of the whistleblower hotline or be indicative of more serious company-wide compliance and ethics issues (Kastiel, 2014). For example, a high volume of calls to a company's hotline when contrasted to peers and its industry may indicate that the company is experiencing significant compliance issues and potentially has an ineffective compliance and ethics program which needs to be addressed so that information is accurately interpreted (Kastiel, 2014). Conversely, a high volume of calls may suggest that the hotline is working as planned and that the company's compliance and ethics employee training program is effective. A high volume may indicate greater awareness of the hotline and increased trust in the company's compliance department, and that the board of directors and management are setting the proper tone in reinforcing internal reporting mechanisms.

On the other hand, silence or a low volume of calls as compared to a company's peers and its industry may not necessarily imply that all is well at the company and unethical or unlawful conduct is not occurring but, to the contrary, may be indicative of an inadequate hotline and overall ineffective corporate compliance and ethics program. It may indicate that employees are aware of the hotline, but are suspicious of being punished for its use given that they may not know how far up the hierarchical ladder the corruption extends. Moreover, third party providers generally have more experience in managing whistleblower calls and may provide company boards and management with insightful hotline data, reports and analyses of the effectiveness of the hotline. Whistleblower hotlines should be evaluated, tested and audited to ensure that the manner in which hotline calls are received, recorded and managed is consistent, confidential, accurate and timely, and the hotline operates as intended by the board and management (Kastiel, 2014).

d. Transaction-level Preventative Procedures

Employees with an interest in outside entities might conduct business transactions that ultimately benefit them at the expense of the organization. Preventative measures to mitigate against misconduct for third party and related party transactions should be reviewed by board of director members. Where business partnering relationships are in place, the risk of fraud, bribery, and corruption increases especially with outside third parties. To mitigate these risks, companies must comply with local and international regulations, but also extend their own antibribery and anticorruption policies, and compliance framework to cover third party relationships. Companies need to ensure that their contracts with third parties explicitly binds them to obey relevant national and international laws and regulations, as well as commitments to comply with and uphold the company's ethical policies (Fordham, 2013). In addition, the contract should give the company the right to audit their third party's conduct to better manage third party risk as well as send a clear message that ethical standards must be upheld on an on-going basis. Contracts that disclose the parties responsibilities are incentivized to avoid non-compliance due to the costs attached to legal liability.

If misconduct is detected and prosecuted, this may demonstrate to the regulator that the company has taken efforts in enforcing its compliance policies, which can potentially minimize potential prosecution and ultimately the severity of the punishment on the company (Fordham, 2013). Using forensic data could potentially identify inappropriate third party activities before they escalate. Typically forensic data enables companies to transform volumes of transactional data into actionable business intelligence quickly by extracting relevant data to create specific third party risk profiles to design tests for analysis. This approach allows companies to continuously evolve and adapt internal policies and procedures to mitigate risk from the onset leading to a proactive response to potential issues rather than reactive investigations after it happens. Performing third party due diligence is critical, as it represents a systematic and consistent effort to disclose business relationships structured by levels of inquiry based on a thorough business inventory and risk assessment. Companies should seek to understand the cultural and business norms, prior incidents of fraud, previous litigation, and adverse press within the industry and geography, or the experience of their peers to develop third party risk profiles when performing due diligence (Fordham, 2013).

e. Performing Background Investigations

An organization's human resource function can play an important role in fraud prevention by implementing the following procedures. A key business and fraud risk in any organization lies in the people hired to operate the business and promoted into positions of trust and authority (CGMA, 2012). For that reason, it is important to know employees in order to evaluate their credentials and competence, match skills to the job requirements, and be aware of any issues of personal integrity that may impact their suitability for the position. Much can be learned about an individual through confirmation of work history, education presented on a job application or résumé and in following-up with references provided. Furthermore, let us not forget the use of integrity assessments in the hiring of new employees and for the promotion of employees within an organization applying for different positions. It is possible to find false, embellished information, or an undisclosed history and reputation that may represent increased, and possibly unacceptable risk (CGMA, 2012). While the organization should establish procedures to obtain sufficient information to assess a job applicant or promotion candidate, the nature and extent of information that can be requested from a prospective or existing employee or obtained independently is governed by applicable employment laws and regulations. Enhanced background checking for criminal record or personal financial situation may only be possible upon receiving the individual's consent. Legal counsel should be sought to advise on what background information can and cannot be obtained and the appropriate procedures to follow. Background checks should also be performed on new and existing suppliers, customers, and business partners to identify any issues of financial health, reputation, and integrity represent an unacceptable risk to the business (CGMA, 2012).

f. Evaluating Performance and Compensation Programs

Human resource managers should be involved in reviewing performance management and compensation programs. Performance management involves the evaluation of employee behavior and performance as well as work-related competence. It is a human trait to want recognition for competence and reward for positive performance and success. Regular and robust assessment of employee performance with timely and constructive feedback goes a long way to preventing potential problems. Employees who are not recognized for what they do and what they have accomplished, especially those bypassed for promotion, may believe their inappropriate and fraudulent conduct is justified as demonstrated by the rationalizations they use and that were covered in chapter one. By conducting compensation surveys and local market analysis, HR can determine whether senior management and employees are compensated appropriately. Managers whose compensation is largely based on short-term performance-related bonuses may be motivated to cut corners or deliberately fabricate financial results to achieve those bonuses (CGMA, 2012).

g. Conducting Exit Interviews

A policy of conducting exit interviews of terminated employees or those who have resigned can help in both prevention and detection efforts. These interviews may help human resource managers determine whether there are issues regarding management's integrity or information regarding conditions conducive to fraud. Human resource should review information contained in resignation letters as they may contain information regarding possible fraud and misconduct existing within the organization (CGMA, 2012).

Fraud Detection

As fraud prevention cannot be 100 percent effective, organizations need to engage in fraud detection. One of the strongest fraud deterrents is the awareness that effective detective controls are in place. Combined with preventive controls, detection controls enhance the effectiveness of a fraud risk management program by demonstrating that preventive controls are working as intended and by detecting and identifying fraud if it does occur (CGMA, 2012). Although detection controls may provide evidence that fraud has occurred or is occurring, they are not intended to prevent fraud. A fraud detection strategy should involve the use of analytical and other

496

procedures to highlight anomalies, and the introduction of reporting mechanisms that provide for communication of suspected fraudulent acts. What do we mean by analytical procedures? For example, if a company states that their sales revenue is increasing, but the overall cash flow is actually negative, how are they able to operate? With this question, we would expand our questions to management to fill in the answers—if they can of course. Fraud detection would also include examining exceptions reporting and trend analysis. When speaking of exceptions reporting, we are referring to why we are not following a reporting process that has been followed in the past. Why is there a deviation from a past practice? What circumstances changed to deviate from past practice and is it justified and disclosed to financial statement users? Below are fraud detection areas to consider.

a. Fraud Detective Controls

There are always people motivated to commit fraud and an opportunity can arise for someone in any organization to override a control or collude with others to do so. Therefore, detection techniques should be flexible, adaptable, and continuously changing to meet the various changes in risk (CGMA, 2012). While preventive measures are apparent and readily identifiable by employees, third parties, and others, detection controls are hidden in nature meaning they operate in a background that are not obvious in an everyday business environment (CIMA, 2008). Moreover, if an organization operates in countries that are identified as having high risks for corruption, it may implement detective controls to identify possible violations of the Foreign Corrupt Practices Act, such as a recurring review of expense reports or consulting fees. Similarly, if an organization has a high frequency of subjective estimates, it may implement detective controls related to regular internal audit review of such activity. In addition, it may behoove an organization to examine unusual or unexpected interpersonal relationships employees establish that would normally not exist especially if there is the potential for corruption to occur such as bribery and kickbacks. On an international level, this examination is especially crucial because of the perception that corruption is perceived as part of the language of doing business abroad.

b. Proactive Fraud Detection Procedures

In addition, organizations may be able to use data analysis, continuous auditing techniques, and other technology tools effectively to detect fraudulent activity. Proactive consideration of how certain fraud schemes may result in identifiable types of transactions or trends enhances an organization's ability to design and implement effective data analysis. Data analysis uses technology to identify financial irregularities, trends, and risk indicators within large populations of transactions (Skalak et al., 2011). Moreover, data analysis allows users to identify relationships among people, organizations, and events. Users of this technology may be able to dig into journal entries looking for suspicious transactions occurring at the end of a period or those that were made in one period and later reversed in the next period (CGMA, 2012). This proactive approach would be of great benefit to the antifraud community such as forensic accountants and fraud examiners. These tools allow users to look for journal entries posted to revenue or expense accounts that improve net income to meet analysts' expectations or incentive compensation targets. Also, some auditors and consulting firms have developed tools, as part of their fraud detection efforts that analyze journal entries to mitigate management override of the internal control system. Evidence of fraud can sometimes be found in e-mails as well, thus the ability of an organization to capture, maintain, and review the communications of any of its employees has led to the detection of numerous frauds (CGMA, 2012). This is accomplished through the use of strict and regular backup programs that capture data, not with the intent of uncovering fraud, but merely as a safeguard in the event that a retrospective search for evidence may be necessary.

c. Fraud Detection Techniques Documentation

An organization should document techniques developed and implemented to detect fraud. This includes documenting processes used to monitor the performance of fraud detective controls or to indicate when such controls are ineffective. Testing procedures conducted to ensure adequate operation of fraud detective controls and the test results should also be documented thoroughly. Integral to this documentation is a detailed description of the elements of the organization's fraud detection techniques, with emphasis placed on the roles and responsibilities of all parties involved. Organizations should designate and document the individuals and departments responsible that include but not limited to: 1) Designing and planning the overall fraud detection process, 2) Designing specific fraud detection controls, 3) Implementing specific fraud detection controls, 4) Receiving and responding to complaints related to possible fraudulent activity, 5) Communicating information about suspected and confirmed fraud to appropriate parties, 6) Investigating reports of fraudulent activity, 7) Monitoring specific fraud detection controls and the overall system of these controls for realization of the process objectives, and 8) Periodically assessing and updating the plan for changes in technology, processes, and organization (Richards et al., n.d.).

Although the organization may want to describe and explain some aspects of its fraud detection techniques to its employees, vendors, and stakeholders to promote deterrence, there will be aspects of the plan that the organization will want to remain confidential (CIMA, 2008). During the fraud detection development phase, participants should be warned to keep such information confidential and there should be a specific list of individuals who are permitted access to the information and define its own level of information access related to fraud detection controls (Skalak et al., 2011). Once the final fraud detection plan is completed, it is necessary to develop a public disclosure regarding the plan and its implementation. Knowledge throughout the organization that a comprehensive fraud detection plan exists is, in and of itself, a strong deterrent. By communicating this to employees, shareholders, and others, the organization affirms that a fraud detection plan is in place and that it takes fraud seriously without revealing all the characteristics of the organization's fraud detection techniques.

d. Independent Monitoring

There is another option to enhance internal compliance management. Rather than rely on a paper compliance system or on internal employees, corporate compliance can also improve through independent monitoring to oversee internal operations. Sometimes firms do so voluntarily, and other times they do so only when forced by prosecutors as part of settlements. One type of independent monitoring is when companies hire a third-party firm to carry out inspections of their operations. This can be beneficial for firms who work with many subcontractors, or who have operations in multiple jurisdictions and who do not trust compliance reports from within their own organization. Such independent inspections can also aid external governmental regulators who themselves do not have the resources to do sufficient inspections and who can now use monitoring data that is arranged by the regulated company themselves (Rorie, 2020). Scholars have also conducted research on a series of studies about these third-party monitors. They find that there is variation in how well monitors do their job. Some monitors may inspect more leniently. They show, for instance, that monitors unearth fewer violations if they have less experience and training, and if they have been at the factory to audit previously.

Furthermore, there may be integrity issues with third-party monitors because they may not be as independent as one would hope. Monitors will be more lenient if directly paid by the firm they inspect, if there is more competition for their monitoring services, if they have a longstanding relationship with said firm, and if they hope that this firm becomes their customer for other non-monitoring goods and services they may supply (Rorie, 2020). Thus, the practice of hiring external monitors may not result in a truly independent audit. Instead, third-party monitoring can become a commercial transaction in which the monitor tries to please the audited firm. The lesson is that the expected win-win for compliance, where the corporation pays for external monitors that can help with independent oversight at less cost to governmental regulators, may often not exist. The more corporations pay for the oversight, the less independent and stringent the monitoring will be. Corporations can also monitor compliance through electronic surveillance technology bypassing individual employees and directly observe whether there is any illegal behavior within their operations. Such electronic monitoring is an attractive way to get better information about compliance behavior in larger organizations.

Electronic monitoring can operate around the clock and in any place the company needs – and all of this at relatively low costs, especially when compared to any human form of monitoring. Electronic surveillance may also directly promote compliance. Employees will know that they are monitored and this in and of itself may reduce wrongdoing. Moreover, the monitoring data may give employees feedback so that they can also learn about their behavior and improve it, especially for behavior that they may be less aware of. There have been a few studies about the effects of electronic monitoring on compliance behavior. Some find positive result such as one study examined what happens when restaurants install a theft monitoring system in order to reduce employee theft. Using data from 392 restaurants, they found that the electronic surveillance works well. In those cases, it not only helped to reduce employee theft, but also improved worker productivity (Rorie, 2020). Other studies warn that monitoring may not always work and may even backfire. In one study, scholars studied how the introduction of electronic monitoring in 71 hospital units affected compliance with hand hygiene rules.

While compliance initially increased when the monitoring was introduced, over the course of three and a half years, it gradually declined. The paper estimates that should they have been able to continue the study, this decline would have completely eroded any positive effects of monitoring on compliance after about 43 months. Researchers explain the reduction that eventually set in as a process of desensitization, meaning that employees simply got used to the monitoring and no longer responded strongly to it. More troubling, when some of the hospital units removed the monitoring, compliance rates even fell below the pre-monitoring period. What may have happened here, they argue, is that the introduction of the monitoring system "crowded out" the social norms and personal morals that sustained individual compliance of the hospital workers studied. Similarly, they note that monitoring is highly dependent on the actual organizational setting in which it is deployed. They hold that organizations looking to build process compliance must think about how electronic monitoring fits within a broader system encompassing not only technology, but also norms, culture, and leadership, among other things. Electronic surveillance is thus a promising way for organizations to create better compliance, particularly in the short term. We realize that such surveillance may not have long-term effects, and also that it may undermine intrinsic motivations that are so vital to building a lasting compliant culture.

The third form of independent monitoring is hiring an external manager to oversee a compliance transformation. This most often happens in the aftermath of a major scandal and prosecutorial settlement. The hope, of course, is that an external monitor with sufficient authority can ensure that the compliance management process is actually effective in creating a lasting behavioral change, and that such a monitor is sufficiently independent from the company to evaluate it critically and act on behalf of protecting the public interest and the law. Prosecutors increasingly impose such monitors on firms caught breaking the law. Siemens, for instance, had to hire a monitor as part of its remedial action following its bribery operation. Citibank, too, was forced to hire a monitor to guarantee that the bank properly returned $2.5 billion in mortgage relief to harmed homeowners with its predatory lending practices. Another example is how HSBC, the British bank, had to hire a monitor after it had been caught moving billions around the financial system for Mexican drug lords, terrorists, and governments on official sanctions lists (Rorie, 2020). Volkswagen was similarly forced to hire an independent monitor following its emissions fraud scandal. So, do these imposed independent monitors work well to create more sustainable compliance?

At present, we still lack an empirical answer to this question, as no one has conducted a rigorous study about the effect of monitorships on compliance. What we have are several studies, mostly by law professors who analyze the history, process, and variation in the operation of monitorships, and extrapolate conclusions about their effectiveness. Rather than provide concrete answers, unfortunately, these studies mostly raise concerns. A first issue is whether monitors actually have a broad enough mandate not just to oversee the surface-level institutionalization of a compliance management process, but to actually seek to go deeper into the organization to try to force a cultural change. A second problem is that monitors often lack sufficient qualifications to manage a compliance transformation process. Many have only very limited and mostly legal experience. Most monitors are former prosecutors that now work for private law firms serving corporate clients. Prosecutorial experience helps prepare them to prosecute wrongdoing, and private practice helps them aid corporations to manage liability; neither experience helps them in making the organization become more compliant and fundamentally alter its behavior.

Also, there is a danger of nepotism, as current prosecutors select former colleagues who have moved to private practice to be monitors, which can be a very lucrative assignment. Meanwhile, monitors operate in organizations that are not necessarily supportive. At the time of the settlement, firms will agree to almost anything if it keeps them from being formally indicted and prosecuted. The monitor is thus forced upon them at a moment of weakness. As soon as the settlement is set, the firm will try to mitigate the burden such monitor imposes on them. Corporations can be very successful at this because private organizations are co-opting the use of monitorships, which may transform the nature of monitorships from a quasi-governmental enforcement mechanism to a privatized reputation remediation tool. Here the core problem is that monitors may lack full independence (Rorie, 2020). The best way to ensure independence is to select monitors who have not had any prior business relationships with the organization, and then enforce a long-term ban on such relationships following the end of the monitorship. In practice, such a rule is not strictly enforced, in part because some deem it overly burdensome on monitors and their firm, and in part because in some specialty areas, there may not be a monitor who both meets such requirements and is willing to serve.

Fraud Investigation Protocol

Potential fraud may come to the organization's attention in many ways, including tips from employees, customers, or vendors, internal audits, process control identification, external audits, or by accident where the organization develops a system for prompt, competent, and confidential review, investigation, and resolution of allegations involving potential fraud or misconduct (CIMA, 2008). Protocols for involvement in such cases, which will vary depending on the nature, potential impact, and seniority of persons involved, should be defined clearly and communicated to management by the board. The process approved by the board should include a tracking or case management system in which all allegations of fraud are logged. The investigation and response system should include a process that is not limited by but includes: 1) Categorizing issues and confirming the validity of the allegation, 2) Defining the severity of the allegation and escalating the investigation when appropriate, 3) Listing types of information that should be kept confidential, 4) Defining how the investigation will be documented and information retained, 5) Conducting the investigation by resolving or closing the investigation (Sharma et al., 2009).

a. Evaluating Fraudulent Misconduct

Once an allegation of misconduct is received, the organization should follow the process that was put in place by management and where applicable, approved by the board of directors (Sharma et al., 2009). The process should include designating an individual or individuals with the necessary authority and skills to conduct an initial evaluation of the allegation and determine the appropriate course of action to resolve it. In cases involving the board or senior management, the board may want to hire outside independent advisers such as legal counsel to assist in this evaluation. Regulators such as the Securities and Exchange Commission (SEC) may have to be involved especially if public companies are the center of the investigation. The allegation should be examined to determine whether it involves a potential violation of law, rules, or company policy. Depending on the nature and severity of the allegation, other departments may need to be consulted, such as HR, internal auditing, IT, security, or loss prevention (Skalak et al., 2011). The organization's external auditor must also be advised of any fraud that could affect the organization's financial statements.

b. Investigation Protocols

Investigations should be performed in accordance with protocols which include a consistent process for conducting investigations that can help the organization mitigate losses and manage risks associated with the investigation (Sharma et al., 2009). Responsibility for overseeing an investigation should be given to an individual with a level of authority at least one level higher than anyone potentially involved in the matter. Investigations of allegations involving senior management should be overseen by the board or a committee of the board designated for that purpose. Legal counsel may be appointed to supervise the investigation. Depending on the specifics of the allegation, the investigation team may need to include members of different departments or disciplines to provide the knowledge and skill sets required. For example, forensic accountants, fraud examiners and attorneys may 1) participate in discussions concerning the scope of the investigation, data resources and data retention, 2) perform data acquisition, processing, review and analysis, 3) conduct interviews, with focus on financial reporting, the control environment, transactions and their particular context, 4) assist company and external auditors with understanding and considering the facts, and 5) quantify damages or prepare financial models for different scenarios (Sharma et al., 2009). Attorneys have additional duties including providing legal advice regarding legal rights and obligations, defending regulatory proceedings and bring claims on behalf of their clients.

The investigation team leader should coordinate the investigation and interface with management as necessary. The roles and responsibilities of each team member should be communicated clearly. All team members should consider whether there is an actual or potential conflict of interest with any of the issues or parties that could be involved. Should the organization not have adequate internal resources and/or if it is determined that internal resources are not sufficiently objective, consideration should be given to retaining outside expertise. Factors to consider in developing the investigation plan include but are not limited to: 1) Investigations may need to be timely conducted due to legal requirements, to mitigate losses or potential harm, or to institute an insurance claim, 2) Notification to regulators, law enforcement, insurers, or external auditors. Information gathered needs to be kept confidential and distribution limited to those with an established need. 3) Protect evidence so that it is not destroyed and admissible in legal proceedings. Involving legal counsel early in the process or, in some cases, in leading the investigation safeguards work product and attorney-client communications. 4) Investigations should comply with applicable laws and rules regarding gathering information and interviewing witnesses.

The investigation team should be removed sufficiently from the issues and individuals under investigation to conduct an objective assessment. 5) Specific issues or concerns should appropriately influence the focus, scope, and timing of the investigation (Richards et al., n.d.). What is often overlooked is how people should be treated during an investigation. Not surprisingly, employees may be upset or nervous about the prospects of being involved in an investigation. As a result, it is important management prepare for their concerns including to be treated fairly, but communicate that their cooperation is expected. Moreover if attorneys are involved in interviews, it may be necessary for the attorney to clarify that he or she represents the company and not the individual employee that may be the subject of an interview. Letting employees know that counsel represents the company and not them are referred to as *UpJohn* warnings named after the legal case.

c. Conducting the Investigation

What initially needs to be determined is whether there is a need for an investigation at all. At times, misconduct is exposed, the culprits identified and the problem is resolved, hopefully with corrective action. However, it is not always apparent whether there needs to be a full-blown investigation and having an independent or objective decision maker can help resolve the issue with clarity (Skalak et al., 2011). Assuming that an investigation is warranted and management is not considered to be targets of the investigation, management oversight might be appropriate with the assistance of investigators including internal and external auditors, fraud examiners, information technology, and attorneys (Sharma et al., 2009). Typically the sponsor of an investigation has the responsibility to retain and direct the investigation, determine the scope and timing of the investigation, monitor the progress of the investigation, take responsibility for its adequacy, assess the results and decide what corrective action to take. That being said, planning is essential to a thorough and competent investigation; the investigation team should establish the investigation tasks and assign each task to the appropriate team members. The plan should prioritize the performance of tasks to provide an interim report of findings, if necessary, and to revise or plan next steps. It is at this stage that appropriate consideration be given to legal issues and constraints in dealing with employees and third parties, obtaining relevant information, and documentation, including seeking assistance from the courts and monitoring the integrity of the results of the investigation thereby maximizing the prospects of success.

Investigation tasks include, but are not limited to the following: 1) Computer forensic examinations especially of computers used by potential suspects. 2) Interviewing including but not limited to: a) neutral third-party witnesses, b) corroborative witnesses who are not suspects but may have insights into the misconduct, c) possible co-conspirators, and d) offenders themselves. 3) Evidence collection, including but not limited to internal documents, such as, personnel files, internal phone records, computer files and e-mails. 4) Collection and analysis of financial records, security camera videos, physical and IT system access records, external records, such as public records, customer/vendor information, media reports, information held by third parties, and private detective reports. 5) Evidence analysis, including but not limited to review and categorization of information collected, computer-assisted data analysis. 6) Development and testing of hypotheses. Here we ask ourselves how could the misconduct have arisen, the methods used to commit fraud, potential motives and who may have been involved. It is also necessary to be fair and ask is it possible that misconduct did not occur. 7) The investigation team should document and track the steps of the investigation, including: privileged or confidential items, documents, electronic data, memoranda of interviews conducted, analysis of documents, data, and interviews and conclusions drawn (Richards et al., n.d.).

Moreover, taking these above issues into account means that an investigation must have qualified people to address these matters. Individuals involved in the investigation must be independent in that there are no conflict of interests that may cloud their sense of independence, due diligence, and professional skepticism. Let us examine some criteria that should not be overlooked. First of all, it is difficult to recognize what is unusual and improper if one has never learned what is normal and customary, thus if the issue to be investigated requires specific industry or subject matter expertise, it is important to include such experts on the team. In the case of fraud, the team needs to understand the accounting and financial reporting issues required to asses which fact patterns are most relevant to financial reporting. Also important is a working knowledge of the company's books and records, business processes, and customs is essential to quickly locate relevant evidence so that it is not destroyed. Furthermore, it is paramount to include an expert on electronic evidence given that for many businesses the primary form of communication and storing information is in the form of electronic evidence. Electronic evidence "has the virtue of being objectively dated and readily available such as e-mails and other electronic also are a source of informal, unguarded, and occasionally highly incriminating communications, precisely because users often believe that such communications are private" (Sharma et al., 2009, p. 193).

d. Regulators Involvement in an Investigation

Often, management is concerned about regulatory scrutiny when there are allegations of corporate misconduct. Depending on the nature and extent of regulatory involvement, management will engage external legal counsel and accountants to respond to regulatory inquiry and conduct fact-finding procedures to determine what remedial actions are needed in the event allegations of fraud are true. We explored how prosecutors view the extent of the misconduct to determine whether just individuals or whether the organization will also be prosecuted for misconduct. If the company makes an early determination during the period of its being investigated that cooperating with regulators is in its best interest until it determines it is not, then some member of the company's investigation team should contact the lead attorney to obtain as much information as possible about the investigation's premise, scope, and planned course of action (Sharma et al., 2009).

The company should work with regulators as reasonably as possible to understand the premise and objectives of the investigation. Moreover, the company should advise both current and former employees about the investigation, and inform them about the scope and purpose of the investigation. Furthermore, they should be apprised of their rights and give them instructions on preserving evidence in their possession or control including electronic evidence such as e-mails. Because the company will want to demonstrate a willingness to cooperate if that is its intent, it would be helpful to obtain the following information as soon as possible. 1) Who does the regulator want to interview? 2) From whom does the regulator plan to request documents for review? 3) What time periods and issues are subject to investigation? 4) How soon does the regulator want to start conducting interviews and review documents? 5) Will or should the company's management and its legal counsel be present for interviews of current and former employees? (Sharma et al., 2009).

e. Reporting the Results

The investigation team should report its findings to the party overseeing the investigation, such as senior management, board of directors, and legal counsel. Where legal counsel is supervising the investigation, counsel will determine the appropriate form of the report, however it is usually in writing and not in an oral form (Sharma et al., 2009). The nature and distribution of the report may be affected by the goals of protecting legal privileges and avoiding defamatory statements. For similar reasons, advice should be sought before the party overseeing the investigation makes public statements or other communications regarding the investigation.

Corrective Action

A reporting process should be in place to solicit input on potential fraud together with a coordinated approach to investigation coupled with any corrective action to help ensure potential fraud is addressed appropriately (Richards et al., n.d.). It is essential that any violations, deviations, or other breaches of the code of conduct or controls, regardless of where in the organization, or by whom they are committed, be reported and dealt with in a timely manner. Appropriate punishment must be imposed provided the same rules are applied at all levels of the organization, including senior management. If there is no penalty for engaging in misconduct, the message is sent that management's antifraud tone at the top is not to be taken seriously. Any findings of actual or potential material impact may need to be reported to the board of directors and the external auditor if they are not receiving investigation reports directly. Notification may also be required to legal and regulatory agencies and the organization's insurers while consultation with legal counsel is strongly recommended before taking disciplinary, civil, or criminal action.

Measurement and Monitoring Risk Management

The scale and complexity of fraud investigations often varies considerably, requiring some flexibility or customization for the measurements adopted and while a variety of measures can be applied, the following may be relatively simple and powerful measurements to track (Sharma, et al., 2009). First, misconduct resolution time should be estimated but hopefully without creating pressure to resolve complex cases in an unrealistically short time. Second, a low rate of repeat incidents can demonstrate effectiveness in promptly remedying business processes and internal controls in response to earlier incidents. Third, fraud investigations are important for their deterrent effect, so their cost-effectiveness should not be judged merely by the assets they help to recover. The organization's plan, approach, and scope of monitoring its fraud prevention techniques should be documented and updated as necessary. With all of the parties involved in the risk assessment process and the subsequent design of the control activities, it is difficult to require that fraud prevention be monitored regularly by an independent entity especially with the costs attached to independent review (Sharma et al., 2009).

Reviews, however, should be conducted separately from any routine or planned audits and should be designed to assure management of the effectiveness of the organization's fraud prevention. Before each program review, issues such as significant changes in the organization and their associated risks, changes in personnel responsible for implementing the activities, and the results of previous assessments will determine if the scope of the current examination needs to be altered (Sharma et al., 2009). Each evaluation should include evidence that 1) management is actively retaining responsibility for oversight of the fraud risk management program, 2) that timely and sufficient corrective measures have been taken with respect to any previously noted control deficiencies or weaknesses, and 3) that the plan for monitoring the program continues to be adequate for ensuring the program's ongoing success (Sharma et al., 2009). One of the most important responsibilities of the board is the ongoing monitoring of the effectiveness of the organization's fraud risk management activities. Continually assessing the performance of the program build on success and addresses areas of weakness.

To aid in monitoring the risk management program, a single point of contact in management to coordinate the program that reports to the board. The single point of contact will coordinate with others that are involved in risk management, but to avoid confusion, the single point of contact can be the one voice that adopts the concerns of others in addition to, 1) incorporating an assessment of the fraud risk management program as a regular agenda item at board meetings, 2) review management's reports on fraud risks, policies, and control activities, 3) assess the effectiveness and corrective results of the organization's response to incidents of fraud, and 4) establish a measurement process to track the program's results (Sharma et al., 2009). In addition, the organization should develop ongoing monitoring and measurements to evaluate, remedy, and continuously improve the organization's fraud detection techniques. If deficiencies are found, management should ensure that improvements and corrections are made as soon as possible. Management should institute a follow-up plan to verify corrective or remedial actions have been taken.

Conclusion

The importance of corporate governance cannot be overstated. So many scandals can be traced to weak corporate governance institutions that did not act as a check on management behaviors. Specifically, the role of the board of directors and their ineffectiveness is directly tied to organizational misconduct. We have observed that when the board does not display independence and is steeped in conflict of interests, it is not surprising they are willing to look the other way even when symptoms associated with misconduct surface. In terms of accountants and auditors, their professions inherently expose them to legal liabilities, both civil and criminal, thus they must familiarize themselves with what factors that are apt to expose them to liabilities.

That being said, there are solutions to mitigate the probability of exposing oneself to legal liabilities. For example, auditors must display with serious respect the role of independence, exercise due diligence beyond what might be expected, engage in professional skepticism, gather real evidence and not rely just on management representations even with a client of many years. Furthermore, they should incorporate a more principle-based approach to their work not just because legally it is expected, but because it is the right thing to do. Professionalism requires the incorporation of virtue into their judgment.

Lastly, even though fraud risk management typically starts with leadership, eventually fraud risk is part of the larger enterprise risk organizations face. Thus, fraud risk management is the responsibility of all those employed within an organization. Quality fraud risk management takes into account a thorough fraud risk assessment, fraud prevention and detection, an investigation and corrective action protocol. However risk management has to be taken into account with the idea that when people come forward to reveal fraud, that they are not alienated and punished because they are following the protocol expected to be applied.

References

Aasland, M. S., Skogstad, A., Notelaers, G., Nielsen, M.B., & Einarsen, S. (2010). The prevalence of destructive leadership behavior. *British Journal of Management, 21*, 438-452.

Abbe A., & Brandon, S.E. (2013). The role of rapport in investigative interviewing: A review. *Journal of Investigative Psychology and Offender Profiling, 10*, 237-249.

Abbot, J.H. (1981). *In the Belly of the Beast*. New York:Vintage Books.

ABC. (2021, September 28). Former theranos board member, investor testifies against elizabeth holmes. Retrieved from www.abc.com.

Abelson, R., & Feudenheim, M. (2003, May 22). The scrushy mix: Strict and so lenient. *New York Times.*
http://www.nytimes.com/2003/04/20/business/the-scrushy-mix-strict-and-so-lenient.html?pagewanted=all&pagewanted=print

Abkowitz, A. (2009, September 9). The informant: I thought I was bullet proof. *Fortune Magazine*. Retrieved from
http://archive.fortune.com/2009/09/24/news/companies/the_informant_mark_whitacre.fortune/index.htm

Ablow, K. (2008, December 17). Inside the minds of rod blagojevich and bernie madoff.
Retrieved from http://health.blogs.foxnews.com/2008/12/17/inside-the-minds-of-rod-blagoyevich-and-bernie-madoff/.

Abraham, Y. (2006). Alleged pyramid scheme offered kinship, a dream. Retrieved from
www.boston.com/news/local/articles/2006/02/19/alleged_pyramid_scheme_offered_kinship_a_dream/.

AFT (2007). Top russian fraud investigator shot dead in Moscow. Retrieved from www.freerepublic.com.

Agnew, R. (2001). An overview of general strain theory. In *Explaining Criminals and Crime*. 161-174, Edited by Raymond Paternoster and Ronet Bachman. CA: Roxbury Publishing Co.

Agrawal, A., Jaffe, J.F., & Karpoff, J.M. (1999). Management turnover and governance changes following the revelation of fraud. *Jounral of Law and Economic, XLII*, 309-342.

Aguilera, R.V., & Vadera, A.K. (2008). The dark side of authority: Antecedents, mechanisms, and outcomes of organizational corruption. *Journal of Business Ethics,77*, 431-449.

Ahmed, A. (2007, November 29). Ex-chicago officer gets 75 yrs for murder plot. Retrieved from www.policeone.com

Alalehto, T., & Azarian, R. (2018). When white collar criminals turn to fatal violence: The impact of narcissism and psychopathy. *Journal of Investigative Psychology and Offender Profiling*. Retrieved from https://onlinelibrary.wiley.com/doi/abs/10.1002/jip.1503

Albrecht, W.S., Albrecht, C.O., Albrecht, C.C., & Zimbelman (2012). *Fraud Examination*. USA: South-Western.

Albrecht, C., Holland, D., Malagueno, R., Dolan, S.L., & Tzafrir, S.S. (2015). Towards a better understanding of financial statement fraud, *Journal of Business Ethics,13*(4), 803-813.

Allen, R. (2015, July 10). Cancer doctor sentenced to 45 years for horrific fraud. Retrieved from
http://www.usatoday.com/story/news/nation/2015/07/10/cancer-doctor-sentenced-years-horrific-fraud/29996107/

Amernic, J., & Craig, R. (2010). Accounting as a facilitator of extreme narcissism. *Journal of Business Ethics, 96*, 79-93.

AML. (1985). *United States v. Automated Medical Laboratories*, 770 F.2d 399 (4th Cir. 1985).

Anand, V., Ashforth, B.E., Joshi, M. (2004). Business as ususal: The acceptance and perpetuation of corruption in organizations. *Academy of Management Executive, 18*(2), 39-53.

Anderson, J.R., & Tirrell, M.E.(2004). Too good to be true: CEOs and financial reporting fraud. *Consulting Psychology Journal: Practice and Research, 56*(1), 35-43.

Antar, S. (2005).Views on white-collar crime. *White Collar Fraud*. Retrieved from http://whitecollarfraud.blogspot.com/p/advice.html

Antar, S. (2007, March, 7). White collar crime: How criminals exploit your humanity.
White Collar Fraud, Retrieved from http://whitecollarfraud.blogspot.com/2007/03/white-collar-crime-how-criminals.html

Antar, S. (2008, December 13). Is there really more white-collar crime today? *White Collar Fraud*. Retrieved from
http://whitecollarfraud.blogspot.com/2008/12/is-there-really-more-white-collar-crime.html

Antar, S. (2009, November 27). Advice from a fraudster, white collar crime and criminals. *White-Collar Fraud*. Retrieved from
http://4closurefraud.org/2009/11/27/advice-from-a-fraudster-white-collar-crime-and-criminals/

Antar, S. (2010). General advice on white collar crime and forensic accounting. *White Collar Fraud*. Retrieved from
http://cleveast.imanet.org/meonske/43010generaladvice.pdf

Antar, S. (2013, January 23). No redemption, (I and II). Market Shawdows, Retrieved from http://ileneca7.tumblr.com/post/135275758913/no-redemption-parts-1-and-2.

Antilla, S. (2012, July 5). Rajat Gupta, other white collar criminals may be better staying on the street. Retrieved from
http://www.huffingtonpost.com/2012/07/05/rajat-gupta-white-collar-criminals_n_1652115.html.

AP. (1989). Minkow of zzzz best gets 25 years. *The New York Times*. Retrieved from
http://www.nytimes.com/1989/03/28/business/minkow-of-zzzz-best-gets-25-years.html

AP. (2010). Jury finds Indian church financier guilty of fleecing investors in Ponzi
scheme, Associated Press, available at: www.allvoices.com/news/7094773-jury-finds-indianachurch-financier-guilty-of-fleecing investors-in-ponzi-scheme.

AP. (2011). Ex-worcester man sentenced for cheating immigrants, *Associated Press*, Retreived from
http://news.bostonherald.com/news/regional/view/20110622ex-worcester_man_sentenced_for_cheating_immigrant/.

APA. (2008). No death penalty in insurance investigators death. Retrieved from www.allvoices.com/news/904758/s/14201993-no-death-penalty-in-insurance-investigator-sdeath.

Apel, R., & Paternoster, R. (2009). Understanding "criminogenic" corporate culture: What white-collar crime researchers can learn from studies of the adolescent employment-crime relationship. The criminology of white-collar crime. 15-33.

Appelbaum, B., Hilzenrath, D.S., & Paley, A.R. (2008, December 13). All just one big lie. *The Washington Post*. Retrieved from
www.washingtonpost.com/wp dyn/content/article/2008/12/12/.

Arendt, H. (1969). *On violence*. San Diego, CA: Harcourt Brace Jovanovich.

Argenti, P.A., & Tait, K. (2001). Arthur Andersen (D). Tuck School of Business at Dartmouth. Retrieved from
http://mba.tuck.dartmouth.edu/pdf/2001-1-0026.pdf

Arjoon, S. (2010). Narcissistic behavior and the economy: The role of virtues. *Journal of Markets and Morality, 13*(1), 59-82.

Arnulf, J.K., & Gottschalk, P. (2013). Heroic leaders as white-collar criminals: An empirical study. *Journal of Investigative Psychology and Offender Profiling, 10,* 96-113.

Ashforth, B., & Anand, V. (2003). The normalization of corruption in organizations. *Research in Organizational Behavior, 25,* 1-52.

Ataiyero, K. (2007, November 15). Chicago man gets 50 years for arranging murder. *The Chicago Tribune*. Retrieved from www. chicagotribune.com.

Auchter, B. (2010). Men who murder their families: What the research tells us. Retrieved from https://www.ncjrs.gov/pdffiles1/nij/230412.pdf

Austin, D. (2004). In god we trust: the cultural and social impact of affinity fraud in the African-American church. *University of Maryland Law Journal of Race, Religion, Gender and Class, 4,* 365-409.

Babiak, P., & Hare, R. (2006). *Snakes in Suits: When Psychopaths Go To Work*. New York: Harper Collins Publishers.

Babiak, P., & Hare, R. D. (2019). *Snakes in Suits: Understanding and Surviving the Psychopaths in Your Office*. Revised and Updated, New York: Harper Collins Publishers.

Babiak, P., Neumann, C.S., & Hare, R.D., (2010). Corporate psychoapthy: Talking the walk. *Behavioral Science and the Law, 28,* 174-193.

Babiak, P., & O'Toole, M., (2012, November 1). The corporate psychopath. Retrieved from https://leb.fbi.gov/articles/featured-articles/the-corporate-psychopath

Bagge, C. L., Glenn, C. R., & Lee, H. (2013). Quantifying the impact of recent negative life events on suicide attempts. *Journal of Abnormal Psychology, 122*(2), 359-368.

Baird, D.G., & Rasmussen, R.K. (2002). Four or five easy lessons from enron. *Vanderbilt Law Review, 55,* 1787-1812.

Baker, R. (2001). United States of America v. Vance Baker and Rosie Baker, 262 F.3d 124.

Bandler, J. & Varchaver, N. (2009, April 30). How bernie did it. *Fortune*. Retrieved from
http://archive.fortune.com/2009/04/24/news/newsmakers/madoff.fortune/index.hm

Barbour, P. (2013, March 12). Criminal thinking. Addiction Technology Transfer Center Network. Retrieved from
http://madcp.dreamhosters.com/sites/default/files/4F_Barbour_Criminal_Thinking.pdf

Barfield, V. (1983). State of North Carolina v. Margie Bullard Barfield, 259 S.E. 2d 510 (1979).

Barnard, A. (1999). Reintegrative shaming in corporate sentencing. *Southern California Law Review, 72,* 959-1007.

Barnard, J. W. (2008a). Securities fraud, recidivism and deterrence. *Penn State Law Review, 113*(1), 189-227.

Barnard, J.W. (2008b). Narcissism, Over-optimism, fear, anger, and depression: The interior lives of corporate leaders. *William and Mary Law School Scholarship Repository, 77,* 405-430.

Barnum, A. (2008a, February 27). Eric Hanson: Man who killed 4 family members had personality disorder, psychologist testifies. *The Chicago Tribune*. Retrieved from http://newsgroups. derkeiler.com/Archive/Alt/alt.true−crime/2008−03/msg00266.html

Barnum, A. (2008b, February 2). Ex-fiance testifies that Eric Hanson, accused of killing 4 relatives, threatened her. *The Chicago Tribune*. Retrieved from http://newsgroups.derkeiler. com/Archive/Alt/alt.true−crime/2008−02/msg00178.html

Barnum, A. (2008c, February 16). Hanson takes stand to deny killing relatives, stealing $140,000. *The Chicago Tribune*. Retrieved from http://www.chicagotribune.com/news/local/ chi-hanson_both.2feb16,1,7546014.story

Barrionuevo, A. (2006a). Enron's Skilling is sentenced to 24 years. *The New York Times*. Retrieved from
http://www.nytimes.com/2006/10/24/business/24enron.html?_r=0

Barrionuevo, A. (2006b). Fastow testifies lay knew of enron's problems. *The New York Times*.
http://www.nytimes.com/2006/10/24/business/24enron.html?_r=0

Barth, S. (2003). *Corporate Ethics: The Business Code of Conduct for Ethical Employees*. Boston, MA: Aspatore.

Basra, R., Neumann, P.R., Brunner, C. (2016). Criminal pasts, terrorist futures: European jihadists and the new crime-terror nexus. *The International Centre for the Study of Radicalization and Political Violence*. Retrieved from http://icsr.info/wp-content/uploads/2016/10/Criminal-Pasts-Terrorist-Futures.pdf

Batson, N. (2003, November 4). Final report of neal batson court-appointed examiner. Case No. 01-16034, United States Bankruptcy Court Southern District of New York. Retrieved from http://www.concernedshareholders.com/CCS_ENRON_Report.pdf

Baumeister, R.F. (1998). The self, in Gilbert, D.T., Fiske, S.T. and Lindzey, G. (Eds), *The Handbook of Social Psychology*, McGraw-Hill, Boston, MA.

Baumeister, R.J., Bushman, B.J., Campbell, W.K., (2000). Self-esteem, narcissism, and aggression: does violence result from low self-esteem or from threatened egotism?, *Current Directions in Psychological Science, 9*(1), 26-29.

Bazerman, M.H., & TenBrunsel, A.E. (2011, April). Ethical breakdowns. *Harvard Business Review*.

Beasley, M.S., Carcello, J.V., & Hermanson, D.R. (2001, March 31). Top 10 audit deficiencies. *Journal of Accountancy*. Retrieved from http://www.journalofaccountancy.com/issues/2001/apr/top10auditdeficiencies.html

Beasley, M.S., Carcello, J.V., & Hermanson, D.R., Neal. T. (2013, May). An analysis of alleged auditor deficiencies in SEC fraud investigations: 1998–2010. 1-36.

Beckner, H.M. (2005). Attachment theory as a predictor of female aggression (Unpublished doctoral dissertation). Texas A & M University.

Beenen, G. & Pinto, J. (2008). Resisting organizational-level corruption: An interview with sherron Watkins. *Academy of Management Learning & Education, 8*(2), 275–289.

Behr, P. (2004, July 9). Lingering anger still directed against Enron's once-trusted chief executive. *Washington Post*, E1.

Bell, R. (2007). Suspect. Retrieved October 22, 2010 from http://www.trutv.com/library/crime/notorious_murders/family/christopher_porco/4.html

Belluz, J. (2018, June 12). How silicon valley got played by theranso. *Vox*. Retrieved from https://www.vox.com/science-and-health/2018/6/12/17448584/theranos-elizabeth-holmes-bad-blood

Belson, K. (2005). Ebbers mounts an 'I never knew' defense. *The New York Times*. Retrieved from
  http://www.nytimes.com/2005/03/01/business/01ebbers.html

Benson, M. (2015). White collar crime: Recent trends and debates. *In International Encyclopedia & Behavioral Sciences*, 2nd Edition. 551-557.

Benson, M., & Simpson, S. (2009). *White Collar Crime: An Opportunity Perspective*. NY: Routledge.

Benson, M., & Manchak, S.M. (2014). The psychology of white-collar offending. *Oxford Handbooks On Line*. Retrieved from
  http://www.oxfordhandbooks.com/view/10.1093/oxfordhb/9780199935383.001.0001/oxfordhb-9780199935383-e-008

Bernstein, A. (2002, August, 24). Enron executive fastow gave away $63,000/feds say former CFO gave away thousands of tainted money. SFGate.
  Retrieved from http://www.sfgate.com/business/article/Enron-executive-Fastow-gave-away-63000-Feds-2806956.php

Bianco, A., Symonds, B., & Byrnes, N. (2002, December 22). The rise and fall of dennis kozlowski. *Bloomberg*. Retrieved from
  http://www.bloomberg.com/news/articles/2002-12-22/the-rise-and-fall-of-dennis-kozlowski

Bierhoff, H., & Vornefeld, B. (2004). The social psychology of trust with applications in the internet. *Analyse & Kritik, 26*, (Lucius & Lucius,
  Stuttgart), 48–62.

Black, J. A., & Cravens, N. M. (2001). Contracts to kill as scripted behavior. In P. H. Blackman, V. L. Leggett, B. Olson, & J. P. Jarvis (Eds.), The
  diversity of homicide: Proceedings of the 2000 annual meeting of the homicide research working group. Washington, D.C.: Federal
  Bureau of Investigation.

Black's Law Dictionary, 1991, 6th Edition. Definition of the word "malicious injury".

Blackburn, R., & Coid, J.W. (1998). Psychopathy and the dimensions of personality disorder in violent offenders. *Personality and Individual
  Differences, 25,* 129-145.

Blair, C., Hoffman, B., & Helland, K. (2008). Narcissism in organizations: A multisource appraisal reflects different perspectives. *Human
  Performance, 21*(3), 254-276.

Blais, J., & Solodukhin, E., & Forth, A. E. (2014, February). A meta-analysis exploring the relationship between psychopathy and instrumental versus
  reactive violence. *Criminal Justice and Behavior, 41,* 797-821.

Blickle, G., Schelgel, A., Fassbender, P. (2006). Some personality correlates of business white collar crime. *Applied Psychology: An International
  Review, 55*, 220-33.

Bloise, K. & Ryan, A. (2013). Affinity fraud and trust within financial markets. *Journal of Financial Crime, 20*(2), 186-202.

Bloomberg News. (2002, October 11). Waksal is accused of forgery. *Los Angeles Times* Retrieved from
  http://articles.latimes.com/2002/oct/11/business/fi-imclone11

Blum, R.H. (1972). Deceivers and the deceived: Observations on confidence men and their victims, informants and their quarry, political and
  industrial spies and ordinary citizens. *Institute of Public Policy Analysis*, Stanford University, Bibliography: 250-256.

Blumenstein, R., & Pullman, S. (2003, June 10). WorldCom fraud was widespread: Ebbers. Many executives conspired to falsify results in late 1990s,
  probes find. *The Wall Street Journal*, A3.

Boduszek, D., & Hyland, P. (2011a). The theoretical model of criminal social identity: Psycho-social perspective. *International Journal of Criminal
  and Sociological Theory, 4*(1), 604-615.

Boduszek, D., McLaughlin, C.G., & Hyland, P.E. (2011b). Criminal attitutdes of ex-prisoners: The role of perosonality, criminal friends and
  recidivism. *Internet Journal of Criminology*, 1-11.

Boduszek, D., & Hyland, P. (2012a). Psycho-sociological review of criminal thinking style. *Journal of Humanistics and Social Sciences, 1*(1), 28-36.

Boduszek, D., Hyland, P., Pedziszczak, J., & Kielkiewicz (2012b). Criminal attitudes, recidivistic behavior and the mediating role of associations with
  criminal friends: An empirical investigation within a prison sample of violent offenders. *Europe's Journal of Psychology, 8*(1), 18-31.

Boddy, C.R. (2006). The dark side of management decisions: Organizational psychopaths. *Management Decisions, 44*(10), 1461-1475.

Boddy, C.R. (2015). Organisational psychopaths: A ten year update. *Management Decision, 53*(10), 2407-2432.

Boddy, C.R. (2016). Unethical 20th century business leaders. *International Journal of Public Leadership, 12*(2), 76-93.

Boddy, C.R., Ladyshewsky, R.K., & Galvin, P. (2010). The influence of corporate psychopaths on corporate social responsibility and organizational
  commitment to employees, *Journal of Business Ethics, 97*(1), 1-19.

Boddy, C., Miles, D., Sanyal, C., & Hartog, M. (2015). Extreme managers, extreme workplaces: Capitalism, organizations and corporate psychopaths.
  Organization, 22(4), 530–551.

Bohlander, G.W., & Snell, S.A. (2007). *Principles of Human Resources Management, 16th Edition*. South-Western. Bologna, G.J. & Lindquist, R.J.
  (1995). *Fraud Auditing and Forensic Accounting, 2nd Edition*. NY: John Wiley & Sons.

Bologna, G.J. & Lindquist, R.J. (1995). *Fraud Auditing and Forensic Accounting: New Tools and Techniques*. N.Y:John Wiley & Sons.

Bond, C.F., & DePaulo, B.M. (2006). Accuracy of deception judgements. *Personality and Social Psychology Review, 10* (3), 214-234.

Boostrom, R. (2011). Tyco international: Leadership crisis. Daniel Funds Ethics Initiative, University of New Mexico. 1-8. Retrieved from
  https://danielsethics.mgt.unm.edu/pdf/Tyco%20Case.pdf

Boudin, M. (2008). Slain insurance investigator family speaks out, Retrieved from www.wcnc.com.

Boudin, M. (2009). Man pleads guilty to embezzlement, will plead to murder. Retrieved from www.wcnc.com/news/topstories/stories/wcnc-052109-
  mw howell_embezzlement_plea.24f90dd. html.

Bovenkerk, F. & Chakra, B.A. (2005). Terrorism and organized crime. Retrieved from https://dspace.library.uu.nl/handle/1874/11952

Braithwaite, V., Ahmed, E., & Brathwaite, J. (2008). Workplace bullying and victimization: The influence of organizational context, shame and pride.
  International Journal of Organisational Behavior, 13(2), 71-94.

Brander, J., & Varchaver, N. (2009, April 30). How Bernie did it. *Fortune Maganzine*. Retrieved from
  http://archive.fortune.com/2009/04/24/news/newsmakers/madoff.fortune/index.htm

Brewer, M.B. (1999). The psychology of prejudice: Ingroup love or outgroup hate? *Journal of Social Issues, 55*(3), 429-444.

Bricker, K. (2009). Over 10,000 dead: Is mexican drug war violence ebbing. Retrieved form http://narcosphere.narconews.com/notebook/kristin-
  bricker/2009/04/over10000-dead-mexican-drug-war-violence-ebbing.

Brickey, K. (2003). From enron to worldcom and beyond:Life and crime after sarbanes-oxley. *Washington University Law Review, 81*, 357-401.

Brief, A.P., Dietz, J., Cohen,R.R., Puch S. D., & Vaslow, J.B. (2000). Just doing business: Modern racism and obedience to authority as explanations for employment discrimination. *Organizational Behavior and Human Decision Processes, 81*(1), 72-97.

Brinkmann, P. (2011, June 20). Minkow seeks leniency in lennar case. *South Florida Business Journal*. Retrieved from http://www.bizjournals.com/southflorida/blog/2011/06/minkow-seeks-leniency-in-lennar-case.html.

Brisard, J. (2002). Terror financing. Report Prepared for the President of the Security Council of the United Nations. 1-34.

Brody, H. (2007*). Hooked: Ethics, the Medical Profession, and the Pharmeceutical Industry*. N.Y: Rowman & Littlefield Publishers Inc.

Brody, R.G. & Kiehl, K.A. (2010). From white-collar crime to red-collar crime. *Journal of Financial Crime,17*(3), 351-364.

Brody, R. G., Melendy S., & Perri, F. S. (2012). Commentary from the American Accounting Association's 2011 Annual Meeting panel on emerging issues in fraud research. *Accounting Horizons, 26*(3), 513-531.

Brody, R.G., Perri, F.S., & Van Buren, H.J. (2015). Further beyond the basic background check: predicting future unethical behavior. *Business and Society Review, 120*(4), 549-576.

Brody, R.G., & Perri, F.S. (2016). Fraud detection suicide: The dark side of white-collar crime. *Journal of Financial Crime, 23*(4), 786-797.

Brody, R.G., & Perri, F.S. (2016). Fraud detection suicide: The dark side of white-collar crime. *Journal of Financial Crime, 23*(4), 786-797.

Brody, R. G., & Kiehl, K. A. (2010). From white-collar to red-collar crime. *Journal of FinancialCrime, 17*(3), 351–364.

Brody, R.G., Melendy S., & Perri, F.S. (2012). Commentary from the American Accounting Association's 2011 Annual Meeting Panel on Emerging Issues in Fraud Research Accounting Horizons. *Accounting Horizons, 26*(3), 513-31.

Bromberg, W. (1948). *Crime of the Mind*. PA: J.P. Lippincott Company.

Bromberg, W. (1965). *Crime of the Mind*. NY: The Macmillan Company.

Brown, B.M. (1996). An examination of severe psychopathy in a female offender (Unpublished doctoral dissertation). The California School of Professional Psychology, San Diego, CA.

Brown, R.P. (2004). Vengeance is mine: Narcissism, vengeance, and the tendency to forgive, *Journal of Research in Personality, 38*, 576-584.

Brown, M.L. (2014, February 4). Former metlife employee pleads guilty in phony expense scheme. *Biz Journals*. Retrieved from https://www.bizjournals.com/boston/news/2014/02/04/metlife-banana-republic-victorias.html

Broyhill, J. (2017). State of North Carolina v. Jonathon Broyhill, No. COA16-841, Retrieved from http://caselaw.findlaw.com/nc-court-of-appeals/1868112.html

Buchard, M. (2011). Ethical dissonance and response to destructive leadership: A proposed model. *Emerging Leadership Journeys, 4*(1), 154-176.

Bucy, P., Formby, E., Raspanti, M., & Rooney, K. (2008). Why do they do it? The motives, mores and character of white collar criminals. *St. John's Law Review, 82*, 401- 571.

Burger, J., Messian, N., Patel, S., del Prado, A. and Anderson, C. (2004). What a coincidence! The effects of incidental similarity on compliance. *Personality and Social Psychology Bulletin, 30*(1), 35-43.

Burgo, J. (2015, September 14). The 5 types of toxic narcissists at work. Retrieved from http://fortune.com/2015/09/14/narcissist-work-toxic/

Burgoon, J.K., Dunbar, N., & Segrin, C. (2002). Nonverbal influence, in Dillard, J.P. and Pfau, M. (Eds), *The Persuasion Handbook: Developments in Theory and Practice*. Thousand Oaks, CA: Sage.

Burke, M. (2018, May 4). I'm not a monster. *Daily Mail*, Retrieved from http://www.dailymail.co.uk/news/article-5691695/Mother-four-leaves-19-page-suicide-letter-explaining-killed-husband-son-herself.html

Burkley, M. (2010). Is dexter a psychopath? *Psychology Today*. Retrieved from https://www.psychologytoday.com/blog/the-social-thinker/201009/is-dexter-successful-psychopath

Burton, F. & Stewart, S. (2008, November 26). *Workplace violence: Myths and mitigation*. Retrieved from https://www.stratfor.com/weekly/20081126_workplace_violence_myths_and_mitigation

Buss, D. & Chiodo, L. (1991). Narcissistic acts in everyday life. *Journal of Personality, 59*(2), 179-215.

Caba, S. (1993, August, 12). Beware of scum on stand, jury told robert b. burke's trial begins. Retrieved from *The Inquirer*.

Cale, E.M., & Lilienfeld, S.O., (2006). Psychopathy factors and risks for aggressive behavior: a test of the "threatened egotism" hypothesis. *Law and Human Behavior, 30*(1), 51-74.

Callahan, D. (2004). Why more Americans are doing wrong to get ahead. Florida: Harcourt, Inc.

Carlsson, R.H. (2011). *Case Studies: Corporations in Crisis*. Wiley.

Carmichael, D. (2018, February-March). Audit v. fraud examination: What's the real difference? *The CPA Journal*.

Carozza, R.H. (2006). An interview with bunny greenhouse, recipient of the 2006 cliff Robertson sentinel award. *Fraud Magazine*. Retrieved from http://www.acfe.com/article.aspx?id=4294967660

Carozza, D. (2007, September/October). An interview with william sanjour. *Fraud Magazine*.

Carozza, D. (2008a). These men know 'snakes in suits'. *Fraud Magazine, 22*(4), 36-43.

Carozza, D. (2008b, November/December). Sentinels we have known. *Fraud Magazine*.

Carozza, D. (2009), Chasing madoff, *Fraud Magazine, 23*(3), 36-40.

Carozza, D. (2010, September/October). Sentinel wins vindication. *Fraud Magazine*.

Carozza, D. (2012, March/April). The real cost of 'choosing truth over self': 2012 Cliff Robertson Sentinel Award Recipient Michael Woodford. *Fraud Magazine*.

Carozza, D. (2013, July). 2013 Keynote speaker: Andrew fastow. *Fraud Magazine*.

Carozza, D. (2014). Fighting a culture of fraud: An interview with dinesh thakur, ACFE's 2014 sentinel award recipient. *Fraud Magazine*.

Carozza, D. (2016, March/April). Truth revealed. *Fraud Magazine*.

Carozza, D. (2018, January/February). Small town, huge fraud, insightful documentary. *Fraud Magazine, 33*(1),40-45.

Carreyrou, J. (2018, May 21). Bad blood: Secrets and lies in a silicon valley. *The New York Times*. Retrieved from https://www.nytimes.com/2018/05/21/books/review/bad-blood-john-carreyrou.html

Carson, T. (2013, June 27). Former bishop Of trumbull church sentenced to 46 months in prison for investment fraud scheme. Retrieved from https://www.justice.gov/usao-ct/pr/former-bishop-trumbull-church-sentenced-46-months-prison-investment-fraud-scheme

Carter, C. (2011). Money manager De Chimay sentenced to three to nine years by New York Judge. *Bloomberg Ness.* Retrieved from www.bloomberg.com/news/2011-03-23/money-manager-dechimay-sentenced-to-3-to-9-years-for-fraud-1-.html#.

Carter, S.A. (2009). Hezbollah uses mexican drug routes into US. *The Washington Times*, Retrieved from www.washingtontimes.com/news/2009/mar/27/hezbollah-uses-mexican-drug-routes-into-us/print/.

Carvajal, A., Monroe, H., Pattillo, C. & Wynter, B. (2009). Ponzi schemes in the caribbean. *IMF Working Paper 09/95*, Washington, DC.

CBS. (2009). The man who figured out Madoff's scheme. Retrieved from www.cbsnews.com/stories/2009/02/27/60minutes/main4833667.shtml.

CBS, (2021, September 23). Theranos trial: Former defense secretary mattis takes stand; it was breathtaking what she was doing. Retrieved from www.cbs.com

Center for Audit Quality. (CAQ). (2010). Deterring and detecting financial reporting fraud: A platform for action. Washington, D.C.: CAQ. Retrieved from http://www.thecaq.org/Anti-FraudInitiative/CAQAnti-FraudReport.pdf

CFPT. (2008). Report to the president corporate fraud task force. Retrieved from https://www.justice.gov/archive/dag/cftf/corporate-fraud2008.pdf

CGAUSS. (2002a, July 8). Committee on Governmental Affairs United States Senate. The role of the board of directors in enron's collapse. Retrieved from https://www.gpo.gov/fdsys/pkg/CPRT-107SPRT80393/pdf/CPRT-107SPRT80393.pdf

CGAUSS. (2002b, October 7). Committee on Governmental Affairs United States Senate. Financial oversight of enron: The sec and private sector watchdogs. Retrieved from https://www.gpo.gov/fdsys/pkg/CPRT-107SPRT82147/pdf/CPRT-107SPRT82147.pdf

CGMA. (2012, January). CGMA report: Fraud risk management. *Chartered Global Management Accountants*. Retrieved from https://www.cgma.org/resources/reports/fraud-risk-management.html

Chancellor, A. S., & Graham, G. D. (2014, January). Staged crime scenes: Crime scene clues to suspect misdirection of the investigation. *Investigative Science Journal, 6*(1), 19-34.

Chandler, D.J. (2009). The perfect storm of leaders' unethical behavior: A conceptual framework. *International Journal of Leadership Studies, 5*(1), 69-93.

Chatterjee, A., & Hambrick, D. C. (2007). It's all about me: Narcissistic chief executive officers and their effects on company strategy and performance. *Administrative Science Quarterly, 52*, 351-386.

Chazan, G. (2006, September 15). Central banker is murdered in Moscow. *The Wall Street Journal.* Retrieved from

Chen, S. (2010). The role of ethical leadership versus institutional constraints: A simulation study of financial misreporting by ceos. *Journal of Business Ethics, 93*, 33-52.

Chepesiuk, R. (2007). Dangerous alliance: terrorism and organized crime. Retrieved from www.globalpolitician.com/23435-crime.

Chernow, R. (2009, March 23). Madoff and his models: Where are the snow jobs of yesteryear? *The New Yorker.* Retrieved from http://www.newyorker.com/magazine/2009/03/23/madoff-and-his-models

Chew, D.H. & Gillan, S.L. (2001). U.S. Corporate Governance. New York: Columbia University Press

Chivers, T. (2014, April 6). *Psychopaths: How to spot one.* Retrieved from http://www.telegraph.co.uk/culture/books/10737827/Psychopaths-how-can-you-spot-one.html

Choi, J.N., & Kim, M.U. (1999). The organizational application of groupthink and its limitations in organizations. *Journal of Applied Psychology, 84*(2), 297-306.

Choo, F., & Tan, K. (2007). The American dream and corporate executive fraud. *Accounting Forum, 31*(2), 203-215.

Christie, R., & Geiss, F. L. (1970). *Studies in Machiavellianism.* New York: Academic Press.

Chugani, S. (2009). Benevolent blood money: Terrorist exploitation of zakat and its complications in the war on terror. *North Carolina Journal of International Law and Commercial Regulation, XXXIV*, 601-655.

Chui, L. & Pike B. (2013). Auditors' responsibility for fraud detection: New wine in old bottles. *Journal of Forensic and Investigative Accounting, 5*(1), 204-233.

Cialdini, R.B. & Goldstein, N.J. (2004). Social influence: Compliance and conformity. *Annual Review of Psychology, 55,* 591-621.

Cialdini, R.B. (2008). *Influence.* U.S.: Pearson.

CIMA. (2008). Fraud risk management: A guide to good practice. *Chartered Institute of Management Accountant.* Retrieved from http://www.cimaglobal.com/Documents/ImportedDocuments/cid_techguide_fraud_risk_management_feb09.pdf.pdf

Cima, M.., Tonnaer, F., & Hauser, M.D. (2010). Psychopaths know right from wrong but don't care. *Social Cognitive and Affective Advance Access.* 1-9.

Cleckley, H. (1941). *The Mask of Sanity*, (1st ed.),St. Louis: Mosby.

Cleckley, H. (1988). *The Mask of Sanity.* St. Louis: Mosby.

Cleff, T., Naderer, G., & Volkert, J. (2013). Motives behind white-collar crime: Results of a quantitative and qualitative study in germany. *Society and Business Review, 8*(2), 145-159.

Cliff, G., & Desilets, C. (2014). White collar crime: What it is and where it's going. *Notre Dame Journal of Law, Ethics & Public Policy, 28*(2). 481-523.

Clinard, M.B., & Meier, R. (2010). *The Sociology of Deviant Behavior.* Belmont, CA:Wadsworth Cengage Learning.

Clinard, M.B., Yeager, P.C., Brisette, J., Petrashek, D., & Harries, E. (1979). *Illegal Corporate Behavior.* Washington, D.C.: U.S. Government Printing Office.

Clinard, M.B. & Yeager, P. (1980). *Corporate Crime.* N.Y.:The Free Press (Macmillan Publishing Company).

Coenen, T.L. (2008). *Essentials of Corporate Fraud.* N.J: John Wiley & Sons.

Cohan, J. (2002). I didn't know and I was only doing my job?: Has corporate governance areened out of control? A case study of Enron's information myopia. *Journal of Business Ethics, 40*, 275-299.

Cohen, M. (2019, February 27). *Full Transcript: Michael Cohen's Opening Statement to Congress.* The New York Times. Retrieved from https://www.nytimes.com/2019/02/27/us/politics/cohen-documents-testimony.html?smid=fb-nytimes&smtyp=cur&fbclid=IwAR283RLXWGDd8JdIHRQ_nMOy_2-EMqFDwLqkkM0VM46jBdYwXsdUQtSFW-w

Cohen, J., Ding, Y., Lesage C., & Stolwy, H. (2010). Corporate fraud and managers' behavior:evidence from the press. *Journal of Business Ethics, 95*, 271-315.

Cohen, A. K., Lindesmith, A., & Schuessler, K. (1956). *The Sutherland Papers.* Bloomington: Indiana University Press.

Cohn, M. (2012, August 20). Ex-IRS agent pleads guilty to ordering hit job on tax clients. Retrieved from
    http://www.accountingtoday.com/news/former-irs-agent-pleads-guilty-hit-job-tax-clients-63698-1.html.

Cohn, M. (2013, June 27). Former enron cfo andrew fastow confronts the fraud examiners, *Accounting Today*, Retrieved from
    http://www.accountingtoday.com/news/Former-Enron-CFO-Andrew-Fastow-Meets-Fraud-Examiners-67263-1.html

Colchester, M. (2017). Compliance officer to leave barclays. *The Wall Street Journal*. p. B11.

Coleman, D. (1990, April, 1). Managing: The dark side of charisma. *The New York Times*. Retrieved from
    http://www.nytimes.com/1990/04/01/business/managing-the-dark-side-of-charisma.html

Coleman, J. W. (1989). *The Criminal Elite: The Sociology of White-collar Crime*. NY: St. Martin's.

Coleman, J.W. (2002). *The Criminal Elite: Understanding White-collar Crime*. New York: Worth Publishers.

Coleman, E. & Bowens, D. (2008, May 19). Police: Enough evidence to file murder charge in angier woman's disappearance, retrieved from
    http://www.wral.com/news/local/story/2905513/.

Coleman, J. W., & Ramos, L. L. (1998). Subcultures and deviant behavior in the organizational context. In P. A. Bamberger and W. J. Sonnenstuhl
    (Eds.), *Research in the Sociology of Organizations: Deviance On and Of Organizations, Volume 15*. Stamford, CT: JAI Press.

Collins. (2010, March 2). USA v. Collins. Retrieved from http://vlex.com/vid/usa-v-collins-77528356.

Collins, J. (2003). Government's amended written proffer in support of its request for detention pending trial. Retrieved from
    www.investigativeproject.org/documents/case_docs/874.pdf

Commission Report of 9/11 (2004). *Commision Report of 9/11*. Retrieved from www.911commission.gov/report/911Report.pdf

Conger, J. (1990). The dark side of leadership. *Organization Dynamics, 19*(2), 44-55.

Continental Vending Case (1969). U.S. v. Simon, 425 F.2d 796 (2d. Cir. 1969).

Cooper, C. (2008). A dark cloud descending. *Fraud Magazine*. Retrieved from http://www.fraud-magazine.com/article.aspx?id=187

Cooper, C. (2009). *Extraordinary Circumstances: The Journey of a Corporate Whistleblower*. Hoboken, NJ: John Wiley & Sons.

Copes, H., Vieraitis, L.M., Cardwell, S.M., & Vasquez, A. (2013). Accounting for identity theft: The roles of lifestyle and enactment. *Journal of
    Contemporary Criminal Justice, 29*(3), 351-368.

Corkery, M. (2016, September 8). Wells fargo fined $185 million for fraudulently opening accounts. *The New York Time*. Retrieved from
    https://www.nytimes.com/2016/09/09/business/dealbook/wells-fargo-fined-for-years-of-harm-to-customers.html

COSO. (2010). Fraudulent financial reporting: 1998-2007. Retrieved from http://www.coso.org/FraudReport.htm.

Covey, S. (2006). *The Speed of Trust*. NY: Free Press.

Credit Alliance. (1985). Credit Alliance v. Arthur Andersen, 65 N.Y.2d 536, 483 N.E.2d 110.

Creswell, J. & Thomas, L. (2009, January 25). The talented mr. madoff. Available at
    http://www.nytimes.com/2009/01/25/business/25bernie.html?_r=1&pagewanted=print .

Crittenden, M.R., & Scannell, K. (2010). Report says regulators missed shots at Stanford., *The Wall Street Journal*, April 17-18, B1, B3, Retrieved
    from http://online.wsj.com/article/SB10001424052702303491304575188220570802084.html.

CRN. (2000, November 10). Joseph Nacchio, chairman and CEO, Qwest. Retrieved from http://www.crn.com/news/channel-
    programs/18811400/joseph nacchio-chairman-andceo-qwest.htm;jsessionid=Ai9FKmyZtZWD4-MZOqI3qA**.ecappj02

Croall, H. (2007a). *Understanding White-collar Crime*. Buckingham, UK: Open University Press.

Croall, H. (2007b). Victims of white collar crime and corporate crime, Retrieved from http://www.uk.sagepub.com/stout/croall_white_collar%20-
    %20vics_crim_soc.pdf.

Croall, H. (2010). Economic crime and victimology: A critical appraisal. *Journal of International Victimology, 8*(2).

Cromwell , P., & Birzer, M. L. (2011). The curious case of George: A case study of a career criminal. *Criminal Justice Review, 37*(4). 512-526.

Cruise, K.R., Colwell, L.H., Lyons, P.M., & Baker, M.D. (2003). Prototypical analysis of adolescent psychopathy: investigating the juvenile justice
    perspective. *Behavioral Sciences and the Law, 21*, 829-846.

Crumbley, D.L., Heitger, L.E., & Smith, G.S. (2011). *Forensic and Investigative Accounting, 5th Edition*. Chicago: CCH.

Cruver, B. (2003). *Enron: Anatomy of Greed*, London: Arrow Books.

Cruz, M. (2006, April 14). Woman plead guilty in highland double slaying. San Bernadino Sun. Retrieved from www.sbsun.com

CTED (2019). Identifying and exploring the nexus between human trafficking, terrorism and terrorism financing. *United Nations Security
    Council Counter-Terrorism Committee Executive Directorate*. 1-59.

Cullen, F.T., Hartman, J.L., & Jonson, C.L. (2009). Bad guy: Why the public supports punishing white collar offenders. *Criminal Law Social Change,
    51*, 31-44.

Cutler, M. (2006). Marriage fraud perpetrated by terrorists and criminals. Counterterrorism Blog. Retrieved from
    http://counterterrorismblog.org/2006/11/marriage fraud_perpetrated_by.php.

Dahling, J.J., Whitaker, B.G., & Levy., P.E. (2009). The development and validation of a new machiavellian scale. *Journal of Management, 35*, 219-
    257.

Daly, K. (1989). Gender and varieties of white collar crime, *Criminology, 27*(4), 769-793.

Daniel, L. (2005). Use personality tests legally and effectively. Retrieved from http://
    www.shrm.org/Publications/StaffingManagementMagazine/EditorialContent/Pages/0504_cover.aspx

Dattner, B. (2004). Narcissism at work. Retrieved from http://dattnerconsulting.com/presentations-files/narcissism.pdf

De Chant, T. (2021a, October, 27). $100 million theranos investor did little vetting for fear of upsetting Elizabeth holmes. www.arstechnica.com.

De Chant, T. (2021a, October, 20). Theranos devices ran null protocol to skip actual demo for investors. www.arstechnica.com.

Delhey, J., & Newton, K. (2003). Who trusts? The origins of social trust in seven societies. *European Societies, 5*(2), 93-137.

Dellaportas, S. (2013). Conversations with inmate accountants: Motivations, opportunity and the fraud triangle. *Accounting Forum, 37*, 29-39.

Demirtas, O. (2015). Ethical leadership influence at organizations: Evidence from the field. *Journal of Business Ethics, 126*, 273-284.

Den Hartog, D.N., & Belschak, F. D. (2012). Work engagement and machiavellianism in the ethical leadership process. *Journal of Business Ethics,
    107* (1), 35-47.

510

Den Nieuwenboer, N., & Kaptein, M. (2008). Spiraling down into corruption: A dynamic analysis of the social identity processes that cause corruption in organizations to grow. *Journal of Business Ethics, 83*,133–146.

DePaulo, B.M., Linday, J.L., Malone, B.E., Muhlenbruck, L., Charlton, K. & Cooper, H. (2003). Cues to deception. *Psychological Bulletin, 129*, 74-118.

Dervan, L.E. & Podgor, E.S. (2016). Investigating and prosecuting white-collar criminals. In Van Slyke, S.R.; Benson, M.L. & Cullen, F.T. (2016). \ *The Oxford Handbook of White-collar Crime.* UK: Oxford University Press.

Deutschman, A. (2005, July 1). Is your boss a psychopath? Retrieved from http://www.fastcompany.com/53247/your-boss-psychopath

Devine, T. & Maassarani, T.F. (2011). *The Corporate Whistleblowers Survival* Guide. California: Berrett-Koehler Publishers

Dhami, M. (2007). White collar prisoners' perceptions of audience reaction. *Deviant Behavior, 28,* 57-77.

Dicksee, L. (1928). *Auditing: A Practical Manual for Auditors.* London: Gee and Co.

DiGiacomo, M. (2009). Convicted murderer's early release opposed, Retrieved from http://www.delcotimey.com/article/DC/20090228/NEWS/302289987

Di Miceli da Silveira, A. (2013). The enron scandal a decade later: Lessons learned? *Homo Oeconomicus, 30*(3), 315-347.

Dodge, M. (2007). From pink to white with various shades of embezzlement: Women who commit white-collar crimes. In *International Handbook of White-collar and Crime.* Pontell, H.N. & Geis, G., 379-404. Springer.

Dodge, M. (2016). Gender construction. In *The Oxford Handbook of White-collar Crime.* Van Slyke, S.R., Benson, M.L., & Cullen, F. T. England: Oxford University Press

DOJ (Department of Justice). (2007). Fact sheet: President's corporate fraud task force marks five years of ensuring corporate integrity. Retrieved from http://www.justice.gov/opa/pr/2007/July/07_odag_507.html

Dorminey, J.W., Fleming, A.S., Kranacher, M., & Riley, R.A. (2010, July). Beyond the fraud triangle. *The CPA Journal,* 17-23.

Douglas, J. E., Burgess, A. W., Burgess, A. G., & Ressler, R. K. (1992). *Crime Classification Manual.* Lanham, MD: Lexington Books.

Duchon, D., & Burns, M. (2008). Organizational narcissism. *Organizational Dynamics, 37*(4), 354-364.

Duchon, D., & B. Drake. (2009). Organizational narcissism and virtuous behavior. *Journal of Business Ethics, 85,* 301–8.

Duffield, G., & Grabosky, P. (2001). The psychology of fraud. Trends and issues in crime and criminal justice. Canberra: *Australian Institute of Criminology, 199.*

Duhigg, C. (2009, September 13). Clean water laws are neglected, at a cost in suffereing. *New York Times.*

Duska, R., Duska, B.S., & Ragatz, J.A. (2011). *Accounting Ethics.* United Kingdom: Wiley-Blackwell

Dutcher, J.S. (2005). From the boardroom to the cellblock: The justifications for harsher punishment of white-collar and corporate crime. *Arizona State Law Journal, 37,* 1295-1319.

Eakin, C.F., Louwers, T., Wheeler, S. (2009). The role of the auditor in managing public disclosures: Potentially misleading information in documents containing audited financial statements. *Journal of Forensic and Investigative Accounting. 1*(2). 1-22.

Eaton, T.V., & Korach, S. (2016). A criminological profile of white-collar crime. *The Journal of Applied Business Research, 32*(1), 129-142.

Economist. (2004, March 4). Bernie's turn. *The Economist.* Retrieved from http://www.economist.com/node/2481701.

Economist, (January 28, 2012). Fleecing the flock. *The Economist.* Retrieved from http://www.economist.com/node/21543526

Egan, M.(2016a, October 25). Wells fargo workers describe mental health nightmares. *CNN Money.* Retrieved from http://money.cnn.com/2016/10/25/investing/wells-fargo-workers-mental-health-nightmares/index.html

Egan, M. (2016b, September 9). Workers tell Wells Fargo horror stories *CNN Money.* Retrieved from http://money.cnn.com/2016/09/09/investing/wells-fargo-phony-accounts-culture/index.html

Egan, M. & Isidore C. (2016, September 22). Wells fargo CEO denies orchestrated fraud in accounts scandal. *CNN Money.* Retrieved from http://money.cnn.com/2016/09/20/news/companies/wells-fargo-ceo-apology/index.html

Ehrenfeld, R. (1990). *Narco-Terrorism.* Basic Books: New York, NY.

Eichenwald, (2005, December, 29). Enron figure may testify,but what will he say? *The New York Times.* Retrieved from https://www.nytimes.com/2005/12/29/business/enron-figure-may-testifybut-what-will-he-say.html

Einarsen, S., Aasland M.S., & Skogstad, A. (2007). Destructive leadership behavior: A definition and conceptual model. *The Leadership Quarterly,18,* 207-216.

Eisenbraun, G. A. (2006). The pros and cons of personality testing in the workplace. Retrieved from http://www.thefreelibrary.com/The+pros+and+cons+of+personality+testing+in+the+workplace.-a0160104861

Elbien, S. (2014). When employees confess, sometimes falsely. *The New York Times,* Retrieved from http://www.nytimes.com/2014/03/09/business/when-employees-confess-sometimes-falsely.html?_r=0

Elderidge, T. (2004). *9/11 and Terrorists Travel: Staff Report of the National Commission onTerrorist Attacks upon the United States.* Retrieved from www.9-11commission.gov/staff_statements/911_TerrTrav_FM.pdf.

Elliott, J. (2010, April 19). Report finds catastrophic failure by the SEC in Stanford Ponzi scheme. Retrieved from http://tpmmuckraker.talkingpointsmemo.com/2010/04/report_sec_failed_massively_in_stanford_alleged_po.php.

Emerson, S. (2002). Fund raising methods and procedures for international terroristOrganizations. Retrieved from www.au.af.mil/au/awc/awcgate/congress/021202se.pdf.

Engel, K.C. and McCoy, P.A. (2011). *The Subprime Virus: Reckless Credit, Regulatory Failure, and Next Steps.* Oxford University Press: Oxford.

Ewens, S., Vrij, A., Jang, M., & Jo, E. (2014). Drop the small talk when establishing baseline behavior in interviewers. *Journal of Investigative Psychology and Offender Profiling, 11,* 244-252.

Fairfax, L.M. (2002-2003). The thin line between love and hate: why affinity-based securities and investment fraud constitutes a hate crime. *U.C. Davis Law Review, 36,* 1073-1143.

Fairfax, L.M. (2010, March 24). Madoff and affinity fraud. Retrieved from www. concurringopinions.com/archives/author/lisa-fairfax.

Farah, D. (2005). The new york book review of the quartermasters of terror. Retrieved from www.patrickraddenkeefe.com/articles/media/NYRB_20050210.pdf.

Farber, D. B. (2005). Restoring trust after fraud: Does corporate governance matter? *The Accounting Review, 80*(2), 539-561.

Farrell, G. (2006). *Corporate Crooks. How Rogue Executives Ripped Off America.* New York: Prometheus Books.

FATF. (2008). Terrorist financing. Retrieved from www.fatf-gafi.org/dataoecd/28/43/40285899.pdf.

FATF (2018, October). *International Standards on Combating Money Laundering and the Financing of Terrorism & Proliferation.* Retrieved from https://www.fatf-gafi.org/media/fatf/documents/recommendations/pdfs/FATF%20Recommendations%202012.pdf

Feeley, D. (2006). Personality, environment, and the causes of white-collar crime. *Law and Psychology Review, 30*(1), 201-213.

Fenton-O'Creevy, M. (2005, November 10). The psychology of deception. Open2.net.

Fersch, E. L. (2006). *Thinking About Psychopaths and Psychopathy.* New York: iUniverse, Inc.

Ferrell, O.C., & Ferrell, L. (2011). The responsibility and accountability of CEOs: The last interview with ken lay. *Journal of Business Ethics, 100*, 209-219.

Ferrell, O.C., Fraedrich, J., & Ferrell, L. (2013). *Business Ethics, Ninth Edition.* U.S.: South-Western.

Fins, A. (2017, January 11). Ex-tyco ceo who served time in prison returns to boca raton. *Palm Beach Post.* Retrieved from http://realtime.blog.palmbeachpost.com/2017/01/11/ex-tyco-ceo-who-served-time-in-prison-returns-to-boca-raton/

Finn, D.W. (2015). Discussant comment on the influence of regulatory approach on tone at the top. *Journal of Business Ethics, 126*, 39-42.

Fisher, D. R., & Nobile, R. J. (n.d). Employee selection: Best practices for reducing legal risk in pre-hire assessments. Retrieved from http://podiaconsulting.com/pdfs/legal_selection_paper_f.pdf

Fishman, S. (2010, June 6). Bernie madoff, free at last. *The New Yorker.* Retrieved from http://nymag.com/news/crimelaw/66468/

Fishman, S. (2011, February 27). The madoff, tapes. *New York Magazine.* Retrieved from http://nymag.com/news/features/berniemadoff-2011-3/

Fitzsimons, E. (2006, April, 19). Wrongly accused in theft, worker awarded millions. SignonSan *Diego.Com.* Retrieved from http://www.sandiegouniontribune.com/uniontrib/20060419/news_1n19autozone.html

Flood, M. (2006, March 7). Fastow testifies about his role in Enron's demise. Retrieved from http://www.chron.com/business/enron/article/Fastow-testifies-about-his-role-in-Enron-s-demise-1856558.php.

Foley, S. (2008, December 31). So where's the money, bernie. *The Independent.* Retrieved from www.independent.co.uk/news/world/americas/madoff-so-wheres-the-money-bernie-1218247.html

Follingstad, D.R., Polek, D.S., Hause, E.S.,Deaton, L.H., Bulger, M.W., & Conway, Z.D. (1989). Factors predicting verdicts in cases where battered women kill their husbands. *Law and Human Behavior, 13*(3), 253-269.

Forbes, W., & Watson, R. (n.d.). Destructive leadership and board loyalty: A case study of michael eisner's long tenure at disney corporation. Retrieved from https://www.cass.city.ac.uk/__data/assets/pdf_file/0005/56372/2A_Forbes.pdf

Ford, M.A. (2008). White-collar crime, social harm, and punishment: A critique and modification of the sixth circuits ruling in united states v. davis. *St. Johns Law Review 82*(1), 383-399

Fordham, C. (2013). Knowing your third party: Asia-pacific fraud survey. Retrieved from http://www.ey.com/Publication/vwLUAssets/EY-Knowing-your-third-party/$FILE/EY-Knowing-your-third-party.pdf

Fox, J. (2008, December 12). Hanging with bernard madoff (it wasn't memorable). Retrieved from http://curiouscapitalist.blogs.time.com/2008/12/12/hanging-with-bernard-madoff-it-wasntmemorable/

Frankel, T. (2012). *The Ponzi Scheme Puzzle: A History and Analysis of Con Artists and Victims.* New York: Oxford University Press.

Frean, A. (2010). SEC suspected Allen Standford of Ponzi scheme a decade ago, report says. Business Times. Retrieved from http://business.timesonline.co.uk/tol/business/industry_sectors/banking_and_finance/article7103091.ece.

Free, C., & Murphy, P.R. (2015). The ties that bind: The decision to co-offend in fraud. *Contemporary Accounting Research, 32*(1), 18-54

Free, C., Stein, M., & Macintosh, N. (July/August, 2007). Management controls: The organizational fraud triangle of leadership, culture and control in enron. *Ivey Business Journal.* Retrieved from http://iveybusinessjournal.com/publication/management-controls-the-organizational-fraud-triangle-of-leadership-culture-and-control-in-enron/

Freiberg, A. (2000, August). Sentencing white collar criminals. *Australian Insitute of Criminology*, Retrieved from http://www.aic.gov.au/events/aic%20upcoming%20events/2000/~/media/conferences/fraud/freiberg.ashx.

Fried, J. (1996, November 2). Michael Burnett, 67, criminal who exposed city corruption. *The New York Times,* Retrieved from http://www.nytimes.com/1996/11/02/nyregion/michael-burnett-67-criminal-who-exposed-city-corruption.html

Friedrichs, D. O. (2007). *Trusted Criminals: White Collar crime in Contemporary Society* (3rd ed.).Belmont, CA: Thomson Wadsworth.

Furnham, A., Richards, S.C., & Paulhus, D.L. (2013). The dark triad of personality: A 10 year review. *Social and Personlity Psychology Compass, 7*(3), 199-216.

Fuse, T. (2017, November 4). Scandal-hit Kobe Steel has a 'look the other way' culture, they say in hometown. *Reuters.* Retrieved from https://www.reuters.com/article/us-kobe-steel-scandal-hometown/scandal-hit-kobe-steel-has-a-look-the-other-way-culture-they-say-in-hometown-idUSKBN1D5011

Gabbay, Z. D. (2007). Exploring the limits of the restorative justice paradigm: restorative justice and white-collar crime. *Cardozo Journal of Conflict Resolutions, 8*, 421-485

Gacono, C. B., & Meloy, J. R. (2012). *The rorhschach assessment of aggressive and psychopathic personalities.* NY: Routledge, Taylor & Francis Group.

Gaede, D. (2007). State of North Dakota v. Dennis James Gaede 2007 ND 125, 736 N.W.2d 418.

Gaetano, C. (2012, March). Reformed fraudster reveals tricks of the trade. *The Trusted Professional.* p. 8. Retrieved from http://www.nysscpa.org/docs/default-source/trusted-professional-archives/3-march-tp---2012.pdf?sfvrsn=4

Gao, J., Greenberg, R., Wing, B. (2015). Whistleblowing intentions of lower-level employees: The effect of reporting channel, bystanders, and wrongdoer power status. *Journal of Business Ethics, 126*, 85-99.

Gao, Y., & Raine, A. (2010). Successful and unsuccessful psychopaths: A neurobiological model. *Behavioral Science and the Law, 28*, 194-210.

Gartenstein, D. & Dabruzzi, K. (2007, March 26). The convergence of crime and terror: Law enforcement opportunities and perils. *Center for Policing Terrorism*, New York, NY, Retrieved from www.rieas.gr/index.php?option¼com_content&view¼article&id¼707& catid¼21&Itemid¼63.

Gaylord, M., & Galliher, J. (1988). *The Criminology of Edwin Sutherland*. USA: Transaction Books.

Gearty, R. (1998, July 31). Mom, son convicted in slaying. *New York Daily News*. Retrieved from
    http://www.nydailynews.com/archives/boroughs/mom- son-convicted-slaying-article-1.819865

Geary, J. (2009, March 5). Nowak gets 30 years in murder for hire plot. Retrieved from
    http://www.theledger.com/article/20090305/NEWS/903050242.

Geberth, V. J. (2013, January). The seven major mistakes in suicide investigation. *Law and Order Magazine, 61*(1) 64-67.

Gedalyahu, T. (2009). Hizbullah's mexican-us drug connection. Retrieved fromwww.freerepublic.com/focus/f-news/2217940/posts.

Geier. (2002, June). *MD businessman pleads guilty to murder for hire*. Retrieved from http://thedailyrecord.com/.

Geis, G. (1968). The heavy electrical equipment antitrust case of 1961, in *White-Collar Criminal,* New York, Atherton

Geis, G. (1995). The heavy electrical equipment anti-trust case of 1961. In Geis, G. Meier, R., & Salinger, L. (eds.), *White Collar Crime*, New York:
    Free Press, 151-165.

Gendar, A. (2009, October, 30). Bernie madoff baffled by sec blunders; compares agency's bumbling actions to Lt. Colombo. *The New York Daily
    News*. Retreived from http://www.nydailynews.com/news/crime/bernie-madoff-baffled-sec-blunders-compares-
    agency-bumbling-actions-lt-colombo-article-1.382446

Gentry, W.A., Cullen, K.L., & Altman, D.G. (2012). The irony of integrity. *Center for Creative Leadership*. 1-21. Retrieved from
    http://insights.ccl.org/wp content/uploads/2015/04/IronyOfIntegrity.pdf

Georgiou, A. (2010, June 14). Skilling speaks: Enron CEO's jailhouse interview.
    Retrieved from http://money.cnn.com/2010/06/14/news/newsmakers/jeffrey_skilling_prison_interview.fortune/index.htm

Gilbert, C.B. (2009, June, 29). Bernie madoff's sentence: Is 150 years for white collar fraud justice or overkill? Retrieved from
    http://www.associatedcontent.com/article/1892592/bernie_madoffs_sentencing_is_150_years.html?cat=3.

Gilbert, J.A., Carr-Ruffino, N., Ivancevich, J.M., & Konopaske, R. (2012). Toxic versus cooperative behaviors at work: The role of organizational
    culture and leadership in creating community centered organizations. *International Journal of Leadership Studies, 7*(1), 29-47.

Gino, F., & Bazerman, M.H. (2009). When misconduct goes unnoticed: The acceptability of gradual erosion in others' unethical behavior. *Journal of
    Experimental Social Psychology, 45,*707-719.

Gitlin, J.M. (2018, July 15). The downfall of Theranos, from the journalist who made it happen**. *ARS Technica***. Retrieved from
    https://arstechnica.com/science/2018/07/the-downfall-of-theranos-from-the-journalist-who-made-it-happen/

Glad, B. (2002). Why tyrants go too far: Malignant narcissism and absolute power. *Political Psychology, 23,*1-37.

Glover, S.M., & Prawitt, D.F. (2012, March). Enhancing board oversight. COSO. 1-20.
    Retrieved from http://www.coso.org/documents/coso-enhancingboardoversight_r8_web-ready%20(2).pdf

Gnau, T. (2013, June 4). Peppel sentenced to two years. Retrieved from http://www.daytondailynews.com/news/business/peppel-sentenced-to-two-
    years/nYBjM/

Gobert, J. & Punch, M. (2007). Because they can. In *International Handbook of White-collar and Corporate Crime*. Pontell, H.N. & Geis, G., New
    York: Springer.

Golding, B., & Fermino, J. (2011). Celeb ponzi schemer kenneth starr sentenced to 71 2 years in prison. Retrieved from
    www.nypost.com/p/news/local/manhattan/fallen_starr_is_forlorn_Bwj1FnXA1Wbk9TlXMlA3TP.

Goldstein, M. (2011a). FBI behavior analysts apply serial killer profiling to white collar
    crime. *Huffington Post*. Retrieved from http://www.huffingtonpost.com/2011/04/20/fbi-white-collar-serial-killers_n_851479.htm

Goldstein, M. (2011b). From Hannibal Lector to Bernie Madoff. *Reuters*. Retrieved from http://www. reuters.com/article/2011/04/20/us-profiling-
    whitecollarcrime-idUSTRE73J2W920110420

Goldstraw, J.E. (2005). Fiddling with accounts: How white-collar offenders account for their actions. Ph.d Dissertation, Department of Criminology,
    Keele University.

Goldfarb, Z. (2010a). At SEC, the system can be deaf to whistle blowing. *The Washingotn Post*. Retrieved from
    www.washingtonpost.com/wpdyn/content/article/2010/01/20/AR2010012005125.html.

Goldfarb, Z. (2010b). SEC inspector raises red flags in new report. *The Washington Post*.
    Retrieved from www.washingtonpost.com/wpdyn/content/article/2010/03/22/AR2010032203820.html .

Golz, J. (2008a, February 20). Hanson found guilty of killing four family members.
    Chicago Sun-Times. Retrieved from http://www.suntimes.com/news/ metro/805558,hansonguilty022008.article

Golz, J. (2008b, February 27). Jury hears Hanson's troubled past. *Chicago Sun-Times*.

Golz, J. (2008c, February 17). Defendant takes the stand, admits to financial problems. *Chicago Sun-Times*.

Golz, J. (2008d, January 13). Suspect charged in killing of four family members. *Chicago Sun-Times*.

Golz, J. (2008e, February 8). Accused killer charged $80,000 on mom's cards. *Chicago Sun-Times*. Retrieved from
    http://www.suburbanchicagonews.com/beaconnews/news/783503,2_1_AU08_HANSON_S1.article

Gomez, J. (2010). A financial profile of the terrorism of al-qaeda and its affiliates. *Perspectives on Terrorism, 4*(4), 3-27.

Goodman, M. (2010, April 15). The embezzler next door. Retrieved from http://abcnews.go.com/Business/white-collar-crime-fraudsters-embezzlers-
    family-friends-neighbors/story?id=10378038

Gornall, W. (2010). Financial fraud: a game of cat and mouse. Retrieved from http://uwspace.uwaterloo.ca/bitstream/10012/5261/1/gornall-will-
    masters-thesis-final.pdf.

Gottfredson, M.R. & Hirschi, T. (1990). *A General Theory of Crime*. Stanford University Press.

Gottschalk, P., & Gunnesdal, L. (2018). White-collar crime in the schadow economy. Palgave Macmillan.

Granhag, W., & Stromwall, L.A. (1999). Repeated interrogations—stretching the deception detection paradigm. *Expert Evidence,7*, 163-174.

Granhag, P.A., Andersson, L.O., Stromwall, L.A., & Hartwig, M. (2004). Imprisoned knowledge: Criminals' beliefs about deception. *Legal and
    Criminological Psychology, 9*, 103-119.

513

Granhag, P.A. & Stromwall, L.A. (2002). Repeated interrogations: Verbal and non-verbal cues to deception. *Applied Cognitive Psychology,16*, 243-257.

Granhag, P.A. & Stromwall, L.A., & Hartwig, M. (2007, January). The sue technique: The way to interview to detect deception. *Forensic Update, 88*, 25-29.

Granhag, P.A., Vrij, A., & Verschuere, B. (2015). *Detecting Deception*. England: John Wiley and Sons.

Grant, P., & McGhee, P. (2012). Organisational narcissism: A case of failed corporate governance. *Issues in Business Ethics, 38*, 97-109.

Green, G. (1990). *Occupational crime*. IL: Nelson-Hall Publishers.

Green, S.P. (2004). Moral ambiguity in white collar criminal law. *Notre Dame Journal of Law,Ethics and Public Policy, 18*, 501-519.

Green, S. P. (2007). The concept o white-collar crime in law and legal theory. *Buffalo Criminal Law Review, 8*(1), 1-34.

Green, S. P., & Kugler, M.B. (2012). Public perceptions of white collar crime culpability: Bribery, perjury, and fraud. *Law and Contemporary Problems, 74*(4), 33-59.

Greeve, H.R. & Palmer, D., & Pozner, J. (2010). Organizations gone wild: The causes, processes and consequences of organizational misconduct. *The Academy of Management Annals. 4*(1), 53-107.

Gregory, T. (2008a, January 14). Jury selection to begin for 2005 quadruple killing. *Chicago Tribune*. Retrieved from http://www.chicagotribune.com/news/chi-hanson_monjan14,1,6222654. story

Gregory, T. (2008b, February 6). Sister of slaying victim testifies about phone calls, threat at brother's murder trial. *Chicago Tribune*. Retrieved from http://www.chicagotribune.com/ news/local/chi-hanson-trial_webfeb06,1,1324846.story

Gregory, T., & Barnum, A. (2008, February 27). Jury in Eric Hanson murder case begins sentencing deliberations. *Chicago Tribune*. Retrieved from http://www.chicagotribune. com/news.local/chi-hanson_web.28feb28,1,7387409. story?track=rss.

Gregory, T., & Barnum, A. (2009, November 6). Brian dugan's brain the subject of sentencing hearing. *Chicago Tribune*. Retrieved from, http://articles.chicagotribune.com/2009-11-06/news/0911050936_1_functional-magnetic-resonance-imaging-sentencing-hearing-fmri

Greisling, D. (2002, March 4). On Andersen the bad apple argument rots. *The Chicago Tribune* Retrieved from http://articles.chicagotribune.com/2002-09-04/business/0209040248_1_arthur-andersen-llp-hubris-auditors

Grondahl, P. (2006, Aug. 13). Porco labeled a psycho killer. *Times Union*. Retrieved from http://www.timesunion.com/AspStories/story.asp?storyID=508011&category=PORCO&BCCode=&newsdate=9/9/2009

Gruner, R.S. (2007). Preventive fault and corporate criminal liability: Transforming corporate organizations into private policing entities. In *International Handbook of White-collar and Crime*. Pontell, H.N. & Geis, G., 279-306. Springer.

Gudmundsson, A., & Southey, G. (2011). Leadership and the rise of the corporate psychopath: What can business schools do about the "snakes inside"? e-*Journal of Social and Behavioral Research in Business, 2*(2), 18-27.

Gunn, J., and Wells, R. (1999).The antisocial personality disorder: strategies for psychotherapy. Chapter 18. *In Forensic Psychotherapy: Crime, Psychodynamics and the Offender Patient*. Philadelphia, PA: Jessica Kingsley Publishers.

Gustafson, J.L. (2007). Cracking down on white collar crime: An analysis of the recent trend of severe sentences for corporate officers, *Suffolk University Law Review, XL*(3), 865-701.

Gutowski, C. (2005, October 2). Fireplace poker could be cru- cial piece of puzzle. *Daily Herald*. Retrieved from http://www.dailyherald.com/story/?id=114677

Gutowski, C. (2008a, January 11). After more than two years, Naperville murder trial set to begin. *Daily Herald*. Retrieved from http://www.dailyherald.com/story/print/?id=111080

Gutowski, C. (2008b, February 27). Fate of killer hangs in balance. *Daily Herald*. Retrieved from http://www.dailyherald.com/story/?id=142858

Gutowski, C. (2008c, February 27). Hanson sentenced to death for murder of 4 family members. *Daily Herald*. Retrieved from http://www.dailyherald. com/story/?id=143146

Gutowski, C. (2008d, January 27). How authorities came to charge Eric Hanson with hisfamily's murder. Retrieved from http://www.dailyherald com/story/?id=122232

Gutowski, C. (2008e, February 16). Hanson denies killings. *Daily Herald*. Retrieved from http://www.dailyherald.com/story/?id=136276

Gutowski, C. (2008f, January 28). Eric hanson: "All I know is, I didn't do it." *Daily Herald*. Retrieved June 17, 2008, from http://www.dailyherald.com/ story/?id=122754

Haberman, C. (2009, July 3). Is 150 years appropriate or just silly, Retrieved from http://www.nytimes.com/2009/07/03/nyregion/03nyc.html.

Haddad, C., Weintraub, A., & Grow, B. (2003, April 14). Too good to be true: Why healthsouth ceo scrushy began deep-frying the chain's books. *Business Week*, p. 70.

Hakkanen-Nyholm, H., & Hare, R. D. (2009). Psychopathy, homicide and the courts: Working the system. *Criminal Justice and Behavior, 36*(8), 761–777.

Ham, C., Lang, M., Seybert, N., & Wang, S. (2017). CFO narcissism and financial reporting quality. *Journal of Accounting Research, 55*(5), 1089-1135.

Hamilton, S. (2008, June). Who controls the ceo? Retrieved from https://www.imd.org/uupload/IMD.WebSite/BoardCenter/Web/129/A%20PRACTICAL%20PERSPECTIVE%20WHO%20CONTROLS%20THE%20CEO.pdf

Haney, R. (1989). 2 former regina officers plead guilty to fraud charges. *The New York Times*. Retrieved from https://www.nytimes.com/1989/02/09/business/2-former-regina-officers-plead-guilty-to-fraud-charges.html

Hanlon, R. (2010, October, 19). Correspondence and interview with Dr. Robert Hanlon.

Hanson, E. (2010). *State of Illinois v. Eric Hanson*, 238 Ill. 2d 74, 939 N.E.2d 238.

Hare, R. (1991). *The Hare Psychopathy Checklist: Revised Manual*. Canada: Multi-Health Systems, Inc.

Hare, R. (1999). *Without conscience: The disturbing world of the psychopaths among us*. New York, NY: Simon & Schuster.

Harms, P.D., & Spain, S.M. (2015). Beyond the bright side: Dark personality at work. *Applied Psychology, 64*(1), 15-24.

Harris, P. (2010). Machiavelli and the global compass: Ends and means in ethics and leadership. *Journal of Business Ethics, 93*, 131-138.

Hart, S. D., & Dempster, R. J. (1997). Impulsivity and psychopathy. In C. D. Webster, & M. A. Jackson, *Impulsivity*. NY: The Guilford Press

Hartwig, M., Granhag, P.A., Stromwall, L.A., & Andersson, L.O. (2004). Suspicious minds: Criminals' ability to detect deception. *Psychology, Crime and Law, 10*(1). 83-95.

Hartwig, M., Granhag, P.A., Stromwall, L.A., & Kronkvist, O. (2006). Strategic use of evidence during police interviews: When training to detect deception works. *Law and Human Behavior, 30*, 603-619.

Harvey, M., Treadway, D., Heames, J.T., & Duke, A. (2008). Bullying in the 21st century global organization: An ethical perspective. *Journal of Business Ethics, 85*, 27-40.

Hasnas, J. (2005). Ethics and the problem of white collar crime. *American University Law School, 54*, 579-660.

Hass, S., Burnaby, P., & Nakashima, M. (2018). Toshiba corporation—how could so much be so wrong? *Journal of Forensic and Investigative Accounting, 10*(2), 267-280.

Haugh, T. (2014). Sentencing the why of white-collar crime. *Fordham Law School, 82*(6), 3143-3188.

Hayes, K.E. (2009). Analyzing and managing deviant organizational leaders. University of Pennsylvania. *Organizational Dynamica Program*. 1-41.

Heath, J. (2008). Business ethics and moral motivation: A criminological perspective. *Journal of Business Ethics, 83*, 595-614.

Heide, K., & Petee, T. (2007, November). Parricide, an empirical analysis of 24 years of U.S. data. *Journal of Interpersonal Violence, 22*, 1382–1399.

Helm, J. & Mietzite, E. (2011). Company bosses committing more fraud. Retrieved from http://www.kpmg.com/LV/en/IssuesAndInsights/ArticlesPublications/Press-releases/Documents/Press_Release_Fraud_EN.pdf.

Helman, G.B. & Ratner, S.R. (2010). Saving failed states. Retrieved from www.foreignpolicy.com/articles/2010/06/21/saving_failed_states?print¼yes&hidecomments¼yes&page¼ full.

Henning, P.J. (2010a, March 24). How not to run an SEC investigation. Retrieved from http://dealbook.blogs.nytimes.com/2010/03/24/how-not-to-run-an-s-e-c-investigation/.

Henning P.J. (2010b, April 12). Sentences get harsher in white-collar cases, Retrievable from http://dealbook.blogs.nytimes.com/2010/04/12/sentences-get-harsher-in-white-collar-cases/.

Henning, P.J. (2014, September 29). Eric holder's mixed legacy on white-collar crime. *New York Times*. Retrieved from https://dealbook.nytimes.com/2014/09/29/eric-holders-mixed-legacy-on-white-collar-crime/

Henriques, D. (2008a). Madoff scheme kept rippling outward, across borders. Retrieved from http://www.adviser.com.au/site/DefaultSite/filesystem/documents/financial_updates/BernieMadoffhistory-22December2008.pdf

Henriques, D. (2008b). *The Wizard of Lies*. NY: St. Martin's Griffin.

Henriques, D. (2011, February 15). From prison, madoff says banks 'had to know' of fraud. *The New York Times*. Retrieved from http://www.nytimes.com/2011/02/16/business/madoff-prison-interview.html

Henry, E., Gordon, E.A., Reed, B., & Louwers, T. (2007). The role of related party transactions in fraudulent financial reporting. Retrieved from https://papers.ssrn.com/sol3/papers.cfm?abstract_id=993532&download=yes

Henry, S., & Lanier, M.M. (2001). *What is Crime*. Rowman & Littlefield Publishers: Boston.

Hercz, R. (2001). Psychopaths among us. *Saturday Night Magazine*. Retrieved from https://therearenosunglasses.wordpress.com/2011/09/03/

Hermanson, H.M. & Rama, D. B. (2016). Pressure on internal auditors to alter findings. *Journal of Forensic and Investigative Accounting, 8*(3), 428-443.

Herve H. (2003). The masks of sanity: A cluster analytical investigation of subtypes of criminal psychopathy. Retrieved from https://open.library.ubc.ca/cIRcle/collections/ubctheses/831/items/1.0099730

Herve, H., & Yuille, J. (2007). *The Psychopath*. Lawrence Erlbaum Associates.

Hesterman, J.L. (2013). *The Terrorist-Criminal Nexus*. London: CRC Press.

Heylar, (2003, July 7). The insatiable king richard. Retrieved from http://archive.fortune.com/magazines/fortune/fortune_archive/2003/07/07/345534/index.htm.

Hicks, B.M., Vaidyanathan, U., & Patrick, C.J. (2010). Validating female psychopathic subtypes: Differences in personality, antisocial and violent behavior, substance abuse, trauma and mental health. *Personality Disorder, 1*(1), 38-57.

Hill, J. (2007, April 4). Fire chief enters not guilty. Retrieved from https://ssristories.org/fire-chief-pleads-not-guilty-in-murder-for-hire-case/

Hirsch, A. (2014). Going to the source: The "new" reid method and false confessions. *Ohio State Journal of Criminal Law, 11*(2), 803-826.

Hobbs, D. & Wright, R. (2006). The sage handbook on fieldwork. CA: Sage Publications.

Hobson, J.L., Mayew, W.J., Peecher, M., Venkatachalam, M. (2017). Improving experienced auditors' detection of deception in ceo narratives. *Journal of Accounting Research, 55*(5), 1137-1166.

Hogan, R. (1994, Winter). Trouble at the Top: Causes and Consequences of Managerial Incompetence. *Consulting Psychology Journal, 46*(1), 9-15.

Hogan, R., & Hogan, J. (2001). Assessing leadership: A view from the dark side. *International Journal of Assessment and Selection, 9*, 40-51.

Hogan, R., & Kaiser, R. (2005). What we know about leadership. *Review of General Psychology, 9*(2), 169-180.

Hogan, C. E., Rezaee, Z., Riley, R. A., & Velury, U. K. (2008). Financial statement fraud: Insights from the academic literature. *Auditing: A Journal of Practice and Theory, 27*(2), 231-252.

Holder, E. (2014, September 14). Attorney general holder remarks on financial fraud prosecutions at NYU school of law. The United States Department of Justice. Retrieved from https://www.justice.gov/opa/speech/attorney-general-holder-remarks-financial-fraud-prosecutions-nyu-school-law

Hollinger, R., & Clark, J. (1983). *Theft by Employees*. Lexington, MA:Heath.

Holtfreter, K. (2005). Is occupational fraud typical white collar crime? A comparison of individual and organizational characteristics. *Journal of Criminal Justice,33*, 353-365.

Holtfreter, K., van Slyke, S., Bratton, J., & Gertz, M (2008). Public perceptions of white-collar crime and punishment. *Journal of Criminal Justice, 36*, 50-60.

Horowitz, S. (2004, June 8). Cigarette smuggling linked to terrorism. *Washington Post*. Retrieved from www.washingtonpost.com/wp-dyn/articles/A23384-2004Jun7.html.

Horowitz, M.J. & Arthur, R.J. (1988). Narcissistic rage in leaders: The intersection of individual dynamics and group processes. *The International Journal of Social Psychiatry, 34*, 135-141.

Howard, A. (2011). Groupthink and corporate governance reform: Changing the formal and informal decision making process of corporate boards. *Southern California Interdisciplinary Law Journal, 20,* 425-457.

Howe, J., Falkenbach, D., & Massey, C. (2014). The relationship among psychopathy, emotional intelligence, and professional success in finance. *International Journal of Forensic Mental Health, 13,* 337-347.

Hoyk, R. & Hersey, P. (2008). *The Ethical Executive*. California: Stanford University Press

Huck, P. (2008, April 12). Hit-and-run grans shock hollywood, Retrieved from http://www.journal-isted.com/peter-huck.

Hulsted, C. (2010, May 22-25). Organi-cultural deviane. *Administrative Sciences Association of Canada Social Responsibility Business Ethics,* 1-12.

ICE. (2009, December 9). Valley man admits soliciting murder of informant helping investigators in bank fraud investigation. Retrieved from https://www.justice.gov/archive/usao/cac/Pressroom/pr2009/142.html

Imoniana, J. O., & Murcia, F. D. (2016). Patterns of similarity of corporate Frauds. *The Qualitative Report, 21*(1), 143-162.

Inbau, F.E., Reid, J.E., Buckley, J.P., & Jayne, B.C. (2001). *Criminal Interrogation and Confessions, 5th ed.* Maryland: Aspen Publishers.

Inbau, F.E., Reid, J.E., Buckley, J.P., & Jayne, B.C. (2013). *Criminal Interrogation and Confessions, 5th ed.* Maryland: Aspen Publishers.

Issa, D. (2010, May 18). *The SEC: Designed for Failure*. Retrieved from http://republicans.oversight.house.gov/images/stories/Reports/20100518SECreport.pdf.

Jack, D.C. (1999). *Behind the mask: destruction and creativity in women's aggression*. Boston:Harvard University Press.

Jacka, M. (2004). An environment for fraud: with jail not yet a distant memory, Walter Pavlo recounts the decisions that led him to hide MCI's bad-debt expenses and embezzle millions. *Internal Auditor, 49.*

Jackson, B. (2012, January 4). Bernard Madoff: The inside story. Retrieved from http://www.princetoninfo.com/index.php?option=com_us1more&Itemid=6&key=01-04-2012_madoff

Jackson, H.E.(2017). One take on the report of the independent directors of wells fargo:vote the bums out. *Harvard Law School Forum on Corporate Governance and Financial Regulation*. Retrieved from https://corpgov.law.harvard.edu/2017/04/22/one-take-on-the-report-of-the-independent-directors-of-wells-fargo-vote-the-bums-out/

Jackson, S. (2021a, November 5). Elizabeth holmes trial week 9 recap: The Kissinger connection and former lab co-director cites lack of clarity. www.yahoo.com.

Jackson, S. (2021b, October 8). Elizabeth holmes trial week 5 recap: A juror leaves over punishment beliefs and former safeway ceo steven burd describes an unusual deal. www.yahoo.com.

Jackson, S. (2021c, October 15). Elizabeth holmes trial week 6 recap. www.yahoo.com.

Jamison, P. (2014, May 14). Avila killer at center of securities fraud scandal. *Tampa Bay News.* Retrieved from http://www.tampabay.com/news/publicsafety/crime/avila-killer-at-center-of-securities-fraud-scandal/2179772

Janis, I. (1982). *Groupthink: Psychological Studies of Policy and Fiascos* (2nd ed.). Boston, MA: Houghton Mifflin.

Javor, I., & Jancsics, D. (2013). The role of power in organizational corruption: An empirical study. *Administration and Society*. Retrieved from http://aas.sagepub.com/content/early/2013/12/10/0095399713514845.abstract

Jenco, M. (2013, September 27). Dixon blames phony invoices, lax auditors for $54M fraud. *Chicago Tribune*. Retrieved from http://articles.chicagotribune.com/2013-09-27/news/chi-attorneys-how-dixon-auditors-missed-54-million-fraud-20130926_1_treasurer-rita-crundwell-auditors-cliftonlarsonallen

Jennings, M. M. (2004). Preventing organizational ethical collapse. *Journal of Government Financial Management, 53*(1), 12-19.

Jennings, M. (2006). *The Seven Signs of Ethical Collapse.* New York, NY: St. Martin's Press.

Jennings, M. (2007). The seven signs of ethical collapse: Taking action that can stop the inexorable march. *New Perspectives*, 21-25.

Jennings, M. (2009, Fall). The sloppiness of business ethics. *Reason Papers.* 109-124.

Jeter, L.W. (2003). *Disconnect: Deceit, and Betrayal at WorldCom.* New York: John Wiley & Sons, Inc.

Johnson, C. (2003). Enron's ethical collapse: Lessons for leadership educators. *Journal of Leadership Education, 2*(1), 45-56.

Johnson, J.M. & Jensen, C. (2010, March). The financing of terrorism. *Journal of the Institute of Justice & International Studies, 10,* 103-115.

Johnson, E.N., Kuhn, J.R., Apostolou, B.A., & Hassell, J.M. (2013). Auditor perceptions of client narcissism as a fraud attitude risk factor. *Auditing: A Journal of Practice and Theory, 32*(1), 203-219.

Jones, S. (2008, July 31), Man held in plot to kill IRS agent. Retrieved from http://www.theledger.com/article/20080731/NEWS/94000367.

Jones, B. (2011). How much do you really know about your background screening process? Retrieved from http://www.articlesbase.com/human-resourcesarticles/how-much-do-you-really-know-about-your-backgroundscreening-process-4261543.html

Jones, S. (2012, April 15). Ex-tyco ceo says "ceo-type bubble" made him feel entitled to steal millions. *The Star-Ledge.* Retrieved from http://www.nj.com/business/index.ssf/2012/04/ex-tyco_ceo_says_ceo-type_bubb.html

Jones, D.M. (2014). Risk in the face of retribution: Psychopathic individuals persist in financial misbehavior among the dark triad. *Personality and Individual Differences, 67,* 109-113.

Jones, R.M. (2017). The irrational actor in the ceo suite: Implications for coroproate governance. *Boston College Law School Faculty Papers, 41*(3), 713-762.

Jones, D.N., & Hare, R. (2015). The mismeasure of psychopathy: A commentary on boddy's PM-MRV. *Journal of Business Ethics, 138*(3), 579-588.

Jones, R.C., & Jones, E.L. (2014). Leadership: A review of the link between effectiveness and behaviors. *Journal of Leadership and Organizational Effectiveness, 2*(1), 4-24.

Jones, D.N., & Neria, A.L. (2015). The dark triad and dispositional aggression. *Personality and Individual Difference, 86,* 360-364.

Judge, T., Scott, B., & Ilies, R. (2006). Hostility, job attitudes, and workplace deviance:Test of a multi-level model. *Journal of Applied Psychology, 91,* 126-138.

Kahan, D.M., & Posner, E.A.. (1999). Shaming white-collar criminals: A proposal for reform of the federal sentencing guidelines. *Journal of Law and Economic, 42.*

Kailemia, M. (2016). Crime and corporate sociopathy: Lessons from the eu meat industry. *International Journal of Business and Applied Social Science, 2*(3), 73-85.

516

Kaiser, R.B., & LeBreton, J.M., & Hogan, J. (2015). The dark side of personality and extreme leader behavior. *Applied Psychology, 64*(1), 55-92.

Kalantarian, K. (2006). Senior tax official killed in car blast. Retrieved from https://www.azatutyun.am/a/1583909.html

Kanazawa, S. (2011, March 13). Criminals look different from non-criminals. *Psychology Today.* Retrieved from
http://www.psychologytoday.com/blog/the-scientific-fundamentalist/201103/criminals-look-different-noncriminals

Kaplan, D. (2005). Paying for terror: how jihadist groups are using organized-crime tactics andprofits – to finance attacks on targets around the globe. Retrieved from www.rtmsd.org/7472208209615587/lib/7472208209615587/Paying_for_Terror.pdf.

Kaplan, R., & Kiron, D. (2004). *Accounting Fraud at WorldCom*. Boston, MA: Harvard Business School Publishing.

Kaptein, M., & Schwartz, M.S. (2007). The effectiveness of business codes: A critical examination of existing studies and the development of an integrated research model. *Journal of Business Ethics, 77*, 111-127.

Karlin, R. (2006, July 24). Forged transcripts center of attention. Retrieved June from
http://www.timesunion.com/AspStories/story.asp?s toryID=502280&category=PORCO&BCCode=&news date=6/18/2008

Kashdan, T. (2014, May 15). Why do people kill themselves? New warning signs. Retrieved from
http://www.psychologytoday.com/blog/curious/201405/why-do-people-kill-themselves-new-warning-signs

Kassin, S. M., & Kiechel, K.L. (1996). The social psychology of false confession: Compliance, internalization and confabulation. *Psychological Science, 7*, 125-128.

Kassin, S.M., Drizin, S.A., Grisso, T., Gudjonsson, G.H., Leo, R.A., Redlich, A.D. (2010). Police-induced confessions: Risk factors and recommendations. *Law and Human Behavior, 34*(1), 3-38.

Kassin, S. M. (2014). False confessions: Causes, consequences, and implications for reform. *Behavioral and Brain Sciences, 1*(1), 112-121.

Kassin, S.M. (2015). The social psychology of false confession. *Social Issues and Police Review, 9*(1), 25-51.

Kassin, S.M., Appleby, S.C., & Perillo, J.T. (2010). Interviewing suspects: Practice, science, and future directions. *Legal and Criminological Psychology 15*, 39-55.

Kassin, S.M., Meissner, C.A., & Norwick, R.J. (2005). I'd know a false confession if I saw one: A comparative study of college students and police investigators. *Law and Human Behavior, 29*(2), 211-227.

Kastiel, K. (2014, October 25). Elements of an effective whistleblower hotline. Harvard Law School Forum on Corporate Governance and Financial Regulation. Retrieved from https://corpgov.law.harvard.edu/2014/10/25/elements-of-an-effective-whistleblowerhotline/

Katz, I. (2009, September 3). Madoff astonished SEC failed to act after interview. Retrieved from
www.bloomberg.com/apps/news?pid¼newsarchive&sid¼aKX2VXWJSeiI.

Keefe, P. R. (2017, July, 31). Why corrupt bankers avoid jail. *The New Yorker*. Retrieved
from https://www.newyorker.com/magazine/2017/07/31/why-corrupt-bankers-avoid-jail

Keith, T.V. (2008, March 18). Jury hears opening statement in trial of women accused of killing homeless men. Retrieved from Knowledgeplex.

Keller, B. (2002, January 26). Enron for dummies. The New York Times. Retrieved from
http://www.nytimes.com/2002/01/26/opinion/enron-for-dummies.html?pagewanted=all&pagewanted=print

Kelley, R. (1988, November/December). In praise of followers. *Harvard Business Review*, 1-8.

Kephart, J. (2005). Immigration and terrorism: moving beyond the 9/11 staff report on terrorist travel. Retrieved from
www.cis.org/articles/2005/kephart.html.

Kessler, R. (1993). *The FBI*. Boston, MA: Pocket Books.

Kets de Vries, M. (2003). Leaders, Foos and Impostors: Essays on the Psychology of Leadership (revised edition), New York: iUniverse.

Khorram, Y. (2021a, December 7). Elizabeth holmes admits she gave journalist incorrect info for theranos cover story. www.cnbc.com.

Khorram, Y. (2021b, November 19). Government rests its case in criminal trial of theranos founder elizabeth holmes. www.cnbc.com.

Kim, S.H. (2005). The banality of fraud:Re-situating the inside counsel as gatekeeper. *Fordham Law School, 74*(3), 984-1075

Kim, V. (2008, April 6). Greed, betrayal are themes in testimony at women's hit and run trial. Retrieved from http://www.latimes.com/news/local/ la-meolgahelen6apr06,0,3960984.story

Kim, V., & Pringle, P. (2008). Woman convicted of murder in homeless men's deaths. Retrievedfrom
http://en.wikipedia.org/wiki/Black_Widow_murders

Kimes, S. (2006). State of California v. Santé Kimes, 2006 WL 1320752, (Cal.App. 2 Dist.).

King, J. (2002). *Dead end: the crime story of thedecade—murder, incest, and high-tech thievery*. New York: M. Evans.

Kinsler, J.S. (2008). Arthur Andersen and the temple of doom. *Southwestern University Law School*, 97-134. Retrieved from
http://www.swlaw.edu/pdfs/lr/37_1kinsler.pdf

Kirtzman, A. (2009). *Betrayal*. New York: Harper.

Klein, G. (2016). *Ethics in Accounting: A Decision Making Approach* N.J:John Wiley & Sons Inc.

Knapp, M. (2009). *Contemporary Auditing*. OH: South-Western.

Knapp, M.C., & Knapp, C.A. (2012). Cognitive biases in audit engagements. *The CPA Journal*. 40-45.

Knapp, M.C. & Knapp, C.A. (2014). Zaiteku + tobashi=olympus accounting fraud. *Journal of Forensic & Investigative Accounting, 6*(3), 236-254.

Koerner, B. (2005, January 28). Terrorist groups relying identity theft for funding and operations. Retrieved from
www.identitytheftsecrets.com/terrorists_using_phishing_sites.html.

Kohn, S.M. (2011). *The Whistleblower Handbook*. Connecticutt: Lyons Press.

Kouwe, Z. (2009, December 1). SEC watchdog outlines internal investigations. Retrieved from http://dealbook.blogs.nytimes.com/2009/12/01/sec-watchdog-outlinesinternal-investigations/

KPMG. (2006). Guide to preventing workplace fraud. Retrieved from http://www.chubb.com/businesses/csi/chubb5305.pdf

KPMG. (2011a). Who is the typical fraudster? *KPMG*. Retrieved from
http://www.kpmg.com/IS/is/utgefidefni/greinarogutgefid/Documents/Who_is_the_typical_fraudster.pdf.

KPMG. (2011b). 2011 Public company audit committee member survey highlights. Retrieved from
https://www.kpmg.com/FR/fr/IssuesAndInsights/ArticlesPublications/Documents/Public-Company-Audit-Committee-Member-Survey-Highlights-2011.pdf

KPMG. (2013). Integrity survey. KPMG Forensic. Retrieved from https://assets.kpmg.com/content/dam/kpmg/pdf/2013/08/Integrity-Survey-2013-O 201307.pdf

Kramer, R.M. (2003, October). The harder they fall. *Harvard Business Review*, 58-66.

Kranacher, M., Riley, R., & Wells, J.T. (2011). *Forensic Accounting and Fraud Examination*. N.J.: John Wiley and Sons.

Kroll. (2015/2016). Global fraud report: Vulnerabilities on the rise. Retieved from http://anticorruzione.eu/wp-content/uploads/2015/09/Kroll_Global_Fraud_Report_2015low-copia.pdf

Kroll. (2016/2017). Global Fraud & Risk Report. Retrieve from http://constructioncitizen.com/sites/constructioncitizen.com/files/blog_attachment s/RPT_KRL_US_Kroll_Global_Fraud_and_Risk_Report_2016.pdf

KTLA. (2009, July 21). Slain Realtor had ties to fraud, homicide case. Retrieved from http://www.ktla.com/news/landing/ktla-real-estate-showing-body,0,1645758.story

Kunduz, A.B. (2009, September 7). How crime pays for the Taliban. *Time Magazine*. Retrieved from www.time.com/time/magazine/article/0,9171,1919154,00.html.

Kyriakos-Saad, N., Vasquez, M., El Khoury C., & El Murr, A. (2016). Islamic finance and antimoney laundering and combating the financing of terrorism. *International Monetary Fund Working Paper*, 1-11.

Lafaive, M.D., Fleenor, P., & Nesbit, T. (2008, December 3). Michigan from 1990 to present. Retrieved from www.mackinac.org/10041

Landsheer, J. A., & Hart, T., & Kox, W. (1994). Delinquent values and victim damage: Exploring the limits of neutralization theory. *British Journal of Criminology 34*, 44–53.

Langbert, M.B. (2010, June 6). Manageing psychopathic employees. *Cornell University ILR School*. 1-5.

Langone, M. (1995). Secular and religious critiques of cults: Complementary visions, not irresolvable conflicts. *Cultic Studies Journal, 12*, 166-186.

Langevoort, D.C. (2009). The sec and the madoff scandal: Three narratives in search of a story. *Michigan State Law Review*, 899-914.

Lau, J. (2005). 4 N.Y.3d 765, 825 N.E.2d 141, 792 N.Y.S.2d 9.

Laub, J. H., & Sampson. (1991). The Sutherland-Glueck debate: On the sociology of criminological knowledge. *American Journal of Sociology, 96*(6), 1402-1440. http://dx.doi.org/10.1086/229691

Laurell, J., & Belfrage, H., & Hellstom, A. (2010). Facets on the psychopathy checklist screening version and instrumental violence in forensic psychiatric patients. *Criminal Behavior and Mental Health, 20*, 285-294.

Le, M.T., Woodworth, M., Gillman, L., Hutton, E., & Hare, R.D. (2017). The linguistic output of psychopathic offenders during a pcl-r interview. *Criminal Journal and Behavior, 44*(4), 1-15.

Lee, G., & Fargher, N. (2014, April 14). Whistle-blowing on financial misconduct: When do companies retaliate against whistle-blowers? 1-29. Retrieved from https://www.researchgate.net/publication/256063586_Whistle Blowing_on_Financial_Misconduct_When_Do_Companies_Retaliate_Against_Whistle-Blowers

Leedom, L.J. (2006). *Just Like His Father*? Healing Arts Press.

Lesha, J. & Lesha, D. (2012). Psychopathy and white collar crime: A review of literature. *SEEU Review, 8*(2), 1-18.

Leung, R. (2003, October 2). Sam waksal: I was arrogant. *60 Minutes*. Retrieved from http://www.cbsnews.com/news/sam-waksal-i-was-arrogant-02-10-2003/.

Leung, R. (2009, February 11). Enron's ken lay: I was fooled. Retrieved from http://www.cbsnews.com/8301-18560_162-679706.html

Levine, D.B. (1991). *Inside Out: An Insider's Account of Wall Street*. New York: Putnam.

Levine, T.R., Serota, K.B., & Shulman, H.C. (2010). The impact of lie to me viewer's actual ability to detect deception. *Communication Research, 37*(6), 847-856.

Levine, M. (2016, September 9). Wells fargo opened a couple million fake accounts. *Bloomberg*. Retrieved from wells-fargo-opened-a-couple-million-fake-accounts

Levitt, M. (2005, May 25). Hezbollah: financing terror through criminal enterprise. Retrieved from www.investigativeproject.org/documents/testimony/313.pdf.

Lewis, A. (2012, March 5). Psychos on wall street. Retrieved from https://www.efxnews.com/story/10863/psychos-wall-street

Lewis, J. (2005a, November 15). Petrick's financee, former girlfriend testify in day 6 testimony. Retrieved from http://www.wral.com/news/local/story/121861/

Lewis, J. (2005b, November 14). Prosecution: Computers map out Petrick's plan to kill wife. Retrieved from http://www.wral.com/news/local/story/121815/

Lewis, J. (2005c, November 28). Petrick prosecutors to reopen case with new computer evidence. Retrieved from http://www.wral.com/news/local/story/122105/

Lewis, M. (2010, April). Greed never left. *Vanity Fair*, 126.

Lewis, L.S. (2010a). Madoff's victims and their day in court. *Culture and Society, 47*, 439-450.

Lewis, L.S. (2011a). After Madoff: Waiting for Justice. *Culture and Society, 48*, 159-173.

Lewis, L.S. (2011b). How Madoff did it: Victims' accountants. *Culture and Society, 48*, 70-76.

Lewis, M.K. (2012). New dogs, old tricks. Why do Ponzi schemes succeed? *Accounting Forum, 36*, 294-309.

Lewis, M.K. (2015). *Understanding Ponzi Schemes*. U.K.: Edward Elgar Publishing.

Liang, C.S. (2011, September). Shadow networks: The growing nexus of terrorism and organized crime. Geneva Centre fo Security Policy. Retrieved from https://www.files.ethz.ch/isn/133082/Policy%20Paper%2020.pdf

Liedtke, M. (2021). Elizabeth holmes gets emotional under fire by prosecutors. www.komonews.com.

Lilien, T.A. (2017). *Defending Criminal Cases: Pretrial Issues, Guilty Pleas, and Defenses*. Illinois, IICLE.

Lilly, J., Cullen, F., & Ball, R. (2011). *Criminological Theory: Context and Consequences*, 5th edition. Thousand Oaks, CA: Sage.

Lingnau, V., Fuchs, F., & Dehne-Niemann (2017). The influence of psychopathic traits on the acceptance of white-collar crime: Do corporate psychopaths cook the books and misuse the news? *Journal of Business Economics, 87*, 1193-1227.

Lipman, F.D. (2012). *Whistleblowers: Incentives, Disincentives and Protection Strategies*. New Jersey: John Wiley & Sons.

Lipman-Blumen, J. (2005). *The Allure of Toxic Leaders*. NY: Oxford University Press.

Listwan, S. J., Piquero, N. L., & Van Voorhis, P. (2010). Recidivism among a white-collar sample: Does personality matter? *Australian and New Zealand Journal of Criminology,43*(1), 156–174.

Livengood, C. (2013, January 8). Michigan supreme court justice hathaway to retire amid Scandal. *The Detroit News.* Retrieved from http://www.detroitnews.com/article/20130108/METRO/301080355/1409/metro Michigan-Supreme-Court-Justice-Hathaway-retire-amid-scandal

Livesley, W.J., & Jang, K. (2005). Differntiating normal, abnormal, and disordered personality. *European Journal of Personality, 19*, 257-268.

Lodder, J. (2012). Narcissism and top management. Retrieved from http://www.poslovni-savjetnik.com/blog/management/john-lodder-narcissism-top-management.

Lohr, S. (1997, October 2). The battle for MCI: The entrepreneur; a long-distance visionary.Retrieved from http://www.nytimes.com/1997/10/02/business/the-battle-for-mci-theentrepreneur- a-long-distance-visionary.html?pagewanted=all&src=pm

Long, C. & Hayes, T. (2010, December 11). Mark Madoff suicide: Bernie Madoff's son found hanged in NYC apartment. Retrieved from http://www.huffingtonpost.com/2010/12/11/mark-madoff-suicide-hanged_n_795342.html

Lopatto, E. (2021a, November 22). Elizabeth holmes tells the jury that at least some of theranos was real. www.theverge.com.

Lopatto, E. (2021a, November 30). Elizabeth holmes admits that she was ceo of theranos, the company she founded.www.theverge.com.

Lormel, D. (2002, July 2). Testimony before the senate judiciary subcommittee on technology, terrorism and government information. Retrieved from www.investigativeproject.org/documents/testimony/234.pdf .

Lowe, J. (2009, May 29). Howell pleads guilty to murder of rohrbach, Retrieved from http://www.news14.com/content/top_stories/609910/howell-pleadsguilty-to-murder-of-rohrbach/Default.aspx.

Luke, T.J., Hartwig, M., Joseph, E., Brimbal, L., Chan, G., Dawson, E., Jordan, S., Donovan, P., & Granhag, P.A. (2016). Training in the strategic use of evidence technique: Improving deception detection accuracy of American enforcement officers. *Journal of Police Criminal Psychology.* Retrieved from https://link.springer.com/article/10.1007/s11896-015-9187-0.

Luo, X., Brody, R., Seazzu, A. & Burd, S. (2011). Social engineering: the neglected human factor for information security management. *Information Resources Management Journal, 24*(3), 1-8.

Lyer, S. (1999, June 28). Software's hardhead. Retrieved from http://m.outlookindia.com/story.aspx?sid=4&aid=207675

Lynch, D.J. (2017, September 14). DOJ revising policy on US white-collar crime prosecutions. *Financial Times.* Retrieved from https://www.ft.com/content/06c6bbb4-9986-11e7-a652-cde3f882dd7b

Lyons, B. (2005a, November 18). E-mails reveal porco family rift. *Times Union.* Retrieved from http://www.timesunion.com/AspStories/story.asp?story ID=420939&category=PORCO&BCCode=&newsdat e=6/18/08

Lyons, B. (2005b, November 4). Unsolved mystery. *Times Union.* Retrieved from http://www.timesunion.com

Lyons, B. (2006a, December 13). Porco draws harsh words, lengthy sentence. *Times Union.* Retrieved from www.timesunion.com/AspStories/story.asp?storyID=4160 81&category=PORCO&BCCode=&newsdate=6/18/08

Lyons, B. (2006b, July 21). E-mails illustrate father, son at odds. Retrieved from http://www.timesunion.com/AspStories/story.asp?story ID=501545&category=PORCO&BCCode=&newsdat e=6/18/2008

Lyons, B. (2006c, August 1). Joan Porco tells of anger. *Times Union.* Retrieved from timesunion.com/AspStories/story.asp?storyID=504489& category=PORCO&BCCode=&newsdate=6/18/2008

Maccoby, M. (2004, January). Narcissistic leaders: The incredible pros the inevitable cons. *Harvard Business Review, 92*-101.

MacDonald, M. (2002, August, 29). Execs should be screened to weed out psychopaths: researcher. Retrieved from http://www.psychopath

Macey, J. (2010). The distorting incentives facing the US securities and exchange commission. *Harvard Journal of Law and Public Policy, 33*(2), 639-70.

Machen R. (2010, September 1). Two district men found guilty in slaying of witness: Victim was to testify in maryland fraud case. Retrieved from http://www.justice.gov/usao/dc/news/2011/jan/11-029.pdf.

Machiavelli, N. (1513). *The Prince.*

Mack, S. (2011). *The End of Normal.* NY: Blue Rider Press

Maclean, T.L. (2001). Thick as thieves: A social embeddedness model of rule breaking in organizations. *Business & Society, 40*(2), 167-196.

Maeda, M. (2010). *Accounting Fraud and Cover-Ups.* Florida: Atlantic Publishing Group.

Mahadeo, S. (2006, January/February). Tone at the top: How management can prevent fraud by example, part one. *Fraud Magazine*

Main, F. (2005, July 16). Cop accused of ordering killing. *Sun Times.* Retrieved from www.suntimes.com.

Makarenko, T. (2004). The crime-terror continuum: tracing the interplay between transnational organized crime and terrorism. *Global Crime, 6*(1), 129-45.

Mann, S.A., Vrij, A., Fisher, R.P., & Robinson, M. (2008). See no lies, hear no lies: Differences in discrimination accuracy and response bias when watching or listening to police suspect interviews. *Applied Cognitive Psychology, 22*, 1062-1071.

Marfo, F. (2014). United States v. Frank Marfo. No. 12-4910. Retrieved from https://www.courtlistener.com/opinion/2675586/united-states-v-frank-marfo/

Margolies, I. (1987). Jacqueline Barbera v. William French Smith, 836 F.2d 96 (1987).

Markopolos, H. (2010). *No One Would Listen.* NJ:Wiley.

Mathieu, C., Hare, R.D., Jones, D.N., Babiak, P., & Neumann, C.S. (2012). Factor structure of the b-scan 360: A measure of corporate psychopathy. *Psychological Assessment, 25*(1), 288-293.

Mathieu, C., Neumann, C., Babiak, P., & Hare, R.D. (2015). Corporate psychopathy and he full-range leadership model. *Assessment, 22*(3), 267-278.

Martin, D. E., & Austin, B. (2010). Validation of the moral competency inventory measurement instrument: Content, construct, convergent and discriminant approaches. *Management Research Review, 33*(5), 437–451.

Martinez, E. (2010, January 11). Ramones manager linda stein murder: Assistant goes to trial. Retrieved from http://www.cbsnews.com/news/ramones-manager-linda- stein-murder-assistant-goes-on-trial/

Martinez, M.A., Zeichner, A., Reidy, D.E., & Miller, J.D. (2008). Narcissism and displaced aggression: Effects of positive, negative and delayed feedback. *Personality Differences,44,*140-149.

Martino, J. (2012, June 20). The mormon madoff: How shawn merriman scammed millions. Retrieved from http://www.cnbc.com/id/47881681

Mauer, D. (1974). *The American Confidence Man.* Illinois: Charles C. Thomas.

Mayer, D.M., Kuenzi, M., Greenbaum, R., Bardes, M., & Salvador, R. (2009). How low does ethical leadership flow? Test of a trickle down model. *Organizational Behavior and Human Decision Processes, 108,* 1-13.

Mayhew, B.W., & Murphy, P.E. (2014). The impact of authority on reporting behavior, rationalization and affect. *Contemporary Accounting Research, 31*(2), 420-443.

McCafferty, J. (2016, November 2). Internal auditors under pressure to alter reports. *MISTI Training Institute.* Retrieved from https://misti.com/internal-audit-insights/internal-auditors-under-pressure-to-alter-reports.

McCartney, L. (2011, March 1). Where there's smoke, there's fraud. CFO. Retrieved from http://ww2.cfo.com/risk-compliance/2011/03/where-theres-smoke-theres-fraud/

McClam, E. (2005, August, 5). Ex-worldcom exec vinson gets prison, house arrest. *USA Today.* Retrieved from http://usatoday30.usatoday.com/money/industries/telecom/2005-08-05-vinson_x.htm

McClure, K.A., Myers, J.J., & Keefauver, K.A. (2013). Witness vetting: What determines detectives' perceptions of witness credibility? *Journal of Investigtive Psychology and Offender Profiling, 10,* 250-267.

McCool, G., & Graybow, M. (2009, March, 12). Madoff pleads guilty, is jailed for $65 billion dollar fraud. *Reuters.* Retrieved from http://www.reuters.com/article/us- usa-consumer paydayloans/new-u-s-rule-on-payday-loans-to-hurt-industry-boost- banks-agency-idUSKBN1CA24K

McCoy, K. (2009, July 1). Appeal of madoff's 150 year sentence wouldn't matter. *USA Today.* Retrieved from http://www.usatoday.com/money/industries/brokerage/2009-06- 30-madoff-sentencing-appeal_N.htm.

McCullough, M.E., Emmons, R.A., Kilpatrick, S.D., & Mooney, C.N. (2003). Narcissists as "victims": The role of narcissism in the perception of transagressions. *Personality and Social Psychology Bulletin, 29,* 885-893.

McDonald, R. (1998). *Secrets Never Lie.* New York: Avon Books.

McFarland, C. (n.d.). United States of America vs. Chalana McFarland, Brief of Appellee, Retrieved from http://lawprofessors.typepad.com/whitecollarcrime_blog/files/mcfarland_reply_0 6.pdf.

McGeehan, J. (2010). Intimidation in the office. *Fraud Magazine.* Retrieved from http://www.fraud-magazine.com/article.aspx?id=2147483746

McGinniss, M.S. (2013). Virtue and advice" Socratic perspectives on lawyer independence and moral counseling. *Texas A & M Law Review, 1*(1), 1-54.

McGinty, T. (2010a). On legal ethics and the SEC's revolving door. *Wall Street Journal* Retrieved from http://blogs.wsj.com/law/2010/04/05/on-legal-ethics-and-the-secs-revolving-door/

McGinty, T. (2010b). SEC lawyer one day, opponent the next. *Wall Street Journal.* Retrieved from http://grassley.senate.gov/about/upload/ICYMI-Wall-St-Journal-4-5-10.pdf.

McGurrin, D., Jarrell, M., Jahn, A., & Cochrane, B. (2013). White collar crime representation in the criminological literature revisited, 2001-2010. *Western Criminology Review, 14*(2), 3-19.

McKnight, D.H., Cummings, I.L. and Chervany, N.L. (1998). Initial trust formation in new organizational relationships. *The Academy of Management Review, 23*(3), 473-490.

McLean, B., & Elkind, P. (2003). *The Smartest Guys in the Room.* NY:Penguin Group.

McNeal, A. (2011, October 21). The role of the board in fraud risk management. *The Conference Board.* Retrieved from board.org/retrievefile.cfm?filename=TCB- DN-V3N21-111.pdf&type=subsite

McNiff, E., & Cuomo, C. (2006). Amid the carnage, a mother's love. Retrieved from http://abcnews.go.com/US/LegalCenter/story?id=2179489&page=1

McRoberts, F. (2002a, September 1). The fall of Andersen. *The Chicago Tribune.* Retrieved from http://www.chicagotribune.com/news/chi-0209010315sep01-story.html

McRoberts, F. (2002b, September 1). Civil war splits andersen. *The Chicago Tribune.* Retrieved from http://www.chicagotribune.com/news/chi-0209020071sep02-story.html

McRoberts, F. (2002c, September 1). Ties to enron blinded andersen. *The Chicago Tribune.* Retrieved from http://www.chicagotribune.com/news/chi-0209030210sep03-story.html

McRoberts, F. (2002d, September 1). Repeat offender gets stiff justice: Sins of past come back to haunt firm. *The Chicago Tribune.* Retrieved from http://articles.chicagotribune.com/2002-09-04/news/0209040368_1_audits-of-enron-corp-enron-investors-andersen

Meloy, J. R. (2002). *The Psychopathic Mind.* Maryland: Rowman & Littlefield Publishers Inc.

Merling, D. (2013, June 13). In faith communities, fraudsters prey on trust. Retrieved from http://www.deseretnews.com/article/865581699/In-faith-communities-fraudsters-prey-on-trust.html

Miceli, M.P., Near, J.P., & Dworkin, T.M. (2009). A word to the wise: How managers and policy-makers can encourage employees to report wrongdoing. *Journal of Business Ethics, 86,* 379-396.

Mikos, R. (2008). United States of America v. Ronald Mikos, Nos. 06-2375, 06-2376 & 06-2421.

Milgram, S. (1974). *Obedience to authority: An experimental view.* New York: Harper & Row.

Miller, J, (2004). Too little, too late: How the government could have prevented the fall of arthur andersen. *Undergraduate Review: Journal of Undergraduate Research, 7*(6), 20-24.

Miller, J.D., Campbell, W.K., Young, D.L., Lakey, C.E., Reidy, D.E., Zeichner, A., Goodie, A.S. (2009). Examining the relations among narcissism, impulsivity, and self-defeating behaviors. *Journal of Personality, 77*(3), 761-793.

Mintz, S.M. & Morris, R.E. (2017). *Ethical Obligations and Decision Making in Accounitng, Fourth Edition,* New York: McGraw-Hill

Mooney, L.A., Knox, D., & Schacht, C. (2009). *Understanding Social Problems.* Wadsworth Cengage Learning, Belmont, CA.

Moore, K.M., Gilman, R., & Kethledge, R. (2013, February 15). United States of America v. Michael E. Peppel. Retrieved from http://www.ca6.uscourts.gov/opinions.pdf/13a0042p-06.pdf

Moran, S., & Kral, R. (2013). *The Board of Directors and Audit Committee Guide to Fiduciary Responsibilities.* New York: AMACOM

Morf, C. C., & Rhodewalt, F. (2001). Unraveling the paradoxes of narcissism: A dynamic self-regulatory processing model. *Psychological Inquiry, 12,* 177-196.

Morgan, G. (1997). *Images of Organization, 2nd Edition.* Thousand Oaks, CA: Sage.

Morgan, E. (2011, January 31). Bills would crack down on affinity fraud in Utah. *Desert News.* Retrieved from www.deseretnews.com/article/700105678/Bills-would-crack-down-on-affinity-fraud-in-Utah.html.

Morgan, E. (2012, December 28). Ex-bishop of Mormon singles ward charged with investment Fraud. Desert News. Retrieved from https://www.deseretnews.com/article/865569589/Ex-bishop-of-Mormon-singles-ward-charged-with-investment-fraud.html

Morrison, A.D., & Wilhelm, W.J. (2010). Computerization and the ABACUS: reputation, trust, and fiduciary responsibility in investment banking, working paper, Said Business School, Oxford.

Moscicki, E. K. (1997). Identification of suicide risk factors using epidemiologic studies. *Psychiatric Clinics of North America, 20*(3), 499-517.

Mullins, S. (2009). Parallels between crime and terrorism: a social psychological perspective.*Studies in Conflict and Terrorism, 32,* 9.

Mullins-Sweat, S.N., Salekin, R. T., & Leistico, A.R. (2006). Psychopathy, empathy and Perspective-taking ability in a community sample: Implications for the successful psychopathy concept. *International Journal of Forensics, 5*(2), 133-149.

Mullins-Sweat, S.N., Glover, N.G., Derefinko, K.J., Miller, J.D., & Widiger, T.A. (2010). The search for the successful psychopath. *Journal of Research in Personality, 44,* 554-558.

Mundy, A. (2001). *Dispensing with the Truth.* St. Martin's Press, New York, N.Y.

Murphy, P.R. (2012). Attitude, machiavellianism, and the rationalization od misreporting. *Accounting, Organization and Society, 37,* 242-259.

Murphy, P.R., & Dacin, T.M. (2011). Psychological pathways to fraud: Understanding and preventing fraud in organizations. *Journal of Business Ethics, 101,* 601-618.

Murphy, C., & Vess, J. (2003). Subtypes of psychopathy: proposed differences between narcissistic, borderline, sadistic and antisocial psychopaths. *Psychiatric Quarterly, 74*(1), 11-29.

Myatt, M. (2012, March 28). 6 tips for making better decisions. *Forbes.* Retrieved from http://www.forbes.com/sites/mikemyatt/2012/03/28/6-tips-for-making-better-decisions/print/

Myers, W.C., Gooch, E., & Meloy, J.R. (2005).The role of psychopathy and sexuality in a female serial killer. *Journal of Forensic Science, 50*(3), 652-657.

NASAA (2011). Top investor traps. North American Securities Administrators Association, Retrieved from www.nasaa.org/investor_education/nasaa_fraud_center/8943.cfm.

Naso, R.C. (2012). When money and morality collide: White-collar crime and the paradox of integrity. *Psychoanalytic Psychology, 29*(2), 241-254.

Navarro, J. (2014). Why predators are attracted to careeers in the clergy, *Psychology Today.* Retrieved from https://www.psychologytoday.com/blog/spycatcher/201404/why-predators-are-attracted-careers-in-the-clergy

Near, J.P., Rhg, M.T., Van Scotter, J.R., & Miceli, M.P. (2004). Does type of wrongdoing affect the whistle-blowing process? *Business Ethics Quarterly, 14*(2), 219-242.

Newcomer, M. (2010, May). Fighting for downward sentencing variances for white collar defendants: Useful post-booker and post-gall trends. *The Champion Magazine, 42.*

Neves, P., & Story, J. (2015). Ethical leadership and reputation: Combined indirect effects on organizational deviance. *Journal of Business Ethics, 127,*165-176.

Nicholls, T.L., & Petrila, J. (2005). Gender and psychopathy: An overview of important issues and introduction to the special issue. *Behavioral Sciences and the Law, 23,* 729-741.

Nocera, J. (2009, March 13). Madoff had accomplices: His victims. *The New York Times.* Retrieved from http://www.nytimes.com/2009/03/14/business/14nocera.html?pagewanted=1&em

NOMS, National Offender Management Service, (2015, September). Working with offenders with personality disorders. Retrieved from https://www.gov.uk/government/uploads/system/uploads/attachment_data/file/468891/NOMSWorking_with_offenders_with_personality_disorder.pdf

Norrismay, F. (2001, May 16). SEC accuses former sunbeam official of fraud. *New York Times.* Retrieved from https://www.nytimes.com/2001/05/16/business/sec-accuses-former-sunbeam-official-of-fraud.html

O'Boyle, E.H., & Forsyth, D.R., Banks, G.C., & McDaniel, M.A. (2012). A meta-analysis of the dark triad and work behavior: A social exchange perspective. *Journal of Applied Psychology, 97*(3), 557-579.

O'Brien, S. (2021, October, 10). What we learned this week in the trial of elizabeth holmes. Retrieved from www.cnn.com.

O'Connor, D.A. (2002). The female psychopath: Validity and factor structure of the revised psychopathy checklist (PCL-R) in women inmates. Unpublished doctoral dissertation, Florida State University Department of Psychology.

O'Connor, M. (2003). The enron board: The perils of groupthink. *University of Cincinnati Law Review, 71,*1233-1320.

Odell, R., & Donnelly, P. (2016). *Bizarre Crimes: Incredible Real-Life Criminal Cases.* England: Robinson.

O'Donnell, J. & Willing, R. (2003, May 12). Prison time gets harder for white collar crooks. *USA Today,* p.1A.

OIG. (2009). Office of the Inspector General, Investigation of failure of the SEC to uncover Bernard madoff's Ponzi scheme. Retrieved from https://www.sec.gov/news/studies/2009/oig-509.pdf

OIG. (2010). Office of the Inspector General, Report of investigation: failure to timely investigate allegations of financial Fraud. Retrieved from www.sec.gov/news/studies/2010/oig-505.pdf.

Olejarz, J.M. (2016, November). Understanding, white-collar crime. *Harvard Business Review.* 110-111, Retrieved from https://hbr.org/2016/11/understanding-white-collar-crime

Oliver, C., Shafiro, M., Bullard, P., &Thomas, J. C. (2012). Use of integrity tests may reduce workers' compensation losses. *Journal of Business and Psychology, 27*(1), 115–122.

521

O'Neil, S. (2007). Terrorist precursor crimes. Retrieved from http://ftp.fas.org/sgp/crs/terror/RL34014.pdf.

Oregan, C. (2002, April 10). The mysterious death of an Enron exec.
Retrieved from http://www.cbsnews.com/news/the-mysterious-death-of-an- enron-exec/

O'Reilly, C.A., Bernadette, B., David F. Caldwell, F., Chatman, J.A. (2014). Narcissistic ceos and executive compensation. *The Leadership Quaterly, 25*(2), 218-231.

Owens, J.B. (2001). Have we no shame?: Thoughts on shaming, white-collar criminals, and the federal sentencing guidelines. *American University LawReview, 49*, 1047-1058.

Padilla, A., Hogan, R., & Kaiser, R. (2007). The toxic triangle: Destructive leaders, susceptible followers, and conducive environments. *The Leadership Quarterly,18,*174-194.

Paine, L.S. (1994, March-April). Managing for organizational integrity. *Harvard Business Review.* 106-117.

Pakaluk, J.H. & Cheffers, A.D. (2011). *Accounting Ethics.* MA: Allen Davis Publishing.

Palazzo, G., Krings, F., & Hoffrage, U. (2012). Ethical Blindness. *Journal of Business Ethics, 109,* 323-338.

Palena, N., Caso, L., Vrij, A., & Orthey, R. (2018). Detecting deception through small talk and comparable truth baselines. *Journal of Investigative Psychology and Offender Profiling.* Retrieved from https://onlinelibrary.wiley.com/doi/abs/10.1002/jip.1495

Palmer, D. (2012). *Normal Organizational Wrongdoing,* NY: Oxford University Press.

Paperny, J.M. (2009). *Lessons from Prison.* CA: APS Publishing.

Paperny, J.M. (2010). *Ethics in Motion.* CA: APS Publishing.

Parcher, A. (2009). Silver Spring man found guilty in murder of Wheaton woman, 83, Retrieved from
http://www.gazette.net/stories/10212009/damanew225632_32535.shtml.

Pardue, A., Robinson, M., & Arrigo, B. (2013a). Psychopathy and corporate crime: A preliminary examination, part 1.
Journal of Forensic Psychology Practice, 13(1), 116-144.

Pardue, A., Robinson, M., & Arrigo, B. (2013b). Psychopathy and corporate crime: A preliminary examination, part 2. *Journal of Forensic Psychology Practice, 13*(2), 145-169.

Paredes, T.A. (2005). Too much pay, too much deference: Behavioral corporate finance, ceos, and corporate governance. *Florida State University Law Review, 32*(2), 673-762.

Parker, M. (2007, November 28). Leak, Jr. sentenced for murder-for-hire. Retrieved from www.CBS2chicago.com

Paternoster, R. & Tibbetts, S.G. (2016). White-collar and perceptual deterrence. In Van Slyke, S.R.; Benson, M.L. & Cullen, F.T. (2016). *The Oxford Handbook of White-collar Crime.* UK: Oxford University Press.

Patterson, S. (2011). Self-described 'fraud consultant' charged with another embezzlement. Retrieved from
http://www.acfe.com/article.aspx?id=4294970224.

Paulhus, D. L., & Williams, K. M. (2002). The dark triad of personality: Narcissism,machiavellianism, and psychopathy. *Journal of Research in Personality, 36,* 556–563.

Paulson, H.M. (2006, November 20). Remarks by treasury Secretary Henry M. Paulson. Retrieved from Remarks by Treasury Secretary Henry M. Paulson.

Payne, B.K. (2013). *White-collar Crime.* California: Sage.

Payne, B.K. (2016). Effects on white-collar defendants of criminal justice attention and sanctions. In Van Slyke, S.R.; Benson, M.L. Cullen, F.T. (2016). *The Oxford Handbook of White-collar Crime.* UK: Oxford University Press.

Pearson, P. (1997). *When she was bad: how and why women get away with murder.* Penguin Books.

Pelley, S. (2005, March 11). Enron's ken lay: I was fooled. Retrieved from http://www.cbsnews.com/news/enrons-ken-lay-i-was-fooled-11-03-2005/

Peltier, T. (2006). Social engineering: concepts and solutions. *Information System Security,15*(3),13-21.

Peppel, M.E. (2013). United States of America v. Michael E. Peppel. Retrieved from http://www.ca6.uscourts.gov/opinions.pdf/13a0042p-06.pdf

Pera, E. & Geary, J. (2008). Suspect in murder plot leaves many people puzzled. Retrieved from
www.theledger.com/article/20080731/NEWS/940003671

Perri, F.S., (2007, June). Principles based accounting and the continental vending case. *The CPA Journal,* 16-17.

Perri, F.S. (2010a). Missing link in the fight against fraud. *Fraud Magazine, 24*(3).

Perri, F.S. (2010b). The fraud-terror link, *Fraud Magazine, 24*(4).

Perri, F.S. (2011a). White-collar criminals: The 'kinder, gentler' offender? *Journal of Investigative Psychology and Offender Profiling, 8,* 217-241.

Perri, F.S. (2011b). White collar crime punishment: Too much or not enough. *Fraud Magazine, 26*(1), 20-22, 43-45.

Perri, F.S. (2011c). The perils of fraud detection at work. *Forensic Examiner, 20*(1), 114-124

Perri, F.S. (2011d). The flawed interview of a psychopathic killer: What went wrong? *Journal of Investigative Psychology and Offender Profiling, 8*(1), 41-57.

Perri, F.S. (2013a). Trust me, I'm just like you: The predatory practice of affinity fraud. *Royal Mounted Canadian Police Gazette, 75*(3), 22-23.

Perri, F.S. (2013b). Visionaries or false prophets. *Journal of Contemporary Criminal Justice, 29*(3), 331-350.

Perri, F.S. (2016). Red collar crime. *International Journal of Psychological Studies, 8*(1).

Perri, F.S., & Brody, R.G. (2011a). Birds of the same feather: The dangers of affinity fraud. *Journal of Forensic Studies in Accounting and Business, 3*(1), 31-44.

Perri, F.S., & Brody, R.G. (2011b). The sleeping watch dog: a.k.a the securities and exchange commission. *Journal of Financial Regulation and Compliance, 19*(3), 208-221.

Perri, F.S., & Brody, R.G. (2011c). The sallie rohrbach story: Lessons for auditors and fraud examiners. *Journal of Financial Crime, 18*(1), 93-104.

Perri, F.S., & Brody, R.G. (2011d). The dark triad: Organized crime, terror and fraud. *Journal of Money Laundering Control, 14*(1), 44-59.

Perri, F.S., & Brody, R.G. (2012). The optics of fraud: Affiliations that enhance offender credibility. *Journal of Financial Crime, 19*(3), 305-320.

Perri, F.S., & Brody, R.G. (2013). Affinity is only skin deep: Insidious fraud of familiarity. *Fraud Magazine, 28*(2), 42-48.

Perri, F.S., & Brody, R.G., & Paperny, J. M. (2014a). Debunking the myth of the out of character offense. *Journal of Forensic & Investigative Accounting, 6*(2), 1-51

Perri, F.S., & Lichtenwald, T.G. (2007a). Fraud detection homicide: A proposed fbi crime classification. *Forensic Examiner, 16*(4), 18-29.

Perri, F.S., & Lichtenwald, T.G. (2007b). Identifying and interviewing red collar criminals. *Fraud Magazine, 21*(4).

Perri, F.S., & Lichtenwald, T.G. (2007c).When white-collar crimes turn red. *Fraud Magazine, 21*(3).

Perri, F.S., & Lichtenwald, T.G. (2008a). A tale of two countries: International fraud detection homicide. *Forensic Examiner, 17*(2), 72-78.

Perri, F.S., & Lichtenwald, T.G. (2008b). The arrogant chameleons: Exposing fraud detection homicide. *Forensic Examiner, 17*(1), 26-33.

Perri, F.S., Lichtenwald, T.G., & MacKenzie, P. (2008c).The lull before the storm: Adult children who kill their parents. *Forensic Examiner, 17*(3), 40-54.

Perri, F.S., Lichtenwald, T.G., & Mackenzie, P. (2009). Evil twins: The crime-terror nexus. *Forensic Examiner, 18*(4), 16-29.

Perri, F.S., & Lichtenwald, T.G. (2010a). The last frontier: Myths and psychopathic women who kill. *Forensic Examiner,* 50-67.

Perri, F.S., Lichtenwald, T.G. & Mieczkowska, E.M. (2014). Sutherland, cleckley and beyond: White-collar crime and psychopathy. *International Journal of Psychological Studies, 6*(4), 71-88.

Perri, F.S., & Mieczkowska, E.M. (2015). I didn't intend to deceive anyone: Fraud rationalizations and the guilty mind. *Fraud Magazine, 30*(2), 43-47

Perry, P. (2010). The revolving door at the SEC compromises investigations. Retrieved from www.investmentfraudlawyerblog.com/2010/04/the_revolving_door_at_the_sec.html.

Petit, V., & Bollaert, H., (2012). Flying too close to the sun? Hubris among ceos and how to prevent it. *Journal of Business Ethics, 108,* 265-283.

Petrick, R. (2007). State of North Carolina v. Robert J. Petrick, No. 03 CRS 49331. Retrieved from http://www.lexisone.com/lx1/caselaw/freecaselaw?action=OCLGetCaseDetail&format=FULL&sourceID=baaib&searchTerm=eScY.ieTa. UYGW.bcgU&searchFlag=y&l1loc=FCLOW.

Petters, T.J. (2010). United States v. Thomas Joseph Petters. Government''s Position Regarding Sentencing. Retrieved fom https://www.justice.gov/sites/default/files/usao-mn/legacy/2010/12/21/Government's%20response.pdf

Phelps, D. & Tevlin, J. (2008, October 26). The collapse of the Petters empire. *Star Tribune.* Retrieved from www.startribune.com/business/33287804.html.

Phillips, M.D., & Kamen, E.A. (2014). Entering the black hole: The taliban, terrorism and organised crime. *Journal of Terrorism Research, 5*(3), 39-48.

Picornell, I. (2013). Analysing deception in written statements: Linguistic evidence in security, *Law and Intelligence, 1*(1), 41-50.

Pierce, L., & Snyder, J.A. (2015). Unethical demand and employee turnover. *Journal of Business Ethics, 131,* 853-869.

Pilch, I., & Turska, E. (2015). Relationships between Machiavellianism, organizational culture, and workplace bullying: Emotional abuse from the target's and the perpetrator's perspective. *Journal of Business Ethics, 128,* 83-93.

Pincus, A.L., & Lukowitsky, M.R. (2009). Pathological narcissism and narcissitic personality disorder. *Annual Review of Clinical Psychology, 6,* 1-26.

Piquero, N.L., Exum, M.L., & Simpson, S.S. (2005). Integrating the desire for control and rational choice in a corporate crime context. *Justice Quarterly, 22*(2), 252-280.

Pleyte, M. (2003, December 1). White collar crime in the twenty first century, Retrieved from http://blj.ucdavis.edu/archives/vol-4-no-1/White-Collar-Crime-in-The-Twenty-First-Century.html.

Plimpton, E. A., & Walsh, D. (2010). Corporate criminal liability. *American Criminal Law Review, 47,* 331–362.

Podgor, E. (2007a). Throwing away the key. *The Yale Law Journal Pocket Part, 116,* 286-291.

Podgor, E. (2007b). The challenge of white collar sentencing. *Journal of Criminal Law and Criminology, 93*(3).

Pontell, H.N. & Geis, G. (2007). *International Handbook of White-collar and Corporate Crime.* New York: Springer.

Pontell, H.N. & Schichor, D., (2001). *Contemporary Issues in Criminal Justice.* N.J.: Prentice Hall.

Poole, P. (2007). Mortgage fraud funding jihad. *Front Page Magazine.* Retrieved from www.FrontPageMagazine.com.

Porco, C. (2011, October 18). *State of New York v. Christopher Porco.* Retrieved from http://www.nycourts.gov/reporter/3dseries/2011/2011_07255.htm

Porter, B. (2004, June 6). A long way down. *The New York Times Magazine,* 50-53.

Porter, S. (2011). The confession interview: Ethical, legal, and psychological implications for the forensic accountant. Association of Certified Fraud Examiners. Retrieved from http://www.acfe.com/uploadedFiles/ACFE_Website/Content/canadian/2013/presentations/5B-Scott-Porter-cpp.pdf

Porter, S., & Woodworth, M. (2006). Psychopathy and aggression. *Clinical and Applied Issues,* 481-494.

Porter, S., & ten Brinke, L. (2010). The truth about lies: What works in detecting high-stakes deception? *Legal and Criminolgical Psychology, 15,* 57-75.

Porter, S., McCabe,S., Woodworth, M., & Peace, K.A. (2007). Genius is 1% inspiration and 99% perspiration…or is it? An investigation of the impact of motivation and feedback on deception detection. *Legal and Criminological Psychology, 12,* 297-309.

Post, J.M. (1997). Narcissism and the quest for political power. *In Omnipotent Fantasies and the Vulnerable Self,* ed. C. S. Ellman and J. Reppen, 195-232. Northvale, NJ: Aronson.

Pressler, J. (2008, December 16). Bernie Madoff: In today's regulatory environment, it's virtually impossible to violate rules. *New York Magazine.* Retrieved from http://nymag.com/daily/intel/2008/12/bernie_madoff_in_todays_regula 1.html

Pressler, J. (2009, February 4). Harry markopolos is testifying in front of congress right now. *New York Magazine.* Retrieved from http://nymag.com/daily/intelligencer/2009/02/harry_markopoulos_is_testifyin.html

Pretty, P. (2010, February 10). Former attorney sentenced to 99 years in prison for Ponzi scheme; Edward S. Digges was a recidivist offender. Retrieved from http://patrickpretty.com/2010/02/20/former-attorney-sentenced-to-99-years-in-prison-for-ponzischeme-edward-s-digges-jr-was-recidivist-offender/.

Price, M. & Norris, D.M.(2009). White collar crime: Corporate and securities and commodities fraud, *Journal of the American Academy of Psychiatry Law, 37*(4), 538-544.

Pringle, P. (2008, April 14). Age, gender could play role in hit-and-run verdict. *Los Angeles Times.* Retrieved from http://www.latimes.com/news/local/la-me olgahelen14apr14,1,7172283.story

Pringle, P., & So, H. (2006, May 31). Two psychopathic old ladies-killers. Retrieved from
    http://friedgreentomatoes.org/articles/psychopathic_old_ladies.php

Pringle, P. & Kim, V. (2008, March 19). Murder case against women outlined. Los Angeles Times. Retrieved from
    http://www.latimes.com/news/local/lame olgahelen19mar19,0,6252440.story

Quayle, J. (2008). Interviewing a psychopathic suspect. *Journal of Investigative Psychology and Offender Profiling, 5,* 79–91.

Rabon, D. (2006). Interviewing the pathological subject. *Fraud Magazine, 20*(3), 53–54.

Rackmill, S.J. (1992). Understanding and sanctioning the white-collar offender. *Federal Probation, 56,* 26-34.

Ragatz, L., & Fremouw, W. (2010). A critical examination of research on the psychological profiles of white-collar criminals. *Journal of Forensic
    Psychological Practice, 10*(5), 373-402.

Ragatz, L., Fremouw, W., & Baker, E. (2012). The psychological profile of white-collar offenders: Demographics, criminal thinking, psychopathic
    traits, and psychopathology. *Criminal Justice and Behavior, 39*(7), 978-997.

Raghavan, A., Kranhold, K., & Barrionuevo, A. (2002, August 26). Full spreed ahead: How enron bosses created a culture of pushing limits. *Wall
    Street Journal*, p. A1.

Raison, C. (2012, August 21). Psychiatrist: I hate suicide but also understand it. Retrieved from http://www.cnn.com/2012/08/21/health/raison-
    suicide-tony-scott/

Ramamoorti, S., & Olsen W. (2007, July-August). Fraud: The human factor. *Financial Executives International,* 53-55.

Ramamoorti, S. (2008). The psychology and sociology of fraud: Integrating the behavioral sciences component into fraud and forensic accounting
    curricula. *Issues in Accounting Education, 23*(4), 521-533.

Ramamoorti, S., Morrison, D.E., Koletar, J.W., Pope, K.R. (2013). *A.B.C.'s of Behavioral Forensics.* New Jersey: Wiley

Ramamoorti, S., Morrison, D., Koletar, J.W. (2014). Bringing freud to fraud: Understanding the state of mind of of the c-level /white-collar offender
    the the a-b-c analysis. *6*(1), 47-81.

Ramirez, M.K. (2016). Oversight and rule making as political conflict. In Van Slyke, S.R.; Benson, M.L. Cullen, F.T. (2016). *The Oxford Handbook
    of White-collar Crime.* UK: Oxford University Press.

Rashbaum, W. K., Ruderman, W., & Secret, M. (2012, December 10). Fallen dean's life, contradictory to its grisly end. *The New York Times.*
    Retrieved from http://www.nytimes.com/2012/12/11/nyregion/a-quick-descent-for-cecilia-chang-dean-at-st-
    johns.html?pagewanted=4&_r=2&hp

Rauthmann, J.F. (2011). The dark triad and interpersonal perception: Similarities and
    differences in the social consequence of narcissism, machiavellianism, and psychopathy. *Social Psychology and Personality Science,* 1-10

Ray, J. (2007). Psychopathy, attitudinal beliefs, and white collar crime. Retrieved from http://www.mendeley.com/research/psychopathy-attitudinal-
    beliefs-white-collar-crime-3/

Ray, J., & Jones, S. (2011). Self-reported psychopathic traits and their relation to intentions to engage in environmental offending. *International
    Journal of Offender Therapy and Comparative Criminology, 55,* 370–391.

Reckard, E.S. (2013, December 21). Wells fargo's pressure-cooker sales culture comes at a cost. *Los Angeles Times.* Retrieved from
    http://www.latimes.com/business/la-fi-wells-fargo-sale-pressure-20131222-story.html

Reed, T.E. (2007). Affinity fraud, Retrieved form http://colonendparenthesis.blogspot.com/2007/05/affinity-fraud-by-trevor-e-reed.html.

Regnaud, D.A. (2011). The relationship between top leaders' observed narcisstic behaviors and workplace bullying. *Walden University Scholarworks.*
    1-184.

Reh, F. (2005, June 2005). Kozlowski, Tyco's ex-ceo, guilty. Retrieved from http://management.about.com/b/2005/06/18/kozlowski-tycos-ex-ceo-
    guilty.htm.

Reid, S., & Lee, J. (2018). Confessions of a criminal psychcopath: An analysis of the robert pinkton cell-plant. *Journal of Police and Criminal
    Psychology,* 1-14. Retrieved from https://link.springer.com/article/10.1007/s11896-018-9256-2

Reidy, D. E., Zeichner, A., & Martinez, M. A. (2008a). Effects of psychopathy traits on unprovoked aggression. *Aggressive Behavior, 34,* 319–328.

Reidy, D. E., Zeichner, A., Foster, J. D., & Martinez, M. A. (2008b). Effects of narcissistic entitlement and exploitativeness on human physical
    aggression. *Personality and Individual Differences, 44,* 865–875.

Reurink, A. (2016). Financial fraud: A literature review. *MPifg Discussion Paper, 16*(5), 1-100.

Reuters. (2007, June 28). Ex-healthsouth ceo scrushy sentenced to prison. *Reuters.* Retrieved from http://www.reuters.com/article/us-usa-scrushy-
    sentence-idUSN2824475720070629

Reynolds, S.J. (2006). Moral awareness and ethical predispositions: Investigating the role of individual differences in the recognition of moral issues.
    Journal of Applied Psychology, 91(1), 233-243.

Rezaee, Z., & Riley, R. (2010). *Financial Statement Fraud: Prevention and Detection, 2nd ed.* New Jersey, John Wiley Inc.

Richards, D.A., Melacion, B.C., & Rately, J.D. (n.d.). Managing the business risk of fraud: A practical guide. Retrieved from
    https://www.acfe.com/uploadedFiles/ACFE_Website/Content/documents/managing-business-risk.pdf

Rieber, R.W. (1997). *Manufacturing Social Distress.* N.Y.: Plenum Press.

Rijsenbilt, A. (2011). CEO narcissism. Retrieved from http://repub.eur.nl/res/pub/23554/EPS2011238STR9789058922816.pdf

Rijsenbilt, A., & Commandeur H. (2013). Narcissus enters the courtroom: CEO narcissism and fraud. *Journal of Business Ethics, 117,* 413-429.

Roberts, B. (2011). Your cheating heart. *HR Magazine, 56*(6), 54–60.

Roberts, S.R. (2016). The crime-terror nexus: Ideology's misleading role in islamist terrorist group. *E-International Relations.* Retrieved from
    http://www.e-ir.info/2016/04/23/the-crime-terror-nexus-ideologys-misleading-role-in-islamist-terrorist-groups/

Robles, J. (2008). Robles v. Autozone. Retrieved from http://reid.com/pdfs/summer2008/robles.pdf

Rodrigues, J. (2019, March 24). Fianance people will eat you for lunch, rajat gupta's wife warned. *Bloomberg.* Retrieved from
    https://www.bloomberg.com/news/articles/2019-03-24/finance-people-will-eat-you-for-lunch-rajat-gupta-s-wife-warned

Roger, B.(2018, May 5). Woman facing life in prison for stealing $1.2 million kills herself in walmart parking lot. WESH News on Demand,
    Retrieved from http://www.wesh.com/article/woman-facing-life-in-prison-for-stealing-dollar12m-kills-herself-in-walmart-parking-
    lot/20195449

Roger, P. (2016). *Auditing and Attestion* 2016. *Roger CPA Review.*

Rollins, J. & Wyler, L.S. (2010, April, 11). International terrorism and transnational crime: security threats, US policy, and considerations for congress. Retrieved from http://fpc.state.gov/documents/organization/141615.pdf.

Romero, S. (2003, March, 21). The rise and fall of richard scrushy, entrepreneur. *The New York Times,* Retrieved from http://www.nytimes.com/2003/03/21/business/the-rise-and-fall-of-richard-scrushy-entrepreneur.html

Rose, A.M., Rose, J.M., & Dibben, M. (2010). The Implications of auditors' dispositional trust and career advancement opportunities for the detection of fraud. *Journal of Forensic & Investigative Accounting, 2*(3), 141-163.

Rosenblatt, J. (2021a, November 29). I adore you: Elizabeth's holmes's romance with sunny balwani resurfaces at trial. Retrieved from www.bloomberg.com

Rosenblatt, J. (2021b, October, 22). Texan 'jackpot' recording of elizabeth holmes played for jury. Retrieved from www.bloomberg.com

Rosenbush, s. (2005). Five lessons of the worldcom debacle. Bloomberg. Retrieved from http://www.bloomberg.com/news/articles/2005-03-15/five-lessons-of-the-worldcom-debacle

Rosenthal, S.A. (n.d.). Narcissism and leadership. *Harvard University Center for Public Leadership.* Retrieved fromhttp://dspace.mit.edu/bitstream/handle/1721.1/55948/cpl_wp_06_04_rosenthal.pdf?sequence=1

Rosenthal, S.A. & Pittinsky, T.L. (2006). Narcissistic leadership. *The Leadership Quarterly, 17,* 617-633.

Ross, E.A. (1907). *Sin and Society: An Analysis of Latter-Day Iniquity.* New York: Houghton, Mifflin.

Ross, E.A. (1977). The criminaloid. In Gilbert Geis and Robert Meier, eds., *White-Collar Crime,* revised ed. 29-37. New York: Macmillan.

Rosoff, S.M. (2007). The role of the mass media in the enron fraud. In *International Handbook of White-collar and Corproate Crime.* NY: Springer.

Rossmo, D.K. (2006). Criminal investigative failures: Avoiding the pitfalls. *FBI Law Enforcement Bulletin.* Retrieved from http://www.au.af.mil/au/awc/awcgate/fbi/cognitive_bias.pdf.

Rothfeld, M. (2012, October 12). Dear judge, gupta is a good man. Retrieved from http://online.wsj.com/article/SB10000872396390444657804578052990875489744.html.

Rothstein, B., & Uslaner, E.M. (2005). All for all: Equality, corruption and social trust. *World Politics, 58,* 41-72.

Rowe, D. & Osgood, D. (1984). Heredity and sociological theories of delinquency: A reconsideration. *American Sociological Review 49,* 526-40.

Rowe, C. A., Walker, K. L., Britton, P. C., & Hirsch, J. K. (2013). The relationship between negative life events and suicidal behavior. *Crisis, 34*(4), 233-241.

Roy, A. (2003). Distal risk factors for suicidal behavior in alcoholics: replications and new findings. *Journal of Affective Disorders, 77*(3), 267-271.

Rozek, D. (2005, November 5). Son charged in quadruple murder: Naperville man killed to hide theft. Chicago Sun-Times Retrieved from http://www.findarticles. com/p/articles/mi_qn4155/is_20051105?pnum=2&opg=n15910884

Rubin, R. (2014, January 3). How the 'wolf of wall street' really did It. *Wall Street Journal.* Retrieved from http://www.wsj.com/articles/SB10001424052702303453004579290450707920302

Ruiz, M. A., Douglas, K. S., Edens, J. F., Nikolova, N. L., & Lilienfeld,S.O.(2012). Co-occurring mental health and substance use problems in offenders: Implications for risk assessment. *Psychological Assessment, 24*(1), 77-87

Rusch, J. (1999). The social engineering of internet fraud, paper presented at the INET 1999 Conference, San Jose, CA. CT.

Russ, E., Shedler, J., Bradley, R., & Westen, D., (2008). Refining the construct of narcissistic personality disorder: Diagnostic criteria and subtypes. *American Journal of Psychiatry, 161*(11).

Rutterschmidt, O. (2009, August 18). The People v. Olga Rutterschmidt. Court of Appeal,Second District, Division 5, California. Retrieved from http://caselaw.findlaw.com/ca-court-of-appeal/1267298.html

Rutterschmidt, O. (2012, October 15). The People v. Olga Rutterschmidt, In the Supreme Court of California. S176213. Retrieved from http://cases.justia.com/california/supreme-court/s176213.pdf?ts=1396114583

Sakuri, Y. & Smith, R.G. (2003). Gambling as a motivation for the commission of financial crime. *Trends and issues in Crime and Criminal Justice, 256,* Canberra: Australian Institute of Criminology.

Salazar, M. (2010, May 9). Ex-Jemez mountain school district embezzler commits suicide before monday's sentencing. *Albuquerque Journal.* Retrieved from http://www.abqjournal.com/news/state/09231923state05-09-10.htm

Sale, R. (2009, February 6). US officials: Hezbollah gaining in Latin America. Middle East Times, Retrieved from www.metimes.com/Politics/2009/02/06/us_officials_hezbollah_gaining_in_latin_america/56857.

Salekin, R.T., Rogers, R. & Sewell, K.W. (1997). Construct validity of psychopathy in a female offender sample. *Journal of Abnormal Psychology,106*(4), 576-585.

Saltzman, J. (2009). Ponzi schemer get 2nd sentence. Retrieved from www.boston.com/news/local/massachusetts/articles/2009/08/14/ponzi_schemer_gets_2d_sentence/.

Sawayda, J. (2011). Arthur Andersen: An accounting confidence crisis. *Daniels Fund Ethics Initiative,* University of New Mexico. Retieved from https://danielsethics.mgt.unm.edu/pdf/Arthur%20Andersen%20Case.pdf

Sawayda, J. (2015). The challenges of expense accounting fraud. *Daniels Fund Ethics Inititative.* Retrieved from https://danielsethics.mgt.unm.edu/pdf/expense-account-fraud.pdf

Samenow, S. (1984). *Inside the Criminal Mind.* New York, NY: Crown Publishers.

Samenow, S. (2009, February 4). What's wrong with Bernie madoff? Retrieved from http://wowowow.com/post/whats-wrong-bernie-madoff-psychologist-stanton-samenow-184867

Samenow, S. (2010, October). The myth of the out of character crime. Concept of the Month

Samenow, S. (2012a, July 7). Armed robber and corporate crook: Similar mentalities. *Psychology Today.* Retrieved from http://www.psychologytoday.com/blog/inside-the-criminal-mind/201207/armed-robber-and-corporate-crook-similar-mentalities.

Samenow, S. (2012b, November 29). The myth of the out of character crime, part 3. *Psychology Today.* Retrieved from https://www.psychologytoday.com/blog/inside-the-criminal-mind/201211/the-myth-the-out-character-crime-part-3

Samenow, S. (2016, April 18). The criminal as a religious person. *Psychology Today*,
    Retrieved from https://www.psychologytoday.com/blog/inside-the-criminal-mind/201604/the-criminal-religious-person

Sauer, R.C. (2010). Why the SEC missed madoff. *Wall Street Journal*, July 17-18, p. A13.

SCCMIGPE. (2009). Assessing the Madoff Ponzi scheme and regulatory failures, Hearing Before the Subcommittee on Capital Markets, Insurance, and Government Sponsored Enterprises of the Committee on Financial Services, US House of Representatives, 111 Congress, First session, Serial No. 111-112, 4 February.

Schaef, A. W., & Fassel, D. (1988, January/February). Hooked on work. *New Age Journal*. 42-63.

Scharff, M.M. (2005). Understanding worldcom's accounting fraud: Did groupthink play a role? *Journal of Leadership and Organizational Studies,11*(3), 109-118.

Schilit, H.M., & Perler, J. (2010). *Financial Shenanigans, 3ʳᵈ Edition*. McGraw-Hill Publishers.

Schlegel, K. &Weisburd, D. (1992). *White-collar Crime Reconsidered*. Boston: Northeastern University Press.

Schlesinger, L.B. (2001). The contract murderer: Patterns, characertistics, and dynamic. *Journal of Forensic Science, (46)*5, 1110-1123.

Schneider, H. (2015). The corporation as victim of white collar crime: Results from a study of german public and private companies. *University of Miami Law School Insitutional Repository, 22*(2), 171-205.

Schoepfer, A., & Carmichael, S., & Piquero, N.L. (2007). Do perceptions of punishment vary between white-collar and street crimes? *Journal of Criminal Justice, 35*, 151-163.

Schoepfer, A., & Tibbetts, S. G. (2012). From early white-collar bandits and robber barons to modern-day white-collar criminals. In D. Shichor, L. Gaines, & A. Shoepfer (Eds.*), In Reflecting on White-Collar andCorporate Crime*. Illinois: Waveland Press Inc.

Schouten, R., & Silver, J. (2012). *Almost a psychopath*. Center City, MN: Hazelden.

Schwartz, J. (2002a, January 21). Enron's collapse: the analyst; man who doubted enron enjoys new recognition. *The New York Times*. Retrieved from https://www.nytimes.com/2002/01/21/business/enron-s-collapse-the-analyst-man-who-doubted-enron-enjoys-new-recognition.html

Schwartz, J. (2002b, February 7). Enron's many strands: Darth Vader, Machiavelli, skilling set intense pace. *The New York Times*. Retrieved from http://www.nytimes.com/2002/02/07/business/enron-s-many-strands-former-ceo-darth-vader-machiavelli-skilling-set-intense.html?pagewanted=all&src=pm

Schwartzman, P. (1999, August 4). Come & get me, jr. Sammy bull sez he doesn't fear revenge. *The Daily News*. Retrieved from http://www.nydailynews.com/archives/news/jr-sammy-bull-sez-doesn-fear-revenge-article-1.849939

Scott, K.H. (2003). MSU lab helping FBI hunt down terrorists. Retrieved from www.allbusiness.com/public-administration/955156-1.html.

Seal, M. (2009, April). Madoff's world. *Vanity Fair*. Retrieved from http://www.vanityfair.com/news/2009/04/bernard-madoff-friends-family-profile

Searcy, D. (2013, September 28-29). Ex-ceo exits prison with a new set of pals. *Wall Street Journal*, A1.

SEC. (2001). Securities and Exchange Commission v. Sunbeam. Securities and Exchange Commission. Retrieved from https://www.sec.gov/litigation/admin/33-7976.htm

SEC. (2003). Report of the investigation by the special investigative committee of the board of directors of worldcom. Securities and Exchange Commission Retrieved from http://www.sec.gov/Archives/edgar/data/723527/000093176303001862/dex991.htmhttp://www.sec.gov/Archives/edgar/data/723527/000093176303001862/dex991.htm

SEC. (2016). Ernst & young to pay $11.8 million for audit failures. Securities and Exchange Commission Retrieved from https://www.sec.gov/news/pressrelease/2016-219.html

SEC. (2018). Securities and Exchange Commission versus Elizabeth Holmes. Securities and Exchange Commission Retrieved from https://www.sec.gov/litigation/complaints/2018/comp-pr2018-41-theranos-holmes.pdf

Security Pacific (1992). Security Pacific Business Credit Inc. v. Peat Marwick & Co., 79 N.Y2d 695, 597 N.E.2d 1080.

Seegull, L., & Caputo, E. (2006). When a test turns into a trial. Retrieved from http://apps.americanbar.org/buslaw/blt/2006-01-02/caputo.html

Sendjaya, S., Pekerti, A., Hartel, C., Hirst, G., & Butarbutar, I. (2014). Are authentic leaders always moral? The role of Machiavellianism in the relationship between authentic leadership and morality. *Journal of Business Ethics, 133*, 125-139.

Sexton, J. (1995, April 19). Longtime informer is accused in killing. *The New York Times*.Retrieved from https://www.nytimes.com/1995/04/19/nyregion/longtime-informer-is-accused-in-killing.html

Shain, R. (2010). Fix the SEC, or abolish it. *Money*. Retrieved from http://money.cnn.com/2010/06/22/news/economy/sec_stanford_madoff_fixes.fortune/index.htm.

Sharma, R., Sherrod, M.H., Corgel, R., & Kuzma, S.J. (2009). *The Guide to Investigating Business Fraud*. N.Y.:American Institute of Certified Public Accountants.

Sharonpande., & Srivastava, M. (2013). The black box of leadership. *International Journal of Business and General Management, 2*(3), 2319-2267.

Sheard. A.G., Kakabadse, N., & Kakabadse, A. (2013). Destructive behaviours and leadership: The source of the shift from a functional to dysfunctional workplace? *International Journal of Social Science Studies,1*(1), 73-89.

Shelley, L. (2006). Growing together, ideological and operational linkages between terrorists and criminal networks. Retrieved from www.fundforpeace.org/web/images/pdf/shelley.pdf.

Shelley, L. & Melzer, S. (2008). The nexus of organized crime and terrorism: two case studies in cigarette smuggling. *International Journal of Comparative & Applied Criminal Justice, 32*(1), 43-63.

Shelley, L.I., Picarelli, J.T., Irby, A., Hart, D.M., Hart, P.A., Williams, P., Simon, S., Abdullaev, N.,Stanislawski, B. & Covisll, L. (2005). Methods and motives: exploring links between transnational organized crime and international terrorism. Retrieved from www.ncjrs.gov/pdffiles1/nij/grants/211207.pdf.

Sherter, A. (2009, September 3). SEC pleads mea culpa on madoff affair. *Money Watch*. Retrieved from https://www.cbsnews.com/news/sec-pleads-mea-culpa-on-madoff-affair/

Shover, N. (2007). Generative worlds of white-collar crime. In *International Handbook of White-collar and Corporate Crime*. New York: Springer.

Shover, N. and Hochstetler, A. (2006). *Choosing White-collar Crime*. New York: Cambridge University Press.

Shover, N. & Wright, J.P. (2001). *Crimes of Privilege*. New York: Oxford University Press

Siddiqui, F. (2021, October 6). Former safeway ceo steven burd testifies about theranos's high flying claims in fraud trial. www.washingtonpost.com

Siegel, N. (2008). United States of America v. Nancy Jean Siegel, No. 07-4551 (2008).

Silverstone, H. & Sheetz, M. (2007). *Forensic Accounting and Fraud Investigation for Non-Experts, 2nd Edition.* NY: John Wiley & Sons.

Simha, A. & Satyanarayan, S. (2016). Straight from the horse's mouth: Auditors' on fraud detection and prevention, roles of technology, and white-collars getting splattered with red! *Journal of Accounting and Finance, 16*(1), 26-44.

Simpson, S. (1986). The decomposition of antitrust: Testing multilevel, longitudinal, model of profit squeeze. *American Sociological Review, 51,* 859-875.

Simpson, S. (1987). Cylcles of illegality: Antitrust violations in corporate America. Social *Forces, 65,* 943-963.

Simpson, S. (2013). White-collar crime: A review of recent developments and promising directions for future research. *Annual Review of Sociology, 39,* 309-331.

Simpson S.S., & Piquero, N.L. (2002). Low self-control, organizational theory, and corporate crime. *Law and Society Review, 36,* 509-547.

Simpson, S.S., & Weisburd, D. (2008). *The Criminolgy of White-collar Crime.* NY: Springer Science.

Sims, R.R. (1992). Linking groupthink to unethical behavior in organizations. *Journal of Business Ethics, 11,* 651-662.

Sims, R.R. (2003). *Ethics and Corporate Social Responsibility: Why Giants Fall.* Connecticut: Praeger.

Sims, R.R., & Brinkmann, J. (2002). Leaders as moral role models: The case of john gutfreund at salomon brothers. *Journal of Business Ethics, 35*(4), 327-339.

Sims, R.R., & Brinkmann, J. (2003). Enron Ethics (Or: culture matters more than codes). *Journal of Business Ethics, 45*(3), 243-256.

Sirota, D. Under Obama administration, federal prosecutions of white-collar crime hits 20-year low. *In These Times.* Retrieved from http://inthesetimes.com/article/18392/federal-prosecution-of-white-collar-crime-hits-20-year-low-under-obama-admi

Skalak, S.L., Golden, T., Clayton, M., & Pill, J. (2011). *A Guide to Forensic Accounting and Investigation.* N.Y: John Wiley & Sons Inc.

Skeem, J., Polaschek, D., Patrick, J., & Lilienfeld, S. (2011). Psychopathic personality: Bridging the gap between scientific evidence and public policy. *Psychological Science in the Public Interest, 12*(3), 95-162.

Smith, D. (2008, August 1). Florida businessman paid hit man to delete irs agent, Retrieved from http://www.efluxmedia.com/news_Fla_Businessman_Paid_Hit_Man_to_Delete_IRS_Agent_21343.html.

Smith, G. (2015a, March). The past, present and future of forensic accounting. *The CPA Journal,*17-21.

Smith, G. (2015b, July 21). Toshiba just lost its CEO to a huge accounting scandal. *Fortune Magazine.* Retrieved from http://fortune.com/2015/07/21/toshiba-just-lost-its-ceo-to-a-huge-accounting-scandal/

Smith, J. (1991, January 4). Accused hit man denied bail in fraud witnesses slaying. Retrieved from http://articles.philly.com/1991-01-04/news/25820873_1_insurance-fraud-fbi-informant-contract-slaying.

Smith, S. & Lilienfeld, S. (2013). Psychopathy in the workplace: The knowns and unknowns. *Aggression and Violent Behavior, 18*(2), 204-218.

Solieri, S.A., Felo, A.J., & Hodowanitz, J. (2008). Richard scrushy: The rise and fall of the 'king of health care'. Retrieved from http://soliericpas.com/attachments/2008MarRichardScrushyTheRise&FalloftheKingofHealthcare.pdf

Soltani, B. (2014). The anatomy of corporate fraud: A comparative analysis of high profile American and European corporate scandals. *Journal of Business Ethics, 120,* 251-274.

Soltes, E. (2016). *Why They Do It.* New York: PublicAffairs

Somerville, H. & Weaver, C. (2021). Romance between homes, balwani continued after he left theranos. www.wsj.com.

Spain, S.M., & Harms, P.D., & Lebreton, J.M. (2013, January 1). The dark side of personality at work. *Management Department Faculty Publications.* 1-21.

Spalek, B. (1999). Exploring the impact of financial crime: A study looking into the effects of the maxwell scandal upon the maxwell pensioner. *International Review of Victimology, 6,* 213-230.

Spalek, B. (2001). White-collar crime vicitms and the issue of trust. *British Society of Criminology. 4.*

Stabile, S. L. (2002). The use of personality tests as a hiring tool: Is the benefit worth the cost? *University of Pennsylvania Journal of Labor and Employment Law, 4*(2), 279–313.

Stachowicz-Stanusch, A. (2011). Destructive sides of charismatic leadership. *Organizational and Management Journal,* 113-125.

State of New Mexico: Office of the State Auditor (2009, August 14). State auditor balderas' special audit reveals over $3.3 million embezzled from the jemez mountain school district. Retrieved from www.saonm.org/media/news_pdf/8-14-09_OSA_PR_Jemez_Mountain_SD_Special_Audit.pdf.

State Street Trust (1938). *State Street Trust Co. v. Ernst.* 278 N.Y. 104.

Steffenmeier, D.J., Schwartz, J., & Roche, M. (2013). Gender and twenty-first-century corporate crime:Female Involvement and the gender gap in enron-era corporate frauds. *American Sociological Review,78*(3), 448-476.

Steinberger, M. (2004). Psychopathic CEO's. *The New York Times.* Retrieved from http://www.nytimes.com/2004/12/12/magazine/12PSYCHO.html.

Sternglanz. R.W. & DePaulo, B.M. (2004). Reading nonverbal cue to emotions: The advantages and liabilities of closeness. *Journal of Nonverbal Behavior, 28*(4), 245-266.

Stewart, G. (1992). *Den of Theives.* NY: Simon and Schuster Inc.

Stotland, E. (1977). White collar criminals. *The Journal of Social Issues, 33*(4), 179–196

Stout, M. (2005). *The Sociopath Next Door.* Random House.

Strader, J.K. (2007). White collar crime and punishment: Reflections on michael, martha and milberg weiss. *George Mason Law Review,15*(1), 45-107.

Streitfeld, D., & Romney, L. (2002, January 27). Enron's run tripped by arrogance, greed. *Los Angeles Times.* Retrieved fromhttp://articles.latimes.com/2002/jan/27/news/mn-25002/3

Strom, S. (2009, February 27). Elie wiesel levels scorn at madoff. Retrieved from http://www.nytimes.com/2009/02/27/business/27madoff.html?_r=0

Stromwall, L.A., & Granhag, P.A. (2003). How to detect deception? Arresting the beliefs of police officers, prosecutors and judges. *Psychology, Crime & Law, 9,* 19-36.

Stromwall, L.A., Hartwig, M., & Granhag, P.A. (2006). To act truthfully: Nonverbal behaviour and strategies during a police interrogation. *Psychology, Crime & Law, 12*(2), 207-219.

Stomwall, L.A., & Willen, R.M. (2011). Inside criminal minds: Offenders' strategies when lying. *Journal of Investigative Psychology and Offender Profiling, 8*, 271-281.

Stuart, C. (2006). FBI worries about mafia-al qaeda links. Retrieved from www.associatedcontent.com/article/68378/fbi_worries_about_mafia_al_qaeda_links.html ?cat¼17.

Stulb, D.L. (2016). Corporate misconduct-individual consequences: 14th global fraud survey. Retrieved from http://www.ey.com/Publication/vwLUAssets/EY-corporate-misconduct-individual-consequences/$FILE/EY-corporate-misconduct-individual-consequences.pdf

Sturman, M.C., & Sherwyn, D. (2007, October, 2). The truth about integrity tests: The validity and utility of integrity testing for the hospitiality industry. Center for Hospitality Research Publications, 7(15), 1-18.

Sullivan, B.A., Chermak, S.M., Chermak., Wilson, J.M., & Feilich, J.D. (2014). The nexus between terrorism and product counterfeiting in the united states. *Global Crime*, 1-22.

Sutherland, E.H. (1924). Criminology, First Edition. Philadelphia: J.B. Lippincott Company.

Sutherland, E.H. (1934). *Principles of Criminology, Second Edition*. Philadelphia: J.B. Lippincott Company.

Sutherland, E.H. (1937). *The Professional Thief*. University of Chicago Press.

Sutherland, E.H. (1940). White-collar criminality. *American Sociological Review, 5*(1), 1-12.

Sutherland, E.H. (1941). Crime and business. *Academy of Political and Social Science, 217*, 112-118.

Sutherland, E. H. (1949). *White collar crime*. NY: Holt, Rinehart & Winston.

Sutherland, E. H. (1983). *White collar crime: The uncut version*. NY: Holt, Rinehart & Winston

Sutherland, E.H., & Cressey, D.R. (1966). *Criminology Seventh Edition*. Philadelphia: J.B. Lippincott Company.

Sutherland, E.H., & Cressey, D.R. (1974). *Criminology Ninth Edition*. Philadelphia: J.B. Lippincott Company.

Sutherland, E.H., & Cressey, D.R. (1978). *Criminology Tenth Edition*. Philadelphia: J.B. Lippincott Company.

Swartz, M., & Watkins, S. (2003). *Power Failure: The Rise and Fall of Enron*. London: Aurum Press.

Sweeney, P. (2002). The travails of tyco. *Financial Executive,18*(4), 20-23.

Sykes G.M. & Matza, D. (1957). Techniques of neutralisation: A theory of delinquency. *American Sociological Review, 22*(1), 664-70.

Sykes, T. (1994). *The Bold Riders: Behind Australia's Corporate Collapse*. Sydney, Australia: Allen & Unwin.

Taibbi, M. (2011, February 11). Why isn't wall street in jail? *Rolling Stone Magazine*. Retrieved from http://www.rollingstone.com/politics/news/why-isnt-wall-street-in-jail-20110216.

Taxman, F., Rhodes, A., & Dumenci, L. (2011). Construct and predictive validity of criminal thinking scales. *Criminal Justice and Behavior, 38*(2), 174-187.

Taylor, E.Z., & Curtis, M.B. (2010). An examination of the layers of workplace influences in ethical judgements: Whistleblowing likelihood and perserverance in public accounting. *Journal of Business Ethics, 93*, 21-37.

Telegraph, (2008, December 20). Bernard madoff: How did he get away with it so long? The Telegraph. Retrieved from http://www.telegraph.co.uk/finance/financetopics/bernard-madoff/3869934/Bernard-Madoff-how-did-he-get-away-with-it-for-so-long.html

Ten Brinke, L. & Porter, S. (2012). Cry me a river. Identifying the behavioral consequences of extremely high stakes interpersonal deception. *Law and Human Behavior, 36*(6), 469-477.

Tenbrunsel, A. E., & Smith-Crowe, K. (2008). Ethical decision making: Where we've been and where we're going. *Academy of Management Annals, 2*, 545-607.

Thibodeau, J.C., & Freier, D. (2014). *Auditing and Accounting Cases*. NY: McGraw-Hill Irwin.

Thiruchelvam, S.(2018,September 6). Theranos: How one woman fooled silicon valley. Raconteur.Retrieved from https://www.raconteur.net/risk-management/theranos-fraud-silicon-valley

Thoroughgood, C.N., Padilla, A., Hunter, S.T., & Tate, B.W. (2012). The susceptible circle: A taxonomy of followers associated with destructive leadership. *The Leadership Quarterly, 23*(5), 897-917.

Toffler, B, & Reingold, J. (2004). *Final Accounting: Ambition, Greed and the Fall of Arthur Andersen*. New York: Doubleday.

Tokars, F. (1996). United States of America v. Fredric W. Tokars, 95 F.2d 1520 (1996).

Tokars, F. (2008, December 8). Infamous murderer, prison snitch-fred tokars. Retrieved from http://bogbuster2.blogspot.com/2008/12/infamous-murderer- prison-snitch-fred.html.

Tomlinson, E.C. & Pozzuto, A. (2016). Criminal decision making in organizational contexts. In Van Slyke, S.R., Benson, M.L., & Cullen, F.T. (2016). *The Oxford Handbook of White-collar Crime*.UK: Oxford University Press.

Torpey, D., & Sherrod, M. (2011, January/February). Who own fraud? *Fraud Magazine*. Retrieved from http://www.fraud-magazine.com/article.aspx?id=4294968975

Tourish D., & Vatcha, N. (2005). Charismatic leadership and corporate cultism at Enron: The elimination of dissent, the promotion of conformity and organizational collapse. *Leadership,1,*455-480.

Traub, J. (1988, July 24). Into the mouths of babes. *New York Times*. Retrieved from http://www.nytimes.com/1988/07/24/magazine/into-the-mouths-of-babes.html?pagewanted=all&pagewanted=print

Trevino, K.L., & Brown, M.E. (2004). Managing to be ethical: Debunking five business ethics myths. *Academy of Management Executive,18*(2), 69-81.

Tsahuridu, E.E., & Vanderlerckhove, W. (2008). Organizational whistleblowing policies: Making employees responsible or liable? *Journal of Business Ethics, 82*, 107-118.

Tse,T.M. (2009, June 30). Madoff sentenced to 150 years. *The Washington Post*. Retrieved from http://www.washingtonpost.com/wpdyn/content/article/2009/06/29/AR2009062902015.html.

Tschakert, N. (2017). Crazy accounting at crazy eddie. *Journal of Forensic and Investigative Accounting, 9*(1). 711-723.

Tucker, E. (2010, April 27). RI man admits to burying parents in backyard cesspool. *CorrectionsOne.com*. Retrieved from
https://www.correctionsone.com/arrests-and-sentencing/articles/2054079-RI-man-admits-to-burying-parents-in-backyard-cesspool/

Tuente, S.K., de Vogel, V., & Stam, J. (2014). Exploring the criminal behavior of women with psychopathy: Results from a multicenter study into psychopathy and violent offending in female psychiatric patients. *International Journal of Forensic Mental Health, 13*, 311-322.

Ueda, K., Matsui, H., Ito, T., & Yamada, K. (2015, July 20). Investigation report: Summary version. Independent Investogation Committee for Toshiba Corporation. Retrieved from https://www.toshiba.co.jp/about/ir/en/news/20150725_1.pdf

Uhl-Bien, M. & Carsten, M. (2007). Being ethical when the boss is not. *Organizational Dynamics, 36*(2),187–201.

Ulrich, S., Farrington, D. P., Coid, J.W. (2008). Psychopathic personality traits and life success. *Personality and Individual Differences, 44*, 1162-1171.

Ultramares. (1932). *Ultramares Corporation v. Touche*, 174 N.E.2d 441.

Umphress, E.E., & Bingham, J.B. (2011). When employees do bad things for good reason: Examining unethical pro-organizational behaviors. *Organization Science, 22*(3), 621-640.

USDL. (2000). Testing and assessment: An employer's guide to good practices. http://www.onetcenter.org/dl_files/empTestAsse.pdf

USDOJ. (2013a, April 12). Ramona tax preparer sentenced for murder for hire, witness tampering, filing false tax returns with the irs, identity theft, money laundering and fraud. Retrieved from https://www.justice.gov/sites/default/files/usao-sdca/legacy/2015/04/30/cas13-0412-MartinezSentPR.pdf

USDOJ. (2013b, February 12). Jacksonville man convicted of orchestrating a scheme to defraud, attempting to murder a witness, and murder for hire. Retrieved from https://www.justice.gov/usao-mdfl/pr/jacksonville-man-convicted-orchestrating- scheme-defraud-attempting-murder-witness-a

Van Herwaarden, M. (2016). The difference between female and male white-collar criminals: Based on personality and positive attitudes with regarf to fraud. 1-28, Retrieved https://docgo.net/philosophy-of-money.html?utm_source=the-difference-between-female-and-male-white-collar-criminals-based-on-personality-and-positive-attitudes-with-regard-to-fraud

Van Slyke, S.R.; Benson, M.L., & Cullen, F.T. (2016). *The Oxford Handbook of White-collar Crime*. UK: Oxford University Press.

Van Slyke, S. R. & Rebovich, D.J. (2016). Public policy on white-collar crime. In *The Oxford Handbook of White-collar Crime*. UK: Oxford Press.

Van Vugt, M., & Hart, C.M. (2004). Social Identity as social glue: The origins of group loyalty. *Journal of Personality and Social Psychology, 86*(4), 585-598.

Vandivier, K. (2002). Why should my conscience bother me? Hiding aircraft break hazards. In Corporate and Governmental Deviance. New York: Oxford University Press.

Vann, R. T. (2007). Statement of rae t. vann. General Counsel, Equal Employment Advisory Council. Meeting of May 16, 2007 on Employment Testing and Screening: The U.S. Equal Employment Opportunity Commission. http://eeoc.gov/eeoc/meetings/archive/5-16-07/vann.html

Vardi, Y., & Weitz, E. (2004). *Misbehavior in Organizations*. London: Lawrence Erlbaum Associates.

Vazire, S., & Funder, D.C.(2006). Impulsivity and the self-defeating behavior of narcissists. *Personality and Social Psychology Review, 10*(2), 154-165.

Votaw, K.Q. (2011, May 24). What if you could measure integrity? TalenTrust. Retrieved from http://www.talentrust.com/blog/what-if-you-could-measure-integrity/

Vronsky, P. (2007). *Female Serial Killers*. New York: The Penguin Group.

Wachter, P. (2010, March 10). Jihad jane and femme fatale fascination. *AOL News*. Retrieved from www.aolnews.com.

Wagner, D. (2017, September 22). Salvatore gravano, aka sammy the bull living fearlessly in arizona. *Azcentral*. Retrieved from https://www.azcentral.com/story/news/local/arizona/2017/09/21/sammy-bull-salvatore-gravano-living-arizona/689289001/

Walker, B.R., & Jackson, C.J. (2016). Moral emotions and corporate psychopathy: A review. *Journal of Business Ethics, 141*(4), 797-810.

Walsh, A., & Hemmens, C. (2008). *Introduction to Criminology*. Beverly Hills, CA: Sage.

Walters, G.D. (2002*). Criminal Belief Systems: An Integrated-Interactive Approach Theory of Lifestyles*. CT: Praeger Publishers.

Walters G.D. & Geyer, M.D. (2004). Criminal thinking and identity in male white collar Offenders. *Criminal Justice and Behavior, 31*(3), 263-281.

Wang, P. (2010). The crime-terror nexus: Transformation, alliance, convergence. *Asian Social Science, 6*(6) 11-20.

Wang, W., & Cheng, H. (2016). The credibility of oversight and aggregate rates of white-collar crime. In Van Slyke, S.R.; Benson, M.L. & Cullen, F.T. (2016). *The Oxford Handbook of White-collar Crime*. UK: Oxford University Press.

Warigon, S. D., & Bowers, B. (2006, September-October). Management by intimidation. *Fraud Magazine*. Retrieved from http://www.fraud magazine.com/article.aspx?id=4294967680

Warren, G.C. (2009). The relationship between psychopathy and indirect aggression in a community sample. Retrieved from http://etheses.whiterose.ac.uk/785/1/thesisfinal.pdf .

Warren, J.I., Burnette, M.L., South, S.C., Chauhan, P., Bale, R., Friend, R., & Van Patten, I. (2003). Psychopathy in women: structural modeling and comorbidity. *International Journal of Law and Psychiatry, 26*, 223-242.

Watch, P.J.(2014, September 29). Eric holder's mixed legacy on white-collar crime. *New York Times*. Retrieved from https://dealbook.nytimes.com/2014/09/29/eric-holders-mixed-legacy-on-white-collar-crime/

Watkins, K., Turtle, J., & Euale, J. (2011). *Interviewing and Investigations*, 2nd Ed. Edmond Montgomery Publishing

WebCPA (2009). SEC admits missed opportunities in madoff case. Retrieved from www.webcpa.com/news/SEC-Admits-Missed-Opportunities-Madoff-Case-5160.html.

Weber, R. (2016, October). The real narcissists. *Psychology Today*. 53-61.

Weigel, J. (2013, January 5). Remarkable woman. *The Chicago Tribune*. Retrieved from http://www.chicagotribune.com/features/life/ct-tribu-remarkable-pope-20130105,0,4731331.story

Weisburd, D., Wheeler, S., Waring, E., & Bode, N. (1991). *Crimes of the Middle Class: White collar Offenders in the Federal Courts*. CT: Yale University Press.

Weisburd, D., Waring, E., & Chayet, E.F. (2001). *White collar Crime and Criminal Careers*. New York: Weisburd Cambridge University Press.

Weiser, B. (2011, June 28). Judge explains 150 year sentence for madoff. The New York Times. Retrieved from
http://www.nytimes.com/2011/06/29/nyregion/judge-denny-chin-recounts-his-thoughts-in-bernard-madoff-sentencing.html

Weissmann, A. & Block, J. (2007, February 21). White collar defendants and white collar crimes. The Yale Law Journal. Retrieved from
http://www.yalelawjournal.org/the-yale-law-journal-pocket-part/scholarship/white-collar-criminals/

Wells, J.T. (2001, May 1). Time is of the essence. Journal of Accountancy. Retrieved from
https://www.journalofaccountancy.com/issues/2001/may/timingisoftheessence.ht\ml

Wells, J.T. (2011). Corporate Fraud Handbook. N.J.: John Wiley & Sons, Inc.

Wells, J.T. (2012, April). The fraudster's mind. Internal Auditor, 53-56.

Wells Fargo. (2017, April 10). Independent directors of the board of wells fargo & company sales practices investigation report. Retrieved from
https://www08.wellsfargomedia.com/assets/pdf/about/investor-relations/presentations/2017/board-report.pdf

Welles, C. (1988, February 22). What led beech-nut down the road of disgrace. Business Week. 124-126.

Wertheimer, L. (2008). Affinity fraud prey's on group's trust. Retrieved from www.npr.org/templates/story/story.php?storyId¼986741.

Westbrook, J. & Scheer, D. (2010, April 16). Report finds SEC dropped the ball in Stanford case. The Wall Street Journal. Retrieved from
http://online.wsj.com/article/SB20001424052702303491304575188220570802084.html.

Wheeler, S., Mann, K., & Sarat, A. (1988). Sitting in Judgement, Yale University Press.

Whelan, C.W., Wagstaff, G.F., & Wheatcroft, J.M. (2014). High-stakes lies: Verbal and nonverbal cues to deception in public appeals for help with missing or murdered relatives. Psychiatry, Psychology and Law, 21(4), 523-537.

Williams, J. (2008, February 23). Victim-impact statement of jennifer williams. Daily Herald. Retrieved from http://www.dailyherald.com/story/?id=140796

Willott, S., Griffin, C., & Torrance, M. (2001). Snakes and ladders: Upper middle class male offenders talk about economic crime. Criminology, 39(2), 441-466.

Wilson, C. (2010, October 12). Indiana church financier faces ponzi scheme trial. Retrieved from
http://theworldlink.com/news/local/article_5f194491
da4d-50f5-90b5-d85c2735a250.html.

Wilson, J.Q. (2011, May, 28-29). Hard times, fewer crimes. Wall Street Journal, C1.

Wilson, K. (2009, June 29). Terrorism and tobacco: how cigarette smuggling finances jihad and insurgency worldwide. Retrieved from
www.thecuttingedgenews.com/index.php?article¼11427.

Winslow, B. (2011, February 2). Bill cracking down on affinity fraud in Utah. Retrieved from www.fox13now.com/news/local/kstu-affinity-fraud-bill,0,3085051.story.

Wolfe, D.T., & Hermanson, D.R. (2004, December). The fraud diamond: Considering the four elements of fraud. The CPA Journal, 38-42.

Woodworth, M., & Porter, S. (2002). In cold blood: Characteristics of criminal homicides as a function of psychopathy, Journal of Abnormal Psychology, 11(3), 436-445.

Wright, G. (2008, May 30). Insurance investigator's death spurs fraud inquiry, The News & Observer. Retrieved from
http://www.allvoices.com/news/547157/s/10270573-death-spurs-fraud-inquiry.

Wright, M. (2013). Homicide detective intuition. Journal of Investigative Psychology and Offender Profiling, 10, 182-199.

Wynn, R., Hoiseth, M. H., & Pettersen, G. (2012). Psychopathy in women: Theoretical and clinical perspectives. International Journal of Women's Heath, 4, 257-263.

Xu, Z.X., & Ma, H.K. (2015). Does honesty result from moral will or moral grace? Why moral identity matters. Journal of Business Ethics,127, 371-384.

Yang, D. (2005, July 29). Florida man convicted in affinity fraud scheme that targeted members of the seventh-day adventist church. Retrieved from www.justice.gov/usao/cac/pressroom/pr2005/111.html.

Yang, C., & Grow, B. (2005, January 13). What did ebbers know? Business Week. Retrieved from http://www.businessweek.com/stories/2005-01-13/what-did-ebbers-know

Yardley, J. (2002, January 26). Critic who quit top Enron post is found dead. New York Times. Retrieved from
http://www.nytimes.com/2002/01/26/business/26HOUS.html?pagewanted=print

Yardley, W. (2011, May 26). A fraud played out on family and friends. New York Times. Retrieved from
http://www.nytimes.com/2011/05/27/us/27ponzi.html

Yasman, V. (2004, July 13). Analysis: American journalist klebnikov gunned down in moscow. Radio Free Europe. Retrieved from
http://www.rferl.org/content/article/1053842.html

Yates, S.Q. (2015). Individual accountability for corporate wrongdoing. U.S. Department of Justice. Retrieved from
https://www.justice.gov/archives/dag/file/769036/download

Yaverbaum, E. (2004). Leadership Secrets of the World's Most Successful CEOs. Chicago, IL:Dearborn Trading.

Yeager, P.C.(2007). Understanding corporate lawbreaking: From profit seeking to law finding. In International Handbook of White-collar and Corporate Crime. New York: Springer

Yeager, P.C. (2016). The practical challenges of responding to corporate crime. In The Oxford Handbook of White-collar Crime. UK: Oxford University Press.

Yildirim, B.O. & Derksen, J.J.L. (2015). Clarifying the heterogeneity in psychopathic samples: Towards a new continuum of primary and secondary psychopathy. Aggression and Violent Behavior, 24, 9-41.

Yochelson, S., & Samenow, S. (1976). The Criminal Personality. NY: Aronson.

Zahra, S.A., Priem, R.L., & Rasheed, A.A. (2005). The antecdents and consequences of top management fraud. Journal of Management, 31(6), 803-824.

Zellner, W. (2002, February 11). Jeff skilling: Enron's missing man. Retrieved from
http://bodurtha.georgetown.edu/enron/jeff_skilling_enrons_missing_man.htm

Zhang, G., & Zhang, L. (2009). An analysis on dealing with audit failure. Journal of Modern Accounting and Auditing, 5(7), 62-65

Zietz, D. (1981). *Women Who Embezzle or Defraud: A Study of Convicted Felons*. N.Y.: Praeger.

Zweig J. & Pilon M. (2010, December 18). When seniors get scammed. *The Wall Street Journal*, Retrieved from http://online.wsj.com/news/articles/SB10001424052748704098304576021600313

Made in the USA
Coppell, TX
30 September 2022

83829263R00307